Banking and Financial Services Law

Banking and Financial Services Law

Cases, Materials, and Problems

Third Edition

Michael P. Malloy
Distinguished Professor and Scholar
University of the Pacific
McGeorge School of Law

Carolina Academic Press
Durham, North Carolina

ISBN: 978-1-61163-097-8
LCCN: 2011933701

Carolina Academic Press
700 Kent Street
Durham, North Carolina 27701
Telephone (919) 489-7486
Fax (919) 493-5668
E-mail: cap@cap-press.com
www.cap-press.com

This book is dedicated to my son
Nicholas Charles Malloy

SUMMARY OF CONTENTS

CONTENTS

TABLE OF CASES

Principal cases, excerpted in the casebook, are indicated by **boldface** type.

PREFACE TO THE THIRD EDITION

In the six years since the second edition of this casebook appeared, the regulation of financial services has confronted one of the most disastrous crises since the Great Depression – and the new century is still young. The expansion of the national and international financial services markets seemed irrepressible, until disaster overtook us in the Fall of 2008, with the collapse of the residential mortgage market. The "securitization" of mortgage-related products spread mortgage risk directly into the securities markets, and this phenomenon linked the collapse of the mortgage market to a meltdown of U.S. capital markets. Hence, much of what was foundational about the regulation of financial services in the last edition has been subjected to agonizing reappraisal – but with no clear resolution in sight. The Dodd-Frank Act, the most significant statutory response to the crisis, touches on virtually every aspect of the regulation of depository institutions, the subject of this book. However, many of the most significant changes mandated by the act will take years to implement fully. This is the result of effective dates of key provisions that stretch out over two years following the enactment of Dodd-Frank, as well as a lengthy and complex process of regulatory implementation of the provisions of the act. Most recently, the Congress itself has begun to question the wisdom of the aggressive restructuring of the regulatory system initiated by Dodd-Frank, and this failure of vision will only complicate the structure even further.

These and other major developments make a challenging field of study even more daunting, if even more thrilling in its complex mix of issues. Hopefully, the problem-oriented approach of this edition, a hallmark of the book from its beginning, will continue to present students with genuine opportunities to confront developments and challenges that are likely to be with us for years to come.

Special thanks are due to many persons for their assistance and encouragement of the completion of this new edition. Many friends and colleagues at other schools have offered useful advice and observations about the previous edition that helped me to rework or replace material in this edition. Ms. Sally Snyder, Supervisor of the Faculty Support Office, and the FSO staff have kept vexing administrative and bureaucratic burdens from my door while I worked on this project. I also acknowledge the encouragement and editorial assistance of my wife, Susie A. Malloy.

Michael P Malloy
London
December 2010

PREFACE TO THE SECOND EDITION

In the five years since the first edition of this casebook appeared, the regulation of financial services has grown in importance and complexity. A wide range of significant legal and financial developments have had a marked impact on the financial services industry. The implications of the collapse of the savings and loan industry in the late 1980s continue to unfold. U.S. banks and bank holding companies have been granted broader authority to participate in activities that are "financial in nature," including securities and insurance activities. Virtual banks and e-banking are becoming a quotidian reality. The federal regulators–particularly the Comptroller of the Currency and the Office of Thrift Supervision–are increasingly aggressive in their efforts to preempt the regulatory authority of individual states. International markets and regulatory developments are ever more significant to the U.S. markets. The terrorist attacks on the United States that occurred in September 2001 have prompted a renewal of U.S. statutory and regulatory interest in both offensive and defensive supervision of the banking system to combat terrorism, and an emerging international consensus has focused on antiterrorism and anti-money laundering in response to international terrorism.

These and other major developments join an even wider variety of traditional regulatory concerns in a complex mix of issues. As with the previous edition, the problem-oriented approach of this new edition focuses on the interactions and crossovers within the financial services industry today. It tries to give students an opportunity to explore the issues that are redefining financial services regulation in a way that will present them coherently and practically.

Special thanks are due to many persons for their assistance and encouragement of the completion of this new edition. Associate Dean John Sprankling has been generous in his support and understanding of the burdens that preparation of even a second edition of a casebook places on an author. Many friends and colleagues at other schools have offered useful advice and observations about the previous edition that helped me to rework or replace material in this edition. I must also acknowledge Ms. Sally Snyder, Supervisor of the Faculty Secretaries' Office, and Ms. Denai Burbank and the rest of the Faculty Secretaries for their singular efforts in keeping administrative burdens from my door while I worked on this project. My student research assistants, Ms. Suzanne Uzelac of the University of the Pacific Class of 1998 and Mr. David Richards of the University of the Pacific Class of 2004, provided invaluable and invariably reliable assistance.

Finally, the original project and the renewed effort of this second edition would have been personally pointless – and very tedious – without the encouragement, inspiration, and devoted editorial assistance of my wife, Susie A. Malloy. She makes all things seem possible.

Michael P Malloy
Dublin
April 2004

PREFACE TO THE FIRST EDITION

This casebook on banking and financial services regulation covers a dynamic, evolving area of law and policy that is still experiencing the kind of dramatic transformation which occurred in securities regulation during 1933 to 1940. Indeed, it is characteristic of banking regulation that it has essentially reinvented or reformulated itself repeatedly in the past 150 years.

By some strange regulatory law of conservation of energy, however, past legal approaches seem to be preserved within each new, fundamental change. The result is that contemporary banking and financial services regulation is remarkably complex, operating in the shadow of its own history. Consider, for example, the fact that the statute that authorizes federal chartering of banks–the National Bank Act–retains many of its original 1864 provisions, but must be reconciled with major statutory developments layered on top of the Act in almost every decade of this century.

This is an area of law and policy that requires an understanding of statutory, regulatory and traditional case law sources of authority. The casebook is based on the belief that the best way to achieve this understanding is to confront directly the practical problems of banking and financial services law. Consequently, in addition to the typical cases and materials found in a traditional course on financial services law, the book includes a wide variety of concrete problems and questions. This problem-oriented approach to the subject, and its focus on the interactions and crossovers within the financial services industry today, are intended to give students an opportunity to explore the issues that are redefining regulation in this area.

Special thanks are due to several persons for their assistance and encouragement of the completion of this book. Dean Gerald Caplan and Associate Dean Kathleen M. Kelly of McGeorge School of Law, University of the Pacific, have provided both moral and material support for this project. My colleague Claude Rohwer has on more than one occasion lifted burdens so that I could concentrate on the work at hand. My student research assistant Ms. Suzanne Uzelac, of the University of the Pacific Class of 1998, has provided invaluable, and invariably thorough, assistance. Finally, this project would have been impossible to finish and of little personal interest without the devoted assistance and encouragement of my wife, Susie A. Malloy.

Michael P. Malloy
Salzburg
July 1998

ACKNOWLEDGMENTS

The author gratefully acknowledges the permission granted to reprint excerpts from the following:

Michael P. Malloy, Banking Law and Regulation (2d ed., 3 vols., Aspen Publishers, 2011).

Michael P. Malloy, Capital Adequacy and Regulatory Objectives, 25 Suffolk Transnational Law Review 299 (2002).

Michael P. Malloy, Principles of Bank Regulation (3d ed., West, 2011).

Michael P. Malloy, Nothing to Fear but FIRREA Itself: Revising and Reshaping the Enforcement Process of Federal Bank Regulation, 50 Ohio St. L.J. 1117 (1989).

Michael P. Malloy, The Sound of Two Hands Flapping: Insurance-Related Activities of National Banks, 41 St. Louis U. L.J. 75 (1996).

Kenneth Scott, In Quest of Reason: The Licensing Decisions of the Federal Banking Agencies, 42 U.Chi. L. Rev. 235 (1975). © 1975 The University of Chicago.

N. Strunk & F. Case, Where Deregulation Went Wrong (1988). Reprinted with permission of U.S. League of Savings Associations.

Weaver and O'Malley, The Depository Institutions Deregulation and Monetary Control Act of 1980: An Overview, 98 Banking L.J. 100 (1981). Reprinted with permission from the Banking Law Journal, February 1981. Warren, Gorham & Lamont Banking/A.S. Pratt, Copyright 1981. All rights reserved.

Banking and Financial Services Law

Chapter 1

The Regulatory Environment for Financial Services

1. Introduction

This chapter briefly examines the history of U.S. banking regulation. It then considers the current regulatory environment within which banking and financial services firms operate in the United States. The chapter concludes with a brief survey of various proposed and enacted reforms of that environment.

These three subjects are only individual aspects of the same overall reality. Contemporary financial services regulation operates in the long shadow of its history; the same issues and polarities repeatedly reemerge in new vocabularies. Efforts to reform the regulatory system regularly confront historically imbedded biases.

The best example of the intererlationships among history, current regulation and reform may be traced out in the early battle over the constitutionality of the Bank of the United States.[1] The positions staked out by Hamilton and Jefferson on this issue represent, on one level, a debate over the constitutional limits of the federal government's power to incorporate a bank. On a more enduring level, however, their positions reflect the opening moves in a continuing dispute over the appropriateness of government (or, at least, federal) intervention in the conduct of commercial and financial activity. Over the years, that dispute has resulted in a regulatory system whose extreme complexity is the byproduct of various compromises between the two sides in the dispute over two centuries. Much of the reform efforts of recent years has been directed at unravelling this complexity.

What is the object of all of this controversy? It is the process of *financial intermediation* performed by banks, securities firms, insurance companies and other similar entities. These entities intervene between capital providers (investors, depositors) and capital users (investments, borrowers). In theory at least, financial intermediaries provide an efficient means for capital to be aggregated and redirected towards productive uses.[2] (*See* Figure 1.1, *infra*.) Individual providers do not have to expend resources identifying, and assessing the appropriateness of, individual investments; the intermediaries can do this for them more

---

1. *See* the material beginning at Note 1.2, *infra* (discussing Bank of the United States).

2. The banking and financial services provided and performed by these intermediaries may now also be available by electronic means over the Internet. *See* The Economist, *A Survey of Online Finance: The virtual threat*, May 20, 2000, at 6, col. 1 (suggesting that traditional banks might eventually be "disintermediated" by Internet financial services).

efficiently on an aggregate basis. Individual capital users do not have to expend resources identifying, aggregating and negotiating with a broad array of individual investors; the intermediaries already represent financial aggregations and are themselves relatively easy to identify.

Figure 1.1
Financial Intermediation

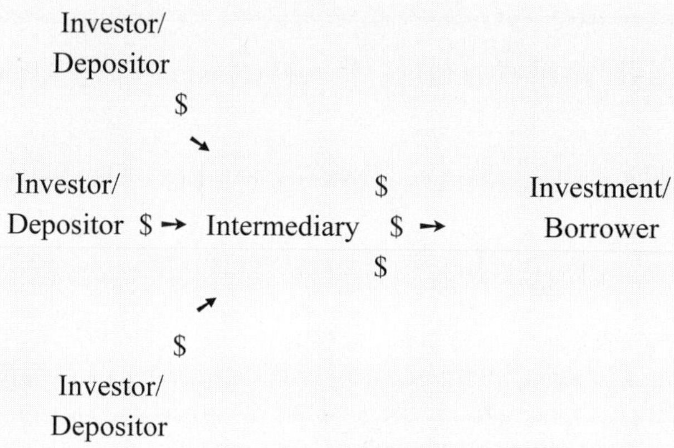

In the case of banks and other depository institutions, another feature of financial intermediation is of particular importance–the credit function. Because depository institutions aggregate financial resources, redistribute them primarily through lending, and usually receive the proceeds of the lending as lendable deposits, the total available amount of *credit* in the banking system can increase exponentially, far beyond the simple aggregation of capital. In other words, banks accept deposits, which are then turned over as loans, which then reenter the banking system as deposits of the borrowers–and *those* deposits are turned over as loans to other borrowers. The deposits and loans are represented by book entries in the system itself. If the process can be kept running without significant net withdrawal of resources from the banking system, credit continues to increase. (*See* Figure 1.2, *infra*.) If the deposit pool begins to contract significantly, or does not continue to increase to fuel further lending, then banks in the system must begin to contract their lending (by calling in loans or refusing new loans), and available credit begins to decrease. What is the deposit itself, as a matter of law? The following excerpt addresses this basic question.

Texas State Bank v. United States

423 F.3d 1370 (Fed. Cir. 2005)
cert. denied, 547 U.S. 1206 (2006)

DYK, CIRCUIT JUDGE

[Texas State Bank brought suit against the United States, claiming that it had a property right in interest income attributable to its statutorily required deposit reserve account at a Federal Reserve Bank, and that transfer of the interest income to the U.S. Treasury

Department therefore violated the Fifth Amendment guarantee against uncompensated government takings. (Detailed excerpts from the case appear in § 3 of this chapter.) In passing, the court had this to say about the deposit relationship.]

. . . Under normal principals [*sic*] of banking law, "the relationship between a bank and its depositor is that of debtor and creditor." *Michie on Banks and Banking,* ch. IX, § 1 (1994). As the Supreme Court put it almost a century ago, when a bank receives deposits, the funds "belong to the bank, become part of its general funds, and can be loaned by it as other moneys.... The general doctrine that upon a deposit made by a customer, ... the title to the money ... is immediately vested in, and becomes the property of, the bank, is not open to question." *Burton v. United States,* 196 U.S. 283, 301-02 (1905) (internal quotations omitted); *see also City of Douglas v. Fed. Reserve Bank of Dallas,* 271 U.S. 489, 492-94 (1926). . . . Texas State conceded during oral argument that "there is no private account to which interest was credited."

Figure 1.2
The Credit Function

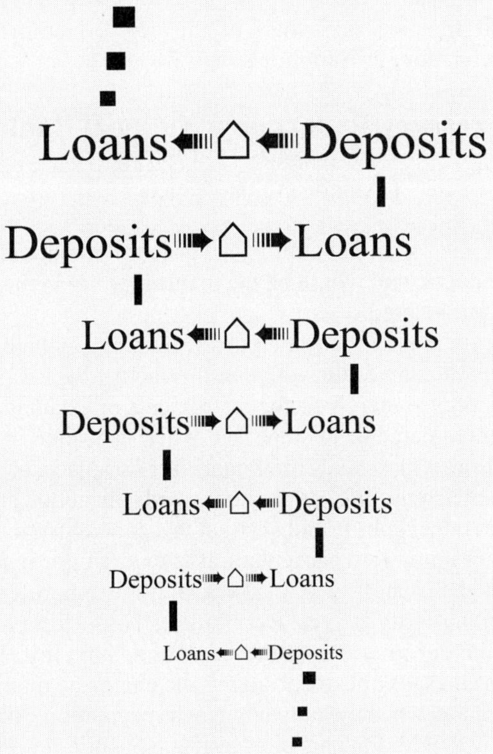

2. History

Notes and Comments 1.1. *The pre-Federal situation.* The English colonies in North America never established a banking system of their own. As a result, an integrated system for the creation and transfer of credit–essential functions of commercial banking–did not exist. This situation was exacerbated by the American Revolution, which created critical problems for the economies of the former colonies. The individual former colonies and their loose "continental" government issued bills of credit–public IOU's–to support their operations and the prosecution of the war of independence, but these issuances proliferated and rapidly devalued. In May 1781 Robert Morris of Philadelphia, the newly appointed Superintendant of Finance presented the Continental Congress with a proposal for chartering a bank as a means of raising money and creating credit. By the end of that year, the Bank of North America was established and began operating in 1782 as a commercial bank. Eventually, it was rechartered by the state of Pennsylvania as a private enterprise, and so the problem of establishing a coherent national credit system reasserted itself.

1.2. *Hamilton's proposal.* In August 1790, the first Congress to meet under the Constitution directed Alexander Hamilton, the Secretary of the Treasury, to formulate recommendations for establishing public credit. Hamilton's proposal was to charter a national bank to engage in the credit function on behalf of the new government. What advantages supported this recommendation, in Hamilton's view?

Treasury Report on a National Bank

December 13, 1790
1 American State Papers 67

[A] national bank is an institution of primary importance to the prosperous administration of the finances, and would be the greatest utility in the operations connected with the support of the public credit. . . .

The following are among the principal advantages of a bank:

First. The augmentation of the active or productive capital of a country. Gold and silver, when they are employed merely as the instruments of exchange and alienation, have not been improperly denominated dead stock; but when deposited in banks, to become the basis of a paper circulation, which takes their character and place, as the signs or representatives of value, they then acquire life, or, in other words, an active and productive quality. This idea, which appears rather subtile and abstract in a general form, may be made obvious and palpable, by entering into a few particulars. It is evident, for instance, that the money which a merchant keeps in his chest, waiting for a favorable opportunity to employ it, produces nothing till that opportunity arrives. But if, instead of locking it up in this manner, he either deposits it in a bank, or invests it in the stock of a bank, it yields a profit during the interval, in which he partakes, or not, according to the choice he may have made of being a depositor or a proprietor; and when any advantageous speculation offers, in order to be able to embrace it, he has only to withdraw his money, if a depositor, or, if a proprietor, to obtain a loan from the bank, or to dispose of his stock–an alternative seldom or never attended with difficulty, when the affairs of the institution are in a prosperous train. His money, thus deposited or invested, is a fund upon which himself and others can borrow to a much larger amount. It is a well-established fact, that banks in good credit can circulate a far greater sum than the actual quantum of their capital in gold and silver. The extent of the possible excess seems indeterminate; though it has been conjecturally stated at the proportions of two and three to one. This faculty is produced in various ways. 1st. A great proportion of the notes which are issued, and pass current as cash, are indefinitely suspended in circulation, from the confidence which each holder has, that he can, at any moment, turn them into gold and silver. 2ndly. Every loan which a bank makes, is, in its first shape, a credit given to the borrower on its books, the amount of which it stands ready to pay, either in its own notes, or in gold or silver, at his option. But, in a great number of cases, no actual payment is made in either. The borrower, frequently, by a check or order, transfers his credit to some other person, to whom he has a payment to make; who, in his turn, is as often content with a similar credit, because he is satisfied that he can, whenever he pleases, either convert it into cash, or pass it to some other hand, as an equivalent for it. And in this manner the credit keeps circulating, performing in every stage the office of money, till it is extinguished by a discount with some person who has a payment to make to the bank, to an equal or greater amount. Thus large sums are lent and paid, frequently through a variety of hands, without the intervention of a single piece of coin. 3dly. There is always a large quantity of gold and silver in the repositories of the bank, besides its own stock, which is placed there, with a view partly to its safekeeping, and partly to the accommodation. These deposits are the immense consequence in the operations of a bank. Though liable to be redrawn at any moment, experience proves, that the money so much oftener changes proprietors than place, and that what is drawn out is generally so speedily replaced, as to authorize the counting upon the sums deposited, as an *effective fund*, which, concurring with the stock of the bank, enables it to extend its loans, and to answer all the demands for coin, whether in consequence of those loans, or arising from the occasional return of its notes.

These different circumstances explain the manner in which the ability of a bank to circulate a greater sum than its actual capital in coin is acquired. This, however, must be gradual, and must be preceded by a firm establishment of confidence–a confidence which may be bestowed on the most rational grounds, since the excess in question will always be bottomed on good security of one kind or another. This, every well-conducted bank carefully requires, before it will consent to advance either its money or its credit, and where there is an auxiliary capital . . . , which, together with the capital in coin, defines the boundary that shall not be exceeded by the engagements of the bank, the security may, consistently with all the maxims of a reasonable circumspection, be regarded as complete. . . .

Secondly. Greater facility as to the government in obtaining pecuniary aids, especially in sudden emergencies. This is another and an undisputed advantage of public banks–one which, as already remarked, has been realized in signal instances among ourselves. The reason is obvious: the capitals of a great number of individuals are, by this operation collected to a point, and placed under one direction. The mass formed by this union, is, in a certain sense, magnified by the credit attached to it; and while this mass is already, and can at once be put in motion, in aid of the government, the interest of the bank to afford that aid, independent of regard to the public safety and welfare is a sure pledge for its disposition to go as far in its compliances as can in prudence be desired. There is, in the nature of things, as will be more particularly noticed in another place, an intimate connection of interest between the government and the bank of a nation.

Thirdly. The facilitating of the payment of taxes. This advantage is produced in two ways. Those who are in a situation to have access to the bank, can have the assistance of loans, to answer, with punctuality, the public calls upon them. . . . The other way in which the effect here contemplated is produced, and in which the benefit is general, is the increasing of the quantity of circulating medium, and the quickening of circulation. The manner in which the first happens has already been traced. The last may require some illustration. When payments are to be made between different places having an intercourse of business with each other, if there happen to be no private bills at market, and there are no bank-notes which have a currency in both, the consequence is, that coin must be remitted.

This is attended with trouble, delay, expense, and risk. If, on the contrary, there are bank-notes current in both places, the transmission of these by the post, or any other speedy or convenient conveyance, answers the purpose; and these again, in the alternations of demand, are frequently returned, very soon after, to the place from which they were first sent: whence the transportation and re-transportation of the metals are obviated and a more convenient and more expeditious medium of payment is substituted. Nor is this all; the metals, instead of being suspended from their usual functions during this process of vibration from place to place, continue in activity, and administer still to the ordinary circulation, which, of course, is prevented from suffering either diminution or stagnation. . . .

The payment of the interest of the public debt at thirteen different places is a weighty reason, peculiar to our immediate situation, for desiring a bank circulation. Without a paper, in general currency, equivalent to gold and silver, a considerable proportion of the specie of the country must always be suspended from circulation, and left to accumulate, preparatory to each day of payment; and as often as one approaches, there must in several cases be an actual transportation of the metals, at both expense and risk, from their natural and proper reservoirs, to distant places. This necessity will be felt very injuriously to the trade of some of the States, and will embarrass not a little the operations of the treasury in those States. It will also obstruct those negotiations, between different parts of the Union, by the instrumentality of treasury bills, which have already afforded valuable accommodations to trade in general. . . .

Considerations of public advantage suggest . . . that the bank could be established upon principles that would cause the profits of it to redound to the immediate benefit of the State. This is contemplated by many who speak of a national bank, but the idea seems liable to insuperable objections. To attach full confidence to an institution of this nature, it appears to be an essential ingredient in its structure, that it shall be under a *private* not a *public* direction–under the guidance of *individual interest*, not of *public policy*; which would be supposed to be, and, in certain emergencies, under a feeble or too sanguine administration, would really be, liable to being too much influenced by *public necessity*. The suspicion of this would, most probably, be a canker that would continually corrode the vitals of the credit of the bank, and would be most likely to prove fatal in those situations in which the public good would require that they should be most sound and vigorous. It would, indeed, be little less than a miracle, should the credit of the bank be at the disposal of the government, if, in a long series of time, there was not experienced a calamitous abuse of it. . . .

The keen, steady, and, as it were, magnetic sense of their own interest as proprietors, in the directors of a bank, pointing invariably to its true pole–the prosperity of the institution,–is the only security that can always be relied upon for a careful and prudent administration. It is, therefore, the only basis on which an enlightened, unqualified, and permanent confidence can be expected to be erected and maintained. . . .

It will not follow, from what has been said, that the state may not be a holder of a part of the stock of a bank, and consequently a sharer in the profits of it. It will only follow that it ought not to desire any participation in the direction of it, and, therefore, ought not to own the whole or a principal part of the stock; for, if the mass of the property should belong to the public, and if the direction of it should be in private hands, this would be to commit the interests of the state to persons not interested, or not enough interested, in their proper management. . . .

Notes and Comments 1.3. *Mr. Jefferson objects.* The congressional bill based on Hamilton's proposal provided for a twenty-year charter for the Bank of the United States. The Bank was to have capital of $10 million, $2 million of which could be subscribed by the federal government. There would be twenty-five directors. While foreign persons were not prohibited from ownership of the stock of the Bank, such persons could not vote their shares by proxy. The Bank would be limited to an interest rate of six percent on its loans and discounts. It was prohibited from buying and selling real estate, except as foreclosed collateral. The bill proved to be highly controversial. It raised fears that the bank's operations would draw funds away from agriculture, increase speculation, and drive "specie" (*i.e.*, gold and silver) out of the country. In February 1791, Representative James Madison voiced opposition to the bill during House debate, claiming among other things that it was unconstitutional.[3] Nevertheless, the bill passed. When the bill reached President Washington, he asked his cabinet for their views. Secretary of State Thomas Jefferson submitted the following critique. What were his reasons for opposing the bill?

Jefferson's Opinion

February 15, 1791

1 H. E. Krooss (ed.), Documentary History of Banking and Currency in the United States 147 (1969 ed.)

. . . [T]he foundation of the Constitution [is] laid on this ground, that, "all powers not delegated to the United States, by the Constitution, nor prohibited by it to the states, are reserved to the states, or to the people" (12th amend.) [*sic*]. To take a single step beyond the boundaries thus specially drawn around the powers of Congress, is to take possession of a boundless field of power, no longer susceptible of any definition.

The incorporation of a bank, and powers assumed by this bill, have not, in my opinion, been delegated to the United States by the constitution.

I. They are not among the powers specially enumerated. . . . [Jefferson then reviewed pertinent enumerated powers, including the power "To regulate commerce with foreign nations, and among the States, and with the Indian Tribes."] To erect a bank, and to regulate commerce, are very different acts. . . . Besides, if this was an exercise of the power of regulating commerce, it would be void, as extending as much to the internal commerce of every State, as to its external. For the power given to Congress by the constitution does not extend to the internal regulation of the commerce of a State . . . which remains exclusively with its own legislature; but to its external commerce only. That is to say, its commerce with another State, or with foreign nations, or with the Indian tribes: accordingly, the bill does not propose this measure as a "regulation of trade", but as "productive of considerable advantage to trade"; still less are these powers covered by any other of the special enumerations.

II. Nor are they within either of the general phrases, which are the two following:

1. "To lay taxes to provide for the general welfare of the United States;" that is to say, to lay taxes *for the purpose* of providing for the general welfare; for the laying of taxes is the *power*, and the general welfare the *purpose* for which the power is to be exercised. They are not to lay taxes *ad libitum, for any purpose they please*, but only *to pay the debts, or provide for the welfare of the Union.* In like manner, they are not *to do anything they please* to provide for the general welfare, but only *to lay taxes* for that purpose. To consider the latter phrase, not as describing the purpose of the first, but as giving a distinct and independent power to do any act they please, which might be for the good of the Union, would render all the preceding and subsequent enumerations of power completely useless: it would reduce the whole instrument to a single phrase, that of instituting a Congress with power to do whatever would be for the good of the United States; and, as they would be the sole judges of the good or evil, it would be also a power to do whatever evil they pleased. . . .

---

3. 3 Annals of Cong. 1944 *et seq*. (1791).

Certainly no such universal power was meant to be given them. . . .

2. The second general phrase is, "to make all laws *necessary* and proper for carrying into execution the enumerated powers." But they can all be carried into execution without a bank. A bank, therefore, is not necessary, and consequently not authorised by this phrase.

It has been much urged, that a bank will give great facility or convenience in the collection of taxes. Suppose this were true, yet the constitution allows only the means which are "necessary," not those which are merely convenient for the effecting the enumerated powers. If such a latitude of construction be allowed to this phrase, as to give any non-enumerated power, it will go to every one; for there is no one which ingenuity may not torture into a *convenience, in some way or other, to some one* of so long a list of enumerated powers: it would swallow up all the delegated powers, and reduce the whole to one phrase, as before observed. Therefore, it was that the constitution restrained them to the *necessary* means; that is to say, to those means, without which the grant of the power would be nugatory. . . .

The [Treasury] report . . . states the only *general* convenience to be preventing the transportation and re-transportation of money between the States and the treasury, (for I pass over the increase of circulating medium, ascribed to it as a merit, and which, according to my ideas of paper money, is clearly a demerit.)

. . . Perhaps, indeed bank bills may be a more *convenient* vehicle than treasury orders [drawn on the State collector]; but a little difference in the degree of convenience cannot constitute the necessity, which the constitution makes the ground for assuming any non-enumerated power.

Besides, the existing [state] banks will, without a doubt, enter into arrangements for lending their agency; and the more favorably, as there will be a competition among them for it; whereas the bill delivers us up bound to the national bank, who are free to refuse all arrangement, but on their own terms, and the public not free, on such refusal, to employ any other bank. . . .

It may be said that a bank, whose bills would have currency all over the States, would be more convenient, than one, whose currency is limited to a single State. So it would be still more convenient that there should be a bank, whose bills should have a currency all over the world; but it does not follow, from this superior conveniency, that there exists any where a power to establish such a bank, or that the world may not go on very well without it.

Notes and Comments 1.4. *Mr. Hamilton responds.* Attorney General Edmund Randolph had also rendered an opinion in opposition to the bill.[4] On February 16, 1791, the President wrote to Hamilton, enclosing the opinions of Jefferson and Randolph and asking Hamilton to respond. Hamilton replied on February 23, 1791. How does his response compare with his original report?

Hamilton's Reply to the President

1 H. E. Krooss (ed.), Documentary History of Banking and Currency in the United States 152 (1969)

The Secretary of the Treasury presents his respects to the President, and sends him the opinion required, which occupied him the greatest part of last night. . . .

In entering upon the argument, it ought to be premised that the objections of the

---

4. *See* M. St. C. Clarke & D. A. Hall, Legislative and Documentary History of the Bank of the United States 86 (1832) (reprinting Randolph's opinion).

Secretary of State and the Attorney-General are founded on a general denial of the authority of the United States to erect corporations. The latter, indeed, expressly admits, that if there be anything in the bill which is not warranted by the Constitution, it is the clause of incorporation.

Now it appears to the Secretary of the Treasury that this *general principle* is *inherent* in the very *definition* of government, and *essential* to every step of the progress to be made by that of the United States, namely: That every power vested in a government is in its nature *sovereign*, and includes, by *force* of the *term*, a right to employ all the *means* requisite and fairly applicable to the attainment of the *ends* of such power, and which are not precluded by restrictions and exceptions specified in the Constitution, or not immoral, or not contrary to the *essential ends* of political society. . . .

[T]he Secretary of State maintains, that no means are to be considered *necessary* but those without which the grant of the power would be nugatory. Nay, so far does he go in his restrictive interpretation of the *word*, as even to make the case of necessity which shall warrant the constitutional exercise of the power to depend on *casual* and *temporary* circumstances; an idea which alone refutes the construction. The *expediency* of exercising a particular power, at a particular time, must, indeed, depend on circumstances; but the constitutional right of exercising it must be uniform and invariable, the same today as tomorrow.

All the arguments, therefore, against the constitutionality of the bill derived from the accidental existence of certain State banks–institutions which happen to exist today, and, for aught that concerns the government of the United States, may disappear tomorrow–must not only be rejected as fallacious, but must be viewed as demonstrative that there is a *radical* source of error in the reasoning. . . .

It is certain, that neither the grammatical nor popular sense of the term requires that construction. According to both, *necessary* often means no more than *needful, requisite, incidental, useful* or *conducive to*. It is a common mode of expression to say, that it is *necessary* for a government or a person to do this or that thing, when nothing more is intended or understood, than that the interests of the government or person require, or will be promoted by, the doing of this or that thing. . . .

[The Secretary of State's] restrictive interpretation of the word *necessary* is also contrary to this sound maxim of construction; namely, that the powers contained in a constitution of government, especially those which concern the general administration of the affairs of a country, its finances, trade, defence, etc., ought to be construed liberally in advancement of the public good. This rule does not depend on the particular form of a government, or on the particular demarcation of the boundaries of its powers, but on the nature and objects of government itself. The means by which exigencies are to be provided for, national inconveniences obviated, national prosperity promoted, are of such infinite variety, extent, and complexity, that there must of necessity be great latitude of discretion in the selection and application of those means. Hence, consequently, the necessity and propriety of exercising the authorities intrusted to a government on principles of liberal construction. . . .

In regard to the clause of the Constitution immediately under consideration, it is admitted by the Attorney-General, that no *restrictive* effect can be ascribed to it. He defines the word *necessary* thus: "To be *necessary* is to be *incidental*, and may be denominated the natural means of executing a power."

. . . [The Attorney General's] first objection is, that the power of incorporation is not *expressly* given to Congress. This shall be conceded, but in *this sense only*, that it is not declared in *express terms* that Congress may erect a corporation. But this cannot mean, that there are not certain *express powers* which *necessarily* include it. . . .

But the argument itself is founded upon an exaggerated and erroneous conception of the nature of the power. It has been shown that it is not of so transcendent a kind as the reasoning supposes, and that, viewed in a just light, it is a means, which ought to have been left to *implication*, rather than an *end*, which ought to have been expressly granted.

Having observed that the power of erecting corporations is not expressly granted to Congress, the Attorney-General proceeds thus:

If it can be exercised by them, it must be:

1. Because the nature of the Federal Government implies it.

2. Because it is involved in some of the specified powers of legislation.

3. Because it is necessary and proper to carry into execution some of the specified powers. . . .

. . . The proposition relied upon is, that the *specified powers of Congress* are in their nature *sovereign*; that it is incident to sovereign power to erect corporations, and that therefore Congress have a right, within the sphere and in *relation* to the *objects of their power*, to *erect corporations*. It shall, however, be supposed that the Attorney-General would consider the two propositions in the same light, and that the objection made to the one would be made to the other.

To this objection an answer has been already given. It is this: that the doctrine is stated with this *express qualification*, that the right to erect corporations does *only* extend to *cases* and *objects* within the *sphere* of the *specified powers* of the *government*. A *general* legislative authority implies a power to erect corporations in *all cases*. A *particular* legislative power implies authority to erect corporations in relation to cases arising under *that power only*. . . .

The Attorney-General undertakes in the next place to show, that the power of erecting corporations is not involved in any of the specified powers of legislation confided to the National Government. In order to do this, he has attempted an enumeration of the particulars, which he supposes to be comprehended under the several heads of the *powers* to lay and collect taxes, etc.; to borrow money on the credit of the United States; to regulate commerce with sovereign nations, between the States, and with the Indian tribes; to dispose of the make all needful rules and regulations respecting the territory or other property belonging to the United States. The design of which enumeration is to show *what* is included under those different heads of power, and negatively, that the power of erecting corporations is not included.

. . . [T]he enumerations which have been attempted by the Attorney-General, are so imperfect as to authorize no conclusion whatever; they therefore have no tendency to disprove that each and every of the powers to which they relate includes that of erecting corporations. . . .

A bank relates to the collection of taxes in two ways–*indirectly*, by increasing the quantity of circulating medium and quickening circulation which facilitates the means of paying[, and directly] by creating a *convenient species* of medium in which they are to be paid.

To designate or appoint the *money* or *thing* in which taxes are to be paid, is not only a proper but a *necessary exercise* of the power of collecting them. . . .

A bank has a direct relation to the power of borrowing money, because it is a usual, and in sudden emergencies an essential, instrument in the obtaining of loans to government. . . .

The institution of a bank has also a natural relation to the regulation of trade between the States, in so far as it is conducive to the creation of a convenient medium of *exchange* between them, and to the keeping up a full circulation, by preventing the frequent displacement of the metals in reciprocal remittances. Money is the very hinge on which commerce turns. And this does not merely mean gold and silver; many other things have served the purpose with different degrees of utility. Paper has been extensively employed.

It cannot, therefore, be admitted, with the Attorney-General, that the regulation of trade between the States, as it concerns the medium of circulation and exchange, ought to be considered as confined to coin. It is even supposable that the whole, or the greatest part, of the coin of the country might be carried out of it . . . .

Notes and Comments 1.5. Jefferson argued that "To erect a bank, and to regulate commerce, are very different acts." Is Jefferson's argument correct with respect to the establishment of a central bank? The Bank of the United States was a primitive prototype of a "central bank"–a quasi-governmental banking entity designed to regulate or control the supply of credit and currency, and to monitor and facilitate transactions in credit and currency. Thus, the regulation of commerce (*i.e.*, transactions in credit in this case) was undertaken not by direct federal regulation of state-chartered banking entities, but by the intervention of a federally chartered entity into the banking system. The federal entity would "regulate" through its participation in and influence over the market for credit. This approach to regulation is a pattern that would repeat itself periodically throughout the history of the federal regulation of banking, as in the case of the Board of Governors of the Federal Reserve System.

1.6. The President signed the bill. The Bank was a modest success, but political bias against it continued. By the time its twenty-year charter expired in 1811, Jefferson's party was in power, and the charter was not renewed.

1.7. *The Second Bank of the United States.* After the demise of the First Bank, the need for central regulation continued to be felt. The number of state-chartered banks continued to grow throughout the period 1784 through 1811, with no failures until 1809. From 1809 through the War of 1812, overextended, inexperienced and undercapitalized state banks frequently failed. Even within Jefferson's party, support was developing for a central bank to stabilize the economy. Congress adopted a plan in 1816 for a Second Bank of the United States, which President Madison approved. However, state banks complained that the Second Bank would expand the economy by liberal loans to the state banks during favorable financial conditions but then force the collapse of the state banks by demands for repayment during periods of financial difficulty.[5] In response, several states passed legislation to curb the activities of the Second Bank.[6] Maryland's law in this regard led to litigation that rehearsed the previous dispute between Hamilton and Jefferson. How does the Supreme Court resolve the dispute?

McCulloch v. Maryland

17 U.S. (4 Wheat.) 316 (1819)

Mr. CHIEF JUSTICE MARSHALL delivered the opinion of the Court.

In the case now to be determined, the defendant [in error], a sovereign state, denies the obligation of a law enacted by the legislature of the Union, and the plaintiff [in error], on his part, contests the validity of an act which has been passed by the legislature of that

---

5. *See* R. C. H. CATTERALL, THE SECOND BANK OF THE UNITED STATES 27-65 (1902) (describing controversy).

6. *See* WARRE, THE SUPREME COURT IN UNITED STATES HISTORY 505-506 (REV. ED. 1923) (discussing state responses).

state.[a] . . .

The first question made in the cause is, has Congress power to incorporate a bank?

It has been truly said that this can scarcely be considered as an open question, entirely unprejudiced by the former proceedings of the nation respecting it. The principle now contested was introduced at a very early period of our history, has been recognized by many successive legislatures, and has been acted upon by the judicial department, in cases of peculiar delicacy, as a law of undoubted obligation. . . .

If any one proposition could command the universal assent of mankind, we might expect it would be this–that the government of the Union, though limited in its powers, is supreme within its sphere of action. This would seem to result necessarily from its nature. It is the government of all; its powers are delegated by all; it represents all, and acts for all. Though any one state may be willing to control its operations, no state is willing to allow others to control them. The nation, on those subjects on which it can act, must necessarily bind its components parts. But this question is not left to mere reason; the people have, in express terms, decided it by saying, "this constitution, and the laws of the United States, which shall be made in pursuance thereof," "shall be the supreme law of the land," and by requiring that the members of the state legislatures, and the officers of the executive and judicial departments of the states shall take the oath of fidelity to it.

The government of the United States, then, though limited in its powers, is supreme; and its laws, when made in pursuance of the constitution, form the supreme law of the land, "anything in the constitution or laws of any state to the contrary notwithstanding."

Among the enumerated powers, we do not find that of establishing a bank or creating a corporation. But there is no phrase in the instrument which . . . excludes incidental or implied powers and which requires that everything granted shall be expressly and minutely described. Even the 10th amendment, which was framed for the purpose of quieting the excessive jealousies which had been excited, omits the word "expressly," and declares only that the powers "not delegated to the United States, nor prohibited to the states, are reserved to the states or to the people;" thus leaving the question, whether the particular power which

---

a. The Maryland statute attempted to limit the Bank's activities by requiring that bank notes be issued on stamped paper as follows:

> If any bank has established, or shall without authority from the State first had and obtained, establish any branch, office of discount and deposit, or office of pay and receipt, in any part of this state, it shall not be lawful for the said branch, office of discount and deposit, or office of pay and receipt, to issue notes in any manner, of any other denomination than five, ten, twenty, fifty, one hundred, five hundred and one thousand dollars, and no note shall be issued except upon stamped paper of the following denominations; that is to say, every five dollar note shall be upon a stamp of ten cents; every ten dollar note upon a stamp of twenty cents; every twenty dollar note, upon a stamp of thirty cents; every fifty dollar note, upon a stamp of fifty cents; every one hundred dollar note, upon a stamp of one dollar; every five hundred dollar note, upon a stamp of ten dollars; and every thousand dollar note, upon a stamp of twenty dollars; which paper shall be furnished by the Treasurer of the Western Shore under the direction of the Governor and Council, to be paid for upon delivery. Provided always, That any institution of the above description may relieve itself from the operation of the provisions aforesaid, by paying annually, in advance, to the Treasurer of the Western Shore, for the use of the State, the sum of fifteen thousand dollars.
>
> The President, Cashier, each of the Directors and officers of every institution established, or to be established as aforesaid, offending against the provisions aforesaid, shall forfeit a sum of five hundred dollars for each and every offence. . . .

1817 Md. Laws c. 156.

may become the subject of contest has been delegated to the one government, or prohibited to the other, to depend on a fair construction of the whole instrument. The men who drew and adopted this amendment had experienced the embarrassments resulting from the insertion of this word in the articles of confederation, and probably omitted it to avoid those embarrassments. A constitution, to contain an accurate detail of all the subdivisions of which its great powers will admit, and of all the means by which they may be carried into execution, would partake of a prolixity of a legal code, and could scarcely be embraced by the human mind. It would probably never be understood by the public. Its nature, therefore, requires, that only its great outlines should be marked, its important objects designated, and the minor ingredients which compose those objects be deduced from the nature of the objectives themselves. That this idea was entertained by the framers of the American constitution, is not only to be inferred from the nature of the instrument but from the language. Why else were some of the limitations, found in the ninth section of the 1st article, introduced? It is also, in some degree, warranted by their having omitted to use any restrictive term which might prevent its receiving a fair and just interpretation. In considering this question, then, we must never forget that it is a constitution we are expounding.

Although, among the enumerated powers of government, we do not find the word "bank" or "incorporation," we find the great powers to lay and collect taxes; to borrow money; to regulate commerce; to declare and conduct a war; and to raise and support armies and navies. The sword and the purse, all the external relations, and no inconsiderable portion of the industry of the nation, are entrusted to its government. It can never be pretended that these vast powers draw after them others of inferior importance, merely because they are inferior. Such an idea can never be advanced. But it may with great reason be contended, that a government, entrusted with such ample powers, on the due execution of which the happiness and prosperity of the nation so vitally depends, must also be entrusted with ample means for their execution. It can never be their interest, and cannot be presumed to have been their intention, to clog and embarrass its execution by withholding the most appropriate means. Throughout this vast republic, from the St. Croix to the Gulf of Mexico, from the Atlantic to the Pacific, revenue is to be collected and expended, armies are to be marched and supported. The exigencies of the nation may require that the treasure raised in the north should be transported to the south, that raised in the east conveyed to the west, or that this order should be reversed. Is that construction of the constitution to be preferred which would render these operations difficult, hazardous, and expensive? Can we adopt that construction (unless the words imperiously require it) which would impute to the framers of that instrument, when granting these powers for the public good, the intention of impeding their exercise by withholding a choice of means? If, indeed, such be the mandate of the constitution, we have only to obey; but that instrument does not profess to enumerate the means by which the powers it confers may be executed; nor does it prohibit the creation of a corporation, if the existence of such a being be essential to the beneficial exercise of those powers. It is, then, the subject of fair inquiry, how far such means may be employed. . . .

But the constitution of the United States has not left the right of Congress to employ the necessary means for the execution of the powers conferred on the government to general reasoning. To its enumeration of powers is added that of making "all laws which shall be necessary and proper, for carrying into execution the foregoing powers, and all other powers vested by this constitution, in the government of the United States, or in any department thereof."

The counsel for the State of Maryland have urged various arguments, to prove that this clause, though in terms a grant of power, is not so in effect; but is really restrictive of the general right, which might otherwise be implied, of selecting means for executing the enumerated powers. . . .

But the argument on which most reliance is placed, is drawn from the peculiar language of this clause. Congress is not empowered by it to make all laws, which may have relation to the powers conferred on the government, but such only as may be "necessary and proper" for carrying them into execution. The word "necessary" is considered as controlling the whole sentence, and as limiting the right to pass laws for the execution of the granted powers to such as are indispensable, and without which the power would be nugatory. That it excludes the choice of means, and leaves to Congress, in each case, that only which is most direct and simple.

Is it true that this is the sense in which the word "necessary" is always used? Does it always import an absolute physical necessity, so strong that one thing, to which another may be termed necessary, cannot exist without the other? We think it does not. If reference be had to its use, in the common affairs of the world, or in approved authors, we find that it frequently imports no more than that one thing is convenient, or useful, or essential to another. To employ the means necessary to an end, is generally understood as employing any means calculated to produce the end, and not as being confined to those single means, without which the end would be entirely unattainable. Such is the character of human language, that no word conveys to the mind, in all situations, one single definite idea; and nothing is more common than to use words in a figurative sense. Almost all compositions contain words, which, taken in their rigorous sense, would convey a meaning different from that which is obviously intended. It is essential to just construction, that many words which import something excessive should be understood in a more mitigated sense–in that sense which common usage justifies. The word "necessary" is of this description. It has not a fixed character peculiar to itself. It admits of all degrees of comparison; and is often connected with other words, which increase or diminish the impression the mind receives of the urgency it imports. A thing may be necessary, very necessary, absolutely or indispensably necessary. To no mind would the same idea be conveyed by these several phrases. This comment on the word is well illustrated by the passage cited at the bar, from the 10th section of the 1st article of the constitution. It is, we think, impossible to compare the sentence which prohibits a state from laying "imposts or duties on imports or exports, except what may be absolutely necessary for executing its inspection laws," with that which authorizes Congress "to make all laws which shall be necessary and proper for carrying into execution" the powers of the general government, without feeling a conviction that the convention understood itself to change materially the meaning of the word "necessary," by prefixing the word "absolutely." This word, then, like others, is used in various senses; and, in its construction, the subject, the context, the intention of the person using them, are all to be taken into view.

Let this be done in the case under consideration. The subject is the execution of those great powers on which the welfare of a nation essentially depends. It must have been the intention of those who gave these powers, to insure, as far as human prudence could insure, their beneficial execution. This could not be done by confiding the choice of means to such narrow limits as not to leave it in the power of Congress to adopt any which might be appropriate and which were conducive to the end. This provision is made in a constitution intended to endure for ages to come, and, consequently, to be adapted to the various crises of human affairs. To have prescribed the means by which government should, in all future time, execute its powers, would have been to change, entirely, the character of the instrument, and give it the properties of a legal code. It would have been an unwise attempt to provide, by immutable rules, for exigencies which, if forseen at all, must have been seen dimly, and which can be best provided for as they occur. . . .

. . . This clause, as construed by the state of Maryland, would abridge, and almost annihilate this useful and necessary right of the legislature to select its means. That this could not be intended, is, we should think, had it not been already controverted, too apparent for controversy. . . .

We admit, as all must admit, that the powers of the government are limited, and that its limits are not to be transcended. But we think the sound construction of the constitution must allow to the national legislature that discretion, with respect to the means by which the powers it confers are to be carried into execution, which will enable that body to perform the high duties assigned to it, in the manner most beneficial to the people. Let the end be legitimate, let it be within the scope of the constitution, and all means which are appropriate, which are plainly adapted to that end, which are not prohibited, but consist with the letter and spirit of the constitution, are constitutional. . . .

If a corporation may be employed indiscriminately with other means to carry into execution the powers of the government, no particular reason can be assigned for excluding the use of a bank, if required for its fiscal operations. To use one, must be within the discretion of Congress, if it be an appropriate mode of executing the powers of government. That it is a convenient, a useful, and essential instrument in the prosecution of its fiscal operations, is not now a subject of controversy. All those who have been concerned in the administration of our finances, have concurred in representing the importance and necessity; and so strongly have they been felt, that statesmen of the first class, whose previous opinions against it had been confirmed by every circumstance which can fix the human judgment have yielded those opinions to the exigencies of the nation. Under the confederation, Congress, justifying the measure by its necessity, transcended perhaps its powers to obtain the advantage of a bank; and our own legislation attests the universal conviction of the utility of this measure. The time has passed away when it can be necessary to enter into any discussion in order to prove the importance of this instrument, as a means to effect the legitimate objects of the government.

But, were its necessity less apparent, none can deny its being an appropriate measure; and if it is, the degree of its necessity, as has been very justly observed, is to be discussed in another place. . . .

After the most deliberate consideration, it is the unanimous and decided opinion of this court that the act to incorporate the bank of the United States is a law made in pursuance of the constitution, and is part of the supreme law of the land. . . .

[The opinion then examined the question "[w]hether the state of Maryland may, without violating the constitution, tax [the Second Bank's Maryland] branch?" The Court found "a total failure of this original right to tax the means employed by the government of the Union, for the execution of its powers. The right never existed, and the question whether it has been surrendered, cannot arise."

[The Court concluded "that the states have no power, by taxation or otherwise, to retard, impede, burden, or in any manner control the operation the powers vested in the general government. This is, we think, the unavoidable consequence of that supremacy which the constitution has declared."]

This opinion does not deprive the states of any resources which they originally possessed. It does not extend to a tax paid by the real property of the bank, in common with the other real property within the state, nor to a tax imposed on the interest which the citizens of Maryland may hold in this institution, in common with other property of the same description throughout the state. But this is a tax on the operations of the bank, and is, consequently, a tax on the operation of an instrument employed by the government of the Union to carry its powers into execution. Such a tax must be unconstitutional. . . .

Notes and Comments 1.8. During oral argument counsel for the State of Maryland argued that, since the Second Bank was primarily privately owned and managed, it was a "Bank of the United States" in name only. *McCulloch*, 17 U.S. (4 Wheat.) at 339-341. Could such an institution benefit from the "power and rights of government," demanding preemption of the laws of a state government? Does *McCulloch* adequately address this question? Does the following case resolve the issue?

Osborn v. The Bank

22 U.S. (9 Wheat.) 738 (1824)

Mr. CHIEF JUSTICE MARSHALL delivered the opinion of the Court.

[State officials seized assets of the Bank for failure to pay the Ohio tax on in-state branches of banks chartered outside the state, despite a federal court injunction to the contrary. The Bank brought suit against the state officials in federal court for return of the assets.]

The foundation of the argument in favour of the right of a State to tax the Bank, is laid in the supposed character of that institution. The argument supposes the corporation to have been originated for the management of an individual concern, to be founded upon contract between individuals, having private trade and private profit for its great end and principal object.

If these premises were true, the conclusion drawn from them would be inevitable. This mere private corporation, engaged in its own business, with its own views, would certainly be subject to the tax power of the State, as any individual would be; and the casual circumstances of its being employed by the government in the transaction of its fiscal affairs, would no more exempt its private business from the operation of that power, than it would exempt the private business of any individual employed in the same manner. But the premises are not true. The Bank is not considered as a private corporation, whose principal object is individual trade and individual profit; but as a public corporation, created for public and national purposes. That the mere business of banking is, in its own nature, a private business, and may be carried on by individuals or companies having no political connexion with the government, is admitted; but the Bank is not such an individual or company. It was not created for its own sake, or for private purposes. It has never been supposed that Congress could create such a corporation. The whole opinion of the Court, in the case of *McCulloch v. The State of Maryland*, is founded on, and sustained by, the idea that the Bank is an instrument which is "necessary and proper for carrying into effect the powers vested in the government of the United States." . . .

It is urged, that Congress has not, by this act of incorporation, created the faculty of trading in money; that it had anterior existence, and may be carried on by a private individual, or company, as well as by a corporation. As this profession or business may be taxed, regulated, or restrained, when conducted by an individual, it may, likewise, be taxed, regulated, or restrained, when conducted by a corporation.

The general correctness of these propositions need not be controverted. Their particular application to the question before the Court, is alone to be considered. We do not maintain that the corporate character of the Bank exempts its operations from the action of State authority. If an individual were to be endowed with the same faculties, for the same purposes, he would be equally protected in the exercise of those faculties. . . .

Notes and Comments 1.9. Considering *McCulloch* and *Osborn*, would it be constitutional for the federal government to incorporate *private* commercial banks, owned and operated by individuals for profit? Does *Osborn* resolve this question?

1.10. *Jacksonian opposition to the Second Bank.* In 1828 Andrew Jackson was elected president. His constituency small merchants, farmers, laborers and other populists were united in their opposition to the Second Bank. In his 1829 message to the Congress, Jackson indicated that he was opposed to extension of the Bank's charter beyond its expiration of 1836. In the face of this opposition, Bank supporters in Congress passed a rechartering bill in 1832, and the President vetoed it.[7] The Congress failed to override the veto, and the Treasury Department began to withdraw federal government funds from the Bank and to deposit them with state banks.[8] Distrusting bank notes, the Jackson Administration undertook to bring specie back into active circulation. For example, it issued in the "Specie Circular" in July 1836, requiring that payment for sales of public land be made only in gold and silver.

1.11. *State banks and the depression of 1837.* Regaining their freedom from discipline with the eclipse of the Second Bank, state banks began to overissue bank notes. This situation of course affected the banks' creditworthiness and was doubtless one of the cause of a depression in 1837. As the effects of the depression spread, a wave of bank failures over a five-year period wiped out hundreds of state banks. In 1837 Martin Van Buren, who had been a close adviser to Jackson, was elected president, and he endorsed a legislative proposal for an independent treasury system to hold all government deposits–effectively withdrawing the federal government from the state banking system. The Independent Treasury Act was signed into law by Van Buren in 1840, and reenacted in 1846.[9] No further intervention of the federal government into banking regulation would be undertaken until the Civil War.[10]

1.12. *Creating a national banking system: Civil War legislation.* Prosecution of the Civil War required not only guns and men to carry them, but money and credit to pay for them. The first conventional efforts by Treasury Secretary Salmon P. Chase to finance the expenses of the war through the sale of government-issued debt proved inadequate as the war dragged on. Eventually Chase developed a plan that called for authorizing the creation of national banks, which would be required to purchase government bonds as a condition of their issuing bank notes. The National Currency Act was passed in 1863 and significantly amended in June 1864,[11] containing the core provisions of what eventually became the National Bank Act ("NBA").[12] Thus, the first step in the creation of a national banking system in the United States was simply a matter of expediency. Another important feature of Chase's plan was to tax the state-chartered banks out of their lead role in banking. This feature was challenged before the Supreme Court–by which time *Chase* was Chief Justice. Based on the Court's opinion in *Veazie Bank*, could the federal government have eliminated state-chartered banks altogether, creating a unified, national banking system?

---

7. Veto Message, July 10, 1832, *reprinted in*, 2 H. E. KROOSS (ED.), DOCUMENTARY HISTORY OF BANKING AND CURRENCY IN THE UNITED STATES 21 (1983 ED.).

8. For an historical discussion of the events following the veto of the rechartering bill, see 1 H. E. KROOSS (ED.), DOCUMENTARY HISTORY OF BANKING AND CURRENCY IN THE UNITED STATES 655-657 (1969 ED.).

9. In the presidential election of November 1840, Van Buren was defeated by William Henry Harrison, and the Independent Treasury Act was repealed in 1841. It was reenacted in 1846, under the Democratic administration of James K. Polk.

10. The system of subtreasuries created by the Independent Treasury Act would continue until subtreasury functions were transferred to the Treasury itself and the Federal reserve banks, after passage of the General Appropriations Act of May 1920.

11. Act of June 3, 1864, c. 106, 13 Stat. 99 (1864) (codified at scattered sections of 12 U.S.C.).

12. Act of June 20, 1874, c. 343, § 1, 18 Stat. 123 (1874) (codified at 12 U.S.C. § 38).

Veazie Bank v. Fenno

75 U.S. 533 (1869)

The CHIEF JUSTICE delivered the opinion of the court.

[Veazie Bank, chartered by Maine, had refused to pay the 10 percent tax applicable to state bank notes in circulation, arguing that the tax was unconstitutional. Fenno, a federal tax collector, levied against the bank, which paid under protest. The bank brought suit against Fenno.]

The necessity of adequate provision for the financial exigencies created by the late rebellion, suggested to the administrative and legislative departments of the government important changes in the systems of currency and taxation which had hitherto prevailed. These changes, more or less distinctly shown in administrative recommendations, took form and substance in legislative acts. We have now to consider, within a limited range, those which relate to circulating notes and the taxation of circulation. . . .

[The opinion describes the various legislative enactments passed between July 1861 through March 1865. The last provided "that every National banking association, State bank, or State banking association, shall pay a tax of ten per centum on the amount of the notes of any State bank, or State banking association, paid out by them after the 1st day of July, 1866." That provision was reenacted, with more extended application, in July 1866.]

The constitutionality of this last provision is now drawn in question. . . .

In support of the position that the act of Congress, so far as it provides for the levy and collection of this tax, is repugnant to the Constitution, two propositions have been argued with much force and earnestness.

The first is that the tax in question is a direct tax, and has not been apportioned among the States agreeably to the Constitution.

The second is that the act imposing the tax impairs a franchise granted by the State, and that Congress has no power to pass any law with that intent or effect.

. . . The tax under consideration is a tax on bank circulation, and may very well be classed under the head of duties [*i.e.*, a type of "indirect," transactional tax]. Certainly it is not, in the sense of the Constitution, a direct tax. It may be said to come within the same category of taxation as the tax on incomes of insurance companies, which this court, as the last term, in the case of *Pacific Insurance Company v. Soule*[a] held not to be a direct tax.

Is it, then, a tax on a franchise granted by a State, which Congress, upon any principle exempting the reserved powers of the States from impairment by taxation, must be held to have no authority to lay and collect?

We do not say that there may not be such a tax. It may be admitted that the reserved rights of the States, such as the right to pass laws, to give effect to laws through executive action, to administer justice through the courts, and to employ all necessary agencies for legitimate purposes of State government, are not proper subjects of the taxing power of Congress. But it cannot be admitted that franchises granted by a State are necessarily exempt from taxation; for franchises are property, often very valuable and productive property; and when not conferred for the purpose of giving effect to some reserved power of a State, seem to be as property objects of taxation as any other property.

But in the case before us the object of taxation is not the franchise of the bank, but property created, or contracts made and issued under the franchise, or power to issue bank bills. A railroad company, in the exercise of its corporate franchises, issues freight receipts,

---

a. 74 U.S. 433 (1868).

bills of lading, and passenger tickets; and it cannot be doubted that the organization of railroads is quite as important to the State as the organization of banks. But it will hardly be questioned that these contracts of the company are objects of taxation within the powers of Congress, and not exempted by any relation to the State which granted the charter of the railroad. And it seems difficult to distinguish the taxation of notes issued for circulation from the taxation of these railroad contracts. Both descriptions of contracts are means of profit to the corporations which issue them; and both, as we think, may properly be made contributory to the public revenue.

It is insisted, however, that the tax in the case before us is excessive, and so excessive as to indicate a purpose on the part of Congress to destroy the franchise of the bank, and is, therefore, beyond the constitutional power of Congress.

The first answer to this is that the judicial cannot prescribe to the legislative departments of the government limitations upon the exercise of its acknowledged powers. The power to tax may be exercised oppressively upon persons, but the responsibility of the legislature is not to the courts, but to the people by whom its members are elected. So if a particular tax bears heavily upon a corporation, or a class of corporations, it cannot, for that reason only, be pronounced contrary to the Constitution.

But there is another answer which vindicates equally the wisdom and the power of Congress.

It cannot be doubted that under the Constitution the power to provide a circulation of coin is given to Congress. And it is settled by the uniform practice of the government and by repeated decisions, that Congress may constitutionally authorize the emission of bills of credit. It is not important here, to decide whether the quality of legal tender, in payment of debts, can be constitutionally imparted to these bills; it is enough to say, that there can be no question of the power of the government to emit them; to make them receivable in payment of debts to itself; to fit them for use by those who see fit to use them in all the transactions of commerce; to provide for their redemption; to make them a currency, uniform in value and description, and convenient and useful for circulation. These powers, until recently, were only partially and occasionally exercised. Lately, however, they have been called into full activity, and Congress had undertaken to supply a currency for the entire country.

. . . [T]his currency . . . now consists of coin, of United States notes, and of the notes of the National banks. Both descriptions of notes may be properly described as bills of credit, for both are furnished by the government; both are issued on the credit of the government; and the government is responsible for the redemption of both; primarily as to the first description, and immediately upon default of the bank, as to the second. When these bills shall be made convertible into coin, at the will of the holder, this currency will, perhaps, satisfy the wants of the community, in respect of a circulating medium, as perfectly as any mixed currency that can be devised.

Having thus, in the exercise of undisputed constitutional powers, undertaken to provide a currency for the whole country, it cannot be questioned that Congress may, constitutionally, secure the benefit of it to the people by appropriate legislation. To this end, Congress had denied the quality of legal tender to foreign coins, and have provided by law against the imposition of counterfeit and base coin on the community. To the same end, Congress may restrain, by suitable enactments, the circulation as money of any notes not issued under its own authority. Without this power, indeed, its attempt to secure a sound and uniform currency for the country must be futile.

Viewed in this light, as well as in the other light of a duty on contracts or property, we cannot doubt the constitutionality of the tax under consideration.

NELSON, J. dissenting.

The tenth amendment to the Constitution is as follows: "The powers not delegated to the United States by the Constitution, nor prohibited by it to the States, are reserved to the States respectively, or to the people." On looking into the Constitution, it will be found that there is no clause or provision which either expressly, or by reasonable implication, delegates this power to the Federal Government, which originally belonged to the States, nor which prohibits it to them. In the discussions on the subject of the creation of the first Bank of the United States, in the first Congress, and in the Cabinet of Washington, in 1790 and 1791, no question was made as to the constitutionality of the State banks. The only doubt that existed, and which divided the opinion of the most eminent statesmen of the day, many of whom had just largely participated in the formation of the Constitution, the government under which they were then engaged in organizing, was, whether or not Congress possessed a concurrent power to incorporate a banking institution of the United States?

Mr. Hamilton, in his celebrated report on a National bank to the House of Representatives, discusses at some length the question, whether or not it would be expedient to substitute the Bank of North America, located in Philadelphia, and which had accepted a charter from the legislature of Pennsylvania, in the place of organizing a new bank. And, although he finally came to the conclusion to organize a new one, there is not a suggestion, or intimation, as to the illegality or unconstitutionality of this State bank. . . .

But, in addition to the above recognition of the State banks, the question of their constitutionality came directly before this court in the case of *Briscoe v. The Bank of the Commonwealth of Kentucky*.[b]

. . . The court, after the fullest consideration, held that the States possessed the power to grant charters to State banks; that the power was incident to sovereignty; and that there was no limitation in the Federal Constitution on its exercise by the States. . . . The decision in this case was affirmed in *Woodruff v. Trapnall*;[c] in *Darrington v. The Bank of Alabama*[d] and in *Curran v. State of Arkansas*.[e]

. . . [T]he power to incorporate banks was not surrendered to the Federal Government, but reserved to the States; and it follows that the Constitution itself protects them, or should protect them, from any encroachment upon this right. As to the powers thus reserved, the States are as supreme as before they entered into the Union, and are entitled to the unrestrained exercise of them. . . .

Notes and Comments 1.13. *Veazie Bank* may resolve the issue of the constitutionality of tax provisions of the Civil War legislation, but what about the constitutionality of federal charters for "national banks"? This issue is addressed in the following excerpted case.

Farmers' National Bank v. Dearing

91 U.S. 29 (1875)

Mr. Justice Swayne delivered the opinion of the Court.

[The case involved interpretation of the NBA provisions imposing penalties for

---

b. 36 U.S. (11 Pet.) 257 (1837).

c. 51 U.S. 190 (1850).

d. 54 U.S. 12 (1851).

e. 56 U.S. 304 (1853).

charging a usurious rate of interest. This question is discussed in Chapter 5, § 2, *infra*. In the course of its discussion, however, the Court made the following observations about the constitutionality of the NBA.]

The constitutionality of the act of 1864 is not questioned. It rests on the same principle as the act creating the second bank of the United States. The reasoning of Secretary Hamilton and of this court in *McCulloch v. Maryland* . . . and in *Osborne v. The Bank of the United States* . . . , therefore, applies. The national banks organized under the act are instruments designed to be used to aid the government in the administration of an important branch of the public service. They are means appropriate to that end. Of the degree of the necessity which existed for creating them Congress is the sole judge.

Being such means, brought into existence for this purpose, and intended to be so employed, the States can exercise no control over them, nor in any wise affect their operation, except insofar as Congress may see proper to permit. Anything beyond this is "an abuse, because it is a usurpation of power which a single State cannot give." Against the national will "the States have no power, by taxation or otherwise, to retard, impede, burthen, or in any manner control, the operation of the constitutional laws enacted by Congress to carry into execution the powers vested in the General Government." *Bank of the United States v. McCulloch, supra*; *Weston and Others v. Charleston*, 27 U.S. (2 Pet.) 466; *Brown v. Maryland*, 25 U.S. (12 Wheat.) 419; *Dobbins v. Erie County*, 41 U.S. (16 Pet.) 435.

The power to create carries with it the power to preserve. The latter is a corollary from the former.

The principle announced in the authorities cited is indispensable to the efficiency, the independence, and indeed to the beneficial existence, of the General Government; otherwise it would be liable, in the discharge of its most important trusts, to be annoyed and thwarted by the will or caprice of every State in the Union. Infinite confusion would follow. The government would be reduced to a pitiable condition of weakness. The form might remain, but the vital essence would have departed. In the complex system of policy which obtains in this country, the powers of government may be divided into four classes:

Those which belong exclusively to the States;

Those which belong exclusively to the National Government;

Those which may be exercised concurrently and independently by both;

And those which may be exercised by the States, but only with the consent, express or implied, of Congress. . . .

The power of the States to tax the existing national banks lies within the category last mentioned.

It must always be born in mind that the Constitution of the United States, "and the laws which shall be made in pursuance thereof," are "the supreme law of the land" (Const., art. 6), and that this law is as much a part of the law of each State, and as binding upon its authorities and people, as its own local constitution and laws.

Notes and Comments 1.14. *Constitutionality of the National Bank Act.* Recall note 1.9, *supra*. *Farmers' National Bank* cites *McCulloch* and *Osborn* as direct authority for the proposition that the NBA is constitutional, but those two cases were considering the constitutionality of the Second Bank of the United States, a quasi-governmental institution carrying many of the responsibilities of a central bank. Is that what is at stake in *Farmers' National Bank*? *See* 1 MICHAEL P. MALLOY, BANKING LAW AND REGULATION §1.03[A] (2d ed. 2011) (discussing *Farmers' National Bank*). Over-extension of the holdings of these two cases–and particularly of *McCulloch*–is a common occurrence. Consider the following excerpt from a recent Supreme Court decision involving preemption of state consumer protection legislation by the NBA and federal regulations. Is the Court accurate in its characterization of *McCulloch*?

Watters v. Wachovia Bank, N.A.

550 U.S. 1 (2007)

Justice GINSBURG delivered the opinion of the Court.

[Wachovia, a national bank, and its state-chartered mortgage company subsidiary sued the Michigan Commissioner of Insurance and Financial Services seeking declaratory and injunctive relief from state registration and inspection requirements, based on preemption of the state law by the NBA.]

II

A

Nearly two hundred years ago, in *McCulloch v. Maryland,* 4 Wheat. 316, 4 L.Ed. 579 (1819), this Court held federal law supreme over state law with respect to national banking. Though the bank at issue in *McCulloch* was short-lived, a federal banking system reemerged in the Civil War era. See *Atherton v. FDIC,* 519 U.S. 213, 221-222 (1997); B. Hammond, Banks and Politics in America: from the Revolution to the Civil War (1957). In 1864, Congress enacted the NBA, establishing the system of national banking still in place today. National Bank Act, ch. 106, 13 Stat. 99; *Atherton,* 519 U.S., at 222, *Marquette Nat. Bank of Minneapolis v. First of Omaha Service Corp.,* 439 U.S. 299, 310 (1978). The Act vested in nationally chartered banks enumerated powers and "all such incidental powers as shall be necessary to carry on the business of banking." 12 U.S.C. § 24 Seventh. To prevent inconsistent or intrusive state regulation from impairing the national system, Congress provided: "No national bank shall be subject to any visitorial powers except as authorized by Federal law ...." § 484(a).

Notes and Comments 1.15. *State taxation of national banks. Farmers' National Bank* indicates that the power of states of tax national banks is one which they may exercise "only with the consent, express or implied, of Congress." Explicit consent is currently contained in 12 U.S.C. § 548.

1.16. *Applicability of other state laws.* To what extent are national banks subject to state laws other than those involving taxation? Consider the following excerpt.

Atherton v. Federal Deposit Insurance Corporation

519 U.S. 213 (1997)

Justice BREYER delivered the opinion of the Court.

[The case involved the proper interpretation of 12 U.S.C. § 1821(k), providing a federal cause of action against directors and officers of federally insured depository institutions for gross negligence.]

[I]n 1870 and thereafter this Court held that federally chartered banks are subject to state law. *See National Bank* v. *Commonwealth*, 9 Wall. 353, 361 (1869). In *National Bank* the Court distinguished *McCulloch* by recalling that Maryland's taxes were "used ... to destroy," and it added that federal banks

> "are subject to the laws of the State, and are governed in their daily course of

> business far more by the laws of the State than of the nation. All their contracts are governed and construed by State laws. Their acquisition and transfer of property, their right to collect their debts, and their liability to be sued for debts, are all based on State law. It is only when the State law incapacitates the banks from discharging their duties to the government that it becomes unconstitutional." 9 Wall., at 362.

The Court subsequently found numerous state laws applicable to federally chartered banks. *See, e.g., Davis* v. *Elmira Savings Bank*, 161 U.S. 275, 290 (1896) ("Nothing, of course, in this opinion is intended to deny the operation of general and undiscriminating state laws on the contracts of national banks, so long as such laws do not conflict with the letter or the general objects and purposes of Congressional legislation"); *First Nat. Bank in St. Louis* v. *Missouri*, 263 U.S. 640, 656 (1924) (national banks "are subject to the laws of a State in respect of their affairs unless such laws interfere with the purposes of their creation, tend to impair or destroy their efficiency as federal agencies or conflict with the paramount law of the United States"); *Wichita Royalty Co.* v. *City Nat. Bank of Wichita Falls*, 306 U.S. 103 (1939) (applying state law to tort claim by depositor against directors of a national bank); *Anderson Nat. Bank* v. *Luckett*, 321 U.S. 233, 248 (1944) ("National banks are subject to state laws, unless those laws infringe the national banking laws or impose an undue burden on the performance of the banks' functions"); *California Fed. Sav. & Loan Assn.* v. *Guerra*, 479 U.S. 272 (1987) (applying state employment discrimination law to federally chartered savings and loan association).

Notes and Comments 1.17. *Modern developments.* The existence of state chartering authorities and of the Comptroller of the Currency, the federal charterer under the NBA, are the only features of contemporary bank regulation that existed prior to the second decade of the twentieth century. From that time forward, the involvement of the federal government in banking regulation became increasingly complex and pervasive. The time line in Figure 1.3, *infra*, gives some indication of these developments.

Figure 1.3
Modern Developments in U.S. Bank Regulation

1907 *Monetary Panic of 1907*

1913 **Federal Reserve Act** *Federal Reserve System created*

1919 **Edge Act** *international banking corporations authorized*

1927 **McFadden Act** *limited branching by national banks permitted*

1929 *stock market collapse*

1932 **Federal Home Loan Act** *Federal Home Loan Bank Board established*

1933—**Banking Act** *(Glass Steagall Act)*

1934—**National Housing Act** **Securities Act**

1935 **Banking Act** **Securities Exchange Act** **Home Owner's Loan Act** **Federal Credit Union Act**

1940—**Investment Company Act**
Investment Advisers Act

Figure 1.3–continued

■1956 **Bank Holding Company Act** *(bank holding companies subject to federal supervision)*

■1960 **Bank Merger Act** *(bank mergers subject to federal approval)*

■1962 **Bank Service Corporation Act** *(certain nonbanking subsidiaries authorized)*

■1964 **Securities Acts Amendments**

■1966—**Bank Merger Act Amendment**
Financial Institutions Supervisory Act
Bank Holding Company Act Amendments

■1968 **Savings and Loan Holding Company Act Amendments**

■1970 **Bank Holding Company Act Amendments**

■1977 **Community Reinvestment Act**

■1978—**International Banking Act**
Regulatory and Interest Rate Control Act

■1980 **Deregulation and Monetary Control Act**; *S&L crisis begins to emerge*

■1982—*international debt crisis emerges*
Garn-St Germain Depository Institutions Act
(deregulation of S&L activities)

■1987 **Competitive Equality Banking Act**

Figure 1.3–continued

□1989 **Financial Institutions Reform, Recovery, and Enforcement Act**
□ *(FHLBB & FSLIC abolished; OTS created)*
■1991——**FDIC Improvements Act**
□ **RTC Improvements Act**
□
■1994——**Interstate Banking and Branching Efficiency Act**
□ **Community Development and Regulatory Improvement Act**
■1996 **Economic Growth and Regulatory Paperwork Reduction Act**
□
■1998 **Credit Union Membership Access Act**
■1999 **Gramm-Leach-Bliley Act**
■2000 **American Homeownership and Economic Opportunity Act**
■2001 *terrorist attack on the United States*; **USA PATRIOT Act**
□2002
□2003
□2004 **Federal Deposit Insurance Reform Act of 2005**
□2005 **Federal Deposit Insurance Reform Conforming Amendments Act of 2005**
■2006—— **Financial Services Regulatory Relief Act of 2006**
□2007
■2008—— *markets collapse*; **Housing and Economic Recovery Act of 2008**
■2009 **Emergency Economic Stabilization Act of 2008**
■2010 **American Recovery and Reinvestment Act**
Dodd-Frank Wall Street Reform and Consumer Protection Act

3. Current Regulatory Environment

Notes and Comments 1.18. *Commercial banks*. This section begins with a survey of the entities subject to the contemporary bank regulation system. This survey cannot be complete, however, until we have also catalogued the regulators with authority over these entities.[13] Traditional categories like *commercial bank*, *savings bank*, *saving and loan association*, and *credit union*–now often referred to generically as *depository institutions*–are as much defined by the regulators to whom they are subject as they are by the type of depository institution that they happen to be. By the same token, the regulators cannot be adequately understood without reference to the institutions that they regulate. To begin with, we may locate *depository institutions* in relation to other types of *financial intermediaries* as illustrated by Figure 1.4, *infra*. Commercial banks are to be distinguished from savings associations (*i.e.*, savings banks and savings and loan associations–sometimes referred to as "thrift institutions" or "thrifts"). Unlike thrifts, commercial banks are authorized to offer the full range of banking services, including demand accounts (*i.e.*, checking accounts) for business and personal use, savings and time deposits, investment and loan services, trust department services, and the like. Commercial banks are also to be distinguished from in-

13. *See* material beginning with Note 1.29, *infra* (discussing depository institution regulators).

vestment banks, financial intermediaries that underwrite and distribute securities and often act as brokers and dealers in securities already distributed. From 1933 to 1999, federal law prohibited most affiliations between commercial and investment banks.[14] Within the depository institutions sector, commercial banks do have the broadest range of powers, overlapping those of other depository institutions. Would it be possible for a state to limit the powers of a commercial bank in order to protect the competitive position of other types of depository institutions? Consider the cases following the next figure.

Figure 1.4
Types of Depository Institutions

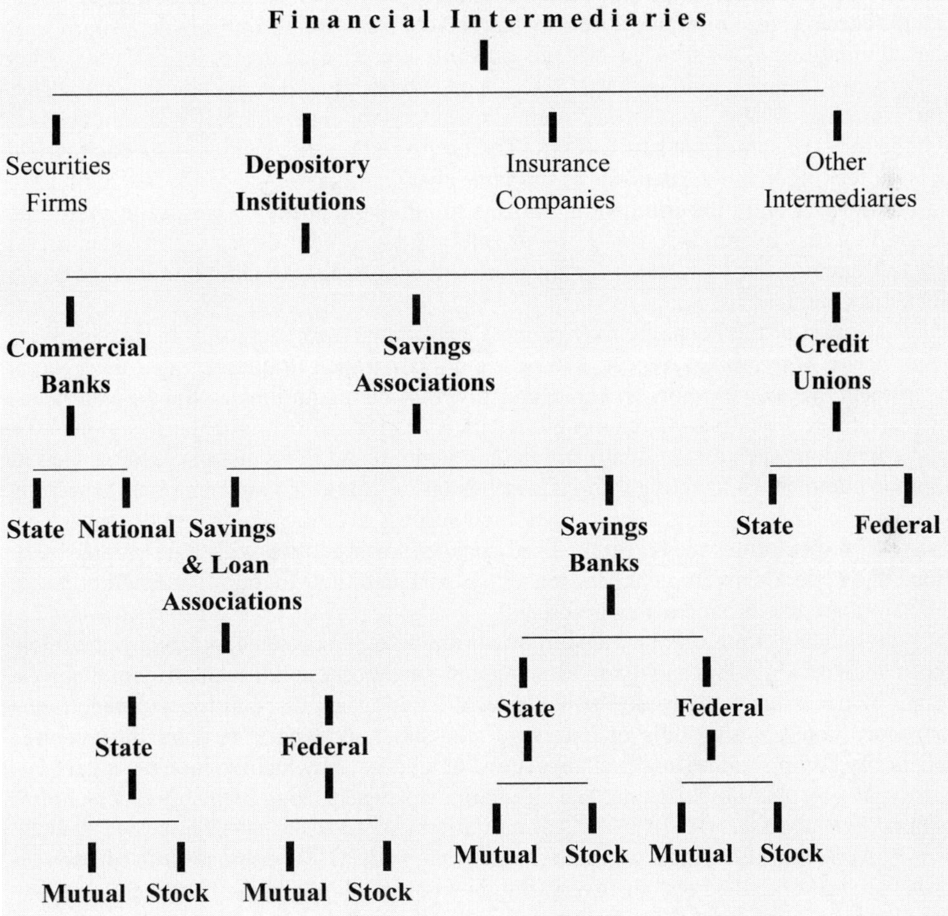

14. The Gramm-Leach-Bliley Act, Pub. L. No. 106-102, Nov. 12, 1999, 113 Stat. 1338 (1999) (codified at scattered sections of 12, 15, 16, 18 U.S.C.) (GLBA), eliminated affiliation prohibitions in most cases. For discussion of the GLBA, see Note 1.60, *infra*.

Franklin Nat. Bank v. New York

347 U.S. 373 (1954)

Opinion of the Court by Mr. Justice JACKSON, announced by Mr. Justice FRANKFURTER.

This appeal . . . presents the narrow question whether federal statutes which authorize national banks to receive savings deposits conflict with New York legislation which prohibits them from using the word "saving" or "savings" in their advertising or business. We think the federal and state statutes are incompatible, and in such circumstances the policy of the State must yield.

It is the policy of New York to charter and foster the mutual savings bank, a nonprofit institution whose earnings inure to the benefit of depositors rather than to stockholders. These institutions have a long history as relatively stable and safe depositaries for the accumulations of thrifty New Yorkers and as a source of credit for limited uses. They have grown to be an important part of New York's banking and economic structure. That State also charters the savings and loan association, an institution of a different type, intended to serve somewhat similar ends. The Legislature was concerned lest commercial banks, in seeking to induce deposits of the same character, so use the word "savings" as to lead uninformed and indiscriminating persons to believe that they were dealing with the chartered savings institutions. Hence, by its Banking Law, New York has forbidden use of the word "savings," or its variants, by any banks other than its own chartered savings banks and savings and loan associations.

However, the Federal Government is a rival chartering authority for banks. Since *McCulloch v. Maryland*, 4 Wheat. 316, it has not been open to question that the Federal Government may constitutionally create and govern such institutions within the states. The United States has set up a system of national banks as federal instrumentalities to perform various functions such as providing circulating medium and government credit, as well as financing commerce and acting as private depositaries. Some of their functions, especially as a source for federal credit, depend upon their success in attracting private deposits. That these federal institutions may be at no disadvantage in competition with state-created institutions, the Federal Government has frequently expanded their functions and authority. Of such nature are the measures now before us.

. . . The National Bank Act authorizes national banks to receive deposits without qualification or limitation, and it provides that they shall possess "all such incidental powers as shall be necessary to carry on the business of banking; by discounting and negotiating promissory notes, drafts, bills of exchange, and other evidences of debt; by receiving deposits; by buying and selling exchange, coin, and bullion; by loaning money on personal security; and by obtaining, issuing, and circulating notes according to the provisions of this chapter."[5]

Appellant believing it was authorized by the Federal Government to do so, used the words "saving" and "savings" in advertising, in signs displayed in the bank, on its deposit and withdrawal slips, and in its annual reports. It is beyond question that appellant violated the State's prohibition if it is a valid one.

The Attorney General of the State initiated this case [in state trial court] by a complaint alleging such violations, seeking a broad injunction. The trial accumulated a large record devoted mainly to the merits and demerits of the New York legislation and its conse-

---

5. R.S. § 5136, 12 U.S.C. (1952 ed.) § 24 (seventh).

quences upon banks and depositors. The trial court found no purposeful deception of the public. It held that the advertising and other use of the forbidden terms were in pursuit of implied and incidental powers conferred upon national banks by the Acts of Congress and that the New York statute in conflict with them must yield. The Appellate Division disagreed and directed a permanent injunction prohibiting the use of the term. The Court of Appeals affirmed. . . . Modern competition for business finds advertising one of the most usual and useful of weapons. We cannot believe that the incidental powers granted national banks should be construed so narrowly as to preclude the use of advertising in any branch of their authorized business. It would require some affirmative indications to justify an interpretation that would permit a national bank to engage in a business but gave no right to let the public know about it.

Appellee does not object to national banks taking savings deposits or even to their advertising that fact so long as they do not use the word "savings." It takes the position that this word is a misnomer in New York because depositors there, as a result of the state statute, have come to think of savings accounts as something entirely different from those to which the Federal Act is referring. Regardless of whether New Yorkers are really misled by the description, the fact is that Congress has given a particular label to this type of account. Whatever peculiar meaning the word may have in New York, it is a word which aptly describes, in a national sense, the type of business carried on by these national banks. They do accept and pay interest on time deposits of people's savings, and they must be deemed to have the right to advertise that fact by using the commonly understood description which Congress has specifically selected. We find no indication that Congress intended to make this phase of national banking subject to local restrictions, as it has done by express language in several other instances.

There appears to be a clear conflict between the law of New York and the law of the Federal Government. We cannot resolve conflicts of authority by our judgment as to the wisdom or need of either conflicting policy. The compact between the states creating the Federal Government resolves them as a matter of supremacy. However wise or needful New York's policy, a matter as to which we express no judgment, it must give way to the contrary federal policy.

Barnett Bank of Marion County, N.A. v. Nelson

517 U.S. 25 (1996)

Justice BREYER delivered the opinion of the Court.

[The case considered whether a federal statute that permitted national banks to sell insurance in small towns preempted Florida statute that forbad them to do so. For the Court's analysis of this issue, see Chapter 5, § 7, *infra*. To answer this question, the Court had to consider both ordinary preemption principles and a special federal anti-preemption rule that applied to federal and state statutes that regulated insurance. This excerpt involves the Court's discussion of ordinary preemption principles.]

We . . . begin by asking whether, in the absence of [the special preemption] rule, we should construe the Federal Statute to pre-empt the State Statute.This question is basically one of congressional intent. Did Congress, in enacting the Federal Statute, intend to exercise its constitutionally delegated authority to set aside the laws of a State? If so, the Supremacy Clause requires courts to follow federal, not state, law. U.S. Const., Art. VI, cl. 2; *see California Fed. Sav. & Loan Assn. v. Guerra*, 479 U.S. 272, 280-281 (1987) (reviewing pre-emption doctrine).

Sometimes courts, when facing the pre-emption question, find language in the federal statute that reveals an explicit congressional intent to pre-empt state law. *E.g., Jones v. Rath Packing Co.*, 430 U.S. 519, 525, 530531 (1977). More often, explicit pre-emption language does not appear, or does not directly answer the question. In that event, courts must consider whether the federal statute's "structure and purpose," or nonspecific statutory language, nonetheless reveal a clear, but implicit, pre-emptive intent. *Id.*, at 525; *Fidelity Fed. Sav. & Loan Assn. v. De la Cuesta*, 458 U.S. 141, 152-153 (1982). A federal statute, for example, may create a scheme of federal regulation "so pervasive as to make reasonable the inference that Congress left no room for the States to supplement it." *Rice v. Santa Fe Elevator Corp.*, 331 U.S. 218, 230 (1947). Alternatively, federal law may be in "irreconcilable conflict" with state law. *Rice v. Norman Williams Co.*, 458 U.S. 654, 659 (1982). Compliance with both statutes, for example, may be a "physical impossibility," *Florida Lime & Avocado Growers, Inc. v. Paul*, 373 U.S. 132, 142-143 (1963); or, the state law may "stan[d] as an obstacle to the accomplishment and execution of the full purposes and objectives of Congress." *Hines v. Davidowitz*, 312 U.S. 52, 67 (1941).

In this case we must ask whether or not the Federal and State Statutes are in "irreconcilable conflict." The two statutes do not impose directly conflicting duties on national banks–as they would, for example, if the federal law said, "you must sell insurance," while the state law said, "you may not." Nonetheless, the Federal Statute authorizes national banks to engage in activities that the State Statute expressly forbids. Thus, the State's prohibition of those activities would seem to "stan[d] as an obstacle to the accomplishment" of one of the Federal Statute's purposes–unless, of course, that federal purpose is to grant the bank only a very *limited* permission, that is, permission to sell insurance *to the extent that state law also grants permission to do so.*

That is what the State of Florida and its supporting amici argue. They say that the Federal Statute grants national banks a permission that is limited to circumstances where state law is not to the contrary. In their view, the Federal Statute removes only federal legal obstacles, not state legal obstacles, to the sale of insurance by national banks. But we do not find this, or the State's related, ordinary pre-emption arguments convincing.

For one thing, the Federal Statute's language suggests a broad, not a limited, permission. That language says, without relevant qualification, that national banks "may ... act as the agent" for insurance sales. 12 U.S.C. §92. It specifically refers to "rules and regulations" that will govern such sales, while citing as their source not state law, but the federal Comptroller of the Currency. . . . It also specifically refers to state regulation, while limiting that reference to licensing–not of banks or insurance agents, but of the insurance companies whose policies the bank, as insurance agent, will sell. . . .

For another thing, the Federal Statute says that its grant of authority to sell insurance is an "addition to the *powers* now vested by law in national [banks]." . . . (emphasis added). In using the word "powers," the statute chooses a legal concept that, in the context of national bank legislation, has a history. That history is one of interpreting grants of both enumerated and incidental "powers" to national banks as grants of authority not normally limited by, but rather ordinarily pre-empting, contrary state law. *See, e.g., First Nat. Bank of San Jose v. California*, 262 U.S. 366, 368-369 (1923) (national banks' "power" to receive deposits pre-empts contrary state escheat law); *Easton v. Iowa*, 188 U.S. 220, 229-230 (1903) (national banking system normally "independent, so far as powers conferred are concerned, of state legislation"). . . .

Thus, this Court, in a case quite similar to this one, held that a federal statute permitting, but not requiring, national banks to receive savings deposits, pre-empts a state statute prohibiting certain state and national banks from using the word "savings" in their advertising. *Franklin Nat. Bank v. New York*, 347 U.S. 373, 375-379 (1954) (Federal Reserve

Act provision that national banks "may continue . . . to receive . . . savings deposits" read as "declaratory of the right of a national bank to enter into or remain in that type of business"). *See also De la Cuesta, supra*, at 154-159 (1982) (federal regulation permitting, but not requiring, national banks to include in mortgage contracts a debt accelerating "due on sale" clause, pre-empts a state law forbidding the use of such a clause); *cf. Lawrence County v. Lead-Deadwood School Dist. No. 40-1*, 469 U.S. 256 (1985) (federal statute providing that local government units "may" expend federal funds for any governmental purpose pre-empts state law restricting their expenditure).

In defining the pre-emptive scope of statutes and regulations granting a power to national banks, these cases take the view that normally Congress would not want States to forbid, or to impair significantly, the exercise of a power that Congress explicitly granted. To say this is not to deprive States of the power to regulate national banks, where (unlike here) doing so does not prevent or significantly interfere with the national bank's exercise of its powers. *See, e.g., Anderson Nat. Bank v. Luckett*, 321 U.S. 233, 247-252 (1944) (state statute administering abandoned deposit accounts did not "unlawful[ly] encroac[h] on the rights and privileges of national banks"); *McClellan v. Chipman*, 164 U.S. 347, 358 (1896) (application to national banks of state statute forbidding certain real estate transfers by insolvent transferees would not "destro[y] or hampe[r]" national banks' functions); *National Bank v. Commonwealth*, 9 Wall. 353, 362 (1870) (national banks subject to state law that does not "interfere with, or impair [national banks'] efficiency in performing the functions by which they are designed to serve [the Federal] Government").

Nor do these cases control the interpretation of federal banking statutes that accompany a grant of an explicit power with an explicit statement that the exercise of that power is subject to state law. *See, e.g.*, 12 U.S.C. §36(c) (McFadden Act) (authorizing national banks to operate branches, but only where state law authorizes state banks to do so); §92a (Comptroller of Currency may grant fiduciary powers "by special permit to national banks applying therefor, when not in contravention of State or local law"). Not surprisingly, this Court has interpreted those explicit provisions to mean what they say. ...

But, . . . where Congress has not expressly conditioned the grant of "power" upon a grant of state permission, the Court has ordinarily found that no such condition applies. In *Franklin Nat. Bank*, the Court made this point explicit. It held that Congress did not intend to subject national banks' power to local restrictions, because the federal power-granting statute there in question contained "no indication that Congress [so] intended ... as it has done by *express language* in several other instances." 347 U.S., at 378, and n. 7 (emphasis added) (collecting examples).

The Federal Statute before us, as in *Franklin Nat. Bank*, explicitly grants a national bank an authorization, permission, or power. And, as in *Franklin Nat. Bank*, it contains no "indication" that Congress intended to subject that power to local restriction. Thus, the Court's discussion in *Franklin Nat. Bank*, the holding of that case, and the other precedent we have cited above, strongly argue for a similar interpretation here–a broad interpretation of the word "may" that does not condition federal permission upon that of the State.

Notes and Comments 1.19. *Federal preemption of state bank regulation.* Federal preemption doctrine has become increasingly important as a tool for consolidation of federal authority over bank regulatory policy.[15] The approach taken in *Franklin National Bank* and

15. *See, e.g., American Bankers Association v. Lockyer*, 239 F.Supp.2d 1000 (E.D.Cal. 2002) (preempting California credit card regulations); *Wells Fargo Bank of Texas NA v. James,* 321 F.3d 488 (5th Cir. 2003) (preempting Texas "par value" statute prohibiting fee for cashing check of non-depositor); *Flager v. Yonkers S&L Assn, FA*, 396 F.3d 178 (2d Cir. 2005) (preempting New York law

followed in *Barnett Bank* is frequently utilized to preempt a widening range of state regulatory law that would otherwise be applicable to national banks and their operating subsidiaries.[16] Since the earlier 2000s, the OCC has been engaged in a concerted effort to pursue a broadly applicable strategy of preemption with respect to such state laws.[17] In *Watters v. Wachovia Bank, N.A.*,[18] the Supreme Court accepted the OCC's conception of broad preemptive power on the part of the federal regulators, even with respect to the regulation of *nonbanking* subsidiaries of federally chartered banking entities. In 2010, however, Title X of the Dodd-Frank Wall Street Reform and Consumer Protection Act appears to repudiate the broad preemptive effect of *Watters* and its progeny.[19] For excerpts from *Watters* and accompanying discussion, see Chapter 5, § 2.d, *infra.*

1.20. *"Savings associations" and FIRREA.* The Financial Institutions Reform, Recovery, and Enforcement Act of 1989 (FIRREA)[20] initiated a number of significant changes in the regulatory environment. Among other things, FIRREA established the use in federal banking law of the generic term "savings associations," defined to include federally chartered S&Ls and savings banks, state-chartered building and loan associations, S&Ls, homestead associations, cooperative banks (other than those that are "State banks" under 12 U.S.C. § 1813(a)(2)) and "any corporation (other than a bank) that the [FDIC] Board of Directors and the Director of the Office of Thrift Supervision jointly determine to be operating in substantially the same manner as a savings association." FIRREA, § 204(b) (codified at 12 U.S.C. § 1813(b)).[21] The term had already made its way into bank regulatory

---

requiring payment of interest on escrow funds); *Am. Bankers Assn v. Gould*, 412 F.3d 1081 (9th Cir. 2005) (preempting affiliate-sharing prohibition of California Financial Information Privacy Act by Fair Credit Reporting Act).

16. For extended discussion of the effects of federal preemption policy on state consumer protection laws, see 1 MICHAEL P. MALLOY, BANKING LAW AND REGULATION § 1.39 (1994 & Cum. Supp).

17. Indeed, a February 2003 notice of proposed rulemaking by the OCC proposes revisions to the interpretive provisions of its regulations that would have the effect of strengthening preemption in this regard, by invoking the exclusive visitorial powers of the federal regulator under 12 U.S.C. § 484. *See Rules, Policies and Procedures for Corporate Activities*, 68 Fed. Reg. 6363 (2003) (to be codified at, *inter alia*, 12 C.F.R. § 7.400(a)(3)(I)-(ii), (b)). It would be fair to say that the discussion of the proposed revisions to § 7.400 in the Supplementary Information section of the notice reads like the final draft of an *amicus* brief in favor of generally applicable preemption of state law with respect to national banks and their operating subsidiaries. *Compare* 68 Fed. Reg. at 6366-6370 (arguing for exclusive, preemptive authority of OCC under visitorial provisions of 12 U.S.C. § 484) *with Wells Fargo Bank, N.A. v. Boutris*, — F.Supp.2d —, 2003 WL 1220131 (E.D.Cal. 2003) (granting preliminary injunction against enforcement of state law against national bank operating subsidiary; discussing OCC *amicus* brief preemption arguments). For analysis and criticism of the OCC preemption policy, see Fisher, *Toward a Basal Tenth Amendment: A Riposte to National Bank Preemption of State Consumer Protection Laws*, 29 HARV. J.L. & PUB. POL'Y 981 (2006); Arthur E. Wilmarth, Jr., *The OCC's Preemption Rules Exceed the Agency's Authority and Present a Serious Threat to the Dual Banking System and Consumer Protection*, 23 Ann. Rev. Banking & Fin. L. 225 (2004).

18. 550 U.S. 1 (2007).

19. *See, e.g.*, Dodd-Frank Act §1044 (codified at 12 U.S.C. §25b(b)) (establishing narrow grounds for federal preemption of state consumer protection laws).

20. Pub. L. No. 101-73, 103 Stat. 183 (1989) (codified at scattered sections of 12 and 15 U.S.C.) (FIRREA).

21. The role of the Director of the Office of Thrift Supervision is discussed in Notes 1.36 and 1.38, *infra.*

law of some states.[22]

1.21. *Traditional powers of savings associations.* For much of their history, savings associations were prohibited from engaging in most of the activities permitted to commercial banks, and were limited to personal savings deposits and personal and home mortgage loans. During the 1980s, the range of services which savings associations were permitted to offer has expanded. For the most part, however, commercial banks remain the leaders in full commercial banking.

1.22. *The S&L crisis and its effect on savings association powers.* Adverse economic conditions during the 1970's impaired the profitability of traditional saving xassociation business, such as home mortgage lending. How did these conditions affect the savings associations? Consider the following excerpt.

United States v. Winstar Corporation

518 U.S. 839 (1996)

Justice SOUTER announced the judgment of the Court and delivered an opinion, in which Justice STEVENS and Justice BREYER join, and in which Justice O'CONNOR joins except as to Parts IV-A and IV-B.

[This case involved the enforceability of contracts between the U.S. Government and savings associations or savings and loan holding companies that were acquiring failed savings associations. The federal regulators agreed to give favorable regulatory treatment the acquiring companies in exchange for their assumption of liabilities that threatened to produce claims against the Government as deposit insurer of the failed institutions. Thereafter, Congress changed the relevant law and barred the Government from honoring the agreements. In a portion of the decision excerpted in Chapter 8, § 3, *infra*, the Court held that the terms assigning the risk of regulatory change to the Government were enforceable, and that the Government was therefore liable in damages for breach of the contracts.]

We said in *Fahey v. Mallonee*, 332 U.S. 245, 250 (1947), that "[b]anking is one of the longest regulated and most closely supervised of public callings." That is particularly true of the savings and loan, or "thrift," industry, which has been described as "a federally-conceived and assisted system to provide citizens with affordable housing funds." H.R. Rep. No. 101-54, pt. 1, p. 292 (1989). . . .

The modern savings and loan industry traces its origins to the Great Depression, which brought default on 40 percent of the Nation's $20 billion in home mortgages and the failure of some 1700 of the nation's approximately 12,000 savings institutions. . . . In the course of the debacle, Congress passed three statutes meant to stabilize the thrift industry. The Federal Home Loan Bank Act created the Federal Home Loan Bank Board (Bank Board), which was authorized to channel funds to thrifts for loans on houses and for preventing foreclosures on them. . . . Next, the Home Owners' Loan Act of 1933 authorized the Bank Board to charter and regulate federal savings and loan associations. . . . Finally, the National Housing Act created the Federal Savings and Loan Insurance Corporation (FSLIC), under the Bank Board's authority, with responsibility to insure thrift deposits and regulate all federally insured thrifts. . . .

The resulting regulatory regime worked reasonably well until the combination of high interest rates and inflation in the late 1970's and early 1980's brought about a second

22. *See* Michael P. Malloy, *Nothing to Fear but FIRREA Itself: Revising and Reshaping the Enforcement Process of Federal Bank Regulation*, 50 Ohio St. L.J. 1117 n. 2 (1989) (discussing California and Florida law).

crisis in the thrift industry. Many thrifts found themselves holding long-term, fixed-rate mortgages created when interest rates were low; when market rates rose, those institutions had to raise the rates they paid to depositors in order to attract funds. . . .

Notes and Comments 1.23. *Broadened powers of savings and loan associations.* The convergence of two factors–relative unprofitability of long-term mortgage loans granted at locked-in interest rates, and increased competition for the investor's funds–caused the S&Ls to search out and develop alternate devices for attracting deposits (or retaining them) and for investing the deposit funds. On March 31, 1980, the Depository Institutions Deregulation and Monetary Control Act of 1980 was signed into law. Title IV of the Act amended the Home Owners' Loan Act of 1933 to provide significant new powers for thrift institutions. Review the provisions of 12 U.S.C. § 1464(b)(4), (c) & (n) for an understanding of the broadened range of powers available to federal savings associations. Consider whether these powers were likely to make a difference to associations that faced the loss of their traditional depositors. Consider also whether these powers significantly blurred the distinction between savings associations and commercial banks.

1.24. *Reassessing expanded savings association powers.* Growing concerns over the crisis in the thrift industry[23] caused a reassessment of the use of expanded powers by savings associations. As part of an effort to return them to their traditional areas of activities, section 104(b) of the Competitive Equality in Banking Act of 1987 ("CEBA"), Pub. L. No. 100-86, 101 Stat. 552, 567 (1987), generally prohibited holding companies of S&Ls ("SLHCs") and their non-S&L subsidiaries from (*a*) commencing business activities, other than those exempted in the Savings and Loan Holding Company Act, 12 U.S.C. § 1730a(c)(2) (1988); and, (*b*) continuing any business activities, other than exempted activities, two years after the enactment of CEBA, or after receiving approval to become an SLHC, whichever was later. These limitations were not applicable to any SLHC or its subsidiary which controlled only one insured institution, or which controlled more than one insured institution through emergency acquisitions, provided that, in either event, the institution or institutions were "qualified thrift lenders" ("QTL's"). 12 U.S.C. § 1730a(c)(3) (1988). The QTL requirements had the effect of forcing many insured institution subsidiaries of SLHCs to concentrate more of their lending activities in the traditional home mortgage market. (On the requirements for treatment of an insured institution as a QTL, see CEBA, § 104(c)(1) (codified at 12 U.S.C. § 1730a(o) (1988)). Essentially, QTL status depended upon the maintenance of "qualified thrift investments" ("QTI's") as at least 60 percent of the total tangible assets of the institution. *See id.* § 1730a(o)(1).[24]

1.25. *Types of savings associations: The savings bank.* In traditional terms, the savings bank, a phenomenon primarily of the eastern portion of the United States, is a bank limited to savings deposits. The "thrift" type of depository function has generally been performed almost entirely by the savings and loan association. There are two basic types of savings banks: (*a*) the mutual savings bank; and, (*b*) the stock savings bank. The former has no capital stock, and it operates as a mutual association for the benefit of its "members," *i.e.*, the depositors, with net earnings accruing to the mutual benefit of those depositors. A board of trustees, instead of a board of directors, guides the policies and activities of the savings bank. The stock savings bank does have capital stock and is organized and operated like any corporation. Until the 1980s, stock savings banks could be chartered only under state law.

---

23. On the crisis and its legislative resolution, see Note 8.46, *infra*.

24. On current QTL rules, see 3 MICHAEL P. MALLOY, BANKING LAW AND REGULATION 8.101-8.103. n.17 (1994 & Cum Supp.).

In 1982, however, the Garn-St Germain Depository Institutions Act[25] amended the Home Owners' Loan Act of 1933 to authorize the conversion of state-chartered savings banks insured by the FDIC into federal savings banks.[26]

1.26. *Types of savings associations: The savings and loan association.* Savings and loan associations ("S&L's"), or building and loan associations as they are known in some states, are savings associations that traditionally were limited to the receipt of savings deposits and the making of home mortgage and related loans. Like savings banks, they can be either mutual or stock in organization. Conversions of mutual S&L's into stock S&L's have been dramatically increasing as more S&L's began to seek increased capital through public offerings of stock. Since at least 1933, S&L's could be state-chartered or federally chartered.[27]

1.27. *Credit unions.* Credit unions, like the other thrift institutions, may be either state or federally chartered. Unlike savings associations, however, they are associational, not stock, entities. Their powers are generally limited to taking personal deposits of members and making personal, typically short-term, loans. What, then, are the differences between credit unions and mutual savings associations? Consider the following cases.

State v. Minnesota Federal Savings & Loan Ass'n

15 N.W.2d 568 (Minn. 1944)

MAGNEY, Justice.

[The case involved a challenge by Minnesota Federal Savings and Loan Association to a provision of the Minnesota Income Tax Act. Minnesota Federal claimed that the provision was invalid because it exempted credit unions and various mutual and cooperative organizations, but not state and federal savings and loan associations, in violation of the uniformity clause of the state constitution and the equal protection clause of the Fourteenth Amendment to the federal constitution. Minnesota Federal was a mutual S&L, and its business consisted of issuing deposit shares and receiving payments thereon, lending to members principally on the security of liens on small homes, and in making other loans to its members. Each share owner and each borrower was a member of the association and entitled to vote at its meetings.]

. . . [C]redit unions make mortgage loans to members. . . .

Credit unions are wholly exempted from the Minnesota income or franchise tax. There are operating in Minnesota large numbers of farmers, fruit growers, and other like associations, farmers mutual insurance companies, and cooperative and mutual rural telephone associations organized and operated on a cooperative basis and paying dividends on shares. These associations are exempted from the Minnesota income or franchise tax. ...

The association contends that credit unions are in every substantial respect like federal savings and loan associations–in purpose, organization, and method of doing business, and there are no substantial differences between them. The state, on the other hand, insists that the differences are so substantial as to warrant discrimination between them for taxation purposes. . . .

The situation presented in each case determines whether or not a particular classification violates the constitutional provisions. It becomes necessary, therefore, in this

---

25. Pub. L. No. 97-320, 96 Stat. 14 (1982).

26. 12 U.S.C. § 1464(o). On conversions, see Chapter 2, § 4 *infra*.

27. *See* 12 U.S.C. § 1464(a) (providing for chartering of federal S&L's).

case to detail the main facts showing in what respects the defendant and credit unions are similar and in what respects they differ. In the first place, both are local, mutual thrift associations. Both receive savings as payments on shares in no set amounts. Both lend money to members on security of liens on homes. In both, persons owning shares in, or borrowing from, the association are entitled to vote. Both may borrow up to 50 percent of assets. Both may lend on security of members' shares. Both are required to set aside substantial reserves. . . .

They differ in the following respects: The association makes its loans principally on security of homes or combinations of homes and business property. It also makes loans on the security of its shares. It may, under certain conditions hereinafter referred to, make loans on other improved real estate. The credit unions make chiefly personal loans. The association deals with members living within 50 miles from the main office in St. Paul, except in certain situations which will be referred to later. The credit unions deal with members united by a common bond of occupation or association, or a group with a well-defined rural district. The average loan made by the association is larger than that made by the credit union. Members of the association are entitled to as many votes as they have shares, up to 50, and may vote by proxy. Each member of the credit union has but one vote and must vote in person.

. . . Credit Unions own no real estate, except as it may be acquired by foreclosure. The credit unions are created especially for the purpose of providing people of moderate means, salaried employees, and wage earners with an institution where they may borrow money for personal needs, such as medical bills and to meet temporary emergencies. Credit unions are under the supervision of the state commissioner of banks. Defendant is under the supervision of the Federal Home Loan Bank Board. . . .

. . . Although many of the credit unions do make loans on the security of homes, their primary purpose is to make personal loans to members. Most of them now make only personal loans, but it is fair to assume that most of them, if not all, will eventually make loans on the security of homes. They have the authority to do so. However, their original purpose and function is to make personal loans in small amounts, payable in installments. The association's principal purpose and function is to make loans upon homes or combinations of homes and business property. . . . The credit unions are authorized to serve only those united by a common bond of occupation or association or by residence within a well- defined rural area. Thus, a credit union organized by public employees serves only public employees. One organized by postal employees serves only postal employees. There is a close, personal touch between the credit union officials and the members. The latter are all in about the same financial situation, at least as to income. Each member knows quite well the problems of the other members. There is a community of interest. There is nothing impersonal in the dealings between the credit union and its members. A credit union in a rural community can serve only those who have their residence within a well-defined area. There each member has a fair knowledge of the other members and individuals and also their financial situations. Defendant, on the other hand, is authorized to serve all persons within 50 miles of its home office in St. Paul and in some circumstances a larger area; that is, it is authorized to serve at least one-third of the population of the state. Within that area its authority is unlimited. The services of the association are available to every one. The ability and willingness of the savings and loan associations to serve every home owner and every investor are evidenced by the numerous advertisements in the newspapers and over the radio. It is purely a business proposition. The personal touch is absent. . . .

In view of the differences between federal savings and loan associations and credit unions, we hold that the classification made by the legislature with reference to them is based on a reasonable ground for making a distinction for purposes of taxation and therefore the legislation in that respect is valid. . . .

Barany v. Buller

670 F.2d 726 (7th Cir. 1982)

CUDAHY, Circuit Judge.

[Members of the credit committee of a federally chartered credit union were removed from the committee by the credit union's board of directors. The removed members sued, arguing that the removal was unauthorized by the Federal Credit Union Act, and that only the supervisory committee of the credit union could remove them. The district court dismissed, on the ground that there was no private right of action, express or implied, for an action of this kind under the Act. On appeal, the Seventh Circuit reversed. In the course of its decision, the Seventh Circuit had the following to say about the historical background of the Act.]

. . . [W]e find that the plaintiffs do not have an implied private right of action under the Act in this case. However, we also conclude that they may bring this action under the federal common law. . . .

An examination of the history of the Act reveals the "uniquely federal interests" which behoove acknowledgement of a federal remedy in this case. The first credit unions were organized in Germany in the middle of the 19th century. In 1898, the first credit union in North American was organized in Quebec, Canada. St. Mary's Bank, the plaintiff in *La Caisse Populaire Ste-Marie v. United States*, 425 F. Supp. 512 (D.N.H. 1976), *aff'd*, 563 F.2d 5050 (1st Cir. 1977), was the first credit union organized in the United States, receiving its charter only six days before the enactment of the first general credit union statute in this country by Massachusetts. 425 F. Supp. at 151. By 1934, when the first federal credit union statute was enacted,[15] thirty-eight states had enacted credit union laws and, in 1932, Congress had passed such a statute for the District of Columbia. . . . Under these statutes, 2,350 credit unions operated in the United States. They had 450,000 members and resources of $50,000,000, and made $65,000,000 in loans annually. . . .

Despite American credit unions' good record during the economic depression of the 1930's, Congress perceived a need for a federal credit union statute:

> At a time when industrial recovery depends on the buying power of the masses of the people, usurious money lending in total amounts which are now figured in billions of dollars annually, obviously destroys vast totals of buying power represented by the difference between what the average worker should pay for credit and what he does pay for credit. It is with this truly national problem that the [Act] is primarily concerned.

S. Rep. No. 555, [73d Cong., 2d Sess. 1 (1934)].

There were several reasons supporting a federal credit union law. First, even where there were local credit unions laws, in many states the laws were inadequate or the state banking department lacked interest in credit unions, thus inhibiting credit union development. Also, in the absence of a federal statute, there were no interstate credit unions. . . . Consequently, one of the purposes of the 1934 Act was the establishment of federal juris-

---

15. Pub. L. No. 73-467, 48 Stat. 1216 (1934).

diction over some credit unions. . . .[17] In addition to permitting the development of credit unions in those jurisdictions without a credit union statute, a federal law was thought to be necessary to insure uniform development of credit unions. . . .

Legislative developments after passage of the initial federal law have increasingly federalized the governance of federal credit unions, lending further support to our conclusion. By 1970, there were 24,000 federal credit unions operating in the United States, with 22 million members and deposits of $14 billion. At that time, credit unions were the only federally chartered thrift institutions without federal insurance protection. . . . Thus, in 1970 Congress required the NCUA to insure federal credit unions and permitted federal insurance of credit unions not chartered under the Act. . . .

Additional support for our conclusion that "uniquely federal interests" require a federal common law remedy in this instance is found in courts' treatment of similar federal institutions. For example, federal credit unions are similar in important respects to federal savings and loan associations. *Cf. Nat'l Alliance of Postal & Federal Employees v. Nickerson*, 424 F. Supp. 323, 325 (D.D.C. 1976) (power of NCUA analogous to that of Federal Home Loan Bank Board). The salient feature of credit unions is their democratic control and management which are buttressed, in part, by the Act's prohibition against proxy voting and its limitation of membership to groups with a common bond. *La Caisse Populaire*, 425 F. Supp. at 517 (citing pertinent statutory provisions). Even state courts acknowledge that a federal savings and loan association "is subject only to state law which does not interfere with the purposes for which it was created, does not destroy its efficiency and does not conflict with paramount federal law." *Bruckner v. Prairie Federal Savings & Loan Ass'n.*, 81 Wis.2d 215, 260 N.W.2d 256, 259 (1977) (quoting *Pearson v. First Federal Savings & Loan Ass'n.*, 149 So.2d 891, 894-5 (Fla. App. 1963));[18] *see also California v. Coast Federal Savings & Loan Ass'n.*, 98 F. Supp. 311, 318 (S.D. Cal. 1951).

Notes and Comments 1.28. *Barany's view of federal common law.* The recognition in *Barany* of a federal common law basis for a cause of action involving a federal credit union has been criticized and rejected by other courts. *See Ridenour v. Andrews Federal Credit Union*, 897 F.2d 715, 719 (4th Cir. 1990); *Heller v. CACL Federal Credit Union*, 775 F.Supp. 839, 843 (E.D. Pa. 1991). The Supreme Court's decision in *Atherton v. Federal Deposit Insurance Corporation*, 519 U.S. 213 (1997), effectively foreclosed federal common law as a source of authority in most federal bank regulatory contexts. For *Atherton*'s discussion of the federal common law issue, see the material following Note 8.41, *infra*.

1.29. *Depository institution regulators.* Each institution is subject to the authority of at least one regulator–the authority that issued its charter. In fact, however, a depository institution is more likely to be subject to the overlapping regulatory jurisdiction of a number of the regulators. For example, a state-chartered bank may be subject to the direct regulatory authority of as many as two federal regulators in addition to its state supervisor. The ma-

---

17. However, the Act did not eliminate state credit unions. Rather, it merely permitted federal chartered credit unions. *See* Vol. 78, Pt. 7 Cong. Rec. 7259 (remarks of Sen. Sheppard). The Act provides for conversion from state to federal charter and vice versa. 12 U.S.C. § 1771.

18. In *Bruckner* the issue was whether a federal savings and loan association could have accounts payable on death, which were expressly permitted by state statute. The federal statute was silent on this issue. The court held that this was strictly a state law question: by what means, other than by will, can property pass upon its owner's death? 260 N.W.2d at 259. Such an issue is appreciably different from the underlying issue presented here–the administration of a federally chartered institution.

terials that follow will examine how that might happen. Figure 1.5, *infra*, illustrates some of the jurisdictional overlaps in U.S. banking regulation. The figure is actually oversimplified, but it may at least give some indication of the complexities of contemporary depository institutions regulation. For example, if *A Bank* is a state-chartered bank that is a member of the Federal Reserve System and is owned by *X Holding Company*, how many agencies have a regulatory interest? What if *A* is a federal stock savings bank, owned by individual shareholders?

Figure 1.5.
U.S. Regulatory Structure
[post-October 2011]

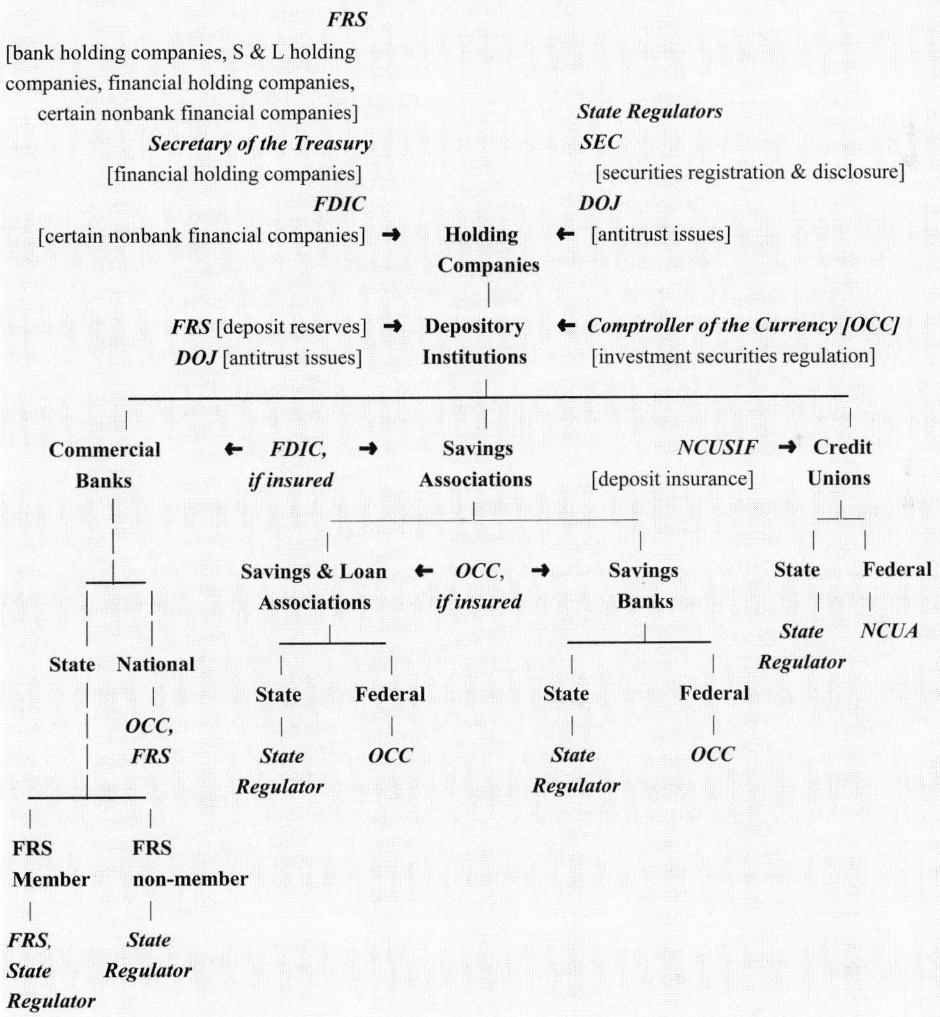

1.30. *The Office of the Comptroller of the Currency ("OCC").* The Comptroller is the supervisor of national banks chartered by him under the National Bank Act. He and the OCC staff are a bureau of the Department of the Treasury, and they are responsible for the administration of virtually all federal laws applicable to national banks, including banks operating in the District of Columbia. Approval by the Comptroller is required for virtually all significant actions to be taken by a national bank–chartering, establishment of branches, changes in corporate control and structure of organization–and the OCC also supervises the day-to-day activities of national banks, including the loan and investment policies of the banks, trust activities, issuance of securities and the like. In addition, under the financial services reform provisions of the Gramm-Leach-Bliley Act of 1999 (GLBA),[28] the Comptroller is responsible for regulating the financial services activities of subsidiaries of national banks,[29] the privacy of nonpublic personal information of customers of national banks,[30] and consumer protection with respect to insurance sales by national banks,[31] among other things. As a matter of administrative law, courts have generally accorded a high degree of deference to the Comptroller's decisions. How far does that insulate the Comptroller and the OCC from judicial review? Consider the following cases.

Ass'n of Data Processing Service Organizations v. Camp

397 U.S. 150 (1970)

Mr. Justice DOUGLAS delivered the opinion of the Court.

Petitioners sell data processing services to businesses generally. In this suit they seek to challenge a ruling by respondent Comptroller of the Currency that, as an incident to their banking services, national banks . . . may make data processing services available to other banks and to bank customers. The District Court dismissed the complaint for lack of standing of petitioners to bring the suit. . . . The Court of Appeals affirmed. . . .

. . . [T]he question of standing in the federal courts is to be considered in the framework of Article III [of the U.S. Constitution] which restricts judicial power to "cases" and "controversies." As we recently stated in *Flast v. Cohen*, 392 U.S. 83, 101, "[I]n terms of Article III limitations on federal court jurisdiction, the question of standing is related only to whether the dispute sought to be adjudicated will be presented in an adversary context and in a form historically viewed as capable of judicial resolution." *Flast* was a taxpayer's suit. The present [case] is a competitor's suit. And while the two have the same Article III starting point, they do not necessarily track one another.

The first question is whether the plaintiff alleges that the challenged action has caused him injury in fact, economic or otherwise. There can be no doubt but that petitioners have satisfied this test. The petitioners not only allege that competition by national banks in the business of providing data processing services might entail some future loss of profits for petitioners, they also allege that respondent American National Bank & Trust Company was performing or preparing to perform such services for two customers for whom petitioner Data Systems, Inc., had previously agreed or negotiated to perform such services. The petitioners' suit was brought not only against the American National Bank & Trust Company,

---

28. Pub. L. No. 106-102, Nov. 12, 1999, 113 Stat. 1338 (1999) (codified at scattered sections of 12, 15, 16, 18 U.S.C.) (GLBA).

29. 12 U.S.C. § 24a.

30. 15 U.S.C. §§ 6801-6809.

31. 12 U.S.C. § 1831x.

but also against the Comptroller of the Currency. The Comptroller was alleged to have caused petitioners injury in fact by his 1966 ruling which stated:

> "Incidental to its banking services, a national bank may make available its data processing equipment or perform data processing services on such equipment for other banks and bank customers." COMPTROLLER'S MANUAL FOR NATIONAL BANKS ¶ 3500 (October 15, 1966). . . .

. . . [T]he question of standing . . . concerns, apart from the "case" or "controversy" test, the question whether the interest sought to be protected by the complainant is arguably within the zone of interests to be protected or regulated by the statute or constitutional guarantee in question. Thus the Administrative Procedure Act grants standing to a person "aggrieved by agency action within the meaning of a relevant statute." 5 U.S.C. § 702 (1964 ed., Supp. IV). . . .

Where statutes are concerned, the trend is toward enlargement of the class of people who may protest administrative action. The whole drive for enlarging the category of aggrieved "persons" is symptomatic of that trend. . . .

[Section] 4 of the Bank Service Corporation Act of 1962,[a] 76 Stat. 1132, 12 U.S.C. § 1864 . . . provides:

> "No bank service corporation may engage in any activity other than the performance of bank services for banks."

The Court of Appeals for the First Circuit held in *Arnold Tours, Inc. v. Camp*, 408 F. 2d 1147, 1153, that by reason of § 4 a data processing company has standing to contest the legality of a national bank performing data processing for other banks and bank customers. . . .

. . . We do think . . . that § 4 arguably brings a competitor within the zone of interests protected by it.

That leaves the remaining question, whether judicial review of the Comptroller's action has been precluded. We do not think it has been. There is great contrariety among administrative agencies created by Congress as respects "the extent to which, and the procedures by which, different measures of control afford judicial review of administrative action." *Stark v. Wickard*, 321 U.S. 288, 312 (Frankfurter, J., dissenting). The answer, of course, depends on the particular enactment under which review is sought. It turns on "the existence of courts and the intent of Congress as deduced from the statutes and precedents." *Id.*, at 308.

The Administrative Procedure Act provides that the provisions of the Act authorizing judicial review apply "except to the extent that–(1) statutes preclude judicial review; or (2) agency action is committed to agency discretion by law." 5 U.S.C. § 701(a) (1964 ed., Supp. IV). . . .

We find no evidence that Congress in either the Bank Service Corporation Act or the National Bank Act sought to preclude judicial review of administrative rulings by the Comptroller as to the legitimate scope of activities available to national banks under those statutes. Both Acts are clearly "relevant" statutes within the meaning of § 702. The Acts do not in terms protect a specified group. But their general policy is apparent; and those whose interests are directly affected by a broad or narrow interpretation of the Acts are easily

---

a. On the Bank Service Corporation Act (since amended as the Bank Service Company Act), see *infra* Chapter 5, § 8.

identifiable. It is clear that petitioners, as competitors of national banks which are engaging in data processing services, are within that class of "aggrieved" persons who, under § 702, are entitled to judicial review of "agency action."

Whether anything in the Bank Service Corporation Act or the National Bank Act gives petitioners a "legal interest" that protects them against violations of those Acts, and whether the actions of respondents did in fact violate either of those Acts, are questions which go to the merits and remain to be decided below. . . .

Camp v. Pitts

411 U.S. 138 (1973)

PER CURIAM.

In its present posture this case presents a narrow, but substantial, question with respect to the proper procedure to be followed when a reviewing court determines that an administrative agency's stated jurisdiction for informal action does not provide an adequate basis for judicial review.

In 1967, respondents submitted an application to the Comptroller of the Currency for a certificate authorizing them to organize a new bank in Hartsville, South Carolina. *See* 12 U.S.C. § 27; 12 CFR § 4.2 (1972). On the basis of information received from a national bank examiner and from various interested parties, the Comptroller denied the application and notified respondents of his decision through a brief letter, which stated in part: "[W]e have concluded that the factors in support of the establishment of a new National Bank in this area are not favorable." No formal hearings were required by the controlling statute or guaranteed by the applicable regulations, although the latter provided for hearings when requested and when granted at the discretion of the Comptroller. Respondents did not request a formal hearing but asked for reconsideration. That request was granted and a supplemental field examination was conducted, whereupon the Comptroller again denied the application, this time stating in a letter that "we were unable to reach a favorable conclusion as to the need factor," and explaining that conclusion to some extent.[2] Respondents then brought an action in federal district court seeking review of the Comptroller's decision. The entire administrative record was placed before the court, and, upon an examination of that record and of the two letters of explanation, the court granted summary judgment against respondents, holding that de novo review was not warranted in the circumstances and finding that "although the Comptroller may have erred, there is substantial basis for his determination, and . . . it was neither capricious nor arbitrary." . . . On appeal, the Court of Appeals did not reach the merits. Rather, it held that the Comptroller's ruling was "unacceptable" because "its basis" was not stated with sufficient clarity to permit judicial review. . . . For the present, the Comptroller does not challenge this aspect of the court's decision. He does, however, seek review here of the procedures that the Court of Appeals specifically

---

2. The letter reads in part:

> "On each application we endeavor to develop the need and convenience factors in conjunction with all other banking factors and in this case we were unable to reach a favorable conclusion as to the need factor. The record reflects that this market area is now served by the Peoples Bank with deposits of $7.2MM, The Bank of Hartsville with deposits of $12.8MM, the First Federal Savings and Loan Association with deposits of $5.4MM, The Mutual Savings and Loan Association with deposits of $.82MM and the Sonoco Employees Credit Union with deposits of $6.5MM. The aforementioned are as of December 31, 1968."

ordered to be followed in the District Court on remand. The court held that the case should be remanded "for a trial de novo before the District Court" because "the Comptroller has twice inadequately and inarticulately resolved the [respondents'] presentation." The court further specified that in the District Court, respondents "will open the trial with proof of their application and compliance with the statutory inquiries, and proffer of any other relevant evidence." Then, "[t]estimony may . . . be adduced by the Comptroller or intervenors manifesting opposition, if any, to the new bank." On the basis of the record thus made, the District Court was instructed to make its own findings of fact and conclusions of law in order to determine "whether the [respondents] have shown by a preponderance of evidence that the Comptroller's ruling is capricious or an abuse of discretion." ...

We agree with the Comptroller that the trial procedures thus outlined by the Court of Appeals for the remand in this case are unwarranted under present law.

Unquestionably, the Comptroller's action is subject to judicial review under the Administrative Procedure Act (APA), 5 U.S.C. § 701. *See Association of Data Processing Service Organizations v. Camp*, 397 U.S. 150, 156-158 (1970). But it is also clear that neither the National Bank Act nor the APA requires the Comptroller to hold a hearing or to make formal findings on the hearing record when passing on applications for new banking authorities. *See* 12 U.S.C. § 26; 5 U.S.C. § 557.[3] Accordingly, the proper standard for judicial review of the Comptroller's adjudications is not the "substantial evidence" test which is appropriate when reviewing findings made on a hearing record, 5 U.S.C. § 706(2)(E). Nor was the reviewing court free to hold a de novo hearing under § 706(2)(F) and thereafter determine whether the agency action was "unwarranted by the facts." . . .

The appropriate standard for review was . . . whether the Comptroller's adjudication was "arbitrary, capricious, an abuse of discretion, or otherwise not in accordance with law," as specified in 5 U.S.C. § 704(2)(A). In applying that standard, the focal point for judicial review should be the administrative record already in existence, not some new record made initially in the reviewing court. . . .

If, as the Court of Appeals held and as the Comptroller does not now contest, there was such failure to explain administrative action as to frustrate effective judicial review, the remedy was not to hold a de novo hearing but . . . to obtain from the agency, either through affidavits or testimony, such additional explanation of the reasons for the agency decision as may prove necessary. We add a caveat, however. . . . [I]n the present case there was contemporaneous explanation of the agency decision. The explanation may have been curt, but it surely indicated the determinative reason for the final action taken: the finding that a new bank was an uneconomic venture in light of the banking needs and the banking services already available in the surrounding community. The validity of the Comptroller's action must, therefore, stand or fall on the propriety of that finding, judged, of course, by the appropriate standard of review. If that finding is not sustainable on the administrative record made, then the Comptroller's decision must be vacated and the matter remanded to him for further consideration.

Notes and Comments 1.31. *The Board of Governors of the Federal Reserve*

---

3. Title 12 U.S.C. § 26 contemplates a wide-ranging ex parte investigation; it reads as follows: [*See* STATUTORY APPENDIX, 12 U.S.C. § 26.]

As to the APA, its requirement of a written statement of "findings and conclusions, and the reasons or basis therefor" (5 U.S.C. § 557(c)(3)(A)), applies only to rulemaking proceedings (§ 553) and to adjudications "required by statute to be determined on the record after opportunity for an agency hearing" (§ 554(a)). By its terms, then, the APA's requirement of formal findings is not relevant since the National Bank Act plainly does not require agency hearings on applications for new banks.

System. A National Monetary Commission was created in 1908 to investigate the causes of the 1907 financial panic and make recommendations for curative legislation. The end result was a proposal for a central banking system to monitor the monetary and credit functions of the U.S. financial system. The Federal Reserve Act of 1913[32] created a system of federal reserve banks, each acting in effect as a central bank for its geographical region and overseen by a board of governors located in Washington, D.C. The Board of Governors of the Federal Reserve System ("the Fed") is charged with the responsibility of monitoring the availability of credit in the financial system, and of intervening when necessary to adjust the availability of credit. In addition, it has had responsibility for administering federal laws concerning interest rates applicable to bank deposits of commercial banks which are members of the Federal Reserve System ("member banks").[33] The Fed also administers federal laws concerning the reserves required to be held by depository institutions against their deposits. The Fed also has the responsibility for administration of federal laws regulating the activities of bank holding companies. Throughout the rest of this book, we shall concentrate on the Fed's supervisory responsibilities, rather than its monetary and credit functions. With respect to the regulation of the activities of depository institutions, the Fed does not perform a chartering function,[34] but it does have supervisory and examination functions with respect to state-chartered member banks.[35] It also administers the Bank Merger Act in mergers in which the acquiring, assuming or resulting bank is a state-chartered member bank.[36] In addition, since 1964 the Fed has had responsibility as the appropriate federal regulatory agency for the administration of the Securities Exchange Act of 1934 with respect to securities issued by state-chartered member banks.[37] Under the 1999 GLBA, the Fed is considered the "umbrella supervisor" of financial services companies (FHCs), diversified holding companies involved in a wide range of financial services activities.[38] It is also responsible for regulating the privacy of nonpublic personal information of customers of bank holding companies, FHCs, and state-chartered banks that are members of the Federal Reserve System,[39] and consumer protection with respect to insurance sales by such entities,[40] among other things.

1.32. What are the regulatory objectives of the Federal Reserve System? In answering this question, consider the following case.

---

32. 38 Stat. 251 (1913) (codified at 12 U.S.C. §§ 221 *et seq.*)

33. *See* 12 U.S.C. § 221.

34. *But cf. id.* 12 U.S.C. § 611 (chartering of Edge Act corporations engaged in international and foreign banking).

35. The member banks include all national banks in the continental United States, as required by law, 12 U.S.C. §§ 221, 222, and those state-chartered banks and trust companies which have chosen to apply for, and have received, membership. *Id.* § 321.

36. *Id.* § 1828(c)(2)(B). On the Bank Merger Act, see *infra* Chapter 4, § 3.

37. 15 U.S.C. § 78*l*(i).

38. 12 U.S.C. § 1848a.

39. 15 U.S.C. §§ 6801-6809.

40. 12 U.S.C. § 1831x.

Texas State Bank v. United States

423 F.3d 1370 (Fed. Cir. 2005)
cert. denied, 547 U.S. 1206 (2006)

DYK, Circuit Judge.

[Texas State Bank brought suit against the United States, alleging that a Fifth Amendment taking had occurred when interest income attributable to its deposit reserve account at the Fed was paid to the U.S. Treasury Department. The U.S. Court of Federal Claims dismissed for lack of jurisdiction, because the actions were those of the Fed, an independent agency, not Treasury. On appeal, the Federal Circuit upheld jurisdiction in the case, but affirmed the decision on the grounds that Texas State Bank did not own a compensable property interest in the earnings generated by the Fed from its investment of the bank's required reserves.]

Appellant Texas State Bank ("Texas State") is a state-chartered bank that holds (and has held) reserves in accordance with the requirements of the Monetary Control Act of 1980, Pub.L. 96-221, Title I, 94 Stat. 132. Texas State claims that a Fifth Amendment taking occurred when the United States allegedly directed the Federal Reserve Board to pay earnings generated by Texas State's mandated reserves to the United States Treasury ("Treasury"). ...

... We hold that the Court of Federal Claims had jurisdiction under the Tucker Act because Texas State's claim is based on actions by the United States and not the Federal Reserve Board. We conclude that the case must nonetheless be dismissed because Texas State has failed to assert a valid takings claim.

BACKGROUND

The Federal Reserve System was established in 1913 pursuant to the Federal Reserve Act ("FRA"). Federal Reserve Act, Pub.L. No. 63-43, 38 Stat. 251, codified as amended at 12 U.S.C. §§ 221 *et seq.* (1913). A principal function of the Federal Reserve System has been to determine and implement monetary policy "so as to promote effectively the goals of maximum employment, stable prices, and moderate long-term interest rates." 12 U.S.C. § 225a. The System is composed of the Board of Governors of the Federal Reserve System and twelve regional Reserve banks ("the Federal Reserve"). Monetary policy is set by the Federal Open Market Committee and is implemented through open market operations, that is, the purchase and sale of government securities. Open market operations are funded with reserves supplied by participating banks, and these operations are profitable for the Federal Reserve. The Federal Reserve banks also provide check clearing and other banking services to financial institutions. *See generally* 12 U.S.C. §§ 221*et seq.*

Before the passage of the Monetary Control Act of 1980, only national banks were required to join the Federal Reserve System and to maintain non-interest bearing, or "sterile" reserves with the Federal Reserve. State-chartered banks could elect to join, but their participation in the system was not mandatory. Member banks did not earn interest on reserves, but were entitled to several free services, including free check-clearing. When inflation rates rose in the late 1970's and interest rates increased, voluntary participation of state-chartered banks in the Federal Reserve System declined as did the level of reserve deposits. . . .

In 1980 Congress sought to reverse this trend through the passage of the Monetary Control Act, and required that all depositary institutions, i.e., all banks, hold sterile reserves, in the form of non-interest bearing deposits at the Federal Reserve Bank, or in the form of Federal Reserve notes (that is, currency) stored at the depository institution. The currency deposits are known as "vault cash." *Id.;* 12 U.S.C. § 461(c). The Federal Reserve has consistently, but unsuccessfully, urged Congress to allow for the payment of a market-rate of interest on required reserves.[1] On the other hand, the Treasury has opposed what it views as "the use of taxpayer resources for this purpose."

The parties have stipulated that the Federal Reserve's open market operations, funded by required reserves, generate substantial income. The parties have also stipulated that the "Federal Reserve notes held as mandatory reserves in the form of vault cash result in earnings for Federal Reserve Banks in the same manner the maintenance of reserve balances in the accounts at the Federal Reserve Banks generate [sic] income for the Federal Reserve Banks." . . . The income generated by the sterile deposits and vault cash is used to pay the expenses of the Federal Reserve, and the remainder is transferred by the Federal Reserve Banks to the Treasury on a yearly basis. This transfer occurs each year by direction of Treasury. In fiscal years 1997, 1998, and 2000, the transfer was statutorily mandated. Omnibus Budget Reconciliation Act of 1993, Pub.L. 103-66 § 3002(a), 107 Stat. 312; Appendix to District of Columbia Appropriations Act, Pub.L. 106-113, § 302, 113 Stat. 1501 (Nov. 29, 1999).

Texas State has maintained sterile reserves and vault cash in accordance with the Monetary Control Act since 1980. . . . In October 2001, Texas State brought suit against the United States in the Court of Federal Claims, alleging jurisdiction under the Tucker Act, 28 U.S.C. § 1491(a)(1). Texas State did not challenge the statutory requirement to maintain reserves pursuant to the Monetary Control Act, nor allege that such a requirement constituted a taking.[4] Rather, in its complaint, Texas State asserted that "[i]ncome on the principal is the property of the owner of the principal. As such, the income on deposits and vault cash belong [sic] to the depository institutions that have maintained required reserves." . . .

DISCUSSION

. . .

III

. . . Although the Court of Federal Claims erred in dismissing the suit for lack of jurisdiction, we conclude that we may appropriately address the merits.

The relevant facts are not in dispute. Texas State does not assert a taking with respect to the requirement that it maintain sterile reserves with the Federal Reserve. This case turns solely on the purely legal question of whether Texas State owned a compensable property interest in the *earnings* generated by the Federal Reserve through investment of its reserves. *See, e.g., Webb's [Fabulous Pharmacies, Inc. v. Beckwith,* 449 U.S. 155,] 161 [(1980)]; *Cermak v. Babbitt,* 234 F.3d 1356, 1361 (Fed.Cir.2000) (holding that the nature of property interests is a question of law); *Coast Indian Cmty. v. United States,* 213 Ct.Cl. 129, 550 F.2d 639, 649 (1977) (determination of plaintiffs' ownership of a compensable property interest was a question of law). . . .

---

1. The Federal Reserve has taken the position that "[n]oninterest-bearing reserve requirements represent a tax on depository institutions that is not borne by other suppliers of financial services [and which] impairs the efficiency of resource allocation.... Paying such interest would circumvent the ill-effects of reserve requirements while preserving their advantages for monetary policy.... [R]eserve requirements provide for a reasonably predictable demand for overall reserve balances [which] is essential for the effective implementation of open market operations." Letter from Alan Greenspan, Chairman, Board of Governors of Federal Reserve System, to Rep. Stephen Neal, Chairman, Subcommittee on Domestic Monetary Policy of House Committee on Banking, Finance, and Urban Affairs (March 6, 1992).

4. Under our decision in *Commonwealth Edison Co. v. United States*, the "mere imposition of an obligation to pay money ... does not give rise to a claim under the Takings Clause of the Fifth Amendment." 271 F.3d 1327, 1340 (Fed.Cir.2001) (en banc).

. . . We . . . conclude that Texas State had no property interest in the income generated by the Federal Reserve through its open market operations, and that the complaint should be dismissed for failure to state a claim. *See, e.g., Helvering v. Gowran,* 302 U.S. 238 (1937).

"It is axiomatic that only persons with a valid property interest at the time of the taking are entitled to compensation." *Chancellor Manor v. United States,* 331 F.3d 891, 901 (Fed.Cir.2003). Indeed, we have previously observed that plaintiffs must identify a property interest cognizable under the Fifth Amendment as a "bedrock requirement" of any successful takings challenge. . . . Here, Texas State has failed to assert a valid property interest.

Texas State argues that its property interest in the share of the net earnings of the Federal Reserve that was generated by the reserve deposits is indistinguishable from the property interests that owners of principal deposited in interest-bearing accounts claim to the interest earned in those accounts, and that decisions by the Supreme Court have held constitutional "property".

The "interest follows principal" cases relied upon by Texas State all involved situations where third parties held plaintiffs' funds in separate interest-bearing accounts. *Webb's,* 449 U.S. at 157-61; *Phillips [v. Washington Legal Foundation,* 524 U.S. 156,] 164 [(1988)]; *Brown [v. Legal Foundation of Washington,* 538 U.S. 216,] 235 [(2003)]. . . .

. . . All of the additional cases relied upon by Texas State in its Supplemental Brief similarly involve claims to interest that was actually generated by specific funds according to the terms of the investment in question.[9]

In contrast to *Webb's, Phillips*, and *Brown,* where the deposited funds were held by third party banks, here Texas State did not provide funds to a third party that were then deposited in an interest-bearing account in a private bank, but entered into a direct depositor relationship with the Federal Reserve. . . . A debtor/creditor relationship also existed with respect to the amounts paid to receive the Federal Reserve notes held as vault cash. Texas State conceded during oral argument that "there is no private account to which interest was credited." Texas State fails to recognize that its reserve deposits, which by their own terms did not generate income, were fundamentally different from the interest-bearing accounts at issue in *Webb's, Brown*, and *Phillips.* And, contrary to Texas State's argument, the mere fact that Texas State was compelled to maintain the reserves on deposit by law-a requirement that is itself not challenged here-did not transform the nature of their underlying property rights. Under such circumstances, even if the funds received by the Federal Reserve were used to earn interest, Texas State did not acquire a property interest in the earnings. . . .

Texas State has failed to state a claim for which relief can be granted, as it had no property interest, cognizable under the Fifth Amendment, in the earnings generated by the Federal Reserve through its investment of required reserves. Texas State's lack of a property interest in the earnings generated by its mandated reserves is fatal not only to its takings claim, but also to its illegal exaction and due process claims. There can be no illegal exaction or due process violation if the money exacted was never the property of Texas State.

NEWMAN, Circuit Judge, concurring in part, dissenting in part.

. . . I must dissent from the panel majority's misapplication of law and its unsupported conclusion. It is beyond debate that money is property, and that the earnings on that

9. *See, e.g., Schneider v. Cal. Dep't of Corr.,* 151 F.3d 1194 (9th Cir.1998); *Hampton v. Hobbs,* 106 F.3d 1281 (6th Cir.1997); *Gillihan v. Shillinger,* 872 F.2d 935 (10th Cir.1989); *Morton Grove Park Dist. v. Am. Nat'l Bank & Trust Co.,* 78 Ill.2d 353, 35 Ill.Dec. 767, 399 N.E.2d 1295 (1980); *Bordy v. Smith,* 150 Neb. 272, 34 N.W.2d 331 (1948).

money are property. In *Webb's Fabulous Pharmacies, Inc. v. Beckwith,* 449 U.S. 155 (1980) the Court stated:

> The earnings of a fund are the incidents of ownership of the fund itself and are property just as the fund itself is property.

449 U.S. at 164. Again in *Phillips v. Washington Legal Foundation,* 524 U.S. 156, 160 (1998) the Court implemented this property right:

> The question presented by this case is whether interest earned on client funds held in [Interest on Lawyers Trust Accounts] is "private property" of either the client or the attorney for purposes of the Takings Clause of the Fifth Amendment. We hold that it is the property of the client.

Again in *Brown v. Legal Foundation of Washington,* 538 U.S. 216, 235 (2003) the Court held that the interest earned on deposits of clients' funds is the property of the client, not of the state. Although the Court recognized that when no interest was earned none had to be paid, it is undisputed that substantial interest is here earned.[1]

Principal and interest are property. The post-argument brief filed by Texas Bank contained expert testimony explaining that placement of a specified percentage of banks' funds in Reserve is compulsory, that minimum deposits must be met or a penalty paid, that the banks own their Reserve deposits, and can withdraw them and trade them in the "Fed funds market." Indeed, it is not disputed that the banks own their reserve deposits. They also own the interest earned by those deposits. "The rule that 'interest follows principal' has been established under English common law since at least the mid-1700's." *Phillips,* 524 U.S. at 165. The Court in *Phillips* cited representative cases from the various states, holding that the interest is the property of the owner of the principal. . . .

Notes and Comments 1.33. Why would Texas State Bank argue that failure to pay interest on deposit reserves was an impermissible taking under the Fifth Amendment, but *not* argue that the deposit reserve requirements were an impermissible taking?

1.34. According to Judge Newman, "the banks own their Reserve deposits, and can withdraw them and trade them in the 'Fed funds market.'" Is his statement true or false?

1.35. *Statutory Changes*. Authority for the Fed pay interest on balances maintained at the Reserve Banks by or on behalf of depository institutions was created in Title II of the Financial Services Regulatory Relief Act of 2006 (FSRRA), Pub. L. No. 109-351, 120 Stat. 1966 (Oct. 13, 2006), with an original effective date of October 1, 2011. The FSRRA Act provides that interest must be paid at least once each quarter at a rate not to exceed the general level of short-term interest rates. The act also provides that the Fed may prescribe regulations concerning the payment of interest, the distribution of earnings to the depository institutions that maintain balances or on whose behalf balances are maintained, and the responsibilities of correspondent banks to distribute and credit earnings on balances maintained by the respondent bank on a pass-through basis with the correspondent. Section 128 of the Emergency Economic Stabilization Act of 2008, (Oct. 3, 2008) accelerated the effective date of the authority to October 1, 2008. On October 9, 2008, the Fed published an interim final rule implementing this authority, effective immediately. 73 Fed. Reg. 59,482 (2008) (codified at 12 C.F.R. § 204.10). The text of § 204.10 is reproduced *infra* at 383.

---

1. In fiscal year 2000 the Federal Reserve was required to transfer net earnings of $3,752 billion to the General fund of the Treasury. . . .

1.36. *Judicial deference to the Fed.* In accordance with *Ass'n of Data Processing Service Organizations, supra*, the Fed's decisions are subject to judicial review under the Administrative Procedure Act. Its actions must be supported by adequate reasoning.[41] In the context of the Bank Holding Company Act, the Fed's factual findings are explicitly subject to review under a "substantial evidence" standard.[42] What are the implications of *Camp v. Pitts, supra*, for judicial review of the Fed's discretionary decisions?

1.37. *The Federal Deposit Insurance Corporation.* The stock market crash of 1929, together with the nationwide series of bank failures that followed, emphasized the need for improved regulation of the nation's banking system. Extensive congressional hearings on the causes of the crash resulted in, among other things, the amendment of the Federal Reserve Act in June of 1933 in order to establish the Federal Deposit Insurance Corporation ("FDIC"), which began insuring bank deposits as of 1934.[43] However, the state banking system continued along with the national banking system, with no attempt to exercise preemptive federal regulatory authority over the activities of the existing state banks. Nevertheless, state member banks of the Federal Reserve System, as well as national banks, were required to obtain insurance from the FDIC. *See* 12 U.S.C. § 1814(b) (1988). What was the supervisory objective of this new system of federal depository insurance? Consider the following case.

FDIC v. Philadelphia Gear Corp.

476 U.S. 426 (1986)

Justice O'Connor delivered the opinion of the Court.

[The case considered whether or not a "standby letter of credit" backed by a contingent promissory note was an insured "deposit" under the Federal Deposit Insurance Act. Standby letters of credit are discussed in Chapter 5, § 4, *infra*.]

When Congress created the FDIC, the Nation was in the throes of an extraordinary financial crisis. . . . More than one-third of the banks in the United States open in 1929 had shut their doors just four years later. . . . In response to this financial crisis, President Roosevelt declared a national banking holiday effective the first business day after he took office. 48 Stat. 1689. Congress in turn responded with extensive legislation on banking, including laws that gave the FDIC its existence.

---

41. *See, e.g., Board of Governors v. Investment Co. Inst.*, 450 U.S. 46 (1981) (upholding Fed's authorization of holding company affiliates to act as investment advisers to closed-end investment companies); *Securities Industry Ass'n v. Board of Governors*, 468 U.S. 207 (1984) (upholding Fed's authorization of acquisition of discount brokerage firm by bank holding company); *First Bank & Trust Co. v. Board of Governors*, 605 F.Supp. 555 (D.Ky. 1984) (upholding Fed's interpretation of application of deposit reserve provisions). *But see Securities Industry Ass'n v. Board of Governors*, 468 U.S. 137 (1984) (rejecting Fed's "post hoc rationalizations" for authorizing distribution of third-party commercial paper by state member bank as "entitled to little deference").

42. *See* 12 U.S.C. § 1848. *See also Bank of Boulder v. Board of Governors*, 535 F.2d 1221 (10th Cir. 1976); *North Hills Bank v. Board of Governors*, 506 F.2d 623 (8th Cir. 1974); *Gravois Bank v. Board of Governors*, 478 F.2d 546 8th Cir. 1973).

43. FDIC regulatory responsibilities have expanded dramatically over the years. Most recently, for example, under the 1999 GLBA the FDIC is responsible for regulating the privacy of nonpublic personal information of customers of state-chartered, FDIC-insured banks that are not members of the Federal Reserve System, 15 U.S.C. §§ 6801-6809, and consumer protection with respect to insurance sales by such banks, 12 U.S.C. § 1831x, among other things.

Congress' purpose in creating the FDIC was clear. Faced with virtual panic, Congress attempted to safeguard the hard earnings of individuals against the possibility that bank failures would deprive them of their savings. Congress passed the 1933 provisions "[i]n order to provide against a repetition of the present painful experience in which a vast sum of *assets and purchasing power* is 'tied up.'" S. Rep. No. 77, 73d Cong., 1st Sess., 12 (1933) (emphasis added). The focus of Congress was therefore upon ensuring that a deposit of "hard earnings" entrusted by individuals to a bank would not lead to a tangible loss in the event of a bank failure. As the chairman of the relevant Committee in the House of Representatives explained on the floor:

> "[T]he purpose of this legislation is to protect the people of the United States in the right to have banks in which their deposits will be safe. They have a right to expect of Congress the establishment and maintenance of a system of banks in the United States where citizens may place their hard earnings with reasonable expectation of being able to get them out again upon demand. ...
>
> "[The purpose of the bill is to ensure that] the community is saved from the shock of a bank failure, and every citizen has been given an opportunity to withdraw his deposits. . . .
>
> "The public . . . demand of you and me that we provide a banking system worthy of this great Nation and banks in which citizens may place the fruits of their toil and know that a deposit slip in return for their hard earnings will be as safe as a Government bond." 77 Cong. Rec. 3837, 3838, 3840 (1933) (remarks of Rep. Steagall).

. . . To prevent bank failure that resulted in the tangible loss of hard assets was therefore the focus of Congress' effort in creating deposit insurance.

Notes and Comments 1.38. *Judicial deference to the FDIC.* To what extent should the discretionary decisions of the FDIC be accorded judicial deference when challenged? Consider the following case.

Magellsen v. Federal Deposit Insurance Corporation

341 F. Supp. 1031 (D. Mont. 1972)

BATTIN, District Judge.

Plaintiff brings this action against these defendants with jurisdiction based on the Federal Deposit Insurance Act, 12 U.S.C. § 1811, *et seq*. Specifically, jurisdiction is based on Section 1819, which makes Federal Deposit Insurance Corporation [(FDIC)] a corporation which can sue and be sued.

Plaintiff was the major shareholder, managing director and creator of two banks. He applied for insurance with FDIC on January 15, 1970. This insurance was not favorably acted upon until November 25, 1970. Plaintiff alleges:

> 1. That defendants FDIC and West delayed arbitrarily and unreasonably in acting upon his applications;
>
> 2. That defendants FDIC and West negligently failed and refused to act on the applications;
>
> 3. That defendant West deliberately aroused suspicion against plaintiff and discriminated against him in applying the rules and regulations of FDIC;
>
> 4. That defendants FDIC and West violated 12 U.S.C. § 1820 by not

> administering these regulations fairly, impartially, and without discrimination; and
>
> 5. That by this procedure defendants FDIC and West violated the Fourteenth Amendment and deprived plaintiff of a fair hearing through selective enforcement of the regulations, oppressive demands, discriminatory policies towards plaintiff, and arbitrary and unfair treatment of plaintiff's application.

Plaintiff also alleges that this action made him vulnerable to various "con artists," including defendant Manuel. Defendants allegedly knew of Manuel's reputation; plaintiff argues that they should have told him of the danger in dealing with Manuel. Plaintiff alleges that had defendants provided him with this information, he would have terminated his dealings with Manuel. As a result of his dealings with Manuel, plaintiff alleges that he suffered the injuries set out in the complaint. Finally, plaintiff alleges that, because of this dealing and his subsequent loss, the FDIC investigated plaintiff and suspended him from banking operations.

Defendant FDIC maintains that the complaint should be dismissed as to it, since plaintiff has not filed a claim with the agency as required by 28 U.S.C. § 2401(b), as amended July 18, 1966, Pub. L. 89-506, Section 7, 80 Stat. 307, and [the Federal Tort Claims Act,] 28 U.S.C. § 2675(a), as amended July 18, 1966, Pub. L. 89-506, Section 2, 80 Stat. 306.

Defendant West maintains that he is immune from suit by virtue of the fact that he was acting within the scope of his office with relation to general matters under his control and supervision by law and by rules and regulations of the FDIC.

It is the opinion of the court that FDIC cannot be sued directly, since it is a federal agency. . . .

Chapter III of 12 C.F.R. sets forth the basic regulations of FDIC. Under 12 C.F.R. § 303.10, upon application by a bank for deposit insurance, the Division of Bank Supervision, FDIC, will cause an investigation to be conducted and an examination to be made of the bank or proposed bank. On this basis, the Board of Directors, FDIC, in accordance with the applicable provisions of law, will act upon the application. Moreover, the Regional Director, FDIC, makes recommendations which are considered by the Board of Directors. The factors to be considered in determining whether to grant an application for insurance are set forth in 12 U.S.C. § 1816. These include:

> "The financial history and condition of the bank, the adequacy of its capital structure, its future earnings prospects, the general character of its management, the convenience and needs of the community to be served by the bank, and whether or not its corporate powers are consistent with the purposes of this chapter [Chapter 967, 64 Stat. 873 *et seq*.]."

Suspension of an officer of a bank for violation of law, rules or regulations of FDIC, or found unsound and unsafe practice with regard to the bank which has or will cause substantial loss to the bank or other damage, is within the power of the Board of Directors under 12 C.F.R. § 308.36.

Examination of the complaint reveals that each one of the actions charged was within the discretion of either the Regional Director, defendant West, or the Board of Directors of FDIC. In Paragraph XI of the complaint, five separate acts are set forth which allegedly injured plaintiff. The first involves the decision as to whether the application should be granted. This decision is relegated to the discretion of the Board. The second alleges a failure to act upon the application. Again, action upon an application is within the discretion of the Board. The third alleges that defendant West aroused resentment, suspicion and hostility towards plaintiff and discriminated against him in applying the rules and regulations of FDIC. Application of the FDIC regulations is a discretionary, regulatory function of the Regional Director and is committed to him by the rules and regulations of FDIC. It is the Regional Director's duty under 12 C.F.R. § 303.10 to make recommendations to the Board of Directors for use in considering applications of proposed banks for deposit insurance. It follows that the Regional Director must make inquiries concerning the bank upon which to base this report. Whether he abused his discretion in making such inquiries is immaterial since he was using his discretion in relation to matters under his supervision and control. ...

The fourth alleges that neither defendant West nor defendant FDIC administered the affairs of the corporation fairly, impartially and without discrimination. Administration of FDIC affairs is committed to these two defendants. . . .

Finally, the fifth alleges that the FDIC procedures violated plaintiff's rights under the Fourteenth Amendment by depriving him of a fair, impartial hearing. The Fourteenth Amendment is inapplicable, since state action is not involved. Section 308, 12 C.F.R. provides for hearings concerning involuntary termination of the insurance status of a bank, issuance of cease and desist orders against any insured non-member bank, and issuance of orders removing or suspending from office, or other specified position, any director or officer of an insured state non-member bank or any other person participating in the conduct of the affairs of such a bank.

When a hearing is permissible, Chapter III, part 308, 12 C.F.R., sets forth procedures to be followed. Plaintiff does not state that these regulations were not followed or that he sought and was refused a hearing. In his uncontroverted affidavit of April 30, 1971, defendant West states that the Board of Directors of the two banks removed Magellsen as officer and employee before December 18, 1970. Defendant West also states that he advised Magellsen to resign from the Board of Directors of the bank on either December 2 or December 4, 1970.

It is the opinion of the court, therefore, that, as a matter of law, the five actions listed in Paragraph XI of the complaint constitute regulatory or discretionary action. . . . With regard to plaintiff's claim that FDIC and West both failed to advise him of George Manuel's bad reputation, there is no statutory duty on the part of either defendant to furnish this information. Moreover, the uncontroverted affidavit of defendant West indicates that neither he nor FDIC had knowledge of the dealings of Magellsen and Manuel until December 4, 1970. The fact that the application for Federal Deposit Insurance was granted by the Board of Directors on November 25, 1970, substantiates West's affidavit in this regard. ...

Plaintiff's second theory is that defendants were under a mandatory duty imposed by law to fairly and justly, and without discrimination, administer the provisions of the FDIC. 12 U.S.C. § 1820(a). Defendant argues that defendant West was acting within the scope of his authority and in matters committed to his discretion and judgment. . . .

It is the opinion of the court that Section 1820(a) of Title 12 does not supersede the Federal Tort Claims Act requirements and in particular 28 U.S.C. § 2680. . . .

Notes and Comments 1.39. *Federal regulation of savings associations pre-1989.* Until the enactment of the FIRREA in 1989 and the abolition of the Federal Home Loan Bank Board ("FHLBB"), the FHLBB was the principal federal regulator of federally chartered S&Ls, and state-chartered S&Ls the deposits of which were federally insured, as well as federally insured mutual savings banks. Chartering, insuring (through the Federal Savings and Loan Insurance Corporation ("FSLIC"), supervisory and examining functions, as well as "central bank" functions, were all performed by the FHLBB or one of its affiliated units. The FHLBB not only performed a chartering function, but also exercised a wide range of supervisory and examination functions with respect to thrift institutions, either directly or through the FSLIC. In addition, the FHLBB had primary responsibility, through the FSLIC, for the administration of the Savings and Loan Holding Company Act ("SLHCA"), regulating the formation and activities of savings and loan holding companies ("SLHC's"). 12 U.S.C. § 1730a (1988). The FHLBB also had responsibility as the appropriate federal regulatory agency for the administration of the Securities Exchange Act of 1934 with respect to securities issued by federally insured S&Ls. 15 U.S.C. § 78*l*(i) (1988).

1.40. *Federal regulation of savings associations after FIRREA.* Losses in the thrift industry reached record heights by the end of 1988.[44] The crisis eventually led to the enactment of FIRREA in August 1989, dramatically restructuring the regulation of savings associations. What did federal regulation of savings associations look like as a result? Something like this:

> FIRREA dramatically changed the regulatory regime which oversees the S & L industry. It abolished the FHLBB and FSLIC and established a new agency–OTS [the Office of Thrift Supervision]–as an office in the Department of the Treasury.... It divided regulatory and insurance responsibilities between OTS (the regulator) and the Savings Association Insurance Fund ("SAIF") (the insurer) [administered by the FDIC].... It removed from OTS certain powers previously exercised by the FHLBB, but placed OTS in the hands of a single Director rather than a three-person board. It vested in the Director responsibility for issuing S & L charters, reviewing proposed changes in control of thrifts, supervising and regulating federally-insured thrifts, and appointing receivers and conservators for ailing thrifts and their officers. . . .[45]

1.41. *Role of the FDIC under FIRREA.* The FDIC has responsibility, among other things, for insurance of deposits of "savings associations." Until 2006, it administered not only a Bank Insurance Fund (BIF)–formerly the Permanent Insurance Fund with respect to deposits of insured banks[46]–but also the SAIF, replacing the functions of the FSLIC.[47] To wrap up the affairs of the FSLIC, an FSLIC Resolution Fund was established, managed and separately maintained by the FDIC, consisting of assets and liabilities transferred from the FSLIC.[48]

1.42. *Merger of Deposit Insurance Funds.* As of March 31, 2006, the FDIC merged the BIF and the SAIF into the new Deposit Insurance Fund (DIF), as required by the Federal Deposit Insurance Reform Act of 2005 (FDIRA), Pub. L. No. 109-171, tit. II, §§ 2101-2109, 120 Stat. 4, 9-21 (Feb. 8, 2006). The FDIRA, and the Federal Deposit Insurance Reform Conforming Amendments Act of 2005 (FDIRCAA), Pub. L. No. 109-173, 119 Stat 3601 (Feb. 15, 2006), necessitated considerable revision and realignment of FDIC insurance regulations, mostly of a technical and conforming nature.

1.43. *Savings Association Regulation post-2010.* In response to the collapse of the capital markets in 2008, the Dodd-Frank Act transferred the functions and responsibilities

---

44. *See, e.g.*, Nash, *Savings Loss Put at $2.3 Billion*, N.Y. Times, Mar. 22, 1989, at D1, col. 6 (reporting 1988 fourth-quarter deficit in savings industry, bringing 1988 total to record $12.1 billion deficit). Deposit withdrawals at thrifts were also at a record high. *See* Nash, *Savings and Loan Withdrawals In December a Record $8.1 Billion*, N.Y. Times, Feb. 11, 1989, at 1, col. 4.

45. *Olympic Federal Savings and Loan Ass'n v. Director, Office of Thrift Supervision*, 732 F.Supp. 1183, 1186 (D.D.C. 1990), *appeal rendered moot*, 903 F.2d 837 (D.C.Cir.).

46. FIRREA, § 211(3) (codified at 12 U.S.C. § 1821(a) (4)-(5)).

47. 12 U.S.C. § 1821(a) (4), (6)).

48. FIRREA, § 215 (codified at 12 U.S.C. § 1821a).

of the OTS to the OCC, particularly as to federal savings associations.[49] Residual authority over state savings associations was transferred to the FDIC.[50] Authority over savings and loan holding companies and affiliate transactions was transferred to the Fed.[51] The transfers were effective July 21, 2011,[52] and the OTS and the position of the DOTS were to be abolished 90 days after that effective date.[53]

1.44. *Judicial deference to the OTS.* Despite the significant structural changes brought about by FIRREA, much of the substance of federal regulation of the savings association industry remained in large part the same.[54] As a result, prior case law examining the essential discretionary authority of the FHLBB continued to be pertinent, at least by analogy to questions concerning the authority of the DOTS. *Cf. Federal Home Loan Bank Board v. Rowe*, 284 F.2d 274 (D.C.Cir. 1960) (deferring to discretionary authority of FHLBB).

1.45. *The National Credit Union Administration.* Federally chartered credit unions are granted their charters by the National Credit Union Administration ("NCUA"). The credit union system is an integrated system of regulation in which the chartering, insuring, supervisory and "central bank" functions[55] are the responsibility of the NCUA and its constitutive units. Insurance of the accounts of credit union members, both state and federally chartered, is provided by the Administrator of the NCUA. Insurance is required for federally chartered credit unions, voluntary in the case of state-chartered credit unions. To what extent are the discretionary decisions of the NCUA accorded judicial deference? Consider the following case.

Nat. Alliance of Postal and Fed. Emp. v. Nickerson

424 F. Supp. 323 (D.D.C. 1976)

WADDY, District Judge.

This action arises under the Federal Credit Union Act of 1934, as amended, 12 U.S.C. § 1751, *et seq.* Plaintiff seeks a declaration that defendant's action in denying its application for a federal credit union charter for its membership was arbitrary, capricious and discriminatory, and in excess of, and contrary to the provisions of the Federal Credit Union Act, more specifically Sections 1754 and 1759 thereof, and the regulations issued thereunder. . . .

Plaintiff, National Alliance of Postal and Federal Employees (National Alliance),

---

49. Dodd-Frank Act §§312(b)(2)(B), 314 (codified at 12 U.S.C. §§1, 4a, 11 5412(b)(2)(B)).

50. Dodd-Frank Act §312(b)(2)(C) (codified at 12 U.S.C. §5412(b)(2)(C)).

51. Dodd-Frank Act §312(b)(1), (2)(A) (codified at 12 U.S.C. 5412(b)(1), (2)(A)).

52. Dodd-Frank Act §311(a) (codified at 12 U.S.C. §5411(a)). The effective date may be extended under certain specified circumstances. 12 U.S.C. §5411(b). Technical details of the transfer are handled by Dodd-Frank Act §§302, 312(a)-(b), 317, 319, 322–327.

53. Dodd-Frank Act §313 (codified at 12 U.S.C. 5413).

54. *See* FIRREA § 401(f) (savings provisions relating to FSLIC), (g) (savings provisions relating to FHLBB), (h)-(i) (continuation of orders, resolutions, determinations and regulations of FSLIC and FHLBB), *id.*, § 402(a)-(b) (continuation and coordination of certain regulations).

55. Established in 1978, the National Credit Union Central Liquidity Facility ("CLF") has assisted credit unions experiencing liquidity problems by granting them loans. Such liquidity assistance is in the nature of a central bank function. Within the credit union system, it is performed by the CLF, a unit of the NCUA.

is a national labor organization with a membership of approximately 40,000, the vast majority of which are black postal employees. . . .

The provisions of the Federal Credit Union Act applicable to the issues raised herein provide in pertinent part: [The court quoted from 12 U.S.C. §§ 1754, 1759.]

In 1971 National Alliance applied to NCUA for a Federal credit union charter to serve its membership on a national basis. The application was referred to an investigator who made a report (Federal Credit Union Investigation Report) and recommended that a charter be granted to the group. The report contained, inter alia, the following information:

> (1) National Alliance applied as a group having an associational common bond;
>
> (2) The proposed field of membership was defined as "Regular and Associate members of the National Alliance of Postal and Federal Employees ...";
>
> (3) There were no factions within the group which may render smooth and efficient credit union operations difficult;
>
> (4) The number of potential members of the proposed National Alliance Credit Union was 37,881;
>
> (5) Organization on an employee basis was not considered because the membership is widely disbursed with many members located in isolated places where it would not be practical to organize a credit union;
>
> (6) 1,500 members had signified their intention of joining and supporting the credit union; and
>
> (7) Space in union publications, a secure office area, clerical assistance, and payroll deductions would be provided by National Alliance.

In an internal memorandum transmitting that report to the Assistant Regional Director of NCUA the investigator referred to the charter meeting of the applicant group, stating that "[a]ll of the persons attending the meeting appear to be highly qualified and all are long-time members of National Alliance." The Acting Regional Director, however, did not recommend the charter to the Administrator because approximately 98 percent of the membership were postal service employees, resulting in a 100 percent overlap with the U.S. Postal Service Federal Credit Union, Charter Number 16402, which serves all postal employees not having credit union service available on a local basis. The Administrator concluded that National Alliance did not qualify for a charter because of this overlap, and because association of members was on a local basis, there being no provisions in the union's constitution or bylaws for association on a national basis through regular annual meetings. By letter dated March 31, 1972, which incorporated the substance of the Administrator's conclusions, National Alliance was advised by the Regional Director that its application was denied.

Plaintiff appealed to the Administrator to reverse the denial pointing to the numerous and continuous contacts among the members of National Alliance, the objectives shared by the membership, and the fact that the National Association of Postmasters of the United States as well as other associations similarly situated to National Alliance had been granted charters by the NCUA. In connection with this review, comments from various divisions and persons within NCUA were solicited. By letter dated June 5, 1972 the denial was affirmed, the Administrator finding there existed no common bond of association, and that the granting of the charter would create overlapping availability of credit union service, contrary to chartering policy set forth in its manual "Organizing a Federal Credit Union," which contained the standards and guidelines relating thereto. Under the circumstances herein, the latter rationale is essentially a denial based on economic advisability.

Plaintiff continued with its appeal efforts through February 8, 1974, when it was informed that NCUA policy had not changed since March 31, 1972, the date of the original rejection. During this period defendant made repeated suggestions that plaintiff apply for separate charters based on its local or district organizational levels.

The discretionary power vested in the Administrator by 12 U.S.C. § 1754 has not heretofore been challenged. The Court is persuaded by defendant's contention that the power of NCUA is analogous to that granted to the Federal Home Loan Bank Board by 12 U.S.C. § 1464(a) and (e), and to the Comptroller of the Currency by 12 U.S.C. § 26 and 27. It is well established that vast discretion has been conferred upon these similar regulatory agencies and that judicial review of discretionary action is necessarily limited. *See, Federal Home Loan Bank Board v. Rowe*, 284 F.2d 274, 277-278 (D.C.Cir. 1960); *Sterling National Bank of Davie v. Camp*, 431 F.2d 514, 516 (5th Cir. 1970). Accordingly, plaintiff must carry the burden of proving that the Administrator's denial of its application for a federal credit union charter was arbitrary, capricious, an abuse of discretion, or otherwise not in accordance with law.

In reviewing the Administrator's denial of the National Alliance application, the Court is confined to the administrative record and such additional explanation of those factors considered as may be necessary to determine if the Administrator's action was unwarranted by the facts. *See Camp v. Pitts*, 411 U.S. 138 (1973); *Citizens to Preserve Overton Park v. Volpe*, 401 U.S. 402 (1971). . . .

Defendant does not question the fact that a common bond exists among plaintiff's membership. Defendant does contend, however, that the Administrator correctly determined that the extent and nature of association was insufficient for issuance of a charter. Plaintiff challenges this conclusion, urging that National Alliance does meet the definition, meaning and purpose of associational common bond. Plaintiff asserts that the Administrator's decision was improperly based on a finding that there was no extensive commingling among National Alliance members on a national scale because only a biennial, rather than an annual, convention with an attendance of approximately 1200 members is held by the union.

Common bond, as it applies to Federal credit union chartering, is defined and explained in the Organization Manual at page 3 as follows:

> "Common bond is a characteristic prerequisite to the fulfillment of group objectives and when present among persons of related interests and purposes, these persons could be expected to effectively operate a credit union."

Associational common bond is further defined as:

> ". . . association resulting from membership in an organization, participation in whose activities develops common loyalties and mutual interests." *Id.*

With respect to applications of associational groups for Federal credit union charters, the Organization Manual further states at pages 10-11:

> "In deciding whether a Federal credit union charter may be issued to an associational group, the extent and nature of association derived from membership should be carefully considered. The effect of common loyalties and mutual interest resulting through participation in organization activities should also be considered. . . .
>
> "The common bond is usually stronger when an association is firmly established. . . .
>
> "The Association should hold regular membership meetings or it should sponsor other activities which provide for commingling of members and

strengthen the bond among them."

Labor unions are specifically listed in the Organization Manual as among those associational groups eligible for a charter. The list of organizational groups which have been granted charters is lengthy and varied. Included are groups such as the National Association of Postmasters, the National Medical Association, the Air Line Pilots Association, the United Mine Workers of America, and the International Arabian Horse Association, whose charters are national in scope. Only a curt explanation was offered by the Administrator as to how National Alliance differed from these, and other chartered associational groups.

As plaintiff points out, the provisions formerly included in definitional statements requiring that members associate together, be extensively acquainted with other members or that they know each other, have been stricken from the current, more liberal standards. Moreover, the current Organization Manual clearly envisions a broad variety of associational activities that can provide the commingling of members, thereby strengthening the bond among them. The suggestion that an annual national gathering should be a requirement is simply not supported.

The Organization Manual does not specifically address national charters. However, it does infer a policy against them. Notwithstanding such a policy, defendant concedes, as it must, that associational groups have been granted nation-wide charters. Defendant views these national charters as exceptions to NCUA policy; plaintiff asserts the granting of such charters to similarly situated organizations is NCUA precedent.

The common bond of association existing among the National Alliance membership grows out of the union's organizational structure as well as the common objectives of improving wages, hours and working conditions. The National Alliance common bond is as strong, if not stronger than the common bond existing among other associations already enjoying a national charter. Continued reliance on a policy against national charters, particularly in light of the existing United Mine Workers' and the National Postmasters' charters, is incongruous. And although the circumstances behind these, and other national charters may be technically distinguishable, their existence supports a finding that whatever policy NCUA had against the granting of national charters when National Alliance was seeking a charter, was either changed, or was not adhered to.

The Court therefore concludes that there was no justification for the disparate treatment of National Alliance, and that the Administrator's action in denying National Alliance a Federal credit union charter for these reasons was arbitrary, capricious and an abuse of discretion. . . .

The Organization Manual defines and explains the meaning of the economic advisability requirement at page 3 as follows:

> "Determination of the economic advisability of establishing a proposed Federal credit union is based on the number of potential members, evidence of group interest, leadership, willingness of persons to serve and participate, and the general characteristics of the sponsor or factors or conditons present in the area."

Additionally, the Organization Manual, at page 22, explains that in order to provide a complete picture of the group planning to organize a Federal credit union, the Investigation Reports contain, inter alia, the following information relating to economic advisability:

> "a. The size and compactness of the group;
> b. The nature of the common bond;
> c. The attitude of . . .

(2) officers in associational groups;
d. The facilities available for credit union operation;
e. The availability of existing credit union service; and
f. Other facts to support a potential for successful operation."

In denying the National Alliance application, the Administrator relied upon a "consistent theme" running throughout the NCUA chartering policy that "overlapping fields of credit union membership will be avoided." Defendant argues that virtually all of plaintiff's members already have a variety of existing credit unions available to provide services to them, and that the likelihood of a new credit union's success is therefore diminished.

Plaintiff points out that it meets each of the factors identified in the Organization Manual as relevant to the economic advisability requirement, and that denial solely on the basis of existing credit union service was arbitrary, particularly since there was no factual investigation concerning economic advisability of actual availability of non-discriminatory credit union service.

Defendant's position is that there is an NCUA policy against overlapping fields of credit union membership and that the U.S. Postal Service Federal Credit Union is already available to serve all postal employees, including plaintiff's members. Plaintiff concedes that granting its application for a national charter would create an overlap.

Plaintiff's members represent about five percent of the total postal workforce. Thus, while nearly all of National Alliance's members would theoretically have two Federal credit unions available to serve them the effect on the stability of the U.S. Postal Service Credit Union would seemingly be minimal.

Moreover, defendant has indicated a willingness to organize Federal credit unions on plaintiff's local or district organizational levels. The Court finds this position inconsistent inasmuch as the granting of such local or district level charters would in no way reduce the overlap situation. Furthermore, overlap situations exist elsewhere in the postal service, the most analogous being the overlap between the U.S. Postal Service Federal Credit Union and the National Postmasters Association Federal Credit Union.

Finally, the record herein fails to reveal any in- depth analysis or investigation with respect to the probable success of a National Alliance Federal credit union on a nationwide basis. The assessment of the economic advisability of such a credit union is found in the following statement by the Deputy Administrator:

> "I would venture a guess that if this FCU was organized–it would not be successful in serving its members–and might well be a casualty within five years."

Under the circumstances presented herein, and plaintiff having met all other economic advisability standards, the Administrator's determination that a National Alliance charter was not economically advisable, and his reliance on overlapping fields of available credit union services was contrary to the National Credit Union Act, and NCUA's own regulations and precedent, and was arbitrary, capricious and an abuse of discretion.

Notes and Comments 1.46. *State regulators of depository institutions.* States play a major role as chartering authorities of state banks and savings associations and as supervisory and examining authorities for the institutions thus created. The state regulator may be an official, variously titled commissioner or superintendent of banking, or a collegial body. The regulator may be independent or may be placed within an executive department of the state government. Beyond these general features, the composition and specific powers and procedures vary from state to state. Such a regulator may or may not have authority over all banks and bank-like entities. In many jurisdictions, a separate regulator will have authority over savings associations or credit unions.

1.47. *State supervisors and federal regulation.* Given the significant role that state regulators play in the examination process, the views of state regulators are included in the process followed by the Federal Financial Institutions Examination Council ("FFIEC") in formulating uniform policy statements. State liaison with the FFIEC is mandated in 12 U.S.C. § 3306. In addition, a 1996 amendment to the Federal Deposit Insurance Act requires that one member of the FDIC Board of Directors have state bank supervisory experience. Economic Growth and Regulatory Paperwork Reduction Act, Pub. L. No. 104-208, title II, § 2243 110 Stat. 3009 (1996) (codified at 12 U.S.C. § 1812(a)(1)(C)).

4. Deregulation, Reregulation, and Structural Realignment

Pervasive regulation of depository institutions is of relatively recent vintage–roughly since 1933. In the 1970's, a deregulation theme emerged that has been primarily concerned with greater efficiency and coherence in regulation. This deregulation movement is not a unitary effort, but involves at least three major objectives: (*a*) deregulation of products (*e.g.*, deposit interest rates, securities activities of banks); (*b*) deregulation of markets (*e.g.*, allowing more freedom to banks to engage in banking on an interstate basis; and, (*c*) structural deregulation, reforming the structure of bank regulation itself. The materials that follow briefly examine each of these objectives.

Notes and Comments 1.48. *Product deregulation: The DIDMCA.* One statutory source of product deregulation can be found in the Depository Institutions Deregulation and Monetary Control Act of 1980 ("DIDMCA"), Pub. L. No. 96-221. In addition to establishing the Depository Institutions Deregulation Committee to remove restrictions on payment of interest on deposits, the act set the tone for banking deregulation for the decade. What were the objectives of the DIDMCA? Consider the following excerpt.

Weaver and O'Malley, The Depository Institutions Deregulation and Monetary Control Act of 1980: An Overview

98 Banking L.J. 100 (1981)

The 1980 Depository Institutions Deregulation and Monetary Control Act (DIDA) became law on March 31, 1980. It is the most significant federal banking legislation since the 1930s.

For over 100 years, the federal government has regulated federal financial institutions. But only since the Depression has that regulation gone further than cursorily protecting bank depositors, shareholders, and the public at large. During the Depression, with widespread bank and savings and loan failures, the federal government intrenvened to protect depositors especially and shareholders as well from imprudent financial institutions and stock manipulations. In the 1960s and early 1970s, however, the federal government further intervened in a much more substantial and less necessary way to protect the bank borrowers and over protect depositors and shareholders as well. Deregulation and equalization of federal financial institutions have become a necessity to return to banking a reasonable and practicable competitive environment.

DIDA addresses nine important new banking issues. Title I, The Monetary Control

Act of 1980, delineates the reserves required on corporate time deposits and all transaction accounts. Title II, the Depository Institutions Deregulation Act of 1980, gradually frees interest rates from any but market restraints, equalizes banks and S&Ls for the first time, and eliminates over a six-year phaseout the current limitations on maximum rates of interest and dividends. Title III, the Consumer Checking Account Equity Act of 1980, permits NOW [negotiable orders of withdrawal] accounts effective December 31, 1980, and immediately increases the FDIC and FSLIC insurance limits on deposits and accounts from $40,000 to $100,000. Title IV, regarding Powers of Thrift Institutions and Miscellaneous Provisions, permits S&Ls to invest up to 20 percent of their assets in consumer loans, commercial paper, and corporate debt securities, and to increase lending limits up to 90 percent of the value of a residence, or more if covered by mortgage insurance. Title V, the State Usury Laws title, preempts state usury laws as they apply to residential mortgages, but can be overriden if states act within three years. This title also preempts state laws as to business and agricultural loans over $25,000 (and more recently, those over $1,000 as well). Title VI, the Truth in Lending Simplification and Reform Act, contains various improvements of the Act's clarity, limits creditor liability, and strengthens administrative restitution enforcement. Title VII, the Amendments to the National Bank Act, changes real estate holding rules, preferred stock dividends, trust powers, bank holidays, shareholder appraisal rights, and bank examinations. Title VIII, the Regulatory Simplification Act, requires periodic review of regulations to promote clarity and eliminate contradictions and duplicity; Title IX, the Foreign Control of United States Financial Institutions Act, imposed a moratorium of takeovers of domestic financial institutions with over $100 million in assets by foreign persons until July 1, 1980. . . .

Federal financial institution deregulaton and equalization are neither complete nor assured in the Act, but federal financial regulation is moving in that direction. The Act did not seriously address interstate banking or preempt all state usury laws, but those more meaningful tools of a truly national financial economy are being debated in the Congress. ...

Notes and Comments 1.49. Initially, the deregulation movement made slow and painful progress. Some advances were made with the enactment of the Garn-St. Germain Depository Institutions Act of 1982.[56] In this act the Congress was already reacting to the financial crisis of the savings associations rather than creating new approaches to deregulation.

1.50. *Product deregulation: The role of the DIDC.* The Depository Institutions Deregulation Committee ("DIDC"), created as a temporary agency by the DIDMCA, had only a specialized role to play in the deregulation movement–removing regulatory restrictions on the interest paid on deposits. Regulatory reform that frees deposit interest rates from artificial restrictions and gradually returns them to "market rates" presumably makes bank deposits more efficient and competitive. On the authority of the DIDC to issue regulations eliminating interest rate ceilings applicable to certain categories of time deposits at federally insured commercial banks and thrift institutions, see *U.S. League of Savings Institutions v. Depository Institutions Deregulation Committee*, 710 F.2d 841 (D.C. Cir. 1983).

1.51. *Judicial approaches to administrative deregulation.* The courts have dealt with other forms of product deregulation that arose from changing administrative interpretations of statutory authority. This has been the case especially as to securities activities

56. Pub. L. 97-320, Oct. 15, 1982, 96 Stat. 1099 (1982) (codified at scattered sections of 11, 12, 15 and 20 U.S.C.).

permissible for commercial banks.[57] Courts have generally been relatively tolerant of deregulation by administrative interpretation, despite apparently constrictive statutory provisions. *See* Langevoort, *Statutory Obsolesence and the Judicial Process: The Revisionist Role of the Courts in Federal Banking Regulation*, 85 Mich. L. Rev. 672 (1987). *See also* Zeppos, *Judicial Candor and Statutory Interpretation*, 78 Geo. L.J. 353, 362-379 (1989).

1.52. *Influence of nonbank competition on product deregulation.* One of the major sources of competition for the deposit account in the 1970s was the money market mutual fund ("MMMF"), a high yield deposit-like product offered by securities firms. *See Centennial Journal: 100 Years in Business, Merrill Lynch CMAs Draw Interest*, 1977, Wall St. J., Nov. 3, 1989, at B1, col. 5 (discussing development of "Cash Management Account"). MMMFs drew a significant amount of deposit business away from depository institutions, especially large-denomination deposits of individual customers of the banks. The banks were anxious to develop a new product that could compete with the MMMFs. This problem was finally resolved directly by Section 327 of the Garn-St Germain Depository Institutions Act of 1982, which amended 12 U.S.C. § 3503 by directing the DIDC to authorize a new deposit account to become known as the money market deposit account ("MMDA"). The MMDA was authorized by the DIDC in 12 C.F.R. § 1204.122 (1984).

1.53. *New products for savings associations.* The now defunct FHLBB was authorized by the Home Owners' Loan Act (HOLA) to issue regulations concerning investments by federally chartered savings & loan associations [S&Ls] in service corporation affiliates. *See* 12 U.S.C. § 1464(c)(4)(B) (1988). These regulations were amended, effective April 30, 1981, to provide increased flexibility in service corporation activities. 46 Fed. Reg. 24,256 (1981) (to be codified at 12 C.F.R. § 545.9-1). New activities added to the list of service corporation activities not requiring specific FHLBB approval ("pre-approved activities") included financial counseling (§ 545.9-1(c)(5), as amended), and "providing liquidity management, investment and advisory services primarily to savings and loan associations. ..." (§ 545.9-1(c)(2) (viii), as amended). The FHLBB's policy was to approve "only service corporation activities reasonably related to [S&L] activities." 46 Fed. Reg. 24,527 (1981). It was not entirely clear what a "reasonably related" activity might be. For example, in an amendment to its service corporation provisions, the FHLBB's remarks might lead one to infer that "reasonably related" simply meant "beneficial to S&Ls:"

> the [FHLBB] also solicited comments on whether service corporations of Federal [S&Ls] should be authorized to operate and manage money market mutual funds. The Board was interested particu larly in determining *whether such authority would enhance the ability of [S&Ls] to attract and maintain deposits and under what conditions the benefits to be realized from such activity would be maximized.*

45 Fed. Reg. at 24,529 (emphasis added). Despite this liberal attitude, the FHLBB did tie the newly authorized preapproved activities to specific powers granted to the S&Ls under the Depository Institutions Deregulation and Monetary Control Act of 1980. The FHLBB explained that this Act:

> authorized [S&Ls] to offer negotiable order of withdrawal accounts, liberalized existing authority . . . to make residential and commercial real estate loans, authorized consumer loan, commercial paper and corporate debt investments, and authorized the providing of trust services.
>
> Since [S&Ls] often implement new investment authority and make investments and provide services related to [S&L's] activities through their service

57. *See infra* Chapter 5, § 9; Chapter 6, § 2.b.

> corporations, *the expanded authority for Federal [S&Ls] under the Act created a need for a corresponding expansion of service corporation authority.*

(Emphasis added.) The authority to invest in service corporation affiliates continues in the HOLA as amended by the Financial Institutions Reform, Recovery, and Enforcement Act of 1989.[58] The regulations of the Office of Thrift Supervision continue the specific authorization of service corporation investments,[59] including a wide range of preapproved activities.[60]

1.54. Review 12 U.S.C. §§ 1464(c)(4)(B), 1467a(c)(3), (m). Do these provisions limit in any significant way the effects of product deregulation for savings associations? Do they contradict the trend towards deregulation so prominent throughout the 1980s?

1.55. Did deregulation go too far? By the end of 1988, with the safety of savings institutions clearly in jeopardy, public perceptions began to turn against the deregulation movement. *See* Berke, *Deregulation Has Gone Too Far, Many Tell the New Administration*, N.Y. Times, Dec. 11, 1988, § 1, at 1, col. 1. What is the relationship between deregulation and the crisis in the savings association industry? Consider the following excerpt.

N. Strunk & F. Case, Where Deregulation Went Wrong

14-16 (1988)

Association failures appear to have occurred in two waves: first, because of the "spread problems," i.e., the costs of funds exceeding the earnings of the assets; and second, because of losses on the asset side of the balance sheet.

Failures for the first reason generally occurred from 1981 through 1984. The second group, far more serious from the standpoint of FSLIC finances, were those in 1985 and 1986, continuing into 1987 and, no doubt, beyond.

A number of factors can be identified as the causes for the failures. The single most important development that precipitated the wave of failures was "deregulation" which first produced operating losses for most institutions and then attracted venturesome entrepreneurs to the business who led savings associations into unfamiliar business activities.

At the same time, supervisory and regulatory staffs were ineffective at supervising the "new" savings and loan business. Unfortunately, the people who worked so hard to deregulate the savings and loan business had failed to realize that there is a basic conflict between deposit insurance and the deregulation of financial institutions–and that by its nature, deregulation requires stronger, not weaker, supervision of the institutions being deregulated. The rate of deregulation required sharp adjustments in regulatory policies and procedures which did not occur. Probably more than anything else, it was this lapse in judgment that brought on the losses now being suffered by the FSLIC.

The following is a detailed summary of the major causes for losses that hurt the business in the 1980s:

> 1. Lack of net worth for many institutions as they entered the 1980s, and a wholly inadequate net worth regulation.
>
> 2. Decline in the effectiveness of Regulation Q [the Federal Reserve regulations that limited the maximum allowable interest to be paid on deposits] in preserving the spread between the cost of money and the rate of return on

---

58. Pub. L. No. 101-73, § 301, 103 Stat. 183, 288 (1989) (codified at 12 U.S.C. § 1464(c)(4)(B)).

59. 12 C.F.R. § 545.74.

60. *Id.* § 545.74(c).

assets, basically stemming from inflation and the accompanying increase in market interest rates.

3. Absence of an ability to vary the return on assets with increases in the rate of interest required to be paid for deposits.

4. Increased competition on the deposit gathering and mortgage origination sides of the business, with a sudden burst of new technology making possible a whole new way of conducting financial institutions generally and the mortgage business specifically.

5. A rapid increase in investment powers of associations with passage of the Depository Institutions Deregulation and Monetary Control Act[,] []the Garn-St Germain Act[], and, more important, through state legislative enactments in a number of important and rapidly growing states. These introduced new risks and speculative opportunities which were difficult to administer. In many instances management lacked the ability or experience to evaluate them, or to administer large volumes of nonresidential construction loans.

6. Elimination of regulations initially designed to prevent lending excesses and minimize failures. Regulatory relaxation permitted lending, directly and through participations, in distant loan markets on the promise of high returns. Lenders, however, were not familiar with these distant markets. It also permitted associations to participate extensively in speculative construction activities with builders and developers who had little or no financial stake in the projects.

7. Fraud and insider transaction abuses were the principal cause for some 20% of savings and loan failures the past three years and a greater percentage of the dollar losses borne by the FSLIC.

8. A new type and generation of opportunistic savings and loan executives and owners–some of whom operated in a fraudulent manner–whose takeover of many institutions was facilitated by a change in FSLIC rules reducing the minimum number of stockholders of an insured association from 400 to one.

9. Deregulation of duty on the part of the board of directors of some savings associations. This permitted management to make uncontrolled use of some new operating authority, while directors failed to control expenses and prohibit obvious conflict of interest situations.

10. A virtual end of inflation in the American economy, together with overbuilding in multifamily, condominium type residences and in commercial real estate in many cities. In addition, real estate values collapsed in the energy states–Texas, Louisiana, Oklahoma particularly–and weakness occurred in the mining and agricultural sectors of the economy.

11. Pressures felt by management of many associations to restore net worth ratios. Anxious to improve earnings, they departed from their traditional lending practices into credits and markets involving higher risks, but with which they had little experience.

12. The lack of appropriate, accurate and effective evaluations of the savings and loan business by public accounting firms, security analysts and the financial community.

13. Organizational structure and supervisory laws, adequate for policing and controlling the business in the protected environment of the 1960s and 1970s, resulted in fatal delays and indecision in the examination/supervision process in the 1980s.

14. Federal and state examination and supervisory staffs insufficient in number, experience and ability to deal with the new world of savings and loan operations.

15. The inability or unwillingness of the [Federal Home Loan] Bank Board and its legal and supervisory staff to deal with problem institutions in a timely manner. Many institutions, which ultimately closed with big losses, were known problem cases for a year or more. Often, it appeared, political considerations

delayed necessary supervisory action.

Notes and Comments 1.56. *Regulation and market discipline.* Contrary to the view expressed by Strunk and Case, is it possible that problems with the savings association industry came about because deregulation did not occur soon enough and thoroughly enough? Some critics have suggested that complete deregulation–and governance by market forces–is the correct approach with respect to certain areas of concern to depository institutions policy.[61] For example, would depository institutions be safer and sounder if, instead of FDIC deposit insurance and financial assistance to troubled institutions, we relied on a system of public disclosure, allowing individual depositors to act upon their assessment of the riskiness of particular depository institutions? The proper role of public disclosure as an instrument of bank regulation is one aspect of the debate over the role of "market discipline" as a means of regulation in a relatively deregulated environment. Market discipline presupposes that investors (and quasi-investors like depositors) can–and would–influence the choice of risk-generating activities of depository institutions by their investment decisions. The assessment of the expected returned and potential investment risk by prospective or current investors might affect an institution's decisions by increasing the expected return offered (thus increasing the cost of relatively risky activities), or by decreasing the potential risk. There are at least two problems with this approach. First, as an empirical matter depositors do not generally contract with depository institutions with the mindset or motivations of investors–nor is it clear that they should. *See* Garten, *Banking on the Market: Relying On Depositors to Control Bank Risks*, 4 Yale J. Reg. 129 (1986) (arguing that market discipline approach to bank regulation is unlikely to work in practice, given behavior of depositors). *See also* Garten, *Still Banking on the Market: A Comment on the Failure of Market Discipline*, 5 Yale J. Reg. 241 (1988) (criticizing market discipline arguments of Macey & Garrett, *supra* note 62); Garten, *Regulatory Growing Pains: A Perspective on Bank Regulation in a Deregulatory Age*, 57 Fordham L. Rev. 501, 558-64 (1989) (discussing increased attention to "market discipline" approach to bank regulation). Second, public disclosure is *already* one instrument of regulation, and its proper role is open to question. *See* Malloy, *Public Disclosure as a Tool of Federal Bank Regulation*, 9 Ann. Rev. Banking L. 229 (1990) (discussing and criticizing current uses of public disclosure in bank regulation). Indeed, the use of public disclosure in depository institutions regulation has created additional ambiguity in the regulatory system, because the system is still essentially committed to a confidential approach to supervision and enforcment. *See, e.g.*, Mathewson, *From Confidential Supervision to Market Discipline: The Role of Disclosure in the Regulation of Commercial Banks*, 11 J. Corp. L. 139, 146-50 (1986) (discussing development of "confidential supervision" as basic principle of federal bank regulation).

1.57. Consider the following excerpt from *Winstar*. Does the Supreme Court link the deregulation of the savings association industry to its eventual collapse?

United States v. Winstar Corporation

518 U.S. 839 (1996)

Justice SOUTER announced the judgment of the Court and delivered an opinion, in which Justice STEVENS and Justice BREYER join, and in which Justice O'CONNOR joins except as to Parts IV-A and IV-B.

---

61. *See, e.g.*, Macey & Garrett, *Market Discipline by Depositors: A Summary of the Theoretical and Empirical Arguments*, 5 Yale J. Reg. 215 (1988) (arguing for increased reliance on market discipline by depositors).

[This case involved the enforceability of contracts between the U.S. Government and savings associations or savings and loan holding companies that were acquiring failed savings associations. The federal regulators agreed to give favorable regulatory treatment the acquiring companies in exchange for their assumption of liabilities that threatened to produce claims against the Government as deposit insurer of the failed institutions. Thereafter, Congress changed the relevant law and barred the Government from honoring the agreements. In a portion of the decision excerpted in Chapter 8, the Court held that the terms assigning the risk of regulatory change to the Government were enforceable, and that the Government was therefore liable in damages for breach of the contracts.]

The first federal response to the rising tide of thrift failures [during 1981-1983] was "extensive deregulation," including "a rapid expansion in the scope of permissible thrift investment powers and a similar expansion in a thrift's ability to compete for funds with other financial services providers." House Report, at 291; *see also id.*, at 295-297; Breeden, *Thumbs on the Scale: The Role that Accounting Practices Played in the Savings and Loan Crisis*, 59 Fordham L.Rev. S71, S72-S74 (1991) (describing legislation permitting nonresidential real estate lending by thrifts and deregulating interest rates paid to thrift depositors).[1] Along with this deregulation came moves to weaken the requirement that thrifts maintain adequate capital reserves as a cushion against losses, *see* 12 CFR § 563.13 (1981), a requirement that one commentator described as "the most powerful source of discipline for financial institutions." Breeden, *supra*, at S75. The result was a drop in capital reserves required by the Bank Board from five to four percent of assets in November 1980, *see* 45 Fed. Reg. 76111, and to three percent in January of 1982, *see* 47 Fed. Reg. 3543; at the same time, the Board developed new "regulatory accounting principles" (RAP) that in many instances replaced generally accepted accounting principles (GAAP) for purposes of determining compliance with its capital requirements.[2] According to the House Banking Committee, "[t]he use of various accounting gimmicks and reduced capital standards masked the worsening financial condition of the industry, and the FSLIC, and enabled many weak institutions to continue operating with an increasingly inadequate cushion to absorb future losses." House Report, at 298. The reductions in required capital reserves, moreover, allowed thrifts to grow explosively without increasing their capital base, at the same time deregulation let them expand into new (and often riskier) fields of investment. *See* Note, *Causes of the Savings and Loan Debacle*, 59 Fordham L.Rev. S301, S311 (1991); Breeden, *supra*, at S74-S75.

Notes and Comments 1.58. *Market deregulation.* Dramatic strides have been made in deregulation of artificial barriers to geographic market expansion in the United States.

---

1. The easing of federal regulatory requirements was accompanied by similar initiatives on the state level, especially in California, Florida, and Texas. The impact of these changes was substantial, since as of 1980 over 50 percent of federally-insured thrifts were chartered by the States. See House Report, at 297.

2. "Regulatory and statutory accounting gimmicks included permitting thrifts to defer losses from the sale of assets with below market yields; permitting the use of income capital certificates, authorized by Congress, in place of real capital; letting qualifying mutual capital certificates be included as RAP capital; allowing FSLIC members to exclude from liabilities in computing net worth, certain contra-asset accounts, including loans in process, unearned discounts, and deferred fees and credits; and permitting the inclusion of net worth certificates, qualifying subordinated debentures and appraised equity capital as RAP net worth." House Report, at 298. The result of these practices was that "[b]y 1984, the difference between RAP and GAAP net worth at S & L's stood at $9 billion," which meant "that the industry's capital position, or . . . its cushion to absorb losses was overstated by $9 billion." *Ibid.*

Historically, it was impermissible for a bank to expand its market geographically beyond the borders of the state in which its principal place of business was located. In some states, the geographic limitations on markets were even more constricted. Given the high degree of public interest on the part of each state in regulating the operation of banks within its borders, the state was given a high degree of control over the establishment of a bank within those borders. For a time, national banks fared even worse. Under the National Bank Act as originally enacted, national banks had no authority to establish branches. Hence, each bank was limited to its "principal" place of business, as set forth in its charter. This situation changed in 1927, when the McFadden Act permitted branching by national banks, but only within the city limits of its "principal" place of business, and then only if pertinent state law permitted state-chartered banks to do so. By 1933, national banks were permitted to branch in any place in the state in which state-chartered banks were permitted to branch.[62] However, these provisions dealt only with *intrastate* branching; *interstate* branching was still generally prohibited. After decades of proposals, study,[63] and litigation,[64] genuine interstate banking and branching was authorized in 1994 by the Interstate Banking and Branching Efficiency Act of 1994 ("IBBEA").[65] Subject to regulatory approvals, the IBBEA authorizes interstate branching, interstate acquisitions of banks by holding companies, and interstate bank mergers.

1.59. *Increased oversight of community involvement by interstate enterprises.* A new form of product regulation (or "reregulation") is emerging, in part as a response to the opening of interstate markets. An increasingly controversial issue in banking regulation is the degree to which banking enterprises should be required to involve themselves in the economic well-being and development of local communities served by their operations.[66] Some of these concerns are addressed by the Community Development and Regulatory Improvement Act of 1994 ("CDRIA").[67] Among other things, the act is intended to create a Community Development and Financial Institutions Fund to promote economic revitalization and community development by investment in and financial assistance to "community development financial institutions."[68] These private institutions will focus on financial activities and transactions intended to promote community development.[69] However, such legislative efforts are relatively specialized, and they avoid rather than resolve the underlying controversy; namely, if banking enterprises enjoy a relatively exclusive advantage in aggregating credit and lendable resources, to what extent should they be required to serve their local communities? In this regard, the IBBEA presents a number of additional, if limited

---

62. 12 U.S.C. § 36(c)(1)-(2). *See infra* Chapter 3, § 2 (discussing national bank intrastate branching).

63. *See, e.g.*, REPORT OF THE PRESIDENT, GEOGRAPHIC RESTRICTIONS ON COMMERCIAL BANKING IN THE UNITED STATES (Department of Treasury, January 1981) (recommending removal of artificial barriers to geographic market expansion).

64. *See, e.g., Northeast Bancorp v. Board of Governors*, 472 U.S. 159 (1985) (upholding interstate arrangements within regional groupings of states).

65. Pub. Law No. 103-328, Sept. 29, 1994, 108 Stat. 2338 (1994) (codified at scattered sections of 12 U.S.C.).

66. *See, e.g.*, Peter Passell, *Redlining Under Attack*, N.Y.Times, Aug. 30, 1994, at D1, col. 1 (discussing Administration efforts for lending to minorities).

67. Pub. L. No. 103-325, Sept. 23, 1994, 108 Stat. 2160 (1994) (codified at scattered sections of 12 U.S.C.) [hereinafter "CDRIA"].

68. CDRIA, §§102(b), 104-105, 108-109, 113-114.

69. *See id.*, §103(5).

responses. These include special notice requirements for closure of branches following an interstate acquisition; regulatory requirements to ensure that the credit needs of communities served by interstate banking enterprises are met; and changes in the Community Reinvestment Act to cover interstate enterprises on a consolidated basis.

1.60. *Structural deregulation.* It should be apparent from the precious discussion of the regulators that supervise depository institutions that the regulatory structure of the depository institutions industry, with its complex, intertwining scheme of regulatory agencies, is neither efficient nor particularly coherent in outline. Structural deregulation–or more precisely, structural realignment–is thus an important objective of the deregulation movement. Proposals for structural realignment can be found almost throughout the modern history of federal bank regulation.[70] In 1984 a presidential task group, chaired by then Vice-President Bush, made significant progress towards the realization of structural realignment in light of the changes which the financial services industry had undergone. Based on the following excerpts from the group's report, how successful would its recommendations have been in making sense of the regulatory structure?

Blueprint for Reform: The Report of the Task Group on Regulation of Financial Services

38-44, 50-64 (September 24, 1984)

. . . [T]he Task Group identified (i) safety and soundness, (ii) consumer protection, and (iii) vigorous competition as the paramount goals of financial regulation. . . .

. . . [T]he recommendations of the Task Group . . . represent the collective judgment of its members[a] as to the best balance and accommodation of the three principal goals that cannot be completely harmonized to negate all conflict between them. More specifically, the Task Group recommendations are predicated on one or more of several specific objectives, each of which is described below. . . .

1. Regulation by Function

Historically, federal regulation of different types of financial institutions has been organized so that a single agency exercised all the different types of regulatory controls applicable to a single type of firm. For example, securities, consumer, antitrust, civil rights and other regulatory provisions applicable to savings and loan associations are centralized today under the authority of the FHLBB, which also administers regulations relating to the safety and soundness of these institutions. To varying degrees a similar pattern of "institutional" regulation exists for other types of financial firms.

Institutional regulation offers the advantage of convenience for regulated firms by permitting "one-stop shopping" for regulatory matters. On the other hand, from a broader public policy standpoint institutional regulation has at least two major disadvantages. First, it involves duplication of effort among the various regulatory agencies. Thus, five separate agencies today regulate the securities activities of banks and thrifts, and five separate agencies handle antitrust review of mergers and acquisitions involving banks or thrifts.

Convenience for regulated firms may therefore be obtained to some extent only

---

70. For history of structural realignment proposals, see Pasley, *Consolidation of the Federal Banking Regulatory Agencies*, 9 Ann. Rev. Banking L. 255 (1990).

a. The members of the Task Group were the Vice President; the Secretary of the Treasury; the Assistant to the President for Policy Development; the Attorney General; the Comptroller of the Currency; the Chairmen of the Fed, the Commodity Futures Trading Commission, the Council of Economic Advisers, the FDIC, the FHLBB, the NCUA and the SEC; and the Director of the Office of Management and Budget.

through greater duplication among government agencies. The second major disadvantage of institutional regulation is that it often results in differential regulation when different types of institutions compete across industry lines. During the era of sharp differentiation in types of products offered by financial firms, institutional regulation operated largely without distorting the competitive balance among firms. . . .

As direct competition among different *types* of financial firms has increased, the problem of regulatory inequities has grown rapidly. As banks, securities firms, thrifts and insurance companies increasingly offer equivalent products and services to the consumer, their ability to be successful competitively may be affected by differences in the regulatory scheme applicable to them based on their historic type of business. . . .

By contrast to institutional regulation, "functional regulation" attempts to regulate each common activity or product by a single agency under a common set of rules, irrespective of the type of institution involved. . . .

In short, functional regulation can serve the public interest by reducing duplication among different government agencies and by promoting equal regulation of competing activities by different types of financial firms. By making regulation "transparent" as to the type of firm involved, functional regulation helps promote the availability of the widest possible range of financial products for the public at the lowest possible cost, with different firms prospering or failing to the greatest degree possible on their efficiency and merits rather than because of arbitrary differences in government regulation.

While functional regulation promotes equality of regulatory treatment and reduces overall government duplication, it can also result in a particular type of firm (*e.g.* a savings and loan, credit union, etc.) having to deal with a variety of special-purpose agencies rather than a single agency. This can result in added regulatory costs for such types of firms because they must deal with more than one agency. Therefore, application of functional regulation in any particular case requires a balancing of costs and benefits that would result, and a recognition that functional regulation may not be suitable in every area. As a result, the overall public interest will most likely be obtained through a mix of institutional and functional regulatory programs, rather than a system consisting exclusively of either type of regulation. Under such a system depository institutions and securities or commodities firms would continue to have most of their internal operations and safety and soundness concerns handled by a single agency, while activities common to many different types of firms or specialized issues would be handled by the appropriate functionally-oriented agency.

2. Removal of Unnecessary Barriers to Competition

. . . Unnecessary barriers to competition inevitably raise prices, reduce alternatives and, ultimately, reduce jobs in the overall economy by preventing the aggregate output of goods and services from reaching its full potential. While many regulatory restraints may be necessary and desirable to prevent excessive concentration of power, to promote safety and soundness, provide disclosure of material business information or otherwise, such restrictions should always be designed to achieve their objectives with the smallest possible restraint on competition.

3. Reduction of Unnecessary Regulatory Costs

. . . Where regulatory programs impose greater transaction or other compliance costs than the benefits they create, the public is ultimately disadvantaged. Therefore, it is never sufficient to inquire only whether a regulation has a desirable objective (*e.g.*, consumer protection, safety and soundness, etc.). In addition, each specific regulatory control should be evaluated to make certain that the manner in which it is applied insures that public benefits outweigh public costs. . . .

4. Maintaining Checks and Balances

. . . [E]limination of unnecessary overlap and duplication among government agencies can produce real savings for the public, and it should be a high priority of any government to eliminate waste and inefficiency. However, unlike the private sector, governmental organizations frequently do not face the same competitive pressures for efficiency and good management that are encountered by private firms. Consequently, there must be checks and balances among the branches of government in order to prevent excessive concentration of government power from developing.

. . . [A]s government agencies become larger and more diverse operationally, more and more internal bureaucratic levels are inevitably created in the agency's chain of responsibility. This can result in slower decision-making, higher personnel costs and reduced public participation than might occur with a smaller agency.

. . . [A]chieving the optimum regulatory organization requires a balancing of the benefits of reducing overlaps and improving consistency and the costs of bureaucratic centralization, which may include excessive rigidity and slowness to adapt to changing situations. . . .

5. Dual Federal and State Financial Regulation

. . . Because it has served the financial needs of the nation so well over time, state participation in the chartering and regulation of financial institutions can genuinely be regarded as one of the finest examples of cooperative federalism in the nation's history. Because the balance of state and federal regulatory participation helps promote the public interest in a safe and competitive financial system, the dual system of chartering financial institutions should be maintained and strengthened wherever possible. . . .

B. Summary of Recommendations to Reform the Bank Regulatory System

. . .

Regulation of Banks. Under the Task Group's plan the number of agencies involved in ordinary day-to-day bank supervision would be reduced from the current three to only two. Although each of the current agencies would continue to exist,[22] the pattern of authority would be greatly simplified. Under the Task Group's proposals, the new Federal Banking Agency ("FBA") would continue the OCC's current responsibilities for supervising all national banks. However, unlike the current system in which the [Fed] and FDIC both regulate state-chartered banks, under the Task Group's recommendations all *federal* regulation of state chartered institutions would be centralized in the [Fed], except for regulation pertaining expressly to deposit insurance.

At the same time that federal regulation of state chartered banks would be consolidated in the [Fed], other proposals of the Task Group would establish a new program under which highly qualified state agencies would assume much of the current federal supervisory role for state-chartered banks, with residual monitoring and standby authority vested in the [Fed]. The "certification" program . . . would permit state agencies to assume exclusive responsibilities for examining and supervising many state-chartered institutions now subject to dual state and federal examinations. . . .

Regulation of Bank Holding Companies. At the same time that federal bank regulation would be consolidated in the FBA for national banks and the [Fed] for state-chartered banks, both the FBA and the [Fed] would have the authority to examine and supervise the parent holding companies of the banks that they otherwise regulate.[23] To the extent "certified", state agencies would examine and supervise the holding companies of banks which they regulate. . . .

---

22. The OCC would, however, be renamed in recognition of its increased responsibilities.

23. In the case of multi-bank holding companies which include subsidiary banks with both national and state charters, holding company authority would be based on the "lead" or largest subsidiary bank in the particular holding company. . . .

As proposed by the Task Group, "international class" holding companies would be defined as those domestic institutions which engage in a domestic banking business in one or more foreign countries or whose size is sufficiently large that supervisory problems affecting any such institution could have a national or even international impact. . . .

Under the Task Group proposals approximately 25 of the largest U.S. bank holding companies and 25 other domestic bank holding companies with significant foreign banking activities would fall under the proposed definition of "international class" institution at the current time. These 50 domestic institutions would remain subject as they are today to [Fed] supervision of their holding companies, although regulation of the subsidiary banks of such firms would not be affected and would continue to be based on charter type. The [Fed] would also maintain jurisdiction over foreign bank holding companies operating in the U.S.

Under the Task Group recommendations, responsibility for interpreting the limitations on non-banking activities contained in the Bank Holding Company Act[a] and for promulgating the list of such permissible activities . . . for all bank holding companies (including "international class") would be transferred from the [Fed] to the FBA. . . .

. . . [T]he [Fed] would retain a right to veto the list of permitted activities or the implementing regulations (together with certain individual orders). . . .

Operation of Deposit Insurance System. Under the Task Group's recommendations, the FDIC would give up all examination, supervision and regulatory responsibilities not directly related to its function of providing deposit insurance. The FDIC would remain an independent corporation, but would be refocused exclusively on providing deposit insurance and administering the deposit insurance system. . . .

. . . [T]he FDIC would have authority to deny insurance, set premium levels related to risk and revoke insurance. It would also have the authority to take enforcement action against violations of federal law regarding unsafe banking practices in any bank examined by it where the primary regulator failed to take such action upon prior request of the FDIC.

Under the revised system, the FDIC would examine all troubled banks (irrespective of charter type) in conjunction with the primary supervisor, together with a sample of non-troubled firms. . . .

C. Summary of Recommendations to Reform the Thrift Regulatory System

. . . As proposed by the Task Group, the FHLBB would continue to regulate thrift institutions, but only to the extent such institutions continued to compete to a significant degree in traditional thrift activities. Individual thrifts would be free to abandon specialization in traditional activities, but in such event the institution would be required to convert to regulation as a bank in recognition of the activities such institution elected to pursue. In addition, the FHLBB would transfer its current examination and supervision of state-chartered firms to state agencies where "certified" under a program similar to that proposed for banks by the Task Group. . . .

D. Summary of General Regulatory Proposals

. . .

Functional Regulation and Streamlining. Under the current system, the OCC, FDIC, [Fed] and FHLBB are each responsible for enforcing the securities and antitrust laws as they may apply to banks or thrifts regulated by such agencies. However, the SEC administers the securities laws for bank and thrift holding companies, and the Justice Department independently reviews all bank and thrift transactions under the antitrust laws. The result is that 5 different federal agencies regulate securities and 5 different federal agencies have a role in antitrust issues, when in each case only 1 agency could handle such responsibilities.

---

a. *See* 12 U.S.C. § 1843. *See also infra* Chapter 6, § 2 (discussing nonbanking activities of holding companies).

The Task Group recommendations would centralize these responsibilities in the SEC and DOJ, respectively.

Notes and Comments 1.61. *Structural realignment under the Financial Institutions Reform, Recovery and Enforcement Act ("FIRREA").* The Task Group recommendation went unheeded, but the emerging crisis in the savings association industry finally turned the attention of policymakers to serious regulatory realignment. In early February 1989 the Bush Administration proposed a dramatic plan for rescuing the savings association industry that would include a significant restructuring of federal regulation of the industry. The FIRREA, introduced in the Senate on February 22, 1989, received relatively swift congressional consideration. The legislation was approved by the Senate, substantially as proposed, on April 19, 1989, and by the House on August 4, 1989. On August 9, 1989, the President signed the bill into law. The principal structural changes brought about by FIRREA are discussed in notes 1.35-1.37, *supra*. How do these changes compare with the Task Group recommendations?

1.62. *"Reregulation" as a reaction to deregulation.* In December 1991, the President signed into law two pieces of legislation intended to reform certain aspects of federal bank regulation: the Resolution Trust Corporation Refinancing, Restructuring, and Improvement Act of 1991 ("RTCIA"),[71] and the Federal Deposit Insurance Corporation Improvement Act of 1991 ("FDICIA").[72] Based on the provisions of the 1991 legislation summarized below, is it fair to say that we have entered an era of "reregulation" after the financial disasters of the 1980s? Does this discredit "deregulation" as a policy? In brief, the principal features of the RTCIA and the FDICIA are as follows:

> **a.** *Resources available to the FDIC and the RTC.* The two acts increased the resources available to the FDIC insurance funds and the Resolution Trust Corporation ("RTC"). The FDICIA increased the borrowing authority of the FDIC from \$5 billion to \$30 billion[73] and mandated recapitalization of the Bank Insurance Fund ("BIF") under specified circumstances.[74] The RTCIA authorized Treasury to provide an increase in funding to the RTC in an amount not to exceed \$25 billion.[75]
>
> **b.** *Improved supervision.* The FDICIA included a series of provisions intended to improve the supervision of insured depository institutions:
>
> > **1.** *Annual examinations.* The FDICIA adopted a general rule requiring annual on-site examinations of all insured depository institutions,[76] effective one year after enactment (December 19, 1991).

---

71. Pub. L. No. 102-233, 105 Stat. 1761 (December 12, 1991) (codified at scattered sections of 12 U.S.C.).

72. Pub. L. No. 102-242, 105 Stat. 2236 (December 19, 1991) (codified at scattered sections of 12 U.S.C.).

73. FDICIA, §101 (codified at 12 U.S.C. §1824(a)). *See also id.* §103 (codified at 12 U.S.C. §§1817(b), 1824(c)) (repayment schedule; emergency assessments on insured depository institutions). *Cf. id.* §102 (codified at 12 U.S.C. §1825(c)(5)-(6)) (limitations on outstanding borrowing of FDIC insurance funds).

74. *Id.* §104 (codified at 12 U.S.C. §1817(b)(1)(A), (C)) (assessment rate changes; rules for recapitalizing the BIF). *See also id.* §1824(d)) (borrowing for BIF from BIF members).

75. RTCIA, §101 (codified at 12 U.S.C. §1441a(i) (3)).

76. FDICIA §111(a) (codified at 12 U.S.C. §1820(d) (1)-(3)). Certain specified small institutions (well-capitalized and well-managed institutions with total assets of less than \$100 million with no recent change in control) are to be examined every eighteen months. *Id.* (codified at 12 U.S.C.

In addition, the federal bank regulatory agencies, acting through the Federal Financial Institutions Examination Council, are required to establish a "comparable examination improvement program,"[77] meeting certain specified requirements.[78]

2. *Independent audits.* As a general rule, the FDICIA requires independent audits of insured depository institutions.[79]

3. *Examination assessments.* Assessments to a federally insured depository institution are authorized to cover the costs of conducting FDIC examinations of the institution.[80] Similar rules apply to examination and supervision of national banks[81] and examination and supervision of savings associations.[82]

4. *Insurance applications.* FDIC insurance of deposits of any depository institution will now generally require a specific application to and approval by the FDIC.[83] New rules also apply to depository institutions that are not insured by the FDIC.[84]

5. *Accounting rules.* The FDICIA established specific accounting objectives, standards and requirements generally applicable to all insured depository institutions.[85] These include uniform standards for accounting of capital.[86]

6. *Prompt "corrective action."* The FDICIA generally requires prompt regulatory action in terms of "corrective action"[87] intended to "resolve the problems of insured depository institutions at the least possible long-term loss to the deposit insurance fund."[88]

7. *Safety and soundness.* The FDICIA focuses on the safety and soundness of insured depository institutions in several ways. It authorizes federal bank regulatory agencies to impose more stringent treatment of capital of institutions that are determined to be in an unsafe and unsound condition or to be engaged in an unsafe and unsound practice.[89] It also requires the creation by the federal bank regulatory agencies of detailed standards for safety and soundness of insured

---

§1820(d)(4)). *But see id.* §111(c) (transition rule).

77. *Id.* §111(d)(1).

78. *See id.* §111(d)(2).

79. *Id.* §112(a) (codified at 12 U.S.C. §1831m).

80. *Id.* §113(a) (codified at 12 U.S.C. §1820(e)).

81. *Id.* §114(a)-(b) (codified at 12 U.S.C. §§481- 482).

82. *Id.* §114(c) (codified at 12 U.S.C. §1467(a)- (b), (k)).

83. *Id.* §115(a) (codified at 12 U.S.C. §1815(a)).

84. *See id.* §151(a)(1), (b) (codified at 12 U.S.C. §1831t) (requiring, inter alia, annual independent audits of private deposit insurers).

85. *Id.* §121(a) (codified at 12 U.S.C. §1831n).

86. *Id.* (codified at 12 U.S.C. §1831n(b)).

87. *Id.* §131 (codified at 12 U.S.C. §1831o(a)(2)).

88. *Id.* (codified at 12 U.S.C. §1831o(a)(1)). *Cf. id.* §141(a), (e) (codified at 12 U.S.C. §1823(c)(4)- (11)) (mandating least-cost resolution of failing institution problems). On principles of early resolution, *see id.* §143. *See also id.* §141(b) (codified at 12 U.S.C. §1821(d)(5)(D)) (authorizing disallowance by receiver of secured claims in excess of collateral); *id.* §142 (codified at 12 U.S.C. §§347a, 347b(a)-(b), (n)) (limiting Federal Reserve discount window advances).

89. *Id.* §131(a) (codified at 12 U.S.C. §1831o(g)).

depository institutions and their holding companies.[90]

8. *Risk-based insurance assessments.* The FDICIA also requires the establishment of a risk-based assessment system for federal deposit insurance.[91]

9. *Activities of insured state banks.* With certain specified exceptions, the FDICIA generally requires that insured state banks not engage in any type of activity not permissible for national banks.[92]

10. *Real estate lending.* The FDICIA requires the agencies to adopt uniform regulations restricting real estate lending by prescribing standards for such extensions of credit in accordance with certain general principles specified in the act.[93]

11. *Extensions of credit to insiders.* The FDICIA also recodified the statutory provisions restricting extensions of credit to insiders of depository institutions.[94] Existing transactions are not affected by these new rules.[95]

c. *Supervision of failing institutions.* The RTCIA made certain structural and substantive changes intended to affect the supervision of failing institutions subject to RTC oversight:

1. *RTC as receiver.* The Office of Thrift Supervision was required to appoint the RTC as receiver for failed thrift institutions through September 30, 1993, rather than the August 9, 1992 date specified in FIRREA.[96]

2. *Structure of the RTC.* The structure of the RTC was realigned. Among other things, the RTC was to be managed by a chief executive officer, rather than by the FDIC.[97]

3. *Structure of the "Oversight Board."* A restructured Thrift Depositor Protection Oversight Board,[98] was charged with the duty, inter alia, of "monitoring" rather than being "accountable for" the RTC.[99]

d. *Mergers and acquisitions.* The FDICIA also contained a series of provisions amending the statutory rules with respect to mergers and acquisitions:

1. *Conversions moratorium.* The FDICIA amended the rule with respect to a five-year moratorium on conversions imposed by the FIRREA.[100] Conversions meeting statutorily specified conditions may

---

90. *Id.* §132(a) (codified at 12 U.S.C. §1831s).

91. *Id.* §302 (codified at 12 U.S.C. §1817(b)).

92. *Id.* §303 (codified at 12 U.S.C. §1831a).

93. *Id.* §304(a) (codified at 12 U.S.C. §1828(o)). *See also id.* §304(b) (codified at 12 U.S.C. §371(a)) (conforming amendment to Federal Reserve Act).

94. *Id.* §306(a) (codified at 12 U.S.C. §375b). Restrictions on transactions with affiliates and insiders apply to insured nonmember insured banks as well as member banks. *See id.* §306(k) (codified at 12 U.S.C. §1828(j)). Corresponding rules apply to savings associations. *See id.* §306(i)-(j) (codified at 12 U.S.C. §§1468(b)(1), 1972(2)(H)(i)).

95. *Id.* §306(n).

96. RTCIA, §103 (codified at 12 U.S.C. §1441a(b) (3)(A)(ii)(II)).

97. *Id.* §201(2) (codified at 12 U.S.C. §1441a(b)(9) (C)).

98. *Id.* §302(a) (codified at 12 U.S.C. §1441a(a)(1)).

99. *Id.* §303(1) (codified at 12 U.S.C. §1441a(a)(2)).

100. *See* 12 U.S.C. §1815(d)(2)(A).

take place with the prior written approval of the responsible agency.[101]

2. *Cross-industry acquisitions.* The FDICIA authorized mergers, consolidations, and other acquisitions by or involving savings associations[102] or national banks[103] with any other insured depository institution. Such transactions are generally subject to the approval or disapproval of the Director of the OTS[104] or the Comptroller of the Currency,[105] respectively, within 60 days of the filing of an application for approval of the transaction.

1.63. *Regulatory simplification.* The Community Development and Regulatory Improvement Act of 1994 ("CDRIA")[106] has undertaken to simplify the regulatory requirements imposed by federal statutory provisions. *See* 1 MICHAEL P. MALLOY, BANKING LAW AND REGULATION §1.4.6 & Figures 1.20-1.22 (1994 & Cum. Supp.) (discussing CDRIA).

1.64. *1996 reform legislation.* This trend towards regulatory simplification has continued with the enactment of the Economic Growth and Regulatory Paperwork Reduction Act ("EGRPRA").[107] The act makes a number of significant changes to the structure of regulation of depository institutions, and also refines or reduces the regulatory requirements applicable to such institutions in a wide variety of statutory provisions.[108] Of particular note are the following provisions:

a. *Amendments to the deposit insurance system.* The EGRPRA imposed a special assessment on insured depository institutions holding SAIF-insured deposits in order to recapitalize the ailing SAIF.[109] It also provided for the merger of the FDIC insurance funds into a new Deposit Insurance Fund ("DIF"), if there were no more savings associations by 1 January 1999.[110]

b. *Amendments to the Bank Service Company Act.* The act formerly known as the Bank Service Corporation Act has been renamed the "Bank Service

---

101. FDICIA §501(a) (codified at 12 U.S.C. §1815(d) (3)).

102. *Id.* §502(a) (codified at 12 U.S.C. §1467a(t)).

103. *Id.* §502(b) (codified at 12 U.S.C. §215c).

104. *Id.* §502(a) (codified at 12 U.S.C. §1467a(t) (2)(A)).

105. *Id.* §502(b) (codified at 12 U.S.C. §215c(b)(1)).

106. Pub. L. No. 103-325, §§ 301-327, 602, 108 Stat. 2160 (1994) (codified at scattered sections of 12 U.S.C.).

107. Pub. L. No. 104-208, 110 Stat. 3009 (1996) (codified at scattered sections of 12, 15, 26, 42 U.S.C.).

108. *See generally* Murray A. Indick, Ronald J. Greene, & Daniel Squire, *The Economic Growth and Regulatory Paperwork Reduction Act of 1996*, 114 Banking L.J. 298 (1997) (surveying provisions of EGRPRA).

109. EGRPRA, § 2702 (to be codified at 12 U.S.C. § 1817 note). *See* Indick, *supra*, at 300-301 (discussing assessment provisions).

110. *Id.*, § 2704 (codified at 12 U.S.C. §§ 24(Eleventh), 338a, 347b(b)(3)(A)(ii), 1431(k), 1441a(b), 1441b(f)(2)(C)(ii), 1464, 1467a, 1723i, 1735f-14, 1813(a)(1), 1813(y), 1815(b) (5), (e), 1816(5), 1817(b)(2)(B)-(E), (*l*)-(m), 1821 note, 1821(a)(4)-(6), 1821a(a), 1823, 1824, 1825 (c)(5), 1827, 1828, 1831e, 1831m(i)(3), 1831o, 1833a(b)(3)(B), 3341(c)(1)(B), 1834(a)(1), 1841(j) (2)) (establishing DIF; repealing former § 1817(*l*) and redesignating former (m)-(n) as (*l*)-(m); repealing former § 1817(b)(2)(B), (F) and redesignating former (C), (E), (G), (H) as (B)-(E); repealing former § 1831h; other technical and conforming amendments changing references to BIF and SAIF to DIF).

Company Act" ("BSCA").[111] As amended, the BSCA now authorizes bank service companies to be organized as limited liability partnerships, as an alternative to corporations.[112] The operative provisions of the BSCA have been amended to conform with this change.[113]

c. *Status of automatic teller machines (ATMs).* The EGRPRA has changed federal law so that ATMs are no longer considered "branches" of depository institutions.[114]

d. *Elimination of duplicative or burdensome regulatory requirements.* Much of the EGRPRA is devoted to the elimination of such requirements.[115]

EGRPRA served as an impetus for all of the banking agencies to review their regulations in depth and to work collaboratively on a number of regulatory burden reduction projects, to develop a consensus on desirable legislative reforms, and to work together with Congress to pass legislation reducing the level of burden on financial institutions.[116] In November 2007, pursuant to EGRPRA § 2222,[117] the Federal Financial Institutions Examination Council (FFIEC) published a report prepared by its constituent agencies (OCC, the Fed, FDIC, OTS, and NCUA) in July 2007.[118] The EGRPRA required the FFIEC to submit a report to Congress that included a summary of the significant issues raised by the review of regulations required by the statute,[119] the relative merits of these issues, and an analysis of whether the appropriate agency is able to address the regulatory burdens associated with these issues by regulation or whether the burdens must be addressed by legislative action.[120] The report describes the actions by FFIEC and each of its member agencies to fulfill the requirements of the EGRPRA. It includes both the agencies' comment summary and their discussion and analysis of significant issues identified during the EGRPRA review process. The report also describes legislative initiatives to reduce unnecessary regulatory burden on

---

111. *Id.*, § 2613(a), 110 Stat. 3009 (1996) (codified at 12 U.S.C. § 1861(a)) (renaming the act).

112. *Id*, § 2613(b) (codified at 12 U.S.C. § 1861(b)).

113. *Id.*, § 2613(d)-(h) (codified at 12 U.S.C. §§ 1862-1867) (conforming amendments).

114. *Id.*, §§ 2204, 110 Stat. 3009 (1996) (codified at 12 U.S.C. §§ 36(j), 1813(o)) (removing ATM from definition of branch in NBA, FDIA).

115. *See, e.g.*, *id.* §§ 2202(d) 2206, 2207(a)-(b), 2214, 2304(a)-(b), 2610, 2612, (codified at 12 U.S.C. §§ 1841(b), (c)(2)(F), (g), (j)(2), (o), 1843(c)(2), (c)(8), (f)(3)(B), (i)-(j)) (qualified family partnerships under BHCA; limited-purpose bank provisions; elimination of approval requirement for divestitures; streamlining procedures for certain nonbanking acquisitions; elimination of duplicative requirements).

116. 72 Fed. Reg. 62,036, 62,062 (2007).

117. 12 U.S.C. § 3311.

118. *Joint Report to Congress on the Economic Growth and Regulatory Paperwork Reduction Act, July 31, 2007*, 72 Fed. Reg. 62,036 (2007). Throughout the EGRPRA process, the NCUA participated in the planning and comment solicitation process with the federal banking agencies. *Id.* at 62,037. However, the NCUA established its own regulatory categories and publication schedule and published its EGRPRA notices separately, though they were consistent and comparable with those published by the federal banking agencies, except on issues unique to credit unions. *Id.* In keeping with this separate approach, the EGRPRA report discussed the NCUA's regulatory burden reduction efforts and analysis of significant issues separately. *Id.* For the summary of comments received by the NCUA, see *EGRPRA Report*, Appendix II-B. *Id.* at 62,097-62,104

119. For an overview of the EGRPRA review process, see 72 Fed. Reg. at 62,038.

120. 12 U.S.C. § 3311(e).

insured depository institutions, including in some cases references to current initiatives being considered by Congress. For a detailed summary of the significant issues raised by the public comments and the responses of the regulators, see 1 MICHAEL P. MALLOY, BANKING LAW AND REGULATION § 1.04[G][3] & Figure 1.13 (2d ed. 2011).

1.65. *The Gramm-Leach-Bliley Act.* On 12 November 1999, the President signed the Gramm-Leach-Bliley Act (GLBA)[121] into law. This financial services reform effort is one of the most significant pieces of federal banking legislation since the Banking Act of 1933. More detailed treatment of specific provisions is provided at appropriate places throughout the casebook. For now, we highlight the major features of the GLBA, which are as follows:

> **a.** *Functional Regulation of Financial Services*: The GLBA generally endorses the principle of functional regulation, positing that similar activities should be regulated by the same regulator. Accordingly, banking activities are regulated by federal and state bank regulators, securities activities by federal and state securities regulators, and insurance activities by state insurance regulators.[122] However, the Fed retains its role of "umbrella supervisor" of bank holding companies ("BHCs"), and it is authorized to examine each holding company and its subsidiaries, including functionally regulated subsidiaries under limited circumstances.[123] The Comptroller, the Fed, and the FDIC are authorized to adopt "prudential safeguards" governing transactions between a depository institution, its subsidiaries and affiliates to avoid, *inter alia*, significant risk to the safety and soundness of the institution.[124]
>
> **b.** *Modernization of the Federal Home Loan Bank System*: The GLBA reforms the FHLBank System in several important respects.[125] Among other things, mandatory FHLBank membership for federal savings associations is eliminated, in favor of a completely voluntary membership.[126] "Community financial institutions" (FDIC-insured depository institutions with assets less than $500 million) are given expanded access to FHLBank advances.[127] Governance of the FHLBanks is decentralized from the Federal Housing Finance Board ("FHFB") to the individual FHLBanks.[128] The Resolution Funding Corporation

---

121. Pub. L. No. 106-102, Nov. 12, 1999, 113 Stat. 1338 (1999) (codified at scattered sections of 12, 15, 16, 18 U.S.C.).

122. *See, e.g.*, GLBA, §§ 111-112, 115, 301 (codified at 12 U.S.C. §§ 1820a, 1831v, 1844 (c)(4)A)-(B), (g), 15 U.S.C. § 6711) (mandating functional regulation of financial services).

123. *Id.*, § 113 (codified at 12 U.S.C. § 1848a).

124. *Id.*, § 114 (codified at 12 U.S.C. § 1828a).

125. In February 2000, effective immediately, the FHFB reorganized and recodified its regulations, 12 C.F.R. ch. IX, in anticipation of the incorporation of new and amended regulations to implement the Federal Home Loan Bank Modernization Act of 1999, Title VI of the GLBA. 65 Fed. Reg. 8253 (2000) (codified at 12 C.F.R. ch. IX).

126. GLBA, § 603 (codified at 12 U.S.C. § 1464(f)).

127. *Id.*, § 604(a) (codified at 12 U.S.C. §§ 1430(a)(1)-(6)).

128. *Id.*, § 606 (codified at 12 U.S.C. §§ 250, 1422b (a)(5)-(7), 1427(a), (d), (g), (i)(1)-(2), 1429, 1430(c)-(d), 1432(a)-(b), 1436(a); striking 1438(b)(4); repealing 12 U.S.C. §§ 1442a, 1447). *See* 64 Fed. Reg. 71,275 (1999) (codified at 12 C.F.R. pts. 932, 934-935) (amending FHFB regulations, devolving certain corporate governance responsibilities from FHFB to FHLBanks). *See also* 65 Fed. Reg. 81 (2000) (to be codified at 12 C.F.R. pt. 917) (proposing new FHFB rules regarding powers and responsibilities of FHLBank boards of directors and senior management); 65 Fed. Reg. 324 (2000) (to be codified at 12 C.F.R. pts. 900, 910, 941) (proposing reorganization of Office of Finance and new authority to issue consolidated obligations of FHLBanks); 65 Fed. Reg. 339 (2000) (proposing

obligation of the FHLBanks, resulting from the savings and loan crisis, is changed from a fixed dollar amount to a fixed percentage of annual net earnings.[129] The GLBA also establishes a new capital structure for the FHLBanks.[130]

c. *Securities Activities of Banking Enterprises*: The GLBA eliminates prohibitions on affiliations between commercial and investment banking enterprises and on interlocking directorates between such enterprises.[131] It also authorizes national banks to deal in, underwrite, and purchase municipal bonds for their own investment accounts.[132]

d. *Financial Services Activities through Financial Holding Companies*: The GLBA freezes in place the "closely related activity" exception of the Bank Holding Company Act (BHCA), as of GLBA enactment.[133] A new provision permits BHCs that qualify as financial holding companies (FHCs) to engage in activities, and acquire companies engaged in activities, that are "financial in nature" or that are incidental to such activities.[134] FHCs are also permitted to engage in activities that are complementary to financial activities, if the Fed determines that the activity does not pose a substantial risk to the safety or soundness of depository institutions or the financial system in general. In determining what activities are financial in nature or incidental, the Fed must notify the Secretary of the Treasury of applications or requests to engage in new financial activities.[135] The Fed may not determine that an activity is financial or incidental to a financial activity if the Secretary objects.[136] The Secretary may also propose to the Fed that the Fed find that a particular activity is financial in nature or incidental.[137] A similar procedure applies to the determination of financial activities and incidental activities for financial subsidiaries of national banks.[138] To engage in the new financial activities and affiliations, a BHC must elect to become an FHC, but it may do so only if all of its subsidiary banks are well capitalized and well managed.[139]

e. *Financial Services Activities through Bank Subsidiaries*: The GLBA permits a bank to engage through a financial subsidiary only in financial activities authorized by the act, with certain exceptions.[140] The act specifically excludes four types of activities for these subsidiaries: insurance or annuity underwriting, insurance company portfolio investments, real estate investment and development, and

---

amended policy statement on financial management policy of Federal Home Loan Bank System and reorganization of Office of Finance).

129. GLBA, § 607(a) (codified at 12 U.S.C. § 1441b(f) (2)(C)). *See* 65 Fed. Reg. 5447 (2000) (to be codified at 12 C.F.R. pts. 951, 997) (proposing new FHFB rules for determination of appropriate present-value factors for payments by FHLBanks to Resolution Funding Corporation).

130. *Id.*, § 608 (codified at 12 U.S.C. § 1426).

131. *See id.*, § 101 (repealing 12 U.S.C. §§ 78, 377).

132. *Id.*, § 151 (codified at 12 U.S.C. § 24).

133. *Id.*, § 102(a) (codified at 12 U.S.C. § 1843(c)(8)).

134. *Id.*, § 103(a) (codified at 12 U.S.C. § 1843(k)).

135. *Id.*, § 103 (codified at 12 U.S.C. § 1843(k)(2)(A)(i)).

136. 12 U.S.C. § 1843(k)(2)(A)(ii).

137. *Id.* § 1843(k)(2)(B)(i).

138. GLBA, § 121 (codified at 12 U.S.C. § 24a(b)(1)(B)).

139. *Id.*, § 103(a) (codified at 12 U.S.C. § 1843(*l*)).

140. *Id.*, §§ 121(a)(2) (codified at 12 U.S.C. § 24a) (authorizing national bank financial subsidiaries), 121(d)(1) (codified at 12 U.S.C. § 1831w) (state bank financial subsidiaries).

merchant banking.[141]

f. *State Insurance Regulation*: While the GLBA permits affiliations among banking, securities and insurance firms, it provides explicitly that the McCarran-Ferguson Act[142] is still operative to require federal deference in most cases to state regulation of the insurance activities carried on by these firms.[143] Subject to special rules concerning permissible affiliations and activities and nondiscrimination in state treatment of affiliated firms, the GLBA requires a state license for any firm to engage in the business of insurance as a principal or agent.[144] Thus, insurance activities of financial services firms are subject to functional regulation by the states, including insurance activities of national banks.[145]

g. *Privacy and Disclosure of Nonpublic Personal Information*: The GLBA requires the federal depository institutions regulators, the Secretary of the Treasury, the SEC and the FTC, after consultation with representatives of state insurance authorities designated by the National Association of Insurance Commissioners (NAIC), to establish comprehensive standards for ensuring the security and confidentiality of consumers' personal information maintained by financial institutions.[146] The act allows customers of financial institutions to opt out of having their personal financial information shared with nonaffiliated third parties, subject to certain exceptions.[147] It bars financial institutions from disclosing customer account numbers or similar forms of access codes to nonaffiliated third parties for telemarketing or other direct marketing purposes.[148] It mandates clear and conspicuous annual disclosure of a financial institution's policies and procedures for protecting customers' nonpublic personal information.[149] The privacy provisions do not supersede any state statutes, regulations, orders, or interpretations, except to the extent that such state provisions are inconsistent, and

---

141. 12 U.S.C. § 24a(a)(2)(B). However, after a five-year period from enactment of the GLBA, the Fed and the Secretary of the Treasury are authorized jointly to adopt rules permitting merchant banking by financial subsidiaries, subject to the conditions that the agencies may jointly determine. GLBA, § 122 (codified at 12 U.S.C. § 1843 note). The GLBA does not define merchant banking. In an interim rule published jointly by the Fed and the Department of the Treasury, implementing merchant banking provisions for financial holding companies, the term is discussed in the following terms:

> [GLBA] section 4(k)(4)(H) and the interim rule permit a financial holding company to acquire or control shares, assets or ownership interests of any company that engages in activities that are not otherwise permissible for a financial holding company. Interests acquired or controlled under the interim rule are referred to as merchant banking investments, and a financial holding company must comply with the requirements of this interim rule in order to make such investments.

65 Fed. Reg. 16,460, 16,463 (2000).

142. 15 U.S.C. §§ 1011 *et seq.*

143. GLBA, § 104(a) (codified at 15 U.S.C. § 6701(a)).

144. *Id.*, § 104(b)-(f) (codified at 15 U.S.C. § 6701(b)-(f)).

145. *Id.*, § 301 (codified at 15 U.S.C. § 6711).

146. *Id.*, § 504 (codified at 15 U.S.C. § 6804).

147. *Id.*, § 502(a)-(b), (e) (codified at 15 U.S.C. § 6802(a)-(b), (e)).

148. *Id.*, § 502(c)-(d) (codified at 15 U.S.C. § 6802(c)-(d)).

149. *Id.* § 503 (codified at 15 U.S.C. § 6803). Nothing in these provisions is to be construed to modify, limit, or supersede the operation of the Fair Credit Reporting Act, 15 U.S.C. §§ 1681-1681u. GLBA, § 506 (codified at 15 U.S.C. §§ 1681s, 6806).

then only to the extent of the inconsistency.[150] A state provision is not considered inconsistent if the protection afforded by the state provision is greater than the protection provided under the privacy provisions, as determined by the FTC in consultation with the federal agency or authority involved.[151]

h. *Effect on Community Reinvestment Act*: The GLBA contains a general provision[152] stating that nothing in the act shall be construed to repeal any provision of the Community Reinvestment Act (CRA),[153] The GLBA amends the CRA to provide that election by a BHC to become an FHC is not effective if the Fed finds that, as of the date of the election, not all of the subsidiary insured depository institutions of the company had received a "satisfactory" or better CRA rating at their most recent CRA examinations.[154] The GLBA also amends the BHCA to require the appropriate federal banking agency to prohibit an FHC (or a bank, through a financial subsidiary) from commencing any new activity or acquiring any company under the BHCA,[155] the National Bank Act,[156] or the FDIA,[157] if the bank or any of its insured depository institution affiliates (or any insured depository institution affiliate of the FHC) fails to have at least a "satisfactory" CRA rating at the time of its last examination.[158] The prohibition ceases to apply once the bank and all of its insured depository institution affiliates (or all of the insured depository institutions controlled by the FHC) have restored their CRA performance rating to at least the "satisfactory" level.[159] The GLBA requires full disclosure of agreements entered into between insured depository institutions or their affiliates and nongovernmental entities or persons made pursuant to or in connection with the fulfillment of the CRA.[160] The federal banking agencies are required to issue regulations mandating procedures reasonably designed to ensure and monitor compliance with the disclosure requirements.[161] The GLBA also amends the CRA to direct that regulated financial institutions with aggregate assets not exceeding $250 million are to be subject to less frequent routine CRA examinations.[162] However, an institution remains fully subject to CRA examination in connection with any application for a deposit facility.[163] In addition, the agencies may subject an institution to more frequent or less frequent examinations for reasonable cause.[164]

1.66. *The Federal Deposit Insurance Reform Act.* The Federal Deposit Insurance

---

150. GLBA, § 507(a) (codified at 15 U.S.C. § 6807 (a)).

151. *Id.*, § 507(b) (codified at 15 U.S.C. § 6807(b)).

152. *Id.*, § 714 (codified at 12 U.S.C. § 1811 note).

153. 12 U.S.C. §§ 2901 *et seq.*

154. GLBA, § 103(b) (codified at 12 U.S.C. § 2903(c)(1)).

155. *Per* 12 U.S.C. § 1843(k), (n).

156. *Per id.* § 24a.

157. *Per id.* § 1831w(a).

158. GLBA, § 103(a) (codified at 12 U.S.C. § 1843(*l*) (2)).

159. *See id.* (referring to "most recent examination" of insured depository institution subsidiary under CRA).

160. *Id.*, § 711 (codified at 12 U.S.C. § 1831y).

161. *Id.* § 1831y(h).

162. GLBA, § 712(a) (codified at 12 U.S.C. § 2908(a)).

163. *Id.*, § 712(b) (codified at 12 U.S.C. § 2908(b)).

164. *Id.*, § 712(c) (codified at 12 U.S.C. § 2908(c)).

Reform Act of 2005 (FDIRA)[165] and the Federal Deposit Insurance Reform Conforming Amendments Act of 2005 (FDIRCAA)[166] together represent a major change in the structure of the Federal Deposit Insurance System. This change has resulted in a considerable revision and realignment of FDIC insurance regulations, mostly of a technical and conforming nature.[167] The principal legislative changes are identified in the discussion that follows.

FDIRA § 2102[168] mandates the merger of the Bank Insurance Fund (BIF) and the Savings Association Insurance Fund (SAIF) into the Depository Insurance Fund (DIF).[169] Thereafter, all assets and liabilities of the BIF and the SAIF are to be transferred to the DIF.[170] The separate existence of the two former funds ceased on the effective date of the merger.[171]

FDIRA § 2103[172] made three important substantive changes to the insurance coverage provisions of the Federal Deposit Insurance Act.[173] First, FDIRA § 2103(a)(2) provides for an inflation index to be applied to the current maximum deposit insurance amount of $100,000,[174] defined in the act as the "standard maximum deposit insurance amount" (SMDIA).[175] Beginning April 1, 2010, and every succeeding five years, subject to approval by the Board of Directors of the FDIC and the National Credit Union Administration Board, the current SMDIA could be increased by a cost-of-living adjustment.[176] Second, the section provides per-participant coverage to employee benefit plan accounts, even if the depository institution at which the deposits are placed is not authorized to accept employee benefit plan deposits.[177] The FDIRA eliminates the former requirement that an insured depository institution meet prescribed capital requirements before employee benefit plan deposits accepted by that institution would be eligible for per-participant coverage. Third, the section increases the deposit insurance limit for "certain retirement accounts" from

---

165. Pub. L. No. 109-171, tit. II, §§ 2101-2109, 120 Stat. 4, 9-21 (Feb. 8, 2006) (FDIRA). *See Regulators Announce Formal Changes Reflecting Reforms, Merger of BIF, SAIF*, BNA BANKING DAILY (April 21, 2006), *available at* http://pubs.bna.com/ip/bna/bbd.nsf/eh/A0B2R3D4M3 (reporting on fund merger).

166. Pub. L. No. 109-173, 119 Stat 3601 (Feb. 15, 2006).

167. For tabular analysis of the provisions of the FDIRA and the FDIRCAA, see 1 MICHAEL P. MALLOY, BANKING LAW AND REGULATION Figures 1.29-1.33 (1994 & Cum. Supp.).

168. 120 Stat. at 9 (codified at 12 U.S.C. § 1821 note; 2 U.S.C. § 905, 12 U.S.C. §§ 24, 338a, 347b, 1431, 1441a, 1441b, 1464, 1467a, 1723i, 1735f-14, 1813, 1815, 1817, 1816, 1821, 1821a, 1823, 1824, 1825, 1827, 1828, 1831a, 1831e, 1831h, 1831m, 1831o, 1833a, 1834, 1841, 3341).

169. FDIRA, § 2102(a)(1) (codified at 12 U.S.C. § 1821 note).

170. *Id.* § 2102(a)(2).

171. *Id.* § 2102(a)(3). *See id.* § 2102(c) (establishing effective date). On risk-based assessment rules and procedures with respect to deposit insurance under the DIF, see *id.* §§ 2104-2106, 120 Stat. at 12-16 (codified at 12 U.S.C. §§ 1817 note, 1817(b)(1)(E)-(F), 1817(b)(2)(A)-(B), (D), (b)(3), (b)(5), (g), 1828(h)). On deposit insurance reserve ratio requirements, see *id.* §§ 2107-2108, 120 Stat. at 16-20 (codified at 12 U.S.C. §§ 1813(y), 1817(b)(3)(E), (e)).

172. *Id.* § 2103, 120 Stat. at 9-12 (codified at 12 U.S.C. §§ 1821(a)(1)(B), (D)-(F), (a)(3)(A), 1821 note).

173. 12 U.S.C. §§ 1813 *et seq.*

174. FDIRA, § 2103(a)(2) (codified at 12 U.S.C. 1821(a)(1)(F)).

175. 12 U.S.C. § 1821(a)(1)(E).

176. *Id.* § 1821(a)(1)(F).

177. FDIRA, § 2103(b) (codified at 12 U.S.C. 1821(a)(1)(D)).

$100,000 to $250,000, also subject to the inflation adjustment described above.[178]

1.67. *The Financial Services Regulatory Relief Act.* On September 27, 2006–more than three years after federal regulators began pushing for a comprehensive financial regulatory relief bill–the House approved a somewhat diluted version of the regulators' and industry representatives' hoped-for legislation,[179] and the Senate followed with its approval two days later.[180] The Financial Services Regulatory Relief Act (FSRRA) was signed into law on October 13, 2006.[181] The FSRRA consists of a wide range of diverse regulatory relief initiatives.[182] In principle at least, these initiatives emerged from the multi-year consensus-gathering process carried out under the Economic Growth and Regulatory Paperwork Reduction Act,[183] which mandated a periodic review of regulations. Looking over the varied and extensive scope of the FSRRA provisions, however, the FSRRA may seem to be a disjointed grab-bag of benefits to federal regulators and industry constituencies alike. Individual provisions are discussed throughout the chapters that follow, but the principal changes brought about by the FSRRA are as follows:

FSRRA § 101 resolves the long-standing dilemma of interpreting the Gramm-Leach-Bliley Act's treatment of securities trading activities traditionally carried out by banks. The Securities and Exchange Commission (SEC) had taken the position that GLBA meant that banks engaging in such activities would need to register with the SEC as broker dealers. Because of intense opposition from affected depository institutions and from federal bank regulatory agencies, the SEC had never been able to issue a final rule implementing such requirements. The FSSRA requires a joint rulemaking by the SEC and the Fed for a revised definition of "broker" in the Securities Exchange Act of 1934.[184] This rulemaking supersedes previous rulemaking efforts undertaken by the SEC.[185] Prior to adopting a joint set of final rules, the SEC and the Fed are required to consult with and seek the concurrence of the "federal banking agencies"[186] concerning the content of the rulemaking.[187] In addition, FSRRA § 401 gives savings association trust activities the same exemptions that are available for bank trust activities under 1934 Act[188] and the Investment Advisors Act of

---

178. *Id.* § 2103(c) (codified at 12 U.S.C. § 1821(a)(3)(A)).

179. H.R. 6062, 109th Cong., 2d Sess. (2006).

180. S. 2856, 109th Cong., 2d Sess. (2006).

181. Pub. L. No. 109-351, 120 Stat. 1966 (2006).

182. For tabular analysis of the provisions of the FSRRA, see MALLOY, *supra*, Figures 1.34-1.36.

183. Pub. L. No. 104-208, title II, 110 Stat. 3009 (1996) (EGRPRA). For discussion of the provisions of the EGRPRA, see Note 1.59, *supra*.

184. FSRRA, § 101(a)(1), 120 Stat. at 1968 (codified at 15 U.S.C. § 78c(a)(4)(F)). Not later than 180 days after the date of the enactment of the FSRRA, the SEC and the Fed are required jointly to issue a proposed single set of rules or regulations to define the term "broker" in accordance with the 1934 Act § 3(a)(4), 15 U.S.C. § 78c(a)(4). FSRRA, § 101(a)(2), 120 Stat. at 1968 (codified at 15 U.S.C. § 78c note).

185. FSRRA, § 101(a)(3), 120 Stat. at 1968 (codified at 15 U.S.C. § 78c note).

186. The term "federal banking agencies" is defined for these purposes as "Office of the Comptroller of the Currency, the Office of Thrift Supervision, and the Federal Deposit Insurance Corporation." *Id.* § 101(c), 120 Stat. at 1968 (codified at 15 U.S.C. § 78c note).

187. *Id.* § 101(b), 120 Stat. at 1968 (codified at 15 U.S.C. § 78c note).

188. *Id.* § 401(a)(1)-(2), 120 Stat. at 1971-1973 (codified at 12 U.S.C. § 78c(a)(6)(A), (C), (a)(34)(A)-(D), (F)-(H)). *See also id.* § 401(a)(3), 120 Stat. at 1973 (codified at 12 U.S.C. § 78w(b)(1)) (conforming exemption to reporting requirement).

1940.[189]

Effective October 1, 2011,[190] the Fed is authorized to pay interest on deposit reserves.[191] The FSRRA also provides the Fed with increased flexibility to establish reserve requirements from 0 percent to 3 percent for the first tranche of total transaction accounts (rather than a required 3 percent) and 0 percent and greater for the second tranche (rather than a required minimum of 8 percent).[192]

Among the many other features of the act that are likely to be of material benefit to various banking constituencies are the following:

a. Elimination of cumulative voting in national bank shareholder elections of the board of directors;[193]

b. Simplification of regulatory requirements with respect to national bank reduction of capital,[194] national bank dividends,[195] insured depository institution reports of condition,[196] depository institution merger applications,[197] and applications for optional conversion of federal savings associations,[198]

c. Enhanced authority for national and state member banks to make community development investments;[199]

d. Repeal of overlapping rules applicable to savings associations with respect to purchased mortgage servicing rights;[200]

e. Clarification of the citizenship of federal savings associations for purposes of federal court jurisdiction, in effect affording federally chartered savings associations the same access to federal courts that national banks have;[201]

f. Repeal of the limitation on loans to one borrower formerly applicable to savings associations;[202]

g. An increase in the general twelve-year limitation of term of federal credit union loans to fifteen years;[203]

h. Authorization of check cashing and money transfer services offered

---

189. *Id.* § 401(b)(1)-(2), 120 Stat. at 1973 (codified at 12 U.S.C. §§ 80b-2(a)(2)(A), (c), 80b-10a(a)(1)(A)(I), (B), (a)(2), (b)). *See also id.* § 401(c), 120 Stat. at 1973 (codified at 12 U.S.C. § 80a-10(c)) (conforming amendment to 1940 Act).

190. *Id.* § 203, 120 Stat. at 1969 (codified at 12 U.S.C. § 461 note).

191. *Id.* § 201(a)-(b), 120 Stat. at 1968-1969 (codified at 12 U.S.C. § 461(b)(4)(C)-(D), (b)(12), (c)(1)(A)).

192. *Id.* § 202, 120 Stat. at 1969 (codified at 12 U.S.C. § 461(b)(2)(A)(I)-(ii)).

193. *Id.* § 301, 120 Stat. at 1969-1970 (codified at 12 U.S.C. § 61).

194. *Id.* § 304, 120 Stat. at 1970 (codified at 12 U.S.C. § 59).

195. *Id.* § 302, 120 Stat. at 1970 (codified at 12 U.S.C. §§ 21, 60).

196. *Id.* § 604, 120 Stat. at 1980-1981 (codified at 12 U.S.C. § 1817(a)(11)).

197. *Id.* § 606, 120 Stat. at 1981-1982 (codified at 12 U.S.C. § 1828(c)(4), (c)(6)).

198. *Id.* § 608, 120 U.S.C. at 1983 (codified at 12 U.S.C. §§ 1464(i)(5), 1814(c)).

199. *Id.* § 305, 120 Stat. 1970-1971 (codified at 12 U.S.C. §§ 24(Eleventh), 338a).

200. *Id.* § 402, 120 Stat. at 1974 (codified at 12 U.S.C. § 1464(t)(9)(A); repealing former § 1464(t)(4)).

201. *Id.* § 403, 120 Stat. at 1974 (codified at 12 U.S.C. § 1464(x)).

202. *Id.* § 404, 120 Stat. at 1974 (codified at 12 U.S.C. § 1464(u)(2)(A)(I), (ii)(I)-(IV)).

203. *Id.* § 502, 120 Stat. at 1975 (codified at 12 U.S.C. § 1757(5)).

by a federal credit union within its field of membership;[204]

i. Repeal of a provision prohibiting nondepository institutions from accepting deposits;[205]

j. Authorization of investments by insured savings associations in bank service companies;[206]

k. Extension of the examination cycle from one year to eighteen months for depository institutions with less than $500 million in assets, in lieu of the previous threshold of $250 million;[207]

l. Inflation adjustment for the small depository institution exception under the Depository Institution Management Interlocks Act,[208] from $20 million to $50 million;[209]

Likewise, among the many features of the FSRRA that are likely to be of significant assistance to the federal regulators are the following:

a. The repeal of an obsolete limitation on the removal authority of the Comptroller of the Currency;[210]

b. Clarifying the definition of net worth under certain circumstances for purposes of prompt corrective action against credit unions;[211]

c. Clarifying the role of state supervisors with respect to nonfederally insured credit unions,[212] and strengthening provisions concerning the disclosures, periodic statements, and account records required of non-federally insured credit unions,[213] as well as advertising and premises,[214] and acknowledgment of disclosure.[215]

d. Enhancing the safety and soundness of insured depository institutions by, *inter alia*, clarifying the authority of the federal regulators to enforce agreements and conditions,[216] protecting the capital of insured depository institutions,[217] targeting golden parachute arrangements

---

204. *Id.* § 503, 120 Stat. at 1975 (codified at 12 U.S.C. § 1757(12)).

205. *Id.* § 505(f), 120 Stat. at 1977 (codified at 12 U.S.C. § 1831t(e)-(f); repealing former subsection (e); redesignating former (f)-(g) as (e)-(f)).

206. *Id.* § 602, 120 Stat. at 1978-1980 (codified at 12 U.S.C. §§ 1861(b)(2)(A)(ii), (B)(ii), (4)-(5), (7)-(9), 1862-1863, 1864(b)-(f), 1865(a)-(c), 1867(b)-(c)).

207. *Id.* § 605, 120 Stat. at 1981 (codified at 12 U.S.C. § 1820(d)(4)(A)).

208. 12 U.S.C. §§ 3201 *et seq*.

209. FSRRA, § 610, 120 Stat. at 1984 (codified at 12 U.S.C. § 3202(1)).

210. *Id.* § 303, 120 Stat. 1970 (codified at 12 U.S.C. § 1818(e)(4)).

211. *Id.* § 504, 120 Stat. at 1975 (codified at 12 U.S.C. § 1790d(o)(2)(E)).

212. *Id.* § 505(a), 120 Stat. at 1975 (codified at 12 U.S.C. § 1831t(a)(3)). *See also id.* § 505(g), 120 Stat. at 1978 (codified at 12 U.S.C. § 1831t(f)) (repealing FTC authority to enforce independent audit requirements; concurrent state enforcement).

213. *Id.* § 505(b), (e), 120 Stat. at 1975, 1977 (codified at 1831t(b)(1), (c)).

214. *Id.* § 505(c), 120 Stat. at 1975-1976 (codified at 12 U.S.C. § 1831t(b)(2)).

215. *Id.* § 505(d), 120 Stat. at 1976-1977 (codified at 12 U.S.C. § 1831t(b)(3)).

216. *Id.* § 702(a), 120 Stat. at 1985 (codified at 12 U.S.C. § 1831aa). *See also id.* § 702(c), 120 Stat. at 1985-1986 (codified at 12 U.S.C. § 1818(b)(3)-(4)) (conforming amendments).

217. *Id.* § 702(b), 120 Stat. at 1985 (codified at 12 U.S.C. § 1828(u)(1)(A), (B)) (striking former subparagraph (B); redesignating former subparagraph (c) as (B)).

involving failing depository institutions or their affiliates,[218] clarifying the extent of suspension, removal, and prohibition authority of federal banking agencies in cases of certain crimes by institution-affiliated parties of insured depository institutions[219] or insured credit unions,[220] extending the automatic prohibition on participation by convicted individuals[221] and enhancing agency discretion to remove convicted individuals,[222] and coordinating home- and host-state examination authority with respect to interstate banking enterprises.[223]

1.68. *The Housing and Economic Recovery Act of 2008*. Effective July 30, 2008, the Housing and Economic Recovery Act of 2008 (HERA)[224] transferred the supervisory and oversight responsibilities of the Office of Federal Housing Enterprise Oversight (OFHEO) over the Federal National Mortgage Association and the Federal Home Loan Mortgage Corporation (respectively, Fannie Mae and Freddie Mac; hereinafter collectively the enterprises)[225] and the oversight responsibilities of the FHFB over the FHLBanks and the

---

218. *Id.* § 704, 120 Stat. at 1986-1987 (codified at 12 U.S.C. § 1828(k)(2)(A)-(B), (F), (3)(A), (4)(A), (5)(A), (D), (6)).

219. *Id.* § 708(a), 120 Stat. at 1988-1989 (codified at 12 U.S.C. § 1818(g)(1)(A), (B)(I), (C)(I), (ii), (D)(I), (E)).

220. *Id.* § 708(b), 120 Stat. at 1989-1990 (codified at 12 U.S.C. § 1786(i)(1)(A), (B)(I), (c), (D)(I), (E)).

221. *Id.* § 710(a), 120 Stat. at 1990-1991 (codified at 12 U.S.C. § 1829(d)-(e)).

222. *Id.* § 710(b), 120 Stat. at 1991 (codified at 12 U.S.C. § 1818(e)(2)(A)).

223. *Id.* § 711, 120 Stat. at 1991-1994 (codified at 12 U.S.C. § 1820(h))

224. Pub. L. 110-289, div. A (Federal Housing Finance Regulatory Reform Act of 2008), §§ 1001-1605, 122 Stat. 2654, 2659-2830 (July 30, 2008) (codified at 5 U.S.C. §§ 3132 note, 3132(a)(1)(B), (D)-(F), 5313, app. 3 § 11, 11 U.S.C. § 783, 12 U.S.C. §§ 250, 1422(11)-(12), 1423-1424, 1426(a)(3)(A), (B), (b)(1), (c)(4)(B), (d)(2), 1426a, 1427(a)-(d), (f), (i)(1), (l), 1428, 1430(a)-(b), (j)(2)(A), (B)-(C), (12)(C)-(D), (k), 1430c, 1431(b)-(c), (f), (l), 1432, 1435, 1436, 1440, 1440a, 1441(b)(5), 1441a-1441b, 1442-1446, 1452 note, 1452(a)(2)(A)-(C), (b)(2), (d)(4), (h)(2), (4), 1454 note, 1454(a)(2), 1455(c)(2), (I), (j)(2), (l), 1456(e)-(f), 1701 note, 1701x note, 1708(e)(5), 1715z-23, 1717 note, 1717(b)(2), 1718(c)(2), 1719(g), 1723 note, 1723(b), 1723a(d)(3)(B), (k)(1), (m)-(n), 1787(c)(10(C)(I), 1813(I), 1820(d)(5)(B), 1821(d)(2)(F), (G), (e)(10)(C)(I), (m)(1), (6), (9), (15)-(16), (18), (n)(1)(A)-(B)(I), (E), (2)(A), (4)(C)-(D), (H), (5)(D), (8)(A)-(B), (11)-(13), (t)(2)(A)(vii), 1822, 1831o(j)(2), 1833(a)(3), (b)-(c), 3413(o), 4501 note, 4502(2), (8)-(11), (13), (19)-(20), (24), (25)-(31), 4511 note, 4511-4513, 4513a, 4513b, 4514, 4514a, 4515(a), (c)-(f), 4516-4521, 4523-4526, 4541-4548, 4561-4569, 4581-4588, 4588(c), 4611, 4612(a)-(f), 4613 note, 4613(a)-(b), 4614 note, 4614(a)-(f), 4615(b)(1)-(2), (c), 4616(a)(2), (b)(5), (7), (c), 4617, 4618, 4619(a)(3), 4622-4623(a)(1), 4624 note, 4624, 4631(a)-(e), 4632(a)-(e), 4633, 4634(a), 4635(a)-(b), 4636(a)-(d), (g), 4636a, 4636b, 4637-4642, 4715(a)(1), (4)-(5), 4716, 5101 note, 5101-5116, 15 U.S.C. §§ 78oo, 1639a, 7215(b)(5)(B)(ii)(II), 18 U.S.C. §§ 212, 657, 1006, 1014, 1905, 26 U.S.C. § 414(l)(2)(G), 42 U.S.C. §§ 1437f note, 4012a(f)(3)(A), 44 U.S.C. § 3502(5); redesignating 12 U.S.C. § 1422(2)-(9), (12)-(13) as § 1422(1)-(10); redesignating 12 U.S.C. § 4502(2)-(7), (8)-(12), (16)-(19) as § 4502(5)-(7), (12), (14)-(18), (21)-(23); redesignating 12 U.S.C. § 4614(c)-(d) as § 4614(d), (f); redesignating 12 U.S.C. § 4616(b)(5) as § 4616(b)(6); redesignating 12 U.S.C. § 4715(a)(1)-(2) as § 4715(a)(2)-(3); repealing 12 U.S.C. §§ 1422(1), (9)-(10), 1422a-1422b, 1427(f)(2), 1438(b), 1451 note, 4502(13)-(15), 4520(b), 4541, 4542, 4547-4548, 4562 note, 4589, 4616(b)(6), 4619-4621, 42 U.S.C. § 3534(d)).

225. *See, e.g.*, 74 Fed. Reg. 2347 (Jan 15, 2009) (codified at 12 C.F.R. pt. 1250) (codifying FHFA authority and responsibility to oversee and enforce statutory requirements affecting flood insurance operations of Federal National Mortgage Association and Federal Home Loan Mortgage

Office of Finance (which acts as the FHLBanks' fiscal agent) to a new independent executive branch agency, the Federal Housing Finance Agency (FHFA). The FHFA is responsible for ensuring that the enterprises and the FHLBanks operate in a safe and sound manner, including maintenance of adequate capital and internal controls, that their activities foster liquid, efficient, competitive and resilient national housing finance markets, and that they carry out their public policy missions through authorized activities.[226] The enterprises and the FHLBanks continue to operate under regulations promulgated by OFHEO and the FHFB until the FHFA issues its own regulations.[227]

The FHFA Director is required to adopt regulations specifying the critical capital level for each FHLBBank.[228] In establishing this requirement, HERA provides that the Director shall take due consideration of the critical capital levels established for the enterprises, with such modifications as the Director determines to be appropriate to reflect the difference in operations between the FHLBanks and the enterprises. HERA also requires the Director to issue regulations establishing the critical capital levels for the banks no later than the expiration of the 180 day period from the date that HERA was enacted.[229] In addition, HERA requires the Director, no later than 180 days from its enactment, to establish for the FHLBanks the following four capital classifications and criteria for each classification: adequately capitalized, undercapitalized, significantly undercapitalized, and critically undercapitalized.[230] HERA specifies that the criteria should be based on the amount and types of capital held by an FHLBank and the risk-based, minimum and critical capital levels for the FHLBanks, taking due consideration of the capital classifications established for the enterprises, with such modifications as the Director determines to be appropriate to reflect the difference in operations between the FHLBanks and the enterprises. HERA also provides the FHFA with prompt corrective action (PCA) authority over the FHLBanks and amends the Federal Housing Enterprises Safety and Soundness Act of 1992[231] so that specific mandatory or discretionary supervisory actions and restrictions under that statute would apply to any FHLBank determined to be undercapitalized, significantly undercapitalized or critically undercapitalized.[232] The general purpose of the PCA framework is to supplement the FHFA's other regulatory and supervisory authority and provide for timely and, in some situations, mandatory intervention by the regulator.

Corporation under the Flood Disaster Protection Act of 1973 (FDPA); implementing congressionally mandated adjustments to the civil money penalties applicable to violations of FDPA; replacing prior HUD regulations, 12 C.F.R. pt. 1773).

226. *See* HERA § 1102, 122 Stat. 2663-64.

227. *See id.* at §§ 1302, 1313, 122 Stat. 2795, 2798.

228. *See id.* at § 1141, 122 Stat. 2730 (codified at 12 U.S.C. § 4613(b)).

229. *See* 74 Fed. Reg. 5595 (2009) (codified at 12 C.F.R. §§ 1229.1-1229.12) (establishing interim capital classifications and critical capital levels for FHLBanks; delineating PCA authority over FHLBanks). The interim final rule was effective January 30, 2009. Id. at 5595. Public comments were due April 30, 2009. *Id.*

230. *See* HERA § 1142, 122 Stat. 2730-32. *See also* 12 C.F.R. §§ 1229.2-1229.4 (concerning determination of criteria for FHLBank capital classification reclassification by Director). *Cf. id.* § 1229.12 (establishing procedures related to capital classification and other actions).

231. Pub.L. 102-550, Title XIII, Oct. 28, 1992, 106 Stat. 3941 (1992) (codified at 12 U.S.C. §§ 4501 *et seq.*).

232. *See* HERA §§ 1143-1145, 122 Stat. 2732-34. *See also* 12 C.F.R. §§ 1229.6-1229.10 (authorizing mandatory and discretionary actions applicable to undercapitalized FHLBanks and applicable to significantly undercapitalized FHLBanks). *Cf. id.* § 1229.11 (concerning capital restoration plans).

1.69. *The Emergency Economic Stabilization Act of 2008.* On October 3, 3008, Title I of the Emergency Economic Stabilization Act of 2008 (EESA)[233] created the Troubled Assets Relief Program for the purchase of troubled assets of financial institutions. From the onset of the TARP, Treasury appeared to be improvising, unsure of even basic issues such as how to price the targeted assets.[234] By mid-October 2008, Treasury shifted direction[235] and began using TARP funds to purchase equity in troubled financial institutions (primarily nine large institutions) rather than purchasing troubled assets. Treasury adopted this approach arguably on the basis of its EESA authority.[236] The new approach prompted criticism[237] that Treasury has failed to require beneficiaries of its funding to use the capital infusions to strengthen the weak credit market.[238] Cluelessly, Treasury officials insisted that the Capital Purchase Program (CPP), under which Treasury was buying shares of preferred stock in selected financial institutions, taking, in most cases, a 5 percent dividend for the first few years, with an increase to 9 percent, would be profitable in the long run.[239] More recently, congressional concern has grown over the excessive levels of executive compensation at

---

233. Pub. L. No. 110-343, tit. I, §§ 101-136. 122 Stat. 3765, 3767-3800 (2008) (codified at 5 U.S.C. § 5315, 12 U.S.C. §§ 461 note, 1715z-23, 1823(c)(11), 1828(a), (c), 5211-5241, 15 U.S.C. § 1638 note, 1638(b)(2), 31 U.S.C. §§ 301, 3101).

234. *See, e.g.*, Stephen Joyce, Treasury Official Discusses Implementation Of $700 Billion Program to Buy Bad Assets, BNA Banking Daily (Oct. 7, 2008), available at http://news.bna.com (reporting on efforts of Treasury to implement TARP).

235. *Cf.* Thecla Fabian, Senate Finance Ranking Member Grassley Hammers Paulson on EESA Implementation, BNA Banking Daily (Nov. 14, 2008), available at http://news.bna.com (criticizing "repeated[] change[s] [of] direction" by Treasury and the Fed under EESA).

236. *Cf.* R. Christian Bruce & Aaron Lorenzo, Banks Receiving Treasury Investments See New Opportunities for Acquisitions, BNA Banking Daily (October 28, 2008), available at http://news.bna.com (discussing allocation of $250 billion of EESA funding for capital injections under Treasury Capital Purchase Program(CPP)). For discussion of the CPP, see Stephen Joyce & Nora Macaluso, Government Officials Say TARP Eligibility May Expand to Additional Types of Firms, BNA Banking Daily (Oct. 29, 2008), available at http://news.bna.com.

237. *See, e.g.*, Levin: Treasury Needs Firm Commitment From Banks to Use New Funds for Loans, BNA Banking Daily, Oct. 20, 2008, available at http://news.bna.com ; Malini Manickavasagam, Pelosi, Reid, Other Lawmakers Share Concern Over Banks' Possible TARP Misuse, BNA Banking Daily (Oct. 30, 2008), available at http://news.bna.com.

238. For contrary studies, arguing that bank lending had increased during the credit crisis, see V. Chari, L. Christiano, & P. Kehoe, *Facts and Myths about the Credit Crisis* (Federal Reserve Bank of Minneapolis Working Paper 666, Oct. 2008), available at http://www.minneapolisfed.org/publications_papers/ pub_display.cfm?id=4062; Octavio Marenzi *et al.*, *Flawed Assumptions about the Credit Crisis: A Critical Examination of US Policymakers* (Celent, Dec. 2009) (arguing that U.S. Government responses to credit crisis based on assumptions contradicted by government's own data), available at http://www.celent.com/PressReleases/ 20081210/CreditCrisis20081212DRAFT.pdf. *But see* Ethan Cohen-Cole, Burcu Duygan-Bump, Jose Fillat, & Judit Montoriol-Gerriga, *Minneapolis: Looking Behind the Aggregates: A Reply to "Facts and Myths About the Financial Crisis of 2008"* (Federal Reserve Bank of Boston Working Paper No. QAU08-5, Nov. 2008) (disputing Minneapolis Fed paper), available at http://www.bos.frb.org/bankinfo/qau/wp/2008/qau0805.htm.

239. The text of prepared remarks on the CPP by Interim Assistant Secretary for Financial Stability Neel Kashkari is available at: http://www.treas.gov/press/releases/hp1314.htm. *See also Capital Purchases Will Turn a Profit For Taxpayers, Treasury's Kashkari Says*, BNA Banking Daily (Dec. 8, 2008), available at http:// news.bna.com (reporting on Assistant Secretary Kashkari's remarks).

institutions benefitting from the CPP.[240] Whether as a result of the intense criticism of its use of the TARP or because of its own meandering approach to responding to the financial crisis, by mid-November 2008, Treasury was publicly moving away from its plan to buy mortgage-related assets; instead, it was reportedly considering other uses for what remained of the original $700 billion in TARP funds.[241] Coincidentally, on November 14, 2008, the Administration reached agreement with congressional leaders to establish a TARP inspector general, and congressional leaders appointed three experts to the Congressional Oversight Panel, another EESA-mandated watchdog.[242]

1.70. *Dodd-Frank Wall Street Reform and Consumer Protection Act.* On July 21, 2010, the President signed into law the Dodd-Frank Wall Street Reform and Consumer Protection Act (Dodd-Frank Act)[243] the most significant structural response so far to the ongoing financial crisis precipitated by the failure of the subprime mortgage market.[244] In many respects the new act, sprawling over 2,300-plus printed pages, is dense, but its basic theme is to mandate new supervision and controls over large and "systemically significant" financial institutions on the one hand, and to create genuine consumer protection mechanisms at the federal level on the other hand. Various provisions of the act will be discussed at appropriate points throughout casebook. The principal features of the act are as follows:

a. *Abolition of the Office of Thrift Supervision.* In a dramatic development, the Dodd-Frank Act transferred the functions and responsibilities of the OTS to the OCC,[245] the FDIC,[246] and the Fed.[247] The transfer was effective July 21, 2011,[248] and the OTS and the position of the DOTS were to be abolished 90 days after that effective date.[249]

---

240. *See Pelosi, Reid Concerned About Excessive CEO Compensation at Banks Getting EESA Funds*, BNA Banking Daily (Oct. 30, 2008), available at http://news.bna.com (reporting on congressional criticism of CEO compensation at EESA-aided firms participating in CPP).

241. Aaron Lorenzo & R. Christian Bruce, *Treasury Pulls Back From TARP Purchase Of Mortgage-Related Assets, Paulson Says*, BNA Banking Daily (Nov. 13, 2008), available at http://news.bna.com.

242. R. Christian Bruce, *Oversight of TARP Comes Into Focus With Action by White House, Pelosi, Reid*, BNA Banking Daily (Nov. 17, 2008), available at http://news.bna.com. The members of the five-member TARP Congressional Oversight Panel are appointed by Speaker of the House (who appointed Richard H. Neiman, the N.Y. Superintendent of Banks), the House Republican Leader (Rep. Jeb Hensarling (R-Texas)), the Senate Majority Leader (Harvard Law Professor Elizabeth Warren, who serves as chair) and the Senate Republican Leader (former Sen. John Sununu) each selecting one member. The fifth member is jointly selected by the Speaker and the Majority Leader (Damon Silvers, AFL-CIO associate general counsel). *See* R. Christian Bruce, *McConnell Names Sununu to TARP Panel; Thacher, Proffitt Tapped to Advise Treasury*, BNA Banking Daily (Dec. 18, 2008) (reporting on TARP panel).

243. Pub. L. No. 111-203, 124 Stat. 1376 (2010) (codified at scattered sections of 2, 5, 7, 11, 12, 15, 18, 20, 22, 26, 28, 31, 42, 44 U.S.C.) (Dodd-Frank Act).

244. For background on the subprime mortgage crisis, *see* MICHAEL P. MALLOY, ANATOMY OF A MELTDOWN (Aspen 2010).

245. Dodd-Frank Act §§312(b)(2)(B), 314 (codified at 12 U.S.C. §§1, 4a, 11 5412(b)(2)(B)).

246. Dodd-Frank Act §312(b)(2)(C) (codified at 12 U.S.C. §5412(b)(2)(C)).

247. Dodd-Frank Act §312(b)(1), (2)(A) (codified at 12 U.S.C. 5412(b)(1), (2)(A)).

248. Dodd-Frank Act §311(a) (codified at 12 U.S.C. §5411(a)). The effective date may be extended under certain specified circumstances. 12 U.S.C. §5411(b). Technical details of the transfer are handled by Dodd-Frank Act §§302, 312(a)-(b), 317, 319, 322–327.

249. Dodd-Frank Act §313 (codified at 12 U.S.C. 5413).

b. *Financial Stability Oversight Council.* The act established the Financial Stability Oversight Council (FSOC), a committee of financial services regulators.[250] The FSOC is intended to identify systemic risks, to promote market discipline, and to respond to emerging threats to the U.S. financial system.[251] For nonbank financial companies identified by the FSOC as systemically significant,[252] the act has expanded and enhanced the authority of the Fed to supervise nonbank financial companies.[253] Dodd-Frank Act also created FDIC authority to supervise resolution of financial crisis – or "orderly liquidation" – with respect to any systemically significant financial company.[254]

c. *Consumer Financial Protection Bureau.* The Dodd-Frank Act established the Consumer Financial Protection Bureau within the Fed to create and enforce effective consumer protection principles with respect to financial services.[255] Title X of the Dodd-Frank Act also appears to repudiate the broad preemptive effect of cases like *Watters*.[256] Despite Title X, the act does not represent a clean break with past preemption practices of the OCC and the OTS.[257] In certain respects, it substantially preserves federal preemption of state regulation of financial services, but with important exceptions in the consumer protection area.[258]

d. *Proprietary Securities Trading.* The Dodd-Frank Act restricts, but does not eliminate, proprietary securities trading by banks.[259]

e. *Mortgage Lending Standards.* The act imposes new mortgage lending stan-

---

250. Dodd-Frank Act §111(a)-(h) (codified at 12 U.S.C. §5321(a)-(h)).

251. Dodd-Frank Act §112(a)(1) (codified at 12 U.S.C. §5322(a)(1)).

252. Dodd-Frank Act §113 (codified at 12 U.S.C. §3523).

253. Dodd-Frank Act §§161–169 (codified at 12 U.S.C. §§5361–5369). *See also id.* §170 (codified at 12 U.S.C. §5370) (providing for safe harbor exemptions for certain types or classes of U.S. nonbank financial companies or foreign nonbank financial companies from supervision by Fed).

254. Dodd-Frank Act §§201–214 (codified at 12 U.S.C. §§4403, 5381–5394; 18 U.S.C. §1032(1)).

255. [4]Dodd-Frank Act §§1001–1067 (codified at 12 U.S.C. §§25b, 1465, 5481, 5491–5497, 5511–5519, 5531–5536, 5551–5587; 20 U.S.C. §9702(c)(1), (d)).

256. [6]*See, e.g.*, Dodd-Frank Act §1044 (codified at 12 U.S.C. §25b(b)) (establishing narrow grounds for federal preemption of state consumer protection laws).

257. *See* 1 MICHAEL P. MALLOY, BANKING LAW AND REGULATION § 1.03[I][2] (2d ed. 2011) (discussing effect of federal preemption policy on state bank regulation).

258. [1]*See generally* R. Christian Bruce, *Dodd-Frank Act's Language on Preemption Forces Some Quick Decisions, Lawyers Say*, BNA Banking Daily (July 23, 2010), *available at* http://www.bna.com (discussing implications for preemption).

259. Dodd-Frank Act §619 (codified at 12 U.S.C. §1851). For these purposes, proprietary trading is defined to mean:

> engaging as a principal for the trading account of the banking entity or nonbank financial company supervised by the [Fed] in any transaction to purchase or sell, or otherwise acquire or dispose of, any security, any derivative, any contract of sale of a commodity for future delivery, any option on any such security, derivative, or contract, or any other security or financial instrument that the appropriate Federal banking agencies, the Securities and Exchange Commission, and the Commodity Futures Trading Commission may, by rule as provided in [§ 1851(b)(2)], determine.

12 U.S.C. § 1851(h)(4).

dards.[260]

f. *Securitization of Financial Instruments*. Prior to the 2008 collapse of the mortgage market, securitization – the process in which interests in a pool of obligations or rights are marketed to investors as pro rata securities – was one of the critical processes for moving risky subprime mortgage obligations into the capital markets as securities. The Dodd-Frank Act imposes new standards with respect to securitization of pools of financial instruments.[261]

g. *SEC Enforcement Powers*. The act enhances the enforcement powers of the Securities and Exchange Commission (SEC).[262] It also provides for the SEC to maintain an additional $100 million of its revenues in a separate fund, which the SEC could use as necessary, with a full accounting to Congress.[263]

h. *Supervision of Hedge Fund and Private Equity Fund Advisers*. The Dodd-Frank Act requires hedge fund and private equity fund advisers[264] to register with the SEC, and will

---

260. Dodd-Frank Act §§1401–1484 (codified at 12 U.S.C. §§1701p-2, 1701x(a)(4), (c)(5)(A)(ii)(III)-(V), (e), (g)-(i), 1701x-1, 2603(c), 2604(a)-(d), 2605(e)-(f), (g), (k)-(m), 3310, 3332(a)(1), (5)-(6), (b), 3335, 3338(a)-(b), 3339, 3341(b), 3342, 3345(c), (e), 3346, 3347(a), (b)(2), 3348(a)(2), 3350(6), (8), (11), 3351(a)(1), (b), (d), (g)-(i), 3353-3355, 5219a-5219b, 5220b; 15 U.S.C. §§1602, 1604(h), 1607(a)(7), 1638(a)(16)-(19), (b)(4), (f), 1638a, 1639(e), (j)-(v), 1639a-1639h, 1640(a), (e), (k)-(l), 1691(e); 42 U.S.C. §3533(g), 8108; repealing 15 U.S.C. §1639(c)(2)).

261. Dodd-Frank Act §§ 941–945 (codified at 15 U.S.C. §§ 77d(5), 77g(c)-(d), 78c(a)(4)(B)(vii)(I), 78c(a)(77), 78o(d), 78o-11). See also DFA § 621(a) (codified at 15 U.S.C. § 77z-2a) (concerning conflicts of interest with respect to securitizations). Cf. Dodd-Frank Act § 619(g)(2) (codified at 12 U.S.C. § 1851(g)(2)) (protecting otherwise authorized sale or securitization of loans by banking entity or systemically significant nonbank financial company from prohibitions on proprietary trading).

262. Dodd-Frank Act §§912, 919, 921–929X (codified at 5 U.S.C. §§3101, 3114(a); 15 U.S.C. §§77h-1(g), 77o, 77s(e), 77t(d)(3)(A), 77v(a), 78d-5, 78g(c)(1)(A), 78i(d)-(j), 78j(a)(1), 78m, 78m(f), 78o(b)(6)(A), (c)(1)(A), (e)-(j), (n)-(o), 78o-4(c)(4), (8), 78o-5(c), 78p(a), 78q(f)(1)-(2), 78q-1(c)(4)(C), (g), 78s(h)(4), 78t(a), (e), 78u(a)(1), 78u-1, 78u-2(a), 78u-6, 78u-7, 78x, 78aa, 78cc(a), 78ddd(d)(1)(C), (h), 78eee(a)(3), 78fff-3(a)(1), (d)-(e), 78jjj(c)-(d), 80a-9(d)(1), 80a-30, 80a-35(a), 80a-41(e)(3)(A), 80a-43, 80a-48, 80b-3(f), (i)(1), 80b-4, 80b-5(a), (f), 80b-9(d)(3)(C)(i), (f), 80b-10(d), 80b-14, 7201(9), 7215(c)(6), 7216, 7217(d)(3), 7246(a)-(b), (h); 18 U.S.C. §§1514A(a), (b)(2), (e)).

263. *See* Dodd-Frank Act §991 (codified at 15 U.S.C. §§77f(b), 78d(i), 78m(e), 78n(g), 78ee(m), 78kk (match funding).

264. A *hedge fund* is an investment fund, usually organized as a private investment partnership, open to a limited number of investors and requiring a very large initial minimum investment committed to the fund for a relatively long period, typically at least one year. The fund's investment strategies are usually very aggressive, making use of leveraged and derivative trading in targeted securities in order to increase the rate of return when the securities perform well. (This also means, of course, that losses can be exacerbated if the securities perform poorly.) A private equity fund is an investment fund that specializes in investments not quoted on public exchanges. The fund typically makes an investment directly into an existing private company or it may buy up a public company and take it private, "delisting" it from public exchanges in the process. Participants in a private equity fund are typically high-end investors (institutions and sophisticated, wealthy individuals) who commit a relatively large amount to the fund for a long period of time. The Dodd-Frank Act treats these definitional issues less helpfully. See Dodd-Frank Act § 619 (codified at 12 U.S.C. § 1851), which defines both terms as follows:

> The terms "hedge fund" and "private equity fund" mean an issuer that would be an investment company, as defined in the Investment Company Act of 1940 (15 U.S.C. 80a-1 et seq.), but for [the Investment Company Act exemptive provisions in 15 U.S.C. § 80a-3(c)(1) or (c)(7)], or such similar funds as the appropriate Federal banking agencies, the Securities and Exchange Commission, and the Commodity Futures Trading Commission may, by rule, as provided in subsection (b)(2), determine.

subject them to SEC inspection and examination.[265]

i. *Regulation of Swaps and Security-Based Swaps*. The act provides for comprehensive regulation of swaps and security-based swaps by the Commodity Futures Trading Commission (CFTC) and the SEC[266] in consultation with the Fed.[267] The SEC and the CFTC have joint responsibility for swap products, to be allocated between the two agencies depending on whether the underlying product is a "security" or not.[268] Institutions deemed to be swap dealers — typically, large banks that make markets in swaps by creating and selling them[269] — as well as "major swap participants" are required to register with either the

---

12 U.S.C. § 1851(h)(2). The exemptive provisions referred to in the quoted excerpt actually provide a more informative description of these types of funds as follows:

> [N]one of the following persons is an investment company within the meaning of [the Investment Company Act]:
>
> (1) Any issuer whose outstanding securities (other than short-term paper) are beneficially owned by not more than one hundred persons and which is not making and does not presently propose to make a public offering of its securities. . .
>
> (7)(A) Any issuer, the outstanding securities of which are owned exclusively by persons who, at the time of acquisition of such securities, are qualified purchasers [i.e., sophisticated investors], and which is not making and does not at that time propose to make a public offering of such securities. . .
>
> (E) For purposes of determining compliance with this paragraph and paragraph (1), an issuer that is otherwise excepted under this paragraph and an issuer that is otherwise excepted under paragraph (1) shall not be treated by the Commission as being a single issuer for purposes of determining whether the outstanding securities of the issuer excepted under paragraph (1) are beneficially owned by not more than 100 persons or whether the outstanding securities of the issuer excepted under this paragraph are owned by persons that are not qualified purchasers. . . .

See Clemente Global Growth Fund, Inc. v. Pickens, 705 F. Supp. 958 (S.D.N.Y. 1989) (interpreting § 80a-3(c)(1)).

265. Id. §§ 401-412, 419 (codified at 15 U.S.C. §§ 80b-2(a)(11), (29)-(30), 80b-3(b), (l)-(n), 80b-3a(a), 80b-4, 80b-10(c), 80b-11, 80b-18b). As a general rule, these registration requirements were effective as of 21 July 2011, but an investment adviser could, in its discretion, register with the SEC under the Investment Advisers Act of 1940 during the one-year transition period, subject to rules to be promulgated by the SEC. 15 U.S.C. § 80b-2 note.

266. Dodd-Frank Act §§711–716, 718 (codified at 7 U.S.C. §§6d(h), 24(c); 15 U.S.C. §§78o(c)(3)(C), 8301–8306).

267. Dodd-Frank Act §712(a)(8) (codified at 15 U.S.C. §8302(a)(8)).

268. Dodd-Frank Act §717 (codified at 7 U.S.C. §2(a)(1)(C)7a-2(c)(1); 15 U.S.C. §§78c-1, 78s(b)(10)). Cf. Dodd-Frank Act §720 (codified at 15 U.S.C. §8308) (memorandum of understanding to be negotiated between CFTC and Federal Energy Regulatory Commission). The SEC and the CFTC have already jointly issued proposed rules "further defining" key terms and regulating "mixed swaps." 75 Fed. Reg. 51,429 (2010) (to be codified at 17 C.F.R. pt. 1 (CFTC rules); id. pt. 240 (SEC rules)).

269. At the same time, a "de minimis" exception from designation as a swap dealer is available to "an entity that engages in a de minimis quantity of swap dealing in connection with transactions with or on behalf of customers." Dodd-Frank Act §721(a)(49)(D) (codified at 7 U.S.C. §1a(a)(49)(D)). This clause is important for regional banks and other smaller financial institutions such as savings associations and credit unions and will enable them to avoid the regulatory burdens likely to be associated with being identified as a swap dealer.

SEC or CFTC, depending on the nature of their products.[270] The Dodd-Frank Act provides for the SEC and the CFTC, in consultation with the Fed, jointly to "further define" certain key terms (specifically, "swap," "security-based swap," "swap dealer," "security-based swap dealer," "major swap participant," "major security-based swap participant," "eligible contract participant," and "security-based swap agreement"), and jointly prescribe regulations regarding "mixed swaps," as that term is used in Dodd-Frank Act Title VII.

j. *Credit Rating Agencies*. Dodd-Frank Act imposes disclosure requirements on credit rating agencies, and requires their registration with and supervision by the SEC.[271] Dodd-Frank Act also expands the availability of private rights of action against credit rating agencies. It eliminates an explicit exclusion of private rights of action arising out of 1934 Act,[272] requiring registration of nationally recognized statistical rating organizations.[273] It also allows for potential liability under the 1933 Act, by eliminating an SEC rule[274] that deemed credit ratings not to be a part of the registration statement "prepared or certified" by a person within the meaning of the private right of action under 1933 Act §11.[275] Hence, credit ratings are now part of the "expertised" portions of a 1933 Act registration statement filed with the SEC, giving rise to an express private right of action against a credit rating agency for materially false or misleading ratings prepared by it and contained in such a statement.[276]

k. *Corporate Governance*. Arguably, extravagant executive compensation practices were a contributing cause of the financial crisis. Dodd-Frank Act requires companies registered pursuant to 1934 Act §12[277] to permit their shareholders to have a nonbinding vote, at least once every three years,[278] on executive compensation.[279] The Dodd-Frank Act also requires disclosure by any person soliciting proxies in favor of a merger or other acquisition of any "golden parachute" compensation agreement or understanding in favor of departing

---

270. 7Dodd-Frank Act §§721–724 (codified at 7 U.S.C. §§1a, 1b, 2(a)(1), (c)(2)(A), (i)-(j), 6(c)(1), (6), 6d(f) 6m, 6q, 6s(l), 7-7a-1, 13-1(a), 16(h), 27; 11 U.S.C. 761; 15 U.S.C. §§78f, 8321-8322).

271. Dodd-Frank Act §§931-939B, 939F (codified at 12 U.S.C. §§24a, 1817(b)(1)(E)(i), 1831e, 4519; 15 U.S.C. §§78a(3)(a), 78c(a)(62), 78o-7(m), (u)-(v), 78o-8, 78u-4(b)(2), 80a-6(a)(5)(A)(iv)(I); 22 U.S.C. §286hh(a)(6)).

272. 15 U.S.C. §78o-7(m)(2) (2009) (foreclosing implication of private right of action resulting from registration of statistical rating agency).

273. Dodd-Frank Act §933(a) (codified at 15 U.S.C. §78o-7(m)) (applying 1934 Act enforcement and penalty provisions to statements made by a credit rating agency).

274. 17 C.F.R. §230.436(g) (2009), nullified by Dodd-Frank Act §939G, 124 Stat. 1376, 1890 (2010).

275. 15 U.S.C. §77k.

276. Pre-Dodd-Frank litigation attempts to impose liability on credit rating agencies that provided misleading favorable ratings for securitized subprime mortgage pools have generally been unsuccessful. See, e.g., Public Employees' Ret. Sys. of Mississippi v. Merrill Lynch & Co., Inc., — F. Supp. 2d —, 2010 WL 2175875 (S.D.N.Y. 2010), at *3-*4 (dismissing 1933 Act §11 action against credit rating agencies; holding agencies not "underwriters" for §11 purposes); Teamsters Allied Benefit. Funds v. McGraw-Hill Cos., Inc., — F. Supp. 2d —, 2010 WL 882883 (S.D.N.Y. 2010) (dismissing derivative suit by shareholders of parent company of credit rating agency for failure to state adequate claim under 1934 Act §10(b)).

277. 15 U.S.C. §78l.

278. The Dodd-Frank Act allows for more frequent nonbinding votes, upon the approval of the shareholders in that regard. See Dodd-Frank Act §951 (codified at 15 U.S.C. §78n-1(a)(2)) (permitting, at least once every six years, shareholder vote on frequency of compensation votes).

279. 15 U.S.C. §78n-1(a)(1).

executives in connection with the merger or acquisition.[280] These provisions of Dodd-Frank Act do not appear to supersede substantive guidance previously issued by the regulators.[281]

280. 15 U.S.C. §78n-1(b)(1). For these purposes, the term "golden parachute" is characterized by the statute as any type of compensation (whether present, deferred, or contingent) that is based on or otherwise relates to the acquisition, merger, consolidation, sale, or other disposition of all or substantially all of the assets of the issuer and the aggregate total of all such compensation that may (and the conditions upon which it may) be paid or become payable to or on behalf of such executive officer." Id.

281. For example, in late June 2010, the OCC, the Fed, the FDIC, and the OTS adopted final guidance designed to ensure that "incentive compensation policies" at banking organizations did not encourage imprudent risk-taking, and that they were consistent with safety and soundness. Guidance on Sound Incentive Compensation Policies, 75 Fed. Reg. 36,395, 36,405–36,414 (2010). The guidance was effective June 25, 2010. 75 Fed. Reg. at 36,395.

Chapter 2

Entry Rules

1. Introduction

This chapter examines the statutory and regulatory requirements applicable to entry into the depository institutions industry. The primary focus here is on the chartering of a commercial bank, and the model followed in that regard is the process of chartering a national bank. The state chartering processes are similar, with the specific requirements governed by the particular state statute involved.

In addition to the chartering process itself, the chapter also examines briefly two secondary entry restrictions. These are membership in the Federal Reserve System and federal deposit insurance.

The chapter concludes with an examination of conversions. There are two distinct types of conversion. One process involves changing the organizational form of an institution, from mutual to stock. The other involves changing from a federal charter to a state charter, or state to federal.

2. Chartering

Notes and Comments 2.1. *National and state bank chartering alternatives.* The choice between a national and a state bank charter is in some respects similar to the choice of state of incorporation for a general business corporation; the goal is to identify a jurisdiction which has sufficiently acceptable–*i.e.*, permissive–rules with respect to activities that are of particular importance to the incorporators. The choice of charter also resembles forum shopping, since the chartering authority is also the administrator that interprets the scope of the statutory powers permissible for the bank. One obvious difference between national and state bank charters is that a national bank is required to be a member of the Federal Reserve System ("the Fed"),[1] while membership of state banks is voluntary. Membership in the Federal Reserve carries with it additional costs, and this can influence the decision of the prospective incorporators. Similarly, national banks and state-chartered Fed-member banks are required by federal law to obtain federal deposit insurance,[2] but federal law generally

1. 12 U.S.C. § 222.

2. *Id.*

does not require nonmember state banks to obtain federal deposit insurance.[3]

2.2. Another difference between national and state charters may involve the scope of a bank's "incidental powers,"[4] but such differences have been significantly narrowed by federal law.[5] Nevertheless, the scope of permissible incidental powers is subject to interpretation by the bank's primary regulator in the first instance–either the Comptroller for a national bank or a state regulator for a state-chartered bank. As a result, the choice of charter may be influenced by the perception that one or the other regulator is a more aggressive chartering authority when it comes to interpretation of the scope of such powers.

2.3. *Formation of a national bank.* The formation of a national bank is governed by the provisions of the National Bank Act ("NBA") and the regulations promulgated by the Comptroller under the NBA. A national bank may be formed by five or more natural persons as incorporators who will be the individuals who enter into and sign the articles of association of the corporate body.[6] A copy of the articles will be submitted to the Comptroller and made part of the OCC's permanent file on the bank. The incorporators are also required to prepare an organization certificate, providing such information as the name of the association, the place of operation, the amount of capital stock and number of shares, the names and residences of the shareholders, and the number of shares held by each.[7] Until 2001, national banks were required to be organized with no less than a statutorily required amount of capital,[8] but now minimum capital requirements for formation are found only in the OCC regulations. How much guidance do you get on this issue from 12 C.F.R. § 5.20(f)(2)(i)(C) (page 90, *infra*) or from § 5.20(h)(4) (page 92, *infra*)?

2.4. *Authority of the Comptroller.* What role is given by the NBA to the Comptroller? To what extent does the Comptroller exercise administrative discretion to approve or disapprove a proposed organization of a national bank? An initial answer can be obtained by reference to 12 U.S.C. §§ 26-27. When the organization certificate is transmitted to the Comptroller, section 26 directs that official to "examine into the condition of such association, ascertain especially the amount of money paid in on account of its capital, . . . and generally whether such association has complied with all provisions . . . required to entitle it to engage in the business of banking; and shall cause to be made . . . a statement of all facts necessary to enable the comptroller to determine whether the association is lawfully entitled to commence the business of banking." Does this mean that the Comptroller is limited to ministerial acts, or does the Comptroller make a substantive determination of the merits of the proposed organization of a national bank? This question is somewhat clarified by the provisions of 12 U.S.C. § 27, requiring the issuance of a certificate of authority from the Comptroller before a national bank may commence banking. Section 27 refers to "a careful examination of the facts so reported, and of any other facts which may come to the knowledge of the comptroller" to determine "that the association is lawfully entitled to commence the business of banking." On the other hand, further language in section 27(a) states that "the comptroller may withhold from [a national bank] his certificate . . . whenever

---

3. *But see* 12 U.S.C. § 1842(c) (requiring federal deposit insurance for bank that is bank holding company and bank that is subsidiary of bank holding company).

4. *See infra* Chapter 5, § 7 (discussing incidental powers).

5. *See* 12 U.S.C. § 1831a (prohibiting generally state bank exercise of powers not permitted for national banks).

6. 12 U.S.C. § 21.

7. 12 U.S.C. § 22.

8. 12 U.S.C. § 51, *repealed*, American Homeownership and Economic Opportunity Act of 2000, Pub. L. No. 106-569, § 1233(c), 114 Stat. 2944 (2000).

he has reason to suppose that the shareholders have formed the same for any other than the legitimate objects contemplated by" the NBA. Is this the only basis on which the Comptroller may disapprove the commencement of banking? Consider the following excerpts.

Camp v. Pitts

411 U.S. 138 (1973)

[Reread the selection from this case reproduced at 44, *supra*.]

Kenneth Scott, In Quest of Reason: The Licensing Decisions of the Federal Banking Agencies

42 U. Chi. L. Rev. 235 (1975)

On its face, the statute does not seem to grant the Comptroller broad discretion to determine whether a community should have a new bank.[11] This fact bothered the district court in *Pitts v. Camp*,[12] and yet that court declared itself "impressed with the long and continued practice of the Comptroller of considering the need of the community [and] with the fact that the weight of authority accepts the consideration by the Comptroller of the need factor without question."[13] The court then cited *Sterling National Bank of Davie v. Camp*,[14] which had asserted: "It has always been recognized that this legislation confers vast discretion on the Comptroller to approve or disapprove a new charter application."[15]

These decisions considerably overstate the matter. It has not "always been recognized" that the National Bank Act confers vast chartering discretion upon the Comptroller, and it has not been his "long and continued practice" to assert such discretion. The dominant views of the mid-nineteenth century favored "free banking," as part of the general trend towards "free incorporation"–the idea that charters to do various kinds of business should be readily available to anyone who complied with relatively simple and specific statutory requirements, rather than be grants of special privilege by the legislature to those who obtained (or bought) its favors. . . . The National Currency Act and the National Bank Act were designed as free-bank laws and with that origin in mind their language becomes perfectly comprehensible.[17] . . .

11.

> The Court has difficulty in seeing language in those sections giving the Comptroller discretion in granting the certificate if the specific requirements of the act are met . . . .
>
> The statutory language, which the defendant contends makes the need of the new bank a proper consideration and commits the determination of that need to the Comptroller's discretion, does not impress the court.

Pitts v. Camp, 329 F. Supp. 1302, 1307 (D.S.C. 1971), *vacated*, 463 F.2d 632 (4th Cir. 1972), *vacated and remanded*, 411 U.S. 138 (1973).

12. *Id.*

13. *Id.* at 1307.

14. 431 F.2d 514 (5th Cir. 1970), *cert. denied*, 401 U.S. 925 (1971).

15. *Id.* at 516.

17. *See generally* [R. ROBERTSON, THE COMPTROLLER AND BANK SUPERVISION] 44-45 [(1968)]. *See also* B. HAMMOND, BANKS AND POLITICS IN AMERICA 727 (1957); 2 F. REDLICH, THE MOLDING OF AMERICAN BANKING 99-105 (1968). In practice, the first Comptrollers tried on occasion to make their own judgments felt, but the legal footing for their efforts was minimal. "The law did not

A shift in position did not begin until 1908, when a new Comptroller took office on the heels of the Panic of 1907,[20] and it did not become established policy until the 1920s.[21] This new approach did not acquire a respectable statutory foundation, however, until the Great Depression led to the creation of the Federal Deposit Insurance Corporation and enactment of the Banking Act of 1935. The latter enactment required the Comptroller, when he chartered a new national bank, which automatically would become an insured bank, to certify to the FDIC that he had "considered" the same six factors that the FDIC was supposed to consider in passing upon the application for insured status of a state nonmember bank:[24] "The financial history and condition of the bank, the adequacy of its capital structure, its future earnings prospects, the general character of its management, the convenience and needs of the community to be served by the bank, and whether or not its corporate powers are consistent with the purposes" of the Federal Deposit Insurance Act.[25] In this somewhat backhanded fashion the law recognized–or, more accurately, created–the Comptroller's chartering discretion. To the extent that there are standards governing that discretion, therefore, they are to be found in the Federal Deposit Insurance Act, not the National Bank Act. . . .

The Comptroller in *Camp v. Pitts* did not challenge before the Supreme Court the Fourth Circuit's holding that his letters of explanation were inadequate for judicial review, but he did attack the procedure of remand to the district court for trial de novo. The Supreme Court agreed. . . .

. . . [T]he proper remedy for an inadequate explanation is to get more, by way of either affidavits or testimony, to add to the administrative record. Since the Comptroller had already indicated the "determinative reason" for his denial,[149] that was the ground that had to be supportable on the record with the aid of the additional explanation.[150] If it was not, then the proper course was to vacate the Comptroller's decision and remand to him for further consideration.

The Supreme Court therefore seemed to take away the only club the Fourth Circuit

---

require the organizers to satisfy the Comptroller that they were qualified to engage in the banking business, that additional banking facilities were needed, or that the proposed bank had reasonable prospects of success." Wyatt, *Federal Banking Legislation*, in BANKING STUDIES 44 (F.R.B. 1941).

20. R. ROBERTSON, *supra* . . . at 66-69.

21. *Id.* at 95-96.

24. 12 U.S.C. § 1814 (1970).

25. *Id.* § 1816.

149. In the Court's rendition, this reason was "the finding that a new bank was an uneconomic venture in light of the banking needs and the banking services already available in the surrounding community." 411 U.S. at 143.

150. The appropriate standard of review for this purpose, the Court also held, was that of section 10(e)(2)(A) of the [Administative Procedure Act]: "whether the Comptroller's adjudication was 'arbitrary, capricious, an abuse of discretion or otherwise not in accordance with law.'" *Id.* at 142, quoting from 5 U.S.C. § 706(2)(A) (1970). The "substantial evidence" test was deemed appropriate for reviewing findings based on a hearing record, which the statutes in question here do not require. 411 U.S. at 141. Presumably, the former standard is a less demanding one affording narrower review, but the distinctions involved have never been very clear. For example, would a finding not supported by evidence that was at least substantial not also be an abuse of discretion? Courts now know which language to use, but it is not evident that they will go about their job much differently; a district court subsequently considered the question in *Grenada Bank v. Watson*, 361 F. Supp. 728, 733 (N.D. Miss. 1973), *aff'd*, 488 F.2d 1056 (5th Cir. 1974), and found "no substantial difference" between the two standards. More recent and authoritative, if not more enlightening, discussion may be found in *Bowman Transp., Inc. v. Arkansas-Best Freight Sys.*, Inc., 95 S. Ct. 438, 441-42 (1974).

had found effective in trying to change the Comptroller's ways–de novo review. That method had always involved a more or less open intrusion upon the functions assigned to the Comptroller by Congress, and was therefore inappropriate, as the Court declared. What was regrettable was the Court's apparent unawareness of the eight years of running struggle between the Comptroller and the lower courts, in which effective judicial review had been frustrated determinedly and continuously.

On the other hand, the Court certainly left the door open for the lower courts to force explanations that they could find comprehensible. Indeed, as *Pitts* made clear, *Overton Park* had limited the rule of *Morgan IV*, about not probing into the mental processes of decision makers by deposition or examination as witnesses, to situations in which the decision maker had made formal findings on a record.[151] That overruled *Warren v. Camp*[152] and other cases holding that the Comptroller could not be examined or deposed, and if litigants pursued the opportunity it would become a new club of some force. If the Comptroller's inevitable objections about the burden on his office were not received sympathetically, he would almost surely move to forestall the embarrassments of cross-examination by providing fuller explanations–if not in contemporaneous opinions then through litigation affidavits. And if he did not, the court was free to remand.

But if the door to more intelligible explanation was still open, the general tenor of the opinion in *Pitts* was not very encouraging. This can best be shown by examining how lower courts have subsequently used or construed *Pitts*. The District of Columbia Circuit vacated *Wood County Bank* and remanded it to the district court for reconsideration in light of *Pitts*, and the district court felt constrained to grant the Comptroller's motion for summary judgment, though not without considerable protest.[153] . . .

In *First National Bank of Homestead v. Watson*,[154] a competitor challenge to a charter approval, the court cited *Pitts* for the proposition that, absent a showing that his action was arbitrary or capricious, the Comptroller was under no obligation to explain his decision.[155] In *Grenada Bank v. Watson*,[156] the Comptroller had without opinion approved a branch on the basis of the usual thick hearing record plus brief and conflicting recommendations from subordinates; the court went back to . . . noting that the record contained evidence that might, on some theory, support [implied findings by the Comptroller]. *Pitts* was cited to the effect that the Comptroller's decision must be upheld unless the record indicates that it is "arbitrary, capricious, an abuse of discretion or otherwise not in accord-

---

151. *See Citizens to Preserve Overton Park v. Volpe*, 401 U.S. 402, 420 (1971).

152. 396 F.2d 52 (6th Cir. 1968). . . .

153.

> [I]n the case at Bar the Comptroller attempted to explain in three short sentences his analysis of 1000 pages of economic data contained in the administrative record. . . .
>
> The Comptroller explained his determinative reasons for the action taken by stating summarily that the new bank would serve the convenience and needs of the relevant market and have no serious effect on the existing institutions now serving the general area. Under present requirements of procedural due process governing the Comptroller's decisions . . . the Court is constrained to deem the Comptroller's explanation sufficient.

Wood County Bank v. Camp, Civil No. 1277-72 (D.D.C., May 24, 1973), *aff'd*, 498 F.2d 1063 (D.C.Cir. 1974). . . .

154. 363 F. Supp. 466 (D.D.C. 1973).

155. *Id.* at 468.

156. 361 F. Supp. 728 (N.D. Miss. 1973), *aff'd*, 488 F.2d 1056 (5th Cir. 1974).

ance with law. . . ."[157]

The plaintiff in *Bank of Commerce of Laredo v. City National Bank of Laredo*[158] requested remand to the district court to obtain from the Comptroller some explanation of his charter approval as a branch substitute for the defendant, but was turned down flatly by the Fifth Circuit in a remarkably obtuse opinion. The court cited *Morgan IV*, and the pre-*Overton Park* banking cases for the proposition that the plaintiff was barred by the "preponderant weight of judicial precedent" from deposing the Comptroller or requiring him to answer interrogatories.[159] *Overton Park* itself was ignored, and *Pitts* was cited as a recent affirmance of this policy, though the opinion had said the exact opposite. The real point in *Laredo* was that the Fifth Circuit did not in that case feel any need for additional explanation to undertake judicial review,[161] and that in turn rested upon a willingness to hold the Comptroller to a generous and undemanding standard–the court was willing to glean from the staff recommendations and a "voluminous record" what "surely" was the determinative reason for the approval.[162]

In *Merchants & Planters Bank v. Smith*[163] the district court applied the limited scope of review of *Pitts* to a branch approval, suggesting it was sufficient if the Comptroller's determination had "a rational basis in fact."[164] Untroubled by the lack of any findings, conclusions, or opinion, the court pieced together conflicting file memoranda and constructed what it felt "the agency thinking" must have been. Needless to say, the Comptroller was sustained.

The only contrary note was *First National Bank of Fayetteville v. Smith*,[165] reversing the Comptroller's approval of a charter. . . . The recommendations of subordinates having gone four to one against approval, the court concluded that the Comptroller must have accepted and relied upon the grounds given in the one favorable recommendation, and that advice became in effect the Comptroller's findings to be tested against the record.[167] After noting that the standard for review was whether the Comptroller's action was arbitrary or capricious, or had no rational basis in the record, the court then waded through the record–considering how much capital would be adequate, choosing one expert over another on the bank's earnings prospects, judging whether the "need" would be better met by branches, and weighing the qualifications of the applicant group and proposed managing officer. Subsequently, however, the Eighth Circuit reversed this decision on the ground that the district judge, though stating the correct standard of review, had actually exercised an independent judgment in place of that of the Comptroller;[168] the failure of the Comptroller to provide even a hint as to how his own judgment had been arrived at occasioned no adverse comment at all. . . .

Notes and Comments 2.5. Hiram Forth, President and principal shareholder of

---

157. *Id.* at 735.

158. 484 F.2d 284 (5th Cir. 1973), *cert. denied*, 416 U.S. 905 (1974).

159. *Id.* at 287.

161. 484 F.2d at 288.

162. *Id.*

163. 380 F. Supp. 354 (E.D. Ark. 1974).

164. *Id.* at 356.

165. 365 F. Supp. 898 (W.D. Ark. 1973).

167. 365 F. Supp. at 904.

168. *First Nat'l Bank of Fayetteville v. Smith*, 508 F.2d 1371 (8th Cir. 1974), *petition for cert. filed*, 43 U.S.L.W. 3439 (U.S. Feb. 4, 1975) (No. 963).

Quartet Real Estate Investment Corp., is interested in organizing a national bank in San Francisco. He anticipates that Quartet will be the primary organizer, along with Hiram and the three other executive officers of Quartet. The initial investment in the new bank, to be called Quarter National Bank ("QNB"), will be $100,000 in common stock and an additional $20,000 in capital surplus. Hiram anticipates that the members of the board of directors will be himself, his son Hiram, Jr. (who graduated from college last Spring), his wife and his accountant. In addition, Hiram expects that he will serve as President of QNB, and he intends to hire Abel, Betta and Carlo, three local bankers with whom he regularly does business, to serve as Executive Vice President, Cashier and Secretary of QNB. Hiram has come to you for advice about organizing QNB. He needs to know what the procedures will be for obtaining a national bank charter and the likelihood that his plans for the organization of QNB will be approved by the Comptroller. Based on the following excerpted material, what advice would you give Hiram?

Comptroller of the Currency

12 C.F.R. pt 5

§ 5.20 Organizing a bank.

(a) Authority. 12 U.S.C. 21, 22, 24(Seventh), 26, 27, 92a, 93a, 1814(b), 1816, and 2903.

(b) Licensing requirements. Any person desiring to establish a national bank shall submit an application and obtain prior OCC approval. . . .

(d) Definitions. For purposes of this section:

(1) Bankers' bank means a bank owned exclusively (except to the extent directors' qualifying shares are required by law) by other depository institutions or depository institution holding companies (as that term is defined in section 3 of the Federal Deposit Insurance Act, 12 U.S.C. 1813), the activities of which are limited by its articles of association exclusively to providing services to or for other depository institutions, their holding companies, and the officers, directors, and employees of such institutions and companies, and to providing correspondent banking services at the request of other depository institutions or their holding companies.

(2) Control means control as used in section 2 of the Bank Holding Company Act, 12 U.S.C. 1841(a)(2).

(3) Final approval means the OCC action issuing a charter certificate and authorizing a national bank to open for business.

(4) Holding company means any company that controls or proposes to control a national bank whether or not the company is a bank holding company under section 2 of the Bank Holding Company Act, 12 U.S.C. 1841(a)(1).

(5) Lead depository institution means the largest depository institution controlled by a bank holding company based on a comparison of the average total assets controlled by each depository institution as reported in its Consolidated Report of Condition and Income required to be filed for the immediately preceding four calendar quarters.

(6) Organizing group means five or more persons acting on their own behalf, or serving as representatives of a sponsoring holding company, who apply to the OCC for a national bank charter.

(7) Preliminary approval means a decision by the OCC permitting an organizing group to go forward with the organization of the proposed national bank. A preliminary approval generally is subject to certain conditions that an applicant must satisfy before the OCC will grant final approval.

(e) Statutory requirements–

(1) General. The OCC charters a national bank under the authority of the National Bank Act of 1864, as amended, 12 U.S.C. 1 et seq. . . . The name of a proposed bank must include the word "national." In determining whether to approve an application to establish a national bank, the OCC verifies that the proposed national bank has complied with the following requirements of the National Bank Act. A national bank shall:

(i) Draft and file articles of association with the OCC;

(ii) Draft and file an organization certificate containing specified information with the OCC;

(iii) Ensure that all capital stock is paid in; and

(iv) Have at least five elected directors.

(2) Community Reinvestment Act. Twelve CFR part 25 requires the OCC to take into account a proposed insured national bank's description of how it will meet its CRA objectives.

(f) Policy–

(1) General. The marketplace is normally the best regulator of economic activity, and competition within the marketplace promotes efficiency and better customer service. Accordingly, it is the OCC's policy to approve proposals to establish national banks, including minority-owned institutions, that have a reasonable chance of success and that will be operated in a safe and sound manner. It is not the OCC's policy to ensure that a proposal to establish a national bank is without risk to the organizers or to protect existing institutions from healthy competition from a new national bank.

(2) Policy considerations.

(i) In evaluating an application to establish a national bank, the OCC considers whether the proposed bank:

(A) Has organizers who are familiar with national banking laws and regulations;

(B) Has competent management, including a board of directors, with ability and experience relevant to the types of services to be provided;

(C) Has capital that is sufficient to support the projected volume and type of business;

(D) Can reasonably be expected to achieve and maintain profitability; and

(E) Will be operated in a safe and sound manner.

(ii) The OCC may also consider additional factors listed in section 6 of the Federal Deposit Insurance Act, 12 U.S.C. 1816, including the risk to the Federal deposit insurance fund, and whether the proposed bank's corporate powers are consistent with the purposes of the Federal Deposit Insurance Act and the National Bank Act.

(3) OCC evaluation. The OCC evaluates a proposed national bank's organizing group and its business plan or operating plan together. The OCC's judgment concerning one may affect the evaluation of the other. An organizing group and its business plan or operating plan must be stronger in markets where economic conditions are marginal or competition is intense.

(g) Organizing group–

(1) General. Strong organizing groups generally include diverse business and financial interests and community involvement. An organizing group must have the experience, competence, willingness, and ability to be active in directing the proposed national bank's affairs in a safe and sound manner. The bank's initial board of directors generally is comprised of many, if not all, of the organizers. The business plan or operating plan and other information supplied in the application must demonstrate an organizing group's collective ability to establish and operate a successful bank in the economic and competitive conditions

of the market to be served. Each organizer should be knowledgeable about the business plan or operating plan. A poor business plan or operating plan reflects adversely on the organizing group's ability, and the OCC generally denies applications with poor business plans or operating plans.

(2) Management selection. The initial board of directors must select competent senior executive officers before the OCC grants final approval. Early selection of executive officers, especially the chief executive officer, contributes favorably to the preparation and review of [a] business plan or operating plan that is accurate, complete, and appropriate for the type of bank proposed and its market, and reflects favorably upon an application. As a condition of the charter approval, the OCC retains the right to object to and preclude the hiring of any officer, or the appointment or election of any director, for a two-year period from the date the bank commences business.

(3) Financial resources.

(i) Each organizer must have a history of responsibility, personal honesty, and integrity. Personal wealth is not a prerequisite to become an organizer or director of a national bank. However, directors' stock purchases, individually and in the aggregate, should reflect a financial commitment to the success of the national bank that is reasonable in relation to their individual and collective financial strength. A director should not have to depend on bank dividends, fees, or other compensation to satisfy financial obligations.

(ii) Because directors are often the primary source of additional capital for a bank not affiliated with a holding company, it is desirable that an organizer who is also proposed as a director of the national bank be able to supply or have a realistic plan to enable the bank to obtain capital when needed.

(iii) Any financial or other business arrangement, direct or indirect, between the organizing group or other insider and the proposed national bank must be on nonpreferential terms.

(4) Organizational expenses.

(i) Organizers are expected to contribute time and expertise to the organization of the bank. Organizers should not bill excessive charges to the bank for professional and consulting services or unduly rely upon these fees as a source of income.

(ii) A proposed national bank shall not pay any fee that is contingent upon an OCC decision. Such action generally is grounds for denial of the application or withdrawal of preliminary approval. Organizational expenses for denied applications are the sole responsibility of the organizing group.

(5) Sponsor's experience and support. A sponsor must be financially able to support the new bank's operations and to provide or locate capital when needed. The OCC primarily considers the financial and managerial resources of the sponsor and the sponsor's record of performance, rather than the financial and managerial resources of the organizing group, if an organizing group is sponsored by:

(i) An existing holding company;

(ii) Individuals currently affiliated with other depository institutions; or

(iii) Individuals who, in the OCC's view, are otherwise collectively experienced in banking and have demonstrated the ability to work together effectively.

(h) Business plan or operating plan--

(1) General.

(i) Organizers of a proposed national bank shall submit [a] business plan or operating plan that adequately addresses the statutory and policy considerations set forth in paragraphs (e) and (f)(2) of this section. The plan must reflect sound banking principles and demonstrate realistic assessments of risk in light of economic and competitive conditions in the market to be served.

(ii) The OCC may offset deficiencies in one factor by strengths in one or more other factors. However, deficiencies in some factors, such as unrealistic earnings prospects, may have a negative influence on the evaluation of other factors, such as capital adequacy, or may be serious enough by themselves to result in denial. The OCC considers inadequacies in [a] business plan or operating plan to reflect negatively on the organizing group's ability to operate a successful bank.

(2) Earnings prospects. The organizing group shall submit pro forma balance sheets and income statements as part of the business plan or operating plan. The OCC reviews all projections for reasonableness of assumptions and consistency with the business plan or operating plan.

(3) Management.

(i) The organizing group shall include in the business plan or operating plan information sufficient to permit the OCC to evaluate the overall management ability of the organizing group. If the organizing group has limited banking experience or community involvement, the senior executive officers must be able to compensate for such deficiencies.

(ii) The organizing group may not hire an officer or elect or appoint a director if the OCC objects to that person at any time prior to the date the bank commences business.

(4) Capital. A proposed bank must have sufficient initial capital, net of any organizational expenses that will be charged to the bank's capital after it begins operations, to support the bank's projected volume and type of business.

(5) Community service.

(i) The business plan or operating plan must indicate the organizing group's knowledge of and plans for serving the community. The organizing group shall evaluate the banking needs of the community, including its consumer, business, nonprofit, and government sectors. The business plan or operating plan must demonstrate how the proposed bank responds to those needs consistent with the safe and sound operation of the bank. The provisions of this paragraph may not apply to an application to organize a bank for a special purpose.

(ii) As part of its business plan or operating plan, the organizing group shall submit a statement that demonstrates its plans to achieve CRA objectives.

(iii) Because community support is important to the long-term success of a bank, the organizing group shall include plans for attracting and maintaining community support.

(6) Safety and soundness. The business plan or operating plan must demonstrate that the organizing group (and the sponsoring company, if any), is aware of, and understands, national banking laws and regulations, and safe and sound banking operations and practices. The OCC will deny an application that does not meet these safety and soundness requirements.

(7) Fiduciary services. The business plan or operating plan must indicate if the proposed bank intends to offer fiduciary services. The information required by § 5.26 shall be filed with the charter application. A separate application is not required.

(i) Procedures–

(1) Prefiling meeting. The OCC normally requires a prefiling meeting with the organizers of a proposed national bank before the organizers file an application. Organizers should be familiar with the OCC's chartering policy and procedural requirements in the Manual before the prefiling meeting. The prefiling meeting normally is held in the district office where the application will be filed but may be held at another location at the request of the applicant.

(2) Business plan or operating plan. An organizing group shall file an business plan

or operating plan that addresses the subjects discussed in paragraph (h) of this section.

(3) Spokesperson. The organizing group shall designate a spokesperson to represent the organizing group in all contacts with the OCC. The spokesperson shall be an organizer and proposed director of the new bank, except a representative of the sponsor or sponsors may serve as spokesperson if an application is sponsored by an existing holding company, individuals currently affiliated with other depository institutions, or individuals who, in the OCC's view, are otherwise collectively experienced in banking and have demonstrated the ability to work together effectively.

(4) Decision notification. The OCC notifies the spokesperson and other interested persons in writing of its decision on an application.

(5) Activities.

(i) Before the OCC grants final approval, a proposed national bank must be established as a legal entity. A national bank becomes a legal entity after it has filed its organization certificate and articles of association with the OCC as required by law. A proposed national bank may offer and sell securities prior to OCC preliminary approval of the proposed national bank's charter application, provided that the proposed national bank has filed articles of association, an organization certificate, and a completed charter application and the bank complies with the OCC's securities offering regulations, 12 CFR part 16. In addition, the organizing group shall elect a board of directors.

(ii) The proposed bank may not conduct the business of banking until the OCC grants final approval.

(iii) For all capital obtained through a public offering a proposed national bank shall use an offering circular that complies with the OCC's securities offering regulations, 12 CFR part 16.

(iv) A national bank in organization shall raise its capital before it commences business. Preliminary approval expires if a national bank in organization does not raise the required capital within 12 months from the date the OCC grants preliminary approval. Approval expires if the national bank does not commence business within 18 months from the date the OCC grants preliminary approval.

(j) Expedited review. An application to establish a full-service national bank that is sponsored by a bank holding company whose lead depository institution is an eligible bank or eligible depository institution is deemed preliminarily approved by the OCC as of the 15th day after the close of the public comment period or the 45th day after the filing is received by the OCC, whichever is later, unless the OCC:

(1) Notifies the applicant prior to that date that the filing is not eligible for expedited review, or the expedited review process is extended, under § 5.13(a)(2); or

(2) Notifies the applicant prior to that date that the OCC has determined that the proposed bank will offer banking services that are materially different than those offered by the lead depository institution. . . .

Camp v. Pitts

411 U.S. 138 (1973)

[Reread the selection from this case reproduced at 44, *supra.*]

Webster Groves Trust Company v. Saxon

370 F.2d 381 (8th Cir. 1966)

GIBSON, Circuit Judge.

Appellant, Webster Groves Trust Company, and others sued James J. Saxon, Comptroller of the Currency, and the West Side National Bank, seeking to enjoin the operation of the newly chartered West Side National Bank and to compel Saxon to grant a formal adversary hearing before finally passing upon the Bank's charter application. ...

Plaintiffs below were eight commercial banking houses (seven state banks and one national bank) doing business in suburban St. Louis County, Missouri, within approximately a four-mile radius of the newly established place of business of defendant West Side National Bank.

On July 31, 1964, defendant West Side National Bank filed an application for a charter as a national bank with Saxon, Comptroller of the Currency, pursuant to the statutes and regulations controlling such applications. . . . Pursuant to these regulations, the Comptroller caused a field investigation to be made of the applicant and the surrounding circumstances. In accordance with the established practice, the agent-examiners of Saxon called upon the competitors of the applicant bank, informed them of West Side's application and ascertained their reaction to the application.

On August 21, 1964, the president of appellent Webster Groves Trust Company wrote the Comptroller, advising him of Webster Groves' opposition to the granting of the charter and requesting a formal hearing on the application. By letter of August 27, 1964, the Deputy Comptroller agreed to discuss the matter, and a meeting was arranged to take place in Washington, D.C. on October 6, 1964. . . . The Deputy Comptroller indicated that the views of the objecting banks would be taken into consideration, but he did not accede to the request for a formal hearing.

On December 12, 1964, the Comptroller approved the application for the establishment of the West Side Bank, without holding any formal hearing.

On January 27, 1965, Webster Groves and seven other banks brought this action against the Comptroller and the West Side National Bank, seeking to have the issuance of the charter declared unlawful, directing the Comptroller to cancel the charter and to conduct a formal hearing prior to the granting of another charter, and to enjoin West Side National Bank from establishing and operating its bank during the interim. Webster Groves Trust Company is the only one of the original eight plaintiffs that is appealing the District Court's judgment.

The appellant acknowledges that this is a case of first impression on the precise issue of whether the Comptroller, in processing an application for a national bank charter, must hold a formal adversary hearing upon request of a competitor bank. Appellant contends it is entitled to a formal hearing at which it and other interested parties my be present, after due notice, and be afforded an opportunity to interrogate and cross-examine the applicants and present evidence in opposition; and, further, that a record be made so that a judicial review can be accorded as set forth in § 10(e) of the Administrative Procedure Act, (A.P.A.) 5 U.S.C. § 1009(e).

We believe that . . . neither the National Banking Act, 12 U.S.C. § 21 *et seq*; the Administrative Procedure Act, nor procedural due process requires a formal hearing of the type sought by appellant.

The National Banking Act is the source of the Comptroller's powers and duties in the granting of a national bank charter. This Act sets forth no requirement of a formal hearing on an application for a charter. The legislative history of the Act clearly indicates that no formal hearing was intended by Congress. After enumerating the detailed requirements, 12 U.S.C. § 27 authorizes the Comptroller to issue a certificate of authority:

> "If, upon a careful examination of the facts so reported, and of any other facts which may come to the knowledge of the comptroller, whether by means of a special commission appointed by him for the purpose of inquiring into the condition of such association, or otherwise, it appears that such association is lawfully entitled to commence the business of banking. . . ."

The Comptroller's practice for over one hundred years has been to proceed informally on these new bank applications. This practice has received the approval of the Attorney General's Committee on Administrative Procedure and has gone unchallenged in at least the appellate courts for the same period of time.

The very nature of the decision required by the Comptroller indicates that a formal adversary type hearing would be of little benefit to him in the discharge of his discretionary powers. There is the further factor present that if bank applicants were subjected to severe public cross-examination, public presentation of unfavorable evidence and were forced to disclose their future plans and programs to competitors, public confidence in the banking system could be adversely affected. . . .

We do not have the prerogative of determining the advisability or the feasibility of a formal adversary hearing in the processing of a charter application for a national bank. Congress has this authority and has not thought it advisable to impose this requirement during the past hundred years. The District Court was correct in not requiring the Comptroller to hold such a hearing. . . .

We agree that the action by the Comptroller is not subject to review by trial de novo, nor does it depend upon a showing of substantial evidence. Likewise, we are precluded from invading the province of the Comptroller's expertise and evaluating the sagacity of, or the policy behind, his actions. The Comptroller, however, must be subordinate to the law from which he received his authority, and is subject to the limitations imposed by that law. Therefore, if he acts in excess of his statutory grant of powers, acts arbitrarily or capriciously, abuses his discretion, or unlawfully discriminates in violation of the Constitution, he is certainly subject to restraint by the courts. Though he may exercise the discretion the expertise of his office affords him, the congressional grant of authority does not empower arbitrary and capricious action, nor does it contemplate abuses of that discretion. Therefore, we do not believe the courts are powerless to protect the public from unconstitutional, illegal, or otherwise arbitrary activities of administrative officials. The Comptroller is free to exercise his discretion in the granting of charters, free from any review on the merits of his action. However, if the Comptroller acts in excess or abuse of his legal authority, to this extent his actions are subject to judicial review, with the burden of proof resting on the party seeking the review. This holding we believe to be consistent with § 10 of the Administrative Procedure Act, 5 U.S.C. § 1009, because no statute precludes judicial review, nor is this the type of agency action that is by law committed to agency discretion so as to be "immunized from review by the exemption in the preface of § 1009". *First National Bank of Smithfield, North Carolina v. Saxon, supra*, at page 270 of 352 F.2d. Therefore, subsection 10(c) of the Act, 5 U.S.C. § 1009(c) would be applicable. This subsection reads:

> "Acts reviewable:
>
> "(c) Every agency action made reviewable by statute and *every final agency action for which there is no other adequate remedy in any court shall be*

subject to judicial review." (Emphasis added.)

The Comptroller is also asserting that a competitor has no standing to object to lawful competition. With this rule we find no fault, but the banks surely have the standing to object to illegal competition. . . . Therefore, when a competitor believes he is being subjected to illegal competition owing to impropriety by the Comptroller, the courts should be open to hear and decide the alleged wrong. The trial court was vested with jurisdiction over the subject matter of this litigation.

The actions of the Comptroller under review, however, are perfectly consistent with his authorized statutory power, they did not violate any due process provisions of the Constitution and there is no indication that there has been any abuse of his discretionary authority. Consequently, for the reasons set forth herein and in the trial court's sound memorandum opinion, we believe the complaint of appellant was properly dismissed.

City National Bank v. Smith

513 F.2d 479 (D.C. Cir. 1975)

SPOTTSWOOD W. ROBINSON, III, Circuit Judge.

Appellant City National Bank filed suit in the District Court challenging the preliminary approval by appellee Comptroller of the Currency of a national bank charter for appellee Meadowbrook National Bank. The court denied City's motion for summary judgment and granted summary judgment for the Comptroller and Meadowbrook. City urges reversal on the grounds that misrepresentations by Meadowbrook's organizers precluded approval of the application, that the Comptroller did not explain his decision sufficiently to permit effective judicial review. We affirm. . . .

The National Bank Act empowers the Comptroller to issue charters for national banks.[3] The dual purpose of the chartering process is to regulate entry into the banking industry on the basis of economic considerations and to assure that national banks are competently and honestly operated. These objectives are reflected in the topics subject to investigation prior to approval of application for charters. . . .

On July 17, 1972, a group of businessmen applied for a character authorizing organization of Meadowbrook National Bank in the eastern section of Fort Worth, Texas. The Regional Administrator of National Banks initiated an investigation, including a four-day field examination. He also notified the 40 existing banks in the county in which Meadowbrook would be located that the application had been filed and invited written comments. City responded in opposition to the proposed charter, expressing the view that there was no economic necessity for a new bank in the area. Later City requested, and was granted, a public hearing on the application at which it might defend that position.

At the hearing Meadowbrook presented evidence of the need for a new bank in east Forth Worth. The testimony of witnesses called by City was directed solely towards the economic considerations generated by the application. Meadowbrook offered further testimony in rebuttal concerning the economic desirability of favorable action on the application.

In closing argument, following Meadowbrook's summation, City's counsel raised

---

3. The present statutory scheme is derived from the Act of June 3, 1864, ch. 106, 13 Stat. 99. A literal reading of the legislation would require the Comptroller to grant an application if the statutory standards are met. *See* 12 U.S.C. § 27 (1970). His discretion to nonetheless deny is, however, unquestioned. *See Sterling Nat'l Bank v. Camp*, 431 F.2d 514, 516 (5th Cir. 1970), *cert. denied*, 401 U.S. 925 (1971); *Webster Groves Trust Co. v. Saxon*, 370 F.2d 381, 387-388 (8th Cir. 1966).

a question regarding a possible lack of full disclosure in the application. This charge had not surfaced in the pre-hearing communications nor had it been the subject of any testimony offered at the hearing. City suggested that Meadowbrook's organizers had concealed the identity of an interested party, and Meadowbrook vigorously denied this allegation.

After the hearing intradepartmental recommendations were submitted to the Comptroller to assist the final decision.[7] The Regional Administrator's report noted the concealment claim, but concluded that "ownership distribution appears satisfactory." The Comptroller approved the application conditionally and stated the following reasons:

> Population of area adequate to support this new entry. Only bank in area is undoubtedly of sufficient size (32 million) to stand competition, the addition of which should redound to the benefit of the consuming public. Subject to aggregate capital of at least one million.[8]

The applicants were notified that the Comptroller had granted preliminary approval subject to a number of conditions, including acceptability of initial management personnel and submission of financial and biographical data by each person who subscribed for 5% of Meadowbrook's shares. The distribution of shares was, as it apparently is in all cases, subject to the Comptroller's approval of the subscribers.

. . . The primary ground for relief stated in City's amended complaint related to the alleged misrepresentation by Meadowbrook's organizers in the application. The Comptroller submitted the full administrative record, and all parties moved for summary judgment. The District Court concluded that "the Comptroller's decision to grant preliminary approval of the charter application of Meadowbrook National Bank is both rationally and substantially supported by the record and the record does not support plaintiff's charge of fraud, misrepresentation, or concealment, and this charge was reasonably and properly rejected by the Comptroller's office." . . .

The Meadowbrook application represented, in the standard form prescribed by the Comptroller, that its organizers were not acting in behalf of any person "undisclosed to the Comptroller" and that there was no "agreement or understanding" providing for purchase of Meadowbrook shares by any person. City claims that the organizers had an understanding with Dee J. Kelley, the principal shareholder of another area bank, that Kelley would be a stockholder and that this understanding suggests that they were acting on his behalf, as well as their own, in filing the application. City contends that the failure to disclose this arrangement–variously termed by City "fraud," "misrepresentation," "omission of material facts" and "lack of candor"–invalidated the Comptroller's approval of the application.

The standard for judicial review of the Comptroller's action in granting or denying a charter application was recently set by the Supreme Court in *Camp v. Pitts*. The test is whether the Comptroller's decision was "arbitrary, capricious, an abuse of discretion, or otherwise not in accordance with law." By this standard, the District Court was clearly justified in rejecting the misrepresentation charge.

The evidence offered by City to substantiate its allegations was, to say the least, far

7. Favorable recommendations were made by the field examiner and a representative of the Department of Economic Banking Research. The Regional Administrator, the Director of the Bank Organization Division and the Deputy Comptroller advised denial of the application. All of these recommendations were based on economic considerations, and the staff summaries did not refer to the misrepresentation charge.

8. These comments were written by hand at the end of staff summaries. *Compare First Nat'l Bank v. Smith*, 365 F. Supp. 898, 904 (W.D. Ark. 1973), *rev'd*, 508 F.2d 1371 (8th Cir. 1974).

from compelling. On the other hand, there was a good deal of evidence indicating that Kelly's proposed participation in Meadowbrook was disclosed to the Comptroller's office, even if the application was not literally accurate in all particulars.[16] Before the filing of the application, the applicants told the Deputy Regional Administrator, in a meeting with Kelly present, that Kelly intended to become a stockholder in the proposed bank. This intention was reaffirmed at the hearing by Meadowbrook's counsel, who also stated that Kelly had recognized throughout the application proceedings that the Comptroller reserved the prerogative of final approval of the stockholders. The field examiner was informed that Kelly intended to subscribe for 5% of the shares, and this fact was contained in the examiner's report, which was a part of the record submitted to the Comptroller. Finally, in a post-hearing letter, Kelly asserted that he always intended to invest in the bank, that he never had any agreement with the organizers and that he realized that any purchase of shares was subject to authorization by the Comptroller. On this record, the approval of the application was not arbitrary, capricious or an abuse of discretion, and the District Court's rejection of the misrepresentation charge must be sustained. . . .

City also asserts that the evidence revealed at the hearing mandated a post-hearing investigation by the Comptroller's office to resolve questions that were yet unanswered. The Comptroller's discretion in the area of investigations and hearings relating to charter applications is plain. Although the Comptroller might have been justified in exercising his discretion in favor of further investigation, City's presentation was not so forceful that he was required to do so. . . .

A related argument posited by City is that the Comptroller's failure to advert to the misrepresentation allegation in his final decision demonstrates that he neither decided nor was aware of the issue. But although the Comptroller did not expressly mention the charge, it was clearly disclosed by the administrative record. Neither the field examiner nor the Regional Administrator, whose reports reflected awareness of the problem, regarded the question as significant enough to merit reference in the summaries of their recommendations. The Comptroller is not obliged to comment personally on every issue, however insignificant, raised in an application proceeding, and in the circumstances presented here we deem the omission inconsequential. . . .

Finally, City argues that the Comptroller's decision does not contain a sufficient contemporaneous explanation of its basis and therefore frustrates effective judicial review. Undoubtedly, judicial review would be a much simpler task were the Comptroller to report his conclusions, and briefly indicate his supporting rationale, on all issues raised in application proceedings. We again note, however, that City's misrepresentation charge was neither compelling nor strongly urged prior to judicial review.

The contention that the Comptroller must make formal findings was flatly rejected by the Supreme Court in *Camp v. Pitts*. What is required is only a contemporaneous explanation of the decision indicating "the determinative reason for the final taken." If the record before us raised a substantial doubt as to whether the Comptroller considered a material issue, we would not permit the approval to stand. Here the alleged concealment was only a minor issue; the agency proceedings centered pivotally on economic factors, which were resolved in Meadowbrook's favor and about which there is no present dispute.

City tries to distinguish *Pitts* by noting that the Comptroller's regulations applicable

16. It is not clear that Kelly's intention to become a subscriber is the type of agreement or understanding referred to in the application. . . . Obviously the organizers were entitled to make exploratory inquiries concerning investor interest before filing. After preliminary application approval, rather than prior to filing the application, is at least arguably the logical time for review of subscribers for acceptability and disclosure of the results of the inquiries and the review. . . .

in that case did not require a hearing, and arguing that the present administrative provision for a hearing mandates formal findings on the record. This argument overlooks the clear language of the Administrative Procedure Act, which calls for formal findings in adjudicative proceedings only when a *statute* mandates a hearing be held on the record. The current hearing requirement for charter applications is stated in the Comptroller's regulations and is not embodied in the National Bank Act.

Klanke v. Camp

320 F. Supp. 1185 (S.D. Tex. 1970)

SEALS, District Judge.

Plaintiffs applied to the Comptroller of the Currency, in accordance with 12 U.S.C. § 21 *et seq*., for permission to organize a new national bank. Following the usual investigation, the Comptroller denied the application. He later explained his denial in an affidavit submitted to the court which stated that he:

> "was convinced, among other reasons, that there was no adequate need for a banking facility at the proposed locations; that the ability and experience of the proposed organizers was insufficient; that the requested new bank would not be successful under its proposed leadership; that the objects contemplated by the National Bank Act would not be served; and that the granting of the charter application would be detrimental to the public interest."

Plaintiffs now allege that the Comptroller's denial was "illegal, arbitrary, capricious and unfairly discriminatory" and seek an order compelling the Comptroller either to grant the charter or "to state the terms upon which plaintiff's application will be granted." . . .

[T]his court has jurisdiction to consider the challenge of the Comptroller's denial to plaintiff's charter application, and that these plaintiff's are within that class of persons whose interest is sufficient to give them standing to sue. But plaintiffs may have gained a hollow victory. For their success depends on a clear showing that the Comptroller exercised his discretion "in excess of his statutory grant of power, acted arbitrarily or capriciously, abused his discretion, or unlawfully discriminated in violation of the constitution. . . ." *Webster Groves Trust Co. v. Saxon*, supra, at 387.

Plaintiff's burden is a heavy one, and they must discharge it without the assistance of many of the vital tools of federal discovery. Plaintiffs may not depose the Comptroller nor require him to answer interrogatories. *United States v. Morgan*, 313 U.S. 409, 422 (1941), *Warren Bank v. Camp*, 396 F.2d 52, 56 (6th Cir. 1968).[a] Accordingly, plaintiffs must rely almost exclusively upon the Comptroller's letters denying their application and upon the affidavits submitted by the Comptroller. In addition, they may obtain the Comptroller's file in this cause. From this relative paucity of evidence, plaintiffs must convince the court that the Comptroller's action was arbitrary and capricious.

Such a test will best protect both the frustrated applicant and the Comptroller as well. An applicant who is the victim of sheer arbitrariness, invidious discrimination, or blatant prejudice should be able to demonstrate the legitimacy of his grievance even without extensive discovery devices. On the other hand, the Comptroller is insulated from judicial

---

a. The Supreme Court's decision in *Camp v. Pitts* essentially eliminates such arguments based on the *Morgan* line of cases. *See* Scott, *supra* (excerpting Scott's discussion of effect of *Pitts* on *Morgan IV*).

interference merely upon evidencing, a minimal basis in reason for his denial. The heavy burden of proof facing potential complainants should help protect the Comptroller from harassment suits by applicants whose sense of outrage exceeds the merits of their claim. ...

Kenneth Scott, In Quest of Reason: The Licensing Decisions of the Federal Banking Agencies

42 U.Chi. L. Rev. 235 (1975)

... The [chartering] process formally begins when an "Application to Organize a National Bank" is filed with the Regional Comptroller.[a] This is a short form containing little more than the proposed name, locations, and initial capital of the new bank, together with rather long and detailed biographical and financial statements by each of the organizers.[204] The applicant is separately required to submit additional information, primarily on the issue of profitability: the location chosen, the population and economic character of the area the bank will serve, competing financial institutions in that area, and projections of deposit and loan growth and of income and expenses. This information is frequently provided in the form of a "market survey" prepared by a consulting firm.

The application is then assigned to a national bank examiner for a filed investigation. His comments and findings are rendered in two parts, the "Examiner's Report of an Investigation," which is available to the public, and the "Confidential Memorandum" to the Comptroller, which is not. The Examiner's Report summarizes some of the application information and gives a brief economic description of the service area and community, but contains little in the way of evaluation. That is provided in the Confidential Memorandum, on a number of topics. The examiner gives his views on how much initial capital the bank should have; he checks on the biographical and financial data furnished by the principal figures in the proposed bank and offers his conclusions about whether they are acceptable persons; and he answers questions such as these:

> 4. Is there a public need for the proposed bank or is the area reasonably well served by existing banks and branches? . . .
>
> 5. Is it reasonable to expect that the available banking business will be adequate to support the proposed bank, if established, together with existing competitive banks and branches, or will an overbanked situation be created? Indicate whether a healthy or unhealthy degree of competition will accrue.

He concludes by recommending either approval or denial of the application. Neither the form nor any standard instructions provide criteria by which these judgments and conclusions are to be reached; consequently, they rest largely on the personal attitudes of the examiner to whom the application was assigned.

The applicant has to publish notice of the filing of the charter application and it is permissible, though uncommon, for objectors to request a hearing.[207] Otherwise, the application simply proceeds along a recommendation chain. The Regional Comptroller adds his comments and recommendation to those of the local examiner, and then application goes

---

a. The organizational structure of the OCC has since been revised. The field organization now consists of six districts, each geographically distinct. 12 C.F.R. § 4.5.

204. . . . The Comptroller customarily also requires these forms from each director, officer and substantial stockholder (holding five percent or more of the stock) of the new bank.

207. 12 C.F.R. §§ 5.2, 5.4 (1974).

to Washington, where three more recommendations are added in turn, those of the Director of the Bank Organization Division, an Economist, and a Deputy Comptroller. These latter three recommendations are usually explained in a few sentences; the basis given for the other two recommendations is summarized in a paragraph or two. When the form arrives at the Comptroller's desk for final decision, he has five recommendations set forth on two pages. The Comptroller signifies his decision by signing on the approval or rejection line, without any statement of reasons. . . .

. . . What can be said about the Comptroller's decision process and grounds for decision, as set forth in the application files? First of all, it is worth noting what factors do not seem significant in most cases. Consider the factors enumerated in section 1816 of title 12 of the United States Code, which constitutes the statutory framework for the Comptroller's exercise of chartering discretion: "[1] The financial history and condition of the bank, [2] the adequacy of its capital structure, [3] its future earnings prospects, [4] the general character of its management, [5] the convenience and needs of the community to be served by the bank, and [6] whether or not its corporate powers are consistent with the purposes of [the statute]."[212]

The first and second factors amount, in the case of a newly chartered bank, to its initial capitalization. In none of the sample cases was inadequate capitalization mentioned as an adverse factor or reason for denial, and for a rather simple reason: the applicants will generally either conform their application to the amount of initial capital which the agency indicates it deems desirable, or abandon the application as not feasible under the circumstances. For an operating bank seeking a branch, these factors have more content. But if there is serious supervisory concern over its management or capital adequacy or operating policies, a bank is made aware that there is no point in its applying for a branch at any location.[213] In effect, in both cases this issue is disposed of at an early stage and is not reflected in the final figures.

The fourth factor, the general character of management, was mentioned in some cases, but in fact was rarely determinative. A lot of the charter application routine bears on this factor–the long biographical and financial questionnaires required of the organizers and principal stockholders and proposed managing offices, and the investigation reports made on them by the field examiner. It is generally understood, however, that if the agency objects to any of these persons, he will be replaced or dropped from the applicant group, so this factor too does not often determine the final outcome.[214]

The sixth factor, corporate powers consistent with the purposes of the act, to the extent it has any meaning at all, is satisfied by the use of a prescribed form of articles of incorporation. It was never referred to in any way in any sample case.

That leaves factors three and five, future earnings prospects and the convenience and needs of the community. . . . [F]or charters the issue [is] more often cast in terms of whether there was a "need" for a new bank. Analytical distinctions between the two factors [are] not clearly made, however. The discussion of community need sometimes, though not

---

212. 12 U.S.C. § 1816 (1970). *See also* 12 C.F.R. § 4.2(b) (1974).

213. This is made quite explicit in the [Federal Home Loan Bank Board's (predecessor to the Office of Thrift Supervision)] treatment of "supervisory clearance"; *see* 12 C.F.R. § 556.5(a)(7) (1974). The withholding of branches is also used as a form of supervisory pressure on an institution to conform to what the agency regards as desirable operating policies and practices.

214. The Comptroller insists that this part of the memorandum section of the examiner's report be kept confidential, to protect the anonymity of sources. The Comptroller's policy carries with it the distinct possibility of personal unfairness, since disqualification may be founded on erroneous or distorted information that is not subject to correction or rebuttal.

often, involve[s] an assertion that the new entry would cause injury to existing banks or branches, but that argument shade[s] into the argument that there [is] not enough business for the new bank . . . to be profitable in the near future.

Most of the Comptroller's decisions, therefore, seem to turn on assessments of "need" and "profitability" and it is these two factors that warrant closer scrutiny. As it stands, each participant in the recommendation chain forms his own judgment as to profitability and reflects his own concept of need; there is no discussion of, or explicit agreement on, the underlying premises. Unless that consideration is systematically undertaken and articulated, the Comptroller's decision process will never be comprehensible, either internally or externally.

Notes and Comments 2.6. According to 12 C.F.R. § 5.20(f)(2)(i)(B), in evaluating a charter application the OCC considers whether the proposed national bank has "competent management." What is the statutory basis for this factor? What does it mean? Would the Comptroller have viable grounds for denying an application on this basis if a proposed director was a recent widower, who had taken to drinking heavily? *Cf. Francis v. United Jersey Bank*, 432 A.2d 814 (N.J. 1981) (incapacitated corporate director liable for failure to prevent misappropriation by other directors; violation of duty of care).

2.7. *Standing to challenge the Comptroller's chartering decision.* Whether or not the Comptroller approves the QNB charter application, who has standing to challenge that decision? As *Pitts* illustrates, if the QNB application is denied, Hiram and the other members of the organizing group have standing to challenge the negative decision. If the application is approved, however, can competing savings associations and state banks in QNB's proposed market challenge the affirmative decision? Consider the following excerpt.

National Credit Union Administration v. First National Bank & Trust Co.

522 U.S. 479 (1998)

Justice THOMAS delivered the opinion of the Court, except as to footnote 6.*

[A bankers' association and competing banks sued the NCUA, seeking to overturn the NCUA'S approval of certain applications filed by a credit union to expand its field of membership to include employees of various small businesses that were unaffiliated with credit union's existing membership base. For the substantive portion of the Court's opinion, striking down the NCUA policy, see the excerpt following Note 2.17, *infra*. In the course of the opinion, the Court discussed the current state of standing doctrine.]

Respondents claim a right to judicial review of the NCUA'S chartering decision under § 10(a) of the APA [Administrative Procedure Act], which provides:

> "A person suffering legal wrong because of agency action, or adversely affected or aggrieved by agency action within the meaning of a relevant statute, is entitled to judicial review thereof." 5 U.S.C. § 702.

We have interpreted § 10(a) of the APA to impose a prudential standing requirement in addition to the requirement, imposed by Article III of the Constitution, that a plaintiff have

---

*. Justice Scalia joins this opinion, except as to footnote 6. [Footnote 6, not reproduced in this excerpt, presented a discussion of the legislative history of § 109, 12 U.S.C. § 1759.]

suffered a sufficient injury-in-fact. *See, e.g., Association of Data Processing Service Organizations, Inc. v. Camp*, 397 U.S. 150, 152 (1970) (*Data Processing*). For a plaintiff to have prudential standing under the APA, "the interest sought to be protected by the complainant [must be] arguably within the zone of interests to be protected or regulated by the statute ... in question." *Id.*, at 153.

Based on four of our prior cases finding that competitors of financial institutions have standing to challenge agency action relaxing statutory restrictions on the activities of those institutions, we hold that respondents' interest in limiting the markets that federal credit unions can serve is arguably within the zone of interests to be protected by § 109. Therefore, respondents have prudential standing under the APA to challenge the NCUA'S interpretation. . . .

Although our prior cases have not stated a clear rule for determining when a plaintiff's interest is "arguably within the zone of interests" to be protected by a statute, they nonetheless establish that we should not inquire whether there has been a congressional intent to benefit the would-be plaintiff. In *Data Processing, supra*, the Office of the Comptroller of the Currency (the Comptroller) had interpreted the National Bank Act's incidental powers clause, Rev. Stat. § 5136, 12 U.S.C. § 24 Seventh, to permit national banks to perform data processing services for other banks and bank customers. *See Data Processing, supra*, at 151. The plaintiffs, a data processing corporation and its trade association, alleged that this interpretation was impermissible because providing data processing services was not, as was required by the statute, "[an] incidental powe[r] . . . necessary to carry on the business of banking." *See* 397 U.S., at 157, n. 2.

In holding that the plaintiffs had standing, we stated that § 10(a) of the APA required only that "the interest sought to be protected by the complainant [be] arguably within the zone of interests to be protected or regulated by the statute . . . in question." *Id.*, at 153. In determining that the plaintiffs' interest met this requirement, we noted that although the relevant federal statutes–the National Bank Act, 12 U.S.C. § 24 Seventh, and the Bank Service Corporation Act, 76 Stat. 1132, 12 U.S.C. § 1864–did not "in terms protect a specified group[,] . . . their general policy is apparent; and those whose interests are directly affected by a broad or narrow interpretation of the Acts are easily identifiable." *Data Processing*, 397 U.S., at 157. "[A]s competitors of national banks which are engaging in data processing services," the plaintiffs were within that class of "aggrieved persons" entitled to judicial review of the Comptroller's interpretation. . . .

Less than a year later, we applied the "zone of interests" test in *Arnold Tours, Inc. v. Camp*, 400 U.S. 45 (1970) (*Arnold Tours*) (per curiam). There, certain travel agencies challenged a ruling by the Comptroller, similar to the one contested in *Data Processing*, that permitted national banks to operate travel agencies. *See* 400 U.S., at 45. In holding that the plaintiffs had prudential standing under the APA, we noted that it was incorrect to view our decision in *Data Processing* as resting on the peculiar legislative history of § 4 of the Bank Service Corporation Act, which had been passed in part at the behest of the data processing industry. *See id.* We stated explicitly that "we did not rely on any legislative history showing that Congress desired to protect data processors alone from competition." . . . We further explained:

> "In *Data Processing* . . . [w]e held that § 4 arguably brings a competitor within the zone of interests protected by it. Nothing in the opinion limited § 4 to protecting only competitors in the data processing field. When national banks begin to provide travel services for their customers, they compete with travel agents no less than they compete with data processors when they provide data-processing services to their customers." *Ibid.* (internal citations and quotation marks omitted).

A year later, we decided *Investment Company Institute v. Camp*, 401 U.S. 617 (1971) (*ICI*). In that case, an investment company trade association and several individual investment companies alleged that the Comptroller had violated, *inter alia*, § 21 of the Glass-Steagall Act[a] by permitting national banks to establish and operate what in essence were early versions of mutual funds. We held that the plaintiffs, who alleged that they would be injured by the competition resulting from the Comptroller's action, had standing under the APA and stated that the case was controlled by *Data Processing*. *See* 401 U.S., at 621. Significantly, we found unpersuasive Justice Harlan's argument in dissent that the suit should be dismissed because "neither the language of the pertinent provisions of the Glass-Steagall Act nor the legislative history evince[d] any congressional concern for the interests of petitioners and others like them in freedom from competition." 401 U.S., at 640.

Our fourth case in this vein was *Clarke v. Securities Industry Assn.*, 479 U.S. 388 (1987) (*Clarke*). There, a securities dealers trade association sued the Comptroller, this time for authorizing two national banks to offer discount brokerage services both at their branch offices and at other locations inside and outside their home States. *See id.*, at 391. The plaintiff contended that the Comptroller's action violated the McFadden Act, which permits national banks to carry on the business of banking only at authorized branches, and to open new branches only in their home States and only to the extent that state-chartered banks in that State can do so under state law. *See id.*, at 391-392.

We again held that the plaintiff had standing under the APA. Summarizing our prior holdings, we stated that although the "zone of interests" test "denies a right of review if the plaintiff's interests are . . . marginally related to or inconsistent with the purposes implicit in the statute," *id.*, at 399, "there need be no indication of congressional purpose to benefit the would-be plaintiff," *id.*, at 399-400 (citing *ICI*). We then determined that by limiting the ability of national banks to do business outside their home States, "Congress ha[d] shown a concern to keep national banks from gaining a monopoly control over credit and money." *Id.*, at 403. The interest of the securities dealers in preventing national banks from expanding into the securities markets directly implicated this concern because offering discount brokerage services would allow national banks "access to more money, in the form of credit balances, and enhanced opportunities to lend money, *viz.*, for margin purchases." . . . The case was thus analogous to *Data Processing* and *ICI*: "In those cases the question was what activities banks could engage in at all; here, the question is what activities banks can engage in without regard to the limitations imposed by state branching law." 479 U.S., at 403. . . .

Our prior cases, therefore, have consistently held that for a plaintiff's interests to be arguably within the "zone of interests" to be protected by a statute, there does not have to be an "indication of congressional purpose to benefit the would-be plaintiff." *Id.*, at 399-400 (citing *ICI*); *see also Arnold Tours, supra*, at 46, (citing *Data Processing*). The proper inquiry is simply "whether the interest sought to be protected by the complainant is arguably within the zone of interests to be protected . . . by the statute." *Data Processing*, 397 U.S., at 153 (emphasis added). Hence in applying the "zone of interests" test, we do not ask whether, in enacting the statutory provision at issue, Congress specifically intended to benefit the plaintiff. Instead, we first discern the interests "arguably . . . to be protected" by the statutory provision at issue; we then inquire whether the plaintiff's interests affected by the agency action in question are among them.

Notes and Comments 2.8. State courts apply similar concepts of standing to judicial review of challenges to state chartering and other administrative decisions. *See, e.g.*,

a. 12 U.S.C. § 378(a). On the application of section 21, see Chapter 5, *infra*.

Pennsylvania Bankers Ass'n v. Pennsylvania Dept. of Banking, 956 A.2d 956 (Pa. 2008), in which competing banks appealed a decision of the Pennsylvania Secretary of Banking dismissing the banks as intervenors in administrative actions in which state-chartered, "group-based" credit unions gave formal notice to the Department of Banking of their intent to expand their fields of membership to "geography-based" community credit unions. The trial court affirmed the dismissal for lack of standing. On appeal, the state supreme court reversed and remanded, holding that dismissal of the banks as intervenors on the ground that they failed to show a "direct interest" in the administrative proceeding offended due process.

2.9. *Ultra vires acts*. National banks are corporate entities, and this fact raises the question whether there are statutory limits to the powers that a national bank may exercise. One aspect of this problem, the scope of "incidental powers," is considered later.[9] At the chartering stage, the problem manifests itself in such traditional corporate law questions as the status of preincorporation contracts, promoter's burdens, obligations of subscribers, and related problems. How are these problems resolved in the context of the NBA? Consider the following cases.

McCormick v. Market Bank

165 U.S. 538 (1897)

Mr. Justice GRAY, after stating the case, delivered the opinion of the court.

By the National Bank Act, . . . ". . . no [national banking] association shall transact any business, except such as is incidental and necessarily preliminary to its organization, until it has been authorized by the Comptroller of the Currency to commence the business of banking." Rev. Stat. § 5136.

The question upon which this case turned was whether a national banking association which, after having duly made and filed its articles of association and organization certificate with the Comptroller of the Currency, but not having received from him a certificate authorizing it to do banking business, enters with the owner of real estate into a contract of lease, for a term of five years determinable at the end of any year by either party, of an office to be occupied by the association as a banking office, is bound by the lease, according to its provisions. . . .

The defendant [bank] contended, and the highest court of the State of Illinois adjudged, that the contract of lease sued on was not incidental and necessarily preliminary to the organization of the corporation, and therefore, by virtue of the last clause of section 5136 of the National Bank Act, . . . having been executed by the defendant before being authorized by the Comptroller of the Currency to commence the business of banking, did not bind the defendant. . . .

[Plaintiff's] first ground [for recovery] was that the execution of the lease by the defendant was "incidental and necessarily preliminary to its organization," and therefore within the exception of the last clause of the section in question.

. . . The plaintiff's second ground . . . was . . . that, taking the whole section together, the defendant, from the date of filing with the Comptroller of the Currency its articles of association and its organization certificate, became a corporation empowered to make contracts appropriate to the business of banking; and that any such contracts were valid as between the parties to them, even if they violated the restriction in the last clause of the section, and therefore might afford a reason for which the United States could enforce a

9. *See* Chapter 5, § 7, infra (discussing incidental powers).

forfeiture of the charter. . . .

Until the association has been authorized by the Comptroller to commence the business of banking, section 5136 peremptorily forbids the corporation to "transact any business" whatever, whether appertaining or not to the business of banking, "except such as is incidental and necessarily preliminary," not to carrying on, or even to commencing, the business of banking, but "to its organization," that is to say, such as is requisite to complete its organization as a corporation, which might doubtless include electing directors and officers, receiving subscriptions and payments for shares, procuring a corporate seal, and a book for recording its proceedings, temporarily hiring a room, and contracting any small debts incidental to the completion of its organization.

To take a lease is certainly to "transact business," within the meaning of the statute; and a lease for a term of years, at a large rent, of offices to be occupied by the bank "as a banking office, and for no other purpose," however necessary it might be for the transacting, or even for the commencing, of banking business by a corporation whose organization had been completed, and which had been completed, and which had been lawfully authorized to commence the business of banking, is in no sense incidental or necessarily preliminary to the organization of the corporation. . . .

The lease sued on, therefore, was clearly prohibited by the very terms of the statute from which the association assumed to derive its power to execute the lease. . . .

Congress, indeed, in establishing the system of national banks, instead of undertaking to grant special charters of incorporation upon its own judgment of the expediency of doing so in each case, has allowed corporations to be organized by voluntary acts of the associates, under the general conditions defined in the statute. But the capacity of these voluntary associations to make contracts and to transact business has not been left to depend upon their own will, however formally expressed, without any public authority having ever passed upon their responsibility and fitness. On the contrary, Congress has entrusted to the Comptroller of the Currency the power and the duty of making a careful examination into the condition of the association, including the amount of its capital stock actually paid in, and its compliance with the requirements of the statute in other respects, and, if the result of his examination is satisfactory, of granting to the association an official certificate that it is authorized to commence the business of banking; and has forbidden the corporation to transact any business whatever, except so far as required to perfect its organization, until it has received the certificate of the Comptroller. . . .

Wise v. Citizens Nat. Bank at Brownwood

107 S.W.2d 715 (Tex. 1937)

Baugh, Justice.

[Wise had unsuccessfully sued the bank for $790, claimed as salary due for services as vice president of said bank during the July, August through September 1934. The bank had been organized in June 1934 to purchase the assets and assume the liabilities of the "Citizens National Bank *in* Brownwood," which had closed and was in the hands of a conservator appointed by the Comptroller of the Currency. The organization certificate had been executed by the organizers and transmitted to the Comptroller of the Currency. According to Wise, he had entered into an agreement with F.S. Abney, as acting executive officer of the new bank on June 12, 1934, under which he was employed at $300 per month. The board of directors not only approved the agreement, but also appointed Wise as a vice president of the new bank.

[Wise began to work for the new bank on July 5, 1934. He purchased and paid cash for $2,800 of the bank's capital stock. In mid-July, the chief bank examiner objected to the new bank's schedule of salaries, and Wise's salary was reduced to $275 per month.

[Wise alleged that his employment was in response to demands of the national bank examiner that an outside executive, not formerly connected with the old bank, be employed as a condition to approval of the organization of the new bank. However, a certificate of authority to commence a banking business was not issued to the new bank until September 28, 1934. The bank opened its doors and began transacting business on October 1, 1934.]

It was further alleged that by virtue of said employment contract said new bank became obligated to pay appellant such salary earned by him during the three months prior to the time it opened for business; that on or about October 15, 1934, appellant withdrew from said bank and deposited to his credit such salary for the months of July, August, and September; that a few days thereafter, at a meeting of the board of directors, F.S. Abney ... raised the question as to whether said bank could legally pay appellant a salary for these three months. Whereupon it was agreed, in effect, that if the Comptroller of the Currency should rule adversely to such payment, then that appellant would forego the collection thereof. That neither the Comptroller nor any of his representatives ever objected to such payment, but, on the contrary, R.H. Collier, examiner for the banking department, advised that no such objection would be made.

Under the first paragraph of section 24, title 12, U.S. Code, appellee bank, upon compliance with the two preceding sections of said title, when its articles of association and certificate were filed with the Comptroller of the Currency, became a body corporate as of the date of the execution of its organization certificate. But under the last paragraph of said section 24 it was expressly forbidden to "transact any business except such as is incidental and necessarily preliminary to its organization, until it has been authorized by the Comptroller of the Currency to commence the business of banking."

... It is the contention of appellee [bank] that the contract here involved, so far as payment to appellant of any salary prior to September 28, 1934, when it was authorized "to commence the business of banking" was not only *ultra vires*, but was expressly prohibited by section 24, and was therefore void.

... Undoubtedly election of its officers and directors in advance would be but steps in perfecting its organization. So the selection of a banking location to be used after authority should be granted to commence business, the selection of future employees, furniture, fixtures, etc., all in advance of actual opening such bank for the transaction of a banking business, might be expedient; but the payment of such things in advance of authority to commence business is clearly not authorized by statute. The organization referred to in the federal statute manifestly refers only to the steps necessary to evolve the association of individuals into a legal entity as a corporation and give it a legal status as such; and does not, under the decisions, contemplate payment of salaries in advance to those who are to serve the corporation, after its organization is completed, as its officers and employees.

Nor does the fact that the contract has been performed prevent the bank, after its organization, from setting up its illegality or *ultra vires* character. As stated in a recent decision of the Supreme Court in *Texas & P. Ry. Co. v. Pottorff*, 291 U.S. 245, 260, "It is the settled doctrine of this court that no rights arise on an *ultra vires* contract, even though the contract has been performed; and that this conclusion cannot be circumvented by erecting an estoppel which would prevent challenging the legality of a power exercised."

... Nor would the question as to whether the bank and Wise would be governed by the determination of the chief banking examiner as to whether he could legally draw his salary for such period affect the legal rights of the bank to deny liability. Clearly appellant did not predicate his cause of action upon any arbitration or award, but upon his contract of employment. Consequently the question of an arbitration is not involved. And if the contract were illegal, as under the rule announced by the Supreme Court of the United States it is held to be, it was not a matter that was subject to arbitration.

Notes and Comments 2.10. *McCormick* and *Wise* have been undermined by the odd disappearance of the statutory provision invoked by each case. Rev. Stat. § 5136, which expressly limited the scope of preincorporation activities, appeared in the codification of the federal statutes as a separate, unnumbered paragraph following the seventh paragraph of 12 U.S.C. § 24. Section 16 of the Banking Act of 1933, known as the Glass-Steagall Act, amended paragraph Seventh, without including that unnumbered paragraph–prior to the decision in *Wise*. *See* 12 U.S.C. § 24 note. It has been excluded from all subsequent codifications of federal statutes. *Wise* seems to suggest that the paragraph is still in effect. Is there any basis for sustaining the result in these two cases under current law?

2.11. Since the chartering process is subject to the supervision of the Comptroller, one might expect that *ultra vires* problems should be containable. Under the Comptroller's current regulations, is it likely that a situation like that in *Wise* or *McCormick* would arise today?

2.12. *Trust powers.* Chartering of a commercial bank does not necessarily include authority to engage in trust activities. Under many chartering systems, there are separate provisions governing the grant of trust powers. Nevertheless, most commercial banks will apply and obtain those powers, incorporating the trust activities within a trust department or division of the bank itself. As with chartering, entry into the trust business is subject to the state chartering authorities for state banks and the Comptroller for national banks. The basic statutory reference for national banks is 12 U.S.C. § 92a. Approval and exercise of trust powers is discussed *infra* in Chapter 5, § 6.

2.13. *State bank chartering: Parallel chartering procedures.* Hiram could, of course, consider a state bank charter.[10] This would require the granting of a charter from an appropriate state official or agency, in accordance with the terms and conditions of the pertinent state statute.[11] The specifics of the chartering process vary broadly from state to state, in keeping with the variety of regulatory structures employed by the states in this area. The chartering decision may be committed to the judgment of a single official, a collegial body, or some combination of the two. In practice, state chartering procedures for the formation of a commercial bank bear obvious similarities to the federal procedures.[12]

2.14. *Savings associations: Parallel chartering procedures.* Entry into the savings association sector of the depository institutions industry is subject to procedures that roughly parallel those applicable to commercial banks. *See generally* 12 U.S.C. § 1464(a).

2.15. *Effect of FIRREA on savings associations.* Significant changes in the federal regulation of savings associations have resulted from the enactment of the Financial Institutions Reform, Recovery, and Enforcement Act of 1989 ("FIRREA").[13] Among the most dramatic changes was the abolition of the Federal Home Loan Bank Board ("FHLBB") and the position of Chairman of the FHLBB, effective 60 days after the enactment of the

---

10. *Cf. supra*, note 2.1 (discussing alternatives).

11. *See, e.g.*, *B.T. Oliphant v. Carthage Bank*, 80 So.2d 63 (Miss. 1955) (discussing chartering).

12. *See* 1 MICHAEL P. MALLOY, BANKING LAW AND REGULATION Figure 2.1 (2d ed. 2011) (presenting finding aid for state bank chartering procedures).

13. Pub. L. No. 101-73, 103 Stat. 183 (1989).

FIRREA.[14] The basic authority for federal chartering of savings associations, the Home Owners' Loan Act ("HOLA")[15] was completely revised by the FIRREA.[16] The Office of Thrift Supervision ("OTS") was established within the Treasury Department,[17] and the Director of the Office of Thrift Supervision ("DOTS")[18] effectively replaced the FHLBB and the Chairman of the FHLBB,[19] except to the extent that any powers of the FHLBB or its Chairman were transferred to other agencies.[20] The DOTS has the authority to charter federal savings associations,[21] "giving primary consideration [to] the best practices of thrift institutions in the United States."[22] A charter may be granted only on satisfaction of the following statutory conditions: (*i*) the persons to whom the charter is issued must be of good character and responsibility; (*ii*) in the judgment of the DOTS, necessity exists for such an institution in the community to be served; (*iii*) there is a reasonable probability of the association's usefulness and success; and, (*iv*) the institution can be established without undue injury to properly conducted existing local savings and home financing institutions.[23] On receiving a federal charter, a savings association automatically becomes a member of the federal home loan bank in the district in which the association is located (or, if convenience requires and the DOTS approves, in an adjoining district).[24]

2.16. Recall Note 2.5, *supra*. Assume that Hiram Forth is interested in organizing a federal savings association, rather than a national bank. What difference would this make to your previous answer? Consider 12 U.S.C. § 1464.[25]

2.17. *Credit unions: Parallel chartering procedures.* How do the chartering procedures for credit unions compare with those for savings associations? To the extent there are differences, can these be explained in policy terms, in light of cases like, for example, *Minnesota Federal Savings & Loan Ass'n, supra*?

2.18. Recall Note 2.5, *supra*. Assume that Hiram Forth is interested in organizing a federal credit union, rather than a national bank. What difference would this make to your original answer? Consider 12 U.S.C. §§ 1753-1754 and the following case.

---

14. FIRREA, § 401(a)(2).

15. 12 U.S.C. §§ 1461 *et seq.*

16. *See id.* § 301 (amending HOLA).

17. 12 U.S.C. § 1462a(a).

18. *See id.* § 1462a(b) (establishing DOTS).

19. *Id.* § 1462a(e)(1).

20. *Id.* § 1462a(e)(2).

21. *Id.* § 1464(a).

22. *Id.*

23. *Id.* § 1464(e)(1)-(4).

24. *Id.* § 1464(f). Newly chartered federal savings association must qualify for membership in same manner as other members under the Home Loan Bank Act. *Id.* On membership, see FIRREA, § 704(a) (codified at 12 U.S.C. § 1424(a)).

25. *Cf. Federal Home Loan Bank Board v. Rowe*, 284 F.2d 274 (D.C. Cir. 1960) (judicial review of chartering authority of Board with respect to savings and loan associations). The statutory authority available to the DOTS is substantially the same as that previously available to the FHLBB. Hence, one may expect that the body of case law concerning the authority and discretion of the FHLBB will remain pertinent to future cases involving the DOTS.

National Credit Union Administration v. First National Bank & Trust Co.

522 U.S. 479 (1998)

Justice THOMAS delivered the opinion of the Court, except as to footnote 6.*

. . .

Section 109 of the Federal Credit Union Act (FCUA), 48 Stat. 1219, 12 U.S.C. § 1759, provides that "[f]ederal credit union membership shall be limited to groups having a common bond of occupation or association, or to groups within a well-defined neighborhood, community, or rural district." Since 1982, the National Credit Union Administration (NCUA), the agency charged with administering the FCUA, has interpreted § 109 to permit federal credit unions to be composed of multiple unrelated employer groups, each having its own common bond of occupation. In this case, respondents, five banks and the American Bankers Association, have challenged this interpretation on the ground that § 109 unambiguously requires that the same common bond of occupation unite every member of an occupationally defined federal credit union. We granted certiorari to answer two questions. First, do respondents have standing under the Administrative Procedure Act to seek federal court review of the NCUA'S interpretation? Second, under the analysis set forth in *Chevron U.S.A. Inc. v. Natural Resources Defense Council, Inc.*, 467 U.S. 837 (1984), is the NCUA'S interpretation permissible? We answer the first question in the affirmative and the second question in the negative. We therefore affirm. . . .

Until 1982, the NCUA and its predecessors consistently interpreted § 109 to require that the same common bond of occupation unite every member of an occupationally defined federal credit union. In 1982, however, the NCUA reversed its longstanding policy in order to permit credit unions to be composed of multiple unrelated employer groups. ... It thus interpreted § 109's common bond requirement to apply only to each employer group in a multiple-group credit union, rather than to every member of that credit union. . . . Under the NCUA'S new interpretation, all of the employer groups in a multiple-group credit union had to be located "within a well-defined area," . . . but the NCUA later revised this requirement to provide that each employer group could be located within "an area surrounding the [credit union's] home or a branch office that can be reasonably served by the [credit union] as determined by NCUA." . . . Since 1982, therefore, the NCUA has permitted federal credit unions to be composed of wholly unrelated employer groups, each having its own distinct common bond. . . .

[The Court held that the respondents had standing under the APA. For that portion of the opinion, see the excerpt following Note 2.7, *supra*.]

. . . [W]e must judge the permissibility of the NCUA'S current interpretation of § 109 by employing the analysis set forth in *Chevron*. . . . Under that analysis, we first ask whether Congress has "directly spoken to the precise question at issue. If the intent of Congress is clear, that is the end of the matter; for the court, as well as the agency, must give effect to the unambiguously expressed intent of Congress." . . . If we determine that Congress has not directly spoken to the precise question at issue, we then inquire whether the agency's interpretation is reasonable. . . . Because we conclude that Congress has made it clear that the same common bond of occupation must unite each member of an occupationally defined federal credit union, we hold that the NCUA'S contrary interpretation is impermissible under the first step of *Chevron*.

---

*. Justice Scalia joins this opinion, except as to footnote 6. [Footnote 6, not reproduced in this excerpt, presented a discussion of the legislative history of § 109, 12 U.S.C. § 1759.]

As noted, § 109 requires that "[f]ederal credit union membership shall be limited to groups having a common bond of occupation or association, or to groups within a well-defined neighborhood, community, or rural district." Respondents contend that because § 109 uses the article "a"–"i.e., one"–in conjunction with the noun "common bond," the "natural reading" of § 109 is that all members in an occupationally defined federal credit union must be united by one common bond. . . . Petitioners reply that because § 109 uses the plural noun "groups," it permits multiple groups, each with its own common bond, to constitute a federal credit union. . . .

. . . [W]e do not think that either of these contentions, standing alone, is conclusive. The article "a" could be thought to convey merely that one bond must unite only the members of each group in a multiple-group credit union, and not all of the members in the credit union taken together. . . . Similarly, the plural word "groups" could be thought to refer not merely to multiple groups in a particular credit union, but rather to every single "group" that forms a distinct credit union under the FCUA. . . . Nonetheless, . . . additional considerations compel the conclusion that the same common bond of occupation must unite all of the members of an occupationally defined federal credit union.

First, the NCUA'S current interpretation makes the phrase "common bond" surplusage when applied to a federal credit union made up of multiple unrelated employer groups, because each "group" in such a credit union already has its own "common bond." . . . [I]n the multiple employer group context, the NCUA has read the statute as though it merely stated that "[f]ederal credit union membership shall be limited to occupational groups," but that is simply not what the statute provides.

Second, the NCUA'S interpretation violates the established canon of construction that similar language contained within the same section of a statute must be accorded a consistent meaning. . . . Section 109 consists of two parallel clauses: Federal credit union membership is limited "to groups having a common bond of occupation or association, or to groups within a well-defined neighborhood, community, or rural district." . . . The NCUA concedes that even though the second limitation permits geographically defined credit unions to have as members more than one "group," all of the groups must come from the same "neighborhood, community, or rural district." . . . The reason that the NCUA has never interpreted, and does not contend that it could interpret, the geographical limitation to allow a credit union to be composed of members from an unlimited number of unrelated geographic units, is that to do so would render the geographical limitation meaningless. Under established principles of statutory interpretation, we must interpret the occupational limitation in the same way.

Petitioners have advanced one reason why we should interpret the occupational limitation differently. They contend that whereas the geographical limitation uses the word "within" and is thus "prepositional," the occupational limitation uses the word "having" and is thus "participial" (and therefore less limiting). . . . There is, however, no reason why a participial phrase is inherently more open-ended than a prepositional one; indeed, certain participial phrases can narrow the relevant universe in an exceedingly effective manner–for example, "persons having February 29th as a wedding anniversary." Reading the two parallel clauses in the same way, we must conclude that, just as all members of a geographically defined federal credit union must be drawn from the same "neighborhood, community or rural district," members of an occupationally defined federal credit union must be united by the same "common bond of occupation."

Finally, by its terms, § 109 requires that membership in federal credit unions "shall be limited." The NCUA'S interpretation–under which a common bond of occupation must unite only the members of each unrelated employer group–has the potential to read these words out of the statute entirely. The NCUA has not contested that, under its current interpretation, it would be permissible to grant a charter to a conglomerate credit union whose members would include the employees of every company in the United States. Nor can it: Each company's employees would be a "group," and each such "group" would have its own "common bond of occupation." Section 109, however, cannot be considered a limitation on credit union membership if at the same time it permits such a limitless result.

Notes and Comments 2.19. Assume that the NCUA has a policy that permits chartering of a credit union for a "community," which is defined for purposes of this policy to mean "a clearly defined geographical area whose residents identify it as a distinct area." A group of local businesses and concerned residents of the Napa Valley in California, an area that consists principally of a string of towns and some 200 wineries stretching northwest along the Napa River, applied to organize the "Napa Valley Federal Credit Union." If the NCUA grants the application as a community-based credit union, and the decision is challenged by Last Country Bank in federal court, what would be the likely result of the litigation, based on your reading of *First National Bank & Trust*?

2.20. *Congressional response to First National Bank & Trust.* Congress responded to *First National Bank & Trust* by amending the FCUA, in effect overruling the result in that case. Credit Union Membership Access Act, Pub. L. No. 105-219, Aug. 7, 1998, 112 Stat. 913 (1998) (codified at scattered sections of 12 U.S.C.) (CUMAA). The act amends the FCUA expressly to allow federal credit unions with multiple common bonds in their fields of membership, CUMAA § 101 (codified at 12 U.S.C. § 1759), while at the same time preserving the integrity and purpose of federal credit unions and enhancing supervisory oversight of insured credit unions. Among other things, the act creates new rules for conversions of insured credit unions, *id.* § 202 (codified at 12 U.S.C. § 1785); imposes new limitations on member business loans' *id.* § 203 (codified at 12 U.S.C. § 1757a); and amends the rules with respect to membership on the NCUA Board. *Id.* § 204 (codified at 12 U.S.C. § 1752a). It also creates new "prompt corrective action" requirements for the supervision of credit unions, *id.* § 301 (codified at 12 U.S.C. § 1790d), and amends the rules with respect to the share insurance fund and liquidity. *Id.* §§ 302, 303 (codified at 12 U.S.C. § 1782). Review the provisions of 12 U.S.C. § 1759. How does it alter the result in *First National Bank & Trust*?

2.21. Considering *First National Bank & Trust*, just how much discretionary authority does the NCUA have in deciding how to implement the amended § 1759? Could it decide to presume eligibility for a multiple common bond charter for applicant groups under 2,500 members? Is it free to decide how the projected membership number would be calculated for these purposes? In considering these questions, review the following case.

American Bankers Association v. National Credit Union Administration

271 F.3d 262 (D.C.Cir. 2001)

TATEL, Circuit Judge.

The American Bankers Association challenges a National Credit Union Administration rule governing chartering and membership standards for federal credit unions. According to the ABA, the rule violates the Credit Union Membership Access Act of 1998, pursuant to which the Administration issued the rule. Except for one claim that we dismiss as moot and another as unripe, we find the ABA's arguments without merit and affirm the district court's dismissal of the case.

I.

The Federal Credit Union Act (FCUA), 12 U.S.C. §§ 1751-1795k, provides for the establishment of federal credit unions and governs their operations. A credit union is a "cooperative association organized in accordance with the provisions of [the FCUA] for the purpose of promoting thrift among its members and creating a source of credit for provident or productive purposes." *Id.* § 1752(1). The National Credit Union Administration "may prescribe rules and regulations for the . . . administration of the [FCUA]," *id.* § 1766(a), and charters, examines, and supervises federal credit unions, *see id.* §§ 1753, 1754, 1756. . . .

As amended, the FCUA permits three types of credit unions, each defined by a different "membership field": single common-bond credit unions, comprised of one group having a common occupational or associational bond; multiple common-bond credit unions, comprised of more than one such group; and community credit unions. 12 U.S.C. § 1759(b)(1)-(3). Pursuant to what the parties call a "grandfather clause," the FCUA exempts certain previously existing "members and groups" from the new membership field provisions. *Id.* § 1759(c)(1). The FCUA also imposes several limitations and conditions on multiple common-bond credit union formation and growth, including: (1) restricting multiple common-bond credit unions to groups with less than 3,000 members, *id.* § 1759(d)(1), unless certain exceptions apply, including where a larger group "could not feasibly or reasonably" form its own credit union, *id.* § 1759(d)(2)(A); (2) directing that the Administration "encourage" a group seeking to join an existing credit union to form its own separately chartered credit union instead, *id.* § 1759(f)(1)(A); (3) requiring that in order to be added to an existing credit union a group be within "reasonable proximity" of that credit union, *id.* § 1759(f)(1)(B); and (4) requiring that where an existing credit union seeks to include an additional group, the credit union must satisfy certain "approval criteria" concerning its financial soundness and administrative capabilities, and that any harmful effect the expansion will have on any other credit union must be "clearly outweighed in the public interest by the probable beneficial effect of the expansion," *id.* § 1759(f)(2). Finally, the 1998 Amendments added the word "local" to the community credit union definition, thus confining such credit unions to "well-defined local communit[ies], neighborhood[s], or rural district[s]." *Id.* § 1759(g)(1).

Following notice and comment, the Administration issued a final rule implementing the 1998 Amendments. *See* IRPS 99-1, 63 Fed.Reg. 71,998 (Dec. 30, 1998). Several of the rule's provisions regarding multiple common-bond credit unions are at issue in this case. First, although the rule allows the immediate family and household of a group member, as well as "[p]ersons retired as pensioners and annuitants," to join the group's multiple common-bond credit union, the rule does not count these persons toward the 3000-member limit. *Id.* at 72,002, 72,037. Second, in determining whether a group with 3000 or more members "could not feasibly or reasonably" form its own credit union, 12 U.S.C. § 1759(d)(2), the Administration considers the group's "desire and intent," 63 Fed.Reg. at 72,002. Third, while the rule requires groups with 3000 or more members to "demonstrate why they cannot satisfactorily form a separate credit union if they want to be added to another credit union," it requires groups with fewer than 3000 members to "demonstrate why they can successfully operate a credit union" in order to be separately chartered. *Id.* at 72,001. Fourth, the rule permits healthy multiple common-bond credit unions comprised of groups with fewer than 3000 members to merge with each other "without regard to the statutory analysis that is required when [such groups] . . . seek to join an existing credit union." *Id.* at 72,003.

Also at issue in this case are the rule's provisions implementing the FCUA's grandfather clause, "reasonable proximity" requirement, and "well-defined local community" standard. *See* 63 Fed.Reg. at 71,998, 72,003, 72,015, 72,037-38. Under the rule, the grandfather clause covers not just individuals who were members of a group at the time the FCUA was amended, but also those who subsequently become members of the group. *Id.* at 72,015. The rule provides that a group is within "reasonable proximity" of a credit union if it is within the "service area of a service facility of the credit union"; a service facility includes a "credit union owned electronic facility" other than an automated teller machine. *Id.* at 72,002-03. Finally, the rule establishes criteria to implement the statute's "well-defined local community" standard and adopts a presumption that certain areas, defined by political jurisdiction and population, meet that standard. *Id.* at 72,037-38.

Alleging that these provisions of the rule violate the FCUA, appellant, the American Bankers Association (ABA), filed suit in the United States District Court for the District of Columbia. . . . Underlying all of the ABA's claims is its belief that the rule is too permissive with respect to credit union formation and growth. Except for the provision regarding pensioners, which the district court found the ABA's amended complaint failed to challenge, the district court concluded that each of the challenged provisions reflects a reasonable interpretation of the FCUA and dismissed the amended complaint. . . .

II.

. . .

Because the ABA argues that the provisions of the rule it challenges violate the FCUA, a statute the Administration is charged with enforcing, we proceed in accordance with *Chevron's* familiar two-part test. *See Chevron U.S.A., Inc. v. Natural Res. Def. Council, Inc.,* 467 U.S. 837 (1984). Although *Chevron* step one analysis begins with the statute's text, we must not "confine [ourselves] to examining a particular statutory provision in isolation. The meaning–or ambiguity–of certain words or phrases may only become evident when placed in context." *FDA v. Brown & Williamson Tobacco Corp.,* 529 U.S. 120, 132 (2000). We must also "exhaust the traditional tools of statutory construction," *Natural Res. Def. Council, Inc. v. Browner,* 57 F.3d 1122, 1125 (D.C.Cir.1995) (internal quotation marks and citation omitted), including examining the statute's legislative history to "shed new light on congressional intent, notwithstanding statutory language that appears superficially clear," *id.* at 1127 (internal quotation marks and citation omitted). And, of course, "we must be guided to a degree by common sense as to the manner in which Congress is likely to delegate a policy decision . . . to an administrative agency." *Brown & Williamson,* 529 U.S. at 121. If, applying these principles, we find that "Congress has directly spoken to the precise question at issue . . . that is the end of the matter; for the court, as well as the agency, must give effect to the unambiguously expressed intent of Congress." *Chevron,* 467 U.S. at 842-43.

Only if we find the statute either silent or ambiguous with respect to "the precise question at issue" do we proceed to *Chevron*'s second step, asking "whether the agency's answer is based on a permissible construction of the statute." *Chevron,* 467 U.S. at 842-44. But not in this case. Although the district court resolved all issues on the basis of *Chevron* step two analysis, . . . the ABA rests its appeal entirely on *Chevron* step one. Throughout its opening brief, the ABA uses only *Chevron* step one language. . . . Moreover, the brief never uses the word "unreasonable" nor any other language suggesting a *Chevron* step two argument. Even after the Administration and Intervenors responded with *Chevron* step one *and* two defenses, the ABA confined its reply brief to straightforward *Chevron* step one arguments. . . . Accordingly, we will evaluate the ABA's claims under *Chevron* step one standards alone.

We begin with the ABA's challenge to the Administration's method for calculating the size of a common-bond group. Under the statute, the "membership field" of a multiple common-bond credit union is limited to groups comprised of persons sharing a common bond, 12 U.S.C. § 1759(b)(2), and "only a group with fewer than 3,000 members shall be eligible to be included in the field of membership category of a [multiple common-bond] credit union. . . ." 12 U.S.C. § 1759(d)(1). Under the rule, the Administration counts only "primary potential members," 63 Fed. Reg. at 72,000, 72,002, *i.e.*, persons sharing the occupational or associational bond that defines the group, toward the 3000-member limit. Although "by virtue of their close relationship to a commonbond group," certain other persons "may be included . . . in the field of membership" of a common-bond credit union–that is, they may join the credit union–such persons are not counted toward the 3000-member limit. *Id.* at 72,037. These persons include immediate family and household members of primary potential members, as well as pensioners and annuitants. *Id.* We consider each category in turn.

[As to the rule's exclusion of family members in calculating the 3000-member limit, the court concluded that it had "no basis for concluding that the FCUA unambiguously requires the Administration to count family and household members toward the 3000-member limit." As to pensioners and annuitants, the court agreed with the district court, which had rejected the ABA's challenge because its amended complaint mentioned only family and household members in the relevant claim. Like its original complaint, the ABA's amended complaint challenged only the exclusion of family and household members.]

III.

The FCUA's grandfather clause provides: "(i) any person or organization that is a member of any Federal credit union as of August 7, 1998 may remain a member of the credit union after August 7, 1998"; and "(ii) a member of any group whose members constituted a portion of the membership of any Federal credit union as of August 7, 1998 shall continue to be eligible to become a member of that credit union, by virtue of membership in that group after August 7, 1998." 12 U.S.C. § 1759(c)(1)(A)(i) and (ii). The Administration interprets the grandfather clause to permit persons who are members of a group that was part of a credit union asof August 7, 1998, the date the 1998 Amendments were enacted, to join the credit union even if they didn't become group members until after that date. *See* 63 Fed.Reg. at 72,015 (grandfather provision applies to "a member, or subsequent new member, of any group, whose membership constituted a portion of the membership of any federal credit union at the date of enactment"). Disagreeing, the ABA argues that the clause's plain language permits only persons who were group members as of August 7, 1998, to join because only they could "continue to be eligible" to become credit union members. 12 U.S.C. § 1759(c)(1)(A)(ii).

. . . The grandfather clause's first part–referring to "a member of any group whose members constituted a portion of the membership of any Federal credit union as of August 7, 1998," 12 U.S.C. § 1759(c)(1)(A)(ii)–suggests, as the Administration argues, that its scope turns not on whether the *individual* was a group member as of August 7, 1998, but on whether the *group* was part of a credit union as of that date. Indeed, if individuals needed to be group members on the date the FCUA was amended, the phrase "as of August 7, 1998" would follow the words "a member of any group."

According to the ABA, the Administration's interpretation of the grandfather clause "has the effect of reading the word 'continue' out of the statute. . . ." We disagree. The Administration plausibly interprets this word to refer to any member of a group that was part of a credit union as of August 7, 1998. To use the statute's language, if a group's "members constituted a portion of the membership of any federal credit union as of August 7, 1998," 12 U.S.C. § 1759(c)(1)(A)(ii), then the group's members, whether they became members before or after August 7, 1998, shall "continue" to be eligible for credit union membership.

Faced with two plausible interpretations of the grandfather clause, we may examine its legislative history, . . . and that history definitively resolves the debate over the grandfather clause's meaning in the Administration's favor. The House Report explains that the "broad grandfather" clause "covers all persons or organizations or successors who were members of a federal credit union on the date of enactment of this Act, as well as anyone who is or becomes a member of a group representing a portion of the credit union's membership," H.R. REP. NO. 105-472, at 19 (1998), U.S. Code Cong. & Admin. News at 334, and "[the provision] grandfathers all current members as well as current groups contained within the membership of a credit union as of the date of enactment of this legislation. The grandfather [provision] will permit such groups to continue accepting new members," *id.* at 11. The Senate Report makes the same point, stating that the clause includes "all current members as well as current groups. . . . The grandfather provision also permits such groups to continue adding new members." S. REP. NO. 105-193, at 3-4 (1998). As the district court put it, this legislative history is "pellucid" on the issue. . . .

IV.

The ABA's next challenge focuses on the FCUA's requirement that in order for a group to be added to a credit union, the group must be within "reasonable proximity" of that credit union. 12 U.S.C. § 1759(f)(1)(B). The rule defines "reasonable proximity" as "within the service area of a service facility of the credit union." 63 Fed. Reg. at 72,002. Although the rule defines a "service facility" as "a credit union owned electronic facility" at which the credit union member is "able to deposit funds, apply for a loan, and obtain funds on approved loans," the rule "excludes . . . ATMs." *Id.* at 72,003. Claiming that an "electronic facility" is similar to an ATM, and that the legislative history of the 1998 Amendments shows that "Congress did not intend for devices similar to ATMs to be considered 'service facilities,' " . . . the ABA argues that the Administration's definition violates the statute. Defending its rule, the Administration argues that the legislative history deals with the term "facility" in the context of a different statutory provision, that *Chevron* step two applies because the FCUA nowhere defines "reasonable proximity," and that the agency's interpretation is reasonable.

Although the parties obviously feel strongly about this issue . . . not one has identified an "electronic facility" that is not also an ATM. The rule doesn't define "electronic facility"; the briefs never define it; and when asked at oral argument, neither counsel could define it, much less tell us whether non-ATM electronic facilities even exist. Under these circumstances, this issue is plainly unripe for judicial review. *See Abbott Labs. v. Gardner,* 387 U.S. 136, 148-49 (1967) (ripeness requires that issue be fit for judicial decision); *Louisiana Envtl. Action Network v. United States Envtl. Prot. Agency,* 172 F.3d 65, 69 (D.C.Cir.1999) (issue not fit for judicial decision where its "[c]onsideration . . . would benefit from a more concrete setting").

V.

The ABA raises several other challenges to the rule's provisions governing multiple common-bond credit unions. None has merit.

First, the ABA argues that the Administration's criteria for determining when a group with 3000 or more members "could not feasibly or reasonably establish a new single common-bond credit union," 12 U.S.C. § 1759(d)(2)(A), and may therefore join an existing credit union, violate the FCUA because the Administration considers the group's "desire and intent" to be "[i]mportant" and "key" in this analysis, 63 Fed. Reg. at 72,002, 72,010. According to the ABA, the statutory phrase "feasibly or reasonably" requires the Administration to determine independently whether the group could operate its own credit union, but the rule "essentially . . . allows the group itself to decide whether it will be allowed to join an existing credit union." . . . The rule specifies, however, that "the intent of the group . . .

[is] *not the sole factor*[ ]. The final decision must be based on an independent regulatory analysis in consideration of the remaining factors in the regulation." 63 Fed. Reg. at 72,002 (emphasis added). Those remaining factors include "the volunteers and resources to support the efficient and effective operations of the credit union, whether the group meets the economic advisability criteria and the demographics of the group." *Id.* at 72,010.

Second, the ABA challenges the portion of the rule that permits voluntary mergers between healthy multiple common-bond credit unions comprised of groups with fewer than 3000 members "without regard to the statutory requirements for non-affiliated groups of [this size] . . . seeking to join an existing credit union." 63 Fed. Reg. at 72,003. These requirements, which apply to multiple common-bond credit union "expansions," include a provision directing the Administration to "encourage the formation of separately chartered credit unions," the "reasonable proximity" requirement, and the "approval criteria" for credit unions seeking to include new groups. 12 U.S.C. § 1759(f). The ABA argues that these requirements "apply on their face whenever a credit union seeks to expand its field of membership by adding new groups–including when it does so through merger." . . . This argument suffers from an obvious defect: Several of the requirements set forth in the "expansions" subsection make no sense in the case of mergers. For example, how can the Administration "encourage the formation of separate credit unions," since mergers, by definition, bring together already-formed credit unions? Or why would Congress have written the "approval criteria" in the singular–"the credit union has not engaged in any unsafe or unsound practice," "is adequately capitalized," and "has the administrative capability . . . and the financial resources . . . to serve the new membership group," 12 U.S.C. § 1759(f)(2)–if it had intended them to apply to mergers of two credit unions? Contrary to the ABA's argument, therefore, subsection 1759(f) does not unambiguously apply to mergers.

Third, the ABA challenges the requirement that groups with fewer than 3000 members "demonstrate why they can successfully operate a credit union" in order to obtain a separate charter. 63 Fed. Reg. at 72,001. According to the ABA, this provision violates the FCUA's requirement that the Administration "encourage the formation of separately chartered credit unions." 12 U.S.C. § 1759(f)(1)(A). Yet the statute only requires the Administration to encourage groups to form their own credit unions "whenever practicable and consistent with reasonable standards for the safe and sound operation of the credit union." *Id.* Requiring that smaller groups show they can operate their own credit unions safely is entirely consistent with this requirement.

VI.

We turn finally to the ABA's challenges to the Administration's approach to the chartering of community credit unions. Pointing out that Congress added the word "local" to the "well-defined community, neighborhood, or rural district" community credit union definition, the ABA argues that although Congress intended the Administration to take a more restricted approach to community credit union charters, the new rule is either the same as, or in some instances, less restrictive than, the prior rule. In support of this proposition, the ABA cites two provisions of the rule: the criteria for determining whether a community qualifies for a charter, *see* 63 Fed. Reg. at 72,038, and the new "presumptive community" standard applicable to a recognized political jurisdiction with no more than 300,000 residents, or multiple contiguous political jurisdictions with no more than 200,000 residents, *see* 63 Fed. Reg. at 72,013, 72,037-38. The ABA contends that the community credit union criteria are substantially unchanged. *Compare* 63 Fed.Reg. at 72,038 (new rule listing political jurisdictions, major trade areas, shared/common facilities, organizations/ clubs, newspapers/other periodicals, maps designating community to be served, common characteristics and background of residents, and other documentation demonstrating common interests or interaction) *with* 59 Fed. Reg. at 29,077 (former rule listing political jurisdictions, major trade areas, shared/common facilities, organizations/clubs, newspapers/other periodicals, census tracts, common characteristics and background of residents, history of area, and other evidence of what distinguishes chosen area and its residents). The ABA also points out that an area benefitting from the "presumptive community" standard is subject to less demanding documentation requirements than ordinarily apply to an area seeking a credit union charter. *See* 63 Fed. Reg. at 72,013, 72,037-38.

Keeping in mind that the ABA limits this appeal to *Chevron* step one, we have little difficulty rejecting these arguments. To begin with, the Administration acknowledges in the rule itself that the addition of the word "local" reflects congressional intent that it take "a more circumspect and restricted approach to chartering community credit unions." 63 Fed. Reg. at 72,012. Moreover, although the Administration left the community credit union criteria substantially unchanged, it has made clear that it intends to apply them more stringently. Specifically, where a community tests the limits of the statutory standard, the Administration will require it "to demonstrate more definitively how it meets the local requirement." *Id.* at 72,012; *see also id.* at 72,037-38 (more documentation required for larger or more densely populated areas). And although the Administration adopted a new presumption, the rule not only requires documentation "describing how the area meets the standards for community interaction or common interests," but also makes clear that the Administration reserves the right to request additional evidence of community interaction or common interests when the community's initial submission falls short. *See id.* at 72,038. At least on its face, therefore, the rule adopts a more circumspect method for applying the community credit union criteria. . . .

3. Secondary Entry Restrictions

Notes and Comments 2.22. *Membership in the Federal Reserve System.* Membership in the Federal Reserve System is an entry requirement for national bank. 12 U.S.C. § 222. For state banks, it is voluntary and subject to approval of the Fed, under the provisions of 12 U.S.C. § 321. For membership, state banks are required to have capital "adequate in relation to the character and condition of its assets and to its existing and prospective deposit liabilities and other corporate responsibilities. . . ." 12 C.F.R. § 208.2(a) (1). For state banks not limited to trust activities, capital must meet the requirements imposed on national banks, or the applicant must either currently be, or have been, approved for deposit insurance by the FDIC. *Id.* § 208.2(a)(1), (b).

2.23. *FDIC deposit insurance.* If Hiram obtains a national bank charter, federal deposit insurance is mandatory. 12 U.S.C. § 222. Is federal deposit insurance automatically granted once QNB is chartered, or must the bank apply for it? *See* 12 U.S.C. §§ 1815-1816. For state-chartered, nonmember banks, federal deposit insurance is voluntary. Is this a feasible option for Hiram? Consider the following excerpt.

Michael P. Malloy, Principles of Bank Regulation

§ 2.10 (3d ed. 2011)

As a matter of federal law, deposit insurance is generally not required for commercial banks that are not members of the Federal Reserve System.[102] As a matter of fact, however, federal deposit insurance is virtually a necessity for all depository institutions.[103] Even for those banks that are required to be FDIC-insured (national banks and state member banks), prior to 1991 there was usually no separate approval process undertaken by the FDIC itself. The Federal Deposit Insurance Corporation Improvement Act of 1991 ("FDICIA")[104] provides that a specific application to, and approval by, the FDIC is required for FDIC insurance of the deposits of all depository institutions.[105]

Every national member bank[106] that receives or will receive non-trust fund deposits is required to obtain FDIC deposit insurance.[107] The situation of state-chartered banks is more complicated. If a state-chartered nonmember bank opts to obtain FDIC insurance – as virtually all such banks do – it must obtain the approval of the Board of Directors of the FDIC.[108] If a state-chartered bank opts to become a member of the Federal Reserve System, FDIC insurance requirements are automatically imposed.[109] If a state-chartered bank is converted into a national member bank, the requirement of FDIC insurance is automatically imposed, in the same way in which FDIC insurance is required for *de novo* national member banks.[110]

In each of the situations described above, an application to and examination by the FDIC is required, with approval of the application by the FDIC Board of Directors.[111] However, if a state-chartered insured bank subsequently becomes a member of the Federal Reserve System, it is not required to reapply for FDIC insurance; its status as an FDIC-insured bank continues despite subsequent acceptance of Fed membership.[112] Similarly, if a state-chartered, FDIC-insured bank subsequently converts to a national charter, its insurance continues without a new application.[113]

Notes and Comments 2.24. If Hiram's bank does apply for federal deposit insurance, how much discretion does the FDIC have in considering the application? Consider the

---

102. 12 U.S.C.A. § 1815(a). However, state-chartered banks that are subsidiaries of bank holding companies, and banks that are themselves holding companies of other banks, are generally required by the Bank Holding Company Act to be FDIC-insured. 12 U.S.C.A. § 1842(e).

103. *See* Helen A. Garten, *Devolution and Deregulation: The Paradox of Financial Reform*, 14 YALE L. & POL'Y REV. 65, 79 n.72 (1996) ("the potential loss of deposits to insured national banks ... may make federal deposit insurance a less costly option for many banks").

104. FDICIA, Pub. L. No. 102-242, 105 Stat. 2236 (Dec. 19, 1991).

105. 12 U.S.C.A. § 1815(a).

106. National banks located in U.S. territories are not required to become members of the Federal Reserve System. 12 U.S.C.A. §§ 282, 1813(d)-(e), 1815(a). However, a national nonmember bank that receives or will receive non-trust fund deposits, and that subsequently opts to become a member bank, is required to be FDIC insured. *Id.* § 1814(b).

107. *Id.* § 1814(b).

108. 12 U.S.C.A. § 1815(a).

109. 12 U.S.C.A. § 1815(a).

110. *Id.* § 1814(b).

111. *Id.* § 1815(a).

112. *Id.* § 1814(b).

113. The same is true for a state-chartered, FDIC-insured bank that results from a merger or consolidation between FDIC-insured banks or between an FDIC-insured bank and an uninsured bank. *Id.*

following case.

Magellsen v. Federal Deposit Insurance Corporation

341 F.Supp. 1031 (D. Mont. 1972)

[Reread the excerpt from this case reproduced at page 52, *supra*.]

Notes and Comments 2.25. *Effect of FIRREA on savings associations.* Prior to 1989, an entirely separate system of federal deposit insurance for savings associations was administered by the Federal Savings and Loan Insurance Corporation ("FSLIC"). Significant changes in the federal regulation of savings associations resulted from the enactment of the Financial Institutions Reform, Recovery, and Enforcement Act of 1989 ("FIRREA").[26]The FSLIC was immediately abolished.[27] The FDIC has been given responsibility for insurance of deposits of "savings associations," *e.g.*, S&Ls and savings banks.[28] It now administers a Bank Insurance Fund ("BIF"), formerly the Permanent Insurance Fund with respect to deposits of insured banks,[29] and a Savings Association Insurance Fund ("SAIF"), replacing the functions of the FSLIC.[30] In addition to BIF and SAIF, the FIRREA also established an FSLIC Resolution Fund, to wind up the affairs of the FSLIC.[31]

2.26. *1996 amendments to the federal deposit system.* In September 1996, the Economic Growth and Regulatory Paperwork Reduction Act ("EGRPRA")[32] was enacted. The act makes a number of significant changes to the structure of regulation of depository institutions,[33] including amendments to the deposit insurance system. The EGRPRA imposed a special assessment on insured depository institutions holding SAIF-insured deposits in order to recapitalize the ailing SAIF.[34] It also provided for the merger of the BIF and SAIF into a new Deposit Insurance Fund ("DIF"), if there were no more savings associations by 1 January 1999.[35]

---

26. Pub. L. No. 101-73, 103 Stat. 183 (1989).

27. FIRREA, § 401(a)(1).

28. FIRREA § 205(1) (codified at 12 U.S.C. § 1814(a)).

29. FIRREA, § 211(3) (codified at 12 U.S.C. § 1821 (a)(4)-(5)).

30. *Id.* § 211(3) (codified at 12 U.S.C. § 1821(a) (4), (6)).

31. *Id.*, § 215 (codified at 12 U.S.C. § 1821a).

32. Pub. L. No. 104-208, title II, 110 Stat. 3009 (1996) (codified at scattered sections of 5, 12, 15, 26, 42 U.S.C.).

33. *See generally* Murray A. Indick, Ronald J. Greene, & Daniel Squire, *The Economic Growth and Regulatory Paperwork Reduction Act of 1996*, 114 Banking L.J. 298 (1997) (surveying provisions of EGRPR Act). Specific features of the EGRPRA are noted at appropriate points throughout this book.

34. EGRPRA, § 2702 (to be codified at 12 U.S.C. § 1817 note). *See* Indick, *supra*, at 300-301 (discussing assessment provisions).

35. EGRPRA, § 2704 (codified at 12 U.S.C. §§ 24(Eleventh), 338a, 347b(b)(3)(A)(ii), 1431(k), 1441a(b), 1441b(f)(2)(C)(ii), 1464, 1467a, 1723i, 1735f-14, 1813(a)(1), 1813(y), 1815(b)(5), (e), 1816(5), 1817(b)(2)(B)-(E), (*l*)-(m), 1821 note, 1821(a)(4)-(6), 1821a(a), 1823, 1824, 1825(c)(5), 1827, 1828, 1831e, 1831m(i)(3), 1831o, 1833a(b)(3)(B), 3341(c)(1)(B), 1834(a)(1), 1841(j) (2)) (establishing DIF; repealing former § 1817(*l*) and redesignating former (m)-(n) as (*l*)-(m); repealing former § 1817(b)(2)(B), (F) and redesignating former (C), (E), (G), (H) as (B)-(E); repealing former § 1831h; other technical and conforming amendments changing references to BIF and SAIF to DIF).

4. Conversions

A depository institution conversion–not a religious experience but regulatory change affecting the institution's charter–can be one of two types. A jurisdictional conversion involves a change from a federal to a state charter, or state to federal. An organizational conversion involves a change from mutual to stock form of ownership, or stock to mutual. *See generally* MICHAEL P. MALLOY, PRINCIPLES OF BANK REGULATION § 2.12 (3d ed. 2003) (discussing conversions of charter and of form).

Notes and Comments 2.27. *Conversions of charter: state to federal.* A national bank can be created by the conversion of a state-chartered bank. The applicable statutory provisions are 12 U.S.C. § 35, as well as the pertinent state law to which the converting institution is subject. Recall Note 2.5, *supra*. Assume that Hiram had organized Quarter State Bank, but now would like to convert it into QNB. What are the applicable procedures and requirements? In answering this question, consider also the regulatory provisions and case excerpted below.

Comptroller of the Currency
12 C.F.R. pt. 5

§ 5.24 Conversion.

(a) Authority. 12 U.S.C. 35, 93a, 214a, 214b, 214c, and 2903.

(b) Licensing requirements. A state bank (including a "state bank" as defined in 12 U.S.C. 214(a)) or a Federal savings association shall submit an application and obtain prior OCC approval to convert to a national bank charter. A national bank shall give notice to the OCC before converting to a state bank (including a "state bank" as defined in 12 U.S.C. 214(a)) or Federal savings association.

(c) Scope. This section describes procedures and standards governing OCC review and approval of an application by a state bank or Federal savings association to convert to a national bank charter. . . .

(d) Conversion of a state bank or Federal savings association to a national bank–

(1) Policy. Consistent with the OCC's chartering policy, it is OCC policy to allow conversion to a national bank charter by another financial institution that can operate safely and soundly as a national bank in compliance with applicable laws, regulations, and policies. The OCC may deny an application by any state bank (including a "state bank" as defined in 12 U.S.C. 214(a)) and any Federal savings association to convert to a national bank charter on the basis of the standards for denial set forth in § 5.13(b),[a] or when conversion would permit the applicant to escape supervisory action by its current regulator.

(2) Procedures.

(i) Prefiling communications. The applicant should consult with the appropriate

---

a. 12 C.F.R. § 5.13(b) provides as follows:

> The OCC may deny a filing if:
>
> (1) A significant supervisory, CRA [community Reinvestment Act] (if applicable), or compliance concern exists with respect to the applicant;
>
> (2) Approval of the filing is inconsistent with applicable law, regulation, or OCC policy thereunder; or
>
> (3) The applicant fails to provide information requested by the OCC that is necessary for the OCC to make an informed decision.

district office prior to filing if it anticipates that its application will raise unusual or complex issues. If a prefiling meeting is appropriate, it will normally be held in the district office where the application will be filed, but may be held at another location at the request of the applicant.

(ii) A state bank (including a state bank as defined in 12 U.S.C. 214(a)) or Federal savings association shall submit its application to convert to a national bank to the appropriate district office. The application must:

(A) Be signed by the president or other duly authorized officer;

(B) Identify each branch that the resulting bank expects to operate after conversion;

(C) Include the institution's most recent audited financial statements (if any);

(D) Include the latest report of condition and report of income (the most recent daily statement of condition will suffice if the institution does not file these reports);

(E) Unless otherwise advised by the OCC in a prefiling communication, include an opinion of counsel that, in the case of a state bank, the conversion is not in contravention of applicable state law, or in the case of a Federal savings association, the conversion is not in contravention of applicable Federal law;

(F) State whether the institution wishes to exercise fiduciary powers after the conversion;

(G) Identify all subsidiaries that will be retained following the conversion, and provide the information and analysis of the subsidiaries' activities that would be required if the converting bank or savings association were a national bank establishing each subsidiary pursuant to § 5.34; and

(H) Identify any nonconforming assets (including nonconforming subsidiaries) and nonconforming activities that the institution engages in, and describe the plans to retain or divest those assets.

(iii) The OCC may permit a national bank to retain such nonconforming assets of a state bank, subject to conditions and an OCC determination of the carrying value of the retained assets, pursuant to 12 U.S.C. 35.

(iv) Approval for an institution to convert to a national bank expires if the conversion has not occurred within six months of the OCC's preliminary approval of the application.

(v) When the OCC determines that the applicant has satisfied all statutory and regulatory requirements, including those set forth in 12 U.S.C. 35, and any other conditions, the OCC issues a charter certificate. The certificate provides that the institution is authorized to begin conducting business as a national bank as of a specified date. . . .

(4) Expedited review. An application by an eligible depository institution to convert to a national bank charter is deemed approved by the OCC as of the 30th day after the filing is received by the OCC, unless the OCC notifies the applicant prior to that date that the filing is not eligible for expedited review under § 5.13(a)(2).[b]

---

b. 12 C.F.R. § 5.13(a)(2) provides as follows:

> The OCC grants eligible banks expedited review within a specified time after filing or commencement of the public comment period, . . . as described in applicable sections of this part.

For these purposes, the term "eligible bank" means a national bank that is well capitalized; has a composite rating of 1 or 2 under the Uniform Financial Institutions Rating System (CAMEL); has a Community Reinvestment Act (CRA), 12 U.S.C. §§ 2901 *et seq.*, rating of "Outstanding" or "Satisfactory;" and, is not subject to formal disciplinary action (unless waived by the OCC). 12 C.F.R. § 5.3(g)(1)-(4).

American Council of Life Insurance v. Ludwig

1 F.Supp.2d 24 (D.D.C. 1998),
vacated as moot and remanded, 194 F.3d 173 (D.C.Cir. 1999)

JUNE L. GREEN, District Judge.

[The American Council, an insurance trade association, brought suit against the Comptroller and the Office of the Comptroller of the Currency (OCC) to contest an OCC decision approving the conversion of a state-chartered bank to a national bank charter and allowing the converted bank to retain certain nonconforming insurance subsidiaries pursuant to 12 U.S.C. § 35. The Comptroller and the OCC moved for summary judgment. The district court first decided that it did have jurisdiction to review the OCC decision, but that the standard of judicial review should be whether the Comptroller's action was arbitrary, capricious, an abuse of discretion, or otherwise not in accordance with law. In the excerpt below, the court applies that standard to the case before it.]

Plaintiff challenges the Comptroller's interpretation of [12 U.S.C. § 35] and states that it is contrary to the National Banking Act ("NBA"), 12 U.S.C. § 1 *et seq*. (1994), which limits the authority of national banks to engage in a wide range of activities. Plaintiffs point specifically to 12 U.S.C. § 92 (1994), which permits national banks to sell insurance, but only if the bank is "located and doing business in any place the population of which does not exceed five thousand inhabitants." 12 U.S.C. § 92. The insurance agencies in this case operate in part in offices situated in communities with populations that exceed 5,000. . . .

The Plaintiff argues that [§ 35] is silent on the issue of whether a converting bank must eventually divest itself of nonconforming assets and, in any event, that interpreting section 35 to allow banks to retain such assets indefinitely would give them privileges beyond other nationally chartered banks. Plaintiff argues that such a result could not have been intended by Congress and cites the first part of section 35 and the NBA in support.

The Plaintiff's interpretation is not correct. There is nothing on the face of the statute or in its legislative history that requires such a narrow reading as Plaintiff suggests. The terms "retain and carry," are plain enough, and given their ordinary meaning, do not suggest to the Court that ultimate divesture of nonconforming assets is a built in, yet unstated component of section 35. The legislative history also supports the Comptroller's interpretation, showing that the purpose of section 35 was to remove impediments from state banks seeking to convert to national bank status by allowing them to retain their nonconforming assets. In fact, the legislative history suggests that encouraging banks to convert (while keeping them financially sound by avoiding divestiture) appears to be an important purpose of section 35.

The Plaintiff makes much of a preceding paragraph of section 35, which states:

> When the Comptroller has given to such bank or banking association a certificate that the provisions of this Act have been complied with, such bank or banking association . . . shall have the same powers and privileges, and shall be subject to the same duties, liabilities, and regulations, in all respects, as shall have been prescribed by the Federal Reserve Act and the National Bank Act for institutions originally organized as national banking associations.

12 U.S.C. § 35. A full reading of the statute, however, makes it clear to the Court that this portion of section 35 is meant to set the baseline for how converting banks are to be regarded once they have completed the conversion process. It comes at the end of a long paragraph on what the bank must do in order to convert. It is compelling to the Court that the "retain

and carry" paragraph, by its placement at the end of the section, was intended to modify the earlier stated provisions by giving the Comptroller the broad discretion to make exceptions with regard to retention of nonconforming assets. To find otherwise would be to imply limitations on section 35 that are not stated on its face. The Court cannot do that.

Under section 35, the Comptroller has the express authority to permit a converting bank to retain its nonconforming assets "subject to such conditions as he may prescribe ..." *Id.* If he so chose, the Comptroller, under this provision, could properly decide that those "conditions" would be the permanent retention of the nonconforming assets.

. . . The Comptroller points to its own policy statements made in 1993 to explain its decision to allow Magna to retain the nonconforming insurance subsidiaries. . . . In these statements, the Comptroller related the disadvantages of reducing the range of products and services of a financial institution as impoverishing the marketplace and the economy by reducing competitiveness and soundness of financial institutions. . . .

In 1994, the Comptroller reinforced this policy in testimony before Congress. The Comptroller explained the need for the OCC's policy to allow banks to participate in providing financial services to the fullest extent permissible under the banking laws. . . . The OCC also proposed rulemaking in 1994 stating the agency's intent to permit converting banks to retain nonconforming assets, including subsidiary corporations, to the full extent permitted by 12 U.S.C. § 35. . . .

The Court considers the Comptroller's interpretation of the last provision in 12 U.S.C. § 35 as reasonable, in light of the language of the statute and the aforementioned evidence of the OCC's policy to approve, where possible, banks' participation in financial services activities. While this policy was not iterated by the Comptroller with specific regard to Magna Bank, the Court can reasonably discern the agency's path toward the Magna Bank decision by looking to the evidence of this policy.

The Plaintiff relies on the Comptroller's decisions in the past 60 years regarding converted banks' retention of nonconforming assets in arguing that the provision in section 35 is intended only for transitional purposes during conversion. In light of the OCC's more recent policy to allow banks to participate in providing financial services to the fullest extent possible, the Court rejects this argument. This change of policy distinguishes the circumstances of the Magna decision from prior OCC decisions that had required converting banks to divest their nonconforming assets.

In addition to this policy to permit banks to engage in the broadest range of services permissible, the record shows that the OCC, in applying section 35, considered whether retention of the nonconforming assets would present any safety and soundness problems, and concluded that it would not. . . . Moreover, it appears that the OCC considered the role the subsidiaries played in Magna's operations and took into account Magna's request to retain them. . . . Finally, the OCC considered whether it had the resources to supervise the retained subsidiaries, and concluded that it had the necessary staff with technical expertise. . . .

This analysis, along with the framework of OCC's publicly articulated policy to permit the expansion of bank activities, convinces the Court that the Comptroller's decision to allow Magna Bank to retain its insurance subsidiaries was neither arbitrary, capricious nor an abuse of discretion. . . .

Notes and Comments 2.28. To what extent do the provisions for conversion and chartering differ? Is it possible that the Comptroller might grant a conversion application even though, all other things being equal, a charter application would have been denied?

2.29. *Savings associations: state to federal conversions.* Recall Note 2.5, *supra.* Assume Hiram had organized a state-chartered savings association, which has now been criticized by state regulators. Hiram is seeking to convert the institution to a federal charter. Is the application likely to be granted? Consider the next case and the notes that follow it.

Hopkins Savings Assn. v. Cleary

296 U.S. 315 (1935)

Mr. Justice CARDOZO delivered the opinion of the Court.

[Hopkins Federal had been a state savings association until it converted. The Wisconsin Banking Commission had challenged the conversion because it did not comply with state law. The Wisconsin Supreme Court annulled the conversion and ordered the directors and officers to continue the business in accordance with Wisconsin law or liquidate.]

The controversy in each of these causes is one as to the meaning and validity of an Act of Congress whereby building and loan associations organized under the laws of a state may be converted into Federal Savings & Loan Associations upon the vote of a majority of the shareholders present at a meeting legally convened. . . .

Building and loan associations organized in Wisconsin are subject to strict supervision by the administrative agencies of the state both in the course of doing business and in that of liquidation. . . . The statute contains provisions governing the consolidation of such association and their voluntary dissolution. Corporations formed thereunder may consolidate with other building and loan associations located in the same county, but only with the consent of the Commissioner of Banking and that of two-thirds of the outstanding shares as well as the consent of a majority of the directors. . . . A vote of approval by two-thirds of the outstanding shares is necessary also for voluntary dissolution. . . . [T]here is nothing in the statutes of Wisconsin whereby building and loan associations chartered in that state may be transmuted into associations chartered by the federal government.

The petitioners insist that without the consent of Wisconsin the transmutation from a state into a federal association has become possible now by virtue of an Act of Congress. The Act relied upon for that purpose is § 5 of the Home Owners' Loan Act of 1933. . . . Subdivision (i), the one that concerns us specially, permits state associations to be converted into federal ones. As amended in April, 1934, its provisions are as follows:

> "(i) Any member of a Federal Home Loan Bank may convert into a Federal Savings and Loan Association under this Act upon a vote of 51 per centum or more of the votes cast at a legal meeting called to consider such action; but such conversion shall be subject to such rules and regulations as the Board may prescribe, and thereafter the converted association shall be entitled to all the benefits of this section and shall be subject to examination and regulation to the same extent as other associations incorporated pursuant to this Act." . . .

Each of the three building and loan associations, the petitioners before us, was a member in good standing of the Federal Home Loan Bank of Chicago, Illinois. After application in proper form each received from the Board permission to convert itself into a federal association under § 5(i) of the Federal Home Loan Act. [Each convened a meeting of its shareholders to consider approval of the conversion, and each conversion proposal was adopted by the respective shareholders' meetings.]

The State of Wisconsin, acting through its Banking Commission, came forward at this point to check the process of conversion. It took the position (1) that § 5(i) of the Home Owners' Loan Act was subject to an implied condition whereby no conversion was to be permitted to contravention of local laws; and (2) that if this reading of the section were to be rejected as erroneous, the statute to that extent was void under the Tenth Amendment as an unconstitutional trespass upon the powers of the states. . . .

The Supreme Court of Wisconsin placed its decision upon the first of these positions to the exclusion of the other. It read the federal statute as subject to the implied condition contended for by the state officials. It did this to avoid embarrassing and doubtful questions of constitutional power, which it described without deciding.

. . . Congress did not mean that the conversion from state associations into federal ones should be conditioned upon the consent of the state or compliance with its laws.

Under § 5(i) as enacted in 1933, the argument could have been obeyed in the process of conversion. The provision then was . . . that the association was to act "upon a vote of its stockholders as provided by the law under which it operates." But Congress would not leave it so. By an amendment of the statute, approved April 27, 1934, there was substituted a provision that conversion would be effective "upon a vote of 51 per centum or more of the votes cast at a legal meeting called to consider such action." Thus Congress erected a standard of its own, which was to be uniform in all the states irrespective of the local laws. A bare majority of the shares voted at a meeting was to be enough to give authority for fundamental changes of policy and power, no matter how many other shares were unrepresented at the meeting. We are unable to accede to the suggestion of the court below that the percentage was meant to be a minimum which the local laws might raise, though they were powerless to reduce it. Nothing in the wording of the statute gives support to that construction. On the contrary, comparison of the act was amended with the act as first adopted impels to the conclusion that Congress had in mind to take possession of the field to the exclusion of other occupants. Thereafter the procedure for conversion and the power to convert were to be governed by a uniform rule, irrespective of repugnant limitations prevailing in the states.

Whatever doubt might exist as to the correctness of this view disappears when other and cognate statutes are subjected to our scrutiny.

The National Banking Act of 1864 (13 Stat. 99, 112, 113) gave permission to the banks incorporated in the states to become national associations upon the consent of the owners of two thirds of the capital stock, the consent to be evidenced by an appropriate certificate. This court in *Casey v. Galli*, 94 U.S. 673, decided in 1876, refused to read into the act a condition that the state as well as the stockholders must consent to the conversion, though no question of constitutional power was necessary to the decision, as will be shown later on. The statute as thus interpreted remained substantially unchanged until 1913, when the percentage was reduced from two thirds to a majority, with the addition of a proviso "that said conversion shall not be in contravention of the state law." R.S. § 5154; 38 Stat. 258; 12 U.S.C. § 35. *Cf.* 12 U.S.C. § 342; *Ex parte Worcester National Bank*, 279 U.S. 347. . . .

The Home Owners' Loan Act, to the extent that it permits the conversion of state associations into federal ones in contravention of the laws of the place of their creation, is an unconstitutional encroachment upon the reserved powers of the states. United States Constitution, Amendment X.

If § 5(i) may be upheld when state laws are inconsistent, any savings bank or insurance company as well as any building and loan association, may be converted into a savings and loan association with a charter from the central government, provided only that 51 percent of the shares represented at a meeting vote approval of the change. Indeed, as counsel for the petitioners insisted at our bar, the power of transformation, if it is adequate in such conditions, is not confined to building and loan associations or savings banks or insurance companies or to members of the Home Loan Bank, except by the adventitious features of this particular enactment. It extends in the view to moneyed corporations generally and even to other corporations, if Congress chooses to convert them into creatures of the federal government. Compulsion, by hypothesis, being lawful, the percentage of assenting shares voted in a given instance or exacted by a given statute assumes the aspect of an accident. Fifty one percent is the minimum required here. Another act may reduce the minimum to ten percent or even one, or dispense with approval altogether. If nonassenting shareholders or creditors were parties to these suits the question would be urgent whether property interests may be so transformed consistently with the restraints of the Fifth Amendment. The Wisconsin courts hold that the protest of a single shareholder will check "a fundamental and radical change" in the powers and purposes of the corporation, though the change be brought about by voluntary amendment. . . .

Shareholders and creditors being absent, we have instead the question whether consistently with Tenth Amendment the change may be made under license of the central government against the protest of the state.

For the purposes of these cases we find it needless to consider whether Congress has the power to create building and loan associations and thereupon to invest them with corporate capacity. As to that we do not indicate an opinion either one way or the other. The critical question here is something very different. The critical question is whether along with such a power there goes the power also to put an end to corporations created by the states and turn them into different corporations created by the nation.

A corporation is a juristic person organized by government to accomplish certain ends, which may be public or quasi-public, though for other purposes of classification the corporation is described as private.

. . . This is true of building and loan associations in Wisconsin and in other states. They have been given corporate capacity in the belief that their creation will advance the common weal. The state, which brings them into being, has an interest in preserving their existence, for only thus can they attain the ends of their creation. They are more than business corporations. They have been organized and nurtured as quasi-public instruments. . . .

They may not divest themselves of a franchise when once it is accepted if the local statutes or decisions command them to retain it. . . .

How they shall be formed, how maintained and supervised, and how and when dissolved, are matters of governmental policy, which it would be an intrusion for another government to regulate by statute or decision, except when reasonably necessary for the fair and effective exercise of some other cognate power explicitly conferred.

Wisconsin, planning these agencies in furtherance of the common good and purposing to preserve them that the good may not be lost, is now informed by the Congress, speaking through a statute, that the purpose and the plan shall be thwarted and destroyed. By the law of state, associations such as these may be dissolved in ways and for causes carefully defined, in which event the assets shall be converted into money and applied so far as adequate, to the payment of the creditors. By the challenged Act of Congress, the same associations are dissolved in other ways and for other causes, and from being creatures of the state become of the nation. In this there is an invasion of the sovereignty or quasi-sovereignty of Wisconsin and an impairment of its public policy, which the state is privileged to redress as a suitor in the courts so long as the Tenth Amendment preserves a field of autonomy against federal encroachment. . . .

Much reliance is placed in behalf of the petitioners upon the decision of this court in *Casey v. Galli, supra.* The Bank of New Orleans, a Louisiana corporation, became a national banking association by vote of its stockholders. The state did not oppose the conversion, thought it was not shown to have consented. The reorganized corporation did business for more than two years when it failed and a receiver was appointed by the Comptroller of the Currency. In an action by the receiver against a shareholder to enforce the individual liability under the provisions of the federal statute, the defendant filed three pleas in abatement, to which the plaintiff demurred. . . . The first plea was abandoned, and the third is without bearing upon the causes now before us. The court sustained the demurrer to the second plea upon two independent grounds. . . . (a) The defendant was estopped from contesting the validity of the change after standing by for over two years without making his objection known; and (b) apart from any estoppel, "no authority from the State was necessary to enable the bank so to change its organization." . . . "The act is silent as to any assent or permission by the State. It was as competent for Congress to authorize the transmutation as to create such institutions originally." . . .

No question of constitutional power was in the case, for nowhere in the record did the defendant invoke the Tenth Amendment or the Fifth or any other provision of the Federal Constitution. The substance of the plea was this, that the change from one form of association to another was to be condemned as ultra vires. The meaning of the statute was thus the pivot of the controversy.

Distinctions may conceivably exist between the power of the Congress in respect of banks of issue and deposit and its power in respect of associations to encourage industry and thrift. Whether that be so or not, all that was said in *Casey V. Galli* as to the condition of consent was unnecessary to the decision if it was meant to do more than define the meaning of the statute. We cannot accept it as determining the constitutional rights and privileges of a party not then before the court, least of all when it appears that constitutional rights and privileges were not invoked or argued.

Notes and Comments 2.30. Can *Hopkins* and *Casey v. Galli*, be reconciled? Does Justice Cardozo adequately explain how he can reach the result in *Hopkins* despite the precedent in *Casey*?

2.31. *FIRREA and state-to-federal conversions.* (a) *General rule.* Under FIRREA, conversion of any savings association that is or is eligible to become a member of a federal home loan bank into a *federal* savings association, and any accompanying conversion from mutual to stock or stock to mutual form,[36] will be subject to regulations prescribed by the DOTS.[37] In addition, any federal savings association may change its designation from a federal savings association to a federal savings bank, or vice versa.[38]

(b) *Converting savings banks.* Conversion of a state savings bank that is a member of the BIF into a federal savings bank is permitted, subject to the provisions of the amended HOLA[39] and pursuant to regulations promulgated by the DOTS.[40] The DOTS is authorized to provide for the organization, incorporation, operation, examination and regulation of such converted savings banks.[41] Such a converted savings bank continues to be a BIF member

---

36. Conversion of any savings association from mutual to stock or stock to mutual form is prohibited except in accordance with regulations promulgated by the DOTS. 12 U.S.C. § 1464(i)(2)(A).

37. *Id.* § 1464(i)(1).

38. *Id.* § 1464(i)(2)(C).

39. *Id.* § 1464(o)(2)(B)-(E).

40. *Id.* § 1464(o)(1).

41. *Id.*

until such time as it changes its status to an SAIF member.[42]

(c) *Hopkins revisited.* FIRREA also authorizes the DOTS, *notwithstanding any other provision of law* (*i*) to approve or (in the case of a federal savings association) to require conversion of a mutual savings association or an FDIC-insured federal mutual savings bank into a federal stock savings association or federal stock savings bank; (*ii*) to charter a federal stock savings association or federal stock savings bank to acquire the assets of such a mutual institution; or, (*iii*) to charter a federal stock savings association or federal stock savings bank to merge with such a mutual institution.[43] The conversion is authorized only if one of the following conditions is met:

> (*i*) The DOTS determines that severe financial conditions exist that threaten the stability of the association to be converted and that the conversion is likely to improve the financial condition of the association.
>
> (*ii*) The FDIC has contracted to provide assistance to the association under 12 U.S.C. § 1823.[44]
>
> (*iii*) The conversion is intended to assist an institution in receivership.[45]

Is the authority granted by the FIRREA with respect to conversions consistent with *Hopkins*? Since that case was decided, the Tenth Amendment may have been all but overwhelmed by the Commerce Clause authority of Congress to make laws, in which case decisions limiting federal regulatory power based upon the amendment may simply be irrelevant. *See* Van Alstyne, *The Second Death of Federalism*, 83 Mich. L. Rev. 1709 (1985) (discussing *San Antonio Metropolitan*); Field, *Garcia v. San Antonio Metropolitan Transit Authority: The Demise of a Misguided Doctrine*, 99 Harv. L. Rev. 84 (1985) (same). *But cf. Garcia v. San Antonio Metropolitan Transit Authority*, 469 U.S. 528, 584 (1984) (O'Connor, J., dissenting) (citing *Hopkins* with approval). How much is left of the Tenth Amendment argument as applied to bank regulation after the Supreme Court's decision in the following case?

Watters v. Wachovia Bank, N.A.

550 U.S. 1 (2007)

Justice GINSBURG delivered the opinion of the Court.

[Wachovia, a national bank, and its state-chartered mortgage company subsidiary sued the Michigan Commissioner of Insurance and Financial Services seeking declaratory and injunctive relief from state registration and inspection requirements, based on preemption of the state law by the NBA and by federal regulations. The Western District of Michigan granted summary judgment for the plaintiffs, and the Sixth Circuit affirmed. On certiorari, the Supreme Court affirmed, principally on the ground that the NBA and federal regulations preempted state regulation of Wachovia's mortgage business, whether conducted by the bank itself or its operating subsidiary. It also considered, however, whether such federal regulation might violate the Tenth Amendment.]

III

---

42. *Id.* § 1464(o)(2)(A).

43. *Id.* § 1464(p)(1).

44. *See, e.g.*, 12 U.S.C. § 1823(c) (providing authority for "open bank assistance" by FDIC to banks in danger of closing).

45. 12 U.S.C. § 1464(p)(2)(A)-(C).

Watters' alternative argument, that 12 CFR § 7.4006 violates the Tenth Amendment to the Constitution, is unavailing. As we have previously explained, "[i]f a power is delegated to Congress in the Constitution, the Tenth Amendment expressly disclaims any reservation of that power to the States." *New York v. United States,* 505 U.S. 144, 156 (1992). Regulation of national bank operations is a prerogative of Congress under the Commerce and Necessary and Proper Clauses. See *Citizens Bank v. Alafabco, Inc.,* 539 U.S. 52, 58 (2003) *(per curiam).* The Tenth Amendment, therefore, is not implicated here. . . .

Justice THOMAS took no part in the consideration or decision of this case.

Justice STEVENS, with whom THE CHIEF JUSTICE and Justice SCALIA join, dissenting. . . .

VI

The novelty of today's holding merits a final comment. Whatever the Court says, this is a case about an administrative agency's power to preempt state laws. I agree with the Court that the Tenth Amendment does not preclude the exercise of that power. But the fact that that Amendment was included in the Bill of Rights should nevertheless remind the Court that its ruling affects the allocation of powers among sovereigns. Indeed, the reasons for adopting that Amendment are precisely those that undergird the well-established presumption against preemption.

With rare exception, we have found preemption only when a federal statute commanded it, see *Cipollone,* 505 U.S., at 517, when a conflict between federal and state law precluded obedience to both sovereigns, see *Florida Lime & Avocado Growers, Inc. v. Paul,* 373 U.S. 132, 142-143 (1963), or when a federal statute so completely occupied a field that it left no room for additional state regulation, see *Napier v. Atlantic Coast Line R. Co.,* 272 U.S. 605, 613 (1926). Almost invariably the finding of preemption has been based on this Court's interpretation of statutory language or of regulations plainly authorized by Congress. Never before have we endorsed administrative action whose sole purpose was to preempt state law rather than to implement a statutory command.

2.32. *Commercial banks: federal to state conversions.* Recall Note 2.5, *supra.* Assume Hiram had organized a national bank, which has now been criticized by the OCC. Hiram is seeking to convert QNB to either a state bank charter or a state savings association charter (a "cross-industry conversion"). State law requirements will of course apply. But what are the federal requirements for such a conversion? Consider the following excerpted material.

Comptroller of the Currency

12 C.F.R. pt. 5

§ 5.24 Conversion.

. . .

(e) Conversion of a national bank to a state bank -- (1) Procedure. A national bank may convert to a state bank, in accordance with 12 U.S.C. 214c, without prior OCC approval. Termination of the national bank's status as a national bank occurs upon the bank's completion of the requirements of 12 U.S.C. 214a, and upon the appropriate district office's receipt of the bank's national bank charter (or copy) in connection with the consummation of the transaction.

(2) Notice of intent. A national bank that desires to convert to a state bank shall submit to the appropriate district office a notice of its intent to convert. The national bank shall file this notice when it first submits a request to convert to the appropriate state authorities. The appropriate district office then provides instructions to the national bank for

terminating its status as a national bank.

(f) Conversion of a national bank to a Federal savings association. A national bank may convert to a Federal savings association without prior OCC approval. The requirements and procedures set forth in paragraph (e) of this section and 12 U.S.C. 214a and 12 U.S.C. 214c apply to a conversion to a Federal savings association, except as follows:

(1) In paragraph (e) of this section references to "appropriate state authorities" mean "appropriate Federal authorities"; and

(2) References in 12 U.S.C. 214c to the "law of the State in which the national banking association is located" and "any State authority" mean "laws and regulations governing Federal savings associations" and "Office of Thrift Supervision," respectively.

Notes and Comments 2.33. *Savings associations: federal to state conversions.* Recall Note 2.5, *supra*. Assume Hiram had organized a federal savings association, which has now been criticized by the OTS. Hiram is seeking to convert the institution to a state charter. Is the application likely to be granted? Consider the next case and the notes that follow it.

Federal Home Loan Bank Board v. Greater Delaware Valley Fed. S. & L. Ass'n.

277 F.2d 437 (3d Cir. 1960)

HASTIE, Circuit Judge.

In this case the Federal Home Loan Bank Board has sought a declaratory judgment that attempted statutory conversion of Greater Delaware Valley Federal Savings and Loan Association from its original status as a federally chartered institution to that of a banking institution chartered by Pennsylvania has been legally ineffective. Officers representing the Commonwealth of Pennsylvania have intervened in opposition to the petition of the Board. On motion of the defendant and the intervenors, the court below found that the Association had lawfully and effectively become a state chartered institution and entered judgement accordingly. . . .

In 1938 the Federal Home Loan Bank Board granted Greater Delaware Valley Federal Savings and Loan Association a federal charter. . . . In 1958 serious differences arose between the Board, which is charged by law with supervision of the local savings and loan association which it has chartered, and the officers and directors of the defendant Association concerning the manner in which the Association had been managed an operated. . . . [T]he Board proposed to take over direct control and management of the affairs of the Association through its own supervisory representative. The Association obtained an injunction against such intervention, but on appeal this court found the proposed action of the Board not to be subject to judicial interdiction, regardless of the merits of the controversy. *Greater Delaware Valley Federal Savings and Loan Association v. Federal Home Loan Bank Board*, 3 Cir., 1958, 262 F.2d 371. In the meantime, the Board made the charges of mismanagement the subject of an administrative proceeding with a view to the appointment of a conservator for the Association.

During the course of the above outlined efforts of the Board, the directors of the Association approved a plan for its conversion into a state chartered institution. The shareholders of the Association were notified of a special meeting to vote on the plan and proxies were solicited for use at that meeting. Neither the notice nor the proxy solicitation said anything about the existing controversy between the Board and the management of the

Association. By means of proxies thus obtained the proponents of conversion were able to poll a large majority vote at the special meeting in favor of the recommended conversion. Articles of conversion were then duly filed with the Department of State of the Commonwealth of Pennsylvania. Thereafter the state Department of Banking approved the conversion and issued a formal certificate of conversion.

This formal conversion was completed while the Board's administrative proceedings were pending and before they could eventuate in any suppression of management by representatives of the Board. Since this conversion the Association has claimed to be and has operated as a state agency. It has denied that it is any longer a federal agency and has refused to recognize any continuing authority of the Board over its activities. . . .

Unquestionably the United States, which incorporated Greater Delaware Valley Federal Savings and Loan Association, had exclusive authority to determine whether and how that corporation could surrender its federal charter and terminate its status and obligations as a federal savings and loan association.

. . . This Congress has undertaken to do in the very statute which provides for the chartering of federal savings and loan associations. Section 5(i) of the Home Owners' Loan Act, as amended, reads in part as follows: [The court quotes language of an earlier version of what became 12 U.S.C. § 1464(i)(3)(A)(i)-(ii).]

The first major contention of the Board is that under the above quoted statute a federal association cannot convert to the status of a Pennsylvania state agency without the approval of the Board. This conclusion is based upon the provision of Section 5(i) which in general terms imposes requirements reciprocally equivalent to the requirements of such State law for the conversion of a State-chartered institution into a Federal association. Therefore, it posits a requirement of Pennsylvania law that approval by the State Department of Banking is prerequisite to conversion of a state association to federal status. However, the Attorney General of Pennsylvania argues forcibly that there is no such requirement of state law. We find it unnecessary to decide this question because we are unable to agree with the Board's basic interpretation of the reciprocating clause of Section 5(i). That subsection lists seven numbered requirements for conversion from a federal to a state charter. The reciprocating clause appears in requirement "(2)" which, in all other respects, relates to the manner of obtaining membership approval of a proposed conversion. Specific essentials of a proper and effective vote for conversion are stated, and their enumeration is followed by the phrase, "and upon compliance with other requirements, reciprocally equivalent to the requirements of such State law for the conversion of a State-chartered institution. . . ." Thus, an analysis of the subject matter of the clause suggests that the mandated compliance with additional state requirements is, like all other specifications of the subsection, concerned only with the way in which membership approval of conversion shall be determined.

The meaning of Section 5(i) is further illuminated by the last paragraph of this subsection. That paragraph authorizes a second or alternative type of conversion, stipulating that "[i]n addition to the foregoing provision for conversion upon a vote of the members only any association chartered as a Federal savings and loan association, including any having outstanding shares held by the Secretary of the Treasury or Home Owners' Loan Corporation, may convert itself into a State institution upon an equitable basis, subject to approval, by regulations or otherwise, by the Federal Home Loan Bank Board and by the Federal Savings and Loan Insurance Corporation." This explicit contrasting of "conversion upon a vote of the members only" with conversion "upon an equitable basis, subject to approval . . . by the Federal Home Loan Bank Board" is in itself a persuasive indication that Congress did not intend that Board approval be a requirement of "conversion upon a vote of the members only".

But quite apart from the reciprocating clause of Section 5(i), it is argued that the pendency of charges of mismanagement and an administrative proceeding and aimed at superseding those in control of a federal savings and loan association preclude a conversion at that time from federal to state status without the consent of the Board. While it is arguable that such a prohibition is desirable, there is simply nothing in the statute, and not even a regulation of the Board, which declares or even suggests its existence. Moreover, as the court below pointed out, during the consideration of this legislation Congress was apprized of the likelihood that an association, displeased by the course of Board monition, would seek to escape federal supervision by acquiring a state charter. Expressing this fear, the then Chairman of the Board recommended that the bill be amended to enable the Board to prevent such conversion. . . . Moreover, during the committee consideration companion Senate bill, controversy between an association and the Federal supervisory agency was suggested as a legitimate reason for desiring to convert to state auspices. . . . This legislative history provides an affirmative reason for not recognizing a restriction which, even without this history, seems a gratuitous gloss on the statute. . . .

Notes and Comments 2.34. *FIRREA and federal-to-state conversions.* Under FIRREA, a federal savings association may convert into a state savings association or savings bank, organized under the laws of the state in which the principal office of the association is located, if the following conditions are met:

> (*i*) The state permits conversion of state savings associations or savings banks into federal savings associations.
>
> (*ii*) The conversion is approved by the requisite vote, in person or by proxy, of members or stockholders of the association in accordance with state law, but in no event by less than 51 percent of the votes cast at the members' or stockholders' meeting, and upon compliance with any other federal requirements equivalent to the requirements of state law for conversion of a state chartered institution into a federal savings association.
>
> (*iii*) Required notice of the meeting is given.[46]
>
> (*iv*) If the converted institution is mutual in form, on any dissolution after conversion the members or shareholders will share on basis in the assets of the association in exact proportion to there relative share or account credits. If the converted institution is stock in form, on any dissolution after conversion the stockholders will share on an equitable basis in the assets of the association.
>
> (*vi*) The conversion is effective on the date on which all provisions of the HOLA have been fully complied with, and upon the issuance of the new charter by the state in which the association is located.[47]

2.35. *GLBA and federal-to-state conversions.* Two provisions of the Gramm-Leach-Bliley Act (GLBA)[48] have altered the rules applicable to conversions of federal savings associations to state charters. Any federal savings association that converts its charter to a national or state bank charter after the enactment of the GLBA is permitted to retain the term "Federal" in its name, if it remains an insured depository institution. GLBA, § 723 (codified at 12 U.S.C. § 30(d)(1)). The GLBA also permits a federal savings association chartered prior to the date of the GLBA enactment to convert into one or more national or state banks,

46. *See id.* § 1464(i)(3)(A)(iii) (concerning notice requirements).

47. *Id.* § 1464(i)(3)(A)(i)-(vi).

48. Pub. L. No. 106-102, Nov. 12, 1999, 113 Stat. 1338 (1999) (codified at scattered sections of 12, 15, 16, 18 U.S.C.).

subject to the approval of the Comptroller or the appropriate state bank supervisor. GLBA, § 739 (codified at 12 U.S.C.A. § 1464(i)(5)). Each of the resulting banks may encompass one or more of the branches of the federal savings association in one or more states. *Id.* Each bank must meet all applicable financial, management, and capital requirements. 12 U.S.C. § 1464(i)(5)(A).

2.36. *Mutual-to-stock conversions.* The provisions with respect to savings association conversion of form have undergone repeated amendment. The following case excerpt provides some background.

Dougherty v. Carver Fed. Sav. Bank

112 F.3d 613 (2d Cir. 1997)

CARDAMONE, Circuit Judge.

[This case involved a federal securities law claim against the conversion of Carver Federal Savings Bank from the mutual to the stock form of ownership. For discussion of the relationship of federal rules against securities fraud and the regulation of depository institutions, see Note 7.5, *infra.*]

. . . The regulatory and legislative environment for [mutual-to-stock] conversions has varied over the years. Initially, all federal savings associations were in mutual form. When Congress first enacted the Home Owners' Loan Act of 1933 (HOLA), 12 U.S.C. § 1461 *et seq.*, permitting the formation of federal savings associations, it provided for only one form of charter–the mutual charter–and provided no mechanism for converting to stock form. This changed in 1948, when the legislature amended HOLA to permit federal mutual associations to convert to state stock associations. *See* [*Charter Fed. Savings & Loan Ass'n* v. *Office of Thrift Supervision*, 912 F.2d 1569, 1571 (11th Cir.1990)].

The initial experience with conversions raised troubling problems. In this initial period, the question of who owned the net worth that had been accumulated over years and how to dispose of it in a conversion to a stock corporation was not well regulated. There was great temptation to raid the billions of dollars in industry accumulation of net worth. In fact, an independent study commissioned by Congress revealed that in the majority of pre-1963 conversions, the group of insiders initiating the conversion appropriated "a large part" of the net worth. S. Rep. No. 93-902 (1974) (additional views of Sen. William Proxmire), *reprinted in* 1974 U.S.C.C.A.N. 6136, 6137. As a result a moratorium was placed on conversions in 1963.

A decade later, Congress began to lift the ban, which was completely eliminated in 1976. *See Charter Fed. Savings & Loan Ass'n*, 912 F.2d at 1571. Conversions resumed under a new set of comprehensive regulations adopted by the Federal Home Loan Bank Board. Initially, concerned with insider abuse, federal regulators were wary of conversions. As time went on these officials became increasingly attracted to the procedure as a means for shoring up the capital position of undercapitalized savings associations. This trend became more pronounced with the advent of the savings and loan crisis of the late 1970s and early 1980s. Faced with the prospect of widespread savings association failures, federal regulators loosened the conversion regulations to make it easier and more attractive for banks to take advantage of the procedure to raise capital. *See Conversions From Mutual to Stock Form*, 59 Fed.Reg. 22,725, 22,725-26 (1994) (to be codified at 12 C.F.R. pts. 563b & 575) (interim final rule with request for comments, May 3, 1994) (discussing evolution of regulatory environment) [hereafter *Proposed 1994 Regulations*].

In this environment, conversions became very popular. Over 300 federal savings institutions converted between 1990 and 1994, raising nearly $5 billion in the process, *see Mutual Depository Institution Conversion Protection Act of 1994: Hearings on S. 1801 Before the Senate Comm. on Banking, Housing and Urban Affairs*, 103 Cong. (1994) (statement of Jonathan L. Fiechter, Acting Director, Office of Thrift Supervision), and in the decade between 1984 and 1994, the number of savings associations in mutual form nationwide dropped by roughly 56 percent. *See Mutual-to-Stock Conversions of State Non-member Savings Banks*, 59 Fed.Reg. 30,357 (1994) (FDIC notice and request for comments) (noting decrease to 1,100 mutual associations in 1994 from more than 2,500 in 1984).

Eventually, Congress passed the Financial Institutions Reform, Recovery, and Enforcement Act of 1989 (FIRREA), Pub.L. No. 101-73, 103 Stat. 183 (1989), which restructured the regulation of the savings association industry by, inter alia, abolishing the Federal Home Loan Bank Board (Bank Board) and vesting many of its functions in the newly-created Office of Thrift Supervision, see FIRREA § 301 (establishing OTS), § 401 (abolishing Bank Board). With time, the thrift undercapitalization problem abated and the industry returned to solvency. With the crisis past, the OTS, concerned anew with insider abuses, tightened its conversion procedures through interim final rules issued in May 1994, *see Proposed 1994 Regulations*, *supra*, 59 Fed.Reg. at 22,725. Those rules were adopted in final form in November 1994. *See Conversions from Mutual to Stock Form*, 59 Fed.Reg. 61,247 (1994) (to be codified at 12 C.F.R. pts. 563b & 575) (final rule, Nov. 30, 1994). ...

Chapter 3

Branch Banking

1. Introduction

The establishment of a branch can be another method of entry for depository institutions; *i.e.*, a means by which an institution can enter another geographic segment of the market. The establishment of a branch is subject to an approval process not unlike the chartering process.

In branching, a depository institution establishes another business office with no separate corporate existence. This is distinguished from "chain banking" and "group banking." Chain banking exists when separate corporate entities that operate as banks are interrelated through common stock control, interlocking directorates,[1] or other similar control devices of a more or less informal nature. The members of the chain may appear to function much like branches operate in relation to a principal office. Functional equivalence notwithstanding, if the members of the chain are in fact independently structured and operated, then they will not be subjected to the legal principles (and limitations) which apply to branch banking.[2] However, if the independence of the chain members is questionable, an analysis akin to "piercing the corporate veil" may be applied to bring the system under the restrictions on branch banking.[3]

Group banking systems also seek to take advantage of a functional equivalence with branch banking while avoiding the restrictions that apply to the branching. Group banking differs from chain banking in that the relationship of control among the group members arises from their corporate structure. Independently chartered banks are controlled, directly or indirectly, by one corporate entity that holds all, or a controlling share of, the stock of each bank in the group. Typically, the controlling entity will be a corporation that acts as a holding company for the group. Group banking run the same risk as chain banking that it may be considered to be an impermissible evasion of branch banking restrictions.[4] In addition, states

---

1. There are statutory limitations on management interlocks between otherwise unaffiliated depository institutions. *See* 12 U.S.C. §§ 3201 *et seq.* (federal Depository Institutions Management Interlocks Act (DIMIA)). *See generally* 2 MICHAEL P. MALLOY, BANKING LAW AND REGULATION § 4.02[A][2] (2d ed., 2011) (discussing DIMIA).

2. *See generally National State Bank, Elizabeth, N.J. v. Howell*, 49 N.J. 330 (1967).

3. *Cf. Bank of North America v. State Banking Board*, 468 S.W.2d 529 (Tex. 1971).

4. *Cf. Commercial Nat'l Bank of Little Rock v. Board of Governors*, 451 F.2d 86 (8th Cir. 1971).

may explicitly prohibit bank holding companies.[5]

This chapter focuses on branch banking. In any given state, both state-chartered and federally chartered depository institutions generally have the power to branch, if either type has it. Where a state statute prohibits a state *bank* from branching, then a national bank located in that state is also prohibited from branching.[6]

Certain state banks will also be subject to the conditions and restrictions on branching that apply to national banks. For example, section 9 of the Federal Reserve Act, as amended, 12 U.S.C. § 321, provides for branching by state member banks to the same extent permissible to national banks. Similarly, 12 U.S.C. § 1828(d) subjects state nonmember insured banks to prior approval by the FDIC before a branch bank can be established. The FDIC's approval is based upon the same factors that the FDIC considers in deciding whether or not to insure a principal office.[7]

2. Intrastate Branching by National Banks

Because the rules concerning intrastate branching by national banks are controlled by reference over to state law, interpretive problems arise concerning the way in which reference over is supposed to operate. These problems include: (*i*) the status of "grandfathered" branches under 12 U.S.C. § 36(a); (*ii*) the scope of the Comptroller's discretion in construing the limitations contained in state statutory provisions concerning branching; (*iii*) the scope of the Comptroller's discretion in construing and applying the definition of "branch" in 12 U.S.C. § 36; and, (*iv*) more specifically, the application of the definition to newer (*i.e.*, post-1927) technologies.

a. "Grandfathered" Branches

Cheshire Nat. Bank v. Smith

427 F.Supp. 277 (D.N.H. 1977)

BOWNES, District Judge.

The plaintiffs, Cheshire National Bank of Keene and Connecticut River National Bank of Charlestown, seek to overturn the Comptroller's approval of an application by the Keene National Bank (Keene) of Keene to relocate its Walpole, New Hampshire, agency from Westminster Street to Main Street. They also challenge an alleged approval by the Comptroller of an expansion of services by Keene.

The issue is whether the Comptroller was correct in finding that Keene's agency in Walpole is a branch and that it qualified under the "grandfather clause" of 12 U.S.C. § 36(a) (The McFadden Act). . . .

Keene was chartered as a national association in 1865 and has continuously conducted banking business in Keene ever since. Despite the fact that national associations were permitted to have offices in only one location, Keene's Board of Directors authorized one Josiah G. Bellows to hold $500 in Walpole for the purpose of cashing checks, making loans, discounting notes, and accepting loan payments as of January 16, 1872. From that time, with

5. *See Whitney National Bank in Jefferson Parish v. James*, 189 So.2d 430 (La. 1966).

6. 12 U.S.C. § 36(c).

7. *See* 12 U.S.C. §§ 1816, 1828(d).

the possible exception of a few months in 1927, Keene employed an agent in Walpole in a similar capacity. From 1898 until May of 1975, this business was conducted at the offices of the Savings Bank of Walpole (Walpole) by an employee paid in part by Walpole and in part by Keene.

Until recently, savings banks in New Hampshire could not offer demand deposit accounts (checking accounts) to their customers while commercial banks, including national associations, could. The arrangement between Keene and Walpole gave the customers of Keene an opportunity to do business with that institution without travelling the seventeen miles from Walpole to Keene and allowed customers of Walpole to have checking accounts conveniently serviced in the same office as was the rest of their business. This mutual convenience provided the basis for a very comfortable relationship between the two banks until 1974 when savings banks in New Hampshire and Massachusetts were granted authority to offer demand deposit accounts called Negotiable Order of Withdrawal (NOW) accounts. . . .

With the advent of NOW accounts in the early 1970's and their express legalization in 1974, Walpole was able to duplicate the checking services offered by Keene. Not surprisingly, Walpole evicted Keene from its premises in May of 1975. By letter of May 16, 1975, Keene notified the Comptroller that it was about to be evicted from Walpole's premises and requested permission to relocate. The Comptroller, by letter dated May 21, 1975, granted Keene temporary permission to relocate pending "the full administrative consideration . . . provided by 12 C.F.R. Part 5. . . ."

The statutory requirements for national banking associations to maintain a branch or branches are at 12 U.S.C. § 36, the codification of the McFadden Act. . . .

The McFadden Act was passed in 1927, according to its chief sponsor, Congressman McFadden, "to restore as nearly as possible the equilibrium between state and national banks within the Federal Reserve System." Cong. Rec., June 7, 1924, p. 1296 ff. Prior to the enactment of this law, several states allowed branch banking for state chartered institutions. National banks, in order to compete in those jurisdictions, were converting from their federal charters to state charters. The McFadden Act allowed national banks to establish branch offices in jurisdictions which permitted it for their own institutions under the same terms and conditions. . . .

One of the requirements of 12 U.S.C. § 36(a) is that a branch to be maintained under the grandfather clause, must have been "continuously . . . operated . . . for a period of more than twenty-five years immediately preceding . . ." February 25, 1927. Another requirement is that the institution wishing to maintain a branch under this authority can have only one branch that qualifies. 12 U.S.C. § 36(a). The Comptroller found that both of these conditions were satisfied. The plaintiffs dispute his findings. This first issue is clearly one of fact, and the Comptroller must be sustained if there is any rational basis for his conclusion. . . .

The second issue is whether the agency at Walpole constituted a branch. The precise practice of Keene's agent in Walpole, which is important in determining whether the Walpole institution operated as a branch, are set out in Keene's Exhibit A to the Comptroller's hearing, a 1954 letter to the Chief National Bank Examiner. . . . It says that there was no sign posted which indicated the existence of the agency, but that the agent kept [Keene] deposit slips at Walpole. Customers of Keene could make deposits at Walpole. ...

According to the testimony of Elliot Snow, the President of Keene, at the Comptroller's hearing on July 9, 1975, new accounts were opened, loans were made, collected and cancelled, and checks drawn on Keene were paid. . . .

Plaintiffs . . . contend that there is a "wide difference" between the "right to establish branch banks at which a general banking business is carried on" and "the mere appointment of agents to receive and collect money and forward it to the bank." . . .

Indeed, were I to look to the law before 1927, I might well have found that this "agency" was not a branch. . . . But, the agency is within the definition of a branch contained at 12 U.S.C. § 36(f) since 1927 when the McFadden Act was passed. That language, which defines a branch, has remained the same since it was passed. The language received little judicial attention at first as it was all most banks could do to hold on to their main offices during the years of the great depression. Recently, however, with the emergence of Electronic Funds Transfer Systems and Bank Holding Companies, the amount of litigation surrounding the definition of a branch bank has become multitudinous.

Notes and Comments 3.1. If national banks lacked authority prior to the McFadden Act to establish branches, how could Keene's Walpole operation have been a branch? Indeed, why should section 36 contain a grandfathering provision at all, if as a matter of law national banks could not have possessed any branches to grandfather in 1927?

3.2. Assuming that there could have been national bank "branches" to grandfather in 1927, why would Congress do so? If federal policy as to intrastate branching by national banks is as specified in section 36(c), what is the justification of grandfathering "branches" that do not comply with that federal policy?

b. Construction of State Law Provisions

Notes and Comments 3.3. *Scope of the "reference over" to state law.* In light of the cases excerpted below, how far is the Comptroller tied to the specific details of state statutory limitations on branching in determining the "whether" "where" and "how" for national bank branching?

First Nat'l Bank of Logan v. Walker Bank & Trust Co.

385 U.S. 252 (1966)

Mr. Justice CLARK delivered the opinion of the Court.

These cases involve the construction of those portions of the National Bank Act, 44 Stat. 1228, 12 U.S.C. § 36(c), which authorize a national banking association, with the approval of the Comptroller of the Currency, to establish and operate new branches within the limits of the municipality in which the bank is located, if such operation is "at the time expressly authorized to State banks by the law of the State in question." Two national banks with their main banking house in Logan and Ogden, Utah, respectively, seek to open branches in those municipalities. The Utah statute prohibits Utah banks, with certain exceptions not here relevant, from establishing branches except by taking over an existing bank which has been in operation for not less than five years. Utah Code Ann., Tit. 7, c. 3, § 6 (1965 Supp.). In No. 51, *First National Bank of Logan v. Walker Bank Trust Co.*, the petitioner seeks to establish a new branch in Logan, where its principal banking house is located, without taking over an established bank. The District Court approved its doing so but the Court of Appeals reversed. . . . In No. 73, *First Security Bank of Utah, N.A. v. Commercial Security Bank*, and No. 88, *Saxon v. Commercial Security Bank*, First Security seeks to establish a new branch in Ogden, in which its home office is situated, without taking over an established bank. The District Court held that state law must be complied with, . . . and the Court of Appeals affirmed. . . . We affirm the judgments. . . .

In No. 51, the petitioner maintains its principal banking house in Logan, Utah, which is a second class city under Utah law (Utah Code Ann., Tit. 10, c. 1, § 1 (1953, as amended)), and is therefore subject to § 7-3- 6 of the Utah Code, *supra*. It applied to the Comptroller of the Currency for a certificate to establish an "inside" branch office in Logan. At the time of the application there were no other banks with their main banking office in Logan. However, there were two branches of banks whose home offices were situated outside of Logan, one of which belonged to respondent, Walker Bank & Trust Co., whose home office was located in Salt Lake City. After a hearing, the Comptroller ordered the certificate issued. The respondent subsequently filed this suit seeking a declaratory judgment and injunctive relief against the Comptroller and First National claiming the action of the Comptroller to be void since the proposed branch was not taking over an established bank in Logan, as required by Utah law. The District Court dismissed the complaint. It found "express authority" under Utah law for state banks to establish branch offices in Logan, relying on the general authority of the statute and holding that the subsequent conditions, such as the acquisition of another bank, did not "change the 'express authority' into a lack of authority on the part of State banks or a lack of a statutory expression of such authority, and [did] not add to the Federal statute a requirement that compliance be made by National banks with all State conditions." . . . The Court of Appeals reversed, holding that the Congress in enacting § 36(c)(1) acceded to state law and created "a competitive equality between state and national banks." Finding that the trial court's interpretation was to the contrary, it declared "the proper approach is for the Comptroller to look at all the State law on branch banking not just part of it." . . .

In Nos. 73 and 88, the First Security Bank of Utah, a national bank, applied for a certificate from the Comptroller to establish a branch in Ogden, where it maintained its principal banking house. Its proposal was to open a new branch and not to take over an existing bank in Ogden. Under Utah law, Ogden is also a second class city and the "take over" provision of § 7-3-6, *supra*, was therefore applicable. Two other banks have their main offices in Ogden. After the Comptroller approved the issuance of the certificate, respondent filed suit in the District Court of the United States for the District of Columbia asking for injunctive and other relief. The District Court imposed all of the restrictions of § 7-3-6 of Utah law on the establishment of national banks and the Court of Appeals for the District of Columbia Circuit affirmed. . . .

It appears clear from . . . the legislative history of § 36(c)(1) and (2) that Congress intended to place national and state banks on a basis of "competitive equality" insofar as branch banking was concerned. Both sponsors of the applicable banking Acts, Representative McFadden and Senator Glass, so characterized the legislation. It is not for us to so construe the Acts as to frustrate this clearcut purpose so forcefully expressed by both friend and foe of the legislation at the time of its adoption. To us it appears beyond question that the Congress was continuing its policy of equalization first adopted in the National Bank Act of 1864. . . .

The Comptroller argues that Utah's statute "expressly authorizes" state banks to have branches in their home municipalities. He maintains that the restriction, in the subsequent paragraph of the statute limiting branching solely to the taking over of an existing bank, is not applicable to national banks. It is a strange argument that permits one to pick and choose what portion of the law binds him. Indeed, it would fly in the face of the legislative history not to hold that national branch banking is limited to those states the laws of which permit it, and even there "only to the extent that the State laws permit branch banking." Utah clearly permits it "only to the extent" that the proposed branch takes over an existing bank.

The Comptroller also contends that the Act supersedes state law only as to "whether" and "where" branches may be located and not the "method" by which this is effected. We believe that where a State allows branching only by taking over an existing bank, it expresses as much "whether" and "where" a branch may be located as does a prohibition or a limitation to the home office municipality. As to the restriction being a "method," we have concluded that since it is part and parcel of Utah's policy, it was absorbed by the provisions of §§ 36(c)(1) and (2), regardless of the tag placed upon it.

Hempstead Bank v. Smith

540 F.2d 57 (2d Cir. 1976)

LUMBARD, Circuit Judge.

Hempstead Bank, a New York state-chartered commercial bank with branches in Nassau and Suffolk Counties, brought his action in the Southern District to set aside as arbitrary and capricious the Comptroller of the Currency's approval of the establishment of a branch of Chase Manhattan Bank, a national bank, in Locust Valley, New York. The district court held that there was an adequate factual basis in the administrative record to support the Comptroller's decision and that it had been made in accordance with New York law that was incorporated by reference into federal law. We find a substantial likelihood that the Comptroller failed to consider the relevant New York law in approving the new branch.We therefore vacate the judgment of the district court with instructions to remand to the Comptroller for further findings.

On August 6, 1974, Chase filed its application for permission to establish a branch banking office in Locust Valley. At the time the application was submitted, the area to be serviced by the branch contained 10,150 persons comprising 2200 families with an average annual income of approximately $20,000. Little room remains in the area for further residential development. Chase proposed to locate its branch at a site adjacent to a shopping center in Locust Valley; the branch would thereby serve the same community currently serviced by appellant, the Nassau Trust Company, and a branch of the Prudential Savings Bank of Manhattan.

Hempstead Bank and the Nassau Trust Company filed with the Office of the Comptroller of the Currency protests opposing Chase's application. Hempstead argued that although the average family income of the area was relatively high, projected population growth was minimal. Hempstead contended with the needs of the community were sufficiently served by existing bank branches, the financial condition of which would be impaired by a drain of funds to the new Chase branch. It pointed out that deposits and loans in its own offices had either remained relatively stable or had diminished since 1970. The Regional Administrator of National Banks denied as untimely the Nassau Trust Company's request for a hearing on the matter, but officers of the competing banks were interviewed with respect to the propriety of approving Chase's application.

Unanimous recommendation to approve the application was made to the Comptroller by the Deputy Comptroller, the Chief National Bank Examiner, the Director of the Bank Organization Division, and the Regional Administrator. The recommendation was based on findings that, although future growth in the area would likely be minimal, (1) establishment of the branch would add a competitive factor to the area; (2) the branch would enable Chase to extend its facilities into an area that it did not currently serve; and (3) the area was sufficiently affluent to support the branch without adversely affecting conditions. The Comptroller approved Chase's application on October 10, 1974, without making additional findings.

Hempstead thereafter instituted this action to have the Comptroller's approval declared null and void as having been made in contravention of law. On February 4, 1976, the district court after reviewing the administrative record upon which the Comptroller based his action, *Camp v. Pitts*, 411 U.S. 138, 142 (1973), held that the Comptroller had complied with the applicable law and that the record supported his decision. The district judge granted summary judgment for the Comptroller and this appeal by Hempstead followed.

Federal law provides that a national bank, such as Chase, may establish branches only under the conditions permitted to state-chartered banks by the law of the state in which it is located. 12 U.S.C. § 36(c). *See First National Bank of Logan v. Walker Bank & Trust Co.*, 385 U.S. 252 (1966). The purpose of incorporating state standards into federal law is to prevent an institution licensed by one governmental entity from expanding into a geographical area forbidden to competing banks licensed by another entity and thereby to maintain competitive equality between state-chartered and federal-chartered banks. *See First National Bank of Logan v. Walker Bank & Trust Co., supra*, 385 U.S. at 258-61. To effectuate this purpose, courts have consistently held that in determining whether to approve branch applications from national banks, the Comptroller not only must consider whether the relevant state allows branching in some form, but must also, in each case, make such specific findings as are required by state law. . . .

In the present case, the Comptroller was required to determine the validity of Chase's application in accordance with the law of New York, which provides that a branch office may be authorized if it is found "upon investigation that the public convenience and advantage will be promoted by the opening of such branch office. . . ." N.Y. Banking Law § 29 (McKinney 1971). Although this language is general and leaves ample room for discretion, presumably it requires that a branch should be established in an area only if the banking structure in the community to be serviced is not adversely affected and that the public will thereby be better served. The administrative record before us allows for substantial doubt whether this criterion was properly considered by the Comptroller.

. . . Nor is the fact that the new branch would add a competitive factor to the are sufficient to show that the Comptroller has properly evaluated "the public convenience and advantage" as that phrase is used in § 29. While the Comptroller need not make explicit findings of fact, the record may not be so paltry and conclusory as to frustrate effective judicial review. 411 U.S. at 142-43. The tautological statement that a new branch would add to competition, is necessary or would promote the public interest, provides no basis for judicial analysis of the reasonableness of the Comptroller's approval of the application. On remand, reliance on competition becomes all the more doubtful, as the New York legislature has recently enacted a law permitting savings banks such as Prudential, which has a branch in the area, to offer checking accounts, a factor that may affect competition in Locust Valley without the addition of another bank branch. *See* 1976 Laws of New York, 199th Session Ch. 225. . . .

An additional rationale for granting Chase's application appears to have been the belief that the community to be serviced was sufficiently affluent to support the proposed branch "without causing greatly adverse conditions." The quoted phrase suggests that the Comptroller's staff was aware that some drain of funds from existing banks to a new branch would occur. Thorough analysis of that possibility would seem to have been essential to a proper determination of whether Chase's presence in Locust Valley would promote the public advantage. The record, however, reveals that the staff fluctuated in its concern over this problem. The National Bank Examiner, in a report also signed by the Regional Administrator, found that the complaints of Hempstead and Nassau that their deposits had remained stable or declined in recent years, and thus that they could not afford additional cash drain, "may have some merit." Nevertheless, in a report signed only by the Regional Administrator, these same objections were summarily dismissed as having "little merit." Despite the existence of this apparent inconsistency, there does not appear to have been any sort of "investigation," required by § 29, to resolve the complaints of the protesting banks and reconcile them with the "public advantage."

The absence of any express findings of public convenience and advantage and our inability to discover consideration of that criterion implicit in the record strongly suggest that the Comptroller's action was not taken "in accordance with law." 5 U.S.C. § 706(2)(A). We conclude, therefore, that we must remand this case so that the Comptroller can provide adequate explanation of his investigation of the applicant's satisfaction of New York's branching requirements.

First Union Bank & Trust Co. v. Heimann

600 F.2d 91 (7th Cir. 1979)

PELL, Circuit Judge.

The plaintiff-appellant, First Union Bank of Winamac, Indiana, (Winamac Bank) brought this action in the district court for declaratory and injunctive relief, seeking to have set aside an order by the defendant Comptroller of the Currency. The order at issue approved the establishment of a branch bank by the defendant First National Bank of Monterey (Monterey Bank) on the east side of U.S. Highway 35 north of Winamac, Indiana. The district court entered summary judgment in favor of the defendants, and the plaintiff Winamac Bank appeals. To decide this case we must determine whether the Comptroller's decision that the proposed site of the branch facility was a "town" within the meaning of the Indiana branch banking law, Ind. Code § 28-1-17, was arbitrary, capricious, an abuse of discretion, or otherwise not in accordance with the law. . . .

The standard applicable to this case is set by Indiana law, which permits banks to open a branch if the branch is within the same county where the bank maintains its principal office, if the branch is in a city or town, and no other bank is located in the city or town.[2] Only the requirement that the branch be located in a "city" or "town" is at issue here. The Comptroller determined that the proposed site of the Monterey Bank branch was a "town." The plaintiff argues vigorously that this determination is contrary to Indiana law.

The proposed site of the Monterey Bank branch is approximately one-eighth mile north of the corporate boundaries of Winamac, Indiana, on the east side of U.S. Highway 35.[3] Also on the east side of the highway, approximately one-quarter mile to the north of the site, is a nursery or garden center. This is the closest business to the proposed branch that is not within the corporate limits of Winamac.[5] A veterinary clinic is located approximately

---

2. This standard appears in Ind. Code § 28-1-17-1 which provides in pertinent part:

> [A]ny bank or trust company may open or establish a branch bank in any city or town within the limits of the county in which the principal office of such bank or trust company is located, if there is no bank or trust company located in such city or town.

3. The record shows that Winamac, Indiana has a population of approximately 2500, approximately 980 residences, over 35 retail stores, 4 schools, 8 churches and some industry. It also has a police department, a fire department, and hospital.

5. The Comptroller's opinion mentions another business, the "Swirly Top" drive-in restaurant, which is also on the east side of U.S. 35, directly to the south of the branch site. Except for a portion of its lot, however, this establishment lies within the corporate boundaries of Winamac, and cannot be considered as a business establishment in the area containing the branch site for purposes

one-quarter mile to the north of the nursery and is also on the east side of U.S. 35. On the west side of U.S. 35, approximately one-half mile to the north of the site, is a farm supply store. Slightly to the north of the supply store on the west side of the highway is a cattle lot. In the area along U.S. 35 north of the corporate boundaries of Winamac, these are they only business establishments within one-half mile of the site.

Also along the highway in the vicinity of the branch site are twenty-five houses with a population of approximately thirty-eight people, eight of whom are minors.[7] The area surrounding the site is not incorporated, nor does it have a name.

We begin our discussion by noting that judicial review of the Comptroller's decision is governed by the APA, 5 U.S.C. § 706(2)(A). We must determine whether the Comptroller's decision was "arbitrary, capricious, an abuse of discretion, or otherwise not in accordance with [the] law." *Camp v. Pitts*, 411 U.S. 138, 142 (1973). We must not set aside the Comptroller's determination if it has a rational basis in the record. *Citizens To Preserve Overton Park v. Volpe*, 401 U.S. 402, 419-20 (1971). The history of these proceedings, however, is somewhat unusual, and the course of the proceedings affects our review. After Winamac Bank brought this action for review of the Comptroller's decision, the district court remanded the case to the agency with directions to reopen the administrative record on the issue whether the proposed branch would be located in a "town" within the meaning of the Indiana statute and to make a written record of the Comptroller's conclusions and the legal basis for those conclusions. This procedure was the proper one for the court to follow when the Comptroller's explanation of its action is inadequate for judicial review. *Camp v. Pitts*, 411 U.S. 138, 143 (1973); *Hempstead Bank v. Smith*, 540 F.2d 57, 58 (2d Cir. 1976); *Central Bank v. Smith*, 532 F.2d 37, 40 (7th Cir. 1976). After consideration of written supplementary materials of the parties, the Comptroller issued a written opinion, explaining why the proposed site satisfied the "town" requirement of Indiana law.[8] Although our review of the

---

of determining whether the area is a town separate from Winamac. According to the local building inspector, the "Swirly Top" building lies entirely within the Winamac corporate boundaries.

7. The plaintiff argues that the area contains 20 houses. We find it virtually impossible to determine from the enlarged map submitted to this court by the Comptroller how the Comptroller reached the figure of 25 residences. We shall assume arguendo, that this finding has support in the record, because the difference between 20 and 25 houses is not material to the outcome of this case. The defendants also argued below that 38 is a "patently absurd" population figure for 25 residences. Other than this conclusory remark, however, no evidence was offered to show a significantly larger population.

8. The portion of the Comptroller's opinion dealing directly with the proposed site said:

> Although there is some dispute as to the exact distance of First National's proposed branch from the boundary of the incorporated town of Winamac, both First National and First Union agree that the proposed office will be located outside the incorporated municipality. At the time of First National's application, there were twenty residences in the vicinity of the proposed branch site. Supplemental information indicates that there are now twenty-five residences within one-half mile of that site. These form a linear cluster along the west side of U.S. Highway 35 north of the corporate limits of Winamac.
>
> In addition to the residential concentration, there are at least four commercial establishments within the linear cluster: a veterinarian, a garden center, a farm supplier, and a stockyard. A fifth commercial establishment apparently straddles the corporate line so that the lot upon which it is situated lies partly within and partly without the corporate boundary.
>
> The supplemental information provided by First National and First Union reveals a dispute as to future development in the area. First National has supplied materials which indicate that the owner of a tract of land along U.S. Highway 35 is in the process of developing his property and has made initial contact with several enterprises in this regard. The

Comptroller's decision would be impossible without it, the explanation before us is to some extent a post hoc rationalization, having been prepared during the course of the litigation, and must be viewed critically. *Citizens to Preserve Overton Park v. Volpe*, 401 U.S. 402, 420 (1971).[9]

We shall now examine the Comptroller's decision with that caveat in mind. The Comptroller's opinion properly considers the three cases in which the definition of "town" under the Indiana branch law is discussed, *First National Bank of Crown Point v. Camp*, 463 F.2d 595 (7th Cir. 1972); *Pendleton Banking Co. v. Department of Financial Institutions*, 355 N.E.2d 873 (Ind. App. 1976).

In *Pendleton*, the Indiana Supreme Court affirmed the determination by the Indiana Department of Financial Institutions that Huntsville, Indiana, was a town, emphasizing that Huntsville had several businesses and a rapidly growing population of 250 or more. In *Pendleton* the court described a town for purposes of the Indiana branch bank law as "a compact area having a number of persons living in close proximity to one another with some degree of business being transacted within the area." 274 N.E.2d at 708.

This definition of the word "town" was repeated by this court in *First National Bank of Crown Point v. Camp*, 463 F.2d 595, 597 n.4 (7th Cir. 1972). In *Crown Point* this court affirmed the Comptroller's determination that an area along a highway containing two or three houses, a retail complex, a saddle club, a veterinarian, and a church was a town for branch banking purposes, although there was an industrial complex one mile to the east, a housing development and restaurant 1.1 miles to the northwest, and a shopping center and mobile home park 1.1 miles to the south.

On the basis of these decisions the Comptroller properly observed that the question whether a site is in a town is for case-by-case determination. Furthermore, the Comptroller properly rejected the notion that "there is a fixed population or number of commercial enterprises which establish minimum requirements for the existence of a 'town.'" Even under this flexible standard, however, the record in this case supplies no rational basis for the Comptroller's conclusion that the site of this branch is in a town within the meaning of the Indiana branch banking law. The decision of the Comptroller must therefore be set aside.

The Indiana branch banking statute uses "town" in its ordinary sense. Ind. Code § 1-1-4-1, First; *Pendleton, supra*. The word "town" denotes an area which serves to some extent as a hub for surrounding communities, that is, a population and commercial center. Thus, it need not be incorporated or have a name, *id.*, but it at least should have a separate

---

materials furnished by First Union indicate that, at this time, there are no definite plans or commitments on the part of any of these enterprises to locate in the area and that the development plans are, at best, in their initial stages. Assuming that the developer's plans ultimately reach fruition, the linear concentration along U.S. Highway 35 will include a bowling alley, Pizza Hut, beauty shop, and home improvement store. As of the filing of the supplemental information, however, no building permits or zoning variances permitting this development had been issued.

(Footnotes omitted).

The opinion also contains a discussion of the relevant cases which we have not quoted here.

9. The plaintiff argues that participation of agency litigation counsel in the Comptroller's decision on remand denied it an impartial arbiter and therefore constitutes arbitrary action. We disagree. The plaintiff was not entitled to the protection inherent in formal adjudicatory proceedings. Furthermore, we read the passage from *Overton Park* cited in the text, *supra*, as an anticipation of this argument, and conclude that participation by agency litigation counsel in the remand proceedings merely should result in critical examination by the reviewing court, but certainly does not in itself require reversal.

identity. From its use of this term, it is apparent that the Indiana legislature intended to impose a general minimum standard for the type of community that it believed could support a branch facility. This qualitative definition of a town as a center of population and commerce sets the limits on what courts have called a "town," not raw numbers of businesses and people. Furthermore, in restricting branches to towns where another bank is not already located, the legislature has expressed opposition to the use of branch banks as a means of competition:

> The policy which seems to underline the Indiana statute is that creation of a branch bank is desirable or justifiable as a means of establishing a new local banking facility in a municipality not already so served, but not desirable or justifiable as a means of promoting competition in a municipality where one or more banks are already located.

Marion National Bank v. Van Buren Bank, 418 F.2d 121, 124 (7th Cir. 1969). We must guard against a definition of "town" that would subvert these policies.

The cases cited by the Comptroller for the applicable standard incorporate these qualitative elements of the definition of "town." . . .

In contrast, the record before the Comptroller contains no basis for the conclusion that the area in question has an identity separate from Winamac or that it serves as a commercial or population center. In fact the record in this case compels the conclusion that placement of the branch at the proposed site would subvert the purpose of the Indiana statute, which would forbid location of the branch in Winamac. We cannot say that twenty-five residences would never be adequate to constitute a town. The area at issue here, however, has only four businesses, all of which specialize in serving agricultural needs. The area does not contain one establishment to serve the daily needs of the general population in the immediate area, such as a grocery store, a gas station, a drug store, a post office, a courthouse, a hospital, or an industrial or shopping center employing a number of area residents. . . .

To conclude on the basis of this record that the site of this branch was a "town" with an identity separate from Winamac, the Comptroller had to ignore the common sense meaning of the word. It is impossible for us to believe that the Indiana legislature intended the term to be defined in the disjointed manner of the Comptroller's opinion:

> It is clear, therefore, that a "town" is a single compact area, regardless of proximity to an incorporated municipality, having a number of persons living in close proximity to one another in something more than three houses, with some degree of business being transacted within the area, and such "town" need not resemble any other "town" with respect to population or commercial activity. In addition, one many look to the future and take account proposed developments, both commercial and residential, when determining whether a particular area is a "town."

The Comptroller's opinion merely incorporated the facts of the cases decided under the Indiana statute, failing to recognize that the legislature had any purpose whatsoever in inserting the word "town." As a result, the term, as applied by the Comptroller, is virtually meaningless.

Notes and Comments 3.4. Would the Comptroller be bound to follow a state law provision which stated: "No bank shall establish or operate any branch in any city or town in which its principal place of business is located except by acquiring an existing bank, trust company or national banking association in such city or town"? Could he, despite this state law provision, authorize a national bank to acquire the existing branches of another national bank in exchange for its existing branches? *See State ex rel. Edward v. Heimann*, 633 F.2d 886 (9th Cir. 1980). Section 36(c) speaks in terms of authorizing the establishment and operation of "new branches," to the extent state banks are so authorized by state statute. Is this authorization sufficient to permit an *exchange* of existing branches? *See id.* at 889-890, arguing that the term "new" can be interpreted to mean "new to the bank," and concluding:

> We find that the strongest argument for interpreting the statute to include acquisition of another bank's branches is to implement the congressional intent to foster competitive equality between national and state banks. . . . If state banks are able to exchange branches under state banking law, federal banks should not be prevented from exchanging branches. We find therefore that the district court correctly determined that section 36(c) applies to the proposed bank exchanges.

3.5. Do competing banks in the area where a proposed national bank branch is to be established have standing to object to the branch application? In considering such applications, should the Comptroller give notice to competing banks? *See Community Bank of Washtenaw v. Smith*, 378 F.Supp. 235 (E.D.Mich. 1974) (failure to notify not a denial of due process).

3.6. Under the cases excerpted above, would the Comptroller be required to determine whether a proposed national bank branch would meet a "solvency of the branch" test under state law, or could the Comptroller confine his determination to capital requirements of federal law? *See First Citizens Bank & Trust Co. v. Camp*, 409 F.2d 1086 (5th Cir. 1969).

3.7. State A prohibits the establishment of any state bank branch in the same village where the branch of another state bank already exists. Last National Bank would like to establish a branch, in an unincorporated area within State *A*, within a mile of a branch of *A State Bank*. The Comptroller determines that the area surrounding the proposed branch site, consisting of 150 homes and a population of 650 persons, and including a church, a service station, a grocery store, and a Swirly Top drive-in, is a "village." He is therefore inclined to approve the application. Would you advise him to do so? *See American Bank & Trust Co. v. Saxon*, 373 F.2d 283 (6th Cir. 1967); *Peoples Bank of Trenton v. Saxon*, 373 F.2d 185 (6th Cir. 1967); *Security Bank v. Saxon*, 298 F. Supp. 991 (E.D.Mich. 1968). Would it make a difference to the outcome if the state banking commissioner had already determined that the area *was* a village? *Cf. Community Bank of Sullivan County v. First Nat. Bank of Jeffersonville*, 125 F.Supp.2d 659 (S.D.N.Y. 2000) (upholding Comptroller's decision).

3.8. Assume State *B* has no explicit provisions for branching of state-chartered commercial banks. However, State *B*'s savings association law allows for branching. Can the Comptroller approve a branch application submitted by a national bank in State *B*? *See Department of Banking v. Clarke*, 809 F.2d 266 (5th Cir.), *cert. denied*, 483 U.S. 1010 (1987).

3.9. State *C* does not permit branching in any town in which the "home office" of another state bank is located. Premier National Bank would like to establish a branch in Homeville, which is the location of Home State Bank. Premier is currently located in Hearthville, some miles east of Homeville. Should the Comptroller approve Premier's branch application? Could the Comptroller achieve the same result by applying 12 U.S.C. §§ 30 and 36? *See Ramapo Bank v. Camp*, 425 F.2d 333 (3rd Cir. 1970), *cert. denied*, 400 U.S. 828.

c. Definition of "Branch"

First Nat'l Bank in Plant City v. Dickinson

396 U.S. 122 (1969)

Mr. Chief Justice BURGER delivered the opinion of the Court.

In these cases we are called upon to construe § 7 of the McFadden Act of 1927, 44 Stat. 1228, as amended, 12 U.S.C. § 36, as it relates to the definition of a branch bank for the purpose of determining the scope of branch banking available to a national bank in a State that prohibits branches for state banks. [The opinion quotes 12 U.S.C. § 36(f), since 1994 recodified as § 36(j).]

Florida prohibits all branch banking by state chartered banks; by statute a Florida bank may "have only one place of doing business," and all the business of the bank is to be carried on at that place "and not elsewhere." The issue must be resolved by determining what constitutes a "branch" or "additional office"; there is a threshold question of the extent to which this is governed by federal law.

The First National Bank in Plant City, Florida, is a national banking association organized and operated pursuant to the National Bank Act, 12 U.S.C. § 21 *et seq.*; it sought and received from the United States Comptroller of the Currency permission to operate two services for the convenience of customers; one was an armored car messenger service and the other an off-premises receptacle for the receipt of packages containing cash or checks for deposit. The Comptroller's letter authorizing the armored car messenger service relied upon paragraph 7490 of the Comptroller's Manual for National Banks,[2] a relatively recent ruling which specifically authorizes such a service. A second letter authorizing construction of an off-premises receptacle authorized such a service "as an incident to" the bank's ordinary business. Both letters contained explicit instructions to First National designed to insure that deposits so received would not become bank liabilities until actually in the hands of the bank teller at the chartered office or regular "banking house"; and that checks cashed for customers would be deemed paid at the bank when the cash was handed to the messenger, not when the cash was delivered to the customer by the armored car teller.

Relying on these letters, First National offered an armored car service and a secured receptacle for receipt of monies intended as deposits. The bank advertised "Full Service Banking at your doorstep . . ." and a "mobile drive in . . . where customers may be served. . . ." A more detailed examination of the services shows that customers having an account with First National could, upon signing a "Comprehensive Dual Control Contract," arrange to have the armored car call at their place of business to pick up cash and checks for deposit, or to bring cash to them in exchange for checks delivered to the armored car teller. The contract provided that in each situation the bank's armored car messenger would be the agent

---

2. Comptroller's Manual for National Banks ¶ 7490.

> "Messenger Service"
>
> "To meet the requirements of its customers, a national bank may provide messenger service by means of an armored car or otherwise, pursuant to an agreement wherein it is specified that the messenger is the agent of the customer rather than of the bank. Deposits collected under this arrangement are not considered as having been received by the bank until they are actually delivered to the teller at the bank's premises. Similarly, a check is considered as having been paid at the bank when the money is handed to the messenger as agent for the customer."

of the customer. Additionally, proffered deposits were accompanied by a transmittal slip upon which the customer itemized the funds being deposited in the same manner as with deposits made at the chartered office of the bank. The transmittal slip contained a "Contract" which provide that in this off-premises transaction the bank was the agent of the customer, and that "the transmittal of said currency, coin and checks, shall not be deemed to be a deposit until delivered into the hands of the bank's tellers at the said banking house." Sums of cash for transmission to the customer were accompanied by a charge slip indicating that the customer's account had been charged for the amount of the order.

The armored car was owned and controlled by the bank; the teller and driver-guard in the car were bank employees. The bank paid the cost of armored car operations and assumed complete responsibility for the monies, checks, and deposits during transit by means of an insurance policy bought and paid for by it to protect the customer six days per week in Plant City and the surrounding trade area in Hillsborough and Polk Counties. The armored car had a plate glass window, a sliding drawer, and a counter on one side where customers might be served. The truck bore the name of the bank and had two-way radiophone communication with the bank. All movements and routing of the armored car were directed by the bank. . . .

The stationary off-premises receptacle for receipt of monies intended for deposit was located in a shopping center one mile from First National's banking house in a space leased by the bank. The facility consisted of a secured receptacle for monies and night bags, together with a writing table supplied with envelopes and transmittal slips identical to those used by the armored car messenger service. The envelopes recited that the funds transported were accepted in accordance with the contract printed on the transmittal slip. A sign at the receptacle recited that the messenger who collected the funds acted as agent for the customer, that funds would not be deemed to have been deposited until delivered at the bank's premises, and that insurance on the funds was provided by the bank. Customers maintaining an account with the bank who had signed the Comprehensive Dual Control Contract were issued a key to open the off-premises depository to drop of the night pouches in the receptacle. The armored car serviced the receptacle daily. The armored car teller, upon making pickups of such night pouches, promptly identified all monies and other items placed in the depository and immediately recorded them by the depositor's number. The driver-guard verified all items collected by the teller and signed the written bank record identifying the monies obtained at the stationary depository. . . .

The parties agree generally that the McFadden Act permits national banks to branch if and only if the host State would permit one of its own banks to branch; the Florida Bank Comptroller insists that the State of Florida unequivocally forbids off-premises banking of any kind. Thus the lines are clearly drawn; the question presented is whether the activities of First National authorized by the United States Comptroller are branch banking. . . .

The policy of competitive equality is . . . firmly embedded in the statutes governing the national banking system. The mechanism of referring to state law is simply one designed to implement that congressional intent and build into the federal statute a self- executing provision to accommodate to changes in state regulation.

We reject the contention made by amicus curiae National Association of Supervisors of State Banks to the effect that state law definitions of what constitutes "branch banking" must control the content of the federal definition of § 36(f) [now § 36(j)]. Admittedly, state law comes into play in deciding how, where, and when branch banks may be operated, *Walker Bank, supra*, for in § 36(c) Congress entrusted to the States the regulation of branching as Congress then conceived it. But to allow the States to define the content of the term "branch" would make them the sole judges of their own powers. Congress did not intend such an improbable result, as appears from the inclusion in § 36 of a general definition of "branch." . . .

Against this background, we turn to the question whether the off-premises business activities conducted by First National amounted to "branch" banking within the meaning of the McFadden Act.Since national banks are "necessarily subject to the paramount authority of the United States," *First National Bank in St. Louis v. Missouri*, 263 U.S. 640, 656 (1924), we consult that part of the McFadden Act that defines the term "branch." . . .

Although the definition may not be a model of precision, in part due to its circular aspect, it defines the minimum content of the term "branch"; by use of the word "include" the definition suggests a calculated indefiniteness with respect to the other limits of the term. However, the term "branch bank" at the very least includes any place for receiving deposits or paying checks or lending money apart from the chartered premises; it may include more. It should be emphasized that, since § 36(f) [now § 36(j)] is phrased in the disjunctive, the offering of any one of the three services mentioned in that definition will provide the basis for finding that "branch" banking is taking place. Thus not only the taking of deposits but also the paying of checks or the lending of money could equally well provide the basis for such a finding. . . .

First National and the Comptroller of the Currency urge that the challenged activity does not amount to branch banking. . . . First National relies heavily, if indeed not entirely, upon carefully drawn contracts with its customers who use armored car or deposit receptacle services. The bank urges that, "deposit" being a word of art, the determination of when a deposit is made is not a casual one inasmuch as that determination fixes important legal relationships of the parties.

The bank also urges that creation of a deposit being purely a matter of intent, the issue is governed exclusively by the private contract. Since these contracts must be interpreted under state law, the argument runs, no "deposit" is actually received as such until monies delivered to the armored car or the receptacle are physically delivered into the hands of a bank teller at the chartered premises. Until such time the bank may not, under the contracts, be held to account for the customer's funds. . . .

We are satisfied, however, that the contracts have no significant purpose other than to remove the possibility that the monies received will become "deposits" in the technical and legal sense until actually delivered to the chartered premises of the bank.

. . . [W]hile the contracting parties are free to arrange their private rights and liabilities as they see fit, it does not follow that private contractual arrangements, binding on the parties under state law, determine the meaning of the language or the reach of § 35(f).

Because the purpose of the statute is to maintain competitive equality, it is relevant in construing "branch" to consider, not merely the contractual rights and liabilities created by the transaction, but all those aspects of the transaction that might give the bank an advantage in its competition for customers. Unquestionably, a competitive advantage accrues to a bank that provides the service of receiving money for deposit at a place away from its main office; the convenience to the customer is unrelated to whether the relationship of debtor and creditor is established at the moment of receipt or somewhat later. . . .

Since the putative deposits are in fact "received" by a bank facility apart from its chartered place of business, we are compelled . . . to view the place of delivery of the customer's cash and checks accompanied by a deposit slip as an "additional office, or . . . branch place of business . . . at which deposits are received."

Mr. Justice DOUGLAS, dissenting.

It will come as a shock, where common sense is the guide, to learn that an armored car picking up merchants' cash boxes and checks is a branch bank. Conceivably a bank could use an armored car as a place of business by stationing it at designated places during designated hours for opening accounts, receiving, deposits, making loans, and the like. But no armored car was so used in these cases.

Federal law stated in the McFadden Act, 12 U.S.C. § 36(f) [now § 36(j)], defines "branch" as any facility "at which deposits are received, or check paid, or money lent." And Congress provided that national banks may establish "branches" whenever, wherever, and however state banks may do so. *First National Bank of Logan v. Walker Bank & Trust Co.*, 385 U.S. 252, 261-262. The opinion of the Court leaves the impression that the McFadden Act created "competitive equality" between national and state banks across the board. But as we stated in the *Walker Bank* case, that Act "intended to place national and state banks on a basis of 'competitive equality' *insofar as branch banking was concerned.*" *Id.*, at 261. (Italics added.) There was no other or additional overriding principle of "competitive equality" that limited off-premises services of national banks to those that state banks could provide.

Among those off-premises activities of national banks was the furnishing of armored car messenger services, which, we are advised by the Comptroller of the Currency, antedated by many years the 1927 McFadden Act. One can read the legislative history of the Act without finding any hint that Congress was providing "competitive equality" as respects armored car messenger services. . . .

The services rendered in these cases were undertaken only after approval by the Comptroller of the Currency who attached a condition that "the messenger is the agent of the customer rather than of the bank." I thought it was elemental law that a bank deposit cannot arise without some unequivocal act whereby both parties express their consent to the creation of the status of debtor. . . . Certainly the Comptroller, who is the supervisory agent for policing § 36, has some authority to define "deposits" . . . , and this case affords no excuse for disparaging him.

Mr. Justice STEWART, dissenting.

I wholly agree with the Court that federal law is to be applied in determining whether the activities of a national bank constitute branch banking under the exclusive definition contained in the National Bank Act, 12 U.S.C. § 36(f) [now 36(j)]. Whether the activities here in question constitute branch banking under that standard seems to me an extremely close question. That being so, I would defer to the determination of the Comptroller of the Currency.

Notes and Comments 3.10. If it is true, as *Camp v. Pitts* appears to hold, that the Comptroller's discretionary decisions are to be given great deference by reviewing courts, why does the Comptroller seem to be losing so many of these branching cases?

Clarke v. Securities Industry Association

479 U.S. 388 (1987)

Justice WHITE delivered the opinion of the Court.

In these cases, we review an application of the so-called "zone of interest" standing test that was first articulated in *Association of Data Processing Service Organizations, Inc. v. Camp*, 397 U.S. 150 (1970). Concluding that respondent is a proper litigant, we also review, and reverse, a judgment that the Comptroller of the Currency exceeded his authority in approving the applications of two national banks for the establishment or purchase of discount brokerage subsidiaries. . . .

In 1982, two national banks, Union Planters National Bank of Memphis (Union Planters) and petitioner Security Pacific National Bank of Los Angeles (Security Pacific), applied to the Comptroller of Currency for permission to open offices that would offer discount brokerage services to the public.[1] Union Planters proposed to acquire an existing discount brokerage operation, and Security Pacific sought to establish an affiliate named Discount Brokerage. Both banks proposed to offer discount brokerage services not only at their branch offices but at other locations inside and outside of their home States.

In passing on Security Pacific's application, the Comptroller was faced with the question whether the operation of Discount Brokerage would violate the National Bank Act's branching provisions.[a] Those limitations, enacted as §§ 7 and 8 of the McFadden Act, 44 Stat. 1228, as amended, are codified at 12 U.S.C. § 36 and 12 U.S.C. § 81. Section 81 limits "the general business" of a national bank to its headquarters and any "branches" permitted by § 36. Section 36(c) provides that a national bank is permitted to branch only in its home State and only to the extent that a bank of the same State is permitted to branch under state law. The term "branch" is defined at 12 U.S.C. § 36(f) [now 36(j)] "to include any branch bank, branch office, branch agency, additional office, or any branch place of business . . . at which deposits are received, or checks paid, or money lent."

The Comptroller concluded that "the non-chartered offices at which Discount Brokerage will offer its services will not constitute branches under the McFadden Act because none of the statutory branching functions will be performed there." He explained that although Discount Brokerage would serve as an intermediary for margin lending, loan approval would take place at chartered Security Pacific offices, so that Discount Brokerage offices would not be lending money within the meaning of § 36(f) [now 36(j)]. Likewise, although Discount Brokerage would maintain, and pay interest on, customer balances created as an incident of its brokerage business, the Comptroller concluded that these accounts differ sufficiently in nature from ordinary bank accounts that Discount Brokerage would not be engaged in receiving deposits.[2] He further observed that treating offices conducting

---

1. Discount brokers execute trades on behalf of their customers but do not offer investment advice. As a result, the commissions they charge are substantially lower than those charged by full-service brokers. *See Securities Industries Assn. v. Board of Governors*, 468 U.S. 207, 209, n. 2 (1984).

a. The permissibility of discount brokerage services by depository institutions under the Glass-Steagall Act, which restricts the securities activities of banks and other depository institutions, is discussed in Chapter 5, *infra*.

2. The Comptroller relied primarily on the fact that banks publicly solicit deposits and use deposited funds in lending, while credit balances maintained by brokers are not, as such, directly solicited from the public, and are subject to regulatory restrictions regarding use by brokers. *See the Securities Investor Protection Act*, 15 U.S.C. § 78aaa *et seq*. (restricting advertising, promotional, and selling practices of brokers regarding interest-bearing free credit balances); 17 CFR § 240.15c3-2 (1986) (regulating the use of credit balances by brokers). Although the Comptroller believed that § 36(f) should be read narrowly to define "branch" only with reference to receiving deposits, making loans, and cashing checks, he recognized that there is authority supporting a broader reading. In *St. Louis County National Bank v. Mercantile Trust Company National Assn.*, 548 F.2d 716 (CA8 1976), *cert. denied*, 433 U.S. 909 (1977), a trust office operated by a national bank was held to be a branch.

brokerage activities as branches under § 36(f) would be inconsistent with the "long-standing and widespread" practice of banks' operating nonbranch offices dealing in United States Government or municipal securities. Accordingly, the Comptroller approved Security Pacific's application.[3]

Respondent, a trade association representing securities brokers, underwriters, and investment bankers . . . contended that bank discount brokerage offices are branches . . . and thus are subject to the geographical restrictions imposed by § 36(c). The Comptroller disputed this position on the merits and also argued that respondent lacks standing because it is not within the zone of interests protected by the McFadden Act. The Comptroller contended that Congress passed the McFadden Act not to protect securities dealers but to establish competitive equality between state and national banks.

The District Court, relying on *Association of Data Processing Service Organizations, Inc. v. Camp*, 397 U.S. 150 (1970), held that respondent has standing and rejected the Comptroller's submission that national banks may offer discount brokerage services at non-branch locations. A divided panel of the Court of Appeals affirmed in a brief *per curiam*, 758 F.2d 739 (1985), and rehearing en banc was denied, with three judges dissenting. 765 F.2d 1196 (1985).

. . . We now affirm the judgment that respondent has standing, but reverse on the merits.

[Part II of the opinion, discussing standing, is omitted.]

"It is settled that courts should give great weight to any reasonable construction of a regulatory statute adopted by the agency charged with the enforcement of that statute. The Comptroller of the Currency is charged with the enforcement of banking laws to an extent that warrants the invocation of this principle with respect to his deliberative conclusions as to the meaning of these laws. *See First National Bank v. Missouri*, 263 U.S. 640. *Investment Company Institute v. Camp*, 401 U.S., at 626-627. *See also, e.g., United States v. Riverside Bayview Homes, Inc.*, 474 U.S. ----, 106 S.Ct. 455 (1985); *Chemical Manufacturers Assn. v. Natural Resources Defense Council, Inc.*, 470 U.S. 116 (1985); *Chevron U.S.A. Inc. v. Natural Resources Defense Council, Inc.*, 467 U.S. 837 (1984).

Respondent contends that the Comptroller's interpretation of the Bank Act is not entitled to deference because it contradicts the plain language of the statute. Respondent relies on 12 U.S.C. § 81. . . .

In respondent's view, the unambiguous meaning of § 81 is that "national banks may locate their business only at their headquarters or licensed branches within the same state." . . . However, § 81 is considerably more ambiguous than respondent allows. The phrase "[t]he general business of each national banking association" in § 81 need not be read to encompass all the business in which the bank engages, but, as we shall explain, can plausibly be read to cover only those activities that are part of the bank's core banking functions.

Prior to 1927, the predecessor of § 81 (Rev.Stat. § 5190) provided that "the usual business of each national banking association shall be transacted at an office or banking-house located in the place specified in its organization certificate." In *Lowry National Bank*, 29 Op. Atty. Gen. 81 (1911), the Attorney General interpreted this statute to permit "a bank [to] maintain an [extra-office] agency, the power of which is restricted to dealing in bills of exchange, or possibly to some other particular class of business incident to the

---

While disagreeing with this holding, the Comptroller took the position that it "should at the very least be limited to those dealings with the public requiring a specialized banking or similar license."

3. A month later, the Comptroller approved without comment the application of Union Planters to acquire an existing brokerage firm.

banking business," but to forbid "a bank [from] establish[ing] a branch for the transaction of a general banking business." *Id.*, at 86. The Attorney General went on to cite cases which he viewed as "recogniz[ing] a vital distinction between a mere agency for the transaction of a particular business and a branch bank wherein is carried on a general banking business." *Id.*, at 87. He summarized the distinction as follows:

> "An agency requires no division of the capital stock, and the details of the business are few and are easily supervised by the officers of the bank, while a branch bank requires, in effect, a division of the capital, the working force is organized, and the business conducted as if it were a separate organization, and it competes in all branches of the banking business with other banks in that locality the same as if it were an independent institution." *Id.*, at 87-88.

The Court subsequently approved this interpretation of § 5190 in *First National Bank v. Missouri*, 263 U.S., at 658.

The *Lowry National Bank* opinion, which is part of the background against which Congress legislated when it passed the McFadden Act in 1927, does not interpret § 5190 as requiring national banks to conduct all of their business at the central office. The opinion equates "the usual business of banking" with "a general banking business," and envisions branching in terms of the performance of core banking functions.

Respondent attempts to sidestep the *Lowry* opinion by arguing that Congress changed the meaning of § 5190 when, in passing the McFadden Act, it changed the words "the usual business of each national banking association" to "the general business of each national banking association." Respondent has pointed to nothing in the legislative history of the McFadden Act, however, indicating that this change in the wording had substantive significance. We find reasonable the Comptroller's position that "the amendment simply codified the accepted notion that the 'usual business' of a bank was the 'general banking business.'"

Respondent's fall-back position from its "plain language" argument is that the phrase "general business" in § 81 at least refers to all activities in which Congress has specifically authorized a national bank to engage, including the trading in securities that the McFadden Act authorized by the amendment of 12 U.S.C. 24 Seventh. *See* McFadden Act, ch. 191, § 2, 44 Stat. 1226. However, petitioner Security National Bank has provided a counter-example to this general thesis: In § 2(b) of the McFadden Act, Congress specifically authorized national banks' involvement in the safe-deposit business, and in doing so deleted language from the bill that arguably would have limited the bank's authority "to conduct a safe deposit business" to activities "located on or adjacent to the premises of such association." 67 Cong. Rec. 3231 (1926). In floor debates, Representative McFadden, in response to the question from Representative Cellar whether the bill as amended would permit "a safe-deposit business [to be] conducted a block away or a mile away from a national banking association," replied that the deletion of the language regarding location "removes the limitations which might be very embarrassing to an institution." *Id.*, at 3232.[18] In view of this exchange, we are not persuaded that Congress intended the locational restriction of § 81 and § 36 to reach all activities in which national banks are specifically authorized to engage. . . .

It is significant that in passing the McFadden Act, Congress recognized and for the

---

18. Representative Wingo then remarked that the locational language that was deleted was to make clear that the limitations on the total amount a bank can invest in the safe-deposit business applies irrespective of whether the business is conducted on or off the bank's premises. 67 Cong. Rec. 3232 (1926).

first time specifically authorized the practice of national banks' engaging in the buying and selling of investment securities. *See* Act of Feb. 25, 1927, ch. 191, § 2, 44 Stat. 1226.[b] Prior to 1927, banks had conducted such securities transactions on a widespread and often interstate basis, without regard to the locational restriction imposed by § 5190 on "the usual business of each national banking association." *See, e.g.*, W. PEACH, THE SECURITY AFFILIATES OF NATIONAL BANKS 74 (1941); Perkins, *The Divorce of Commercial and Investment Banking: A History*, 88 Banking L.J. 483, 492, 494, n. 26 (1971).[21] We find it unlikely that Congress, in recognizing and explicitly authorizing this practice, would have undertaken to limit its geographic scope through the branching law without specifically noting the restriction on the prior practice.[22]

For the foregoing reasons, we conclude that Congress did not intend to subject a bank's conduct of a securities business to the branching restrictions imposed by 12 U.S.C. § 36(f) [now 36(j)]. We do not view our decision today as inconsistent with our prior decisions interpreting 12 U.S.C. § 36(f) as embodying a policy of "competitive equality" between state and national banks. *See, e.g., First National Bank in Plant City v. Dickinson*, 396 U.S. 122 (1969). The Comptroller reasonably interprets the statute as requiring "competitive equality" only in core banking functions, and not in all incidental services in which national banks are authorized to engage.[23] . . .

Notes and Comments 3.11. Assuming that section 36(c) embodies a congressional intention to establish competitive equality with respect to the "whether," "where" and "how" of state and national bank branching, should that rationale also be read into section 36(j)? Is that what *Plant City* did? To the extent that the Court does rely upon the competitive equality

---

b. On investment securities, see 12 U.S.C. § 24(Seventh).

21. Respondent treats these prior practices as "immaterial to the issue here" because in the 1920's national banks generally carried out such transactions through affiliates rather than directly owned subsidiaries. . . . However, it appears doubtful that such securities affiliates were functionally distinguishable from subsidiaries. Various devices were used to achieve identity of stock ownership between the affiliate and the bank, *see* W. PEACH, THE SECURITY AFFILIATES OF NATIONAL BANKS (1941), at 66-68, and as a Senate Subcommittee later commented, "it goes without saying that, through identity of stock ownership, there is identity of real control." *Operation of the National and Federal Reserve Banking Systems: Hearings Pursuant to S.Res. 71 before a Subcommittee of the Senate Committee on Banking and Currency*, 71st Cong., 3d Sess., 1052, 1057 (1931). Moreover, at the time it passed the McFadden Act, Congress did not appear to place any particular weight on the affiliate-subsidiary distinction; thus, the legislative history contains references to securities trading as "a type of business which national banks are now conducting under their incidental charter powers." S. Rep. No. 473, 69th Cong., 1st Sess., 7 (1926); H.R. Rep. No. 83, 69th Cong., 1st Sess., 3 (1926).

22. Congress did of course later restrict the types of securities transactions in which national banks could engage, through passage of the Glass-Steagall Act in 1933. *See* 12 U.S.C. § 24 (1982 ed. and Supp. III); 12 U.S.C. §§ 78, 377, 378. However, Congress showed no intention of placing geographic restrictions on the location of those securities transactions in which banks could still engage. Rather, Congress emphasized that the Glass-Steagall Act permitted banks "to purchase and sell investment securities for their customers to the same extent as heretofore." S. Rep. No. 77, 73d Cong., 1st Sess., 16 (1933).

23. If the "competitive equality" principle were carried to its logical extreme, the ability of a national bank to carry on an incidental activity such as the safe-deposit business would be limited to the same extent as a state bank's ability to do so under state law. However, as we have noted, the legislative history of the McFadden Act rather clearly indicates that Congress intended national banks to be able to carry on a safe-deposit business without locational restrictions.

rationale, how does it justify it?

3.12. Is *Clarke* consistent with *Plant City*? Does the *Clarke* give any indication of how it reconciles the relatively broad interpretation of *Plant City* with its rather narrow reading of the term "branch" in considering the status of the brokerage outlets?

3.13. Recall that *Cheshire National Bank, supra*, considered Keene's Walpole operation to be a "branch." Is this conclusion consistent with federal policy under section 36(j) as articulated in *Plant City*? In *Clarke*?

d. Branching and Technological Innovation

Notes and Comments 3.14. The emergence of customer-bank communications terminals, or automated teller machines ("ATMs"), in the 1970s raised some interesting problems with respect to the definition of "branch" as interpreted by the Supreme Court in *Plant City*. The materials that follow deal with these conceptual problems. Note, however, that the specific issue of the status of ATMs has been resolved by statute. The Economic Growth and Regulatory Paperwork Reduction Act ("EGRPRA"), Pub. L. No. 104-208, § 2204 (a), 110 Stat. 3009 (1996) (codified at 12 U.S.C. § 36(j)), excluded ATMs from the federal definition of "branch." However, the EGRPRA leaves *Plant City* and its progeny untouched. Hence, that case, and the cases discussed in this subsection, remain important authority for future technological developments with respect to the remote delivery of banking services.

3.15. Assume that Quarter National Bank wants to establish a new service for its customers.[8] It proposes to provide each customer with a special telephone apparatus, wired directly to the bank and containing a small viewing screen. The customer will be able to press a series of buttons at any time of day or night and receive information on the screen concerning account balances, credits and debits, interest rates and similar information. The customer may also press buttons to direct transfers and payments to and from accounts. (A receipt for such transactions is automatically mailed to the customer on the following banking day.) During banking hours, the customer may also pick up the receiver and, by pressing another button, contact directly an "account executive" at the bank for further information about the customer's accounts. The telephone apparatus is leased by the customer from an affiliate of Quarter National and is installed at the customer's expense. Would this proposal require approval by the Comptroller under section 36?

Independent Bankers Ass'n of America v. Smith

534 F.2d 921 (D.C. Cir. 1976),
cert. denied, 429 U.S. 862

WILKEY, Circuit Judge.

This is an appeal by the Comptroller of the Currency from a judgment . . . declaring unlawful and enjoining an interpretive ruling of the Comptroller relating to the use of electronic funds transfer systems by national banks. . . .

On 11 December 1974 the Comptroller of Currency issued an interpretive ruling in which he construed the National Bank Act as permitting national banks to establish customer-bank communication terminals (CBCT's) apart from their main offices and

8. *See generally* Guenther, *Citicorp Skips Computer In New Home-Banking Plan*, Wall St. J., Feb. 28, 1990, at B1, col. 5.

branches. The Comptroller's ruling required national banks to give the Comptroller written notice of proposed CBCT operations thirty days before terminals were established, and a later amendment imposed a fifty mile geographical restriction on exclusive (unshared) terminals.

CBCT's are manned or unmanned electronic terminals which, depending on how the machines are programmed, permit an existing bank customer to accomplish various financial transactions, including the deposit and withdrawal of funds and the transfer of funds between accounts. These automated tellers may be installed off bank premises in shopping centers, supermarkets, stores, factories, office buildings, etc., and any approved bank customer with a plastic "key card" can effect transactions at these terminals. Some CBCT's are connected directly to their bank's central computer, while others record transactions on electronic tapes which are later decoded or read by a machine at the bank. Most CBCT's which accept deposits and dispense funds require some periodic transportation of funds to and from the bank.

The central, substantive issue in this case is whether CBCT's are bank "branches" under the National Bank Act. If they are, then CBCT's are subject to the restrictions of the Act governing branching; if they are not, national banks can install and operate CBCT's anywhere (even across the state lines) subject only to the thirty day filing requirement and the fifty mile geographical limitation of the Comptroller's ruling. . . .

The Comptroller's ruling states that CBCT's are not "branches" within the meaning of section 36(f) [now 36(j)] of the National Bank Act. Under this interpretation, the restrictions of sections 36(c), 36(d), and 51 are totally circumvented. The ruling would permit national banks to install and operate CBCT's without reference to, or limitation by, state laws regulating or prohibiting branching by state-chartered banks. Also, insofar as CBCT's are concerned, it would permit national banks to ignore the minimum capital requirements established by sections 36(d) and 51. The ruling does not provide for public notice of the thirty days filings; nor is there any requirement of a traditional branch. As of 9 July 1975 twenty-eight national banks in seventeen states had filed notices of intention to establish 155 CBCT's in accordance with the Comptroller's ruling. . . .

If "deposits are received, checks paid, or money lent" at CBCT's, then CBCT's are "branches" within the meaning of section 36(f) of the National Bank Act. Hence, the substantive issue in this case is whether all CBCT's exhibit at least one of these indicia of branchness. After a careful review of the record, we agree with the district court's conclusion that the legislative history of the National Bank Act, the plain language of section 36(f), and the Supreme Court's decision in *First National Bank In Plant City v. Dickinson* (hereinafter referred to as "*Plant City*"), requires this court to find that all CBCT's do perform one of these three branch services and are, indeed, branch banks. . . .

When Congress established our dual banking system it wisely placed at one cornerstone the principle of competitive equality between state and national banks. In furtherance of this principle, the National Bank Act incorporates certain fundamental aspects of each state's banking regulations into the statute governing the federal banking system. . . .

If allowed to stand, the Comptroller's ruling would probably not destroy competitive equality or irreparably injure our dual banking system. At worst, the ruling would only temporarily disturb the competitive balance between state and national banks. If national banks were suddenly allowed to establish CBCT's without undoubtedly react to protect the interests of their state banking systems by enacting legislation permitting state banks to install and operate off-premises CBCT's. In fact, several states have already reacted to the

Comptroller's ruling in this fashion.[45]

This court must decide whether the National Bank Act gives the Comptroller the power to initiate this technological revolution in banking or whether this initiative falls within the province of the states. Hence, the question we face is more of federalism and statutory interpretation than of sound banking practice or competitive equality. The Comptroller's decision to classify CBCT's as non-branches may be technologically a step in the right direction–that is not for us to decide. Legally, however, we conclude that it was a step beyond the authority vested in him by Congress.

All parties and the district court agree that the definition of "branch" as it appears in section 36(f) is exclusive, *i.e.*, what constitutes a national bank "branch" is a threshold question of federal law to be determined without resort to state law. . . .

In the statement accompanying his ruling, the Comptroller correctly cites *Plant City* as supporting the exclusivity of the federal definition of "branch." He misapprehends, however, the remainder of Chief Justice Burger's reasoning and analysis when he states,

> Consideration . . . of the competitive aspects referred to by the Court in *Plant City* does not require CBCT's to be viewed as branches. Additionally, an analysis of the contractual rights and liabilities under which a CBCT is operated shows that–even if a CBCT is considered to be a branch office, branch agency, or branch place of business–it is not receiving deposits, paying checks, or making loans within the meaning of 12 U.S.C. 36(f). . . . The[se] contractual rights and liabilities arise from the usual operating procedures of a CBCT, and have significant purposes other than structuring the technical and legal aspects of the transaction to avoid the branch banking statutes. *Compare Plant City, supra* 396 U.S. at 126, 136-137.

To the contrary, *Plant City* clearly supports (in fact, requires) the district court's conclusion that all CBCT's are branches for purposes of federal law.

. . . The utility of CBCT's is obvious; several states permit state-chartered banks to use this eminently sensible mode of operations, but the policy of those states who choose to prohibit CBCT's is not open to judicial review or to modification by the Comptroller. The policy of competitive equality defers to state standards, not to standards prescribed by the Comptroller. Since 1927 Congress has made it clear that the Comptroller lacks the authority "to allow a national bank to establish as many agencies for receiving deposits and paying checks as he [the Comptroller] sees fit. . . ."[59]

---

45. In the statement accompanying the amendment to his original ruling, the Comptroller states,

> [S]ince the December 1974 ruling, the states of North Dakota, Maryland, Kansas, and Nebraska each have passed statutes authorizing the equivalent of CBCT's to be established and used by state banks and declaring that such terminals are not deemed to be branch banks.

40 Fed. Reg. 21701 (1975). Additionally, in a statement officially adopted by the Oklahoma State Banking Board, the Bank Commissioner of Oklahoma has stated, "[I]f . . . CBCTs are not branches and may lawfully be utilized by national banks, [I] will permit state banks to also use CBCTs." *Oklahoma ex rel. State Banking Bd. v. Utica Nat'l Bank & Trust Co.*, 409 F. Supp. 71, 88 (N.D.Okl., 1975), *notice of appeal filed*, 10th Cir., 23 Feb. 1976.

59. 66 Cong. Rec. 1627 (1925). During the House debates over the McFadden Act, Representative Stevenson of South Carolina explained:

> [Y]ou have branches in the Federal reserve system established by the dictum of the

. . . The appendix to the Comptroller's ruling draws several rather fine distinctions between banking transactions executed at a CBCT and similar activities conducted at a bank's main office or a traditional branch. In essence, the Comptroller argues that "[c]ommunications between customers and their banks through CBCT's involve instructions to consummate . . . transactions" and not "transactions" themselves. This is so, we are told, because CBCT's are not yet sophisticated enough to carry out certain procedures, *e.g.*, to verify the authenticity of the documents they receive. Thus, the consummation of a CBCT transaction and the attachment of contractual rights and obligations must await the main bank's verification and approval. Additionally, as to manned, point-of-sale CBCT's, the Comptroller insists that "the customer's direct transactions are not with the bank at all, but with a bona fide third party." According to the Comptroller and one federal district court in Oklahoma,[66] telephones are not facilities supplied by banks for the added convenience of their customers and designed to retain and attract patronage. these carefully drawn distinctions prove that deposits can be received, checks can be paid, and loans can be made only by the main bank, not by CBCT's. We disagree on all three counts. . . .

Besides the ordinary deposit into a customer's checking or savings account, two other types of CBCT transactions properly are characterized as "deposits" within the meaning of section 36(f); (1) transfers of funds between two accounts of the same customer and (2) payments on installment loans or credit card accounts.

In the first of these transactions, CBCT's enable bank customers to transfer funds between two or their accounts at a place remote from the bank's main premises. Hence, under the rationale of *Plant City*, these off-premises CBCT's are bank facilities where deposits are received when customers withdraw money from their checking, savings, or credit card accounts and deposit these funds into one of their other accounts. The Comptroller's attempt to analogize these account transfers to banking-by-mail and banking-by-telephone breaks down because, in the case of a mailbox or a telephone, no place or facility established (*i.e.*, owned or rented) by a bank is involved. Mailboxes and telephones are not facilities supplied by banks for the added convenience of their customers and designed to retain and attract

---

> Comptroller of the Currency, who has assumed [*sic*] to say that he can allow a national bank to establish as many agencies for receiving deposits and paying checks as he sees fit. . . . I will show presently that we cut that out, root and branch.

Id.

We note that federally-chartered savings and loan associations and federally-chartered credit unions are presently permitted to establish and operate CBCT's (referred to as remote service units or RSU's) without regard to state or federal branching restrictions under regulations promulgated by the Federal Home Loan Bank Board and the National Credit Union Administration, respectively. 12 C.F.R. § 545 4-2 (1975) (savings and loan associations), amended by 40 Fed. Reg. 27477 (30 June 1975) (extends termination date to 31 July 1976); 12 C.F.R. § 721.3 (1975) (credit unions). Both of these regulations are of a temporary, experimental nature. These "pilot projects" are possible because Congress has not defined "branching" in the area of federal savings and loan associations and federal credit unions, but has left it to the discretion of the governing agencies to regulate what constitutes a "branch." In contrast, section 36(f) of the National Bank Act did not leave it to the Comptroller to determine by regulation what constitutes a "branch" of a national bank. If the Federal Home Loan Bank Board and the National Credit Union Administration decide to authorize RSU's on a permanent basis, each state (not the Comptroller) will have to decide whether the resulting competitive advantage for savings and loan associations and credit unions necessitates a change in the state's posture toward bank-operated CBCT's.

66. *Oklahoma ex rel. State Banking Bd. v. Utica Nat'l Bank & Trust Co.*, 409 F. Supp. 71 (N.D. Okl. 1975), *notice of appeal filed*, 23 Feb. 1976.

patronage.

Similarly, we conclude that banks which provide the service of receiving payments on installment loans or credit card accounts at a place away from their main banking premises are receiving deposits within the meaning of section 36(f). The competitive advantage accruing to a bank that accepts conventional deposits at various conveniently located CBCT's is difficult to distinguish from the advantage that accrues to a bank from permitting its customers to deposit their monthly credit card or installment loan payments in the same CBCT's. Again, the bank is providing a customer convenience and is thereby gaining a competitive advantage over banks that do not furnish this service. . . .

. . . [T]he Comptroller divides CBCT's into two classifications, manned and unmanned terminals. The Comptroller then lists three reasons why a cash withdrawal from the later classification of CBCT's does not constitute paying a check:

> First, if the withdrawal is from a savings account, no check can be involved because savings deposits by definition are not subject to withdrawals by check. Second, whatever the nature of the deposit account, the CBCT is activated by a card or similar device and no check is involved. The required form of a check is specified in section 3-104 of the Uniform Commercial Code. Nothing resembling a check is used in withdrawals using an unmanned CBCT. Third, all withdrawals are subject to verification. If the CBCT is online, the verification takes place instantaneously at the bank. . . . If the CBCT is offline, the transaction is verified at the bank when the tape or other record is retrieved from the CBCT.

In the case of manned units, the Comptroller does not rely on the second argument above since manned CBCT's do cash conventional paper checks. Instead, he repeats his contention that "the customer's direct transactions are not with the bank at all, but with a bona fide third party."

To determine what constitutes paying a "check" under section 36(f) this court must balance the technical commercial definition of a "check" against the method of statutory interpretation prescribed by the Supreme Court in *Plant City*. The Uniform Commercial Code defines a "check" as a "negotiable instrument" (*i.e.*, a "draft") "drawn on a bank and payable on demand." Admittedly, it would be difficult to fit under the UCC definition, or the standard dictionary definition, of "check" anything involved in an unmanned CBCT withdrawal transaction. Fortunately, such semantical exercises have become unnecessary since the *Plant City* Court instructed that "the definition of 'branch' in § 36(f), must not be given a restrictive meaning which [would] frustrate the congressional intent . . . found to be plain in *Walker Bank*."

. . . Like the form of the check, the form of the account from which funds are withdrawn is also without significance. If the CBCT withdrawal is from a savings account, while no "check" could have been drawn on the account, the cash disbursement by the CBCT is nonetheless a routine transaction like those generally carried on at the main banking office or an authorized branch. We conclude that Congress envisioned all account withdrawals when it used the shorthand phrase "checks paid" in section 36(f) will still include within its broad standard those facilities that permit bank customers to perform the traditional banking funds from their accounts. . . .

With regard to the lending function of CBCT's, the Comptroller asserts,

> [A] cash withdrawal from an open end credit account, such as a credit card or approved overdraft account, does not constitute making a loan at the CBCT. Such withdrawals are from an already approved line of credit, and are subject to verification that the withdrawal is within the approved line. With most unmanned

> CBCT's this verification takes place at the bank, either immediately with an online CBCT, or later with an off-line CBCT. In these circumstances the revolving credit agreement may be viewed as an original contract which establishes the loan relationship between the customer and bank. Each request by the customer for a cash advance must be verified and accepted by the bank. The transaction thus is consummated, and the loan made, when the bank verifies as its office that the credit agreement conditions are satisfied . . . . Thus no loan is made at the CBCT.

These are essentially the same arguments the Comptroller advances on behalf of the other two previously discussed services performed by CBCT's. Here again he attaches great importance to the "conclusion[s] of ordinary contract law" and to subsequent (or instantaneous) verification at the bank.

As we continue to point out, the same arguments were made and rejected in *Plant City*. Specifically, *Plant City* rejects the idea that "private contractual arrangements, binding on the parties under state law, [can somehow] determine the meaning of the language or the reach of § 36(f). . . ."

The net result of the above analysis is as follows: If a state permits its state chartered banks to establish CBCT's for the purpose of (1) receiving deposits, or (2) paying checks, or (3) lending money, then national banks in that state also can establish CBCT's limited to the functions permitted under state law.

This result would hold true even in a state that prohibits branch, but permits the use of CBCT's since they are not considered "branches" under state law. Since we hold that off-premises CBCT's are "branches" within the meaning and intent of section 36(f)'s federal definition, for each CBCT a national bank wishes to establish it must (1) file a branch application with the Comptroller, (2) secure the Comptroller's approval, and (3) satisfy the capital and surplus requirements for branches found in (a) sections 36(d) and 51 of the National Bank Act and (b) the state banking statutes.

State Bank of Fargo v. Merchants Nat. Bank & Trust

593 F.2d 341 (8th Cir. 1979)

HENLEY, Circuit Judge.

The plaintiff in the district court was the State Bank of Fargo, a banking institution chartered under the laws of North Dakota and governed by state statutes and regulations.... The defendants were The Merchants National Bank and Trust Company of Fargo (Merchants), a national bank, and the Comptroller of the Currency. Merchants is subject to the provisions of the National Bank Act, 12 U.S.C. § 21 et seq., and is subject to the regulatory jurisdiction of the Comptroller.

The object of the suit is to prohibit Merchants from operating in the City of Fargo two CBCT's under initial authority granted by the Comptroller in 1976 and under branch bank authority issued by him in 1977. . . .

. . . As the law stood when Judge Benson decided the case and as it stands today, a national bank is permitted to operate at the discretion of the Comptroller one of more CBCT's. However, the right or privilege of a national bank to operate such a machine at a given place or in a given state is limited by the branch banking provisions appearing in 12 U.S.C. § 36(c). That statute provides generally that a national bank may not operate a branch in circumstances or at locations within a state in or at which a state chartered bank would not be permitted under state law to operate a branch.

. . . State Bank contends that in view or relevant provisions of North Dakota law the

Comptroller was forbidden by 12 U.S.C. § 36(c) to authorize the maintenance and operation of the CBCT's involved in the case. The district court rejected that contention, and the district court also found with respect to the particular machines in question that the Comptroller did not act arbitrarily or capriciously or abuse his administrative discretion when he authorized the maintenance and use of the machines.

. . . Whether a national bank may establish and operate a branch in a given state or at a particular point in that state is governed by state law. *First Nat'l Bank of Logan v. Walker Bank & Trust Co.*, 385 U.S. 252 (1966). But the question of whether a particular operation or facility of a national bank constitutes a "branch bank" is a question of federal law. *First Nat'l Bank in Plant City v. Dickinson*, 396 U.S. 122 (1969).

Recent years have been characterized by increasing competition between banks and between banks and other types of financial institutions. Those years have also been characterized by tremendous advances in electronic technology including the development of CBCT's and similar machines.

Efforts on the part of national banks to establish branches are frequently opposed both by state bank and other national banks, and problems connected with branch banking have frequently come before this court, and others, in recent years. . . .

Ever since CBCT's came on the scene, the Comptroller has claimed and exercised the power to limit and regulate their use by national banks. However, he did not prior to mid or late 1976 consider the machines to be "branch banks." In *Independent Bankers Ass'n of America v. Smith*, 534 F.2d 921, *cert. denied*, 429 U.S. 862 (1976), it was held that in view of the fact that a CBCT can accept deposits and disburse funds, it falls within the definition of a branch bank that appears in 12 U.S.C. § 36(f) [now 36(j)]. This court came to the same conclusion in *State of Missouri ex rel. Kostman v. First Nat'l Bank.* Following the holding in *Independent Bankers, supra*, the Comptroller abandoned his original position, and it is now settled beyond question that when a national bank makes use of a CBCT, it is engaging in "branch banking," at least where the CBCT is located away from the bank's main business premises, which is the case here.

The ultimate question before the district court was, and the ultimate question before us is whether under North Dakota law a state bank chartered by the State of North Dakota could lawfully operate the machines that Merchants has been authorized to operate. While that question is one of state law, it is complicated by the fact that the relevant North Dakota statute presently to be mentioned makes reference to federal law to some extent, and that the National Bank Act refers to state banking law. . . .

As pointed out by Judge Benson, the public policy of North Dakota with respect to branch banking has been restrictive, and generally North Dakota banks are not permitted to engage in off premises operations except to a limited extent; and as of 1975 the powers of banks chartered under North Dakota law did not permit them to operate CBCT's. . . .

As we have seen, the original position taken by the Comptroller was that the maintenance and operation of a CBCT by a national bank did not constitute branch banking, and, therefore, national banks could be authorized to use CBCT's without regard to state laws dealing with branch banking by state chartered banks. That position seems to have caused understandable concern among "state bankers" in North Dakota fearing competition with national banks which might be permitted to use CBCT's while state chartered banks would not be permitted to use them. The state bankers may also have been concerned by the use or possible use of RSU's [remote service units] by federal savings and loan associations and by federal credit unions.[4]

That concern or apparent concern generated a response by the North Dakota Legislature which in 1975 adopted what now appears as Subsection 8 of N.D. Cent. Code § 6-03-02.

That section defines the powers of banks chartered under North Dakota law, and Subsection 8 provides that state banks may provide services to its customers involving electronic transfers of funds "to the same extent that other financial institutions chartered and regulated by any agency of the federal government are permitted to provide such services within this state. . . ." The subsection stipulates that a CBCT is not to be considered a "branch," a "paying and receiving station," or a "separate facility," but simply as a "customer electronic funds transfer center" which may be established subject to rules and regulations that the state banking board may adopt. The subsection also states that if a bank establishes an off premises CBCT, the facility must be available to customers of any other bank which may request that the facility be made available to its customers with the cost of the operation to be shared between the banks involved. . . .

The district judge found that when Merchants' branching application was approved in 1977, both federal savings and loan associations and federal credit unions were being permitted to use RSU's in their operations. . . . And he found that at the time of decision in 1978 federal credit unions were still being permitted to use RSU's. . . .

To the finding last mentioned we will add with respect to federal savings and loan associations that the regulations permitting them to use RSU's were theoretically temporary during earlier years; however, the authorizations were periodically continued in force and were finally made permanent in late May, 1978. 43 Fed. Reg. 22929. And as far as we know, the original "temporary" authority to federal credit unions to use RSU's has never been revoked.

We accept the district court's construction of the North Dakota statute here involved, and since federal savings and loan associations and federal credit unions are still permitted to use RSU's in North Dakota, it follows that North Dakota state banks may use CBCT's. Hence, the Comptroller was not forbidden by 12 U.S.C. § 36(c) to authorize Merchants to maintain and operate its Fargo CBCT's as "branch banks."

Independent Bankers Ass'n of New York v. Marine Midland Bank

757 F.2d 453 (2d Cir. 1985)

FEINBERG, Chief Judge.

Defendant Marine Midland Bank, N.A. (Marine) appeals from a judgment of the United States District Court for the Western District of New York, . . . enjoining it from using an automated teller machine (ATM) owned and operated by Wegmans Food Markets Inc. (Wegmans) and located in Wegmans' store in Canandaigua, New York. . . .

Marine is a federally chartered bank. Wegmans owns a chain of grocery stores, including 31 at which it has installed an ATM. Wegmans made these electronic banking services available in order to attract customers and support a high-volume grocery business. In January 1983, Marine entered into an agreement with Wegmans that permitted Marine depositors to use the ATM located in the Wegmans Canandaigua store. Canandaigua has a

---

4. There can be no question that federal savings and loan associations operate in North Dakota, and Judge Benson took judicial notice of the fact that federal credit unions also operate there. 451 F.Supp. at 790, n.32.

population of approximately 11,000, and is the principal office of plaintiff Canandaigua National Bank.

The ATM in the Canandaigua store has Wegmans' logo on it, is under Wegmans' control and is a shared ATM, that is, it may be used by many financial institutions. Marine's account-holders may use the ATM to make deposits and cash withdrawals, obtain cash advances against credit cards, transfer funds between accounts, pay bills and obtain account balance information.

Wegmans is obligated under the agreement with Marine to load the machine with cash, provide deposit envelopes and other customer forms, issue transaction receipts, unload and deliver deposit containers and provide security, insurance and maintenance services.

To use the machine, a customer inserts an encoded plastic card and enters a personal identification number on the machine's keyboard. The customer then enters the desired transaction and amount. Deposits are placed in envelopes marked "Wegmans Electronic Teller Deposit/Payment Envelope" and dropped through a slot in the machine into a secured deposit box maintained by Wegmans. The customer receives a receipt marked "Electronic Teller Wegmans," which reflects the amount indicated on the keyboard. Account withdrawals must first be approved electronically, and cash is then disbursed by the machine.

Marine, Wegmans and several financial institutions are members of a shared ATM network known as HarMoney. HarMoney's members share the use of central computer processing facilities–a "switch"–owned by Marine. Customers of the member institutions can use other members' ATM's to transact business with their own institutions. Wegmans also belongs to another shared ATM network, Metroteller, which has 45 financial institution members in New York and other states. The crediting and debiting of the accounts of customers who use the Wegmans machine occurs through a series of transactions involving the relevant switch.

Plaintiff Bankers Association is a non-profit association of over 90 member banks, including plaintiff Canandaigua National Bank. Plaintiffs brought suit in the Western District in September 1983, alleging that Marine's use of Wegmans' ATM constituted branch banking under the McFadden Act, 12 U.S.C. § 36(f), and thus violated section 36(c) of the Act, which incorporates by reference the restriction on branch banking contained in New York Banking Law § 105.[a] This section prohibits a bank from opening a branch in any community with a population of 50,000 or less that is the principal office of another bank (home office protection). . . .

. . . [T]he district court . . . permanently enjoined Marine from utilizing the Wegmans ATM in Canandaigua for Marine bank account and credit card account transactions; the court held that such use constituted unlawful branch banking under the applicable provisions of the McFadden Act. . . .

Determination of whether a particular banking practice constitutes "branching" under sections 36(c) and (f) [now (i)] is . . . the task of the federal courts, and it has proved to be a thorny one. Banking, like other industries, has changed radically since the McFadden Act was passed in 1927. "Brick and mortar" banking, with a single physical locus of

---

a. Section 105 provides in pertinent part:

1. No bank . . . shall transact any part of its usual business of banking at any place other than its principal office, except that a bank or trust company may open and occupy one or more branch offices at any location in the state, provided: . . . (ii) that, except for the city or village in which its principal office is located, in no event shall a branch be opened and occupied pursuant to this subdivision in a city or village with a population of fifty thousand or less in which is already located the principal office of another bank, trust company or national banking association. . . .

bank-customer transactions, has been supplemented by many other forms of communication that could not have been contemplated in 1927. In the past two decades in particular, the industry has been transformed by the advent of computer technology. N. PENNEY & D. BAKER, THE LAW OF ELECTRONIC FUND TRANSFER SYSTEMS ¶ 1.01 (1980); Fraser, *Structural and Competitive Implications of Interstate Banking*, 9 J.Corp.L. 643 (1984). . . .

Shortly after the Supreme Court denied certiorari in [*Independent Bankers*], 429 U.S. 862 (1976), the Comptroller issued regulations governing the establishment of CBCT's. In the introduction to the amendments, the Comptroller stated that they were based upon the holding in [*Independent Bankers*] that a CBCT owned or rented by a national bank is subject to the branching restrictions of the McFadden Act. 41 Fed. Reg. 48,333 (Nov. 3, 1976). But, equally important, the introduction also stated that these restrictions did not apply to CBCT's that banks do not "own or rent," and have thus not "established." *Id.* Thereafter, the Comptroller's staff issued a series of interpretive letters along similar lines. Finally, in July 1981, the Comptroller published a proposed regulation formally incorporating his 1976 interpretation that an ATM is not a branch of a national bank unless the bank owns or rents it. 46 Fed. Reg. 38,925 (July 30, 1981). In July 1982, the Comptroller adopted the regulation (the Regulation). It provides in relevant part:

> A "CBCT branch" is an automated device, established (*i.e.*, owned or rented) by a national bank at a location separate from the main office or a domestic branch, that:
>
> 1. Takes deposits, or
> 2. Disburses cash drawn against:
> (i) A customer's deposit account, or
> (ii) A customer's pre-approved loan account.

12 C.F.R. § 5.31(b) (1984). . . . Defendant Marine entered into the agreement with Wegmans not long after the Regulation was adopted, obviously on the assumption that by sharing the use of an ATM owned and operated by Wegmans, Marine would not "establish" a "branch" in Canandaigua. . . .

With this background in mind, we turn to the issues raised by defendant Marine's appeal. It is clear that whether a particular facility is a branch established and operated by a national bank under the McFadden Act is a question of federal law, that home office protection is one of New York State's restrictions as to location incorporated by reference in the McFadden Act, that plaintiff Canandaigua National Bank enjoys such protection and that Marine is therefore barred from establishing and operating a branch in Canandaigua. Thus, the key issue is whether the shared ATM in the Wegmans store in Canandaigua is a branch established and operated by Marine.

Marine argues that an electronic connection to a machine that is owned and operated by a supermarket and shared by numerous other financial institutions is not what Congress meant by "establishment" of a "branch." Marine alleges that its customers' use of Wegmans' ATM is not significantly different from their use of Wegmans' manual check cashing services, or banking by mail or telephone. Plaintiffs Banking Association and Canandaigua National Bank argue that use of Wegmans' ATM by Marine customers is a kind of electronic branch banking that falls squarely within the McFadden Act's definition of a branch, since Wegmans' ATM functions for Marine's account holders as a "place of business . . . at which deposits are received [and] checks paid." 12 U.S.C. § 36(f). . . . Both Marine and plaintiffs find support in the decision in [*Independent Bankers*]. Plaintiffs say that the District of Columbia Circuit used a functional analysis to determine the nature of a branch, and that the same method compels the conclusion here that Wegmans' ATM is a Marine branch. Marine claims that the Comptroller's Regulation used the precise language of [*Independent Bankers*] in exempting from the definition of "branch" an ATM not "owned or rented" by a national bank. Plaintiffs respond by characterizing this phrase as merely a "three-word parenthetical comment"; Marine answers that the "owned or rented" standard was central to the holding in [*Independent Bankers*] and was intended to provide a bright line test.

Resolution of these issues is not simple. The question before us is one of statutory construction. Therefore, we start with the language of 12 U.S.C. § 36(c) and (f) to divine the meaning of the phrase "establish and operate" a "branch." The parties argue that the plain meaning of these terms requires a particular result, but such arguments, by focusing on different phrases in the relevant sections, seem to balance each other off. As indicated, plaintiffs say that the Wegmans ATM is a place at which deposits are received and checks paid for Marine account holders, within the meaning of subsection (f). But it is pointed out in response that, in the words of subsection (c), Marine did not "establish" and does not "operate" the ATM in Canandaigua; Wegmans did, and does. We do not believe that the issue can be resolved for either side so simply. The meaning of the phrase "establish and operate" is affected by the ambiguity of the definition of its object, "branch." More fundamentally, Congress in 1927 could not possibly have foreseen the current revolution in banking practices. The McFadden Act pre-dated the invention of computers as well as their application to banking through electronic funds transfer systems. Banking is no longer confined to physical transactions. A rigid application of the language of 1927 to the new technology fails to confront the economic realities facing a court, and leads to anomalous results.

We see no way neatly to categorize all of the various modern ways of accomplishing banking transactions so that it will be clear (or logically distinct) which ones constitute branch banking within the meaning of 12 U.S.C. § 36(f) and which ones do not. If Wegmans' supermarket cashes a check and at the same time telephones the bank to guard against insufficiency of funds in the customer's account, apparently there is no branch; if the same functions are instantly performed by an automated teller, plaintiffs claim that there is a branch. Furthermore, the ATM networks at issue here are not even the cutting edge of the new technology. The wave of the future includes point-of-sale terminal systems (POS) and home computer banking. In the use of POS's, funds are electronically transferred directly from the customer's account to the retailer's account without the use of cash or checks. N. PENNEY & D. BAKER, *supra*, ¶ 7.01, at 7-2. It would defy common sense to consider a personal computer a branch, yet home banking by computer is already available and may soon offer some of the functions performed by Wegmans' ATM, including those arguably covered by the definition in section 36(f). The technology for such systems already exists. Frieder, *Legislating for Interstate Bank Expansion: Financial Deregulation and Public Policy*, 9 J.Corp.L. 673, 739 (1984).

Since the language of the statute is not determinative, we turn to two alternate sources of guidance–first, legislative intent at the time the McFadden Act was passed, ... and second, the views of the executive agency charged with the Act's enforcement. As to the former, it is clear that the governing principle behind the McFadden Act was to strengthen national banks and achieve approximate competitive equality between the state and national banking systems. In the words of Representative McFadden, the Act's major sponsor,

> As a result of the passage of this act . . . the national banks are able to meet the needs of modern industry and commerce and competitive equality has been established among all member banks of the Federal reserve system.

68 Cong. Rec. 5815 (1927). Indeed, the parties before us agree that the Act sought to insure

rough competitive equality between state and national banks. They disagree, however, about the impact on this objective of defining a shared ATM system as a branch.

Plaintiffs insist that failure to characterize the Wegmans-Marine arrangement as a branch gives national banks a significant competitive advantage over state banks, since the latter are barred by the New York Banking Law from using ATM's in home office protected communities. An amendment to New York Banking Law, section 105-a, was passed after the opinion below was issued, and became effective on October 8, 1984. It authorizes banks to conduct banking at ATM's, point-of-sale terminals and "similar facilities," and states generally that "[s]uch facilities shall not be deemed to be branches," but with the proviso that in home office protected communities they "shall be deemed to be branches."[3]

On the other hand, Marine argues that if we affirm the district court's ruling that the ATM at Wegmans is a Marine branch, state banks will gain a competitive advantage. Marine claims that New York State banks are authorized to use ATM's in any state in the nation that permits their use; national banks, however, will be barred from offering ATM access across state lines, since the McFadden Act allows the establishment of branches only "within the State in which said association is situated." 12 U.S.C. § 36(c)(2). Some state-chartered members of plaintiff Bankers Association, for example, would thus be insulated from competition in their home communities, yet might be free to offer ATM services in other states without competition from national banks. This could be a considerable marketing advantage, not merely a theoretical one, since numerous states have issued rulings or passed legislation permitting ATM usage, in some instances excluding it from the usual limitations on branch banking.[4] Thus, it appears that if shared ATM usage is deemed the "establishment" of a "branch" for purposes of federal law, national banks will be prohibited from the interstate activities facilitated by such laws, for the reasons given above. This will limit the ability of national banks to compete in the use of major technological developments in this industry, contrary to Congressional purpose.

We would feel uneasy, however, resting our decision primarily on a determination of economic impact that we are ill-equipped to assess. Accordingly, we turn to the interpretation of the McFadden Act by the administrative agency charged with its enforcement. Ordinarily, the agency's view would be entitled to "considerable respect," . . . and we believe that this is particularly appropriate here. Fashioning policies in response to events that were unforeseeable when the legislation was written is one of the primary functions of executive agencies. . . . The Comptroller has determined that an ATM that is not "owned or rented" by

---

3. Section 105-a, as amended, provides:

> A bank or trust company, pursuant to resolution duly adopted by a majority of its board of directors, may conduct a banking business, at automated teller machines, point-of-sale terminals, and similar facilities subject to regulations which may be promulgated by the banking board. Such facilities shall not be deemed to be branches and shall not be subject to any of the provisions of this chapter applicable to branches; provided however that notwithstanding the foregoing, for purposes of clause (ii) of subdivision one of section one hundred five of this chapter, such facilities shall be deemed to be branches, and such facilities shall be subject to the terms and conditions of section one hundred five, and for purposes of section twenty-eight-b of this chapter, such facilities shall be deemed to be branches. . . .

4. Of the approximately 40 states that have enacted special legislation authorizing state-chartered institutions to use electronic terminals, more than 20, including New York, consider them not to be "branches." Like New York, however, some of these states do impose geographic restrictions on the deployment of the terminals. N. PENNEY & D. BAKER, *supra*, ¶ 22.01[2], at 22-12 to 22-14, n. 44 (1980 & 1983 Cum.Supp.).

a national bank is not a branch under sections 36(c) and (f) of the Act. We think that considerable deference should be accorded to this view. . . . This construction need not be the only permissible one, nor the one that we necessarily would have adopted in an initial review. . . . But absent compelling evidence that the agency's regulation is erroneous, arbitrary, or clearly unsupported by the statute, judicial deference is appropriate. . . . Here, as best we can tell, the agency's interpretation in fact appears to promote the purposes of the McFadden Act.

Courts should be particularly cautious where the regulated parties have relied on the agency's ruling and would be harmed by a reversal. . . . Marine and numerous amici inform us of the substantial growth of shared ATM networks in the past decade, . . . and the reliance by national banks and other parties on the Comptroller's post-[*Independent Bankers*] rulings. Congress has passed several pieces of banking legislation since 1976 when [*Independent Bankers*] was decided, but has not overruled the Comptroller's contemporaneous interpretation of that decision. Nor has Congress moved to further define the permissible scope of national bank participation in electronic funds transfer systems, despite numerous suggestions that it do so. Such inaction lends further weight to our inclination to defer to the Comptroller's view. . . .

It is true that the Regulation uses a distinction that is perhaps arbitrary, even if it does track the language of [*Independent Bankers*]. Whether an ATM is "owned" or "rented" or simply "used" by a bank may be more a matter of how agreements are structured than a reliable determinant of whether or not the ATM constitutes a "branch." On the other hand, the differences between a Wegmans machine and a Marine branch office are significant. Marine determines where a branch office will be located in light of its own judgment concerning banking needs; Marine owns or rents the facility and maintains it; Marine controls customer access and publicly identifies the facility as its own. With Wegmans' ATM, however, Wegmans decided to install it to attract customers for its store; Wegmans owns the machine and maintains it; Wegmans apparently decides whether to allow customers of different banks to use it; and customers do not view the machine as belonging to Marine. Moreover, the [*Independent Bankers*] court's use of the "owned or rented" phraseology seems to have been more than an off-handed parenthetical, as alleged by plaintiffs. The phrase is used not just once in the [*Independent Bankers*] opinion, but twice. . . . In addition, the [*Independent Bankers*] court apparently recognized . . . that without the requirement that a facility be "established (*i.e.*, owned or rented)," the definition of "branch" would be broad enough to include almost any means of communicating instructions to a bank and in theory could bar such accepted conveniences as banking by mail and banking by telephone. Finally, definitions that draw a line between what is permitted and what is not are frequently arbitrary, but lines still must be drawn and this one has the advantage of being a bright one. For these reasons, the Comptroller's definition of "branch" in the 1982 Regulation is a reasonable construction of the McFadden Act.

. . . Plaintiffs also contend, however, and the district court agreed, that Marine has established a branch in Canandaigua even under the Comptroller's Regulation on the theory that the transaction fees Marine paid to Wegmans for each use of the ATM by Marine customers constitute "rent." We do not agree that this is "rent" in any colloquial or legal sense of the word. The fees do not grant Marine, or the other participating financial institutions, any proprietary or leasehold interest in the machine–even on a temporary basis. The transaction fee is more akin to the charge incurred for a phone call. It is a per unit cost for electronic access, by multiple parties, to equipment owned and operated by another party.

The Comptroller made a similar determination in a 1981 interpretive letter, which states that:

> a national bank which makes regular use of a facility but has no property interest in the facility has not established a branch. Thus, banks only paying a transaction fee for the use of a facility need not file branch applications; the use of the facility is analogous to the use of a mail box or post office. . . .

Comptroller Staff Interpretive Letter No. 188 (May 12, 1981), [1981-82 Transfer Binder] Fed. Banking L.Rep. (CCH) ¶ 85,269. This view, which was codified in the Comptroller's Regulation, 12 C.F.R. § 5.31(g)(4), appears to be eminently sensible. Plaintiffs argue, in effect, that all of the financial institutions that join shared ATM networks are simultaneously renting all of the ATM's electronically connected to those networks. This makes the word "rent" so broad as to be meaningless.

Notes and Comments 3.16. As is made clear in *State Bank of Fargo*, Judge Wilkey's decision in *Independent Bankers* definitively resolved the problem of the status of CBCT's, at least as a practical matter. As *Marine Midland Bank* noted, the Comptroller revised his policy in light of Judge Wilkey's decision and began treating CBCT's as branches for application purposes, and most states have amended their statutory provisions to take CBCT's into account. Nevertheless, the situation under many state statutes remained ambiguous at best. Consider the following hypothetical case. Assume that the national bank in *Plant City* is now utilizing a CBCT rather than an armored car and shopping center receptacle. Assume further that, since the decision in *Plant City*, there has been only one change in Florida law: the Florida bank administrator has issued an interpretive letter to the effect that CBCT's are not considered "branches" for purposes of state law. Florida statutory law does not specifically and affirmatively grant state banks the authority to establish and operate CBCT's. Under section 36(c), can the Comptroller approve the use of the CBCT by the national bank in Florida? *See Independent Bankers Ass'n*, 534 F.2d at n.104. *See also First Nat'l Bank v. Camp*, 465 F.2d 586, 597 (D.C. Cir. 1972).

3.17. Under the amended OCC regulations discussed in *Marine Midland Bank*, shared ATM networks directly among banks are increasingly in vogue, both regionally and nationally. Has Judge Wilkey's "cornerstone principle" of competitive equality finally been displaced? Who, if anyone, must obtain section 36 approval for a bank-shared ATM network?

3.18. *State Bank of Fargo* alludes to the relatively unrestricted branching permitted to federally chartered thrift institutions and holds that national banks in North Dakota are permitted to use CBCT's to the extent that thrift institutions are permitted to use them in the state, since state-chartered banks are so permitted. As a general matter, thrifts are not subject to any of the "competitive equality" impedimenta found in section 36. However, federally chartered thrifts have long been required to obtain approval from their regulator before establishing and operating branches. *See generally* Scott, *In Quest of Reason: The Licensing Decisions of the Federal Banking Agencies*, 42 U. Chi. L. Rev. 235, 239-242 (1975) (contrasting approval processes of Comptroller and FHLBB, since replaced by Office of Thrift Supervision).

3.19. If an office is not a "branch," what is it? It may be an operation specializing in certain aspects of one of the functions associated with a branch, but not others. Thus, it may be, for example, an agency of the institution that originates loans, preparing the paperwork and passing the file along to a branch or to headquarters for approval and disbursement (a "loan production office" or LPO), or it may be a location limiting to the servicing of loans originated in a branch or headquarters. In December 1989, the OTS published a final rule, effective January 8, 1990, that removed restrictions against any federal savings association from establishing agency offices outside the state of its home office or that of any branch. 54 Fed. Reg. 50,613 (1989) (codified at 12 C.F.R. § 545.96(a), (d)). Does this give federal savings associations a competitive advantage?

3.20. In an interpretive ruling and policy statement published in July 1989, the NCUA took a sharp departure from *Independent Bankers*. In discussing NCUA policy with respect to chartering of a federal credit union to serve a combination of distinct occupational and associational groups (a "multiple-group charter"), Interpretive Ruling and Policy Statement 89-1 stated:

> All groups must be within the operational area of a planned home or branch office of the proposed Federal credit union. . . . For chartering purposes, "branch office" means any office of a Federal credit union where an employee accepts payment on shares and disburses loans. An ATM or similar cash disbursing machine does not qualify as a "branch office."

54 Fed. Reg. 31,165, 31,170 (1989). How can the NCUA justify this position in light of *Independent Bankers*?

3.21. *Rise of nondepositor ATM fees*. In 1996, ATM networks first allowed network members to impose transaction fees. A national survey conducted by the Public Interest Research Group indicates that the cost of using another bank's ATM has since almost tripled, from an average of $1.01 in 1996 to $2.86 in 2001. *See* Joyce E. Cutler & Richard Cowden, *ATMS: U.S. PIRG Survey Finds Rising Costs for Non-Customers Using Banks' ATMS*, BNA Banking Daily, Apr. 2, 2001, at d4. The survey included 333 banks and 43 credit unions. Have costs of operating ATMs tripled in the past five years?

3.22. *GLBA and ATM fees*. With the passage of the Gramm-Leach-Bliley Act[9] (GLBA) in 1999, the Congress stepped back into ATM policy in response to a new issue that has emerged with respect to ATMs, the legitimacy of fees charged by a bank for the use of its ATM by noncustomers.[10] The GLBA requires ATM operators who impose a fee for use of an ATM by a noncustomer to post a notice on the machine and on the ATM screen that a fee will be charged and the amount of the fee.[11] When ATM cards are issued, the GLBA also requires a notice that surcharges may be imposed by other parties when transactions are initiated from ATMs not operated by the card issuer.[12]

3.23. Under the GLBA amendments and implementing regulations, ATM operators "who impose[ ] a fee on any consumer for providing host transfer services to such consumer" are required "to provide notice ... to the consumer (at the time the service is provided) of (i) the fact that a fee is imposed by such operator for providing the service; and (ii) the amount of any such fee." 15 U.S.C. § 1693b(d)(3)(A). Webster National Bank has decided to charge some but not all non-customers a fee, depending, *inter alia*, on the type of transaction, frequency of use and the home bank of the non-customer. Webster's notice on its ATM states that a fee "may" be charged. Since it is likely that *some* non-customers *will* be charged, is Webster's notice inadequate? *See Morrissey v. Webster Bank, N.A.*, 417 F.Supp.2d 183 (D.Mass. 2006) (rejecting plaintiff's interpretation of statute as requiring notice that fee "will" be charged if any non-customer would be charged as "ridiculous" and "bordering on the

---

9. Pub. L. No. 106-102, Nov. 12, 1999, 113 Stat. 1338 (1999) (codified at scattered sections of 12, 15, 16, 18 U.S.C.)

10. GLBA, § 702 (codified at 15 U.S.C. § 1693b(d)(3)).

11. GLBA, § 702 (codified at 15 U.S.C. § 1693b(d) (3)). The GLBA grants a temporary exemption from the screen notice requirement (through 31 December 2004) for older machines that are unable to provide such a notice. 15 U.S.C. § 1693(d)(3)(B)(ii).

12. GLBA, § 703 (codified at 15 U.S.C. § 1693c(a)(10)).

frivolous").

3.24. *Challenges to nondepositor ATM fees*. Nondepositor ATM fees have created controversy and have already attracted significant litigation as states, local governments and consumers attempt to thwart initiatives by banks to generate fee income from the use of their ATM networks by nondepositors.[13] Unlike state and local laws that sought to prohibit the imposition of such fees, however, the GLBA merely requires ATM operators who impose a fee for the use of an ATM by a noncustomer to post a notice on the machine and on the screen that a fee will be charged and the amount of the fee. The issue may be with us for a while before it is definitively resolved. Do the GLBA provisions have a preemptive effect as to the prohibitory provisions of state and local laws, or otherwise affect the merits of these challenges to the surcharges? Consider the following cases.

Bank One, Utah v. Guttau

190 F.3d 844 (8th Cir. 1999)
cert. denied sub nom. Foster v. Bank One, Utah,
529 U.S. 1087 (2000)

WOLLMAN, Chief Judge.

Bank One, Utah, N.A. (Bank One) appeals from the district court's denial of a preliminary injunction that would prevent the state of Iowa (the State) from enforcing Iowa statutes restricting Bank One's operation of automated teller machines (ATMs). Because we find that certain provisions of the Iowa Electronic Funds Transfer Act (EFTA), . . . are preempted by section 36 of the National Bank Act (NBA), 12 U.S.C. §§ 21-216d, we reverse the district court's order and remand for the entry of a permanent injunction prohibiting enforcement of the relevant sections.

I.

Bank One is a national bank organized under the NBA. Its main office is located in Salt Lake City, Utah, and it has no branch offices in Iowa. In 1997, Bank One installed ATMs at twenty-four retail store locations in Iowa, including eleven at Sears, Roebuck & Co. (Sears) stores throughout the state.

In October of 1997, the Iowa Superintendent of Banking ordered Sears to cease operation of the ATMs, citing multiple violations of the Iowa EFTA. On December 26, 1997, the State filed an action in state court against Sears to prevent the operation of the ATMs and to assess a fine. As a result, Sears instructed Bank One to remove all of its ATMs from Sears stores in Iowa. Bank One complied with Sears's request and placed the ATMs in storage pending the outcome of this litigation.

Bank One filed suit in district court, seeking a declaration that provisions of the Iowa EFTA restricting out-of-state banks from operating ATMs within Iowa are preempted by the NBA and praying for the issuance of a preliminary and permanent injunction. Bank One's complaint also alleged that the restrictions violate several provisions of the United States Constitution. The district court denied Bank One's motion for a preliminary injunction, finding that the challenged provisions of Iowa law were not preempted and concluding that Bank One was unlikely to succeed on any of its constitutional claims.

---

13. *See, e.g., Bank of America v. City & County of San Francisco*, 309 F.3d 551, 559 (9th Cir. 2002) (preempting San Francisco and Santa Monica ordinances prohibiting banks from charging ATM fees).

II.

Although Bank One's motion asked for a preliminary injunction, we may consider it as a motion for a permanent injunction. *See generally Minnesota Dep't of Econ. v. Riley*, 107 F.3d 648, 649 (8th Cir.1997) (reviewing a district court grant of a preliminary injunction and granting a permanent injunction because all issues were questions of law). Because Bank One and the State disagree only on questions of law, nothing remains for the district court to resolve regarding the underlying facts. Accordingly, we must determine whether a permanent injunction is appropriate. . . .

A.

The Iowa EFTA contains several provisions relevant to the placement and operation of ATMs within the state. Among other things, it contains an in-state office requirement for the establishment of ATMs:

> A satellite terminal shall not be established within this state except by a financial institution whose principal place of business is located in this state, one which has a business location licensed in this state under chapter 536A, or one which has an office located in this state and which meets the requirements of subsection 4.

Iowa Code § 527.4(1) (citing *id.* § 527.4(4), which sets various restrictions on the operation of ATMs). All banks, including national banks, must file an informational statement with the Iowa Superintendent of Banking (the administrator) stating the name of the business, the location of the terminal, a schedule of required charges, and an agreement that the bank will maintain the terminal in compliance with the Iowa EFTA. *See id.* § 527.5(3). If the administrator does not respond to the informational statement within thirty days of its filing, the informational statement is deemed to have been expressly approved. *See id.* § 527.5(7).

In addition to the in-state office and approval requirements, the Iowa EFTA limits the advertising that may be placed on an ATM. It provides:

> A satellite terminal in this state shall bear a sign or label identifying each type of financial institution utilizing the terminal. A satellite terminal location in this state shall not be used to advertise individual financial institutions or a group of financial institutions. However, a satellite terminal shall bear a sign or label no larger than three inches by two inches identifying the name, address, and telephone number of the owner of the satellite terminal. The administrator may authorize methods of identification the administrator deems necessary to enable the general public to determine the accessibility of a satellite terminal.

Id. § 527.5(5).

The NBA grants national banks the authority to exercise "all such incidental powers as shall be necessary to carry on the business of banking." . . . [12 U.S.C. § 24 (Seventh).] Bank One argues that the NBA implicitly authorizes the placement of ATMs without restriction by the states. The provisions of the Iowa EFTA, it argues, impair the ability of a national bank to place its ATMs and to advertise thereon.

"[G]rants of both enumerated and incidental 'powers' to national banks [are] grants of authority not normally limited by, but rather ordinarily preempting, contrary state law." *Barnett Bank v. Nelson*, 517 U.S. 25 (1996). Where state law stands "as an obstacle to the accomplishment and execution of the full purposes and objectives of Congress," it may be found to be preempted. *Id.* (quoting *Hines v. Davidowitz*, 312 U.S. 52, 67 (1941)). State regulations are not preempted, however, when Congress "accompan[ies] a grant of an explicit power with an explicit statement that the exercise of that power is subject to state law." *Id.* Congress predicated the establishment of national bank branches upon compliance with state regulations. *See* 12 U.S.C. § 36(c). Therefore, in order to determine whether the NBA preempts the Iowa regulations, we must determine whether an ATM is a "branch" as defined in section 36.

In 1996, Congress amended section 36 to read, "[t]he term 'branch', as used in this section, does not include an automated teller machine or a remote service unit." *See* 12 U.S.C. § 36(j). Thus, whatever regulatory authority the states may retain with respect to national bank branches, the 1996 amendment clearly expresses Congress's intent that that authority no longer extends to national bank ATMs.

That intent is made even clearer in light of the assumption that Congress enacts legislation with knowledge of relevant judicial decisions. . . . Prior to the 1996 amendment, courts had held that because ATMs were branches they were subject to state restrictions. . . . By excluding ATMs from the definition of "branch," Congress eliminated the contingency that formed the basis of those decisions and thus signaled its intention to foreclose the states from imposing location and approval restrictions on a national bank's ATMs.

Likewise, the legislative history of the 1996 amendment makes clear Congress's intent in adopting the amendment, which was enacted as part of the Economic Growth and Regulatory Paperwork Reduction Act of 1996. The purpose of this act was to "strengthen our nation's financial institutions and to increase their competitiveness." S.Rep. No. 104-185, at 1 (1996). The legislation was intended to "allow financial institutions to devote additional resources to productive activities, such as making loans, rather than to compliance with unnecessary regulations." *Id.* "Section [36(j)] clarifies that an 'ATM' or 'remote service unit' is not considered a 'branch' for purposes of federal bank branching law and is therefore not subject to prior approval requirements or geographic restrictions." *Id.* at 24.

Finally, the interpretation given the 1996 amendment by the Office of the Comptroller of the Currency (OCC), which appears in this action as an *amicus* supporting Bank One, supports a finding that the relevant Iowa regulations are preempted. . . . [T]he Supreme Court has made it clear that the Comptroller's interpretation of the NBA is entitled to great weight. . . . *Clarke v. Securities Indus. Ass'n*, 479 U.S. 388 (1987). *See also Smiley v. Citibank (South Dakota), N.A.*, 517 U.S. 735 (1996); *Independent Bankers Ass'n of America v. Clarke*, 917 F.2d 1126, 1128 (8th Cir.1990). The OCC has ruled that "[a] national bank may perform, provide, or deliver through electronic means and facilities any activity, function, product, or service that it is otherwise authorized to perform, provide, or deliver." *See* 12 C.F.R. § 7.1019 (1998); *see also* OCC Interpretative Letter No. 821, 1998 LEXIS 15 at *10 (Feb. 17, 1998) (stating that section 36 preempts state geographic restrictions of ATMs). We conclude that the OCC's interpretation is a reasonable one. ...

Given the clear language of the 1996 amendment, its legislative history and the judicial decisions that formed the backdrop against which it was adopted, and the interpretation of the regulatory body charged with the responsibility of administering the national banking laws, we conclude that Bank One's ATMs are not subject to the restrictions contained in Iowa Code § 527.4(1).

Bank One also challenges that provision of Iowa law which states that ATMs "shall not be used to advertise individual financial institutions or a group of financial institutions." Iowa Code § 527.5(5). Assuming that this section has any validity as against a national bank ATM in light of our holding with respect to section 527.4(1), we conclude that it is preempted by the NBA. In *Franklin National Bank v. New York*, 347 U.S. 373 (1954), the Supreme Court held that a state law prohibiting national banks from using the word "saving" or "savings" was preempted by the NBA. In so holding, the Court noted that "[m]odern competition for business finds advertising one of the most usual and useful of weapons. We cannot believe that the incidental powers granted to national banks should be construed so narrowly as to preclude the use of advertising in any branch of their authorized business." *Id.* at 377 (referring to the incidental powers granted in 12 U.S.C. § 24 (Seventh)). In light of *Franklin*, we conclude that the State's attempt to regulate the advertisements on Bank One's ATMs is preempted. *See Barnett Bank* (stating that grants of incidental powers to national banks normally preempt contrary state law).

Moreover, the OCC considered a similar Colorado EFTA provision requiring banks to remove their names from ATMs or to place the names of all other banks whose customers may use the machines. It declared in an interpretative letter that these regulations created a "significant burden on a national bank's right to engage in the business of banking by means of an ATM, as authorized by the [NBA]." OCC Interpretative Letter No. 789 [1997 Transfer Binder] Fed. Banking L.Rep. (CCH) ¶ 81-216 at 90,244 (June 27, 1997) (citing 12 U.S.C. § 24 (Seventh)). Once again giving deference to the OCC's interpretation of the national banking laws, we conclude that this provision of Iowa law must be held invalid as against national bank ATMs.

The State argues that the federal Electronic Funds Transfer Act, 15 U.S.C. §§ 1693-1693r permits the states to regulate the electronic transfer of funds. The federal EFTA was enacted in 1978 "to provide a basic framework establishing the rights, liabilities, and responsibilities of participants in electronic fund transfer systems." 15 U.S.C. § 1693(b). The primary objective of the federal EFTA "is the provision of individual consumer rights." *Id.* To achieve that goal, the act allows the states to retain control over electronic transfers:

> This subchapter does not annul, alter, or affect the laws of any State relating to electronic funds transfers, except to the extent that those laws are inconsistent with the provisions of this subchapter, and then only to the extent of the inconsistency. A State law is not inconsistent with this subchapter if the protection such law affords any consumer is greater than the protection afforded by this subchapter.

15 U.S.C. § 1693q. Despite the State's claims, this anti-preemption provision is specifically limited to the provisions of the federal EFTA, and nothing therein grants the states any additional authority to regulate national banks. State regulation of national banks is proper where "doing so does not prevent or significantly interfere with the national bank's exercise of its powers." *Barnett Bank*. Congress has made clear in the NBA its intent that ATMs are not to be subject to state regulation, and thus the provisions of the Iowa EFTA that would prevent or significantly interfere with Bank One's placement and operation of its ATMs must be held to be preempted.

B.

To be entitled to the grant of an injunction, Bank One must establish the existence of irreparable harm. We conclude that it has done so, for in the absence of an injunction the continued enforcement of the relevant provisions of the Iowa EFT would result in irreparable economic loss to Bank One. Accordingly, Bank One is entitled to the entry of a permanent injunction enjoining the enforcement of those provisions.

BRIGHT, Circuit Judge, dissenting.

The court today reverses the district court and orders it to enjoin the State from enforcing Iowa Code Chapter 527, in its entirety, against Bank One–or against any other national bank for that matter. The court does so because it concludes that, following Congress's 1996 changes to the statutory definition of "branch," as found in 12 U.S.C. § 36(j),

Automated Teller Machines ("ATMs") are exempt from geographical branching requirements based in state law. While it is true that such requirements no longer pertain to ATMs, I cannot agree that this exemption controls the disposition of the case before us. Even if a national bank's ATMs need not comply with state law geographic restrictions, that does not mean other relevant and permissible state law restrictions are preempted thereby. Many of the sections of Iowa law at issue here are simply not geographical restrictions and ought not be analyzed as though they were.

In my view, those statutory restrictions imposed under Chapter 527 which are valid, evenhanded consumer protections are not preempted by federal law. Thus, I believe that the Superintendent is entitled to enforce them against banks, both state and national alike. I therefore respectfully dissent.

Iowa Code, Chapter 527, titled Electronic Transfer of Funds, has a number of subsections. Many of these subsections are simply not geographical branching restrictions. For example, § 527.5(5) indicates that, "[An ATM] terminal shall bear a sign or label no larger than three inches by two inches identifying the name, address, and telephone number of the owner." Thus, by its terms, this subsection is a straightforward consumer protection measure. . . .

Protection of the consumer is well within the power of States to render and is not preempted by federal law. In the recent case of *Barnett Bank of Marion County, N.A. v. Nelson*, 517 U.S. 25 (1996), the Supreme Court had reason to consider the contours of preemption in the context of federal banking law. There the Court noted that, "[i]n defining the preemptive scope of statutes and regulations granting a power to national banks . . . normally Congress would not want States to forbid, or to impair significantly, the exercise of a power that Congress explicitly granted." *Id.* at 33. The Court went on to add, however, that "[t]o say this is not to deprive States of the power to regulate national banks, where (unlike here) doing so does not prevent or significantly interfere with the national bank's exercise of its powers." *Id.* (parenthetical in original). . . . Thus, when a State attempts to regulate the activities of a national bank within its jurisdiction, the State's laws are not preempted if they create no significant interference with the national bank's exercise of its due powers.

A subsection of Chapter 527, such as § 527.5(5), which does no more than protect innocent Iowans through the imposition of a *de minimus* labeling requirement creates no significant interference with any legitimate power vested in national banks, explicit or otherwise. Thus, in my view, these subsections are simply not preempted.

Moreover, it is important to note that the statute before us applies with equal force against both state and national banks. Every bank is required to comply and no advantage is gained by state chartered institutions in the process. This latter point is critically important because the questions raised by consumerism might warrant a different analysis if Iowa's statute were constructed so as to favor state banks, giving them an advantage over their national bank counterparts in the ongoing competition for borrowers, deposits, and fees. After all, the National Bank Act ("NBA") has been repeatedly interpreted to prevent such competitive imbalances and to insure that national banks are allowed to compete on an even footing with state banks. *See First Nat'l Bank of Logan, Utah v. Walker Bank & Trust Co.*, 385 U.S. 252, 261 (1966) ("Congress intended to place national and state banks on a basis of 'competitive equality'. . . ."); *First Nat'l Bank in Plant City, Florida v. Dickinson*, 396 U.S. 122, 131 (1969) (The NBA "respond[s] to the competitive tensions inherent in a dual banking structure ... [and] reflects the congressional concern that neither system have advantages over the other. . . .").

Ironically, the court's conclusion in this case is at odds with this important principle of competitive equality. State chartered banks remain bound by Iowa's consumer protection laws. To the extent that the court's decision today means that national banks are given a free pass, national banks thereby achieve a distinct and favored position under the law. Competitive equality this is not.

First Union Nat. Bank v. Burke

48 F.Supp.2d 132 (D.Conn. 1999)

ARTERTON, District Judge.

These motions present the deceptively simple question of who has the authority to administratively enforce state banking laws against in-state branches of national banks. The answer requires analysis of the requirements of the national banking regulatory scheme with respect to the Connecticut Banking Commissioner's ("Commissioner") recent issuance of administrative cease and desist orders against the plaintiff banks, requiring that they cease imposing on non-depositor customers a surcharge fee for transactions at the banks' automated teller machines ("ATMs").

These now consolidated actions were originally brought by two out-of-state national banks with branches in Connecticut, joined subsequently by the Office of the Comptroller of the Currency ("OCC") whose request to file an intervening complaint was granted without objection. In its intervening complaint, the OCC claims that by the National Banking Act and related federal banking statutes, Congress intended the OCC to have exclusive administrative enforcement authority over national banks for all laws, including state banking laws related to ATM transaction fees. The OCC seeks a preliminary injunction to enjoin the Commissioner from proceeding with its pending administrative action against the two plaintiff national banks. . . . The Commissioner seeks to dismiss the OCC's intervening complaint claiming: lack of subject matter jurisdiction, that abstention is required, that the OCC fails to state a claim, and that the regulatory scheme urged by the OCC violates the Tenth Amendment.

For the following reasons, the Commissioner's Motion to Dismiss the OCC's Intervening Complaint is DENIED and the OCC's Motion for a Preliminary Injunction is GRANTED, enjoining the Commissioner from proceeding with his pending administrative enforcement proceeding against Fleet Bank and First Union National Bank pending final disposition of the OCC's complaint. This order does not address the Commissioner's interpretation of the ATM statute in dispute, Conn. Gen. Stat. § 36a-156, nor does it preclude either the OCC from initiating its own administrative proceeding related to Conn. Gen. Stat. § 36a-156 or the Commissioner from further seeking enforcement through judicial means.

Introduction

A. Prior Litigation

Although this action arises within the context of the ongoing dispute between Fleet Bank and the Connecticut Banking Commissioner over whether a national bank may impose surcharge or "convenience" fees on non-depositors who access Fleet's ATMs in the state of Connecticut, the current posture of the case raises an issue not previously before this Court or the Second Circuit in *Fleet Bank, Nat'l Ass'n v. Burke*, 23 F.Supp.2d 196, *vacated* 160 F.3d 883 (2d Cir.1998) (hereafter "*Fleet I*"): whether the Commissioner's cease and desist order unlawfully interferes with the OCC's exclusive regulatory and enforcement authority over national banks on this subject.

In *Fleet I*, Fleet sought a declaratory judgment asserting the preemptive effect of the national banking laws over the Banking Commissioner's interpretation of Conn. Gen. Stat.

§ 36a-156. The Second Circuit vacated this Court's ruling that interpreted state law as the predicate step for determining whether the state law conflicted with federal law so as to be preempted. The Second Circuit articulated the principle that Fleet's defensive preemption claim was inadequate to confer subject matter jurisdiction and remanded the case for dismissal. In denying Fleet's motion for reconsideration, the Second Circuit made clear that raising the OCC's claim of exclusive authority over national banks as grounds for reconsideration "is presented too late to warrant consideration in this litigation; moreover, that claim is currently pending in separate litigation now pending in the District Court. Our opinion in this litigation is not intended to deny the District Court any jurisdiction, otherwise available over a complaint that omits a claim requiring construction of state law." *Fleet Bank, Nat'l Ass'n v. Burke*, 160 F.3d 883 (2d Cir.1998) (order denying Fleet's petition for rehearing).

B. Current Litigation

Immediately following issuance of the Second Circuit's decision on November 9, 1998, the Commissioner issued cease and desist orders directing Fleet, First Union and a third national bank to immediately stop imposing surcharge fees or subject themselves to fines of up to $7,500 per violation. On the same day, Fleet and First Union separately filed these actions under 42 U.S.C. § 1983, seeking injunctive relief prohibiting the Commissioner from enforcing his cease and desist order. Simultaneously, Fleet and First Union sought and were denied a temporary injunction in Connecticut superior court in which they sought to enjoin the Commissioner's temporary cease and desist orders on state law grounds expressly reserving their federal law claims for adjudication in federal district court. *See Fleet Nat'l Bank v. Burke*, 1998 WL 892258 (Conn. Super. Nov. 20, 1998) (Teller, J.). After initially filing an *amicus* brief in this action, the OCC intervened to preserve what it claims to be its exclusive authority to enforce all banking laws, state and federal, against national banks. By agreement of all parties at oral argument, further administrative proceedings on the cease and desist orders were stayed pending the Court's ruling on the plaintiffs' motions for a preliminary injunction and the Commissioner's motions to dismiss. . . .

Jurisdictional Challenges

The Commissioner has moved to dismiss the OCC's intervening complaint on the following four grounds: 1) this Court lacks jurisdiction over the OCC's intervening complaint in the absence of jurisdiction over the plaintiff national banks' complaints; 2) abstention is required under the *Younger* doctrine; 3) the OCC's intervening complaint fails to state a cause of action, and 4) even if the OCC does have exclusive administrative enforcement authority for Connecticut's ATM law as applied to national banks, such a role violates the Tenth Amendment.

A. Subject Matter Jurisdiction

The Court must initially satisfy itself that it has subject matter jurisdiction over the OCC's intervening complaint before considering any request for relief based upon the merits of the case. . . .

1. Relation between jurisdiction over the OCC's intervening complaint and national banks' complaints

The Commissioner contends that if the Court lacks jurisdiction over the plaintiff banks' original complaints, it necessarily lacks jurisdiction over the OCC's intervening complaint and thus the Court must first determine whether it has jurisdiction over the banks' complaints before determining whether its jurisdiction over the OCC's intervening complaint. The Commissioner relies upon "[t]he longstanding and clear rule is that 'if jurisdiction is lacking at the commencement of [a] suit, it cannot be aided by intervention of a plaintiff with a sufficient claim.'" *Pressroom Unions-Printers League Income Sec. Fund v. Continental*

Assurance Co., 700 F.2d 889, 893 (2d Cir.) *cert. denied* 464 U.S. 845 (1983) (quoting *Pianta v. H.M. Reich Co.*, 77 F.2d 888, 890 (2d Cir.1935)). *See also* 7C CHARLES A. WRIGHT, ARTHUR R. MILLER, & MARY KAY KANE, FEDERAL PRACTICE AND PROCEDURE § 1917, at 457 (2d ed.1986) (intervention cannot cure any jurisdictional defect that would have barred the federal court from hearing the original action).

The Commissioner is only partially correct. While the existence of a properly asserted federal claim by the OCC does not and could not cure the absence of jurisdiction over the banks' complaint, such alleged deficiency does not divest this Court of jurisdiction over the OCC's complaint since a trial court has discretion to consider the intervenor's complaint and corresponding motion for a preliminary injunction as a separate action if jurisdiction is proper with respect to the intervenor's complaint, avoiding the unnecessary and overly formalistic procedure of dismissing the pending action and requiring the OCC to refile the matter. . . . Therefore, while reserving judgment on the issue of its jurisdiction over the banks' complaints, the Court will treat the OCC's intervening complaint as a separate action for the purpose of considering subject matter jurisdiction.

2. Jurisdiction over OCC's Intervening Complaint

In its intervening complaint dated December 1, 1998, the OCC asserts jurisdiction under 28 U.S.C. § 1331 and § 1337 as an action arising under the Supremacy Clause of the United States Constitution and federal statutes, 12 U.S.C. § 24 (Seventh) and § 484. . . . The OCC claims authority to bring this action pursuant to 12 U.S.C. § 93(d) authorizing the OCC to enforce any provision of the banking title, or any other law or regulation or any action suit or proceeding to which the OCC is a party.

In its complaint, the OCC contends that the pending enforcement action by the Commissioner directly interferes with its exclusive authority to regulate and supervise the banking activities of national banks pursuant to its "visitorial power" under 12 U.S.C. § 484. At this stage, the OCC does not challenge the Commissioner's interpretation of Conn. Gen. Stat. § 36a-156, nor its applicability to these national banks, but instead disputes the Commissioner's administrative enforcement authority to issue cease and desist orders against national banks, claiming the Commissioner's actions abrogate the OCC's exclusive administrative enforcement authority provided in 12 U.S.C. § 24 (Seventh), 12 U.S.C. § 484, and/or 15 U.S.C. § 1693(o).

Thus, neither interpretation of state banking law (Conn. Gen. Stat. § 36a- 156), nor its preemption by federal banking law is put in issue by the OCC's complaint and motion. The narrow issue presented is whether the Commissioner's pending cease and desist order violates the OCC's claimed right of exclusive regulatory authority over these plaintiff national banks.

Exercising its discretion to consider the OCC's intervening complaint as a separate action brought under federal law, the Court concludes that it has subject matter jurisdiction under 28 U.S.C. §§ 1331 and 1337 to determine the OCC's claim of exclusive authority.

B. Abstention Arguments

The Court next considers the Commissioner's contention that the Court must nonetheless abstain under the *Younger* doctrine, in that the "normal thing to do when federal courts are asked to enjoin pending proceedings in state courts is not to issue such injunctions." *Younger v. Harris*, 401 U.S. 37, 45 (1971).

The test of whether *Younger* abstention is appropriate is "(1) whether there is an ongoing state proceeding; (2) whether an important state interest is involved; and (3) whether the federal plaintiff has an adequate opportunity for judicial review of his [federal] constitutional claims during or after the proceeding." *University Club v. City of New York*, 842 F.2d 37, 39 (2d Cir. 1988). Although the *Younger* doctrine emerged in the context of criminal proceedings, subsequent decisions have liberally expanded it, to the point that abstention may now be proper even if the ongoing state proceeding is administrative and the plaintiff must wait for state court review to have its constitutional claim heard. . . .

The OCC argues that the Court has an unflagging obligation to exercise the jurisdiction given to it and that the *Younger* doctrine is inapplicable when the United States is a party to the action. However, the Supreme Court in *Colorado River Water Conservation District v. United States*, 424 U.S. 800, 816 n. 23, expressly left open this question of "when, if at all, abstention would be appropriate where the Federal Government seeks to invoke federal jurisdiction." The OCC contends that *Younger*'s policy of avoiding conflicts between the state and federal courts is more appropriate in the case of private litigants but that by "the time the United States brings suit in federal court against a state, any attempt to avoid a federal-state conflict would be futile." . . .

In contrast, the Commissioner urges this Court to follow the Sixth Circuit's approach in *United States v. Ohio*, 614 F.2d 101, 105 (6th Cir.1979), applying the *Younger* abstention doctrine notwithstanding the presence of a federal agency as a federal plaintiff. In *United States v. Ohio*, the Government filed a declaratory action against the State of Ohio alleging that the imposition of state taxes on government contractors was improper under state law. Notwithstanding the anticipation that the issue of the constitutionality of the state tax assessments would inevitably be raised in the course of the challenge to the state tax, the Sixth Circuit found abstention appropriate under either [*Railroad Commission v.*] *Pullman* [*Co.*, 312 U.S. 496 (1941)] [or] *Younger*, reasoning that the constitutional issue could be raised in the state forum and there was no indication that the United States could not intervene and raise its constitutional claims in the state proceeding. Analogously, the Commissioner argues that the "question of whether the OCC has the exclusive authority under the National Banking Act to interpret and enforce Connecticut's ATM law can be properly litigated in the presently ongoing state proceedings, either by the national banks or the OCC itself." . . . *United States v. Ohio* is, however, distinguishable since the sole basis for federal jurisdiction was the status of the United States as plaintiff and the only issue raised on the face of the complaint was a challenge to the state's interpretation of state law. In contrast, the OCC is not only the intervening plaintiff in this case, but alleges solely a federal claim–its exclusive enforcement authority under national banking law–not the state's interpretation of its banking law. Therefore, no questions of state law affect the OCC's federal claim of exclusive enforcement authority of that state law.

Moreover, the OCC is not a party to the pending administrative enforcement proceeding,[3] and neither national bank has yet raised the OCC's claim of exclusive authority as a defense in that proceeding. . . . Although the national banks are the subjects of the pending cease and desist orders and their interest in raising the OCC's exclusive enforcement authority overlaps to some extent with OCC's claim in this action, the OCC's interest in preserving what it perceives to be its exclusive regulatory authority over national banks extends far beyond the plaintiff banks' particular interest in imposing surcharge fees, with probable ramifications beyond the current dispute, to the national regulatory scheme over national banks. . . . The OCC argues that it would be futile for this Court to abstain and force it to intervene in precisely the state proceeding that it claims the Commissioner lacks authority to conduct in order to raise its claim of exclusive enforcement authority. The OCC's complaint makes no claim that the state banking law, Conn. Gen. Stat. § 36a-156, is preempted by federal law, but rather that state proceeding interferes with its exclusive

3. The OCC filed an *amicus* brief in the banks' unsuccessful state court proceeding seeking a temporary injunction. The Commissioner contends that the OCC would be permitted to intervene in the state administrative proceedings under state law. . . .

regulatory enforcement authority over national banks. Without needing to resolve the larger issue of whether abstention is ever appropriate when the federal government raises a federal claim against a state in federal court, the Court finds that under these circumstances abstention is not appropriate given that the OCC is not a litigant in the pending state proceeding, its interests are broader than those of the respondent national banks, the strong federal interest in a uniform enforcement mechanism over national banks is at least as important as the State's interest in enforcing its banking laws, the OCC's interest in asserting its regulatory authority to enforce state law is not necessarily antithetical to the state's interest in insuring compliance with state law, and that the precise nature of this dispute–jurisdictional–indicates the inadequacy of the opportunity for state judicial review. Accordingly, the Court declines to abstain on these grounds. . . .

Merits of OCC Motion for Preliminary Injunctive Relief

A. Likelihood of Success

The OCC claims that the pending cease and order issued by the Commissioner interferes with or violates the OCC's exclusive authority to regulate national banks through regulation and administrative enforcement actions as provided for under federal banking law. In opposition, the Commissioner maintains that: 1) the state has the implicit authority to enforce state ATM laws directly against national banks under the Electronic Funds Act, 15 U.S.C. § 1693(q); 2) ATM transactions involving non-depositors do not fall within the "business of banking," and 3) any federal regulatory scheme impairing state authority to enforce state banking laws against national banks violates the Tenth Amendment of the United States Constitution. . . .

1. "Visitorial powers"

The OCC contends that the pending state administrative enforcement of the Commissioner's cease and desist order represents an intrusion on its statutory visitorial and enforcement powers and does not fall within any of the narrow exceptions provided under 12 U.S.C. § 484. The Commissioner disputes the OCC's interpretation of its visitorial authority as overbroad and contrary to precedent establishing State authority to enforce state banking laws against national banks and maintains that he may directly enforce against national bank branches the state banking statute, which he interprets as prohibiting the imposition of ATM surcharge fees on non-depositors, without interfering with the regulatory and enforcement authority over national banks conferred by Congress on the OCC.

Title 12, § 484 of the United States Code states in pertinent part:

> (a) No national bank shall be subject to any visitorial powers except as authorized by Federal law, vested in the courts of justice or such as shall be, or have been exercised or directed by Congress or by either House thereof or by any committee of Congress or of either House duly authorized.
>
> (b) Notwithstanding subsection (a) of this section, lawfully authorized state auditors and examiners may, at reasonable times and upon reasonable notice to a bank, review its records solely to ensure compliance with applicable State unclaimed property or escheat laws upon reasonable cause to believe that the bank has failed to comply with such laws.

12 U.S.C. § 484. Although section 484 does not contain an explicit grant of exclusive regulatory or visitorial power over national banks to the OCC, the OCC contends that section 484 precludes states from any visitorial power over national banks unless authorized by federal law, court order or within the narrow exception created under section 484(b).

The OCC has interpreted federal visitorial power under section 484 as extending to ensuring the bank's compliance with state banking laws. Faced with three state statutes imposing certain credit card requirements on national banks and enforceable by state agencies, the OCC concluded that it alone was vested with enforcement authority:

> The enforcement authority of the Office of the Comptroller of Currency has not been limited to the enforcement of federal law. Although states have an important interest in ensuring that their laws are obeyed, the Office of the Comptroller of Currency is the exclusive regulator of national banks. It is, therefore, the province of the Office of the Comptroller of Currency, not state regulators to examine national banks compliance with state laws. . . . *See generally* 12 U.S.C. § 1818(b) *et seq.* . . . Congress has delegated to the Office of the Comptroller of Currency the authority to issue cease and desist orders and to take other enforcement actions, including levying civil money penalties, against national banks to ensure that they comply with the laws applicable to them, including state laws. . . . In light of the foregoing legal authority, the Office of the Comptroller of Currency has consistently maintained that state attempts to exercise supervisory authority over national banks are preempted. [citation to prior interpretive letters omitted].

Interpretive Letter No. 614, [1992-1993 Transfer Binder] Fed. Banking L. Rep. ¶ 83,454 (January 15, 1993). . . .

. . . The OCC's concept of its exclusive enforcement authority is drawn from *Nat'l State Bank, Elizabeth, N.J. v. Long*, 630 F.2d 981 (3rd Cir.1980), in which the Third Circuit held that the state banking commissioner was precluded from enforcing the state anti-redlining law against national banks by means of a cease and desist order even though the state anti-redlining statute was not preempted by a federal anti-redlining provision. In reaching its conclusion, the Third Circuit noted:

> Questions about the applicability of state legislation to national banks must be distinguished from the related inquiry of who is responsible for enforcing national bank compliance. In analyzing the latter issue, we find that important federal interests take precedence over competing state concerns. Thus, we find ourselves unable to agree with the district court's determination that state officials have the power to issue cease and desist orders against national banks for violations of the antiredlining statute.

Id. at 987-88. Recognizing the potential for state law applicability to national banks under federal regulatory control, the Third Circuit observed:

> Whatever may be the history of federal-state relations in other fields, regulation of banking has been one of dual control since the passage of the first National Bank Act in 1863. . . . In only a few instances has Congress explicitly preempted state regulation of national banks. More commonly, it has been left to the courts to delineate the proper boundaries of federal and state supervision.

Id. at 986. . . .

The Commissioner views *Long* as an aberration and contrary to precedent he claims recognizes state authority to enforce state banking laws against national banks. In so arguing, he relies on *Brown v. Clarke*, 878 F.2d 627 (2d Cir.1989) (suit brought by Commissioner against national bank in federal court after the OCC refused to enforce state law against national banks); *First Nat'l Bank v. Dickinson*, 396 U.S. 122 (1969) (declaratory and injunctive action brought by national bank with OCC as intervening plaintiff against state comptroller following his letter "requesting" bank to cease and desist operations of services which violated state branch banking laws);[5] *Jackson v. Valdosta*, 349 F.2d 71 (5th Cir. 1965) (declaratory judgment action by state superintendent of banks seeking declaration that bank could not operate a drive-in banking facility under federal banking law that incorporates state law limits on branching laws); *First Nat'l Bank of Bay City v. Fellows*, 244 U.S. 416 (1917) (state commissioner could initiate a *quo warranto* proceeding in state court to test the authority of national bank to engage in trust services).

While these cases indeed involved disputes between state banking authorities and national banks over the application of state law to national banks, they are all actions seeking judicial declaratory or injunctive relief, and do not involve state administrative cease and desist orders. Thus, these cases should be seen as falling within the "visitorial powers" recognized in Section 484 as "vested in the courts of justice." While these cases illustrate ways in which a state may seek enforcement of its state banking laws in either federal or state court, they do not stand for the proposition that states may directly enforce state law against national banks.

The OCC's view of its exclusive administrative enforcement authority for all banking laws, state and federal is consistent with 12 U.S.C. § 36(f), making certain types of state laws applicable to interstate branches of national banks. The Riegle-Neal Interstate Banking Act of 1994, amending section 36(c) of the McFadden Act to permit interstate branching, explicitly subjects interstate branches of national banks to "the laws of the host State regarding community reinvestment, consumer protection, fair lending, and establishment of interstate branches." 12 U.S.C. § 36(f)(1)(A). However, at the same time, Congress also made clear that "the provisions of any State law to which a branch of a national bank is subject under this paragraph shall be enforced with respect to the such branch by the Comptroller of the Currency." 12 U.S.C. § 36(f)(1)(B). . . .

Although the legislative history of the Riegle-Neal Interstate Banking Act contains some Congressional expression of concern that the OCC historically may have been too willing to find state laws preempted and not enforceable, Congress granted the OCC exclusive enforcement authority over interstate branches' compliance with state banking laws and required it to maintain a report of its preemption determinations for Congressional review under 12 U.S.C. § 36(f)(C). Although ATMs are expressly excluded from the definition of "branches" under Section 36(j), the regulatory structure of Section 36(f)(1)(B) reflects Congressional intent that the existing regulatory scheme remain unchanged in further corroboration of the OCC's view of its exclusive regulatory role.

2. Electronic Funds Transfer Act

The Commissioner claims that the Electronic Funds Transfer Act, 15 U.S.C. § 1693 *et seq.* (EFTA), which specifically governs ATM transactions and thus controls the analysis, preserves the state's right to enforce state banking laws against national banks where the state law is a consumer protection measure and is not inconsistent with the Electronic Funds Transfer Act. The statutory section relied on states:

> This subchapter does not annul, alter or affect the laws of any State relating to electronic fund transfers, except to the extent that those laws are inconsistent with the provisions of this subchapter, and then only to the extent of the inconsistency. A State law is not inconsistent with this subchapter if the

5. The national bank's request for federal injunctive relief in *Dickinson* arose after the state had "requested" the national banks to cease and desist from the disputed activity. Even though the OCC intervened to assert federal preemption of state law, nothing in the opinion suggests that the issue of the OCC's exclusive enforcement authority was raised by the parties or even considered by the Supreme Court in its determination that the state's interpretation of its law was correct.

> protection such law affords any consumer is greater than the protection afforded by this subchapter.

15 U.S.C. § 1693(q). The Commissioner's claim of authority under the EFTA to enforce Conn. Gen. Stat. § 36a-156 is based on his contention that it is a state "consumer protection" statute that affords consumers greater protection and is not inconsistent with the EFTA. He reasons that since the state ATM statute is unaffected by the EFTA, national banks that violate it cannot be said to have violated the EFTA because state law was not substantively incorporated into the EFTA and thus the OCC's EFTA enforcement authority is inapplicable.

Without conceding the applicability of the EFTA, the OCC argues that the EFTA, far from displacing OCC exclusive enforcement authority, preserves federal authority to take administrative enforcement actions through cease and desist orders against national banks for violations of state law pursuant to 12 U.S.C. § 1818(b). Section 1693(o) of the Electronic Funds Transfer Act provides:

> Compliance with the requirements imposed under this title shall be enforced . . . , in the case of (a) national banks, and federal branches and Federal agencies of foreign banks, by the Office of the Comptroller of the Currency. . . .

This OCC enforcement authority is exercised by means of cease and desist orders directed against national banks if any such institution "is about to violate, a law, rule, or regulation, or any condition imposed in writing . . . or any written agreement entered into with the agency." 12 U.S.C. § 1818(b)(1). The OCC further argues that the Commissioner's position that he implicitly retains enforcement authority would render the above EFTA administrative enforcement provision nugatory. The language of the EFTA simply does not support the Commissioner's interpretation and does not contain language from which it can be reasonably inferred that Congress intended to disrupt other federal laws including the National Banking Act by an implicit reservation of the power to administratively regulate banks to the states. Thus, the Court concludes that an independent state enforcement power for state consumer protection laws against national banks cannot be read into the EFTA.

3. "Business of Banking"

The Commissioner next takes the position that the type of ATM transaction involving a national bank and a non-depositor falls outside "banking business," and therefore outside the scope of the OCC's exclusive regulatory authority. He analogizes the bank's ATMs used to conduct the transaction with a non-depositor to a vending machine that distributes cash instead of sodas, and thus the service has no relation to the business of banking, and constituting a matter over which he retains regulatory authority. This theory, that determination of state regulatory authority over national banks' ATM services is predicated on who accesses the national bank's branches' ATMs, is without legal authority or sound rationale. The ATM service offered to these non-depositors enables them to access their accounts at their own banks from a different geographic location and logically constitutes part of banking business. The fact that the EFTA designates the OCC as responsible for enforcing the law on national banks relative to such electronic transfers further supports the premise that such transactions may reasonably be considered the business of banking when the ATMs are owned and operated by national banks. OCC interpretative letters and regulation give further support to the inclusion of ATM related activity as within the business of banking. "The establishment of ATMs by national banks is authorized by section 24 (Seventh)" since they serve as an instrumentality for performing activities that are incidental to business of banking. Interpretative Letter, No. 789, 1997 WL 402489 (finding that provisions of the Colorado state EFT Act were preempted by federal law). The OCC has also promulgated the following regulation:

> A national bank may perform, provide, or deliver through electronic means and facilities any activity, function or product, or service that it is otherwise authorized to perform, provide or deliver. A national bank may also, in order to optimize the use of the bank's resources, market and sell to third parties electronic capacities acquired or developed by the bank in good faith for banking purposes.

12 C.F.R. § 7.1019.

Finally, the Commissioner's argument that these ATM services do not constitute the business of banking seems disingenuous in light of the actions of the state banking commissioner to enjoin fees imposed by banks on such transactions as violative of state banking laws.

4. Tenth Amendment Challenge

Lastly, the Commissioner challenges the OCC's likelihood of success on the grounds that the OCC's expansive reading of the enforcement procedures under the National Banking Act and EFTA, specifically 12 U.S.C. §§ 484 and 36(f), intrudes on Connecticut's constitutional sovereignty under the Tenth Amendment and amounts to "strip[ping] away the sovereign function of state officials to interpret and enforce state laws," thus overstepping the boundary between federal and state authority.... In *Printz v. United States*, 521 U.S. 898 (1997), the Supreme Court held unconstitutional the enforcement provisions of the Brady Handgun Violence Prevention Act requiring local chief law enforcement officers to perform background checks on gun purchasers. "[T]he whole object of the law [is] to direct the functioning of the state executive, and hence to compromise the structural framework of dual sovereignty.... It is the very principle of separate state sovereignty that such a law offends. . . ."). *Id.* Similarly, in *New York v. United States*, 505 U.S. 144, 178 (1992), which found unconstitutional the "take title" provision of the Low Level Radioactive Waste Policy Amendments Act of 1985, the Court observed that "[n]o matter how powerful the federal interest involved, the Constitution simply does not give Congress the authority to require states to regulate."

However, *Printz* and *New York* have no applicability to the national bank regulatory scheme, which does not compel the Commissioner to enact or enforce a particular regulatory scheme, but rather has carved out from state control supervisory authority over these federal instrumentalities. Article I, Section 8 of the Constitution authorizes Congress to establish national banks and "to enact legislation for the protection, preservation and regulation of such institutions." *Clark v. United States*, 184 F.2d 952, 953 (10th Cir. 1950). Under the national banking regulatory scheme, Congress does not direct the state executive to affirmatively function in any particular way, nor does the OCC's exercise of exclusive visitorial powers over national banks preclude the state statutory enactments from being applied to national banks, provided they are not in conflict with and thus preempted by federal banking laws.

By creating such a scheme, Congress has not seized the machinery of state government to achieve federal purposes. The relegation of regulatory and supervisory authority over federal instrumentalities to a single federal regulator does not interfere with the Commissioner's enforcement of state law against state banks, does not interfere with the state's enactment of non-preempted state banking laws applicable to national banks, does not preclude the Commissioner from seeking OCC enforcement of state laws, and expressly leaves available judicial remedies to compel national bank compliance with state law.

Accordingly, the Court finds no basis for concluding that this federal regulatory scheme over federally created instrumentalities violates the Tenth Amendment. The dual banking system is such that when the states seek to enact laws affecting national banks, they do so subject to the enforcement limitation imposed by Congress for the purpose of protecting against a state's use of its legislative authority to restrict, limit or otherwise penalize national banks.

In light of the persuasive authority that the OCC, not the Commissioner, is empowered to directly enforce state banking law against national banks through administrative orders, the federal bank regulatory structure authorized by the National Banking Act and the EFTA, and the conclusion that ATM transactions with non-depositors relate to the business of banking, the Court concludes that the OCC has demonstrated a likelihood of success on the merits of its claim that the Commissioner's cease and desist order interferes with its exclusive enforcement authority over national banks.

Notes and Comments 3.25. *ATM nondepositor fees under state laws and the NBA.* State laws prohibiting banks from charging fees to non-account holders have continued to fall in the face of preemption arguments based on the NBA. *See, e.g., Metrobank, N.A. v. Foster*, 193 F.Supp.2d 1156 (S.D.Iowa 2002) (holding NBA preempted Iowa ATM statute from prohibiting fees to non-accountholders who used national bank ATMs). *Cf. Wells Fargo Bank Texas, N.A. v. James*, 184 F.Supp.2d 588 (W.D.Tex. 2001) (holding NBA preempted Texas statute from prohibiting fees to non-account holders who cashed checks drawn on national bank).

3.26. *The status of e-banking.* In the GLBA, Congress has expressed concern over the pertinence of current banking regulations to the delivery of financial services on-line.[14] The GLBA required the banking agencies by November 2001 to submit a report on e-banking.[15] For now, however, activities in the e-banking line continue to advance[16] without specifically applicable policy.[17] Essentially, e-banking as a sector of e-commerce is currently manifesting itself in three ways. First, e-banking may simply represent the use of electronic means as a more efficient medium of communication.[18] This may be characterized as e-banking as an efficiency device. It is of practical significance but unremarkable as a matter of

---

14. *See* GLBA, § 729(a) (codified at 12 U.S.C. § 4801 note) (mandating study of regulations).

15. *Id.*, § 729(b). *See, e.g.*, Office of the Comptroller of the Currency, *Electronic Banking*, 65 Fed. Reg. 4895 (February 2, 2000); Board of Governors of the Federal Reserve System, *Study of Banking Regulations Regarding the Online Delivery of Financial Services*, (May 21, 2001); Office of Thrift Supervision, *Request for Comment on Study of Banking Regulations Regarding the Online Delivery of Financial Services*, 66 Fed. Reg. 31,186 (June 11, 2001); Federal Deposit Insurance Corporation, *Request for Comment on Study of Banking Regulations Regarding the Online Delivery of Banking Services*, 66 Fed. Reg. 37,029 (July 16, 2001).

16. For example, the Comptroller has reported that, as of September 1999, 541 national banks had already established transactional Web sites. 65 Fed. Reg. 4895, 4895 n.1 (2000).

17. *See* 65 Fed. Reg. 4895 (2000) (announcing Comptroller proposed rulemaking on electronic banking). *See generally* Gary Rice, *Selected Issues Relating to Banking and the Internet*, in 1999 Strategies for Financial Institutions in the New E-Commerce Economy (Prac. L. Inst., Dec. 1999) (surveying e-banking issues).

18. *See* 65 Fed. Reg. at 4895 ("Telecommunications advances offer banks faster and more efficient communication and data transmission"). *Cf., e.g.*, Jeanette Borzo, *B2B Holds Big Promise in Russia*, Wall. St. J. Europe, May 3, 2000, at 27, col. 1 (detailing use of e-commerce media to overcome communications inefficiencies).

policy, though it may raise important safety and soundness and related issues.[19]

Second, e-banking may manifest itself as the establishment of specialized fora for transactions in specific types of products.[20] This may be characterized as e-banking as a "trading platform," in which traditional banking participants create an electronic locus for transactions.[21] The use of e-banking trading platforms is already well developed in practice. It requires the adaptation of bodies of transactional law (*e.g.*, contract law) and regulatory law to the medium of electronic trading,[22] with due attention to operational safety and soundness.[23]

Third, e-banking may manifest itself as an independent banking market, in which banking participants may "exist" as on-line participants.[24] This may be characterized as core e-banking, that is, e-banking by principals, not merely as a medium or a platform for real-time participants. Virtual banks are already being approved,[25] and it is core e-banking that is likely to raise the greatest challenges for regulatory policy as we approach the next

---

19. *See, e.g.*, *Reporting Computer-Related Crimes*, OCC Advisory Letter No. 97-9 (Nov. 19, 1997); *Technology Risk Management*, OCC Bulletin 98-3 (Feb. 4, 1998); *Guidance on Electronic Financial Services and Consumer Compliance*, OCC Bulletin 98-31, (July 30, 1998); *Technology Risk Management: PC Banking*, OCC Bulletin 98-38 (Aug. 24, 1998); *Guidance to National Banks on Web Site Privacy Statements*, OCC Advisory Letter No. 99-6 (May 4, 1999); *Infrastructure Threats from Cyber-Terrorists*, OCC Bulletin 99-9 (Mar. 5, 1999); *Certification Authority Systems*, OCC Bulletin 99-20 (May 6, 1999); Comptroller's Handbook, Other Income Producing Activities, Internet Banking (Oct. 1999) (offering guidance on safety and soundness and other supervisory issues; all documents available on OCC Web site at www.occ.treas.gov). *See generally* 65 Fed. Reg. at 4896 (recognizing fluid, fast-evolving nature of bank use of technology and potential effects on safety and soundness).

20. *See, e.g.*, Simon Targett, *State Street to launch multibank trading*, Fin. Times, May 4, 2000, at 16, col. 1 (reporting on plans to launch multi-bank electronic foreign exchange trading system).

21. *See* 65 Fed. Reg. at 4895, in which the Comptroller noted:

> Improvements in computer hardware and software are opening up new banking applications. These rapid developments in new technologies are causing banks to reevaluate existing delivery channels and business practices and to develop new products and services.

22. *See, e.g.*, 12 C.F.R. § 7.1019 (authorizing national banks to conduct through electronic means or facilities any activity otherwise authorized). *See also* David Church *et al.*, *Recent Developments Regarding U.S. and EU Regulation of Electronic Commerce*, 33 Int'l Law. 347 (1999) (surveying international legal developments).

23. *See* 65 Fed. Reg. at 4897 (providing OCC discussion of operational flexibility and safety and soundness).

24. As the Comptroller has observed:

> The explosive growth of the Internet also is prompting banks to reconsider business strategies and adopt alternative distribution and marketing systems. The recent chartering of Internet-only banks that operate without a conventional brick and mortar physical presence . . . present[s] new opportunities and challenges for national banks.

65 Fed. Reg. at 4895.

25. *See, e.g.*, OCC Conditional Approval No. 253 (Aug. 20, 1997) (chartering a national bank to deliver products and services to customers primarily through electronic means) (document available on OCC Web site at www.occ.treas.gov). One may expect these developments to continue apace. The Comptroller has indicated that his office "will not delay making changes to its rules or supervisory policies during the pendency of the [GLBA] §729 study and report." 65 Fed. Reg. at 4896 n.7.

century.[26]

3.27. *"Location" of a national e-bank.* Where is an e-bank "located" for regulatory purposes? Traditional legal analysis of the location of a national bank is not particularly helpful. The NBA indicates that a national banks are deemed "citizens of the States in which they are respectively located." But where is a national bank "located"? *See, e.g., Firstar Bank, N.A. v. Faul*, 253 F.3d 982 (7th Cir. 2001) (holding that national bank is citizen of state of its principal place of business *and* state listed in organization certificate). Presumably, the organization certificate of a national e-bank will tell us the listed state, but where is its "principal place of business? A conflict in the circuits emerged on this issue. *Compare Horton v. Bank One, N. A.*, 387 F.3d 426, 429, 431 (5th Cir. 2004) (holding that, for diversity purposes, "a national bank is not 'located' in, and thus [is] not a citizen of, every state in which it has a branch"), *and Firstar Bank, N.A., supra* (looking to principal place of business and state listed in organization certificate) *with Wachovia Bank v. Schmidt*, 388 F.3d 414, 432 (4th Cir. 2005) (considering national bank to be citizen of both state of main office and every state with branch operations), *and World Trade Center Properties, LLC v. Hartford Fire Ins. Co.*, 345 F.3d 154, 161 (2d Cir. 2003) (dictum) (same). In *Wachovia Bank v. Schmidt*, 546 U.S. 303 (2006), the Supreme Court resolved the conflict, indicating that in answering the question where a national bank is located–at least for purposes of determining diversity jurisdiction–the determinant is the state designated in its articles of association as locus of its main office, *not* every state where it has branch offices. The Court did not address the issue of where a national bank's "principal place of business" is.

3.28. *e-Banking and branching.* Trading platform and core e-banking raise serious issues of construction and interpretation with respect to the NBA branching provisions. The experience of the OCC in litigation over the branching provisions is not encouraging in this regard. In virtually every significant case involving branching, the courts have repudiated OCC attempts to regulate around the strictures of the branching provision. This was particularly true as to the ATM, a new technology unanticipated by the NBA. If the OCC attempts to create a regulatory solution without affirmative congressional intervention,[27] it is likely that the newest technology will confront the same problem. If you were advising the Comptroller on this issue, how would you suggest that he proceed?

3.29. *e-Banking failures.* There have been few failures of stand-alone e-banks, but those that have failed raise some serious concerns. Many core e-banks have relatively specialized business plans, and may not be good prospects for recovery if the market for their particular services fails. In what may be the first significant core e-bank failure, the FDIC received no bids in 2002 for the deposits of NextBank, National Association, a failed Internet-only bank that had no brick-and-mortar branches. NextBank solicited only certificates of deposit of $100,000 or more (jumbo CDs) and had no checking or savings accounts. NextBank had total assets of $700 million and total deposits of $554 million, of which $29.4 million in 2,075 accounts exceeded the federal deposit insurance limit at the time. As a result, the FDIC would be required to pay off the insured amount of deposits, leaving a portion of the jumbo CD holders as general creditors of the failed bank. *See FDIC Approves the Payout of Insured Deposits of Nextbank, National Association, Phoenix, Arizona* (PR-16-2002, Feb. 7, 2002), *available at* http://www.fdic.gov/news/news/press/

---

26. *See* Pres. Memorandum on Facilitating the Growth of Electronic Commerce, Nov. 29, 1999, 35 Weekly Comp. Pres. Doc. 2457-2458 (1999) (announcing initiative to update laws and regulations developed before advent of Internet that may have unintended negative effects on electronic commerce).

27. There are some indications that the OCC may make such an attempt. *See* 65 Fed. Reg. at 4897 (providing OCC discussion of branching implications of e-banking).

2002/pr1602.html, (FDIC press release discussing disposition of NextBank). In September 2007, the OTS appointed the FDIC as receiver for NetBank Inc., an online savings association with $2.5 billion in assets, because of NetBank's unsustainable level of mortgage defaults. Office of Thrift Supervision, *NetBank, Alpharetta, GA; Notice of Appointment of Receiver*, 72 Fed. Reg. 57,100 (2007). NetBank thus became the first significant depository institution closed because of burgeoning defaults in sub-prime mortgage loans, a problem that had previously occurred only among non-depository mortgage lenders . *See Online Bank Fails, and Regulators Shut It*, N.Y. TIMES, Sept. 29, 3007, at C9 (discussing failure of NetBank). This time, however, the FDIC was able to arrange the assumption of $1.5 billion of NetBank's insured deposits (out of a total of $2.3 billion in deposits) by ING Bank, an e-bank that is a unit of the Dutch financial conglomerate ING Groep. *Id.* Approximately $109 million in deposits exceeded the federal deposit insurance limit, and NetBank depositors would to that extent. become general creditors in the NetBank receivership. *Id.*

3. State Branching Laws

By the mid-1980s, state law restrictions on branching could be broadly divided into three general categories: (*i*) "unit banking," in which banks would not be permitted to establish branches; (*ii*) limited branch banking, in which banks would be permitted to establish and operate branches, but only within certain limited geographical areas or with only a maximum number of branches allowed; (*iii*) full branch banking, in which no absolute geographical or numerical limitations would be imposed upon the authority of banks to establish and operate branches. The distinctions delineating each of these categories are of course equally pertinent to the situation of national banks as well as state-chartered banks, since 12 U.S.C. § 36(c) requires reference over to state law to determine the authority of national banks to establish branches.

The significance of these distinctions was somewhat reduced by the emergence of a new trend in geographic expansion–the rise of regional interstate banking arrangements among groups of states.[28] This trend established itself as the dominant method of geographic expansion, until the passage of federal interstate banking legislation in 1994.[29] Indeed, by 1991, the leading trend among the states was clearly in favor of full-service regional or national interstate banking.[30]

4. Interstate Branching

On September 29, 1994, the President signed the Riegle-Neal Interstate Banking and Branching Efficiency Act of 1994 ("IBBEA")[31] into law. IBBEA permits geographic expansion by banks without regard to artificial barriers to interstate expansion heretofore

28. *See Northeast Bancorp v. Board of Governors*, 472 U.S. 159 (1985) (upholding regional interstate banking arrangement).

29. *See infra* § 4 (discussing interstate banking and branching).

30. Saulsbury, *Interstate Banking, reprinted in* 1 Fed. Banking L. Rep. (CCH) ¶ 3106B (June 14, 1991).

31. Pub. Law No. 103-328, Sept. 29, 1994, 108 Stat. 2338 (1994) ("IBBEA").

imposed by the Douglas Amendment[32] to the Bank Holding Company Act (BHCA)[33] and the branching provisions of state law and the National Bank Act (NBA).[34]

Notes and Comments 3.30. *State "opt-in" provisions permitting de novo interstate branching: National banks.* The Comptroller of the Currency has the authority to approve the establishment and operation of a *de novo* national bank branch[35] in a state other than the home state[36] of the bank, in which the bank does not maintain a branch.[37] However, this authority is available only if the host state[38] has in effect a law that applies equally to all banks, and that expressly permits all out-of-state banks to establish branches in the state.[39] Approval of a *de novo* interstate national bank branch is also subject to two conditions. First, the application is subject to the same requirements and conditions applicable to interstate merger transactions[40] concerning state filing requirements,[41] community reinvestment,[42] and adequacy of capital and management.[43] Second, as to each *de novo* interstate national bank branch that is approved under this authority, the branch is subject to state and federal antitrust laws[44] and limitations on the operation of additional branches,[45] as such laws and limitations would apply to a branch resulting from an interstate merger transaction.[46]

3.31. *State "opt-in" provisions permitting de novo interstate branching: Insured state nonmember banks.* The FDIC is authorized to approve *de novo* interstate branches of insured state nonmember bank branching, subject to rules that correspond to those applicable to national banks.[47] Thus, approval of such branches are subject to corresponding rules

---

32. 12 U.S.C. § 1842(d) (1988). On the Douglas Amendment, see 3 MICHAEL P. MALLOY, BANKING LAW AND REGULATION §§ 10.02[A], 10.07[A][1] (2d ed., 2011).

33. 12 U.S.C. §§ 1841 *et seq.*

34. *See, e.g., id.* § 36(c) (NBA provision limiting branching by national banks).

35. For these purposes, "*de novo* branch" is defined to mean a national bank branch that

> (i) is originally established by the national bank as a branch; and
> (ii) does not become a branch of such bank as a result of --
> (I) the acquisition by the bank of an insured depository institution or a branch of an insured depository institution; or
> (II) the conversion, merger, or consolidation of any such institution or branch.

12 U.S.C. § 36(g)(3)(A)(i)-(ii), *as amended.*

36. For these purposes, "home state" is defined to mean "the State in which the main office of a national bank is located." *Id.* § 36(g)(3)(B).

37. *Id.* § 36(g)(1).

38. For these purposes, "host state" is defined to mean "with respect to a bank, a State, other than the home State of the bank, in which the bank maintains, or seeks to establish and maintain, a branch." *Id.* § 36(g)(3)(C).

39. *Id.* § 36(g)(1)(A)(i)-(ii).

40. On regulation of interstate mergers under IBBEA, see Notes 4.47-4.51, *infra.*

41. *See id.* § 1831u(b)(1).

42. *See id.* § 1831u(b)(3).

43. *Id.* § 36(g)(2)(A). *See id.* § 1831u(b)(4).

44. *See id.* § 1831u(c).

45. *See id.* § 1831u(d)(2).

46. *Id.* § 36(g)(2)(B).

47. *Id.* § 1828(d)(4)).

requiring a state "opt-in" statute expressly permitting such branches,[48] applying the requirements and conditions applicable to interstate merger transactions concerning state filing requirements, community reinvestment, and adequacy of capital and management,[49] and applying state and federal antitrust laws and limitations on the operation of additional branches to the approved *de novo* interstate branch.[50]

3.32. IBBEA expressly provides for interstate branching by national banks and by insured state nonmember banks. What about state member banks? Consider 12 U.S.C. §§ 36, 335.

3.33. *GLBA and interstate banking*: The GLBA alters the rules with respect to interest rates that may be charged by state banks competing with interstate branches of out-of-state banks. For discussion of the new rules, see Note 5.22, *infra*.

3.34. For 125 years, *A National Bank* has had its headquarters in Jolly, West Dakota. It has branch offices in West Dakota and other states. Five years ago, *A* purchased the assets of *B State Bank* of Holly, East Dakota, which is less than thirty miles from Jolly, and *A* moved its headquarters to Holly. (After relocating its main office to Holly, *A* received approval from the OCC to open two new branches in East Dakota. Late last year, *A*'s board of directors approved a merger with *C National Bank*, which has its headquarters office in Folly, West Dakota. Under the terms of the proposed merger, *A* will be the surviving bank, *C*'s charter will be dissolved, and *A*'s headquarters will be relocated to Folly. Upon learning of the proposed merger between *A* and *C*, the Director of the East Dakota Division of Finance notified the OCC of East Dakota's opposition to the merger. The Director claims that the merger violates provisions of IBBEA, specifically 12 U.S.C. §§ 36(d), 215a-1, 1831u. East Dakota's "minimum-age" law, adopted six years ago, prohibits mergers between out-of-state banks and in-state banks that have been in existence for less than five years. (An amendment adopted four years ago counts the age of a bank that relocates to East Dakota from another state from the date of the relocation.) If you were on the OCC Chief Counsel's staff, would you advise the Comptroller that the proposed merger was permitted by IBBEA? Consider the following case in preparing your answer.

TeamBank, N.A. v. McClure

279 F.3d 614 (8th Cir. 2002)

RILEY, Circuit Judge.

TeamBank, N.A. (TeamBank) sued the Director of the Missouri Division of Finance (the Director) to prevent the State of Missouri from interfering with TeamBank's merger with the First National Bank and Trust Company of Parsons, Kansas (First National Bank). The district court granted an injunction prohibiting the Director from taking any action on the State's claim that the merger violates state and federal law. The Director appeals, and we affirm.

I. BACKGROUND

TeamBank is a national bank that was founded in 1874. For most of its history,

---

48. *Compare* 12 U.S.C. § 36(g)(1) (NBA provision) *with id.* § 1828(d)(4)(A) (corresponding FDIA provision).

49. *Compare id.* § 36(g)(1)(B), (2)(A) (NBA provision) *with id.* § 1828(d)(4)(A)(ii), (B)(i) (corresponding FDIA provision.

50. *Compare id.* § 36(g)(2)(B) (NBA provision) *with id.* § 1828(d)(4)(B)(ii) (corresponding FDIA provision).

TeamBank has had its headquarters in Paola, Kansas. It has branch offices in Kansas and other states. In 1997, TeamBank purchased the assets of a bank in Freeman, Missouri, which is less than thirty miles from Paola, and TeamBank moved its headquarters there. After relocating its main office to Freeman, TeamBank opened two new offices in Missouri.

On March 23, 2000, TeamBank's board of directors approved a merger with First National Bank, which had its main office in Parsons, Kansas. Both banks were wholly owned subsidiaries of Team Financial Acquisition Subsidiary, Inc., which is itself a wholly owned subsidiary of a Kansas bank holding company, Team Financial, Inc. Under the terms of the proposed merger, TeamBank was to be the surviving entity and First National Bank's charter was to be dissolved. In addition, TeamBank's main office was to return to Paola, Kansas, and TeamBank's branches in Kansas, Missouri, and Nebraska were to be part of the new bank.

On March 24, 2000, TeamBank filed an application for approval of the merger with the Office of the Comptroller of the Currency (OCC). The State of Missouri, through the Director, notified the OCC of its opposition to the merger and its position that the merger violates the Riegle-Neal Interstate Banking and Branching Efficiency Act of 1994 (Riegle-Neal Act), 12 U.S.C. §§ 215a-1, 1831u & 36(d). The Riegle-Neal Act allows states to prohibit mergers between out-of-state banks and in-state banks which have been in existence for less than five years. Missouri's "minimum-age" law, Mo.Rev.Stat. §§ 362.077 & 362.610, adopted in 1997, prohibits such mergers. A Missouri amendment, adopted in 1999, counts the age of a bank that relocates to Missouri from another state from the date of the relocation. Mo.Rev.Stat. § 362.077.2.The Director advised the OCC that these statutes prohibit the proposed merger.

On May 26, 2000, before the merger was approved, the Director sent TeamBank a letter notifying the bank of the State's position that the merger was illegal. "The Division of Finance," he wrote, "requests that your institution honor our state laws by refraining from relocating out of Missouri until the five-year threshold is met." In the same letter, the Director also wrote of his office's "plan to meet with the Missouri Attorney General's Office shortly to discuss our legal options in this matter."

On June 20, 2000, the OCC approved the proposed merger. In so doing, the OCC issued an opinion which addressed and rejected the Director's legal arguments against the merger. On June 26, 2000, TeamBank and First National Bank merged.

TeamBank filed this lawsuit on the same day as the merger, seeking a declaration that the merger is lawful and an injunction preventing the Director from "taking any action upon [his] claim that [TeamBank] is in violation of applicable federal and state laws." The district court ruled in favor of TeamBank and granted the injunction on cross-motions for summary judgment.

On appeal, the Director raises the same arguments he made informally to the OCC. He also argues that the OCC's ruling will have the effect of allowing other banks to evade restrictions on interstate branching that Missouri has enacted in accordance with the Riegle-Neal Act. . . .

III. DISCUSSION

The Riegle-Neal Act generally permits interstate bank mergers in participating states, but prohibits such mergers that:

> would have the effect of permitting an out-of-State bank or out-of-State bank holding company to acquire a bank in a host State that has not been in existence for the minimum period of time, if any, specified in the statutory law of the host State.

12 U.S.C. § 1831u(a)(5)(A). The "minimum period of time" enforceable under the Riegle-Neal Act cannot exceed five years. 12 U.S.C. § 1831u(a)(5)(B).

In 1997, Missouri amended its banking statutes to add a minimum-age statute as authorized by the Riegle-Neal Act. Missouri's minimum-age statute permits out-of-state banks to merge with banks in Missouri if the bank being acquired was at least five years old. Mo.Rev.Stat. §§ 362.077.1, 362.610 (Supp.2001). In 1999 Missouri supplemented its minimum-age statute with a statute on bank relocation:

> Any state bank, trust company or national bank, already in existence in another state, which is relocated to Missouri de novo shall calculate the age of its bank charter for Missouri purposes as of the date such charter is moved to Missouri, and may not engage in an interstate acquisition or merger with the result that such charter is merged or relocated to another state with Missouri branches of such charter remaining in Missouri, until such bank or trust company's charter is at least five years old.

Mo.Rev.Stat. § 362.077.2 (Supp.2001). The Director invokes both the minimum-age statute and the bank-relocation statute in opposition to the merger of TeamBank and First National Bank.

The Director argues that the merger violates the Riegle-Neal Act because its effect is to permit a Kansas bank to acquire a Missouri bank that is less than five years old. Under the Director's theory, the Kansas bank is either the new TeamBank entity with its main office in Paola, Kansas, or the old First National Bank with its main office in Parsons, Kansas. According to the Director, the Missouri bank is the old TeamBank at its former headquarters in Freeman, Missouri. TeamBank has been in existence since 1874, but it only moved to Missouri in 1997. The Director argues that, at the time of the merger, TeamBank was less than five years old under Missouri's bank-relocation statute. . . . Thus, the argument goes, TeamBank's acquisition by a Kansas bank violates Missouri's minimum-age statute which was enacted pursuant to the Riegle-Neal Act.

The OCC rejected the Director's argument on three grounds. First, the OCC concluded Missouri's minimum-age statute does not apply to TeamBank's merger. In accordance with Riegle-Neal, the Missouri statute only protects Missouri banks that are being acquired. . . . According to the OCC, TeamBank, as the surviving bank, is the acquiring bank, and First National Bank is the bank being acquired. Since First National Bank's home state is Kansas, the only minimum-age statute that potentially applies is that of Kansas, and Kansas does not have any minimum-age requirement.

Second, the OCC concluded that even if Missouri's minimum-age statute does apply, its bank-relocation statute does not. In reaching this conclusion, the OCC applied the general presumption against construing statutes retroactively. TeamBank moved its main office to Missouri in 1997. The bank-relocation statute was not adopted until 1999, and applies to a bank "which *is* relocated to Missouri," . . . (emphasis added), in contrast to a bank "which *has* relocated to Missouri." This language, the OCC reasoned, was not intended to apply to a bank which, like TeamBank, relocated to Missouri before the statute was enacted. Because the statute did not reset TeamBank's age to zero as of the date it moved to Missouri, TeamBank is more than five years old. Thus, even if TeamBank were to be acquired by First National Bank, the merger would not violate Missouri's minimum-age statute.

Third, the OCC found that even if the bank-relocation statute does apply retroactively, it conflicts with and is preempted by the Riegle-Neal Act. Riegle-Neal, the OCC pointed out, calculates a bank's age according to the time it has been "in existence," not the time it has been in a particular state. *See* 12 U.S.C. § 1831u(a)(5)(A). The OCC also relied upon the congressional policies it found to underlie the Riegle-Neal Act. Citing a House Conference Report, the OCC found that Riegle-Neal embodies a policy that a bank which has moved its main offices into a new state should be treated the same as other banks with main offices in that state. *See* H.R. Conf. Rep. No. 651, 103d Cong., 2d Sess. 57 (1994). Missouri's bank-relocation statute, the OCC reasoned, treats relocated banks differently by requiring them to calculate their age based upon the time they have been in Missouri rather than the time they have been in existence. Since this requirement conflicts with the OCC's interpretation of Riegle-Neal, the OCC found it preempted.

The OCC, participating *amicus curiae* in this case, argues that its decision is entitled to deference under *Chevron U.S.A. Inc. v. Natural Resources Defense Council, Inc.*, 467 U.S. 837 (1984). *Chevron* deference applies when Congress has, either explicitly or implicitly, left a gap in a statute to be filled by a particular agency. *Chevron,* 467 U.S. at 843-45. In appropriate cases, *Chevron* requires courts to give "considerable weight . . . to an executive department's construction of a statutory scheme it is entrusted to administer." *Id.* at 844. Under *Chevron,* such decisions are controlling "unless they are arbitrary, capricious, or manifestly contrary to the statute." *Id.* . . .

Chevron does not apply to every interpretation of a statute by an agency. As the Supreme Court recently explained, *Chevron* deference is generally reserved for interpretations reached through "relatively formal" administrative procedures, such as "notice-and-comment rulemaking or formal adjudication." *United States v. Mead Corp.,* 533 U.S. 218 (2001); *see also Central S.D. Coop. Grazing Dist. v. Secretary of U.S. Dep't. of Ag.,* 266 F.3d 889, 894 (8th Cir.2001).[4] The decisions of the Comptroller of the Currency, however, present an exception to this general rule. Such decisions merit deference "even when no such administrative formality was required and none was afforded." . . .

The Riegle-Neal Act's provisions on state minimum-age laws left a space for the OCC to fill through interpretation. In enacting Riegle-Neal, Congress prohibited mergers that "have the effect" of violating certain state minimum-age statutes. 12 U.S.C. § 1831u(a)(5)(A). Congress did not give any explicit guidance on what kinds of mergers fall within this rather imprecise statutory prohibition. As the agency charged with implementing Riegle-Neal, the OCC is entitled to fill this gap in the statute through informal adjudication.

The opinion issued by the OCC in this case is thorough and well enough reasoned to merit deference under *Chevron.* The OCC's interpretation of the Riegle-Neal Act in this case is particularly suited for *Chevron* deference because it involves "reconciling conflicting policies" and depends "upon more than ordinary knowledge" about interstate banking. *See Chevron,* 467 U.S. at 844 (quoting *United States v. Shimer,* 367 U.S. 374, 382 (1961)). The district court agreed with the OCC's reasoning. We find the OCC's reasoning persuasive to the extent it interprets and applies the Riegle-Neal Act to the facts and specific issues raised in this case. While the OCC's reasoning may be open to challenge on certain points, it is not arbitrary, capricious, or manifestly contrary to law.

The Director also opposes the merger on the grounds it would permit other banks to evade Riegle-Neal's limits on interstate banking. *See McQueen v. Williams,* 177 F.3d 523, 530-35 (6th Cir.1999) (invalidating "sham" relocation of a bank's main office to another state under the law prior to Riegle-Neal). However, the Director does not contend, nor does the record reflect, that TeamBank's initial relocation to Freeman, Missouri, was part of a scheme to evade federal law. We need not decide, in this case, whether the reasoning employed by

---

4. Agency interpretations that are not the result of such formal administrative procedures are generally entitled to a lesser degree of deference under *Skidmore v. Swift & Co.,* 323 U.S. 134 (1944). . . .

the OCC in approving TeamBank's merger would also apply to a merger involving a bank's sham relocation to another state.

Chapter 4

Control Transactions

1. Introduction

An entrepreneur might seek to enter the depository institutions industry not by obtaining a new charter, but by creating a non-banking corporation which in turn would acquire a controlling interest in a bank. One depository institution may seek to merge another into it, thus expanding its reach into other markets. Or an entrepreneur might individually buy a controlling interest in the outstanding stock of an existing bank. Any of these transactions would represent a control transaction, one in which the ownership or direct or indirect control of a depository institution is acquired. These transactions are the subject of this chapter.

There are good business reasons which might lead one to structure corporate control of a depository institution in a holding-company pattern; for example, added flexibility in managing operations, "leverage" in financing the operations of the overall enterprise, and diversification of corporate activities, both intrastate and interstate. Hence, in § 2 of this chapter, we examine limitations on the creation of holding companies, primarily under the Bank Holding Company Act (BHCA).[1] Regulation of holding company activities will be considered in a later chapter.[2]

While creation of a holding company may represent a type of *de novo* entry into the regulated industry, mergers and acquisitions between existing depository institutions represent a method of secondary entry into the industry.In this respect, mergers and acquisition can be said to be akin to branching; that is, not a *de novo* entry into the industry but an expansion into new market segments of the industry. Today such secondary entries are controlled by the Bank Merger Act of 1966 (BMA).[3] In § 3 of this chapter, we examine limitations on mergers and acquisitions.

Finally, in § 4 we briefly examine the effect of the Change in Bank Control Act[4] on acquisition of control by persons not covered by the BHCA or the BMA.

Notes and Comments 4.1. Essentially, both holding company formation and merger involve some form of acquisition activity directed at a target depository institution.

---

1. 12 U.S.C. §§ 1841 *et seq*. Holding company formation with respect to savings associations is governed by the holding company provisions of the Home Owners' Loan Act. *See id.* § 1467a.

2. *See infra* Chapter 6 (discussing activities of bank holding companies).

3. 12 U.S.C. § 1828(c). Despite its name, since August 1989 the BMA has applied not only to bank mergers but also to mergers of savings associations. *Id.*

4. *Id.* § 1817(j).

It is therefore appropriate to begin with preliminary consideration of typical acquisition methods. Tax consequences aside, the most obvious and straightforward method for acquiring a target depository institution would be the purchase of the outstanding stock or capital shares of the institution, or the exchange of short-term debt instruments of the acquiror for the stock shares. Presumably, the exchange would be a taxable event for the former owners. If the acquiror wanted to make the acquisition more attractive to the target's owners, it would structure the holding company transaction to conform with rules under the Internal Revenue Code providing for nontaxable treatment of certain forms of corporate reorganization.[5]

4.2. *Typical acquisition methods*. The holding company structure is "a dominant trend in the corporate law and practice of depository institutions."[6] In many cases, a depository institution may "spin up" a holding company of its own. The resulting formation of the holding company "amounts to a reorganization of the corporate structure of a preexisting enterprise."[7] In other cases, a company may become a holding company of a depository institution through *de novo* chartering of a depository institution subsidiary.[8] Finally, a holding company enterprise may be created (expanded) through the acquisition of a preexisting, independent depository institution.[9] In these last two circumstances, the formation of the holding company enterprise may be viewed as a method of entry into the regulated industry by the holding company.

2. Holding Company Acquisitions

Federal regulation of the formation of holding companies of depository institutions is principally based on two sets of statutory provisions: the Bank Holding Company Act of 1956, as amended (BHCA),[10] and the savings and loan holding company provisions of the Home Owners' Loan Act (SLHCA).[11] In overall outline, and in many of their specific details, the provisions of the BHCA and the SLHCA are parallel. The major focus of the material that follows will be on the BHCA.

---

5. *See* 26 U.S.C. §§ 351 *et seq*. For discussion of these rules, see MICHAEL P. MALLOY, PRINCIPLES OF BANK REGULATION § 4.2 (3d ed. 2011).

6. MALLOY, *supra* at 109.

7. *Id. S.ee, e.g., Board of Governors v. First Lincolnwood Corp.*, 439 U.S. 234 (1978) (providing example of spin-up establishment of bank holding company).

8. *See, e.g., Deerbrook State Bank v. Conover*, 568 F. Supp. 696 (N.D. Ill. 1983) (involving challenge to chartering of 31 national banks by Dimension Financial Corp.). *See also Board of Governors v. Dimension Fin. Corp.*, 474 U.S. 361 (1986) (upholding acquisitions despite contrary Fed regulations). On this "nonbank bank" controversy, later resolved by statute (*see* Competitive Equality Banking Act, Pub. L. No. 100-86, § 101, 101 Stat. 552, 554 (1987) (*codified at* 12 U.S.C. § 1841(c)), see generally 3 MICHAEL P. MALLOY, BANKING LAW AND REGULATION §§ 10.02[E]-10.02[E][3] (2d ed. 2011). *Cf. Synovus Fin. Corp., v. Board of Governors,* 952 F.2d 426 (D.C. Cir. 1991) (finding no Fed authority over "acquisition" by relocation of subsidiary bank from one state to another); *State of Idaho, Dep't of Fin. v. Clarke*, 994 F.2d 1441 (9th Cir. 1993) (declining to follow *Synovus*).

9. *See, e.g., Commercial Nat'l Bank of Little Rock v. Board of Governors*, 451 F.2d 86 (8th Cir. 1971) (involving challenge to acquisition of preexisting bank by one-bank holding company); *Centerre Bancorporation v. Kemper*, 682 F. Supp. 459 (E.D. Mo. 1988).

10. 12 U.S.C. §§ 1841 *et seq.*

11. *Id.* § 1467a

Notes and Comments 4.3. *GLBA and the Financial Holding Company.* The Gramm-Leach-Bliley Act (GLBA)[12] overhauls the U.S. financial services system by, among other things, allowing affiliations between banks, securities firms, and insurance companies through "financial holding companies" (FHCs) that are regulated by the Fed. 12 U.S.C. § 1843(k). While FHCs primarily raise concerns with respect to the nonbanking activities of holding companies, to be discussed in the next chapter, the FHC provisions of the GLBA do affect some of the details of federal law with respect to the formation of holding companies. For example, the GLBA eliminates duplicative application and filing requirements for BHCs that elect to become FHCs.[13] It streamlines BHC report and examination requirements.[14] It limits the authority of the Fed to impose source-of-strength financial requirements,[15] in favor of a depository institution subsidiary, on BHCs that are insurance companies or that are broker-dealers, investment advisers or investment companies where the state insurance regulator or the SEC, respectively, objects.[16] Finally, It limits the Fed's discretionary authority to regulate, supervise or discipline a BHC subsidiary that is functionally regulated by a state insurance regulator or the SEC.[17]

4.4. While the GLBA holding company provisions looked as if they were intended to authorize the expansion of bank holding company enterprises into other financial services like securities and insurance, in the current financial crisis the GLBA has provided authority for *investment* banking enterprises to transform themselves into bank holding companies. As the securities markets were imploding in late 2008, two major investment banks, Goldman Sachs and Morgan Stanley, reorganized their operations to convert to bank holding company status, with a full service bank as an operating subsidiary. *See* Stephen Joyce, *Last Two Investment Banks Receive Charters, Foreshadow Regulatory Debate*, BNA BANKING DAILY (Dec. 1, 2008), *available at* http://news.bna.com (discussing approvals of reorganizations and conversions by state and federal authorities). Goldman Sachs converted some of its operations to full service bank approved by New York State, and Morgan Stanley similarly converted some of its operations to a national bank approved by the Comptroller of the Currency. At the same time, each firm sough approval under the BHCA, reorganizing as bank holding companies.

4.5. *Basic outline of the BHCA provisions.* Review the provisions of 12 U.S.C. § 1842, together with the applicable definitional provisions of § 1841. The BHCA identifies a series of actions that are prohibited unless the Fed has given prior approval. Among the actions covered by these prohibition are: (*i*) actions that cause any company to become a bank holding company (BHC); (*ii*) any action that causes a bank to become a subsidiary of a BHC; (*iii*) acquisition by a BHC of direct or indirect ownership or control of any voting shares of any bank, resulting in the BHC's ownership or control of more than five percent of the bank's voting shares; (*iv*) acquisition by a BHC or a BHC non-banking subsidiary of all

---

12. Pub. L. No. 106-102, Nov. 12, 1999, 113 Stat. 1338 (1999) (codified at scattered sections of 12, 15, 16, 18 U.S.C.). For further information concerning the GLBA, see Note 1.60, *supra*.

13. GLBA, § 116, 113 Stat. at 1372 (codified at 12 U.S.C. § 1844(a), (e)(1)).

14. *Id.*, § 111, 113 Stat. at 1362-1365 (codified at 12 U.S.C. § 1844(c)).

15. Under the source-of-strength doctrine, the Fed imposes an obligation on each bank holding company to act as a source of financial strength for its operating bank subsidiaries. *See* James F. Groth, Comment, *Can Regulators Force Bank Holding Companies to Bail Out Their Failing Subsidiaries?–An Analysis of the Federal Reserve Board's Source-of-Strength Doctrine*, 86 Nw. U.L. Rev. 112 (1991) (discussing doctrine).

16. GLBA, § 112(a), 113 Stat. at 1365-1367 (codified at 12 U.S.C. § 1844(g)).

17. *Id.*, § 113, 113 Stat. at 1368-1369 (codified at 12 U.S.C. § 1848a).

or substantially all of the assets of a bank; and, (*v*) mergers and consolidations between BHCs. *Id.* § 1842(a)(1)-(5). The procedures for application for approval of any of these otherwise prohibited actions are provided in section 3(b) of the BHCA, *id.* § 1842(b). In determining whether or not to approve the application, the Fed must consider the factors identified in section 3(c), *id.* § 1842(c). While the Fed is given full authority at the federal level to regulate BHCs (*see id.* § 1844), the states retain their individual authority to regulate banks, BHC's and subsidiaries thereof, to the extent they had this power prior to the enactment of the act. *See id.* § 1846. Furthermore, although the Fed is required to consider the competitive effects of proposed acquisitions under the BHCA, the Justice Department retains its role in administering the antitrust laws. Under 12 U.S.C. § 1849(b), the Fed is required to notify the Attorney General of any approval by it pursuant to § 1842. In most cases, the approved transaction cannot be consummated until the expiration of thirty days after approval. Within that time, the Justice Department may initiate an action to enjoin the consummation of the transaction under the federal antitrust laws. If such an action is initiated, the Fed and any appropriate state banking regulator may appear as a party by its own motion as of right. *See id.* § 1849(c). The action by the Justice Department is subject to the "convenience and needs" defense afforded by § 1842(c)(2). *See id.* § 1849(e).[18]

4.6. *Basic outline of the SLHCA provisions.* Review the provisions of 12 U.S.C. § 1467a, together with the applicable definitional provisions of § 1461. The SLHCA provides for a substantially similar, though relatively more complicated regulatory regime for the formation of a savings and loan holding company (SLHC), with the approval of the Director of the Office of Thrift Supervision (DOTS) – after July 21, 2011, approval of the Fed. As with the BHCA, the SLHCA identifies a series of actions that are prohibited by the act unless the regulator has given prior approval. Among the actions covered by this prohibition are: (*i*) acquisition by an SLHC of control of a savings association or an SLHC, or to retain such control in violation of the SLHCA, *id.* § 1467a(e)(1)(A)(i); (*ii*) acquisition, by merger, consolidation, or purchase of assets, of a savings association or an SLHC, *id.* § 1467a(e)(1)(A)(ii); and, (*iii*) with certain exceptions, direct or indirect acquisition by a company that is not an SLHC (non-SLHC) of control of one or more savings associations. *Id.* § 1467a(e)(1)(B). Furthermore, acquisition, or retention for more than one year, of control of an uninsured institution is generally prohibited. *Id.* § 1467a(e)(1)(A)(iv). As to acquisitions by SLHCs (*i.e.*, acquisitions described in *i.* and *ii.* above), or acquisitions of more than one savings associations by a non-SLHC,[19] the regulator is required to take into consideration such factors as the financial and managerial resources and future prospects of the company and association involved, the insurance risk to the Deposit Insurance Fund, and the convenience and needs of the community to be served. *Id.* § 1467a(e)(2).

4.7. *Impact of Dodd-Frank Act.* **a.** *Supervision of Savings and Loan Holding Companies.* On July 21, 2011, the functions and authority of the DOTS and the OTS over

---

18. The significance of the availability of this defense will become apparent after reading of *United States v. Philadelphia Nat'l Bank, infra*, an antitrust action decided three years before the enactment of the amendments to the BHCA that created the defense.

19. In general, an acquisition of one or more savings associations by a non-SLHC must be approved by the DOTS unless he or she finds that

> the financial and managerial resources and future prospects of the company and association involved to be such that the acquisition would be detrimental to the association or the insurance risk of the Savings Association Insurance Fund or Bank Insurance Fund. . . .

12 U.S.C. § 1467a(e)(1)(B).

SLHCs are first exercised by the Fed.[20] Under Dodd-Frank Act § 313,[21] the OTS and the position of the DOTS are scheduled to be abolished 90 days after the "transfer date" 21 July 2011.

b. *"Intermediate Holding Company" and the SLHCA*. Post-2010, the term "savings and loan holding company" (SLHC) does not include a bank holding company (BHC) that is registered under, and subject to, the Bank Holding Company Act (BHCA) and any *company* directly or indirectly controlled by a BHC (other than a savings association), a company that controls a savings association that functions solely in a trust or fiduciary capacity as described in BHCA § 2(c)(2)(D) (12 U.S.C.A. 1841(c)(2)(D)), or a company that is an existing unitary SLHC solely by virtue of its control of an *intermediate holding company.*[22] An intermediate holding company can be established under Dodd-Frank Act § 626,[23] if and when an existing grandfathered unitary SLHC conducts activities other than financial activities, and the Fed requires the company to establish and conduct all or some specified portion of its financial activities in or through an intermediate holding company created for that purpose.[24] The intermediate company becomes the SLHC, and at that point the parent company is no longer considered an SLHC under the exemptive provision in the HOLA.[25] To date, the Fed has not published proposals for implementing regulations.

c. *Supervision of Mutual Holding Companies*. The scope of the SLHCA includes the authority, currently exercised by the DOTS, to approve reorganization of a mutual savings association into a mutual holding company and operating subsidiary.[26] The Dodd-Frank Act adds a requirement of prior notice to the appropriate regulator (eventually, the Fed) of dividends to be declared by a savings association subsidiary of mutual SLHC.[27] To date, proposals for implementing regulations have not been published.

4.8. Forth Corp. has just purchased twenty percent of the outstanding shares of common stock of Quarter National Bank. The Chairman of Forth Corp., Hiram Forth, who is also the president of Quarter National, intends to buy five percent of the outstanding shares of common stock of Quarter National from the bank's former president. Do these transactions raise any problems? Review 12 U.S.C. §§ 1841(a)(1), (2)(A)-(B), 1842(a)(1). Do you need any other information to answer the question?

4.9. Assume that Forth Corp. and its chairman have not yet made their stock purchases. They are preparing a BHCA application, which will include the disclosure that Forth Corp. expects that in the near future it may diversify into other activities that would require more capital. Would this disclosure make a difference to the Fed's consideration of the application? Review 12 U.S.C. § 1842(c).

4.10. Would it make any difference in either of the two previous questions if Forth Corp. and its chairman had or were about to acquire shares in Quarter Federal Savings Association? *See, e.g., id.* § 1467a(a)(2), (e)(1)(B).

4.11. *Holding company regulation after FIRREA: SLHC regulation.* From 1959

---

20. *See* Dodd-Frank Act §312(b) (codified at 12 U.S.C. §5412(b)) (mandating transfer of functions).

21. Dodd-Frank Act §313, 124 Stat. at 1523 (codified at 12 U.S.C. §5413) (DFA).

22. 12 U.S.C. § 1467a(a)(1)(D)(ii)(I)-(III).

23. Dodd-Frank Act §626, 124 Stat. at 1638-1640 (codified at 12 U.S.C. § 1467b).

24. 12 U.S.C. § 1467b(b)(1)(A).

25. 12 U.S.C. § 1467a(1)(D)(ii)(III).

26. 12 U.S.C. §1467a(o)

27. Dodd-Frank Act § 625, 124 Stat. at 1636-1638 (codified at 12 U.S.C.A. § 1467a(o)(11)).

until 1989, SLHCs were subject to a statutory scheme of regulation under the Savings and Loan Holding Company Act (SLHCA),[28] similar to that established for BHCs in 1956. The Financial Institutions Reform, Recovery, and Enforcement Act of 1989[29] drew the provisions governing the regulation of SLHCs into the amended Home Owners' Loan Act (HOLA).[30] For these purposes, an SLHC is defined to mean any company that directly or indirectly controls a "savings association" (*e.g.*, a savings and loan association or savings bank) or that controls any other company which is an SLHC.[31]

4.12. *Holding company regulation after FIRREA: BHC regulation.* The FIRREA also amends section 4 of the BHCA,[32] expressly to facilitate thrift acquisitions by BHCs, not limited to acquisitions of failing thrifts.[33] In addition, FIRREA indicates that no special restrictions on transactions between such acquired institutions and their holding company affiliates are to be imposed by the Fed beyond those restrictions generally applicable.[34] The FIRREA also makes technical amendments to the BHCA, conforming the act's definitional and approval provisions to the generic use in the FIRREA of the terminology "savings association"[35] and "depository institution."[36] Similarly, it makes substantive and technical amendments to BHCA provisions with respect to passive investments by companies controlling certain nonbank banks,[37] and permits the purchase of minority interests in undercapitalized savings associations by BHCs.[38] The FIRREA also amends section 205 of the Depository Institutions Management Interlocks Act to exempt certain specified interlocks by a single management official in connection with the purchase of a minority interest in an undercapitalized savings association by a savings and loan holding company.[39]

4.13. *Treatment of unitary holding companies.* As originally enacted, the BHCA only applied to multibank holding companies. This changed under 1970 amendments to the BHCA, which extended the scope of the act to one-bank holding companies. As to SLHCs, however, review 12 U.S.C. § 1467a(e)(1)(B)(ii) (acquisitions); *id.* § 1467a(c)(3)(A) (permissible activities). To what extent do these provisions give relatively more favorable treatment under the SLHCA to unitary SLHCs?

4.14. *GLBA and unitary savings & loan holding companies.* The GLBA prohibits new unitary savings and loan holding companies from engaging in nonfinancial activities or

---

28. 12 U.S.C. § 1730a (1982).

29. Pub. L. No. 101-73, 103 Stat. 183 (1989) (FIRREA).

30. 12 U.S.C. §§ 1461 *et seq. See* FIRREA §§ 301, 303, 407, 103 Stat. at 318-342, 343-350, 363 (codified at 12 U.S.C. § 1467a; repealing, *inter alia*, § 1730a) (regulation of holding companies moved from National Housing Act to the HOLA and revised).

31. 12 U.S.C. § 1467a(a)(1)(D).

32. 12 U.S.C. § 1843.

33. FIRREA, § 601(a), 103 Stat. at 408-409 (codified at 12 U.S.C. § 1843(i)(1)).

34. *Id.*, § 601(a), 103 Stat. at 409 (codified at 12 U.S.C. § 1843(i)(2)). The Fed is required to remove any such restrictions on pre-FIRREA thrift acquisitions. *Id.* § 601(b).

35. *See id.* § 602(a), 103 Stat. at 409 (codified at 12 U.S.C. § 1841(j)(1)-(2)) (BHCA definition of "savings association" and "insured institution").

36. *See id.* § 602(b), 103 Stat. at 409 (codified at 12 U.S.C. § 1842(e)) (substituting "insured depository institution as defined in section 3" for "insured bank as defined in section 3(h)").

37. *See id.* § 603, 103 Stat. at 409-410 (codified at 12 U.S.C. § 1843(f)(2)(A)(ii), (10)-(11)).

38. *See id.* § 604(b), 103 Stat. at 411 (codified at 12 U.S.C. § 1843(f)(2)(A), (12)-(13)).

39. *Id.* § 604(a), 103 Stat. at 410-411 (codified at 12 U.S.C. § 3204(9)).

affiliating with nonfinancial entities.[40]

4.15. *"Qualified thrift lenders" and the SLHCA.* Review 12 U.S.C. § 1467a(c)(3), (m). To what extent are "qualified thrift lenders" and their holding companies given relatively more favorable treatment under the SLHCA? Based particularly on your review of the provisions of section 1467a(m), what policy is served by this differential treatment?

4.16. *Banks, nonbank banks, and nonbank nonbank banks.* Perhaps the most troublesome definitional issue under the BHCA has been the provision defining, for purposes of the BHCA, "bank," the acquisition of which might trigger the requirements and prohibitions of the act. The term was amended in 1966, 1970 and 1989. Assume that First Credulity Bank of California, a state-chartered, FDIC-insured nonmember bank, does not accept demand deposits (*i.e.*, checking accounts), but does accept NOW accounts.[41] It does make commercial loans. Would First Holdulity Company be required to comply with the BHCA if it wanted to acquire control of First Credulity? Consider the following two cases.

Wilshire Oil Co. v. Board of Governors

668 F.2d 732 (3d Cir. 1981)

VAN DUSEN, Senior Circuit Judge.

This matter comes before us as a petition for review of a cease and desist order[a] of the Board of Governors of the Federal Reserve System (the "Board"). The Board found petitioner, Wilshire Oil Company of Texas ("Wilshire"), to be in violation of the Bank Holding Company Act of 1956, *as amended*, 12 U.S.C. §§ 1841-1850 (1976) (the "BHC Act"). The only contested issue is whether Wilshire's subsidiary, the Trust Company of New Jersey ("TCNJ"), is a "bank" under the BHC Act. Wilshire concedes that if TCNJ is a "bank," then Wilshire is a "bank holding company" engaged in both banking and non-banking activities in violation of § 4(a)(2) of the Act, 12 U.S.C. § 1843(a)(2). We affirm the Board's conclusion that TCNJ is a "bank" under the BHC Act, and deny the petition for review seeking to terminate the cease and desist order against Wilshire. . . .

The Bank Holding Company Act . . . was enacted to prevent the concentration of commercial banking activities and to separate banking from commerce. Section 4 of the BHC Act generally restricts the non-banking activities of "bank holding companies,"[b] defined in § 2(a)(1) as companies which have "control over any bank." As originally enacted, the BHC Act restricted the non-banking activities of only companies that controlled more than one bank, but in 1970 Congress amended the Act so as to apply also to one-bank holding companies. Under § 4(a)(2), these one-bank holding companies were given 10 years, until December 31, 1980, either to divest their non-banking operations or to cease being bank

---

40. GLBA, § 401(a) (codified at 12 U.S.C. § 1467a(c)(9)). The prohibition applies to a company that becomes a unitary savings and loan holding company pursuant to an application filed with the OTS after 4 May 1999. 12 U.S.C. § 1467a(c)(9)(A). A grandfathered unitary thrift holding company retains its authority to engage in nonfinancial activities. *Id.* § 1467a(c)(9)(C). The new prohibition also does not apply to corporate reorganizations. *Id.* § 1467a(c)(9)(D).

41. On NOW accounts, see 12 U.S.C. § 1832.

a. On the cease and desist order, the administrative equivalent of an injunction, see Chapter 8, § 2, *infra*.

b. On the regulation of nonbanking activities of BHCs and their subsidiaries, see Chapter 6, *infra*.

holding companies. 12 U.S.C. § 1843(a)(2) (1976).

Congress has twice modified the definition of "bank" under the BHC Act.[c] The original definition included all national banks, State banks, and savings banks. . . . In 1966, the definition was narrowed to encompass only those domestic institutions which "[accept] deposits that the depositor has a legal right to withdraw on demand." . . . The current definition was enacted in 1970:

> "(c) 'Bank' means any institution . . . which (1) accepts deposits that the depositor has a legal right to withdraw on demand, and (2) engages in the business of making commercial loans."

12 U.S.C. § 1841(c) (1976).

The Board of Governors of the Federal Reserve System is charged with the administration of the BHC Act, and § 5(b) authorizes the Board "to issue such regulations and orders as may be necessary to enable it to administer and carry out the purpose of this chapter and prevent evasions thereof." 12 U.S.C. § 1844(b) (1976). Under §§ 8(b)(1) & (3) of the Financial Institutions Supervisory Act of 1966 ("FISA"), 12 U.S.C. §§ 1818(b)(1) & (3) (Supp. 1980), the Board also has the power to institute cease and desist proceedings whenever it has reason to believe that the BHC Act is about to be violated. . . .

Wilshire Oil Company of Texas . . . is engaged in the production of oil and natural gas, both directly and through its subsidiaries. Until November 1980, Trust Company of New Jersey, one of Wilshire's subsidiaries,[2] was concededly a "bank" under the BHC Act's current definition; TCNJ "(1) accept[ed] deposits that the depositor [had] a legal right to withdraw on demand, and (2) engage[d] in the business of making commercial loans." 12 U.S.C. § 1841(c) (1976). Because Wilshire controlled a "bank," it was a bank holding company required by § 4(a)(2) either to divest its oil and gas business or to cease being a bank holding company before December 31, 1980.

Beginning in 1977, the Board frequently urged Wilshire to decide how it would come into compliance with the BHC Act before the December 31, 1980, deadline. Wilshire suggested several possible ways of complying with the Act, but made no firm proposal until November 1980. On November 3, 1980, less than two months before the final deadline, Wilshire notified the Board that it intended to keep both its oil and gas business and its interest in TCNJ. Wilshire announced that it would comply with the BHC Act by changing TCNJ into a "non-bank" under the Act.

On November 5, 1980, TCNJ sent a notice to its depositors that:

> "The Trust Company of New Jersey, beginning November 20, 1980 reserves the right to require 14 days notice prior to withdrawal from its transactional accounts. The Trust Company has never exercised its right to require notice and has no intention of exercising a notice provision on any type of account."

. . . TCNJ also modified its account agreement forms for its newly-named "transactional accounts" to include this reservation of the right to require notice for withdrawal. Except for this reservation, TCNJ has not changed any of its banking operations, and the reservation has had no practical effect on the institution. Specifically, TCNJ has not altered

---

c. The BHCA definition of "bank" has since been amended yet again, specifically to resolve the problem of the "nonbank bank" such as TCNJ tried to become. *See infra* Note 4.17.

2. Wilshire owns 90% of the shares of TCNJ. . . .

its commercial lending activities.

Wilshire claims that this reservation of a right to require notice means that TCNJ's depositors no longer have "a legal right to withdraw [their deposits] on demand," and therefore TCNJ is not a "bank" under the BHC Act definition in § 2(c) and Wilshire is not a "bank holding company" under § 2(a)(1). The Board disagreed and issued a Notice of Charges against Wilshire, its directors, and certain officers on December 9, 1980, pursuant to §§ 8(b)(1) & (3) of FISA, 12 U.S.C. §§ 1818(b)(1) & (3). The Board also directed that a formal administrative hearing be held to determine whether Wilshire would be in violation of the BHC Act on January 1, 1981. . . .

Wilshire argues that TCNJ's reservation of the right to require 14 days' notice of withdrawal means that the holders of its "transactional accounts" no longer have a legal right to withdraw their deposits on demand. Because the depositors lack this legal right, Wilshire contends, TCNJ does not fit within the literal definition of a "bank" in § 2(c) of the Act, and Wilshire is not a bank holding company subject to the Board's regulatory powers.

The Board concluded in its Final Order and Decision that "TCNJ is a 'bank' within the meaning of the section 2(c) of the BHC Act because it accepts deposits that the depositor has the legal right to withdraw on demand and engages in the business of making commercial loans . . ." The Board considered the statement sent by TCNJ to its depositors reserving the right to require notice of withdrawal, and noted that this announcement stated that TCNJ "has no intention of exercising" this reserved right. The purpose of this disclaimer of intention, the Board assumed, was to induce TCNJ's checking account customers not to withdraw their deposits from TCNJ. Referring to § 90 of the Restatement (Second) of Contracts on promissory estoppel, the Board stated "it appears that a depositor who relies to his detriment on TCNJ's representation of intent not to invoke the prior notice requirement may have a legally enforceable right in a court of law (on a breach of contract theory or on general equitable principles) to prevent TCNJ from asserting any prior notice requirement". . . .

Wilshire disagrees and asserts that TCNJ's letter to its depositors of November 5, 1980, was effective in reserving a right to require advance notice. It argues that no promise was made by TCNJ that it would never exercise the right, nor was there any voluntary waiver of the right. Wilshire supports this contention by noting that the disclaimer of any intention to exercise the right we sent to the depositors in the same notice that reserved the right in the first place. This makes clear to depositors, Wilshire argues, that TCNJ did not promise to forego its right, but merely stated its intention not to exercise the right in the foreseeable future. Wilshire also points to the documents used by TCNJ to open new accounts since November 1980 which contain the reserved right to require notice, but not the disclaimer of intention to exercise that right. . . . TCNJ has not given the holders of these accounts any assurance that it will not require them at some point in the future to give 14 days' advance notice of withdrawal.

We do not need to decide, however, if the Board was correct in its conclusion that TCNJ's depositors still have a legal right to withdraw their funds on demand despite TCNJ's reservation of the right to require advance notice. While the language of the BHC Act may be the starting point in construing the statute, we may look beyond the plain language, if necessary, to ensure that application of the literal terms does not destroy the practical operation of the statute. . . .

The legislative history . . . shows that Congress intended to include an institution such as TCNJ under the definition of "bank" in the BHC Act. Congress enacted the BHC Act "to prevent possible abuses related to the control of commercial credit" by separating commercial banking from commerce. S.Rep. No. 91-1084, 91st Cong., 2d Sess. 24 (1970), *reprinted in* [1970] U.S. Code Cong. & Ad. News 5519, 5541. Congress found it necessary to amend the definition of "bank" twice, as it sought a definition that would serve the purposes of the statute, without unnecessarily restricting banks that did not engage in commercial credit transactions.

The legislative history indicates that the original definition of "bank" in the BHC Act considered too broad, and the 1966 amendment to the definition, which generated the first half of the current definition, was passed to remedy this problem. . . . S. Rep. No. 1179, 89th Cong., 2d Sess. 7 (1966), *reprinted in* [1966] U.S. Code Cong. & Ad. News 2385, 2391.

The Senate Report shows that the 1966 definition of a "bank" as "any institution . . . which accepts deposits that the depositor has a legal right to withdraw on demand" was meant to include those institutions that accept "deposits payable on demand (checking accounts)." *Id.* Traditionally, the ability to withdraw deposits on demand has been associated with non-interest bearing checking accounts, while a reservation of a right to require advance notice of withdrawals has been a condition of interest-bearing savings accounts. . . .[8] It is reasonable to conclude, as did the Board, that the reason why Congress did not consider in its definition of "bank" an institution such as TCNJ that offers accounts that are non-interest bearing and not accessible on demand was simply because such accounts were not commonly used.[9] Congress did not choose the words "accepts deposits that the depositor has a legal right to withdraw on demand" because it was concerned with the distinction between a depositor's legal right to withdraw on demand and the ability in practice to withdraw on demand. The more reasonable interpretation of why Congress selected those terms is that stated in the Senate Report, supra: Congress was merely adopting "the commonly accepted test of whether an institution is a commercial bank." *Id.*

This interpretation of the legislative history is reinforced by the Senate Report to the 1970 amendment of the BHC Act, which once again changed the definition of "bank" in § 2(c) of the Act. This amendment added the second element of the current definition: whether the institution "engages in the business of making commercial loans." 12 U.S.C. § 1841(c)(2). The Senate Report shows clearly that, in framing the definition of "bank," Congress was not as concerned with the precise legal rights of a bank's depositors as it was with the practical effect of the Act on commercial lending practices:

> "The definition of 'bank' adopted by Congress in 1966 was designed to include commercial banks and excludes those institutions not engaged in commercial banking, since the purpose of the act was to restrain undue concentration of commercial banking resources and to prevent possible abuses related to the control of commercial credit. However, the Federal Reserve Board has noted that this definition may be too broad and may include institutions which are not in fact engaged in the business of commercial banking in that they do not make commercial loans. The committee, accordingly, adopted a provision which would exclude institutions that are not engaged in the business of making commercial loans from the definition of 'bank.'"

---

8. Even though the 1980 Deregulation Act, 12 U.S.C. § 1832 (Supp. 1981), allows financial institutions to offer to individuals and non-profit corporations interest-bearing accounts that are accessible by negotiable instrument, the regulations mandate that the institutions still reserve the right to require advance notice for withdrawals. *See* 12 C.F.R. Parts 217, 329 (1981). We note that this reservation of a right to require advance notice is once again associated with interest-bearing accounts, unlike TCNJ's non-interest bearing transactional accounts.

9. The Board . . . recognized that federal law does not require the payment of interest on savings accounts that are subject to a reservation of the right to require notice of withdrawal. . . . We emphasize the financial institutions typically do pay interest on accounts subject to this reservation, because it indicates the factual context in which Congress defined the term "bank."

S. Rep. No. 91-1084, 91st Cong., 2d Sess. 24 (1970), *reprinted in* [1970] U.S. Code Cong. & Ad. News 5519, 5541.

This legislative history shows that TCNJ falls within the category of institutions that Congress intended to include in its definitions of "bank" in the BHC Act. In practice, TCNJ's "transactional accounts" are "demand deposits," because, as TCNJ has notified its customers, it has no intention of exercising its right to require advance notice of withdrawals. There is no dispute that TCNJ makes commercial loans. Together, these factors indicate that the possibility of abuse of commercial credit exists, and TCNJ is the type of institution that Congress meant to include with the definition of a "bank" under § 2(c). ...

Congress specifically instructed the Board to look to the purposes of the BHC Act in administering its terms. [The opinion quotes 12 U.S.C. § 1844(b) (1976).]

The Board found, and Wilshire does not contest on appeal, that TCNJ has made no functional change in its banking operations, and the reservation of a right to require notice has had no practical effect on the bank's deposits. Given that the Act admittedly applied to TCNJ before November 1980 because of its commercial activities, the Board appropriately determined that it must continue to apply the Act to TCNJ to "carry out the purpose" of the BHC Act.

Section 5(b) also permits the Board to act to "prevent evasions" of the BHC Act. Wilshire admitted at oral argument that the purpose of the reservation of the right to require advance notice was to take TCNJ outside the BHC Act. Because we approve the Board's finding that the reservation of the right to advance notice served no banking purpose, but was made merely to withdraw TCNJ from the coverage of the BHC Act, we accept the Board's order as necessary to "prevent evasion" of the Act. The Board explained its conclusion:

> "[A]ny determination by the Board to the effect that TCNJ's notice to its demand deposits customers terminates TCNJ's status as a bank under the BHC Act would serve to nullify the entire regulatory framework of that Act. If a bank holding company is permitted to escape its obligations under the Act without making any functional change in its operations simply by causing its subsidiary bank(s) to send a notice to customers holding demand deposits reserving a right to notice of prior withdrawal, circumvention of the Act's substantive requirements on a large scale is likely." . . .

Since acceptance of Wilshire's position would allow evasion of the Act, we agree with the Board that § 5(b) "enables the Board to prohibit activities that are technically outside the literal terms of the Act in order to prevent a clear evasion of the purposes of the Act." . . .

Notes and Comments 4.17. *Developments after Wilshire.* The establishment of more sophisticated versions of the "nonbank bank" at issue in *Wilshire Oil* led to a major crisis in bank regulation, and to conflict among the regulators, in the first half of the 1980s. *See generally* Malloy, *Nonbanks and Nondefinitions: New Challenges in Bank Regulatory Policy*, 10 Seton Hall Leg. J. 1 (1986) (discussing the "nonbank bank" controversy and the emergence of "nonbank nonbank banks" and proposing solutions). In effect taking a cue from *Wilshire Oil*, the Fed finally expanded its definitions of what constituted a "demand deposit" or a "commercial loan" under the BHCA, so as to capture the nonbank banks. The Supreme Court responded in the following case.

Board of Governors v. Dimension Fin. Corp.

474 U.S. 361 (1986)

Chief Justice BURGER delivered the opinion of the Court.

We granted certiorari to decide whether the Federal Reserve Board acted within its statutory authority in defining "banks" under § 2(c) of the Bank Holding Company Act of 1956, 12 U.S.C. § 1841 *et seq.*, as any institution that (1) accepts deposits that "as a matter of practice" are payable on demand and (2) engages in the business of making "any loan other than a loan to an individual for personal, family, household, or charitable purposes" including "the purchase of retail installment loans or commercial paper, certificates of deposit, bankers' acceptances, and similar money market instruments." 12 CFR § 225.2(a)(1) (1985). . . .

Section 2(c) of the Bank Holding Company Act defines "bank" as any institution "which (1) accepts deposits that the depositor has a legal right to withdraw on demand, and (2) engages in the business of making commercial loans." 70 Stat. 133, *as amended*, 12 U.S.C. § 1841(c).

This case is about so-called "nonbank banks"–institutions that offer services similar to those of banks but which until recently were not under Board regulation because they conducted their business so as to place themselves arguably outside the narrow definition of "bank" found in § 2(c) of the Act. Many nonbank banks, for example, offer customers NOW (negotiable order of withdrawal) accounts which function like conventional checking accounts but because of prior notice provisions do not technically give the depositor a "legal right to withdraw on demand." 12 U.S.C. § 1841(c)(1). Others offer conventional checking accounts, but avoid classification as "banks" by limiting their extension of commercial credit to the purchase of money market instruments such as certificates of deposit and commercial paper.

In 1984, the Board promulgated rules providing that nonbank banks offering the functional equivalent of traditional banking services would thereafter be regulated as banks. 49 Fed. Reg. 794. The Board accomplished this by amending its definition of a bank, found in "Regulation Y," in two significant respects. First, the Board defined "demand deposit" to include deposits, like NOW accounts, which are "as a matter of practice" payable on demand. 12 CFR § 225.2(a)(1)(A) (1985). Second, the Board defined the "making of a commercial loan" as "any loan other than a loan to an individual for personal, family, household, or charitable purposes," including "the purchase of retail installment loans or commercial paper, certificates of deposit, bankers' acceptances, and similar money market instruments." 12 CFR § 225.2(a)(1)(B) (1985). . . .

Cases challenging the amended Regulation Y were commenced in three Circuits and were consolidated in the United States Court of Appeals for the Tenth Circuit. The Court of Appeals set aside both the demand deposit and commercial loan aspects of the Board's regulation. 744 F.2d 1402 (1984). The court did not discuss the demand deposit regulation in detail, relying instead on the holding of an earlier Tenth Circuit case, *First Bancorporation v. Board of Governors*, 728 F.2d 434 (1984). In *First Bancorporation*, the court noted that the statutory definition of demand deposit is a deposit giving the depositor "a legal right to withdraw on demand." The court recognized that "withdrawals from NOW accounts are in actual practice permitted on demand." *Id.*, at 436. But, since the depositary institution retains a technical prior notice requirement it does not, for the purposes of Congress' definition of "bank," accept "deposits that the depositor has a legal right to withdraw on demand."

The Court of Appeals also concluded that the Board's new definition of "commercial loan" was at odds with the Act. The legislative history revealed that in passing § 2(c) Congress intended to exempt from Board regulation institutions whose only commercial credit activity was the purchase of money market instruments. Although agencies must be "able to change to meet new conditions arising within their sphere of authority," any expansion of agency jurisdiction must come from Congress and not the agency itself. 744 F.2d, at 1409. Accordingly, the Court of Appeals invalidated the amended regulations. ...

The Bank Holding Company Act of 1956, 12 U.S.C. § 1841 *et seq.*, vests broad regulatory authority in the Board over bank holding companies "to restrain the undue concentration of commercial banking resources and to prevent possible abuses related to the control of commercial credit." S. Rep. No. 91-1084, p. 24 (1970), U.S. Code Cong. & Admin. News 1970, pp. 5519, 5541. The Act authorizes the Board to regulate "any company which has control over any bank." 12 U.S.C. § 1841(a)(1).

The breadth of that regulatory power rests on the Act's definition of the word "bank." The 1956 Act gave a simple and broad definition of bank: "any national banking association or any State bank, savings bank, or trust company." 12 U.S.C. § 1841(c) (1964 ed.). Experience soon proved that literal application of the statute had the unintended consequence of including within regulation industrial banks offering limited checking account services to their customers. These institutions accepted "'funds from the public that are, in actual practice, repaid on demand.'" *Amend the Bank Holding Company Act of 1956: Hearings on S. 2253, S. 2418, and H.R. 7371 before a Subcommittee of the Senate Committee on Banking and Currency*, 89th Cong., 2d Sess., 447 (1966) (letter to the Committee from J.L. Robertson, Member, Federal Reserve Board). Although including these institutions within the bank definition was the "correct legal interpretation" of the 1956 statute, the Board saw "no reason in policy to cover such institutions under this act." . . . Congress agreed, and accordingly amended the statutory definition of a bank in 1966, limiting its application to institutions that accept "deposits that the depositor has a legal right to withdraw on demand."[2]

The 1966 definition proved unsatisfactory because it too included within the definition of "bank" institutions that did not pose significant dangers to the banking system. Because one of the primary purposes of the Act was to "restrain undue concentration of ... commercial credit," it made little sense to regulate institutions that did not, in fact, engage in the business of making commercial loans. S. Rep. No. 91-1084, p. 24 (1970), U.S. Code Cong. & Admin. News 1970, p. 5541. Congress accordingly amended the definition, excluding all institutions that did not "engag[e] in the business of making commercial loans." . . .

In 1984, the Board initiated rulemaking to respond to the increase in the number of nonbank banks. After hearing views of interested parties, the Board found that nonbank banks pose three dangers to the national banking system. First, by remaining outside the reach of banking regulations, nonbank banks have a significant competitive advantage over regulated banks despite the functional equivalence of the services offered. Second, the proliferation of nonbank banks threatens the structure established by Congress for limiting the association of banking and commercial enterprises. *See* 12 U.S.C. § 1843(c)(8) (bank holding company can purchase nonbanking affiliate only if entity "closely related to banking"). Third, the interstate acquisition of nonbank banks undermines the statutory proscription on interstate banking without prior state approval. 49 Fed. Reg. 794, 835-836 (1984). Since the

---

2. The Senate Report explained, "the bill redefines 'bank' as an institution that accepts deposits payable on demand (checking accounts), the commonly accepted test of whether an institution is a commercial bank so as to exclude institutions like industrial banks and nondeposit trust companies." S. Rep. No. 1179, 89th Cong., 2d Sess., 7 (1966), U.S. Code Cong. & Admin. News 1970, pp. 2385, 2391.

narrowed statutory definition required that both the demand deposit and the commercial loan elements be present to constitute the institution as a bank, the Board proceeded to amend Regulation Y redefining both elements of the test. We turn now to the two elements of this definition. . . .

The Board amended its definition of "demand deposit" primarily to include within its regulatory authority institutions offering NOW accounts. A NOW account functions like a traditional checking account–the depositor can write checks that are payable on demand at the depository institution. The depository institution, however, retains a seldom exercised but nevertheless absolute right to require prior notice of withdrawal. Under a literal reading of the statute, the institution–even if it engages in full scale commercial lending–is not a "bank" for the purposes of the Holding Company Act because the prior notice provision withholds from the depositor any "legal right" to withdraw on demand. The Board in its amended definition closes this loophole by defining demand deposits as a deposit, not that the depositor has a "legal right to withdraw on demand," but a deposit that "as a matter of practice is payable on demand."

In determining whether the Board was empowered to make such a change, we begin, of course, with the language of the statute. If the statute is clear and unambiguous "that is the end of the matter, for the court, as well as the agency, must give effect to the unambiguously expressed intent of Congress." *Chevron U.S.A. Inc. v. National Resources Defense Council, Inc.*, 467 U.S. 837, 842-843 694 (1984). The traditional deference courts pay to agency interpretation is not to be applied to alter the clearly expressed intent of Congress.

Application of this standard to the Board's interpretation of the "demand deposit" element of § 2(c) does not require extended analysis. By the 1966 amendments to § 2(c), Congress expressly limited the Act to regulation of institutions that accept deposits that "the depositor has a legal right to withdraw on demand." 12 U.S.C. § 1841(c). The Board would now define "legal right" as meaning the same as "a matter of practice." But no amount of agency expertise–however sound may be the result–can make the words "legal right" mean a right to do something "as a matter of practice." A legal right to withdraw on demand means just that: a right to withdraw deposits without prior notice or limitation. Institutions offering NOW accounts do not give the depositor a legal right to withdraw on demand; rather, the institution itself retains the ultimate legal right to require advance notice of withdrawal. The Board's definition of "demand deposit," therefore, is not an accurate or reasonable interpretation of § 2(c). . . .

Section 2(c) of the Act provides that, even if an institution accepts deposits that the depositor has a legal right to withdraw on demand, the institution is not a bank unless it "engages in the business of making commercial loans." Under Regulation Y, "commercial loan" means "any loan other than a loan to an individual for personal, family, household, or charitable purposes," including "the purchase of retail installment loans or commercial paper, certificates of deposit, bankers' acceptances, and similar money market instruments."

The purpose of the amended regulation is to regulate as banks institutions offering "commercial loan substitutes," that is, extensions of credit to commercial enterprises through transactions other than the conventional commercial loan. In its implementing order, the Board explained that "it is proper to include these instruments within the scope of the term commercial loan as used in the Act in order to carry out the Act's basic purposes: to maintain the impartiality of banks in providing credit to business, to prevent conflicts of interest, and to avoid concentration of control of credit." 49 Fed. Reg., at 841.

As the Board's characterization of these transactions as "commercial loan substitutes" suggests, however, money market transactions do not fall within the commonly accepted definition of "commercial loans." The term "commercial loan" is used in the financial community to describe the direct loan from a bank to a business customer for the purpose of providing funds needed by the customer in its business. The term does not apply to, indeed is used to distinguish, extensions of credit in the open market that do not involve close borrower-lender relationships. *Cf.* G. MUNN & F. GARCIA, ENCYCLOPEDIA OF BANKING AND FINANCE 607 (1983). These latter money market transactions undoubtedly involve the indirect extension of credit to commercial entities but, because they do not entail the face-to-face negotiation of credit between borrower and lender, are not "commercial loans."

This common understanding of the term "commercial loan" is reflected in the Board's own decisions. Throughout the 1970's the Board applied the term "commercial loan" to exclude from regulation institutions engaging in money market transactions. For example, in *D.H. Baldwin Co.*, 63 Fed. Res. Bull. 280 (1977), the Board noted that although savings and loans participated in the Federal funds market and issued certificates of deposit, they were not "technically 'banks' for the purposes of the Act" because they did not make commercial loans. . . . The Board recognized that savings and loans resembled banks but concluded that "the decision should be left to Congress whether, in light of the policies underlying the Bank Holding Company Act, such 'near-banks' should be treated as 'banks' or 'nonbanks.'" . . . *See also American Fletcher Corp.*, 60 Fed. Res. Bull. 868, 869, and n. 8 (1974) (savings and loans participate in the federal funds market and offer certificates of deposit but may not be deemed "banks" within the meaning of the Act). In 1976, the Board's Legal Division found that broker call loans "do not appear to have the close lender-borrower relationship that is one of the characteristics of commercial loans." . . .

The Board now contends that the new definition conforms with the original intent of Congress in enacting the "commercial loan" provision. The provision, the Board argues, was a "technical amendment to the Act designed to create a narrowly circumscribed exclusion from the Act's coverage." . . . The Board supports this revisionist view of the purpose of the "commercial loan" provision by citing a comment in the "legislative history" indicating that at the time the provision was enacted, it operated to exclude only one institution, the Boston Safe Deposit & Trust Co. The Board does not go so far as to claim that the commercial loan amendment was a private bill, designed only to exempt Boston Safe. It suggests, however, that because the amendment was prompted by the circumstances of one particular institution, the language "commercial loan" should be given something other than its commonly accepted meaning.

The statute by its terms, however, exempts from regulation all institutions that do not engage in the business of making commercial loans. The choice of this general language demonstrates that, although the legislation may have been prompted by the needs of one institution, Congress intended to exempt the class of institutions not making commercial loans. Furthermore, the legislative history supports this plain reading of the statute. . . .

The only reference to Boston Safe is in a lengthy banking journal article that Representative Gonzalez entered into the Congressional Record. *See* 116 Cong. Rec. 25846, 25848 (1970) (indicating that Boston Safe was "[v]irtually the only bank that does no commercial lending"). Such a passage is not "legislative history" in any meaningful sense of the term and cannot defeat the plain application of the words actually chosen by Congress to effectuate its will. Finally, even if the legislative history evidenced a congressional intent to exclude only Boston Safe, which it does not, the Board's expansive definition of "commercial loan" would be an unreasonable interpretation of the statute. At the time the commercial loan provision was enacted, Boston Safe did not "make commercial loans," but did purchase money market instruments such as certificates of deposit and commercial paper. Recognizing the common usage of the term "commercial loan" and the purpose of the 1970 amendment, the Board in 1972 advised Boston Safe that it was not, in fact, a bank for the purposes of the Bank Holding Company Act. . . .

Nothing in the statutory language or the legislative history, therefore, indicates that the term "commercial loan" meant anything different from its accepted ordinary commercial usage. The Board's definition of "commercial loan," therefore, is not a reasonable interpretation of § 2(c). . . .

Unable to support its new definitions on the plain language of § 2(c), the Board contends that its new definitions fall within the "plain purpose" of the Bank Holding Company Act. Nonbank banks must be subject to regulation, the Board insists, because "a statute must be read with a view to the 'policy of the legislation as a whole' and cannot be read to negate the plain purpose of the legislation." The plain purpose of the legislation, the Board contends, is to regulate institutions "functionally equivalent" to banks. Since NOW accounts are the functional equivalent of a deposit in which the depositor has a legal right to withdraw on demand and money market transactions involve the extension of credit to commercial entities, institutions offering such services should be regulated as banks.[6]

The "plain purpose" of legislation, however, is determined in the first instance with reference to the plain language of the statute itself. . . . Application of "broad purposes" of legislation at the expense of specific provisions ignores the complexity of the problems Congress is called upon to address and the dynamics of legislative action. Congress may be unanimous in its intent to stamp out some vague social or economic evil; however, because its Members may differ sharply on the means for effectuating that intent, the final language of the legislation may reflect hard fought compromises. Invocation of the "plain purpose" of legislation at the expense of the terms of the statute itself takes no account of the processes of compromise and, in the end, prevents the effectuation of congressional intent.

Without doubt there is much to be said for regulating financial institutions that are the functional equivalent of banks. NOW accounts have much in common with traditional payment-on-demand checking accounts; indeed we recognize that they generally serve the same purpose. Rather than defining "bank" as an institution that offers the functional equivalent of banking services, however, Congress defined with specificity certain transactions that constitute banking subject to regulation. The statute may be imperfect, but the Board has no power to correct flaws that it perceives in the statute it is empowered to administer. Its rulemaking power is limited to adopting regulations to carry into effect the will of Congress as expressed in the statute.

If the Bank Holding Company falls short of providing safeguards desirable or necessary to protect the public interest, that is a problem for Congress, and not the Board or the courts, to address. . . .

Notes and Comments 4.18. Does *Dimension Financial* repudiate *Wilshire Oil*? How do the two cases compare on the issue of statutory interpretation?

4.19. With the Supreme Court's rejection of the Fed's expanded regulatory response to the growing use of "nonbank banks," it was not until late the following year that the legislative deadlock over "nonbank banks" was broken, with the enactment of section 101 of the Competitive Equality Banking Act of 1987. Pub. L. No. 100-86, § 101, 101 Stat. 552, 554 (1987) (codified at 12 U.S.C. § 1841(c)). Review the current provisions of section

---

6. In a related argument, the Board contends that it has the power to regulate these institutions under § 5(b), which provides that the Board may issue regulations "necessary to enable it to administer and carry out the purposes of this chapter and prevent evasions." 12 U.S.C. § 1844(b). But § 5 only permits the Board to police within the boundaries of the Act; it does not permit the Board to expand its jurisdiction beyond the boundaries established by Congress in § 2(c).

1841(c). How do they resolve the problem of "nonbank banks"? To what extent would it affect your answer to the question in note 4.14, *supra*?

4.20. Within the limits established by *Dimension Financial*, how much room is there for the exercise of administrative discretion and judgment under the BHCA? Consider the following two cases.

Board of Governors v. First Lincolnwood Corp.

439 U.S. 234 (1978)

Mr. Justice MARSHALL delivered the opinion of the Court.

Section 3(a) of the Bank Holding Company Act of 1956, 12 U.S.C. § 1842(a), prohibits any company from acquiring control of a bank without prior approval by the Board of Governors of the Federal Reserve System (Board). Under § 3(c)(1) of the Act, 12 U.S.C. § 1842(c)(1), the Board may not approve a transaction that would create a monopoly or further an attempt to monopolize the business of banking. In addition, it must disapprove a transaction that would generate anticompetitive effects not clearly outweighed by beneficial effects upon the bank's ability to serve the community. § 1842(c)(2). . . . The threshold question before us is whether this final sentence authorizes the Board to disapprove a transaction on grounds of financial unsoundness in the absence of any anticompetitive impact. If so, we must decide whether the Board can only exercise that authority when the transaction would cause or exacerbate the financial unsoundness of the holding company or a subsidiary bank. . . .

The First National Bank of Lincolnwood, Ill., is controlled by four individuals who hold 86% of its stock in a voting trust. These individuals organized respondent, the First Lincolnwood Corp., to serve as a bank holding company. They planned to exchange their shares in the bank for shares of respondent and, in addition, to have respondent assume a $3.7 million debt they had incurred in acquiring control of the bank. Respondent intended to use the dividends it would receive on the bank's shares to retire this debt over a 12-year period. Further, in order to augment the bank's capital, respondent would issue $1.5 million in capital notes and then use the proceeds to purchase new shares issued by the bank. The purpose of restructuring ownership interests in this fashion was to enable the holding company and the bank to file a consolidated tax return and thereby realize substantial tax savings.

Because under the proposed transaction respondent would become a bank holding company, § 3(a) of the Act required that the proposal be submitted for the Board's approval. . . . Respondent filed its application with the Federal Reserve Bank of Chicago, as specified by Board regulations. The Chicago Reserve Bank concluded that the Lincolnwood bank's capital position–in essence, the difference between its assets and its liabilities–was inadequate and, under respondent's proposal, was unlikely to improve enough to attain the minimum level the Board had determined necessary to protect the bank's depositors.[6] Nonetheless, the Lincolnwood bank's favorable earnings prospects and strong management led the Chicago Reserve Bank to recommend that the transaction be approved. The Comptroller of the Currency, however, independently reviewed respondent's application and con-

---

6. The Board uses several measures of capital adequacy. One is the ratio of equity capital to total liabilities less cash on hand, known as the invested- asset ratio. Another is the ratio of total capital (debt and equity) to total assets, known as the capital-asset ratio. . . . The Board regards an invested-asset ratio of 9% . . . , and a capital-asset ratio of 8% . . . , as their minimal levels of capital necessary to maintain financial soundness. Respondent has not specifically challenged the validity of these standards as measures of bank safety.

cluded that it should be denied unless the bank's capital position was strengthened.

Respondent thereupon modified its proposal to accommodate the Comptroller's objections. Instead of issuing $1.5 million in capital notes and using the proceeds to purchase new bank stock, respondent proposed that the bank itself sell $1 million in long-term capital notes and $1.1 million in new common stock. In addition, respondent proposed a substantial reduction in the dividends to be paid on the bank stock. Upon review of the modified proposal, the Chicago Reserve Bank adhered to its original recommendation, finding the modification salutary insofar as it increased the total addition to the bank's capital, though "slightly unfavorable" insofar as it decreased the addition to the bank's equity capital from $1.5 to $1.1 million.[7] The Comptroller considered the revised plan superior to the original proposal; therefore, he, too, recommended approval.

The Board staff independently evaluated the application and determined that the bank's projected capital position would fall below the Board's requirements. The staff also found that respondent had not established its ability to raise the additional capital without the individual shareholders' incurring more debt. Although acknowledging that the bank's management was capable, the staff concluded that

> "it would appear desirable that Bank's overall capital position should be materially improved and that financing arrangements for the proposed capital injections into Bank [should] be made more definite."

The Board concurred. It reviewed each of the elements enumerated in § 3(c), determining first that the proposal had no anticompetitive impact because the transaction merely transferred control of the bank "from individuals to a corporation owned by the same individuals." . . . Similarly, the Board found that the proposal would effect no significant changes in the services offered by the bank to customers, so factors relating to the convenience and needs of the community militated neither for nor against approval. . . . Thus, the financial and managerial considerations specified in the final sentence of § 3(c) were dispositive of respondent's application.

Addressing these considerations, the Board ruled that a bank holding company "should provide a source of financial and managerial strength to its subsidiary bank(s)." ... Here, the Board found, even if the bank's optimistic earnings projections were realized, respondent would lack the financial flexibility necessary both to service its debt and to maintain adequate capital at the bank. This, as well as the uncertainty regarding the proposed source of the capital injections, raised serious doubts as to respondent's financial ability to resolve unforeseen problems that could arise at the bank. The Board therefore concluded that

> "it would not be in the public interest to approve the formation of a bank holding company with an initial debt structure that could result in the weakening of Bank's overall financial condition."

A divided panel of the Court of Appeals for the Seventh Circuit affirmed, the majority finding substantial evidence to support the denial of respondent's application. ... On rehearing *en banc*, the court unanimously set aside the Board's order. The court recognized that Congress had empowered the Board "to deny approval of a bank acquisition upon finding

7. While the Board considers capital notes that are subordinated to depositors' demands to be part of a bank's overall capital, it regards them as a less desirable financial cushion than equity. . . . *[S]ee, e.g., Clayton Bancshares Corp.*, 50 Fed. Res. Bull. 1261, 1264 (1964); *Mid-Continent Bancorporation*, 52 Fed. Res. Bull. 198, 200 (1966).

it not to be in the public interest for reasons other than an anticompetitive tendency." . . . However, in the court's view, § 3(c) of the Act did not permit the Board to withhold approval because of financial or managerial deficiencies unless those deficiencies were "caused or enhanced by the proposed transaction." . . . This transaction, the court observed, merely reshuffled ownership interests in the bank. Apart from the proposed addition to capital and the tax advantage, which could accelerate reduction of the $3.7 million debt, respondent's proposal was without financial consequence. The court therefore held that the Board had overstepped its authority under § 3(c) in denying respondent's application. . . .

. . . We conclude that the court below improperly restricted the Board's authority, and, accordingly, we reverse. . . .

Respondent contends that the Court of Appeals misinterpreted the legislative history of the Bank Holding Company Act in sustaining the Board's authority to deny applications for holding-company status solely on grounds of financial or managerial unsoundness. As respondent reads the legislative history, Congress' only concern in passing the Act was with the anticompetitive potential in the concentration of banking resources and the combination of banking and nonbanking enterprises. . . . This focus on competitive considerations was reflected in the amendment of the Act in 1966 to conform § 3(c) with the standards enunciated in the Bank Merger Act amendments of the same year. . . . The amended standards in the Bank Merger Act were intended to provide an exception to the antitrust laws for those bank mergers in which the benefits to the community outweighed the anticompetitive impact. . . . By incorporating these same standards into the Bank Holding Company Act, respondent infers, Congress intended to authorize the Board to consider financial and managerial resources only as counterweights to a transaction's anticompetitive impact. We do not agree that the Board's authority under the Bank Holding Company Act is so limited.

The language of the statute supports the Board's interpretation of § 3(c) as an authorization to deny applications on grounds of financial and managerial unsoundness even in the absence of any anticompetitive impact. Section 3(c) directs the Board to consider the financial and managerial resources and future prospects of the applicants and banks concerned "[i]n every case," not just in cases in which the Board finds that the transaction will have an anticompetitive effect.

Moreover, the Board's interpretation of § 3(c) draws support from the legislative history. Section 19 of the original version of the Banking Act of 1933, 48 Stat. 186, authorized the Board to regulate the financial and managerial soundness of bank holding companies and their banking subsidiaries. Holding companies were required to obtain a permit from the Board before voting the shares of a national bank. Section 19 directed the Board to consider, in acting upon an application for a voting permit, the financial condition of the company and the general character of its management. . . . In addition, an applicant had to submit to financial examination by the Board and to maintain a prescribed reserve of liquid assets. . . . However, the voting-permit provisions applied only if the bank was a member of the Federal Reserve System and the holding company sought to exercise control by actually voting the bank shares. Because of this limitation, § 19 ultimately proved of little value in ensuring the financial responsibility of bank holding companies and their subsidiaries. . . .

To ameliorate this deficiency, Congress expanded the Board's authority by enacting the Bank Holding Company Act of 1956. Section 3(c) of the Act enumerated five factors for the Board to consider whenever a company sought to acquire control of a bank:

> "(1) the financial history and condition of the company or companies and the banks concerned; (2) their prospects; (3) the character of their management; (4)

> the convenience, needs, and welfare of the communities and the area concerned; and (5) whether or not the effect of such acquisition or merger or consolidation would be to expand the size or extent of the bank holding company system involved beyond limits consistent with adequate and sound banking, the public interest, and the preservation of competition in the field of banking." 70 Stat. 135.

The House Report on the Act noted the similarity between these factors and those specified in other banking statutes as the basis for admitting state banks to membership in the Federal Reserve System and for granting federal deposit-insurance coverage. . . . In both instances, the adequacy of the bank's capital is an important factor to be considered by the reviewing agency. *See* 12 U.S.C. §§ 329, 1816.

In amending § 3(c) to conform to the language of the Bank Merger Act in 1966, . . . Congress did not intend to confine the Board's consideration of financial and managerial soundness only to transactions that would have an anticompetitive impact. The sole reason given for the change was "the interests of uniform standards" in regulating both mergers and acquisitions in the banking industry. . . .

In 1970, Congress amended the Bank Holding Company Act to extend its coverage to holding companies that controlled only one bank. . . . Previously, the Act had applied only to multibank holding companies. The principal purpose of this change was to prevent one-bank holding companies from entering businesses not related to banking. . . . Nothing in the legislative history of the 1970 amendments suggests that in extending the Act, Congress intended to depart from its prior understanding of the Board's authority or to establish a different rule for one-bank holding companies. . . .

While the Court of Appeals recognized the Board's authority to treat financial or managerial unsoundness as a dispositive consideration, it held that this authority was limited to instances in which the unsoundness was caused or exacerbated by the proposed transaction. The Court of Appeals rejected the Board's argument that permission to form a holding company is "a reward which it may withhold until the applicant's financial status fulfills the Board's standard of desirability." . . . The legislative history, the court held, revealed nothing that would allow the Board to disapprove formation of a bank holding company where the transaction would not weaken a subsidiary bank's financial condition. In addition, the already extensive regulation of the financial integrity of banks by the Comptroller of the Currency and state regulatory agencies persuaded the court that Congress could not have intended to extend identical authority to the Federal Reserve Board. . . .

We perceive no basis for the limitation the Court of Appeals imposed. Certainly, it is not compelled by the language of the statute. By its terms, § 3(c) requires the Board to consider financial and managerial factors in "every case." Just as we observed earlier that this language encompasses cases in which the proposed transaction would have no anti-competitive effect, . . . so, too, it encompasses cases in which the transaction would not weaken the bank or the bank holding company. Indeed, the Court of Appeals' construction of the statute would require the Board to approve formation of a bank holding company with corrupt management simply because management would become no more corrupt by virtue of the transaction. We hesitate to adopt a construction that would yield such an anomalous result.

Furthermore, the legislative record does provide support for the Board's actions. In deliberations on the Bank Holding Company Act [in 1978], and in subsequent inquiries into banking regulation, . . . Congress has evinced substantial concern for the financial soundness of the banking system. And Congress has long regarded capital adequacy as a measure of bank safety. . . . To rule that the Board could not require applicants for holding-company status and their subsidiary banks to meet minimum capital-adequacy requirements would be inconsistent with this general legislative mandate.

Nor can we accept the conclusion that Congress intended to reserve questions of bank safety to the Comptroller or state agencies except where a transaction would harm the financial condition of an applicant or the bank. The history of the Bank Holding Company Act nowhere suggests that Congress sought to delineate such a jurisdictional boundary. Indeed, our decision in *Whitney Nat. Bank v. Bank of New Orleans*, 379 U.S. 411 (1965), indicates that the Board's jurisdiction is paramount. We ruled there that the Comptroller could not deny a new bank a license to do business–a decision normally within his competence, *see* 12 U.S.C. §§ 26, 27–once the Board approved a bank holding company transaction that entailed formation of the new bank. . . . It follows that the Federal Reserve Board's actions here are not invalid merely because the powers exercised duplicate those of other regulators. . . .

Respondent contends that the Board's denial of its application was arbitrary and capricious. We have already determined that the Board's "source of strength" requirement is consistent with the language, purpose, and legislative history of the Bank Holding Company Act. Our only remaining inquiry is whether substantial evidence supports the Board's finding that respondent fell short of this standard. 12 U.S.C. § 1848.

The Court of Appeals panel had "no difficulty" in finding substantial evidence to sustain the Board's decision, . . . and respondent did not press this issue in its petition for rehearing *en banc*. We, too, find in this record more than the amount of evidence "a reasonable mind might accept as adequate to support [the Board's] conclusion." . . . The application failed to establish that respondent could raise the $2.1 million in additional capital in the manner proposed. Moreover, it revealed that even with this infusion, the bank's capital would have been well below the level the Board had determined necessary to sustain the financial soundness of the enterprise. Thus, the Board was entitled to conclude that respondent would not be a sufficient source of financial and managerial strength to its subsidiary bank. Having so determined, the Board was entitled to deny the application.

MCorp Financial, Inc. v. Board of Governors

900 F.2d 852 (5th Cir. 1990)
affirmed in part and reversed in part on other grounds
502 U.S. 32 (1991)

W. EUGENE DAVIS, Circuit Judge.

[MCorp, a bank holding company, was a Bankruptcy Chapter 11 debtor. It moved to enjoin the Fed from prosecuting an administrative proceeding against it based upon the "source of strength" policy. The district court granted the motion, and the Fed appealed. Although the Fifth Circuit opinion held that the district court had no jurisdiction, pursuant to its authority over bankruptcy matters, to enjoin administrative proceedings by federal bank regulators, the opinion applied an exception for administrative actions exceeding statutory authority. It held, among other things, that the Fed was without authority under the BHCA to require MCorp to transfer funds to its troubled subsidiary banks under the "source of strength" policy. Excerpts from the opinion dealing with the relationship between federal bankruptcy and banking regulation and with the meaning of "unsafe or unsound practice" under federal banking regulation are set forth in Chaper 8, § 4, *infra*. Excerpts dealing with the "source of strength" policy are set forth below.]

We consider first whether the authority the Board assumed under its regulation and policy statement exceeds its statutory grant. The Bank Holding Company Act of 1956

(BHCA), 12 U.S.C. § 1841 *et seq.*, grants the Board supervisory control over the formation, structure and operation of bank holding companies and their nonbank subsidiaries. Section 3(a) of the Act, 12 U.S.C. § 1842(a), provides that no company may acquire control of a bank without prior approval by the Board. In determining whether to approve an application, S 3(c) of the Act, 12 U.S.C. § 1842(c), directs the Board to consider "the financial and managerial resources and future prospects of the company or companies and the banks concerned."

In 1984, as part of its comprehensive revision of Regulation Y, the Board added 12 C.F.R. § 225.4(a)(1), which provides:

> § 225.4 Corporate practices.
>
> (a) Bank holding company policy and operations. (1) A bank holding company shall serve as a source of financial and managerial strength to its subsidiary banks and shall not conduct its operations in an unsafe or unsound manner. [*sic*]

Revision of Regulation Y, 49 Fed.Reg. 820 (1984) (codified at 12 C.F.R. § 225.4(a)(1)).

In April 1987, the Board published a policy statement in the Federal Register, which further provided:

> It is the policy of the Board that in serving as a source of strength to its subsidiary banks, a bank holding company should stand ready to use available resources to provide adequate capital funds to its subsidiary banks during periods of financial stress or adversity and should maintain the financial flexibility and capital-raising capacity to obtain additional resources for assisting its subsidiary banks. . . .
>
> A bank holding company's failure to meet its obligation to serve as a source of strength to its subsidiary bank(s), including an unwillingness to provide appropriate assistance to a troubled or failing bank, will generally be considered an unsafe and unsound banking practice or a violation of Regulation Y, or both.
>
> . . .

Policy Statement, 52 Fed. Reg. 15707, 15708 (1987). . . . This policy statement was effective April 24, 1987. The Board solicited comments on the policy, with a view to revising the statement in light of such comments. No subsequent revision has been published.

The Board also relies on the broad language of § 5(b) of the BHCA, 12 U.S.C. § 1844(b), for authority to issue the above regulation and policy statement. . . .

The Board finds support for its authority to enforce its source of strength requirements in *Board of Governors v. First Lincolnwood Corp.*, 439 U.S. 234 (1978). In this case the Court considered whether the BHCA authorized the Board to disapprove an application of a proposed bank holding company solely on grounds of financial unsoundness, and in the absence of any anticompetitive effects resulting from the transaction. The Supreme Court answered this question in the affirmative and upheld the Board's rejection of a proposed holding company's application. This holding was based on the statutory language of 12 U.S.C. § 1842(c), as well as the legislative history of the BHCA. . . .

. . . In *First Lincolnwood* . . . the Court relied upon the express provisions of § 3(c) that required the Board to consider financial soundness of the subsidiary bank in determining whether to approve a holding company's application. The Court made it clear that it did not read the BHCA to grant the Board authority to regulate the day-to-day financial soundness of the subsidiary banks.

The Supreme Court in *Board of Governors v. Dimension Financial Corp.* . . . found that the BHCA "vests broad regulatory authority in the Board over bank holding companies 'to restrain the undue concentration of commercial banking resources and to prevent possible abuses related to the control of commercial credit.'" . . . The Board's new definitions did not fall within the plain purposes of the BHCA, the Court concluded. The Court added that "§ 5 only permits the Board to police within the boundaries of the Act. ..."

First Lincolnwood and *Dimension Financial* together teach that the primary purposes of the BHCA are to prevent the concentration of control of banking resources, and to separate banking from nonbanking enterprises. *First Lincolnwood* is narrowly written and expressly limits the Board's authority to consider financial and managerial soundness of subsidiary banks to the Board's decision to grant or deny a holding company's application. Section 3(c) of the BHCA specifically grants this authority to the Board. The BHCA does not grant the Board authority to consider the financial and managerial soundness of the subsidiary banks after it approves the application, and *First Lincolnwood* finds this regulatory authority lacking in the day-to-day operations of a subsidiary bank. For these reasons, we conclude that the Board is without authority under the BHCA to require MBank to transfer its funds to its troubled subsidiary bank.

Notes and Comments 4.21. Is *MCorp* consistent with *First Lincolnwood*? Based upon your reading of *First Lincolnwood* and *Dimension Financial*, would you consider *MCorp*'s use of these authorities to be well founded? On certiorari, the Supreme Court reversed the Fifth Circuit's decision enjoining the "source of strength" proceeding, on narrow grounds that did not determine the validity of the doctrine. Rather, the Court focused on the independence of these administrative proceedings from judicial intervention. Excerpts from the Court's opinion are set forth in Chapter 8, § 4, *infra*.

4.22. The logical result of the position taken by *MCorp* would seem to be that, although the Fed could insist that a BHCA applicant have sufficient financial resources to support the proposed subsidiary bank, the Fed could do nothing to insist upon the provision of support as needed by the subsidiary, once the BHCA application had been approved. However, could the Fed make it a condition of approval in the first place that the holding company formally agree to provide such support? In fact, the now defunct Federal Home Loan Bank Board (FHLBB), through the defunct Federal Savings and Loan Insurance Corporation (the regulator of S&L holding companies until 1989), had long followed such a practice in approving S&L holding company applications. *Cf. Kaneb Services, Inc. v. Federal Sav. & Loan Ins. Corp.*, 650 F.2d 78 (5th Cir. 1981) (approving FSLIC practice). In this regard, the statutory authority was essentially identical to the Fed's authority under the BHCA.[42] The OTS, the post-FIRREA federal regulator of S&L holding companies, appears to have continued this practice.[43] *MCorp* itself suggested that this practice might be a viable alternative for the Fed's enforcement of a "source of strength" policy. *MCorp Financial*, 900 F.2d at 862 n. 5. How can the Fed impose a condition of approval that it could not impose directly as a matter of statutory authority?

4.23. *GLBA and the "Source of Strength" Doctrine*. The GLBA gives some strong support for the legality of the Fed's source of strength doctrine under the BHCA. It limits the authority of the Fed to impose source-of-strength requirements on BHCs that are insurance

42. *See, e.g.*, 12 U.S.C. §§ 1730(e)(1), (e)(3), 1730a(e)(2) (1988); *Regulatory Capital Maintenance Obligations of Acquirers of Insured Institutions*, 53 Fed. Reg. 31,761 (1988); *Acquisition of Control of Insured Institutions*, 54 Fed. Reg. 32,959 (1989) (to be codified at 12 C.F.R. § 574.7(a)(2), (a)(3)).

43. *See Transfer and Recodification of Regulations Pursuant to Financial Institutions Reform, Recovery and Enforcement Act*, 54 Fed. Reg. 49,411 (1989).

companies or that are broker-dealers, investment advisers or investment companies if the state insurance regulator or the SEC, respectively, objects. GLBA, § 112(a), 113 Stat. at 1365-1367 (codified at 12 U.S.C. § 1844(g)). By inference, this would seem to indicate that Congress otherwise recognizes the Fed's source-of-strength authority under the BHCA.

4.24. *Capital standards and capital adequacy as considerations in regulatory approvals.* The requirements of capital standards and the capital adequacy of applicants have become increasingly significant considerations in regulatory approvals. A relatively early example of this phenomenon is afforded by *First Lincolnwood.* The federal bank regulators are currently in the process of implementing additional capital-assets ratio guidelines that take into account the relative risk of assets, guidelines implementing a multilateral undertaking among the bank regulators of the principal industrialized Western democracies. *See generally* Malloy, *Capital Adequacy and Regulatory Objectives*, 25 SUFFOLK TRANSNAT'L L. REV. 299 (2002) (discussing rules).

4.25. *Capital standards and savings associations.* As amended by the FIRREA, the HOLA now directs the DOTS, consistent with the purposes of section 908 of the International Lending Supervision Act of 1983, 12 U.S.C. § 3907, and the capital requirements established thereunder by the federal banking regulators, to require all savings associations to achieve and maintain adequate capital by establishing minimum capital levels and by using other methods as determined to be appropriate by the DOTS. 12 U.S.C. § 1464(s)(1) (A)-(B). Consistent with provisions concerning capital standards, *see id.* § 1464(t), the DOTS may establish minimum capital levels on a case-by-case basis, by amount or at a capital-to-assets ratio. *Id.* § 1463(s)(2). Failure by a savings association to maintain capital at or above the minimum level may be treated by the DOTS as an unsafe or unsound practice. *Id.* § 1464(s)(3). The DOTS is also authorized to issue capital directives, *id.* § 1464(s) (4)(A), and to enforce directives and capital plans approved thereunder in the same manner as outstanding, final orders issued under the general enforcement provisions of the Federal Deposit Insurance Act. *Id.* § 1464(s)(4)(B). *See id.* § 1818 (FDIA enforcement provisions). Progress in complying with any capital plan may be taken into account by the DOTS in considering any other proposal by a savings association or affiliate that would have the effect of diverting earnings, diminishing capital, or otherwise impeding progress with respect to the capital plan. *id.* § 1464(s)(5)(A). Such a proposal may be disapproved if the DOTS determines that it would adversely affect the ability of the association to comply with a capital plan. *Id.* § 1464(s)(5)(B). The amended HOLA also requires the DOTS to prescribe by regulation and maintain uniformly applicable capital standards for savings associations. *Id.* § 1464(t)(1)(A). The prescribed capital standards must include (*i*) a "leverage limit" of "core capital" in an amount not less than three percent of a savings association's total assets, *id.* § 1464(t)(1)(A)(i), (2)(A); (*ii*) a "tangible capital" requirement in an amount not less than 1.5 percent of a savings association's total assets, *id.* § 1464(t)(1)(A)(ii), (2) (B); and, (*iii*) a risk-based capital requirement. *Id.* § 1464(t)(1)(A)(iii), (2)(C). A savings association is not in compliance with the statutory capital standards unless it complies with all three prescribed standards. *Id.* § 1464(t)(1)(B). The prescribed standards must be no less stringent than those applicable to national banks. *Id.* § 1464(t)(1)(C).

4.26. *Antitrust considerations.* Reconsider note 4.14, *supra.* In reviewing First Holdulity's BHCA application, to what extent must the Fed consider the possible anticompetitive effects of First Holdulity's acquisition of control over First Credulity? Consider 12 U.S.C. § 1842(c) and the following case.

Mercantile Texas Corp. v. Board of Governors

638 F. 2d 1255 (5th Cir. 1981)

ALVIN B. RUBIN, Circuit Judge.

Mercantile Texas Corporation is a bank holding company operating nine banks throughout Texas. PanNational Group, Inc., a smaller bank holding company, operates five banks in El Paso and Waco, cities not presently served by Mercantile. Mercantile seeks review of a Federal Reserve Board order denying approval to a proposed merger between the two companies. The Board held that elimination of potential competition between the two companies would have a substantially adverse effect on competition in El Paso and Waco without countervailing benefits to those communities.

On review, the Board argues that Section 1842(c) of the Bank Holding Company Act, U.S.C. § 1842(c), grants it broad discretion to reject proposed mergers upon finding that a merger would have an anticompetitive effect detrimental to the convenience and needs of the community even if the merger would not have violate the explicit antitrust standards included in Section 1842(c). We conclude that the statute denies the Board the broad discretion it claims. If the Board rejects a proposed merger on anticompetitive grounds, it must find a violation of the Sherman[, 15 U.S.C. §§ 1, 2,] and Clayton Act[, *id.* § 18,] standards written into the statute.

Anticipating our interpretation, the Board argues that the merger would violate the Clayton Act standard by eliminating potential competition in the two markets. Because the Board failed to make several important findings of fact (and because we can affirm the Board's decision only on the basis of the findings that the Board actually made), we cannot determine whether the merger would violate the potential competition doctrine. Without adequate findings, we are also unwilling to decide whether the elimination of potential competition constitutes a violation of the Clayton Act standard. . . .

Mercantile Texas Corporation is the fifth largest bank holding company in Texas. Its nine banks have aggregate deposits of $2.8 billion, representing 4.2 per cent of the total commercial bank deposits in the state. PanNational controls five banks with deposits of $620 million, representing 0.9 per cent of the commercial bank deposits in Texas. The merged corporation would have 5.1 per cent of Texas commercial bank deposits. Mercantile would remain the fifth largest banking organization, but its total deposits would increase by approximately 22 per cent.

PanNational operates four banks in El Paso; the nearest market served by Mercantile is San Antonio, more than 500 miles away. PanNational also owns one bank in Waco; the nearest market served by Mercantile is Dallas, 95 miles away. Because of these distances, the Board found that the proposed merger would not eliminate any significant present competition between the two companies.

The Board found, instead, the future potential competition in Waco and El Paso between the two companies would probably be eliminated by the merger. It predicted that, if the proposed merger were rejected, Mercantile would nevertheless enter the two markets, but in a manner resulting in greater competition. The Board stated this conclusion after only a limited discussion of the relevant economic data. . . .

Section 1842(c) of the Bank Holding Company Act, 12 U.S.C. § 1842(c), forbids Board approval of any merger that would foster a monopoly or "whose effect . . . may be substantially to lessen competition" unless "it finds that the anticompetitive effects are clearly outweighed in the public interest." The phrase "substantially to lessen competition" is, of course, borrowed from Section 7 of the Clayton Act, 15 U.S.C. § 18. Because this repetition was purposeful, the principles developed under the Clayton Act are applicable to mergers of bank holding companies under Section 1842(c), *Mid-Nebraska Bancshares, Inc. v. Board of Governors*, 627 F. 2d 266 (D.C. Cir. 1980), as well as to mergers of banks under Section 1828(c)(5)(B) of the Bank Merger Act, which uses the same language. *See United States v. Marine Bancorporation*, 418 U.S. 602 (1974); *United States v. First City National Bank*, 386 U.S. 361 (1967).

If the antitrust consequences of the merger do not require Board disapproval, then the statute commands the Board to "take into consideration . . . the convenience and needs of the community." Counsel for the Board argues that this second provision enables it to reject proposed mergers if it finds that the anticompetitive effects of the merger would thwart the "convenience and needs" of the community even if these effects are insufficient to violate the antitrust standards. While an agency's interpretation of its own governing statutes is entitled to great deference, *Board of Governors v. First Lincolnwood Corp.*, 439 U.S. 234 (1978), we are not persuaded that Congress intended the Board to have nearly unlimited discretion to reject proposed mergers on anticompetitive grounds beyond Clayton Act violations.

Two circuits have already rejected the Board's contention. In *Washington Mutual Savings Bank v. F.D.I.C.*, 482 F.2d 459 (9th Cir. 1973), the Ninth Circuit considered this argument in the context of the identical language of the Bank Merger Act provision, 12 U.S.C. § 1828(c)(5). The court held that Congress intended to impose a uniform antitrust standard for consideration of bank mergers, thereby enabling the agencies and courts to develop a "discernible body of law." . . . The community's "convenience and needs," which the Board must also consider, was found to refer exclusively to banking (as distinguished from competitive) factors. . . . In *County National Bancorporation v. Board of Governors*, No. 79-1783 (8th Cir. Sept. 3, 1980), *rehearing granted*, the Eighth Circuit followed *Washington Mutual* and held that the Clayton Act standard was the exclusive test for evaluating anticompetitive effects under the Bank Holding Company Act provision, 12 U.S.C. § 1842(c).

The legislative history of the two provisions establishes that Congress did not intend for the Board to apply a more stringent standard than ordained by Section 7 of the Clayton Act. Above all, Congress sought to establish "uniform standards" for consideration of anticompetitive effects of bank mergers and acquisitions by bank holding companies. ... Allowing the Board to employ a more stringent standard tailored to the "convenience and needs" of each community would destroy that uniformity.

The House Banking and Currency Committee designed the language of the statute as a compromise between those seeking the most vigorous possible application of the antitrust laws to banks and those seeking to exempt banks from their operation. The two sides compromised by applying the established principles of the antitrust laws to bank mergers, but allowing those mergers whose anticompetitive effects are outweighed by "the convenience and needs of the community." By applying standards more stringent than the antitrust laws, the Board would go beyond the terms of the compromise to gain a victory that Congressional antitrust proponents may not have sought and certainly did not obtain.

The Board argues that Congress established standards that would be uniform only when the Board is required to reject a proposed merger, but did not limit the Board's discretion to apply a standard stricter than the Clayton Act if the "convenience and needs" of the community warrant. This construction, however, gives "convenience and needs" an additional meaning unknown to the bill's proponents.

The statute twice uses the same term, "convenience and needs" only a few lines apart. The term is first used to state circumstances that may outweigh even Clayton Act anticompetitive effects. It is next used to state a criterion to be applied "in every case." There is some indication in the congressional debate that the two phrases are intended to reflect the same values. . . . The Board's interpretation would require the clause to be given a different effect the second time it is used. . . .

Finding that the Board's interpretation of Section 1842(c) contradicts the antitrust policy embodied in the statute, we hold that the Board may not deny approval to a proposed merger of bank holding companies without finding a violation of the antitrust standards explicitly incorporated into the statute.

[The court's discussion, in *dicta*, of the Fed's use on appeal of the controversial and unresolved "actual potential competition" doctrine is excerpted later in this chapter. *See* § 3, *infra*. The court expressed the view that, since the Fed had made no findings with respect to the doctrine in its consideration of the application, the issue of the validity of the doctrine was not properly before it.]

Notes and Comments 4.27. What, then, is the substantive content of the "convenience and needs" approval factor? Is it the same as that contained in the "convenience and needs" defense in 12 U.S.C. § 1842(c)(2)? In national bank chartering standards?[44]

4.28. How broad a role for state regulation is preserved by 12 U.S.C. § 1846? Assume Forth Corp. owns Quarter National Bank, a large bank in the state of York, and would like to acquire a controlling interest in Lee State Bank, organized under the laws of the state of Jersey and doing business there. Lee State Bank would continue to be operated as a separate banking operation, entirely independent of Quarter National's business. The Jersey Banking Code prohibits "acquisition of control of any [Jersey] state[-chartered] bank by any company [as defined in Jersey law, to include Forth Corp.] controlling, at the time of the proposed acquisition, any other bank."[45] Consider § 1846 and the following case.

Commercial Nat. Bank of Little Rock v. Board of Gov.

451 F. 2d 86 (8th Cir. 1971)

HEANEY, Circuit Judge.

The First Arkansas Bankstock Corporation (FABCO), a one-bank holding company, owned ninety-nine percent of the voting shares of the Worthen Bank and Trust Company (Worthen). It applied to the Federal Reserve Board seeking prior approval to become a bank holding company by acquiring eighty percent or more of the voting shares of the Arkansas First National Bank (AFNB).[a] FABCO and Worthen are located in Little Rock, Arkansas, and AFNB in Hot Springs, Arkansas.

The Comptroller of the Currency recommended approval of the Application. At least two of the protestants filed responses to the application and requested a trial-type hearing before the Board. The Board denied the request and instead ordered a public oral pre-

44. *See* 12 C.F.R. § 5.20(f)(2)(i)(C) (setting forth OCC chartering policy; indicating that OCC considers whether proposed national bank "has capital that is sufficient to support the projected volume and type of business"). *Cf. Bank of Boulder v. Board of Governors*, 535 F.2d 1221 (10th Cir. 1976) (BHC application includes same factors as charter application under National Bank Act).

45. It is unlikely that this prohibition would be struck down under the Commerce Clause of the U.S. Constitution, despite its effects on interstate commerce. *See Northeast Bancorp, Inc. v. Board of Governors*, 424 U.S. 159 (1985) (upholding regional banking compact).

a. At the time of the events leading to this case, only multibank holding companies were covered by the BHCA. Since the 1970 amendments to the act, even a one-bank holding company would be covered by the BHCA. *See Wilshire Oil, supra*.

sentation. Following the oral presentation, FABCO and the protestants submitted additional briefs.

The Board approved FABCO's application. Four of the protestant banks have filed this petition for review on the Federal Reserve Board's order.

The protestants' first contention is that Arkansas branch banking laws prohibit the formation of multi-bank holding companies. While these statutes do not, by their terms, specifically apply to holding companies, it is argued that a multi-bank holding company such as FABCO is, in effect, engaged in branch banking and should come under Arkansas's branch banking restrictions.

Pursuant to the Bank Holding Company Act of 1956, 12 U.S.C. § 1846, Arkansas is free to prohibit, by specific legislation, the formation of bank holding companies. *See, Whitney Nat. Bank in Jefferson Parish v. Bank of New Orleans*, 379 U.S. 411, n. 5 (1965); *Trans-Nebraska Co.*, 49 Fed. Res. Bull. 633 (1963). However, the legislative history indicates that Congress did not intend that the Bank Holding Company Act automatically make state branch banking restrictions applicable to bank holding companies. . . .

Nevertheless, a banking institution cannot avoid state branch banking restrictions merely because it is organized as a holding company, if it is in fact carrying out branch banking. *Whitney Nat. Bank in Jefferson Parish v. Bank of New Orleans & Trust Co.*, 323 F. 2d 290 (1963), *rev'd on other grounds*, 379 U.S. 411 (1965); *First National Bank in Billings v. First Bank Stock Corp.*, 306 F. 2d 937, 942 (9th Cir. 1962). In *Billings*, the Court found that holding company banking is branch banking when one of the subsidiary banks of the holding company is, ". . . in substance, . . . doing business through the instrumentality of . . ." another subsidiary bank. *First National Bank in Billings v. First Bank Stock Corp., supra* at 942. There must exist ". . . the unitary type of operation characteristic of branch banking. . . ." *Ibid.* at 943.

In this case, there is substantial evidence in the record to indicate that the relationship between FABCO and its subsidiaries did not represent the kind of unitary operation that was unlawful under Arkansas branch banking laws. Worthen and AFNB had no common directors. They will continue to have separate and independent board of directors, no members of which are common to both boards. Both banks will continue to be managed by local officers. Each bank is a separate corporation with its own capital, surplus, and undivided profit. Each will have its own loan limits based on its own capital and surplus. Worthen will be supervised by the Arkansas Bank Commissioner, AFNB by the Comptroller of the Currency, and FABCO by the Federal Reserve Board. Although Worthen and AFNB are located in the same state, they are a considerable distance apart. Finally, there is nothing to indicate that they will be identified as one institution by the public. These basic facts are undisputed.

It is clear that Worthen and AFNB will cooperate in the future. But ". . . it is not enough . . . to show that common control, through stock ownership by [a bank which] participates actively in the management of its subsidiaries, produces cooperation . . . between the subsidiaries. This is a usual, although not necessary, result of common ownership and control." *First National Bank in Billings v. First Bank Stock Corp., supra* at 942.

The protestants suggest that this situation is not comparable to that in *Billings*, but is rather controlled by *Whitney*, where the Fifth Circuit found a holding company organization to be engaged in branch banking. We do not think *Whitney* is comparable. In *Whitney*, a "parent" bank, in an intricate financial arrangement, established both a holding company and a new bank. The holding company's only subsidiaries were to be the parent bank and the new bank. It was clear from the statements of management and the Comptroller of the Currency that the intention was to run the two banks as a unitary operation under the direction of the parent bank. Thus, the transaction was a subterfuge for the establishment of a branch office in the same market area as the present bank.

In the present case, FABCO is acquiring AFNB, an old, established bank with its own capital structure, and there is substantial evidence to indicate the independence of AFNB and Worthen.

Notes and Comments 4.29. *Interstate acquisitions by BHCs.* Reconsider the Forth Corp. situation in Note 4.26, *supra.* Assume that the laws of the state of Jersey do *not* contain the prohibition quoted in that note. Can the Fed approve the acquisition of Lee State Bank under the Riegle-Neal Interstate Banking and Branching Efficiency Act of 1994 (IBBEA)?[46] The provisions of IBBEA permit geographic expansion by banks without regard to artificial barriers to interstate expansion heretofore imposed by the Douglas Amendment[47] to the BHCA and the branching provisions of state law and of the National Bank Act (NBA).[48] Beginning one year after the enactment of IBBEA in September 1994,[49] the Fed is authorized to approve BHCA applications for acquisition of control[50] of out-of-state banks[51] "without regard to whether such transaction is prohibited under the law of any State."[52] This authority is limited to acquisitions by banks that are adequately capitalized and adequately managed.[53] Permitted "acquisitions" include acquisition of a *de novo* bank chartered to establish a presence of the acquiring BHC within the target state.[54] Certain state law restrictions affecting interstate acquisitions will continue to have effect. The Fed is generally not permitted to approve an acquisition that would contravene applicable state statutory law requiring a bank

---

46. Pub. Law No. 103-328, Sept. 29, 1994, 108 Stat. 2338 (1994) (IBBEA).

47. 12 U.S.C. § 1842(d) (1988).

48. *See, e.g.*, 12 U.S.C. § 36(c) (NBA provision limiting branching by national banks to branching permitted to state banks in same state). *See generally* Chapter 3, § 2, *supra* (discussing § 36).

49. 12 U.S.C. § 1842 note (effective date provision).

50. "Acquisition of control" means "to acquire control of, or acquire all or substantially all of the assets of." *See id.* § 1842(d)(1)(A).

51. For these purposes, "out-of-state bank" means "a bank located in a State other than the home State of [the acquiring] bank holding company." *Id. See also id.* § 1841(o)(6) (IBBEA definition). For these purposes, the IBBEA defines "home State" to mean:

> (A) with respect to a national bank, the State in which the main office of the bank is located;
> (B) with respect to a State bank, the State by which the bank is chartered; and
> (C) with respect to a bank holding company, the State in which the total deposits of all banking subsidiaries of such company are the largest on the later of --
> (i) July 1, 1966; or
> (ii) the date on which the company becomes a bank holding company under [the BHCA].

Id. §1841(o)(4)(A)-(C).

52. *Id.*

53. *Id.* "Adequately capitalized" means "a level of capitalization [that] meets or exceeds all applicable Federal regulatory capital standards." *Id.* § 1841(o)(1). The term "adequately managed" is undefined by the IBBEA.

54. *See, e.g., id.* § 1842(d)(1)(A), (C) (acquisitions of "shell banks" included within new rules).

to be in existence for a minimum period of time before acquisition.[55] However, the Fed may approve such an acquisition if the target bank has been in existence for at least five years, notwithstanding any longer minimum period in the statutory law of the host state.[56]

4.30. *Continuing state law authority over BHCs.* Prior to the enactment of the IBBEA, the provisions of the BHCA generally did not affect the authority of states to regulate banks and BHCs subject to their jurisdiction.[57] Aside from the explicit limitations on state authority contained in the IBBEA, the act not only confirms this authority, but also explicitly provides that nothing in the act is to be construed as affecting the authority of states and their political subdivisions to subject banks, BHCs, foreign banks, and affiliates thereof to state taxation.[58] Under IBBEA, state law requirements that a portion of the assets of a target bank be held available for call by a state-sponsored housing entity remain applicable to such acquisitions, if four conditions are met. First, the state law must not have the effect of discriminating against out-of-state banks, BHCs and their subsidiaries.[59] Second, the state law must have been in effect prior to September 29, 1994.[60] Third, the FDIC has not made a determination that compliance with the state law would result in an unacceptable risk to the BIF or SAIF.[61] Fourth, the "appropriate Federal banking agency"[62] of the target bank has not made a determination that compliance with the state law would place the bank in an unsafe or unsound condition.[63] Certain nationwide and statewide concentration limits apply to the newly authorized interstate BHC acquisitions. First, the Fed is not permitted to approve an interstate acquisition if the applicant (including its affiliates) controls, or would control upon consummation of the acquisition, more than ten percent of the total amount of deposits

---

55. *Id.* § 1842(d)(1)(B)(i). For these purposes, a "shell" or "phantom" bank, created to be controlled by the acquiring BHC and to receive an existing target bank, is deemed to have been in existence for as long as the target bank has been. *Id.* § 1842(d)(1)(C).

56. *Id.* § 1842(d)(1)(B)(ii). For these purposes, the IBBEA defines the term "host state" to mean:

> (A) with respect to a bank, a State, other than the home State of the bank, in which the bank maintains, or seeks to establish and maintain, a branch; and
>
> (B) with respect to a bank holding company, a State, other than the home State of the company, in the company controls, or seeks to control, a bank subsidiary.

Id. § 1841(o)(5).

57. *See* 12 U.S.C. § 1846 (1988) (pre-IBBEA BHCA provision; state authority preserved), *redesignated by* IBBEA, § 101(b)(1), 108 Stat. at 2341 (codified at 12 U.S.C. § 1846(a)).

58. 12 U.S.C. § 1846(b). This state authority is confirmed "to the extent that such tax or tax method is otherwise permissible by or under the Constitution of the United States or other Federal law." *Id. See also* IBBEA, § 111 (codified at 12 U.S.C. § 1811 Note) (restatement of existing law with respect to state taxation of banking enterprises).

59. *Id.* § 1842(d)(1)(D)(i). "Out-of-State bank holding company" means "with respect to any State, a bank holding company whose home State is another State." *Id.* §1841(o)(7).

60. *Id.* § 1842(d)(1)(D)(ii).

61. *Id.* § 1842(d)(1)(D)(iii).

62. For these purposes, the term "appropriate Federal banking agency" has the same meaning as in section 3 of the FDIA, *id.* §1813(q). 12 U.S.C. § 1841(n)).

63. *Id.* § 1842(d)(1)(D)(iv).

of insured depository institutions in the United States.[64] Second, as to acquisitions other than initial entry into the target state, the Fed is not permitted to approve an acquisition if (*a*) immediately before the proposed acquisition, the applicant (or an affiliate) controls an insured depository institution or any branch of such an institution in the home state of the target bank, or in any host state in which the target bank maintains a branch; and, (*b*) upon consummation of the proposed acquisition the applicant would control 30 percent or more of the total amount of deposits of insured depository institutions in any such state.[65] The nationwide and statewide concentration provisions do not affect the authority of any state to limit, by statute, regulation or order, the percentage of the total amount of deposits of insured depository institutions in the state held or controlled by a bank, BHC and subsidiaries thereof.[66]

4.31. *Interstate BHC acquisitions: Compliance with other laws.* Approval of interstate acquisitions are fully subject to compliance with the Community Reinvestment Act (CRA).[67] The Fed must also take into account the record of the applicant BHC in complying with applicable state community reinvestment laws.[68] Similarly, approval of interstate acquisitions are fully subject to applicable antitrust laws.[69] The Fed must also take into account the applicability of any similar state anticompetitive laws.[70]

4.32. *Interstate BHC acquisitions: Banks in default or in danger of default.* An exception from the generally applicable IBBEA rules exists for acquisitions of banks in default or in danger of default.[71] Notwithstanding the restrictions discussed above, the Fed may approve an interstate acquisition of one or more banks in default or in danger of default,[72] or an interstate acquisition as to which financial assistance is provided by the FDIC under section 13(c) of the FDIA.[73]

4.33. *Interstate BHC acquisitions: Intracompany agency activities.* Pre-IBBEA, questions sometimes arose as a matter of state law as to whether or not a depository institution subsidiary of a BHC could undertake transactions as an agent for an affiliate in-

---

64. "Deposit" has the same meaning as in section 3(*l*) of the FDIA, 12 U.S.C. § 1813(*l*). 12 U.S.C. § 1842(d)(2)(E). *See generally FDIC v. Philadelphia Gear Corp*, 476 U.S. 426 (1986) (construing the term "deposit" under § 1813(*l*)). The term "insured depository institution" has the same meaning as in section 3 of the FDIA, 12 U.S.C. § 1813. 12 U.S.C. § 1841(n).

65. *Id.* § 1842(d)(2)(B)(i)-(ii). *See id.* § 1841(o)(3) ("branch" for BHCA purposes). IBBEA provides certain exceptions to the statewide concentration limit. The acquisition will be permitted if there is state deposit cap limitation that permits a bank or BHC (and affiliates thereof) to control a greater percentage of total deposits in the target state. *Id.* § 1842(d)(2)(D)(i). Alternatively, the acquisition will be permitted if it is approved by the appropriate state bank supervisor of the host state, and the applicable standard of approval does not have the effect of discriminating against out-of-state banks, BHCs and subsidiaries thereof. *Id.* § 1842(d)(2)(D)(ii).

66. *Id.* § 1842(d)(2)(C). These state deposit caps are given effect so long as they do not discriminate against out-of-state banks, BHCs and subsidiaries thereof. *Id.*

67. *Id.* § 1842(d)(3)(A). *See id.* §§ 2901 *et seq.* (CRA requirements).

68. *Id.* § 1842(d)(3)(B).

69. *Id.* § 1842(d)(4)(A). *Cf. id.* § 1841(o)(2) (IBBEA definition of "antitrust laws").

70. *Id.* § 1842(d)(4)(B).

71. The terms "default" and "in danger of default" have the same meaning as in section 3 of the FDIA, 12 U.S.C. § 1813. *Id.* § 1841(n).

72. *Id.* § 1842(d)(5)(A).

73. *Id.* § 1842(d)(5)(B).

stitution.[74] Under IBBEA, a bank subsidiary is generally permitted to "receive deposits, renew time deposits, close loans, service loans, and receive payments on loans and other obligations as an agent for a depository institution affiliate."[75] A bank acting in this capacity "shall not be considered to be a branch of the affiliate."[76] Any such agency relationship must be consistent with safe and sound banking practices, and all applicable regulations of any appropriate federal banking agency.[77] Similarly, an insured savings association that was an affiliate of a bank on July 1, 1994, is permitted to act as agent for the bank, in the same manner as an insured bank affiliate could act.[78] However, the agency activities must be conducted only (*a*) in a state in which the bank is not prohibited from operating a branch,[79] and the savings association maintained an office or branch and conducted business as of July 1;[80] or, (*b*) in a state in which the bank is not expressly prohibited from operating a branch under a state law prohibiting interstate bank mergers,[81] and the savings association maintained a main office and conducted business as of July 1, 1994.[82] Any such agency relationship must be consistent with safe and sound banking practices, and all applicable regulations of any appropriate federal banking agency.[83] Certain prohibitions apply to agency activities of depository institutions. The institution may not conduct on an agency basis any activity prohibited to it as principal under any applicable federal or state law.[84] By the same token, the institution, as principal, may not authorize an agent to conduct any activity on its behalf that it is prohibited from conducting under applicable federal or state law.[85]

4.34. Based upon the material in this section, consider the following problem. Carl Skeeting is the chairman and president of Pull Savings and Loan Association ("Pull"), a state-chartered savings association located in a southwestern state of the United States. Pull has been experiencing a loss of deposits that has been increasing over the past few months. Skeeting has been looking for a way to increase Pull's deposit base and diversify into a broader range of financial services. He does not think that Pull can accomplish these objectives on its own since, among other things, it has a relatively weak capital base and little surplus. Skeeting recently had lunch with several members of the board of directors of Small

---

74. *See, e.g., Commercial Nat'l Bank of Little Rock, supra* (discussing use of bank as functional branch of affiliated bank).

75. 12 U.S.C. § 1828(r)(1). The question may be raised whether the list of permitted agency activities is intended to be exclusive. According to the IBBEA, the list is not to be construed as limiting the authority of the bank to act in such a capacity "under any other provision of law." *Id.* §1828(r)(4)(A).

76. *Id.* § 1828(r)(2). However, if the bank acts in an agency capacity under another provision of law, the IBBEA does not affect the question of whether or not the bank so acting is to be considered a branch of the principal. *See id.* § 1828(r)(4)(B).

77. *Id.* § 1828(r)(5).

78. *Id.* § 1828(r)(6).

79. *Id.* § 1828(r)(6)(A)(i).

80. *Id.* § 1828(r)(6)(A)(ii).

81. *Id.* § 1828(r)(6)(B)(i). *See* IBBEA, § 102(a), 108 Stat. at 2343 (codified at 12 U.S.C. § 1831u(a)(2)) (state election to prohibit interstate merger transactions). *See also* Note 4.50, *infra* (discussing permitted state law prohibitions on interstate mergers under IBBEA).

82. *Id.* § 1828(r)(6)(B)(ii).

83. *Id.* § 1828(r)(5).

84. *Id.* § 1828(r)(3)(A).

85. *Id.* § 1828(r)(3)(B).

National Bank ("Small"), which is located in the same southwestern state. The directors indicated to Skeeting that Small might be interested in merging. In terms of deposits and loans, the relative size of all depository institutions in their state, if taken together in the aggregate, is set forth in Figure 4.1, *infra.*

Figure 4.1
Pull-Small Market Data

Institution	Deposits		Loans	
	demand	time	commercial	consumer
Snitty Bank, N.A.	35%	30%	40%	30%
Chimerical Bank	30%	25%	35%	25%
Pull S&L	----	25%	----	20%
Medium State Bank	20%	3%	15%	3%
Small National Bank	15%	10%	10%	15%
First Federal S&L	----	4%	----	4%
Second Federal S&L	----	2%	----	2%
First State S&L	----	1%	----	1%

After discussing the situation, Pull's board of directors has developed a proposal for effecting the acquisition of Small. They would create a company, to be called Stranglehold Corp., that would make tender offers for the outstanding voting stock of both Pull and Small, exchanging Stranglehold stock for the respective stock of Pull and Small. What regulatory procedures and requirements are involved in obtaining approval of this proposal? What is the likelihood that the proposal would succeed? Is there any other information that you would need to answer these questions?

3. Mergers and Consolidations

Notes and Comments 4.35. *The scope of the Bank Merger Act.* Broadly speaking, the Bank Merger Act (BMA)[86] prohibits mergers, consolidations, or purchases of assets and assumption of liabilities involving insured banks or savings associations, unless the prior written approval of the appropriate federal bank regulatory agency has been obtained. Authority to administer the BMA is divided up among the "responsible agencies" identified in the act. As to a merger, consolidation or purchase and assumption between an insured and

86. 12 U.S.C. § 1828(c).

an uninsured depository institution, the FDIC is the responsible agency.[87] As to any such transaction between insured banks, the Comptroller is the responsible agency if the acquiring, assuming or resulting bank is a national bank.[88] If the acquiring, assuming or resulting bank is to be a state member bank, the Fed is the responsible agency.[89] If the acquiring, assuming or resulting bank is a nonmember insured state bank, the FDIC is the responsible agency.[90] If the acquiring, assuming or resulting institution were an insured savings association, the Director of Thrift Supervision (DOTS) was the responsible agency, at least until July 2011.[91] A notice of the proposed transaction covered by the BMA must be published prior to approval at appropriate intervals during the review of the proposal.[92] Upon receipt of a proposal, the responsible agency is required to request reports on the competitive aspects of the proposal from the Attorney General and from the other responsible agencies, before acting on the proposal (unless an emergency merger is required to salvage a failing bank).[93]

4.36. Section 606(a) of the Financial Services Regulatory Relief Act of 2006 (FSRRA), Pub. L. No. 109-351, 120 Stat. 1966, 1981 (2006) (codified at 12 U.S.C. § 1828(c)(4)), eliminated the requirement in the Bank Merger Act that each federal banking agency request a "competitive factors" report from the other three agencies as well as from the Attorney General. The FSRRA requires only a request to the Attorney General and a copy of the request to the FDIC. Do you think that this streamlining was appropriate? Why did the former version of § 1828(c)(4) require requests to all three agencies, as well as the Attorney General? Are there different reasons under the current legislation for requesting and copying the Attorney General and the FDIC respectively? Notice that the Attorney General is still subject to the 30-day/10-day alternative deadlines. 12 U.S.C. § 1828(c)(4)(B).

4.37. The responsible agency still has the authority to act immediately on the application with requesting a report if it finds that that is necessary to prevent the probable failure of an insured depository institution involved in the merger. *Id.* § 1828(c)(4)(C)(i). However, FSSRA adds a new exception from requesting reports for cases in which "the merger transaction involves solely an insured depository institution and 1 or more of the affiliates of such depository institution." *Id.* § 1828(c)(4)(C)(ii). Why would the act add such an exception?

4.38. Assume that Quarter National Bank is seeking to acquire Teensy Federal Savings Bank by merger. The application has been filed, and the prior notice has been published. Reports have been requested under section 1828(c)(4). What is the approval process applicable to this merger? *See* 12 U.S.C. § 1828(c)(5)-(7).

4.39. *Changes under the FDICIA.* The Federal Deposit Insurance Corporation Improvement Act of 1991 (FDICIA)[94] includes provisions amending certain statutory rules

---

87. *See* 12 U.S.C. § 1828(c)(1).

88. *See id.* § 1828(c)(2)(A).

89. *See id.* § 1828(c)(2)(B).

90. *See id.* § 1828(c)(2)(C).

91. *See id.* § 1828(c)(2)(D) (2009). Under the Dodd-Frank Act, in July 2011 the functions and authority of the DOTS and the OTS over mergers in which the surviving party is a savings association were first exercised by the OCC and the FDIC for federal and state savings associations, respectively. DFA § 363(7)(A)(i), (iii) (codified at 12 U.S.C.A. § 1828(c)(2)(A), (C)) (transferring to OCC and FDIC OTS responsibility for mergers in which federal or state savings association survives).

92. *See id.* § 1828(c)(3).

93. *See id.* § 1828(c)(4).

94. Pub. L. No. 102-242, 105 Stat. 2236 (December 19, 1991) (codified at scattered sections of 12 U.S.C.).

with respect to mergers and acquisitions. The FDICIA authorizes mergers, consolidations, and other acquisitions by or involving savings associations[95] or national banks[96] with any other insured depository institution. Thus, cross-industry acquisitions now appear to be explicitly authorized, as they are under certain state statutory schemes. Under the FDICIA, such transactions are generally subject to the approval or disapproval of the Director of the OTS[97] or the Comptroller of the Currency,[98] respectively, within 60 days of the filing of an application for approval of the transaction. The approval process is subject to the general requirements of the BMA as well as the specific requirements of the FDICIA.[99] In addition, certain specified acquisitions that involve a conversion from BIF membership to SAIF membership are authorized, subject to special rules with respect to the deposit fund conversion.[100]

4.40. Mergers and consolidations are subject to a wider range of requirements than those contained in the Bank Merger Act. The requirements for national banks involved in mergers and consolidations are found in 12 U.S.C. §§ 215, 215a, 215a-3. State laws contain corresponding requirements for state banks involved in mergers and consolidations. Review the national bank provisions and consider the following questions:

> **a.** Hiram Forth and certain other shareholders hold a majority of the shares of Quarter National Bank (QNB). They form a corporation, QuarterCorp, and apply to state authorities to charter a bank that will be a subsidiary of QuarterCorp. They also propose and vote in favor of a consolidation between QNB and the new state bank. The resulting bank will be called Quarter National Bank and will be almost wholly owned by QuarterCorp. (Former shareholders of QNB will now be shareholders of QuarterCorp.) Is this transaction, known as "a reverse

---

95. FDICIA, § 502(a) (codified at 12 U.S.C. § 1467a(t)).

96. *Id.* § 502(b) (codified at 12 U.S.C. § 215c).

97. *Id.* § 502(a) (codified at 12 U.S.C. § 1467a(t)(2) (A)).

98. *Id.* § 502(b) (codified at 12 U.S.C. § 215c(b)(1)).

99. 12 U.S.C. §§ 215c(a), 1467a(t)(1).

100. *Id.* § 1815(d)(3). The FIRREA had imposed a five-year moratorium on such conversions. *See id.* § 1815(d) (2)(A). The FDICIA permits such conversions, subject to the following conditions:

> (i) The conversion must be approved by the responsible agency under the BMA. *Id.* § 1815(d) (3)(A)(i). *See id.* § 1828(c)(2). (On the conditions for approval by the responsible agency, see *id.* § 1815(d)(3)(E).)
>
> (ii) If the acquiring, assuming or resulting depository institution is a BIF member that is a subsidiary of a bank holding company, prior written approval of the Fed is also required. *Id.* § 1815 (d)(3)(A)(ii), (F).
>
> (iii) Appropriate insurance assessments on deposits attributable to the acquired depository institution must be made in accordance with rules applicable to BIF or SAIF members, depending on whether the acquired institution was formerly a BIF or SAIF member. *Id.* § 1815(d)(3)(B), (D). (On the determination of this attributable deposit amount, see *id.* §1815(d)(3)(C). On the allocation of costs between the two funds in relation to any subsequent default of the acquiring, assuming, or resulting institution, or in relation to such institution being in danger of default, see *id.* §1815(d)(3) (H).)

Expedited approval of such conversions is mandated by FDICIA. *See id.* § 1815(d)(3)(G).

triangular merger,"[101] authorized by the NBA? *See Boone v. Carlsbad Bancorporation, Inc.*, 972 F.2d 1545, 1551-1552 (10th Cir. 1992); *Martin v. Kilgore First Bancorp, Inc.*, 747 F.2d 1024 (5th Cir. 1984).

b. Quarter National Bank (QNB) and Fifth State Bank are merging, with QNB the surviving bank. A number of QNB shareholders have dissented, demanded appraisal of their shares, and eventually have asked the Comptroller to determine the value of their shares. The Comptroller applies the "Delaware Block Method" to value the shares.[102] The dissenting shareholders argue, however, that the Delaware Block Methodology cannot reasonably be used, because the Delaware Supreme Court itself has repudiated this method as the exclusive method of valuing shares.[103] If the dissenting shareholders bring suit challenging the Comptroller's appraisal, what is the likelihood that they will succeed? *See Boone v. Carlsbad Bancorporation, Inc.*, 972 F.2d 1545, 1553 (10th Cir. 1992). *See also Beerly v. Department of the Treasury*, 768 F.2d 942, 945-46 (7th Cir. 1985), *cert. denied*, 475 U.S. 1010 (1986).

c. The majority of Fourth State Bank common stock is owned by Hiram Forth and members of his family. They have proposed to merge Fourth into First Bank, N.A., a newly formed national bank in which all shares are currently owned by the Forth family. Under the terms of the merger agreement, Fourth State Bank's minority shareholders are to receive cash for their shares, while the majority shareholders are to receive common stock in the merged bank. Can the minority shareholders of Fourth successfully challenge this merger, on the grounds that the NBA does not authorize a "freeze out" of minority shareholders by requiring them to take cash instead of shares? *See Lewis v. Clark [sic]*, 911 F.2d 1558 (11th Cir. 1990), *rehearing denied*, 972 F.2d 1351 (11th Cir. 1991); *NoDak Bancorporation v. Clarke*, 998 F.2d 1416 (8th Cir. 1993).

4.41. *Judicial review and the "convenience and needs" defense.* Assume that QNB has entered into a consolidation agreement with First Bank N.A., which will result in an increased share of deposits and loans in the banks' market from QNB's 30 and 27 percent to 48 and 40 percent for First Quarter National Bank. If the Antitrust Division of the Justice Department challenges the merger as substantially lessening competition in QNB's market, could QNB successfully defend the merger on the grounds that it would enable QNB to increase the efficiency and ability of the bank in meeting the credit needs of its market, and to compete more effectively with large New York banks that are attempting to attract the lending business of some of QNB's largest commercial customers? Consider the following materials.

---

101. In a triangular bank merger, an existing bank is merged *into* an interim or "phantom" bank that is wholly owned by a BHC. In a reverse triangular merger, the original bank is the survivor. In either case, the surviving bank is wholly owned by the BHC, and the shareholders of the original bank are required to exchange their original bank shares for shares of the BHC. *See Boone v. Carlsbad Bancorporation, Inc.*, 972 F.2d 1545, 1549 (10th Cir. 1992) (discussing triangular mergers).

102. The Delaware Block Method of appraisal requires the consideration and relative weighting of four factors, which are treated as independent "blocks": book value, adjusted book value, market value, and investment value. *See Northern Acceptance Trust 1065 v. Amfac, Inc.*, 59 F.R.D. 116, 125 (D.Haw. 1973) (discussing Delaware block method).

103. *See Weinberger v. UOP, Inc.*, 457 A.2d 701, 712 (Del. 1983) (rejecting exclusive use of method).

United States v. Philadelphia Nat. Bank

374 U.S. 321 (1963)

Mr. Justice BRENNAN delivered the opinion of the Court.

The United States, appellant here, brought this civil action . . . under § 4 of the Sherman Act, 15 U.S.C. § 4, and § 15 of the Clayton Act, 15 U.S.C. § 25, to enjoin a proposed merger of The Philadelphia National Bank (PNB) and Girard Trust Corn Exchange Bank (Girard), appellees here. The complaint charged violations of § 1 of the Sherman Act, 15 U.S.C. § 1, and § 7 of the Clayton Act, 15 U.S.C. § 18. From a judgment for appellees after trial, . . . the United States appealed to this Court. . . . We reverse the judgment of the District Court. We hold that the merger of appellees is forbidden by § 7 of the Clayton Act and so must be enjoined; we need not, and therefore do not, reach the further question of alleged violation of § 1 of the Sherman Act. . . .

The Philadelphia National Bank and Girard Trust Corn Exchange Bank are, respectively, the second and third largest of the 42 commercial banks with head offices in the Philadelphia metropolitan area, which consists of the City of Philadelphia and its three contiguous counties in Pennsylvania. The home county of both banks is the city itself; Pennsylvania law, however, permits branching into the counties contiguous to the home county, . . . and both banks have offices throughout the four-county area. PNB, a national bank, his assets of over $1,000,000,000, making it (as of 1959) the twenty-first largest bank in the Nation. Girard, a state bank, is a member of the [Federal Reserve System] and is insured by the FDIC; it has assets of about $750,000,000. Were the proposed merger to be consummated, the resulting bank would be the largest in the four-county area, with (approximately) 36% of the area banks' total assets, 36% of deposits, and 34% of net loans. It and the second largest (First Pennsylvania Bank and Trust Company, now the largest) would have between them 59% of the total assets, 58% of deposits, and 58% of the net loans, while after the merger the four largest banks in the area would have 78% of total assets, 77% of deposits, and 78% of net loans. . . .

In November 1960 the boards of directors of the two banks approved a proposed agreement for their consolidation under the PNB charter. By the terms of the agreement, PNB's stockholders were to retain their share certificates, which would be deemed to represent an equal number of shares in the consolidated bank, while Girard's stockholders would surrender their shares in exchange for shares in the consolidated bank, receiving 1.2875 such shares for each Girard share. Such a consolidation is authorized, subject to the approval of the Comptroller of the Currency, by 12 U.S.C. (1958 ed., Supp. IV) § 215. But under the Bank Merger Act of 1960, 12 U.S.C. (1963 ed., Supp. IV) § 1828(c), the Comptroller may not give his approval until he has received reports from the other two banking agencies and the Attorney General respecting the probable effects of the proposed transaction on competition. All three reports advised that the proposed merger would have substantial anticompetitive effects in the Philadelphia metropolitan area. However, on February 24, 1961, the Comptroller approved the merger. No opinion was rendered at that time. But as required by § 1828(c), the Comptroller explained the basis for his decision to approve the merger in a statement to be included in his annual report to Congress. As to effect upon competition, he reasoned that "[s]ince there will remain an adequate number of alternative sources of banking service in Philadelphia, and in view of the beneficial effects of this consolidation upon international and national competition it was concluded that the overall effect upon competition would not be unfavorable." He also stated that the consolidated bank "would be far better able to serve the convenience and needs of its community by being of material assistance to its city and state in their efforts to attract new industry and to retain existing industry." The day after the Comptroller approved the merger, the United States commenced the present action. No steps have been taken to consummate the merger pending the outcome of this litigation. . . .

The Government's case in the District Court relied chiefly on statistical evidence bearing upon market structure and on testimony by economists and bankers to the effect that, notwithstanding the intensive governmental regulation of banking, there was a substantial area for the free play of competitive forces; that concentration of commercial banking, which the proposed merger would increase, was inimical to that free play; that the principal anticompetitive effect of the merger would be felt in the area in which the banks had their offices, thus making the four-county metropolitan area the relevant geographical market; and that commercial banking was the relevant product market. The defendants, in addition to offering contrary evidence on these points, attempted to show business justifications for the merger. They conceded that both banks were economically strong and had sound management, but offered the testimony of bankers to show that the resulting bank ... would be able to compete with large out-of-state (particularly New York) banks, would attract new business to Philadelphia, and in general would promote the economic development of the metropolitan area. . . .

By its terms, the present § 7 reaches acquisitions of corporate stock or share capital by any corporation engaged in commerce, but it reaches acquisitions of corporate assets only by corporations "subject to the jurisdiction of the Federal Trade Commission." The FTC, under § 5 of the Federal Trade Commission Act, has no jurisdiction over banks. 15 U.S.C. § 45(a)(6). Therefore, if the proposed merger be deemed an assets acquisition, it is not within § 7. Appellant argues vigorously that a merger is crucially different from a pure assets acquisition, and appellees argue with equal vigor that it is crucially different from a pure stock acquisition. Both positions, we think, have merit; a merger fits neither category neatly. Since the literal terms of § 7 thus do not dispose of our question, we must determine whether a congressional design to embrace bank mergers is revealed in the history of the statute. The question appears to be one of first impression. . . .

. . . Congress contemplated that the 1950 amendment would give § 7 a reach which would bring the entire range of corporate amalgamations, from pure stock acquisitions to pure assets acquisitions, within the scope of § 7. Thus, the stock-acquisition and assets-acquisition provisions, *read together*, reach mergers, which fit neither category perfectly but lie somewhere between the two ends of the spectrum. . . . So construed, the specific exception for acquiring corporations not subject to the FTC's jurisdiction excludes from the coverage for § 7 only assets acquisitions by such corporations when not accomplished by merger. . . .

. . . When Congress enacted the Bank Merger Act, the applicability of § 7 to bank mergers was still to be authoritatively determined; it was a subject of speculation. Thus, this is not a case in which our "earlier decisions are part of the arch on which the new structure rests, [and] we [must] refrain from disturbing them lest we change the design that Congress fashioned." *State Board of Ins. v. Todd Shipyards Corp.*, 370 U.S. 451, 458. . . . The design fashioned in the Bank Merger Act was predicated upon uncertainty as to the scope of § 7, and we do no violence to that design by dispelling the uncertainty. . . .

Appellees contended below that the Bank Merger Act, by directing the banking agencies to consider competitive factors before approving mergers, 12 U.S.C. (1958 ed., Supp. IV) § 1828(c), . . . immunizes approved mergers from challenge under the federal antitrust laws. We think the District Court was correct in rejecting this contention. No express immunity is conferred by the Act. . . .

Nor did Congress, in passing the Bank Merger Act, embrace the view that federal regulation of banking is so comprehensive that enforcement of the antitrust laws would be either unnecessary, in light of the completeness of the regulatory structure, or disruptive of that structure. On the contrary, the legislative history of the Act seems clearly to refute any suggestion that applicability of the antitrust laws was to be affected. Both the House and Senate Committee Reports stated that the Act would not affect in any way the applicability of the antitrust laws to bank acquisitions. . . .

It should be unnecessary to add that in holding as we do that the Bank Merger Act of 1960 does not preclude application of § 7 of the Clayton Act to bank mergers, we deprive the later statute of none of its intended force. Congress plainly did not intend the 1960 Act to extinguish other sources of federal restraint of bank acquisitions having anticompetitive effects. For example, Congress certainly knew that bank mergers would continue subject to the Sherman Act, . . . as well as that pure stock acquisitions by banks would continue subject to § 7 of the Clayton Act. If, in addition, bank mergers are subject to § 7, we do not see how the objectives of the 1960 Act are thereby thwarted. It is not as if the Clayton and Sherman Acts embodies approaches to antitrust policy inconsistent with or unrelated to each other. The Sherman Act, of course, forbids mergers effecting an unreasonable restraint of trade. . . .

. . . To be sure, not every violation of § 7, as amended, would necessarily be a violation of the Sherman Act; our point is simply that since Congress passed the 1960 Act with no intention of displacing the enforcement of the Sherman Act against bank mergers–or even of § 7 against pure stock acquisitions by banks–continued application of § 7 to bank mergers cannot be repugnant to the design of the 1960 Act. It would be anomalous to conclude that Congress, while intending the Sherman Act to remain fully applicable to pure stock acquisitions by banks, nevertheless intended to § 7 to be completely inapplicable to bank mergers. . . .

The statutory test is whether the effect of the merger "may be substantially to lessen competition" in any line of commerce in any section of the country." We analyzed the test in detail in *Brown Shoe Co. v. United States*, 370 U.S. 294, and that analysis need not be repeated or extended here, for the instant case presents only a straightforward problem of application to particular facts.

We have no difficulty in determining the "line of commerce" (relevant product or services market) and "section of the country" (relevant geographical market) in which to appraise the probable competitive effects of appellees' proposed merger. We agree with the District Court that the cluster of products (various kinds of credit) and services (such as checking accounts and trust administration) denoted by the term "commercial banking," ... composes a distinct line of commerce. Some commercial banking products or services are so distinctive that they are entirely free of effective competition from products or services of other financial institutions; the checking account is in this category. Others enjoy such cost advantages as to be insulated within a broad range from substitutes furnished by other institutions. For example, commercial banks compete with small-loan companies in the personal-loan market; but the small-loan companies' rates are invariable much higher than the banks', in part, it seems, because the companies' working capital consists in substantial part of bank loans. Finally, there are banking facilities which, although in terms of cost and price they are freely competitive with the facilities provided by other financial institutions, nevertheless enjoy a settled consumer preference, insulating them, to a marked degree, from competition; this seems to be the case with savings deposits. In sum, it is clear that commercial banking is a market "sufficiently inclusive to be meaningful in terms of trade realities." *Crown Zellerbach Corp. v. Federal Trade Comm'n*, 296 F.2d 800, 81 (C.A. 9th

Cir. 1961).

We part company with the District Court on the determination of the appropriate "section of the country." The proper question to be asked in this case is not where the parties to the merger do business or even where they compete, but where, within the area of competitive overlap, the effect of the merger on competition will be direct and immediate. . . . This depends upon "the geographic structure of supplier-customer relations." KAYSEN AND TURNER, ANTITRUST POLICY (1959), 102. In banking, as in most service industries, convenience of location is essential to effective competition. Individuals and corporations typically confer the bulk of their patronage on banks in their local community; they find it impractical to conduct their banking business at a distance. See *Transamerica Corp. v. Board of Govs. of Fed. Res. Sys.*, 206 F.2d 163, 169 (C.A. 3d Cir. 1953). The factor of inconvenience localizes banking competition as effectively as high transportation costs in other industries. . . .

Therefore, since, as we recently said in a related context, the "area of effective competition in the known line of commerce must be charted by careful selection of the market area in which the seller operates, and to which the purchaser can practicably turn for supplies," *Tampa Elec. Co. v. Nashville Coal Co.*, 365 U.S. 320, 327 (emphasis supplied); *see Standard Oil Co. v. United States*, 337 U.S. 293, 299 and 300, n.5, the four-county area in which appellees' offices are located would seem to be the relevant geographical market. . . . In fact, the vast bulk of appellee's business originates in the four-county area.[36] Theoretically, we should be concerned with the possibility that bank offices on the perimeter of the area may be in effective competition with bank offices within; actually; this seems to be a factor of little significance.

We recognize that the area in which appellees have their offices does not delineate with perfect accuracy an appropriate "section of the country" in which to appraise the effect of the merger upon competition. Large borrowers and large depositors, the record shows, may find it practical to do a large part of their banking business outside their home community; very small borrowers and depositors may, as a practical matter, be confined to bank offices in their immediate neighborhood; and customers of intermediate size, it would appear, deal with banks within an area intermediate between these extremes. . . . So also, some banking services are evidently more local in nature than others. But that in banking the relevant geographical market is a function of each separate customer's economic scale means simply that a workable compromise must be found; some fair intermediate delineation which avoids the indefensible extremes of drawing the market either so expansively as to make the effect of the merger upon competition seem insignificant, because only the smallest

36. The figures of PNB and Girard respectively are: 54% and 63% of the dollar volume of their commercial and industrial loans originate in the four-county area; 75% and 70%, personal loans; 74% and 84%, real estate loans; 41% and 62%, lines of credit; 94% and 72%, personal trusts; 81% and 94%, time and savings deposits; 56% and 77%, demand deposits; 93% and 87%; demand deposits of individuals. Actually, these figures may be too low. The evidence discloses that most of the business done outside the area is with large borrowers and large depositors; appellees do not, by and large, deal with small businessmen and average individuals not located in the four-county area. For example, of appellees' combined total business demand deposits under $10,000, 94% originate in the four-county area. This reinforces the thesis that the smaller the customer, the small is his banking market geographically. . . .

The appellees concede that the four-county area has sufficient commercial importance to qualify, under *Brown Shoe Co., supra*, at 336-337, as a "section of the country" within the meaning of § 7. *See Maryland & Va. Milk Producers Assn. v. United States*, 362 U.S. 458, 469; *cf. United States v. Yellow Cab Co.*, 332 U.S. 218, 226; *Indiana Farmer's Guide Publishing Co. v. Prairie Farmer Publishing Co.*, 293 U.S. 268, 279.

customers are considered. We think that the four-county Philadelphia metropolitan area, which state law apparently recognizes as a meaningful banking community in allowing Philadelphia banks to branch within it, and which would seem roughly to delineate the area in which bank customers that are neither very large nor very small find it practical to do their banking business, is a more appropriate "section of the country" in which to appraise the instant merger than any larger or smaller or different area. . . . We are helped to this conclusion by the fact that the three federal banking agencies regard the area in which banks have their offices as an "area of effective competition." Not only did the FDIC and FRB, in the reports they submitted to the Comptroller of the Currency in connection with appellees' application for permission to merge, so hold, but the Comptroller, in his statement approving the merger, agreed: "With respect to the effect upon competition,, there are three separate levels and effective areas of competition involved. These are the national level for national accounts, the regional or sectional area, and the local area of the City of Philadelphia and the immediately surrounding area."

Having determined the relevant market, we come to the ultimate question under § 7: whether the effect of the merger "may be substantially to lessen competition" in the relevant market. Clearly, this is not the kind of question which is susceptible of a ready and precise answer in most cases. It requires not merely an appraisal of the immediate impact of the merger upon competition, but a prediction of its impact upon competitive conditions in the future; this is what is meant when it is said that the amended § 7 was intended to arrest anticompetitive tendencies in their "incipiency." . . . Such a prediction is sound only if it is based upon a firm understanding of the structure of the relevant market; yet the relevant economic data are both complex and elusive. . . . So also, we must be alert to the danger of subverting congressional intent by permitting a too-broad economic investigation. *Standard Oil Co. v. United States*, 337 U.S. 293, 313. And so in any case in which it is possible, without doing violence to the congressional objective embodies in § 7, to simplify the test of illegality, the courts out to do so in the interest of sound and practical judicial administration. *See Union Carbide Corp.*, Trade Reg. Rep., FTC Complaints and Orders, 1961-1963, ¶ 15503, at 20375-20376 (concurring opinion). This is such a case.

. . . [W]e think that a merger which produces a firm controlling an undue percentage share of the relevant market, and results in a significant increase in the concentration of firms in that market, is so inherently likely to lessen competition substantially that it must be enjoined in the absence of evidence clearly showing that the merger is not likely to have such anticompetitive effects. *See United States v. Koppers Co.*, 202 F. Supp. 437 (D.C.W.D. Pa. 1962).

Such a test lightens the burden of proving illegality only with respect to mergers who size makes them inherently suspect in light of Congress' design in § 7 to prevent undue concentration. Furthermore, the test is fully consonant with economic theory. That "[c]ompetition is likely to be greatest when there are many sellers, none of which has any significant market share," is common ground among most economists, and was undoubtedly a premise a congressional reasoning about the antimerger statute.

The merger of appellees will result in a single bank's controlling at least 30% of the commercial banking business in the four-county Philadelphia metropolitan area. Without attempting to specify the smallest market share which would still be considered to threaten undue concentration, we are clear that 30% presents that threat. Further, whereas presently the two largest banks in the area (First Pennsylvania and PNB) control between them approximately 44% of the area's commercial banking business, the two largest after the merger (PNB Girard and First Pennsylvania) will control 59%. Plainly, we think, this increase of more than 33% in concentration must be regarded as significant. . . .

We turn now to three affirmative justifications which appellees offer for the proposed merger. The first is that only through mergers can banks follow their customers to the suburbs and retain their business. This justification does not seem particularly related to the instant merger, but in any event it has no merit. There is an alternative to the merger route: the opening of new branches in the areas to which the customers have moved– so-called de novo branching. Appellees do not contend that they are unable to expand thus, by opening new offices rather than acquiring existing ones, and surely one premise of an antimerger statute such as § 7 is that corporate growth by internal expansion is socially preferable to growth by acquisition.

Second, it is suggested that the increased lending limit of the resulting bank will enable it to compete with the large out-of-state banks, particularly the New York banks, for very large loans.[a] We reject this application of the concept of "countervailing power." *Cf. Kiefer-Stewart Co. v. Joseph E. Seagram & Sons*, 340 U.S. 211. If anticompetitive effects in one market could be justified by procompetitive consequences in another, the logical upshot would be that every firm in an industry could, without violating § 7, embark on a series of mergers that would make it in the end as large as the industry leader. For if all the commercial banks in the Philadelphia area merged into one, it would be smaller than the largest bank in New York City. This is not a case, plainly, where two small firms in a market propose to merge in order to be able to compete more successfully with the leading firms in that market. Nor is it a case in which lack of adequate banking facilities is causing hardships to individuals or businesses in the community. The present two largest banks in Philadelphia have lending limits of $8,000,000 each. The only businesses located in the Philadelphia area which find such limits inadequate are large enough readily to obtain bank credit in other cities.

This brings us to appellees' final contention, that Philadelphia needs a bank larger than it now has in order to bring business to the area and stimulate its economic development. . . . We are clear, however, that a merger the effect of which "may be substantially to lessen competition" is not saved because, on some ultimate reckoning of social or economic debits and credits, it may be deemed beneficial. A value choice of such magnitude is beyond the ordinary limits of judicial competence, and in any event had been made for us already, by Congress when it enacted the amended § 7. Congress determined to preserve our traditionally competitive economy. It therefore proscribed anticompetitive mergers, the benign and the malignant alike, fully aware, we must assume, that some price might have to be paid.

3 Michael P. Malloy, Banking Law and Regulation

§ 12.02[A] (2d ed. 2011)

[A]s originally enacted, the BMA had only an approximate focus on the factor of anticompetitiveness with respect to bank mergers and acquisitions. Any more precise attention to such factors, and the opportunity for direct, public consideration of proposed acquisitions . . . were rejected. Further, the relationship between the regulatory framework of the BMA and the general antitrust laws was correspondingly unclear.

It should therefore not be surprising that by 1965 it was apparent that the BMA was in need of modification. Two major aspects of the act required particular attention. First, the

---

a. The lending limit of a national bank is calculated as a statutorily specified percentage of capital and surplus. Hence, the larger the capital/surplus base of a national bank, the higher the lending limit that applies to the aggregate of all its loans and extensions of credit to any one borrower. *See infra* Chapter 5, § 2.a (discussing lending limits).

standards applied in reviewing applications appeared to be in need of strengthening. A major purpose of the BMA, the reduction of the hectic pace of bank mergers, had not been realized. The federal banking agencies had approved more than 90 percent of the merger applications filed since 1960.[38]

Second, there was confusion and controversy surrounding the applicability of the general antitrust laws to bank mergers.[39] The Justice Department had begun to challenge bank mergers under the antitrust laws, particularly section 7 of the Clayton Act, despite the fact that federal banking agencies had approved the mergers under the BMA.[40] . . .

[I]n *United States v. First National Bank & Trust Co. of Lexington*,[51] the Court held that such mergers were also subject to the Sherman Act.[52] In both *Philadelphia National Bank* and *First National Bank*, the Court went on to apply traditional antitrust analysis without regard to the "convenience and needs" of the community to be served by the surviving bank.[53]

Clearly, then, the time was ripe for congressional action. Six merger transactions were pending in the courts. Three had been consummated prior to *Philadelphia National Bank*; three had been consummated after that decision. At least 30 more merger applications were before the federal banking agencies. On September 13, 1965, over eighteen bills dealing with the amendment of the BMA were introduced in the House. However, congressional attention was focused on two bills, the Robertson-Proxmire bill in the Senate and the Patman bill in the House.

On April 5, 1965, Senator Robertson had introduced S. 1698. This bill presented a rather simple answer to the problem of the applicability of the antitrust laws to bank mergers. It exempted all past, pending and future bank mergers from the Sherman and Clayton Acts.[58] The sole test for approval of bank mergers would be the original test incorporated in the BMA itself. The bill was referred to the Senate Banking Committee.

In committee the bill was extensively modified by the addition of an amendment drafted by Senator Proxmire. It exempted all past mergers, including those currently the subject of litigation, from the antitrust laws. With regard to future mergers, the amendment required, as did the original bill, that the mergers meet the standards established by the BMA. Even after obtaining approval of the appropriate banking agency, however, the involved banks were required to wait thirty days before consummating the merger. During that time, the transaction was subject to challenge under the Sherman and Clayton Act, measured by the traditional antitrust analysis used in *Philadelphia National Bank* and *First National Bank*. If suit were brought within the thirty-day period, the merger could not be consummated until the conclusion of the litigation. After the merger was consummated, however, it was exempt from challenge under either the Sherman or the Clayton Act.

---

38. *See* 112 Cong. Rec. 2442 (1966) (statement of Rep. Patman). *See also id.* at 2660.

39. *Id.* at 2652 (statement of Sen. Robertson).

40. *See* H. R. Rep. No. 1221, 89th Cong. 2d Sess. 4 (1966), *reprinted* in 1966 U.S. Code Cong. & Ad. News 1860.

51. 376 U.S. 665 (1964).

52. *Id.* at 666. As Justice Harlan noted, however, with the Court's decision in *Philadelphia National Bank* opening the way to Clayton Act challenges to bank mergers, the government would not in the future need to rely, as it did in *First National Bank*, solely on Sherman Act arguments. *See id.* at 673.

53. *See, e.g., Philadelphia National Bank*, 374 U.S. at 371 (Clayton Act "proscribed anticompetitive mergers, the benign and the malignant alike").

58. [111 Cong. Rec.] at 6920; 112 Cong. Rec. 2657 (1966).

The Robertson-Proxmire bill was reported out of the Senate Banking Committee on June 9, 1965. During limited debate, only one amendment was offered. That amendment, by Senator Hart, would have removed the provisions that exempted past mergers from the antitrust laws. The amendment was defeated, and the bill was approved by the Senate.

The bill was then referred to the House Banking Committee on June 14, 1965, and it was reported out of the committee with amendments on October 19. No further action was taken on that bill.

Representative Patman introduced H. R. 12173 in the House on January 19, 1966.[66] This bill was significantly different from the earlier Senate bill. It abandoned the standards for approval then contained in the BMA. It provided instead certain standards for *disapproval*. For example, it incorporated, in substantially identical language, the monopoly prohibition of section 2 of the Sherman Act. This standard was to be applied to bank mergers without exception. In addition, a second standard for disapproval incorporated, in substantially identical language, the "restraint of trade" prohibition of section 1 of the Sherman Act, and the prohibition of section 7 of the Clayton Act against transactions that may substantially lessen competition. This second standard was subject to an exception, however, for merger transactions in which "anticompetitive effects [were] clearly outweighed in the public interest by the probable effect in meeting the needs of the community to be served." Furthermore, in every case the appropriate federal agency was to consider financial and managerial resources, future prospects of the surviving bank, and the convenience and needs of the community to be served.

There was no reference in the bill to the concept of the "relevant market" for purposes of applying the prohibitions. This issue was discussed by the House Committee Report, which stated that "effects outside the section of the country involved may be relevant to the capacity of the institution to meet the convenience and needs of the community to be served."[73]

Under the House bill, the merger could not be completed for thirty days following approval, during which time it was subject to challenge under the antitrust laws. The standards to be applied by the trial court in such a challenge would be identical to those applied by the banking agencies. If litigation commenced within that time period, the merger could not be consummated until the conclusion of the litigation, unless the trial court specifically allowed otherwise. The bill also provided that in any such litigation, federal and state banking agencies were entitled to appear as of right. Finally, if a challenge was not brought within the period, the merger could be consummated, and it would then be exempted from challenge under either section 1 of the Sherman Act or section 7 of the Clayton Act. The merger would, however, remain subject to possible challenge under the monopoly provisions of section 2 of the Sherman Act.

With the exception of the monopoly provisions of section 2 of the Sherman Act, the bill exempted past mergers from the antitrust laws. The bill also dealt with the six merger transactions which were the subject of pending litigation. It exempted the three mergers which had been consummated prior to the Court's decision in *Philadelphia National Bank*. . . .

However, the bill did not exempt the three post-*Philadelphia National Bank* mergers that were involved in pending litigation. These mergers were to be analyzed in accordance with the same standards for disapproval that would apply generally to future mergers.

After minor discussion, the House inserted the text of H. R. 12173 in place of the

---

66. 112 Cong. Rec. 586 (1966).

73. H. R. Rep. No. 1221 at 3.

text of S. 1698. S. 1698 as amended was subsequently approved by the House on February 8, 1966. The following day the Senate agreed to the House amendments. The BMA of 1966 was signed into law on February 21, 1966.

Notes and Comments 4.42. *Philadelphia National Bank* sees a natural connection between the structure of bank regulation (and the limitations on geographic and product markets traditionally implicit in that structure) and antitrust analysis. This inclination to parallel the regulatory structure in antitrust analysis sets the tone for many of the cases in the bank merger area. *See, e.g., United States v. Marine Bancorporation, infra.* The opinion in *Philadelphia National Bank* begins with an overview of bank regulation, as follows:

> Because this is the first case which has required this Court to consider the application of the antitrust laws to the commercial banking industry, and because aspects of the industry and of the degree of government regulation of it will recur throughout our discussion, we deem it appropriate to begin with a brief background description. . . .
>
> Federal supervision of banking has been called "[p]robably the outstanding example in the federal government of regulation of an entire industry through methods of supervision. . . . The system may be one of the most successful [systems of economic regulation], if not the most successful." . . . To the efficacy of this system we may owe, in part, the virtual disappearance of bank failures from the American economic scene.[6]

Philadelphia Nat. Bank, 374 U.S. at 324, 330 & n. 6. In light of the dramatic increase in bank failures in the 1980s, the authorization of interstate bank markets in 1994, and the increased blurring of markets among financial services firms, does it still make sense to focus on the regulatory structure of banks alone in beginning analysis of a bank merger problem?

4.43. What does the regulator–or, ultimately, a court hearing an antitrust suit brought by the Justice Department–look for as the basis of a "convenience and needs" defense? Should they rely on some version of the affirmative defenses raised in *Philadelphia National Bank*? *See United States v. Marine Bancorporation*, 418 U.S. 602 (1974); *United States v. Phillipsburg Nat. Bank & Trust Co.*, 399 U.S. 350 (1970); *United States v. Third Nat. Bank in Nashville*, 390 U.S. 171 (1968); *United States v. First Nat. Bank of Md.*, 310 F. Supp. 157 (D.Md. 1970); *United States v. Provident Nat. Bank*, 280 F. Supp. 1 (E.D. Pa. 1968); *United States v. Crocker-Anglo Nat. Bank*, 277 F. Supp. 133 (N.D.Cal. 1967). OCC regulations identify the following factors that might outweigh anticompetitive effects:

> For purposes of weighing against anticompetitive effects, a business combination may have favorable effects in meeting the convenience and needs of the community if the depository institution being acquired has limited long-term prospects, or if the resulting national bank will provide significantly improved, additional, or less costly services to the community.

---

6. In 1967, for example, there were three bank suspensions in the entire country by reason of financial difficulties; in 1960, two; and in 1961, nine. Of these nine, four involved state banks which were neither members of the FRS nor insured by the FDIC. 1961 Annual Report of the Comptroller of the Currency 286. In a typical year in the 1920's, roughly 600 banks failed throughout the country, about 100 of them national banks. *See* S. Rep. No. 196, *Regulation of Bank Mergers*, 86th Cong., 1st Sess. 17-18.

12 C.F.R. § 5.33(e)(1)(i)(B). The regulations also indicate that a bank's performance in helping to meet the credit needs of the relevant communities, including low- and moderate-income neighborhoods, consistent with safe and sound banking practices, is a factor in deciding on a merger application. *Id.* § 5.33(e)(1)(iv).

4.44. *Measuring concentration of the market.* Assume that the pertinent geographic and product markets affected by a proposed merger have been determined. What degree of concentration is impermissible? Consider the following excerpt.

3 Michael P. Malloy, Banking Law and Regulation

§ 12.02[D] (2d ed. 2011)

. . . Once the relevant product and geographic markets are established, the next step is to determine whether the proposed merger would result in a substantial lessening of competition, or would tend to create a monopoly, with respect to those markets,[25] now or in the future. A proposed merger resulting in control of a significant percentage of these markets is perforce impermissibly anticompetitive.[27] In particular geographic markets where market shares are already highly concentrated,[28] mergers between market participants are highly likely to be anticompetitive.[29] This is especially true in markets in which there has been a trend towards increasing concentration, with few new entrants into the market.[30]

Notes and Comments 4.45. *Indexing concentration within a market.* In discussing the measurement of concentration, the OCC merger regulations make no reference to the Herfindahl-Hirschman Index (HHI) utilized in the Merger Guidelines. *See* 12 C.F.R. § 5.33 (b)(3)(ii). *But see Comptroller's Manual for Corporate Activities* § 20.3 (including HHI worksheet). *Cf.* 12 C.F.R. § 303.7(c)(5)(iii) (1987) (FDIC merger regulations; use of HHI as condition of delegated approval authority).[104] *See generally New Hampshire Sav. Bank Corp,*

---

25. 15 U.S.C. § 18.

27. *See, e.g., Phillipsburg Nat'l Bank, supra* . . . (75 - 85 percent of relevant line of commerce in the market); *Third Nat'l Bank in Nashville, supra* . . . (40 percent market share). The benchmark has been considered to be a 30 percent market share. *See Philadelphia Nat'l Bank, supra.* . . .

28. Concentration is now likely to be judged through the methodology of the Justice Department's 1982 Merger Guidelines, as revised. *See* Department of Justice, Merger Guidelines, 49 Fed. Reg. 26,824 (1984), *reprinted in* 2 Trade Reg. Rep. (CCH) ¶ 4490 (June 14, 1984), 57 Fed. Reg. 41,552 (1992), *reprinted in* 4 Trade Reg. Rep. ¶ 13,104 (May 5, 1992) (hereinafter Merger Guidelines). *See* Joseph & Mountz, *The Justice Department Guidelines: Impact on Horizontal Mergers between Commercial Banks*, 72 Ky. L. J. 505 (1983-84). Although the Merger Guidelines are expressly intended only to articulate the considerations that Justice will consult in deciding whether to challenge a merger, it is likely that "the courts [will] tend to give deference to the Guidelines' approach in actual merger cases." Cohen & Sullivan, [*The Herfindahl-Hirschman Index and the New Antitrust Merger Guidelines: Concentrating on Concentration*, 62 Texas L. Rev. 453,] 455 [(1983)].

29. *See, e.g., United States v. Citizens & S. Nat'l Bank*, 422 U.S. 86 (1975).

30. *See, e.g., Philadelphia Nat'l Bank, supra. . . . See also [United States v.] Provident Nat'l Bank*, [280 F. Supp. 1 (E.D.Pa. 1968)]. *Cf.* [*United States v.*] *First Nat'l Bank of Md.*, [310 F. Supp. 157 (D.Md. 1970)]; [*United States v.*] *First Nat'l Bank of Jackson*, [301 F. Supp. 1161 (S.D.Mass. 1969)].

104. The deleted FDIC provision was substantially replaced by a discussion in a recently released FDIC Policy Statement, which also invokes the HHI methodology.

April 18, 1988, *reprinted in* [1988-1989 Transfer Binder] Fed. Banking L. Rep. (CCH) ¶ 87,337 (May 6, 1988), at 93,817-93,818 (Fed order approving acquisition of bank resulting from a conversion of non-failing federal savings bank; applying HHI to competitiveness analysis). Despite the relative inattention of the bank regulators to the HHI methodology of the Merger Guidelines, judicial evaluation of a bank merger may be expected to subject the merger to analysis in light of the Merger Guidelines. *Cf., e.g., Vial v. First Commerce Corp.*, 564 F. Supp. 650 (E.D.La. 1983). The HHI represents concentration in a market by the sum of the squares of the market share percentage of each market participant. The higher the sum, the more concentrated the market. Consider the following examples.

a. In a market with ten participants, each having a ten percent share of the market, the HHI would be:

$$10^2 \cdot 10,$$

or an HHI of 1000. If two of these banks were to merge, and the surviving bank retained their aggregate percentage share of the market, the HHI for the post-merger market would be:

$$20^2 + (10^2 \cdot 8),$$

or an HHI of 1200.

b. On the other hand, if in the pre-merger version of this market, two banks each held a 22 percent market share, five each held a 10 percent share, and two each held a 3 percent share, then the HHI for the market would be:

$$22^2 + 22^2 + (10^2 \cdot 5) + 3^2 + 3^2,$$

or an HHI of 1486. If one of the two largest and one of the two smallest banks merged, the post-merger market would have an HHI of:

$$25^2 + 22^2 + (10^2 \cdot 5) + 3^2,$$

or an HHI of 1618.

c. If instead the two largest banks merged, the post-merger market would have an HHI of:

$$44^2 + (10^2 \cdot 5) + 3^2 + 3^2,$$

or an HHI of 2454.

d. Finally, if the two smallest banks merged, the post-merger market would have an HHI of:

$$22^2 + 22^2 + (10^2 \cdot 5) + 6^2,$$

or an HHI of 1504.

Thus, variations in the distribution of market share or in the size of the banks merging will have markedly different effects on the pre- and post-merger HHI. The Merger Guidelines establish a series of presumptions about the significance of particular HHIs. Generally, a post-merger HHI below 1,000 is viewed as unconcentrated, and the merger will not be challenged. Merger Guidelines, § 3.11(a). A post-merger HHI of 1,000-1,800 evidences concentration in the market, but if the change from pre- to post-merger HHI is less than 100 points, the merger will probably not be challenged. *Id.* § 3.11(b). A post-merger HHI above 1,800 indicates a highly concentrated market, but if the change from pre- to post-merger HHI is less than 50 points challenge is unlikely. *Id.* § 3.11(c). Of the four examples set forth above, which are likely to raise the most serious competitiveness concerns?

4.46. *Defining the product market.* How should the regulators–and ultimately the courts–define the product market of banks involved in a proposed merger? Is it the deposit and lending market of commercial banks? The deposit and lending market generally? The financial services market generally? Consider the following materials.

United States v. Connecticut National Bank

418 U.S. 656 (1974)

Mr. Justice POWELL delivered the opinion of the Court.

This case concerns the legality of a proposed consolidation of two nationally chartered commercial banks operating in adjoining regions of Connecticut. The United States brought a civil antitrust action challenging the consolidation under § 7 of the Clayton Act, 38 Stat. 731, as amended, 15 U.S.C. § 18. Following a lengthy trial and on the basis of extensive findings and conclusions, the United States District Court for the District of Connecticut dismissed the Government's complaint. . . . The Government brought a direct appeal. . . .

The banks desiring to consolidate, Connecticut National Bank (CNB) and First New Haven National Bank (FNH), have offices in contiguous areas in the southwestern portion of Connecticut. CNB maintains its headquarters in the town of Bridgeport, which is situated on the Long Island Sound approximately 60 miles from New York City. CNB is the fourth largest commercial bank in the State. At year-end 1972, it held 6.2% of the deposits in commercial banks in Connecticut. CNB operates 51 offices located in Bridgeport and nearby towns in the extreme southwest section of Connecticut.

FNH has its headquarters in the town of New Haven, approximately 19 miles to the northeast of Bridgeport along the Long Island Sound. FNH is the eighth largest commercial bank in Connecticut. At the end of 1972, it held 4.1% of commercial bank deposits in the State. FNH operates 22 bank offices in New Haven and surrounding towns.

In Connecticut as a whole at the end of 1971, the five largest commercial banks held 83% of the deposits in such banks in the State. Two large commercial banks based in Hartford, Connecticut Bank & Trust Co. of Hartford and Hartford National Bank, operate essentially statewide. At year-end 1972, they had 41% of the total commercial bank deposits held by Connecticut banks.

CNB and FNH both have offices and are in direct competition in a so-called "four-town area" located between Bridgeport and New Haven. The banks assured the District Court, however, that in implementing the consolidation they would divest themselves of a sufficient number of offices in the four-town area to render insignificant the degree of overlap of their areas of actual operation. The District Court held that this divestiture plan eliminated any antitrust difficulties presented by the merger of direct competitors. . . . The United States has not pursued the point on appeal. Accordingly, the case has been presented to us strictly as a geographic market extension merger on the part of both banks. The proposed consolidation would join the banks under FNH's national charter (with headquarters in Bridgeport). It would have no effect on the number of banks operating in either the Bridgeport or New Haven area. In that posture, the case presents potential-competition issues similar to those raised in *United States v. Marine Bancorporation, Inc.*[a] . . .

. . . In our view, the District Court erred in its definition of [properly defined product and geographic markets], and it is not possible to ascertain the degree, if any, to which those errors may have influenced its conclusions with regard to the Government's potential-competition arguments. Accordingly, the District Court's judgment must be vacated and the

---

a. On the potential competition doctrine, see *Marine Bancorporation, infra.*

case remanded for reconsideration. . . .

The District Court concluded that the appropriate "line of commerce" within the meaning of § 7 included both commercial banks and savings banks. . . . The court recognized that its conclusion departed from this Court's holdings in, *e.g., United States v. Phillipsburg National Bank*, 399 U.S. 350, 359-362 (1970), and *United States v. Philadelphia National Bank*, 374 U.S. 321, 356-357 (1963). But in the District Court's view the pronouncements in *Phillipsburg National Bank* and *Philadelphia National Bank* "were not intended to be ironclad, hard and fast rules which require a court to don blinders to block out the true competitive situation existing in every set of circumstances." . . .

Several factors led the District Court to the conclusions that "savings banks are in direct and substantial competition with commercial banks in providing product-services to the banking consumers in Connecticut . . . ," and that "[t]he cold, hard realities of the situation are that saving and commercial banks are fierce competitors in this state." . . . The court noted that under state law savings banks in the near future will be permitted to offer one of the traditional indicia of commercial banks, personal checking accounts. . . . It pointed out that savings banks in Connecticut compete with commercial banks for real estate mortgages, personal loans, IPC (individual, partnership, and corporate) deposits, and, the court found, commercial loans. . . . It cited *United States v. Continental Can Co.*, 378 U.S. 441 (1964), for the proposition that "complete industry overlap" is not required to establish a relevant line of commerce under § 7. . . . It also relied on the omission of the "in any line of commerce" phrase from the Bank Merger Act of 1966, 12 U.S.C. § 1828(c)(5) (B), an Act which in other essential respects tracks the language of § 7 of the Clayton Act. Finally, it distinguished *Philadelphia National Bank, supra*, by pointing to the absence of significant competition by savings banks in the relevant geographic markets in those cases. . . . The District Court's conclusion on the appropriate line of commerce caused it to "shade" (*i.e.*, to reduce) the Government's concentration ratios to take into account the presence of savings banks. . . .

We are in complete agreement with the District Court that *Phillipsburg National Bank* and *Philadelphia National Bank* do not require a court to blind itself to economic realities. Similarly, we have no doubt on this record that savings banks and commercial banks in Connecticut are "fierce competitors," . . . to the degree that they offer identical or essentially fungible services. The District Court was also correct that "complete inter-industry competitive overlap need not be shown." . . . As the Court declared in *Continental Can*, "we must recognize meaningful competition where it is found to exist." 378 U.S., at 449. Nonetheless, we hold for several reasons that the District Court was mistaken in including both savings and commercial banks in the same product market for purposes of this case.

Two of the District Court's reasons may be dealt with briefly. The court erred as a matter of law in concluding that the absence of a "line of commerce" phrase in the Bank Merger Act of 1966 alters traditional standards under § 7 of the Clayton Act for defining the relevant product market in a bank merger case. *United States v. Third National Bank*, 390 U.S. 171, 182 n. 15 (1968). *See Phillipsburg National Bank*, 399 U.S., at 359-362. Moreover, the absence of significant competition from savings banks in *Philadelphia National Bank, supra*, and *Phillipsburg National Bank, supra*, is not determinative. The commercial banks in both of those cases faced significant competition from savings and loan associations and other credit institutions. *See, e.g.*, 374 U.S., at 357 n. 34; *United States v. Phillipsburg National Bank*, 306 F. Supp. 645, 649 (NJ 1969). The Court in both instances nevertheless viewed the business of commercial banking as sufficiently distinct from other credit institutions to merit treatment as a separate "line of commerce" under § 7. Analogous distinctions, although perhaps not as sharply defined, are controlling here.

We believe that the District Court overestimated the degree of competitive overlap that in fact exists between savings banks and commercial banks in Connecticut. To be sure, there is a large measure of similarity between the services marketed by the two categories of banks.[3] . . . In our view, however, the overlap is not sufficient at this state in the development of savings banks in Connecticut to treat them together with commercial banks in the instant case. Despite the strides that savings banks in that State have made toward parity with commercial banks, the latter continue to be able to provide a cluster of services that the former cannot, particularly with regard to commercial customers, and this Court has repeatedly held that it is the unique cluster of services provided by commercial banks that sets them apart for purposes of § 7.

The Court declared in *Phillipsburg National Bank, supra*, at 360:

> "*Philadelphia Bank* emphasized that it is the *cluster* of products and services that full-service banks offer that as a matter of trade reality makes commercial banking a distinct line of commerce. Commercial banks are the only financial institutions in which a wide variety of financial products and services–some unique to commercial banking and others not–are gathered together in one place. The clustering of financial products and services in banks facilitates convenient access to them for all banking customers. . . ." (Emphasis in original.)

From the vantage point of at least one significant consumer of bank services–the commercial enterprise–commercial banks in Connecticut offer a "cluster of products and services" that their savings bank counterparts do not. The facts of this case indicate that the difference in what commercial banks in the State can offer to that important category of bank customers are sufficient to establish commercial banking as a distinct line of commerce.

The District Court concluded that "meaningful competition" existed between commercial and savings banks for commercial loans. . . . This conclusion is not supported by the record. Commercial loans, generally speaking, are relatively short-term loans to business enterprises of all sizes, usually for purposes of inventory or working capital. At the end of 1971 commercial banks in Connecticut had outstanding $1.03 billion in commercial loans. Savings banks, by comparison, had $26 million in such loans at that time. The disparity in these figures demonstrates that the commercial bank-loan business in Connecticut is controlled almost exclusively by commercial banks. Moreover, commercial banks in the State offer credit-card plans, loans for securities purchases, trust services, investment services, computer and account services, and letters of credit. Savings banks do not.

It is true that under state law savings banks soon will be able to provide some checking account services. . . . This will increase the degree of direct competition between savings banks and commercial banks, because demand deposits have traditionally been a unique attribute of the latter institutions. But even this new authority for savings banks will not allow them to serve commercial customers, who constitute a significant percentage of the clientele of commercial banks. The state law empowering savings banks to offer demand

3. As we have noted, the District Court identified some of the services offered by both savings and commercial banks, including real estate mortgages, personal loans, and time deposits. As the District Court put it in another context, it would be "ostrich-like," . . . to assume that the two types of banks are not in direct and vigorous competition with regard to the services they share or are not viewed by many bank customers as more or less fungible for purposes of those services. *Cf. United States v. Phillipsburg National Bank*, 399 U.S. 350, 360 (1970). That savings and commercial banks are direct competitors in some submarkets, however, is not the end of the inquiry, as *Phillipsburg* makes clear.

deposits forbids those banks from marketing the service to anyone "for the purpose of, or in connection with, the carrying on of any business, trade, occupation or profession." . . . Thus, under the new Act, savings banks will be restricted to offering personal checking accounts. . . .

We do not say, and *Phillipsburg National Bank, supra*, and *Philadelphia National Bank, supra*, do not say, that in a case involving a merger of commercial banks a court may never consider savings banks and commercial banks as operating in the same line of commerce, no matter how similar their services and economic behavior. At some stage in the development of savings banks it will be unrealistic to distinguish them from commercial banks for purpose of the Clayton Act. In Connecticut, that point may well be reached when and if savings banks become significant participants in the marketing of bank services to commercial enterprises. But, in adherence to the tests set forth in our earlier bank merger cases, which we are constrained to follow, we hold that such a point has not yet been reached. Accordingly, on remand the District Court should treat commercial banking as the relevant product market.

3 Michael P. Malloy, Banking Law and Regulation

§ 12.02[D] (2d ed. 2011)

. . . The tendency of a proposed merger between two banks (a "horizontal merger") to lessen competition substantially requires the identification of the "line of commerce"[14] in which competition may be affected. Presumably, this product market will be constituted of the core "cluster of products and services denoted by the term 'commercial banking.'"[15] The related products and services of other financial institutions are not included within this "line of commerce."[16] Despite resistance to this circumscription of the line of commerce in bank merger cases in the lower courts,[17] and questions raised about this approach in the secondary

14. 15 U.S.C. § 18.

15. *Philadelphia Nat'l Bank*, 374 U.S. at 356. *See United States v. Connecticut Nat'l Bank*, 418 U.S. 656 (1974) (thrift products and services not included in "line of commerce"). *See generally* Katz, *The Determination of the Line of Commerce for Bank Mergers: a Contemporary View*, 5 J. L. & Com. 155 (1984); Comment, *Bank Mergers: Agency Review and the Changing Line of Commerce*, 11 Fordham Urb. L.J. 307 (1982/83); Via, *Commercial Banking as the "Line of Commerce" in Bank Amalgamations: A Reexamination*, 99 Banking L.J. 326 (1982); Bleier & Eisenbeis, *Commercial Banking as the "Line of Commerce" and the Role of Thrifts*, 98 Banking L. J. 374 (1981); Friedlander & Slayton, *Determination of the Relevant Product Market in Bank Mergers: a Time for Reassessment?* 36 Bus. Law. 1537 (1981); Alcorn, *Merger Analysis for Banks and Others–Marine Bancorporation and Connecticut National Bank*, 12 Houston L. Rev. 539 (1975); Weston & Hoskins, *"Line of Commerce" and Commercial Banking*, So. Cal. L. Rev. 225 (1969).

16. *See United States v. Phillipsburg Nat'l Bank & Trust Co.*, 399 U.S. 350 (1970). *See generally* Alcorn, *Phillipsburg and Beyond–Developing Trends in Substantive Standards for Bank Mergers*, 9 Houston L. Rev. 417 (1972); Darnell, *Phillipsburg National Bank*, 16 Antitrust Bull. 33 (1971).

17. *See, e.g., United States v. Idaho First Nat'l Bank*, 315 F. Supp. 261 (D.Idaho 1970); *United States v. First Nat'l Bank of Md.*, 310 F. Supp. 157 (D.Md. 1970); *United States v. Phillipsburg Nat'l Bank & Trust Co.*, 306 F. Supp. 645 (D.N.J. 1969); *United States v. First Nat'l Bank of Jackson*, 301 F. Supp. 1161 (S.D.Mass. 1969); *United States v. Provident Nat'l Bank*, 280 F. Supp. 1 (E.D.Pa. 1968).

literature,[18] the Supreme Court has maintained this delimitation of the "line of commerce" with respect to bank mergers.[19]

Notes and Comments 4.47. Given the consolidation of federal regulation of depository institutions mergers under the BMA in 1989, the emerging significance of "depository institution" and "savings association" as generic regulatory terms, and the increased competition among financial service firms generally, is it time to reassess the strict distinction between commercial banks and thrift institutions upheld in *Connecticut National Bank*?

4.48. *Defining the geographic market.* Defining the geographic market would seem to be a relatively straightforward undertaking, at least under traditional analysis in *Philadelphia National Bank*. However, the deregulation of geographic limits has complicated the situation. How would *Philadelphia National Bank* or *Marine Bancorporation, infra*, delimit the geographic market of a bank in a regionalized banking system, or one in which banks are branching nationwide?

United States v. Marine Bancorporation

418 U.S. 602 (1974)

Mr. Justice POWELL delivered the opinion of the Court.

The United States brought this civil antitrust action under § 7 of the Clayton Act, 38 Stat. 731, as amended, 15 U.S.C. § 18, to challenge a proposed merger between two commercial banks. The acquiring bank is a large, nationally chartered bank based in Seattle, Washington, and the acquired bank is a medium-size, state-chartered bank located at the opposite end of the State in Spokane. The banks are not direct competitors to any significant degree in Spokane or any other part of the State. They have no banking offices in each other's home cities. The merger agreement would substitute the acquiring bank for the acquired bank in Spokane and would permit the former for the first time to operate as a direct participant in the Spokane market.

The proposed merger would have no effect on the number of banks in Spokane. The United States bases it case exclusively on the potential-competition doctrine under § 7 of the Clayton Act. It contends that if the merger is prohibited, the acquiring bank would find an alternative and more competitive means for entering the Spokane area and that the acquired bank would ultimately develop by internal expansion or mergers with smaller banks into an actual competitor of the acquiring bank and other larger banks in sections of the State outside Spokane. The Government further submits that the merger would terminate the alleged procompetitive influence that the acquiring bank presently exerts over Spokane banks due to the potential for its entry into that market.

---

18. *See, e.g.*, Rosenblum, O'Brien & DiClemente, *On Banks, Non Banks, and Overlapping Markets: A Reassessment of Commercial Banking as a Line of Commerce*, 51 Tenn. L. Rev. 401 (1984); Alcaly & Nelson, *Will Including Thrifts in the Banking Market Affect Mergers?* 97 Banking L.J. 346 (1980). *See also* note 14, *supra*. *See generally* Rhoades, *Interstate Banking and Product Line Expansion: Implications from Available Evidence*, 18 Loy.-L.A. L. Rev. 1115 (1985); Klebaner, *Recent Changes in United States' Commercial Banking Structure in Perspective*, 18 Antitrust Bull. 759 (1973).

19. *See, e.g., Connecticut Nat'l Bank, supra* note 14. However, some lower courts have further refined the delimitation, in cases involving large banks in money center markets, by distinguishing between retail and wholesale commercial banking. *See, e.g., Provident Nat'l Bank, supra* note 16; *United States v. Manufacturers Hanover Trust Co.*, 240 F. Supp. 867 (S.D.N.Y. 1965).

After a full trial, the District Court held against the Government on all aspects of the case. We affirm that court's judgment. We hold that in applying the potential-competition doctrine to commercial banking, courts must take into account the extensive federal and state regulation of banks, particularly the legal restraints on entry unique to this line of commerce. The legal barriers to entry in the instant case, notably state-law prohibitions against de novo branching, against branching from a branch office, and against multibank holding companies, compel us to conclude that the challenged merger is not in violation of § 7. . . .

The acquiring bank, National Bank of Commerce (NBC), is a national banking association with its principal office in Seattle, Washington. Located in the northwest corner of the State, Seattle is the largest city in Washington. NBC is a wholly owned subsidiary of a registered bank holding company, Marine Bancorporation, Inc. (Marine), and in terms of assets, deposits, and loans is the second largest banking organization with headquarters in the State of Washington. At the end of 1971, NBC had total assets of $1.8 billion, total deposits of $1.6 billion; and total loans of $881.3 million. It operates 107 branch banking offices within the State, 59 of which are located in the Seattle metropolitan area and 31 of which are in lesser developed sections of eastern Washington. In order of population, the four major metropolitan areas in Washington are Seattle, Tacoma, Spokane, and Everett. NBC has no branch offices in the latter three areas.

The target bank, Washington Trust Bank (WTB), founded in 1902, is a state bank with headquarters in Spokane. Spokane is located in the extreme eastern part of the State, approximately 280 road miles from Seattle. It is the largest city in eastern Washington, with a population of 170,000 within the corporate limits and of approximately 200,000 in the overall metropolitan area. The city has a substantial commercial and industrial base. The surrounding region is sparsely populated and is devoted largely to agriculture, mining, and timber. Spokane serves as a trade center for this region. NBC, the acquiring bank, has had a longstanding interest in securing entry into Spokane.

WTB has seven branch offices, six in the city of Spokane and one in Opportunity, a Spokane suburb. WTB is the eighth largest banking organization with headquarters in Washington and the ninth largest banking organization in the State. At the end of 1971, it had assets of $112 million, total deposits of $95. million, and loss of $57.6 million. It controls 17.4% of the 46 commercial banking offices in the Spokane metropolitan area. It is one of 12 middle-size banks in Washington (*i.e.*, banks with assets in the $30 million to $250 million range).

WTB is well managed and profitable. From December 31, 1966, to June 30, 1972, it increased its percentage of total deposits held by banking organizations in the Spokane metropolitan area from 16.6% to 18.6%. The amount of its total deposits grew by approximately 50% during that period, a somewhat higher rate of increase than exhibited by all banking organizations operating in Spokane at the same time. Although WTB has exhibited a pattern of moderate growth, at no time during its 70-year history has it expanded outside the Spokane metropolitan area.

As of June 30, 1972, there were 91 national and state banking organizations in Washington. The five largest in the State held 74.3% of the State's total commercial bank deposits and operated 61.3% of its banking offices. At that time, the two largest in the State, Seattle-First National Bank and NBC, held 51.3% of total deposits and operated 36.5% of the banking offices in Washington. There are six banking organizations operating in the Spokane metropolitan area. One organization, Washington Bancshares, Inc., controls two separate banks and their respective branch offices. As of midyear 1972, this organization in the aggregate held 42.1% of total deposits in the area. Seattle-First National Bank, by comparison, held 31.6%. The target bank held 18.6% of total deposits at that time, placing it third in the Spokane area behind Washington Bancshares, Inc., and Seattle-First National Bank and WTB hold approximately 92% of total deposits in the Spokane area. None of the remaining three commercial banks in Spokane holds a market share larger than 3.1%. One of these banks, Farmers & Merchants Bank, has offices in a Spokane suburb.

The degree of concentration of the commercial banking business in Spokane may well reflect the severity of Washington's statutory restraints on de novo geographic expansion by banks. Although Washington permits branching, the restrictions placed on that method of internal growth are stringent. Subject to the approval of the state supervisor of banking, Washington banks with sufficient paid-in capital may open branches in the city or town in which their headquarters are located, the unincorporated areas of the county in which their headquarters are located, and incorporated communities which have no banking office. . . . But under state law, no state-chartered bank "shall establish or operate any branch . . . in any city or town outside the city or town in which its principal place of business is located in which any bank, trust company or national banking association regularly transacts a banking or trust business, except by taking over or acquiring an existing bank, trust company or national banking association . . . ." Since federal law subjects nationally chartered banks to the branching limitations imposed on their state counterparts, national and state banks in Washington are restricted to mergers or acquisitions in order to expand into cities and towns with pre-existing banking organizations.

The ability to acquire existing banks is also limited by a provision of state law requiring that banks incorporating in Washington include in their articles of incorporation a clause forbidding a new bank from merging with or permitting its assets to be acquired by another bank for a period of at least 10 years, without the consent of the state supervisor of banking. . . . In addition, once a bank acquires or takes over one of the banks operating in a city or town other than the acquiring bank's principal place of business, it cannot branch from the acquired bank. . . . Thus, an acquiring bank that enters a new city or town containing banks other than the acquired bank is restricted to the number of bank offices obtained at the time of the acquisition. Moreover, multibank holding companies are prohibited in Washington. Under state law, no corporation in Washington may own, hold, or control more than 25% of the capital stock of more than one bank. . . . Violations of the one-bank holding company statute are gross misdemeanors carrying a possible penalty of forfeiture of a corporate charter. . . . Accordingly, it is not possible in Washington to achieve the rough equivalent of free branching by aggregating a number of unit banks under a bank holding company. . . .

In February 1971, Marine, NBC, and WTB agreed to merge the latter into NBC. NBC, as the surviving bank, would operate all eight banking offices of WTB as branches of NBC. In March 1971, NBC and WTB applied to the Comptroller of the Currency pursuant to the Bank Merger Act of 1966 for approval of the merger. As required by the Act, *see* 12 U.S.C. § 1828(c)(4), the Comptroller requested "reports on the competitive factors involved" from the Attorney General, the Federal Deposit Insurance Corporation, and the Board of Governors of the Federal Reserve System. Each of these agencies submitted a negative report on the competitive effects of the merger. The Attorney General relied on the reasons advanced in the instant case. The latter two agencies based their conclusions primarily on the degree of concentration in commercial banking in Washington as a whole.

The Comptroller approved the merger in a report issued September 24, 1971. He concluded that state law precluded NBC from branching in Spokane and "effectively prevented" NBC from causing a new Spokane bank to be formed which could later be treated as a merger partner. He noted that state law prevented the only independent small bank with offices located within the city boundaries of Spokane from merging with NBC, since that bank was state chartered, had been founded in 1965, and was subject to the minimum 10-year restriction against sale of a new bank set out in [Washington banking statutes]. The Comptroller relied heavily on the view that the merger would contribute to the convenience and needs of bank customers in Spokane by bringing to them services not previously provided by WTB.

Acting within the 30 day limitation period set out in the Bank Merger Act of 1966, 12 U.S.C. § 1828(c)(7), the United States then commenced this action in the United States District Court for the Western District of Washington, challenging the legality of the merger under § 7 of the Clayton Act. As a result, the merger was automatically stayed. 12 U.S.C. § 1828(c)(7)(A). Pursuant to 12 U.S.C. § 1828(c)(7)(D), the Comptroller intervened in support of the merger as a party defendant.

Prior to trial the United States dropped all allegations concerning actual competition between the merger partners. The remainder of the complaint addressed the subject of potential competition. . . .

According to the District Court, Washington law forbade NBC from establishing de novo branches in Spokane, and the Government had failed to establish that there was any existing bank in Spokane other than WTB "available for acquisition by NBC on any reasonably acceptable basis at any time in the foreseeable future, or at all." Moreover, any attempt by NBC to enter de novo by assisting in the formation of and then acquiring a newly chartered bank in Spokane "even if it could be legally accomplished," or to undertake a foothold acquisition, would not be economically feasible. In addition to noting the past and projected slow growth of the Spokane area, the court found that the ability to branch in a metropolitan area was essential to effective competition in the banking business. Under state law, NBC would be unable to open new branch offices in Spokane if it made a foothold acquisition or helped form and then acquired a new bank. These and other factors rendered "negative" the prospects for growth of a foothold acquisition or of a sponsored bank started from scratch. This was confirmed by the experience of another large banking organization not based in Spokane that had entered the city through a foothold acquisition in 1964 and subsequently had been unable to expand the market share of the acquired bank.

The court found no perceptible procompetitive effect deriving from NBC's premerger presence on the fringe of the Spokane market. It also held that the Government had failed to carry its burden of proving a reasonable probability that WTB, absent the merger, would expand beyond the Spokane market by de novo growth or through combination with another medium-size bank. It found no probability that NBC would be "entrenched as a dominant bank in the Spokane metropolitan area" as a result of the merger, and it could find no likelihood that the merger would trigger a series of defensive mergers by other banks in the State.

On the basis of its findings, the District Court dismissed the Government's complaint. The Government thereupon brought this direct appeal.

[The parties did not dispute the trial court's determination that the relevant product market was the "business of commercial banking (and the cluster of products and services denoted thereby). . . ." The Court considered that determination to be "in full accord with our precedents." The Court then turned to the determination of the relevant geographic market.]

The District Court found that the relevant geographic market is the Spokane metropolitan area, "consisting of the City of Spokane and the populated areas immediately adjacent thereto, including the area extending easterly through the suburb of Opportunity toward the Idaho border. . . ." This area extends approximately five miles to the west and south and 10 miles to the north and east of the center of the city. It is wholly within and considerably smaller than Spokane County and is surrounded by a sparsely populated region, with no nearby major metropolitan centers. It contains all eight of the target bank's offices. On the basis of the record, we have no reason to doubt that it constitutes a reasonable approximation of the "localized" banking market in which Spokane banks offer the major part of their services and to which local consumers can practicably turn for alternatives. . . .

Prior to trial the Government stipulated that the Spokane area is a relevant geographic market in the instant case, and there is no dispute that it is the only banking market in which WTB is a significant participant. Nevertheless, the Government contends that the entire State is also an appropriate "section of the country" in this case. It is conceded that the State is not a banking market. But the Government asserts that the State is an economically differentiated region, because its boundaries delineate an area within which Washington banks are insulated from most forms of competition by out-of-state banking organizations. The Government further argues that this merger, and others it allegedly will trigger, may lead eventually to the domination of all banking in the State by a few large banks, facing each other in a network of local, oligopolistic banking markets. This assumed eventual statewide linkage of local markets, it is argued, will enhance statewide the possibility of parallel, standardized, anticompetitive behavior. . . .

The Government's proposed reading of the "any section of the country" phrase of § 7 is at variance with this Court's § 7 cases, and we reject it. Without exception the Court has treated "section of the country" and "relevant geographic market" as identical, and it has defined the latter concept as the area in which the goods or services at issue are marketed to a significant degree by the acquired firm. *E.g., Philadelphia National Bank, supra*, at 357-362. In cases in which the acquired firm markets its products or services on a local, regional, and national basis, the Court has acknowledged the existence of more than one relevant geographic market. But in no previous § 7 case has the Court determined the legality of a merger by measuring its effects on areas where the acquired firm is not a direct competitor. In urging that the legality of this merger be gauged on a statewide basis, the Government is suggesting that we take precisely that step, because, as it concedes, the section of the country in which WTB markets by far the greatest portion of its services, due to the predominantly localized character of commercial banking, is the Spokane metropolitan area. Under the precedents, we decline the Government's invitation. We hold that in a potential-competition case like this one, the relevant geographic market or appropriate section of the country is the area in which the acquired firm is an actual, direct competitor. . . .

The term "potential competitor" appeared for the first time in a § 7 opinion of this Court in *United States v. El Paso Natural Gas Co.*, 376 U.S. 651, 659 (1964). *El Paso* was in reality, however, an actual-competition rather than a potential-competition case. The potential-competition doctrine has been defined in major part by subsequent cases, particularly *United States v. Falstaff Brewing Corp.*, 410 U.S. 526 (1973). Unequivocal proof that an acquiring firm actually would have entered de novo but for a merger is rarely available. Thus, as *Falstaff* indicates, the principal focus of the doctrine is on the likely effects of the premerger position of the acquiring firm on the fringe of the target market. . . .

Since *United States v. Philadelphia National Bank*, 374 U.S. 321 (1963), the Court has taken the view that, as a general rule, standard § 7 principles applicable to unregulated industries apply as well to mergers between commercial banks. *See also United States v. First National Bank*, 376 U.S. 665 (1964). . . .

Although the Court's prior bank merger cases have involved combinations between actual competitors operating in the same geographic markets, an element that distinguishes them factually from this case, they nevertheless are strong precedents for the view that § 7 doctrines are applicable to commercial banking. In accord with the general principles of those cases, we hold that geographic market extension mergers by commercial banks must pass muster under the potential-competition doctrine. We further hold, however, that the application of the doctrine to commercial banking must take into account the unique federal and state regulatory restraints on entry into that line of commerce. Failure to do so would produce misconceptions that go to the heart of the doctrine itself. . . .

Unlike, for example, the beer industry, *see Falstaff Brewing Corp., supra*, entry of new competitors into the commercial banking field is "wholly a matter of governmental grace . . ." and "far from easy." *Philadelphia National Bank, supra*, at 367, and n. 44. ... Reflecting this country's bitter experience of four decades ago that "[a] bank failure is a community disaster. . . ," entry into and exit from the commercial banking business have been extensively regulated by the Federal and State Governments. The regulatory barriers to entry include federal and state supervisory controls over the number of bank charters to be granted, designed to limit the number of banks operating in any particular market and thus to prevent bank failures. *See id.*, at 328. In addition, no branch, no matter how small, may be opened without prior approval of the appropriate bank regulatory agency. Moreover, there are state-law restrictions, such as those in force in Washington, on de novo geographic expansion through branching and multibank holding companies. As noted earlier, Washington statutes forbid branching into cities and towns where the expanding bank does not maintain its headquarters and other banks operate, and they forbid branching from a branch in such areas. . . . Similarly, Washington permits only one-banking holding companies. . . .

In *Philadelphia National Bank, supra*, the Court relied on regulatory barriers to entry to support its conclusion that mergers between banks in direct competition in the same market must be scrutinized with particular care under § 7. . . . But the same restrictions on new entry render it difficult to hold that a geographic market extension merger by a commercial bank is unlawful under the potential-competition doctrine. Such limitations often significantly reduce, if they do not eliminate, the likelihood that the acquiring bank is either a perceived potential de novo entrant or a source of future competitive benefits through de novo or foothold entry. Similarly, the Court noted in *Philadelphia National Bank* that under applicable state law de novo branching in the relevant market was permissible and presented an "alternative to the merger route. . . ." In this case, by contrast, there are serious questions whether an "alternative to the merger route" through branching or a functional equivalent is a legal or feasible method of entry by NBC into the Spokane market. . . .

Since the legality of the challenged merger must be judged by its effects on the relevant product and geographic markets, commercial banking in the Spokane metropolitan area, it is imperative to determine the competitive characteristics of commercial banking in that section of the country. . . .

We conclude that by introducing evidence of concentration ratios of the magnitude of those present here the Government established a prima facie case that the Spokane market was a candidate for the potential-competition doctrine. On this aspect of the case, the burden was then upon appellees to show that the concentration ratios, which can be unreliable indicators of actual market behavior, *see United States v. General Dynamics Corp.*, 415 U.S. 486 (1974), did not accurately depict the economic characteristics of the Spokane market. In our view, appellees did not carry this burden, and the District Court erred in holding to the contrary. Appellees introduced no significant evidence of the absence of parallel behavior in the pricing or providing of commercial bank services in Spokane. ...

The third step in the Government's argument, resolution of the question reserved in *Falstaff*, was the primary basis on which the case was presented to the District Court and to us. The Government contends that the challenged merger violates § 7 because it eliminates the alleged likelihood that, but for the merger, NBC would enter Spokane de novo or through a foothold acquisition. Utilization of one of these methods of entry, it is argued, would be likely to produce deconcentration of the Spokane market over the long run or other procompetitive effects, because NBC would be required to compete vigorously to expand its initially insignificant market share. . . .

It is undisputed that under state law NBC cannot establish de novo branches in Spokane and that its parent holding company cannot hold more than 25% of the stock of any other bank. Entry for NBC into Spokane therefore must be by acquisition of an existing bank. The Government contends that NBC has two distinct alternatives for acquisition of banks smaller than WTB and that either alternative would be likely to benefit the Spokane commercial banking market.

First, the Government contends that NBC could arrange for the formation of a new bank (a concept known as "sponsorship"), insure that the stock for such a new bank is placed in friendly hands, and then ultimately acquire that bank. Appellees respond that this approach would violate the spirit if not the letter of state-law restrictions on bank branching. They note that this method would require the issuance of either a state or a national charter, and they assert that neither state nor federal banking authorities would be likely to grant a charter for a new bank in a static, "well-banked" market like Spokane. . . .

In its findings and conclusions, the District Court did not resolve the question of the status of the Government's proposed sponsorship-acquisition approach under Washington's banking statutes. We similarly decline to decide this issue. Although we note that the intricate procedure for entry by sponsorship espoused by the Government can scarcely be compared to the de novo entry opportunities available to unregulated enterprises such as beer producers, *see Falstaff, supra*, we will assume, arguendo, that NBC conceivably could succeed in sponsoring and then acquiring a new bank in Spokane at some indefinite time in the future. It does not follow from this assumption, however, that this method of entry would be reasonably likely to produce any significant procompetitive benefits in the Spokane commercial banking market. To the contrary, it appears likely that such a method of entry would not significantly affect that market.

State law would not allow NBC to branch from a sponsored bank after it was acquired. NBC's entry into Spokane therefore would be frozen at the level of its initial acquisition. . . .

As a second alternative method of entry, the Government proposed that NBC could enter by a foothold acquisition of one of two small, state-chartered commercial banks that operate in the Spokane metropolitan area. Appellees reply that one of those banks is located in a suburb and has no offices in the city of Spokane, that after an acquisition NBC under state law could not branch from the suburb into the city, and that such a peripheral foothold cannot be viewed as an economically feasible method of entry into the relevant market. Appellees also point out that the second small bank was chartered in 1965 and thus under state law would not have been available for acquisition until at least four years after the 1971 NBC-WTB merger agreement. . . .

The Government's failure to establish that NBC has alternative methods of entry that offer a reasonable likelihood of producing procompetitive effects is determinative of the fourth step of its argument. Rational commercial bankers in Spokane, it must be assumed, are aware of the regulatory barriers that render NBC an unlikely or an insignificant potential entrant except by merger with WTB. In light of those barriers, it is improbable that NBC exerts any meaningful procompetitive influence over Spokane banks by "standing in the wings.". . .

In the final step of its argument, the Government challenges the merger on the ground that it will eliminate the prospect that WTB may expand outside its base in Spokane and eventually develop into a direct competitor with large Washington banks in other areas of the State. The District Court found, however, that the Government had "failed to establish . . . that there is any reasonable probability that WTB will expand into other banking markets. . . ." The record amply supports this finding. At no time in its 70-year history has WTB established branches outside the Spokane metropolitan area. Nor has it ever acquired another bank or received a merger offer other than the one at issue here. In sum, the Government's argument about the elimination of WTB's potential for expansion outside Spokane is little more than speculation. It provides no sound basis for overturning the District Court's holding.

Notes and Comments 4.49. Why is the potential competition doctrine so unpalatable for courts? And why has it yet to be rejected? Could part of the answer to both questions be the indeterminate nature of some of its basic premises? The potential competition doctrine has arisen in the Bank Holding Company Act context as well. Has its treatment there been any more favorable than in the merger context? Consider the following excerpt.

Mercantile Texas Corp. v. Board of Governors

638 F. 2d 1255 (5th Cir. 1981)

ALVIN B. RUBIN, Circuit Judge.

[For the background and facts of this case, see the excerpt following Note 4.24, *supra.*]

In rejecting Mercantile's application, the Board concluded that the merger would violate the Clayton Act standard by eliminating "actual potential competition" between Mercantile and PanNational. The Board relied on a controversial doctrine whose validity remains a current subject of debate. . . .

In a concentrated market, a small number of firms can dominate the market through their ability to manipulate the supply of a given product or service. Collusion is difficult to prove, but easy to accomplish either by agreement or through consciously parallel action. In banking, for example, a concentrated market enables dominant banks to avoid cutting interest rates, offering new services or extending credit to all but the safest credit risks, secure in the knowledge that their customers cannot go to a competitor and get better service.

Seeing the possibility of significant profits, companies outside of the market will desire to enter it. One way to enter easily is to acquire a successful company already in the market. Thus, the new entrant does not add to the number of competitors and yet enjoys the opportunity to enjoy the oligopolistic profits that result from the noncompetitive environment.

The potential competition doctrine postulates two benefits if outside firms are prevented from acquiring dominant firms within a concentrated market. "Perceived potential competition" describes the effect exerted on a concentrated market by large firms outside of the market who are "perceived" as likely entrants. The threatened entry of a powerful new competitor may intimidate already dominant firms into maintaining nearly competitive prices to avoid enticing the outside "midget killer" into the market by the prospect of oligopoly profits. . . .

The Board now maintains that Mercantile was also a perceived potential competitor. Because the Board made no finding to that effect in its decision, we cannot consider this post hoc rationalization on appeal. . . .

While perceived potential competition describes a present procompetitive effect, "actual potential competition" describes the future procompetitive benefit that occurs when an effective new competitor "actually" enters the market on its own. (Hereafter, "potential competition" and "potential competitor" refer exclusively to the actual potential competition doctrine.) The potential competition doctrine holds that, if a strong outsider is prevented from acquiring a dominant insider, the outsider will still enter the market independently, either de novo or through the purchase of a small (*i.e.* not dominant) company to establish a "toehold" in the market. If the outsider is forced to enter independently, it is more likely to become an aggressive price-cutting competitor as it attempts to increase its share of the market. The addition of a new effective competitor to the band of dominant firms will also make collusion or conscious parallelism more difficult. Had the outsider been allowed to merge with a successful insider, it would have assumed the role of the insider and continued the anti-competitive practices. Because the outsider's full competitive force will never be felt, the merger is said to substantially lessen competition for purposes of the Clayton Act standard. . . .

The Supreme Court has twice refused to decide whether the elimination of "actual potential competition" violates the Clayton Act. *See United States v. Marine Bancorporation*, 418 U.S. 602 (1974) (decided under the Bank Merger Act provision); *United States v. Falstaff Brewing Corp.*, 410 U.S. 526 (1973). This circuit has not yet passed on the issue. As the Second Circuit noted in *BOC International Ltd. v. FTC*, 557 F.2d 24 (2d Cir. 1977), we are on the frontiers of antitrust law in attempting to determine the validity and applicability of the theory to specific mergers. . . .

In the absence of necessary findings by the Board, however, we will not decide whether the doctrine adequately describes a violation of the Clayton Act standard. . . .

To establish a violation of the doctrine, the Board must make explicit findings as to the degree of concentration in the market, the existence of other potential competitors, the probability that the potential competitor will enter the market independently and the probability that the potential competitor's entry will have a significant procompetitive impact in either El Paso or Waco. The Board made an adequate finding only as to the degree of concentration in El Paso and Waco.

Notes and Comments 4.50. The OCC regulations give the following general guidance on the issue of anticompetitive effects of proposed mergers:

> In order to determine the effect of a proposed merger upon competition, it is necessary to identify the relevant geographic market. The delineation of such a market can seldom be precise. Applicant have two options for delineating the relevant market.
>
> (i) Under the first option, the applicant may use standardized market definitions specified by the [OCC] in its Quick Check Merger Screen (a sample screen is included in section 20 of the Comptroller's Manual for Corporate Activities [and contains an HHI worksheet]). The use of the Quick Check Merger Screen enables the [OCC] to assess quickly whether the proposed merger meets the [OCC]'s standards for mergers which clearly have no anticompetitive effects. . . . [F]ailure to meet these standards does not indicate that a merger raises competitive concerns. However, the [OCC] generally will require additional information in applications that do not meet the standards and will perform a more in-depth competitive analysis of those applications.
>
> (ii) If the applicant[] find[s] that the markets specified in the [OCC]'s Quick Check Merger Screen are not applicable, [it] may apply under the second option. Under the second option, the applicant defines the geographic market

> using realistic limits so that the effect of the merger upon competition can be analyzed. The applicant should define the market to encompass an area where the effect upon competition will direct and immediate. The [OCC] recognizes that different banking services may have different relevant geographic markets. Although the largest borrowers and depositors may find it convenient and practical to conduct part of their banking business outside the relevant geographic market, the applicant should not define the market so expansively as to cause the competitive effect of the merger to seem insignificant because only the largest customers are considered. Conversely, the applicant should not define the market so narrowly as to place competitors in different [geographic] markets because only the smallest customers are considered. A fair definition of the relevant geographic market should take into account the demands of most customers for the bank's services. After the relevant geographic market has been defined, the competitive effects of the proposed merger can be analyzed. The [OCC] will consider both the definition of the market and the intensity of competition within the market. . . .

12 C.F.R. § 5.33(b)(3)(i)-(ii). On the delineation of the geographic market, see generally *United States v. Phillipsburg Nat. Bank & Trust Co.*, 399 U.S. 350 (1970); *Southwest Mississippi Bank v. Federal Deposit Ins. Corp.*, 499 F. Supp. 1 (D.Miss. 1979); *Washington Mut. Sav. Bank v. Federal Deposit Ins. Corp.*, 347 F. Supp. 790 (W.D.Wash. 1972), *affirmed*, 482 F.2d 459 (9th Cir. (1973).

4.51. Reread Note 4.32, *supra*, first paragraph, and Figure 4.1. Based upon the material in this section 3, consider the following problem. After discussing the situation, Pull's board of directors has developed an alternative proposal for effecting the acquisition of Small. This alternative would involve a merger between Pull and Small, in which Small would be merged into Pull. What regulatory procedures and requirements are involved in obtaining approval of this proposal? What is the likelihood that the proposal would succeed? Is there any other information that you would need to answer these questions?

4.52. *Other aspects of bank antitrust law: Management interlocks.* While the major impact of U.S. antitrust law on depository institutions has been with respect to monopoly and anticompetitiveness in mergers and acquisitions, a broader range of concerns under generally applicable antitrust law is relevant in the depository institutions context.[105] One important antitrust-related concern that has been incorporated into federal bank regulatory policy is the problem of interlocking management between competitors. The interlocking directorate is a problem addressed by the Clayton Act, but the act has been narrowly applied by the Supreme Court in *BankAmerica Corporation v. United States*, 462 U.S. 122 (1983), so that interlocks between competing financial services firms such as insurance companies and bank holding companies is not covered by the act.[106] As to interlocks between banks, in the view of the Fed the Clayton Act provisions have been "supplanted by the revised and more comprehensive prohibitions on management official interlocks between depository organizations"[107] contained in the Depository Institutions Management Interlocks Act

---

105. For guidance on these broader aspects, see generally Gruis, *Antitrust Laws and Their Application to Banking*, 24 Geo. Wash. L. Rev. 89 (1955); Carter, *Commercial Banking and the Antitrust Laws*, 11 Antitrust Bull. 141 (1966); Lifland, *Banking Practices and the Antitrust Laws*, 42 Notre Dame L. Rev. 465 (1967); Austin & Solomon, *New Antitrust Problem: Vertical Integration in Correspondent Banking*, 122 U. Pa. L. Rev. 366 (1973).

106. For discussion of *BankAmerica Corporation*, see Note, *Antitrust Law–The Clayton Act–The Regulation of Interlocking Directorates between Competing Banks and Insurance Companies, BankAmerica Corporation v. United States*, 51 Tenn. L. Rev. 599 (1984).

107. 12 C.F.R. § 212.7.

(DIMIA), 12 U.S.C. §§ 3201 *et seq.*, as amended. Review the DIMIA and consider the following problems.

> **a.** Quarter Corp. is the holding company of Quarter National Bank. The current board of directors of Quarter Corp. has asked Carl Skeeting, chairman and president of Pull Savings and Loan Association, if he would be interested in serving on Quarter Corp.'s board. Quarter Corp. is headquartered in Quartertown, and Pull is located 150 miles away in Phonics. Is it legally permissible for Skeeting to serve on Quarter Corp.'s board?
>
> **b.** Would it make any difference to your answer to the previous question if Skeeting had been serving on the Pull and Quarter Corp. boards since December 1975?
>
> **c.** Pull Savings and Loan Association is now losing deposits at such an alarming rate, that the its state supervisor has expressed serious concern over its continuing existence. The state supervisor would like to persuade Herman Vierte, executive vice president of Quarter National Bank, to serve temporarily as chief executive officer of Pull to assist in its recovery. Is it legally permissible for Vierte to serve in this capacity?
>
> **d.** Antoine Lyonnais is the chair of the executive committee of the Confectioners' Union Credit Union. Is it legally permissible for him to serve on a management committee of the Gourmet Society Credit Union? Both the Confectioners' Union and the Gourmet Society are located in the same metropolitan area.
>
> **e.** If any of the situations discussed in the previous questions did involve a violation of the DIMIA, what agency would have the authority to enforce the provisions of the act?
>
> **f.** If any of the situations discussed in the previous questions did involve a violation of the DIMIA, does that preempt the Justice Department's authority under the Clayton Act, even if the latter were otherwise applicable?

4.53. *Other aspects of bank antitrust law: Tying arrangements.* Consider the competitive implications if a bank requires a customer who seeks a financial service offered by the bank (*e.g.*, a loan) to purchase some other service from the bank as well (*e.g.*, credit life insurance).[108] Similarly, what if a bank refused to extend credit to a customer unless the customer agreed not to maintain any deposits at other banks? These kinds of requirements or conditions imposed in the extension of financial services are known as tying arrangements. They are subject to the antitying provisions of the Bank Holding Company Act, 12 U.S.C. §§ 1971 *et seq.* Review these provisions and consider the following problems.

> **a.** Push Mutual Savings Bank is permitted by its chartering state to offer credit life insurance to cover the life of any customer obtaining a loan from the savings bank. The vice president in charge of lending has issued a directive to loan officers indicating that loans "should generally be denied" unless the applicant also "applie[s] for [credit life insurance] from [Push]." George Borrow, a depositor of the bank has just applied for a loan from Push, but declined to apply for credit life insurance, because he already has, in his view, more than sufficient life

---

108. The antitying provisions of federal banking law make certain specified practices in effect *per se* violations, with no specific showing of antitcompetitiveness required. *See Sharkey v. Security Bank & Trust Co.*, 651 F. Supp. 1231 (D.Minn. 1987). Nor is the plaintiff required to show market power of the bank and the foreclosure of a substantial volume of commerce, as would be required under general antitrust law principles. *See Bruce v. First Federal Sav. and Loan Ass'n of Conroe, Inc.*, 837 F.2d 712 (5th Cir. 1988).

insurance to cover the amount of the loan. Borrow's loan application is denied, by letter from the vice president that states in part that "credit risk considerations regretfully require us to deny your application at this time." Has Push violated the antitying provisions? Can Borrow obtain any relief?

b. Would it make any difference to your answer to the previous question if Borrow had not been a depositor of Push, the loan application being his first contact with the bank? *See Swerdloff v. Miami Nat. Bank*, 584 F.2d 54 (5th Cir. 1978).

c. Would it make any difference to your answer to question a. if the loan application had been made on behalf of Borrow's business, Neither Corporation, and not Borrow himself, while the credit life insurance was to be obtained by Borrow and his wife personally? *Cf. Swerdloff, supra*; *Delta Diversified, Inc. v. Citizens & Southern Nat. Bank*, 171 Ga. App. 625, 320 S.E.2d 767 (1984).

d. Assume that, after being turned down by Push, Borrow has applied for a loan from Quarter National Bank, at the then prevailing rate of 18 percent. Borrow now learns that Hugh Roller, president of Solid State Bank, has just obtained a loan from Quarter at the rate of 15 percent. Solid maintains a correspondent account with Quarter. Has Quarter violated the antitying provisions? Can Borrow obtain any relief?

e. Assume that when Borrow applied for a loan from Quarter, the loan officer told him that it would "enhance his application" if he included an updated credit review from "a reputable credit agency." She then told Borrow that Quarter Corp. has another subsidiary, Quarter Credit Co., that would do a "very fine job" in this regard. Borrow declined to use Quarter Credit for his credit review, because he thought that its fee was too high. Borrow's loan application is denied, and the letter informing Borrow of the denial states in part that "regretfully, credit risk considerations require us to deny your application." Has Quarter National violated the antitying provisions? Can Borrow obtain any relief?

f. Would it make any difference to your answer to question e. if the loan officer had instead insisted that Borrow hire a financial adviser, in order to protect Quarter's interest as creditor in the prospective loan? *Cf. B.C. Recreational Industries v. First Nat. Bank of Boston*, 639 F.2d 828 (1st Cir. 1981); *Freidco of Wilmington, Del., Ltd. v. Farmers Bank of the State of Del.*, 499 F.Supp. 995 (D.Del. 1980).

g. If any of the situations discussed in the previous questions did involve a violation of the antitying provisions, what agency would have the authority to enforce the provisions?

h. Assume that the situation discussed in a., *supra*, did involve a violation of the antitying provisions, but the vice president has since been dismissed for unrelated violations of the Push's internal rules and procedures. In light of this development, would the pertinent agency still have authority to enforce the antitying provisions?

4.54. *Interstate mergers: Bank-bank mergers.* Reconsider the QNB appplication to merge with Teensy Federal Savings Bank in note 4.34, *supra*. Assume that QNB and Teensy are located in different states. Can the Comptroller approve the merger under the Interstate Banking and Branching Efficiency Act of 1994 (IBBEA)?[109] As of June 1, 1997,[110] the

109. Pub. Law No. 103-328, Sept. 29, 1994, 108 Stat. 2338 (1994).

110. An interstate merger could have been approved by the responsible federal agency prior to June 1, 1997, if the home State of each bank involved in the transaction has already elected to permit interstate mergers. 12 U.S.C. § 1831u(a)(3)(A). The state law must apply equally to all out-of-state banks, *id.* § 1831u(a)(3)(A) (i). and it must expressly permit such transactions with all

responsible federal agencies are generally permitted to approve interstate merger transactions under the BMA[111] between insured banks with different home states, regardless of state law prohibitions.[112] This authority is subject to election by the home state of a merging bank to enact a law expressly prohibiting merger transactions involving out-of-state banks.[113] Any such state law must be applicable to all out-of-state banks.[114] State election has no effect on merger transactions approved before the effective date of the state law.[115] The responsible federal agency is generally not permitted to approve an interstate merger that would contravene applicable state statutory law requiring a bank to be in existence for a minimum period of time before a merger.[116] However, the agency may approve such a merger if the target bank has been in existence for at least five years, notwithstanding any longer minimum period specified in the statutory law of the host state.[117]

---

out-of-state banks. *Id.* § 1831u(a)(3)(A)(ii). In early merger situations, the host state is permitted by the IBBEA to impose certain conditions on in-state branches of the resulting bank in an interstate merger transaction. *Id.* § 1831u(a)(3)(B). For these purposes, the term "branch" is defined to mean a domestic branch only. *Id.* § 1831u(f)(3). The term "resulting bank" is defined to mean "a bank that has resulted from an interstate merger transaction under [12 U.S.C. § 1831u]." *Id.* § 1831u(f)(11). Any such conditions must not have the effect of discriminating against out-of-state banks, BHCs or subsidiaries thereof. *Id.* § 1831u(a)(3)(B)(i). For these purposes, the term "out-of-state bank holding company" is defined to mean "with respect to any State, a bank holding company whose home State is another State." *Id.* § 1831u(f)(9). The restriction against discriminatory conditions would not apply to a nationwide reciprocal treatment requirement. *Id.* § 1831u(a)(3)(B)(i). The imposition of the conditions must not otherwise be preempted by federal law. *Id.* § 1831u(a)(3)(B)(ii). Finally, any such conditions must lapse after May 31, 1997. *Id.* § 1831u(a)(3)(B)(iii).

111. "Responsible agency" means "the agency determined in accordance with [§ 1828(c)(2)] with respect to a merger transaction." *Id.* § 1831u(f)(10). That is, the responsible agency is for these purposes (*a*) with respect to a merger in which a national bank results, the Comptroller; (*b*) with respect to a merger in which a state member bank results, the Fed; and, (*c*) with respect to a merger in which an insured state nonmember bank results, the FDIC.

In addition, for these purposes the term "interstate merger transaction" is defined to mean "any merger transaction approved pursuant to [12 U.S.C. § 1831u(a)(1)]." *Id.* § 1831u(f)(6). The term "merger transaction" is itself defined to have "the meaning determined under [§ 1828(c)(3)]," *id.* § 1831u(f)(7), that is, a merger, consolidation or purchase of substantially all the assets of a target.

112. *Id.* § 1831u(a)(1). "Home state" means:

> (i) with respect to a national bank, the State in which the main office of the bank is located; and
>
> (ii) with respect to a State bank, the State by which the bank is chartered. . . .

Id. § 1831u(f)(4)(A)(i)-(ii). With respect to a BHC, "home state" has the meaning ascribed to it in the BHCA, as amended by the IBBEA. *Id.* § 1831u(f)(4)(B).

113. *Id.* § 1831u(a)(2)(A)(ii). "Out-of-state bank" means "with respect to any State, a bank whose home State is another State." *Id.* § 1831u(f)(8).

114. *Id.* § 1831u(a)(2)(A)(i).

115. *Id.* § 1831u(a)(2)(B).

116. *Id.* § 1831u(a)(5)(A). For these purposes, a "shell" or "phantom" bank, created to be controlled by the acquiring BHC and to receive an existing target bank, is deemed to have been in existence for as long as the target bank has been. *Id.* § 1831u(a)(6).

117. *Id.* § 1831u(a)(5)(B). "Host state" means "with respect to a bank, a State, other than the home State of the bank, in which the bank maintains, or seeks to establish and maintain, a branch." *Id.* § 1831u(f)(5).

4.55. *Interstate mergers: Bank-branch mergers.* An interstate merger transaction may involve the acquisition of a branch[118] of an insured bank without the acquisition of the entire target bank.[119] Such acquisitions will be permitted only if the law of the state in which the target branch is located permits out-of-state banks to acquire a branch without acquisition of the entire target bank.[120]

4.56. *Interstate mergers: Application and approval process.* Any interstate merger involving insured depository institutions is subject to the application and approval requirements of the BMA.[121] In addition, the IBBEA requires compliance with certain state filing requirements.[122] Material failure to comply with these state filing requirements bars approval of the BMA application.[123] A bank that files a BMA application for an interstate merger transaction must comply with filing requirements of any host state of the resulting bank, to the extent that the requirements do not have the effect of discriminating against out-of-state banks, BHCs or subsidiaries thereof.[124] The applicant must submit a copy of the BMA application to the state bank supervisor of the host state.[125] In addition, certain nationwide and statewide concentration limits will apply to interstate merger transactions, except for transactions involving only affiliated banks.[126] Approval of an interstate merger is also subject to the following considerations specified in the IBBEA:

---

118. Where an interstate transaction involves acquisition of a branch of an insured bank, without acquisition of the bank itself, the branch will be treated as an insured bank, the home state of which is the state in which the branch is located. *Id.* § 1831u(a)(4)(B).

119. *Id.* § 1831u(a)(4)(A).

120. *Id.*

121. *See id.* § 1828(c).

122. *See id.* § 1831u(b)(1).

123. *Id.* § 1831u(b)(1)(B).

124. *Id.* § 1831u(b)(1)(A)(i)(I). The state filing requirements must also be similar in effect to any requirement imposed by the host state on out-of-state nonbanking corporations engaging in business in the host state. *Id.* § 1831u(b)(1)(A)(i)(II). In other words, the filing requirement applicable to the out-state-bank must essentially be similar to generally applicable corporate law provisions requiring registration of foreign corporations doing business within the state. *See, e.g.*, N.Y. Bus. Corp. Law art. 13 (foreign corporations).

125. 12 U.S.C. § 1831u(b)(1)(A)(ii).

126. *Id.* § 1831u(b)(2)(E). First, the responsible federal agency is not permitted to approve an interstate merger transaction if the resulting bank (including affiliates) would control upon consummation of the transaction more than ten percent of the total amount of deposits of insured depository institutions in the United States. *Id.* § 1831u(b)(2)(A). Second, as to transactions other than initial entry into the host state, the agency is not permitted to approve a transaction if (*a*) any bank involved in the transaction (or its affiliate) has a branch in any state in which any other bank involved in the transaction has a branch, *id.* § 1831u(b)(2)(B)(i); and, (*b*) upon consummation the resulting bank would control 30 percent or more of the total amount of deposits of insured depository institutions in any such state. *Id.* § 1831u(b)(2)(B)(ii). However, the transaction will be permitted if a state deposit cap limitation (*see infra*) permits a bank or BHC (and affiliates thereof) to control a greater percentage of total deposits. *Id.* § 1831u(b)(2)(D)(i). The transaction will also be permitted if approved by the appropriate state bank supervisor of the host state under a standard that does not have the effect of discriminating against out-of-state banks, BHCs and subsidiaries thereof. *Id.* § 1831u(b)(2)(D)(ii).

These concentration provisions do not affect state authority to limit the percentage of the total amount of deposits of insured depository institutions in the state held or controlled by any bank, BHC and subsidiaries thereof. *Id.* § 1831u(b)(2)(C). These state deposit caps are given effect so long as they do not discriminate against out-of-state banks, BHCs and subsidiaries thereof. *Id.*

a. If the merger would give the resulting bank a branch or bank affiliate in a state in which the acquiring bank had no branch or bank affiliate, the responsible federal agency must apply the Community Reinvestment Act (CRA)[127] in its consideration of the application.[128] It must take into account the most recent written CRA evaluation of any bank that would be an affiliate of the resulting bank.[129] The agency must also take into account the record of any applicant bank in complying with applicable state community reinvestment laws.[130]

b. The responsible federal agency must take into account adequacy of capital and management. The agency is permitted to approve an interstate merger transaction only if each bank involved is adequately capitalized as of the date on which the application is filed.[131] It must also determine that the resulting bank will continue to be adequately capitalized and adequately managed upon consummation of the transaction.[132]

c. Interstate transactions remain fully subject to applicable antitrust laws.[133] The agency must also take into account the applicability of any similar state anticompetitive laws.[134]

4.57. *Interstate mergers: Banks in default or in danger of default.* A general exception exists for interstate merger transactions involving banks in default or in danger of default. Notwithstanding the restrictions discussed above,[135] the responsible federal agency may approve an application for an interstate merger in which one or more banks in default or in danger of default are involved, or as to which financial assistance is provided by the FDIC under section 13(c) of the FDIA.[136]

4.58. *Interstate mergers: Effect on branching.* One consequence of interstate merger transactions is to create new interstate patterns of branch ownership and control. The IBBEA includes certain conforming amendments to other provisions of federal law concerning branches, as follows:

a. Domestic branching by national banks is governed by 12 U.S.C. § 36.[137] The IBBEA amends this provision of the National Bank Act (NBA) in several respects.[138] Under the amended NBA, a national bank that results from an interstate merger transaction is permitted to maintain and operate a branch in a

---

127. 12 U.S.C. §§ 2901 *et seq.*

128. 12 U.S.C. § 1831u(b)(3)(A).

129. *Id.* § 1831u(b)(3)(B).

130. *Id.* § 1831u(b)(3)(C).

131. *Id.* § 1831u(b)(4)(A).

132. *Id.* § 1831u(b)(4)(B).

133. *Id.* § 1831u(c)(2)(A).

134. *Id.* § 1831u(c)(2)(B).

135. Specifically, in these situations the IBBEA waives the following requirements: (*a*) state election to prohibit interstate merger transactions; (*b*) branch acquisition provisions; (*c*) state law provisions concerning required minimum years of existence prior to merger; (*d*) compliance with state filing requirements; (*e*) concentration limits; (*f*) community reinvestment compliance; and, (*g*) adequacy of capital and management. *Id.* § 1831u(e).

136. *Id.* § 1831u(e). *See id.* § 1823(c) (financial assistance under FDIA).

137. *See* Chapter 3, § 2, *supra* (discussing § 36).

138. *See* 12 U.S.C. § 36(d)-(f), (h)-(*l*).

host state, in accordance with the interstate merger transaction provisions.[139] Effective June 1, 1997, a national bank generally may acquire, establish or operate a branch in a host state (including a host state in which it already has a branch) only if authorized by the amended NBA, the emergency acquisition provisions of the FDIA,[140] or the new interstate merger provision.[141] If a national bank relocates its main office from one state to another after May 31, 1997,[142] the bank may retain and operate its branches within its former home state only to the extent that the bank would be authorized to acquire, establish or commence operation of a branch in such a state.[143] In general, any host state branch of an out-of-state national bank will be subject to host state laws concerning community reinvestment, consumer protection, fair lending, and establishment of intrastate branches to the same extent as a state-chartered bank would be.[144] However, this rule does not apply if federal law preempts the application of any such state law to a national bank.[145] The rule also does not apply if the Comptroller of the Currency determines that application of any such state law would have a discriminatory effect on the national bank branch, as compared to its effect on branches of state-chartered banks.[146] All other laws of the host state, except for the application or administration of any tax or method of taxation, apply to the in-state branches of an out-of-state national bank to the same extent such laws would apply if the in-state branch were itself a national bank with its main office in the host state.[147]

b. The Federal Deposit Insurance Act (FDIA) has been amended to apply to branches of state nonmember banks in host states rules that correspond to those applicable to branches of national banks in host states.[148] Thus, these state nonmember banks will be subject to corresponding exclusive rules with respect

---

139. *Id.* § 36(d). However, IBBEA has required the federal banking agencies to promulgate regulations, effective June 1, 1997, prohibiting any out-of-state bank from using any authority to engage in interstate branching primarily for the purpose of deposit production. 12 U.S.C. § 1835a.

140. *See* 12 U.S.C. § 1823(f), (k).

141. *Id.* § 36(e)(1).

142. *Cf.* 12 U.S.C. § 30(c) (coordinating NBA relocation provision with new § 36(e)(2) governing retention of branches).

143. *Id.* § 36(e)(2). In determining whether the national bank would have been authorized "to acquire, establish or commence to operate" such a branch, the provision contemplates a situation in which:

> (*a*) the bank had no branches in the former home state (*i.e.*, where it had previously operated only a main office in the former home state); or,
>
> (*b*) the branch resulted from either an interstate merger transaction under section 1831u, or a transaction after May 31, 1997, pursuant to which the bank received financial assistance from the FDIC under section 1823(c).

Id. § 36(e)(2)(A)-(B).

144. *Id.* § 36(f)(1)(A). Enforcement of these state laws with respect to national bank branches is the responsibility of the Comptroller of the Currency, not the applicable state authority. *Id.* § 36(f)(1)(B).

145. *Id.* § 36(f)(1)(A)(i). This provision does not affect the generally applicable legal standards with respect to preemption of the application of state law to national banks. *Id.* § 36(f)(3). On notice requirements for federal bank agency decisions preempting state law, see *id.* § 43.

146. *Id.* § 36(f)(1)(A)(ii).

147. *Id.* § 36(f)(2).

148. *Id.* §§ 1828(d)(3), 1831a(j)).

to the acquisition, establishment and operation of host state branches,[149] retention of branches upon out-of-state relocation of the main office,[150] and applicability of host state law to the activities of the in-state branch.[151] In addition, the FDIA has been amended to prohibit an in-state branch of an out-of-state state nonmember bank from conducting any activity that is not permissible for a state-chartered bank in the host state.[152]

4. Change-in-Control Transactions

Notes and Comments 4.59. If Quarter Holding Company seeks to acquire the outstanding shares of Forth State Bank, it is likely that the BHCA will intervene.[153] On the other hand, if Quarter National Bank and Forth State Bank seek to merge, it is likely that the BMA will be invoked.[154] What if Hiram Forth decides to purchase a controlling interest in Forth State Bank personally? At both the state and federal level, special statutory provisions may be involved.[155] What do these provisions add to regulatory policy that is not already treated by holding company and merger regulation? Consider the following excerpt.

Michael P. Malloy, Principles of Bank Regulation

§ 4.19 (3d ed. 2011)

The Change in Bank Control Act ("CBCA")[1] was enacted in 1978 to provide the "statutory authority . . . needed to give financial institution regulators authority over . . . transfers"[2] of control by individuals.[3] An acquisition of control by any person of an existing

---

149. *Compare id.* § 36(e)(1) (NBA provision) *with id.* § 1828(d)(3)(A) (corresponding FDIA provision applicable to state nonmember banks).

150. *Compare id.* § 36(e)(2) (NBA provision) *with id.* § 1828(d)(3)(B) (corresponding FDIA provision applicable to state nonmember banks).

151. *Compare id.* § 36(f)(1)(A) (NBA provision) *with id.* § 1831a(j)(1) (corresponding FDIA provision applicable to state nonmember banks). However, the limitations and exceptions applicable to in-state branches of out-of-state national banks discussed in ¶ a., *supra*, have no corresponding provision in the FDIA.

152. 12 U.S.C. § 1831a(j)(2).

153. 12 U.S.C. § 1842.

154. *Id.* § 1828(c).

155. On state law governing acquisition by an individual of control of a bank or other depository institution, see 1 MICHAEL P. MALLOY, BANKING LAW AND REGULATION §§ 5.05-5.05[C] (2d ed. 2011).

1. 12 U.S.C.A. § 1817(j).

2. H.R. Rep. No. 1383, 95th Cong., 1st Sess. (1978), *reprinted in*, 1978 U.S. Code Cong. & Admin. News 9273, 9292.

3. On changes in control, see generally *Sletteland v. Federal Deposit Ins. Corp.*, 924 F.2d 350 (D.C. Cir. 1991); *Citibank, Fed. Sav. Bank v. Federal Deposit Ins. Corp.*, 836 F. Supp. 3 (D.D.C. 1993). A persuasive case has been made for the proposition that the statute is not intended to grant a private right of action. *See Indiana Nat'l Corp v. Rich*, 712 F.2d 1180 (7th Cir. 1983) (reviewing CBC Act legislative history); *Quaker City Nat'l Bank v. Hartley*, 533 F. Supp. 126 (S.D. Ohio 1981) (rejecting *First Alabama, infra* this note); *but see First Alabama Bancshares, Inc. v. Lowder*, [1981 Transfer Binder] Fed. Sec. L. Rep. (CCH) ¶ 98,015 (N.D. Ala. 1981) (finding private right of action);

FDIC-insured depository institution or of a holding company[4] is subject to the CBCA's relatively passive disapproval process.[5] The scope of the CBCA was significantly expanded in 1989, with the passage of the Financial Institutions Reform, Recovery, and Enforcement Act ("FIRREA").[6] As amended, the CBCA now applies to insured depository institutions rather than insured banks.[7] Until July 2011, the OTS is the "appropriate Federal banking agency" for these purposes with respect to savings associations.[8] Thereafter, the OCC and the FDIC are the appropriate federal banking agencies for federal and state savings associations, respectively.[9]

The CBCA prohibits any person,[10] directly or indirectly or through or in concert with one or more other persons, from acquiring "control"[11] of an insured depository institution or holding company through the purchase, assignment, transfer, pledge, or other disposition of the target's voting stock, unless: (1) the person has given prior notice to the "appropriate Federal banking agency;" and (2) the agency has not disapproved the acquisition within the statutory time period.[12]

Mid-Continent Bancshares, Inc. v. O'Brien, [1981 Transfer Binder] Fed. Sec. L. Rep. (CCH) ¶ 98,734 (E.D. Mo. 1981) (relying on *First Alabama*); *CityFed Fin. v. Federal Home Loan Bank Bd.*, 615 F. Supp. 1122 (D.D.C. 1985) (interpreting prior statutory language; finding SLHC to be "party aggrieved").

4. By its own terms, the CBCA applied to acquisitions of control of FDIC-insured depository institutions, but it defined "insured depository institution" for these purposes to include "any depository institution holding company" and any other company that controls an insured depository institution. 12 U.S.C.A. § 1817(j)(18)(A)-(B).

5. *See* 12 U.S.C.A. § 1817(j)(1) (affirmative regulatory approval of change in control not required).

6. Pub. L. No. 101-73, 103 Stat. 183 (1989), §§ 201(a)(1), 201(b), 208(8)-(13), 905(c), 907(d), 103 Stat. at 187-188, 213, 460, 468-469 (*codified at* 12 U.S.C.A. § (j)(2)(A), (j)(2)(D), (j)(7)(F), (j)(15), (j) (16)-(18)).

7. *See* FIRREA § 201(a)(1), 103 Stat. at 187 (*codified at* 12 U.S.C.A. § 1817).

8. 12 U.S.C.A. 1813(q)(4) (2009).

9. 12 U.S.C.A. § 1813(q), *as amended*, Dodd-Frank Wall Street Reform and Consumer Protection Act (DFA) § 312(c)(1), Pub. L. No. 111-203, 124 Stat. 1376, 1522-1523 (2010) (codified at 12 U.S.C.A. § 1813(q)(1)-(3); striking (q)(4)).

10. For these purposes, "person" is defined to mean "an individual or a corporation, partnership, trust, association, joint venture, pool, syndicate, sole proprietorship, unincorporated organization, or any other form of entity not specifically listed herein." *Id.* § 1817(j)(8)(A). *But cf. id.* § 1817(j)(17) (acquisitions subject to 12 U.S.C.A. §§ 1467a, 1828(c), 1842 not subject to CBCA).

11. For these purposes, the term "control" is defined to mean "the power, directly or indirectly, to direct the management or policies of an insured depository institution or to vote 25 per centum or more of any class of voting securities of an insured depository institution." *Id.* § 1817(j)(8) (B). On the meaning of "control" under the CBCA, see *Zinman v. Federal Deposit Ins. Corp.*, 567 F. Supp. 243 (E.D. Pa. 1983); *Citizens First Bancorp v. Harreld*, 559 F. Supp. 867 (W.D. Ky. 1982); *Southeast Banking Corp. v. Adler*, [1982-1983 Transfer Binder] Fed. Sec. L. Rep. (CCH) ¶ 99,183 (S.D. Fla. 1982); *Riggs Nat'l Bank v. Albritton*, 516 F. Supp. 164, 179 (D.D.C. 1981).

12. 12 U.S.C.A. § 1817(j)(1). For these purposes, until July 2011, the term "appropriate Federal banking agency" is defined to mean: [quoting 12 U.S.C.A. § 1813(q)(1)-(4)].

. . . As to the statutory time period for disapproval of changes in control, the appropriate federal banking agency generally has 60 days from the submission of a CBCA notice to decide whether to disapprove the change in control. *Id.* § 1817(j)(1). In the agency's discretion, this time period may be extended "for an additional 30 days during which such a disapproval may issue." *Id.*

Notes and Comments 4.60. Hiram Forth enters into a contract with Major Shareholder, under which Hiram has the right of first refusal if the Major should decide to sell his shares in Other State Bank. (The Major currently owns 20 percent of the outstanding shares of common stock in Other State Bank.) The contract also provides that the Major must give Hiram his proxy to vote the shares each year in connection with the bank's annual meeting for the election of directors. Is this contract subject to the Change in Bank Control Act?

4.61. Assume that Hiram already owns three percent of the outstanding common stock of Last National Bank. He has become dissatisfied with the management of the bank, and is preparing to wage a proxy fight to elect a slate of directors. Does this trigger the Change in Bank Control Act?

The period of disapproval "may be extended not to exceed 2 additional times for not more than 45 days each time," *id.*, but on the explicit condition that

> (A) the agency determines that any acquiring party has not furnished all the information [required under 12 U.S.C. § 1817(j)(6), discussed *infra*];
>
> (B) in the agency's judgment, any material information submitted is substantially inaccurate;
>
> (C) the agency has been unable to complete the investigation of an acquiring party under paragraph (2)(B) because of any delay caused by, or the inadequate cooperation of, such acquiring party; or
>
> (D) the agency determines that additional time is needed to investigate and determine that no acquiring party has a record of failing to comply with the requirements of [31 U.S.C.A. §§ 5311-5324].

12 U.S.C. § 1817(j)(1)(A)-(D).

Chapter 5

Transactional Rules

1. Introduction

As a practical matter, state and national banks are both equally and entirely subject to state transactional law governing, for example, collection of debts, commercial paper, bank deposits, contracts, and the like.[1] For national banks, however, there is at least one important exception to this rule.[2] Federal law, primarily that administered by the Office of the Comptroller of the Currency ("OCC"), defines the rights and obligations of national banks as corporate entities.[3] It is this balance of generally applicable state transactional law and the federal corporate law of banks – plus any other federal law that might preempt otherwise applicable state law – that defines the framework in which banks operate. Attempts by state authority to intrude into the fundamental governance of federally chartered depository institutions have generally been held to be constitutionally preempted.[4]

Federal law is playing an increasingly important role in the powers of depository

---

1. It has long been recognized, for example, that national banks

> are subject to the laws of the State, and are governed in their daily course of business far more by the laws of the State than of the Nation. . . . It is only when the state law incapacitates the banks from discharging their duties to the government that it becomes unconstitutional.

First Nat'l Bank v. Kentucky, 76 U.S. (9 Wall.) 353, 362 (1870). *See also Davis v. Elmira Sav. Bank*, 161 U.S. 276, 283 (1896); *McClellan v. Chipman*, 164 U.S. 347, 356-357 (1896).

2. Arguably, another exception is provided by the constitutional doctrine of preemption, under which federal law applicable to national banks might replace otherwise generally applicable state transactional law. *See* § 2.d., *infra* (discussing federal preemption of state state consumer protection statutes).

3. *See, e.g.*, 12 U.S.C. § 24 (concerning powers of national banking associations). *See also Easton v. Iowa*, 188 U.S. 220 (1903) (recognizing sole power of Congress to define powers of national banks); *Bullard v. National Eagle Bank*, 85 U.S. 589 (1873); *Coon v. Smith*, 4 F. Supp. 960 (D. Ill. 1933).

4. *See, e.g., Franklin Nat'l Bank v. New York*, 347 U.S. 373 (1954) (preempting state law governing advertisement of accounts in light of national bank powers under 12 U.S.C. § 24); *Fidelity Fed. Sav. & Loan Ass'n v. De la Cuesta*, 458 U.S. 141 (1982) (preempting state law governing due-on-sale clauses applicable to savings associations).

institutions, state and federal, to engage in particular types of transactions, for a number of reasons. Despite the dual nature of the depository institutions industry,[5] it has become markedly federalized, primarily due to the fact that virtually all depository institutions are subject to federal supervision through the federal deposit insurance system.[6]

In addition, standards of conduct in banking transactions are subject to a distinctive federal regime. The authority of state-chartered banks to engage in activities not permitted to national banks has been significantly curtailed by the enactment of the Federal Deposit Insurance Corporation Improvements Act ("FDICIA").[7] With certain specified exceptions, FDICIA generally requires that insured state banks not engage in any type of activity not permissible for national banks.[8]

In the sections that follow, the focus will be primarily on regulation at the federal level, focusing on national banks. The chapter considers the regulation of core banking functions–lending and deposit-taking–as well as other typical activities, such as guarantees and letters of credit, real property transactions and trust powers. Finally, the chapter offers extended analysis of three areas of special interest: the incidental powers doctrine, which has been the key to commercial bank penetration into a number of related product markets; bank service companies, a newly revised method of diversification for commercial banks; and securities activities, the growth industry for commercial bank diversification for the past 30 years.

Notes and Comments 5.1. *Effect of the GLBA.* The 1999 Gramm-Leach-Bliley Act (GLBA)[9] generally endorses the principle of functional regulation, positing that similar activities should be regulated by the same regulator. Accordingly, banking activities are regulated by federal and state bank regulators, securities activities–even if engaged in by banks–are regulated by federal and state securities regulators, and insurance activities by state insurance regulators.[10] However, the Fed retains its role of "umbrella supervisor" of bank holding companies, a subject that will be explored in greater detail in the next chapter. The GLBA has also created a new power, operation of direct financial subsidiaries of national banks,[11] that seems to exist somewhere between national bank incidental powers (discussed in § 7, *infra*) and the use of bank service companies (discussed in § 8, *infra*), and

---

5. *See, e.g.*, Lovett, *Federalism, Boundary Conflicts and Responsible Financial Regulation*, 18 Loy.-L.A. L. Rev. 1053 (1985); Scott, *Patchwork Quilt: State and Federal Roles in Bank Regulation*, 32 Stan. L. Rev. 687 (1980); Scott, *Dual Banking System: Model of Competition in Regulation*, 30 Stan. L. Rev. 1 (1977); Golembe, *Our Remarkable Banking System*, 53 Va. L. Rev. 1091 (1967); Redford, *Dual Banking: A Case Study in Federalism*, 31 Law & Contemp. Prob. 749 (1966) (discussing dual nature of state and federal bank regulation).

6. *See, e.g.*, Malloy, *Seeing the Light: Savings Association Conversions and Federal Regulatory Realignment*, 10 Ann. Rev. Banking L. 189 (1991) (arguing that federal deposit insurance has already minimized effects of dual banking system).

7. Pub. L. No. 102-242, 105 Stat. 2236 (Dec. 19, 1991) (codified at scattered sections of 12 U.S.C.).

8. FDICIA § 303 (codified at 12 U.S.C. § 1831a).

9. Pub. L. No. 106-102, Nov. 12, 1999, 113 Stat. 1338 (1999) (codified at scattered sections of 12, 15, 16, 18 U.S.C.) (GLBA).

10. *See, e.g.*, GLBA, §§ 111-112, 115, 301 (codified at 12 U.S.C. §§ 1820a, 1831v, 1844(c)(4)A)-(B), (g), 15 U.S.C. § 6711).

11. GLBA § 121(a)(2) (codified at 12 U.S.C. § 24a). *See also id.* § 121(d)(1) (codified at 12 U.S.C. § 1831w) (concerning state bank financial subsidiaries).

yet is neither of these.[12] The GLBA permits a national bank to engage through a financial subsidiary in "financial activities"[13] authorized by the act,[14] subject to specified conditions. First, a national bank may control such a subsidiary (or hold an interest therein) only if the financial subsidiary engages only in activities that are financial in nature or incidental to a financial activity, and activities that are permitted for national banks to engage in directly (subject to the same terms and conditions that govern the conduct of the activities by a national bank).[15] The GLBA provisions concerning activities that are "financial in nature" is discussed in § 10, *infra*.

5.2. *The business of banking.* Depository institutions are creatures of their constitutive statutes, a condition that courts have traditionally interpreted as limiting their transactional powers to whatever is provided for in such a statute.[16] Depository institutions generally have authority only to exercise express statutory powers and powers necessarily incident to those express powers.[17] Among the typical express powers found in these statutes is the power to carry on the "business of banking."[18] But what *is* the business of banking? Consider the following excerpt.

Michael P. Malloy, Principles of Bank Regulation

§ 5.1 (3d ed. 2011)

Carrying on the business of banking . . . has become a complicated undertaking. The statutory language that supports it is complex. In the case of national banks, the language begins simply enough, with the mandate that a national bank has the power "[t]o exercise by

---

12. *See* 12 U.S.C. § 24a(g)(3), which defines "financial subsidiary" to mean a company controlled by one or more insured depository institutions *other than a subsidiary* that:

> (A) engages solely in activities that national banks are permitted to engage in directly and are conducted subject to the same terms and conditions that govern the conduct of such activities by national banks; or
>
> (B) a national bank is specifically authorized . . . to control . . . by . . . the Bank Service Company Act.

13. On the meaning of the term "financial activity" for these purposes, see *id.* §§ 24a(b), 1843(k)(4).

14. *Id.* § 24a(a)(1).

15. *Id.* § 24a(a)(2)(A)(i)-(ii).

16. *See, e.g., City of Yonkers v. Downey*, 309 U.S. 590 (1940) (using statutory provisions as measure of bank's powers); *Texas & Pac. Ry. Co. v. Pottorff*, 291 U.S. 245 (1934), *rehearing denied*, 292 U.S. 600 (using statutory provisions as measure of bank's powers); *First Nat'l Bank of St. Louis v. Missouri*, 263 U.S. 640 (1924) (limiting national banks to express statutory powers and necessary incidental powers); *Easton v. Iowa*, 188 U.S. 220 (1903); *California Sav. Bank v. Kennedy*, 167 U.S. 362 (1897) (limiting banks to express statutory powers and necessary incidental powers); *Logan County Nat'l Bank v. Townsend*, 139 U.S. 67 (1891) (limiting national banks to express statutory powers and necessary incidental powers); *Kimen v. Atlas Exch. Nat'l Bank of Chicago*, 92 F.2d 615 (7th Cir. 1937), *cert. denied sub nom. Awotin v. Healy*, 303 U.S. 650 (1938); *Berylwood Inv. Co. v. Graham*, 111 P.2d 467 (Cal. App. 1941); *Commonwealth Trust Co. v. First-Second Nat'l Bank*, 103 A. 598 (Pa. 1918), *cert. denied*, 246 U.S. 675.

17. *Williams v. Merchants' Nat'l Bank of St. Cloud*, 42 F.2d 243 (D. Minn. 1930); *Suburban Trust Co. v. National Bank of Westfield*, 211 F. Supp. 694 (D.N.J. 1962); *Bank of California v. Portland*, 69 P.2d 273 (Ore. 1937), *cert. denied*, 302 U.S. 765.

18. 12 U.S.C. § 24(Seventh).

its board of directors or duly authorized officers or agents, subject to law, all such incidental powers as shall be necessary to carry on the business of banking."[1] This seems inverted; the statute expressly grants the incidental powers before the express powers of which they are incidental are even specified. There follows a disjointed list of five activities that appear to represent "the business of banking,"[2] though the text does not so identify them:

> by discounting and negotiating promissory notes, drafts, bills of exchange, and other evidences of debt; by receiving deposits; by buying and selling exchange, coin, and bullion; by loaning money on personal security; and by obtaining, issuing, and circulating notes. . . .[3]

By a later amendment of the section, we are told that "[t]he business of dealing in securities and stock by the association shall be limited to purchasing and selling such securities and stock without recourse, solely upon the order, and for the account of, customers, and in no case for its own account, and [a national bank] shall not underwrite any issue of securities or stock,"[4] with certain exceptions with respect to eligible "investment securities."

2. Lending

Once entry into the regulated industry of banking has been achieved, the next question that arises is the extent of the powers available to the depository institution under its charter. Typically, the charter or articles of the institution will say very little about the powers available. Unlike general business corporations operating under typical modern business corporation statutes, however, depository institutions remain, in a very real sense, creatures of the statute under which their charters were granted. It is in the pertinent banking or depository institutions statute that the extent of available powers will be found.

In this section, we shall examine the typical regulatory restrictions on loan activities of depository institutions. These restrictions include: (*i*) limitations on aggregate amounts of loans to any one borrower ("lending limitations"); (*ii*) limitations on certain types of loans, apart from or in addition to general lending limitations; and, (*iii*) prohibitions against usurious rates of interest charged on loans. For purposes of discussion, the model which will be used is the regulation of loan activities of national banks.

---

1. [12 U.S.C. § 24(Seventh).]

2. *See, e.g., First Nat'l Bank v. Nat'l Exch. Bank*, 92 U.S. (2 Otto) 122 (1875) (construing language not as limitation on incidental powers, but as description of "banking").

3. 12 U.S.C.A. § 24(Seventh). On discounting and negotiating, see *National Bank v. Johnson*, 104 U.S. (14 Otto) 271 (1881); *National Bank of the Republic v. Price*, 234 P. 231 (Utah 1923). *Cf. Cooper v. National Bank of Savannah*, 94 S.E. 611 (Ga. 1917), *aff'd sub nom. Evans v. National Bank of Savannah*, 251 U.S. 108 (1918) (holding power to discount includes power to take interest in advance). On the power to accept deposits, see *Eastern Townships Bank v. Vermont Nat'l Bank*, 22 F. 186 (D. Vt. 1884). On the power to make loans, see *First Nat'l Bank v. Harris*, 27 F.2d 117 (8th Cir. 1928); *Murphy v. Hanna*, 164 N.W. 32 (N.D. 1917).

4. 12 U.S.C. § 24(Seventh). On the meaning of "without recourse" for these purposes, see *Awotin* [*v. Atlas Exch. Nat'l Bank of Chicago*, 295 U.S. 209 (1935)]; *Genessee Trustee Corp. v. Smith*, 102 F.2d 125 (6th Cir. 1939).

a. Lending Limitations

In the absence of general limitations on the aggregate amount of loans which may be extended to any one borrower, it is not inconceivable that a depository institution might begin to experience an undue concentration of loans to a single borrower or group of borrowers. The end result would be that, to a significant extent, the stability of the institution would become more and more tied to the financial soundness and success of its borrower. Delays by the borrower in fulfilling its payment obligations might then have a serious effect on the institution's liquidity. Such delays, coupled with a sudden demand for withdrawal from depositors could quickly move the institution into a "troubled" status.[19] In the worst case, where the major borrower actually collapses financially and defaults on the loans, it is possible that this could result in a "run" on the bank by its depositors and the collapse of the bank itself. The damage to public confidence in the banking system as a whole which may result from the situation of a "failed" bank[20] also cannot be ignored. Accordingly, one of the core purposes of general lending limitations is to require a bank to diversify the risks attendant upon its lending activities, by limiting the extent to which its fate can be tied to the continuing stability of any single borrower or group of borrowers.

For national banks, the key provision in this regard is 12 U.S.C. § 84. The lending limitation applied to aggregate outstanding loans and extensions of credit of any given borrower is determined as a percentage of the bank's unimpaired capital and surplus, not its total deposits. Thus, commercial risk with respect to each borrower is linked to the bank's capital liquidity; shareholders, rather than depositors are expected to bear the risk of a bank failure.

Section 84 provides two basic percentage limitations. As to total loans and extensions of credit[21] outstanding to any one person[22] at any one time, where the loans and extensions of credit are not fully secured, the total must not exceed 15 percent of the unimpaired capital and surplus of the bank.[23]

As to total loans and extensions of credit outstanding to any one person at any one time, where the loans or extensions of credit are fully secured "by readily marketable collateral having a market value . . . at least equal to the amount of the funds outstanding," the total must not exceed 10 percent of the unimpaired capital and surplus of the bank.[24] This percentage limitation is calculated separately from and in addition to the percentage limitation for loans and extensions not fully secured by § 84(a)(2)-type collateral.[25]

The Comptroller is given full authority to prescribe rules and regulations, not only to administer the lending limitations, but also to "define and further define" the terms of the section, and even to establish limits or requirements other than those set forth in the section for any category of loans and extensions of credit.[26] In addition, the Comptroller is given authority to determine when loans purportedly extended to different "persons" should be aggregated as loans to a single person for purposes of determining compliance with the

---

19. The concept of a "troubled" depository institution is discussed in Chapter 8, § 2, *infra*.

20. "Failed" banks are discussed in Chapter 8, § 3, *infra*.

21. For the definition of "loans and extensions of credit," see 12 U.S.C. § 84(b)(1).

22. For the definition of "person," see *id.* § 84(b)(2).

23. *Id.* § 84(a)(1).

24. *Id.* § 84(a)(2).

25. *Id.*

26. *Id.* § 84(d)(1).

limitations.[27]

While the two basic percentage limitations would seem to be fairly mechanical and definite restrictions on loan activities, they may be often swallowed by the exceptions provided in section 84(c). These exceptions should be examined carefully, as much of counsel's interpretive efforts may be taken up with determining whether or not an exception applies to a particular loan or extension of credit. As a general rule, the exceptions seem to concern situations in which the risk to the lender-bank does not present the dangers typically manifested in the usual commercial loan or extension of credit. In reviewing the exceptions, consider in what way, and to what extent, this general rule is illustrated in each exception.

Enforcement of the lending limitations may occur in several ways. Keep in mind that national banks are subject to periodic examination by national bank examiners. Failure to follow the requirements of section 84, or failure to correct deficiencies in accordance with the directives of the Comptroller's Office once uncovered, may result in the application of the sanctions authorized by 12 U.S.C. § 1818. In addition, 12 U.S.C. § 93(a) is also available, and may result in personal liability of any director who participated in or assented to the granting of a loan or other extension of credit in violation of section 84.

Acting under the authority granted him by 12 U.S.C. § 84, the Comptroller has issued a series of interpretive rulings concerning the application of the lending limitations. These were originally collected in 12 C.F.R. pt. 7. However, Section 401(a) of the Garn-St Germain Depository Institutions Act, Pub. L. No. 97-320, October 15, 1982, substantially revised section 84. Accordingly, the Comptroller amended his regulations, revoking most of the applicable provisions in part 7, and promulgating a new set of rules codified at 12 C.F.R. pt. 32.

Notes and Comments 5.3. Review the following excerpts from the Comptroller's regulations with a view to answering the questions posed in the Notes appearing after the excerpts.

Office of the Comptroller of the Currency
National Bank Lending Limits

12 C.F.R. pts. 3, 32

§ 3.100 Capital and surplus.

For purposes of determining statutory limits that are based on the amount of bank's "capital" and/or "surplus," the provisions of this section are to be used. . . .

(a) Capital. The term "capital" as used in provisions of law relating to the capital of national banking associations shall include the amount of common stock outstanding and unimpaired plus the amount of perpetual preferred stock outstanding and unimpaired.

(b) Capital Stock. The term "capital stock" as used in provisions of law relating to the capital stock of national banking associations, other than 12 U.S.C. 101, 177 and 178, shall have the same meaning as the term "capital" set forth in paragraph (a) of this section.

(c) Surplus. The term "surplus" as used in provisions of law relating to the surplus of national banking associations means the sum of paragraphs (c) (1), (2), (3) and (4) of this section:

(1) Capital surplus; undivided profits; reserves for contingencies and other capital reserves (excluding accrued dividends on perpetual and limited life preferred stock); net worth certificates issued pursuant to 12 U.S.C. 1823(i); minority interests in consolidated

27. *Id.* § 84(d)(2).

subsidiaries; and allowances for loan and lease losses; minus intangible assets;

(2) Mortgage servicing rights;

(3) Mandatory convertible debt to the extent of 20% of the sum of paragraphs (a) and (c) (1) and (2) of this section;

(4) Other mandatory convertible debt, limited life preferred stock and subordinated notes and debentures to the extent set forth in paragraph (f)(2) of this section.

(d) Unimpaired Surplus Fund. The term "unimpaired surplus fund" as used in provisions of law relating to the unimpaired surplus fund of national banking associations shall have the same meaning as the term "surplus" set forth in paragraph (c) of this section.

(e) Definitions.

(1) "Allowance for loan and lease losses" means the balance of the valuation reserve on December 31, 1968, plus additions to the reserve charged to operations since that date, less losses charged against the allowance net of recoveries.

(2) "Capital surplus" means the total of those accounts reflecting:

(i) Amounts paid in excess of the par or stated value of capital stock;

(ii) Amounts contributed to the bank other than for capital stock;

(iii) Amounts transferred from undivided profits pursuant to 12 U.S.C. 60; and

(iv) Other amounts transferred from undivided profits.

(3) "Intangible assets" means those purchased assets that are to be reported as intangible assets in accordance with the "Instructions -- Consolidated Reports of Condition and Income" (Call Report).

(4) "Limited Life preferred stock" means preferred stock which has a maturity or which may be redeemed at the option of the holder.

(5) "Mandatory convertible debt" means subordinated debt instruments which unqualifiedly require the issuer to exchange either common or perpetual preferred stock for such instruments by a date at or before the maturity of the instrument. The maturity of these instruments must be 12 years or less. In addition, the instrument must meet the requirements of paragraph (f)(1)(i) through (v) of this section for subordinated notes and debentures or other requirements published by the OCC.

(6) "Minority interest in consolidated subsidiaries" means the portion of equity capital accounts of all consolidated subsidiaries of the bank that is allocated to minority shareholders of such subsidiaries.

(7) "Mortgage servicing rights" means the bank-owned rights to service for a fee mortgage loans that are owned by others.

(8) "Perpetual preferred stock" means preferred stock that does not have a stated maturity date and cannot be redeemed at the option of the holder.

(f) Requirements and restrictions: Limited life preferred stock, mandatory convertible debt, and other subordinated debt --

(1) Requirements. Issues of limited life preferred stock and subordinated notes and debentures (except mandatory convertible debt) shall have original weighted average maturities of at least five years to be included in the definition of surplus. In addition, a subordinated note or debenture must also:

(i) Be subordinated to the claims of depositors;

(ii) State on the instrument that it is not a deposit and is not insured by the FDIC;

(iii) Be unsecured;

(iv) Be ineligible as collateral for a loan by the issuing bank;

(v) Provide that once any scheduled payments of principal begin, all scheduled payments shall be made at least annually and the amount repaid in each year shall be no less than in the prior year; and

(vi) Provide that no prepayment (including payment pursuant to an acceleration clause or redemption prior to maturity) shall be made without prior OCC approval. . . .

(2) Restrictions. The total amount of mandatory convertible debt not included in paragraph (c)(3) of this section, limited life preferred stock, and subordinated notes and debentures considered as surplus is limited to 50 percent of the sum of paragraphs (a) and (c) (1), (2) and (3) of this section.

(3) Reservation of authority. The OCC expressly reserves the authority to waive the requirements and restrictions set forth in paragraphs (f)(1) and (2) of this section, in order to allow the inclusion of other limited life preferred stock, mandatory convertible notes and subordinated notes and debentures in the capital base of any national bank for capital adequacy purposes or for purposes of determining statutory limits. The OCC further expressly reserves the authority to impose more stringent conditions than those set forth in paragraphs (f)(1) and (2) of this section to exclude any component of Tier 1 or Tier 2 capital, in whole or in part, as part of a national bank's capital and surplus for any purpose.

(g) Transitional rules.

(1) Equity commitment notes approved by the OCC as capital and issued prior to April 15, 1985, may continue to be included in paragraph (c)(3) of this section. All other instruments approved by the OCC as capital and issued prior to April 15, 1985, are to be included in paragraph (c)(4) of this section.

(2) Intangible assets (other than mortgage servicing rights) purchased prior to April 15, 1985, and accounted for in accordance with OCC instructions, may continue to be included as surplus up to 25% of the sum of paragraphs (a) and (c)(1) of this section.

§ 32.1 Authority, purpose and scope.

(a) Authority. This part is issued pursuant to 12 U.S.C. 1 et seq., 12 U.S.C. 84, and 12 U.S.C. 93a.

(b) Purpose. The purpose of this part is to protect the safety and soundness of national banks by preventing excessive loans to one person, or to related persons that are financially dependent, and to promote diversification of loans and equitable access to banking services.

(c) Scope.

(1) This part applies to all loans and extensions of credit made by national banks and their domestic operating subsidiaries. This part does not apply to loans made by a national bank and its domestic operating subsidiaries to the bank's "affiliates," as that term is defined in 12 U.S.C. 371c(b)(1) and (e), as implemented by section 223.2(a) of Regulation W to the bank's operating subsidiaries. . . .

(2) The lending limits in this part are separate and independent from the investment limits prescribed by 12 U.S.C. 24 (Seventh), and a national bank may make loans or extensions of credit to one borrower up to the full amount permitted by this part and also hold eligible securities of the same obligor up to the full amount permitted under 12 U.S.C. 24 (Seventh) and 12 CFR part 1.

(3) Extensions of credit to executive officers, directors and principal shareholders of national banks, and their related interests are subject to limits prescribed by 12 U.S.C. 375a and 375b in addition to the lending limits established by 12 U.S.C. 84 and this part.

(4) In addition to the foregoing, loans and extensions of credit made by national banks and their domestic operating subsidiaries must be consistent with safe and sound banking practices.

§ 32.2 Definitions.

(a) Borrower means a person who is named as a borrower or debtor in a loan or extension of credit, or any other person, including a drawer, endorser, or guarantor, who is deemed to be a borrower under the "direct benefit" or the "common enterprise" tests set forth in § 32.5. . . .

(c) Close of business means the time at which a bank closes its accounting records for the business day.

(d) Consumer means the user of any products, commodities, goods, or services, whether leased or purchased, but does not include any person who purchases products or commodities for resale or fabrication into goods for sale.

(e) Consumer paper means paper relating to automobiles, mobile homes, residences, office equipment, household items, tuition fees, insurance premium fees, and similar consumer items. Consumer paper also includes paper covering the lease (where the bank is not the owner or lessor) or purchase of equipment for use in manufacturing, farming, construction, or excavation.

(f) Contractual commitment to advance funds.

(1) The term includes a bank's obligation to–

(i) Make payment (directly or indirectly) to a third person contingent upon default by a customer of the bank in performing an obligation and to make such payment in keeping with the agreed upon terms of the customer's contract with the third person, or to make payments upon some other stated condition;

(ii) Guarantee or act as surety for the benefit of a person;

(iii) Advance funds under a qualifying commitment to lend, as defined in paragraph (l) of this section; and

(iv) Advance funds under a standby letter of credit as defined in paragraph (p) of this section, a put, or other similar arrangement.

(2) The term does not include commercial letters of credit and similar instruments where the issuing bank expects the beneficiary to draw on the issuer, that do not guarantee payment, and that do not provide for payment in the event of a default by a third party.

(g) Control is presumed to exist when a person directly or indirectly, or acting through or together with one or more persons–

(1) Owns, controls, or has the power to vote 25 percent or more of any class of voting securities of another person;

(2) Controls, in any manner, the election of a majority of the directors, trustees, or other persons exercising similar functions of another person; or

(3) Has the power to exercise a controlling influence over the management or policies of another person.

(h) Current market value means the bid or closing price listed for an item in a regularly published listing or an electronic reporting service.

(i) Eligible bank means a national bank that:

(1) Is well capitalized . . . ; and

(2) Has a composite rating of 1 or 2 under the Uniform Financial Institutions Rating System in connection with the bank's most recent examination or subsequent review, with at least a rating of 2 for asset quality and for management.

(j) Financial instrument means stocks, notes, bonds, and debentures traded on a national securities exchange, OTC margin stocks as defined in Regulation U, 12 CFR part 221, commercial paper, negotiable certificates of deposit, bankers' acceptances, and shares in money market and mutual funds of the type that issue shares in which banks may perfect a security interest. Financial instruments may be denominated in foreign currencies that are freely convertible to U.S. dollars. The term "financial instrument" does not include mortgages.

(k) Loans and extensions of credit means a bank's direct or indirect advance of funds to or on behalf of a borrower based on an obligation of the borrower to repay the funds or repayable from specific property pledged by or on behalf of the borrower.

(1) Loans or extensions of credit for purposes of 12 U.S.C. 84 and this part include–

(i) A contractual commitment to advance funds, as defined in paragraph (f) of this section;

(ii) A maker or endorser's obligation arising from a bank's discount of commercial paper;

(iii) A bank's purchase of securities subject to an agreement that the seller will repurchase the securities at the end of a stated period, but not including a bank's purchase of Type I securities, as defined in part 1 of this chapter, subject to a repurchase agreement, where the purchasing bank has assured control over or has established its rights to the Type I securities as collateral;

(iv) A bank's purchase of third-party paper subject to an agreement that the seller will repurchase the paper upon default or at the end of a stated period. The amount of the bank's loan is the total unpaid balance of the paper owned by the bank less any applicable dealer reserves retained by the bank and held by the bank as collateral security. Where the seller's obligation to repurchase is limited, the bank's loan is measured by the total amount of the paper the seller may ultimately be obligated to repurchase. A bank's purchase of third party paper without direct or indirect recourse to the seller is not a loan or extension of credit to the seller;

(v) An overdraft, whether or not prearranged, but not an intra-day overdraft for which payment is received before the close of business of the bank that makes the funds available;

(vi) The sale of Federal funds with a maturity of more than one business day, but not Federal funds with a maturity of one day or less or Federal funds sold under a continuing contract; and

(vii) Loans or extensions of credit that have been charged off on the books of the bank in whole or in part, unless the loan or extension of credit --

(A) Is unenforceable by reason of discharge in bankruptcy;

(B) Is no longer legally enforceable because of expiration of the statute of limitations or a judicial decision; or

(C) Is no longer legally enforceable for other reasons, provided that the bank maintains sufficient records to demonstrate that the loan is unenforceable.

(2) The following items do not constitute loans or extensions of credit for purposes of 12 U.S.C. 84 and this part–

(i) Additional funds advanced for the benefit of a borrower by a bank for payment of taxes, insurance, utilities, security, and maintenance and operating expenses necessary to preserve the value of real property securing the loan, consistent with safe and sound banking practices, but only if the advance is for the protection of the bank's interest in the collateral, and provided that such amounts must be treated as an extension of credit if a new loan or extension of credit is made to the borrower;

(ii) Accrued and discounted interest on an existing loan or extension of credit, including interest that has been capitalized from prior notes and interest that has been advanced under terms and conditions of a loan agreement;

(iii) Financed sales of a bank's own assets, including Other Real Estate Owned, if the financing does not put the bank in a worse position than when the bank held title to the assets;

(iv) A renewal or restructuring of a loan as a new "loan or extension of credit," following the exercise by a bank of reasonable efforts, consistent with safe and sound banking practices, to bring the loan into conformance with the lending limit, unless new funds are advanced by the bank to the borrower (except as permitted by § 32.3(b)(5)), or a new borrower replaces the original borrower, or unless the OCC determines that a renewal or restructuring was undertaken as a means to evade the bank's lending limit;

(v) Amounts paid against uncollected funds in the normal process of collection; and

(vi)(A) That portion of a loan or extension of credit sold as a participation by a bank on a nonrecourse basis, provided that the participation results in a pro rata sharing of credit risk proportionate to the respective interests of the originating and participating lenders. Where a participation agreement provides that repayment must be applied first to the portions sold, a pro rata sharing will be deemed to exist only if the agreement also provides that, in the event of a default or comparable event defined in the agreement, participants must share in all subsequent repayments and collections in proportion to their percentage participation at the time of the occurrence of the event.

(B) When an originating bank funds the entire loan, it must receive funding from the participants before the close of business of its next business day. If the participating portions are not received within that period, then the portions funded will be treated as a loan by the originating bank to the borrower. If the portions so attributed to the borrower exceed the originating bank's lending limit, the loan may be treated as nonconforming subject to § 32.6, rather than a violation, if:

(1) The originating bank had a valid and unconditional participation agreement with a participating bank or banks that was sufficient to reduce the loan to within the originating bank's lending limit;

(2) The participating bank reconfirmed its participation and the originating bank had no knowledge of any information that would permit the participant to withhold its participation; and

(3) The participation was to be funded by close of business of the originating bank's next business day.

(*l*) Person means an individual; sole proprietorship; partnership; joint venture; association; trust; estate; business trust; corporation; limited liability company; not-for-profit corporation; sovereign government or agency, instrumentality, or political subdivision thereof; or any similar entity or organization.

(m) Qualifying commitment to lend means a legally binding written commitment to lend that, when combined with all other outstanding loans and qualifying commitments to a borrower, was within the bank's lending limit when entered into, and has not been disqualified.

(1) In determining whether a commitment is within the bank's lending limit when made, the bank may deduct from the amount of the commitment the amount of any legally binding loan participation commitments that are issued concurrent with the bank's commitment and that would be excluded from the definition of "loan or extension of credit" under paragraph (j)(2)(vi) of this section.

(2) If the bank subsequently chooses to make an additional loan and that subsequent loan, together with all outstanding loans and qualifying commitments to a borrower, exceeds the bank's applicable lending limit at that time, the bank's qualifying commitments to the borrower that exceed the bank's lending limit at that time are deemed to be permanently disqualified, beginning with the most recent qualifying commitment and proceeding in reverse chronological order. When a commitment is disqualified, the entire commitment is disqualified and the disqualified commitment is no longer considered a "loan or extension of credit." Advances of funds under a disqualified or non-qualifying commitment may only be made to the extent that the advance, together with all other outstanding loans to the borrower, do not exceed the bank's lending limit at the time of the advance, calculated pursuant to § 32.4.

(n) Readily marketable collateral means financial instruments and bullion that are salable under ordinary market conditions with reasonable promptness at a fair market value determined by quotations based upon actual transactions on an auction or similarly available daily bid and ask price market.

(o) Readily marketable staple means an article of commerce, agriculture, or industry, such as wheat and other grains, cotton, wool, and basic metals such as tin, copper and lead, in the form of standardized interchangeable units, that is easy to sell in a market with sufficiently frequent price quotations.

(1) An article comes within this definition if–

(i) The exact price is easy to determine; and

(ii) The staple itself is easy to sell at any time at a price that would not be considerably less than the amount at which it is valued as collateral.

(2) Whether an article qualifies as a readily marketable staple is determined on the basis of the conditions existing at the time the loan or extension of credit that is secured by the staples is made.

(p) Residential real estate loan means a loan or extension of credit that is secured by 1-4 family residential real estate.

(q) Sale of Federal funds means any transaction between depository institutions involving the transfer of immediately available funds resulting from credits to deposit balances at Federal Reserve Banks, or from credits to new or existing deposit balances due from a correspondent depository institution.

(r) Small business loan means a loan or extension of credit "secured by nonfarm nonresidential properties" or "a commercial or industrial loan" as defined in the instructions for preparation of the Consolidated Report of Condition and Income. . . .

(t) Standby letter of credit means any letter of credit, or similar arrangement, that represents an obligation to the beneficiary on the part of the issuer:

(1) To repay money borrowed by or advanced to or for the account of the account party;

(2) To make payment on account of any indebtedness undertaken by the account party; or

(3) To make payment on account of any default by the account party in the performance of an obligation.

§ 32.3 Lending limits.

(a) Combined general limit. A national bank's total outstanding loans and extensions of credit to one borrower may not exceed 15 percent of the bank's capital and surplus, plus an additional 10 percent of the bank's capital and surplus, if the amount that exceeds the bank's 15 percent general limit is fully secured by readily marketable collateral, as defined in § 32.2(m). To qualify for the additional 10 percent limit, the bank must perfect a security interest in the collateral under applicable law and the collateral must have a current market value at all times of at least 100 percent of the amount of the loan or extension of credit that exceeds the bank's 15 percent general limit.

(b) Loans subject to special lending limits. The following loans or extensions of credit are subject to the lending limits set forth below. When loans and extensions of credit qualify for more than one special lending limit, the special limits are cumulative.

(1) Loans secured by bills of lading or warehouse receipts covering readily marketable staples.

(i) A national bank's loans or extensions of credit to one borrower secured by bills of lading, warehouse receipts, or similar documents transferring or securing title to readily marketable staples, as defined in § 32.2(n), may not exceed 35 percent of the bank's capital and surplus in addition to the amount allowed under the bank's combined general limit. The market value of the staples securing the loan must at all times equal at least 115 percent of the amount of the outstanding loan that exceeds the bank's combined general limit.

(ii) Staples that qualify for this special limit must be nonperishable, may be refrigerated or frozen, and must be fully covered by insurance if such insurance is customary. Whether a staple is non-perishable must be determined on a case-by-case basis because of differences in handling and storing commodities.

(iii) This special limit applies to a loan or extension of credit arising from a single transaction or secured by the same staples, provided that the duration of the loan or extension of credit is:

(A) Not more than ten months if secured by nonperishable staples; or

(B) Not more than six months if secured by refrigerated or frozen staples.

(iv) The holder of the warehouse receipts, order bills of lading, documents qualifying as documents of title under the Uniform Commercial Code, or other similar documents, must have control and be able to obtain immediate possession of the staple so that the bank is able to sell the underlying staples and promptly transfer title and possession to a purchaser if default should occur on a loan secured by such documents. The existence of a brief notice period, or similar procedural requirements under applicable law, for the disposal of the collateral will not affect the eligibility of the instruments for this special limit.

(A) Field warehouse receipts are an acceptable form of collateral when issued by a duly bonded and licensed grain elevator or warehouse having exclusive possession and control of the staples even though the grain elevator or warehouse is maintained on the premises of the owner of the staples.

(B) Warehouse receipts issued by the borrower-owner that is a grain elevator or warehouse company, duly-bonded and licensed and regularly inspected by state or Federal authorities, may be considered eligible collateral under this provision only when the receipts are registered with an independent registrar whose consent is required before the staples may be withdrawn from the warehouse.

(2) Discount of installment consumer paper.

(i) A national bank's loans and extensions of credit to one borrower that arise from the discount of negotiable or nonnegotiable installment consumer paper, as defined at § 32.2(e), that carries a full recourse endorsement or unconditional guarantee by the person selling the paper, may not exceed 10 percent of the bank's capital and surplus in addition to the amount allowed under the bank's combined general limit. An unconditional guarantee may be in the form of a repurchase agreement or separate guarantee agreement. A condition reasonably within the power of the bank to perform, such as the repossession of collateral, will not make conditional an otherwise unconditional guarantee.

(ii) Where the seller of the paper offers only partial recourse to the bank, the lending limits of this section apply to the obligation of the seller to the bank, which is measured by the total amount of paper the seller may be obligated to repurchase or has guaranteed.

(iii) Where the bank is relying primarily upon the maker of the paper for payment of the loans or extensions of credit and not upon any full or partial recourse endorsement or guarantee by the seller of the paper, the lending limits of this section apply only to the maker. The bank must substantiate its reliance on the maker with --

(A) Records supporting the bank's independent credit analysis of the maker's ability to repay the loan or extension of credit, maintained by the bank or by a third party that is contractually obligated to make those records available for examination purposes; and

(B) A written certification by an officer of the bank authorized by the bank's board of directors or any designee of that officer, that the bank is relying primarily upon the maker to repay the loan or extension of credit.

(iv) Where paper is purchased in substantial quantities, the records, evaluation, and certification must be in a form appropriate for the class and quantity of paper involved. The bank may use sampling techniques, or other appropriate methods, to independently verify the reliability of the credit information supplied by the seller.

(3) Loans secured by documents covering livestock.

(i) A national bank's loans or extensions of credit to one borrower secured by shipping documents or instruments that transfer or secure title to or give a first lien on livestock may not exceed 10 percent of the bank's capital and surplus in addition to the amount allowed under the bank's combined general limit. The market value of the livestock securing the loan must at all times equal at least 115 percent of the amount of the outstanding loan that exceeds the bank's combined general limit. For purposes of this subsection, the term "livestock" includes dairy and beef cattle, hogs, sheep, goats, horses, mules, poultry and fish, whether or not held for resale.

(ii) The bank must maintain in its files an inspection and valuation for the livestock pledged that is reasonably current, taking into account the nature and frequency of turnover of the livestock to which the documents relate, but in any case not more than 12 months old.

(iii) Under the laws of certain states, persons furnishing pasturage under a grazing contract may have a lien on the livestock for the amount due for pasturage. If a lien that is based on pasturage furnished by the lienor prior to the bank's loan or extension of credit is assigned to the bank by a recordable instrument and protected against being defeated by some other lien or claim, by payment to a person other than the bank, or otherwise, it will qualify under this exception provided the amount of the perfected lien is at least equal to the amount of the loan and the value of the livestock is at no time less than 115 percent of the portion of the loan or extension of credit that exceeds the bank's combined general limit. When the amount due under the grazing contract is dependent upon future performance, the resulting lien does not meet the requirements of the exception.

(4) Loans secured by dairy cattle. A national bank's loans and extensions of credit to one borrower that arise from the discount by dealers in dairy cattle of paper given in payment for the cattle may not exceed 10 percent of the bank's capital and surplus in addition to the amount allowed under the bank's combined general limit. To qualify, the paper–

(i) Must carry the full recourse endorsement or unconditional guarantee of the seller; and

(ii) Must be secured by the cattle being sold, pursuant to liens that allow the bank to maintain a perfected security interest in the cattle under applicable law.

(5) Additional advances to complete project financing pursuant to renewal of a qualifying commitment to lend. A national bank may renew a qualifying commitment to lend, as defined by § 32.2(l), and complete funding under that commitment if all of the following criteria are met–

(i) The completion of funding is consistent with safe and sound banking practices and is made to protect the position of the bank;

(ii) The completion of funding will enable the borrower to complete the project for which the qualifying commitment to lend was made; and

(iii) The amount of the additional funding does not exceed the unfunded portion of the bank's qualifying commitment to lend.

(c) Loans not subject to the lending limits. The following loans or extensions of credit are not subject to the lending limits of 12 U.S.C. 84 or this part.

(1) Loans arising from the discount of commercial or business paper.

(i) Loans or extensions of credit arising from the discount of negotiable commercial or business paper that evidences an obligation to the person negotiating the paper. The paper–

(A) Must be given in payment of the purchase price of commodities purchased for resale, fabrication of a product, or any other business purpose that may reasonably be expected to provide funds for payment of the paper; and

(B) Must bear the full recourse endorsement of the owner of the paper, except that paper discounted in connection with export transactions, that is transferred without recourse, or with limited recourse, must be supported by an assignment of appropriate insurance covering the political, credit, and transfer risks applicable to the paper, such as insurance provided by the Export-Import Bank.

(ii) A failure to pay principal or interest on commercial or business paper when due does not result in a loan or extension of credit to the maker or endorser of the paper; however, the amount of such paper thereafter must be counted in determining whether additional loans or extensions of credit to the same borrower may be made within the limits of 12 U.S.C. 84 and this part.

(2) Bankers' acceptances. A bank's acceptance of drafts eligible for rediscount under 12 U.S.C. 372 and 373, or a bank's purchase of acceptances created by other banks that are eligible for rediscount under those sections; but not including–

(i) A bank's acceptance of drafts ineligible for rediscount (which constitutes a loan by the bank to the customer for whom the acceptance was made, in the amount of the draft);

(ii) A bank's purchase of ineligible acceptances created by other banks (which constitutes a loan from the purchasing bank to the accepting bank, in the amount of the purchase price); and

(iii) A bank's purchase of its own acceptances (which constitutes a loan to the bank's customer for whom the acceptance was made, in the amount of the purchase price).

(3)(i) Loans secured by U.S. obligations. Loans or extensions of credit, or portions thereof, to the extent fully secured by the current market value of:

(A) Bonds, notes, certificates of indebtedness, or Treasury bills of the United States or by similar obligations fully guaranteed as to principal and interest by the United States;

(B) Loans to the extent guaranteed as to repayment of principal by the full faith and credit of the U.S. government, as set forth in paragraph (c)(4)(ii) of this section.

(ii) To qualify under this paragraph, the bank must perfect a security interest in the collateral under applicable law.

(4) Loans to or guaranteed by a Federal agency.

(i) Loans or extensions of credit to any department, agency, bureau, board, commission, or establishment of the United States or any corporation wholly owned directly or indirectly by the United States.

(ii) Loans or extensions of credit, including portions thereof, to the extent secured by unconditional takeout commitments or guarantees of any of the foregoing governmental entities. The commitment or guarantee–

(A) Must be payable in cash or its equivalent within 60 days after demand for payment is made;

(B) Is considered unconditional if the protection afforded the bank is not substantially diminished or impaired if loss should result from factors beyond the bank's control. Protection against loss is not materially diminished or impaired by procedural requirements, such as an agreement to take over only in the event of default, including default over a specific period of time, a requirement that notification of default be given within a specific period after its occurrence, or a requirement of good faith on the part of the bank.

(5) Loans to or guaranteed by general obligations of a State or political subdivision. (i) A loan or extension of credit to a State or political subdivision that constitutes a general obligation of the State or political subdivision, as defined in part 1 of this chapter, and for which the lending bank has an opinion of counsel or the opinion of that State Attorney General, or other State legal official with authority to opine on the obligation in question, that

the loan or extension of credit is a valid and enforceable general obligation of the borrower; and

(ii) A loan or extension of credit, including portions thereof, to the extent guaranteed or secured by a general obligation of a State or political subdivision and for which the lending bank has an opinion of counsel or the opinion of that State Attorney General, or other State legal official with authority to opine on the guarantee or collateral in question, that the guarantee or collateral is a valid and enforceable general obligation of that public body.

(6) Loans secured by segregated deposit accounts. Loans or extensions of credit, including portions thereof, to the extent secured by a segregated deposit account in the lending bank, provided a security interest in the deposit has been perfected under applicable law.

(i) Where the deposit is eligible for withdrawal before the secured loan matures, the bank must establish internal procedures to prevent release of the security without the lending bank's prior consent.

(ii) A deposit that is denominated and payable in a currency other than that of the loan or extension of credit that it secures may be eligible for this exception if the currency is freely convertible to U.S. dollars.

(A) This exception applies to only that portion of the loan or extension of credit that is covered by the U.S. dollar value of the deposit.

(B) The lending bank must establish procedures to revalue foreign currency deposits to ensure that the loan or extension of credit remains fully secured at all times.

(7) Loans to financial institutions with the approval of the Comptroller. Loans or extensions of credit to any financial institution or to any receiver, conservator, superintendent of banks, or other agent in charge of the business and property of a financial institution when an emergency situation exists and a national bank is asked to provide assistance to another financial institution, and the loan is approved by the Comptroller. For purposes of this paragraph, financial institution means a commercial bank, savings bank, trust company, savings association, or credit union.

(8) Loans to the Student Loan Marketing Association. Loans or extensions of credit to the Student Loan Marketing Association.

(9) Loans to industrial development authorities. A loan or extension of credit to an industrial development authority or similar public entity created to construct and lease a plant facility, including a health care facility, to an industrial occupant will be deemed a loan to the lessee, provided that–

(i) The bank evaluates the creditworthiness of the industrial occupant before the loan is extended to the authority;

(ii) The authority's liability on the loan is limited solely to whatever interest it has in the particular facility;

(iii) The authority's interest is assigned to the bank as security for the loan or the industrial occupant issues a promissory note to the bank that provides a higher order of security than the assignment of a lease; and

(iv) The industrial occupant's lease rentals are assigned and paid directly to the bank.

(10) Loans to leasing companies. A loan or extension of credit to a leasing company for the purpose of purchasing equipment for lease will be deemed a loan to the lessee, provided that–

(i) The bank evaluates the creditworthiness of the lessee before the loan is extended to the leasing corporation;

(ii) The loan is without recourse to the leasing corporation;

(iii) The bank is given a security interest in the equipment and in the event of default, may proceed directly against the equipment and the lessee for any deficiency resulting from the sale of the equipment;

(iv) The leasing corporation assigns all of its rights under the lease to the bank;

(v) The lessee's lease payments are assigned and paid to the bank; and

(vi) The lease terms are subject to the same limitations that would apply to a national bank acting as a lessor.

§ 32.4 Calculation of lending limits.

(a) Calculation date. For purposes of determining compliance with 12 U.S.C. 84 and this part, a bank's lending limit shall be calculated as of the most recent of the following dates --

(1) When the bank's Consolidated Report of Condition and Income is required to be filed; or

(2) When there is a change in the bank's capital category for purposes of 12 U.S.C. 1831o. . . .

(b) Authority of OCC to require more frequent calculations. If the OCC determines for safety and soundness reasons that a bank should calculate its lending limit more frequently than required by paragraph (a) of this section, the OCC may provide written notice to the bank directing the bank to calculate its lending limit at a more frequent interval, and the bank shall thereafter calculate its lending limit at that interval until further notice.

§ 32.5 Combination rules.

(a) General rule. Loans or extensions of credit to one borrower will be attributed to another person and each person will be deemed a borrower–

(1) When proceeds of a loan or extension of credit are to be used for the direct benefit of the other person, to the extent of the proceeds so used; or

(2) When a common enterprise is deemed to exist between the persons.

(b) Direct benefit. The proceeds of a loan or extension of credit to a borrower will be deemed to be used for the direct benefit of another person and will be attributed to the other person when the proceeds, or assets purchased with the proceeds, are transferred to another person, other than in a bona fide arm's length transaction where the proceeds are used to acquire property, goods, or services.

(c) Common enterprise. A common enterprise will be deemed to exist and loans to separate borrowers will be aggregated:

(1) When the expected source of repayment for each loan or extension of credit is the same for each borrower and neither borrower has another source of income from which the loan (together with the borrower's other obligations) may be fully repaid. An employer will not be treated as a source of repayment under this paragraph because of wages and salaries paid to an employee, unless the standards of paragraph (c)(2) of this section are met;

(2) When loans or extensions of credit are made–

(i) To borrowers who are related directly or indirectly through common control, including where one borrower is directly or indirectly controlled by another borrower; and

(ii) Substantial financial interdependence exists between or among the borrowers. Substantial financial interdependence is deemed to exist when 50 percent or more of one borrower's gross receipts or gross expenditures (on an annual basis) are derived from transactions with the other borrower. Gross receipts and expenditures include gross revenues/expenses, intercompany loans, dividends, capital contributions, and similar receipts or payments;

(3) When separate persons borrow from a bank to acquire a business enterprise of

which those borrowers will own more than 50 percent of the voting securities or voting interests, in which case a common enterprise is deemed to exist between the borrowers for purposes of combining the acquisition loans; or

(4) When the OCC determines, based upon an evaluation of the facts and circumstances of particular transactions, that a common enterprise exists.

(d) Special rule for loans to a corporate group.

(1) Loans or extensions of credit by a bank to a corporate group may not exceed 50 percent of the bank's capital and surplus. This limitation applies only to loans subject to the combined general limit. A corporate group includes a person and all of its subsidiaries. For purposes of this paragraph, a corporation or a limited liability company is a subsidiary of a person if the person owns or beneficially owns directly or indirectly more than 50 percent of the voting securities or voting interests of the corporation or company.

(2) Except as provided in paragraph (d)(1) of this section, loans or extensions of credit to a person and its subsidiary, or to different subsidiaries of a person, are not combined unless either the direct benefit or the common enterprise test is met.

(e) Special rules for loans to partnerships, joint ventures, and associations–

(1) Partnership loans. Loans or extensions of credit to a partnership, joint venture, or association are deemed to be loans or extensions of credit to each member of the partnership, joint venture, or association. This rule does not apply to limited partners in limited partnerships or to members of joint ventures or associations if the partners or members, by the terms of the partnership or membership agreement, are not held generally liable for the debts or actions of the partnership, joint venture, or association, and those provisions are valid under applicable law.

(2) Loans to partners.

(i) Loans or extensions of credit to members of a partnership, joint venture, or association are not attributed to the partnership, joint venture, or association unless either the direct benefit or the common enterprise tests are met. Both the direct benefit and common enterprise tests are met between a member of a partnership, joint venture or association and such partnership, joint venture or association, when loans or extensions of credit are made to the member to purchase an interest in the partnership, joint venture or association.

(ii) Loans or extensions of credit to members of a partnership, joint venture, or association are not attributed to other members of the partnership, joint venture, or association unless either the direct benefit or common enterprise test is met.

(f) Loans to foreign governments, their agencies, and instrumentalities–

(1) Aggregation. Loans and extensions of credit to foreign governments, their agencies, and instrumentalities will be aggregated with one another only if the loans or extensions of credit fail to meet either the means test or the purpose test at the time the loan or extension of credit is made.

(i) The means test is satisfied if the borrower has resources or revenue of its own sufficient to service its debt obligations. If the government's support (excluding guarantees by a central government of the borrower's debt) exceeds the borrower's annual revenues from other sources, it will be presumed that the means test has not been satisfied.

(ii) The purpose test is satisfied if the purpose of the loan or extension of credit is consistent with the purposes of the borrower's general business.

(2) Documentation. In order to show that the means and purpose tests have been satisfied, a bank must, at a minimum, retain in its files the following items:

(i) A statement (accompanied by supporting documentation) describing the legal status and the degree of financial and operational autonomy of the borrowing entity;

(ii) Financial statements for the borrowing entity for a minimum of three years prior to the date the loan or extension of credit was made or for each year that the borrowing entity has been in existence, if less than three;

(iii) Financial statements for each year the loan or extension of credit is outstanding;

(iv) The bank's assessment of the borrower's means of servicing the loan or extension of credit, including specific reasons in support of that assessment. The assessment shall include an analysis of the borrower's financial history, its present and projected economic and financial performance, and the significance of any financial support provided to the borrower by third parties, including the borrower's central government; and

(v) A loan agreement or other written statement from the borrower which clearly describes the purpose of the loan or extension of credit. The written representation will ordinarily constitute sufficient evidence that the purpose test has been satisfied. However, when, at the time the funds are disbursed, the bank knows or has reason to know of other information suggesting that the borrower will use the proceeds in a manner inconsistent with the written representation, it may not, without further inquiry, accept the representation.

(3) Restructured loans–

(i) Non-combination rule. Notwithstanding paragraphs (a) through (e) of this section, when previously outstanding loans and other extensions of credit to a foreign government, its agencies, and instrumentalities (i.e., public-sector obligors) that qualified for a separate lending limit under paragraph (f)(1) of this section are consolidated under a central obligor in a qualifying restructuring, such loans will not be aggregated and attributed to the central obligor. This includes any substitution in named obligors, solely because of the restructuring. Such loans (other than loans originally attributed to the central obligor in their own right) will not be considered obligations of the central obligor and will continue to be attributed to the original public-sector obligor for purposes of the lending limit.

(ii) Qualifying restructuring. Loans and other extensions of credit to a foreign government, its agencies, and instrumentalities will qualify for the non-combination process under paragraph (f)(3)(i) of this section only if they are restructured in a sovereign debt restructuring approved by the OCC, upon request by a bank for application of the non-combination rule. The factors that the OCC will use in making this determination include, but are not limited to, the following:

(A) Whether the restructuring involves a substantial portion of the total commercial bank loans outstanding to the foreign government, its agencies, and instrumentalities;

(B) Whether the restructuring involves a substantial number of the foreign country's external commercial bank creditors;

(C) Whether the restructuring and consolidation under a central obligor is being done primarily to facilitate external debt management; and

(D) Whether the restructuring includes features of debt or debt-service reduction.

(iii) 50 percent aggregate limit. With respect to any case in which the non-combination process under paragraph (f)(3)(i) of this section applies, a national bank's loans and other extensions of credit to a foreign government, its agencies and instrumentalities, (including restructured debt) shall not exceed, in the aggregate, 50 percent of the bank's capital and surplus.

§ 32.6 Nonconforming loans.

(a) A loan, within a bank's legal lending limit when made, will not be deemed a violation but will be treated as nonconforming if the loan is no longer in conformity with the bank's lending limit because–

(1) The bank's capital has declined, borrowers have subsequently merged or formed a common enterprise, lenders have merged, the lending limit or capital rules have changed; or

(2) Collateral securing the loan to satisfy the requirements of a lending limit

exception has declined in value.

(b) A bank must use reasonable efforts to bring a loan that is nonconforming as a result of paragraph (a)(1) of this section into conformity with the bank's lending limit unless to do so would be inconsistent with safe and sound banking practices.

(c) A bank must bring a loan that is nonconforming as a result of circumstances described in paragraph (a)(2) of this section into conformity with the bank's lending limit within 30 calendar days, except when judicial proceedings, regulatory actions or other extraordinary circumstances beyond the bank's control prevent the bank from taking action.

. . .

Notes and Comments 5.4. In the following problems, determine whether section 84 would prohibit the loan or extension of credit involved. Indicate any other facts or information you may need to make the determination. In each problem, assume that Quarter National Bank has a balance sheet resembling the Consolidated Statement of Condition reproduced in Figure 5.1, *infra*.

Figure 5.1

Quarter National Bank
Consolidated Statement of Condition
June 1, __

Assets		Liabilities		
Cash and Due from Banks	$1,027,982,743	Deposits:		
Securities:		Demand		$ 874,983,331
U.S. Government	172,697,255	Savings		583,568,421
Federal Agency	16,345,250	Other Time		489,972,393
Obligations of States and		Foreign Offices		1,315,167,129
Political Subdivisions	213,284,376	Federal Funds Purchased and Other		
Other	12,572,302	Borrowings		466,653,654
Trading Account	61,979,557	Accrued Taxes and Other Expenses		51,925,354
Loans:		Other Liabilities		16,183,468
Federal Funds Sold and Securities Purchased		Reserve for Possible		
Under Agreements to Resell	231,900,000	Loan Losses		30,877,610
Other Money Market	536,599,490	Capital Accounts:		
Other Loans	1,607,839,442	Capital Notes–6-3/4%, June 1, __	30,000,000	
Direct Lease Financing	13,547,381	Shareholder's Equity:		
Buildings and Equipment	66,637,655	Capital Stock ($20 Par Value)	60,000,000	
Other Assets	49,169,391	Surplus	74,000,000	
		Undivided Profits	18,673,458	
		Reserve for Contingencies	16,550,024	
		Total Shareholder's Equity		169,223,482
TOTAL ASSETS	$4,010,554,842	TOTAL LIABILITIES AND CAPITAL		$4,010,554,842

a. Harry N. St. George has applied to Quarter National Bank for a loan. Harry is the head of Agincourt Travel Services, and he wishes to purchase a fleet of tour buses. If Quarter will grant him a loan of $28,150,000 to make the purchase, he will give the bank a perfected security interest in the buses. Can the bank make this loan consistent with the requirements of section 84?

b. Assume that the bank has made a preliminary decision to grant the loan described in paragraph a, subject to your answer. May it grant a loan of

$21,000,000 to Mrs. St. George, to purchase a portion of the Crown Jewels of England, being auctioned by Richard Plant, Agent of the Crown, if she puts up collateral consisting of U.S. Treasury bills worth $5,000,000 and Long Island Lighting Company bonds worth $16,000,000?

c. Barry "Spin" Oza, former star pitcher for Tick Technological Institute, is the president of Liebniz Laboratories, Inc. He is negotiating a loan with the bank of $30,000,000, for the purchase of refracting monads, optical devices which are used in satellites to illuminate all points of view. Can the bank grant the loan?

5.5. Assume that Last National Bank has a lending limit under section 84(a)(1) of $1,500,000. Among others, the bank has the following loans outstanding:

Bosworth Partners:	$750,000
Egbert Catesby:	100,000
Percival Ratcliff:	20,000
T. Smythe Lovell:	10,000

Catesby, Ratcliff and Lovell are the sole partners of Bosworth Partners. The loans to each of them individually were used for purposes unrelated to the activities of the partnership. Richard Plant, agent of Bosworth Partners, has asked you what additional amount of funds the partnership may borrow from the bank.

5.6. As to lending limitations for savings associations, section 301 of the Financial Institutions Reform, Recovery, and Enforcement Act of 1989 (FIRREA)[28] generally requires the section 84 lending limitations to be applied to savings associations as well. However, certain variant rules applicable to savings associations are specified in FIRREA.[29] In addition, the Director of the Office of Thrift Supervision (DOTS) is given statutory authority to impose more stringent restrictions on a savings association, if necessary to protect the association's safety and soundness.[30]

b. Limitations on Types of Loans

Beyond the straightforward policy interest reflected in the lending limitations of section 84, there are other limitations placed upon the loan activities of depository institutions that relate to the type of loan, rather than the aggregate dollar amount of lender exposure. These limitations reflect other regulatory policies, such as limitations placed upon the types of loans considered too risky for thrift institutions and credit unions.

Other restrictions on types of loans are concerned with the appropriateness of the type of loan. The most obvious example of this sort of restriction is the criminal prohibition of loans to bank examiners.[31] In addition, loans to a member bank's affiliates are significantly restricted by 12 U.S.C. § 371c. Loans to executive officers of a member bank itself are also restricted, under 12 U.S.C. § 375a.

Notes and Comments 5.7. Review the provisions of 12 U.S.C. §§ 371c, 371c-1, 375a and 375b. Are the provisions of these sections duplicative, or do they supplement each other? What does each section cover?

---

28. Pub. L. No. 101-73, § 301, 103 Stat. 183, 310 (1989) (codified at 12 U.S.C. § 1464(u)(1)).

29. *See id.*, 103 Stat. at 310-311 (codified at 12 U.S.C. § 1464(u)(2)).

30. *Id.*, 103 Stat. at 311 (codified at 12 U.S.C. § 1464(u)(3)).

31. 18 U.S.C. § 212.

5.8. If a violation of one of these sections occurs, would the bank (or its shareholders, or anyone else) have a private right of action? If so, against whom? Consider the following case.

Adato v. Kagan

599 F.2d 1111 (2d Cir. 1979)

VAN GRAAFEILAND, Circuit Judge.

Fifty-nine foreign nationals appeal from orders of the United States District Court for the Southern District of New York dismissing their complaint against appellees under Federal Rule of Civil Procedure 12(b)(6) for failure to state claims under either the federal securities law or banking laws. We reserve as to all claims except those predicated upon alleged violations of section 11(m) of the Federal Reserve Act, 12 U.S.C. § 248(m). . . .

Until September 15, 1976, American Bank & Trust Co. (ABT) was a New York chartered commercial bank and a member of the Federal Reserve System. Its deposits were insured by the Federal Deposit Insurance Corporation. All of ABT's outstanding capital stock was owned by the defendant American B & T Corp. (ABT Corp.) and constituted almost all of the assets of that corporation. Approximately seventy-six percent of ABT Corp.'s stock was held by defendant Continental Trade Bank, a Swiss banking corporation, and an additional nine percent was owned by nine of the individual defendants, each of whom was an officer of ABT.

On November 25, 1975, defendant Juan Graiver agreed to buy the stock owned by Continental and the nine individual defendants for $32,604,000, which was almost double the stock's book value. Only $9,100,000 of this amount was paid in cash; the balance was to be paid over a five-year period. Two months prior to the execution of this agreement, state and federal regulatory authorities had warned ABT that it was in hazardous financial condition due to its large proportion of high-risk loans and the lack of supervision by directors and senior management. The New York Superintendent of Banks had issued a cease and desist order directing ABT to remedy this condition and to discontinue certain unsafe and unauthorized practices. Appellants allege that Continental and the nine individual defendants, knowing of ABT's shaky financial condition and the exorbitant price paid by Graiver, were put on notice that improper financial machinations involving ABT were in the offing.

Such machinations did take place. Pending approval by the New York Superintendent of Banks of Juan Graiver's acquisition of ABT Corp. (which was never given), Continental was authorized by the purchase agreement to nominate three representatives to the board of ABT Corp. Graiver was authorized to nominate the remaining members and given voting control of the stock. Juan's son, David,[2] was elected first to the board of ABT Corp. and then to the board of ABT, Juan succeeding him as director of ABT Corp. Both were provided with offices in the bank, and David was given authority to act as a bank executive officer.

In 1974, the Graivers had organized a bank in Brussels, Belgium, known as Banque Pour L'Amerique du Sud (BAS). In 1975, the Graivers had organized a Panamanian corporation known as New Loring, Inc., which was a corporate shell with no assets and no operations. Between September 30, 1975, and May 31, 1976, ABT extended credit in various forms to the Graivers and Graiver-controlled corporations, including the foregoing, in amounts ranging from $10 million to $22.4 million. This was between 43.1% and 88.5%

2. David Graiver was reportedly killed in the crash of a private plane in Acapulco, Mexico, on August 7, 1976.

of ABT's book capital. The proceeds of the loans were funneled back to the Graivers and used to finance their purchase of ABT Corp. Because these extensions of credit resulted in substantial overdrafts and violated federal and state banking laws as well as the cease and desist order of the State Superintendent of Banks, defendants searched for ways to reduce the unfavorable balances in the Graiver-controlled accounts. The plan that evolved was supervised by David Graiver, who had been placed in charge of ABT's International Division, including its Mexican operations.

David induced ABT's Mexican representative to conduct a concerted drive for new deposits. Appellants were among those who responded, delivering new funds to ABT as time deposits and renewing existing time deposits; their total financial commitment exceeded $5 million. However, these funds were not entered in ABT's books as time deposits. Instead, they were credited to the accounts of BAS, New Loring, and ABT Corp., with bookkeeping entries showing that the money had been invested in "time deposits" of BAS, "certificates" of New Loring, and "commercial paper" of ABT Corp. ABT gave appellants receipts showing that they were depositors of ABT but followed this up by sending them confirmations of their "investments" in BAS, New Loring, and ABT Corp.

On September 15, 1976, ABT was put into receivership by the New York Superintendent of Banks. The FDIC was appointed receiver and arranged for the sale of ABT to Bank Leumi Trust Company of New York, which assumed certain liabilities of ABT, including its time deposits. Appellants were informed thereafter that, because their funds were not represented on ABT's books as deposits, they would not be repaid by Bank Leumi. Appellants could expect little or no payment from the corporations in which their funds had been "invested." New Loring never had any assets; BAS was closed by Belgian authorities on September 1, 1976, and subsequently placed in receivership; ABT Corp. was insolvent and filed in Chapter XI reorganization on December 2, 1976.

This unhappy situation led to the present suit for rescission and damages. . . .

Appellants' first claim under the federal banking laws is based upon alleged violations of section 22(g) of the Federal Reserve Act, 12 U.S.C. § 375(a), which limits to $5,000 the amount of credit a member of the Federal Reserve may extend to any of its executive officers. Section 22(f), 12 U.S.C. § 503, provides that any officer who knowingly participates in or assents to a violation of section 22(g) shall be personally liable for all damages "which the member bank, its shareholders, or any other persons shall have sustained in consequence of such violation."

Appellants allege that excessive loans were made to the Graivers and Graiver-affiliated corporations and to at least one other executive officer, and that the diversion of appellants' funds to the Graiver-controlled corporations was for the benefit of the Graivers, enabling them to gain control of ABT. Appellants claim that they suffered damage "in consequence of such violation." Again, we are met with problems that are difficult to solve on a Rule 12(b)(6) motion.

We can find no case that has considered the question whether an excessive loan to a corporate alter ego of a bank officer for his personal use and benefit violates section 22(g). However, it has been held to be a violation for a bank president to borrow $10,000 from the bank by using the accommodation note of a third party. *See FDIC v. Vest*, 122 F.2d 765 (6th Cir.), *cert. denied*, 314 U.S. 696 (1941).[6] Having in mind the salutary purposes of the statute,

---

6. Regulations of the Board of Governors of the Federal Reserve System provide that loans to a partnership in which a bank's executive officer has a majority interest shall be treated as a loan to the executive officer. 12 C.F.R. §§ 215.3, 215.4. Under FDIC rules relating to unsafe and unsound banking practices, policy-making officers come within the definition of "insiders," and an "insider transaction" is defined as one between the bank and "[a]ny other person where the transaction inures

we are not prepared to reject out of hand the possibility that ABT officers violated section 22(g). Appellants should be permitted to present their proof.

A second obstacle which appellants must surmount, the one that prompted the district court to dismiss, concerns appellants' right to predicate their individual causes of action upon the alleged statutory violation. As a general rule, wrongdoing by bank officers that adversely affects all depositors creates a liability which is an asset of the bank, and only the bank or its receiver may sue for its recovery. *Michelsen v. Penney*, 10 F. Supp. 537, 539 (S.D.N.Y. 1934); . . . *see* 12 U.S.C. § 1821(d). Individual depositors may sue in their own right, however, if they have suffered a wrong that is distinctly theirs and not common to all. *Harmsen v. Smith*, 542 F.2d 496, 500 (9th Cir. 1976). . . . We see no reason why this exception to the general rule should not apply to section 22(g) violation.

It can hardly be denied that, as of now, appellants stand in a different position from that of the other depositors. Their right to be treated as depositors has been disputed by both the FDIC and Bank Leumi, and appellants have a suit pending against the FDIC. Under the circumstances, the FDIC is hardly the proper party to represent them in this proceeding. If appellants have a claim, it is not common to those of other depositors whose interests are represented by the FDIC.

Finally, appellants are confronted with the task of establishing causal relation between the illegal loans and their own loss. The existence of causal relation may depend perhaps upon whether the misappropriation of appellants' money was an integral part of the allegedly illegal lending or was simply an attempted cover-up for illegal acts that had already been committed. Proving causal relation will not be an easy task. However, "difficulty of proof provides no reason for dismissing the complaint." *Harmsen v. Smith, supra*, 542 F.2d at 502. Tenuous theories of liability are better assayed in the light of actual facts than in pleader's supposition. *Shull v. Pilot Life Insurance Co.*, 313 F.2d 445, 447 (5th Cir. 1963). We believe that the making of an intelligent decision on this issue requires prior development of the facts. . . . We conclude that appellants' claim under section 22(g) should not have been dismissed. In so holding, we do not in any way predetermine the merits of appellants' contentions.

Appellants' second claim under the federal banking laws alleges a violation of section 11(m) of the Federal Reserve Act, 12 U.S.C. § 248(m), which prohibits the making of a loan to any person which is in excess of ten percent of the bank's unimpaired capital and surplus. A private right of action for violation of this section is not provided for by statute. However, appellants contend that the district court erred in refusing to imply one. We disagree.

Section 11 deals with the powers of the Board of Governors of the Federal Reserve System. Subsection (m) empowers the Board to fix the percentage of member banks' capital and surplus represented by secured loans, but imposes a ten percent ceiling on individual loans as described above. There is nothing to indicate that Congress contemplated a private cause of action against bank officers for exceeding this limitation. Support for this conclusion is found in the failure of Congress to include section 11 among those for the violation of which individual liability is prescribed in section 22(f).

A similar ten percent limitation is contained in 12 U.S.C. § 84, and Congress has provided that bank directors may be held personally liable for the knowing violation of this section. 12 U.S.C. § 93. However, sections 84 and 93 are applicable only to national banks. It seems quite clear that, in this area, Congress intended the liability of state bank officials to be determined under state banking laws. Measured by the criteria found significant in *Cort v. Ash*, 422 U.S. 66 (1975), the refusal of the district court to imply a cause of action was

---

to the tangible economic benefit of an insider . . ." 12 C.F.R. § 337.3(a)(6)(iv).

correct. . . .

TIMBERS, Circuit Judge, concurring in part and dissenting in part.

Judge Van Graafeiland has written his usual thoughtful, perceptive majority opinion. I agree with it in part and disagree with it in part. . . .

I concur with the majority's refusal to imply a private right of action under Section 11(m) of the Federal Reserve Act, 12 U.S.C. § 248(m) (1976), and I concur with its affirmance of the district court's dismissal of appellants' claims under that section. To the extent, however, that the majority reverses the district court's dismissal of appellants' claims under Sections 22(f) and 22(g)(4) of the Federal Reserve Act, I respectfully dissent.

Section 22(g)(4) prohibits a member bank of the Federal Reserve System from extending credit to any of its executive officers in excess of an aggregate amount of $5,000 outstanding at any one time. Section 22(f) expressly provides for a private right of action against those directors or officers of a member bank "participating in or assenting to" violations of certain sections of the Act, including Section 22(g). Such private action permits recovery "for all damages . . . sustained in consequence of such violations."

The district court correctly held that appellants' complaint failed to allege all of the essential elements of a cause of action under Section 22(f); in particular, the complaint failed to allege a causal relationship between the asserted violations and the losses appellants claimed to have sustained. Although no court, so far as we know, has passed on what sort of causation is required under this section, the language "in consequence of such violation" clearly requires a showing of some causal connection.

Section 93 of the National Bank Act, 12 U.S.C. § 93 (1976), which provides for a private right of action for violations of Chapter 2 of Title 12 and contains language similar to Section 22(f), has been construed to require a showing of some causal connection. . . .

In cases arising under Section 93, courts uniformly have required proof of a causal relationship between a director's alleged violation and the damage that a plaintiff asserts. In some instances, courts have required that the plaintiffs allege that they "relied upon reports . . . falsely indicating compliance with [the section violated] to their injury." *Harmsen v. Smith*, 542 F.2d 496, 502 (9 Cir. 1976); *Michelsen v. Penney*, 10 F. Supp. 537, 540 (S.D.N.Y. 1934). *Cf. Chesbrough v. Woodworth*, 244 U.S. 72, 77 (1917) (showing of reliance on statement of bank's condition required for Section 93 suit). Alternatively, plaintiffs have been required to show that the illegal loan was the primary factor resulting in the diminution of the value or the demise of their investment. *Holman v. Cross, supra*, 75 F.2d at 911-12. *Compare Corsicana National Bank v. Johnson*, 251 U.S. 68, 87-88 (1919), *with First National Bank of Lincolnwood v. Keller*, 318 F.Supp. 339, 346-47 (N.D.Ill. 1970). In the absence of allegations that the director's wrongdoing was the primary cause of the plaintiff's loss, no recovery has been permitted under Section 93.

Applying this analysis to the present case, the complaint clearly is insufficient. Appellants do not allege detrimental reliance on any misrepresentations with respect to compliance with Section 22(g)(4),[12] nor do they allege that the loans led to the failure of their

12. Appellants do allege that in March of 1976, Juan Graiver submitted an affidavit to the Superintendent of Banks, in which he represented that he would not borrow from ABT to finance his pending purchase of Holding Company stock. Appellants, however, do not allege that they relied on this misrepresentation.

investments.[13] Instead, they attempt to avoid the causation requirement by suggesting that executive officers also are liable for a failure to disclose violations actionable under Section 22(f). Since reliance on material omissions has been held unnecessary in other related contexts, *see, e.g., Affiliated Ute Citizens of Utah v. United States*, 406 U.S. 128 (1972), appellants argue that it likewise should not be required here.

Appellants' reliance on *Affiliated Ute* and its progeny is misplaced. Those cases involved Section 10(b) of the [Securities] Exchange Act [of 1934, 15 U.S.C. § 78j(b)], an antifraud provision intended to encourage disclosure of information material to investors; it does not prescribe any substantive standards apart from disclosure. *See Santa Fe Industries, Inc. v. Green*, 430 U.S. 462, 476-77 (1977). The rationale behind the elimination of the causation element in *Affiliated Ute* was that, because it is so difficult to prove reliance on a nondisclosure or material omission, private enforcement of an action under Section 10(b) would have been intolerably encumbered in cases involving omissions. The Supreme Court accordingly thought it desirable to eliminate the reliance requirement[14] in order to foster the principal purpose of the statute -- disclosure. 406 U.S. at 152-54.

The harm that Section 22(f) of the Reserve Act guards against is quite different and calls for a different approach to private enforcement. Section 22(f) permits private claims to enforce certain enumerated provisions of the Act and thereby promote their objectives. None of these enumerated provisions demands disclosure. Rather they prescribe adherence to certain well defined substantive requirements. It is not nearly as difficult to show the causal relationship required by Section 22(f) as it is to show that one would have acted differently had certain information been disclosed. Thus, requiring a causal relationship between the violation and the loss will not frustrate the purposes for which Section 22(f) was enacted.

Notes and Comments 5.9. The issue of the existence of a private right of action under 12 U.S.C. § 503 has continued to receive the attention of the courts. *See Fitzpatrick v. Federal Deposit Insurance Corp.*, 765 F.2d 569 (6th Cir. 1985) (discussing private rights of action and civil money penalties); *Marx v. Centran Corp.*, 747 F.2d 1536 (6th Cir. 1984), *cert. denied*, 471 U.S. 1125 (1985) (finding private right of action); *Lode v. Leonardo*, 557 F. Supp. 675 (N.D.Ill. 1982) (finding no private right of action relating to nonmember, federally insured bank).

5.10. Hiram Forth is the chairman and president of Quarter National Bank. He wants to obtain a $5,000 loan from Quarter to finance Hiram, Jr.'s world tour upon graduation from high school. He is willing to put up his Quarter National Bank common stock as security for the loan, which is expected to carry an interest rate equivalent to the current rate that Quarter would charge on an automobile loan. Is the loan permissible on the terms indicated? *See* 12 U.S.C. §§ 83, 375a, 375b.

5.11. Hiram Forth is also an investor in Reel Estate Development Corp. of Los

---

13. Indeed, since the extensions of credit were made to BAS, New Loring and Holding Company–the very entities in which appellants' funds were invested–it would seem that the illegal loans buttressed their investments rather than undermining them.

14. While this difficulty of proof relieves the plaintiff of the burden of establishing causation, in order to protect against windfalls to such litigants the courts have not foreclosed defendants from presenting direct evidence of nonreliance in order to rebut the presumption and thereby disprove causation. *See Chris-Craft Industries, Inc. v. Piper Aircraft Corp.*, 480 F.2d 341, 375 (2 Cir.), *cert. denied*, 414 U.S. 910 (1973). *Accord, Chelsea Associates v. Rapanos*, 527 F.2d 1266, 1272 (6 Cir. 1975); *Thomas v. Duralite Co.*, 524 F.2d 577, 585-86 (3 Cir. 1975); *Carras v. Burns*, 516 F.2d 251, 257 (4 Cir. 1975).

Angeles (Reel), which specializes in the construction and sale of homes that are facsimiles of homes of famous cinema personalities. The president of Reel has applied to Quarter for a long-term loan in the amount of $30,000,000. Is the loan permissible? Are there any other facts or information you require in order to answer the question? Quarter's balance sheet resembles that set forth in Figure 5.1, *supra*. *See* 12 U.S.C. § 371c, 375b. *See also Fitzpatrick, supra* (collateral requirement).

5.12. Would it make any difference to your answer to the previous question if Quarter was considering charging Reel an interest rate substantially the same as that which it charges for its most creditworthy longstanding customers? *See* 12 U.S.C. § 371c-1.

5.13. Would it make any difference to your answers to the two previous questions if Quarter was a state-chartered, nonmember, FDIC-insured bank? If it was a savings association? *See* 12 U.S.C. §§ 1468, 1828(j), (v).

5.14. *Extensions of Credit to Insiders under the FDICIA.* In December 1991, the President signed into law the Federal Deposit Insurance Corporation Improvement Act of 1991 (FDICIA).[32] The FDICIA recodifies the statutory provisions restricting extensions of credit to insiders of depository institutions.[33] Among other things, normal credit underwriting procedures must be followed by depository institutions extending credit to insiders in accordance with these provisions.[34] Limits on loans to one borrower are applicable to directors.[35] Aggregate extensions of credit to insiders are also limited.[36] Knowing receipt by an insider of an unauthorized extension of credit is prohibited.[37] The insider transaction rules will apply to any holding company of a depository institution (not just one defined as a bank holding company),[38] subsidiaries of member banks,[39] and to all principal shareholders.[40] Existing transactions are not affected by these new rules.[41]

c. Prohibitions against Usury

The prohibition against usury, an outgrowth of moral concerns, is a legal restriction on loan activities that prohibits interest rates greater than a statutory maximum. For national banks, the governing provisions are those contained in 12 U.S.C. §§ 85-86.

A review of the language of these two sections will indicate that interpretive problems. Complicating matters is the fact that section 85 contains rather confusing "reference over" provisions, directing attention to usury provisions of state law under certain conditions. Basically, loans made by national banks are limited to either (*i*) the rate allowed by state law

---

32. Pub. L. No. 102-242, 105 Stat. 2236 (December 19, 1991) (codified at scattered sections of 12 U.S.C.).

33. FDICIA, §306(a) (codified at 12 U.S.C. §375b). Restrictions on transactions with affiliates and insiders apply to insured nonmember insured banks as well as member banks. *See id.* §306(k) (codified at 12 U.S.C. §1828(j)). Corresponding rules apply to savings associations. *See id.* §306(i)-(j) (codified at 12 U.S.C. §§1468(b)(1), 1972(2)(H)(i)).

34. *Id.* §306(b) (codified at 12 U.S.C. §375b(2)).

35. *Id.* §306(c) (codified at 12 U.S.C. §375b(4)).

36. *Id.* §306(d)(1) (codified at 12 U.S.C. §375b(5)).

37. *Id.* §306(e) (codified at 12 U.S.C. §375b(7)).

38. *See id.* §306(f) (codified at 12 U.S.C. §375b(8)).

39. *See id.* §306(g) (codified at 12 U.S.C. §375b(9) (E)).

40. *See id.* §306(h) (codified at 12 U.S.C. §306(9) (F)).

41. *Id.* §306(n).

where the bank is located; or (*ii*) a rate one percent over the Fed discount rate on 90-day commercial paper, whichever is greater. However, if state law stipulates a different rate for state-chartered banks (*i.e.*, different from that applying to other lenders), then the state bank rate is applied to national banks in the state as well. *However*, if state law has "fixed" no rate at all, then national banks are limited to seven percent or one percent above the Fed 90-day discount rate, whichever is greater.

The situation is rendered even more complicated–if that is at all possible–by the fact that section 85 does not indicate how one is to calculate the "rate" as applying to any given principal amount. That is, is a simple, stated rate in the loan agreement to be used (the "nominal" rate), or is the "effective interest rate" (*e.g.*, the actual interest charged when compounding is taken into effect) to be used?[42] Should the computation of the rate take into account so-called "add-on" charges, such as finance charges or late-payment fees, however they might be designated in the loan agreement? In referring over to state law, which of several possible interest rates should be applied? These and other interpretive questions are not resolved by the language of section 84, and have consequently been the subject of extensive litigation over the years.

Notes and Comments 5.15. *Underlying policy of the usury provisions.* The underlying policy of the federal usury provisions might assist us in answering some of these interpretive questions. Is it supposed to ensure, as in the case of branching policy,[43] that national banks operate at the same level of competition as state banks? Is it supposed to give a competitive advantage to national banks? Or is some other policy responsible for the complicated structure of section 85? Consider the following cases.

Tiffany v. National Bank of Missouri

85 U.S. (18 Wall.) 409 (1873)

Mr. Justice STRONG delivered the opinion of the court.

. . . The question . . . is whether the thirtieth section of the act of Congress of June 3d, 1864, [12 U.S.C. § 85,] relative to National banking associations, clearly prohibits such associations in the State of Missouri from reserving and taking a greater rate of interest than 8 per cent., the rate limited by the laws of that State to be charged by the banks of issue organized under its laws. . . . What, then, were the rates of interest allowed in Missouri when the loans were made by the defendants that are alleged to have been usurious? It is admitted to have been 10 per cent. per annum, allowed to all persons, except banks of issue organized under the laws of the State, and they were allowed to charge and receive only 8 per cent.

The position of the plaintiff is, that the general provision of the act of Congress that National banking associations may charge and receive interest at the rate allowed by the laws of the State where they are located, has no application to the case of these defendants, and that they are restricted to the rate allowed to banks of issue of the State, that is, to 8 per cent. This, we think, cannot be maintained. The act of Congress is an enabling statute, not a restraining one, except so far as it fixes a maximum rate in all cases where State banks of issue are not allowed a greater. There are three provisions in section thirty, each of them

42. The two may well be different. *See, e.g. First National Bank in Mena v. Nowlin, infra* (illustrating difference between nominal and effective rates).

43. *See* Chapter 3, § 2, *supra* (discussing "competitive equality" with respect to branching by national banks).

enabling. If no rate of interest is defined by State laws, 7 per cent. is allowed to be charged. If there is a rate of interest fixed by State laws for lenders generally, the banks are allowed to charge that rate, but no more, except that if State banks of issue are allowed to reserve more, the same privilege is allowed to National banking associations. Such, we think, is the fair construction of the act of Congress, entirely consistent with its words and with its spirit. It speaks of allowances to National banks and limitations upon State banks, but it does not declare that the rate limited to State banks shall be the maximum rate allowed to National banks. There can be no question that if the banks of issue of Missouri were allowed to demand interest at a higher rate than 10 per cent. National banks might do likewise. And this would be for the reason that they would then come within the exception made by the statute, that is, the exception from the operation of the restrictive words "no more" than the general rate of interest allowed by law. But if it was intended they should in no case charge a higher rate of interest than State banks of issue, even though the general rule was greater, if the intention was to restrict rather than to enable, the obvious mode of expressing such an intention was to add the words "and no more," as they were added to the preceding clause of the section. The absence of those words, or words equivalent, is significant. Couple with the general spirit of the act, and of all the legislation respecting National banks, it is controlling. It cannot be doubted, in view of the purpose of Congress in providing for the organization of National banking associations, that it was intended to give them a firm footing in the different States where they might be located. It was expected they would come into competition with State banks, and it was intended to give them at least equal advantages in such competition. In order to accomplish this they were empowered to reserve interest at the same rates, whatever those rates might be, which were allowed to similar State institutions. This was considered indispensible to protect them against possible unfriendly State legislation. Obviously, if State statutes should allow to their banks of issue a rate of interest greater than the ordinary rate allowed to natural persons, National banking associations could not compete with them, unless allowed the same. On the other hand, if such associations were restricted to the rates allowed by the statutes of the State to banks which might be authorized by the State laws, unfriendly legislation might make their existence in the State impossible. A rate of interest might be prescribed so low that banking could not be carried on, except at a certain loss. The only mode of guarding against such contingencies was that which, we think, Congress adopted. It was to allow to National associations the rate allowed by the State to natural persons generally, and a higher rate, if State banks of issue were authorized to charge a higher rate. This construction accords with the purpose of Congress, and carries it out. It accords with the spirit of all the legislation of Congress. National banks have been national favorites. They were established for the purpose, in part, of providing a currency for the whole country, and in part to create a market for the loans of the General government. It could not have been intended, therefore, to expose them to the hazard of unfriendly legislation by the States, or to ruinous competition with State banks. On the contrary, much has been done to insure their taking the place of State banks. The latter have been substantially taxed out of existence. A duty has been imposed upon their issues so large as to manifest a purpose to compel a withdrawal of all such issues from circulation. In harmony with this policy is the construction we think should be given to the thirtieth section of the act of Congress we have been considering. It gives advantages to National banks over their State competitors. It allows such banks to charge such interest as State banks may charge, and more, if by the laws of the State more may be charged by natural persons.

The result of this is that the defendants, in receiving 9 per cent. interest upon the loans made by them, have not transgressed the act of Congress, consequently they are under no liability to the plaintiff.

Marquette Nat'l Bank v. First of Omaha Serv. Corp.

439 U.S. 299 (1978)

Mr. Justice BRENNAN delivered the opinion of the Court.

The question for decision is whether the National Bank Act, Rev. Stat. S 5197, as amended, 12 U.S.C. § 85, authorizes a national bank based in one State to charge its out-of-state credit card customers an interest rate on unpaid balances allowed by its home State, when that rate is greater than that permitted by the State of the bank's nonresident customers. The Minnesota Supreme Court held that the bank is allowed by § 85 to charge the higher rate. . . . We affirm. . . .

The First National Bank of Omaha (Omaha Bank) is a national banking association with its charter address in Omaha, Neb. Omaha Bank is a card issuing member in the BankAmericard plan. This plan enables cardholders to purchase goods and services from participating merchants and to obtain cash advances from participating banks throughout the United States and the world. Omaha Bank has systematically sought to enroll in its BankAmericard program the residents, merchants, and banks of the nearby State of Minnesota. The solicitation of Minnesota merchants and banks is carried on by respondent First of Omaha Service Corporation (Omaha Service Corporation), a wholly owned subsidiary of Omaha Bank.

Minnesota residents are obligated to pay Omaha Bank interest on the outstanding balances of their BankAmericards. Nebraska law permits Omaha Bank to charge interest on the unpaid balances of cardholder accounts at a rate of 18% per year on the first $999.99, and 12% per year on amounts of $1,000 and over.[3] Minnesota law, however, fixes the permissible annual interest rate on such accounts at 12%. To compensate for the reduced interest, Minnesota law permits banks to charge annual fees of up to $15 for the privilege of using a bank credit card.

The instant case began when petitioner Marquette National Bank of Minneapolis (Marquette) itself a national banking association, enrolled in the BankAmericard plan,[7] brought suit in the District Court of Hennepin County, Minn., to enjoin Omaha Bank an Omaha Service Corporation from soliciting in Minnesota for Omaha Bank's BankAmericard program until such time as that program complied with Minnesota law. Marquette claimed to be losing customers to Omaha Bank because, unlike the Nebraska bank, Marquette was forced by the low rate of interest permissible under Minnesota law to charge a $10 annual fee for the use of its credit cards. . . .

Marquette named as defendants Omaha Bank, Omaha Service Corporation, which is organized under the laws of Nebraska but qualified to do business and doing business in Minnesota,[9] and the Credit Bureau of St. Paul., Inc., a corporation organized under the laws of Minnesota having its principal office in St. Paul, Minn. Omaha Service Corporation participates in Omaha Bank's BankAmericard program by entering into agreements with banks and merchants necessary to the operation of the BankAmericard scheme. . . . At the time Marquette filed its complaint, Omaha Service Corporation had not yet entered into any such agreements in Minnesota, although it intended to do so. . . . For its services, Omaha Service Corporation receives a fee from Omaha Bank, but it does not itself extend credit or

---

3. *See* Rev. Stat. Neb. §§ 8-815-8-823, 8-825-8-829 (1974). . . .

7. The principal banking offices of Marquette are located in the County of Hennepin in the State of Minnesota. . . .

9. The principal offices of Omaha Service Corporation are located in Omaha, Neb.

receive interest.[10] . . . It was alleged that the Credit Bureau of St. Paul, Inc., solicited prospective cardholders for Omaha Bank's BankAmericard program in Minnesota. . . .

. . . Marquette . . . moved for partial summary judgment to have Omaha Bank's BankAmericard program declared in violation of Minnesota usury statute, Minn. Stat. § 47.175, and permanently to enjoin the remaining defendants from engaging in any activity in connection with the offering or operation of that program in further violation of Minnesota law. Defendants argued that the National Bank Act, Rev. Stat. § 5197, as amended, 12 U.S.C. § 85, preempted Minn. Stat. § 48.185 and enforcement of that statute against Omaha Bank's BankAmericard program. . . .

The District Court of Hennepin County granted plaintiffs' motion for partial summary judgment, holding in an unreported opinion that "nothing contained in the National Bank Act, 12 U.S.C. § 85, precludes or preempts the application and enforcement of Minnesota Statutes, § 48.185 to the First National Bank of Omaha's BankAmericard program as solicited and operated in the State of Minnesota." . . . The Court enjoined Omaha Service Corporation, "as agent of the First National Bank of Omaha," from "engaging in any solicitation of the residents of the State of Minnesota or other activity in connection with the offering or operation of a bank credit card program in the State of Minnesota in violation of Minnesota Statutes, § 48.185." . . .

On appeal, the Minnesota Supreme Court reversed. Noting that . . . a recent decision of the Court of Appeals for the Eighth Circuit had made it plain that in its judgment the usury laws of Nebraska rather that Minnesota should govern the operation of Omaha Bank's BankAmericard program in Minnesota, *see Fisher v. First National Bank of Omaha*, 548 F.2d 255 (C.A.8 1977),[16] the Minnesota Supreme Court concluded that it would be "inappropriate for this court to permit the use of procedural devised to obtain a result inconsistent with the existing doctrine in the Eighth Circuit." Minn., 262 N.W.2d, at 365 (1977).[17] . . .

In the present posture of this case Omaha Bank is no longer a party defendant. The federal question presented for decision is nevertheless the application of 12 U.S.C. § 85 to the operation of Omaha Bank's BankAmericard program. There is no allegation in petitioners' complaints that either Omaha Service Corporation or the Minnesota merchants and banks participating in the BankAmericard program are themselves extending credit in violation of Minn. Stat. § 48.181, and we therefore have no occasion to determine the application of the National Bank Act in such a case.

Omaha Bank is a national bank; it is an "instrumentalit[y] of the federal government, created for a public purpose, and as such necessarily subject to the paramount authority of the United States." *Davis v. Elmira Savings Bank*, 161 U.S. 275, 283 (1896). The interest rate that Omaha Bank may charge in its BankAmericard program is thus governed by federal law. *See Farmers' and Mechanics' National Bank v. Dearing*, 91 U.S. 29, 34 (1875). . . .

Section 85 . . . plainly provides that a national bank may charge interest "on any loan" at the rate allowed by the laws of the State in which the bank is "located." The questions before us is therefore narrowed to whether Omaha Bank and its BankAmericard program are "located" in Nebraska and for that reason entitled to charge its Minnesota cus-

---

10. Omaha Service Corporation does, however, accept assignments of delinquent accounts from Omaha Bank and, as an incident to collecting these accounts, does collect interest. . . .

16. In its opinion the Eighth Circuit relied upon the decision of the Court of Appeals for the Seventh Circuit in *Fisher v. First National Bank of Chicago*, 538 F.2d 1284 (C.A.7 1976).

17. The Supreme Court of Iowa has since reached a contrary conclusion. *See Iowa v. First of Omaha Service Corporation*, (Iowa 1978), appeal docketed, No. 78-846.

tomers the rate of interest authorized by Nebraska law.[19]

There is no question but that Omaha Bank itself, apart from its BankAmericard program, is located in Nebraska. Petitioners concede as much. . . . The National Bank Act requires a national bank to state in its organization certificate "[t]he place where its operations of discount and deposit are to be carried on, designating the State, Territory, or District, and the particular county and city, town, or village." Rev. Stat. § 5134, 12 U.S.C. § 22. The charter address of Omaha Bank is in Omaha, Douglas County, Nebraska. The Bank operates no branch banks in Minnesota, *cf. Seattle Trust and Savings Bank v. Bank of California*, 492 F.2d 48 (CA9 1974), nor apparently could it under federal law. See 12 U.S.C. § 36(c).[21]

The State of Minnesota, however, contends that this conclusion must be altered if Omaha Bank's BankAmericard program is considered: "In the context of a national bank which systematically solicits Minnesota residents for credit cards to be used in transactions with Minnesota merchants the bank must be deemed to be 'located' in Minnesota for purposes of this credit card program." . . .

We disagree. Section 85 was originally enacted as § 30 of the National Bank Act of 1864, 13 Stat. 108 (1864).[23] The congressional debates surrounding the enactment of § 30 were conducted on the assumption that a national bank was "located" for purposes of the section in the State named in its organization certificate. *See* Cong. Globe, 38th Cong., 1st Sess., 2123-2127 (1864). Omaha Bank cannot be deprived of its location merely because it is extending credit to residents of a foreign State. Minnesota residents were always free to visit Nebraska and receive loans in that State. It has not been suggested that Minnesota usury laws would apply to such transactions. Although the convenience of modern mail permits Minnesota residents holding Omaha Bank's BankAmericards to receive loans without visiting Nebraska, credit on the use of their cards is nevertheless similarly extended by Omaha Bank

---

19. We have no occasion in this case to parse the meaning of the phrase in § 85 "associations *organized or existing* in any such State. . . ." (Emphasis added.) This phrase occurs in the "except" clause of § 85, which, at least since *Tiffany v. National Bank of Missouri*, 19 Wall. 409 (1873), has been interpreted as an "enabling" clause. "If there is a rate of interest fixed by State laws for lenders generally, the banks are allowed to charge that rate, but no more, except that if State banks of issue are allowed to reserve more, the same privilege is allowed to National banking associations." *Id.*, at 411. Since there is in this case no allegation or proof that Minnesota state banks are "allowed to reserve more" than the rate of interest "for lenders generally," we need not determine the relationship of the phrase "organized or existing" to the term "located."

21. Last Term *Citizens and Southern National Bank v. Bougas*, 434 U.S. 35 (1977), held that, with respect to the venue provision of the National Bank Act, 12 U.S.C. § 94, . . . a national bank is "located" either in the place designated in its "organization certificate," 12 U.S.C. § 22, ... or in the places in which it has established authorized branches. Omaha Bank is thus also "located" in Nebraska for the purposes of 12 U.S.C. § 94. [Note that, with the enactment of the IBBEA in 1994, interstate branching now is possible for national banks. *See* Chapter 3, § 4, *supra* (discussing interstate branching).]

23. Section 30 is, in its pertinent parts, virtually identical with the current § 85. . . .

Section 30 was preceded by § 46 of the Currency Act of 1863, 12 Stat. 678-679 (1863), which provided:

> "[E]very association may take, reserve, receive, and charge on any loan, or discount made, or upon any note, bill of exchange, or other evidence of debt, such rate of interest or discount as is for the time the established rate of interest for delay in the payment of money, in the absence of contract between the parties, by the laws of the several States in which the associations are respectively located, and no more. . . ."

in Nebraska by the Bank's honoring of the sales drafts of participating Minnesota merchants and banks. Finance charges on the unpaid balances of cardholders are assessed by the Bank in Omaha, Neb., and all payments on unpaid balances are remitted to the Bank in Omaha, Neb. Furthermore, the Bank issues its BankAmericards in Omaha, Neb., after credit assessments are made by the Bank in that city. . . .

Nor can the fact that Omaha Bank's BankAmericards are used "in transactions with Minnesota merchants" be determinative of the Bank's location for purposes of § 85. The Bank's BankAmericard enables its holder "to purchase goods and services from participating merchants and obtain cash advances from participating banks throughout the United States and the world." . . . Minnesota residents can thus use their Omaha Bank BankAmericards to purchase services in the State of New York or mail-order goods from the State of Michigan. If the location of the Bank were to depend on the whereabouts of each credit card transaction, the meaning of the term "located" would be so stretched as to throw into confusion the complex system of modern interstate banking. A national bank could never be certain whether its contacts with residents of foreign States were sufficient to alter its location for purposes of § 85. We do not choose to invite these difficulties by rendering so elastic the term "located." The mere fact that Omaha Bank has enrolled Minnesota residents, merchants, and banks in its BankAmericard program thus does not suffice to "locate" that bank in Minnesota for purposes of 12 U.S.C.A. § 85.[25] *See Second National Bank of Leavenworth v. Smoot*, 9 D.C. 371, 373 (1876). . . .

Since Omaha Bank and its BankAmericard program are "located" in Nebraska, the plain language of § 85 provides that the Bank may charge "on any loan" the rate "allowed" by the State of Nebraska. Petitioners contend, however, that this reading of the statute violates the basic legislative intent of the National Bank Act. *See Train v. Colorado Public Interest Research Group, Inc.*, 426 U.S. 1, 9-10 (1976). At the time Congress enacted § 30 of the National Bank Act of 1864, 13 Stat. 108, so petitioners' argument runs, it intended "to insure competitive equality between state and national banks in the charging of interest." . . . This policy could best be effectuated by limiting national banks to the rate of interest allowed by the States in which the banks were located. Since Congress in 1864 was addressing a financial system in which incorporated banks were "local institutions," it did not "contemplate a national bank soliciting customers and entering loan agreements outside of the state in which it was established." . . . Therefore to interpret § 85 to apply to interstate loans such as those involved in this case would not only enlarge impermissibly the original intent of Congress, but also undercut the basic policy foundations of the statute by upsetting the competitive equality now existing between state and national banks.

We cannot accept petitioners' argument. Whatever policy of "competitive equality" has been discerned in other sections of the National Bank Act, *see, e.g., First National Bank v. Dickinson*, 396 U.S. 122, 131 (1969); *First National Bank of Logan v. Walker Bank & Trust Co.*, 385 U.S. 252, 261-262 (1966), § 30 and its descendants have been interpreted for over a century to give "advantages to National banks over their State competitors." *Tiffany v. National Bank of Missouri*, 18 Wall. 409, 413 (1873). "National banks," it was said in *Tiffany*, "have been National favorites." The policy of competitive equality between state and national banks, however, is not truly at the core of this case. Instead we are confronted by the inequalities that occur when a national bank applies the interest rates of its home State

---

25. Similarly, the mere fact that a national bank "transacts business" or even violates the Securities Exchange Act of 1934 in a State other than that of its "organization certificate," . . . does not suffice to locate the bank in the foreign State for purposes of venue under the National Bank Act, 12 U.S.C. § 94, *Radzanower v. Touche Ross & Co.*, 426 U.S. 148 (9176); *see Bank of America v. Whitney Central National Bank*, 261 U.S. 171 (1923); *cf. Cope v. Anderson*, 331 U.S. 461, 467 (1947).

in its dealing with residents of a foreign State. These inequalities affect both national and state banks in the foreign State. Indeed, in the instant case Marquette is a national bank claiming to be injured by the unequal interest rates charged by another national bank. Whether the inequalities which thus occur when the interest rates of one State are "exported" into another violate the intent of Congress in enacting § 30 in part depends on whether Congress in 1864 was aware of the existence of a system of interstate banking in which such inequalities would seem a necessary part.

Close examination of the National Bank Act of 1864, its legislative history, and its historical context makes clear that, contrary to the suggestion of petitioners, Congress intended to facilitate what Representative Hooper termed a "national banking system." Cong. Globe, 38th Cong., 1st Sess., 1451 (1864). *See also* Report of the Comptroller of the Currency 4 (1864). Section 31 of the Act, for example, fully recognized the interstate nature of American banking by providing that three fifths of the 15% of the aggregate amount of their notes in circulation that national banks were required to "have on hand, in lawful money" could

> "consist of balances due to an association available for the redemption of its circulation notes from associations approved by the comptroller of the currency, organized under this act, in the cities of Saint Louis, Louisville, Chicago, Detroit, Milwaukie [*sic*], New Orleans, Cincinnati, Cleveland, Pittsburgh, Baltimore, Philadelphia, Boston, New York, Albany, Leavenworth, San Francisco, and Washington City." 13 Stat. 109 (1864).[29]

The debates surrounding the enactment of this section portray a banking system of great regional interdependence. Senator Chandler of Michigan, for example, noted that

> "[T]he banking business of the Northwest is done upon bills of exchange. The wool clip of Michigan, the wheat crop of Michigan, the hog crop of Iowa, are all purchased with drafts drawn chiefly upon [New York, Philadelphia, and Boston]. The wool clip is chiefly bought by drafts upon Boston. I put in the three cities

---

29. Section 31 also provided:

> "That the cities of Charleston and Richmond may be added to the list of cities in the national associations of which other associations may keep three fifths of their lawful money, whenever, in the opinion of the comptroller of the currency, the condition of the southern states will warrant it." 13 Stat. 109 (1964).

See also § 32 of the National Bank Act of 1864, 13 Stat. 109 (1864).

Senator Sherman, sponsor of the Act in the Senate, described in the following terms the purpose of § 31:

> "The first important provision of this bill is, that it provides centers of redemption. Under the old bill, a bank was not bound to redeem its issues except at its own counter. If it failed to redeem there, then provision was made for winding it up. Under the present bill, certain cities of the United States are designated where the banks are required to redeem their issues. Each bank is to redeem its issue at its center of redemption as prescribed by the Comptroller of the Currency. The cities named are the principal cities along the Atlantic coast, Cincinnati, Louisville, Chicago, Detroit, and two or three other places. That will strengthen the system very much by relieving the noteholder from the trouble of going away from any part of the United States to a remote village or city, and there demanding redemption at the counter of the bank." Cong. Globe, 38th Cong., 1st Sess., 1865 (1864).

> because it is convenient to the customer, to the broker, to the merchant, to be enabled to purchase a draft upon either one of these three places." Cong. Globe, 38th Cong., 1st Sess., 2144 (1864).

See also id., at 1343, 1376, 2143-2145, 2181-2182. Similarly, the debates surrounding the enactment of § 41 of the Act, which provided that the shares of a national bank could be taxed as personal property "in the assessment of taxes imposed by or under state authority at the place where such bank is located, and not elsewhere," 13 Stat. 112, demonstrated a sensitive awareness of the possibilities of interstate ownership and control of national banks. *See, e.g.*, Cong. Globe, 38th Cong., 1st Sess., 1271, 1898-1899 (1864).

Although in the debates surrounding the enactment of § 30 there is no specific discussion of the impact of interstate loans, these debates occurred in the context of a developed interstate loan market. As early as 1839 this Court had occasion to note that "Money is frequently borrowed in one state, by a corporation created in another. . . . These usages of commerce and trade have been so general and public, and have been practiced for so long a period of time, and so generally acquiesced in by the states, that the Court cannot overlook them. . . ." *Bank of August v. Earle*, 13 Pet. 519, 590-591 (1839). Examples of this interstate loan market have been noted by historians of American banking. *See, e.g.*, 1 F. REDLICH, THE MOLDING OF AMERICAN BANKING 49 (1968); 1 F. JAMES, THE GROWTH OF CHICAGO BANKS 546 (1938); Breckenridge, *Discount Rates in the United States*, 13 Pol. Sci. Q. 119, 136-138 (1898). Evidence of this market is to be found in the numerous judicial decisions in cases arising out of interstate loan transactions. *See, e.g., Woodcock v. Campbell*, 2 Port. 456 (Ala. 1835); *Clarke v. Bank of Mississippi*, 10 Ark. 516 (1850); *Planters Bank v. Bass*, 2 Lou. Ann. R. 430 (1847); *Knox v. Bank of United States*, 27 Miss. 65 (1854); *Bard v. Pole*, 12 N.Y. 495 (1855); *Curtis v. Leavitt*, 15 N.Y. 9 (1857). After passage of the National Bank Act of 1864, cases involving interstate loans begin to appear with some frequency in federal courts. *See, e.g., In re Wild*, Fed. Cas. No. 17,645 (S.D.N.Y. 1873); *Cadle v. Tracy*, Fed. Cas. No. 2,279 (S.D.N.Y. 1873); *Farmers' National Bank v. McElhinney*, 42 F. 801 (S.D.Iowa 1890); *Second National Bank of Leavenworth v. Smoot*, 9 D.C. 371 (1876).

We cannot assume that Congress was oblivious to the existence of such common commercial transactions. We find it implausible to conclude, therefore, that Congress meant through its silence to exempt interstate loans from the reach of § 30. We would certainly be exceedingly reluctant to read such a hiatus into the regulatory scheme of § 30 in the absence of evidence of specific congressional intent. Petitioners have adduced no such evidence.

Petitioners' final argument is that the "exportation" of interest rates, such as occurred in this case, will significantly impair the ability of States to enact effective usury laws. This impairment, however, has always been implicit in the structure of the National Bank Act, since citizens of one State were free to visit a neighboring State to receive credit at foreign interest rates.[31] *Cf.* 38 Cong. Globe, 38th Cong., 1st Sess., 2123 (1864). This impairment may in fact be accentuated by the ease with which interstate credit is available by mail through the use of modern credit cards. But the protection of state usury laws is an

---

31. When the National Bank Act of 1864 originally passed the House, it imposed a uniform maximum rate of interest of 7% on all national banks. *See* Cong. Globe, 38th Cong., 1st Sess., 1866 (1864) (remarks of Sen. Sherman); J. KNOX, A HISTORY OF BANKING IN THE UNITED STATES 238-239, 248, 255-256 (1969). Such a provision, of course, would have eliminated interstate inequalities among national banks resulting from differing state usury rates.

. . . To the extent the enumerated federal rates of interest are greater than permissible state rates, state usury laws must of course give way to the federal statute.

issue of legislative policy, and any plea to alter § 85 to further that end is better addressed to the wisdom of Congress than to the judgment of this Court.

Notes and Comments 5.16 Recall the discussion in Notes 4.38, 4.42-4.43, *supra*, of the delineation of product markets in assessing the likely anticompetitive effects of bank mergers.Should merging banks view as favorable to them *Marquette Nat. Bank*'s recognition of a "national banking system," and its acknowledgement of "a banking system of great regional interdependence" with a "developed interstate loan market"?

5.17. *Marquette revisited.* The following case develops some of the implications of *Marquette Nat'l Bank*. What is the combined practical effect of *Marquette Nat'l Bank* and *Smiley*?

Smiley v. Citibank (South Dakota), N. A.

517 U.S. 735 (1996)

Justice SCALIA delivered the opinion of the Court.

Section 30 of the National Bank Act of 1864, Rev. Stat. § 5197, as amended, 12 U.S.C. § 85, provides that a national bank may charge its loan customers "interest at the rate allowed by the laws of the State . . . where the bank is located." In *Marquette Nat. Bank of Minneapolis v. First of Omaha Service Corp.*, 439 U.S. 299 (1978), we held that this provision authorizes a national bank to charge out-of-state credit-card customers an interest rate allowed by the bank's home State, even when that rate is higher than what is permitted by the States in which the cardholders reside. The question in this case is whether § 85 also authorizes a national bank to charge late-payment fees that are lawful in the bank's home State but prohibited in the States where the cardholders reside–in other words, whether the statutory term "interest" encompasses late-payment fees. . . .

Petitioner, a resident of California, held two credit cards–a "Classic Card" and a "Preferred Card"–issued by respondent, a national bank located in Sioux Falls, South Dakota. The Classic Card agreement provided that respondent would charge petitioner a late fee of $15 for each monthly period in which she failed to make her minimum monthly payment within 25 days of the due date. Under the Preferred Card agreement, respondent would impose a late fee of $6 if the minimum monthly payment was not received within 15 days of its due date; and an additional charge of $15 or 0.65% of the outstanding balance on the Preferred Card, whichever was greater, if the minimum payment was not received by the next minimum monthly payment due date. Petitioner was charged late fees on both cards.

These late fees are permitted by South Dakota law, *see* S.D. Codified Laws §§ 54-3-1, 54-3-1.1 (1990 and Supp.1995). Petitioner, however, is of the view that exacting such "unconscionable" late charges from California residents violates California law, and in 1992 brought a class action against respondent on behalf of herself and other California holders of respondent's credit cards, asserting various statutory and common-law claims.[1] Respondent moved for judgment on the pleadings, contending that petitioner's claims were pre-empted by § 85. The Superior Court of Los Angeles County initially denied respondent's motion, but the California Court of Appeal, Second Appellate District, issued a writ of man-

---

1. By way of common-law claims, petitioner's complaint alleged breach of duty of good faith and fair dealing; unjust enrichment; fraud and deceit; negligent misrepresentation; and breach of contract. It also alleged violation of Cal. Bus. & Prof. Code Ann. § 17200 (West Supp.1996) (prohibiting unlawful business practices) and Cal. Civ. Code Ann. § 1671 (West 1985) (invalidating unreasonable liquidated damages).

date directing the Superior Court to either grant the motion or show cause why it should not be required to do so. The Superior Court chose the former course, and the Court of Appeal affirmed its dismissal of the complaint, 26 Cal.App.4th 1767, 32 Cal.Rptr.2d 562 (1994). The Supreme Court of California granted review and affirmed, two Justices dissenting. 11 Cal.4th 138, 44 Cal.Rptr.2d 441, 900 P.2d 690 (1995). We granted certiorari. . . .

In light of the two dissents from the opinion of the Supreme Court of California, . . . and in light of the opinion of the Supreme Court of New Jersey creating the conflict that has prompted us to take this case,[2] it would be difficult indeed to contend that the word "interest" in the National Bank Act is unambiguous with regard to the point at issue here. It is our practice to defer to the reasonable judgments of agencies with regard to the meaning of ambiguous terms in statutes that they are charged with administering. . . .

On March 3, 1995, which was after the California Superior Court's dismissal of petitioner's complaint, the Comptroller of the Currency noticed for public comment a proposed regulation dealing with the subject before us, *see* 60 Fed.Reg. 11924, 11940, and on February 9, 1996, which was after the California Supreme Court's decision, he adopted the following provision: "The term 'interest' as used in 12 U.S.C. § 85 includes any payment compensating a creditor or prospective creditor for an extension of credit, making available of a line of credit, or any default or breach by a borrower of a condition upon which credit was extended. It includes, among other things, the following fees connected with credit extension or availability: numerical periodic rates, late fees, not sufficient funds (NSF) fees, overlimit fees, annual fees, cash advance fees, and membership fees. It does not ordinarily include appraisal fees, premiums and commissions attributable to insurance guaranteeing repayment of any extension of credit, finders' fees, fees for document preparation or notarization, or fees incurred to obtain credit reports." 61 Fed.Reg. 4869 (to be codified in 12 CFR § 7.4001(a)).

[Smiley proposed several reasons why the traditional judicial deference to the administering agency's interpretation should not apply to the interpretation in question. The Court rejected each of the reasons, in a portion of the opinion excerpted *infra*.]

Since we have concluded that the Comptroller's regulation deserves deference, the question before us is not whether it represents the best interpretation of the statute, but whether it represents a reasonable one. The answer is obviously yes.

Petitioner argues that the late fees charged by respondent do not constitute "interest" because they "do not vary based on the payment owed or the time period of delay." We do not think that such a limitation must be read into the statutory term. Most legal dictionaries of the era of the National Bank Act did not place such a limitation upon "interest." . . . The definition of "interest" that we ourselves set out in *Brown v. Hiatts*, 15 Wall. 177, 185 (1873), decided shortly after the enactment of the National Bank Act, likewise contained no indication that it was limited to charges expressed as a function of time or of amount owing: "Interest is the compensation allowed by law, or fixed by the parties, for the use or forbearance of money or as damages for its detention." *See also Hollowell v. Southern Building & Loan Assn.*, 120 N.C. 286, 26 S.E. 781 (1897) ("[A]ny charges made against [the borrower] in excess of the lawful rate of interest, whether called 'fines,' 'charges,' 'dues,' or 'interest,' are in fact interest, and usurious").

Petitioner suggests another source for the asserted requirement that the charges be

2. *Sherman v. Citibank (South Dakota), N. A.*, 143 N.J. 35, 668 A.2d 1036 (1995). The Supreme Court of Colorado and the United States Court of Appeals for the First Circuit have adopted the same interpretation as the Supreme Court of California. *See Copeland v. MBNA America Bank, N. A.*, 907 P.2d 87 (Colo.1995); *Greenwood Trust Co. v. Massachusetts*, 971 F.2d 818, 829-831 (C.A.1 1992) (dictum), *cert. denied*, 506 U.S. 1052 (1993).

time- and rate-based: What is authorized by § 85, she notes, is the charging of interest "at the rate allowed" by the laws of the bank's home State. This requires, in her view, that the interest charges be expressed as functions of time and amount owing. It would be surprising to find such a requirement in the Act, if only because it would be so pointless. Any flat charge may, of course, readily be converted to a percentage charge–which was indeed the basis for 19th-century decisions holding that flat charges violated state usury laws establishing maximum "rates." *See, e.g., Craig v. Pleiss*, 26 Pa. 271, 272-273 (1856); *Hollowell, supra*, at 286, 26 S. E., at 781. And there is no apparent reason why home-state-approved percentage charges should be permissible but home-state-approved flat charges unlawful. In any event, common usage at the time of the National Bank Act prevents the conclusion that the Comptroller's refusal to give the word "rate" the narrow meaning petitioner demands is unreasonable. . . .

Finally, petitioner contends that the late fees cannot be "interest" because they are "penalties." To support that dichotomy, she points to our opinion in *Meilink v. Unemployment Reserves Comm'n of Cal.*, 314 U.S. 564, 570 (1942). But *Meilink* involved a provision of the Bankruptcy Act that disallowed debts owing to governmental entities "as a penalty," except for "the amount of the pecuniary loss sustained by the act . . . out of which the penalty . . . arose, with . . . such interest as may have accrued thereon according to law." *Id.*, at 566. Obviously, this provision uses "interest" to mean only that interest which is exacted as commercial compensation, and not that interest which is exacted as a penalty. . . . More relevant than *Meilink* is our opinion in *Citizens' Nat. Bank of Kansas City v. Donnell*, 195 U.S. 369 (1904), which did involve § 85. . . . There, a bank argued that a 12% charge on overdrafts did not violate a state law setting an 8% ceiling on interest rates because, *inter alia*, the overdraft charge "was a penalty because of a failure to pay a debt when due." *Id.*, at 373-374. We dismissed the argument out of hand. . . .

. . . Because the [Comptroller's] regulation is entitled to deference, and because the Comptroller's interpretation of § 85 is not an unreasonable one, the decision of the Supreme Court of California must be affirmed.

Notes and Comments 5.18. There is also a federal statutory provision prohibiting usury by federally insured, state-chartered depository institutions. Review 12 U.S.C. § 1831d, and consider the following questions:

a. Section 85 was intended to keep the "national favorites" competitive with state banks. What is the purpose or rationale of § 1831d? (*See* 12 U.S.C. § 1831d(a).)

b. What are the usury limits under § 1831d? How do they compare with § 85?

c. Should a court interpret and apply § 1831d in accordance with cases interpreting and applying § 85? Consider the approach taken by the court in the following excerpt with a rather unusual set of facts for a usury case.

Mamot Feed Lot and Trucking v. Hobson

539 F.3d 898 (8th Cir. 2008)

HANSEN, Circuit Judge.

[Customers and parties who had been sued by a bank filed a class action against the bank, its holding company, and its shareholders, directors, officers, and employees, after the criminal indictment of the bank's president for defrauding the bank of nearly $1 million. The plaintiffs asserted, *inter alia*, usury claims under § 1831d. The district court granted the defendants' motion to dismiss. On appeal, the Eighth Circuit affirmed.]

I.

Exchange Bank is a federally-insured, state-chartered bank located in Nebraska. [A]pparently (and allegedly) Scott Hobson, as the President of the Bank, misappropriated assets of the Bank, misstated the value of collateral on loans, misstated the Bank's assets on its balance sheet, and diverted loan payments made by customers to other accounts. . . .

Following Hobson's indictment on fraud charges, the Appellants filed this action in federal court claiming that the Bank Defendants had charged them usurious interest. The basis for the usurious interest claim was that "Hobson, without permission, contrary to the documents, but with the full approval of Defendant Exchange Bank of Gibbon, et. al. deliberately and intentionally misstated or took collateral of Plaintiffs, for his or others [*sic*] benefits, misstated the value of the collateral on the books and records of Defendant Exchange Bank, and that all amounts misappropriated, stolen, misstated, diverted, by Defendant Scott Hobson shall be deemed excessive interest paid by plaintiff/borrower. . . ." The complaint also alleged that Hobson "routinely, systematically and deliberately overstated the statements of financial condition of said borrower so that the loan could be 'booked' as a legitimate asset on the books and records of defendant Exchange Bank," and that Hobson "deliberately converted collateral of said Plaintiffs and deliberately diverted payments on loans to his own account thereby again misstating the books and records of the bank, thereby triggering a default and thereby triggering phoney acceleration clauses and attorney's fees clauses, all of which constitute interest which is excessive." . . .

II. . . .

The appellants . . . claimed that the Bank Defendants' actions violated 12 U.S.C. § 1831d, which, by its explicit terms, [applies] to federally-insured state-chartered banks. *See Discover Bank,* 489 F.3d at 604 (noting that § 1831d "is to state-chartered banks" as the National Bank Act "is to national banks"). Section 1831d allows state-chartered banks to charge up to a specified interest rate and explicitly preempts state laws that set lower ceilings. *See* § 1831d(a). It also provides a civil cause of action for a person who is charged a rate higher than that allowed in subsection (a), specifying the remedy of forfeiture of the entire interest charged as well as damages in the amount of twice the interest unlawfully paid. § 1831d(b).

The forfeiture and damages remedies of § 1831d(b) apply to "the taking, receiving, reserving, or charging [of] a greater rate of interest than is allowed by subsection (a)." A rather obvious prerequisite to a claim of usurious interest under § 1831d is that the overcharge relate to a charge of interest. Regulations interpreting § 85 of the National Bank Act define "interest" to "include[ ] any payment compensating a creditor or prospective creditor for an extension of credit, making available of a line of credit, or any default or breach by a borrower of a condition upon which credit was extended."12 C.F.R. § 7.4001(a)[3].

Appellants pick out the term "compensating" from the definition of "interest" and assert that they state a claim for usurious interest because "the bank was compensated by Defendant Hobson's ... misallocation and theft." . . . We sincerely doubt that benefitting (assuming that the Bank would in some way benefit from Hobson's alleged action of misallocating nearly $1 million from the Bank) from another's fraudulent activity amounts to compensation. In any event, it is not just any "compensation," however broadly construed, that meets the definition of interest. The compensation must relate to the extension of credit. The regulation lists examples, including late fees, insufficient funds fees, overlimit fees, annual fees, cash advance fees, and membership fees as included within the definition of "interest." § 7.4001(a). Although read broadly, the term "interest" is not without limitation.

3. Courts construe the parallel provisions of § 85 and § 1831d similarly, as § 1831d was modeled after § 85. *See Discover Bank,* 489 F.3d at 606.

The regulation explicitly excludes from the definition of "interest" such fees as appraisal fees, credit insurance premiums, finders fees, document or notary fees, or fees charged for obtaining a credit report. *Id.* These fees are surely compensation to the bank, certainly more closely tied to the extension of credit than the Appellants' claim that benefitting from fraudulent activity is compensation related to the extension of credit. Yet, such fees, not directly tied to the extension of credit, are excluded from the definition of interest to which the federal usury laws apply. *See Smiley v. Citibank (S.D.), N.A.,* 517 U.S. 735, 745 (1996) (concluding that the regulation's distinction between charges assigned to specific expenses and charges "assessed for simply making the loan" was a rational distinction entitled to deference even though "in the broadest sense *all* payments connected in any way with the loan ... can be regarded as compensating the creditor for the extension of credit" (internal marks omitted)). It goes without saying that if appraisal fees and credit reporting fees are excluded from the term interest, so too is a claimed benefit from the misallocation and theft of collateral and loan payments. *See Doe v. Norwest Bank Minn., N.A.,* 107 F.3d 1297, 1302 (8th Cir.1997) ("We have little difficulty concluding that the Comptroller's interpretation of 'interest' as excluding insurance premiums is reasonable."). The first amended complaint, alleging broadly that the Bank Defendants received compensation from Hobson's fraudulent acts, simply fails to state a claim under § 1831d. The district court properly dismissed this claim under Rule 12(b)(6).

Notes and Comments 5.19. *Mamot Feed Lot* relies on *Discover Bank v. Vaden*, 489 F.3d 594 (4th Cir. 2007), on the issue of the meaning § 1831d and its relation to § 85. While that interpretive issue remains sound, it should be noted that the Fourth Circuit's decision in *Discover Bank* was reversed and remanded by the Supreme Court on other grounds. In *Vaden v. Discover Bank*, — U.S. —, 129 S.Ct.1262 (2009), a federally insured bank/credit card issuer and the issuer's collection services affiliate filed suit to compel arbitration of state law counterclaims asserted by a credit cardholder against the affiliate in its state court action seeking past due charges. The district court ordered arbitration, and the cardholder appealed. The Fourth Circuit vacated and remanded, holding that the district court had to decide in the first instance whether it had subject matter jurisdiction over the petition to compel arbitration. On remand, the district court again ordered arbitration, and the cardholder appealed. The Fourth Circuit affirmed, in the decision later cited by *Mamot Feed Lot*. On certiorari, the Supreme Court reversed the Fourth Circuit and remanded, holding that (*i*) a federal court may "look through" a petition to compel arbitration to determine whether it has jurisdiction over the petition; and, (*ii*) the district court lacked jurisdiction to entertain the petition to compel arbitration.

5.20 Since this is another area of federal statutory "reference over" to state law, why does the policy of "competitive equality"–so prominent in branching law–not control in federal usury law as well? *But cf. Roper v. Consurve, Inc.*, 578 F.2d 1106 (5th Cir. 1978), *affirmed*, 445 U.S. 326 (1980), *rehearing denied*, 446 U.S. 947 (discussing "competitive equality" rationale). Should competitive equality apply at least to interpret the meaning of a state rate and how its is calculated? Consider the following cases.

Northway Lanes v. Hackley U. Nat'l Bank & Trust Co.

464 F.2d 855 (6th Cir. 1972)

CARL B. RUBIN, District Judge.

Sections 85 and 86 of the National Bank Act, 12 U.S.C. §§ 85 and 86, prescribe the rates of interest that may be charged by national banking associations and declare that the receiving of a rate of interest greater than that allowed, when knowingly done, shall give rise to a statutory proceeding for double that amount of interest.

Appellants herein, Northway Lanes, a co-partnership consisting of Ralph Kuris and Bessie Shull, and Marshull, Inc., the successor corporation, brought this action under section 86 in the United States District Court for the Western District of Michigan, to recover from appellee the penalty imposed by that section. From an adverse judgment, . . . they appeal.

This controversy began on November 10, 1967, when the appellee bank, a national banking association, loaned to appellants Kuris and Shull, both individually and doing business as a co-partnership under the name of "Northway Lanes," $600,000.00 for the construction and operation of an eight lane bowling alley. Because banking associations in Michigan are subject to limitations as to the amount they may loan on real estate, two separate loans were arranged in the following manner: first, a mortgage note in the fact amount of $350,000.00 secured primarily by the underlying real estate with the bowling alley equipment as additional collateral; and second, an installment note in the face amount of $337,500.00 of which latter amount $87,500.00 was interest reserved by the bank in advance. The primary security for this installment loan was the bowling alley equipment and a second lien was granted upon the improved real estate.

By the terms of the mortgage note, the appellants obligated themselves to pay the principal sum of $350,000.00, with interest at the rate of 7% per year for a term of seven years. The mortgage note was payable in monthly installments of $5,283.00, with the payments to be applied first to interest and then to principal. The mortgage note also reserved to the borrower the privilege of prepayment, subject to a 5% prepayment charge if prepaid during the year 1968, and reserved to the lender the right to charge a 4% late charge on any delinquent installment.

Interest on the installment note amounted to $7.00 per $100.00 per year. The note was payable in forty monthly installments of $8,437.50 each, commencing November 20, 1987, and continuing on the same day of each month except May, June, July and August of each year. It contained no specific provision allocating a specific principal or interest factor to each installment payment, but did contain provisions similar to the mortgage note with respect to prepayment and late charges. With regard to both the mortgage note and the installment note, the reservation by the lender of 7% interest was the maximum permitted under Michigan law.[4]

---

4. In Michigan the limit of interest on commercial real estate mortgage loans exceeding five years in duration is 7%. M.S.A. § 19.15(1), M.C.L.A. § 438.31 provides in part that:

> [T]he interest of money shall be at the rate of $5.00 upon $100.00 for a year, and at the same rate for a greater or less sum, and for a longer or shorter time, except that in all cases it shall be lawful for the parties to stipulate in writing for the payment of any rate of interest, not exceeding 7% per annum.

The limit on interest on industrial discount, or "add-on" loans is likewise 7% per year, subject to certain other restrictions. The relevant sections of M.S.A. § 23.766, M.C.L.A. § 487.38, provide that banks shall have the power:

> (a) To loan money and deduct interest thereof in advance at the rate of 7% per annum, or less, on the entire amount of the loan from the date of disbursement thereof to the date of maturity of the last maturing installment thereof, and in addition to receive uniform weekly, semi-monthly or monthly repayment installments on said loan, herein called "industrial loans," with or without an allowance of interest on such installments. If necessary, the amount of the final installment may be less than the amount of any previous

In addition to the above terms, the appellants obligated themselves to pay all out-of-pocket expenses incurred by the appellee bank in connection with both the real estate mortgage and the installment loans, and to furnish the bank with a land survey and a commitment of title insurance satisfactory to it. Pursuant to this agreement, the appellee bank charged the borrowers $1,595.00 to cover the expenses of the loan. . . .

The partnership, in the latter part of 1967 and the early part of 1968, made one payment on the mortgage note in the amount of $5,448.50 and four payments on the installment note of $8,437.50 each. On February 27, 1968, appellant corporation, Marshull, Inc., a Michigan corporation, was organized with the former partners as officers and sole stockholders thereof. On March 1, 1968, the partnership conveyed the business real estate to the corporation by deed, subject to the real estate mortgage to the appellee bank, which mortgage the appellant corporation assumed and agreed to pay. The personal property covered by the security agreement was also conveyed by the partnership to the corporation, by bill of sale executed the same day. However, no arrangement was made between the appellee bank and the corporation to relieve the co-partners Kuris and Shull individually from liability on the existing indebtedness.

Subsequent to March 1, 1968, the record shows that at least one payment, in the amount of $8,437.50, was made by the newly formed corporation on a Marshull, Inc. check. On April 16, 1968, both notes were paid off in full. Included in the final payment amount of $592,073.04 was a prepayment charge of $30,000.00, of which $17,500.00 was attributable to the mortgage note and $12,500.00 to the installment note.

Having discharged their indebtedness to the bank in full, appellants Kuris and Shull, in their capacity as partners of Northway Lanes, and Marshull, Inc., filed a complaint in the United States District Court for the Western District of Michigan under the provisions of Sections 85 and 86 of the National Bank Act, alleging that the deduction by the appellee bank of interest in advance, the assessment against the appellants of $1,595.00 in so-called "closing charges," and the imposition of a $30,000.00 prepayment charge separately and collectively constituted usurious interest, for which they sought double damages under 12 U.S.C. § 86, or twice the following amount:

Interest at 7% for 158 days	$25,071.62
Prepayment charges	30,000.00
Title insurance on mortgage's interest only	876.00
Land survey	125.00
Bank's attorney fees	575.00
Recording new mortgage (2 counties)	14.00
Financing search	3.00
Security instrument filing fee	2.00
TOTAL	$56.666.62

The District Court, by order of July 12, 1971, concluded that none of appellants'

installment. No such loan shall exceed 3% or $10,000 whichever is greater of the capital and surplus of the bank, nor be made for a longer period than 60 months from the date thereof, and the aggregate principal amount of such loans at any time shall not exceed 25% of the total deposits of the bank, whichever is the greater. Upon proper showing and consistent with sound banking practice, the commission may waive said restrictions.

(b) To charge the borrower in connection with loans made pursuant to this section $1.00 for each $50.00 or fraction thereof for expenses, including any examination or investigation of the character and circumstances of the borrower, co-maker or surety and the drawing and taking acknowledgement of necessary papers. No charge shall be collected unless a loan shall have been made and no charge shall exceed $15.00.

contentions were meritorious and dismissed the action after a trial upon the merits. From this order, appellants have prosecuted a timely appeal.

Appellants' first contention, that the appellee's reservation in advance of $87,500.00 interest on the $250,000.00 installment note constituted usurious interest, requires little discussion. The figure $87,500.00 was reached by the bank in the usual manner: the maximum legal interest rate of 7% was applied to the principal amount of the loan $250,000.00, to yield a yearly interest figure of $17,500.00. Since the term of the loan was for five years, this yearly interest was multiplied by a factor of five to obtain the total interest on the loan, $87,500.00. This figure was then added in advance to the principal amount of the loan, yielding a face amount of $337,500.00, to be amortized in forty equal installments over a five year period.

It has long been established that the taking of interest in advance at the legal rate, upon discounting a note at a bank, is not usurious. *See, Fleckner v. United States Bank*, 21 U.S. 338, 8 Wheat 338 (1823); *Evans v. National Bank of Savannah*, 251 U.S. 108 (1919). . . . This device, variously called "discounting" or "add-on" loaning, is permitted by statute in a number of states, and is expressly allowed to National Banks organized and operated under Title 12, United States Code. *See* 12 U.S.C. § 85 . . . ; *see, also*, 12 U.S.C. § 24.

These statutory provisions have been broadly construed. In *Evans v. National Bank of Savannah, supra* by a 6-3 decision, the Court approved the taking of interest in advance at the maximum legal interest rate by national banks even if located in states which prohibited their own state banks, competing in a limited loan market, from doing the same. The Court noted that discounting is an "ancient and commonly accepted doctrine," sanctioned by common law custom and not dependent upon federal statute or state law. *Id.*, at 114.

Appellants acknowledge that, under Michigan statute as well, appellee might have reserved interest in advance, but maintain that in order to do so, it had to comply with the other restrictions of the Michigan enabling statue, including limitations on the amount of the loan and the charging of closing expenses. *See* M.S.A. § 23.766, M.C.L.A. § 487.38. . . . This argument misses the point. Under the reasoning of *Evans, supra*, appellee's right to charge interest in advance arises independent of state laws which are binding upon state banks. Appellants' first contention, therefore, is not meritorious.

Appellants' second contention is that $1,595.00 in closing costs were properly the charges of the lender and that under Michigan law where the maximum legal interest rate is charged, the imposition of the additional burden of these charges upon the borrower is tantamount to usury.

There is no question that if a national banking association were to be held solely to the standard of a state bank (other than a savings and loan association), such add-ons would be usurious. In November of 1967, at the time this transaction was entered into, state banks generally in Michigan were prohibited from charging expenses incurred in the making of loans in an amount greater than $15.00. *See*, M.S.A. § 23.766(b), M.C.L.A. § 487.38(b) . . . ; *see also, Panos v. Smith*, 116 F.2d 576 (6th Cir. 1940), and Michigan cases cited therein. But the Michigan legislature, by statute enacted in 1965, specifically amended its law to permit a specific class of state lenders, savings and loan associations, to charge to its borrowers all reasonable and necessary expenses incurred in connection with the making or closing of real estate loans. The question raised by this appeal is whether national banking associations, organized and operated pursuant to Title 12, United States Code, may do likewise.

The National Bank Act of 1864, 13 Stat. 99, substantially amended and replaced the National Currency Act of 1863, 12 Stat. 665. The paramount intention of both of these statutes was to ". . . give every possible support to the public credit . . ." by a uniform currency ". . . furnished by national associations, organized under a general act of Congress. . . ." *See*, Abraham Lincoln, *Special Message on Financing the War*, Senate Journal, pp. 121-122 (37th Cong., 3rd Sess., Jan. 17, 1863). The legislative history of this statute indicates a Congressional intent to give national banks special competitive advantages over state banks, by permitting national banks to charge interest at the highest rate available to lenders generally in each respective state. *See* Cong. Globe, 38th Cong., 1st Sess., pp. 2123-2127. The operative clause of the statute, permitting national banking associations to "take, receive, reserve and charge . . . interest at the rate allowed by the law of the state . . . where the bank is located," was construed by Senator Sherman, a principal drafter of the act, as follows:

> I know that the amendment as agreed upon in the Committee on Finance was well and carefully considered, and was intended to confer on these national banks the same privileges that are conferred by the laws of the States on other *associations and individuals*, and therefore, to avoid the controversy, I will move to consider the vote on the amendment proposed by the Senator from Iowa which was adopted, and let us have the original amendment stand just as it was reported from the committee, which I know was considered carefully, and which *will allow those national banks the same rate of interest as is provided for by the local law for the people within their own States*. If the State choose to change their law, they can change it at any time. My own preference, however, as I have already stated, is to establish a uniform rate of interest by our law; but having been overruled on that point, *I prefer now to place the national banks in each state on precisely the same footing with individuals and persons doing business in the State by its laws*. [emphasis added] (*Id.* at 2126).

Appellants contend that 12 U.S.C. § 85 restricts the rate of interest national banks may charge to the rate established by state law for state "banks"; that savings and loan associations are not "banks"; and that national banks, accordingly, may not charge a borrower interest which a savings and loan concededly could charge under Michigan law on the same type of loan. The legislative history of the act simply does not support this construction. Indeed, an amendment to Section 30 (the predecessor to the present Section 85) of the Act, designed to put national banks "on precisely the same footing with the state banks so far as this matter of taking interest is concerned," was expressly rejected by the Senate. *See* Cong. Globe, 37th Cong., 1st Sess., p. 2126 (remarks of Sen. Doolittle). The reference in Section 30 to the "rate allowed by the laws of the State," was not intended to include any exceptions to that rate established for special transactions or special classes of lenders. *See*, Cong. Globe, 38th Cong., 1st Sess., pp. 2123-2126 (remarks of Sen. Grimes). The legislative history of Section 85 therefore requires the conclusion that national banks may charge as much interest as savings and loan associations are allowed to charge on equivalent transactions by Michigan law.

This conclusion is clearly supported by the judicial constructions that the act has received. [The opinion discusses *Tiffany v. National Bank of Missouri*, 85 U.S. (19 Wall.) 409 (1873).]

If . . . it was the purpose of the Banking Act to protect national banks from potentially discriminatory legislation by state legislatures, that principle is of controlling significance in the case at bar. In 1965, the Michigan legislature amended its laws to permit savings and loan associations to: "require borrowing members to pay all reasonable and necessary charges incurred in connection with the making, closing, disbursing, expending, readjusting, or renewing of real estate loans, property improvement loans, and educational loans," further providing that such charges "shall be in addition to interest authorized by law and shall not be deemed to be a part of interest collected or agreed to be paid . . . within the meaning of the law of this state. . . ." *See*, M.S.A. § 23.540(379), M.C.L.A. § 489.779. During the same period in 1965, savings and loan associations organized in the state of Michigan were granted broad authority to participate in the industrial real estate loan market, subject only to the restriction that such real estate loans not exceed in value 80% of the appraised value of the underlying security. *See* M.C.L.A. § 489.769 (P.A. 1967, No. 96, § 1, Eff. June 21, 1967, repealing § 489.755). Since the above provisions operate to give Michigan savings and loan associations, a specific class of lender, a competitive advantage in the commercial real estate mortgage market, it is the opinion of this Court that national banking associations organized in the State of Michigan and making similar commercial real estate loans, should be accorded the same treatment.

In this regard, the Court notes that although the loan in the instant case was separated into two parts, both were in fact commercial real estate loans within the meaning of Michigan law. Similarly, the expenses charged in this case to the borrower, including the cost of obtaining title insurance, land survey, mortgage recording, financing search and reasonable attorney's fees, were never allocated as between the so-called "industrial" loan and the real estate mortgage loan and in fact constitute the ordinary charges which are made in connection with commercial real estate mortgage loans. Had not the appellee bank styled part of its loan as an "industrial" loan, the conflict between the restrictive closing costs provisions of M.S.A. § 23,766(b), M.C.L.A. § 487.38(b), . . . and the provisions of the Savings & Loan Associations Act, M.S.A. § 23.540(379), M.C.L.A. § 489.779, would not have arisen. In this Court's view, given the nature of the expenses charged, the former statute cannot be considered controlling.

In interpreting the meaning and intent of 12 U.S.C. § 85, the District Court below concluded that:

> "Since a savings and loan associations can in fact charge 7% interest and in addition thereto . . . require a borrower to pay all reasonable and necessary charges incurred in connection with the making, closing and disbursing of real estate loans, it is the opinion of the court that a national banking association operating within the State of Michigan may do so also. To construe the Act otherwise would place a national bank in a competitively inferior position not contemplated by the federal statute."

The District Court's ruling is supported by the administrative interpretations of Comptrollers of the Currency over many years. We note in passing Ruling 7.7310, 12 C.F.R. § 7.7310, 36 F.R. 17015, which provides as follows:

> "A national bank may charge interest at the maximum rate permitted by state law to any competing state-chartered or licensed lending institution. If state law permits a higher interest rate on a specified class of loans, a national bank making such loans at such higher rate is subject only to the provisions of state law reliant to such class of loans that are material to the determination of the interest rate. For example, a national bank may lawfully charge the highest rate permitted to be charged by a state-licensed small loan company or Morris plan bank, without being so licensed."

The above interpretations, made by an office charged with the responsibility of promulgating reasonable regulations pursuant to the National Banking Act, and supported by the legislative history of the Act and by the Supreme Court's decision in *Tiffany, supra*, are entitled to deference by this Court. . . . The fact that savings and loan associations may be organized and operated in a manner different from banks generally does not, contrary to appellant's suggestions, alter the fact that such associations should be treated as "competing state-chartered or licensed lending institution[s]," within the meaning of Ruling 7.7310, supra. The conclusion is inescapable that the National Bank Act accorded national banks the right to charge the interest rate afforded their state competitors whether the competitor was a state bank or other non-bank lender. *See, Tiffany v. National Bank of Missouri, supra.* Accordingly, appellants' second contention is without merit.

Appellants argue finally that the assessment by the appellee bank of $30,000.00 in prepayment penalties constituted usury, because taken on an otherwise usurious loan. Appellants concede that prepayment penalties are not generally considered interest and that when charged in addition to maximum interest do not make an *otherwise nonusurious* loan usurious. . . . Since the Court has concluded that the loans herein were not usurious, this question need not be considered.

First National Bank in Mena v. Nowlin

509 F.2d 872 (8th Cir. 1975)

GIBSON, Chief Judge.

Is a note which is usurious under state law also usurious when made to a national bank? With the limited exception of a short-term single payment note, we think it is. The central issue presented by this litigation is whether the National Bank Act, 12 U.S.C. § 21 *et seq*., permits a national bank in Arkansas to reserve interest in advance on installment loans calculated at a numerical rate not in excess of the statutory Arkansas usury limits but yielding an effective rate of return substantially in excess of the state limit.

The First National Bank in Mena (Bank), Mena, Arkansas, an association organized and operating pursuant to the National Bank Act, appeals from a judgment of the District Court finding two installment loans usurious and granting the bank recovery only on the principal of the notes and denying recovery of any interest. The debtor defendant, Jack A. Nowlin, cross-appeals, seeking more extensive relief in the form of forfeiture of the principal due on the notes or, in the alternative, recovery of double the interest reserved on the notes.

In this diversity action the Bank sought declaratory relief and a money judgment for principal and interest due it as payee on the two notes executed January 11, 1974, by Nowlin, a Tennessee citizen. One note evidenced an installment loan of $11,000 payable in twelve equal monthly installments, from which the bank had discounted 8% annual interest, thus making an effective yield of 16.05% per annum; the other evidenced a $2,000 loan payable in thirty-six equal monthly installments to which the bank had added 8% interest in advance, raising the face of the note to $2,480, resulting in an effective interest rate of 15.57%.

Nowlin made no payments and renounced his obligations by letters dated January 15, 1974, claiming both notes were usurious and void under Arkansas law. After the Bank accelerated both notes and filed suit, Nowlin counter-claimed for forfeiture of both the principal of the notes and interest paid, pursuant to the sanctions of 12 U.S.C. § 86 (1970).

The District Court in this non-jury trial determined that if these installment loans yielding in excess of 10% annually had been made by any Arkansas lender other than a national bank, they would have been usurious under the Arkansas constitution and Arkansas cases construing the constitutional provision. The court further held that because the purpose of 12 U.S.C. § 85 (1970) is to permit national banks to charge as much, but no more, interest than the most favored lenders operating under state laws, a loan by a national bank is usurious under federal law if usurious under state law were it made by such a favored state lender. Consequently, the court held that both Nowlin notes were usurious and thus void with respect to interest but not principal. Nowlin's counterclaim under § 86 was denied because he had not in fact paid any interest. The Bank does not contest that the loans, as evidenced by the notes, would be usurious if made by any lender operating solely under state law.

Under 12 U.S.C. § 85 (1970), national banks may charge "interest at the rate allowed by the laws of the State . . . where the bank is located . . . and no more. . . ." The penalty under 12 U.S.C. § 86 for knowingly charging a rate of interest greater than allowed by law is a forfeiture of double the amount of interest if it actually has been paid on the usurious loan.

The pertinent Arkansas law incorporated by reference in § 85 is a constitutional provision restricting interest rates to an amount not greater than 10% per annum,[5] and the statutory law implementing that constitutional provision setting the maximum state interest rate at 10% per annum.[6] Other state statutory provisions prohibit usurious interest and make all notes and evidence of indebtedness or contracts violative of the usury prohibition void.[7] The test for ascertaining whether a loan or transaction is usurious in Arkansas is a simple one of comparing the amount the borrower is required to pay with the total amount he could be required to pay at the maximum rate of interest (10%), figured at simple interest per annum for the term.[8] . . .

The Bank contends that the term "rate" of interest "allowed by the laws of the

---

5. Ark. Const. art. 19, § 13, reads:

> Usury -- Legal Rate. -- All contracts for a greater rate of interest than ten percent per annum shall be void, as to principal and interest, and the General Assembly shall prohibit the same by law; but when no rate of interest is agreed upon, the rate shall be six per centum per annum.

6. Ark. Stat. Ann. § 68-602 (1957 repl.) reads:

> Maximum rate of interest by contract. -- The parties to any contract, whether the same be under seal or not, may agree in writing for the payment of interest not exceeding ten per centum . . . per annum on money due or to become due.

7. The applicable state statutory provisions read:

> § 68-603 Usurious interest prohibited.–No person or corporation shall, directly or indirectly, take or receive in money, goods, things in action, or any other valuable thing, any greater sum or value for the loan or forbearance of money or goods, things in action, or any other valuable thing, than is in section one [§ 68-602] of this act prescribed.
>
> . . .
>
> § 68-608 Bonds, bills and notes, conveyances, contracts or securities void when interest excessive.–All bonds, bills, notes, assurances, conveyances, and all other contracts or securities whatever, whereupon or whereby there shall be reserved, taken or secured, or agreed to be taken or reserved, any greater sum, or greater value for the loan or forbearance of any money, gods, things in action, or any other valuable thing than is prescribed in this act . . . shall be void.

8. *Davidson v. Commercial Cred. Equip. Corp.*, 255 Ark. 127, 499 S.W.2d 68, 70-71 (1973). In Arkansas the term "rate," therefore, is to be read as "effective yield."

Prior to 1952 the test for determining usury was not so simple. *See, e.g., Strickler v. State Auto Finance Co.*, 220 Ark. 565, 249 S.W.2d 307, 310-311 (1952). *See generally Sloan v. Sears, Roebuck & Co.*, 228 Ark. 464, 308 S.W.2d 802, 804-805 (1958).

State," as used in 12 U.S.C. § 85 should be construed not to apply the maximum "effective rate" or "yield" allowed by state law, but rather merely to incorporate the numerical rate permitted the most favored state lender, as it appears in the state statutes, applying it on a discount basis without taking notice of the state's cases construing those statutes. The Bank does not dispute that lenders under Arkansas law are prohibited from adding-on or discounting interest to increase the yield on installment notes above the 10% limit. It argues, however, that the 1919 Supreme Court decision in *Evans v. National Bank*, 251 U.S. 108 (1919), permits national banks to discount loans at the maximum state rate without regard to state prohibitions on discounting which prevent yields in excess of the maximum state rate.

We think that determination of the "rate allowed by the laws of the State" can only be accomplished with reference to state court interpretations of the state's own constitution and statutes. The primary principle of construction of 12 U.S.C. § 85, to which *Evans* might be considered a narrow exception, is that the federal Act adopts the entire case law of the state interpreting the state's limitations on usury; it does not merely incorporate the numerical rate adopted by the state. *Citizens' National Bank v. Donnell*, 195 U.S. 369, 374 (1904); *Daggs v. Phoenix National Bank*, 177 U.S. 549, 555 (1900). As expressed by Mr. Justice McKenna for a unanimous court in *Daggs*:

> The intention of the national law is to adopt the state law, and permit to national banks what the state law allows to its citizens and to the banks organized by it. *Tiffany v. National Bank of Missouri*, [85 U.S. (18 Wall.) 409 (1973)].

Daggs, supra at 555.

The rationale of *Evans*, based on the long standing mercantile practice of discounting short-term single payment commercial paper, should not now be extended to permit usurious discounting practices on installment loans. While many question the soundness of the *Evans* 6-3 holding and feel that Mr. Justice Pitney's dissent, concurred in by Justices Brandeis and Clarke, presents a more rational view, we cannot overrule *Evans*, but we do feel that *Evans* should be confined to its own facts of single payment short-term paper. To extend *Evans*' rationale, as the Bank urges, in order to allow discounting of installment paper would be to extend it to a materially different factual situation and into a new economic setting.

Installment credit as it is extended and utilized today was for all practical purposes nonexistent at the time of *Evans*. The discounting of short-term *single payment* commercial paper, however, was a prevalent and widespread practice at that time and has continued to the present time. The now common practice of lending on *installment* paper of varying terms, including long-terms, and of figuring the interest rate on a discount basis is of fairly recent origin. The practice has only become widespread with the advent of consumer credit, making almost anyone without an extremely dismal credit record eligible to purchase almost any item or service on a comparatively long-term installment credit basis. This practice has only recently found widespread acceptance, increasingly so in the last two decades.

Evans was a 1919 lawsuit by receivers of a state bank to recover the federal usury penalty from a national bank lender which had reserved interest in advance at 8%, the maximum rate permitted in Georgia, to achieve a slightly higher effective yield. Each loan was paid at maturity. The Supreme Court affirmed judgment on the pleadings for the defendant national bank, holding that by discounting "short-time" notes at the maximum 8% rate allowed by Georgia statute, the national bank did not act usuriously under the federal statute. The majority of the Court took note of, but chose not to follow, the current Georgia court-made rule[9] which prohibited the taking of interest in advance at the maximum rate because it inevitably increased the effective yield above the 8% limit. The unsuccessful plaintiff in *Evans* argued, as does Nowlin in the instant case, that the federal statute applied the same usury rule to national banks as Georgia law applied to individuals and state banks.

The *Evans*' Court majority disagreed, however, relying upon *Fleckner v. Bank of the United States*, 21 U.S. (8 Wheat.) 338, 354 (1923),[10] and a line of American and English authorities, recognizing that discounting of "short-time" commercial paper in the ordinary course of business was a long settled commercial tradition, and concluding that doing so at the maximum state rate could therefore not be usurious. 251 U.S. at 113-114. The majority reasoned that because "Congress intended to endow national banks with the power . . . of discounting notes reserving charges at the highest rate permitted for interest," federal law empowers the national bank in Georgia to retain interest at the maximum 8% allowed by Georgia statute, "referring to the state law only to determine the maximum permitted rate," not to determine the proper means for calculating that rate. 251 U.S. at 114.

However, in his well-reasoned dissent in *Evans*, Mr. Justice Pitney argued that the federal courts, in determining the maximum interest rate "allowed by the laws of the State," must consider not only the multiplier figure but all state cases interpreting and construing the state statute which might reveal the proper arithmetical use of that figure.[11] Specifically, he stated:

> The section has regard to substance, not merely to form; and in determining what is in substance the local rate of interest it is fallacious, I submit, to regard the multiplier only (say, 8 per cent.), and ignore the multiplicand, since both factors have equal influence in producing the result. As in other cases of testing state laws by a federal standard, the question is, what is the effect and operation of those laws, as construed and applied by the state court of last resort? *Evans, supra*, 251 U.S. at 118.

In conclusion, quoting from Mr. Justice Holmes speaking for the Court in *Citizens' National Bank v. Donnell*, 195 U.S. 369, 373-374 (1904), Mr. Justice Pitney stated that in applying the National Bank Act "on the question whether what was done amounted to . . . [usury] within the meaning of the [state] statute, we follow the state court"; therefore, given the existing Georgia court rule, the national bank in *Evans* "charged more than 'interest at the rate allowed by the laws of the State.'" 251 U.S. at 120.

The *Evans* case dealt with "short-time" single payment notes. The 1823 *Fleckner* case, a bank charter violation case, upon which the *Evans* majority relied, dealt with a single payment 23-month note of $10,000. The Court's holding in *Evans* that the practice of discounting is not usurious even if it raises the effective yield above the state ceiling, is based essentially on the Court's recognition that discounting on single payment commercial paper

9. *Loganville Banking Co. v. Forrester*, 143 Ga. 302, 84 S.E. 961 (1915).

10. *Fleckner* is not a sound precedent for a usury case, as the rate limitation of 6% was imposed in the federal charter of United States Banks, and a violation of the limit at best constitutes a charter violation of which only the Government might complain.

11. Citing *Farmers' and Mechanics' Nat'l Bank v. Dearing*, 91 U.S. 29, 32 (1875); *Union Nat'l Bank v. Louisville, N.A. & C. Ry.*, 163 U.S. 325, 331 (1896); *Haseltine v. Central Bank*, 183 U.S. 132, 134 (1901).

was then widely practiced.[12] It is widely practiced on *short-term single payment* paper as well today, *i.e.*, United State Treasury Bills of 90 days, 180 days, and one year duration. It is doubtful, however, that the Supreme Court would as readily hold the discounting of installment paper by a national bank to be as acceptable today, 150 years after *Fleckner*, in view of the enhanced economic aspect of discounting installment paper as compared to short-term single payment paper and the obvious discrimination in allowing national banks to charge almost double the effective rate charged by state financial institutions.[13] What affects the borrower's pocketbook is the effective rate, not semantics dealing with figures.

The Bank's reliance on *Northway Lanes v. Hackley Union National Bank & Trust Co.*, 464 F.2d 855 (6th Cir. 1972), is not persuasive for two reasons. First, for reasons stated above, we disagree with the Sixth Circuit's extension of *Evans* and *Fleckner* as its basis for approving the Michigan national bank's reservation of interest in advance on a five-year 7% chattel mortgage installment note with an effective annual yield of approximately 13-1/2%. Michigan's limit on commercial mortgages and industrial discount or add-on loans was apparently 7%. The *Northway* court relied upon *Fleckner* and *Evans* for the proposition that the taking of interest in advance at the maximum rate, when discounting a note at a bank, is not usurious. 464 F.2d at 860. Quoting the *Evans* Court's statement that discounting is an "ancient and commonly accepted doctrine," the Sixth Circuit affirmed a judgment for the national bank denying the debtor its 12 U.S.C. § 86 statutory penalty without distinguishing between the historically accepted practice of discounting "short-time" *single payment*

---

12. The *Evans* Court's long quotation of dictum from *Fleckner v. Bank of the United States*, 21 U.S. (8 Wheat.) 338, 354 (1923), supports this conclusion:

> [T]his court, through Mr. Justice Story, said: "If a transaction of this sort [discounting a single payment 2 year note at the maximum 6% nominal rate] is to be deemed usurious, the same principle must apply with equal force to bank discounts, generally, for the practice is believed to be universal; and, probably, few, if any, charters, contain an express provision, authorizing, in terms, the deduction of the interest in advance upon making loans or discounts. It has always been supposed, that an authority to discount, or make discounts, did, from the very force of the terms, necessarily include an authority to take the interest in advance. And this is not only the settled opinion among professional and commercial men, but stands approved by the soundest principles of legal construction. Indeed, we do not know in what other sense the word 'discount' is to be interpreted. Even in England, where no statute authorizes bankers to make discounts, it has been solemnly adjudged, that the taking of interest in advance by bankers, upon loans, in the ordinary course of business, is not usurious." 251 U.S. at 113.

The plaintiff bank's reliance on *Bank of Newport v. Cook*, 60 Ark. 288, 30 S.W. 35 (1895), ited by the *Evans* majority as well, is likewise misplaced for the same reason as its reliance on *Evans*. Both cases dealt with single payment, not installment, obligations discounted in the ordinary course of business. Moreover, recent Arkansas cases apply the usury laws more strictly than did those in prior years. *See* note 7, *supra*.

13. As an example, a $1,000 single payment one-year note discounted at 8% yields 8.70%. The same note yields 16.05% if principal and interest are repaid in twelve monthly installments. The increase in yield is almost as substantial when the interest is added-on in advance rather than discounted. *See* AMERICAN BOOK OF SIMPLE INTEREST YIELDS 6, 14, 35 (1958).

The inherent vice in discounting is readily apparent when carried to its extreme. A $10,000 ten year installment note at 10% interest would leave the maker zero dollars and the ten year discount at 10% would make the discount $10,000, equal to the face of the note. As noted by an early English case, "if the practice [of discounting] be carried to a great length, the interest will annihilate the principal." Lord Alvanley, *quoted in Bank of Newport v. Cook*, 60 Ark. 288, 299, 30 S.W. 35, 38 (1895) (Battle, J., dissenting).

commercial paper and reserving advance interest on *installment* notes. We believe the vast difference between the actual interest charged in discounting installment paper over that charged in discounting short-term single payment notes precludes such a smooth extension of *Evans*. Although the national bank's "right to charge interest in advance arises independent of state laws", *Northway, supra* at 860-861 of 464 F.2d, that independence is necessarily limited by the Act's adoption of the state's law, including its case law, to set the maximum rate. While the validity of the legislative history relied on in *Northway* has been questioned, we need not face that debatable issue in this appeal.[15]

Second, the *Northway* case is distinguishable from the instant case in that the reservation of interest in advance at the maximum statutory rate by the national bank in that case was not so clearly prohibited by Michigan law as is the instant practice by Arkansas law, the court utilizing the most favored lender doctrine created in *Tiffany v. National Bank*, 85 U.S. (18 Wall.) 409 (1873), to find the interest and other charges permissible under state law.

A construction of 12 U.S.C. § 85 which takes full notice of the state's case law is consistent with the Act's legislative history. The Act reflects a congressional compromise giving national banks full and complete parity of interest rate regulation with state banks while guarding against unfriendly anti-federal state legislation or ruinous competition with state banks. Speaking with respect to a prior unsuccessful proposed version of the legislation, Senator Sherman, a principal supporter of national bank interests, stated:

> I prefer now to place the national banks in each state on precisely the same footing with individuals and persons doing business in the State by its own laws.[17]

The policy of the pro-national bank faction in Congress in fashioning the Act was to place national banks in a position of limited advantage over state banks by allowing them to charge interest at the highest rate applicable under state law to lenders generally in each respective state, not necessarily at the rate applicable to state banks which might be lower. While it has been questioned whether Congress in the final version of the Act actually intended to adopt the policy of giving national banks most favored lender status rather than parity with state banks, it has been established in the law since *Tiffany v. National Bank, supra*. The most favored lender policy has not, however, been extended to give national banks superiority over all state lenders, corporate and individual, including banks, as is contended by the Bank in the instant case.

Further support for construing 12 U.S.C. § 85 so as to incorporate the state's interpretation of its own law can be found in *Union National Bank v. Louisville, N.A. & C. Ry.*, 163 U.S. 325, 331 (1896), cited by the *Evans* dissenters, and in the Supreme Court's recognition of a general policy of state-federal equalization and "competitive equality" under various twentieth century amendments to the Act in different but related contexts. [The court quotes *First National Bank v. Walker Bank & Trust Co.*, 385 U.S. 252, 261 (1966).]

The policy of competitive state-federal equality in the context of usury regulation is supported by the District Court's construction of § 85 which imposes the same interest ceiling on national banks as on the most favored lenders in the state, and thereby puts

15. *See* Comment, 58 Iowa L. Rev. 1240, 1265-66 (1973). This comment suggests with documentation that *Tiffany v. Nat'l Bank*, 85 U.S. (18 Wall.) 409 (1873), and cases such as *Northway* following it find no support in, and directly oppose, the policy of strict national and state bank interest rate parity enunciated in the legislative history of the 1864 Act.

17. [Cong. Globe, 38th Cong., 1st Sess.] 2126 [(1864)].

national banks on an equal footing with the most favored lenders in the state without giving them an unconscionable and destructive advantage over all state lenders. Whether the state banks will enjoy parity in interest regulation with national banks is thus left to the states to decide. The federal statute merely prevents state legislation which purports to give state banks or possibly any state lender advantages over national banks.

Notes and Comments 5.21. What if National Bank, N.A., operates only in a state that does not make exceptions in its usury laws for any loan-related fees. National Bank charges an "overdraft item fee" on every overdrawn check that the bank honors. According to the bank, this fee is intended to cover "the administrative cost of processing checks drawn in excess of the collected balance in a depositor's account." The bank also charges the depositor interest on the overdrawn amount, at the maximum allowable interest rate. Has National Bank committed usury under the NBA? In answering this question, see *Video Trax, Inc. v. NationsBank, N.A.*, 33 F.Supp.2d 1041 (S.D.Fla. 1998), *affirmed*, 205 F.3d 1358 (11th Cir. 2000), *cert. denied*, 531 U.S. 822.

5.22. *Northway* and *Nowlin* clash over the proper application of section 85. Which presents the better argument? Is the difference in the two cases simply a difference between an historically-rooted approach to the provision and one that attempts to fashion a contemporary reading of the provision in light of factual developments during the century following its enactment?

5.23. Can *Nowlin*, with its reliance on the "competitive equality rationale," be satisfactorily squared with *Tiffany*? With *Marquette Nat. Bank*? Is *Nowlin* consistent with the approach taken by the Court in *Smiley*? Is *Northway*?

5.24. *GLBA and interstate banks*. In light of *Marquette Nat. Bank* and *Smiley*, if a national bank in state *A* has an interstate branch[44] in state *B*, which state usury rate is used in referencing over under § 85? Presumably, it is the rate that applies to the bank's home office. In response to this situation, the GLBA provides that if an interstate bank can charge a particular interest rate, then a local bank in the state into which the interstate bank has branched may charge a comparable rate. GLBA, § 731 (codified at 12 U.S.C. § 1831u(f)). The legislative history of the act indicates that this amendment was intended to "provide[] loan pricing parity among interstate banks." *Conference Report on S. 900, reprinted in* 145 Cong. Rec. H11255-01, 11302 (1999) (discussing congressional intent concerning GLBA section 731). Does section 731 preempt contrary state usury law? *See Johnson v. Bank of Bentonville*, 122 F.Supp.2d 994 (W.D.Ark. 2000) (overriding Arkansas usury law).

5.25. Quarter National Bank is located in a state that has enacted the following statutory provisions concerning usury:

> § 1. a. No person may take or receive interest on any loan or extension of credit in excess of 10 per centum per annum.
>
> b. For purposes of this section, the term "person" means any individual, partnership, corporation, or other association.
>
> § 2. Notwithstanding any other provision of law, no bank may take or receive interest on any loan or extension of credit in excess of 8 per centum per annum.
>
> § 3. Notwithstanding any other provision of law, a savings association may take or receive interest on any loan or extension of credit in an amount not to exceed 15 per centum per annum.
>
> § 4. a. Notwithstanding any other provision of law, any person engaged in the provision of consumer credit may take or receive interest on any loan or

44. On interstate branching, see Chapter 3, § 4, *supra*.

extension of credit in an amount not to exceed 20 per centum per annum.

b. For purposes of this section, the term "person" means any individual, partnership, corporation, or other association.

c. For purposes of this section, the term "consumer credit" means the provision of a loan or other extension of credit, whether in a single transaction or in a series of transactions, or by the establishment of a revolving line of credit, for the purpose of financing the purchase by an individual of products or services for personal consumption and not for resale.

Quarter is negotiating the terms of a loan with Bosworth Partners, which has applied for a line of credit to finance its periodic purchases of inventory for its chain of high-fashion boutiques, the Henry Shoppes. Bosworth has recently opened Henry VI and Henry VII and has found that the volume of business at the boutiques has reached the point where it can no longer comfortably finance inventory out of current receipts. Quarter has evaluated the credit risk in making the loan, and it would like to price the loan at an annual rate of approximately 18 percent of the outstanding balance on the line of credit. How would you advise Quarter with respect to the legality of this interest rate? *Cf. Fisher v. First Nat. Bank of Chicago*, 538 F.2d 1284 (7th Cir. 1976), *cert. denied*, 429 U.S. 1062 (1977); *Acker v. Provident Nat. Bank*, 512 F.2d 729 (3d Cir. 1975); *First Bank of Cadillac v. Miller*, 347 N.W.2d 715, 131 Mich. App. 764 (1984); *Attorney General of Maryland v. Equitable Trust Co.*, 450 A.2d 1273, 294 Md. 385 (1982).

5.26. Would it make any difference to your answer to the previous question if none of the other lenders in the state charged the maximum allowable rate of interest under the statutory provisions quoted above? *Cf. United Missouri Bank of Kansas City, N.A. v. Danforth*, 394 F. Supp. 774 (W.D.Mo. 1975).

5.27. *Federal preemption of state usury laws.* Title V of the Depository Institutions Deregulation and Monetary Control Act of 1980 preempted state law provisions concerning usury with respect to certain specified types of loans. *See generally* Weaver and O'Malley, *The Depository Institutions Deregulation and Monetary Control Act of 1980: An Overview*, 98 Banking L. J. 100, 110-111 (1980). On a prospective basis only, the effect of state usury provisions on certain first mortgage loans made by depository institutions and other mortgage lenders was permanently preempted, unless the state enacted legislation overriding the preemption within three years of April 1, 1980. 12 U.S.C. § 1735f-7a & note. In addition, similar preemptive provisions applied prospectively to business and agricultural loans of $1,000 or more, for a three-year period. 12 U.S.C. § 86a (1982). Finally, as to all loans made by federally insured depository institutions, state usury provisions imposing interest rate limitations lower than the federal rate (*i.e.*, 1% above the 90-day commercial paper discount rate charged by the Fed) were permanently preempted, subject to state law override at any time. *See, e.g.*, 12 U.S.C. §§ 1785(g), 1831d.

5.28. *State overriding legislation.* Despite the political volatility of state usury policy–or perhaps because of it–few states took advantage of the provisions permitting state override of federal preemption. These were Colorado, Georgia, Hawaii, Idaho, Iowa, Kansas, Massachusetts, Minnesota, Nebraska, Nevada, North Carolina, South Carolina, South Dakota and Wisconsin, plus Puerto Rico. *See* 6 Fed. Banking L. Rep. (CCH) ¶¶ 64-005, at 73,602, 64-053 *passim* (discussing state overrides of federal preemption).

5.29. *Penalties applicable to usurious loans.* Assume that Quarter National Bank has made the loan to Bosworth discussed in note 5.23, *supra*, at an annual rate of 21 percent. The state in which Quarter is located provides as follows in its Banking Code:

§ 5. a. Any person who charges a rate of interest on any loan or extension of credit in violation of the provisions of the Usurious Loan Act [§§ 1-3, *supra*] shall . . . forfeit to the borrower the original principal amount of such loan or extension of credit.

b. Any person who knowingly charges a rate of interest on any loan or extension of credit in violation of the provisions of the Usurious Loan Act shall . . . be liable to the borrower in an amount equal to twice the amount of any interest actually paid by the borrower on account of such loan or extension of credit.

6. Any person who, making a loan or extension of credit subject to the Consumer Credit Act [§ 4, *supra*], charges a rate of interest on such loan or extension of credit in violation of the provisions of the act shall . . . be liable to the borrower an amount equal to three times the amount of the average daily balance of such loan or extension of credit from the date the loan or extension of credit was made until the date the suit for damages under this section is filed.

If Quarter is found to have charged a usurious rate of interest on the Bosworth loan in a suit brought by Bosworth, what will be the amount of its liability? Consider the following cases.

Farmer's Nat. Bank v. Dearing

91 U.S. 29 (1875)

Mr. Justice SWAYNE delivered the opinion of the court.

The question presented for our determination involves the construction of the provisions of the national bank act of Congress of the 3d of June, 1864, 13 Stat. 99, upon the subject of the interest taken by the institutions organized under that act. [The Court quotes 12 U.S.C. § 86.] . . .

The facts of the case are few and simple. On the 2d of September, 1874, it was agreed between the parties that Dearing should make his promissory note to one Deitman for $2,000, payable one month from date, and that the bank should discount the note for Dearing at the rate of interest of ten per cent per annum. This agreement was carried out. The bank received the note, and paid to Dearing the sum of $1,981.67. The discount reserved and taken was $18.33. The rate of interest which the bank was legally authorized to take was seven per cent per annum. The excess reserved over that rate was $5.50. Dearing failed to pay the note at maturity. The bank thereupon sued him in the Superior Court of Buffalo. He answered, that the agreement touching the discount was usurious, corrupt, and illegal; that it avoided the note; and that he was in no wise liable to the plaintiff. The court sustained this defence, and gave judgment for the defendant. . . .

These clauses [§ 86 of the National Bank Act], examined by their own light, seem to us too clear to admit of doubt as to any thing to which they relate. They form a system of regulations. All the parts are in harmony with each other, and cover the entire subject.

But it is contended that the phrase, "a rate of interest greater than aforesaid," as it stands in the context, has reference only to the preceding sentence, which relates to banks where no rate of interest is fixed by law; and that hence it leaves the consequences of usury, where such rate is fixed, to be governed wholly by the local law upon the subject. This, in the State of New York, would, in all such cases, render the contract a nullity, and forfeit the debt. Such the Court of Appeals held to be the law of this case, and adjudged accordingly.

Neither of these views can be maintained. The collocation of the terms in question does not grammatically require such a construction. Viewed in this light, the phrase is as much applicable to both the foregoing clauses as to the next preceding one. The point to be sought is the intent of the law-making power. The offense of usury under this section is as great where the local law does not, as where it does, define the rate of interest. The same considerations apply in both cases. Why should Congress punish in one class of cases, and, so far as its action is concerned, exempt in the other? Why such discrimination? The result would be, that in Pennsylvania, where the contract would be void only as to the unlawful excess, the bank would lost nothing but such excess; while in New York, under a contract precisely the same, except as to the identity of the lender, the entire debt would be lost to the bank. This would be contrary to the plainest principles of reason and justice.

A purpose to produce or permit such a state of things ought not to be imputed to Congress, unless the circumstances are so cogent as to render that result inevitable.

We find nothing within the scope of the subject of that character. . . .

It must always be borne in mind that the Constitution of the United States, "and the laws which shall be made in pursuance thereof," are "the supreme law of the land" (Const., art. 6), and that this law is as much a part of the law of each State, and as binding upon its authorities and people, as its own local constitution and laws.

In any view that can be taken of the thirtieth section, the power to supplement it by State legislation is conferred neither expressly nor by implication. There is nothing which gives support to such a suggestion.

There was reason why the rate of interest should be governed by the law of the State where the bank is situated; but there is none why usury should be visited with the forfeiture of the entire debt in one State, and with no penal consequence whatever in another. This, we think, would be unreasonable, and contrary to the manifest intent of Congress. . . .

The thirtieth section is remedial as well as penal, and is to be liberally construed to effect the object which Congress had in view in enacting it. . . .

Beneficial National Bank v. Anderson

539 U.S. 1 (2003)

Justice STEVENS delivered the opinion of the Court.

I

[Borrowers who obtained secured "tax refund anticipation loans" brought a state court action against, *inter alia*, the lending national bank seeking damages for violations of a common law usury doctrine and an Alabama usury statute. The action was removed to federal court, and the borrowers moved to remand. The district court denied the motion, and the borrowers appealed. The Eleventh Circuit reversed and remanded. On certiorari, the Supreme Court reversed, holding that: (*i*) the National Bank Act provided the exclusive cause of action for usury against national banks, and (*ii*) under the "complete preemption" doctrine, the cause of action arose only under federal law and could therefore be removed. The applicability of the "complete preemption" doctrine depended upon whether or not the federal statute at issue wholly displaced the state law cause of action through complete preemption. In the following excerpts from the decision, the Court considers whether the NBA usury provisions completely preempt state law.]

Respondents are 26 individual taxpayers who made pledges of their anticipated tax refunds to secure short-term loans obtained from petitioner Beneficial National Bank, a national bank chartered under the National Bank Act. Respondents brought suit in an Alabama court against the bank and the two other petitioners that arranged the loans, seeking compensatory and punitive damages on the theory, among others, that the bank's interest rates were usurious. . . . Their complaint did not refer to any federal law.

Petitioners removed the case to the United States District Court for the Middle

District of Alabama. In their notice of removal they asserted that the National Bank Act, Rev. Stat. § 5917, as amended, 12 U.S.C. § 85, is the exclusive provision governing the rate of interest that a national bank may lawfully charge, that the rates charged to respondents complied with that provision, that § 86 provides the exclusive remedies available against a national bank charging excessive interest, and that the removal statute, 28 U.S.C. § 1441, therefore applied. . . . The District Court denied respondents' motion to remand the case to state court but certified the question whether it had jurisdiction to proceed with the case to the Court of Appeals pursuant to 28 U.S.C. § 1292(b).

A divided panel of the Eleventh Circuit reversed. *Anderson v. H & R Block, Inc.*, 287 F.3d 1038 (2002). The majority held that under our "well-pleaded complaint" rule, removal is generally not permitted unless the complaint expressly alleges a federal claim and that the narrow exception from that rule known as the "complete preemption doctrine" did not apply because it could "find no clear congressional intent to permit removal under §§ 85 and 86." *Id.*, at 1048. Because this holding conflicted with an Eighth Circuit decision, *Krispin v. May Dept. Stores Co.*, 218 F.3d 919 (2000), we granted certiorari. . . .

III

Count IV of respondents' complaint sought relief for "usury violations" and claimed that petitioners "charged ... excessive interest in violation of the common law usury doctrine" and violated "Alabama Code. § 8-8-1, *et seq.* by charging excessive interest." . . . Respondents' complaint thus expressly charged petitioners with usury. . . . Does the National Bank Act provide the exclusive cause of action for usury claims against national banks? If so, then the cause of action necessarily arises under federal law and the case is removable. If not, then the complaint does not arise under federal law and is not removable.

Sections 85 and 86 serve distinct purposes. The former sets forth the substantive limits on the rates of interest that national banks may charge. The latter sets forth the elements of a usury claim against a national bank, provides for a 2-year statute of limitations for such a claim, and prescribes the remedies available to borrowers who are charged higher rates and the procedures governing such a claim. If, as petitioners asserted in their notice of removal, the interest that the bank charged to respondents did not violate § 85 limits, the statute unquestionably pre-empts any common-law or Alabama statutory rule that would treat those rates as usurious. The section would therefore provide the petitioners with a complete federal defense. Such a federal defense, however, would not justify removal. . . . Only if Congress intended § 86 to provide the exclusive cause of action for usury claims against national banks would the statute be comparable to the provisions that we construed in [*Avco Corp. v. Machinists,* 390 U.S. 557 (1968) (involving § 301 of Labor Management Relations Act of 1947, 29 U.S.C. § 185)] and [*Metropolitan Life Ins. Co. v. Taylor,* 481 U.S. 58 (1987) (involving Employee Retirement Income Security Act of 1974, 29 U.S.C. § 1001 *et seq.*)].[5]

In a series of cases decided shortly after the Act was passed, we endorsed that approach. In *Farmers' and Mechanics' Nat. Bank v. Dearing,* 91 U.S. 29, 32-33 (1875), we rejected the borrower's attempt to have an entire debt forfeited, as authorized by New York law, stating that the various provisions of §§ 85 and 86 "form a system of regulations ... [a]ll the parts [of which] are in harmony with each other and cover the entire subject," so that "the State law would have no bearing whatever upon the case." We also observed that "[i]n any view that can be taken of [§ 86], the power to supplement it by State legislation is conferred neither expressly nor by implication." *Id.*, at 35. In *Evans v. National Bank of Savannah,* 251

5. Because the proper inquiry focuses on whether Congress intended the federal cause of action to be exclusive rather than on whether Congress intended that the cause of action be removable, the fact that these sections of the National Bank Act were passed in 1864, 11 years prior to the passage of the statute authorizing removal, is irrelevant, contrary to respondents' assertions.

U.S. 108, 114 (1919), we stated that "federal law ... completely defines what constitutes the taking of usury by a national bank, referring to the state law only to determine the maximum permitted rate." See also *Barnet v. National Bank,* 98 U.S. 555, 558 (1879) (the "statutes of Ohio and Indiana upon the subject of usury ... cannot affect the case" because the Act "creates a new right" that is "exclusive"); *Haseltine v. Central Bank of Springfield,* 183 U.S. 132, 134 (1901) ("[T]he definition of usury and the penalties affixed thereto must be determined by the National Banking Act and not by the law of the State").

In addition to this Court's longstanding and consistent construction of the National Bank Act as providing an exclusive federal cause of action for usury against national banks, this Court has also recognized the special nature of federally chartered banks. Uniform rules limiting the liability of national banks and prescribing exclusive remedies for their overcharges are an integral part of a banking system that needed protection from "possible unfriendly State legislation." *Tiffany v. National Bank of Mo.,* 18 Wall. 409, 412 (1874). The same federal interest that protected national banks from the state taxation that Chief Justice Marshall characterized as the "power to destroy," *McCulloch v. Maryland,* 4 Wheat. 316, 431 (1819), supports the established interpretation of §§ 85 and 86 that gives those provisions the requisite pre-emptive force to provide removal jurisdiction. In actions against national banks for usury, these provisions supersede both the substantive and the remedial provisions of state usury laws and create a federal remedy for overcharges that is exclusive, even when a state complainant, as here, relies entirely on state law. Because §§ 85 and 86 provide the exclusive cause of action for such claims, there is, in short, no such thing as a state-law claim of usury against a national bank. Even though the complaint makes no mention of federal law, it unquestionably and unambiguously claims that petitioners violated usury laws. This cause of action against national banks only arises under federal law and could, therefore, be removed under § 1441. . . .

Justice SCALIA, with whom Justice THOMAS joins, dissenting.

Today's opinion takes the view that because § 30 of the National Bank Act, 12 U.S.C. §§ 85, 86, provides the exclusive cause of action for claims of usury against a national bank, all such claims–even if explicitly pleaded under state law–are to be construed as "aris[ing] under" federal law for purposes of our jurisdictional statutes. . . . This view finds scant support in our precedents and no support whatever in the National Bank Act or any other Act of Congress. I respectfully dissent. . . .

. . . [E]ven if the Court is correct that the National Bank Act obliterates entirely any state-created right to relief for usury against a national bank, that does not explain how or why the claim of such a right is transmogrified into the claim of a federal right. Congress's mere act of creating a federal right and eliminating all state-created rights *in no way* suggests an expansion of federal jurisdiction so as to wrest from state courts the authority to decide questions of pre-emption under the National Bank Act.

d. Federal Preemption and State Consumer Protection Statutes

As *Marquette* and *Smiley* have illustrated, federal usury provisions applicable to national banks have the effect of preempting inconsistent state law. Nevertheless, the traditional norm is that banking and commercial transactions involving national banks are governed by state law, not federal.[45] Contemporary state consumer protection statutes may, by their own terms, apply to such transactions. Do these statutes come under the traditional norm, or are they vulnerable to preemption arguments? In answering this question, consider the following case.

Watters v. Wachovia Bank, N.A.

550 U.S. 1 (2007)

Justice GINSBURG delivered the opinion of the Court.

[Wachovia, a national bank, and its state-chartered mortgage company subsidiary sued the Michigan Commissioner of Insurance and Financial Services seeking declaratory and injunctive relief from state registration and inspection requirements, based on preemption of the state law by the NBA. The Western District of Michigan granted summary judgment for the plaintiffs, and the Sixth Circuit affirmed. On certiorari, the Supreme Court affirmed, holding, *inter alia*, that under the NBA Wachovia's mortgage business–whether conducted by the bank itself or through its operating subsidiary–was subject to supervision by the OCC, and was not subject to the licensing, reporting, and visitorial regimes of the states in which the subsidiary operated.]

Business activities of national banks are controlled by the National Bank Act (NBA or Act), 12 U.S.C. § 1 *et seq*., and regulations promulgated thereunder by the Office of the Comptroller of the Currency (OCC). See §§ 24, 93a, 371(a). As the agency charged by Congress with supervision of the NBA, OCC oversees the operations of national banks and their interactions with customers. See *NationsBank of N. C., N.A. v. Variable Annuity Life Ins. Co.,* 513 U.S. 251, 254, 256 (1995). The agency exercises visitorial powers, including the authority to audit the bank's books and records, largely to the exclusion of other governmental entities, state or federal. See § 484(a); 12 CFR § 7.4000 (2006). . . .

Respondent Wachovia Bank, a national bank, conducts its real estate lending business through Wachovia Mortgage Corporation, a wholly owned, state-chartered entity, licensed as an operating subsidiary by OCC. It is uncontested in this suit that Wachovia's real estate business, if conducted by the national bank itself, would be subject to OCC's superintendence, to the exclusion of state registration requirements and visitorial authority. The question in dispute is whether the bank's mortgage lending activities remain outside the governance of state licensing and auditing agencies when those activities are conducted, not by a division or department of the bank, but by the bank's operating subsidiary. In accord with the Courts of Appeals that have addressed the issue,[1] we hold that Wachovia's mortgage business, whether conducted by the bank itself or through the bank's operating subsidiary, is subject to OCC's superintendence, and not to the licensing, reporting, and visitorial regimes of the several States in which the subsidiary operates.

I

Wachovia Bank is a national banking association chartered by OCC. Respondent Wachovia Mortgage is a North Carolina corporation that engages in the business of real estate lending in the State of Michigan and elsewhere. Michigan's statutory regime exempts banks, both national and state, from state mortgage lending regulation, but requires mortgage

45. *See, e.g.*, § 1, *supra* (discussing the traditional principle).

1. *National City Bank of Indiana v. Turnbaugh,* 463 F.3d 325 (C.A.4 2006); *Wachovia Bank, N.A. v. Burke,* 414 F.3d 305 (C.A.2 2005); 431 F.3d 556 (C.A.6 2005) (case below); *Wells Fargo Bank N.A. v. Boutris,* 419 F.3d 949 (C.A.9 2005.

brokers, lenders, and servicers that are subsidiaries of national banks to register with the State's Office of Insurance and Financial Services (OIFS) and submit to state supervision. Mich. Comp. Laws Ann. §§ 445.1656(1), 445.1679(1)(a) (West 2002), 493.52(1), and 493.53a(d) (West 1998).[2] From 1997 until 2003, Wachovia Mortgage was registered with OIFS to engage in mortgage lending. As a registrant, Wachovia Mortgage was required, *inter alia,* to pay an annual operating fee, file an annual report, and open its books and records to inspection by OIFS examiners. §§ 445.1657, 445.1658, 445.1671 (West 2002), 493.54, 493.56a(2), (13) (West 1998).

Petitioner Linda Watters, the commissioner of OIFS, administers the State's lending laws. She exercises "general supervision and control" over registered lenders, and has authority to conduct examinations and investigations and to enforce requirements against registrants. See §§ 445.1661, 445.1665, 445.1666 (West 2002), 493.58, 493.56b, 493.59, 493.62a (West 1998 and Supp.2005). She also has authority to investigate consumer complaints and take enforcement action if she finds that a complaint is not "being adequately pursued by the appropriate federal regulatory authority." § 445.1663(2) (West 2002).

On January 1, 2003, Wachovia Mortgage became a wholly owned operating subsidiary of Wachovia Bank. Three months later, Wachovia Mortgage advised the State of Michigan that it was surrendering its mortgage lending registration. Because it had become an operating subsidiary of a national bank, Wachovia Mortgage maintained, Michigan's registration and inspection requirements were preempted. Watters responded with a letter advising Wachovia Mortgage that it would no longer be authorized to conduct mortgage lending activities in Michigan.

Wachovia Mortgage and Wachovia Bank filed suit against Watters, in her official capacity as commissioner, in the United States District Court for the Western District of Michigan. They sought declaratory and injunctive relief prohibiting Watters from enforcing Michigan's registration prescriptions against Wachovia Mortgage, and from interfering with OCC's exclusive visitorial authority. The NBA and regulations promulgated thereunder, they urged, vest supervisory authority in OCC and preempt the application of the state-law controls at issue. Specifically, Wachovia Mortgage and Wachovia Bank challenged as preempted certain provisions of two Michigan statutes-the Mortgage Brokers, Lenders, and Services Licensing Act and the Secondary Mortgage Loan Act. The challenged provisions (1) require mortgage lenders-including national bank operating subsidiaries but not national banks themselves-to register and pay fees to the State before they may conduct banking activities in Michigan, and authorize the commissioner to deny or revoke registrations, §§ 445.1652(1) (West Supp.2006), 445.1656(1)(d) (West 2002), 445.1657(1), 445.1658, 445.1679(1)(a), 493.52(1) (West 1998), 493.53a(d), 493.54, 493.55(4), 493.56a(2), and 493.61; (2) require submission of annual financial statements to the commissioner and retention of certain documents in a particular format, §§ 445.1657(2) (West 2002), 445.1671, 493.56a(2) (West 1998); (3) grant the commissioner inspection and enforcement authority over registrants, §§ 445.1661 (West 2002), 493.56b (West Supp.2005); and (4) authorize the commissioner to take regulatory or enforcement actions against covered lenders, §§ 445.1665 (West 2002), 445.1666, 493.58-59, and 493.62a (West 1998).

In response, Watters argued that, because Wachovia Mortgage was not itself a national bank, the challenged Michigan controls were applicable and were not preempted. She also contended that the Tenth Amendment to the Constitution of the United States prohibits OCC's exclusive superintendence of national bank lending activities conducted

---

2. Michigan's law exempts subsidiaries of national banks that maintain a main office or branch office in Michigan. Mich. Comp. Laws Ann. §§ 445.1652(1)(b) (West Supp.2006), 445.1675(m) (West 2002), 493.53a(d) (West 1998). Wachovia Bank has no such office in Michigan.

through operating subsidiaries.

The District Court granted summary judgment to the banks in relevant part. . . . Invoking the two-step framework of *Chevron U.S.A. Inc. v. Natural Resources Defense Council, Inc.,* 467 U.S. 837 (1984), the court deferred to the Comptroller's determination that an operating subsidiary is subject to state regulation only to the extent that the parent bank would be if it performed the same functions[,] citing, *e.g.,* 12 CFR §§ 5.34(e)(3), 7.4006 (2004)). The court also rejected Watters' Tenth Amendment argument. . . .

II

A

. . . The Act vested in nationally chartered banks enumerated powers and "all such incidental powers as shall be necessary to carry on the business of banking." 12 U.S.C. § 24 Seventh. To prevent inconsistent or intrusive state regulation from impairing the national system, Congress provided: "No national bank shall be subject to any visitorial powers except as authorized by Federal law ...." § 484(a).

In the years since the NBA's enactment, we have repeatedly made clear that federal control shields national banking from unduly burdensome and duplicative state regulation. See, *e.g., Beneficial Nat. Bank v. Anderson,* 539 U.S. 1, 10 (2003) (national banking system protected from "possible unfriendly State legislation" (quoting *Tiffany v. National Bank of Mo.,* 18 Wall. 409, 412 (1874))). Federally chartered banks are subject to state laws of general application in their daily business to the extent such laws do not conflict with the letter or the general purposes of the NBA. *Davis v. Elmira Savings Bank,* 161 U.S. 275, 290 (1896). See also [*Atherton v. FDIC,* 519 U.S. 213, 223 (1997)]. For example, state usury laws govern the maximum rate of interest national banks can charge on loans, 12 U.S.C. § 85, contracts made by national banks "are governed and construed by State laws," *National Bank v. Commonwealth,* 9 Wall. 353, 362 (1870), and national banks' "acquisition and transfer of property [are] based on State law," *ibid.* However, "the States can exercise no control over [national banks], nor in any wise affect their operation, except in so far as Congress may see proper to permit. Any thing beyond this is an abuse, because it is the usurpation of power which a single State cannot give." *Farmers' and Mechanics' Nat. Bank v. Dearing,* 91 U.S. 29, 34 (1875) (internal quotation marks omitted).

We have "interpret[ed] grants of both enumerated and incidental 'powers' to national banks as grants of authority not normally limited by, but rather ordinarily pre-empting, contrary state law." *Barnett Bank of Marion Cty., N.A. v. Nelson,* 517 U.S. 25, 32 (1996). See also *Franklin Nat. Bank of Franklin Square v. New York,* 347 U.S. 373, 375-379 (1954). States are permitted to regulate the activities of national banks where doing so does not prevent or significantly interfere with the national bank's or the national bank regulator's exercise of its powers. But when state prescriptions significantly impair the exercise of authority, enumerated or incidental under the NBA, the State's regulations must give way. *Barnett Bank,* 517 U.S., at 32-34 (federal law permitting national banks to sell insurance in small towns preempted state statute prohibiting banks from selling most types of insurance); *Franklin Nat. Bank,* 347 U.S., at 377-379 (local restrictions preempted because they burdened exercise of national banks' incidental power to advertise).

The NBA authorizes national banks to engage in mortgage lending, subject to OCC regulation. [The Court quotes 12 U.S.C. § 371(a).]

Beyond genuine dispute, state law may not significantly burden a national bank's own exercise of its real estate lending power, just as it may not curtail or hinder a national bank's efficient exercise of any other power, incidental or enumerated under the NBA. See *Barnett Bank,* 517 U.S., at 33-34; *Franklin,* 347 U.S., at 375-379. See also 12 CFR § 34.4(a)(1) (2006) (identifying preempted state controls on mortgage lending, including licensing and registration). In particular, real estate lending, when conducted by a national bank, is immune from state visitorial control: The NBA specifically vests exclusive authority to examine and inspect in OCC. 12 U.S.C. § 484(a) ("No national bank shall be subject to any visitorial powers except as authorized by Federal law.").

Harmoniously, the Michigan provisions at issue exempt national banks from coverage. Mich. Comp. Laws Ann. § 445.1675(a) (West 2002). This is not simply a matter of the Michigan Legislature's grace. . . . For, as the parties recognize, the NBA would have preemptive force, *i.e.,* it would spare a national bank from state controls of the kind here involved. . . . State laws that conditioned national banks' real estate lending on registration with the State, and subjected such lending to the State's investigative and enforcement machinery would surely interfere with the banks' federally authorized business: National banks would be subject to registration, inspection, and enforcement regimes imposed not just by Michigan, but by all States in which the banks operate.[6] Diverse and duplicative superintendence of national banks' engagement in the business of banking, we observed over a century ago, is precisely what the NBA was designed to prevent: "Th[e] legislation has in view the erection of a system extending throughout the country, and independent, so far as powers conferred are concerned, of state legislation which, if permitted to be applicable, might impose limitations and restrictions as various and as numerous as the States." *Easton v. Iowa,* 188 U.S. 220, 229 (1903). Congress did not intend, we explained, "to leave the field open for the States to attempt to promote the welfare and stability of national banks by direct legislation .... [C]onfusion would necessarily result from control possessed and exercised by two independent authorities." *Id.*, at 231-232.

Recognizing the burdens and undue duplication state controls could produce, Congress included in the NBA an express command: "No national bank shall be subject to any visitorial powers except as authorized by Federal law... ." 12 U.S.C. § 484(a). . . . "Visitation," we have explained "is the act of a superior or superintending officer, who visits a corporation to examine into its manner of conducting business, and enforce an observance of its laws and regulations." *Guthrie v. Harkness,* 199 U.S. 148, 158 (1905) (internal quotation marks omitted). See also 12 CFR § 7.4000(a)(2) (2006) (defining "visitorial" power as "(i) [e]xamination of a bank; (ii) [i]nspection of a bank's books and records; (iii) [r]egulation and supervision of activities authorized or permitted pursuant to federal banking law; and (iv)[e]nforcing compliance with any applicable federal or state laws concerning those activities"). Michigan, therefore, cannot confer on its commissioner examination and enforcement authority over mortgage lending, or any other banking business done by national banks.[7]

---

6. See 69 Fed.Reg. 1908 (2004) ("The application of multiple, often unpredictable, different state or local restrictions and requirements prevents [national banks] from operating in the manner authorized under Federal law, is costly and burdensome, interferes with their ability to plan their business and manage their risks, and subjects them to uncertain liabilities and potential exposure.").

7. Ours is indeed a "dual banking system." . . . But it is a system that has never permitted States to license, inspect, and supervise national banks as they do state banks. The dissent repeatedly refers to the policy of "competitive equality" featured in *First Nat. Bank in Plant City v. Dickinson,* 396 U.S. 122, 131 (1969). . . . Those words, however, should not be ripped from their context. *Plant City* involved the McFadden Act (Branch Banks), 44 Stat. 1228, 12 U.S.C. § 36, in which Congress expressly authorized national banks to establish branches "only when, where, and how state law would authorize a state bank to establish and operate such [branches]." 396 U.S., at 130. See also *id.*, at 131 ("[W]hile Congress has absolute authority over national banks, the [McFadden Act] has incorporated by reference the limitations which state law places on branch banking activities by state banks. Congress has deliberately settled upon a policy intended to foster competitive equality. ... [The] Act reflects the congressional concern that neither system ha[s] advantages over the other in the use of branch banking." (quoting *First Nat. Bank of Logan v. Walker Bank & Trust Co.,* 385 U.S. 252, 261

B

While conceding that Michigan's licensing, registration, and inspection requirements cannot be applied to national banks, . . . Watters argues that the State's regulatory regime survives preemption with respect to national banks' operating subsidiaries. Because such subsidiaries are separately chartered under some State's law, Watters characterizes them simply as "affiliates" of national banks, and contends that even though they are subject to OCC's superintendence, they are also subject to multistate control. . . . We disagree.

Since 1966, OCC has recognized the "incidental" authority of national banks under § 24 Seventh to do business through operating subsidiaries. See 31 Fed.Reg. 11459-11460 (1966); 12 CFR § 5.34(e)(1) (2006) ("A national bank may conduct in an operating subsidiary activities that are permissible for a national bank to engage in directly either as part of, or incidental to, the business of banking...."). That authority is uncontested by Michigan's commissioner. . . . OCC licenses and oversees national bank operating subsidiaries just as it does national banks. § 5.34(e)(3) ("An operating subsidiary conducts activities authorized under this section pursuant to the same authorization, terms and conditions that apply to the conduct of such activities by its parent national bank.");[8] United States Office of the Comptroller of the Currency, Related Organizations: Comptroller's Handbook 53 (Aug.2004) (hereinafter Comptroller's Handbook) ("Operating subsidiaries are subject to the same supervision and regulation as the parent bank, except where otherwise provided by law or OCC regulation.").

. . . For supervisory purposes, OCC treats national banks and their operating subsidiaries as a single economic enterprise. . . . OCC oversees both entities by reference to "business line," applying the same controls whether banking "activities are conducted directly or through an operating subsidiary." . . .[10]

As earlier noted, Watters does not contest the authority of national banks to do

---

(1966))). "[W]here Congress has not expressly conditioned the grant of 'power' upon a grant of state permission, the Court has ordinarily found that no such condition applies." *Barnett Bank of Marion Cty., N.A. v. Nelson,* 517 U.S. 25, 34 (1996). The NBA provisions before us, unlike the McFadden Act, do not condition the exercise of power by national banks on state allowance of similar exercises by state banks. . . .

8. The regulation further provides:

> "If, upon examination, the OCC determines that the operating subsidiary is operating in violation of law, regulation, or written condition, or in an unsafe or unsound manner or otherwise threatens the safety or soundness of the bank, the OCC will direct the bank or operating subsidiary to take appropriate remedial action, which may include requiring the bank to divest or liquidate the operating subsidiary, or discontinue specified activities." 12 CFR § 5.34(e)(3) (2006).

10. For example, "for purposes of applying statutory or regulatory limits, such as lending limits or dividend restrictions," *e.g.,* 12 U.S.C. §§ 56, 60, 84, 371d, "[t]he results of operations of operating subsidiaries are consolidated with those of its parent." Comptroller's Handbook 64. Likewise, for accounting and regulatory reporting purposes, an operating subsidiary is treated as part of the member bank; assets and liabilities of the two entities are combined. See 12 CFR §§ 5.34(e)(4)(i), 223.3(w) (2006). OCC treats financial subsidiaries differently. A national bank may not consolidate the assets and liabilities of a financial subsidiary with those of the bank. Comptroller's Handbook 64. It cannot be fairly maintained "that the transfer in 2003 of [Wachovia Mortgage's] ownership from the holding company to the Bank" resulted in no relevant changes to the company's business. . . . On becoming Wachovia's operating subsidiary, Wachovia Mortgage became subject to the same terms and conditions as national banks, including the full supervisory authority of OCC. This change exposed the company to significantly more federal oversight than it experienced as a state nondepository institution.

business through operating subsidiaries. Nor does she dispute OCC's authority to supervise and regulate operating subsidiaries in the same manner as national banks. Still, Watters seeks to impose state regulation on operating subsidiaries over and above regulation undertaken by OCC. But just as duplicative state examination, supervision, and regulation would significantly burden mortgage lending when engaged in by national banks, . . . so too would those state controls interfere with that same activity when engaged in by an operating subsidiary.

We have never held that the preemptive reach of the NBA extends only to a national bank itself. Rather, in analyzing whether state law hampers the federally permitted activities of a national bank, we have focused on the exercise of a national bank's *powers,* not on its corporate structure. See, *e.g., Barnett Bank,* 517 U.S., at 32. And we have treated operating subsidiaries as equivalent to national banks with respect to powers exercised under federal law (except where federal law provides otherwise). . . . See also *Clarke v. Securities Industry Assn.,* 479 U.S. 388 (1987) (national banks, acting through operating subsidiaries, have power to offer discount brokerage services).[11]

Security against significant interference by state regulators is a characteristic condition of the "business of banking" conducted by national banks, and mortgage lending is one aspect of that business. See, *e.g.,* 12 U.S.C. § 484(a); 12 CFR § 34.4(a)(1) (2006). . . . That security should adhere whether the business is conducted by the bank itself or is assigned to an operating subsidiary licensed by OCC whose authority to carry on the business coincides completely with that of the bank. See *Wells Fargo Bank, N.A. v. Boutris,* 419 F.3d 949, 960 (C.A.9 2005) (determination whether to conduct business through operating subsidiaries or through subdivisions is "essentially one of internal organization").

Watters contends that if Congress meant to deny States visitorial powers over operating subsidiaries, it would have written § 484(a)'s ban on state inspection to apply not only to national banks but also to their affiliates. She points out that § 481, which authorizes OCC to examine "affiliates" of national banks, does not speak to state visitorial powers. This argument fails for two reasons. *First,* one cannot ascribe any intention regarding operating subsidiaries to the 1864 Congress that enacted §§ 481 and 484, or the 1933 Congress that added the provisions on examining affiliates to § 481 and the definition of "affiliate" to § 221a. That is so because operating subsidiaries were not authorized until 1966. . . . Over the past four decades, during which operating subsidiaries have emerged as important instrumentalities of national banks, Congress and OCC have indicated no doubt that such subsidiaries are "subject to the same terms and conditions" as national banks themselves.

Second, Watters ignores the distinctions Congress recognized among "affiliates." The NBA broadly defines the term "affiliate" to include "any corporation" controlled by a national bank, including a subsidiary. See 12 U.S.C. § 221a(b). An operating subsidiary is therefore one type of "affiliate." But unlike affiliates that may engage in functions not authorized by the NBA, *e.g.,* financial subsidiaries, an operating subsidiary is tightly tied to its parent by the specification that it may engage only in "the business of banking" as authorized by the Act. § 24a(g)(3)(A); 12 CFR § 5.34(e)(1) (2006). . . .

C

Recognizing the necessary consequence of national banks' authority to engage in mortgage lending through an operating subsidiary "subject to the same terms and conditions that govern the conduct of such activities by national banks," 12 U.S.C. § 24a(g)(3)(A), see also § 24 Seventh, OCC promulgated 12 CFR § 7.4006 (2006): "Unless otherwise provided

---

11. Cf. *Marquette Nat. Bank of Minneapolis v. First of Omaha Service Corp.,* 439 U.S. 299, 308, and n. 24 (1978) (holding that national bank may charge home State's interest rate, regardless of more restrictive usury laws in borrower's State, but declining to consider operating subsidiaries).

by Federal law or OCC regulation, State laws apply to national bank operating subsidiaries to the same extent that those laws apply to the parent national bank." See Investment Securities; Bank Activities & Operations; Leasing, 66 Fed.Reg. 34784, 34788 (2001). Watters disputes the authority of OCC to promulgate this regulation and contends that, because preemption is a legal question for determination by courts, § 7.4006 should attract no deference. . . . This argument is beside the point, for under our interpretation of the statute, the level of deference owed to the regulation is an academic question. Section 7.4006 merely clarifies and confirms what the NBA already conveys: A national bank has the power to engage in real estate lending through an operating subsidiary, subject to the same terms and conditions that govern the national bank itself; that power cannot be significantly impaired or impeded by state law. See, *e.g., Barnett Bank,* 517 U.S., at 33-34; 12 U.S.C. §§ 24 Seventh, 24a(g)(3)(A), 371.[13]

The NBA is thus properly read by OCC to protect from state hindrance a national bank's engagement in the "business of banking" whether conducted by the bank itself or by an operating subsidiary, empowered to do only what the bank itself could do. . . . The authority to engage in the business of mortgage lending comes from the NBA, § 371, as does the authority to conduct business through an operating subsidiary. See §§ 24 Seventh, 24a(g)(3)(A). That Act vests visitorial oversight in OCC, not state regulators. § 484(a). State law (in this case, North Carolina law), all agree, governs incorporation-related issues, such as the formation, dissolution, and internal governance of operating subsidiaries.[14] And the laws of the States in which national banks or their affiliates are located govern matters the NBA does not address. . . . But state regulators cannot interfere with the "business of banking" by subjecting national banks or their OCC-licensed operating subsidiaries to multiple audits and surveillance under rival oversight regimes. . . .

Justice THOMAS took no part in the consideration or decision of this case.

Justice STEVENS, with whom THE CHIEF JUSTICE and Justice SCALIA join, dissenting.

Congress has enacted no legislation immunizing national bank subsidiaries from compliance with nondiscriminatory state laws regulating the business activities of mortgage brokers and lenders. Nor has it authorized an executive agency to preempt such state laws whenever it concludes that they interfere with national bank activities. Notwithstanding the absence of relevant statutory authority, today the Court endorses an agency's incorrect determination that the laws of a sovereign State must yield to federal power. The significant impact of the Court's decision on the federal-state balance and the dual banking system makes it appropriate to set forth in full the reasons for my dissent. . . .

II

Although the dual banking system has remained intact, Congress has radically transformed the national bank system from its Civil War antecedent and brought considerably more federal authority to bear on state-chartered institutions. Yet despite all the changes Congress has made to the national bank system, and despite its exercise of federal power over state banks, it has never preempted state laws like those at issue in this case.

---

13. Because we hold that the NBA itself-independent of OCC's regulation-preempts the application of the pertinent Michigan laws to national bank operating subsidiaries, we need not consider the dissent's lengthy discourse on the dangers of vesting preemptive authority in administrative agencies. . . .

14. Watters does not assert that Wachovia Mortgage is out of compliance with any North Carolina law governing its corporate status.

Most significantly, in 1913 Congress established the Federal Reserve System to oversee federal monetary policy through its influence over the availability of credit. Federal Reserve Act §§ 2, 9, 38 Stat. 252, 259. The Act required national banks and permitted state banks to become Federal Reserve member banks, and subjected all member banks to Federal Reserve regulations and oversight. *Ibid.* Also of signal importance, after the banking system collapsed during the Great Depression, Congress required all member banks to obtain deposit insurance from the newly established Federal Deposit Insurance Corporation. Banking Act of 1933 (or Glass-Steagall Act), § 8, 48 Stat. 168; see also Banking Act of 1935, 49 Stat. 684. Although both of these steps meant that many state banks were subjected to significant federal regulation, "the state banking system continued along with the [national] banking system, with no attempt to exercise preemptive federal regulatory authority over the activities of the existing state banks." M. Malloy, Banking and Financial Services Law 48 (2d ed.2005).

In addition to these systemic overhauls, Congress has over time modified the powers of national banks. The changes are too various to recount in detail, but two are of particular importance to this case. First, Congress has gradually relaxed its prohibition on mortgage lending by national banks. . . . While these changes have enabled national banks to engage in more evenhanded competition with state banks, they certainly reflect no purpose to give them any competitive advantage.[9]

Second, Congress has over the years both curtailed and expanded the ability of national banks to affiliate with other companies. In the early part of the century, banks routinely engaged in investment activities and affiliated with companies that did the same. . . .

A scant two years later, Congress forbade national banks from owning the shares of any company because of a similar fear that such ownership could undermine the safety and soundness of national banks. . . . That provision remains on the books today. See 12 U.S.C. § 24 Seventh.

These congressional restrictions did not forbid all affiliations, however, and national banks began experimenting with new corporate forms. One of those forms involved the national bank ownership of "operating subsidiaries." In 1966, the Comptroller of the Currency took the position "that a national bank may acquire and hold the controlling stock interest in a subsidiary operations corporation" so long as that corporation's "functions or activities ... are limited to one or several of the functions or activities that a national bank is authorized to carry on." 31 Fed.Reg. 11459 (1966). The Comptroller declined to read the categorical prohibition on national bank ownership of stock to foreclose bank ownership of operating subsidiaries, finding authority for this aggressive interpretation of national bank authority in the "incidental powers" provision of 12 U.S.C. § 24 Seventh. See 31 Fed.Reg. 11460.

III

It is familiar learning that "[t]he purpose of Congress is the ultimate touchstone of pre-emption analysis." *Cipollone v. Liggett Group, Inc.,* 505 U.S. 504, 516 (1992) (internal quotation marks omitted). In divining that congressional purpose, I would have hoped that the Court would hew both to the NBA's text and to the basic rule, central to our federal system, that "[i]n all pre-emption cases ... we 'start with the assumption that the historic police powers of the States were not to be superseded by the Federal Act unless that was the

---

9. It is noteworthy that the principal cases that the Court cites to support its conclusion that the federal statute itself preempts the Michigan laws were decided years before Congress authorized national banks to engage in mortgage lending and years before the Office of the Comptroller of the Currency (OCC) authorized their use of operating subsidiaries. . . .

clear and manifest purpose of Congress.' " *Medtronic, Inc. v. Lohr,* 518 U.S. 470, 485 (1996) (quoting *Rice v. Santa Fe Elevator Corp.,* 331 U.S. 218, 230 (1947)). Had it done so, it could have avoided the untenable conclusion that Congress meant the NBA to preempt the state laws at issue here.

The NBA in fact evinces quite the opposite congressional purpose. It provides in 12 U.S.C. § 484(a) that "[n]o national bank shall be subject to any visitorial powers except as authorized by Federal law." Although this exemption from state visitorial authority has been in place for more than 140 years, . . . it is significant that Congress has never extended 12 U.S.C. § 484(a)'s preemptive blanket to cover national bank *subsidiaries*. . . .

V . . .

In my view, the most pressing questions in this case are whether Congress has delegated to the Comptroller of the Currency the authority to preempt the laws of a sovereign State as they apply to operating subsidiaries, and if so, whether that authority was properly exercised here. See 12 CFR § 7.4006 (2006) ("State laws apply to national bank operating subsidiaries to the same extent that those laws apply to the parent national bank"). Without directly answering either question, the Court concludes that preemption is the "necessary consequence" of various congressional statutes. . . . Because I read those statutes differently, I must consider (as did the four Circuits to have addressed this issue) whether an administrative agency can assume the power to displace the duly enacted laws of a state legislature.

Notes and Comments 5.30. The OCC and the OTS adopted policies targeting state transactional and consumer protection laws that affect national bank and federal savings association operations. Do you think such policies go too far? At a September 2005 meeting of the American Bankers Association, the FDIC Chairman criticized the OCC initiative to assert preemptive powers as a symptom of the problem threatening the viability of the dual banking system. *See* Richard Cowden, *Powell Says Falling State Bank Asset Share Highlights Inequities in Dual Banking System*, BNA BANKING DAILY (Sept. 27, 2005), *available at* http://pubs.bna.com/ip/BNA/bbd.nsf/is/A0B1M9Z5H3 (reporting on speech). For a vigorous critiques of OCC preemption policies, see Fisher, *Toward a Basal Tenth Amendment: A Riposte to National Bank Preemption of State Consumer Protection Laws*, 29 HARV. J.L. & PUB. POL'Y 981 (2006); Arthur E. Wilmarth, Jr., *The OCC's Preemption Rules Exceed the Agency's Authority and Present a Serious Threat to the Dual Banking System and Consumer Protection*, 23 Ann. Rev. Banking & Fin. L. 225 (2004). What is the attitude of the majority in *Watters* towards this threat to the viability of the dual banking system? What is attitude of the dissent?

5.31. Do you think that *Watters* threatens the dual banking system? The dissent repeatedly emphasized the "dual banking system" as an important feature of the structure of U.S. banking. Does this feature seem to favor or disfavor aggressive preemption of state law as applied to national banks and their affiliates? Does it survive *Watters*?

5.32. What was "unduly burdensome and duplicative" about the state regulation involved in this case? Is it at all significant, as the dissent re[eatedly stressed, that the state law was "nondiscriminatory"?

5.33. What is it that is preempting the Michigan mortgage lending statute – federal statutes or federal regulations? Does it matter which?

5.34. In note 13 to its opinion, *supra*, the majority insists that, because it holds that the NBA itself preempts the application of Michigan law to national bank operating subsidiaries, it does not need to consider "the dissent's lengthy discourse on the dangers of vesting preemptive authority in administrative agencies." Does this mean that the majority takes no position on that preemptive authority as applied to the facts of the case? What are the dangers, if any, of this purported authority? *Cf.* Ann Graham, *Searching for* Chevron *in Muddy*

Watters: *The Roberts Court and Judicial Review of Agency Regulations,* 60 Admin. L.Rev. 229 (2008) (exploring the absence of judicial deference analysis in *Watters*).

5.35. Not surprisingly, the aggressive preemption initiative endorsed by *Watters* continued apace. *See, e.g., State Farm Bank v. Reardon,* 539 F.3d 336 (6th Cir. 2008) (holding that OTS preemption regulation, 12 C.F.R. § 560.2, preempted application of Ohio Mortgage Broker Act to federal savings association independent contractor agent). At a broader level, however, in May 2009 President Obama signed a Memorandum directed to the heads of executive departments and agencies stating "the general policy of [his] Administration that preemption of State law by executive departments and agencies should be undertaken only with full consideration of the legitimate prerogatives of the States and with a sufficient legal basis for preemption." *Presidential Memorandum: Preemption,* 74 Fed. Reg. 24,693 (May 20, 2009).By its own terms, the Memorandum does not revoke any rules or policies, including the current OCC and OTS preemption policies. Furthermore, the Memorandum states that it "is not intended to, and does not, create any right or benefit, substantive or procedural, enforceable at law or in equity by any party against the United States, its departments, agencies, or entities, its officers, employees, or agents, or any other person. and does not give any party grounds to challenge the validity of an agency action. Any repeal of preemptive actions that the OCC or OTS have taken will have to come from the agencies themselves." *Id.* There has been some speculation that state officials and consumer advocates might use the Memorandum as an argumentative basis for lobbying federal financial services agencies to roll back the preemption initiative. *See* David L. Beam, *Obama Order on Preemption Could Expose Banks to State Regulation,* BNA BANKING DAILY (May 29, 2009), *available at* http://news.bna.com ("state officials, consumer advocates, and other preemption critics will no doubt encourage the agencies to scale back their preemption regulations"). Beam's view, however, is that the Memorandum does not "require either the OCC or the OTS to repeal or reverse any preemptive actions they have taken in the past." *Id.*

5.36. Mortgage lending has been experiencing a serious downturn in the wake of the subprime mortgage crisis – the near-collapse of the mortgage market linked to an aggressive policy of lending to relatively uncreditworthy home owners and buyers. Is there a connection between the subprime mortgage crisis and federal preemption of state consumer protection laws applicable to mortgage lending? In responding to this question, consider the following excerpt.

Malloy, The Subprime Mortgage Crisis and Bank Regulation

27 Banking & Fin.Services Pol'y Rep. 1 (2008)

The financial crisis that has erupted around the growing failures in the subprime mortgage market[1] has already gone through the typical initial stages that usually greet such a crisis in the United States – denial, bargaining, capitulation, and forgetfulness. Both the Fed and the Congress seem genuinely engaged in trying to determine the appropriate shape of the bailout for market participants and even, perhaps, to create some relief for mortgagors at the retail level. What seems missing, unfortunately, is any realistic attempt to reevaluate and reform the structural anomalies that have contributed to the problem. There is every reason to believe that when the current crisis bottoms out and relief has been bestowed on

---

1. For background on the subprime mortgage crisis and a discussion of the initial congressional reaction to the Administration's proposed responses, see Richard Cowden, *Banking Panel Members Show Impatience With White House's Mortgage Rescue Moves*, BNA BANKING DAILY (Feb. 1, 2008), *available at* http://pubs.bna.com/ip/ bna/bbd.nsf/eh/A0B5U2B5B8.

whomever the Congress has decided to rescue, the structural flaws that helped to precipitate the crisis in the first place will persist.

At the heart of the problem of dealing with the crisis is a problem of perspective. It is tempting to think about the crisis in terms of specific manifestations – the wave of foreclosures affecting individual homeowners, the effects on lenders and the mortgage market as well as credit markets generally, the meltdown of securitized mortgage portfolios held by institutional investors – and to treat those manifestations separately. Yet the subprime mortgage crisis is systemic, and understanding it requires an appreciation of the system that developed around the subprime mortgage business to sustain its funding and dramatic expansion. This system may be illustrated in simple terms by ***Figure 1****, infra.*

This market involves an "origination-to-distribution" model of debt securitization, a mark-to-market system, believed to be a more robust way of spreading risk than the more conservative investment analysis of the 1960s. While the subprime mortgage market emerged as a result of aggressive marketing by non-bank lenders such as "lightly regulated" mortgage finance companies (MFCs)[2] to less credit-worthy borrowers, larger depository institutions responded to the increased MFC market share by began easing credit standards, often through state-chartered MFC subsidiaries. Lenders of all types vigorously sold these loan products to subprime mortgagors, and then packaged the portfolios of mortgages into such securitized products as collateralized debt obligations (CDOs) that were analyzed and rated by credit rating agencies and marketed to institutional investors by investments banks. Securitization of these portfolios ameliorated lending risk, and the net proceeds of CDO placements provided lenders with funding to expand the subprime mortgage market itself. The cycle continued to operate, expanding as it drew more investors into the system and encouraged ever-increasing competition for subprime products and programs. When the cycle eventually wobbled – as the inherent counterparty risk manifested itself in the inability of the mortgagors to sustain markedly increasing levels of indebtedness – the system began to break down as the value of the CDO portfolios dramatically contracted.

---

2. Thecla Fabian, *Regulatory Lapses Spurred Crisis, Bair Says; Reform Effort Should Restore Common Sense*, BNA BANKING DAILY (Feb. 25, 2008), *available at* http://pubs.bna.com/ip/bna/ bbd.nsf/eh/A0B6B5J7X3 (quoting FDIC Chairman Sheila Bair).

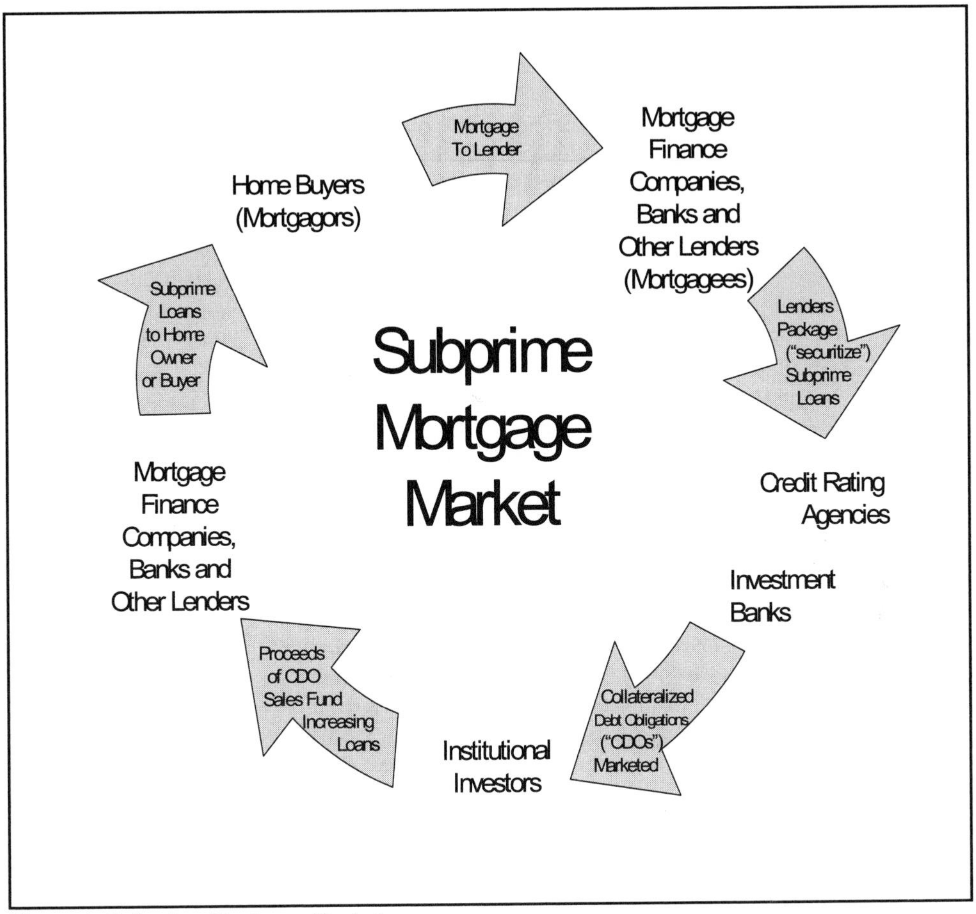

Figure 1: Subprime Mortgage Market

The results of this systemic breakdown have been dramatic. CDOs have been the source of significant losses across the U.S. banking sector. In November 2008, for example, Citibank announced losses of $8 billion to $11 billion on its sub-prime investments.[3] The recent losses have been so striking that the Chair of the Basel Committee on Banking Supervision at the Bank for International Settlements[4] has suggested that the newly revised capital adequacy rules[5] may have to be reevaluated in light of the risk from CDO downgrad

3. *See, e.g.*, Daniel Pruzin, *Subprime Crisis Signals Need for More Work On Capital Accord, Basel Panel Head Says*, BNA BANKING DAILY (Mar. 6, 2008), *available at* http://pubs.bna.com/ip/bna/bbd.nsf/eh/A0B6D7Y0T7 (reporting on Citibank experience).

4. On the role of the Basel Committee, particularly in the establishment of international capital adequacy standards, see 3 MICHAEL P. MALLOY, BANKING LAW AND REGULATION § 15.02[C][1] (2d ed., Aspen Publishers, 2011).

5. For the revised rules, see Committee on Banking Supervision, Bank for International Settlements, *International Convergence of Capital Measurement and Capital Standards: A Revised Framework* (June 26, 2004), *available at* http://www.bis.org/publ/bcbs107.htm. In December 2007 the Office of the Comptroller of the Currency, the Federal Reserve, the FDIC, and the Office of Thrift

ing.[6] There is serious question "whether the capital charges for these types of exposures are calibrated appropriately in relation to their risks and complexity."[7] Quite simply, the crisis precipitated by the contraction of CDO values was unanticipated. As the Basel Chair observed, "when [CDO portfolios] start experiencing losses, these can build very rapidly, producing a real cliff effect. . . . This explains the unprecedented downgrades we have seen on triple-A super senior tranches, which exceed anything we have seen in traditional corporate bonds."[8]

Denial

Faced with the downturn in the housing market, the view of the Administration and the regulators was to deny that this was a crisis. Rather, it was a temporary pause, or a slowdown. Indeed, as late as April 2008, Federal Reserve chairman Ben Bernanke was still touting the joys of the CDO market. At worst, he acknowledged that the risk management capacity of debt securitization "proved to be much less extensive than many believed."[9] Although the subprime mortgage market had emphatically broken down at virtually every stage – mortgage lending, underwriting, credit rating, investor due diligence – the Chairman blithely proclaimed that, "[t]hese problems notwithstanding, the originate-to-distribute model has proven effective in the past and with adequate repairs, could be so in the future."[10] In March 2008 hearings, members of the Senate Banking Committee excoriated the federal regulators for failing to anticipate the risks involved in the burgeoning CDO market.[11] Yet, even after the crisis had begun to unfold, the Administration and the regulators had seemed reluctant to acknowledge that the subprime crisis was a regulatory issue.

Instead, an administration-backed "HOPE NOW Alliance," formed in October 2007 by a wide group of lenders, loan servicing firms, and institutional investors focused on aiding subprime borrowers through loan modifications or repayment plans. By late January 2008,

---

Supervision jointly published final rules implementing the revised Basel rules for the largest, internationally active U.S. banks. 72 Fed. Reg. 69,288 (2007) (codified at 12 C.F.R. pts. 3 (OCC rules), 208, 225 (Fed rules), 325 (FDIC rules), 559-560, 563, 567 (OTS rules)). For simplicity, the final rule uses the term "bank" to include banks, savings associations, and bank holding companies (BHCs). 72 Fed. Reg. at 69,288 n.1. The terms "bank holding company" and "BHC" do not include savings and loan holding companies regulated by the OTS. *Id.* The final rules were effective April 1, 2008. 72 Fed. Reg. at 69,288. While U.S. banking institutions are expected to begin a preliminary phase of implementation early in 2008, compliance with the revised Basel rules is not required until January 1, 2009, when the new standards will begin to be phased in over a three-year period. R. Christian Bruce, *Fed's Governors, Eyeing Credit Turmoil, Welcome New Capital Rules Under Basel II*, BNA BANKING DAILY (Nov. 5, 2007), *available at* http://pubs.bna.com/ip/bna/bbd.nsf/eh/ A0B5H8M7E8. However, the overwhelming majority of U.S. banking institutions will be required either to continue to apply the original 1988 Basel standards, or a new and more risk-sensitive version of the 1988 standards expected to be promulgated by the regulators within the next few months. *Id.*

6. *See, e.g.*, Daniel Pruzin, *Subprime Crisis, supra* (discussing public remarks by Basel Committee Chair Nout Wellink).

7. *Id.*

8. *Id.* (quoting public remarks of Wellink).

9. Jeff Day, *Bernanke Touts Fed's Action in Credit Crunch, Contrasts It With 1929's Passive Central Bank*, BNA BANKING DAILY (Apr. 11, 2008), *available at* http://pubs.bna.com/ip/bna/bbd.nsf/eh/A0B6H3F9T2.

10. *Id.*

11. Richard Cowden, *Senators Grill Financial Regulators on Failure To Supervise Banks During Mortgage Crisis*, BNA BANKING DAILY (Mar. 5, 2008), *available at* http://pubs.bna.com/ip/bna/bbd.nsf/eh/ A0B6D6Q7U1

however, members of the Senate Banking Committee were criticizing this private approach to the crisis and were demanding new public initiatives to respond to the rising home mortgage foreclosures.[12] The apparent response from the Administration was to increase proposed Fiscal 2009 Budget resources for mortgagor counseling and education.[13]

Regulatory responses on the subprime crisis have so far been inconsequential. In July 2007, for example, the OCC, the Fed, the FDIC, the OTS, and the NCUA issued an interagency *Statement on Subprime Mortgage Lending*[14] providing "guidance" developed to clarify how depository institutions could offer certain adjustable rate mortgage (ARM) products in a safe and sound manner, and in a way that clearly discloses the risks that borrowers may assume. The statement was effective July 10, 2007.[15] The guidance is thin at best; among other shortcomings, it steadfastly refuses to define the term "subprime mortgage," which is the supposed focus of the statement, beyond general characteristics that might lead to "payment shock."[16] It tends to focus on adjustable rate mortgage (ARM) products, as typifying subprime mortgages, but also considers ARM products as offered to non-subprime borrowers.

Bargaining

Significantly, it was not the mortgage crisis itself, as it affected borrowers, that prodded the regulators into action, but rather the near-failure of investment firms involved in the CDO market that focused the attention of policy makers. This focus reached its most intense moment on March 13, 2008, Bears Stearns & Cos. Inc. saw its liquidity fall from approximately $12.4 billion to $2 billion, as a result of the dissipation of the market's confidence in the firm and the refusal of its counterparties to act. Bear Stearns informed the Federal Reserve Bank of New York and the Commission that it was on the brink of bankruptcy. Swiftly the Federal Reserve and the Treasury Department facilitated a loan to Bears Stearns through bank holding company JPMorgan Chase & Co., followed by a loan to JPMorgan to support its outright acquisition of Bears Stearns at a price of $2.00 per share (later raised to $10.00).[17]

Attention to the dire circumstances threatening home mortgage borrowers did not receive such swift attention. It was not until the very end of March 2008 that negotiations over H.R. 3221, a bipartisan housing stimulus package, reached the stage where a final Senate floor vote could be scheduled for April 8.[18] Even so, the Senate Banking Committee Chair emphasized that the bill would be only the first step in addressing the housing finance

---

12. Richard Cowden, *Banking Panel Members Show Impatience With White House's Mortgage Rescue Moves*, BNA BANKING DAILY (Feb. 1, 2008), *available at* http://pubs.bna.com/ip/bna/ bbd.nsf/eh/A0B5U2B5B8.

13. *See* Richard Cowden, *Several Federal Agencies Slated to Get Boost In FY 2009 Budget Related to Housing Issues*, BNA BANKING DAILY (Feb. 5, 2008), *available at* http://pubs.bna.com/ip/bna/bbd.nsf/eh/ A0B5X4F4F7 (discussing proposed budget increases).

14. 72 Fed. Reg. 37,569 (2007).

15. *Id.* at 37,569.

16. *Id.* at 37,571.

17. Aaron Lorenzo, *Regulators Defend Bear Stearns Decision; Senators Ask If Fed Needs Additional Powers*, BNA BANKING DAILY (Apr. 4, 2008), *available at* http://pubs.bna.com/ip/bna/ bbd.nsf/eh/A0B6G6Y8J1

18. Thecla Fabian, *Senate Starts Housing Stimulus Debate; Bankruptcy Amendment on Indefinite Hold*, BNA BANKING DAILY (Apr. 7, 2008), *available at* http://pubs.bna.com/ip/bna/ bbd.nsf/eh/A0B6G7Z5T7.

crisis and the wave of foreclosures looming on the financial horizon.[19] In the interim, the House Ways and Means Committee endorsed a different approach to the crisis in the housing market, emphasizing home-buyer tax credits,[20] while the House Financial Services Committee considered a foreclosure prevention bill, H.R. 3221, that included authorization for wholesale refinancing of mortgages in danger of default, a provision much maligned by White House policy advisers.[21]

Capitulation: Regulatory Responses

Of course, the subprime mortgage crisis is not just about the personal financial tragedies triggered by improvident mortgage lending. Fueling the dramatic expansion of this sector was the facility of the investment markets in securitizing these mortgages into CDOs sold to a wide range of institutional investors. The existence of the CDO market had the apparent effect of moderating the risk of lenders and feeding their liquidity levels, with the result that the subprime mortgage market experienced growth at significant rates. The poor quality of the underlying mortgage obligations has now had serious adverse effects on the value of CDO portfolios, to the great distress of many institutional investors. The Chairman of the Securities and Exchange Commission made it clear during remarks at the annual *SEC Speaks* conference in February 2008[22] that the Commission was investigating possible securities fraud and breaches of fiduciary duty in the marketing of CDOs.[23] In its investigation, the Commission may be expected to consider whether the banking enterprises that packaged the mortgages and the securities firms that marketed the CDOs made appropriate public disclosures concerning the valuation of CDOs and the risks involved.[24]

Nevertheless, it was not until a March 2008 Senate Banking Committee hearing that the regulators grudgingly admitted that they had not "fully appreciated all [the] risks out there"[25] and acknowledged the gravity of the dramatic reductions in bank earnings, the mounting foreclosures, and the difficulties still to be faced in restoring liquidity in the credit markets.[26] At that point, capitulation to the need for regulatory responses to the crisis was becoming complete.

The broadened responses of the Administration and the regulators still tend to be somewhat unfocused. With much fanfare, the Administration announced in mid-March 2008 proposed measures intended to prevent *future* financial crisis, rather than to respond to the

---

19. *Id.*

20. Heather M. Rothman, *Ways and Means Set to Consider $11 Billion Housing Tax Measure*, BNA BANKING DAILY (Apr. 9, 2008), *available at* http://pubs.bna.com/ip/bna/bbd.nsf/eh/A0B6H0V4J3.

21. Richard Cowden, *Frank, White House Advisers Exchange Barbs Over Features of Foreclosure Prevention Bill*, BNA BANKING DAILY (Apr. 11, 2008), *available at* http://pubs.bna.com/ip/bna/bbd.nsf/eh/ A0B6H3F9X6.

22. For the text of the speech by Commission Chairman Christopher Cox, see http://www.sec.gov/news/speech/2008/spch020808cc.htm.

23. Rachel McTague, *Cox Outlines SEC Agenda for 2008, Including Initiatives Related to Subprime*, BNA BANKING DAILY (Feb. 11, 2008), *available at* http://pubs.bna.com/ip/bna/bbd.nsf/eh/A0B5X8X3F5.

24. *Id.* In addition, one can expect the Commission to consider whether broker-dealers complied with suitability requirements in selling CDOs and other debt-related derivatives to their customers. *Id.*

25. Richard Cowden, *Senators Grill Financial Regulators, supra* (quoting Federal Reserve Governor Donald Kohn).

26. *Id.*

present one.[27] These measures represent a call to states and market participants to tighten market supervision. Thus, states are urged to establish nationwide licensing standards for MFCs, while lenders would be required to improve the quality of the disclosure that they provide to borrowers about payment terms and stronger conflict of interest rules would apply to credit rating agencies that assess the risk of CDO offerings. The proposals were widely dismissed as ineffective and limited, though they were praised by industry representatives.[28]

Also in March, the President's Working Group on Financial Markets (PWG), chaired by the Treasury Secretary, offered a broader and more detailed set of proposals.[29] In its report the PWG identified short-term recommendations, designed to be implemented immediately;[30] intermediate-term recommendations, designed to be implemented in the intermediate term, to increase the efficiency of financial regulation;[31] and, a long-term "Optimal Regulatory Structure," intended to reform and strengthen the regulation of U.S. financial institutions.[32] . . .

The Treasury recommendations are ambitious and complex, but they ultimately feed into the recommended long-term "optimal regulatory structure." This structure is itself a model of simplicity, based upon fundamental principles of functional regulation.[33] In contrast to the current thicket of institutional regulators that now supervise financial services in the United States,[34] the recommended structure would include a relatively small core group of specialized regulators, as is illustrated in ***Figure 5**, infra*.

---

27. *See* Stephen Labaton, *White House Offers Plan To Ward Off Credit Crisis*, N.Y. TIMES, Mar. 14, 2008, at A1, col.5 (reporting on prospective plan).

28. *Id.* at A17, col. 2.

29. U.S. Department of the Treasury, *Blueprint for a Modernized Financial Regulatory Structure* (Mar. 2008), *available at* http://www.treas.gov/press/releases/reports/Blueprint.pdf.

30. *Id.* at 75-86.

31. *Id.* at 89-133.

32. *Id.* at 137-179.

33. On functional regulation, which establishes regulatory structures relating to functions and activities to be regulated rather than the nature of the particular institution being regulated, see *Report of the Task Group on Financial Services* 39-40 (1984). *See generally* 1 MICHAEL P. MALLOY, BANKING LAW AND REGULATION §§ 1.04[A]-[B] (2d ed., Aspen Publishers, 2011) (discussing and contrasting institutional and functional regulation).

34. For a description and critique of the current regulatory system, see 1 MICHAEL P. MALLOY, BANKING LAW AND REGULATION §§ 1.03, 1.04 (2d ed., Aspen Publishers, 2011).

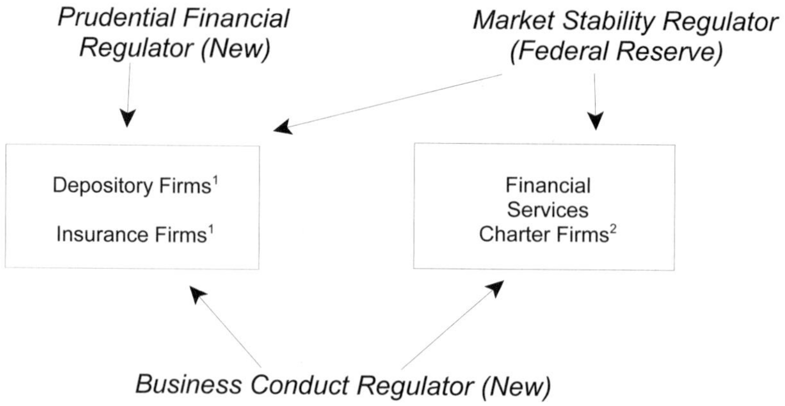

[1]Includes depository firms with access to federal deposit insurance and insurance firms with access to an insurance guaranty fund.

[2]Includes securities firms, futures firms, exchanges, investment advisors, privates pools of capital, and surplus lines insurers.

Figure 5: Objectives-Based Regulatory Structure

Forgetfulness: Lessons from the Past

Unfortunately, the Treasury *Blueprint* follows in a long tradition of over-arching studies of financial services regulatory structure that have never come to fruition.[35] Particularly for a study that emerges in the last months of a presidential term, the prospects for adoption of its recommendations seem rather limited. What we are left with are the current responses to the subprime mortgage crisis as they now exist, responses that to date have done little to assuage the markets or bring significant relief to borrowers.

One implication of the Treasury *Blueprint* is quite striking, however. The burgeoning subprime mortgage crisis is linked to issues of regulatory realignment. There is no single regulator accountable for the U.S. banking system, let alone a phenomenon like the subprime mortgage market, and this allows for a certain amount of "regulatory arbitrage," in which participants in the market can exploit the gaps in the multi-regulator system. As I argued in a December 2007 interview with Reuters, "A trend toward something as questionable as subprime mortgages can easily develop because there are too many cooks,

---

35. *See, e.g., Blueprint for Reform: The Report of the Task Group on Regulation of Financial Services* (1984) (recommending fundamental changes to U.S. regulatory structure); *Modernizing the Financial System: Recommendations for Safer, More Competitive Banks* (1991) (same). *See also* 1 MICHAEL P. MALLOY, BANKING LAW AND REGULATION §§ 1.04[A], [D] (2d ed., Aspen Publishers, 2011) (discussing *Task Group* and *Modernizing*, respectively). The Treasury *Blueprint* itself notes:

> Over the past forty years, a number of Administrations have presented important recommendations for financial services regulatory reforms. Most previous studies have focused almost exclusively on the regulation of depository institutions as opposed to a broader scope of financial institutions. These studies served important functions, helping shape the legislative landscape in the wake of their release.

Blueprint for a Modernized Financial Regulatory Structure, supra at 3 (footnote omitted). For background on the prior Administration studies referred to in the quotation, see *Id.*, Appendix B, at 197-206.

too many supervisors and no one is really coordinating."[36] By the end of February 2008, this view was echoed in a speech by FDIC Chairman Bair,[37] who argued that for the future "the home mortgage market needs strong rules."[38]

One unresolved issue with which policy makers are still struggling is whether the regulatory response to the subprime mortgage crisis should be distinct and independent of generally applicable supervisory requirements.[39] Comments from many financial institutions and industry groups on the interagency *Statement on Subprime Mortgage Lending*[40] urged that responsive consumer protection goals could be accomplished more effectively through amendments to generally applicable regulations, such as Regulation Z, concerning the Truth in Lending Act,[41] or Regulation X, mandating real estate settlement procedures).[42] Other comments questioned the efficacy of additional required disclosures and expressed concern that the *Statement* would contribute to "consumer information overload."[43] The agencies essentially split the difference, determining that "given the growth in the market for the products covered by the Statement and the heightened legal, compliance, and reputation risks associated with these products, guidelines are needed now to ensure that consumers will receive the information they need about the material features of these loans."[44] Unfortunately, there is little that is new and nothing that is binding in the *Statement.*

The fact remains that perennial attempts at structural reform–often prompted by disasters like the collapse of the savings associations sector in the 1980's or the subprime mortgage crisis of the late 2000's–are always vulnerable to political attack by interested constituencies. In June 2007, for example, the Treasury Department announced a major "capital markets competitiveness plan" that would, *inter alia*, modernize the regulatory structure of U.S. financial institutions.[45] This might include merging operations of the OCC and the OTS,[46] a recommendation included in the Treasury *Blueprint* approach along with the elimination of thrift charters. In response, the American Bankers Association and America's Community Bankers wrote Treasury Secretary Henry Paulson in July 2007, urging

---

36. John Poirier, *Mortgage woes spotlight U.S. bank regulation*, GUARDIAN UNLIMITED (Dec. 7, 2007), *available at*, http://www.guardian.co.uk/ feedarticle?id=7135495 (quoting Malloy). *Cf.* U.S. Government Accountability Office, *Industry Trends Continue to Challenge the Federal Regulatory Structure* (GAO-08-32, Oct. 12, 2007), *reprinted at*, 2007 WL 3015229 (identifying need to modernize financial regulatory system; criticizing difficulties of multiple specialized regulators in identifying and responding to risks that traditional cross industry lines).

37. *See* Thecla Fabian, *Regulatory Lapses Spurred Crisis, Bair Says; Reform Effort Should Restore Common Sense*, BNA BANKING DAILY (Feb. 25, 2008), *available at*, http://pubs.bna.com/ip/bna/bbd.nsf/eh/ A0B6B5J7X3 (quoting Bair as saying "Weaknesses and holes in our bank regulatory structure lie at the heart of our current housing predicament").

38. *Id.*

39. *See Statement on Subprime Mortgage Lending*, 72 Fed. Reg. 37,569, 37,573 (2007) (discussing controversy over regulatory responses).

40. *Id.*

41. 12 C.F.R. pt. 226.

42. 24 C.F.R. pt. 3500.

43. *Id.* at 37,573.

44. *Id.*

45. Richard Cowden, *ABA, ACB Urge Treasury Not to Merge Thrift, National Bank Regulatory Agencies*, BNA BANKING DAILY (July 10, 2007), *available at* http://pubs.bna.com/ip/bna/bbd.nsf/eh/ A0B4W3E4B3.

46. *Id.*

him not to merge the operations.[47]

The sad irony is that the Administration's March 13 plan to prevent future credit crises relies upon two basic elements that are simply no longer reliable. One is the notion of market discipline and voluntary restraint as a protection against disaster,[48] features that have obviously not been very efficacious in the present crisis. The other is the assumption that state regulation of MFCs and the mortgage markets can be harnessed to "tighten their oversight of financial markets."[49] In the wake of the sweeping preemption of state consumer protection-based supervision of mortgage bankers resulting from longstanding preemption initiatives of the Office of the Comptroller of the Currency[50] and the decision of the Supreme Court in *Watters v. Wachovia Bank, N.A.*[51] broadly confirming the Comptroller's policy, it would be foolish to expect state-based supervision of MFCs and mortgage banking to be effective in the current legal environment. We may agree with the Treasury *Blueprint* that vigorous change is needed, but the roots of the subprime mortgage crisis are to be found in the aggressively preemptive, market-oriented policies of the current Administration.

Notes and Comments 5.37. Watters *under the Bridge*. Post-*Watters*, preemption continued to roil the lower courts until the Supreme Court returned to the issue in *Cuomo v. Clearing House Ass'n, L.L.C.*, excerpted below. *Cuomo* holds that an OCC regulation interpreting the NBA visitorial powers provision was not a reasonable interpretation, since it appeared to preclude state officials from using the courts to enforce compliance by national banks with non-preempted state law. Can the two cases be reconciled?

Cuomo v. Clearing House Ass'n, L.L.C.

— U.S. —, 129 S.Ct. 2710 (2009)

JUSTICE SCALIA delivered the opinion of the Court.

In 2005, Eliot Spitzer, Attorney General for the State of New York, sent letters to several national banks making a request "in lieu of subpoena" that they provide certain non-public information about their lending practices. He sought this information to determine whether the banks had violated the State's fair-lending laws. Spitzer's successor in office, Andrew Cuomo, is the petitioner here. Respondents, the federal Office of the Comptroller of the Currency ("Comptroller" or "OCC") and the Clearing House Association, a banking trade group, brought suit to enjoin the information request, claiming that the Comptroller's

---

47. *Id.*

48. The Treasury *Blueprint* itself looks favorably on market discipline as a complement to supervisory policy. At one point, it notes that the "PWG, the Federal Reserve Bank of New York, and the OCC have previously stated that market discipline is the most effective tool to limit systemic risk." *Blueprint for a Modernized Financial Regulatory Structure, supra* at 15 n.2, *citing Agreement among PWG and U.S. Agency Principals on Principles and Guidelines Regarding Private Pools of Capital* (Feb. 2007). See also PWG, HEDGE FUNDS, LEVERAGE, AND THE LESSONS OF LONG-TERM CAPITAL MANAGEMENT 24-25, 30 (Apr. 1999); PWG, OVER-THE-COUNTER DERIVATIVES MARKETS AND THE COMMODITY EXCHANGE ACT 34-35 (Nov. 1999).

49. Labaton, *White House Offers Plan, supra* at A1, col. 5.

50. *See, e.g.*, 69 Fed. Reg. 1895 (2004) (codified at 12 C.F.R. § 7.4000(a)(3), (b)) (adopting regulations asserting broad preemptive authority).

51. 550 U.S. 1 (2007). For discussion of *Watters* and its implications for state regulation of financial services, see 1 MICHAEL P. MALLOY, BANKING LAW AND REGULATION § 1.03[I][2] (2d ed., Aspen Publishers, 2011).

regulation promulgated under the National Bank Act prohibits that form of state law enforcement against national banks.

The United States District Court for the Southern District of New York entered an injunction in favor of respondents, prohibiting the attorney general from enforcing state fair-lending laws through demands for records or judicial proceedings. The United States Court of Appeals for the Second Circuit affirmed. . . . The question presented is whether the Comptroller's regulation purporting to pre-empt state law enforcement can be upheld as a reasonable interpretation of the National Bank Act.

I . . .

Section 484(a) of Title 12, U.S.C., a provision of the National Bank Act, 13 Stat. 99, reads as follows:

> "No national bank shall be subject to any visitorial powers except as authorized by Federal law, vested in the courts of justice or such as shall be, or have been exercised or directed by Congress or by either House thereof or by any committee of Congress or of either House duly authorized."

The Comptroller, charged with administering the National Bank Act, adopted, through notice-and-comment rulemaking, the regulation at issue here designed to implement the statutory provision. Its principal provisions read as follows:

> § 7.4000 Visitorial powers.
>
> "(a) General rule. (1) Only the OCC or an authorized representative of the OCC may exercise visitorial powers with respect to national banks, except as provided in paragraph (b) of this section. State officials may not exercise visitorial powers with respect to national banks, such as conducting examinations, inspecting or requiring the production of books or records of national banks, or prosecuting enforcement actions, except in limited circumstances authorized by federal law. However, production of a bank's records (other than non-public OCC information under 12 CFR part 4, subpart C) may be required under normal judicial procedures.
>
> "(2) For purposes of this section, visitorial powers include:
>
> "(i) Examination of a bank;
>
> "(ii) Inspection of a bank's books and records;
>
> "(iii) Regulation and supervision of activities authorized or permitted pursuant to federal banking law; and
>
> "(iv) Enforcing compliance with any applicable federal or state laws concerning those activities." 12 CFR § 7.4000 (2009).

By its clear text, this regulation prohibits the States from "prosecuting enforcement actions" except in "limited circumstances authorized by federal law."

Under the familiar *Chevron* framework, we defer to an agency's reasonable interpretation of a statute it is charged with administering. *Chevron U.S.A. Inc. v. Natural Resources Defense Council, Inc.*, 467 U.S. 837 (1984). There is necessarily some ambiguity as to the meaning of the statutory term "visitorial powers," especially since we are working in an era when the prerogative writs – through which visitorial powers were traditionally enforced – are not in vogue. The Comptroller can give authoritative meaning to the statute within the bounds of that uncertainty. But the presence of some uncertainty does not expand Chevron deference to cover virtually any interpretation of the National Bank Act. We can discern the outer limits of the term "visitorial powers" even through the clouded lens of history. They do not include, as the Comptroller's expansive regulation would provide, ordinary enforcement of the law. Evidence from the time of the statute's enactment, a long line of our own cases, and application of normal principles of construction to the National Bank Act make that clear.

A

Historically, the sovereign's right of visitation over corporations paralleled the right of the church to supervise its institutions and the right of the founder of a charitable institution "to see that [his] property [was] rightly employed," 1 W. Blackstone, Commentaries on the Laws of England 469 (1765). By extension of this principle, "[t]he king [was] by law the visitor of all civil corporations," ibid. A visitor could inspect and control the visited institution at will.

When the National Bank Act was enacted in 1864, "visitation" was accordingly understood as "[t]he act of examining into the affairs of a corporation" by "the government itself." 2 J. Bouvier, A Law Dictionary 790 (15th ed. 1883). Lower courts understood "visitation" to mean "the act of a superior or superintending officer, who visits a corporation to examine into its manner of conducting business, and [to] enforce an observance of its laws and regulations." *First Nat. Bank of Youngstown v. Hughes*, 6 F. 737, 740 (C.C.N.D.Ohio 1881). A State was the "visitor" of all companies incorporated in the State, simply by virtue of the State's role as sovereign: The "legislature is the visitor of all corporations founded by it." *Guthrie v. Harkness*, 199 U.S. 148, 157 (1905) (internal quotation marks omitted).

This relationship between sovereign and corporation was understood to allow the States to use prerogative writs – such as mandamus and quo warranto – to exercise control "whenever a corporation [wa]s abusing the power given it, . . . or acting adversely to the public, or creating a nuisance." H. Wilgus, Private Corporations, in 8 American Law and Procedure § 157, pp. 224-225 (1910). State visitorial commissions were authorized to "exercise a general supervision" over companies in the State. I. Wormser, Private Corporations § 80, pp. 100, 101, in 4 Modern American Law (1921).

B

Our cases have always understood "visitation" as this right to oversee corporate affairs, quite separate from the power to enforce the law. In the famous Dartmouth College case, Justice Story, describing visitation of a charitable corporation, wrote that Dartmouth was "subject to the controlling authority of its legal visitor, who . . . may amend and repeal its statutes, remove its officers, correct abuses, and generally superintend the management of [its] trusts," and who are "liable to no supervision or control." *Trustees of Dartmouth College v. Woodward*, 4 Wheat. 518, 676, 681, 4 L.Ed. 629 (1819) (concurring opinion). This power of "genera[l] superintend[ence]" stood in contrast to action by the court of chancery, which acted "not as itself possessing a visitorial power . . . but as possessing a general jurisdiction . . . to redress grievances, and frauds." Id., at 676.

In *Guthrie, supra*, we held that a shareholder acting in his role as a private individual was not exercising a "visitorial power" under the National Bank Act when he petitioned a court to force the production of corporate records, id., at 159. "[C]ontrol in the courts of justice," we said, is not visitorial, and we drew a contrast between the nonvisitorial act of "su[ing] in the courts of the State" and the visitorial "supervision of the Comptroller of the Currency," *id.*, at 159, 157, 26 S.Ct. 4.

In *First Nat. Bank in St. Louis v. Missouri*, 263 U.S. 640 (1924), we upheld the right of the Attorney General of Missouri to bring suit to enforce a state anti-bank-branching law against a national bank. We said that only the United States may perform visitorial administrative oversight, such as "inquir[ing] by quo warranto whether a national bank is acting in excess of its charter powers." Id., at 660, 44 S.Ct. 213. But if a state statute of general applicability is not substantively pre-empted, then "the power of enforcement must rest with the [State] and not with" the National Government, ibid.

Our most recent decision, *Watters v. Wachovia Bank, N.A.*, 550 U.S. 1 (2007), does not, as the dissent contends, . . . "suppor[t] OCC's construction of the statute." To the contrary, it is fully in accord with the well established distinction between supervision and law enforcement. Watters held that a State may not exercise " 'general supervision and control' " over a subsidiary of a national bank, 550 U.S., at 8, because "multiple audits and surveillance under rival oversight regimes" would cause uncertainty, id., at 21. "[G]eneral supervision and control" and "oversight" are worlds apart from law enforcement. All parties to the case agreed that Michigan's general oversight regime could not be imposed on national banks; the sole question was whether operating subsidiaries of national banks enjoyed the same immunity from state visitation. The opinion addresses and answers no other question.

The foregoing cases all involve enforcement of state law. But if the Comptroller's exclusive exercise of visitorial powers precluded law enforcement by the States, it would also preclude law enforcement by federal agencies. Of course it does not. See, e.g., *Bank of America Nat. Trust & Sav. Assn. v. Douglas*, 105 F.2d 100, 105-106 (CADC 1939) (Securities Exchange Commission investigation of bank fraud is not an exercise of "visitorial powers"); *Peoples Bank of Danville v. Williams*, 449 F.Supp. 254, 260 (W.D.Va.1978) (same).

In sum, the unmistakable and utterly consistent teaching of our jurisprudence, both before and after enactment of the National Bank Act, is that a sovereign's "visitorial powers" and its power to enforce the law are two different things. There is not a credible argument to the contrary. And contrary to what the Comptroller's regulation says, the National Bank Act pre-empts only the former.

C

The consequences of the regulation also cast doubt upon its validity. No one denies that the National Bank Act leaves in place some state substantive laws affecting banks. . . . But the Comptroller's rule says that the State may not enforce its valid, non-pre-empted laws against national banks. Ibid. The bark remains, but the bite does not. . . .

. . . As the Court said in *St. Louis*:

> "To demonstrate the binding quality of a statute but deny the power of enforcement involves a fallacy made apparent by the mere statement of the proposition, for such power is essentially inherent in the very conception of law." 263 U.S., at 660.

In sharp contrast to the "unusual" reading propounded by the Comptroller's regulation, reading "visitorial powers" as limiting only sovereign oversight and supervision would produce an entirely commonplace result – the precise result contemplated by our opinion in *St. Louis*, which said that if a state statute is valid as to national banks, "the corollary that it is obligatory and enforceable necessarily results." Id., at 659-660 (emphasis added). Channeling state attorneys general into judicial law-enforcement proceedings (rather than allowing them to exercise "visitorial" oversight) would preserve a regime of exclusive administrative oversight by the Comptroller while honoring in fact rather than merely in theory Congress's decision not to pre-empt substantive state law. This system echoes many other mixed state/federal regimes in which the Federal Government exercises general oversight while leaving state substantive law in place. See, e.g., *Wyeth v. Levine,* 555 U.S. —, 129 S.Ct. 1187 (2009).

This reading is also suggested by § 484(a)'s otherwise inexplicable reservation of state powers "vested in the courts of justice." As described earlier, visitation was normally conducted through use of the prerogative writs of mandamus and quo warranto. The exception could not possibly exempt that manner of exercising visitation, or else the exception would swallow the rule. Its only conceivable purpose is to preserve normal civil and criminal lawsuits. To be sure, the reservation of powers "vested in the courts of justice" is phrased as an exception from the prohibition of visitorial powers. But as we have just discussed, it cannot possibly be that, and it is explicable only as an attempt to make clear that the courts' ordinary powers of enforcing the law are not affected.

On a pragmatic level, the difference between visitation and law enforcement is clear. If a State chooses to pursue enforcement of its laws in court, then it is not exercising its power of visitation and will be treated like a litigant. An attorney general acting as a civil litigant must file a lawsuit, survive a motion to dismiss, endure the rules of procedure and discovery, and risk sanctions if his claim is frivolous or his discovery tactics abusive. Judges are trusted to prevent "fishing expeditions" or an undirected rummaging through bank books and records for evidence of some unknown wrongdoing. In New York, civil discovery is far more limited than the full range of "visitorial powers" that may be exercised by a sovereign. Courts may enter protective orders to prevent "unreasonable annoyance, expense, embarrassment, disadvantage, or other prejudice," N.Y. Civ. Prac. Law Ann. § 3103(a) (West 2005), and may supervise discovery sua sponte, § 3104(a). A visitor, by contrast, may inspect books and records at any time for any or no reason.

II

The Comptroller's regulation, therefore, does not comport with the statute. Neither does the Comptroller's interpretation of its regulation, which differs from the text and must be discussed separately.

Evidently realizing that exclusion of state enforcement of all state laws against national banks is too extreme to be contemplated, the Comptroller sought to limit the sweep of its regulation by the following passage set forth in the agency's statement of basis and purpose in the Federal Register:

> "What the case law does recognize is that 'states retain some power to regulate national banks in areas such as contracts, debt collection, acquisition and transfer of property, and taxation, zoning, criminal, and tort law.' [citing a Ninth Circuit case.] Application of these laws to national banks and their implementation by state authorities typically does not affect the content or extent of the Federally-authorized business of banking . . . but rather establishes the legal infrastructure that surrounds and supports the ability of national banks . . . to do business." 69 Fed.Reg. 1896 (2004) (footnote omitted).

This cannot be reconciled with the regulation's almost categorical prohibition in 12 CFR § 7.4000(a)(1) of "prosecuting enforcement actions." . . .

III

The dissent fails to persuade us. Its fundamental contention – that the exclusive grant of visitorial powers can be interpreted to preclude state enforcement of state laws – rests upon a logical fallacy. The dissent establishes, . . . (and we do not at all contest), that in the course of exercising visitation powers the sovereign can compel compliance with the law. But it concludes from that . . . that any sovereign attempt to compel compliance with the law can be deemed an exercise of the visitation power. That conclusion obviously does not follow. . . .

States . . . have always enforced their general laws against national banks – and have enforced their banking-related laws against national banks for at least 85 years, as evidenced by *St. Louis*, in which we upheld enforcement of a state anti-bank-branching law, 263 U.S., at 656, 44 S.Ct. 213. See also *Anderson Nat. Bank v. Luckett*, 321 U.S. 233, 237 (1944) (state commissioner of revenue may enforce abandoned-bank-deposit law against national bank through "judicial proceedings"); *State by Lord v. First Nat. Bank of St. Paul,*

313 N.W.2d 390, 393 (Minn.1981) (state treasurer may enforce general unclaimed-property law with "specific provisions directed toward" banks against national bank); *Clovis Nat. Bank v. Callaway*, 69 N.M. 119, 130-132, 364 P.2d 748, 756 (1961) (state treasurer may enforce unclaimed-property law against national bank deposits); *State v. First Nat. Bank of Portland*, 61 Or. 551, 554-557, 123 P. 712, 714 (1912) (state attorney general may enforce bank-specific escheat law against national bank). . . .

IV

Applying the foregoing principles to this case is not difficult. "Visitorial powers" in the National Bank Act refers to a sovereign's supervisory powers over corporations. They include any form of administrative oversight that allows a sovereign to inspect books and records on demand, even if the process is mediated by a court through prerogative writs or similar means. The Comptroller reasonably interpreted this statutory term to include "conducting examinations [and] inspecting or requiring the production of books or records of national banks," § 7.4000, when the State conducts those activities in its capacity as supervisor of corporations.

When, however, a state attorney general brings suit to enforce state law against a national bank, he is not acting in the role of sovereign-as-supervisor, but rather in the role of sovereign-as-law-enforcer. Such a lawsuit is not an exercise of "visitorial powers" and thus the Comptroller erred by extending the definition of "visitorial powers" to include "prosecuting enforcement actions" in state courts, § 7.4000. . . .

JUSTICE THOMAS, with whom the CHIEF JUSTICE, JUSTICE KENNEDY, and JUSTICE ALITO join, concurring in part and dissenting in part.

The Court holds that the term "visitorial powers" as used in the National Bank Act (NBA), 12 U.S.C. § 484(a), refers only "to a sovereign's supervisory powers over corporations," which are limited to "administrative oversight" including "inspect[ion of] books and records on demand." . . . Based on this definition, the Court concludes that § 484(a) does not pre-empt a "state attorney general['s] . . . suit to enforce state law against a national bank." Ibid. I would affirm the Court of Appeals' determinations that the term "visitorial powers" is ambiguous and that it was reasonable for the Office of the Comptroller of the Currency (OCC) to interpret the term to encompass state efforts to obtain national bank records and to enforce state fair lending laws against national banks. Accordingly, I respectfully concur in part and dissent in part.

Notes and Comments 5.38. How should we reconcile the holdings in *Watters* and *Cuomo*? In *Cuomo*, Justice Scalia argues that the two decisions are in harmony – "[*Watters*] is fully in accord with the well established distinction between supervision and law enforcement." This suggests that *Watters* concerned a question of "supervision" – and thus the state statute was preempted, whereas *Cuomo* involved "law enforcement," and state law properly pursued in state courts would not be preempted. The following case seems to pit the two cases against each other, with the majority using *Watters* to preempt a state garnishment statute and the dissent using *Cuomo* to insulate the statute from preemption. Which opinion seems persuasive to you?

Monroe Retail, Inc. v. RBS Citizens, N.A.

589 F.3d 274 (6th Cir. 2009)
motion to vacate denied sub nom. Monroe Retail, Inc. v. Charter One Bank NA,
— F. Supp.2d —, 2010 WL 4181424 (N.D.Ohio 2010)

JULIA SMITH GIBBONS, Circuit Judge.

[Judgment creditors in Ohio had sought to collect on their judgments by garnishing the judgment debtors' deposits at various banks. The banks routinely imposed garnishment fees on customer accounts prior to full recovery of the amounts owed. The garnishor-creditors brought suit against the banks in state court. After removal, the U.S. district court granted the banks' motions to dismiss. The Sixth Circuit affirmed the dismissal, holding that: (i) the garnishors had standing; (ii) NBA preempted the garnishor-creditors' conversion claims brought pursuant to Ohio garnishment statutes; and, (iii) the principle of setoff, invoked by the district court, did not apply as between the banks and the garnishors.]

Plaintiffs-appellants Monroe Retail, Inc.; Jerome Phillips, Esq.; and Leo Marks, Inc. ("the Garnishors") appeal the district court's dismissal of their claim against defendants-appellees RBS Citizens, N.A. (formerly known as Charter One Bank, N.A.); The Huntington National Bank; Huntington Bancshares, Inc.; JPMorgan Chase Bank, N.A .; JPMorgan Chase & Co.; Keybank; N.A.; Keycorp; National City Bank; National City Corporation; Sky Bank; U.S. Bank, N.A.; and U.S. Bancorp ("the Banks"). . . .

I.

The relevant facts are not in dispute. The Garnishors are garnishor-creditors in Ohio who obtain judgments against debtors when debts are not repaid. The Garnishors often collect these judgments by garnishing the debtors' bank accounts. Ohio Revised Code ("ORC") § 2716.12 provides that a garnishment action must be accompanied by a one dollar fee to the garnishee, in this case, the Banks who hold the debtors' funds in customer accounts. The Banks charge an additional $25 to $80 service fee to the debtors for the garnishment process. When debtors have insufficient funds to satisfy both the service fee and the garnishment order, the Banks extract the service fees from the garnished funds before releasing the remainder of the funds to the Garnishors.

The Garnishors filed a class action suit against the Banks in the Court of Common Pleas of Lucas County, Ohio, on August 31, 2006, alleging three causes of action against the Banks. First, the Garnishors claimed that the service fees charged by the Banks amount to additional garnishment fees beyond the one dollar fee authorized by ORC § 2716.12 and therefore violate that section, causing the Garnishors to have lost at least $5,000,000. Second, the Garnishors claimed that by deducting these service fees, the Banks were illegally converting funds belonging to the Garnishors for their own use in violation of the garnishment process prescribed by ORC § 2716.13(B) and § 2716.21(D). Third, the Garnishors sought injunctive relief to prevent the Banks from continuing to deduct service fees from funds in the debtors' accounts. The Banks all responded by filing dispositive motions. . . .

III. . . .

[T]he only issue before us is whether the Garnishors' conversion claim can survive a motion for judgment on the pleadings and a motion to dismiss. The Garnishors claim that the Banks have wrongfully converted $25 to $80 per garnishment to their own use in violation of ORC § 2716.13(B) and ORC § 2716.21(D). . . . The Garnishors interpret these regulations [sic] to require the Banks to relinquish debtors' funds before deducting service fees for the garnishment process. The Banks argue that the Garnishors do not state a claim because the National Bank Act, 12 U.S.C. § 24 (Seventh) ("NBA"), permits them to charge fees and preempts any claim to the contrary.

Ordinarily, a presumption against preemption applies. *See United States v. Locke*, 529 U.S. 89, 108 (2000). . . . In the context of national banking, however, the Supreme Court has held that the general presumption against preemption does not apply. *See Watters v. Wachovia Bank, N.A.*, 550 U.S. 1, 12 (2007); *Locke*, 529 U.S. at 108 ("[A]n 'assumption' of nonpre-emption is not triggered when the State regulates in an area where there has been a history of significant federal presence."); *Barnett Bank of Marion County, N.A. v. Nelson*, 517 U.S. 25, 32 (1996).

. . . The Officer [sic] of the Comptroller of the Currency ("OCC"), which has regulatory and supervisory power over national banks, has issued regulations defining the "incidental powers" a national bank may exercise without state interference. *See, e.g., NationsBank of N.C., N.A. v. Variable Annuity Life Ins. Co.*, 513 U.S. 251, 25658 (1995). The OCC's interpretation of the NBA is entitled to substantial deference:

> It is settled that courts should give great weight to any reasonable construction of a regulatory statute adopted by the agency charged with the enforcement of that statute. The [OCC] is charged with the enforcement of banking laws to an extent that warrants the invocation of this principle with respect to [its] deliberative conclusions as to the meaning of these laws.

Clarke v. Secs. Indus. Ass'n, 479 U.S 388, 403-04 (1987) (citation omitted) (quoting *Investment Co. Institute v. Camp*, 401 U.S. 617, 62627 (1971), and collecting cases).

The OCC has specifically defined the ability to charge fees as an "incidental power" of a national bank. The OCC promulgated § 7.4002(a) of Title 12 of the Code of Federal Regulations, which gives national banks explicit "[a]uthority to impose charges and fees." 12 C.F.R. § 7.4002(a). Both parties have stipulated that the Banks have authority pursuant to such federal regulation to charge contractual fees to their customers. They disagree, however, as to whether the NBA's grant of authority to charge fees includes the service fees for the garnishment process and preempts the Garnishors' conversion claim.

The Banks contend that the NBA permits them to charge the Garnishors the service fees when debtors have insufficient funds in their accounts to satisfy the fees. According to the OCC's regulations, a national bank is authorized to "charge its customers non-interest charges and fees, including deposit account service charges." Id. The Banks argue that this language permits them to collect service fees from debtors' accounts, even if the funds in the accounts are subject to garnishment by the Garnishors. In response, the Garnishors argue that their right to the funds is protected by Ohio's garnishment statute, see ORC §§ 2716.13(B), 2716.21(D), and that Ohio garnishment law is explicitly exempt from preemption and the Banks' broad authority under 12 C.F.R. § 7.4007(c)(4), which exempts state laws governing the "rights to collect debts" from preemption. The Banks contend that this language exempts only state laws governing the Banks' rights to collect debts from preemption, not the Garnishors' rights, and further argue that any interpretation of Ohio debt collection law that would allow the Garnishors' claim to proceed is preempted by the NBA.

We find that the NBA does not preempt general state laws governing the rights of all entities, not just Banks, to collect debts; but we conclude that the Garnishors' specific conversion claim pursuant to the Ohio garnishment statute is nevertheless preempted by the NBA's grant of authority to the Banks to charge and collect fees.

A. "Rights to Collect Debts"

. . . The first question before us is whether the NBA saves all state laws governing "rights to collect debts" from preemption, or, as the Banks contend, merely laws governing the Banks' rights to collect debts. The text of the pertinent regulation states:

> State laws that are not preempted. State laws on the following subjects are not inconsistent with the deposit-taking powers of national banks and apply to national banks to the extent that they only incidentally affect the exercise of national banks' deposit-taking powers:
>
> (1) Contracts;
> (2) Torts;
> (3) Criminal law;
> (4) Rights to collect debts;
> (5) Acquisition and transfer of property;
> (6) Taxation;
> (7) Zoning;
> (8) Any other law the effect of which the OCC determines to be incidental to the deposit-taking operations of national banks or otherwise consistent with the powers set out in paragraph (a) of this section.

12 C.F.R. § 7.4007(c) (footnote omitted).

The Banks claim that this language clearly refers only to the Banks' rights to collect debts and thus that all other laws governing the rights to collect debts, including ORC § 2716.13(B) and § 2716.21(D), are preempted by the NBA. . . .

[The court reasoned that the NBA did not purport to preempt state laws of general applicability that did not target banks. It rejected the banks' narrow interpretation.]

B. Banks' Authority to Charge Fees

This finding, however, does not end our inquiry. We must now examine whether the Garnishors' specific conversion claim pursuant to Ohio's garnishment statute is preempted. As mentioned above, state laws, including those governing "rights to collect debts," are only exempted from preemption "to the extent that they only incidentally affect the exercise of national banks' deposit-taking powers." 12 C.F.R. § 7.4002(c)(4). The Supreme Court has held that states may not "prevent or significantly interfere with the national bank's exercise of its powers." *Barnett Bank*, 517 U.S. at 33. When state laws "significantly impair the exercise of authority, enumerated or incidental under the NBA," the state laws "must give way." *Watters*, 550 U.S. at 12. We have found that the level of "interference" that gives rise to preemption under the NBA is not very high. *See Ass'n of Banks in Ins., Inc. v. Duryee*, 270 F.3d 397, 409 (6th Cir.2001) (rejecting as "unpersuasive" an "attempt to redefine 'significantly interfere' as 'effectively thwart'"). Although the Garnishors have withdrawn their statutory claim, the Banks argue that any interpretation of Ohio's garnishment laws that would allow the Garnishors' conversion claim to proceed would interfere with their ability to collect fees, as authorized by 12 C.F.R. § 7.4002(a), and is thus preempted.

The Banks . . . solicited the OCC's opinion on this matter. In [an] opinion letter, the OCC declared that the service fee for the garnishment process was a "fee" within the meaning of 12 C.F.R. § 7.4002 and therefore that the Banks were authorized to collect these fees. ... Attendant to this authority to charge fees is the authority and discretion to determine the amount and method of charging those fees. See 12 C.F.R. § 7.4002(b)(2) ("The establishment of non-interest charges and fees, their amounts, and the method of calculating them are business decisions to be made by each bank, in its discretion, according to sound banking judgment and safe and sound banking principles."). By preventing the banks from exacting a fee for processing the garnishment orders through freezing the accounts, the Ohio garnishment laws "significantly interfere" with this fundamental national bank function by de facto mandating a $1 fee and the method by which that fee is extracted.

Moreover, the OCC stated that a "bank's authorization to establish fees pursuant to § 7.4002(a) includes the authorization to determine the order in which the fees are posted to a depositor's account." . . . As explained by the OCC, "[t]he garnishment fee and the Bank's process of debiting it first are intended to reduce the Bank's costs and compensate the Bank for other potential risks in connection with the legal requirement to process garnishments served on the Bank." . . . Accordingly, if the Banks are authorized to charge the service fee and similarly authorized to post the service fee in whatever order they determine, the OCC argued that the Banks are consequently authorized to collect the service fee even if this process has the effect of reducing the funds that the Garnishors receive. . . .

We find this argument persuasive. The requirement that banks freeze accounts immediately upon receipt of a garnishment order is unduly burdensome on national banks because it mandates the order in which those banks carry out their daily account-balancing and account-management functions. The OCC has consistently interpreted § 7.4002(a) as including the authorization to determine the order in which banks may post fees to an account. . . . Likewise, we note that this proposition is consistent with Ohio law, which grants state banks the power to decide that "items may be accepted, paid, certified, or charged to the indicated account of its customer in any order." Ohio Rev.Code, § 1304.29(B).

We find the OCC's interpretation sensible as it permits the Banks to complete the daily account-balancing tasks that all banks must undertake, both as a general operational matter and specifically in the context of responding to a garnishment notice served on debtors' accounts. The Garnishors cite the Ohio garnishment statute, which states that garnishees are liable "at the time of service of the order" of garnishment. ORC § 2716.21(D). Relying on this statutory language, the Garnishors claim that Ohio law requires the Banks to freeze the funds in the debtors' accounts at the time of service of the garnishment order and thus that Ohio law prohibits them from further deducting service fees after receiving the garnishment order. We agree with the Banks that the Garnishors' contention that the Banks must immediately "freeze" the garnished accounts is overly simplistic as the Banks must first undertake a number of procedures to assess what funds are available to be garnished.

Thus the Garnishors' interpretation would allow ORC § 2716.13(B) and § 2716.21(D) to "significantly interfere" not only with the Banks' ability to collect and set their service fees, but also with the Banks' federal authority to complete other transactions and balance their accounts. *See Duryee*, 270 F.3d at 409. We therefore find that any interpretation of the Ohio garnishment statute that would allow the Garnishors' claim to proceed is preempted by the NBA's grant of authority to the Banks to collect fees without interference. The Garnishors have thus failed to state a claim upon which relief can be granted. See Fed.R.Civ.P. 12(b)(6), (c). . . .

COLE, Circuit Judge, dissenting.

. . . The garnishment law at issue is a law of general applicability that only incidentally affects national banks, with negligible effect on their ability to perform their business. Both Supreme Court precedent and the plain language of the OCC regulation's savings clause strongly suggest that preemption is inappropriate here.

A. Supreme Court precedent clearly weighs against preemption

The majority opinion rests on several cases that it claims support a finding of preemption, but it does not discuss the substance of those cases, nor does it address the two Supreme Court decisions on which Monroe Retail principally relies. The cases cited by the majority do not weigh in favor of preemption here because those cases involved much more significant intrusions into the business of national banks – intrusions that bear little resemblance to the Ohio statute before us. On the other hand, the cases cited by Monroe

Retail dealt with state statutes similar to Ohio's garnishment law, and both held those statutes not to be preempted by national banking laws.

The majority relies on *Watters v. Wachovia Bank, N.A.*, 550 U.S. 1, 21 (2007), in which the Court held that state regulators could not exercise corporate visitorial powers, such as the right to inspect books and records, over national banks' operating subsidiaries. The state conceded that the NBA preempts state visitorial powers over the national banks themselves, but claimed that the same was not true of bank subsidiaries (specifically at issue were subsidiaries in the mortgage-lending business). Id. at 15. The Court disagreed and held that the NBA preempted the state from exercising its visitorial powers over the subsidiaries: "[S]tate regulators cannot interfere with the 'business of banking' by subjecting national banks or their OCC-licensed operating subsidiaries to multiple audits and surveillance under rival oversight regimes." *Id.* at 21. Thus, the intrusion into the business of banking at issue in Watters – "multiple audits [by state regulators] and surveillance under rival oversight regimes" – was far more significant than Ohio's garnishment law. . . .

[T]he cases cited by the majority offer limited guidance because they entail far more significant intrusions into the business of national banks than the statute before us. The majority does not mention two cases raised by Monroe Retail in which the Supreme Court declined to find preemption with respect to state statutes similar to the one at issue here. Those decisions held that such statutes are not preempted because they do not significantly impair national banks' functions.

In *Anderson National Bank v. Luckett*, 321 U.S. 233, 236 (1944), the Supreme Court found that a state law directing banks, both state and national, to "turn over to the state, deposits which have remained inactive and unclaimed for a specified period" was not preempted by national banking laws. The Court stated: "This Court has often pointed out that national banks are subject to state laws, unless those laws infringe the national banking laws or impose an undue burden on the performance of the banks' functions." *Id.* at 248. With respect to the requirement that banks, including national banks, turn over abandoned funds, the Court stated: "It has never been suggested that non-discriminatory laws of this type are *so burdensome* as to be inapplicable to the accounts of depositors in national banks." *Id.* (emphasis added). We are not at liberty to ignore the holding of this binding authority. I doubt the majority would contend that if the state law at issue in Luckett had also specified that banks were required to turn over all of the abandoned property, without first deducting an "abandoned-property-turnover fee," like the one at issue in the present case, the Luckett Court would have changed course and deemed the state law to be preempted. Luckett was cited by the Supreme Court several months ago, and there is no indication that it is no longer good law. *See Cuomo v. Clearing House Ass'n, L.L. C.*, 129 S.Ct. 2710, 272122 (2009). In light of Luckett, I fail to see how we can fairly hold that Ohio's garnishment law is preempted.

The Supreme Court engaged in similar analysis and reached the same result in *McClellan v. Chipman*, 164 U.S. 347, 358 (1896). In that case, a national bank argued that a federal statute that allowed national banks to accept real property in satisfaction of a debt preempted a state statute that forbade preferential transfers of property to creditors on the eve of insolvency. The Court rejected this argument, stating:

> [There is nothing] in the statutes of the State of Massachusetts, here considered, which in any way impairs the efficiency of national banks or frustrates the purpose for which they were created. No function of such banks is destroyed or hampered by allowing the banks to exercise the power to take real estate, provided only they do so under the same conditions and restrictions to which all the other citizens of the State are subjected, one of which limitations arises from

> the provisions of the state law which in case of insolvency seeks to forbid preferences between creditors.

Id. This case, too, presents a much more analogous state law to the one under our consideration than any of the cases upon which the majority relies, further demonstrating that preemption should not apply here.

The above cases stand for the following proposition: a non-discriminating state law of general applicability that has an incidental effect on national banks but does not "frustrate[ ] the purpose for which they were created," *McClellan*, 164 U.S. at 358, "impose an undue burden on the performance of [their] functions," Luckett, 321 U.S. at 248, or "prevent or significantly interfere with the [ ] exercise of [their] powers," *Barnett*, 517 U.S. at 33, is not preempted by federal banking laws. . . .

3. Deposits

The other side of the credit function equation is the acceptance of deposits. In substance, the law of bank collections and deposits is the law of the Uniform Commercial Code, Article 4. Overlaying this body of commercial law, however, is a system of federal regulation calculated to serve such policy interests as the stability of the nation's banking system, the maintenance of sound monetary policy, and the protection of depositors. To a large extent, this aspect of bank regulation, like others we have already encountered, represents the cumulative reaction to several major financial crises during the first third of this century.

In this section, we consider several aspects of federal regulation of deposit-taking activities: (*i*) the requirement that depository institutions maintain reserves against the deposits that they hold; (*ii*) restrictions on rates of interest to be paid on deposits; and, (*iii*) administration of the federal deposit insurance system. The enactment of the Depository Institutions Deregulation and Monetary Control Act of 1980[46] threw both reserve requirements[47] and interest rate restrictions into extended periods of transition.[48] Hence, we shall also examine the specific effects of the act on these areas of regulation.

a. Reserve Requirements

Reserve requirements, administered by the Board of Governors of the Federal Reserve System (Fed), theoretically operate as a cushion against sudden demands for withdrawals of deposits. Since, through the credit function, funds deposited almost immediately go out into the market–several times over–as loans, a bank faced with a sudden demand for withdrawals would obviously face a serious liquidity problem in the absence of reserves.[49] This purpose of reserve requirements relates directly to the public policy of main-

46. Pub. L. No. 96-221, March 31, 1980, 94 Stat. 132 (1980) (codified at various sections of 12 U.S.C.).

47. *See* 12 U.S.C. § 461 *et seq.*

48. *See, e.g.*, 12 U.S.C. § 461(b)(8) (providing transitional rules concerning reserve requirements).

49. *See generally* Mathewson, *From Confidential Supervision to Market Discipline: The Role of Disclosure in the Regulation of Commercial Banks*, 11 J. Corp. L. 139, 139-142 (1986) (discussing bank run phenomenon as concern of traditional bank regulation).

tenance of a safe and sound banking system.

In addition, reserve requirements indirectly serve a broader public policy purpose, namely, monetary control. By raising or lowering the percentage of deposits to be reserved, the Fed could affect the availability of money in the credit markets. The higher the percentage of deposits required to be reserved, the less deposit funds are available for the credit function; the lower the reserve requirement, the more deposit funds are available to the credit market. Under the new reserve provisions established by the Monetary Control Act, Title I of the Depository Institutions Deregulation and Monetary Control Act of 1980, this public policy purpose would appear to be the sole statutory basis for Fed action adjusting the reserve requirements.[50]

Perhaps the most significant change effected by the act has been the assertion of federal jurisdiction to set reserve requirements for *all* depository institutions, a jurisdictional scope far greater than traditional federal statutory reliance on the "appropriate regulatory agency" approach that we have seen in other contexts.

Notes and Comments 5.39. The key statutory provision with respect to the current federal reserve requirements is 12 U.S.C. § 461, the terms of which should be reviewed carefully. The broad jurisdictional scope of the new reserve requirements can be seen in the provisions of § 461(b)(1)(A), defining the term "depository institution,"[51] and § 461(b)(2), imposing the reserve requirements on depository institutions as so defined. The Fed is given statutory authority to implement and enforce the reserve requirements. *See id.* § 461(a), (b)(2)-(5), (c). Only limited consultation with other federal agencies is required.[52] What does the statute require with respect to deposit reserves, and how much discretion does the Fed have to vary the statutory requirements? Review 12 U.S.C. § 461(b)(2)(A)-(B), (b)(3), (b)(4), and the following excerpt.

Weaver and O'Malley, The Depository Institutions Deregulation and Monetary Control Act of 1980: An Overview

98 Banking L. J. 102-105 (1981)

The FRB is authorized to prescribe the amount of reserves required to be maintained by depository institutions against transaction accounts (including demand deposits, NOW accounts, savings deposits subject to automatic transfer, share draft accounts, corporate time deposits, time deposits and accounts representing funds deposited to the credit of a depositor that is not a natural person, or a time deposit or account in which any beneficial interest is held by a depositor that is not a natural person).

For transaction accounts of $25 million or less, reserves of 3 percent must be maintained.

For transaction accounts in excess of $25 million, initial reserves of 12 percent must be maintained. The FRB is authorized to fix the reserves between 8 and 14 percent.

Nonpersonal time deposits. An initial reserve of 3 percent must be maintained for all such deposits. The FRB is authorized to fix such reserves between zero and 9 percent.

---

50. *See* 12 U.S.C. § 461(b)(2)(A), (B).

51. *Compare* 12 U.S.C. § 461(b)(1)(A) (defining "depository institution" for purposes of reserve requirements) *with id.* § 1813(c)(1) (defining term for purposes of Federal Deposit Insurance Act).

52. *See id.* § 461(b)(1)(F). *Cf. id.* § 461(c)(1)(B), (2).

Base level of $25 million. The $25 million base level for reserves will be adjusted each year by 80 percent of the change in the total transaction deposits for the preceding year.

Waiver

The FRB may waive maximum reserve limits and under extraordinary circumstances may impose reserve requirements in excess of the above-stated limits, for a period of up to 180 days. (Five members of the FRB must find such extraordinary circumstances to exist, and the FRB must consult with appropriate committees of Congress and inform Congress of the exercise of these powers and reasons for their exercise.)

Supplemental Reserves

A supplemental reserve requirement of not more than 4 percent of a depository institution's total transaction accounts may be imposed by the FRB if: (1) the action is approved by five members of the Board; (2) before acting, the Board consults with the Boards of the Federal Deposit Insurance Corporation, the Federal Home Loan Bank Board, and the National Credit Union Administration; (3) the action is justified by the FRB in a report to Congress; and (4) supplemental reserves are maintained by the FRB in an earnings participation account.

Reserves on Foreign Obligations or Assets

Nonmember foreign branches, subsidiaries, and international banking facilities of depository institutions must maintain the same reserves required of foreign member banks.

However, reserve requirements are not applicable to deposits payable outside the United States.

Discount and Borrowing

Depository institutions with transaction accounts are now afforded the same discount and borrowing privileges as member banks.

Phase-In of the Reserve Requirements

Reserve requirements for nonmember banks (as of July 1, 1979) will be phased in over an eight-year period in amounts of one-eighth per year of these reserves. Immediate reserve requirements will apply, however, to any category of deposits or accounts that are authorized pursuant to federal law in any state after March 31, 1980, for example, NOW accounts other than those previously authorized in the northeastern United States and New York.

Reserve requirements for member banks may be adjusted over a four-year period by the FRB. Reserve requirements for banks that withdrew from the FRB after July 1, 1979 are the same as for member banks. They must maintain reserves in an amount equal to the amount of reserves they would have been required to maintain had they been members on the day before the March 31, 1980, effective date of the Monetary Control Act.

Nonmember institutions outside the United States are not required to maintain reserves against their deposits until the sixth year after the effective date of the Monetary Control Act. At that time, reserves must be maintained in an amount equal to one-eighth of those discussed above. In the seventh year, they must equal one-fourth of those otherwise required, and so on in each successive year until the full reserves are set aside.

Exemption

Reserve requirements are not applicable to an institution that (1) is organized solely to do business with other financial institutions, (2) is organized primarily by financial institutions with which it does business, and (3) does no business with the general public.

Waiver

Required reserves can be in either of the following forms:

(1) Balances maintained by a depository institution for reserve purposes in the FRB of which it is a member or at which it maintains an account;

(2) Balances maintained by a nonmember depository institution in a depository

institution that maintains required reserve balances at a Federal Reserve Bank, in a Federal Home Loan Bank, or in the central liquidity facility for credit unions, if such depository institution, Federal Home Loan Bank, or central liquidity facility maintains such funds in the form of balances in a FRB Bank.

Balances maintained to meet reserve requirements may also be used to satisfy liquidity requirements under legal provisions.

Notes and Comments 5.40. Consider the following excerpts from the Fed's reserve requirements, Regulation D, 12 C.F.R. pt. 204. As to each regulatory provision, what is the specific statutory provision it is intended to implement?

Reserve Requirements of Depository Institutions

12 C.F.R. pt. 204

§ 204.2 Definitions.

For purposes of this part, the following definitions apply unless otherwise specified:

(a)(1) "Deposit" means:

(i) The unpaid balance of money or its equivalent received or held by a depository institution in the usual course of business and for which it has given or is obligated to give credit, either conditionally or unconditionally, to an account, including interest credited, or which is evidenced by an instrument on which the depository institution is primarily liable;

(ii) Money received or held by a depository institution, or the credit given for money or its equivalent received or held by the depository institution in the usual course of business for a special or specific purpose, regardless of the legal relationships established thereby, including escrow funds, funds held as security for securities loaned by the depository institution, funds deposited as advance payment on subscriptions to United States government securities, and funds held to meet its acceptances;

(iii) an outstanding teller's check, or an outstanding draft, certified check, cashier's check, money order, or officer's check drawn on the depository institution, issued in the usual course of business for any purpose, including payment for services, dividends or purchases;

(iv) Any due bill or other liability or undertaking on the part of a depository institution to sell or deliver securities to, or purchase securities for the account of, any customer (including another depository institution), involving either the receipt of funds by the depository institution, regardless of the use of the proceeds, or a debit to an account of the customer before the securities are delivered. A deposit arises thereafter, if after three business days from the date of issuance of the obligation, the depository institution does not deliver the securities purchased or does not fully collateralize its obligation with securities similar to the securities purchased. A security is similar if it is of the same type and if it is of comparable maturity to that purchased by the customer;

(v) Any liability of a depository institution's affiliate that is not a depository institution, on any promissory note, acknowledgment of advance, due bill, or similar obligation (written or oral), with a maturity of less than one and one half years, to the extent that the proceeds are used to supply or to maintain the availability of funds (other than capital) to the depository institution, except any such obligation that, had it been issued directly by the depository institution, would not constitute a deposit. If an obligation of an affiliate of a depository institution is regarded as a deposit and is used to purchase assets from the depository institution, the maturity of the deposit is determined by the shorter of the maturity of the obligation issued or the remaining maturity of the assets purchased. If the proceeds from an affiliate's obligation are placed in the depository institution in the form of a reservable deposit, no reserves need be maintained against the obligation of the affiliate since reserves are required to be maintained against the deposit issued by the depository institution. However, the maturity of the deposit issued to the affiliate shall be the shorter of the maturity of the affiliate's obligation or the maturity of the deposit;

(vi) Credit balances;

(vii) Any liability of a depository institution on any promissory note, acknowledgment of advance, bankers' acceptance, or similar obligation (written or oral), including mortgage-backed bonds, that is issued or undertaken by a depository institution as a means of obtaining funds, except any such obligation that:

(A) Is issued or undertaken and held for the account of:

(1) An office located in the United States of another depository institution . . . ;

(2) The United States government or an agency thereof; or

(3) The Export-Import Bank of the United States, Minbanc Capital Corporation, the Government Development Bank for Puerto Rico, a Federal Reserve Bank, a Federal Home Loan Bank, or the National Credit Union Administration Central Liquidity Facility;

(B) Arises from a transfer of direct obligations of, or obligations that are fully guaranteed as to principal and interest by, the United States Government or any agency thereof that the depository institution is obligated to repurchase;

(C) Is not insured by a Federal agency, is subordinated to the claims of depositors, has a weighted average maturity of five years or more, and is issued by a depository institution with the approval of, or under the rules and regulations of, its primary Federal supervisor;

(D) Arises from a borrowing by a depository institution from a dealer in securities, for one business day, of proceeds of a transfer of deposit credit in a Federal Reserve Bank or other immediately available funds (commonly referred to as "Federal funds"), received by such dealer on the date of the loan in connection with clearance of securities transactions; or

(E) Arises from the creation, discount and subsequent sale by a depository institution of its bankers' acceptance of the type described in paragraph 7 of section 13 of the Federal Reserve Act (12 U.S.C. 372).

(viii) Any liability of a depository institution that arises from the creation after June 20, 1983, of a bankers' acceptance that is not of the type described in paragraph 7 of section 13 of the Federal Reserve Act (12 U.S.C. 372) except any such liability held for the account of an entity specified in § 204.2(a)(1)(vii)(A). . . .

(2) "Deposit" does not include:

(i) Trust funds received or held by the depository institution that it keeps properly segregated as trust funds and apart from its general assets or which it deposits in another institution to the credit of itself as trustee or other fiduciary. If trust funds are deposited with the commercial department of the depository institution or otherwise mingled with its general assets, a deposit liability of the institution is created;

(ii) An obligation that represents a conditional, contingent or endorser's liability;

(iii) Obligations, the proceeds of which are not used by the depository institution for purposes of making loans, investments, or maintaining liquid assets such as cash or "due from" depository institutions or other similar purposes. An obligation issued for the purpose of raising funds to purchase business premises, equipment, supplies, or similar assets is not a deposit;

(iv) Accounts payable;

(v) Hypothecated "deposits" created by payments on an installment loan where (A) the amounts received are not used immediately to reduce the unpaid balance due on the loan until the sum of the payments equals the entire amount of loan principal and interest; (B) and where such amounts are irrevocably assigned to the depository institution and cannot be reached by the borrower or creditors of the borrower;

(vi) Dealer reserve and differential accounts that arise from the financing of dealer installment accounts receivable, and which provide that the dealer may not have access to the funds in the account until the installment loans are repaid, as long as the depository institution is not actually (as distinguished from contingently) obligated to make credit or funds available to the dealer;

(vii) A dividend declared by a depository institution for the period intervening between the date of the declaration of the dividend and the date on which it is paid;

(viii) An obligation representing a "pass through account," as defined in this section;

(ix) An obligation arising from the retention by the depository institution of no more than a 10 per cent interest in a pool of conventional 1-4 family mortgages that are sold to third parties;

(x) An obligation issued to a State or municipal housing authority under a loan-to-lender program involving the issuance of tax exempt bonds and the subsequent lending of the proceeds to the depository institution for housing finance purposes;

(xi) Shares of a credit union held by the National Credit Union Administration or the National Credit Union Administration Central Liquidity Facility under a statutorily authorized assistance program; and

(xii) Any liability of a United States branch or agency of a foreign bank to another United States branch or agency of the same foreign bank, or the liability of the United States office of an Edge Corporation to another United States office of the same Edge Corporation.

(b)(1) "Demand deposit" means a deposit that is payable on demand, or a deposit issued with an original maturity or required notice period of less than seven days, or a deposit representing funds for which the depository institution does not reserve the right to require at least seven days' written notice of an intended withdrawal. Demand deposits may be in the form of:

(i) Checking accounts;

(ii) certified, cashier's, teller's, and officer's checks (including such checks issued in payment of dividends);

(iii) Traveler's checks and money orders that are primary obligations of the issuing institution;

(iv) Checks or drafts drawn by, or on behalf of, a non-United States office of a depository institution on an account maintained at any of the institution's United States offices;

(v) Letters of credit sold for cash or its equivalent;

(vi) Withheld taxes, withheld insurance and other withheld funds;

(vii) Time deposits that have matured or time deposits upon which the contractually required notice of withdrawal as given and the notice period has expired and which have not been renewed (either by action of the depositor or automatically under the terms of the deposit agreement); and

(viii) An obligation to pay, on demand or within six days, a check (or other instrument, device, or arrangement for the transfer of funds) drawn on the depository institution, where the account of the institution's customer already has been debited.

(2) The term "demand deposit" also means deposits or accounts on which the depository institution has reserved the right to require at least seven days' written notice prior to withdrawal or transfer of any funds in the account and from which the depositor is authorized to make withdrawals or transfers in excess of the withdrawal or transfer limitations specified in paragraph (d)(2) for such an account and the account is not a NOW account, or an ATS account or other account that meets the criteria specified in either

paragraph (b)(3)(ii) or (iii) of this section.

(3) "Demand deposit" does not include:

(i) Any account that is a time deposit or a savings deposit under this part;

(ii) Any deposit or account on which the depository institution has reserved the right to require at least seven days' written notice prior to withdrawal or transfer of any funds in the account and either --

(A) Is subject to check, draft, negotiable order of withdrawal, share draft, or similar item, such as an account authorized by 12 U.S.C. 1832(a) ("NOW account") and a savings deposit described in § 204.2(d)(2), provided that the depositor is eligible to hold a NOW account; or

(B) From which the depositor is authorized to make transfers by preauthorized transfer or telephonic (including data transmission) agreement, order or instruction to another account or to a third party, provided that the depositor is eligible to hold a NOW account;

(iii) Any deposit or account on which the depository institution has reserved the right to require at least seven days' written notice prior to withdrawal or transfer of any funds in the account and from which withdrawals may be made automatically through payment to the depository institution itself or through transfer of credit to a demand deposit or other account in order to cover checks or drafts drawn upon the institution or to maintain a specified balance in, or to make periodic transfers to such other account, such as accounts authorized by 12 U.S.C. 371a (automatic transfer account or ATS account), provided that the depositor is eligible to hold an ATS account. . . .

(c)(1) "Time deposit" means:

(i) A deposit that the depositor does not have a right and is not permitted to make withdrawals from within six days after the date of deposit unless the deposit is subject to an early withdrawal penalty of at least seven days' simple interest on amounts withdrawn within the first six days after deposit. A time deposit from which partial early withdrawals are permitted must impose additional early withdrawal penalties of at least seven days' simple interest on amounts withdrawn within six days after each partial withdrawal. If such additional early withdrawal penalties are not imposed, the account ceases to be a time deposit. The account may become a savings deposit if it meets the requirements for a saving deposit; otherwise it becomes a transaction account. "Time deposit" includes funds–

(A) Payable on a specified date not less than seven days after the date of deposit;

(B) Payable at the expiration of a specified time not less than seven days after the date of deposit;

(C) Payable only upon written notice that is actually required to be given by the depositor not less than seven days prior to withdrawal;

(D) Held in "club" accounts (such as "Christmas club" accounts and "vacation club" accounts that are not maintained as "savings deposits") that are deposited under written contracts providing that no withdrawal shall be made until a certain number of periodic deposits have been made during a period of not less than three months even though some of the deposits may be made within six days from the end of the period; or

(E) Share certificates and certificates of indebtedness issued by credit unions, and certificate accounts and notice accounts issued by savings and loan associations;

(ii) A "savings deposit;" . . .

(iv) Borrowings, regardless of maturity, represented by a promissory note, an acknowledgment of advance, or similar obligation described in § 204.2(a)(1)(vii) that is issued to, or any bankers' acceptance (other than the type described in 12 U.S.C. 372) of the depository institution held by–

(A) Any office located outside the United States of another depository institution or Edge or agreement corporation organized under the laws of the United States;

(B) Any office located outside the United States of a foreign bank;

(C) A foreign national government, or an agency or instrumentality thereof, engaged principally in activities which are ordinarily performed in the United States by governmental entities;

(D) An international entity of which the United States is a member; or

(E) Any other foreign, international, or supranational entity specifically designated by the Board.

(2) A time deposit may be represented by a transferable or nontransferable, or a negotiable or nonnegotiable, certificate, instrument, passbook, or statement, or by book entry or otherwise.

(d)(1) "Savings deposit" means a deposit or account with respect to which the depositor is not required by the deposit contract but may at any time be required by the depository institution to give written notice of an intended withdrawal not less than seven days before withdrawal is made, and that is not payable on a specified date or at the expiration of a specified time after the date of deposit. The term "savings deposit' includes a regular share account at a credit union and a regular account at a savings and loan association.

(2) The term "savings deposit" also means: A deposit or account, such as an account commonly known as a passbook savings account, a statement savings account, or as a money market deposit account (MMDA), that otherwise meets the requirements of § 204.2(d)(1) and from which, under the terms of the deposit contract or by practice of the depository institution, the depositor is permitted or authorized to make no more than six transfers and withdrawals, or a combination of such transfers and withdrawals, per calendar month or statement cycle (or similar period) of at least four weeks, to another account (including a transaction account) of the depositor at the same institution or to a third party by means of a preauthorized or automatic transfer, or telephonic (including data transmission) agreement, order or instruction, or by check, draft, debit card, or similar order made by the depositor and payable to third parties. A preauthorized transfer includes any arrangement by the depository institution to pay a third party from the account of a depositor upon written or oral instruction (including an order received through an automated clearing house (ACH)) or any arrangement by a depository institution to pay a third party from the account of the depositor at a predetermined time or on a fixed schedule. Such an account is not a transaction account by virtue of an arrangement that permits transfers for the purpose of repaying loans and associated expenses at the same depository institution (as originator or servicer) or that permits transfers of funds from this account to another account of the same depositor at the same institution or permits withdrawals (payments directly to the depositor) from the account when such transfers or withdrawals are made by mail, messenger, automated teller machine, or in person or when such withdrawals are made by telephone (via check mailed to the depositor) regardless of the number of such transfers or withdrawals.[4]

---

4. In order to ensure that no more than the permitted number of withdrawals or transfers are made, for an account to come within the definition of "savings deposit," a depository institution must either:

(a) Prevent withdrawals or transfers of funds from this account that are in excess of the limits established by paragraph (d)(2) of this section, or

(b) Adopt procedures to monitor those transfers on an ex post basis and contact customers who exceed the established limits on more than occasional basis. For customers who continue to violate those limits after they have been contacted by the depository institution, the depository institution must either close the account and place the funds in another account that the depositor is eligible to maintain or take away the transfer and draft capacities of the account. An account that authorizes withdrawals or transfers in excess of the permitted number is a transaction account

(3) A deposit may continue to be classified as a savings deposit even if the depository institution exercises its right to require notice of withdrawal.

(4) "Savings deposit" does not include funds deposited to the credit of the depository institution's own trust department where the funds involved are utilized to cover checks or drafts. Such funds are "transaction accounts."

(e) "Transaction account" means a deposit or account from which the depositor or account holder is permitted to make transfers or withdrawals by negotiable or transferable instrument, payment order of withdrawal, telephone transfer, or other similar device for the purpose of making payments or transfers to third persons or others or from which the depositor may make third party payments at an automated teller machine ("ATM") or a remote service unit, or other electronic device, including by debit card, but the term does not include savings deposits or accounts described in paragraph (d)(2) of this section even though such accounts permit third party transfers. "Transaction account" includes:

(1) Demand deposits;

(2) Deposits or accounts on which the depository institution has reserved the right to require at least seven days' written notice prior to withdrawal or transfer of any funds in the account and that are subject to check, draft, negotiable order of withdrawal, share draft, or other similar item, except accounts described in paragraph (d)(2) of this section (savings deposits), but including accounts authorized by 12 U.S.C. 1832(a) (NOW accounts).

(3) Deposits or accounts on which the depository institution has reserved the right to require at least seven days' written notice prior to withdrawal or transfer of any funds in the account and from which withdrawals may be made automatically through payment to the depository institution itself or through transfer or credit to a demand deposit or other account in order to cover checks or drafts drawn upon the institution or to maintain a specified balance in, or to make periodic transfers to such accounts, except accounts described in paragraph (d)(2) of this section, but including accounts authorized by 12 U.S.C. 371a (automatic transfer accounts or ATS accounts).

(4) Deposits or accounts on which the depository institution has reserved the right to require at least seven days' written notice prior to withdrawal or transfer of any funds in the account and under the terms of which, or by practice of the depository institution, the depositor is permitted or authorized to make more than six withdrawals per month or statement cycle (or similar period) of at least four weeks for the purposes of transferring funds to another account of the depositor at the same institution (including "transaction account") or for making payment to a third party by means of a preauthorized transfer, or telephonic (including data transmission) agreement, order or instruction, except accounts described in paragraph (d)(2) of this section. An account that authorizes more than six such withdrawals in a calendar month, or statement cycle (or similar period) of at least four weeks, is a "transaction account" whether or not more than six such transfers are made during such period. A "preauthorized transfer" includes any arrangement by the depository institution to pay a third party from the account of a depositor upon written or oral instruction (including an order received through an automated clearing house (ACH)), or any arrangement by a depository institution to pay a third party from the account of the depositor at a predetermined time or on a fixed schedule. Such an account is not a "transaction account" by virtue of an arrangement that permits transfers for the purpose of repaying loans and associated expenses at the same depository institution (as originator or servicer) or that permits transfers

---

regardless of whether the authorized number of transactions is actually made. For accounts described in paragraph (d)(2) of this section, the institution at its option may use, on a consistent basis, either the date on the check, draft, or similar item, or the date the item is paid in applying the limits imposed by that section.

of funds from this account to another account of the same depositor at the same institution or permits withdrawals (payments directly to the depositor) from the account when such transfers or withdrawals are made by mail, messenger, automated teller machine or in person or when such withdrawals are made by telephone (via check mailed to the depositor) regardless of the number of such transfers or withdrawals.

(5) Deposits or accounts maintained in connection with an arrangement that permits the depositor to obtain credit directly or indirectly through the drawing of a negotiable or nonnegotiable check, draft, order or instruction or other similar device (including telephone or electronic order or instruction) on the issuing institution that can be used for the purpose of making payments or transfers to third persons or others or to a deposit account of the depositor.

(6) All deposits other than time and savings accounts, including those accounts that are time and savings deposits in form but that the Board has determined, by rule or order, to be transaction accounts.

(f)(1) "Nonpersonal time deposit" means:

(i) A time deposit, including an MMDA or any other savings deposit, representing funds in which any beneficial interest is held by a depositor which is not a natural person;

(ii) A time deposit, including an MMDA or any other savings deposit, that represents funds deposited to the credit of a depositor that is not a natural person, other than a deposit to the credit of a trustee or other fiduciary if the entire beneficial interest in the deposit is held by one or more natural persons;

(iii) A transferable time deposit. A time deposit is transferable unless it contains a specific statement on the certificate, instrument, passbook, statement or other form representing the account that it is not transferable. A time deposit that contains a specific statement that it is not transferable is not regarded as transferable even if the following transactions can be effected: a pledge as collateral for a loan, a transaction that occurs due to circumstances arising from death, incompetency, marriage, divorce, attachment, or otherwise by operation of law or a transfer on the books or records of the institution; and

(iv) A time deposit represented by a promissory note, an acknowledgment of advance, or similar obligation described in paragraph (a)(1)(vii) of this section that is issued to, or any bankers' acceptance (other than the type described in 12 U.S.C. 372) of the depository institution held by:

(A) Any office located outside the United States of another depository institution or Edge or agreement corporation organized under the laws of the United States;

(B) Any office located outside the United States of a foreign bank;

(C) A foreign national government, or an agency or instrumentality thereof, engaged principally in activities which are ordinarily performed in the United States by governmental entities;

(D) An international entity of which the United States is a member; or

(E) Any other foreign, international, or supranational entity specifically designated by the Board.

(2) Nonpersonal time deposit does not include nontransferable time deposits to the credit of or in which the entire beneficial interest is held by an individual pursuant to an individual retirement account or Keogh (H.R. 10) plan under 26 U.S.C. 408, 401, or non-transferable time deposits held by an employer as part of an unfunded deferred-compensation plan established pursuant to subtitle D of the Revenue Act of 1978 (Pub. L. 95-600, 92 Stat. 2763), or a "401(k) plan" under 26 U.S.C. 401(k).

(g) "Natural person" means an individual or a sole proprietorship. The term does not mean a corporation owned by an individual, a partnership or other association.

(h) "Eurocurrency liabilities" means:

(1) For a depository institution or an Edge or Agreement Corporation organized under the laws of the United States, the sum, if positive, of the following:

(i) Net balances due to its non-United States offices and its international banking facilities ("IBFs") from its United States offices;

(ii)(A) For a depository institution organized under the laws of the United States, assets (including participations) acquired from its United States offices and held by its non-United States offices, by its IBF, or by non-United States offices of an affiliated Edge or Agreement Corporation; or

(B) For an Edge or Agreement Corporation, assets (including participations) acquired from its United States offices and held by its non-United States offices, by its IBF, by non-United States offices of its U.S. or foreign parent institution, or by non-United States offices of an affiliated Edge or Agreement Corporation; and

(iii) Credit outstanding from its non-United States offices to United States residents (other than assets acquired and net balances due from its United States offices), except credit extended (A) from its non-United States offices in the aggregate amount of $100,000 or less to any United States resident, (B) by a non-United States office that at no time during the computation period had credit outstanding, to United States residents exceeding $1 million, (C) to an international banking facility, or (D) to an institution that will be maintaining reserves on such credit pursuant to this part. Credit extended from non-United States offices or from IBFs to a foreign branch, office, subsidiary, affiliate of other foreign establishment ("foreign affiliate") controlled by one or more domestic corporations is not regarded as credit extended to a United States resident if the proceeds will be used to finance the operations outside the United States of the borrower or of other foreign affiliates of the controlling domestic corporation(s). . . .

(i)(1) "Cash item in process of collection" means:

(i) Checks in the process of collection, drawn on a bank or other depository institution that are payable immediately upon presentation in the United States, including checks forwarded to a Federal Reserve Bank in process of collection and checks on hand that will be presented for payment or forwarded for collection on the following business day;

(ii) Government checks drawn on the Treasury of the United States that are in the process of collection; and

(iii) Such other items in the process of collection, that are payable immediately upon presentation in the United States and that are customarily cleared or collected by depository institutions as cash items, including:

(A) Drafts payable through another depository institution;

(B) matured bonds and coupons (including bonds and coupons that have been called and are payable on presentation);

(C) Food coupons and certificates;

(D) Postal and other money orders, and traveler's checks;

(E) Amounts credited to deposit accounts in connection with automated payment arrangements where such credits are made one business day prior to the scheduled payment date to insure that funds are available on the payment date;

(F) Commodity or bill of lading drafts payable immediately upon presentation in the United States;

(G) Returned items and unposted debits; and

(H) Broker security drafts.

(2) "Cash item in process of collection" does not include items handled as noncash collections and credit card sales slips and drafts.

(j) "Net transaction accounts" means the total amount of a depository institution's transaction accounts less the deductions allowed under the provisions of § 204.3.

(k)(1) Vault cash means United States currency and coin owned and booked as an asset by a depository institution that may, at any time, be used to satisfy claims of that depository institution's depositors and that meets the requirements of paragraph (k)(2)(i) or (k)(2)(ii) of this section.

(2) Vault cash must be either:

(i) Held at a physical location of the depository institution (including the depository institution's proprietary ATMs) from which the institution's depositors may make cash withdrawals; or

(ii) Held at an alternate physical location if--

(A) The depository institution claiming the currency and coin as vault cash at all times retains full rights of ownership in and to the currency and coin held at the alternate physical location;

(B) The depository institution claiming the currency and coin as vault cash at all times books the currency and coin held at the alternate physical location as an asset of the depository institution;

(C) No other depository institution claims the currency and coin held at the alternate physical location as vault cash in satisfaction of that other depository institution's reserve requirements;

(D) The currency and coin held at the alternate physical location is reasonably nearby a location of the depository institution claiming the currency and coin as vault cash at which its depositors may make cash withdrawals (an alternate physical location is considered "reasonably nearby" if the depository institution that claims the currency and coin as vault cash can recall the currency and coin from the alternate physical location by 10 a.m. and, relying solely on ground transportation, receive the currency and coin not later than 4 p.m. on the same calendar day at a location of the depository institution at which its depositors may make cash withdrawals); and

(E) The depository institution claiming the currency and coin as vault cash has in place a written cash delivery plan and written contractual arrangements necessary to implement that plan that demonstrate that the currency and coin can be recalled and received in accordance with the requirements of paragraph (k)(2)(ii)(D) of this section at any time. The depository institution shall provide copies of the written cash delivery plan and written contractual arrangements to the Federal Reserve Bank that holds its account or to the Board upon request.

(3) "Vault cash" includes United States currency and coin in transit to a Federal Reserve Bank or a correspondent depository institution for which the reporting depository institution has not yet received credit, and United States currency and coin in transit from a Federal Reserve Bank or a correspondent depository institution when the reporting depository institution's account at the Federal Reserve or correspondent bank has been charged for such shipment.

(4) Silver and gold coin and other currency and coin whose numismatic or bullion value is substantially in excess of face value is not vault cash for purposes of this part.

(*l*) Pass-through account means a balance maintained by a depository institution with a correspondent institution under § 204.5(d). . . .

(q) "Affiliate" includes any corporation, association, or other organization:

(1) Of which a depository institution, directly or indirectly, owns or controls either a majority of the voting shares or more than 50 percent of the numbers of shares voted for the election of its directors, trustees, or other persons exercising similar functions at the preceding election, or controls in any manner the election of a majority of its directors, trustees, or other persons exercising similar functions;

(2) Of which control is held, directly or indirectly, through stock ownership or in

any other manner, by the shareholders of a depository institution who own or control either a majority of the shares of such depository institution or more than 50 percent of the number of shares voted for the election of directors of such depository institution at the preceding election, or by trustees for the benefit of the shareholders of any such depository institution;

(3) Of which a majority of its directors, trustees, or other persons exercising similar functions are directors of any one depository institution; or

(4) Which owns or controls, directly or indirectly, either a majority of the shares of capital stock of a depository institution or more than 50 percent of the number of shares voted for the election of directors, trustees or other persons exercising similar functions of a depository institution at the preceding election, or controls in any manner the election of a majority of the directors, trustees, or other persons exercising similar functions of a depository institution, or for the benefit of whose shareholders or members all or substantially all the capital stock of a depository institution is held by trustees. . . .

(s) "United States resident" means (1) any individual residing (at the time of the transaction) in the United States; (2) any corporation, partnership, association or other entity organized in the United States ("domestic corporation"); and (3) any branch or office located in the United States of any entity that is not organized in the United States.

(t) "Any deposit that is payable only at an office located outside the United States" means (1) a deposit of a United States resident[9] that is in a denomination of $100,000 or more, and as to which the depositor is entitled, under the agreement with the institution, to demand payment only outside the United States or (2) a deposit of a person who is not a United States resident as to which the depositor is entitled, under the agreement with the institution, to demand payment only outside the United States. . . .

(v) Clearing balance means the average balance held in an account at a Federal Reserve Bank by an institution over a reserve maintenance period to satisfy its contractual clearing balance with a Reserve Bank.

(w) Clearing balance allowance means the greater of $25,000 or two percent of an institution's contractual clearing balance.

(x) Contractual clearing balance means an amount that an institution agrees or is required to maintain in its account at a Federal Reserve Bank in addition to any reserve balance requirement. An institution that has a reserve balance requirement of zero may still have a contractual clearing balance.

(y) Eligible institution means–

(1) Any depository institution as described in § 204.1(c) of this part;

(2) Any trust company;

(3) Any corporation organized under section 25A of the Federal Reserve Act (12 U.S.C. 611 et seq.) or having an agreement with the Board under section 25 of the Federal Reserve Act (12 U.S.C. 601 et seq.); and

(4) Any branch or agency of a foreign bank (as defined in section 1(b) of the International Banking Act of 1978, 12 U.S.C. 3101(b)).

(z) Excess balance means the average balance held in an account at a Federal Reserve Bank by or on behalf of an institution over a reserve maintenance period that exceeds the sum of the required reserve balance and any clearing balance.

(aa) Excess balance account means an account at a Reserve Bank pursuant to § 204.10(d) of this part that is established by one or more eligible institutions through an agent

9. A deposit of a foreign branch, office, subsidiary, affiliate or other foreign establishment ("foreign affiliate") controlled by one or more domestic corporations is not regarded as a deposit of a United States resident if the funds serve a purpose in connection with its foreign or international business or that of other foreign affiliates of the controlling domestic corporation(s).

and in which only excess balances of the participating eligible institutions may at any time be maintained. An excess balance account is not a "pass-through account" for purposes of this part.

(bb) Required reserve balance means the average balance held in an account at a Federal Reserve Bank by or on behalf of an institution over a reserve maintenance period to satisfy the reserve requirements of this part.

(cc) Targeted federal funds rate means the federal funds rate established from time to time by the Federal Open Market Committee.

(dd) Term deposit means those funds of an eligible institution that are maintained by that institution for a specified maturity at a Federal Reserve Bank pursuant to section 204.10(e) of this part.

§ 204.3 Reporting and location.

(a) Every depository institution, U.S. branch or agency of a foreign bank, and Edge or Agreement corporation shall file a report of deposits (or any other form or statement that may be required by the Board or by a Federal Reserve Bank) with the Federal Reserve Bank in the Federal Reserve District in which it is located, regardless of the manner in which it chooses to maintain required reserve balances.

(b) A foreign bank's U.S. branches and agencies and an Edge or Agreement corporation's offices operating within the same State and the same Federal Reserve District shall prepare and file a report of deposits on an aggregated basis.

(c) For purposes of this part, the obligations of a majority-owned (50 percent or more) U.S. subsidiary (except an Edge or Agreement corporation) of a depository institution shall be regarded as obligations of the parent depository institution.

(d) A depository institution, a foreign bank, or an Edge or Agreement corporation shall, if possible, assign the low reserve tranche and reserve requirement exemption prescribed in § 204.4(f) to only one office or to a group of offices filing a single aggregated report of deposits. The amount of the reserve requirement exemption allocated to an office or group of offices may not exceed the amount of the low reserve tranche allocated to such office or offices. If the low reserve tranche or reserve requirement exemption cannot be fully utilized by a single office or by a group of offices filing a single report of deposits, the unused portion of the tranche or exemption may be assigned to other offices or groups of offices of the same institution until the amount of the tranche (or net transaction accounts) or exemption (or reservable liabilities) is exhausted. The tranche or exemption may be reallocated each year concurrent with implementation of the indexed tranche and exemption, or, if necessary during the course of the year to avoid underutilization of the tranche or exemption, at the beginning of a reserve computation period. . . .

(f) The Board and the Federal Reserve Banks will not hold a pass-through correspondent responsible for guaranteeing the accuracy of the reports of deposits submitted by its respondents.

(g)(1) For purposes of this section, a depository institution, a U.S. branch or agency of a foreign bank, or an Edge or Agreement corporation is located in the Federal Reserve District that contains the location specified in the institution's charter, organizing certificate, license, or articles of incorporation, or as specified by the institution's primary regulator, or if no such location is specified, the location of its head office, unless otherwise determined by the Board under paragraph (g)(2) of this section.

(2) If the location specified in paragraph (g)(1) of this section, in the Board's judgment, is ambiguous, would impede the ability of the Board or the Federal Reserve Banks to perform their functions under the Federal Reserve Act, or would impede the ability of the institution to operate efficiently, the Board will determine the Federal Reserve District in

which the institution is located, after consultation with the institution and the relevant Federal Reserve Banks. The relevant Federal Reserve Banks are the Federal Reserve Bank whose District contains the location specified in paragraph (g)(1) of this section and the Federal Reserve Bank in whose District the institution is proposed to be located. In making this determination, the Board will consider any applicable laws, the business needs of the institution, the location of the institution's head office, the locations where the institution performs its business, and the locations that would allow the institution, the Board, and the Federal Reserve Banks to perform their functions efficiently and effectively.

§ 204.4 Computation of required reserves.

(a) In determining the reserve requirement under this part, the amount of cash items in process of collection and balances subject to immediate withdrawal due from other depository institutions located in the United States (including such amounts due from United States branches and agencies of foreign banks and Edge and Agreement corporations) may be deducted from the amount of gross transaction accounts. The amount that may be deducted may not exceed the amount of gross transaction accounts.

(b) United States branches and agencies of a foreign bank may not deduct balances due from another United States branch or agency of the same foreign bank, and United States offices of an Edge or Agreement Corporation may not deduct balances due from another United States office of the same Edge or Agreement Corporation.

(c) Balances "due from other depository institutions" do not include balances due from Federal Reserve Banks, pass-through accounts, or balances (payable in dollars or otherwise) due from banking offices located outside the United States. An institution exercising fiduciary powers may not include in balances "due from other depository institutions" amounts of trust funds deposited with other banks and due to it as a trustee or other fiduciary.

(d) For institutions that file a report of deposits weekly, required reserves are computed on the basis of the institution's daily average balances of deposits and Eurocurrency liabilities during a 14-day computation period ending every second Monday.

(e) For institutions that file a report of deposits quarterly, required reserves are computed on the basis of the institution's daily average balances of deposits and Eurocurrency liabilities during the 7-day computation period that begins on the third Tuesday of March, June, September, and December.

(f) For all depository institutions, Edge and Agreement corporations, and United States branches and agencies of foreign banks, required reserves are computed by applying the reserve requirement ratios below to net transaction accounts, nonpersonal time deposits, and Eurocurrency liabilities of the institution during the computation period.

Reservable liability	Reserve requirement ratio
NET TRANSACTION ACCOUNTS:	
$0 to reserve requirement exemption amount ($10.7 million)	0 percent of amount.
Over reserve requirement exemption amount ($10.7 million) and up to low reserve tranche ($55.2 million)	3 percent of amount.
Over low reserve tranche ($55.2 million)	$1,335,000 plus 10 percent of amount over $55.2 million.
Nonpersonal time deposits	0 percent.
Eurocurrency liabilities	0 percent.

§ 204.5 Maintenance of required reserves.

(a)(1) A depository institution, a U.S. branch or agency of a foreign bank, and an Edge or Agreement corporation shall maintain required reserves in the form of vault cash and, if vault cash does not fully satisfy the institution's required reserves, in the form of a balance maintained

(i) Directly with the Federal Reserve Bank in the Federal Reserve District in which the institution is located, or

(ii) With a pass-through correspondent in accordance with § 204.5(d).

(2) Each individual institution subject to this part is responsible for satisfying its reserve balance requirement, if any, either directly with a Federal Reserve Bank or through a pass-through correspondent.

(b)(1) For institutions that file a report of deposits weekly, the balances that are required to be maintained with the Federal Reserve shall be maintained during a 14-day maintenance period that begins on the third Thursday following the end of a given computation period.

(2) For institutions that file a report of deposits quarterly, the balances that are required to be maintained with the Federal Reserve shall be maintained during each of the 7-day maintenance periods during the interval that begins on the fourth Thursday following the end of the institution's computation period and ends on the fourth Wednesday after the close of the institution's next computation period.

(c) Cash items forwarded to a Federal Reserve Bank for collection and credit shall not be counted as part of the reserve balance to be carried with the Federal Reserve until the expiration of the time specified in the appropriate time schedule established under Regulation J, "Collection of Checks and Other Items by Federal Reserve Banks and Funds Transfers Through Fedwire" (12 CFR Part 210). If a depository institution draws against items before that time, the charge will be made to its account if the balance is sufficient to pay it; any resulting impairment of reserve balances will be subject to the penalties provided by law and to the reserve-deficiency charges provided by this part. However, the Federal Reserve Bank may, at its discretion, refuse to permit the withdrawal or other use of credit given in an account for any time for which the Federal Reserve Bank has not received payment in actually and finally collected funds.

(d)(1) A depository institution, a U.S. branch or agency of a foreign bank, or an Edge or Agreement corporation required to maintain reserve balances ("respondent") may select only one pass-through correspondent institution to pass through its required reserve balances, unless otherwise permitted by the Federal Reserve Bank in whose District the respondent is located. Eligible pass-through correspondent institutions are Federal Home Loan Banks, the National Credit Union Administration Central Liquidity Facility, depository institutions, U.S. branches or agencies of foreign banks, and Edge and Agreement corporations that maintain required reserve balances, which may be zero, at a Federal Reserve Bank. In addition, the Board reserves the right to permit other institutions, on a case-by-case basis, to serve as pass-through correspondents. The correspondent chosen must subsequently pass through the required reserve balances of its respondents directly to a Federal Reserve Bank. The correspondent placing funds with a Federal Reserve Bank on behalf of respondents will be responsible for account maintenance as described in paragraph (d)(4) of this section.

(2) Respondents or correspondents may institute, terminate, or change pass-through agreements for the maintenance of required reserve balances by providing all documentation required for the establishment of the new agreement or termination of the existing agreement to the Federal Reserve Banks involved within the time period provided for such a change by those Reserve Banks.

(3) A correspondent that passes through required reserve balances of respondents shall maintain such balances, along with the correspondent's own required reserve balances (if any), in a single commingled account at the Federal Reserve Bank in whose District the correspondent is located. The balances held by the correspondent in an account at a Reserve Bank are the property of the correspondent and represent a liability of the Reserve Bank solely to the correspondent, regardless of whether the funds represent the reserve balances of another institution that have been passed through the correspondent.

(4)(i) A pass-through correspondent shall be responsible for assuring the maintenance of the appropriate aggregate level of its respondents' required reserve balances. A Federal Reserve Bank will compare the total reserve balance required to be maintained with the total actual reserve balance held in such account for purposes of determining required-reserve deficiencies, imposing or waiving charges for deficiencies in required reserves, and for other reserve maintenance purposes. A charge for a deficiency in the aggregate level of the required reserve balance will be imposed by the Reserve Bank on the correspondent maintaining the account.

(ii) Each correspondent is required to maintain detailed records for each of its respondents in a manner that permits Reserve Banks to determine whether the respondent has provided a sufficient required reserve balance to the correspondent. A correspondent passing through a respondent's required reserve balance shall maintain records and make such reports as the Board or Reserve Bank requires in order to ensure the correspondent's compliance with its responsibilities for the maintenance of a respondent's reserve balance. Such records shall be available to the Reserve Banks as required.

(iii) The Federal Reserve Bank may terminate any pass-through agreement under which the correspondent is deficient in its recordkeeping or other responsibilities.

(iv) Interest paid on supplemental reserves (if such reserves are required under § 204.7) held by a respondent will be credited to the account maintained by the correspondent.

(e) Any excess or deficiency in an institution's required reserve balance shall be carried over and applied against the balance maintained in the next maintenance period as specified in this paragraph. The amount of any such excess or deficiency that is carried over shall not exceed the greater of:

(1) The amount obtained by multiplying 0.04 times the sum of depository institution's required reserves and the depository institution's contractual clearing balance, if any, and then subtracting from this product the depository institution's clearing balance

allowance, if any; or

(2) $50,000, minus the depository institution's clearing balance allowance, if any. Any carryover not offset during the next period may not be carried over to subsequent periods.

§ 204.6 Charges for reserve deficiencies.

(a) Deficiencies in a depository institution's required reserve balance, after application of the carryover provided in § 204.5(e), are subject reserve-deficiency charges. Federal Reserve Banks are authorized to assess charges for deficiencies in required reserves at a rate of 1 percentage point per year above the primary credit rate, as provided in § 201.51(a) of this chapter, in effect for borrowings from the Federal Reserve Bank on the first day of the calendar month in which the deficiencies occurred. Charges shall be assessed on the basis of daily average deficiencies during each maintenance period. Reserve Banks may, as an alternative to levying monetary charges, after consideration of the circumstances involved, permit a depository institution to eliminate deficiencies in its required reserve balance by maintaining additional reserves during subsequent reserve maintenance periods.

(b) Reserve Banks may waive the charges for reserve deficiencies except when the deficiency arises out of a depository institution's gross negligence or conduct that is inconsistent with the principles and purposes of reserve requirements. Decisions by Reserve Banks to waive charges are based on an evaluation of the circumstances in each individual case and the depository institution's reserve maintenance record. For example, a waiver may be appropriate for a small charge or once during a two-year period for a deficiency that does not exceed a certain percentage of the depository institution's required reserves. If a depository institution has demonstrated a lack of due regard for the proper maintenance of required reserves, the Reserve Bank may decline to exercise the waiver privilege and assess all charges regardless of amount or reason for the deficiency.

(c) In individual cases, where a Federal supervisory authority waives a liquidity requirement, or waives the penalty for failing to satisfy a liquidity requirement, the Reserve Bank in the District where the involved depository institution is located shall waive the reserve requirement imposed under this part for such depository institution when requested by the Federal supervisory authority involved.

(d) Violations of this part may be subject to assessment of civil money penalties by the Board under authority of Section 19(1) of the Federal Reserve Act (12 U.S.C. 505) as implemented in 12 CFR part 263. In addition, the Board and any other Federal financial institution supervisory authority may enforce this part with respect to depository institutions subject to their jurisdiction under authority conferred by law to undertake cease and desist proceedings.

§ 204.7 Supplemental reserve requirement.

(a) Finding by Board. Upon the affirmative vote of at least five members of the Board and after consultation with the Board of Directors of the Federal Deposit Insurance Corporation, the Federal Home Loan Bank Board, and the National Credit Union Administration Board, the Board may impose a supplemental reserve requirement on every depository institution of not more than 4 percent of its total transaction accounts. A supplemental reserve requirement may be imposed if:

(1) The sole purpose of the requirement is to increase the amount of reserves maintained to a level essential for the conduct of monetary policy;

(2) The requirement is not imposed for the purpose of reducing the cost burdens resulting from the imposition of basic reserve requirements;

(3) Such requirement is not imposed for the purpose of increasing the amount of

balances needed for clearing purposes; and

(4) On the date on which supplemental reserve requirements are imposed, the total amount of basic reserve requirements is not less than the amount of reserves that would be required on transaction accounts and nonpersonal time deposits under the initial reserve ratios established by the Monetary Control Act of 1980 (Pub.L. 96-221) in effect on September 1, 1980.

(b) Term.

(1) If a supplemental reserve requirement has been imposed for a period of one year or more, the Board shall review and determine the need for continued maintenance of supplemental reserves and shall transmit annual reports to the Congress regarding the need for continuing such requirement.

(2) Any supplemental reserve requirement shall terminate at the close of the first 90-day period after the requirement is imposed during which the average amount of supplemental reserves required are less than the amount of reserves which would be required if the ratios in effect on September 1, 1980, were applied.

(c) Earnings Participation Account. A depository institutions's supplemental reserve requirement shall be maintained by the Federal Reserve Banks in an Earnings Participation Account. Such balances shall receive earnings to be paid by the Federal Reserve Banks during each calendar quarter at a rate not to exceed the rate earned on the securities portfolio of the Federal Reserve System during the previous calendar quarter. Additional rules and regulations maybe prescribed by the Board concerning the payment of earnings on Earnings Participation Accounts by Federal Reserve Banks.

(d) Report to Congress. The Board shall transmit promptly to the Congress a report stating the basis for exercising its authority to require a supplemental reserve under this section.

(e) Reserve requirements. At present, there are no supplemental reserve requirements imposed under this section. . . .

§ 204.9 Emergency reserve requirement.

(a) Finding by Board. The Board may impose, after consulting with the appropriate committees of Congress, additional reserve requirements on depository institutions at any ratio on any liability upon a finding by at least five members of the Board that extraordinary circumstances require such action.

(b) Term. Any action taken under this section shall be valid for a period not exceeding 180 days, and may be extended for further periods of up to 180 days each by affirmative action of at least five members of the Board for each extension.

(c) Reports to Congress. The Board shall transmit promptly to Congress a report of any exercise of its authority under this paragraph and the reasons for the exercise of authority.

(d) Reserve requirements. At present, there are no emergency reserve requirements imposed under this section.

§ 204.10 Payment of interest on balances.

(a) Payment of interest. The Federal Reserve Banks shall pay interest on balances maintained at Federal Reserve Banks by or on behalf of an eligible institution as provided in this section and under such other terms and conditions as the Board may prescribe.

(b) Rate. Except as provided in paragraph (c) of this section, Federal Reserve Banks shall pay interest at the following rates–

(1) For required reserve balances, at 1/4 percent;

(2) For excess balances, at 1/4 percent; or

(3) For required reserve balances, excess balances, and term deposits, at any other rate or rates as determined by the Board from time to time, not to exceed the general level of short-term interest rates. For purposes of this subsection, "short-term interest rates" are rates on obligations with maturities of no more than one year, such as the primary credit rate and rates on term federal funds, term repurchase agreements, commercial paper, term Eurodollar deposits, and other similar instruments.

(c) Pass-through balances. A pass-through correspondent that is an eligible institution may pass back to its respondent interest paid on balances held on behalf of that respondent. In the case of balances held by a pass-through correspondent that is not an eligible institution, a Reserve Bank shall pay interest only on the required reserve balances held on behalf of one or more respondents, and the correspondent shall pass back to its respondents interest paid on balances in the correspondent's account. Any passing back of interest by a correspondent to a respondent under this subsection is not a payment of interest on a demand deposit for purposes of Part 217 of this chapter (Regulation Q).

(d) Excess balance accounts. (1) A Reserve Bank may establish an excess balance account for eligible institutions under the provisions of this paragraph (d). Notwithstanding any other provisions of this part, the excess balances of eligible institutions in an excess balance account represent a liability of the Reserve Bank solely to those participating eligible institutions.

(2) The participating eligible institutions in an excess balance account shall authorize another institution to act as agent of the participating institutions for purposes of general account management, including but not limited to transferring the excess balances of participating institutions in and out of the excess balance account. An excess balance account must be established at the Reserve Bank where the agent maintains its master account, unless otherwise determined by the Board. The agent may not commingle its own funds in the excess balance account.

(3) No required reserve balances or clearing balances may be maintained at any time in an excess balance account, and balances maintained in an excess balance account will not satisfy any institution's reserve balance requirement or contractual clearing balance.

(4) An excess balance account must be used exclusively for the purpose of maintaining the excess balances of participants and may not be used for general payments or other activities.

(5) Interest shall be paid on excess balances of eligible institutions maintained in an excess balance account in accordance with paragraph (b)(2) or (b)(3) of this section.

(6) A Reserve Bank may establish additional terms and conditions consistent with this part with respect to the operation of an excess balance account, including, but not limited to, terms of and fees for services, conditions under which an institution may act as agent for an account, restrictions on the agent with respect to account management, penalties for noncompliance with this section or any terms and conditions, and account termination.

(e) Term deposits. (1) A Federal Reserve Bank may accept term deposits from eligible institutions under the provisions of this paragraph (e) subject to such terms and conditions as the Board may establish from time to time, including but not limited to conditions regarding the maturity of the term deposits being offered, maximum and minimum amounts that may be maintained by an eligible institution in a term deposit, the interest rate or rates offered, early withdrawal of term deposits, pledging term deposits as collateral and, if term deposits are offered through an auction mechanism, the size of the offering, maximum and minimum bid amounts, and other relevant terms.

(2) A term deposit will not satisfy any institution's required reserve balance or contractual clearing balance.

(3) A term deposit may not be used for general payments or settlement activities.

Notes and Comments 5.41. Quarter National Bank (QNB) is currently holding deposits as reflected in Figure 5.1, *supra*. Applying the preceding excerpts from the Fed's regulations concerning reserve requirements, what dollar amount of reserves is QNB currently required to maintain? If assumptions must be made, or additional facts or other information are required to arrive at an answer, specify what the assumptions, facts or information are, and explain what difference they would make to the answer.

5.42. Altered State Bank, an FDIC-insured, nonmember bank, is a correspondent of QNB. What effect do the Fed's reserve requirements have on Altered?

5.43. What would be the possible consequences to QNB if it were discovered that the bank had inadvertently failed to maintain sufficient reserves against deposits? What if the deficiency were caused by the fact that no one in a supervisory capacity within the bank ever reviewed these matters, and funds were being embezzled through false electronic transfers, rather than being maintained as reserves? What if the board of directors of QNB, caught in a sudden liquidity shortage, simply decided that they would withhold the reserves, although they knew that the reserves were required?

5.44. If the Fed determined that QNB's real estate lending activities were too speculative, could the Fed impose an additional, emergency reserve requirement on the bank's deposits, in order to tighten the bank's credit activities? Could the Fed impose a supplemental reserve requirement on the bank's deposits for this purpose?

b. Restrictions on Rates of Interest

Until the enactment of Title II of the Depository Institutions Deregulation and Monetary Control Act of 1980, rates of interest on deposits were strictly regulated, principally under regulations promulgated by the Fed. *See* 12 C.F.R. pt. 217 (1979). With respect to demand deposits in fact, no interest could be paid. *See* 12 U.S.C. § 1832 (Supp. 1973). As competition for deposits increased, particularly with the inroads of nondepository institutions such as money market mutual funds (MMMFs), the federal prohibition began to fray about the edges. In February 1976, federal law was amended to permit negotiable orders of withdrawal accounts (NOW accounts), interest-bearing deposits from which transfers to third parties could be ordered by the depositor by negotiable or transferable instruments. *See* Pub. L. No. 94-222, § 2, 90 Stat. 197 (1976) (codified at 12 U.S.C. § 1832(a)). This experimental change was limited to withdrawals from depository institutions in Connecticut, Maine, Rhode Island and Vermont. *Id.*

In November 1978, New York was added to the list of favored jurisdictions. *See* Pub. L. No. 95-630, § 1301, 92 Stat. 3712 (1978) (codified at 12 U.S.C. § 1832(a)). New Jersey was added in December 1979. *See* Pub. L. No. 96-161, § 106, 93 Stat. 1235 (1979) (codified at 12 U.S.C. § 1832(a)).

Notes and Comments 5.45. This issue was particularly important for savings associations. These institutions wished to offer services to their depositors similar to the services available from competing commercial banks. Yet the demand deposits of commercial banks were subject to well developed regulations concerning the holding of reserves against deposits, among other things. Demand deposits were considered more volatile, being subject to withdrawal at any time. There was a greater risk to the institution holding such deposits than is the case with interest-bearing savings and time deposits, since the latter are generally withdrawable subject to a waiting period, at least in principle. Was it permissible for the federal government to restrict deposit taking by savings associations, while at the same time it selectively allowed NOW accounts to be offered in a few states? Consider the following cases.

Otero Sav. & Loan Ass'n v. Board of Governors

497 F. Supp. 370 (D.Colo. 1980)

KANE, District Judge.

This case is before me on plaintiff's and plaintiffs-intervenor's motions for a preliminary injunction restraining defendants from refusing to accept or process their drafts through the federal reserve clearing and collection system in the same manner as said checks have been cleared and collected prior to August 18, 1980. A temporary restraining order to this effect was issued August 15, 1980 and extended on August 25, 1980.

Plaintiff, Otero Savings and Loan Association initiated a program to provide its customers with checking account services, through the use of funds in their regular savings accounts. The Check-In Program involved the opening of a checking account and a savings account, along with a savings to checking transfer agreement authorizing Otero to transfer automatically funds from the savings account to the checking account for the purpose of honoring checks presented to Otero for payment. Checks issued by Otero customers are cleared and collected through the federal reserve system by virtue of an agreement between Otero and United Bank of Denver which is a member of the federal reserve system and has the right to use its clearing and collection services. Otero maintains an account with United Bank for the purpose of effecting final settlement of checks issued by Otero customers. Plaintiffs-intervenors have initiated similar programs. However Sun Savings & Loan Association has an additional program which authorizes Sun to honor nonnegotiable instruments drawn by the depositor on a savings account. . . .

Plaintiff and plaintiffs-intervenors have established that they will suffer irreparable harm if the defendants' proposed actions are not enjoined. In the absence of reasonable alternative clearinghouse services, they will be forced to interrupt the banking services of almost 19,000 customers. While defendants have shown that some alternative means of clearing and processing these checks are available, it is unrealistic to suggest that in the current commercial milieu financial institutions such as the plaintiff can clear checks outside the clearinghouse system and it is abundantly clear that the federal reserve bank is the linchpin of the system. The precipitous cessation of the participation in the system by Otero and the plaintiffs-intervenors would result in dire and probably devastating consequences to them in the marketplace. Such consequences include severe confusion of processes and loss of good will and customer confidence in these institutions. . . . Also, I take into consideration that administrative proceedings before the Federal Home Loan Bank Board are currently pending. They were initiated by the Federal Savings and Loan Insurance Corporation ("FSLIC") pursuant to 12 U.S.C. § 1730(e)(1) to compel Otero to cease and desist the Check-In Program.[j] The defendants' proposed actions would in effect render these proceedings moot. Otero would have to dismantle its programs prior to a determination by an administrative body. This would impair the agency's ability to grant an effective remedy and deny Otero the notice and hearing procedures accorded to it by law pursuant to 12 U.S.C. § 1730(e)(1). . . .

12 U.S.C. § 1832(a) prohibits depository institutions from allowing the owners of a deposit or account on which interest or dividends are paid to make withdrawals by negotiable or transferable instruments for the purpose of making transfers to third parties, ex-

j. Use of administrative cease and desist orders is discussed in Chapter 8, Note 8.4, *infra*, and materials following the note.

cept in eight states.[4] Otero and plaintiffs-intervenors claim that § 1832 is unconstitutional because activity is prohibited in some states while expressly allowed in others, that their activities do not come within its prohibitions, and that in any case the Federal Reserve Board has no power to enforce this provision. In addition they allege a violation of their due process rights since § 1832 is already being enforced by the FSLIC and those proceedings would be rendered moot by defendants proposed actions.

The legislative history of § 1832 indicates that Congress was concerned about the effect of Negotiable Order of Withdrawal accounts on the competitive balance between various financial institutions and the serious disruptions which could result from their use. However, testimony from the Federal Reserve Bank, among others, indicated that at that time, 1973, the evidence of disruption was not sufficient to warrant their total prohibition. Therefore, they were allowed in the states where they were currently permitted by state law, namely New Hampshire and Massachusetts. However Congress did want to monitor these accounts and therefore included in the bill a section giving the FDIC authority to monitor the effects of Negotiable Order of Withdrawal accounts and take swift corrective action where necessary. The legislative history indicates that the actual legality of such accounts is determined by the laws, banking regulations, and judicial decisions of the individual states. S.R. No. 93-149, 93rd Cong., 1st Sess., *reprinted in* (1973) U.S. Code Cong. & Admin. News pp. 2014, 2015-6. Thus, there appears to be a rational basis for allowing these accounts in some states but not others, rendering plaintiff's equal protection claims weak although not defeated. The legislative history does raise the question of whether these accounts are prohibited by Colorado law.

C.R.S. § 11-6-102(1) provides that the payment of interest, directly or indirectly, on demand accounts is prohibited. However it is open to question whether plaintiffs come within this section since they do not pay interest on demand accounts, but on savings accounts. Plaintiff-intervenor Sun seems to come within this prohibition. C.R.S. § 11-6-102(2) provides that savings deposits shall be repaid to the depositor under such regulations as the board of directors of the state bank shall prescribe. Similar statutory provisions have been held to permit Negotiable Order of Withdrawal accounts, *Savings Bank of Baltimore v. Bank Commissioner*, 248 Md. 461, 237 A.2d 45 (1968), *Consumers Savings Bank v. Commissioner of Banks*, 361 Mass. 717, 282 N.E.2d 416 (Mass. 1972), while other courts have held the opposite, *N.Y.S. Bankers Assoc. v. Albright*, 46 A.D.2d 269, 361 N.Y.S.2d 949 (1974). In the instant case the Colorado State Savings and Loan Commissioner, in consultation with the Colorado Attorney General, approved Sun's program prior to its initiation. Thus this issue should be developed further rather than curtailed by the issuance of a preliminary injunction. In *U.S. League of Savings Assoc. v. Board of Governors of the Federal Reserve Board*, 463 F. Supp. 342 (D.D.C. 1978), *vacated and set aside without opinion, American Bankers Association v. Connell*, 595 F.2d 887, 888 (C.A.D.C.), the court emphasized the existence of two accounts in holding that the automatic fund transfer service, from savings to checking accounts, offered by commercial banks did not violate § 1832. The court held that two accounts are required to operate the AFT service and therefore no negotiable orders are drawn on, or third party payment made from, a savings deposit. It is probable that plaintiff's activities do not fall within the statute. This issue is currently being litigated before an administrative body. The probability of success on the merits is further support for the issuance of a preliminary injunction.[6]

---

4. Mass., Conn., R.I., Maine, Vermont, N.Y., N.J., and N.H.

6. Defendants' principal thrust is that the two account system is a sham and that I must pierce the form and look at the substance. I agree wholeheartedly, but I need a trial with its panoply of discovery, research and preparation in order to undertake such a probe. The exigencies attendant upon

Enforcement of § 1832 seems to fall within the authority of the FDIC, 12 U.S.C. § 1811, *et seq.* The legislative history indicates that the FDIC is to keep watch on such deposits and their effect on other institutions. The Federal Reserve Bank regulates member banks pursuant to 12 U.S.C. § 221. However Otero, Majestic, Sun, and Golden are not members of the Federal Reserve System, but are simply institutions whose deposits are insured by the FDIC. The FSLIC is presently enforcing the statute against Otero. The defendants have no apparent enforcement power over this provision. The probability of plaintiff succeeding on this issue is further support for the issuance of this injunction.

The defendants have the power to establish and regulate clearinghouses pursuant to 12 U.S.C. § 248(o) and 12 C.F.R. 210.2 *et seq.* (Regulation J) thereunder. 12 U.S.C. § 342, § 347, and § 360 further regulate these activities as to member and nonmember banks. Pursuant to Regulation J, the Federal Reserve Bank has defined "item" and plaintiff and plaintiffs-intervenors claim that since they fall within that definition, defendants cannot refuse to process their checks. In *Independent Banker Assoc. of America v. Board of Governors of the Federal Reserve System*, 500 F.2d 812 (C.A.D.C. 1974) in deciding whether a new rule within regulation J was arbitrary and capricious, the court found that such regulations were subject to judicial review. The court further held that having established such services for member and non-member banks, the board could not unreasonably jeopardize or prejudice operations by alterations in the way service is administered to either. That non-members can choose not to use this service does not relieve the board of this obligation, particularly as there remains no comparable alternative in terms of speed and efficiency. Adequate provisions must be made for non-member banks. In the instant case however, plaintiff and plaintiffs-intervenors will in effect be put out of business as to these particular accounts if the defendants are allowed to proceed. They will also be denied a meaningful hearing on a statute the Federal Reserve Bank has no authority to enforce. In the absence of strong statutory authority to the contrary, defendants' actions should be enjoined. . . .

Otero Sav. & Loan Ass'n v. Federal Home Loan Bank Board

665 F.2d 279 (10th Cir. 1981)

Before HOLLOWAY, MCKAY and LOGAN, Circuit Judges.*

[Otero Savings and Loan Association (Otero) challenged an order of the Federal Savings and Loan Insurance Corporation (FSLIC) and the Federal Home Loan Bank Board (Bank Board) finding that Otero's "Check-In" program, as operated prior to December 31, 1980, violated 12 U.S.C. § 1832(a). The order required Otero to close all checking accounts held by for-profit corporations and partnerships and to stop offering new customer Check-In or related automatic transfer system accounts (ATS) or negotiable order of withdrawal (NOW) accounts for a period of 268 days following the effective date of the order. Otero argued on appeal that it had not violated § 1832, and that the Board and the FSLIC had no power to order the closing of the accounts and prohibit account offerings for 282 days. A

---

a preliminary hearing do not permit me to proceed with such an effort at this point.

*. There is a divergence of views on some issues before us. The various separate opinions which follow express those views and the concurrence of a majority of the panel in the conclusion stated, *infra*. Our opinion in a related case is being filed today in No. 80-1946, *Otero Savings and Loan Association, et al. v. The Federal Reserve Bank of Kansas City, Missouri*, 665 F.2d 275 (10th Cir. 1981).

temporary stay of the order pending final decision was issued by a panel of the Tenth Circuit.]

The FSLIC instituted an administrative proceeding against Otero pursuant to 12 U.S.C. § 1730(e) (1980) which culminated in the Bank Board's decision that the operation of Otero's Check-In program before December 31, 1980, violated 12 U.S.C. § 1832, although it would be legal to offer such accounts to depositors other than for-profit corporations and partnerships after December 31, 1980.[1] The Bank Board, claiming authority under 12 U.S.C. § 1730(e) (1980), entered an order permitting Otero to maintain its existing Check-In accounts, except for those held by for-profit organizations, but directing Otero to cease opening any new Check-In or equivalent accounts for a period of 268 days following the effective date of the order. This penalty was conceived to be the most equitable under the circumstances, since Otero had achieved a 268 day competitive advantage by offering such accounts before being permitted to do so by law. . . .

LOGAN, Circuit Judge.

. . .

Because its accounts are insured by the FSLIC, Otero is deemed an "insured institution" within the meaning of 12 U.S.C. § 1724, and is therefore a "depository institution" by definition under 12 U.S.C. § 1832(b)(5). As such, Otero is subject to § 1832(a), which provides:

> (a) No depository institution shall allow the owner of a deposit or account on which interest or dividends are paid to make withdrawals by negotiable or transferable instruments for the purpose of making transfers to third parties, except that such withdrawals may be made in the States of Massachusetts, Connecticut, Rhode Island, Maine, Vermont, New York, New Jersey, and New Hampshire.

Otero argues that its two-account ATS system does not violate 12 U.S.C. § 1832(a), reading that section as applying only to NOW accounts, that is, single account systems in which interest or dividends are paid directly upon savings accounts from which withdrawals by negotiable instruments are permitted.

We believe a fair reading of the language of 12 U.S.C. § 1832(a) indicates that no depository institution may offer an interest bearing demand deposit account, whether operated directly as a one-account NOW system or indirectly as a two-account ATS system. The statutory language is broad enough to apply to both types of accounts. We have found nothing in the legislative history of this provision, enacted in 1973, to indicate that Congress intended to differentiate between the two types of accounts. It is true that Congress treated ATS and NOW systems separately in later legislation. But the legislative history of subsequent acts is of dubious value in interpreting an act passed six years earlier. *See Haynes v. United States*, 390 U.S. 85, 87 n.4 (1968); *United States v. Price*, 361 U.S. 304, 313 (1960); *United States v. United Mine Workers*, 330 U.S. 258, 282 (1947).

It is also a fact that the congressional reports treating the original enactment of 12 U.S.C. § 1832 refer only to NOW accounts, and it may be, as represented to us at oral argument, that no savings and loan was using anything but NOW accounts at the time of that legislation. No doubt the NOW account development in New England and the threat of competitive inequality between savings and loan associations and commercial banks was the

---

1. In view of the disposition we make of this issue, we do not decide whether Colorado law permits Otero and other state-chartered savings and loans to offer ATS accounts.

impetus to congressional action. This does not, however, limit the general language of § 1832 which we construe as forbidding depositor withdrawals from interest bearing accounts via negotiable or transferable instruments payable to third parties, whether accomplished directly under the NOW format or indirectly under the ATS format.

Otero's strongest argument focuses on the interrelationship between 12 U.S.C. §§ 371a and 1832(a) after 1979 legislation. It argues that § 1832(a) must not be read to prohibit ATS accounts because such an interpretation would nullify the 1979 amendments to § 371a. The 1979 amendments expressly allow member banks to offer ATS accounts after December 31, 1979, while § 1832(a) prohibits all depository institutions from offering such accounts until after December 31, 1980.[2] Thus, Otero contends we must reject the broad reading of section 1832 to avoid rendering a legislative enactment a nullity. . . .

We find no fatal inconsistency between section 371a, as amended, and the broad reading of section 1832, however. The general language in section 1832, prohibiting any depository institution from offering interest bearing demand deposit accounts or their equivalents, either NOW or ATS accounts, must give way to the specific language of section 371a, granting federal reserve member banks authority to offer ATS accounts after December 31, 1979. . . . The legislative history of the Depository Institutions Deregulation Act of 1980 offers no explanation for Congress' disparate treatment of granting federal reserve member banks ATS privileges one year earlier than all other federally insured depository institutions. The underlying policy reasons for granting member banks a one year head start do not concern us.

At oral argument no constitutional arguments were made against the application of 12 U.S.C. § 1832 to this Colorado-based savings and loan association. Such arguments were made to the Bank Board, however, in administrative proceedings and in briefs filed there, and the constitutional issue was treated in the Bank Board's decision. Any constitutional argument must be based upon the exception provided for eight northeastern states from the prohibitions in 12 U.S.C. § 1832, or the inconsistency between the treatment of commercial banks and savings and loan associations during 1980. We agree with the Bank Board that the governing principle is stated in *New Orleans v. Dukes*, 427 U.S. 297 (1976); a rational basis classification test is applicable. Here there is no inherently suspect classification, nor is a fundamental interest involved; this is solely an economic regulation governing financial institutions. Congress has undisputed authority to legislate in this area and may make reasonable distinctions between its treatment of commercial banks and savings and loans. It may also experiment by allowing particular types of accounts in one region of the country before extending the rule to others. We think there is no constitutional problem here.

Thus we hold 12 U.S.C. § 1832(a) applies to prohibit Otero's "Check-In" ATS type account during 1980, and that section is constitutional.

[Part II of the court's opinion, authored by Judge Holloway, dealt with the issue of the validity of the remedial aspects of the administrative order. It is excerpted in Chapter 8, § 2, *infra*. Judge Logan dissented from the portion of Part II holding that the Board could not prohibit Otero from opening new Check-In, NOW, or similar accounts for a 268-day period.]

---

2. The 1979 amendment to § 371a was only effective December 31, 1979 to March 31, 1980. On March 31, 1980, Congress enacted the Depository Institutions Deregulation and Monetary Control Act of 1980, Pub. L. No. 96-221, 94 Stat. 132 *et seq.*, (amending scattered sections of Title 12 U.S.C.). The Act extended the effect of the 1979 amendment to § 371a indefinitely and modified § 1832(a) by allowing all depository institutions to permit withdrawals from interest bearing accounts, except accounts of for-profit corporations, by negotiable or transferable instruments payable to third parties after December 31, 1980.

MCKAY, Circuit Judge, concurring.

No explanation of the legislation governing what amounts to, in one form or another, third party check withdrawals from savings accounts is entirely satisfactory, and delving too deeply into the legislative history of these sections raises, perhaps, more questions than it answers. Therefore, it seems appropriate to state separately my reasons for agreeing with the result reached by the court. The mischief probably is rooted in the fact that a debating body such as Congress could not respond swiftly enough with regulations to accommodate the sophisticated devices designed by depository institutions to circumvent comprehensive legislation. Therefore, the congressional legislation evolved in a piecemeal fashion so that sometimes one enactment overlapped or did not quite match another. In order to elicit a rational marketplace meaning of the various acts and amendments, it is necessary to avoid the usual detailed refinements of comparative statutory history that have normally been the hallmark of judicial work. Instead, we must emphasize the objectives of Congress without over-emphasizing the individual steps taken to achieve those ends. While the general objectives of Congress remain elusive, they can reasonably be derived from the legislative history, statutory language, and overall structure of the legislation. In the Acts at issue here, too much attention to precision in the use of statutory language would lead to the unwise effect of holding that Congress failed in the one objective that seems clearest, that is, the objective of putting all regulated financial institutions on an equal competitive footing in offering what amounts to, in whatever form, check withdrawals from interest-bearing accounts. The title of the 1980 Depository Institutions Deregulation and Monetary Control Act evidences this overriding objective.

The 1980 Act represented a reversal of the previous legislative position, first manifested in 1933 with the enactment of 12 U.S.C. § 371a, which prohibited all check withdrawals from interest-bearing accounts. That section expressly forbade federally-insured banks from granting demand access to interest-bearing accounts either "directly or indirectly, by any device whatsoever." Sometime thereafter, in a handful of northeastern states, state-chartered financial institutions began offering what are currently known as Negotiable Order of Withdrawal (NOW) accounts to accomplish this objective. Responding to those developments, Congress enacted 12 U.S.C. § 1832(a) in 1973. While it did not use the sweeping "directly or indirectly" language of § 371a, it is reasonable in light of the history of the Act to conclude that no negative pregnant was intended. The purpose of § 1832(a) was to prevent all such devices explicitly, except in the states where local competitive advantage had to be met because state-chartered institutions were already offering such accounts. By 1979 Congress had concluded that banks generally should be permitted to allow check access to savings accounts. While it is true that the description of devices used in the 1979 amendment to 12 U.S.C. § 371a spoke of what commonly are referred to as Automatic Fund Transfer (AFT) accounts, Congress' apparent intent was simply to permit instant access to savings accounts through the checking device. That amendment was effective only until March 31, 1980. In the meantime, Congress was forced to deal comprehensively with the regulations authorizing various banking services, after the United States Court of Appeals for the District of Columbia, in an unpublished opinion, struck down Federal Reserve Board regulations that authorized a variety of innovative banking services. The court stayed the effectiveness of its action to allow Congress time to act. In response, Congress adopted the Depository Institutions Deregulation and Monetary Control Act of 1980, Pub. L. No. 96-221, § 303, 94 Stat. 146 (1980). Under this Act, an amendment to 12 U.S.C. § 1832, effective December 31, 1980, allowed all depository institutions to "permit the owner of a deposit or account on which interest or dividends are paid to make withdrawals by negotiable or transferable instruments for the purpose of making transfers to third parties." Congress also extended the 1979 amendments to 12 U.S.C. § 371a, which gave federally-insured banks authority to offer AFT accounts. These amendments would have expired by their own terms on March 31, 1980, leaving a gap between that date and the effective date of the sweeping new legislation.

One can rationally argue that it is significant that the amendment to § 371a was extended indefinitely rather than merely until December 31, 1980, when § 1832, authorizing all depository institutions to offer check access to savings accounts, became effective. Considered out of the context of the overall scheme, this suggests that § 371a dealt only with AFT accounts, while § 1832 covered only NOW accounts. However, to credit this argument ignores Congress' obvious overall purpose of eliminating competitive advantage among financial institutions in providing check access to savings accounts. When considered in context, I am satisfied that when Congress originally enacted § 1832, it intended to permit savings and loan institutions in certain named states to offer special programs not generally allowed in order that they could compete with state-chartered institutions. I am also satisfied that for whatever reason, when Congress amended § 371a in 1979, it intended to grant that same competitive advantage to federally-insured banks, without extending that advantage to other institutions. The language and chronological sequence of the statutory sections dealing with check access to savings accounts suggests that the disparities arising from this type of piecemeal legislation caused Congress eventually to conclude that it should reverse its original position, which prevented essentially all checking access to savings accounts, and instead to authorize such services for all financial institutions under its control, effective December 31, 1980.

From this history we glean the following: Prior to 1973, no federally-regulated financial institutions were authorized to permit check access to savings accounts. After 1973 only the depository institutions in the states expressly exempted in the 1973 enactment of § 1832(a) were permitted check access to savings accounts. Beginning with the 1979 amendments, federally-insured banks were added to the limited list of those permitted check access to savings accounts. Finally, on December 31, 1980, all remaining federally-regulated financial institutions were added to the list. At least from the enactment of § 1832(a) in 1973 and in all probability by implication before that date, all federally-regulated financial institutions were forbidden from offering check access to savings accounts unless expressly exempted under that section or its subsequent amendments, or under S 371a. Thus, at least from 1973 until December 31, 1980, Otero was forbidden by § 1832(a) from offering any program that effectively allowed check access to savings accounts. . . .

Notes and Comments 5.46. In March 1980, the federal statutory provision with respect to NOW accounts was expanded to authorize such accounts throughout the United States. Pub. L. No. 96-221, § 303, 94 Stat. 146 (1980) (codified at 12 U.S.C. § 1832(a)(1)). This expanded authority was effective December 31, 1980. *See* 12 U.S.C. § 371a note. This development was but one feature of a broader program of product deregulation undertaken by the 1980 legislation. For a discussion of some of the implementation activities of the Depository Institutions Deregulation Committee (DIDC) in this regard, see DiNuzzo, *The Depository Institutions Deregulation Committee: Did it Achieve the Goal?*, 101 Banking L.J. 100 (1984).

5.47. *Note on "deposit substitutes."* Throughout the period immediately preceding the enactment of the Depository Institutions Deregulation and Monetary Control Act of 1980, depository institutions were becoming increasingly concerned about the rise of competition which they were experiencing from other investment media, such as the MMMFs. The institutions felt hampered in their efforts to compete effectively with the MMMFs, since funds taken in as "deposits" were subject to, inter alia, the reserve requirements and the interest rate restrictions, neither of which applied to MMMF's. Even after the enactment of the Act and the efforts of DIDC, the institutions were still subject to the reserve requirements. Consequently, depository institutions were interested in developing "deposit substitutes." A deposit substitute is structured as the functional equivalent of a "deposit"–*i.e.*, the creation of an obligation to pay on the bank's part, preferably at a set rate, at a set time or after a minimum period of notice of withdrawal–but without the regulatory restrictions that apply to deposits as defined. Typically, such deposit substitutes are not insured. The depository institutions were repeatedly frustrated in their search for a deposit substitute. The First National Bank of Chicago developed a program involving bankers' acceptances,[53] but these were determined to be subject to the reserve requirements of the Fed's Regulation D and the interest rate restrictions of the Fed's Regulation Q.[54] Union National Bank of Little Rock, Arkansas, developed a NOW account with a feature for transferring funds above a stated amount into a pool to buy large denomination certificates of deposit, but the Federal Reserve discouraged the use of this device.[55] The Bank of California proposed to avoid deposit restrictions by accepting funds from U.S. depositors "at" the bank's London branch, for investment at higher Eurodollar rates. The Fed squelched the proposal, indicating that it would look through the technical formulation of the transaction and treat the "deposit" as being accepted within the United States for purposes of Regulations D and Q.[56]

5.48. *Treatment of pooled investments.* What was common to many of these deposit substitute proposals was that funds "deposited" would be "pooled" for investment by the depository institution in investment media that often required a larger minimum investment than the small depositor/investor could afford on his or her own. In this respect, the proposed deposit substitutes operated much as the MMMFs themselves operated. Furthermore, even with "deposits" as defined by the Fed's regulations, much the same investment activity might be going on, but the characterization of the customer's investment as a "deposit" triggered not only the benefits of insurance but also the burdens of reserve and interest restrictions. Faced with continuing competition from the MMMFs and the slow pace of interest rate deregulation, the depository institutions remained assiduous in their search for deposit substitutes. One device which was permitted as a deposit substitute by the regulators was the "retail repurchase agreement" (retail repo). The idea of the "repurchase agreement" did not arise in the first instance as a deposit substitute. Under a repurchase agreement, an investor, typically a large institutional investor, may generate some short-term liquid funds on the strength of securities in its portfolio without liquidating the investment. The transaction looks like a sale of securities: (*i*) Institutional Investor *A* needs to generate cash, possibly for only a day or two. (*ii*) *A* holds a $1 million government-issued debt security, but does not want to sell the security outright for short term purposes. (*iii*) *A* goes to Institutional Investor *B* (*e.g.*, a bank, insurance company, brokerage firm) and offers to "sell" the debt security to *B* for $800,000, on the condition that "seller" *A* is to "repurchase" the security from "buyer" *B* in two days at an agreed premium. (*iv*) In fact, it is possible that the security may not even change hands. Though typically treated as a "sale" by the parties, the agreement has been characterized by the courts as being, in economic reality, a loan collateralized by the secur-

53. On bankers' acceptances, see 12 U.S.C. § 372 (concerning regulation of bankers' acceptances).

54. *See Short Term High Yield Instruments in Small Denominations are Subject to Regulations D and Q*, [1978-1979 Transfer Binder] Fed. Banking L. Rep. (CCH) ¶ 85,227.

55. *See Fed Pressures Union into Altering Account*, Arkansas Gazette, Mar. 21, 1982, at 1F (citing Letter of February 2, 1982, from Fed General Counsel to Acting Chief Counsel, OCC).

56. *Small Deposits at Foreign Offices of Depository Institutions Subject to Regulations D and Q*, [1981 Transfer Binder] Fed. Banking L. Rep. (CCH) ¶ 98,731.

ity.[57] Prior to 1979, Regulations D and Q contained exclusions from their respective definitions of "deposit" for any obligation that "evidences an indebtedness arising from the transfer of direct obligations of, or obligations that are fully guaranteed as to principal and interest by the United States or any agency or any agency thereof that the bank if obligated to repurchase." 12 C.F.R. §§ 204.1(f)(2) and 217.1(f)(2) (1979). It was assumed that this exclusion allowed large, institutional transactions in repurchase agreements, now called "wholesale repo's." Eventually, however, depository institutions decided to try marketing repo's at the "retail" level, *i.e.*, in small amounts to individual bank customers, whose investments would be pooled, and which would involve "participations" by the small investors in the larger, underlying securities.[58] These retail repo's gained a modest following by 1981, but they eventually were usurped by the advent of such DIDC-endorsed instruments as the Money Market Deposit Account.

c. Deposit Insurance

Notes and Comments 5.49. Deposit insurance is perhaps the most prominent feature of the contemporary landscape of federal regulation of depository institutions. The bold move to offer deposit insurance in the midst of the Depression is now virtually commonplace for depositors; they have come to accept it–and expect it–from the depository institutions with which they do business. Furthermore, it is the federal insurance of accounts at state chartered institutions that is the typical, often the exclusive, basis of federal regulatory jurisdiction over such institutions.[59] In Chapter 8 we shall examine the role of the deposit insurance system, and the Federal Deposit Insurance Corporation (FDIC), in the ultimate–but hopefully avoidable–responsibilities of assisting troubled institutions and of resolving the crisis created by a failure. For present purposes, however, we examine another fundamental problem: the inclusion of a "deposit" within the protection of FDIC insurance. How broad is the eligibility rule for deposit insurance? Consider the following case.

FDIC v. Philadelphia Gear Corp.

476 U.S. 426 (1986)

Justice O'CONNOR delivered the opinion of the Court.

We granted certiorari to consider whether a standby letter of credit backed by a contingent promissory note is insured as a "deposit" under the federal deposit insurance program. We hold that, in light of the longstanding interpretation of petitioner Federal Deposit Insurance Corporation (FDIC) that such a letter does not create a deposit and, in light of the fact that such a letter does not entrust any noncontingent assets to the bank, a standby letter of credit backed by a contingent promissory note does not give rise to an insured deposit. . . .

---

57. *See, e.g., Securities and Exchange Commission v. Miller*, 495 F. Supp. 465 (S.D.N.Y. 1980) (holding that large denomination repurchase agreements are, in reality, secured borrowings).

58. *See generally* Malloy & Pitts, *Post-Mortem on Retail Repurchase Agreements: Where Were the Regulators?*, 3 Ann. Rev. Banking L. 89 (1984) (discussing legal implications of retail repo's).

59. *See, e.g.*, 12 U.S.C. § 1818(b)(1) (cease and desist authority against unsafe and unsound practices based on insured status).

Orion Manufacturing Corporation (Orion) was, at the time of the relevant transactions, a customer of respondent Philadelphia Gear Corporation (Philadelphia Gear). On Orion's application, the Penn Square Bank, N.A. (Penn Square) issued a letter of credit for the benefit of Philadelphia Gear in the amount of $145,200. The letter of credit provided that a draft drawn upon the letter of credit would be honored by Penn Square only if accompanied by Philadelphia Gear's "signed statement that [it had] invoiced Orion Manufacturing Corporation and that said invoices have remained unpaid for at least fifteen (15) days." Because the letter of credit was intended to provide payment to the seller only if the buyer of the invoiced goods failed to make payment, the letter of credit was what is commonly referred to as a "standby" or "guaranty" letter of credit. *See, e.g.*, 12 CFR § 337.2(a), and n. 1 (1985) (defining standby letters of credit and mentioning that they may "'guaranty' payment of a money obligation"). A conventional "commercial" letter of credit, in contrast, is one in which the seller obtains payment from the issuing bank without looking to the buyer for payment even in the first instance. *See id.*, n. 1 (distinguishing standby letters of credit from commercial letters of credit).[a]

On the same day that Penn Square issued the standby letter of credit, Orion executed an unsecured promissory note for $145,200 in favor of Penn Square. The purpose of the note was listed as "Back up Letter of Credit." Although the face of the note did not so indicate, both Orion and Penn Square understood that nothing would be considered due on the note, and no interest charged by Penn Square, unless Philadelphia Gear presented drafts on the standby letter of credit after nonpayment by Orion. . . .

On July 5, 1982, Penn Square was declared insolvent. Petitioner Federal Deposit Insurance Corporation (FDIC) was appointed its receiver. Shortly thereafter, Philadelphia Gear presented drafts on the standby letter of credit for payment of over $700,000 for goods delivered before Penn Square's insolvency. The FDIC returned the drafts unpaid. . . . Philadelphia Gear sued the FDIC in the Western District of Oklahoma. Philadelphia Gear alleged that the standby letter of credit was an insured deposit under the definition of "deposit" set forth at 12 U.S.C. § 1813(l)(1), and that Philadelphia Gear was therefore entitled to $100,000 in deposit insurance from the FDIC. *See* 12 U.S.C. § 1821(a)(1) (setting forth $100,000 as the maximum amount generally insured by the FDIC for any single depositor at a given bank). In apparent hopes of obtaining additional funds from the FDIC in the latter's capacity as receiver rather than as insurer, respondent also alleged that terms of the standby letter of credit allowing repeated reinstatements of the credit made the letter's total value more than $145,200.

The District Court held that the total value of the standby letter of credit was $145,200; that the letter was an insured deposit on which the FDIC was liable for $100,000 in deposit insurance; and that Philadelphia Gear was entitled to prejudgment interest on that $100,000. The FDIC appealed from the District Court's ruling that the standby letter of credit backed by a contingent promissory note constituted a "deposit" for purposes of 12 U.S.C. § 1813(l)(1) and its ruling that Philadelphia Gear was entitled to an award of prejudgment interest. Philadelphia Gear cross-appealed from the District Court's ruling on the total value of the letter of credit.

The Court of Appeals for the Tenth Circuit reversed the District Court's award of prejudgment interest, . . . but otherwise affirmed the District Court's decision. As to the definition of "deposit," the Court of Appeals held that a standby letter of credit backed by a promissory note fell within the terms of 12 U.S.C. § 1813(l)(1)'s definition of "deposit," and was therefore insured. . . . We granted the FDIC's petition for certiorari on this aspect of the Court of Appeals' ruling. . . . We now reverse. . . .

---

a. On the power of commercial banks to issue letters of credit, see *infra* § 4.

Title 12 U.S.C. § 1813(l)(1) provides:

> "The term 'deposit' means–
>
> "(1) the unpaid balance of money or its equivalent received or held by a bank in the usual course of business and for which it has given or is obligated to give credit, either conditionally or unconditionally, to a commercial . . . account, or which is evidenced by . . . a letter of credit or a traveler's check on which the bank is primarily liable: Provided, That, without limiting the generality of the term 'money or its equivalent,' any such account or instrument must be regarded as evidencing the receipt of the equivalent of money when credited or issued in exchange for checks or drafts or for a promissory note upon which the person obtaining any such credit or instrument is primarily or secondarily liable. . . ."

Philadelphia Gear successfully argued before the Court of Appeals that the standby letter of credit backed by a contingent promissory note constituted a "deposit" under 12 U.S.C. § 1813(l)(1) because that letter was one on which the bank was primarily liable, and evidenced the receipt by the bank of "money or its equivalent" in the form of a promissory note upon which the person obtaining the credit was primarily or secondarily liable. The FDIC does not here dispute that the bank was primarily liable on the letter of credit. . . . Nor does the FDIC contest the fact that the backup note executed by Orion is, at least in some sense, a "promissory note." . . . The FDIC argues rather that it has consistently interpreted § 1813(l)(1) not to include standby letters of credit backed only by a contingent promissory note because such a note represents no hard assets and thus does not constitute "money or its equivalent." Because the alleged "deposit" consists only of a contingent liability, asserts the FDIC, a standby letter of credit backed by a contingent promissory note does not give rise to a "deposit" that Congress intended the FDIC to insure. Under this theory, while the note here may have been labeled a promissory note on its face and may have been a promissory note under state law, it was not a promissory note for purposes of the federal law set forth in 12 U.S.C. § 1813(l)(1). *See D'Oench, Duhme & Co. v. FDIC*, 315 U.S. 447, 456 (1942) (holding that liability on a promissory note acquired by the FDIC is a federal question); *First National Bank v. Dickinson*, 396 U.S. 122, 133-134 (1969) (holding that federal law governs the definition of branch banking under the McFadden Act).

The Court of Appeals quite properly looked first to the language of the statute. ... Finding the language of the proviso in § 1813(l)(1) sufficiently plain, the Court of Appeals looked no further. But as the FDIC points out, the terms "letter of credit" and "promissory note" as used in the statute have a federal definition, and the FDIC has developed and interpreted those definitions for many years within the framework of the complex statutory scheme that the FDIC administers. The FDIC's interpretation of whether a standby letter of credit backed by a contingent promissory note constitutes a "deposit" is consistent with Congress' desire to protect the hard earnings of individuals by providing for federal deposit insurance. Since the creation of the FDIC, Congress has expressed no dissatisfaction with the FDIC's interpretation of "deposit"; indeed, Congress in 1960 adopted the FDIC's regulatory definition as the statutory language. When we weigh all these factors together, we are constrained to conclude that the term "deposit" does not include a standby letter of credit backed by a contingent promissory note. . . .

Despite the fact Congress revisited the deposit insurance statute in 1935, 1950, and 1960, [the initial congressional comments with respect to the purpose of deposit insurance] remain the best indication of Congress' underlying purpose in creating deposit insurance. The reports on the 1935 amendments presented the definition of "deposit" without any specific comment. . . . The floor debates centered around changes in the Federal Reserve

System made in the same bill, not on deposit insurance. . . . Indeed, in light of the fact that instruments denominated "promissory notes" seem at the time to have been considered exclusively uncontingent, . . . it is unlikely that Congress would have had occasion to refer expressly to contingent notes such as the one before us here even if Congress had turned its attention to the definition of "deposit" when it first enacted the provision treating "money or its equivalent."

The legislative history of the 1950 amendments is similarly unhelpful, as one would expect given that the relevant provisions were re-enacted but unchanged. . . . The Committee Reports on the 1960 amendments likewise give no indication that the amendments' phrasing was meant to effect any fundamental changes in the definition of deposit; those Reports state only that the changes are intended to bring into harmony the definitions of "deposit" used for purposes of deposit insurance with those used in reports of condition, and that the FDIC's rules and regulations are to be incorporated into the new definition. . . .

Congress' focus in providing for a system of deposit insurance–a system that has been continued to the present without modification to the basic definition of deposits that are "money or its equivalent"–was clearly a focus upon safeguarding the assets and "hard earnings" that businesses and individuals have entrusted to banks. Congress wanted to ensure that someone who put tangible assets into a bank could always get those assets back. The purpose behind the insurance of deposits in general, and especially in the section defining deposits as "money or its equivalent," therefore, is the protection of assets and hard earnings entrusted to a bank.

This purpose is not furthered by extending deposit insurance to cover a standby letter of credit backed by a contingent promissory note, which involves no such surrender of assets or hard earnings to the custody of the bank. Philadelphia Gear, which now seeks to collect deposit insurance, surrendered absolutely nothing to the bank. The letter of credit is for Philadelphia Gear's benefit, but the bank relied upon Orion to meet the obligations of the letter of credit and made no demands upon Philadelphia Gear. Nor, more importantly, did Orion surrender any assets unconditionally to the bank. The bank did not credit any account of Orion's in exchange for the promissory note, and did not treat its own assets as increased by its acceptance of the note. The bank could not have collected on the note from Orion unless Philadelphia Gear presented the unpaid invoices and a draft on the letter of credit. In the absence of a presentation by Philadelphia Gear of the unpaid invoices, the promissory note was a wholly contingent promise, and when Penn Square went into receivership, neither Orion nor Philadelphia Gear had lost anything except the ability to use Penn Square to reduce Philadelphia Gear's risk that Philadelphia Gear would go unpaid for a delivery of goods to Orion. . . .

Congress' actions with respect to the particular definition of "deposit" that it has chosen in order to effect its general purpose likewise lead us to believe that a standby letter of credit backed by a contingent promissory note is not an insurable "deposit." In 1933, Congress amended the Federal Reserve Act to authorize the creation of the FDIC and charged it "to insure . . . the deposits of all banks which are entitled to the benefits of [FDIC] insurance." § 8, Banking Act of 1933, ch. 89, 48 Stat. 168. Congress did not define the term "deposit," however, until the Banking Act of 1935, in which it stated:

> "The term 'deposit' means the unpaid balance of money or its equivalent received by a bank in the usual course of business and for which it has given or is obligated to give credit to a commercial, checking, savings, time or thrift account, or which is evidenced by its certificate of deposit, and trust funds held by such bank whether retained or deposited in any department of such bank or deposited in another bank, together with such other obligations of a bank as the

> board of directors [of the FDIC] shall find and shall prescribe by its regulations to be deposit liabilities by general usage. . . ." § 101, Banking Act of 1935, ch. 614, 49 Stat. 684, 685-686.

Less than two months after this statute was enacted, the FDIC promulgated a definition of "deposit," which provided in part that "letters of credit must be regarded as issued for the equivalent of money when issued in exchange for . . . promissory notes upon which the person procuring [such] instruments is primarily or secondarily liable." *See* 12 CFR § 301.1(d) (1939) (codifying Regulation I, rule 1, Oct. 1, 1935), revoked after incorporation into statutory law, 12 CFR 234 (Supp. 1962).

In 1950, Congress revisited the provisions specifically governing the FDIC in order to remove them from the Federal Reserve Act and place them into a separate Act. *See* Act of Sept. 21, 1950, ch. 967, 64 Stat. 874. The new provisions did not modify the definition of "deposit." In 1960, Congress expanded the statutory definition of "deposit" in several categories, and also incorporated the regulatory definition that the FDIC had employed since 1935 into the statute that remains in force today. . . .

At no point did Congress disown its initial, clear desire to protect the hard assets of depositors. . . . At no point did Congress criticize the FDIC's longstanding interpretation . . . that a standby letter of credit backed by a contingent promissory note is not a "deposit." In fact, Congress had re-enacted the 1935 provisions in 1950 without changing the definition of "deposit" at all. . . . When the statute giving rise to the longstanding interpretation has been re-enacted without pertinent change, the "congressional failure to revise or repeal the agency's interpretation is persuasive evidence that the interpretation is the one intended by Congress." *NLRB v. Bell Aerospace*, 416 U.S. 267, 275 (1974). *See Zenith Radio Corp. v. United States*, 437 U.S. 443, 457 (1978). Indeed, the current statutory definition of "deposit," added by Congress in 1960, was expressly designed to incorporate the FDIC's rules and regulations on "deposits." . . . Congress, therefore, has expressly incorporated into the statutory scheme the regulations that the FDIC devised to assist it in determining what constitutes a "deposit" within the statutory scheme. Under these circumstances, we must obviously give a great deal of deference to the FDIC's interpretation of what these regulations do and do not include within their definition of "deposit." . . .

Although the FDIC does not argue that it has an express regulation excluding a standby letter of credit backed by a contingent promissory note from the definition of "deposit" in 12 U.S.C. § 1813(l)(1), that exclusion by the FDIC is nonetheless longstanding and consistent. . . .

Because Penn Square apparently never reflected the letter of credit here as a noncontingent liability, and because the interwoven financial instruments at issue here can be viewed most accurately as the extension of a line of credit by Penn Square to Orion, this transcript lends support to the FDIC's contention that its longstanding policy has been to exclude standby letters of credit backed by contingent promissory notes from 12 U.S.C. § 1813(l)(1)'s definition of "deposit."

The FDIC's contemporaneous understanding that standby letters of credit backed by contingent promissory notes do not generate a "deposit" for purposes of 12 U.S.C. § 1813(l)(1) has been fortified by its behavior over the following decades. The FDIC has asserted repeatedly that it has never charged deposit insurance premiums on standby letters of credit backed by contingent promissory notes, and Philadelphia Gear does not contest that assertion. . . . Congress requires the FDIC to assess contributions to its insurance fund at a fixed percentage of a bank's "deposits" under 12 U.S.C. § 1813(l)(1). *See* 12 U.S.C. §§ 1817(a)(4), (b)(1), (b)(4)(A). By the time that this suit–the first challenge to the FDIC's treatment of standby letters of credit backed by contingent promissory notes–was brought, almost $100 billion in standby letters of credit was outstanding. . . . The FDIC's failure to levy premiums on standby letters of credit backed by contingent promissory notes therefore clearly demonstrates that the FDIC has never considered such letters to reflect deposits.

Although the FDIC's interpretation of the relevant statute has not been reduced to a specific regulation, we conclude nevertheless that the FDIC's practice and belief that a standby letter of credit backed by a contingent promissory note does not create a "deposit" within the meaning of 12 U.S.C. § 1813(l)(1) is entitled in the circumstances of this case to the "considerable weight [that] should be accorded to an executive department's construction of a statutory scheme it is entrusted to administer." *Chevron U.S.A. Inc. v. Natural Resources Defense Council, Inc.*, 467 U.S. 837, 844 (1984). As we have stated above, the FDIC's interpretation here of a statutory definition adopted wholesale from the FDIC's own regulation is consistent with congressional purpose, and may certainly stand. . . .

Philadelphia Gear essentially seeks to have the FDIC guarantee the contingent credit extended to Orion, not assets entrusted to the bank by Philadelphia Gear or by Orion on Philadelphia Gear's behalf. With a standard "commercial" letter of credit, Orion would typically have unconditionally entrusted Penn Square with funds before Penn Square would have written the letter of credit, and thus Orion would have lost something if Penn Square became unable to honor its obligations. As the FDIC concedes, deposit insurance extends to such a letter of credit backed by an uncontingent promissory note. . . . But here, with a standby letter of credit backed by a contingent promissory note, Penn Square was not in possession of any of Orion's or Philadelphia Gear's assets when it went into receivership. Nothing was ventured, and therefore no insurable deposit was lost. We believe that, whatever the relevant State's definition of "letter of credit" or "promissory note," Congress did not by using those phrases in 12 U.S.C. § 1813(l)(1) intend to protect with deposit insurance a standby letter of credit backed only by a contingent promissory note. We thus hold that such an arrangement does not give rise to a "deposit" under 12 U.S.C. § 1813(l)(1).

. . .

Justice MARSHALL, with whom Justice BLACKMUN and Justice REHNQUIST join, dissenting.

There is considerable common sense backing the Court's opinion. The standby letter of credit in this case differs considerably from the savings and checking accounts that come most readily to mind when one speaks of an insured deposit. Nevertheless, to reach this common-sense result, the Court must read qualifications into the statute that do not appear there. We recently recognized that even when the ingenuity of businessmen creates transactions and corporate forms that were perhaps not contemplated by Congress, the courts must enforce the statutes that Congress has enacted. *See Board of Governors, FRS v. Dimension Financial Corp.*, 474 U.S. ----, ----, 106 S.Ct. 681 (1986). Congress unmistakably provided that letters of credit backed by promissory notes constitute "deposits" for purposes of the federal deposit insurance program, and the Court's attempt to draw distinctions between different types of letter of credit transactions forces it to ignore both the statute and some settled principles of commercial law. Here, as in *Dimension*, the inflexibility of the statute as applied to modern financial transactions is a matter for Congress, not the FDIC or this Court, to remedy. It cannot be doubted that the standby letter of credit in this case meets the literal definition of a "deposit" contained in 12 U.S.C. § 1813(l) (1). It is "a letter of credit . . . on which the bank is primarily liable . . . issued in exchange for . . . a promissory note upon which [Orion] is primarily or secondarily liable." The Court, however, holds that the note in this case, whether or not it is a promissory note under the Uniform Commercial Code (UCC) and Oklahoma law, is not a promissory note for purposes of the Federal Deposit Insurance Act. We should assume, absent convincing evidence to the contrary, that Congress intended for the term "promissory note" to derive its meaning from the ordinary sources of commercial law. I believe that there is no such evidence in this case.

The Court justifies its restrictive reading of the term "promissory note" in large part by arguing that Congress would not have wanted to include in that term any obligation that was not the present equivalent of money. The keystone of the FDIC's arguments, and of the Court's decision, is that Orion did not entrust "money or its equivalent" to the bank. The note in this case, however, was the equivalent of money, and the Court's reading of Congress' intent is therefore largely irrelevant.

FDIC concedes, as it must, that Congress has determined that a promissory note generally constitutes money or its equivalent. Moreover, that statutory definition comports with economic reality. Promissory notes typically are negotiable instruments and therefore readily convertible into cash. The FDIC argues, and the Court holds, that the promissory note in this case is "contingent" and therefore not the equivalent of money. However, while the FDIC argues strenuously that Orion's note is not a promissory note in the usual sense of the word, one could more plausibly state that it is not a "contingent" obligation in the usual sense of that word. On its face the note is an unconditional obligation of Orion to pay the holder $145,200 plus accrued interest on August 1, 1982. It sets out no conditions that would affect the negotiability of the note, and therefore is fully negotiable for purposes of the UCC, U.C.C. § 3-104(1) (1977); Okla. Stat., Tit. 12A, § 3-104(1) (1981).

The Court therefore misses the point when it states that at the time of the original banking Acts, the term "promissory note" was not understood to include a contingent obligation.... The note at issue in this case is an unconditional promise to pay, and satisfies all the requisites of a negotiable promissory note, either under the UCC or the common law as it existed in the 1930's. The only contingencies attached to Orion's obligation arise out of a separate contract. As to such contingencies, the law was well settled long before 1930:

> "[I]n order to make a note invalid as a promissory note, the contingency to avoid it must be apparent, either upon the face of the note, or upon some contemporaneous written memorandum on the same paper; for, if the memorandum is not contemporaneous, or if it be merely verbal in each case, whatever may be its effect as a matter of defence between the original parties, it is not deemed to be a part of the instrument, and does not affect, much less invalidate, its original character." J. THORNDIKE, STORY ON PROMISSORY NOTES 34 (7TH ED. 1878) (footnotes omitted).[1]

It is far from a matter of semantics to state that while Orion and the bank may have an oral understanding concerning the bank's treatment of Orion's note, that note itself is unconditional, and equivalent to money. The Court correctly observes that the bank would have breached its oral contract had it attempted to sue on the note; nevertheless, Orion would have had separately to plead and prove a breach of contract in that case, because parol evidence that the contract between the parties differed from the written instrument would have been inadmissible in the bank's action to collect the debt.... Similarly, should the note have found its way into the hands of a third party, Orion would have had no choice but to honor it, again being left with only the right to sue the bank for breach of the oral contract. Orion's entrustment of the note to the bank was not, therefore, completely risk free.

---

1. We would have a very different case if the conditions put upon Orion's obligation to the bank were reflected on the face of the note, as they were in *Allen v. FDIC*, 599 F. Supp. 104 (ED Tenn. 1984), *appeal pending*, No. 85-5003 (CA6), a case raising the same issue as the present one. Because such a note is not negotiable, it is much more plausible to argue that Congress would not have considered it "money or its equivalent." The note in this case, however, is in no sense a contingent note.

The risk taken on by Orion may not differ substantially from the risk assumed by one who hands over money to the bank to guaranty repayment of funds paid out on a letter of credit. The bank typically undertakes to put such cash collateral into a special account, where it never enters into the general assets of the bank. *See* U.C.C. § 5-117, comment (1977). Should the bank cease operations, the customer will enjoy a preference in bankruptcy, entitling it to receive its money back before general unsecured creditors of the bank are paid. U.C.C. § 5-117; Okla. Stat., Tit. 12A, § 5-117 (1981). Like Orion, then, that hypothetical customer has little to fear absent misconduct by the bank or a third party. If the federal deposit insurance program should not protect Philadelphia Gear, therefore, it probably should not protect any holder of a letter of credit, whether commercial, standby, funded, or unfunded.[2] That, however, is clearly a matter for Congress to determine.

While the Court purports to examine what Congress meant when it said "promissory note," in fact the Court's opinion does not rest on any special attributes of Orion's note. Rather, the Court rules that when an individual entrusts a negotiable instrument to a bank, that instrument is not "money or its equivalent" for purposes of § 1813(l)(1) so long as the bank promises not to negotiate it or collect on it until certain conditions are met. That is a proviso that Congress might have been well-advised to include in the Act, but did not. . . .

Notes and Comments 5.50. Whose argument is more persuasive on the issue of the inclusion of these instruments within the concept of a "deposit," the majority or the dissent? Is it significant that, as illustrated by the dissent's discussion, the instruments are subject to article 5 of the Uniform Commercial Code (dealing with letters of credit), and not article 4 (dealing with deposits)?

5.51. Review the language of 12 U.S.C. § 1813(*l*). Assume that Altered State Bank is one of the banks participating in a syndicated loan to a customer of Chaste Madhatter Bank, N.A. In order to fund the loan, Altered electronically transfers money to Chaste, which is the lead or managing bank for the loan. Are these funds a "deposit" at Chaste Madhatter? *See Seattle-First National Bank v. FDIC*, 619 F. Supp. 1351 (W.D. Okla. 1985).

5.52. The Federal Deposit Insurance Reform Act of 2005 (FDIRA)[60] and the Federal Deposit Insurance Reform Conforming Amendments Act of 2005 (FDIRCAA)[61] are responsible for major changes in the structure of the Federal Deposit Insurance System.[62] Among other things, FDIRA provides for an inflation index to be applied to the current maximum deposit insurance amount of $100,000[63] – with this new, indexed maximum called the "standard maximum deposit insurance amount" (SMDIA).[64] Beginning April 1, 2010, and

---

2. It seems odd that Philadelphia Gear's status as an insured depositor should depend on the terms of the repayment agreement between Orion and the bank. Ordinarily, Philadelphia Gear would be indifferent to the agreement between Orion and the bank, and might not even be aware of the terms of that agreement. The Court, therefore, is not necessarily bringing greater rationality to this area of the law by creating distinctions between types of letters of credit for purposes of federal deposit insurance coverage.

60. Pub. L. No. 109-171, tit. II, §§ 2101-2109, 120 Stat. 4, 9-21 (Feb. 8, 2006) (FDIRA). *See Regulators Announce Formal Changes Reflecting Reforms, Merger of BIF, SAIF*, BNA BANKING DAILY (April 21, 2006), *available at* http://pubs.bna.com/ip/bna/bbd.nsf/eh/A0B2R3D4M3 (reporting on fund merger).

61. Pub. L. No. 109-173, 119 Stat 3601 (Feb. 15, 2006).

62. For discussion of the FDIRA and the FDIRCA, see note 1.61, *supra*.

63. FDIRA, § 2103(a)(2) (codified at 12 U.S.C. 1821(a)(1)(F)).

64. 12 U.S.C. § 1821(a)(1)(E).

every succeeding five years, subject to approval by the Board of Directors of the FDIC and the National Credit Union Administration Board, the SMDIA can be increased by a cost-of-living adjustment.[65] There are also a host of technical and conforming amendments that needed to be made as the deposit insurance terminology shifted from a stated maximum to the more flexible concept of the SMDIA. In September 2009, the FDIC published a number of amendments to its deposit insurance regulations, excerpted below, to implement these FDIRA changes.

Federal Deposit Insurance Corporation
Deposit Insurance Regulations;
Temporary Increase in Standard Coverage Amount;
Mortgage Servicing Accounts;
Revocable Trust Accounts . . .
12 CFR Part[] 330 . . .
74 Fed. Reg. 47,711 (Sept. 17, 2009)

The FDIC is adopting a final rule amending its deposit insurance regulations to: Reflect Congress's extension, until December 31, 2013, of the temporary increase in the standard maximum deposit insurance amount ("SMDIA") from $100,000 to $250,000;[a] finalize the interim rule, with minor modifications, on revocable trust accounts;[b] and finalize the interim rule on mortgage servicing accounts.[c] . . .
DATES: Effective Date: The final rule is effective October 19, 2009.

. . .

PART 330--DEPOSIT INSURANCE COVERAGE

. . .

2. In § 330.1, paragraph (n) is revised to read as follows:

§ 330.1 Definitions.
* * * * *

(n) Standard maximum deposit insurance amount, referred to as the "SMDIA" hereafter, means $250,000 from October 3, 2008, until December 31, 2013. Effective January 1, 2014, the SMDIA means $100,000 adjusted pursuant to subparagraph (F) of section 11(a)(1) of the FDI Act (12 U.S.C. 1821(a)(1)(F)). All examples in this part use $250,000 as the SMDIA.
* * * * *

3. In § 330.7, paragraph (d) is revised to read as follows:

§ 330.7 Account held by an agent, nominee, guardian, custodian or conservator.
* * * * *

(d) Mortgage servicing accounts. Accounts maintained by a mortgage servicer, in a custodial or other fiduciary capacity, which are comprised of payments by mortgagors of principal and interest, shall be insured for the cumulative balance paid into the account by

---

65. *Id.* § 1821(a)(1)(F).

a. 12 C.F.R. §§ 330.1(n), § 330.9(b).

b. *Id.* § 330.10.

c. *Id.* § 330.7(d).

the mortgagors, up to the limit of the SMDIA per mortgagor. Accounts maintained by a mortgage servicer, in a custodial or other fiduciary capacity, which are comprised of payments by mortgagors of taxes and insurance premiums shall be added together and insured in accordance with paragraph (a) of this section for the ownership interest of each mortgagor in such accounts. This provision is effective as of October 10, 2008, for all existing and future mortgage servicing accounts.
* * * * *

4. In § 330.9, paragraph (b) is revised to read as follows:

§ 330.9 Joint ownership accounts.
* * * * *

(b) Determination of insurance coverage. The interests of each co-owner in all qualifying joint accounts shall be added together and the total shall be insured up to the SMDIA. (Example: "A&B" have a qualifying joint account with a balance of $150,000; "A&C" have a qualifying joint account with a balance of $200,000; and "A&B&C" have a qualifying joint account with a balance of $375,000. A's combined ownership interest in all qualifying joint accounts would be $300,000 ($75,000 plus $100,000 plus $125,000); therefore, A's interest would be insured in the amount of $250,000 and uninsured in the amount of $50,000. B's combined ownership interest in all qualifying joint accounts would be $200,000 ($75,000 plus $125,000); therefore, B's interest would be fully insured. C's combined ownership interest in all qualifying joint accounts would be $225,000 ($100,000 plus $125,000); therefore, C's interest would be fully insured.
* * * * *

5. Section 330.10 is revised to read as follows:

§ 330.10 Revocable trust accounts.

(a) General rule. Except as provided in paragraph (e) of this section, the funds owned by an individual and deposited into one or more accounts with respect to which the owner evidences an intention that upon his or her death the funds shall belong to one or more beneficiaries shall be separately insured (from other types of accounts the owner has at the same insured depository institution) in an amount equal to the total number of different beneficiaries named in the account(s) multiplied by the SMDIA. This section applies to all accounts held in connection with informal and formal testamentary revocable trusts. Such informal trusts are commonly referred to as payable-on-death accounts, in-trust-for accounts or Totten Trust accounts, and such formal trusts are commonly referred to as living trusts or family trusts. (Example 1: Account Owner "A" has a living trust account with four different beneficiaries named in the trust. A has no other revocable trust accounts at the same FDIC-insured institution. The maximum insurance coverage would be $1,000,000, determined by multiplying 4 times $250,000 (the number of beneficiaries times the SMDIA). (Example 2: Account Owner "A" has a payable-on-death account naming his niece and cousin as beneficiaries, and A also has, at the same FDIC-insured institution, another payable-on-death account naming the same niece and a friend as beneficiaries. The maximum coverage available to the account owner would be $750,000. This is because the account owner has named only three different beneficiaries in the revocable trust accounts--his niece and cousin in the first, and the same niece and a friend in the second. The naming of the same beneficiary in more than one revocable trust account, whether it be a payable-on-death account or living trust account, does not increase the total coverage amount.) (Example 3: Account Owner "A" establishes a living trust account, with a balance of $300,000, naming his two children "B" and "C" as beneficiaries. A also establishes, at the same FDIC-insured institution, a payable-on-death account, with a balance of $300,000, also naming his children B and C as beneficiaries. The maximum coverage available to A is $500,000, determined by multiplying 2 times $250,000 (the number of different beneficiaries times the SMDIA). A is uninsured in the amount of $100,000. This is because all funds that a depositor holds in both living trust accounts and payable-on-death accounts, at the same FDIC-insured institution and naming the same beneficiaries, are aggregated for insurance purposes and insured to the applicable coverage limits.)

(b) Required intention and naming of beneficiaries. (1) The required intention in paragraph (a) of this section that upon the owner's death the funds shall belong to one or more beneficiaries must be manifested in the "title" of the account using commonly accepted terms such as, but not limited to, "in trust for," "as trustee for," "payable-on-death to," or any acronym therefor. For purposes of this requirement, "title" includes the electronic deposit account records of the institution. (For example, the FDIC would recognize an account as a revocable trust account even if the title of the account signature card does not designate the account as a revocable trust account as long as the institution's electronic deposit account records identify (through a code or otherwise) the account as a revocable trust account.) The settlor of a revocable trust shall be presumed to own the funds deposited into the account.

(2) For informal revocable trust accounts, the beneficiaries must be specifically named in the deposit account records of the insured depository institution.

(c) Definition of beneficiary. For purposes of this section, a beneficiary includes a natural person as well as a charitable organization and other non-profit entity recognized as such under the Internal Revenue Code of 1986, as amended.

(d) Interests of beneficiaries outside the definition of beneficiary in this section. If a beneficiary named in a trust covered by this section does not meet the definition of beneficiary in paragraph (c) of this section, the funds corresponding to that beneficiary shall be treated as the individually owned (single ownership) funds of the owner(s). As such, they shall be aggregated with any other single ownership accounts of such owner(s) and insured up to the SMDIA per owner. (Example: Account Owner "A" establishes a payable-on-death account naming a pet as beneficiary with a balance of $100,000. A also has an individual account at the same FDIC-insured institution with a balance of $175,000. Because the pet is not a "beneficiary," the two accounts are aggregated and treated as a single ownership account. As a result, A is insured in the amount of $250,000, but is uninsured for the remaining $25,000.)

(e) Revocable trust accounts with aggregate balances exceeding five times the SMDIA and naming more than five different beneficiaries. Notwithstanding the general coverage provisions in paragraph (a) of this section, for funds owned by an individual in one or more revocable trust accounts naming more than five different beneficiaries and whose aggregate balance is more than five times the SMDIA, the maximum revocable trust account coverage for the account owner shall be the greater of either: five times the SMDIA or the aggregate amount of the interests of each different beneficiary named in the trusts, to a limit of the SMDIA per different beneficiary. (Example 1: Account Owner "A" has a living trust with a balance of $1 million and names two friends, "B" and "C" as beneficiaries. At the same FDIC-insured institution, A establishes a payable-on-death account, with a balance of $1 million naming his two cousins, "D" and "E" as beneficiaries. Coverage is determined under the general coverage provisions in paragraph (a) of this section, and not this paragraph (e). This is because all funds that A holds in both living trust accounts and payable-on-death accounts, at the same FDIC-insured institution, are aggregated for insurance purposes. Although A's aggregated balance of $2 million is more than five times the SMDIA, A names only four different beneficiaries, and coverage under this paragraph (e) applies only if there are more than five different beneficiaries. A is insured in the amount of $1 million (4 beneficiaries times the SMDIA), and uninsured for the remaining $1 million.) (Example 2: Account Owner "A" has a living trust account with a balance of $1,500,000. Under the terms of the trust, upon A's death, A's three children are each entitled to $125,000, A's friend is entitled to $15,000, and a designated charity is entitled to $175,000. The trust also provides that the remainder of the trust assets shall belong to A's spouse. In this case, because the balance of the account exceeds $1,250,000 (5 times the SMDIA) and there are more than five different beneficiaries named in the trust, the maximum coverage available to A would be the greater of: $1,250,000 or the aggregate of each different beneficiary's interest to a limit of $250,000 per beneficiary. The beneficial interests in the trust for purposes of determining coverage are: $125,000 for each of the children (totaling $375,000), $15,000 for the friend, $175,000 for the charity, and $250,000 for the spouse (because the spouse's $935,000 is subject to the $250,000 per-beneficiary limitation). The aggregate beneficial interests total $815,000. Thus, the maximum coverage afforded to the account owner would be $1,250,000, the greater of $1,250,000 or $815,000.)

(f) Co-owned revocable trust accounts. (1) Where an account described in paragraph (a) of this section is established by more than one owner, the respective interest of each account owner (which shall be deemed equal) shall be insured separately, per different beneficiary, up to the SMDIA, subject to the limitation imposed in paragraph (e) of this section. (Example 1: A and B, two individuals, establish a payable-on-death account naming their three nieces as beneficiaries. Neither A nor B has any other revocable trust accounts at the same FDIC-insured institution. The maximum coverage afforded to A and B would be $1,500,000, determined by multiplying the number of owners (2) times the SMDIA ($250,000) times the number of different beneficiaries (3). In this example, A would be entitled to revocable trust coverage of $750,000 and B would be entitled to revocable trust coverage of $750,000.) (Example 2: A and B, two individuals, establish a payable-on-death account naming their two children, two cousins, and a charity as beneficiaries. The balance in the account is $1,750,000. Neither A nor B has any other revocable trust accounts at the same FDIC-insured institution. The maximum coverage would be determined (under paragraph (a) of this section) by multiplying the number of account owners (2) times the number of different beneficiaries (5) times $250,000, totaling $2,500,000. Because the account balance ($1,750,000) is less than the maximum coverage amount ($2,500,000), the account would be fully insured.) (Example 3: A and B, two individuals, establish a living trust account with a balance of $3.75 million. Under the terms of the trust, upon the death of both A and B, each of their three children is entitled to $600,000, B's cousin is entitled to $380,000, A's friend is entitled to $70,000, and the remaining amount ($1,500,000) goes to a charity. Under paragraph (e) of this section, the maximum coverage, as to each co-owned account owner, would be the greater of $1,250,000 or the aggregate amount (as to each co-owner) of the interest of each different beneficiary named in the trust, to a limit of $250,000 per account owner per beneficiary. The beneficial interests in the trust considered for purposes of determining coverage for account owner A are: $750,000 for the children (each child's interest attributable to A, $300,000, is subject to the $250,000-per-beneficiary limitation), $190,000 for the cousin, $35,000 for the friend, and $250,000 for the charity (the charity's interest attributable to A, $750,000, is subject to the $250,000 per-beneficiary limitation). As to A, the aggregate amount of the beneficial interests eligible for deposit insurance coverage totals $1,225,000. Thus, the maximum coverage afforded to account co-owner A would be $1,250,000, which is the greater of $1,250,000 or the aggregate of all the beneficial interests attributable to A (limited to $250,000 per beneficiary), which totaled slightly less at $1,225,000. Because B has equal ownership interest in the trust, the same analysis and coverage determination also would apply to B. Thus, of the total account balance of $3.75 million, $2.5 million would be insured and $1.25 million would be uninsured.)

(2) Notwithstanding paragraph (f)(1) of this section, where the owners of a co-owned revocable trust account are themselves the sole beneficiaries of the corresponding trust, the account shall be insured as a joint account under § 330.9 and shall not be insured under the provisions of this section. (Example: If A and B establish a payable-on-death account naming themselves as the sole beneficiaries of the account, the account will be insured as a joint account because the account does not satisfy the intent requirement (under paragraph (a) of this section) that the funds in the account belong to the named beneficiaries upon the owners' death. The beneficiaries are in fact the actual owners of the funds during the account owners' lifetimes.)

(g) For deposit accounts held in connection with a living trust that provides for a life-estate interest for designated beneficiaries, the FDIC shall value each such life estate interest as the SMDIA for purposes of determining the insurance coverage available to the account owner under paragraph (e) of this section. (Example: Account Owner "A" has a living trust account with a balance of $1,500,000. Under the terms of the trust, A provides a life estate interest for his spouse. Moreover, A's three children are each entitled to $275,000, A's friend is entitled to $15,000, and a designated charity is entitled to $175,000. The trust also provides that the remainder of the trust assets shall belong to A's granddaughter. In this case, because the balance of the account exceeds $1,250,000 ((5) five ***47718** times the SMDIA) and there are more than five different beneficiaries named in the trust, the maximum coverage available to A would be the greater of: $1,250,000 or the aggregate of each different beneficiary's interest to a limit of $250,000 per beneficiary. The beneficial interests in the trust considered for purposes of determining coverage are: $250,000 for the spouse's life estate, $750,000 for the children (because each child's $275,000 is subject to the $250,000 per-beneficiary limitation), $15,000 for the friend, $175,000 for the charity, and $250,000 for the granddaughter (because the granddaughter's $310,000 remainder is limited by the $250,000 per-beneficiary limitation). The aggregate beneficial interests total $1,440,000. Thus, the maximum coverage afforded to the account owner would be $1,440,000, the greater of $1,250,000 or $1,440,000.)

(h) Revocable trusts that become irrevocable trusts. Notwithstanding the provisions in section 330.13 on the insurance coverage of irrevocable trust accounts, if a revocable trust account converts in part or entirely to an irrevocable trust upon the death of one or more of the trust's owners, the trust account shall continue to be insured under the provisions of this section. (Example: Assume A and B have a trust account in connection with a living trust, of which they are joint grantors. If upon the death of either A or B the trust transforms into an irrevocable trust as to the deceased grantor's ownership in the trust, the account will continue to be insured under the provisions of this section.)

(i) This section shall apply to all existing and future revocable trust accounts and all existing and future irrevocable trust accounts resulting from formal revocable trust accounts. . . .

Notes and Comments 5.53. May Aculpa and her husband Maxim have established a trust for their four children at Chaste Madhatter, in the amount of $400,000. May and Maxim are the trustees. The trust is revocable at any time until the death of either of the two trustees. May and Maxim also have a joint savings account with a current balance of $153,000, and each of them owns certificates of deposit, payable only to the named certificate holder in the respective amounts of $90,000 and $101,000. In light of the FDEIA and the regulatory provisions excerpted above:

a. Are the equal interests of the four children separately insured by the

FDIC?

b. To what extent are May's deposit accounts insured by the FDIC?

c. To what extent are Maxim's deposit accounts insured by the FDIC?

4. Guarantees and Letters of Credit

The power of a commercial bank to issue guarantees on behalf of third parties, or to issue letters of credit, is based upon its express or incidental corporate powers. The source of the general corporate powers of national banks, for example, is to be found in 12 U.S.C. § 24, Seventh. Under this provision, the courts have generally found no power to *guarantee* the obligations of third parties, but they can issue letters of credit, even though letters of credit are "in essence only guarantees." *Dunn v. McCoy*, 113 F.2d 587, 588 (3d Cir. 1940).

Notes and Comments 5.54. The cases excerpted below trace the development of judicial responses to the question of the power to issue third-party guarantees. What exactly are the limitations on the issuance of such guarantees? Is the distinction made between third-party guarantees and letters of credit a credible one?

People's Bank v. National Bank

101 U.S. 181 (1879)

Mr. Justice SWAYNE delivered the opinion of the court.

On the 8th of August, 1873, Henry E. Picket made his ten promissory notes of that date, each for $5,000, all payable one year from date to his own order, indorsed by him, and bearing interest at the rate of ten per cent, payable semi-annually. . . . Picket delivered the notes to the defendant [Manufacturers' National Bank of Chicago] to be negotiated to the plaintiff [People's Bank of Belleville], pursuant to a prior agreement between him and the defendant, that the latter should so negotiate the notes and apply the proceeds to the cancellation of other indebtedness then due from him to the defendant. On the 8th of August, 1873, M. D. Buchanan, vice-president, and one of the directors of the defendant, with the knowledge and consent of the president and cashier of the defendant, who were also directors, but without any authority from the board of directors as a board, or of a majority of them individually, or any notification to the board of directors as a board, transmitted the notes to the plaintiff with a letter, in which occurs the following language: 'In accordance with your telegram I herewith hand you ten notes of $5,000 each, &c. . . . We debit your account $50,000. . . . This bank hereby guarantees the payment of the principal sum and interest of said notes.' This letter was written below one of defendant's letter-heads, and signed 'M. D. Buchanan, vice-president.' The notes were also indorsed, 'Pay to the order of the People's Bank of Belleville. Henry E. Picket;' and below, 'This bank hereby guarantees the payment of this note, principal and interest, at maturity. M. D. Buchanan, Vice-President Manufacturers' National Bank of Chicago.' The defendant was the plaintiff's correspondent at Chicago, and the plaintiff's account with the defendant was debited with $50,000 on account of the notes. At the same time, Picket's paper in the defendant's hands was cancelled to the same amount. All the notes were protested at maturity for non-payment, and due notice was given to the defendant. Nothing has been paid on either of the notes. . . .

The National Banking Act . . . gives to every bank created under it the right 'to exercise by its board of directors, or duly authorized agents, all such incidental powers as shall be necessary to carry on the business of banking, *by discounting and negotiating promissory notes, drafts, bills of exchange, and other evidences of debt*, by receiving deposits,' &c. Nothing in the act explains or qualifies the terms italicised. To hand over with an indorsement and guaranty is one of the commonest modes of transferring the securities named. Undoubtedly a bank might indorse, 'waiving demand and notice,' and would be bound accordingly. A guaranty is a less onerous and stringent contract than that created by such an indorsement. We see no reason to doubt that, under the circumstances of this case, it was competent for the defendant to give the guaranty here in question. It is to be presumed the vice-president had rightfully the power he assumed to exercise, and the defendant is estopped to deny it. Where one of two innocent parties must suffer by the wrongful act of a third, he who gave the power to do the wrong must bear the burden of the consequences.

All the parties engaged in the transaction and the privies were agents of the defendant. If there were any defect of authority on their part, the retention and enjoyment of the proceeds of the transaction by their principal constituted an acquiescence as effectual as would have been the most formal authorization in advance, or the most formal ratification afterwards. These facts conclude the defendant from resisting the demand of the plaintiff. . . .

Whether, if the guaranty were void, the fund received by the defendant as its consideration moving from the plaintiff could be recovered back in this action upon the common count, is a point which we do not find it necessary to consider. *See United States v. State Bank*, 96 U.S. 33.

Border National Bank of Eagle Pass v. American National Bank of San Francisco

282 F. 73 (5th Cir. 1922)
dismissed for want of jurisdiction cert. denied, 260 U.S. 701 (1922)

BRYAN, Circuit Judge.

This is a suit by the American National Bank of San Francisco, Cal., herein called plaintiff, against the Border National Bank of Eagle Pass, Tex., herein called defendant. After the exchange of several telegrams, defendant's obligation to plaintiff, which is the basis of the suit, assumed the following form:

> 'We guarantee irrevocably payment for account Joseph De Bona covering purchase 200 long tons Orient white granulated sugar from Maldonado & Co. f.o.b. Frisco twenty-two cents pound duty paid San Francisco public weigher's certificates of weights July, August, September shipment drawing on us with railroad bills lading and/or warehouse receipts attached.'

Besides a general denial, the defendant interposed special defenses to the effect that its undertaking was entered into as an accommodation, without security or consideration, and amounted to a guaranty of De Bona's obligation to Maldonado & Co.; that if De Bona and Maldonado & Co. ever entered into a contract, which is denied, it was a materially different one from the contract covered by defendant's guaranty; that De Bona repudiated his contract with Maldonado & Co. while it was wholly executory, and that defendant thereupon revoked its said guaranty; and that defendant had never received any benefit or thing of value out of the whole transaction. The court sustained exceptions to the special defenses.

April 22, 1920, De Bona, a broker at Eagle Pass, requested Maldonado & Co., brokers at San Francisco, to quote prices on refined granulated cane sugar for immediate or later delivery. April 23 Maldonado & Co. replied, and offered, subject to confirmation, from 100 to 200 long tons of Java white granulated sugar, for July, August, and September shipment from the Orient, at 22 cents per pound, f.o.b. San Francisco, upon being furnished with 'irrevocable letter of credit by wire.' April 24 De Bona informed Maldonado & Co. that in all probability he would accept their offer of 200 tons, and inquired if they would confirm sale. Maldonado & Co. replied that, before they would confirm sale, 'you must have your bank wire American National Bank irrevocable letter of credit with order.' Thereupon De Bona accepted Maldonado & Co.'s offer, and stated: 'Border National Bank this city guaranteeing.' During these negotiations the Border Bank notified Maldonado & Co. that it would guarantee De Bona's contract for July, August, and September delivery, but, upon Maldonado & Co. notifying De Bona that their offer provided for shipment, instead of delivery, during the months mentioned, the Border Bank modified its undertaking with the American Bank accordingly. In pursuance of the negotiations and contract between De Bona and Maldonado & Co., the Border Bank sent to the American Bank the obligation sued on. The entire correspondence was carried on by telegram.

Thereupon Maldonado & Co. contracted with Amsinck & Co. for the purchase of sugar with which to fill their contract with De Bona. Amsinck & Co. required of them a letter of credit, which was furnished by the American Bank to the amount of $96,300, in reliance upon its contract with the Border Bank. June 19, 1920, De Bona undertook to cancel his contract with Maldonado & Co., and June 22, 1920, the Border Bank gave notice of the revocation of its obligation to the American Bank. But both Maldonado & Co. and the American Bank insisted upon performance.

The sugar was shipped from Java in September, 1920, and the American Bank paid out on its letter of credit $96,310.11, and on November 22, 1920, presented Maldonado & Co.'s draft for $98,594.88, payable to itself, with bill of lading, warehouse receipts, and other documents attached, to the Border Bank. The bill of lading called for the sugar described in defendant's obligation. Payment of the draft was refused, and thereafter the sugar was sold at public auction for $28,534.46.

The court sustained objections to defendant's offer to prove that De Bona had no funds, assets, or security on deposit with it at any time during the year 1920 or since; that during all said time De Bona was insolvent; and that defendant had at no time applied to the Federal Reserve Board for enlargement of its powers as to bankers' acceptances or otherwise. At the conclusion of the evidence the court directed a verdict for plaintiff, and entered judgment thereon for $72,368.84, which, it was calculated, represented the difference between the proceeds of sale of the sugar and the amount paid out by plaintiff on its letter of credit, together with interest and expenses incident to storage and sale.

The defendant assigns error and contends: (1) That the obligation sued on is *ultra vires*, because it is in legal effect a guaranty or lending of credit, and not a letter of credit; it contemplates a nonbankable transaction; and it contravenes certain provisions of the Federal Reserve Act, relating to bankers' acceptances. . . .

A guaranty is a promise to answer for the payment of some debt, or the performance of some obligation, in case of the default of another person, who is in the first instance liable for such payment or performance. A letter of credit confers authority upon the person to whom it is addressed to advance money or furnish goods on the credit of the writer. . . . It is well settled that the guaranty of a national bank is *ultra vires*. . . . But a national bank is bound by its letter of credit. *Decatur Bank v. St. Louis Bank*, 21 Wall. 294, 22 L.Ed. 560.

The defendant insists upon a strict construction of the word 'guarantee,' contained in its contract. If there were nothing to limit, qualify, or explain its meaning, that word might reasonably be construed to imply a promise to pay De Bona's debt in the event he failed to do so. But to ignore the circumstances in which it was used is to attach too much importance to it. It is a word which is frequently employed in business transactions, which do not provide for securing the promise or debt of another, to express an original, primary obligation. The promise, in which the word appears, is to be construed in the light of the evidence and as a whole.

It was the intention of the parties to the sugar contract to secure it by a letter of credit. Maldonado & Co. required that form of security as a condition precedent to their offer. That offer was accepted by De Bona as made. The American Bank was also making the same requirement. The Border Bank was fully cognizant of the correspondence between the parties to the sugar contract. It therefore knew of the requirement that a letter of credit be furnished. It would be imputing bad faith to the Border Bank to conclude that it deliberately attempted to substitute a guaranty for a letter of credit. But clearly that was not the case. The Border Bank readily consented to every suggestion of change, and evidenced an intention to comply with every requirement made by the American Bank. The only reasonable conclusion from the evidence is that the banks, as well as the parties to the sugar contract, contemplated and intended a letter of credit. The defendant's obligation is consistent with the intention of the parties. It does not purport to secure payment by De Bona, but for his account. The promise is not that defendant would pay if De Bona did not, but that defendant would pay in the first instance.

A construction which renders a contract valid is to be preferred to one which renders it void. . . . We are therefore of opinion that defendant's obligation, tested by its terms and by the intention of the parties, as shown by the circumstances preceding and surrounding it, is not a guaranty, but is a direct, independent promise, and constitutes in legal effect a letter of credit. . . .

A letter of credit is not required to be in any particular form. Even a formal letter of credit rarely, if ever, discloses on its face that the bank issuing it is secured. A bank is liable on its certified check to one who takes it upon the faith of its certification, though the drawer has nothing to his credit in the bank. *Thompson v. St. Nicholas National Bank*, 146 U.S. 240. Likewise the acceptance of a draft 'affords a presumption of funds of the drawer in the hands of the acceptor.' *Raborg v. Peyton*, 2 Wheat. 385, 4 L.Ed. 268. And a promise to accept a draft is equivalent to an acceptance of it. *Coolidge v. Payson*, 2 Wheat. 66, 4 L.Ed. 185. There is no difference in principle between defendant's promise and the everyday acceptance of, or agreement to accept, a draft. The presumption that a bank will require security arises in one case as well as in the other; and that presumption is conclusive in favor of an innocent party, who changes his position in reliance upon it. *Scudder v. Union National Bank*, 91 U.S. 406, 414, 23 L.Ed. 245. . . .

If it be conceded or assumed that defendant violated the provisions of the Federal Reserve Act relating to bankers' acceptances . . . , it is not perceived that any advantage would be gained by it in this suit. Penalties for violations of the act are prescribed, but none of them include the invalidation of contracts. *Thompson v. St. Nicholas Bank*, 146 U.S. 240; *Hanover National Bank v. First National Bank*, 109 Fed. 421, 48 C.C.A. 482.

Dunn v. McCoy

113 F.2d 587 (3d Cir. 1940)

CLARK, Circuit Judge.

We seem to be still picking up the pieces. A small state chartered bank in the suburbs (Shillington) of Reading, Pennsylvania, begins to feel the pinch of 1929 in 1932. To secure its statute prescribed cash it sells some of its assets (inferentially at least not otherwise marketable) to a pool comprising the clearing house (seven) banks of Reading. Title was taken in the name of one Snyder, secretary of that Association. This proved only a stop-gap an further help was indicated. So one of the all too frequent rescue parties of that era was organized. The stretcher bearers were the same clearing house banks with the addition of a trust company from another suburb of Reading, Wyomissing.

The terms and conditions of rescue are embodied in a formal agreement dated March 29, 1932. . . . It provided inter alia for a fund of $100,000, to be furnished the Shillington Bank, to restore its vanished capital and surplus and impaired (to the extent of $38,000) deposits. This fund was furnished in eight equal installments by the assisting banks and was by each of them placed to the credit of the distressed bank in their own institutions. This credit was evidenced by pass books for $12,500 each. In return for this credit, the Shillington Bank turned over 689 of its 1,000 shares to Mr. Snyder as trustee under an option agreement. These shares were all owned by the directors of the embarrassed bank and by another bank in the affected suburb. The agreement also gave the Trustee these significant powers. We quote:

> '1. The 'Trustee' shall have power at any and all times during reasonable hours to make an examination, either by himself or/and such representatives, as he may designate in writing, of the affairs of the 'Beneficiary' and for this purpose 'Beneficiary' hereby covenants to lend all possible assistance and to disclose any and all information concerning the affairs of the 'Beneficiary' to enable the 'Trustee' to be fully informed in regards to all of the financial affairs of the 'Beneficiary'.
>
> '2. The 'Trustee' shall have the right under the authority granted him by the 'Beneficiary' to at any time discuss the financial affairs of the institution with the Secretary of Banking provided he is acceptable to the said Secretary of Banking'. . . .

So the Shillington Bank was allowed to remain open.

Events moved too fast for the members of this, as well as of other banking fraternities. All the banks concerned were closed at or about the time of the banking holiday. Two of them, at least, the litigants here, did not reopen. Three liquidating Trustees were appointed for the plaintiff Shillington Bank and a conservator and receiver successively for the defendant clearing house bank, the Farmers National Bank and Trust Company, a national bank.

The state bank has paid its depositors 83%, will pay them in full, and may have some money left over for its stockholders. The national bank, originally the big brother, was not so fortunate and has paid its depositors only 60% with no predictions as to the future. It seems to have been the experience that the sooner they fail the higher they pay. In other words, swim with the tide not against it. The clearing house banks exercised their option and now own the 689 shares of the old (it is being reorganized) Shillington Bank. These shares are, of course, assessable but, by the same token, are not going to be assessed when the assets of the bank indicate a surplus due stockholders.

The plaintiff-appellee, the Shillington Bank, received its dividends ($5,343.75) up to March 15, 1937. On that date another dividend of $1,187.50 was declared by the defendant-appellant, Farmers National Bank & Trust Company. This, it refused to pay and on this suit being brought therefore counterclaimed for the already paid dividends on the theory of a mistake of law. As we think there was no such mistake, we are not concerned with the unsatisfactory complications in the 'payments under mistake of law' doctrine. ...

The question for our decision has been considerably litigated. The cases are not in accord. It may be stated in broad terms as follows. What is the power of cooperative banking action prompted by the common interest in preventing the impact upon public confidence in the banking group of a failure of a member of the group? It is conceded that legislative bodies do not seem to have foreseen the necessity for any such cooperative action. We must fall back then on the always difficult interpretation of words. The words here are 'all such incidental powers as shall be necessary to carry on the business of banking', 12 U.S.C. 24, . . . and are simply a legislative recognition of the impracticability of complete prevision in the field of expressly delegated powers. A similar recognition has made work for the courts in a subdivision of constitutional law. The cooperative action fostered by the banking events of this and similar cases lies in the field and takes the form of a guaranty. This is so, actually if not technically, irrespective of the legal garments put on by the rescue party as they set out on their errand of mercy. A form so extreme as perhaps not to be a form at all would include donations. . . .

A general power to make guaranties is rarely included in the statutory list of general powers granted to banks. . . . Pennsylvania at one time authorized banks to guarantee bonds secured by mortgages on real estate. . . . The experience seems to have been unfortunate for the grant was expressly repealed by the Act of April 22, 1937. . . . In many states, however, the power to issue letters of credit forms an exception to this general rule. . . . Such letters are in essence only guaranties. . . . The absence of an express grant of power, however, has not prevented the enforcement of guaranties which the courts would characterize as having been entered into by banks for the furtherance of their own rights or as an incident to the transaction of their own business. Under the applications of this flexible rule, it is clear that in order to protect authorized loans, a bank may ordinarily guarantee to its debtors' other creditors that their preexisting or subsequently created loans will be paid. A bank may also guarantee the quality of its debtor's goods in order to realize on collateral security already obtained;[g] or guarantee payment of a note which is the obligation of another, if this is necessary to dispose of its own paper and securities;[h] and the guaranty of the liabilities of another bank, if accompanied by a receipt of assets, may be upheld as incidental to the exercise of the power either to purchase and discount paper and securities or to buy and sell coin and bullion."[i] On the other hand, banks are not permitted to guarantee the business accounts of their customers.[j]

There can be no doubt as to the impact on confidence, of which we spoke earlier. A closed bank is as surely followed by withdrawals from open banks as is the day by night. This happens not only from apprehension but also from altruism–friends may have frozen funds. Should the depositors and stockholders fortunate enough to escape either the *vis major* of the financial world or the folly of those who practice its arts endanger their own security? An analogy to the flood, fire, and pestilence of the physical world seems more than persuasive because here there is an element of self-interest. There the individual must yield to the community and accept his losses philosophically. So the bank owner and creditor must make some sacrifices at least.

The criteria governing the extent of that sacrifice come readily to mind. Is the

---

g. *Gotham National Bank v. Sharood Co.*, 2 Cir., 23 F.2d 567; *Taylor v. Hemphill*, Tex. Civ. App., 238 S.W. 986.

h. *International Harvester Co. v. State Bank of Upham*, 38 N.D. 632, 166 N.W. 507; *Collings v. Guarantee Trust Co.*, D.C., 10 F.Supp. 462; *People's Bank v. Manufacturers' Bank*, 101 U.S. 181, 25 L.Ed. 907.

i. *Schofield v. State National Bank*, 8 Cir., 97 F. 282.

j. *Rice & Hutchins Atlanta Co. v. Commercial Nat. Bank*, 18 Ga.App. 151, 88 S.E. 999; *Healey & Son v. Stewardson Nat. Bank*, 285 Ill.App. 290, 1 N.E.2d 858; contra: *Wasson v. American Can Co.*, 189 Ark. 354, 72 S.W.2d 241.

guaranty bare, *i.e.* unsecured or is it in return for tangible benefit? Is that benefit proportionate to the risk of loss? Is the guarantee limited in amount? Does it entail, go beyond, the loss of the guaranty and endanger the solvency of the guarantor?

Searching for these criteria in the principal case, what do we find? There is no real tangible benefit because the value of the collateral shares depends on the outcome of the original risk. There is a provision for supervision and appellant's denial thereof moved us to quote it. The guarantee is exactly limited to the rather negligible sum of $12,500. There is no evidence of how far that negligible sum affected the stability of an institution that afterwards did in fact fail. The record is also bare of testimony as to the banking posture in Reading and its environs and so the superfluity of the plaintiff and the consequent unwisdom of its continuance do not appear.

On that showing we uphold the contract and so align ourselves with those courts which deprecate the arguments of hindsight. It is perhaps significant that only those institutions whose custodial status requires judicial advice seem to seek to repudiate this type of contracts. Those who survive stick to their bargains and so give an intimation of the judgment of the banking world. We accept that judgment in the principal case.

We need hardly add our agreement to the view of appellant's counsel that the possibility of benefit to the Shillington Bank's other stockholders (outside the 689 shares pledged and finally bought by the defendant) is a bridge that should not be crossed until arrival thereat.

FDIC v. Freudenfeld

492 F.Supp. 763 (E.D.Wisc. 1980)

WARREN, District Judge.

In January of 1975, the defendant, Bernard A. Freudenfeld, applied to the American City Bank & Trust Company (American) for an Irrevocable Standby Letter of Credit up to an amount of $10,000.00 available by drafts drawn at sight. The application named the Miami National Bank (MNB) of Miami, Florida as beneficiary and specified that the requested letter of credit was to be for the account of James and Jill Weinberg d/b/a James Lee, Inc. The Weinbergs were seeking to borrow $10,000.00 from the MNB and the letter of credit satisfied a requirement of the MNB. Under the agreement between Freudenfeld and American, Freudenfeld agreed to pay a fee for issuance of the letter of credit and to reimburse American the amount of any draft on the credit presented to American for payment. On January 23, 1975, American issued Irrevocable Standby Letter of Credit No. 1629 for a sum not exceeding $10,000.00 and for the account of the Weinbergs with the MNB as beneficiary. The stated sum was:

> Available by (a) draft at sight accompanied by the following documents:
> Beneficiary's signed certificate that loan to account party is past due for an amount in principal and interest equal to, or greater than amount claimed on attached sight draft.

On October 21, 1975, before the MNB drew on Letter of Credit No. 1629, American City Bank was declared insolvent by the Comptroller of the Currency and the Federal Deposit Insurance Corporation (FDIC) was appointed receiver of American. Title to the asset represented by the agreement between Freudenfeld and American, and all liability under Letter of Credit No. 1629, passed to the FDIC. The FDIC, however, took the position that the Letter of Credit was still contingent at the time American was declared insolvent and that it could, therefore, avoid liability on the letter of credit. Pursuant to that posture, on October 28, 1975, the FDIC advised the MNB and the Weinbergs d/b/a James Lee, Inc. by letter that it was cancelling and terminating the Letter of Credit No. 1629 as of October 21, 1975.

Notwithstanding the October 28, 1975 letter from the FDIC, the MNB sent a sight draft for $10,000.00 with the appropriate required certificate attached showing that the loan by the MNB to James Lee, Inc. was past due in the amount of $10,000.00. These documents were received by the FDIC on November 28, 1975 and, consistent with its previously stated position, it refused to honor the draft of the MNB. Consequently, on May 18, 1977, the MNB commenced an action in this district against the FDIC, as receiver of American, to require funding of Letter of Credit No. 1629. This action was stayed by agreement of the parties because a case, *First Empire Bank New York v. FDIC*, involving standby letter of credit issues substantially similar to those in the MNB v. FDIC case, was pending in the Southern District of California. The MNB and the FDIC agreed to abide by the judicial determination in the *First Empire* case. This agreement was never disclosed to defendant Freudenfeld.

On April 6, 1978, the Ninth Circuit Court of Appeals decided the *First Empire* case, 572 F.2d 1361 (9th Cir. 1978), holding that standby letters of credit still contingent at the time of the bank's closing cannot be avoided or terminated by the FDIC and, furthermore, that under a purchase and assumption agreement as used in the American closing, *i. e.*, whereby another bank assumes liabilities and purchases assets of the closed bank including commercial letters of credit, a standby letter of credit must be treated like commercial letters of credit and thus either be included in the purchase and assumption agreement or be paid in full by the FDIC. Mr. Freudenfeld was advised of the MNB's lawsuit against the FDIC and of the decision of the Ninth Circuit Court of Appeals in the FDIC's letter of May 18, 1978. The letter advised defendant Freudenfeld that if the Supreme Court affirmed the Ninth Circuit and the FDIC was required to pay the MNB, the FDIC would look to Freudenfeld for reimbursement. . . . Subsequently, the FDIC sought and on October 16, 1978 was denied certiorari of the *First Empire* case in the Supreme Court. 439 U.S. 919. Consequently, on January 12, 1979, the FDIC paid $10,000.00 plus interest to the MNB and by letter of February 6, 1979, advised Freudenfeld of payment under the letter of credit and demanded reimbursement pursuant to the application agreement. . . Freudenfeld refused payment and the FDIC commenced this litigation.

In addition to these events leading to the commencement of this litigation by the FDIC, certain actions were taken by the MNB with respect to its loan with the Weinbergs. Later in 1975, September 22, 1975, the MNB loaned an additional $13,000.00 to James Lee, Inc., as borrower with Jill Weinberg nee Freudenfeld as guarantor. In October of 1975, James Lee, Inc. defaulted on the $10,000.00 note and, notwithstanding the FDIC's notice of cancellation, the MNB perfected its interest in the standby Letter of Credit. Thereafter, the MNB commenced its action against the FDIC in May of 1977, but Freudenfeld was not advised of this lawsuit or the settlement agreement.

At about the same time the MNB commenced its action against the FDIC, it also filed an action against James and Jill Weinberg in a Florida circuit court to recover on both the $10,000.00 and $13,000.00 loans. Subsequently, the Weinbergs were divorced and James filed for personal bankruptcy. On her own behalf, Jill Weinberg negotiated a stipulation of dismissal of the Florida action in consideration of which she paid the MNB $1,500.00. Because Jill Weinberg lacked the money, Mr. Freudenfeld supplied the $1,500.00 necessary for the settlement agreement.

According to defendant, he first learned of the action by the MNB against the FDIC on May 18, 1978 when he received the FDIC's explanatory letter. On that same day, he made the last payment under his daughter's settlement agreement with the MNB. However, it was not until July 13, 1978, that the MNB drafted a release and caused the stipulation of dismissal to be filed in the Florida court resulting in the entry of a judgment of dismissal. The release dated July 13, 1980 provides that the $1,499.00 satisfies Jill Weinberg's obligation for the $13,000.00 debit of James Lee, Inc. to the MNB and $1.00 releases her duty on the $10,000.00 loan. The agreement further provides:

> Nothing herein shall in any way effect, discharge, waive or disclaim the rights, claims and actions of the (MNB) as against any other guarantors, sureties, indemnities or the maker of the aforementioned promissory notes.

Based upon the foregoing facts, the FDIC claims that it is entitled to summary judgment. . . .

At the outset, it is important to note that Freudenfeld admits execution of the agreement, issuance of the Letter of Credit, payment by the FDIC of $10,000.00 to MNB, and non-payment of the FDIC's demand for repayment. Furthermore, the record is clear that as the applicant for the letter of credit, and pursuant to paragraph 5 of the agreement ... , Freudenfeld is obliged to reimburse the FDIC, unless his defenses and the purported supporting facts present a valid issue for trial.

The first defense raised by Freudenfeld is that the standby Letter of Credit was a guaranty contrary to the authority of the American City Bank as a national banking association. In order to establish this defense, the FDIC asserts that Freudenfeld must prove three points: 1) that a national bank does not have authority to make a guaranty; 2) that a standby letter of credit should be characterized as a guaranty; and 3) that if American's issuance of the letter of credit was ultra vires, that Freudenfeld is entitled to assert the lack of authority in order to avoid his liability to reimburse the FDIC which disbursed the funds under the terms of the Letter of Credit. The Court agrees that these are the points defendant must establish and holds that, as a matter of law, Freudenfeld cannot establish two of them.

The FDIC, citing 12 U.S.C. § 24, concedes that a national bank lacks authority to make a guaranty. However, based upon the court's holding in *Prudential Insurance Co. v. Marquette National Bank of Minneapolis*, 419 F.Supp. 734, 735-36 (D.Minn.1976), and the court's comments in *First Empire Bank New York v. FDIC*, 572 F.2d 1361, 1366-67 (9th Cir. 1978), the FDIC argues that a "standby" letter of credit is not a guaranty.

Furthermore, it argues that only the United States, which has chosen to regulate the affairs of national banks, and not a private individual, can challenge a national bank action as being *ultra vires*.

Although in the *Prudential* case the court did not undertake extensive reasoning, the opinion is rational and will be followed here. A standby letter of credit is simply not a guaranty even though it has some of the same characteristics.

Even if the Letter of Credit was, however, a guaranty, only the United States can challenge a national bank's actions as *ultra vires*. *Thompson v. St. Nicholas National Bank*, 146 U.S. 240, 251 (1892). In *Thompson* the Court held:

> It has been held repeatedly by this court that where the provisions of the national banking act prohibit certain acts by banks or their officers, without imposing any penalty or forfeiture applicable to particular transactions which have been executed, their validity can be questioned only by the United States and not by private parties. *Id.*

Since only the federal government can challenge the actions of American, defendant Freudenfeld will not be permitted to challenge the bank's actions. To do so would clearly work an injustice. The Letter of Credit was issued at Freudenfeld's behest and he benefited from it because the MNB loaned funds to the account party designated by defendant in the Letter of Credit. The FDIC, by force of law, rightfully paid the MNB under the Letter of Credit, and to deny it recovery from Freudenfeld on the ultra vires ground, would be unfair.

Notes and Comments 5.55. Assume that Borderline National Bank has agreed to pay checks of a customer in unlimited amounts. Is this permissible in light of the cases excerpted above? *See, e.g., Border National Bank*, 282 F. at 79 (distinguishing similar factual situations and giving citations). *But see* 12 C.F.R. § 7.7015 (1995), which provided:

> An arrangement whereby a bank holds out to the public that it will honor checks drawn on it up to a certain amount by a depositor displaying a so-called "check guaranty card," is in essence an agreement by the bank with its depositor to extend credit to the depositor, if necessary, to honor his checks. Such an arrangement is essentially a commitment to lend and is within the power of a national bank.

5.56. Borderline has written to Mr. Peer and stated that it would "guarantee" the payment of "any bill of goods which our customer, Mr. Webb, may buy of you in Chicago during the current week." The letter does not appear to be subject to any dollar limit. Will Borderline's undertaking be enforceable against it? *See, e.g., Border National Bank*, 282 F. at 79 (distinguishing similar factual situations and giving citations).

5.57. Borderline has written to Baggers, Inc. and stated that it would "guarantee" any obligations, over the next twelve months, of its customer, the Des Moines Paper Bag Company, "to the extent of the cost of a carload of bag paper." Will Borderline be liable for such obligations? *See, e.g., Border National Bank*, 282 F. at 79 (distinguishing similar factual situations and giving citations).

5.58. *Freudenfeld* asserts that only the federal government (presumably, in the case of a national bank, the Comptroller of the Currency) can challenge a bank that attempts to issue a third-party guaranty. Under what circumstances would it do so? Consider the following excerpt from the Comptroller's regulations. How does this interpretive provision compare with the cases excerpted above?

Comptroller of the Currency

12 C.F.R. pt. 7

§ 7.1017 National bank as guarantor or surety on indemnity bond.

(a) A national bank may lend its credit, bind itself as a surety to indemnify another, or otherwise become a guarantor . . . , if:

(1) The bank has a substantial interest in the performance of the transaction involved (for example, a bank, as fiduciary, has a sufficient interest in the faithful performance by a cofiduciary of its duties to act as surety on the bond of such cofiduciary); or

(2) The transaction is for the benefit of a customer and the bank obtains from the customer a segregated deposit that is sufficient in amount to cover the bank's total potential liability. A segregated deposit under this section includes collateral:

(i) In which the bank has perfected its security interest (for example, if the collateral is a printed security, the bank must have obtained physical control of the security, and, if the collateral is a book entry security, the bank must have properly recorded its security interest); and

(ii) That has a market value, at the close of each business day, equal to the bank's total potential liability and is composed of:

(A) Cash;

(B) Obligations of the United States or its agencies;

(C) Obligations fully guaranteed by the United States or its agencies as to principal and interest; or

(D) Notes, drafts, or bills of exchange or bankers' acceptances that are eligible for rediscount or purchase by a Federal Reserve Bank; or

(iii) That has a market value, at the close of each business day, equal to 110 percent of the bank's total potential liability and is composed of obligations of a State or political subdivision of a State.

(b) In addition to paragraph (a) of this section, a national bank may guarantee obligations of a customer, subsidiary or affiliate that are financial in character, provided the amount of the bank's financial obligation is reasonably ascertainable and otherwise consistent with applicable law.

5. Real Property

Notes and Comments 5.59. As with most state banks, the power of national banks to acquire interests in real property is statutorily based. Their power to hold real property is outlined and limited by the provisions of 12 U.S.C. § 29. The power to extend loans against real estate is found in *id.* § 371. National banks also have the authority to spin off mortgage lending activities into separate operating subsidiaries. *Id.* §§ 24(Seventh), 24a. Although the majority and dissent in the following case disagreed about the authority of state regulators to supervise such subsidiaries, do they agree on the authority of national banks to engage in mortgage banking?

Watters v. Wachovia Bank, N.A.

550 U.S. 1 (2007)

Justice GINSBURG delivered the opinion of the Court.

Business activities of national banks are controlled by the National Bank Act (NBA or Act), 12 U.S.C. § 1 *et seq*., and regulations promulgated thereunder by the Office of the Comptroller of the Currency (OCC). See §§ 24, 93a, 371(a). . . .

. . . A national bank has the power to engage in real estate lending through an operating subsidiary, subject to the same terms and conditions that govern the national bank itself; that power cannot be significantly impaired or impeded by state law. See, *e.g., Barnett Bank,* 517 U.S., at 33-34; 12 U.S.C. §§ 24 Seventh, 24a(g)(3)(A), 371. . . .

Justice STEVENS, with whom THE CHIEF JUSTICE and Justice SCALIA join, dissenting.

. . . In 1913, Congress permitted national banks to make loans secured by farm land, Federal Reserve Act, § 24, 38 Stat. 273, and in succeeding years, their mortgage-lending power was enlarged to cover loans on real estate in the vicinity of the bank, Act of Sept. 7, 1916, 39 Stat. 754, and loans "secured by first liens upon forest tracts which are properly managed in all respects," Act of Aug. 15, 1953, ch. 510, 67 Stat. 614. Congress substantially expanded national banks' power to make real estate loans in 1974, see Housing and Community Development Act, Title VII, § 711, 88 Stat 716, and in 1982 it enacted the broad language, now codified at 12 U.S.C. § 371(a), authorizing national banks to make "loans ...

secured by liens on interests in real estate." Garn-St Germain Depository Institutions Act of 1982, Title IV, § 403, 96 Stat. 1510. . . .

5.60. Consider the following case and excerpts from the Comptroller's regulations concerning real property in preparing to answer 5.61-5.63, *infra.*

First National Bank of Bellaire v. Comptroller of the Currency

697 F.2d 674 (5th Cir. 1983)

GARZA, Circuit Judge.

The petitioner, First National Bank of Bellaire, (hereinafter the Bank), seeks to have the Cease and Desist Order issued by the Comptroller of the Currency (hereinafter the Comptroller) set aside.[a] . . . [T]he Acting Comptroller of the Currency, Charles E. Lord, issued a Cease and Desist Order on May 28, 1981. . . .

On October 19, 1972 the Bank acquired a tract of land, the Dashwood property, for the purpose of future expansion. The Bank paid $42,914 for the property and it was not held under mortgage nor was it purchased to secure any debts due the Bank. The Dashwood property was being held in the Banking House account on the Bank's books. In 1974 the Bank acquired additional property for the purpose of expansion. On May 1, 1974, the Bank transferred the Dashwood property from the Banking House account to the account entitled "Real Estate Owned Other Than Bank Premises." The Dashwood property was held in this account until 1981 when it was sold.

In the Notice of Charges the Comptroller alleged the Bank violated 12 U.S.C. § 29. The Cease and Desist Order commands the Bank to take such actions as are necessary to correct the violation and to implement adequate policies and procedures to insure that similar violations do not occur in the future. We hold that the Comptroller's finding of a violation of 12 U.S.C. § 29 was supported by substantial evidence and the Cease and Desist Order in this regard was proper.

The purpose of 12 U.S.C. § 29 is "to keep the capital of the banks flowing in the daily channels of commerce; to deter them [banks] from embarking in hazardous real-estate speculations; and to prevent the accumulation of large masses of such property in their hands, to be held as it were, in mortmain." *National Bank v. Matthews*, 98 U.S. 621, 626 (1878). . . .

The statute sets forth the four exclusive categories of real property a bank can purchase, hold or convey. Furthermore, if real property falls in one of the four permissible categories and the property is held under mortgage or the property was purchased to secure debts due the bank the property cannot be held more than five years. If the property does not fall in one of the four permissible categories the five-year limitation on real estate obtained through mortgage foreclosure or the like does not apply. . . . If the five-year limitation is applied to property outside the four permissible categories (to property which the bank is not authorized to hold) the effect would be to allow the bank to hold unauthorized property, which is held under mortgage or was purchased to secure debts due the bank, for five years. Such a construction would clearly be contrary to the intent of Congress. The five-year category was meant to limit the four permissible categories and not to expand them.

The Dashwood property was originally acquired for future expansion. Property held for future expansion is that which is necessary for the accommodation and furtherance of

---

a. On cease and desist orders, see Chapter 8, § 2, *infra.*

banking business. . . . The Bank was properly holding the property until 1974. In 1974, however, when the property was moved to the "Real Estate Owned Other Than Bank Premises" account the property was no longer being held within the four permissible categories of 12 U.S.C. § 29. The Bank, therefore, was under a duty to divest itself of the property in a reasonable time. In view of the entire record we find that as a matter of law the Bank did not divest itself of the Dashwood property in a reasonable time.[8] The Bank, therefore, violated 12 U.S.C. § 29 and the Cease and Desist Order was proper.

Comptroller of the Currency

12 C.F.R. pts. 5, 7

§ 5.37 Investment in bank premises.

(a) Authority. 12 U.S.C. 29, 93a, and 371d.

(b) Scope. This section sets forth the procedures governing OCC review and approval of applications by national banks to invest in bank premises or in certain bank premises related investments, loans, or indebtedness, as described in paragraph (d)(1)(i) of this section.

(c) Definition -- Bank premises for purposes of this section includes the following:

(1) Premises that are owned and occupied (or to be occupied, if under construction) by the bank, its branches, or its consolidated subsidiaries;

(2) Capitalized leases and leasehold improvements, vaults, and fixed machinery and equipment;

(3) Remodeling costs to existing premises;

(4) Real estate acquired and intended, in good faith, for use in future expansion; or

(5) Parking facilities that are used by customers or employees of the bank, its branches, and its consolidated subsidiaries.

(d) Procedure–

(1) Application.

(i) A national bank shall submit an application to the appropriate supervisory office to invest in bank premises, or in the stock, bonds, debentures, or other such obligations of any corporation holding the premises of the bank, or to make loans to or upon the security of the stock of such corporation, if the aggregate of all such investments and loans, together with the indebtedness incurred by any such corporation that is an affiliate of the bank, as defined in 12 U.S.C. 221a, will exceed the amount of the capital stock of the bank.

(ii) The application must include:

(A) A description of the bank's present investment in bank premises;

(B) The investment in bank premises that the bank intends to make, and the business reason for making the investment; and

(C) The amount by which the bank's aggregate investment will exceed the amount

---

8. In light of the Comptroller's expertise in the area of banking and the Comptroller's power to promulgate regulations under 12 U.S.C. § 25a(e), we are inclined to leave the task of establishing guidelines for determining reasonableness to the Comptroller. The only guidance we provide is that the facts of this case establish unreasonableness. Here the property was held for approximately seven years; Houston incurred tremendous growth during these seven years; and expert testimony established that a market existed for the property. These facts establish without question that the Bank could have sold the property in a much shorter time if it had exercised due diligence. The Bank argues that due to a street widening project during part of this period, by holding the property, the Bank was able to make a substantial profit on the property. This argument only establishes that the Bank was holding the property for speculative purposes in violation of the intent of 12 U.S.C. § 29.

of the bank's capital stock.

(2) Approval. An application for national bank investment in bank premises or in certain bank premises' related investments, loans or indebtedness, as described in paragraph (d)(1)(i) of this section, is deemed approved as of the 30th day after the filing is received by the OCC, unless the OCC notifies the bank prior to that date that the filing presents a significant supervisory, or compliance concern, or raises a significant legal or policy issue. An approval for a specified amount under this section remains valid up to that amount until the OCC notifies the bank otherwise.

(3) Notice process. Notwithstanding paragraph (d)(1)(i) of this section, a bank that is rated 1 or 2 under the Uniform Financial Institutions Rating System (CAMELS) may make an aggregate investment in bank premises up to 150 percent of the bank's capital and surplus without the OCC's prior approval, provided that the bank is well capitalized as defined in 12 CFR part 6 and will continue to be well capitalized after the investment or loan is made. However, the bank shall notify the appropriate supervisory office in writing of the investment within 30 days after the investment or loan is made. The written notice must include a description of the bank's investment. . . .

§ 7.1000 National bank ownership of property.

(a) Investment in real estate necessary for the transaction of business --

(1) General. Under 12 U.S.C. 29 (First), a national bank may invest in real estate that is necessary for the transaction of its business.

(2) Type of real estate. For purposes of 12 U.S.C. 29 (First), this real estate includes:

(i) Premises that are owned and occupied (or to be occupied, if under construction) by the bank, its branches, or its consolidated subsidiaries;

(ii) Real estate acquired and intended, in good faith, for use in future expansion;

(iii) Parking facilities that are used by customers or employees of the bank, its branches, and its consolidated subsidiaries;

(iv) Residential property for the use of bank officers or employees who are:

(A) Located in remote areas where suitable housing at a reasonable price is not readily available; or

(B) Temporarily assigned to a foreign country, including foreign nationals temporarily assigned to the United States; and

(v) Property for the use of bank officers, employees, or customers, or for the temporary lodging of such persons in areas where suitable commercial lodging is not readily available, provided that the purchase and operation of the property qualifies as a deductible business expense for Federal tax purposes.

(3) Permissible means of holding. A national bank may acquire and hold real estate under this paragraph (a) by any reasonable and prudent means, including ownership in fee, a leasehold estate, or in an interest in a cooperative. The bank may hold this real estate directly or through one or more subsidiaries. The bank may organize a bank premises subsidiary as a corporation, partnership, or similar entity (e.g., a limited liability company).

(b) Fixed assets. A national bank may own fixed assets necessary for the transaction of its business, such as fixtures, furniture, and data processing equipment.

(c) Investment in bank premises–

(1) Investment limitation; approval. 12 U.S.C. 371d governs when OCC approval is required for national bank investment in bank premises. A bank may seek approval from the OCC in accordance with the procedures set forth in 12 CFR 5.37.

(2) Option to purchase. An unexercised option to purchase bank premises or stock in a corporation holding bank premises is not an investment in bank premises. A national

bank must receive OCC approval to exercise the option if the price of the option and the bank's other investments in bank premises exceed the amount of the bank's capital stock.

(d) Other real property–

(1) Lease financing of public facilities. A national bank may purchase or construct a municipal building, school building, or other similar public facility and, as holder of legal title, lease the facility to a municipality or other public authority having resources sufficient to make all rental payments as they become due. The lease agreement must provide that the lessee will become the owner of the building or facility upon the expiration of the lease.

(2) Purchase of employee's residence. To facilitate the efficient use of bank personnel, a national bank may purchase the residence of an employee who has been transferred to another area in order to spare the employee a loss in the prevailing real estate market. The bank must arrange for early divestment of title to such property.

Notes and Comments 5.61. Hiram Forth, Chairman of Quarter National Bank (QNB), wants QNB to purchase a large tract of swamp land in Florida for possible future development as a "Southern banking center" for QNB. While QNB is located in a state some 1,000 miles from Florida, Harry believes that "some day, we may want to take advantage of the possibilities of interstate banking, and I just want the bank to be ready." The board of directors has asked for legal advice on the permissibility of this proposed purchase. How would you advise the board?

5.62. Ten years ago, Hiram's nephew had obtained a loan from QNB to finance an amusement park project in Florida. The large tract of Florida land on which the project was to be built was collateral for the loan. The nephew has since defaulted on the loan. In the view of QNB's Vice President in charge of real estate lending, the Florida real estate market is now "soft," and she has recommended that QNB foreclose on the property and hold onto it "for a number of years, until there's an upturn in the market." May QNB:

a. Hold onto the property for five to ten years, awaiting an upturn?

b. Create a real estate finance subsidiary and sell the property to the subsidiary for future development?

c. Pay off a second mortgage on the property, amounting to approximately one-third of the original appraised value of the property?

5.63. Three years ago, QNB purchased a large tract of land within two miles of its headquarters. It had planned to move its headquarters to a new high-rise building that it proposed to build on the site. Since then, QNB has tried unsuccessfully to obtain the necessary zoning variances to permit construction. It is now unclear whether QNB will be able to proceed with the project at any time in the foreseeable future. What are the consequences of these developments for QNB?

6. Trust Powers

Notes and Comments 5.64. *Authorization of trust powers.* Statutory authority to engage in the business of commercial banking does not necessarily include the authority to engage in trust activities as well. Under many chartering systems, there are distinct provisions governing the application for a grant of trust powers; in other systems, trust authority may be included in the chartering process itself. Nevertheless, most commercial banks will apply and obtain those powers, incorporating the trust activities within a trust department or division of the bank itself. Trust activities are governed by state law principles of the law of trusts, as they would affect any fiduciary. Overlaying the operation of these principles, however, is a system of federal regulation of trust activities. The Comptroller will in the first instance supervise and examine the trust departments of national banks; the Fed will do the same for state member banks, and the FDIC state nonmember insured banks. However, in terms of entry into the trust business itself, the relevant authorities are those exercised by state chartering authorities for state banks and the Comptroller for national banks. The basic statutory reference for national banks is 12 U.S.C. § 92a. To what extent does the procedure for obtaining trust powers parallel the procedure for obtaining a charter?[61] What is the scope of the Comptroller's discretion in this regard? Consider § 92a and the following excerpts.

Office of the Comptroller of the Currency

12 C.F.R. pt. 5

§ 5.20 Organizing a bank.

. . .

(*l*) Special purpose banks. An applicant for a national bank charter that will limit its activities to fiduciary activities . . . shall adhere to established charter procedures with modifications appropriate for the circumstances as determined by the OCC. . . . In addition to the other requirements in this section, a bank limited to fiduciary activities . . . may not conduct that business until the OCC grants final approval for the bank to commence operations. . . .

§ 5.26 Fiduciary powers.

(a) Authority. 12 U.S.C. 92a.

(b) Licensing requirements. A national bank must submit an application and obtain prior approval from, or in certain circumstances file a notice with, the OCC in order to exercise fiduciary powers. No approval or notice is required in the following circumstances:

(1) Where two or more national banks consolidate or merge, and any of the banks has, prior to the consolidation or merger, received OCC approval to exercise fiduciary powers and that approval is in force at the time of the consolidation or merger, the resulting bank may exercise fiduciary powers in the same manner and to the same extent as the national bank to which approval was originally granted; and

(2) Where a national bank with prior OCC approval to exercise fiduciary powers is the resulting bank in a merger or consolidation with a state bank.

(c) Scope. This section sets forth the procedures governing OCC review and approval of an application, and in certain cases the filing of a notice, by a national bank to exercise fiduciary powers. A national bank's fiduciary activities are subject to the provisions of 12 CFR part 9.

(d) Policy. The exercise of fiduciary powers is primarily a management decision of the national bank. The OCC generally permits a national bank to exercise fiduciary powers if the bank is operating in a satisfactory manner, the proposed activities comply with applicable statutes and regulations, and the bank retains qualified fiduciary management.

(e) Procedure–

(1) General. The following institutions must obtain approval from the OCC in order to offer fiduciary services to the public:

(i) A national bank without fiduciary powers;

(ii) A national bank without fiduciary powers that desires to exercise fiduciary

---

61. *See* Chapter 2, § 2, *supra* (excerpting OCC chartering regulations).

powers after merging with a state bank or savings association with fiduciary powers; and

(iii) A national bank that results from the conversion of a state bank or a state or Federal savings association that was exercising fiduciary powers prior to the conversion.

(2) Application.

(i) Except as provided in paragraph (e)(2)(ii) of this section, a national bank that desires to exercise fiduciary powers shall submit to the OCC an application requesting approval. The application must contain:

(A) A statement requesting full or limited powers (specifying which powers);

(B) A statement that the capital and surplus of the national bank is not less than the capital and surplus required by state law of state banks, trust companies, and other corporations exercising comparable fiduciary powers;

(C) Sufficient biographical information on proposed trust management personnel to enable the OCC to assess their qualifications;

(D) A description of the locations where the bank will conduct fiduciary activities; and

(E) If requested by the OCC, an opinion of counsel that the proposed activities do not violate applicable Federal or State law, including citations to applicable law.

(ii) If approval to exercise fiduciary powers is desired in connection with any other transaction subject to an application under this part, the applicant covered under paragraph (e)(1)(ii) or (e)(1)(iii) of this section may include a request for approval of fiduciary powers, including the information required by paragraph (e)(2)(i) of this section, as part of its other application. The OCC does not require a separate application requesting approval to exercise fiduciary powers under these circumstances.

(3) Expedited review. An application by an eligible bank to exercise fiduciary powers is deemed approved by the OCC as of the 30th day after the application is received by the OCC, unless the OCC notifies the bank prior to that date that the filing is not eligible for expedited review under § 5.13(a)(2).

(4) Permit. Approval of an application under this section constitutes a permit under 12 U.S.C. 92a to conduct the fiduciary powers requested in the application.

(5) Notice of fiduciary activities in additional states. No further application under this section is required when a national bank with existing OCC approval to exercise fiduciary powers plans to engage in any of the activities specified in § 9.7(d) of this chapter or to conduct activities ancillary to its fiduciary business, in a state in addition to the state described in the application for fiduciary powers that the OCC has approved. Instead, unless the bank provides notice through other means (such as a merger application), the bank shall provide written notice to the OCC no later than ten days after it begins to engage in any of the activities specified in § 9.7(d) of this chapter in the new state. The written notice must identify the new state or states involved, identify the fiduciary activities to be conducted, and describe the extent to which the activities differ materially from the fiduciary activities that the bank was previously authorized to conduct. No notice is required if the bank is conducting only activities ancillary to its fiduciary business through a trust representative office or otherwise.

(7) Expiration of approval. Approval expires if a national bank does not commence fiduciary activities within 18 months from the date of approval.

National State Bank of Elizabeth, N.J. v. Smith

591 F.2d 223 (3d Cir. 1979)

MARIS, Circuit Judge.

This civil action was brought in the District Court for the District of New Jersey on July 29, 1976, by National State Bank of Elizabeth, N.J., (herein National State), against the Comptroller of the Currency (herein Comptroller), the Federal Home Loan Bank Board (herein Board), City Federal Savings and Loan Association (herein City Federal), City Consumer Services, Inc. (herein City Consumer) and Gilbert G. Roessner, Gerald R. Rupp, Alfred H. Hedden, David W. Matchett, Ronald J. Tell and John W. Atherton, Jr. (herein the individual defendants). The complaint sought a declaratory Judgment that the actions of the Board and the Comptroller in approving the creation of City Trust Services, N.A. (herein City Trust) were invalid as contrary to the Home Owners' Loan Act of 1933, 12 U.S.C. § 1461 *et seq.*, the National Bank Act, 12 U.S.C. § 21 *et seq.*, the Bank Holding Company Act, 12 U.S.C. § 1841 *et seq.*, the Sherman Antitrust Act, 15 U.S.C. § 1, and the Clayton Act, 15 U.S.C. § 19. The complaint also sought orders enjoining the Comptroller from issuing a certificate of authority to commence business to City Trust and enjoining City Federal, City Consumer and the individual defendants from engaging in the business of banking. . . .

The court (1) adjudged the Comptroller's actions in approving the creation of City Trust to be invalid, (2) ordered him to revoke the certificate of authority which he had issued to City Trust, and (3) dismissed as moot the claims against the other defendants. ... From the portion of the final judgment against him adjudging his approval of the creation of City Trust to be invalid and directing him to revoke the certificate of authority issued to City Trust the Comptroller appealed. . . . City Federal, City Consumer and the individual defendants likewise appealed from that part of the final judgment . . . .

The facts are not in dispute and will be briefly stated. Central to them was the creation of City Trust as a national bank which was to conduct only the business of a commercial bank trust department and which was to be a wholly-owned subsidiary of City Consumer which in turn is a wholly-owned subsidiary of City Federal. It seems clear that the intention was to operate City Trust as, in effect, a trust department of City Federal. In order to create this subsidiary City Federal, as a savings and loan association organized pursuant to the laws of the United States, had to obtain the approval of the Board as the agency in charge of regulating federal savings and loan associations. . . .

On April 14, 1975, while its application to the Board was pending, City Federal, having on April 3, 1975, requested authority for City Trust to offer fiduciary services without the customary authority of a national bank to receive deposits and make loans, made application to the Comptroller for permission to organize a national banking association to be known as City Trust Services, N.A. The application was accepted for filing on July 3, 1975. Twelve banks, including National State, together with Bankers filed objections to the application. A hearing was held on the application on October 28, 1975, by the Regional Administrator of National Banks following which, on June 28, 1976, City Federal was notified that the Comptroller had granted preliminary approval of its application to organize a national bank and exercise fiduciary powers. The approval was given subject to certain stated conditions, among them

> ". . . that Article Eighth of the Articles of Association should be adopted to read as follows:
> 'The corporate existence of the Association shall continue until terminated in accordance with the laws of the United States. The purpose of the Association shall be to carry on the general business of a commercial bank trust department

> and to engage in such activities as are necessary, incident or related to such business. This Article shall not be amended, or any other provision added elsewhere in these Articles expending the powers of the Association, without the prior approval of the Comptroller of the Currency.'"

. . . We turn then to consider the defendant- appellant's contention that the district court erred in its judgment declaring the Comptroller's approval of the creation of City Trust to be invalid and ordering him to revoke the certificate of authority which he had issued to it.

. . . [T]he Comptroller required City Trust in its articles of association and elsewhere to agree to limit its activities to the business of a commercial bank trust department and such activities as are necessary, incident or related to that business. It is this restriction upon the operations of City Trust amounting to a prohibition against its engaging in the general banking business of receiving deposits and making loans, which the district court held to invalidate the creation of City Trust, action which the defendant-appellants urge as error.

This issue was fully presented to us by the parties at the argument of the appeals on October 18, 1978, on the basis of the then existing law. On November 10, 1978, however, the Financial Institutions Regulatory and Interest Rate Control Act of 1978, Pub.L. 95-630, 92 Stat. 3641, was enacted by Congress.

Section 1504 of that Act amended the National Bank Act, Sec. 5169 R.S., 12 U.S.C. § 27, by adding thereto the following sentence:

> "A National Bank Association, to which the Comptroller of the Currency has heretofore issued or hereafter issues such certificate, is not illegally constituted solely because its operations are or have been required by the Comptroller of the Currency to be limited to those of a trust company and activities related thereto."

This new statutory provision validates retroactively as well as prospectively the action of the Comptroller in limiting to the business of a trust company the operation of a national banking association to which he has granted a certificate of authority to commence business. It seems clear, therefore, that pursuant to this statutory mandate, the Comptroller's action limiting the business of City Trust to the operations of a commercial bank trust department must now be held to be valid if the statutory phrase "trust company" may be read as limited in meaning to the trust or fiduciary operations of such a company. Unless we so read the statute, it becomes virtually meaningless since, in most states, and certainly in New Jersey where City Trust is to do business, trust companies are authorized to and ordinarily do conduct the general banking business of receiving deposits and making loans in addition to their fiduciary activities. Indeed, in New Jersey a trust company is incorporated under the banking laws and as a practical matter is actually a bank which has specially qualified itself to exercise fiduciary powers. *See* N.J.S.A. 17:9A-28. Thus, restricting to the exercise of trust company powers the operations of a national bank which has been empowered under the Act of September 28, 1962, 12 U.S.C. § 92a, to exercise also fiduciary powers would in practice often amount to no restriction at all. And this would certainly be so in the present case if, as seems logical, the powers of a New Jersey trust company are to be taken as the statutory standard in the case of a national bank authorized to operate in that state.

We assume, of course, that Congress intended its enactment to have meaningful effect. We must accordingly, if possible, construe it so as to give it such effect.

. . . We find no legislative history to assist us in this task. But we do have the background fact that Congress by the Act of September 28, 1962, 12 U.S.C. § 92a, had empowered the Comptroller by special permit to authorize a national banking association to exercise certain fiduciary powers in addition to its normal banking functions. We think that it must have been these specially permitted fiduciary powers to which Congress intended to refer when by its recent enactment it authorized the Comptroller to restrict the operations of a national bank to those of a trust company and activities related thereto. In other words, it was the fiduciary operations carried on in the trust department to which reference must have been intended. Only by being so read does the statute have full meaningful effect and we so read it. It follows that regardless of whether the district court's judgment declaring the Comptroller's action invalid and ordering him to revoke it was correct when it was entered (a question we need not now consider), the amendment made by the Act of November 10, 1978, to § 5169 R.S., 12 U.S.C. § 27, has validated the Comptroller's action and requires the reversal of the judgment of the district court on these issues.

It remains for us to consider the last clause of the judgment, which ordered the suit dismissed as moot as to all defendants other than the Comptroller. It will be recalled that the complaint also seeks a declaratory judgment that the actions of the Board were invalid in approving the creation of City Trust and its acquisition by City Federal as a sub-subsidiary and further seeks an injunction against City Federal, City Consumer and the individual defendants from engaging in the business of banking through City Trust. In this connection, violations of the Home Owners' Loan Act, the Bank Holding Company Act, the Sherman Antitrust Act, and the Clayton Act are alleged. In the light of our conclusion that under the recent statute the creation of City Trust as a national banking association and its restriction to fiduciary business must now be held to be valid, it is clear that the issues raised as to the other defendants are no longer moot. These issues, however, have not been adjudicated by the district court. While they all involve City Trust in one way or another, they raise a number of questions with respect to the application of the statutes referred to which are quite distinct from and unrelated to the issues involved in the plaintiff's claim against the Comptroller. They must, therefore, now be reinstated and remanded to the district court for trial and adjudication, . . . if the plaintiff, National State, has standing to prosecute them. Obviously, the bank has standing to sue City Federal, City Consumer and the individual defendants on its Sherman and Clayton Acts claim. The more difficult question is whether it has standing to sue the Board on its claim that the Board violated the Home Owners' Loan Act and the Bank Holding Company Act in approving the creation of City Trust and authorizing the acquisition of the institution by City Federal as a sub-subsidiary.

. . . [W]e are satisfied that a sufficient showing of prospective injury as the result of the Board's action has been made. . . . [W]hether the interests National State seeks to protect fall arguably within the zone of interests intended to be protected by the Home Owner's Loan Act, presents a more difficult question. In deciding this question we are not limited to the particular provisions of the statute allegedly violated but may look to the entire statutory scheme. . . .

The Home Owner's Loan Act of 1933 authorized the Board to provide for the organization of federal savings and loan associations to make available ". . . local mutual thrift institutions in which people may invest their funds and in order to provide for the financing of homes. . . ." 12 U.S.C. § 1464(a). The Act provides that "No charter shall be granted . . . unless the same can be established without undue injury to properly conducted existing local thrift and home-financing institutions." 12 U.S.C. § 1464(e). This provision obviously expresses the congressional concern to protect the interests of existing state institutions which compete with federal savings and loan associations. Banks with trust departments, such as National State, arguably may be included in this competing group since they frequently invest trust funds in home mortgage loans. We do not agree with what we regard as the unduly narrow view of the arguable scope of this provision of the statute which was taken in *Union National Bank of Clarksburg v. Home Loan Bank Board*, 233 F.2d 695 (1956), upon which the Board relies. The Act also authorizes federal savings and loan associations to create subsidiary service corporations. 12 U.S.C. § 1464(c). However, the general statutory scheme, as well as its legislative history, supports the view that Congress intended that the corporation in which federal savings and loan associations invest will be limited to the performance of services and functions related to the business of savings and loan associations.

Here, City Federal has sought through its subsidiary, City Consumer, to invest in City Trust, a national bank trust company which is, it is argued, not merely not limited to the performance of functions related to the savings and loan business, but is likely to be in competition for trust business with its near neighbor, National State.

In *Data Processing Services v. Camp*, 397 U.S. 150, 155-156, (1970), the Supreme Court, noting that section 4 of the Bank Service Corporation Act, 12 U.S.C. § 1864, restricts the activities of bank service corporations to the performance of bank services for banks, held that the section arguably brought within the zone of interests protected by the Act a competitor of the bank in the furnishing of data processing services to the bank's customers. Here it may reasonably be argued that 12 U.S.C. § 1464(c) restricts savings and loan services related to the savings and loan business, the limitation being arguably, *inter alia*, for the protection of institutions such as National State with which they might otherwise be in competition. We conclude that the plaintiff, National State, has standing to prosecute the present suit against the Board.

Notes and Comments 5.65. *Federal savings association trust powers.* It is unlikely that a case like *National State Bank* would arise again since the passage of the Depository Institutions Deregulation and Monetary Control Act of 1980. Under the act, savings associations were granted express statutory authority to exercise trust powers. 12 U.S.C. § 1464(n).

5.66. *Effect of FIRREA.* Under the Financial Institutions Reform, Recovery, and Enforcement Act of 1989 ("FIRREA"), Pub. L. No. 101-73, 103 Stat. 183 (1989) (codified at scattered sections of 12 U.S.C.), a federal savings association (*i.e.*, a federally chartered S&L or savings bank) may still act as a trustee, executor, administrator, guardian, or in any other fiduciary capacity in which a state bank, trust company, or other corporation that competes with federal savings associations is permitted to act under the laws of the state in which the federal savings association is located, upon the issuance of a special permit by the Director of the Office of Thrift Supervision ("DOTS"), the successor to the FHLBB. FIRREA, § 301 (codified at 12 U.S.C. § 1464(n)(1)). Subject to regulations to be promulgated by the DOTS, a service corporation subsidiary of a federal savings association may invest in federally or state chartered corporations, located in the state in which the home office of the federal savings association is located, that are engaged in trust activities. *Id.* In reviewing trust applications, the DOTS may consider the following statutory factors:

> (*i*) The amount of capital of the applicant federal savings association. (A permit may not be issued if the applicant has capital in an amount less than required by state law of state chartered banks, trust companies and corporations exercising such trust powers *Id.* (codified at 12 U.S.C. § 1464(n)(8)).)
>
> (*ii*) The sufficiency of the association's capital under the circumstances.
>
> (*iii*) The needs of the community to be served.
>
> and,
>
> (*iv*) Other facts and circumstances that the DOTS deems to be proper.

Id. (codified at 12 U.S.C. § 1464(n)(8)(A)-(D)). On surrender or revocation of trust powers, *see id.* (codified at 12 U.S.C. § 1464(n)(9), (10), respectively).

5.67. The exercise of trust powers is also statutorily defined. For national banks, provisions concerning trust powers are found in 12 U.S.C. § 92a. These provisions are implemented in the Comptroller's regulations, 12 C.F.R. pt. 9. Review section 92a and consider whether the Comptroller's regulations (excerpts from which are set forth below) properly interpret and implement that provision.

Comptroller of the Currency

12 C.F.R. pt. 9

§ 9.1 Authority, purpose, and scope.

(a) Authority. The Office of the Comptroller of the Currency (OCC) issues this part pursuant to its authority under 12 U.S.C. 24 (Seventh), 92a, and 93a, and 15 U.S.C. 78q, 78q-1, and 78w.

(b) Purpose. The purpose of this part is to set forth the standards that apply to the fiduciary activities of national banks.

(c) Scope. This part applies to all national banks that act in a fiduciary capacity, as defined in § 9.2(e). This part also applies to all Federal branches of foreign banks to the same extent as it applies to national banks.

§ 9.2 Definitions.

For the purposes of this part, the following definitions apply:

(a) Affiliate has the same meaning as in 12 U.S.C. 221a(b).

(b) Applicable law means the law of a state or other jurisdiction governing a national bank's fiduciary relationships, any applicable Federal law governing those relationships, the terms of the instrument governing a fiduciary relationship, or any court order pertaining to the relationship.

(c) Custodian under a uniform gifts to minors act means a fiduciary relationship established pursuant to a state law substantially similar to the Uniform Gifts to Minors Act or the Uniform Transfers to Minors Act as published by the American Law Institute.

(d) Fiduciary account means an account administered by a national bank acting in a fiduciary capacity.

(e) Fiduciary capacity means: trustee, executor, administrator, registrar of stocks and bonds, transfer agent, guardian, assignee, receiver, or custodian under a uniform gifts to minors act; investment adviser, if the bank receives a fee for its investment advice; any capacity in which the bank possesses investment discretion on behalf of another; or any other similar capacity that the OCC authorizes pursuant to 12 U.S.C. 92a.

(f) Fiduciary officers and employees means all officers and employees of a national bank to whom the board of directors or its designee has assigned functions involving the exercise of the bank's fiduciary powers.

(g) Fiduciary powers means the authority the OCC permits a national bank to exercise pursuant to 12 U.S.C. 92a.

(h) Guardian means the guardian or conservator, by whatever name used by state law, of the estate of a minor, an incompetent person, an absent person, or a person over whose estate a court has taken jurisdiction, other than under bankruptcy or insolvency laws.

(i) Investment discretion means, with respect to an account, the sole or shared authority (whether or not that authority is exercised) to determine what securities or other assets to purchase or sell on behalf of the account. A bank that delegates its authority over investments and a bank that receives delegated authority over investments are both deemed to have investment discretion. . . .

§ 9.3 Approval requirements.

(a) A national bank may not exercise fiduciary powers unless it obtains prior approval from the OCC to the extent required under 12 CFR 5.26. . . .

§ 9.4 Administration of fiduciary powers.

(a) Responsibilities of the board of directors. A national bank's fiduciary activities shall be managed by or under the direction of its board of directors. In discharging its responsibilities, the board may assign any function related to the exercise of fiduciary powers to any director, officer, employee, or committee thereof.

(b) Use of other personnel. The national bank may use any qualified personnel and facilities of the bank or its affiliates to perform services related to the exercise of its fiduciary powers, and any department of the bank or its affiliates may use fiduciary officers, employees, and facilities to perform services unrelated to the exercise of fiduciary powers, to the extent not prohibited by applicable law.

(c) Agency agreements. Pursuant to a written agreement, a national bank exercising fiduciary powers may perform services related to the exercise of fiduciary powers for another bank or other entity, and may purchase services related to the exercise of fiduciary powers from another bank or other entity.

(d) Bond requirement. A national bank shall ensure that all fiduciary officers and employees are adequately bonded.

§ 9.5 Policies and procedures.

A national bank exercising fiduciary powers shall adopt and follow written policies and procedures adequate to maintain its fiduciary activities in compliance with applicable law. Among other relevant matters, the policies and procedures should address, where appropriate, the bank's:

(a) Brokerage placement practices;

(b) Methods for ensuring that fiduciary officers and employees do not use material inside information in connection with any decision or recommendation to purchase or sell any security;

(c) Methods for preventing self-dealing and conflicts of interest;

(d) Selection and retention of legal counsel who is readily available to advise the bank and its fiduciary officers and employees on fiduciary matters; and

(e) Investment of funds held as fiduciary, including short-term investments and the treatment of fiduciary funds awaiting investment or distribution.

§ 9.6 Review of fiduciary accounts.

(a) Pre-acceptance review. Before accepting a fiduciary account, a national bank shall review the prospective account to determine whether it can properly administer the account.

(b) Initial post-acceptance review. Upon the acceptance of a fiduciary account for which a national bank has investment discretion, the bank shall conduct a prompt review of all assets of the account to evaluate whether they are appropriate for the account.

(c) Annual review. At least once during every calendar year, a bank shall conduct a review of all assets of each fiduciary account for which the bank has investment discretion to evaluate whether they are appropriate, individually and collectively, for the account. ...

§ 9.8 Recordkeeping.

(a) Documentation of accounts. A national bank shall adequately document the establishment and termination of each fiduciary account and shall maintain adequate records for all fiduciary accounts.

(b) Retention of records. A national bank shall retain records described in paragraph (a) of this section for a period of three years from the later of the termination of the account or the termination of any litigation relating to the account.

(c) Separation of records. A national bank shall ensure that records described in paragraph (a) of this section are separate and distinct from other records of the bank.

§ 9.9 Audit of fiduciary activities.

(a) Annual audit. At least once during each calendar year, a national bank shall arrange for a suitable audit (by internal or external auditors) of all significant fiduciary activities, under the direction of its fiduciary audit committee, unless the bank adopts a continuous audit system in accordance with paragraph (b) of this section. The bank shall note the results of the audit (including significant actions taken as a result of the audit) in the minutes of the board of directors.

(b) Continuous audit. In lieu of performing annual audits under paragraph (a) of this section, a national bank may adopt a continuous audit system under which the bank arranges for a discrete audit (by internal or external auditors) of each significant fiduciary activity (i.e., on an activity-by-activity basis), under the direction of its fiduciary audit committee, at an interval commensurate with the nature and risk of that activity. Thus, certain fiduciary activities may receive audits at intervals greater or less than one year, as appropriate. A bank that adopts a continuous audit system shall note the results of all discrete audits performed since the last audit report (including significant actions taken as a result of the audits) in the minutes of the board of directors at least once during each calendar year.

(c) Fiduciary audit committee. A national bank's fiduciary audit committee must consist of a committee of the bank's directors or an audit committee of an affiliate of the bank. However, in either case, the committee:

(1) Must not include any officers of the bank or an affiliate who participate significantly in the administration of the bank's fiduciary activities; and

(2) Must consist of a majority of members who are not also members of any committee to which the board of directors has delegated power to manage and control the fiduciary activities of the bank.

§ 9.10 Fiduciary funds awaiting investment or distribution.

(a) In general. With respect to a fiduciary account for which a national bank has investment discretion or discretion over distributions, the bank may not allow funds awaiting investment or distribution to remain uninvested and undistributed any longer than is reasonable for the proper management of the account and consistent with applicable law. With respect to a fiduciary account for which a national bank has investment discretion, the bank shall obtain for funds awaiting investment or distribution a rate of return that is consistent with applicable law.

(b) Self-deposits–

(1) In general. A national bank may deposit funds of a fiduciary account that are awaiting investment or distribution in the commercial, savings, or another department of the bank, unless prohibited by applicable law. To the extent that the funds are not insured by the Federal Deposit Insurance Corporation, the bank shall set aside collateral as security, under the control of appropriate fiduciary officers and employees, in accordance with paragraph (b)(2) of this section. The market value of the collateral set aside must at all times equal or

exceed the amount of the uninsured fiduciary funds.

(2) Acceptable collateral. A national bank may satisfy the collateral requirement of paragraph (b)(1) of this section with any of the following:

(i) Direct obligations of the United States, or other obligations fully guaranteed by the United States as to principal and interest;

(ii) Securities that qualify as eligible for investment by national banks pursuant to 12 CFR part 1;

(iii) Readily marketable securities of the classes in which state banks, trust companies, or other corporations exercising fiduciary powers are permitted to invest fiduciary funds under applicable state law;

(iv) Surety bonds, to the extent they provide adequate security, unless prohibited by applicable law; and

(v) Any other assets that qualify under applicable state law as appropriate security for deposits of fiduciary funds.

(c) Affiliate deposits. A national bank, acting in its fiduciary capacity, may deposit funds of a fiduciary account that are awaiting investment or distribution with an affiliated insured depository institution, unless prohibited by applicable law. A national bank may set aside collateral as security for a deposit by or with an affiliate of fiduciary funds awaiting investment or distribution, unless prohibited by applicable law.

§ 9.11 Investment of fiduciary funds.

A national bank shall invest funds of a fiduciary account in a manner consistent with applicable law.

§ 9.12 Self-dealing and conflicts of interest.

(a) Investments for fiduciary accounts–

(1) In general. Unless authorized by applicable law, a national bank may not invest funds of a fiduciary account for which a national bank has investment discretion in the stock or obligations of, or in assets acquired from: the bank or any of its directors, officers, or employees; affiliates of the bank or any of their directors, officers, or employees; or individuals or organizations with whom there exists an interest that might affect the exercise of the best judgment of the bank.

(2) Additional securities investments. If retention of stock or obligations of the bank or its affiliates in a fiduciary account is consistent with applicable law, the bank may:

(i) Exercise rights to purchase additional stock (or securities convertible into additional stock) when offered pro rata to stockholders; and

(ii) Purchase fractional shares to complement fractional shares acquired through the exercise of rights or the receipt of a stock dividend resulting in fractional share holdings.

(b) Loans, sales, or other transfers from fiduciary accounts–

(1) In general. A national bank may not lend, sell, or otherwise transfer assets of a fiduciary account for which a national bank has investment discretion to the bank or any of its directors, officers, or employees, or to affiliates of the bank or any of their directors, officers, or employees, or to individuals or organizations with whom there exists an interest that might affect the exercise of the best judgment of the bank, unless:

(i) The transaction is authorized by applicable law;

(ii) Legal counsel advises the bank in writing that the bank has incurred, in its fiduciary capacity, a contingent or potential liability, in which case the bank, upon the sale or transfer of assets, shall reimburse the fiduciary account in cash at the greater of book or market value of the assets;

(iii) As provided in § 9.18(b)(8)(iii) for defaulted investments; or

(iv) Required in writing by the OCC.

(2) Loans of funds held as trustee. Notwithstanding paragraph (b)(1) of this section, a national bank may not lend to any of its directors, officers, or employees any funds held in trust, except with respect to employee benefit plans in accordance with the exemptions found in section 408 of the Employee Retirement Income Security Act of 1974 (29 U.S.C. 1108).

(c) Loans to fiduciary accounts. A national bank may make a loan to a fiduciary account and may hold a security interest in assets of the account if the transaction is fair to the account and is not prohibited by applicable law.

(d) Sales between fiduciary accounts. A national bank may sell assets between any of its fiduciary accounts if the transaction is fair to both accounts and is not prohibited by applicable law.

(e) Loans between fiduciary accounts. A national bank may make a loan between any of its fiduciary accounts if the transaction is fair to both accounts and is not prohibited by applicable law.

§ 9.13 Custody of fiduciary assets.

(a) Control of fiduciary assets. A national bank shall place assets of fiduciary accounts in the joint custody or control of not fewer than two of the fiduciary officers or employees designated for that purpose by the board of directors. A national bank may maintain the investments of a fiduciary account off-premises, if consistent with applicable law and if the bank maintains adequate safeguards and controls.

(b) Separation of fiduciary assets. A national bank shall keep the assets of fiduciary accounts separate from the assets of the bank. A national bank shall keep the assets of each fiduciary account separate from all other accounts or shall identify the investments as the property of a particular account, except as provided in § 9.18.

§ 9.14 Deposit of securities with state authorities.

(a) In general. If state law requires corporations acting in a fiduciary capacity to deposit securities with state authorities for the protection of private or court trusts, then before a national bank acts as a private or court-appointed trustee in that state, it shall make a similar deposit with state authorities. If the state authorities refuse to accept the deposit, the bank shall deposit the securities with the Federal Reserve Bank of the district in which the national bank is located, to be held for the protection of private or court trusts to the same extent as if the securities had been deposited with state authorities. . . .

§ 9.15 Fiduciary compensation.

(a) Compensation of bank. If the amount of a national bank's compensation for acting in a fiduciary capacity is not set or governed by applicable law, the bank may charge a reasonable fee for its services.

(b) Compensation of co-fiduciary officers and employees. A national bank may not permit any officer or employee to retain any compensation for acting as a co-fiduciary with the bank in the administration of a fiduciary account, except with the specific approval of the bank's board of directors.

§ 9.17 Surrender or revocation of fiduciary powers.

(a) Surrender. In accordance with 12 U.S.C. 92a(j), a national bank seeking to surrender its fiduciary powers shall file with the OCC a certified copy of the resolution of its board of directors evidencing that intent. If, after appropriate investigation, the OCC is satisfied that the bank has been discharged from all fiduciary duties, the OCC will provide written notice that the bank is no longer authorized to exercise fiduciary powers.

(b) Revocation. If the OCC determines that a national bank has unlawfully or unsoundly exercised, or has failed for a period of five consecutive years to exercise its fiduciary powers, the Comptroller may, in accordance with the provisions of 12 U.S.C. 92a(k), revoke the bank's fiduciary powers.

Notes and Comments 5.68. In addition to the generally applicable rules governing the basic activities of trust management, Part 9 also includes provisions concerning the "collective investment" of trust assets. See 12 C.F.R. § 9.18. However, management of collective investments by a national bank raises the issue of whether or not the bank would thereby be engaged in securities activities prohibited by certain provisions of the Glass-Steagall Act.[62]

5.69. Quarter National Bank (QNB) is planning to apply for trust powers. It is beginning to make preparations for the organization of a trust department within the bank. Since the department will likely be buying, selling and holding securities for its trust accounts, it is considering using Forth Securities, a local securities broker, to handle all of these transactions. What procedures must QNB establish concerning its dealings with the broker?

5.70. Would it make any difference if Forth Securities were substantially owned by Hiram Forth, Jr., the son of the chairman of the board of QNB and himself a member of the board?

5.71. At present, QNB does not have anyone on its banking staff or in its general counsel's office with background or experience with respect to running a trust department. Could QNB enter into a contract with a local investment advisory firm to manage the trust accounts? The firm has indicated that it could market QNB's trust services nationwide, signing up trust accounts at an estimated average rate of $50,000 a day for the first year of operation. On delegations of authority from the trustee bank, see OCC Trust Interpretation No. 168, Aug. 3, 1988, *reprinted in* [1988-1989 Transfer Binder] Fed. Banking L. Rep. (CCH) ¶ 84,935 (Sept. 30, 1988); OCC Trust Interpretation No.169, Aug. 5, 1988, *reprinted in* [1988-1989 Transfer Binder] Fed. Banking L. Rep. (CCH) § 84,936 (Sept. 30, 1988); OCC Trust Interpretation No. 176, Sept. 14, 1988, *reprinted in* [1988-1989 Transfer Binder] Fed Banking L. Rep. (CCH) § 84,943 (Nov. 11, 1988).

5.72. If it does decide to manage the trust department internally, could QNB achieve certain economies of scale by simply assigning additional trust department duties to the personnel of the commercial loan department? These individuals have sophisticated business experience, and the audit and recordkeeping units of the commercial loan department could also efficiently handle all such functions for the trust department. On the dangers of this practice under federal securities law with respect to "insider trading" in securities, see Malloy, *Can 10b-5 for the Banks? The Effect of an Antifraud Rule on the Regulation of Banks*, 61 FORDHAM L. REV. S23 (Survey Issue 1993), *reprinted in* 8 BANKING L. ANTH. 257 (1994).

5.73. QNB board members are somewhat concerned about the amount of capital the bank currently maintains, given the likely expansion of its business resulting from the operation of a trust department. Could QNB invest trust funds in its own securities? For administrative interpretations involving financial benefits to a trustee bank from trust department investments and transactions, see, *e.g.*, OCC Trust Interpretation No. 195, Jan. 13, 1989, *reprinted in* [1988-1989 Transfer Binder] Fed. Banking L. Rep. (CCH) § 84,962 (February 24, 1989).

---

62. *See, e.g.*, 12 U.S.C. § 24 (Seventh).

5.74. We have seen the rules that apply when a national bank wishes to engage in trust services. What if a national bank wanted to operate trust services on an *interstate* basis? This possibility raises a number of technical issues:

> **a.** Is a national bank permitted to operate an interstate trust service?
>
> **b.** If it can do so, do the laws of the bank's home office govern those operations? The laws of the state where the interstate trust services are offered? The laws of both states?
>
> **c.** Must the bank submit a new application for trust services for every new state it enters?
>
> **d.** Is such an interstate trust service operation a "branch" for purposes of 12 U.S.C. § 36, thus requiring a branch application?

In July 2001, the Office of the Comptroller of the Currency (OCC) published a final rule, effective 1 August 2001, regarding the authority and standards for national banks to conduct multistate trust operations. The amendments were intended to provide specfic guidance to national banks engaging in fiduciary activities. What answers do the amendments offer to the questions posed above?

Excerpts from 66 Fed. Reg. 34,792 (2001)
Office of the Comptroller of the Currency
12 C.F.R. Parts 5 and 9
Fiduciary Activities of National Banks

PART 5--RULES, POLICIES, AND PROCEDURES FOR CORPORATE ACTIVITIES

. . .

2. Paragraph (e)(5) of § 5.26 is revised to read as follows:

§ 5.26 Fiduciary powers.

* * * * *

(e) * * *

(5) Notice of fiduciary activities in additional states. No further application under this section is required when a national bank with existing OCC approval to exercise fiduciary powers plans to engage in any of the activities specified in § 9.7(d) of this chapter or to conduct activities ancillary to its fiduciary business, in a state in addition to the state described in the application for fiduciary powers that the OCC has approved. Instead, unless the bank provides notice through other means (such as a merger application), the bank shall provide written notice to the OCC no later than ten days after it begins to engage in any of the activities specified in § 9.7(d) of this chapter in the new state. The written notice must identify the new state or states involved, identify the fiduciary activities to be conducted, and describe the extent to which the activities differ materially from the fiduciary activities that the bank was previously authorized to conduct. No notice is required if the bank is conducting only activities ancillary to its fiduciary business through a trust representative office or otherwise.

PART 9--FIDUCIARY ACTIVITIES OF NATIONAL BANKS

. . .

2. § 9.2 is amended by removing the second sentence in paragraph (g) and adding new paragraphs (j) and (k) as follows:

§ 9.2 Definitions.

* * * * *

(j) Trust office means an office of a national bank, other than a main office or a branch, at which the bank engages in one or more of the activities specified in § 9.7(d). Pursuant to 12 U.S.C. 36(j), a trust office is not a "branch" for purposes of 12 U.S.C. 36, unless it is also an office at which deposits are received, or checks paid, or money lent.

(k) Trust representative office means an office of a national bank, other than a main office, branch, or trust office, at which the bank performs activities ancillary to its fiduciary business, but does not engage in any of the activities specified in § 9.7(d). Examples of ancillary activities include advertising, marketing, and soliciting for fiduciary business; contacting existing or potential customers, answering questions, and providing information about matters related to their accounts; acting as a liaison between the trust office and the customer (e.g., forwarding requests for distribution or changes in investment objectives, or forwarding forms and funds received from the customer); inspecting or maintaining custody of fiduciary assets or holding title to real property. This list is illustrative and not comprehensive. Other activities may also be "ancillary activities" for the purposes of this definition. Pursuant to 12 U.S.C. 36(j), a trust representative office is not a "branch" for purposes of 12 U.S.C. 36, unless it is also an office at which deposits are received, or checks paid, or money lent.

3. § 9.3 is amended by revising paragraph (b) and adding paragraph (c) to read as follows:

§ 9.3 Approval requirements.

* * * * *

(b) A national bank that has obtained the OCC's approval to exercise fiduciary powers is not required to obtain the OCC's prior approval to engage in any of the activities specified in § 9.7(d) in a new state or to conduct, in a new state, activities that are ancillary to its fiduciary business. Instead, the national bank must follow the notice procedures prescribed by 12 CFR 5.26(e).

(c) A person seeking approval to organize a special-purpose national bank limited to fiduciary powers shall file an application with the OCC pursuant to 12 CFR 5.20.

4. A new § 9.7 is added to read as follows:

§ 9.7 Multi-state fiduciary operations.

(a) Acting in a fiduciary capacity in more than one state. Pursuant to 12 U.S.C. 92a and this section, a national bank may act in a fiduciary capacity in any state. If a national bank acts, or proposes to act, in a fiduciary capacity in a particular state, the bank may act in the following specific capacities:

(1) Any of the eight fiduciary capacities expressly listed in 12 U.S.C. 92a(a), unless the state prohibits its own state banks, trust companies, and other corporations that compete with national banks in that state from acting in that capacity; and

(2) Any other fiduciary capacity the state permits for its own state banks, trust companies, or other corporations that compete with national banks in that state.

(b) Serving customers in other states. While acting in a fiduciary capacity in one state, a national bank may market its fiduciary services to, and act as fiduciary for, customers located in any state, and it may act as fiduciary for relationships that include property located in other states. The bank may use a trust representative office for this purpose.

(c) Offices in more than one state. A national bank with fiduciary powers may establish trust offices or trust representative offices in any state.

(d) Determination of the state referred to in 12 U.S.C. 92a. For each fiduciary relationship, the state referred to in section 92a is the state in which the bank acts in a fiduciary capacity for that relationship. A national bank acts in a fiduciary capacity in the state in which it accepts the fiduciary appointment, executes the documents that create the fiduciary relationship, and makes discretionary decisions regarding the investment or distribution of fiduciary assets. If these activities take place in more than one state, then the state in which the bank acts in a fiduciary capacity for section 92a purposes is the state that the bank designates from among those states.

(e) Application of state law. (1) State laws used in section 92a. The state laws that apply to a national bank's fiduciary activities by virtue of 12 U.S.C. 92a are the laws of the state in which the bank acts in a fiduciary capacity.

(2) Other state laws. Except for the state laws made applicable to national banks by virtue

of 12 U.S.C. 92a, state laws limiting or establishing preconditions on the exercise of fiduciary powers are not applicable to national banks.

5. Section 9.14(b) is revised to read as follows:

§ 9.14 Deposit of securities with state authorities

* * * * *

(b) Acting in a fiduciary capacity in more than one state. If a national bank acts in a fiduciary capacity in more than one state, the bank may compute the amount of securities that are required to be deposited for each state on the basis of the amount of assets for which the bank is acting in a fiduciary capacity at offices located in that state. If state law requires a deposit of securities on a basis other than assets (e.g., a requirement to deposit a fixed amount or an amount equal to a percentage of capital), the bank may compute the amount of deposit required in that state on a pro-rated basis, according to the proportion of fiduciary assets for which the bank is acting in a fiduciary capacity at offices located in that state.

5.75. Could QNB invest trust funds in its own long-term certificates of deposit? What if it limited this practice to situations in which trust property has been sold and the proceeds of the sale are being held by the trust department in trust accounts? Consider the following case.

Humane Society of Austin and Travis County v. Austin National Bank

531 S.W.2d 574 (Tex. 1975), *cert. denied*, 425 U.S. 976 (1976)

DOUGHTY, Justice.

This is a case in which petitioner, the Humane Society of Austin and Travis County, is challenging commissions and attorneys' fees claimed by Austin National Bank as dependent executor of the estate of Mary Mayfield Gutsch, deceased. The probate court allowed the claims as submitted and disallowed all offsets claimed by the Humane Society, and the Court of Civil Appeals affirmed. . . .

[T]he Humane Society contends that the Bank was guilty of self-dealing in investing the estate's funds in its own certificates of deposit pending distribution of those funds. [It also] contends that the Bank incurred unnecessary expenses for maintenance and storage of property in the estate. [It] contends that the Bank is not entitled to claim attorneys' fees incurred in a prior suit seeking a construction of decedent's will because the work performed by the attorneys was of no benefit to the estate. We overrule all points of error and affirm the judgment of the Court of Civil Appeals.

Mary Mayfield Gutsch died on October 19, 1971, in Travis County, Texas, leaving a holographic will in which Austin National Bank was named executor. The will was probated in Travis County on November 1, 1971, and the Bank qualified as dependent executor. The Bank instituted suit seeking a declaratory judgment to determine the rights of the named beneficiaries under the will. The outcome of that suit was finally determined by this Court in our decision of December 13, 1973, *City of Austin v. Austin National Bank*, Tex., 503 S.W.2d 759. As it was finally construed, the will devised to a godchild all tangible personal property found in Mrs. Gutsch's house at her death; the house and the land upon which it was located was devised to the City of Austin to be used as a public park; and the remainder of the estate (approximately two-thirds) was devised to the Humane Society in fee.

On September 11, 1972, the Bank made an application to the probate court, joined by the Humane Society, to sell certain bank and other stock of the estate and re-invest the funds in other securities yielding a better return, pending the outcome of the will construction suit. On September 15, 1972, the probate court entered an order authorizing such sale and listing the types of securities in which the Bank could re-invest the proceeds, including certificates of deposit in banks and savings and loan institutions. Pursuant to this order the Bank sold the estate's stock and, in September and November of 1972, purchased certificates of deposit from its own commercial department with the proceeds. These certificates, in the total amount of $883,000.00, were renewed from time to time over the succeeding sixteen months.

The Humane Society contends that under the common law of trusts and the provisions of the Texas Trust Act, the Texas Banking Code, and the regulations of the Federal Comptroller of Currency, the Bank was absolutely prohibited from investing funds of the estate with itself. For this alleged breach of the Bank's fiduciary duty the Humane Society seeks to deny the bank its commission as executor and to recover any profits made by the bank from use of the money invested in the certificates of deposit.

First, it is clear that the Texas Trust Act, Tex. Rev. Civ. Stat. Ann. articles 7425b--1 through 7425b--47, is not applicable here. Article 7425b--2 states that a 'trust' for purposes of the Act 'means an express trust only, . . .' In *City of Austin v. Austin National Bank*, . . . we held that Mrs. Gutsch's will did not create a perpetual charitable trust, but vested the residuary estate in the Humane Society in fee. Even though the estate's funds were held by the Bank in a fiduciary capacity for the benefit of the Humane Society as beneficiary of the estate, the duties of the Bank arose by reason of its position as executor of the estate, not as trustee of any express trust created by the will. An express devise of property to another as trustee for named beneficiaries is required for creation of an express trust. . . . Moreover, the trustee of an express trust is given authority, absent limiting provisions in the instrument creating the trust, to exchange and invest property of the trust, article 7425b-25; a dependent executor of an estate has no such power absent an authorization from the probate court or an express grant of authority from testator. . . .

Even though the Texas Trust Act is not applicable, the executor of an estate is held to the same fiduciary standards in his administration of the estate as a trustee. Section 37 of the Probate Code provides, in part, that the executor 'shall recover possession of and hold such estate in trust to be disposed of in accordance with law.' As trustee of the property of the estate, the executor is subject to the high fiduciary standards applicable to all trustees. In *Slay v. Burnett Trust*, 143 Tex. 621, 187 S.W.2d 377 (1945), this Court quoted with approval the following excerpt from *Magruder v. Drury*, 235 U.S. 106, 119 (1914):

> 'It is a well-settled rule that a trustee can make no profit out of his trust. The rule in such cases springs from his duty to protect the interests of the estate, and not to permit his personal interest to in any wise conflict with his duty in that respect. The intention is to provide against any possible selfish interest exercising an influence which can interfere with the faithful discharge of the duty which is owing in a fiduciary capacity.'

By purchasing its own certificates of deposit with funds of the Gutsch estate which it held in trust as executor, the Bank in effect borrowed the funds for its own use. Austin National Bank contends that it was expressly authorized to invest the estate's funds in its own certificates of deposit by the provisions of 12 U.S.C. § 92a (Supp.1975), and Tex. Rev. Civ. Stat. Ann. art. 342--604 (1973). 12 U.S.C. § 92a provides that the Comptroller of the Currency shall be authorized to grant to national banks the power to act as executor of estates to the same extent that state banks are permitted such power. The statute requires national banks to segregate all assets held in a fiduciary capacity, and provides that

> . . . funds deposited or held in trust by the bank awaiting investment shall be carried in a separate account and shall not be used by the bank in the conduct of its business unless it shall first set aside in the trust department United States bonds or other securities approved by the Comptroller of the Currency.

12 U.S.C. § 92a(d).

The Comptroller of the Currency has issued regulations pursuant to section 92a granting to national banks power to act as executor coextensive with the authority of state banks. . . . Thus federal law allows a national bank to deposit trust funds with itself when such funds are 'awaiting investment,' provided that (1) it sets aside in its trust department approved securities equal in face value to the amount of the fund, and (2) local law authorizes such a deposit.

Article 342-604 of the Texas Banking Code provides:

> Unless the trust instrument provides otherwise, funds received in trust by a state bank awaiting investment shall be carried in a separate account and shall not be used by the bank in the conduct of its business, unless it shall first set aside in the trust department United States government bonds or other securities eligible under the laws of this State for the investment of funds by guardians or trustees of a market value equivalent to the amount so used. . . .

'(F)unds received in trust' within the meaning of this statute includes funds received by a bank as executor. Under these state and federal statutes, a bank may temporarily deposit with itself funds of an estate 'awaiting investment' provided it sets aside adequate security. It is undisputed that Austin National Bank complied with the security requirement by setting aside in its trust department qualified securities equal in value to the certificates of deposit. The question to be decided, therefore, is whether the funds used to purchase the certificates of deposit were 'awaiting investment' within the meaning of Article 342--604 and the corresponding federal law.

[The court quoted the then current version of 12 C.F.R. § 9.10.]

It is apparent from this regulation that the Comptroller has interpreted the term 'awaiting investment' in § 92a to mean 'awaiting investment or distribution.' The Comptroller's broad interpretation of § 92a comports with the interpretation of Article 342-604 urged by the Bank in this case.

In *American Legion Post No. 90 of Village of Mamaroneck v. First National Bank and Trust Co. of Mamaroneck*, 113 F.2d 868 (2nd Cir. 1940), the Court construed the term 'awaiting investment' in the statute from which § 92a was derived, 12 U.S.C. § 248(k). In that case some investors had placed proceeds from the sale of land with the bank pending their distribution to the investors. Because of litigation concerning the proper allocation of taxes arising from the sale, the proceeds remained in the bank's trust department for several years, during which time the bank paid three percent interest on the funds. The bank had set aside securities to secure the trust fund as required by § 248(k) and the corresponding regulations. When the bank became insolvent the investors attempted to claim their lien on the securities so set aside, and the general creditors of the bank challenged the lien, contending that the funds were not 'awaiting investment' within the meaning of § 248(k). The Court agreed with the investors, stating, at page 872:

> Perhaps more serious is the further claim that these were not funds held in trust 'awaiting investment' and hence without the statute. We think, however, that this is too narrow a construction of the statute, and really defeats its intent. If trust funds held for investment are subject to the statute, but trust funds held for

> distribution are only general assets of the bank, then we find a serious difference in result following from a very slight, even formalistic, change in the relations of the parties. It would be no great stretch to term this a fund held 'for investment,' particularly since the desire of the subscribers for some increment on their funds was made so clear. . . .

We agree with the construction placed upon § 92a by the Court of Appeals for the Second Circuit and by the Comptroller, and we believe that the same interpretation should be placed upon article 342--604 of the Banking Code. The Gutsch estate's funds were held by the Bank in its fiduciary capacity as executor of the estate, and the Bank was required to keep the funds segregated from its general assets. The Bank held the funds temporarily, pending the outcome of litigation which would determine whether it would place them in a charitable trust or distribute them to the beneficiaries. We hold that these were funds 'awaiting investment' within the meaning of article 342--604 and 12 U.S.C. § 92a, and that the Bank was thereby authorized to invest the funds in its own certificates of deposit pending final determination of their proper dispersal. This interpretation most fully effectuates the purpose of the statute to allow efficient temporary investment of funds held in trust by a bank pending their ultimate disposition, while providing maximum security for those funds.

Notes and Comments 5.76. The substantive law governing trusts and the fiduciary duties of trustees is state law. A national bank is authorized to exercise trust powers only to the extent not inconsistent with "local law." To what does "local law" refer in this context? To what extent can an individual state control the provision of trust services within its borders? One court has noted:

> Undoubtedly, [each state] has a legitimate interest in assuring that corporate fiduciaries serve the public faithfully. Laws prescribing the fiduciaries' financial resources, governing their conduct, and defining their responsibilities are appropriate means of controlling trust companies. The difficulty with the state's argument is that the challenged statutes do not bear a fair and substantial relation to the objectives that the state seeks.

American Trust Company, Inc. v. South Carolina State Board of Bank Control, 381 F. Supp. 313, 320 (D.S.C. 1974). In light of these interests, could a state bar the provision of trust services by out-of-state trust companies? By in-state trust companies controlled by out-of-state holding companies? Consider the following excerpts from *American Trust Company, Inc.*

American Trust Company, Inc. v. South Carolina State Board of Bank Control

381 F.Supp. 313 (D.S.C. 1974)

BUTZNER, Circuit Judge.

The NCNB Corporation, a North Carolina bank holding company, and two of its wholly owned subsidiaries, North Carolina National Bank and American Trust Company, Inc., brought this action against the South Carolina State Board of Bank Control and various state officials for a declaration that South Carolina Code 8-580, and portions of 19-592 and 67-53(a)(3) and (4) (1972 Supp.) are unconstitutional and for an injunction restraining their enforcement. . . .

After deferring decision of a motion for summary judgment, the court tried the case on a full evidentiary record. We hold that the second paragraph of 19-592, which prohibits a foreign controlled domestic corporation from serving as an executor and administrator in the state, violates the equal protection clause of the 14th amendment.[1] Similarly, we hold unconstitutional under the equal protection clause those portions of 67-53(a)(3) and (4), which bar South Carolina domestic corporations from serving as testamentary trustees because they are controlled by corporations domiciled or licensed in states contiguous to South Carolina.[2] However, we conclude that 67-53(a)(4) does not violate the due process

---

1.

19-592. Foreign corporation or officer, etc., thereof, or person controlled by such corporation, not to act as representative.–No corporation created by another state of the United States or by any foreign state, kingdom or government, and no corporation created under the laws of the United States and not having a business in this State shall be eligible or entitled to qualify or serve in this State as executor or administrator of the estate of any person domiciled in this State at the time of his death, whether the decedent shall die testate or intestate. No officer, employee, or agent of such foreign corporation shall be eligible to serve as executor or administrator in this State, whether the officer, employee, or agent is a resident or a non-resident of this State, if such officer, employee, or agent is acting as executor or administrator on behalf of such corporation.

No corporation, partnership or organization controlled, directly or indirectly, by such a foreign corporation shall be eligible or entitled to serve as executor or administrator in this State.

The 1972 amendment added the second paragraph.

2.

67-53. Foreign corporation, etc., or non-resident as trustee.–(a) No corporation created by another state of the United States or by any foreign state, kingdom, or government, and no corporation created under the laws of the United States and not having a place of business in the State of South Carolina shall be eligible or entitled to qualify, serve, or hold title to property in this State as testamentary trustee of an estate of any person domiciled in this State at the time of his death, whether the decedent shall die testate or intestate, except, however, such foreign corporations may act as testamentary trustee in this State if:

(1) It has a bona fide capital of at least two hundred fifty thousand dollars actually paid in;

(2) It is authorized to act as testamentary trustee in the state in which it is incorporated or if such foreign corporation be a national banking association in the state in which it has its principal place of business; and

(3) Any bank or other corporation organized under the laws of this State or a national banking association having its principal place of business in this State is permitted by law to act as testamentary trustee in the state in which such foreign corporation seeking to act in this State is organized or in which it has its principal place of business if it is a national banking association without further showing or qualification other than that it is authorized to act in such fiduciary capacity in this State and upon compliance with the laws of such other state, if any, concerning service of process on nonresident fiduciaries. . . . No officer, employee or agent of any such foreign corporation shall be eligible or entitled to serve as testamentary trustee in this State whether such officer, employee, or agent is a resident or a nonresident of this State if such officer, employee, or agent is acting as testamentary trustee on behalf of such foreign corporation except when such foreign corporation itself shall be eligible to so serve.

No corporation, partnership or other organization controlled, directly or indirectly, by such a foreign corporation shall be eligible or entitled to serve as testamentary trustee in this State, except when such foreign corporation itself shall be eligible to so serve.

(4) Such foreign corporation is not domiciled or licensed to do business in a state contiguous to the State of South Carolina.

The 1970 amendment added subdivision (4). The 1972 amendment added the second paragraph of subdivision (3).

clause or the commerce clause by excluding North Carolina National from serving as a testamentary trustee of estates of South Carolina decedents. Finally, we hold constitutional 8-580, which, with certain exceptions, requires the State Board's approval for conducting a trust business.[3]

NCNB Corporation is organized under the laws of North Carolina as a bank holding company within the meaning of the Bank Holding Company Act. 12 U.S.C. 1841 *et seq.* (1970). It owns all of the stock, except the directors' qualifying shares of North Carolina National Bank, which is organized under the laws of the United States and maintains its principal offices in Charlotte, North Carolina. In addition to being one of the largest commercial banks in the southeastern part of the country, North Carolina National operates an extensive trust department. Its customers include a number of residents of South Carolina, who, in conformity with South Carolina law in effect at the time, named North Carolina National as their testamentary trustee. However, in 1970, South Carolina excluded otherwise qualified corporations that are domiciled or licensed in North Carolina or Georgia from serving as testamentary trustees of estates of South Carolina decedents.

NCNB Corporation then formed a South Carolina corporation, American Trust Company, to transact trust business in South Carolina. Before NCNB could launch its proposal to provide trust services in South Carolina through American Trust, it was required by federal law to obtain the approval of the Board of Governors of the Federal Reserve System. Despite opposition from South Carolina banking interests, the Board of Governors concluded that it would be in the public interest for NCNB to engage in the trust business in South Carolina through its subsidiary, American Trust.[6] The Board, however, was unable

---

3.

> 8-580. Written approval from State Board of Bank Control required; exceptions.-- No corporation, partnership or other person shall conduct a trust business in this State without first making a written application to the State Board of Bank Control and receiving written approval from the Board. Before any such application shall be approved, the Board shall make an investigation to determine whether or not the applicant has complied with all the provisions of law, whether in the judgment of the Board the applicant is qualified to conduct such a business and whether the conduct of such a business would serve the public interest, taking into consideration local circumstances and conditions at the place where such applicant proposes to do business; provided, however, that any person actively engaged in conducting a trust business in this State on January 1, 1972, shall not be required to make the application and receive the approval provided for herein. Provided, further, that nothing contained in this section shall prevent a natural person or a national banking association having its principal place of business in this State from qualifying and acting as trustee, executor, administrator, guardian, committee or in any other fiduciary capacity.

This section was enacted in 1972.

6. The Board stated in part:

> Further, the Board questions the characterization of the entry of additional competitors into South Carolina trust markets as undesirable. The record in this matter discloses sufficient evidence for the Board to conclude reasonably that corporate-held personal trust assets are highly concentrated in the hands of the three largest South Carolina banks. The entry of NCNB into South Carolina may serve to reduce this concentration by the introduction of an additional alternative source for personal trust services; this would constitute, in the Board's view, a substantial public benefit.
>
> . . . The Board considers as wholly speculative allegations contained in the record that the proposal will lead to undue concentration of economic resources or will result in decreased or unfair competition.

Statement by Board of Governors of the Federal Reserve System Regarding Proposal by NCNB Corporation to Operate A Trust Company in South Carolina through American Trust Company at 3, to give its unqualified approval because, while NCNB's application was pending American Trust was prohibited by newly enacted laws from serving as an executor, administrator, or testamentary trustee. Accordingly, the Board approved NCNB's request to the extent permitted by South Carolina law. This litigation was then instituted to test the constitutionality of South Carolina's restrictive statutes.

At the outset it may be well to clarify the scope of the attack on South Carolina's statutes. The plaintiffs do not question the power of South Carolina to prohibit foreign corporations from serving as executors or administrators of the estates of South Carolina decedents. Nor do they challenge any South Carolina statutes governing the conduct of fiduciaries and prescribing their duties. The plaintiff's attack is directed against those portions of South Carolina statutes that (I) bar foreign controlled domestic corporations from serving as executors, administrators (19-592) and testamentary trustees (67-53(a)(3) and (4)); (II) exclude corporations domiciled or licensed in contiguous states, *i.e.*, North Carolina and Georgia, from serving as testamentary trustees (67-53(a)(4)); and (III) require approval of the State Board to engage in the trust business (8-580). . . .

American Trust principally relies on the equal protection clause in attacking 19-592 and 67-53(a)(3) and (4) which prohibit it, as a domestic corporation, from serving as executor, administrator, or testamentary trustee because it is controlled by a North Carolina corporation.[8] It charges that the classification of domestic corporations by the domicile of their corporate owners is irrelevant to any constitutionally permissible exercise of South Carolina's police powers. South Carolina asserts that the prohibition of foreign controlled domestic trust companies assures local control over fiduciaries and prevents destructive competition to native controlled corporations for the ultimate benefit of the public. The state emphasizes that South Carolina's estates and trusts should be administered by persons trained in South Carolina law, that trust companies should serve small as well as large accounts, and that it is to the advantage of South Carolina's economy to retain within the state both commercial and trust deposits. All of these objectives, the state contends, will be impaired by the operation of foreign controlled domestic trust companies.

We start by accepting three of the state's propositions: the classification of domestic trust companies according to the domicile of their corporate owners is not inherently suspect, and the state, therefore, need not justify the classification by proving a compelling state interest; the trust business, like banking, is subject to pervasive state control; and the statutes are presumptively constitutional. . . .

No similar case dealing with the application of the equal protection clause to a trust company has been called to our attention, but we perceive no reason for exempting this type of business. . . . Moreover, several courts have held that the classification of domestic corporations according to the residence or domicile of their controlling stockholders bears no relation to the legitimate objective of state control over companies engaged in various aspects of financing. Consequently, courts dealing with the problem have ruled that classification by domicile of the owners is a form of invidious discrimination that violates the equal protection clause. *Mid-Penn National Mtge. Co. v. Hughes*, 258 A.2d 291 (Del.Super.Ct. 1969), *aff'd per curiam*, 268 A.2d 876 (Del.Sup.1970) (mortgage company); *Oxford Consumer Discount Co. v. Stefanelli*, 102 N.J.Super. 549, 246 A.2d 460 (1968), *aff'd per curiam*, 55 N.J. 489, 262 A.2d 874, *appeal dismissed*, 400 U.S. 808 (1970) (mortgage company); *Miskell v. Termplan, Inc.*, 381 S.W.2d 129 (Tex. Civ. App. 1964) (small loan

---

4 (March 9, 1973).

8. American Trust and NCNB also contend that the statutes violate the due process and the commerce clauses. Since we find the statutes unconstitutional under the equal protection clause, it is unnecessary to discuss the alternative allegations of unconstitutionality. . . .

company).[12]

. . . A domestic trust company, whether it be native or foreign owned, can be required to retain licensed South Carolina attorneys to conduct those aspects of its business which the state includes in the practice of law. But the challenged statutes do not contain this requirement. Similarly, nothing in the challenged statutes would prevent a native owned domestic corporation from seeking investment or legal advice from persons who have offices in other states. A native owned domestic corporation is not barred from refusing small, uneconomic accounts, or from transferring funds out of the state if this is in the best interests of a trust's beneficiaries. The challenged statutes address none of these business practices. Contrary to the state's contention, the record fails to establish that a domestic trust company owned by a corporation domiciled or licensed in a state contiguous to South Carolina would be a less suitable testamentary trustee than a domestic company owned by a corporation domiciled in some other state. Nor does the proof demonstrate that a locally owned domestic trust company would better serve the public, or be more amenable to regulation, than a domestic company owned by a foreign corporation. Classification of domestic trust companies by the domicile or licensing of their corporate ownership bears no rational relation to the lawful discharge of their fiduciary duties or to the state's control over them.

The state also argues that the statute serves the public interest by preventing competition that would injure South Carolina's existing corporate fiduciaries. While the equal protection clause denies a state the power to arbitrarily favor one domestic corporation over a competitor, the state can curb competition when the public interest will be served. . . . Accordingly, we accept the legal premise on which the state bottoms its argument: a state may limit competition in the trust business if the public interest will be served. *Philadelphia Savings Fund Soc'y v. Myers*, 406 Pa. 438, 179 A.2d 209 (1962). *Cf. Noble State Bank v. Haskell*, 219 U.S. 104 (1911). But we reject the factual basis of the state's claim that foreign corporate control of domestic trust companies inherently creates competition that is detrimental to the public interest. The claim is based on speculative opinions that are directly in conflict with the conclusions reached by the Board of Governors of the Federal Reserve System. Moreover, we find no rational relationship between the state's classification of domestic trust companies and the protection of the public from competition. If the public welfare will suffer from injurious competition, nothing in the challenged statutes prevents such competition from native owned domestic trust companies. . . .

North Carolina National, claiming that it is otherwise qualified as a foreign corporation to serve as a testamentary trustee for South Carolina decedents, charges that the exclusion of corporations domiciled or licensed in states contiguous to South Carolina causes 67-53(a)(4) to violate both the due process and commerce clauses of the Constitution.[13] These contentions require only brief comment. . . .

It is undisputed that the Bank is a foreign corporation. Therefore, without violating the fourteenth amendment, South Carolina can exclude it from doing business in the state. ... Moreover, the Constitution commits to the states the power to control the administration

12. Cases dealing with other types of exclusion are instructive. A state's excessive license fee that lacks a reasonable basis for being levied only against fishing boats owned by citizens of other states violates the privileges and immunities clause. *Toomer v. Whitsel*, 334 U.S. 385 (1948). Exclusion of aliens from a state's fisheries violates the equal protection clause. *Takahashi v. Fish and Game Commission*, 334 U.S. 410 (1948). And closer to the mark, a statute excluding a domestic corporation from state fishing grounds because it is owned by nonresidents violates the equal protection clause. *Edwards v. Leaver*, 102 F.Supp. 698 (D.R.I.1952) (three-judge court).

13. As a foreign corporation that is not 'within [South Carolina's] jurisdiction,' as specified by the 14th amendment, North Carolina National does not rely on the equal protection clause.

of their citizens' estates. . . . Because the due process clause no longer offers a substantive bar to state regulation of a business subject to state control, . . . we conclude that 67-53(a)(4) does not deprive North Carolina National of due process of law. . . .

North Carolina National places a value in excess of $32,000,000 on the estates of South Carolina residents who have requested it to act as testamentary trustee or as trustee of pour-over trusts into which the customers may eventually devise their estates. The Bank explained that it formerly transacted this business 'through use of the mails, telephone, and personal visits between its trust officers and South Carolina residents establishing the trusts, the beneficiaries of such trusts, or their attorneys.' We hold, for the purpose of this case, that the Bank's interstate activities as testamentary trustee for South Carolina decedents constituted interstate commerce. *Cf. United States v. Philadelphia National Bank*, 374 U.S. 321, 336 n.12 (1963). This aspect of the case, therefore, turns on the question whether the ban against the Bank is an impermissible burden on interstate commerce.

National banks can exercise only the authority that has been expressly or impliedly granted to them by Congress. *Investment Company Institute v. Camp*, 401 U.S. 617, 628 (1971). Federal law, 12 U.S.C. 92a(a) and (b), authorizes a national bank to act as a fiduciary only 'when not in contravention of State or local law.' But a national bank does not act in contravention of state or local law if a competing state bank can serve as a fiduciary. In this event, the national bank's authority is coextensive with the state bank's, but it is not enlarged. *New Hampshire Bankers' Ass'n v. Nelson*, 336 F. Supp. 1330 (D.N.H.), *aff'd* 460 F.2d 307 (1st Cir.1972). The term, 'local law,' as used in 92a is defined as 'the law of the state . . . governing the fiduciary relationship,' 12 C.F.R. 9.1(f) (1974), which in this instance is the law of South Carolina. . . . Section 67-53(a)(4) prohibits both North Carolina state banks and national banks located in North Carolina from serving as testamentary trustees of South Carolina decedents. In this respect it treats both types of banks equally.

Congress has paramount authority over national banks. *McCulloch v. Maryland*, 17 U.S. (4 Wheat.) 316 (1819). It can exercise its authority by incorporating restrictions found in state law. In 1927, when the McFadden Act, 12 U.S.C. 36 (1970), authorized national banks to operate branches to the same extent that a state bank located in the same state could operate them, it intended to create 'competitive equality' between state and national banks located in the same state. *First Nat'l Bank v. Walker Bank and Trust Co.*, 385 U.S. 252, 261 (1966). It is apparent that in enacting 92a, Congress intended to create the same kind of 'competitive equality' with regard to trust services. Since South Carolina's ban on foreign testamentary trustees operates equally against state and national banks located in North Carolina, the exclusion of North Carolina National is not an impermissible burden on interstate commerce; Congress has allowed it by enacting 92a. Furthermore, because the commerce clause is a grant, not a restriction, on the power of Congress 'to regulate Commerce . . . among the several States . . .' the exclusion is constitutionally valid. *Cf. Prudential Insurance Co. v. Benjamin*, 328 U.S. 408, 423 (1946).[16] . . .

---

16. The Comptroller of the Currency, who is charged by 12 U.S.C. 92a(a) (1970) with determining whether a national bank may act as a fiduciary, has inferentially indicated that a national bank cannot exercise this power in a foreign jurisdiction which excludes nonresident fiduciaries. The Comptroller's opinion is as follows:

> Exercise of Fiduciary Powers in Jurisdiction Other than the One in Which the Principal Office of the Bank is Located
>
> This Office is of the opinion that a national bank authorized to exercise fiduciary powers may, without additional authority from this Office, exercise such power in other jurisdictions, the laws of which do not exclude nonresident fiduciaries. Accordingly, a national bank with

South Carolina Code 8-580 (1972 Supp.) requires, with certain exceptions, every corporation engaged in the trust business before January 1, 1972, to receive approval of the State Board of Bank Control before commencing operations. American Trust particularly objects to the Board's authority to determine 'whether the conduct of such a business would serve the public interest, taking into consideration local circumstances and conditions at the place where such applicant proposes to do business.' Recalling the opposition to NCNB's Federal Reserve application, American Trust contends that the clause will serve as a device to exclude it at the behest of its competitors.

The statute, however, is not unique. For example, it resembles, in many respects, federal law and regulations that pertain to applications from national banks seeking permission to exercise fiduciary powers.[18] . . . [I]t does not violate the due process clause. The statute's grandfather clause and exemptions have not been proved to be unreasonable classifications. *Braeburn Securities Corporation v. Smith*, 15 Ill.2d 55, 153 N.E.2d 806, 810 (1958). Therefore the statute, on its face, does not violate the equal protection clause.

NCNB contends that the statute unlawfully suppresses commercial intercourse between it and American Trust in contravention of the commerce and supremacy clauses.

We find no merit in NCNB's contentions. [The court quoted section 7 of the Bank Holding Company Act, 12 U.S.C. 1846 (1970).]

While this statute does not enlarge a state's powers over trust companies owned by bank holding companies, neither does it diminish them. Accordingly, for the reasons stated . . . , we conclude that the statute does not unconstitutionally burden NCNB's interstate commercial activities. . . .

American Trust correctly contends that a valid statute may be applied in violation of the equal protection clause. . . . But its attack on this ground is premature because it has not yet sought approval from the State Board of Bank Control. Accordingly, we deny the request for an injunction against 8-580.

Notes and Comments 5.77. For an interesting treatment by the Supreme Court of a challenge to state banking regulation based on commerce clause and equal protection grounds, among others, see *Northeast Bancorp, Inc. v. Board of Governors*, 472 U.S. 159 (1985) (upholding regional banking compact limiting entry by banking enterprises to those based in designated states within region).

7. Incidental Powers

a. Introduction

The concept of incidental powers serves as the basis for many traditional banking activities beyond the core functions of taking deposits and making loans.[63] However, the concept is also the basis for the exercise of many "nontraditional activities" that intersect

---

fiduciary powers may exercise them in another State or country if the bank conforms to the laws of that jurisdiction.

Comptroller's Trust Examiners' Manual, Opinion Section, G-1 (1969). *See also Current Legal and Regulatory Developments*, 1 National Banking Review 599, 610 (1964).

18. *See* 12 U.S.C. 92a(i) (1970); 12 C.F.R. 9.3 (1974).

63. *See, e.g., supra* § 4 (discussing guarantees as incidental powers).

banking with, for example, securities and insurance. In this section, we explore some of the outer limits of the concept.

Just as the banking and trust powers of depository institutions are statutorily based, so also are nonbanking and other nontraditional activities of these institutions.[64] These powers are supposed to have an affinity to the other traditional, banking activities. However, as many of the cases that follow will illustrate, the movement of banks into the securities and insurance sectors have strained this affinity almost to the breaking point.

For national banks, the statutory authority for the incidental powers is 12 U.S.C. § 24(Seventh).[65] This provision has been repeatedly amended, but the key passage for present purposes is the initial clause which gives the national bank the power "[t]o exercise by its board of directors . . . all such incidental powers as shall be necessary to carry on the business of banking. . . ."[66]

Notes and Comments 5.78. Should the incidental powers concept be viewed as a positive source of authority to engage in activities beyond, or other than the core activities of banking? Or is it a limiting concept, restricting possible implied powers of banks? Consider the following case.

First Nat. Bank v. Nat. Exchange Bank

92 U.S. 122 (1875)

Mr. Chief Justice WAITE delivered the opinion of the court.

[For factual discussion, see excerpt in § 7.b, *infra*.]

Dealing in stocks is not expressly prohibited; but such a prohibition is implied from the failure to grant the power. In the honest exercise of the power to compromise a doubtful debt owing to a bank, it can hardly be doubted that stocks may be accepted in payment and satisfaction, with a view to their subsequent sale or conversion into money so as to make good or reduce an anticipated loss. Such a transaction would not amount to a dealing in stocks. It was, in effect, so decided in *Fleckner v. Bank*, 8 Wheat. 351, where it was held that a prohibition against trading and dealing was nothing more than a prohibition against engaging in the ordinary business of buying and selling for profit, and did not include purchases resulting from ordinary banking transactions. For this reason, among others, the acceptance of an indorsed note in payment of a debt due was decided not to be a "dealing" in notes. Of course, all such transactions must be compromises in good faith, and not mere

---

64. *See, e.g.*, 12 U.S.C. § 24(Seventh) (providing for incidental powers of national banks). The concept of "incidental powers" is also a part of state regulation of banking. For a functional analysis of the scope of a state-chartered bank's incidental powers, see *Block v. Pennsylvania Exchange Bank*, 253 N.Y. 222 (1930). Since even state banks are generally limited to the powers available to national banks (*see* 12 U.S.C. § 1831a(a) (1)), this section uses the incidental powers of national banks as the basis for discussion.

65. This provision is also of direct significance with respect to the limitations on securities activities of financial institutions generally. *See infra* § 9 (discussing securities activities). *See also infra* Chapter 7 (discussing securities regulation as applied to financial institutions).

66. Some of these "incidental powers" may be utilized in a bank service company, in which certain operations are "spun off" into a non-banking subsidiary of the bank. Such spin-offs are governed by the Bank Service Company Act, 12 U.S.C. §§ 1861 *et seq*. On bank service companies, see § 8, *infra*.

cloaks or devices to cover unauthorized practices.

Notes and Comments 5.79. How does Chief Justice Waite's approach to analysis of "incidental powers" compare with that reflected in Judge Sneed's opinion in *M & M Leasing, infra*?

5.80. The following excerpt describes some of the relatively traditional activities that have been upheld under the "incidental powers" concept. Is there an organizing principle of decision that explains the results in the cases described?

Arnold Tours, Inc. v. Camp,

472 F.2d 427 (1st Cir. 1972)

HAMLEY, Circuit Judge.

. . . [W]hen one looks at past decisions it becomes apparent that the activities of national banks which have been held to be permissible under the "incidental powers" provision have been those which are directly related to one or another of a national bank's express powers.

Thus, in *Merchants' Bank v. State Bank*, 77 U.S. (10 Wall.) 604 (1870), the Supreme Court held that national banks may, as an incidental power, engage in the practice of certifying checks. The Court there recognized the great similarity between the activity of certifying checks and the express power granted by the National Bank Act to discount and negotiate bills of exchange.

In *First National Bank v. National Exchange Bank*, 92 U.S. 122, 127 (1875), the Court held that the power to acquire stock in settlement of a claim arising out of a legitimate banking transaction is an incidental power of national banks. In *Wyman v. Wallace*, 201 U.S. 230, 243 (1906), the Court held that national banks may, as an incidental power, borrow money. The Court referred to a line of cases which trace back to *Auten v. United States Nat. Bank*, 174 U.S. 125, 141, 142 (1899), in which the Court had noted that a greater part of banking practice was "in strict sense borrowing" and that several of the express powers granted to banks created a debtor-creditor relationship.

In *Miller v. King*, 223 U.S. 505, 510-511 (1912), the Court held that national banks may, as an incidental power, collect a judgment on behalf of a depositor. Similarly, in *Clement National Bank v. Vermont*, 231 U.S. 120, 139-140 (1913), the Supreme Court held that national banks may, as an incidental power, pay taxes on behalf of depositors. As the Court there indicated, this activity is directly related to the express power of national banks to receive deposits.

In *First National Bank v. Hartford*, 273 U.S. 548, 559-560 (1927), the Court found that the sale of mortgages and other evidences of debt, acquired in the exercise of the express power to loan money and to discount and negotiate other evidences of debt, was permissible under the bank's incidental powers. In *Colorado Nat. Bank v. Bedford*, 210 U.S. 41, 49 (1940), the Court held that the operation of a safe deposit business was embraced within the bank's incidental powers because the operation of a safe deposit business is virtually identical to the express statutory authority of banks to accept special deposits. . . .

Finally, in *Franklin Nat. Bank v. New York*, 347 U.S. 373, 375-377 (1957), the Court held that national banks were entitled to advertise the word "savings" because such advertising was incidental to the express power of such banks to receive time and savings deposits and to pay interest thereon.

Notes and Comments 5.81. Incidental powers are supposed to be *incidental* to something else. The text of 12 U.S.C. § 24(Seventh) requires that these powers be incidental to "the business of banking," but it does not explain what that "business" is. The following excerpt offers an explanation. Is it convincing?

M & M Leasing Corp. v. Seattle First Nat'l Bank,

563 F.2d 1377 (9th Cir. 1977), *cert. denied*, 436 U.S. 956 (1978)

SNEED, Circuit Judge.

[The case concerned national bank involvement in automobile leasing. *See* § 7.b, *infra.*]

While the importance of leasing to the business of national banks is relevant to determining the extent to which such activity is useful and convenient, it does not alone establish that leasing is within the "business of banking" as authorized by 12 U.S.C. § 24 (Seventh). In construing the scope of the authority established by this statutory provision, we adopt the approach employed by the First Circuit in *Arnold Tours, Inc. v. Camp*, 472 F.2d 427, 431-32 (1st Cir. 1972). That is, for an activity to be pursuant to an incidental power "necessary to carry on the business of banking" it must be "convenient or useful in connection with the performance of one of the bank's established activities pursuant to its express powers under the National Bank Act." *Id.* at 432. Thus, leasing must be convenient or useful to business *expressly* authorized by 12 U.S.C. § 24 (Seventh). [W]e hold that leasing, when in the light of all relevant circumstances the transaction constitutes a loan of money secured by the leased property, . . . is incidental to the "loan of money on personal security," an activity expressly authorized by the National Bank Act.

In reaching this conclusion we draw comfort from the fact that commentators uniformly have recognized that the National Bank Act did not freeze the practices of national banks in their century forms. Indeed, many contend that the powers of national banks "are not confined to the powers specified in the National Bank Act and those necessary to carry out those specific powers." Trimble, *The Implied Power of National Banks to Issue Letters of Credit and Accept Bills*, 58 Yale L.J. 713, 721 (1949). *See* Huck, *What Is the Banking Business?* 21 Bus. Lawyer 537, 541 (1966); Note, *Diversification by National Banks*, 21 Stan. L. Rev. 650, 651- 53 (1969). We prefer, however, the *Arnold Tours, Inc.* formulation of the scope of "incidental" powers; but, whatever the scope of such powers may be, we believe the powers of national banks must be construed so as to permit the use of new ways of conducting the very old business of banking. . . .

. . . A loan secured by a chattel mortgage or a conditional sales contract provides the proper means, [appellants] insist, by which a "loan of money on personal security" ought to be accomplished. A lease which serves the same purpose is impermissible. Particularly this is true, they assert, when both the lessor bank and the lessee customer distinguish the lease from a loan, and third parties, including various government agencies, treat the two quite differently. Appellants are correct in stating that functionally interchangeable leases and secured loans are regarded as distinct in both the rhetoric and regulation of this form of commerce. However, it is their functional interchangeability that is the touchstone of our decision. . . . Whether third parties in other contexts should treat leases that are equivalent to loans as nonetheless distinct and separate is not at present before us. Whatever might be the proper dispositions of such issues, they should not influence our opinion in this case.

b. The Evolving Concept of "Incidental Powers"

Notes and Comments 5.82. How do we test the "incidental" nature of incidental powers? Should they be related to powers expressly granted to the bank? Directly or indirectly related? Consider the following cases.

First Nat. Bank v. Nat. Exchange Bank
92 U.S. 122 (1875)

Mr. Chief Justice WAITE delivered the opinion of the court.

The question presented for our consideration in this case is, whether a national bank, organized under the National Banking Act, may, in a fair and bona fide compromise of a contested claim against it growing out of a legitimate banking transaction, pay a larger sum than would have been exacted in satisfaction of the demand, so as to obtain by the arrangement a transfer of certain stocks in railroad and other corporations; it being honestly believed at the time, that, by turning the stocks into money under more favorable circumstances than then existed, a loss, which would otherwise accrue from the transaction, might be averted or diminished. . . .

Authority is . . . given to transact such a banking business as is specified [by 12 U.S.C. § 24(Seventh)], and all incidental powers necessary to carry it on are granted. These powers are such as are required to meet all the legitimate demands of the authorized business, and to enable a bank to conduct its affairs, within the general scope of its charter, safely and prudently. This necessarily implies the right of a bank to incur liabilities in the regular course of its business, as well as to become the creditor of others. Its own obligations must be met, and debts due to it collected or secured. The power to adopt reasonable and appropriate measures for these purposes is an incident to the power to incur the liability or become the creditor. Obligations may be assumed that result unfortunately. Loans or discounts may be made that cannot be met at maturity. Compromises to avoid or reduce losses are oftentimes the necessary results of this condition of things. These compromises come within the general scope of the powers committed to the board of directors and the officers and agents of the bank, and are submitted to their judgment and discretion, except to the extent that they are restrained by the charter or by-laws. Banks may do, in this behalf, whatever natural persons could do under like circumstances. . . .

It is difficult to see how a debt due from, or a contested obligation resting upon, a bank, occupies any different position in respect to this power of adjustment and compromise from that of a debt owing to it. The object in both cases is to get rid of or reduce an apprehended loss growing out of legitimate business; and it would seem that whatever might be done in the one case ought not to be excluded form the other under the same circumstances. Often a discharge by a bank of its own obligation created a debt due to it from another. Such was the case here. Bayne, without authority, transferred to the defendant, as collateral security for his indebtedness, a certificate of deposit issued to him by the plaintiff, and afterwards collected the money due upon the certificate from the plaintiff without disclosing the transfer. Any payment buy the plaintiff to the defendant, therefore, in discharge of its liability upon the certificate, became a lawful charge against Bayne. He was insolvent. It was, on this account, not only the right, but the duty, of the officers and agents of the plaintiff to protect by their arrangements, as far as possible, the stockholders who se interests they represented. This was necessarily left to their judgment and discretion. No question of good faith is involved. The transaction for all the purposes of this suit must be taken to have been, in fact, what it purports to be, -- a fair and honest compromise of an outstanding claim, with a view to ultimate protection against an impending loss. As such, we think it was within the corporate powers of the bank, and that the Court of Appeals did not err in so holding.

Texas & Pacific Ry. v. Pottorff

291 U.S. 245 (1934), *amended*, 291 U.S. 649, *rehearing denied*, 292 U.S. 600

Mr. Justice BRANDEIS delivered the opinion of the Court.

The main question for decision is whether a national bank has power to pledge a part of its assets to secure a private deposit.

The First National Bank of El Paso, Texas, failed on September 4, 1931, and S.O. Pottorff was appointed receiver. The Texas & Pacific Railway Company was then, and long had been, a depositor. To secure it as such the bank had, in January, 1931, pledged $50,000 Liberty Bonds and held them for the Railway in the Trust Department of the bank. The balance in the Railway's regular checking account at the time of the failure was $54,646.94. Of this claim it made proof as a secured creditor. The receiver approved the amount of the claim, but denied the validity of the pledge; and he tendered a dividend check only for the amount to which the Railway would have been entitled as an unsecured creditor. Thereupon, the Railway brought, in the federal court for western Texas, this suit against the receiver, praying, in the alternative, that the bonds be delivered to it; or that they be sold for its benefit; or that the claim be paid in full with interest. The receiver filed a cross-bill praying that the bank's title to the bonds be quieted.

. . . [T]he court dismissed the bill and entered a decree for the receiver upon the cross-bill, holding that the pledge was void and that the Liberty Bonds constituted assets to be administered for the benefit of the general creditors of the bank. The Circuit Court of Appeals affirmed the decree. . . . The Railway contends that the bank had power to make the pledge; that even if the bank did not have such power, the receiver is not in a position to question the validity of the pledge; and that even if he is not estopped from doing so, he may not disaffirm it without returning the consideration therefor received by the bank. We are of the opinion that none of these contentions is sound.

The District Court found the following additional facts. The relation between the Railway and the bank began in 1922 when the Railway was in receivership. Then, an order was entered appointing the bank a depositary upon condition that it should furnish a bond with solvent sureties. An acceptable bond was then given in the sum of $25,000. When, in 1924, the receivership terminated, the Railway continued its deposit account; and a bond in like amount was given with the National Surety Company as surety. When, in 1927, the average deposits had increased to about $50,000, an additional bond of $25,000 was given with the Maryland Casualty Company as surety. While these bonds were in full force and effect and the bank was solvent, it requested the Railway to accept, in substitution for the surety bonds, the pledge of $50,000 in Liberty Bonds, giving as its reason for the request that the premiums payable on the surety bonds were a burden from which it wished to be relieved. The Railway expressed willingness to assent to the substitution, but only on condition that thereby it would be as fully protected as by the surety bonds. The bank and its attorney gave this assurance; and thereupon the pledge was substituted for the surety bonds and these were cancelled. Without that assurance, the Railway would not have consented to the cancellation of the surety bonds; or if they had been cancelled without its consent, would have immediately withdrawn all of its deposits. In reliance upon the assurances and the pledge, the Railway continued until the failure to make deposits; and in fact increased its deposits.

National bank examiners commenced on August 6, 1931, an examination of the bank. Within a few days, they learned from the bank's books that the pledge had been made; but neither the examiners nor the Comptroller of the Currency advised the bank's officers that the pledge was beyond the powers of the bank or that it was irregular or otherwise objectionable. The bank had frequently secured private deposits by surety bonds; but never before by a pledge of assets. The examiners concluded their investigation on August 20, 1931. The failure occurred on September 4, 1931.

. . . National banks lack power to pledge their assets to secure a private deposit. The measure of their powers is the statutory grant; and powers not conferred by Congress are denied. For the Act under which national banks are organized constituted a complete system for their government, *Cook County National Bank v. United States*, 107 U.S. 445, 448; *California Bank v. Kennedy*, 167 U.S. 362, 366; *First National Bank v. Missouri*, 263 U.S. 640. Confessedly the power to pledge assets to secure a private deposit was not granted in specific terms. The contention is that this power is incidental to the general grant of powers "necessary to carry on the business of banking . . . by receiving deposits"; and, hence, is implied.

There is no basis for the claim that the power to pledge assets is necessary to deposit banking. The record is barren of evidence that the practice of so pledging assets has ever prevailed among national banks. And facts of which we take judicial notice indicate that among national banks such action must have been deemed contrary to good banking practice.[3] From the establishment of the system in 1864 to March 1, 1933, 2159 national banks failed and there has been much litigation arising from their insolvency; but only two other reported cases have been found involving a pledge of assets to secure a private deposit, and in those cases, very recent ones, the existence of the power was denied.[6] *Smith v. Baltimore & O. R. Co.*, 48 F. (2d) 861; 56 F. (2d) 799; *Illinois Central R. Co. v. Rawlings*, 66 F. (2d) 146. In the case at bar, there is a specific finding that the transaction challenged was the only instance in which this bank had ever pledged assets to secure a private deposit. Surely action cannot be deemed a *necessary incident*[a] of a business when only a single incident has been found in which it was taken. Moreover, even a practice commonly pursued may not be a necessary one.[7]

To permit the pledge would be inconsistent with many provisions of the National Bank Act which are designed to ensure, in case of disaster, uniformity in the treatment of

---

3. No mention of securing a private deposit in a national bank by a pledge of assets or otherwise has been found in any published report of the Comptroller . . . ; or in any of the 52 available treatises or textbooks on banks and banking practice published since 1900; in any of the annual proceedings of the American Bankers Association or in any issue of the American Banker's Journal; or in any issue of The Commercial and Financial Chronicle since 1900; or in the New York Times Index since 1913. *Compare* "Contemporary Banking," by Willis, Chapman & Robey (1933), p. 336.

6. In that case the parties stipulated, and the District Court found . . . that "during, before, and after the said period of February 23, 1928, to July 31, 1930, when the said Comptroller was requested by national banks or others for an opinion upon the power of national banks to pledge securities to secure a private depositor, in every instance the Comptroller disapproved of such pledges by stating that in his opinion national banks had no such power."

a. (Emphasis added by editor.) Is "necessary incident" the same thing as "incidental to"?

7. *Compare Federal Reserve Bank v. Malloy*, 264 U.S. 160, 167. A practice is not within the incidental powers of a corporation merely because it is convenient in the performance of an express power. *Merrill v. Monticello*, 138 U.S. 673, 692; *compare Beaty v. Knowler's Lessee*, 4 Pet. 1542, 168-171.

depositors and a ratable distribution of assets. *Compare Davis v. Elmira Savings Bank*, 161 U.S. 275, 290. This policy of equal treatment was held to preclude, in case of a national bank, even the preference under § 3466 of the Revise Statutes which otherwise is accorded to the United States when its debtor becomes insolvent. *Cook County National Bank v. United States*, 107 U.S. 445. The effect of a pledge is to withdraw for the benefit of one depositor part of the fund to which all look for protection. Thereby the legitimate expectations of a great body of the depositors are defeated and confidence in the fairness of the national banking laws and administration is impaired. It is no answer to say that the other depositors are benefited by the increased resources which the pledge brings to the bank, or at least are not harmed, since the new funds take the place of the securities pledges and are available to meet liabilities.[8] The immediate safety of unsecured creditors depends on the bank remaining open and solvent; the pledge reduces the fund of quick assets available to meet unusual demands without any assurance that the deposit will be used to replenish this fund.

The fact that this bank had frequently secured private deposits by surety bonds lends no support to the contention that the power to pledge assets is necessary to carrying on the business of deposit banking. Such a practice would likewise be a departure from the policy of equal treatment of depositors; but the loss to other depositors resulting from such action would be far less serious. A pledge withdraws capital assets, while the giving of a surety bond merely increases the bank's expenses. There is, however, no finding that among national banks there exists the practice of securing by surety bonds some private deposits. If there has been such a practice, it must have been a secret one; for reference to it has not been found in either official reports, or the books on banking or other publications dealing with financial affairs. Whether a national bank could legally engage in such a practice we have no occasion to decide.

The Railway insists that Congress in providing that the Secretary of the Treasury might deposit public money in national banks upon receiving satisfactory security by "the deposit of United States bonds or otherwise," . . . assumed a general power in national banks to pledge their assets to secure deposits; and that the assumption indicates that it intended this power to be among the "incidental" powers granted. . . . But without such assumption, the duty of the Secretary to demand a pledge authorizes a national bank to make it. . . . Moreover, if the Railway's argument were sound it would have been unnecessary to amend § 45 as was done by the Act of June 25, 1930, c. 604, 46 Stat. 809, which provides:

---

8. These arguments seem to ignore the realities of the banking business. The primary interest of a depositor is that the bank shall be able to pay as and when he demands payment. The ability to do so depends not on the bulk of the assets but on their liquidity. The law applicable to national banks requires them to maintain as reserves in the form of cash or of cash balances with a federal reserve bank, fixed percentages of their demand deposits in order to assure ability to meet probable demands as they arise; but such reserve is commonly deemed insufficient to meet possible emergencies. Because of this, soundly managed banks maintain so-called "secondary reserves," usually in the form of government obligations which can be liquidated quickly with little or no loss. The effect of pledging quick assets for particular deposits is to reduce the fund available for meeting currency demands of an unexpected nature. The funds received from the deposit are not necessarily an equivalent for the securities withdrawn from available resources. In the first place the deposit, in the process of clearing and collection, may serve merely to cancel liabilities against the bank. This may mean that there will be fewer competing claims in case of insolvency, but it will still be true that the reserves have been depleted considerably beyond what would be justified by reason of the cancellation of the liability. In the second place, to the extent that the deposit represent free funds, it is not probable that the deposit will be used to buy other low yield quick assets to take the place of those which have been pledged.

> "Any [national banking] association may, upon the deposit with it of public money of a State or any political subdivision thereof, give security for the safe-keeping and prompt payment of the money so deposited, of the same kind as is authorized by the law of the State in which such association is located in the case of other banking institutions in the State."

This amendment indicates that Congress believed that the original Act had not granted general power to pledge assets to secure deposits." The fact that the amendment was made to § 45 indicates that the power to pledge was granted only as an incident of the public officer's duty to demand a pledge. If, as is suggested, the 1930 amendment was passed merely in order to settle doubts as to the power of a national bank to pledge its assets to secure deposits, the amendment would naturally have been made not to § 45, but to [§ 24(Seventh)] which contains the grant of "incidental" powers.

The Railway urges also that since the relation of the bank to its depositors is that of debtor to creditor, and since a national bank may borrow money, . . . and pledge its assets therefor, . . . it may likewise pledge assets to secure a private deposit. The fallacy of this contention has been many times exposed.[14] The difference between deposits and loans is fundamental and far-reaching. The amount of the deposits is commonly accepted as a measure of the bank's success; and increase of deposits as evidence of increased prosperity. The depositor does not think of himself as lending money to the bank. The modern deposit grew out of the older form of deposit in which the fund was held separate and intact, and the sole purpose of the deposit was safe-keeping. Safe-keeping is still a very important function of deposit banking; and from the point of view of most depositors the chief one. Borrowing by a bank (as distinguished from a re-discount) is commonly regarded as evidence of weakness. Often the loan is made in the hope of averting insolvency. Loans made by one bank to another commonly involve a pledge of assets, since only upon such a condition is the transaction possible. . . .

Notes and Comments 5.83. Considering note 7 in *Pottorff*, if convenience in performance of an express power is not a sufficient connection to make a power "incidental," what sort of connection is required? Must it be a "necessary incident"? (*See supra* at note a.) How close a connection does the following case require?

Houston v. Drake

97 F.2d 863 (9th Cir. 1938)

WILBUR, Circuit Judge.

[Consolidated National Bank of Tucson had obtained the assignment of a lease of bank premises from Arizona National Bank (ANB), which was failing. In connection with the assignment, the lessor reduced the rent paid by Consolidated. Some seven years later, Consolidated was itself in liquidation. The appellant in this case was the voluntary liquidating agent of Consolidated, appointed under 12 U.S.C. § 181. He gave notice to the appellee, the lessor of the ANB premises, that he rejected the lease. Eventually, he brought an action against the appellee for a declaratory judgment determining the rights of the bank

---

14. *Farmers & Merchants Bank v. Consolidated School District*, 174 Minn. 286, 291; 219 N.W. 163; *State Bank of Commerce v. Stone*, 261 N.Y. 175; 184 N.E. 750; *Divide County v. Baird*, 55 N.D. 45, 52; 212 N.W. 236; *Commercial Banking & Trust Co. v. Citizens Trust & Guaranty Co.*, 153 Ky. 566, 574; 156 S.W. 160. . . .

in liquidation and the owner of the premises under the terms of the rejected lease. The appellee countered for all rentals due under the terms of the lease and for a declaration that the lease was binding against the bank. The District Court decreed that the assumption of the lease by Consolidated was valid. The Supreme Court held that Consolidated's original 1925 agreement was *ultra vires* and void as to the unexecuted part of the lease by the liquidator, and that upon the surrender of the premises to the appellee, or the offer so to do, the obligations under the lease as to rents not yet accrued were terminated.]

Appellee . . . predicates the authority of the Bank to take the assignment of the lease upon the provisions of [12 U.S.C. § 24(Seventh)]. It is argued that one of the incidental powers of a national bank as established by the decisions is to take over the assets of another bank upon a pledge to secure its assumption of the obligations of the bank whose assets are thus acquired. . . . It is contended, therefore, that as the assumption of the lease by the Consolidated Bank was pursuant to the agreement of February 9, 1925, between the Consolidated Bank and the Arizona Bank, such assumption was within the power of the Consolidated Bank. Under the terms of this agreement the assets transferred to the Consolidated Bank were to be placed in a liquidation account and upon liquidation and payment of the debts of the Arizona Bank the remaining assets were to be reconveyed to the Arizona Bank.

It is further contended by appellee that the legal effect of the agreement of February 9, 1925, was to create a creditor debtor relationship between the Consolidated Bank and the Arizona Bank; that in effect the Consolidated loaned the Arizona Bank money to pay its liabilities and took as security a pledge of the assets of the latter bank. Except as it may have reference to the lease, we may assume that the transaction of February 9, 1925 was in legal effect a loan by the Consolidated Bank to the Arizona Bank with a pledge of the assets of the latter bank as security. As to the lease, however, a different situation is presented. Even though it be assumed that the lease was assigned to the Consolidated Bank pursuant to the option given that bank in the agreement of February 9, 1925, it is clear that by the transaction of May, 1, 1925 the Arizona Bank was discharged from all obligations arising from privity of estate and the Consolidated Bank became liable as tenant under the lease. . . .

The liability of the Consolidated Bank was not only by reason of privity of estate but also by privity of contract because in the tri-party agreement of May 1, 1925, it expressly assumed all the covenants of the lease. . . . It may be true that the assignment of the lease by the Arizona Bank to the consolidated Bank was in pursuance of the option contained in the agreement of February 9, 1925, whereby the Consolidated Bank took over the assets of the Arizona Bank, and that had the assets of the Arizona Bank been sufficient to pay its debts without recourse to the lease it could have compelled a reassignment of the lease from the Consolidated Bank. As between them that question is not free from doubt. However that may be, there is no escape from the proposition that in legal effect the Consolidated Bank, by the assignment of the lease to it and the assumption of the obligations contained therein, by the contract of May 1, 1925 became the lessee of the premises and a reassignment of the lease would not have terminated the liability of the Consolidated Bank arising from privity of contract. . . . It follows that the transaction of May 1, 1925 cannot be regarded as a mere pledge of the lease by the Arizona Bank as security for a loan authorized by [12 U.S.C. § 24(Seventh)], or by 12 U.S.C. 29.

Notes and Comments 5.84. Recall that in *Pottorff*, Justice Brandeis relied in part on the position taken by the Comptroller in rejecting pledging of assets against deposits as an incidental power. Would Justice Brandeis's analysis have been significantly affected by a contrary view being expressed by the Comptroller? A modern, revisionist view of incidental powers on the part of the Comptroller in fact began to emerge in the early 1960s. In

1963, then Comptroller James J. Saxon radically expanded the range of activities authorized by administrative interpretation under the incidental powers concept. *See Arnold Tours, Inc. v. Camp, infra* at 215, n. 9 (discussing 1963 rulings). How do the approaches taken by the courts in the following cases compare with the traditional approach taken in the previous cases?

Arnold Tours, Inc. v. Camp,

472 F.2d 427 (1st Cir. 1972)

HAMLEY, Circuit Judge.

This class action involves the authority of national banks to engage in the travel agency business. The plaintiffs are Arnold Tours, Inc., and forty-one other independent travel agents of Massachusetts engaged in the travel agency business.

One of the defendants is William B. Camp, Comptroller of the Currency (Comptroller), whose office has issued rulings and regulations to the effect that national banks may engage in that business. The other defendant is South Shore National Bank (South Shore), a national banking association chartered by the United States Government, with a principal place of business in Quincy, Massachusetts, and with twenty-seven branch offices throughout Massachusetts. South Shore has been engaged in the travel agency business, operating it as a department of the bank, since November, 1966, after having bought out the fourth largest travel bureau in New England. Plaintiffs asked for declaratory and injunctive relief, the effect of which would be to force South Shore out of the travel business.

. . . The district court . . . declared that the Comptroller's regulation set out in 12 C.F.R. § 7.1 (1959), now superseded by 12 C.F.R. § 7.7475 (1972), is invalid to the extent that it is construed by the Comptroller as authorizing a national bank to operate a full-scale travel agency. In addition, the court permanently enjoined South Shore from engaging in the travel agency business and ordered the bank to divest itself of its travel department within six months. *Arnold Tours, Inc. v. Camp*, 338 F.Supp. 721 (D.Mass. 1972).

. . . [W]e affirm, but with one qualification. . . .

The Comptroller relied upon [12 U.S.C. §24(Seventh)] in his 1963 ruling that national banks could engage in the travel agency business. Thus, . . . 12 C.F.R. § 7.7475, reads:

> "§ 7.7475 National banks acting as travel agents.
>
> "Incident to those powers vested in them under 12 U.S.C.A. § 24, national banks may provide travel services for their customers and receive compensation therefor. Such services may include the sale of trip insurance and the rental of automobiles as agent for a local rental service. In connection therewith, national banks may advertise, develop, and extend such travel services for the purpose of attracting customers to the bank."

In holding that 12 U.S.C. § 24, Seventh, did not authorize national banks to engage in the travel agency business the district court, in its opinion, first focused attention on the nature of South Shore's travel agency operation. The court relied upon the graphic description of a modern agency operation given by Charles F. Heartfield. Heartfield had served as vice-president of South Shore, in charge of its travel department, from November 1, 1966 to 1970. . . .

The district court then observed that

"To say that conduct of a business of the nature and type described by Mr. Heartfield is a *sine qua non* to the successful operation of a national bank is a self-refuting proposition, especially in view of the fact that on the defendants' own claim only 122 national banks out of the many hundreds if not thousands in existence were providing travel agency services in 1967." 338 F. Supp. at 723.

The Comptroller argues that the district court applied an erroneous legal standard in reviewing the Comptroller's construction of the "incidental powers" clause of the National Bank Act . . . as indicated by the court's above-quoted use of the term *sine qua non*.

We are in agreement with the Comptroller that a *sine qua non* standard would be an inappropriate measure of a national bank's incidental powers under 12 U.S.C. § 24, Seventh. While the pertinent language of that section refers to all such incidental powers "as shall be necessary to carry on the business of banking," we do not believe that "necessary" was there used to connote that which is indispensable.

But we believe that, read in context with its entire opinion, the district court's reference to the concept of *sine qua non* was not intended to state the test for determining whether a particular bank activity is authorized as an incidental power. What seems to us to be a more reliable gauge of the district court's rationale is its discussion immediately following the sine qua non statement. . . .

The district court therein indicated that its chief concern was whether a travel agency business primarily involves the performance of financial transactions pertaining to money or substitutes therefor. If not, the court in effect ruled, that business was not within the normal and traditional range of the monetary activities of a national bank, and thus not encompassed by the "incidental powers" provision of 12 U.S.C. § 24, Seventh. It was on this basis that the district court distinguished the travel agency business from such approved "incidental powers" of national banks as those employed in selling travelers' checks or foreign currency, issuing letters of credit, or making travel loans.

But the Comptroller and South Shore do not agree that the "incidental powers" of national banks should even be restricted to the performance of financial transactions pertaining to money or substitutes therefor or that only such transactions lie within the normal traditional range of the activities of a national bank. The Comptroller and South Shore, for example, refer to *McCulloch v. Maryland*, 17 U.S. (4 Wheat.) 316 (1819), which upheld the constitutionality of the first Bank of the United States, as laying down the broad principle that the word "necessary" may include that which is convenient, or useful.

McCulloch v. Maryland was concerned not with statutory construction but with the power of Congress, under Article I, § 8 of the Constitution, "to make all Laws which shall be necessary and proper." . . . Almost the identical argument defendants here make concerning *McCulloch v. Maryland* was made in *Texas & P. Ry. Co. v. Pottorff*, 291 U.S. 245, 247, 249, 253, 259 (1934), and it was rejected or ignored by the Supreme Court.

. . . It may be convenient and useful for a national bank to carry on any number of activities. But one of the critical questions here is whether a convenient and useful activity be within the incidental powers of a bank if it is not directly related to what 12 U.S.C. § 24, Seventh, refers to as "the business of banking."

The most reliable guides as to what is encompassed in the term "the business of banking" are the express powers of national banks as set out in the National Bank Act. And when one looks at past decisions it becomes apparent that the activities of national banks which have been held to be permissible under the "incidental powers" provision have been those which are directly related to one or another of a national bank's express powers. . . .

In our opinion, . . . a national bank's activity is authorized as an incidental power, "necessary to carry on the business of banking," within the meaning of 12 U.S.C. § 24,

Seventh, if it is convenient or useful in connection with the performance of one of the bank's established activities pursuant to its express powers under the National Bank Act. If this connection between an incidental activity and an express power does not exist, the activity is not authorized as an incidental power. . . .

While the Comptroller and South Shore do not concede a relationship between an incidental and an express power must exist, they suggest ways in which they believe a travel agency business is directly related to a national bank's normal banking operations. In presenting this view, they pursue two lines of argument. One of these is an effort to equate the basic functions performed by travel agencies with functions which have historically been performed by banks. The other is based on the premise that a substantial number of banks have, for a long time, been providing travel agency services.

With regard to the first of these contentions, defendants assert that the basic functions performed by travel agencies consist of: (1) procuring carrier passage and other travel accommodations by acting as agent for passengers and carriers, and (2) providing various informational services to the traveler. Defendants then assert that both of these "basic" travel agency functions are only particular applications of the broad agency and informational services which banks traditionally offer among their "congeries of services."

In our view this analysis unrealistically minimizes the basic functions of a travel agency business and unjustifiably exalts the agency and informational functions of national banks.

The operation of a travel agency in the United States today is a highly complex activity. . . . Some of the aspects of that business are closely regulated under the supervision of the Civil Aeronautics Board, the Interstate Commerce Commission, and the Federal Maritime Commission. It is true that a travel agent acts as an agent for the traveler, but it also acts as an agent for carriers. A travel agency provides informational services for the traveler, but it also solicits travel business, advertises and in general promotes the interests of its carrier principals. More importantly, the agency and informational services a bank travel agency renders are pursuant to its own interest in making its travel department profitable, wholly apart from the bank's normal banking operations.

On the other hand, while national banks provide certain agency and informational services they are normally of a kind which are germane to the financial operations of the bank in the exercise of its express powers. There are, of course, instances in which banks have, as a convenience to their regular customers, and without additional compensation, obtained railroad, steamship or airline tickets for such customers, or provided information helpful to such customers in connection with their travels. But incidental good-will service of this kind cannot reasonably be equated with the operation of a modern travel agency for profit. In short, there is a difference between supplying customers with financial and informational services helpful to their travel plans and developing a clientele which looks to the bank not as a source of general financial advice and support but as a travel management center.

The Comptroller asserts that one of the central purposes of the National Bank Act, enacted during the Civil War, was to serve as a unifying force to the nation and that the draftsmen of the Act contemplated that the Act would fulfill its unifying purpose by, among other things, facilitating interstate commerce and "facilitating travel."

As a reading of these documents demonstrates, the objective of establishing a "unifying force" and "facilitating travel" were viewed in those early years, not as being attainable through the operation of a banking travel service, but as being attainable through the establishment and circulation of a national currency. Prior to the National Currency Act of 1863, now also known as the National Bank Act, there was no national currency and financial transactions were largely conducted through the medium of bank notes issued by state banks. The establishment of a national currency provided a form of legal specie acceptable throughout the country, and it was this which provided the desired "unifying force" and assisted in "facilitating travel."

South Shore asserts that banks in the United States have been offering travel services to their customers since at least 1865, when the Security National Bank in Sheboygan, Wisconsin, formally established its bank travel department. According to South Shore, in the ensuing years of the nineteenth century and the period preceding World War I, numerous other banks began to offer travel services largely to accommodate the great number of immigrants arriving in this country. The travel service then rendered by banks involved assisting immigrants in remitting money to families in their native lands, obtaining steamship tickets for relatives, and transmitting these prepaid tickets to foreign addresses. Immigrants during this period made periodic trips "home" and needed travelers' checks, letters of credit, foreign currency and other banking assistance.

The limited and largely uncompensated services of this kind, rendered by banks during this period, bear very little resemblance to the functioning of a modern travel agency. Moreover, it was not until 1959 that the Comptroller of the Currency ruled that national banks could engage in a regular travel agency business.

On December 11, 1935, in answer to an inquiry, the Comptroller's office issued a letter stating that it would not be lawful for a national bank to invest its funds in tickets for travel of any kind for the purpose of reselling them. Continuing, the Comptroller stated that:

> "There is no legal objection, however, to a national bank acting as collection agent for a steamship, railroad or other company, its sole duty being to deliver tickets and place the amount collected to the credit of the company."

It is apparent that the travel services rendered by a bank, as thus envisioned, were relatively limited as compared to those rendered by a travel agency today, and that they were services closely related to a bank's normal functions under its express powers.

In 1949, the Comptroller issued his Rule 67, indicating that at that time national banks were deemed to be without power to operate a travel agency business.

In 1957 and 1958, the Comptroller studied and reevaluated the subject of travel services vis-a-vis national banks. At that time there were apparently about forty national banks which were engaged in the performance of travel services. On the basis of his survey, the Comptroller, in January, 1959, determined that national banks could properly continue to provide travel services "as they have been doing for many years. . . ." The quoted words apparently have reference to the activities of the forty or so national banks, out of several thousand then in operation, some of which had reported they were then rendering general travel agency services. This 1959 ruling became 12 C.F.R. § 7.1 and Paragraph 9700 of the Comptroller's Digest of Opinions.

In 1963, Paragraph 7475 of the Comptroller's Manual for National Banks was issued, and later became 12 C.F.R. § 7.7475, and 12 C.F.R. § 7.1 was deleted as unnecessary. It was in 12 C.F.R. § 7.7475 that the Comptroller finally sanctioned full travel agency operations by national banks.

Despite the Comptroller's sanction, since 1959, of the operation of travel agency business by national banks, only one hundred twenty-two out of about four thousand seven hundred national banks were engaged in that business in 1967, when this action was brought. This is far from persuasive evidence that the operation of travel service departments is useful and convenient to the functioning of normal banking services under the express powers granted by the National Bank Act.

The Comptroller and South Shore urge us, on the authority of *Inland Waterways*

Corp. v. Young, 309 U.S. 517, 524-525 (1940), and *Investment Co. Institute v. Camp*, 401 U.S. 617, 626-627 (1971), and other cases, to accord great weight to the Comptroller's construction, in 12 C.F.R. § 7.7475, of the "incidental powers" provision, 12 U.S.C. § 24, Seventh.

We fully recognize the principle to which defendants refer. But, as the Supreme Court said in *Zuber v. Allen*, 396 U.S. 168, at 192-193 (1969):

> "While this Court has announced that it will accord great weight to a departmental construction of its own enabling legislation, especially a contemporaneous construction . . . it is only one input in the interpretational equation. . . .
> "The Court may not, however, abdicate its ultimate responsibility to construe the language employed by Congress."[9]

In view of the many considerations which lead to a contrary conclusion, as reviewed above, the lack of essential articulation supporting the Comptroller's 1963 ruling, issued without opinion or accompanying statement, and in the light of the lack of uniformity in the Comptroller's own interpretation of the statute, we conclude that the Comptroller's current interpretation, as embodied in 12 C.F.R. § 7.7475, is not entitled to dispositive deference.

Defendants urge that Congress has long been aware of the Comptroller's regulation authorizing national banks to provide travel agency services and has often considered, but failed to enact, proposed legislation which would have amended the Act expressly to prohibit

---

9. A particularly pertinent application of this view is found in *Webster Groves Trust Co. v. Saxon*, 370 F.2d 381 (8th Cir. 1966), where the Eighth Circuit, in upholding the right of judicial review of the Comptroller's action in issuing a new national bank charter, said:

> "'The courts, however, have held that judicial cognizance of a controversy with the Comptroller may be taken and judicial power exercised to keep the Comptroller within statutory bounds. . . . This rule keeps the Comptroller from being a free-wheeling agency dispensing federal favors; and it gives some assurance that he will render principled decisions within the rule of law laid down by Congress.'" *Id.* at 387, quoting *Whitney National Bank v. Bank of New Orleans*, 379 U.S. 411, 427-428 (1965) (Douglas, J., dissenting).

The reference in this excerpt from the *Webster Groves Trust Co.* opinion to the need for keeping the Comptroller from being a "free-wheeling" agency, calls to mind the fact that, in 1963, when James J. Saxon, then the Comptroller, promulgated the ruling which was later to become 12 C.F.R. § 7.7475, he, in the same year, forced a number of bold and radical changes in established bank policy and, as plaintiffs correctly put it, "opened up new avenues of exploration for national banks." During that year, Comptroller Saxon, in addition to authorizing national banks to engage in the travel agency business, allowed them to enter the insurance business, underwriting business, mutual investment fund business and the armored car and courier business. Every one of these other 1963 rulings which have been challenged on their merits have subsequently been struck down by the courts. Saxon's 1963 ruling that national banks could enter the insurance business was overturned in *Georgia Ass'n of Independent Ins. Agents, Inc. v. Saxon*, 268 F. Supp. 236 (N.D.Ga. 1967), *aff'd*, 399 F.2d 1010 (5th Cir. 1968). Saxon's 1963 ruling that national banks could underwrite government securities was invalidated in *Baker, Watts & Co. v. Saxon*, 261 F. Supp. 247 (D.D.C. 1966), *aff'd* 392 F.2d 497 (D.C.Cir. 1968). His 1963 ruling that national banks could operate a mutual investment fund was set aside in *Investment Company Institute v. Camp*, 401 U.S. 617 (1971). His 1963 ruling that national banks could set up an armored car service and deposit receptacles at various locations deposits state branch banking was overturned in *First National Bank v. Dickinson*, 396 U.S. 122 (1969). In none of these cases, despite the fact that agency expertise was more directly involved than it is here, was the ruling of the Comptroller permitted to control over what the court thought was the correct construction of the relevant statute.

national banks from providing such services.

As the Supreme Court said in *Zuber v. Allen*, 396 U.S. 168, 185 (1969), "[l]egislative silence is a poor beacon to follow in discerning the proper statutory route." From the materials which are before us we cannot determine whether any committee or subcommittee of Congress rejected, on the merits, the proposal to overturn the Comptroller's ruling that national banks could engage in the travel agency business. It may very well have been that this ruling was simply viewed as an inconsequential aberration which would probably involve very few national banks and hence was not deserving of legislative attention. We think that, under the circumstances, a much more reliable guide to the correct statutory construction of 12 U.S.C. § 24, Seventh, is to be found in what the national banks, as a whole, were doing about the travel agency business. As indicated above, all but a tiny fraction of them have avoided this activity. . . .

The subsequent decision of the Supreme Court in *Investment Co. Institute v. Camp*, 401 U.S. 617, 620-621 (1971) indicates to us that the sole question for the merits is whether Congress has permitted the travel agency business as presented here. This would seem to indicate that further establishment of harm was not necessary.

But, in the event it is, we think harm to plaintiff was amply established here. . . .

[T]he district court did not err in permanently enjoining South Shore from engaging in the travel agency business and in requiring South Shore to divest itself of its travel department.

The district court ordered that divestiture be complete within six months after this judgment becomes final. South Shore complains that six months is far too short a time for it to divest itself of its travel department without substantial loss and extreme difficulty. We see possible merit in South Shore's representations as to this although we do not accept the bank's suggestion that ten years be allowed for divestiture.

Notes and Comments 5.85. Does *Arnold Tours* mean that a direct connection between the asserted incidental power and a core banking power is required? What kind of direct connection? Could an incidental power involve a *nonbanking* activity that is the *functional equivalent* of an activity that banks do engage in? Consider the following case.

M & M Leasing Corp. v. Seattle First Nat's Bank,

563 F.2d 1377 (9th Cir. 1977), *cert. denied*, 436 U.S. 956 (1978)

SNEED, Circuit Judge.

Appellees, Seattle First National Bank (Seafirst) and Peoples National Bank of Washington, are engaged in the leasing of motor vehicles and other personal property. Appellants, M & M Leasing Corporation, Goodway Leasing, Inc., Bill Pierre Leasing, Inc., and Budget Rent-a-Car of Washington-Oregon, Inc., are independent corporations engaged principally in motor vehicle leasing. Defendant-cross-appellant is the Comptroller of Currency of the United States.

Appellants, plaintiffs in the trial court, sought a declaration that the appellees' leasing of motor vehicles and other personal property was not authorized by 12 U.S.C. § 24 (Seventh), despite the fact that it is sanctioned by the Comptroller of the Currency.[2] . . .

---

2. The authorization appears in 12 C.F.R. § 7.3400 and is as follows:

"A national bank may become the owner or lessor of personal property acquired upon the specific request and for the use of a customer and may incur such additional

The trial court . . . enjoined the appellees "from engaging in motor vehicle lease transactions in which the banks assume the risk of residual value fluctuation upon termination of the lease" . . . and declared the Comptroller's interpretive rulings, 12 C.F.R. §§ 7.3400 and 7.7376, invalid to the extent they authorized such leases.

None of the parties was entirely satisfied by this disposition of their dispute. The appellee banks moved to clarify the opinion and judgment to remove "closed end" leases in which there is to be a "full payout" prior to termination of the lease from the scope of the trial court's injunction and to delete the words "motor vehicle" from the language of the injunction. The appellants thought the court's injunction should embrace all leasing and the Comptroller of Currency indicated displeasure with the restrictiveness of the trial court's opinion and injunction.

The trial court in due course amended its injunction to delete the words "motor vehicle" so that it currently reads "from engaging in lease transactions in which the banks assume the risk of residual value fluctuation upon termination of the lease." . . . Also, by order, the trial court construed its opinion and judgment as follows:

> "Lease transactions in which the lessor bank, during the initial lease term, is repaid the cost of financing the transaction, in the form of rentals, tax benefits and/or the guarantee of a financially responsible guarantor, are neither disapproved in the Court's opinion nor enjoined by the judgment entered herein." ...

These modifications satisfied the appellees but, of course, neither the appellants nor the Comptroller. Hence, this appeal was taken by them. We affirm in part and reverse in part.

In essence, we view the trial court's holding as correct, so far as it goes, but somewhat more restrictive than the law requires. As we see it, the "business of banking," which 12 U.S.C. § 24 (Seventh) authorizes the appellees to conduct, includes leases of personal property when, in the light of all relevant circumstances, the transactions constitute the loan of money secured by the properties leased. A transaction may be so characterized, in our opinion, even if it is designed so that the lessor bank does not recover during the initial lease term every penny of the cost of the leased property plus its financing costs. A lease ceases to be a secured loan when the lessor assumes material burdens other than those of a lender of money and is subject to significant risks not ordinarily incident to a secured loan. The bright line traced by the trial court provides a sound guide by which leases can be kept within the scope of the "business of banking." We are not, however, prepared to say that the trial court's bright line constitutes the precise outer limit of the "business of banking." . . .

. . . [T]he role of national banks . . . in personal property leasing generally is essentially that of a financing agency. To illustrate this it is useful to divide personal property leases into motor vehicle leases and leases of aircraft, ships and other so-called "big ticket" items.

Motor vehicle leases usually, but not invariably, are generated by automobile dealers. Particular dealers will enter into an agreement with a bank under which banks will lease automobiles to their customers. The major terms of a lease, *i.e.*, make, model, accessories, term, and payment schedule, are fashioned by the dealer in a manner that fits his and

---

> obligations as may be incident to becoming an owner and lessor of such property. Lease transactions do not result in obligations for the purpose of 12 U.S.C. 84. Since the lease payments are in the nature of rent rather than interest, 12 U.S.C. 85 and 86 are not applicable."

12 C.F.R. § 7.7376 authorizes an operating subsidiary of a national bank to "lease property."

the customer's interests and conforms to the lease design envisioned by the dealer's arrangement with the bank. To protect itself against improvident leases the bank possesses the right to review both the substantive terms of a lease and the credit-worthiness of the lessee before accepting the lease. The crucial items reviewed are the credit rating of the customer and the vehicle's residual value. Upon accepting the lease the lessee-customer is notified and instructed to make lease payments to the bank. The title of the vehicle shows the bank as the legal owner, while the customer is listed as registered owner and lessee. Customers who approach the bank initially are usually referred to dealers with whom the bank has leasing arrangements.

The bank functions somewhat differently with respect to "big ticket" items. With respect to them, generally the customer calls the bank directly and expresses an interest in leasing particular personal property. This contact essentially is to inquire about the availability of credit. The bank performs no procurement function. The customer chooses the property he wishes to lease, selects a vendor and negotiates with him the terms of the purchase. Assuming the bank finds the customer an acceptable credit risk, it then purchases the property and leases it to the customer. Delivery by the seller is made directly to the customer-lessee who makes the lease payments to the bank.

Both motor vehicle leases and "big ticket" leases provide that the burdens of operating costs and risks are borne by the lessee. Thus, the lessee agrees to purchase insurance sufficient to cover the bank's interest, to pay all repairs and maintenance, and to assume the risk of loss or damage.

Motor vehicle leases and "big ticket" leases frequently differ, however, in certain important respects. Foremost is the difference in the lessee's responsibility at the expiration of the initial term of the lease. Motor vehicle leases, for example, include a guarantee by the lessee that the vehicle will have a certain residual value at the expiration of the usual two or three year term.

This residual value is simply the anticipated resale value of the vehicle at the lease's termination. Should resale value in fact be less than the guaranteed residual value, the lessee must pay the difference. Should it be more, the excess when realized is refunded to the lessee. "Big ticket" item leases, on the other hand, normally impose no residual value guarantee on the lessees. The need for such guarantees is reduced, if not eliminated, by the fact that such leases typically are for a term which approximates the economic life of the properties. Leases in which there is a residual value guarantee are designated, in the language of commerce, as "open end" leases, while those in which no such guarantee exists are designated "closed end" leases.

Closed end leases, therefore, do impose on the lessor bank a risk not borne in the case of open end leases. In the former the lessor bank must absorb any difference between the estimated residual value at the end of the lease and a lesser actual resale price. In the open end lease, on the other hand, any such difference is guaranteed by the lessee. It is this distinction between the two types of lease that . . . strongly influenced the trial court's disposition of this case.

Notwithstanding this difference between open end and closed end leases, the lessor bank under each type of lease realizes on the property at the expiration of the lease in a substantially similar manner. Thus, at the lease's end the lessor bank will dispose of the property in the simplest possible manner. Should the lessee not purchase the item, either for the estimated residual value or for a mutually agreeable price, the lessor bank will dispose of it by sale or by way of a new lease. Motor vehicles not sold to the lessee, for example, are either resold to the dealer, sold in the wholesale market, or leased to another customer. Moreover, the record of this case does not reveal that closed end leases as a class impose significantly more onerous economic burdens on banks than do open end leases. This is not surprising because leases of "big ticket" items, leased under closed end terms, generally provide for the bank's investment plus interest to be returned by way of lease payments prior to the expiration of the lease.

From the standpoint of a bank the advantages of leasing, as opposed to traditional lending on chattel security, are said to be numerous. Certain tax benefits pertaining to depreciation and the investment tax credit are said to be available under leasing but not under lending. Leasing . . . permits the avoidance of usury laws and increases the demand for credit by eliminating the need for down payments by the customer.

Lessees also may derive advantages from leasing not available when conventional borrowing is employed. A lease obligation may be reflected on the balance sheet more favorably than an indebtedness, and leasing may permit avoidance of limitations on the lessee's ability to borrow. . . .

In any event, leasing yields to the banks a rate of return that compares favorably to that of lending. A portfolio of prudently-arranged leases imposes no greater risks than one of equally prudently-arranged loans. It is small wonder, therefore, that today over 1000 national banks are engaged in the leasing of personal property which has an aggregate value in excess of $2 billion. Thus, although much of this growth has occurred in the 1970's and resulted from the entrance of national banks into the field of motor vehicle leasing, it is clear that leasing at present is a significant part of the business of national banks.

[The court expressly adopted the *Arnold Tours* test of what constituted an "incidental power," and emphasized the "functional interchangeabilty" of leases and loans as "the touchstone of [its] decision," in essentially upholding the Comptroller's interpretation. It then turned to a discussion of the limits of its understanding of the concept "business of banking."]

It should be clear that our holding is not without limits. It does not embrace the view that national banks may compete with appellants in the daily or short-term car rental business. Nor does it permit national banks to become self-financing automobile dealers, utilizing their position to acquire an inventory of automobiles at advantageous prices to lease at going market rates to customers. Neither activity is a means by which a bank makes a "loan of money on personal security." Each is a business distinct from banking.

A national bank also leaves the business of banking when it undertakes, as a "service" to its customers, to pass on to them any price reductions which its marketing power can extract from seller of automobiles or other personal property. There may be a place for a "buyer's cooperative" in automobile marketing, but that place is not in a national bank. Such a cooperative, whether in substance or in form, is not the business of banking.

It is also clear that national banks cannot provide operational services such as repairs, maintenance, spare parts, insurance coverage, license renewals, etc. Such services are not those of a bank. This proscription shapes the duration of a lease that a national bank properly can employ. Short term leases which inescapably thrust upon the bank significant service responsibilities impose non-banking responsibilities. As previously indicated, leases of automobiles for two or three years do not necessarily entail nonbanking responsibilities; and, of course, a lease for the economic life of the property also does not.

Proscribed operational services, also, do not include the functions incident to the disposal of the property at the expiration of the lease. . . . So long as these activities constitute only the orderly liquidation of the bank's security they remain within the business of banking.

Finally, our holding manifestly is not intended to authorize leases which impose significant financial risks on national banks more onerous than those incident to loans. Therefore, it is necessary that the lessor bank look primarily to the obligations of the lessee for the entire return of its advances. It is the lessee's credit worthiness, not primarily the market value of the leased property, to which the bank must look for its return. No banker, however, ignores the borrower's collateral; nor must he when the loan is cast in lease form. Our point, put differently, is that a lease, which from its inception inevitably must be repeated or extended to enable the bank to recover its advances plus profit, is not a "loan of money on personal security." Such leases indicate a rental business, not the business of banking. To engage in the business of renting personal property would permit the assumption of risks not permitted national banks. An impermissible assumption of risks is not indicated, however, either by an open end lease, in which the bank's entire advance is guaranteed by the lessee, or a closed end lease, in which the residual value of the leased property at the expiration of the lease contributes insubstantially to the bank's recovery of its advances plus interest. . . .

KOELSCH, Circuit Judge, concurring in part, dissenting in part:

I concur in much of Judge Sneed's able effort to introduce a degree of coherence into the rapidly developing (and judicially uncharted) field of bank "lease financing." Shorn of the "language of commerce," I understand the majority to sanction two forms of lease transactions . . . : either the bank as lessor recovers all of its investment and profit in the form of rental payments from the lessee over a lease term spanning the substantial economic life of the chattel, or at the expiration of a lease term less than that of the approximate economic life of the asset, looks to the lessee to guarantee any "residual value," that is, the bank's investment and profit less the sum of rentals collected over the term of the lease. (Parenthetically, I read the majority opinion as invalidating short-term lease transactions which make no provision for the lessee's guarantee of the chattel's residual value–the so-called "closed-end lease"–except where the "residual value of the leased property at the expiration date of the lease contributes *insubstantially* to the bank's recovery of its advances plus interest." . . .

The majority approves the former transaction (typically employed, in banker's jargon in the financing of so-called "big ticket" items) because the lessor-bank, having recovered its investment over the term of the lease, assumes no risk not incidental to one aspect of the "business of banking": the "loaning of money on personal property" (12 U.S.C. § 24 (Seventh)), albeit cast in the form of a lease. Accordingly, I concur in that part of the majority opinion holding that such transactions constitute the "business of banking" within the meaning of the statute. The bank recovers its advances plus interest in the form of rentals over the term of the lease, and the record indicates that as a matter of practice in such arrangements, the bank bears no risk of having to recover its investment by regaining possession of the chattel for the purpose of further realizing on its security. I agree with the majority that such transactions are functionally indistinguishable from purchase money loans secured by a lien-like interest in the chattel.

The majority upholds the use of short-term leases, however–Typically employed in the "financing" of motor vehicles and like consumer items–on the ground that in such transactions the bank looks to the creditworthiness of the lessee to guarantee the anticipated resale value of personal property leased for a term less than that of its approximate economic life, thus freeing the bank of any obligation to realize further on the chattel by repeated leasings or comparable means of recovering its investment. The majority appears to reach this result by analogizing the bank's recovery and disposition of the chattel at the expiration of the lease to "the orderly liquidation of the bank's security. . . ."

I agree, of course, with the proposition that a "lessor"-national bank may properly engage in functions incident to the orderly liquidation of its security. That is a traditional incident of the "business of banking" necessitated when any borrower defaults on a loan. But

I do not regard that rule as in any way relevant to the present inquiry. In my view, the short-term lease arrangement entered into between the bank and the lessee contemplates at the outset that the bank will inevitably gain or regain possession of the subject matter of the so-called lease and that the amount reserved as rent does not reflect the full value (or price) of the chattel plus interest. In such cases, the transaction is not, in my view, to be deemed one which constitutes the "business of banking" within the meaning of the statute. For in every such instance the fact is manifest that the bank itself will ultimately become the owner of the chattel.

In such a short-term lease transaction, it matters not whether the bank secures the guarantee of the lessee as to the residual value of the chattel at the expiration of the lease or must itself bear the risk of a downward fluctuation in value. On whomever the risk of a downward market falls, the bank as lessor must–if the lessee himself does not agree to purchase the property–look to the market in the first instance in order to realize the full value of its investment. The majority concedes as much . . . in noting that "[s]hould the lessee not purchase the item . . . the lessor bank will dispose of it by sale or by way of a new lease." The bank is thus drawn ineluctably into the business of disposing of used chattels–not in pursuit of the lender's traditional remedy of foreclosure and sale incident to the borrower's default–but pursuant to the terms of the lease agreement itself. In my view, the resultant preordained participation of national banks in the market disposition of personal property is neither a part of the "business of banking" nor an incident thereto. I accordingly dissent from that part of the majority opinion holding short-term lease financing by national banks to be within the purview of 12 U.S.C. § 24 (Seventh).

Notes and Comments 5.86. What is the majority in *M & M Leasing* authorizing national banks to do with respect to leasing? To what extent does Judge Koelsch disagree, and why?

5.87. Does "functional interchangeability" add anything to traditional notions of "incidental powers"?

5.88. Why should it be "clear" that the holding in *M & M Leasing* "does not embrace the view that national banks may compete with appellants in the daily or short-term car rental business"? The court insists that this activity would not be "a means by which a bank makes a 'loan of money on personal security.'" Is there any meaningful difference for these purposes between long-term and short-term leasing, other than the length of time the bank is exposed to risk that its contracting party will not faithfully perform its part of the bargain?

5.89. *Functional equivalence as a test of incidental powers*. One recent case, involving complex issues of the relationship between the NBA incidental powers provision and the Bank Holding Company Act "closely related" activities test suggested that "functional equivalence" may be important in determining whether an activity is incidental to the business of banking. Does the following case adopt functional equivalence as the test of incidental powers?

American Insurance Ass'n v. Clarke

865 F.2d 278 (D.C.Cir. 1989)[a]

BUCKLEY, Circuit Judge:

. . . Appellant challenges the Comptroller of the Currency's concurrence in a

---

a. The court's original opinion, 854 F.2d 1405 (D.C. Cir. 1988), was withdrawn.

proposal by Citibank to form a subsidiary to offer municipal bond insurance. We affirm the district court's rejection of appellant's claim that the Comptroller's action violates the National Bank Act, but we reverse the court's dismissal of appellant's challenge under the Bank Holding Company Act. . . .

Citibank, N.A. ("Citibank"), a national bank chartered under 12 U.S.C. §21 (1982), is a wholly-owned subsidiary of Citicorp, a registered bank holding company. On January 30, 1985, Citibank notified the Comptroller of the Currency ("Comptroller") under 12 C.F.R. §5.34(d)(1) (1988) of its intention to establish a subsidiary to offer municipal bond insurance. As Citibank's subsidiary, the American Municipal Bond Assurance Corporation ("AMBAC") is subject to the same restrictions applicable to national banks. 12 C.F.R. §5.34(d)(2)(i) (1988).

The service offered by AMBAC under Citibank's proposal would operate as follows. A municipality wishing to issue bonds would apply to AMBAC for insurance. (We will refer to AMBAC's service as "insurance" without deciding whether it meets the legal criteria for insurance under various regulatory schemes.) After engaging in a traditional credit analysis (determining the ability of the issuer to satisfy the claims in the event of default), AMBAC would offer the insurance in the form of a "standby credit." If the issuer defaults, the bondholders would present documentary proof of nonpayment to AMBAC, which would pay the interest and principal due the bondholders. AMBAC would then be subrogated to the rights of the bondholders against the issuer. . . .

The Comptroller concurred in Citibank's proposal, concluding that AMBAC's activities were permissible under the National Bank Act ("NBA") . . . , and the Bank Holding Company Act ("BHCA") . . . . AMBAC began operations shortly thereafter. The American Insurance Association ("AIA"), a trade group representing property and casualty insurance companies, then repaired to the district court, seeking declaratory and injunctive relief to set aside the Comptroller's order. Citibank intervened as a party defendant. The district court eventually entered summary judgment for the Comptroller, . . . and the AIA appealed. . . .

The Supreme Court recently reaffirmed that the principles concerning judicial deference to an agency's interpretation of its governing statute apply to the Comptroller's interpretation of the NBA. *Clarke v. Securities Indus. Ass'n*, 479 U.S. 388 (1987). Those principles, of course, were outlined by *Chevron, U.S.A. Inc. v. NRDC, Inc.*, 467 U.S. 837 (1984). If Congress has spoken directly to the precise question at issue, we must enforce that unambiguously expressed intent. *Id.* at 842-43. If congressional intent is unclear, however, we will defer to the agency's permissible construction, *id.* at 843, *i.e.*, one that is "rational and consistent with the statute." *NLRB v. United Food & Commercial Workers Union, Local 23*, --- U.S. ----, 108 S.Ct. 413, 421 (1987). . . .

Appellant first argues that the Comptroller's approval of the Citibank proposal violates the NBA. As the NBA does not specifically prohibit AMBAC's municipal bond insurance, congressional intent is unclear, and we will defer to the Comptroller's decision if it is rational and consistent with the statute. . . .

Appellant argues that a bank may engage only in those activities specifically mentioned and others incident (i.e., convenient or useful) to the expressly authorized activities. . . .

We agree with the district court, however, that this reflects "a narrow and artificially rigid view of both the business of banking and the [NBA]." Rather than attempt to correlate municipal bond insurance to a specific power mentioned in section 24 (Seventh), the Comptroller focused on the essence of AMBAC's service: the provision of credit. We agree with the district court that

> the business of banking involves the substitution of the "[bank's] own credit,

> which has general acceptance in the business community, for the individual's credit, which has only limited acceptability. . . . It is the end for which a bank exists." Indeed, the extension of credit on both a secured and unsecured basis is such a long-standing practice under the [NBA] that credit is today viewed as one of "[t]he principal banking 'products.'" Banks provide this "product" in a variety of forms not specifically enumerated in the [NBA]: they offer irrevocable lines of credit, standby and mercantile letters of credit, and check guaranty and credit card programs. See e.g., 12 C.F.R. §§7.7017, 7.7016, 7.378, 32.3 (1985).

656 F.Supp. at 408 (citations omitted; ellipsis original).

We do not think the Comptroller acted irrationally in concluding that AMBAC's municipal bond insurance was part of the business of banking, sufficiently similar to credit services routinely performed by banks. The Comptroller, in his expert financial judgment, concluded that AMBAC's proposed use of standby credits to insure municipal bonds was functionally equivalent to the issuance of a standby letter of credit, a device long recognized as within the business of banking.

To understand the Comptroller's comparison of AMBAC's standby credits with standby letters of credit, we begin with a brief review of the operation of letters of credit, which come in two basic forms: commercial and standby. A basic function of the commercial letter of credit is to make it possible for a seller to ship goods to a buyer whose creditworthiness is unknown to him in confidence that the goods will be paid for.

> Stripped to its essentials, the [commercial letter of credit] transaction runs as follows: the buyer arranges for a bank–whose credit the seller will accept–to issue a letter of credit in which the bank agrees to pay drafts drawn on it by the seller if, but only if, such drafts are accompanied by specified documents, such as bills of lading or air freight receipts, representing title to the goods that are the subject matter of the transaction between buyer and seller. The bank undertakes this obligation for a specified period of time.

Verkuil, *Bank Solvency and Guaranty Letters of Credit*, 25 Stan. L. Rev. 716, 718 (1973). The obligation created by the letter of credit is absolute. Upon the presentation of the stipulated documents by the seller, the bank is required to make the payment irrespective of any counterclaims the buyer might have against the seller.

A standby letter of credit represents the other side of the commercial letter of credit coin. Whereas the latter is used to guarantee payment upon performance, the former guarantees payment upon a failure to perform. Thus, by way of illustration, if a purchaser is concerned over the seller's ability to deliver the contracted goods on schedule, the seller may ask his bank to open a standby letter of credit in favor of the buyer. If the buyer subsequently presents documents showing that the seller has failed to deliver the goods, his bank is obliged to pay the buyer the amount specified in the standby letter. The bank will be reimbursed by the seller.

Although the two varieties of letters of credit differ, they serve the same essential purpose: to facilitate transactions by substituting the credit of the bank for that of one of the contracting parties. Banks have long been permitted to provide this form of credit. *See, e.g.*, 12 C.F.R. §7.7016 (1988) (letters of credit); *First Empire Bank-New York v. FDIC*, 572 F.2d 1361, 1367 (9th Cir.) (standby credits), *cert. denied*, 439 U.S. 919 (1978); 12 C.F.R. §32.2(e) (1988) (recognizing standby letters of credit as service provided by banks). As one commentator has explained:

> The nature of the banking business implies the lawful power to make loans. A

> necessary incident of that power is the power to commit to make the loan at a future date. If that future commitment is made to a third party, it amounts to a present loan of credit. So long as the bank's promise is made for the account of its customer, and is a money promise, its characterization or form should be immaterial in determining its validity. . . .

H. Harfield, Bank Credits and Acceptances 165-66 (5th ed. 1974).

The Comptroller concluded that AMBAC's municipal bond insurance was sufficiently similar to a standby letter of credit to qualify as part of the business of banking. The Comptroller noted that the insurance met all but one of the guidelines ordinarily imposed on letters of credit "[a]s a matter of sound banking practice," 12 C.F.R. §7.7016 (1988): AMBAC's standby credits are for a definite term, limited in amount, oblige AMBAC to pay upon presentation of documents (the unpaid bond or notice from the trustee), and result in an unqualified obligation of the issuer to reimburse the bank (through subrogation). *See id.* The AMBAC insurance departs from the guidelines only in that it is not labelled "letter of credit." The Comptroller observed, however, that the regulation does not establish an inflexible definition of letters of credit, each element of which must be satisfied in every case. Rather, it provides a guideline for sound banking practice that may be waived in part when appropriate. *See, e.g.*, Comptroller of the Currency, Interpretive Letter No. 214. . . . Moreover, the Comptroller's lending limits refer to a standby letter of credit as

> any letter of credit, or similar arrangement, *however named or described*, which represents an obligation on the part of the issuer . . . (3) to make payment on account of any default by the account party in the performance of an obligation.

12 C.F.R. §32.2(e) (1988) (emphasis added). The Comptroller's conclusion that AMBAC's standby credits satisfy this standard is well within his discretion.

. . . [T]he Comptroller also concluded that AMBAC's service was functionally equivalent to a standby letter of credit because AMBAC will engage in a financial rather than an actuarial analysis. In other words, AMBAC will not rely on an estimate of the likelihood of default, but on the issuer's financial strength in the event of default. The district court correctly concluded that the Comptroller's expert judgment in this regard should not be overturned. . . .

Appellant's final claim is that AMBAC's standby credits are impermissible guarantees because AMBAC is reimbursed by means of subrogation. But the means of reimbursement is not essential in distinguishing a guaranty from a standby letter of credit. The "central distinction" between the two is that the standby credit

> creates a primary liability on an original obligation–to pay on the presentation of documents–whereas the contract of guaranty creates a secondary liability on the pre-existing obligation of another–to pay in the event that the other does not.

Bank of North Carolina, N.A. v. Rock Island Bank, 570 F.2d 202, 206 n. 7 (7th Cir.1978). The Comptroller properly classified AMBAC's insurance as a standby credit because AMBAC's obligation to pay arises upon the presentation of documents (the unpaid bond or notice from the trustee), not upon actual proof of the issuer's default. The means of reimbursement is not controlling in this classification.

Appellant correctly notes that the Comptroller's regulations provide that "the bank's customer should have an *unqualified* obligation to reimburse the bank for payment under the letter of credit." 12 C.F.R. §7.7016 (e) (1988) (emphasis added). This requirement, however, ordinarily is imposed "[a]s a matter of sound banking practice," 12 C.F.R. §7.7016, not as a means of distinguishing a permissible banking practice from an impermissible guaranty. See Comptroller of the Currency, Interpretive Letter No. 295 . . . (five requirements of section 7.7016 "are 'merely' matters of 'sound banking practice;' they do not circumscribe the limits of the 'no guaranty' rule"). . . .

Appellant nevertheless challenges the Comptroller's determination that AMBAC's credits satisfy the sound banking practice requirement. AMBAC's right to reimbursement from the issuer is not unqualified, argues appellant, because AMBAC is merely subrogated to the rights of the bondholders. Its right to repayment is therefore subject to whatever defenses that issuer would have against the bondholder. . . .

Appellant claims that the Comptroller's treatment of subrogation here is inconsistent with his decision in Interpretive Letter No. 295. The Comptroller there rejected a bank's application to offer political risk insurance to other banks making offshore loans. Among his concerns was that the bank offering the insurance would be subrogated to the loaning bank in the event of default, thus potentially involving the insuring bank in disputes between the debtor and the loaning bank. . . . Of greater significance, however, was the complete absence of credit evaluation by the insuring bank, which relied totally on actuarial estimates of the likelihood of the political risks causing default. *Id.* Such actuarial assessments are problematic generally, and especially so when the bank proposes to insure against highly speculative risks. In the present case, the Comptroller concluded that the marginal increase in risk caused by AMBAC's method of reimbursement was insufficient to create an unsound banking practice, in view of the totality of the circumstances. . . .

Notes and Comments 5.90. *American Insurance Ass'n* is one of several important recent inroads of national banks into the insurance sector of the financial services industry, each involving the incidental powers concept. Consider the following case.

NationsBank of North Carolina, N.A. v. Variable Annuity Life Insurance Co.

513 U.S. 251 (1995)

Justice GINSBURG delivered the opinion of the Court.

These consolidated cases present the question whether national banks may serve as agents in the sale of annuities. The Comptroller of the Currency . . . determined that federal law permits such annuity sales as a service to bank customers. Specifically, the Comptroller considered the sales at issue "incidental" to "the business of banking" . . . . The Comptroller further concluded that annuities are not "insurance" within the meaning of §92; that provision, by expressly authorizing banks in towns of no more than 5,000 people to sell insurance, arguably implies that banks in larger towns may not sell insurance. The United States District Court for the Southern District of Texas upheld the Comptroller's conclusions as a permissible reading of the National Bank Act, but the United States Court of Appeals for the Fifth Circuit reversed. We are satisfied that the Comptroller's construction of the Act is reasonable and therefore warrants judicial deference. Accordingly, we reverse the judgment of the Court of Appeals. . . .

Petitioner NationsBank of North Carolina, N.A., a national bank based in Charlotte, and its brokerage subsidiary sought permission from the Comptroller of the Currency, pursuant to 12 CFR §5.34 (1994), for the brokerage subsidiary to act as an agent in the sale of annuities. Annuities are contracts under which the purchaser makes one or more premium payments to the issuer in exchange for a series of payments, which continue either for a fixed period or for the life of the purchaser or a designated beneficiary. When a purchaser invests in a "variable" annuity, the purchaser's money is invested in a designated way and payments to the purchaser vary with investment performance. In a classic "fixed" annuity, in contrast, payments do not vary. Under the contracts NationsBank proposed to sell, purchasers could direct their payments to a variable, fixed, or hybrid account, and would be allowed periodically to modify their choice. The issuers would be various insurance companies. *See* Letter from J. Michael Shepherd, Senior Deputy Comptroller, to Robert M. Kurucza (Mar. 21, 1990) . . . (Comptroller's Letter).

The Comptroller granted NationsBank's application. He concluded that national banks have authority to broker annuities within "the business of banking" under 12 U.S.C. §24 Seventh. He further concluded that §92 . . . did not impede his approval; for purposes of that provision, the Comptroller explained, annuities do not rank as "insurance." . . .

Respondent Variable Annuity Life Insurance Co. (VALIC), which sells annuities, challenged the Comptroller's decision. . . . Relying on its decision in *Saxon v. Georgia Assn. of Independent Ins. Agents, Inc.*, 399 F.2d 1010 (1968), the Fifth Circuit first held that §92 bars banks not located in small towns from selling insurance, and then rejected the Comptroller's view that annuities are not insurance for purposes of §92. . . .

Authorizing national banks to "carry on the business of banking," the National Bank Act provides that such banks shall have power -- "To exercise . . . all such incidental powers as shall be necessary to carry on the business of banking; by discounting and negotiating promissory notes, drafts, bills of exchange, and other evidences of debt; by receiving deposits; by buying and selling exchange, coin, and bullion; by loaning money on personal security; and by obtaining, issuing, and circulating notes. . . . The business of dealing in securities and stock by the [bank] shall be limited to purchasing and selling such securities and stock without recourse, solely upon the order, and for the account of, customers, and in no case for its own account, and the [bank] shall not underwrite any issue of securities or stock. . . ." 12 U.S.C. §24 Seventh (1988 ed. and Supp. V).

As the administrator charged with supervision of the National Bank Act, . . . the Comptroller bears primary responsibility for surveillance of "the business of banking" authorized by §24 Seventh. We have reiterated: "'It is settled that courts should give great weight to any reasonable construction of a regulatory statute adopted by the agency charged with the enforcement of that statute. The Comptroller of the Currency is charged with the enforcement of banking laws to an extent that warrants the invocation of this principle with respect to his deliberative conclusions as to the meaning of these laws.'" *Clarke v. Securities Industry Assn.*, 479 U.S. 388, 403-404 (1987) (quoting *Investment Company Institute v. Camp*, 401 U.S. 617, 626-627 (1971)). Under the formulation now familiar, when we confront an expert administrator's statutory exposition, we inquire first whether "the intent of Congress is clear" as to "the precise question at issue." *Chevron U.S.A. Inc. v. Natural Resources Defense Council, Inc.*, 467 U.S. 837, 842 (1984). If so, "that is the end of the matter." *Ibid.* But "if the statute is silent or ambiguous with respect to the specific issue, the question for the court is whether the agency's answer is based on a permissible construction of the statute." *Id.*, at 843. If the administrator's reading fills a gap or defines a term in a way that is reasonable in light of the legislature's revealed design, we give the administrator's judgment "controlling weight." *Id.*, at 844.

In authorizing NationsBank to broker annuities, the Comptroller invokes the "power [of banks] to broker a wide variety of financial investment instruments," . . . which the Comptroller considers "part of [banks'] traditional role as financial intermediaries," ... and therefore an "incidental powe[r] . . . necessary to carry on the business of banking." 12 U.S.C. §24 Seventh. . . . The Comptroller construes the §24 Seventh authorization of "incidental powers . . . necessary to carry on the business of banking" as an independent grant of authority; he reads the specific powers set forth thereafter as exemplary, not exclusive.

VALIC argues that the Comptroller's interpretation is contrary to the clear intent of Congress because the banking power on which the Comptroller relies–"broker[ing] financial investment instruments"–is not specified in §24 Seventh. . . . According to VALIC, the five specific activities listed in §24 Seventh after the words "business of banking" are exclusive–banks are confined to these five activities and to endeavors incidental thereto. . . . VALIC thus attributes no independent significance to the words "business of banking." We think the Comptroller better comprehends the Act's terms.

The second sentence of §24 Seventh, in limiting banks' "dealing in securities," presupposes that banks have authority not circumscribed by the five specifically listed activities. Congress' insertion of the limitation decades after the Act's initial adoption makes sense only if banks already had authority to deal in securities, authority presumably encompassed within the "business of banking" language which dates from 1863. VALIC argues, however, that the limitation was imposed by the GlassSteagall Act of 1933, and that the power Glass-Steagall presupposed was specifically granted in the McFadden Act of 1927. . . . While the statute's current wording derives from the Glass-Steagall Act, . . . the earlier McFadden Act does not bolster VALIC's case, for that Act, too, limited an activity already part of the business national banks did. *See* Act of Feb. 25, 1927, §2(b), 44 Stat. 1226 ("Provided, That the business of buying and selling investment securities shall hereinafter be limited to buying and selling without recourse. . . ."); *see also Clarke v. Securities Industry Assn., supra*, 479 U.S., at 407-408 (even before the McFadden Act, banks conducted securities transactions on a widespread basis). . . .[2]

[T]he Comptroller . . . then reasonably concluded that the authority to sell annuities qualifies as part of, or incidental to, the business of banking. National banks, the Comptroller observed, are authorized to serve as agents for their customers in the purchase and sale of various financial investment instruments, . . . and annuities are widely recognized as just such investment products. . . .

By making an initial payment in exchange for a future income stream, the customer is deferring consumption, setting aside money for retirement, future expenses, or a rainy day. For her, an annuity is like putting money in a bank account, a debt instrument, or a mutual fund. Offering bank accounts and acting as agent in the sale of debt instruments and mutual funds are familiar parts of the business of banking. *See, e.g., Securities Industry Assn. v. Board of Governors, FRS*, 468 U.S. 207, 215 ("Banks long have arranged the purchase and sale of securities as an accommodation to their customers."); *First Nat. Bank of Hartford v. Hartford*, 273 U.S. 548, 559-560 (1927) (banks have authority to sell mortgages and other debt instruments they have originated or acquired by discount).

In sum, modern annuities, though more sophisticated than the standard savings bank deposits of old, answer essentially the same need. By providing customers with the opportunity to invest in one or more annuity options, banks are essentially offering financial investment instruments of the kind congressional authorization permits them to broker. Hence, the Comptroller reasonably typed the permission NationsBank sought as an "incide-

2. We expressly hold that the "business of banking" is not limited to the enumerated powers in §24 Seventh and that the Comptroller therefore has discretion to authorize activities beyond those specifically enumerated. The exercise of the Comptroller's discretion, however, must be kept within reasonable bounds. Ventures distant from dealing in financial investment instruments–for example, operating a general travel agency–may exceed those bounds.

ntal powe[r] . . . necessary to carry on the business of banking."[4] . . .

In the alternative, VALIC argues that 12 U.S.C. §92 (1988 ed., Supp. V) bars NationsBank from selling annuities as agent. . . .

The parties disagree about whether §92, by negative implication, precludes national banks located in places more populous than 5,000 from selling insurance. We do not reach this question because we accept the Comptroller's view that, for the purpose at hand, annuities are properly classified as investments, not "insurance."

Again, VALIC contends that the Comptroller's determination is contrary to the plain intent of Congress, or else is unreasonable. In support of its position that annuities are insurance, VALIC notes first that annuities traditionally have been sold by insurance companies. But the sale of a product by an insurance company does not inevitably render the product insurance. For example, insurance companies have long offered loans on the security of life insurance, . . . but a loan does not thereby become insurance.

VALIC further asserts that most States have regulated annuities as insurance and that Congress intended to define insurance under §92 by reference to state law. Treatment of annuities under state law, however, is contextual. States generally classify annuities as insurance when defining the powers of insurance companies and state insurance regulators. *See, e.g.*, 998 F.2d, at 1300, n. 2 (citing statutes). But in diverse settings, States have resisted lump classification of annuities as insurance. *See, e.g., In re New York State Assn. of Life Underwriters, Inc. v. New York State Banking Dept.*, 83 N.Y.2d 353, 363, 610 N.Y.S.2d 470, 475, 632 N.E.2d 876, 881 (1994) (rejecting "assertion that annuities are insurance which [state-chartered] banks are not authorized to sell," even though state insurance law "includes 'annuities' in its description of 'kinds of insurance authorized' "); *In re Estate of Rhodes*, 197 Misc. 232, 237, 94 N.Y.S.2d 406, 411 (Surr.Ct.1949) (annuity contracts do not qualify for New York estate tax exemption applicable to insurance); *Commonwealth v. Metropolitan Life Ins. Co.*, 254 Pa. 510, 513- 516, 98 A. 1072, 1073 (1916) (annuities are not insurance for purposes of tax that insurance companies pay on insurance premiums received within the State); *State ex rel. Equitable Life Assurance Soc. of United States v. Ham*, 54 Wyo. 148, 159, 88 P.2d 484, 488 (1939) (same).

As our decisions underscore, a characterization fitting in certain contexts may be unsuitable in others. Moreover, the federal banking law does not plainly require automatic reference to state law here. The Comptroller has concluded that the federal regime is best served by classifying annuities according to their functional characteristics. Congress has not ruled out that course . . . ; courts, therefore, have no cause to dictate to the Comptroller the state law constraint VALIC espouses.

VALIC further argues that annuities functionally resemble life insurance because some annuities place mortality risk on the parties. Under a classic fixed annuity, the purchaser pays a sum certain and, in exchange, the issuer makes periodic payments throughout, but not beyond, the life of the purchaser. In pricing such annuities, issuers rely on actuarial assumptions about how long purchasers will live.

While cognizant of this similarity between annuities and insurance, the Comptroller points out that mortality risk is a less salient characteristic of contemporary products. Many annuities currently available, both fixed and variable, do not feature a life term. Instead they provide for payments over a term of years; if the purchaser dies before the term ends, the balance is paid to the purchaser's estate. Moreover, the presence of mortality risk does not necessarily qualify an investment as "insurance" under §92. For example, VALIC recognizes

---

4. Assuring that the brokerage in question would not deviate from traditional bank practices, the Comptroller specified that NationsBank "will act only as agent, . . . will not have a principal stake in annuity contracts and therefore will incur no interest rate or actuarial risks." . . .

that a life interest in real property is not insurance, although it imposes a mortality risk on the purchaser. . . . Some conventional debt instruments similarly impose mortality risk. . . .

VALIC also charges the Comptroller with inconsistency. As evidence, VALIC refers to a 1978 letter from a member of the Comptroller's staff describing annuity investments as insurance arrangements. . . . *[S]ee* Letter from Charles F. Byrd, Assistant Director, Legal Advisory Services Division, Office of the Comptroller of the Currency (June 16, 1978) . . . (Byrd Letter). We note, initially, that the proposal disfavored in the 1978 letter did not clearly involve a bank selling annuities as an agent, rather than as a principal. *See* Byrd Letter . . . ("[T]he bank would purchase a group annuity policy from an insurer and then sell annuity contracts as investments in trust accounts."). Furthermore, unlike the Comptroller's letter to NationsBank here, the 1978 letter does not purport to represent the Comptroller's position. *Compare* Byrd Letter . . . ("It is my opinion . . .") *with* Comptroller's Letter . . . ("The OCC's legal position on this issue was announced in a [prior 1990 letter]. Since I find neither policy nor supervisory reasons to object to this proposal, the Subsidiary may proceed."). Finally, any change in the Comptroller's position might reduce, but would not eliminate, the deference we owe his reasoned determinations. . . .

The Comptroller's classification of annuities, based on the tax deferral and investment features that distinguish them from insurance, in short, is at least reasonable. . . . A key feature of insurance is that it indemnifies loss. . . . As the Comptroller observes, annuities serve an important investment purpose and are functionally similar to other investments that banks typically sell. . . . And though fixed annuities more closely resemble insurance than do variable annuities, fixed annuities too have significant investment features and are functionally similar to debt instruments. *See ibid.* Moreover, mindful that fixed annuities are often packaged with variable annuities, the Comptroller reasonably chose to classify the two together.

Notes and Comments 5.91. *NationsBank* is one of the Supreme Court's latest statements on judicial deference to the discretionary judgments of federal banking agencies. What test does Justice Ginsburg apply in deciding whether to defer to the Comptroller's judgment? How does this test compare with, for example, the test applied in *Camp v. Pitts, supra*? How does the *Camp* test compare with the following excerpt?

Smiley v. Citibank (South Dakota), N. A.

517 U.S. 735 (1996)

Justice SCALIA delivered the opinion of the Court.

[The case involved the proper interpretation of the term "interest" in the NBA usury provision, 12 U.S.C. § 85, and specifically whether that term included late payment charges. If it did include such charges, then state law attempting to regulate the charges would be preempted. (These substantive aspects of the case are discussed in § 2, *supra.*) During the pendency of the litigation in *Smiley*, the Comptroller promulgated an interpretation of section 85 that included late charges within the meaning of the term interest.]

. . . It is our practice to defer to the reasonable judgments of agencies with regard to the meaning of ambiguous terms in statutes that they are charged with administering. *See Chevron U.S.A. Inc. v. Natural Resources Defense Council, Inc.*, 467 U.S. 837, 842-845 (1984). As we observed only last Term, that practice extends to the judgments of the Comptroller of the Currency with regard to the meaning of the banking laws. "The Comptroller of the Currency," we said, "is charged with the enforcement of banking laws to an extent that warrants the invocation of [the rule of deference] with respect to his deliberative conclusions as to the meaning of these laws." *NationsBank of N. C., N.A. v. Variable Annuity Life Ins. Co.*, 513 U.S. ----, ----, 115 S.Ct. 810, 813 (1995) (citations and internal quotation marks omitted). . . .

Petitioner proposes several reasons why the ordinary rule of deference should not apply to this regulation. First, petitioner points to the fact that this regulation was issued more than 100 years after the enactment of § 85, and seemingly as a result of this and similar litigation in which the Comptroller has participated as amicus curiae on the side of the banks. The 100-year delay makes no difference. To be sure, agency interpretations that are of long standing come before us with a certain credential of reasonableness, since it is rare that error would long persist. But neither antiquity nor contemporaneity with the statute is a condition of validity. We accord deference to agencies under *Chevron*, not because of a presumption that they drafted the provisions in question, or were present at the hearings, or spoke to the principal sponsors; but rather because of a presumption that Congress, when it left ambiguity in a statute meant for implementation by an agency, understood that the ambiguity would be resolved, first and foremost, by the agency, and desired the agency (rather than the courts) to possess whatever degree of discretion the ambiguity allows. *See Chevron, supra*, at 843-844. Nor does it matter that the regulation was prompted by litigation, including this very suit. Of course we deny deference "to agency litigating positions that are wholly unsupported by regulations, rulings, or administrative practice," *Bowen v. Georgetown Univ. Hospital*, 488 U.S. 204, 212 (1988). The deliberateness of such positions, if not indeed their authoritativeness, is suspect. But we have before us here a full-dress regulation, issued by the Comptroller himself and adopted pursuant to the notice-and-comment procedures of the Administrative Procedure Act designed to assure due deliberation, *see* 5 U.S.C. § 553; *Thompson v. Clark*, 741 F.2d 401, 409 (C.A.D.C. 1984). That it was litigation which disclosed the need for the regulation is irrelevant.

Second, petitioner contends that the Comptroller's regulation is not deserving of our deference because "there is no rational basis for distinguishing the various charges [it] has denominated interest . . . from those charges it has denominated 'non-interest.'" . . . We disagree. As an analytical matter, it seems to us perfectly possible to draw a line, as the regulation does, between (1) "payment compensating a creditor or prospective creditor for an extension of credit, making available of a line of credit, or any default or breach by a borrower of a condition upon which credit was extended," and (2) all other payments. To be sure, in the broadest sense all payments connected in any way with the loan–including reimbursement of the lender's costs in processing the application, insuring the loan, and appraising the collateral–can be regarded as "compensating [the] creditor for [the] extension of credit." But it seems to us quite possible and rational to distinguish, as the regulation does, between those charges that are specifically assigned to such expenses and those that are assessed for simply making the loan, or for the borrower's default. In its logic, at least, the line is not "arbitrary [or] capricious," and thereby disentitled to deference under *Chevron, see* 467 U.S., at 844. . . .

Finally, petitioner argues that the regulation is not entitled to deference because it is inconsistent with positions taken by the Comptroller in the past. Of course the mere fact that an agency interpretation contradicts a prior agency position is not fatal. Sudden and unexplained change, . . . or change that does not take account of legitimate reliance on prior interpretation . . . may be "arbitrary, capricious [or] an abuse of discretion," 5 U.S.C. § 706(2)(A). But if these pitfalls are avoided, change is not invalidating, since the whole point of *Chevron* is to leave the discretion provided by the ambiguities of a statute with the implementing agency.

In any case, we do not think that anything which can accurately be described as a change of official agency position has occurred here. The agency's Notice of Proposed Rulemaking asserted that the new regulation "reflect[s] current law and [Office of the Comptroller of the Currency (OCC)] interpretive letters," 60 Fed. Reg. 11929 (1995), and the Statement of Basis and Purpose accompanying the final adoption stated that "[t]he final ruling is consistent with OCC interpretive letters in this area . . . and reflects the position the OCC has taken in amicus curiae briefs in litigation pending in many state and Federal courts," 61 Fed. Reg. 4859 (1996) (citing OCC interpretive letters). Petitioner points only to (1) a June 1964 letter from the Comptroller to the President's Committee on Consumer Interests, which states that "[c]harges for late payments, credit life insurance, recording fees, documentary stamp are illustrations of charges which are made by some banks which would not properly be characterized as interest," . . . and (2) a 1988 opinion letter from the Deputy Chief Counsel of the OCC stating "it is my position that [under § 85] the laws of the states where the banks are located . . . determine whether or not the banks can impose the foregoing fees and charges [including late fees] on Iowa residents," OCC Interpretive Letter No. 452, *reprinted in* 1988-1989 Transfer Binder, CCH Fed. Banking L. Rep. ¶ 85,676 p. 78,064 (1988). We doubt whether either of these statements was sufficient in and of itself to establish a binding agency policy–the former, because it was too informal, and the latter because it only purported to represent the position of the Deputy Chief Counsel in response to an inquiry concerning particular banks. Nor can it even be argued that the two statements reflect a prior agency policy, since, in addition to contradicting the regulation before us here, they also contradict one another–the former asserting that "interest" is a nationally uniform concept, and the latter that it is to be determined by reference to state law. What these statements show, if anything, is that there was good reason for the Comptroller to promulgate the new regulation, in order to eliminate uncertainty and confusion.

In addition to offering these reasons why 12 CFR § 7.4001(a) in particular is not entitled to deference, petitioner contends that no Comptroller interpretation of § 85 is entitled to deference, because § 85 is a provision that pre-empts state law. . . . [T]here is no doubt that § 85 pre-empts state law. In *Marquette Nat. Bank of Minneapolis v. First of Omaha Service Corp.*, 439 U.S. 299 (1978), we dismissed petitioners' argument that the "exportation" of interest rates from the bank's home State would "significantly impair the ability of States to enact effective usury laws" with the observation that "[t]his impairment . . . has always been implicit in the structure of the National Bank Act. . . . [T]he protection of state usury laws is an issue of legislative policy, and any plea to alter § 85 to further that end is better addressed to the wisdom of Congress than to the judgment of this Court." *Id.*, at 318-319. What is at issue here is simply the meaning of a provision that does not . . . deal with pre-emption, and hence does not bring into play the considerations petitioner raises.

Notes and Comments 5.92. Both *NationsBank* and *Smiley* are also of interest for their treatment of an alleged inconsistency between the Comptroller's current position and an earlier OCC interpretive position purportedly at odds with the current position. Temporal inconsistency in interpretive positions might conceivably lead to a conclusion that an agency's current interpretation is not entitled to deference. *See, e.g., National Alliance of Postal & Fed. Employees v. Nickerson, supra* at 58 (challenging inconsistency in NCUA interpretation of chartering requirements). How does Justice Ginsburg's treatment of this issue in *NationsBank* compare with Judge Waddy's approach in *Nickerson*? How does Justice Scalia's treatment of this issue in *Smiley*, compare with *NationsBank* and *Nickerson*?

5.93. *NationsBank* authorizes a national bank to act as an agent (through its securities subsidiary) in the sale of annuities within "the business of banking" under 12 U.S.C. § 24(Seventh). For a discussion of this aspect of the decision, see 2 MICHAEL P. MALLOY, BANKING LAW AND REGULATION § 7.02[C] (2d ed., Aspen Publishers, 2011). In this context, the Court examined the proper construction of the provision itself. How does the Court understand the term "business of banking"? How does its understanding compare with that found in *Arnold Tours*? In *M & M Leasing*? In the *AMBAC* decision?

5.94. *Insurance activities and national banks. NationsBank* avoids the issue of the scope of permissible insurance powers of national banks by accepting the Comptroller's interpretation that variable annuities are not "insurance" for purposes of § 92. The Supreme Court subsequently addressed the issue of insurance activities under § 92 in *Barnett Bank of Marion County, N.A. v. Nelson*, parts of which are also excerpted *supra* at 31. If *Barnett Bank* had been decided first, would *NationsBank* have been easier to decide?

Barnett Bank of Marion County, N.A. v. Nelson

517 U.S. 25 (1996)

Justice BREYER delivered the opinion of the Court.

[For the background of the case, see Chapter 1, § 3, *supra*. In the second part of the opinion, the Court concluded that, under ordinary preemption principles, 12 U.S.C. § 92 would preempt a Florida statute that prohibited banks (including national banks) from selling insurance in Florida. For excerpts from the Court's opinion in this regard, see the previous excerpt from the opinion.]

We now must decide whether ordinary legal principles of pre-emption, or the special McCarran-Ferguson Act anti-pre-emption rule, governs this case. The lower courts held that the McCarran-Ferguson Act's special anti-pre-emption rule applies, and instructs courts not to "construe" the Federal Statute to "invalidate, impair, or supersede" that of the State. 15 U.S.C. §1012(b). By its terms, however, the Act does not apply when the conflicting federal statute "*specifically relates to* the business of insurance." *Ibid.* (emphasis added). In our view, the Federal Statute in this case "specifically relates to the business of insurance"–therefore the McCarran-Ferguson Act's special anti-pre-emption rule does not apply.

Our conclusion rests upon the McCarran-Ferguson Act's language and purpose, taken together. Consider the language–"specifically relates to the business of insurance." In ordinary English, a statute that says that banks may act as insurance agents, and that the Comptroller of the Currency may regulate their insurance-related activities, "*relates*" to the insurance business. The word "relates" is highly general, and this Court has interpreted it broadly in other pre-emption contexts. . . .

More importantly, in ordinary English, this statute "*specifically*" relates to the insurance business. "Specifically" can mean "explicitly, particularly, [or] definitely," Black's Law Dictionary 1398 (6th ed.1990), thereby contrasting a *specific* reference with an *implicit* reference made by more general language to a broader topic. The general words "business activity," for example, will sometimes include, and thereby implicitly refer, to insurance; the particular words "finance, banking, and insurance" make that reference explicitly *and specifically*.

Finally, using ordinary English, one would say that this statute specifically relates to the "*business of insurance*." The statute explicitly grants national banks permission to "act as the agent for any fire, life, or other insurance company," to "solici[t] and sel[l] insurance," to "collec[t] premiums," and to "receive for services so rendered . . . fees or commissions," subject to Comptroller regulation. 12 U.S.C. §92. It also sets forth certain specific rules prohibiting banks from guaranteeing the "payment of any premium on insurance policies issued through its agency . . ." and the "truth of any statement made by an assured in filing his application for insurance." *Ibid.* The statute thereby not only focuses directly upon industry-specific selling practices, but also affects the relation of insured to insurer and the spreading of risk–matters that this Court, in other contexts, has placed at the core of the McCarran-Ferguson Act's concern. . . .

Consider, too, the McCarran-Ferguson Act's basic purposes. The Act sets forth two mutually reinforcing purposes in its first section, namely that "continued regulation and taxation by the several States of the business of insurance is in the public interest," and that "*silence* on the part of the Congress shall not be construed to impose any barrier to the regulation or taxation of such business by the several States." 15 U.S.C. §1011 (emphasis added). The latter phrase, particularly the word "silence," indicates that the Act does not seek to insulate state insurance regulation from the reach of all federal law. Rather, it seeks to protect state regulation primarily against *inadvertent* federal intrusion–say, through enactment of a federal statute that describes an affected activity in broad, general terms, of which the insurance business happens to comprise one part.

The circumstances surrounding enactment of the McCarran-Ferguson Act suggest the same. Just prior to the law's enactment, this Court, in *United States v. South-Eastern Underwriters Assn.*, 322 U.S. 533 (1944), held that a federal antitrust law, the Sherman Act, applied to the business of insurance. The Sherman Act's highly general language said nothing specifically about insurance. See 15 U.S.C. §1 (forbidding every "contract, combination . . . or conspiracy, in restraint of trade or commerce among the several States"). The Sherman Act applied only to activities in or affecting interstate commerce. . . . Many lawyers and insurance professionals had previously thought, (relying, in part, on this Court's opinion in *Paul v. Virginia*, 8 Wall. 168, 183 (1869), and other cases), that the issuance of an insurance policy was not a "transaction of commerce," and therefore fell outside the Sherman Act's scope. *South-Eastern Underwriters* told those professionals that they were wrong about interstate commerce, and that the Sherman Act did apply. And *South-Eastern Underwriters*' principle meant, consequently, that other generally phrased congressional statutes might also apply to the issuance of insurance policies, thereby interfering with state regulation of insurance in similarly unanticipated ways.

In reaction to *South-Eastern Underwriters*, Congress "moved quickly," enacting McCarran-Ferguson "to restore the supremacy of the States in the realm of insurance regulation." . . . But the circumstances we have just described mean that "*restor[ation]*" of "supremacy" basically required setting aside the unanticipated effects of *South-Eastern Underwriters*, and cautiously avoiding similar unanticipated interference with state regulation in the future. It did not require avoiding federal pre-emption by future federal statutes that indicate, through their "specific relat[ion]" to insurance, that Congress had focused upon the insurance industry, and therefore, in all likelihood, consciously intended to exert upon the insurance industry whatever pre-emptive force accompanied its law. . . .

The language of the Federal Statute before us is not general. It refers specifically to insurance. Its state regulatory implications are not surprising, nor do we believe them inadvertent. . . . Consequently, considerations of purpose, as well as of language, indicate that the Federal Statute falls within the scope of the McCarran-Ferguson's "specifically relates" exception to its anti-pre-emption rule. . . .

. . . Florida says that the Federal Statute "specifically relates" to banking, not to insurance. But, a statute may specifically relate to more than one thing. Just as an ordinance forbidding dogs in city parks specifically relates to dogs and to parks, so a statute permitting banks to sell insurance can specifically relate to banks and to insurance. Neither the McCarran-Ferguson Act's language, nor its purpose, requires the Federal Statute to relate *predominantly* to insurance. To the contrary, specific detailed references to the insurance industry in proposed legislation normally will achieve the McCarran-Ferguson Act's objectives, for they will call the proposed legislation to the attention of interested parties, and thereby normally guarantee, should the proposal become law, that Congress will have focused upon its insurance-related effects.

. . . Many federal statutes with potentially preemptive effect, such as the bankruptcy statutes, use general language that does not appear to "specifically relate" to insurance; and where those statutes conflict with state law that was enacted "for the purpose of regulating the business of insurance," the McCarran-Ferguson Act's anti-pre-emption rule will apply. . . .

The lower courts argued that the Federal Statute's 1916 date of enactment was significant, because Congress would have then believed that state insurance regulation was beyond its "Commerce Clause" power to affect. The lower courts apparently thought that Congress therefore could not have intended the Federal Statute to pre-empt contrary state law. The short answer to this claim is that there is no reason to think that Congress believed state insurance regulation beyond its constitutional powers to affect–insofar as Congress exercised those powers to create, to empower, or to regulate, national banks. ... We have explained . . . why we conclude that Congress indeed did intend the Federal Statute to pre-empt conflicting state law.

Notes and Comments 5.95. Must a power be implicit to be incidental? Must it be derived from § 24 to be incidental? Consider *Barnett Bank, supra.*

5.96. Where does federal policy stand currently on the intersection of banking and insurance? Consider the following excerpts.

Michael P. Malloy, The Sound of Two Hands Flapping: Insurance-Related Activities of National Banks

41 St. Louis U. L.J. 75, 87-91 (1996)[a]

A number of implications are readily apparent when the Court's decisions in *NationsBank* and *Barnett Bank* flap together. These implications make it clear that the controversy surrounding these cases is not simply a matter of whether or not banks–small town or otherwise–are going to be permitted to offer insurance services to their customers. To the contrary, what is at stake are the contours of the financial services industry in the foreseeable future.

First, and most obviously, *Barnett Bank* resolves the question of the scope of section 92 itself. Contrary to the position taken by Florida in *Barnett Bank*,[1] the authorization contained in section 92 is not limited by reference over to state law.[2] The section itself, properly construed, controls the extent of national bank involvement in insurance services,[3] beyond the variable annuities brokerage permitted by *NationsBank*.

Second, the extent of that involvement will be far broader than the bare language and sparse legislative history of the NBA provisions involved in the two cases might otherwise suggest. For example, in *Barnett Bank* Florida had argued that the "special cir-

---

a. Footnotes have been renumbered in this excerpt.

1. [*Barnett Bank*, 116 S.Ct.] at 1110 (discussing argument that section 92 "grant[ed] only a limited permission (subject to State approval)").

2. *Id.* at 1109.

3. *Id.* at 1109-1110. *See also Owensboro Nat. Bank* [*v. Stephens*, 44 F.3d 388 (6th Cir. 1994)] (despite contrary Kentucky statute, section 92 controls national bank sale of insurance in small towns).

cumstances surrounding the enactment of [section 92] . . . demonstrate[d] Congress' intent to grant only a limited permission"[4] to engage in insurance services (and that subject to state approval in any event). The "special circumstances" concern the apparently modest scope intended by the Comptroller in recommending the enactment of section 92 in 1916, *i.e.*, the assistance of "small town" banks.[5]

While the Court was not willing to concede that the Comptroller's 1916 letter was relevant to the question before it,[6] it noted that, in any event, "the letter does not significantly advance [Florida's] case."[7] The Court chose to ignore the "small town" orientation of section

---

4. *Barnett Bank*, 116 S.Ct. at 1110.

5. The Court repeatedly referred to the "small town" focus of the Comptroller's recommendation in discussing Florida's argument in this regard. In a letter to Congress in 1916,

> [t]he Comptroller attached a draft of what became [section 92], and the letter explains to Congress why the Comptroller wants Congress to enact his proposal. The letter says that, since 1900, many *small town national banks* had failed; that some States had authorized *small town state banks* to sell insurance; that providing *small town national banks* with authority to sell insurance would help them financially; and that doing so would also improve their competitive position vis-a-vis state banks.

Id. at 1110 (emphasis added). The relevant language in the letter stated that since 1900, of 3,084 small national banks, 438:

> have either failed or gone into liquidation. . . . [T]here are many banks located in [small towns] . . . where the small deposits which the banks receive may make it somewhat difficult [to earn] . . . a satisfactory return. . . . For some time I have been giving careful consideration to the question as to how the powers of these small national banks might be enlarged so as to provide them with additional sources of revenue and place them in a position where they could better compete with local State banks and trust companies which are sometimes authorized under the law to do a class of business not strictly that of commercial banking. . . .

Id. The federal banking laws, while granting national banks certain "incidental powers," did not give them

> either expressly nor by necessary implication the power to act as agents for insurance companies. . . . My investigations lead me respectfully to recommend to Congress an amendment to the national-bank act by which national banks located in [small towns] . . . may be permitted to act as agents for insurance companies. . . . It seems desirable from the standpoint of public policy and banking efficiency that this authority should be limited to banks in small communities. This additional income will strengthen them and increase their ability to make a fair return. . . . I think it would be unwise and therefore undesirable to confer this privilege generally upon banks in large cities where the legitimate business of banking affords ample scope for the energies of trained and expert bankers. . . . I inclose [*sic*] . . . a draft . . . designed to empower national banks located in [small] towns . . . under such regulations and restrictions as may from time to time be approved and promulgated by the Comptroller of the Currency, to act as agents for the placing of insurance policies. . . ." 53 Cong. Rec. 11001 (1916) (Letter from Comptroller Williams to the Chairman of the Senate Bank and Currency Committee).

Id. at 1110.

6. *See id.* ("Assuming for argument's sake that this letter is relevant").

7. *Id.*

92,[8] and instead focused on "a broad insurance-selling authority that is not limited by state law."[9] This approach actually misses the point of the underlying controversy before the Court in *Barnett Bank*–the ability of national banks to use the small town outpost authorized by section 92 as the point of entry into state-wide (or possibly wider[10]) participation in the insurance services market.[11] This development in itself will likely transform the financial services market, as state banks follow the lead of the national banks into variable annuities and other insurance products.[12]

Third, *NationsBank* and *Barnett Bank* are significant as part of the suite of developments expanding the involvement of banking enterprises in insurance services. Despite the modest limitations on bank holding company involvement in insurance services suggested by *Alabama Ass'n of Ins. Agents v. Board of Governors*,[13] a range of insurance activities were later imbedded in the amended Bank Holding Company Act[14] as closely related to banking, and as such permissible in principle for bank holding companies.[15] The Court's decision in *NationsBank* extended the reach of national banks into insurance services by upholding the Comptroller's authorization of sales of variable annuities as an "incidental power" under the NBA.[16] In this perspective, *Barnett Bank* confirms the direction and quickens the speed of the march of commercial banks into insurance services.

Fourth, the two cases also underscore the expansive nature of the Court's reading of incidental powers doctrine, in line with its considerable deference to administrative decision making. It was already evident from *NationsBank* that insurance as a form of financial intermediation might be broadly included within the grant of "incidental powers" to national banks. *Barnett Bank* confirms this suggestion. Considering the implications of the Comptroller's 1916 letter, the Court observed:

> The letter makes clear that authority to sell insurance in small towns is an added "incidental power" of a national bank -- a term that, in light of this Court's

---

8. *See supra* note 5 (discussing emphasis on "small town" character of banks benefiting from enactment of section 92).

9. *Barnett Bank*, 116 S.Ct. at 1110.

10. *See, e.g., Barnett Bank of Marion County, N.A. v. Gallagher*, 43 F.2d at 633 (posing question, unanswered by Supreme Court, "whether Barnett Marion is located and doing business in a place with fewer than five thousand people, and if so, whether the bank may sell insurance nationally or only within this small town").

11. Since the Comptroller's 1986 interpretation authorizing national banks to use small-town branches to sell insurance state-wide, OCC Interpretive Letter No. 366, [1986 Transfer Binder] Fed. Banking L. Rep. (CCH) ¶ 85,536, approximately 200 national banks have entered the insurance services market. Greenhouse, [*Ruling Backs Banks' Sales Of Insurance*, N.Y. Times, Mar. 27, 1996, at D1]. It is expected that, following *Barnett Bank*, "virtually all" national banks are likely to enter that market in their respective states. *Id.* (citing an interview with Michael Crotty of the American Bankers Association).

12. Most states have laws permitting state-chartered banks to exercise the same powers as national banks. Greenhouse, *supra* note 11.

13. 533 F.2d 224 (5th Cir. 1976), *amended*, 558 F.2d 729 (1977), *cert. denied*, 435 U.S. 904 (1978) (questioning authorization by Federal Reserve of general insurance agency activities by bank holding companies).

14. 12 U.S.C. § 1843(c)(8)(A)-(G).

15. *But cf. id.* § 1843(c)(8) ("closely related" activity subject to showing that activity is "proper incident" of banking).

16. 12 U.S.C. § 24 (Seventh).

then-existing cases, suggested freedom from conflicting state regulation. See *Easton* [*v. Iowa*, 188 U.S. [220], at 229-230 [1903]; *First Nat. Bank* [*of San Jose v. California*], 262 U.S. [366], at 368-369 [(1923)].[17] . . .

Thus, in a painfully deliberate fashion, the Court has moved the broad sector of financial services closer to a consolidated structure. At present, however, legislative policy with respect to the permissible insurance activities of banking enterprises is in disarray.[18] It remains to be seen whether Congress will undertake any significant review of this area.

In decisions like *NationsBank* and *Barnett Bank*, commercial banks have already made extensive inroads into the insurance business. They may well expect that the implications of these decisions may lead to nationwide participation in the insurance business.[19] In light of these prospects, one may expect the banking industry to resist any attempts by Congress to rationalize the relationship between the banking and insurance sectors.[20] As in the case of the relationship between the banking and securities sectors,[21] commercial banks may conclude that it is not in their best interest to compromise the gains they have won in the courts in favor of congressional efforts to delimit the pace and direction of change in the financial intermediary industry. If this position is maintained by banks, the Court's expansive reading of incidental powers doctrine will, as a tactical matter, ultimately make it more difficult for the Congress to make sense of federal policy with respect to the confluence of banking and insurance.

American Council of Life Insurance v. Ludwig

1 F.Supp.2d 24 (D.D.C. 1998),
vacated as moot and remanded, 194 F.3d 173 (D.C.Cir. 1999)

[Reread the excerpt in Chapter 1, § 4, *supra*.]

Notes and Comments 5.97. *GLBA and insurance activities*. The GLBA has expanded the involvement of banking enterprises in the insurance sector (and *vice versa*). However, it requires functional regulation of insurance activities, *i.e.*, insurance activities are to be regulated by state insurance regulators regardless of the type of financial firm that is engaged in the activity. What does this rule of functional regulation do to the results in *NationsBank* and *Barnett Bank*? How will bank insurance activities be regulated under the GLBA? Consider the following excerpt and the statutory provisions that it cites in answering these questions.

---

17. *Barnett Bank*, 116 S.Ct. at 1110-1111.

18. *See, e.g.*, Keith Bradsheer, *Plan Would Assess Fees on Federal Home-Loan Agencies*, N.Y. Times, Oct. 23, 1995, at D3, col. 1 (reporting that House proposal to ease restrictions on commercial bank involvement in securities is opposed by banks because of proposed limits on insurance activities).

19. *See supra* note 10 and accompanying text (suggesting that decisions may allow nationwide expansion from section 92 small-town outpost).

20. *See* Bradsheer, *supra* note 18 (discussing such resistance by banks).

21. *See* M. P. Malloy, *U.S. International Banking Policy: Prospects and Problems in a New Millennium*, 15 Ann. Rev. Banking L. 277, 290-291 (1996) (discussing difficulties of congressional proposal to rationalize banking and securities).

2 Michael P. Malloy, Banking Law and Regulation

§ 6.11 (2d ed., Aspen Publishers, 2011)

The GLBA takes federal regulatory policy with respect to insurance activities into a new regime. It generally endorses the principle of functional regulation, positing that similar activities should be regulated by the same regulator. Accordingly, insurance activities, whether carried out by affiliates of banks, securities firms or insurance companies, are regulated under the GLBA by state insurance regulators.[1] However, the GLBA directs the federal banking agencies and the state insurance regulators to coordinate efforts to supervise companies that control both depository institutions and insurance firms, and to share, on a confidential basis, supervisory information including financial health and business unit transactions.[2] The GLBA also directs the agencies to provide notice to and consultation with the state regulators before taking actions that would affect any affiliates engaging in insurance activities.[3] However, the GLBA does not require a banking regulator to provide confidential information to a state insurance regulator, unless the state regulator agrees to keep the information in confidence and to make all reasonable efforts to oppose disclosure of such information.[4] Similarly, GLBA directs federal banking regulators to treat as confidential any information received from a state regulator that is entitled to confidential treatment under applicable state law, and to make similar reasonable efforts to oppose disclosure of the information.[5]

While GLBA permits affiliations among banking, securities and insurance firms, it provides explicitly that the McCarran-Ferguson Act[6] is still operative to require federal deference in most cases to state regulation of the insurance activities carried on by these firms.[7] Subject to special rules concerning permissible affiliations and activities and nondiscrimination in state treatment of affiliated firms, GLBA requires a state license for any firm to engage in the business of insurance as a principal or agent.[8] Functional regulation of insurance activities of financial services firms by the states, including insurance activities of national banks, is subject to these permissibility and nondiscrimination rules. Under the GLBA, national banks and their subsidiaries are prohibited from underwriting insurance, except for authorized products.[9] To prevent evasion of state insurance regulation through the use of non-U.S. reinsurance subsidiaries or offices of U.S. banks, the GLBA explicitly states that providing insurance (including reinsurance) *outside* the United States to indemnify an insurance product or firm *within* a state is considered to be providing insurance as principal

1. *See* GLBA, § 301, 113 Stat. at 1407 (codified at 15 U.S.C. § 6711) (mandating functional regulation of insurance activities).

2. GLBA, § 307(a)-(b), 113 Stat. at 1415 (codified at 15 U.S.C. § 6716(a)-(b)).

3. GLBA, § 307(c), 113 Stat. at 1415 (codified at 15 U.S.C. § 6716(c)).

4. GLBA, § 307(e)(1), 113 Stat. at 1415 (codified at 15 U.S.C. § 6716(e)).

5. *Id.*

6. 15 U.S.C. §§ 1011 *et seq.*

7. GLBA, § 104(a), 113 Stat. at 1352 (codified at 15 U.S.C. § 6701(a)). Cf. 70 Fed. Reg. 60,019 (2005) (to be codified at 12 C.F.R. pts. 331, 362) (providing, inter alia, that home state law of state bank applies to interstate activities of the bank and operating subsidiaries thereof to same extent that NBA applies to interstate activities of national bank and operating subsidiaries thereof; addressing interest charged by FDIC-insured state banks and insured U.S. branches of foreign banks).

8. GLBA, § 104(b)-(f), 113 Stat. at 1352 (codified at 15 U.S.C. § 6701(b)-(f)).

9. GLBA, § 302, 113 Stat. at 1407 (codified at 15 U.S.C. § 6712).

in that state.[10]

National banks are prohibited from engaging in any activity involving underwriting or sale of title insurance, except that they may sell title insurance products in any state in which state-chartered banks are authorized to do so (other than through a state "wild card" provision).[11] Sales by national banks must be undertaken in the same manner, to the same extent, and under the same restrictions as apply to state-chartered banks. Certain extant, lawfully conducted title insurance activities of banks are grandfathered.[12] Preexisting state laws prohibiting all persons from providing title insurance are preserved.[13] As to conflicts between federal and state regulators regarding insurance issues, GLBA establishes an expedited and equalized dispute resolution mechanism, originating in the federal courts of appeals, to guide the courts in deciding such conflicts.[14]

The GLBA preempts state laws that prevent or otherwise significantly interfere with[15] the ability of an insurer to affiliate, become an FHC, or demutualize.[16] The GLBA also preempts state laws limiting the investment of an insurer's assets in a depository institution, except to the extent that the GLBA permits an insurer's domicile state to limit such investments.[17]

The GLBA allows mutual insurance companies to "redomesticate" to another state and reorganize into a mutual holding company or stock company.[18] This rule is preemptive as to states that have not established reasonable terms and conditions for allowing mutual insurance companies to reorganize into a mutual holding company consistent with the purpose and intent of the GLBA provisions.[19]

In a redomestication, all licenses of the insurer are preserved.[20] All outstanding policies, contracts, and forms remain in effect.[21] A redomesticating insurer must provide notice to the state insurance regulators of each state for which the company is licensed.[22]

A mutual insurer may redomesticate under this rule only if the state insurance regulator of the new domicile affirmatively determines that the company's reorganization

---

10. 15 U.S.C. § 6712(d).

11. GLBA, § 303, 113 Stat. at 1408 (codified at 15 U.S.C. § 6713).

12. 15 U.S.C. § 6713(c).

13. *Id.* § 6713(e).

14. GLBA, § 304, 113 Stat. at 1409 (codified at 15 U.S.C. § 6714).

15. For a case considering what constitutes significant interference for these purposes, see *Association of Banks-in-Insurance v. Duryee*, 55 F.Supp2d 799 (S.D.Ohio 1999), *affirmed and remanded*, 270 F.3d 397 (6th Cir. 2001) (preempting state "principal purpose" licensing restrictions; preempting state statute requiring life insurance agent be organized for that purpose; preempting state licensing requirements for foreign corporations as applied to national banks; remanding to determine preemptive effect of new federal nondiscrimination standards affecting depository institutions).

16. GLBA, § 306, 113 Stat. at 1415 (codified at 15 U.S.C. § 6715). This restriction does not affect the state's authority to require licensing as a condition to participation in insurance activities, *per id.* § 104 (codified at 15 U.S.C. § 6701).

17. *Id.*

18. GLBA, § 312(a)-(b), 113 Stat. at 1417 (codified at 15 U.S.C. § 6732(a)-(b)).

19. *Id.*, § 313, 113 Stat. at 1419 (codified at 15 U.S.C. § 6733).

20. *Id.*, § 312(c), 113 Stat. at 1417 (codified at 15 U.S.C. § 6732(c)).

21. GLBA, § 312(d), 113 Stat. at 1417-1418 (codified at 15 U.S.C. § 6732(d)).

22. GLBA, § 312(e), 113 Stat. at 1418 (codified at 15 U.S.C. § 6732(e)).

plan meets certain reasonable terms and conditions.[23] The reorganization must be approved by a majority of the insurer's board of directors and voting policyholders (after notice and disclosure of the reorganization and its effects on contract rights of policyholders).[24] The policyholders must have equivalent voting rights in the new mutual holding company, and all contractual rights of the policyholders must be preserved.[25] Any initial public offering of stock must be in accordance with applicable securities laws, and under the supervision of the state insurance regulator of the new domicile.[26] The new mutual holding company may not award any stock options or grants to its elected directors or officers for six months.[27] The reorganization must be approved as fair and equitable to the policyholders by the insurance regulator of new domicile.[28] The GLBA generally preempts state laws that otherwise restrict redomestication.[29]

The GLBA encourages the states to establish uniform or reciprocal requirements for the licensing of insurance agents.[30] If a majority of the states do not establish uniform or reciprocal licensing provisions within a three-year period, as determined by the National Association of Insurance Commissioners (NAIC), then the National Association of Registered Agents and Brokers (NARAB) would be established as a private, non-profit entity managed and supervised by the state insurance regulators.[31] State insurance laws and regulations apparently are not affected, except to the extent that they are inconsistent with any specific requirement of these rules.[32]

If the NAIC determines that the states have not met the uniformity or reciprocity requirements,[33] then the NAIC has two years to establish the NARAB.[34] The NAIC is to appoint the NARAB board of directors, some of whom must have significant experience with the regulation of commercial insurance lines in the twenty states with the most commercial lines business.[35] If within the time period allotted for creation of the NARAB, the NAIC has still not appointed the initial board of directors for NARAB, then the initial directors shall be the state insurance regulators of the seven states with the greatest amount of commercial lines insurance.[36] NARAB bylaws are required to be filed with the NAIC, taking effect 30

---

23. GLBA, § 312(f), 113 Stat. at 1418-1419 (codified at 15 U.S.C. § 6732(f)).

24. 15 U.S.C. § 6732(f)(1).

25. *Id.* § 6732(f)(2).

26. *Id.*

27. *Id.* § 6732(f)(3).

28. *Id.* § 6732(f)(5).

29. *Id.* § 6733.

30. GLBA, § 321, 113 Stat. at 1422 (codified at 15 U.S.C. § 6751).

31. GLBA, § 322, 113 Stat. at 1424 (codified at 15 U.S.C. § 6752). Significant progress has been made on licensing. See U.S. Government Accountability Office, Insurance Reciprocity and Uniformity: NAIC and State Regulators Have Made Progress in Producer Licensing, Product Approval, and Market Conduct Regulation, but Challenges Remain (GAO-09-372, Apr. 6, 2009), available at 2009 WL 1262871.

32. GLBA, § 321(f), 113 Stat. at 1423 (codified at 15 U.S.C. § 6751(f)).

33. GLBA, § 321(d)(1), 113 Stat. at 1423 (codified at 15 U.S.C. § 6751(d)(1)).

34. GLBA, § 321(e), 113 Stat. at 1423 (codified at 15 U.S.C. § 6751(e)).

35. GLBA, § 326(c)(1)-(2), 113 Stat. at 1426 (codified at 15 U.S.C. § 6756(c)(1)-(2)). On the NARAB board of directors and officers, see GLBA, §§ 326-327, 113 Stat. at 1426-1427 (codified at 15 U.S.C. § 6756-6757).

36. GLBA, § 326(c)(3)(A), 113 Stat. at 1426 (codified at 15 U.S.C. § 6756(c)(3)(A)).

days after filing unless disapproved by the NAIC as being contrary to the public interest or requiring a public hearing.[37] The NAIC may require NARAB to adopt or repeal additional bylaws or rules as it determines appropriate to the public interest.[38] The NAIC is given the responsibility of overseeing the NARAB, and is authorized to examine and inspect NARAB records, and to require the NARAB to furnish it with any reports.[39]

If at the end of the two years after the NARAB is required to be established, a majority of the states representing at least 50 percent of the total commercial lines insurance premiums in the United States have not established uniform or reciprocal licensing regulations, or the NAIC has not approved NARAB bylaws or is unable to operate or supervise the NARAB (or if the NARAB is not conducting its activities under the GLBA), then the NARAB is to be created and supervised by the President, and would exist without NAIC oversight.[40] The President would be required to appoint the NARAB board, with the advice and consent of the Senate, from lists of candidates submitted by the NAIC.[41] If the President determines that the NARAB board is not acting in the public interest, the President may replace the entire board with new members (subject to the advice and consent of the Senate).[42] The President may also suspend the effectiveness of any rule or action by the NARAB that the President determines to be contrary to the public interest.[43] The NARAB would be required to report annually to the President and Congress on its activities.[44]

Membership in the NARAB is voluntary and does not affect the rights of a firm under each individual state license.[45] Any state-licensed insurance firm whose license has not been suspended or revoked is eligible to join the NARAB.[46] The NARAB is required to base its membership criteria on the highest qualification levels set by the states on standards such as integrity, personal qualification, education, training, and experience.[47] NARAB members must continue to pay the appropriate fees required by each state in which they are licensed, and must renew their membership annually.[48] The NARAB may inspect member records, and revoke membership where appropriate.[49] The NARAB must establish an Office

37. GLBA, § 328, 113 Stat. at 1427 (codified at 15 U.S.C. § 6758).

38. GLBA, § 328(b)(5)(B), 113 Stat. at 1429 (codified at 15 U.S.C. § 6758(b)(5)(B)).

39. GLBA, § 324, 113 Stat. at 1424 (codified at 15 U.S.C. § 6754).

40. GLBA, § 332, 113 Stat. at 1431 (codified at 15 U.S.C. § 6762). During a hearing on March 31, 2004, members of the Subcommittee on Capital Markets, Insurance and Government Sponsored Enterprises of the House Financial Services Committee expressed impatience with state efforts to achieve uniformity in some aspects of insurance regulation, and suggested that congressional intervention may be needed. Karen L. Werner, Congressional Mandate Needed to Spur State Progress in Uniformity, Members Say, BNA Banking Daily, Apr. 1, 2004, available athttp://pubs.bna.com/ip/BNA/bbd.nsf/is/A0A8H2D7P8. Critical areas of insurance regulation that were cited as insufficiently uniform included company licensing, approval of new products, duplicative reviews, price controls, and compliance with GLBA licensing reciprocity provisions. *Id.*

41. GLBA, § 332(b)(1), 113 Stat. at 1431 (codified at 15 U.S.C. § 6762(b)(1)).

42. GLBA, § 332(b)(2)(C)(i), 113 Stat. at 1431-1432 (codified at 15 U.S.C. § 6762(b)(2)(C)(i)).

43. GLBA, § 332(b)(2)(C)(ii), 113 Stat. at 1432 (codified at 15 U.S.C. § 6762(b)(2)(C)(ii)).

44. GLBA, § 332(c), 113 Stat. at 1432 (codified at 15 U.S.C. § 6762(c)).

45. GLBA, § 325(a)(1), 113 Stat. at 1424 (codified at 15 U.S.C. § 6755(a)(1)).

46. GLBA, § 325(a), 113 Stat. at 1424 (codified at 15 U.S.C § 6755(a)).

47. GLBA, § 325(b), (d), 113 Stat. at 1424 (codified at 15 U.S.C § 6755(b), (d)).

48. GLBA, § 325(e)-(f), 113 Stat. at 1424 (codified at 15 U.S.C § 6755(e)-(f)).

49. GLBA, § 325(h), 113 Stat. at 1424 (codified at 15 U.S.C § 6755(h)).

of Consumer Complaints to receive and investigate consumer complaints and recommend disciplinary actions.[50] The Office must maintain records of such complaints, and these records must be made available to the NAIC and individual state insurance regulators.[51] The NARAB must refer complaints where appropriate to the regulators.[52]

The GLBA preempts state laws regulating insurance licensing that discriminate against NARAB members based on non-residency, and state laws and regulations that impose additional licensing requirements on non-resident NARAB members beyond those established by the NARAB board.[53] However, state unfair trade practice and consumer protection laws are protected from preemption.[54] The NARAB is required to coordinate its multistate licensing with the various states, and to coordinate with the states on establishing a central clearinghouse for license issuance and renewal and for the collection of regulatory information on insurance firm activities.[55] The NARAB is also required to coordinate with the NASD to facilitate joint membership.[56]

Any dispute involving the NARAB must be brought in the appropriate U.S. District Court under federal law.[57] All administrative remedies through the NARAB and the NAIC must first be exhausted.[58]

8. Bank Service Companies

Notes and Comments 5.98. Standing to challenge the Comptroller's interpretation that a particular activity is permitted as an incidental power is especially significant as financial services sectors of banking, securities and insurance increasingly overlap. The following cases examine standing. To what extent have these cases changed the contours of the "incidental powers" concept?

Association of Data Processing Service Organizations v. Camp

397 U.S. 150 (1970)

[Reread the excerpt in Chapter 1, § 3, *supra.*]

Arnold Tours v. Camp

400 U.S. 45 (1970)

Per Curiam.

Petitioners are 42 independent travel agents doing business in Massachusetts. They ask for declaratory and injunctive relief against the Comptroller of the Currency and the

---

50. GLBA, § 325(i), 113 Stat. at 1425 (codified at 15 U.S.C § 6755(i)).

51. GLBA, § 325(i)(2)(A), 113 Stat. at 1426 (codified at 15 U.S.C § 6755(i)(2)(A)).

52. GLBA, § 325(i)(2)(B), 113 Stat. at 1426 (codified at 15 U.S.C § 6755(i)(2)(B)).

53. GLBA, § 333, 113 Stat. at 1432 (codified at 15 U.S.C. § 6763).

54. GLBA, § 333(c), 113 Stat. at 1432-1433 (codified at 15 U.S.C. § 6763(c)).

55. GLBA, § 334(a), 113 Stat. at 1433 (codified at 15 U.S.C. § 6764(a)).

56. GLBA, § 334(b), 113 Stat. at 1433 (codified at 15 U.S.C. § 6764(b)).

57. GLBA, § 335(a), (c), 113 Stat. at 1433 (codified at 15 U.S.C. § 6765(a), (c)).

58. GLBA, § 335(b), 113 Stat. at 1433 (codified at 15 U.S.C. § 335(b)).

South Shore National Bank. They seek to invalidate a ruling by the Comptroller that, incidental to their banking services, national banks may provide travel services for their customers. Petitioners allege that as a result they have lost substantial business and profits and stand to lose even greater business in the future. They contend the Comptroller exceeded his authority when he authorized national banks to provide travel services.

The District Court dismissed the complaint for lack of standing and the Court of Appeals affirmed. . . . Following our decisions last Term in *Association of Data Processing Service Organizations, Inc. v. Camp*, 397 U.S. 150, and *Barlow v. Collins*, 397 U.S. 159, we vacated and remanded the case for reconsideration (397 U.S. 315) and the Court of Appeals reaffirmed its decision.

Here, as in *Data Processing*, we are concerned with § 4 of the Bank Service Corporation Act, 76 Stat. 1132, 12 U.S.C. § 1864. In *Data Processing* we did not rely on any legislative history showing that Congress desired to protect data processors alone from competition. Moreover, we noted a growing trend "toward enlargement of the class of people who may protest administrative action." 397 U.S., at 154. We held that § 4 "arguably brings a competitor within the zone of interests protected by it." *Id.*, at 156. Nothing in the opinion limited § 4 to protecting only competitors in the data-processing field. When national banks begin to provide travel services for their customers, they compete with travel agents no less than they compete with data processors when they provide data-processing services to their customers.

Notes and Comments 5.99. Does it make a difference in *Arnold Tours* that the Bank Service Company Act ("BSCA"), 12 U.S.C. §§ 1861 *et seq.*,[59] may itself authorize nonbanking activities carried out through a separate entity controlled by a national bank? Assume Quarter National Bank wishes to establish a subsidiary, Quarter Travel Service, Inc., that will operate as a travel agency. Even if not authorized for Quarter National under 12 U.S.C. § 24 (Seventh), could the activity be authorized for Quarter Travel under the BSCA?

5.100. What is the relationship between the "incidental powers" provision of 12 U.S.C. § 24 (Seventh) and the BSCA? If the Court's decisions in *Data Processing* and *Arnold Tours* are based upon its reading of § 4, are these decisions distinguishable in situations in which a challenge is being made to the power of a national bank to engage directly in an activity under the "incidental powers" provisions? What if Quarter National Bank decided to establishment a department within the bank to handle travel services for customers? Could that be an "incidental power" of Quarter, despite *Data Processing* and *Arnold Tours*?

9. Securities Activities

a. Introduction

The securities sector is, even more than the insurance sector, one area of the

59. At the time *Arnold Tours* was decided, the act was known as the Bank Service Corporation Act, and only authorized the creation of a corporate subsidiary of a national bank. The act was amended in 1996 to authorize bank service "companies" to be organized as limited liability partnerships. *See* Economic Growth and Regulatory Paperwork Reduction Act, Pub. L. No. 104-208, title II, § 2613, 110 Stat. 3009 (1996) (codified at 12 U.S.C. §§ 1861-1867) (renaming Bank Service Corporation Act as Bank Service Company Act; authorizing bank service companies to organize as limited liability partnerships; conforming amendments).

financial services industry in which there has been significant crossover of depository institutions. Depository institutions may also be securities market professionals, that is, persons who underwrite, purchase, sell and otherwise deal in securities in the securities markets. These activities have been significantly limited, until relatively recently, by the Glass-Steagall Act,[60] but these limitations have been progressively narrowed by administrative interpretation and court decisions. Most recently, the GLBA eliminated the Glass-Steagall Act prohibitions on affiliations between commercial and investment banking enterprises and on interlocking directorates between such enterprises by repealing 12 U.S.C. §§ 78 & 377.[61]

In this section, the focus will be the Glass-Steagall Act, since that has been the major concern of much recent litigation and congressional consideration. Securities activities are, for the most part, only another specific example of the trend towards integration of the components of the financial services industry that has already been encountered in the previous two sections. However, to be understood adequately, securities activities of depository institutions need to be seen in conjunction with the overall federal policy on securities regulation, which in part applies to depository institutions, as well as to all other securities issuers and securities professionals. We shall therefore return to this subject, but from another angle, in Chapter 7.

b. The Glass-Steagall Act Restrictions

The Glass-Steagall Act[62] was enacted in the wake of the financial crisis that burgeoned during the period 1929 to 1933. As *Investment Company Institute v. Camp, infra*, explains, close affiliation between investment and commercial banks resulted in a great potential for harm in the activities of each. The congressional solution was a radical break between the two, in many cases involving divestiture of the investment banking affiliates of major commercial banks.[63] In the years since its enactment in 1933, and particularly since the 1960s, banks and bank regulators have been crossing over into investment banking and the securities business with increasing vigor. The line of cases excerpted in this section track that slow development.

Congress has also assisted this development, although perhaps inadvertently. One of the key provisions of the Glass-Steagall Act, codified in 12 U.S.C. § 24(Seventh), has been amended repeatedly to allow more and more exceptions to the basic rule that depository institutions are generally prohibited from underwriting, purchasing and dealing in securities. Most recently, the GLBA eliminated the Glass-Steagall Act prohibitions on affiliations between commercial and investment banking enterprises and on interlocking directorates between such enterprises by repealing 12 U.S.C. §§ 78 & 377.[64]

---

60. 48 Stat. 162 (1933) (codified at scattered sections of 12 U.S.C.).

61. GLBA, § 101.

62. 48 Stat. 162 (1933) (codified at scattered sections of 12 U.S.C.).

63. *See United States v. Morgan*, 118 F. Supp. 621, 646 (S.D.N.Y. 1953):

> Institutions which had previously engaged both in commercial and deposit banking on the one hand and investment banking on the other were required to elect prior to June 16, 1934, which of the two functions they would pursue to the exclusion of the other. This resulted in the complete elimination of the commercial banks and trust companies from the investment banking business; and the various bank affiliates were dissolved and liquidated.

64. GLBA, § 101.

Notes and Comments 5.101. Review 12 U.S.C. §§ 24(Seventh), 378. What are the limitations on the securities activities of national banks? Of member banks?[65] Of depository institutions of all types? Can a bank offer brokerage services to its customers? To the public at large?[66]

5.102. For an interesting interpretation of the meaning and applicability of 12 U.S.C. § 24(Seventh), see *NationsBank of North Carolina, N.A. v. Variable Annuity Life Insurance Co.*, in § 7.b, *supra*. This decision permits the Comptroller to authorize national banks to broker annuities issued by insurance companies. To what extent does the decision broaden the possible range of securities activities in which banks may engage? Consider the following excerpt.

2 Michael P. Malloy, Banking Law and Regulation

§ 7.02[C] (2d ed., Aspen Publishers, 2011)

The Supreme Court offered interpretive guidance with respect to the application of section 16 in its 1995 decision in *NationsBank of North Carolina, N.A. v. Variable Annuity Life Insurance Co.* Writing for a unanimous Court, Justice Ginsberg gave great deference to the Comptroller's interpretation of the provision as authorizing a national bank to act as an agent (through its securities subsidiary) in the sale of annuities within "the business of banking" under 12 U.S.C. §24 (Seventh). In this context, the Court examined the proper construction of the provision itself.

The Comptroller had concluded that acting as an agent in the sale of annuities issued by insurance companies was within the "business of banking" authorized by section 16, relying on the "power [of banks] to broker a wide variety of financial investment instruments," which, in the Comptroller's view, were "part of [banks'] traditional role as financial intermediaries."[1] Hence, the inquiry under section 16 would appear to be whether or not the proposed activity were within the "business of banking" (and not prohibited by the section's restriction on securities activities). Under this reading of section 16, the authorization of "incidental powers...necessary to carry on the business of banking" is viewed as "an independent grant of authority"[2] with the five specific powers set forth in the language that follows in the section[3] being viewed "as exemplary, not exclusive."[4]

In contrast, the Variable Annuity Life Insurance Company (VALIC) read the authorization of power in section 16 as unitary and exclusive. The five specific powers enumerated following the reference to the "business of banking" (and any powers incidental thereto) are to be viewed as exhaustive of the business of banking; VALIC would attribute

---

65. 12 U.S.C. § 335 expressly imposes the same limitations on state member banks that apply to national banks.

66. *See generally* Michael P. Malloy, *The Regulation of Bank Brokerage Activities: Was Rule 3b-9 Benign?* 6 Ann. Rev. Banking L. 181 (1987) (discussing brokerage activities of commercial banks).

1. [*NationsBank of North Carolina, N.A. v. Variable Annity Life Ins. Co.*, 513 U.S. 251, 258 (1995) (quoting OCC interpretive letter).]

2. *NationsBank*, 513 U.S. at 258.

3. "[B]y discounting and negotiating promissory notes, drafts, bills of exchange, and other evidences of debt; by receiving deposits; by buying and selling exchange, coin, and bullion; by loaning money on personal security; and by obtaining, issuing, and circulating notes...." 12 U.S.C. § 24 (Seventh).

4. *NationsBank*, 513 U.S. at 258.

"no independent significance to the words 'business of banking."[5] The limitation on "dealing in securities" that follows the enumerated list would apparently stand on its own as a restriction imposed by the Glass-Steagall Act amendment of the prior version of section 24 (Seventh).[6]

The Court resolved this controversy by focusing on the significance of the Glass-Steagall Act's amendment of section 24 (Seventh) that added the limitation on "dealing in securities." In the Court's view,

> The second sentence of §24 Seventh, in limiting banks' "dealing in securities," presupposes that banks have authority not circumscribed by the five specifically listed activities. Congress' insertion of the limitation decades after the [National Bank] Act's initial adoption makes sense only if banks already had authority to deal in securities, authority presumably encompassed within the "business of banking" language which dates from 1863.[7]

Hence, the "business of banking" language of section 24 (Seventh) should be read to cover "brokerage of financial investment instruments, and is not confined to the examples specifically enumerated."[8] Under section 24 (Seventh), therefore, there are only two limitations on the power of a national bank to involve itself in securities activities. One is the necessity of demonstrating that the activities is within the general rubric of powers incidental to the "business of banking." The other is the extent to which the Glass-Steagall Act may restrict the bank's involvement in activities otherwise encompassed by the "business of banking."

Notes and Comments 5.103. Note that the cases in this section focus on the effect of sections 16 and 21 of the Glass-Steagall Act, 12 U.S.C. §§ 24(Seventh), 378, on depository institutions. Until the passage of the GLBA in November 1999, restrictions might also have applied to an affiliate of a bank under section 20 of the Glass-Steagall Act, 12 U.S.C. § 377 (1998), repealed by the GLBA, and section 4(c)(8) of the Bank Holding Company Act (BHCA), *id.* § 1843(c)(8), now significantly limited by the GLBA. Such affiliation questions are now subject to section 4(k) of the BHCA, 12 U.S.C. § 1843(k), which was added by the GLBA. The effect of section 4(k) is discussed in the next chapter.

5.104. First Credulity Savings Association wants to act as a dealer in equity securities, buying and selling them for its own account. First Credulity is a state-chartered savings association, insured by the FDIC. Does 12 U.S.C. § 24(Seventh) limit its power to do so? *See* 12 U.S.C. § 378.

5.105. Quarter National Bank would like to organize an "investment fund" within its trust department. The fund would accept "contributions" from the general public, and invest the total proceeds in a range of securities and other investments in which the bank's trust accounts are also invested. The fund would be supervised by the head of the trust department. Will Quarter have any problem establishing this proposed fund under the Glass-Steagall Act? Consider the following case.

---

5. *Id.*

6. *See id.* ("VALIC argues...that the limitation was imposed by the Glass-Steagall Act of 1933").

7. *Id.*

8. *Id.* at 259.

Investment Company Institute v. Camp

401 U.S. 617 (1971)

Mr. Justice STEWART delivered the opinion of the Court.

[The case involved two challenges to portions of 12 C.F.R. pt. 9, regulations promulgated by the Comptroller governing trust and related activities of national banks, on the ground that the regulation, in authorizing national banks to establish and operate "collective investment" funds, permitted national banks to operate open-end investment companies, prohibited to national banks and their affiliates by the Glass-Steagall Act. The Comptroller had approved the application of First National City Bank of New York (now Citibank) to establish and operate a collective investment fund. In addition, the National Association of Securities Dealers had challenged a related order of the Securities and Exchange Commission that partially exempted Citibank's collective investment fund from various provisions of the Investment Company Act of 1940, 15 U.S.C. §§ 80a-1 *et seq.*]

... For the reasons that follow, we hold Regulation 9 invalid insofar as it authorizes the sale of interests in an investment fund of the type established by First National City Bank pursuant to the Comptroller's approval. This disposition make it unnecessary to consider the propriety of the action of the Securities and Exchange Commission in affording this fund exemption from certain of the provisions of the Investment Company Act of 1940. . . .

II.

The issue before us is whether the Comptroller of the Currency may, consistently with the banking laws, authorize a national bank to offer its customers the opportunity to invest in a stock fund created and maintained by the bank. Before 1963 national banks were prohibited by administrative regulation from offering this service. . . .

In 1962 Congress transferred jurisdiction over most of the trust activities of national banks from the Board of Governors of the Federal Reserve System to the Comptroller of the Currency, without modifying any provision of substantive law. Pub.L. 87-722. 76 Stat. 668, 12 U.S.C. § 92a. The Comptroller thereupon solicited suggestions for improving the regulations applicable to trust activities. Subsequently, new regulations . . . were officially promulgated in 1963. . . . In 1965 the First National City Bank of New York submitted for the Comptroller's approval a plan for the collective investment of managing agency accounts. The Comptroller promptly approved the plan, and it is now in operation. This plan, which departs in some respects from the plan envisaged by the Comptroller's Regulation, is expected . . . to be a model for other banks which decide to offer their customers a collective investment service.

Under the plan the bank customer tenders between $10,000 and $500,000 to the bank, together with an authorization making the bank the customer's managing agent. The customer's investment is added to the fund, and a written evidence of participation is issued which expresses in "units of participation" the customer's proportionate interest in fund assets. Units of participation are freely redeemable, and transferable to anyone who has executed a managing agency agreement with the bank. The fund is registered as an investment company under the Investment Company Act of 1940. The bank is the underwriter of the fund's units of participation within the meaning of that Act. The fund has filed a registration statement pursuant to the Securities Act of 1933. The fund is supervised by a five-member committee elected annually by the participants pursuant to the Investment Company Act of 1940. The Securities and Exchange Commission has exempted the fund from the Investment Company Act to the extent that a majority of this committee may be affiliated with the bank, and it is expected that a majority always will be officers in the bank's trust and investment division. The actual custody and investment of fund assets is carried out by the bank as investment advisor pursuant to a management agreement. Although the Investment Company Act requires that this management agreement be approved annually by the committee, including a majority of the unaffiliated members, or by the participants, it is expected that the bank will continue to be investment advisor.

III.

Section 16 of the Glass-Steagall Act as amended, 12 U.S.C. § 24, Seventh provides that the "business of dealing in securities and stock [by a national bank] shall be limited to purchasing and selling such securities and stock without recourse, solely upon the order, and for the account of, customers, and in no case for its own account. . . . Except as hereinafter provided or otherwise permitted by law, nothing herein contained shall authorize the purchase by [a national bank] for its own account of any shares of stock of any corporation." The petitioners contend that a purchase of stock by a bank's investment fund is a purchase of stock by a bank for its own account in violation of this section [and] . . . that the creation and operation of an investment fund by a bank which offers to its customers the opportunity to purchase an interest in the fund's assets constitutes the issuing, underwriting, selling, or distributing of securities or stocks in violation of these sections.

The questions raised by the petitioners are novel and substantial. National banks were granted trust powers in 1913. Federal Reserve Act, § 11, 38 Stat. 261. The first common trust fund was organized in 1927, and such funds were expressly authorized by the Federal Reserve Board by Regulation F promulgated in 1937. *Report on Commingled or Common Trust Funds Administered by Banks and Trust Companies*, H.R. Doc. No. 476, 76th Cong., 2d Sess., 4-5 (1939). For at least a generation, therefore, there has been no reason to doubt that a national bank can, consistently with the banking laws, commingle trust funds on the one hand, and act as a managing agent on the other. No provision of the banking law suggests that it is improper for a national bank to pool trust assets, or to act as a managing agent for individual customers. But the union of these powers gives birth to an investment fund whose activities are of a different character. The differences between the investment fund that the Comptroller has authorized and a conventional open-end mutual fund are subtle at best, and it is undisputed that this bank investment fund finds itself in direct competition with the mutual fund industry. One would suppose that the business of a mutual fund consists of buying stock "for its own account" and of "issuing" and "selling" stock or "other securities" evidencing an undivided and redeemable interest in the assets of the fund. On their face, §§ 16 and 21 of the Glass-Steagall Act [12 U.S.C. §§ 24, 378] appear clearly to prohibit this activity by national banks.

But we cannot come lightly to the conclusion that the Comptroller has authorized activity that violates the banking laws. . . .

[T]he Comptroller adopted no expressly articulated position at the administrative level as to the meaning and impact of the provisions of §§ 16 and 21 as they affect bank investment funds. The Comptroller promulgated [Part 9] without opinion or accompanying statement. His subsequent report to Congress did not advert to the prohibitions of the Glass-Steagall Act. . . . Quite obviously the Comptroller should not grant new authority to national banks until he is satisfied that the exercise of this authority will not violate the intent of the banking laws. If he faces such questions only after he has acted, there is substantial danger that the momentum generated by initial approval may seriously impair the enforcement of the banking laws that Congress enacted.

IV.

There is no dispute that one of the objectives of the Glass-Steagall Act was to prohibit commercial banks, banks that receive deposits subject to repayment, lend money, discount and negotiate promissory notes and the like, from going into the investment banking business. Many commercial banks were indirectly engaged in the investment banking business when the Act was passed in 1933. Even before the passage of the Act it was generally believed that it was improper for a commercial bank to engage in investment banking directly. But in 1908 banks began the practice of establishing security affiliates that engaged in, inter alia, the business of floating bond issues and, less frequently, underwriting stock issues. The Glass-Steagall Act confirmed that national banks could not engage in investment banking directly, and in addition made affiliation with an organization so engaged illegal. One effect of the Act was to abolish the security affiliates of commercial banks.

It is apparent from the legislative history of the Act why Congress felt that this drastic step was necessary. The failure of the Bank of United States in 1930 was widely attributed to that bank's activities with respect to its numerous securities affiliates. Moreover, Congress was concerned that commercial banks in general and member banks of the Federal Reserve System in particular had both aggravated and been damaged by stock market decline partly because of their direct and indirect involvement in the trading and ownership of speculative securities. The Glass-Steagall Act reflected a determination that policies of competition, convenience, or expertise which might otherwise support the entry of commercial banks into the investment banking business were outweighed by the "hazards" and "financial dangers" that arise when commercial banks engage in the activities proscribed by the Act.

The hazards that Congress had in mind were not limited to the obvious danger that a bank might lose its investments in frozen or otherwise imprudent stock or security investments. For often securities affiliates had operated without direct access to the assets of the bank. This was because securities affiliates had frequently been established with capital paid in by the bank's stockholders, or by the public, or through the allocation of a legal dividend on bank stock for this purpose. The legislative history of the Glass-Steagall Act shows that Congress also had in mind and repeatedly focused on the more subtle hazards that arise when a commercial bank goes beyond the business of acting as fiduciary or managing agent and enters the investment banking business either directly or by establishing an affiliate to hold and sell particular investments. This course places new promotional and other pressures on the bank which in turn create new temptations. For example, pressures are created because the bank and the affiliate are closely associated in the public mind, and should the affiliate fare badly, public confidence in the bank might be impaired. And since public confidence is essential to the solvency of a bank, there might exist a natural temptation to shore up the affiliate through unsound loans or other aid. Moreover, the pressure to sell a particular investment and to make the affiliate successful might create a risk that the bank would make its credit facilities more freely available to those companies in whose stock or securities the affiliate has invested or become otherwise involved. Congress feared that banks might even go so far as to make unsound loans to such companies. In any event, it was thought that the banks' salesman's interest might impair its ability to function as an impartial source of credit.

Congress was also concerned that bank depositors might suffer losses on investments that they purchased in reliance on the relationship between the bank and its affiliate. This loss of customer good-will might "become an important handicap to a bank during a major period of security market deflation." More broadly, Congress feared that the promotional needs of investment banking might lead commercial banks to lend their reputation for prudence and restraint to the enterprise of selling stocks and securities, and that this could not be done without that reputation being undercut by the risks necessarily incident to the investment banking business. There was also perceived the danger that when commercial banks were subject to the promotional demands of investment banking, they might be tempted to make loans to customers with the expectation that the loan would facilitate the purchase of stocks and securities. There was evidence before Congress that loans for investment written by commercial banks had done much to feed the speculative fever of the late 1920's. Senator Glass-made it plain that it was "the fixed purpose of Congress" not to see the facilities of commercial banking diverted into speculative operations by the aggressive and promotional character of the investment banking business.

Another potential hazard that very much concerned Congress arose from the plain conflict between the promotional interest of the investment banker and the obligation of the commercial banker to render disinterested investment advice. . . . Congress had before it evidence that security affiliates might be driven to unload excessive holding through the trust department of a sponsor bank. Some witnesses at the hearings expressed the view that this practice constituted self-dealing in violation of the trustee's obligation of loyalty, and indeed that it would be improper for a bank's trust department to purchase anything from the banks's securities affiliate.

In sum, Congress acted to keep commercial banks out of the investment banking business largely because it believed that the promotional incentives of investment banking and the investment banker's pecuniary stake in the success of particular investment opportunities was destructive of prudent and disinterested commercial banking and of public confidence in the commercial banking system. . . .

V.

The language that Congress chose to achieve this purpose includes the prohibitions of § 16 that a national bank "shall not underwrite any issue of securities or stock" and shall not purchase "for its own account . . . any shares of stock of any corporation," and the prohibition of § 21 against engaging in "the business of issuing, underwriting, selling, or distributing . . . stocks, bonds, debentures, notes, or other securities." In this litigation the Comptroller takes the position that the operation of a bank investment fund is consistent with these provisions, because participating interests in such a fund are not "securities" within the meaning of the Act. It is argued that a bank investment fund simply makes available to the small investor the benefit of investment management by a bank trust department which would otherwise be available only to large investors, and that the operation of an investment fund creates no problems that are not present whenever a bank invests in securities for the account of customers.

But there is nothing in the phrasing of either § 16 or § 21 that suggests a narrow reading of the word "securities." To the contrary, the breadth of the term is implicit in the fact that the antecedent statutory language encompasses not only equity shares but also securities representing debt. And certainly there is nothing in the language of these provisions to suggest that the sale of an interest in the business of buying, holding, and selling stocks for investment is to be distinguished from the sale of an interest in a commercial or industrial enterprise.

Indeed, there is direct evidence that Congress specifically contemplated that the word "security" includes an interest in an investment fund. . . .

[W]e are persuaded that the purposes for which Congress enacted the Glass-Steagall Act leave no room for the conclusion that a participation in a bank investment fund is not a "security" within the meaning of the Act. From the perspective of competition, convenience, and expertise, there are no arguments to be made in support of allowing commercial banks to enter the investment banking business. But Congress determined that the hazards outlined above made it necessary to prohibit this activity to commercial banks. Those same hazards are clearly present when a bank undertakes to operate an investment fund.

A bank that operates an investment fund has a particular investment to sell. It is not a matter of indifference to the bank whether the customer buys an interest in the fund or makes some other investment. If its customers cannot be persuaded to invest in the bank's investment fund, the bank will lose their investment business and the fee which that business would have brought in. . . . When interests in the fund were redeemed, the bank would be effectively faced with the choice of selling stocks from the fund's portfolio or of selling new participations to cover redemptions. The bank might have a pecuniary incentive to choose the latter course in order to avoid the cost of stock transactions undertaken solely for redemption purposes.

Promotional incentives might also be created by the circumstance that the bank's fund would be in direct competition with mutual fund that, from the point of view of the investor, offered an investment opportunity comparable to that offered by the bank. The bank would want to be in a position to show to the prospective customer that its fund was more attractive than the mutual funds offered by others. The bank would have a salesman's stake in the performance of the fund, for if the fund were less successful than the competition the bank would lose the business and the resulting fees.

A bank that operated an investment fund would necessarily put its reputation and facilities squarely behind that fund and the investment opportunity that the fund offered. The investments of the fund might be conservative or speculative, but in any event the success or failure of the fund would be a matter of public record. Imprudent or unsuccessful management of the bank's investment fund could bring about a perhaps unjustified loss of public confidence in the bank itself. If imprudent management should place the fund in distress, a bank might find itself under pressure to rescue the fund through measures inconsistent with sound banking.

The promotional and other pressures incidental to the operation of an investment fund, in other words, involve the same kinds of potential abuses that Congress intended to guard against when it legislated against bank security affiliates. It is not the slightest reflection on the integrity of the mutual fund industry to say that the traditions of that industry are not necessarily the conservative traditions of commercial banking. The needs and interests of a mutual fund enterprise more nearly approximate those of securities underwriting, the activity in which bank security affiliates were primarily engaged. When a bank puts itself in competition with mutual funds, the bank must make an accommodation to the kind of ground rules that Congress firmly concluded could not be prudently mixed with the business of commercial banking.

And there are other potential hazards of the kind Congress sought to eliminate with the passage of the Glass- Steagall Act. The bank's stake in the investment fund might distort its credit decisions or lead to unsound loans to the companies in which the fund had invested. The bank might exploit its confidential relationship with its commercial and industrial creditors for the benefit of the fund. The bank might undertake, directly or indirectly, to make its credit facilities available to the fund or to render other aid to the fund inconsistent with the best interests of the bank's depositors. The bank might make loans to facilitate the purchase of interests in the fund. The bank might divert talent and resources from its commercial banking operation to the promotion of the fund. Moreover, because the bank would have a stake in a customer's making a particular investment decision–the decision to invest in the bank's investment fund–the customer might doubt the motivation behind the bank's recommendation that he make such an investment. If the fund investment should turn out badly there would be a danger that the bank would lose the good-will of those customers who had invested in the fund. It might be unlikely that disenchantment would go so far as to threaten the solvency of the bank. But because banks are dependent on the confidence of their customers, the risk would not be unreal. . . .

The Glass-Steagall Act was a prophylactic measure directed against conditions that the experience of the 1920's showed to be great potentials for abuse. The literal terms of that Act clearly prevent what the Comptroller has sought to authorize here. Because the potential hazards and abuses that flow from a bank's entry into the mutual investment business are the same basic hazards and abuses that Congress sought to eliminate almost 40 years ago, we cannot but apply the terms of the federal statute as they were written. We conclude that the operation of an investment fund of the kind approved by the Comptroller involves a bank in the underwriting, issuing, selling, and distributing of securities in violation of §§ 16 and 21 of the Glass-Steagall Act.

Notes and Comments 5.106. Does *Investment Company Institute* ("*ICI I*") create a subtle hazards "test" under the Glass-Steagall Act? If it does, then could Quarter National Bank argue that it should permitted to sponsor a open-end investment company, if it agrees to conditions that minimize or eliminate the subtle hazards through regulation?[67]

5.107. A second generation of the Comptroller regulations challenged in *ICI I* was later promulgated, authorizing common trust funds, 12 C.F.R. § 9.18(a)(1) (collective investment and reinvestment of funds contributed to a common trust fund maintained by a national bank) and "collective investment funds," *id.* § 9.18(a)(2) (collective investment in a fund consisting solely of assets of retirement, pension, profit-sharing, stock bonus or other trusts exempt from federal income taxation). Does the following regulation conform with *ICI I*?

Comptroller of the Currency

12 C.F.R. pt. 9

§ 9.18 Collective investment funds.

(a) In general. Where consistent with applicable law, a national bank may invest assets that it holds as fiduciary in the following collective investment funds:[1]

(1) A fund maintained by the bank, or by one or more affiliated banks,[2] exclusively for the collective investment and reinvestment of money contributed to the fund by the bank, or by one or more affiliated banks, in its capacity as trustee, executor, administrator, guardian, or custodian under a uniform gifts to minors act.

(2) A fund consisting solely of assets of retirement, pension, profit sharing, stock bonus or other trusts that are exempt from Federal income tax.

(i) A national bank may invest assets of retirement, pension, profit sharing, stock bonus, or other trusts exempt from Federal income tax and that the bank holds in its capacity as trustee in a collective investment fund established under paragraph (a)(1) or (a)(2) of this section.

(ii) A national bank may invest assets of retirement, pension, profit sharing, stock bonus, or other employee benefit trusts exempt from Federal income tax and that the bank holds in any capacity (including agent), in a collective investment fund established under this

---

67. *ICI I* notwithstanding, commercial banks, directly or indirectly through holding company affiliates, have continued to involve themselves in investment management. *See generally* Martin Lybecker, *Bank-Sponsored Investment Management Services: A Legal History and Statutory Interpretive Analysis*, 5 Sec. Reg. L.J. (1977).

1. In determining whether investing fiduciary assets in a collective investment fund is proper, the bank may consider the fund as a whole and, for example, shall not be prohibited from making that investment because any particular asset is nonincome-producing.

2. A fund established pursuant to this paragraph (a)(1) that includes money contributed by entities that are affiliates under 12 U.S.C. 221a(b), but are not members of the same affiliated group, as defined at 26 U.S.C. 1504, may fail to qualify for tax-exempt status under the Internal Revenue Code. See 26 U.S.C. 584.

paragraph (a)(2) if the fund itself qualifies for exemption from Federal income tax.

(b) Requirements. A national bank administering a collective investment fund authorized under paragraph (a) of this section shall comply with the following requirements:

(1) Written plan. The bank shall establish and maintain each collective investment fund in accordance with a written plan (Plan) approved by a resolution of the bank's board of directors or by a committee authorized by the board. The bank shall make a copy of the Plan available for public inspection at its main office during all banking hours, and shall provide a copy of the Plan to any person who requests it. The Plan must contain appropriate provisions, not inconsistent with this part, regarding the manner in which the bank will operate the fund, including provisions relating to:

(i) Investment powers and policies with respect to the fund;

(ii) Allocation of income, profits, and losses;

(iii) Fees and expenses that will be charged to the fund and to participating accounts;

(iv) Terms and conditions governing the admission and withdrawal of participating accounts;

(v) Audits of participating accounts;

(vi) Basis and method of valuing assets in the fund;

(vii) Expected frequency for income distribution to participating accounts;

(viii) Minimum frequency for valuation of fund assets;

(ix) Amount of time following a valuation date during which the valuation must be made;

(x) Bases upon which the bank may terminate the fund; and

(xi) Any other matters necessary to define clearly the rights of participating accounts.

(2) Fund management. A bank administering a collective investment fund shall have exclusive management thereof, except as a prudent person might delegate responsibilities to others.[3]

(3) Proportionate interests. Each participating account in a collective investment fund must have a proportionate interest in all the fund's assets.

(4) Valuation–(i) Frequency of valuation. A bank administering a collective investment fund shall determine the value of the fund's readily marketable assets at least once every three months. A bank shall determine the value of the fund's assets that are not readily marketable at least once a year.

(ii) Method of valuation–

(A) In general. Except as provided in paragraph (b)(4)(ii)(B) of this section, a bank shall value each fund asset at market value as of the date set for valuation, unless the bank cannot readily ascertain market value, in which case the bank shall use a fair value determined in good faith.

(B) Short-term investment funds. A bank may value a fund's assets on a cost, rather than market value, basis for purposes of admissions and withdrawals, if the Plan requires the bank to:

(1) Maintain a dollar-weighted average portfolio maturity of 90 days or less;

(2) Accrue on a straight-line basis the difference between the cost and anticipated

3. If a fund, the assets of which consist solely of Individual Retirement Accounts, Keogh Accounts, or other employee benefit accounts that are exempt from taxation, is registered under the Investment Company Act of 1940 (15 U.S.C. 80a-1 et seq.), the fund will not be deemed in violation of this paragraph (b)(2) as a result of its compliance with section 10(c) of the Investment Company Act of 1940 (15 U.S.C. 80a-10(c)).

principal receipt on maturity; and

(3) Hold the fund's assets until maturity under usual circumstances.

(5) Admission and withdrawal of accounts–

(i) In general. A bank administering a collective investment fund shall admit an account to or withdraw an account from the fund only on the basis of the valuation described in paragraph (b)(4) of this section.

(ii) Prior request or notice. A bank administering a collective investment fund may admit an account to or withdraw an account from a collective investment fund only if the bank has approved a request for or a notice of intention of taking that action on or before the valuation date on which the admission or withdrawal is based. No requests or notices may be canceled or countermanded after the valuation date.

(iii) Prior notice period for withdrawals from funds with assets not readily marketable. A bank administering a collective investment fund described in paragraph (a)(2) of this section that is invested primarily in real estate or other assets that are not readily marketable, may require a prior notice period, not to exceed one year, for withdrawals.

(iv) Method of distributions. A bank administering a collective investment fund shall make distributions to accounts withdrawing from the fund in cash, ratably in kind, a combination of cash and ratably in kind, or in any other manner consistent with applicable law in the state in which the bank maintains the fund.

(v) Segregation of investments. If an investment is withdrawn in kind from a collective investment fund for the benefit of all participants in the fund at the time of the withdrawal but the investment is not distributed ratably in kind, the bank shall segregate and administer it for the benefit ratably of all participants in the collective investment fund at the time of withdrawal.

(6) Audits and financial reports–

(i) Annual audit. At least once during each 12-month period, a bank administering a collective investment fund shall arrange for an audit of the collective investment fund by auditors responsible only to the board of directors of the bank.[4]

(ii) Financial report. At least once during each 12-month period, a bank administering a collective investment fund shall prepare a financial report of the fund based on the audit required by paragraph (b)(6)(i) of this section. The report must disclose the fund's fees and expenses in a manner consistent with applicable law in the state in which the bank maintains the fund. This report must contain a list of investments in the fund showing the cost and current market value of each investment, and a statement covering the period after the previous report showing the following (organized by type of investment):

(A) A summary of purchases (with costs);

(B) A summary of sales (with profit or loss and any other investment changes);

(C) Income and disbursements; and

(D) An appropriate notation of any investments in default.

(iii) Limitation on representations. A bank may include in the financial report a description of the fund's value on previous dates, as well as its income and disbursements during previous accounting periods. A bank may not publish in the financial report any predictions or representations as to future performance. In addition, with respect to funds described in paragraph (a)(1) of this section, a bank may not publish the performance of

---

4. If a fund, the assets of which consist solely of Individual Retirement Accounts, Keogh Accounts, or other employee benefit accounts that are exempt from taxation, is registered under the Investment Company Act of 1940 (15 U.S.C. 80a-1 et seq.), the fund will not be deemed in violation of this paragraph (b)(6)(i) as a result of its compliance with section 10(c) of the Investment Company Act of 1940 (15 U.S.C. 80a-10(c)), if the bank has access to the audit reports of the fund.

individual funds other than those administered by the bank or its affiliates.

(iv) Availability of the report. A bank administering a collective investment fund shall provide a copy of the financial report, or shall provide notice that a copy of the report is available upon request without charge, to each person who ordinarily would receive a regular periodic accounting with respect to each participating account. The bank may provide a copy of the financial report to prospective customers. In addition, the bank shall provide a copy of the report upon request to any person for a reasonable charge.

(7) Advertising restriction. A bank may not advertise or publicize any fund authorized under paragraph (a)(1) of this section, except in connection with the advertisement of the general fiduciary services of the bank.

(8) Self-dealing and conflicts of interest. A national bank administering a collective investment fund must comply with the following (in addition to § 9.12):

(i) Bank interests. A bank administering a collective investment fund may not have an interest in that fund other than in its fiduciary capacity. If, because of a creditor relationship or otherwise, the bank acquires an interest in a participating account, the participating account must be withdrawn on the next withdrawal date. However, a bank may invest assets that it holds as fiduciary for its own employees in a collective investment fund.

(ii) Loans to participating accounts. A bank administering a collective investment fund may not make any loan on the security of a participant's interest in the fund. An unsecured advance to a fiduciary account participating in the fund until the time of the next valuation date does not constitute the acquisition of an interest in a participating account by the bank.

(iii) Purchase of defaulted investments. A bank administering a collective investment fund may purchase for its own account any defaulted investment held by the fund (in lieu of segregating the investment in accordance with paragraph (b)(5)(v) of this section) if, in the judgment of the bank, the cost of segregating the investment is excessive in light of the market value of the investment. If a bank elects to purchase a defaulted investment, it shall do so at the greater of market value or the sum of cost and accrued unpaid interest.

(9) Management fees. A bank administering a collective investment fund may charge a reasonable fund management fee only if:

(i) The fee is permitted under applicable law (and complies with fee disclosure requirements, if any) in the state in which the bank maintains the fund; and

(ii) The amount of the fee does not exceed an amount commensurate with the value of legitimate services of tangible benefit to the participating fiduciary accounts that would not have been provided to the accounts were they not invested in the fund.

(10) Expenses. A bank administering a collective investment fund may charge reasonable expenses incurred in operating the collective investment fund, to the extent not prohibited by applicable law in the state in which the bank maintains the fund. However, a bank shall absorb the expenses of establishing or reorganizing a collective investment fund.

(11) Prohibition against certificates. A bank administering a collective investment fund may not issue any certificate or other document representing a direct or indirect interest in the fund, except to provide a withdrawing account with an interest in a segregated investment.

(12) Good faith mistakes. The OCC will not deem a bank's mistake made in good faith and in the exercise of due care in connection with the administration of a collective investment fund to be a violation of this part if, promptly after the discovery of the mistake, the bank takes whatever action is practicable under the circumstances to remedy the mistake.

(c) Other collective investments. In addition to the collective investment funds authorized under paragraph (a) of this section, a national bank may collectively invest assets that it holds as fiduciary, to the extent not prohibited by applicable law, as follows:

(1) Single loans or obligations. In the following loans or obligations, if the bank's only interest in the loans or obligations is its capacity as fiduciary:

(i) A single real estate loan, a direct obligation of the United States, or an obligation fully guaranteed by the United States, or a single fixed amount security, obligation, or other property, either real, personal, or mixed, of a single issuer; or

(ii) A variable amount note of a borrower of prime credit, if the bank uses the note solely for investment of funds held in its fiduciary accounts.

(2) Mini-funds. In a fund maintained by the bank for the collective investment of cash balances received or held by a bank in its capacity as trustee, executor, administrator, guardian, or custodian under a uniform gifts to minors act, that the bank considers too small to be invested separately to advantage. The total assets in the fund must not exceed $1,000,000 and the number of participating accounts must not exceed 100.

(3) Trust funds of corporations and closely-related settlors. In any investment specifically authorized by the instrument creating the fiduciary account or a court order, in the case of trusts created by a corporation, including its affiliates and subsidiaries, or by several individual settlors who are closely related.

(4) Other authorized funds. In any collective investment authorized by applicable law, such as investments pursuant to a state pre-need funeral statute.

(5) Special exemption funds. In any other manner described by the bank in a written plan approved by the OCC.[5] In order to obtain a special exemption, a bank shall submit to the OCC a written plan that sets forth:

(i) The reason that the proposed fund requires a special exemption;

(ii) The provisions of the proposed fund that are inconsistent with paragraphs (a) and (b) of this section;

(iii) The provisions of paragraph (b) of this section for which the bank seeks an exemption; and

(iv) The manner in which the proposed fund addresses the rights and interests of participating accounts.

Notes and Comments 5.108. The validity of the regulation was challenged by the Investment Company Institute, on the strength of *ICI I*. Is Judge Starr's opinion consistent with *ICI I*?

Investment Company Institute v. Conover

790 F.2d 925 (D.C. Cir. 1986),
cert. denied sub nom. Investment Company Institute v. Clarke, 479 U.S. 939[a]

STARR, Circuit Judge.

. . . The Institute brought an action for declaratory and injunctive relief in the District Court, challenging a decision by the Comptroller of the Currency allowing Citibank to establish and market a "Collective Investment Trust" for assets of Individual Retirement

---

5. Any institution that must comply with this section in order to receive favorable tax treatment under 26 U.S.C. 584 (namely, any corporate fiduciary) may seek OCC approval of special exemption funds in accordance with this paragraph (c)(5).

a. *Accord Investment Company Institute v. Clarke*, 789 F.2d 175 (2d Cir. 1986), *cert. denied*, 479 U.S. 940; *Investment Company Institute v. Clarke*, 793 F.2d 220 (9th Cir. 1986), *cert. denied*, 479 U.S. 939.

Accounts, commonly known as "IRAs." The Institute contended that Citibank's Trust is functionally equivalent to a mutual fund, and that Citibank could not operate the Trust without running afoul of the 1933 Glass-Steagall Act. . . .

The District Court granted the Comptroller's motion for summary judgment, . . and the Institute appealed. The sole issue before us is whether "units of beneficial interest," or shares, in Citibank's Trust constitute "securities" within the meaning of sections 16 and 21 of the Glass-Steagall Act, 12 U.S.C. §§ 24 (Seventh), 378(a)(1) (1982) ("the Act"). The Comptroller concluded that the units are not "securities" for purposes of the Act, and that Citibank could therefore lawfully offer the units to the public. The District Court agreed with the Comptroller, thereby disagreeing with the then only other judicial decision on this issue, *Investment Co. Institute v. Conover*, 593 F.Supp. 846 (N.D.Cal.1984) (Schwarzer, J.), [*reversed, Investment Company Institute v. Clarke*, 793 F.2d 220 (9th Cir. 1986), *cert. denied*, 479 U.S. 939].[1] Guided by the deference principles enunciated in *Chevron U.S.A., Inc. v. Natural Resources Defense Council, Inc.*, 467 U.S. 837 (1984), we uphold the Comptroller's interpretation of the Act and affirm.

I

An understanding of the specific dispute before us requires familiarity with a portion of the elaborate federal statutory scheme governing national banking activities and the newer provision of federal law permitting IRAs, an acquaintance with the structure of Citibank's Trust, and an appreciation of the procedural history of this case.

A

. . . Also of relevance in this case is the Employee Retirement Income security Act (ERISA), enacted by Congress at 1974. Among other things, ERISA added a provision to the Internal Revenue Code permitting qualified individuals to deduct investments in IRAs from taxable income up to a specified amount, currently $2,000 annually. 26 U.S.C. § 408(a)(1) (1982). Such contributions, together with earnings on IRA assets, are not taxed until distribution or withdrawal, *id.* § 408(d)(1), but a ten percent tax penalty is imposed if the account holder withdraws the funds before reaching the age of 59-1/2, *id.* § 408(f)(1). Section 408(a)(2), moreover, requires specific approval by the Secretary of the Treasury before a bank or other institution may serve as trustee for IRA trust assets. These assets may only be commingled in a common investment fund or trust fund. *Id.* § 408(a)(5).

B

In 1982, Citibank established a common trust fund for IRA investors. A common trust fund is a device, long known to the banking industry, by which a bank commingles the assets of individual trusts and invests those assets collectively. The assets of each participating trust are exchanged for an undivided ownership interest in the common trust fund, with the ownership interest being proportionate to the assets contributed by each trust to the fund's total assets. This device obviously permits each participating trust to enjoy greater diversification and wider investment opportunities than would otherwise exist. It also permits banks, acting as trustees, to manage trusts that are too small to be managed individually. National banks have operated such funds since at least 1936. . . .

Styled a "Collective Investment Trust," the Citibank trust fund at issue here consists of four separate investment portfolios into which an individual may instruct Citibank to place his or her IRA trust assets. This is accomplished by means of a written trust agreement, which is freely revocable save for the ten percent penalty imposed by I.R.C. § 408. An

---

1. Subsequent to the District Court's decision, the U.S. District Court in Connecticut agreed with the court below, holding that Citibank's Trust does not run afoul of the Glass-Steagall Act. *See Investment Company Institute v. Clarke*, 630 F.Supp. 593 (D.Conn. 1986) (Cabranes, J.), *aff'd mem. per curiam*, 789 F.2d 175 (2d Cir. 1986).

individual's ownership interest in the entire trust fund is expressed in terms of "units of beneficial interest," which are available only to Citibank IRA-holders and are non-transferable. IRA assets may, however, be freely transferred among the four portfolios, as well as among any of Citibank's other IRA programs. Citibank serves as trustee and investment advisor to the trust fund and receives a monthly fee based in part on the net value of the fund's portfolios. In order to comply with SEC requirements, however, Citibank has placed the fund under the ultimate control of an independent five-member "supervisory committee," which essentially serves as a board of directors. Citibank has marketed its fund as an alternative to, or a competitor of, similar programs now being offered by mutual funds.

C

Citibank first sought approval of its Collective Investment Trust from the Securities and Exchange Commission, which has in the past opined that ownership interests in collective trust funds are "securities" for purposes of the federal securities laws. Although not conceding the correctness of the SEC's interpretation, Citibank registered the Trust as an investment company under the Investment Company Act of 1940, [15 U.S.C. §§ 80a-1 *et seq.*] and registered the units of beneficial interest as securities under the 1933 Securities Act[, *id.* §§ 77a *et seq.*].[4]

Citibank then sought approval of the Trust from the Comptroller of the Currency. . . . Citibank asked the Comptroller to determine that its operation of the Trust did not violate the Glass-Steagall Act; it also asked for exemptions from those regulations that Citibank feared might conflict with requirements imposed by the SEC pursuant to the Investment Company Act.

. . . The Comptroller found Citibank's operation of the Trust to be authorized by applicable trust regulations and granted the requested exemptions. Importantly for present purposes, the Comptroller provided a lengthy analysis of the applicability of the Glass-Steagall Act to the Trust, concluding that "there is no Glass-Steagall Act impediment to a bank collectively investing IRA trust assets."

Much of the Comptroller's discussion of the Glass-Steagall Act centered on the Supreme Court's 1971 decision in [*ICI I*]. After noting certain "general similarities" between the present Trust and the Citibank fund at issue in [*ICI I*], the Comptroller offered two reasons why the units of beneficial interest in the Trust should not be considered "securities" for purposes of Glass-Steagall. First, unlike the arrangement in [*ICI I*], Citibank receives the IRA assets in trust rather than in a "managing agent" capacity. The Comptroller observed that, as [*ICI I*] had recognized, national banks have long enjoyed authority to commingle funds received in trust. . . . In light of this long established authority, the Comptroller concluded that "when, as in the present case, the 'securities' merely represent the formal manifestation of a traditional banking service, . . . the prohibitions of the Glass-Steagall Act are not applicable." . . . According to the Comptroller, moreover, "the meaning of the term securities under the securities law [is] not necessarily synonymous with its meaning under the Glass-Steagall Act." . . . Second, the Comptroller concluded that Citibank's operation of the Trust entails none of the "hazards and potential abuses" identified by the Supreme Court in [*ICI I*]. The Comptroller explained in detail his reasons for so believing, concluding that "because the potential for abuse is non-existent or negligible here, and because this is essentially a traditional banking service, it would be inappropriate to conclude that there is any security here for purposes of the Glass-Steagall Act." . . .

. . . [T]he District Court held that the Comptroller's decision was entitled to "great weight," and that the Comptroller had acted reasonably in interpreting Glass-Steagall as not

---

4. Citibank asserts that these actions were taken merely to avoid a potentially expensive, protracted dispute with the SEC.

prohibiting Citibank's Trust. . . .

II

. . . [W]e first examine the Institute's vigorously pressed contention that [*ICI I*] itself disposes of this case, requiring invalidation of Citibank's latter-day efforts to compete with the mutual fund industry. As we understand its argument, the Institute asserts two independent grounds for this position. First, [*ICI I*] makes it unlawful for national banks to operate a mutual fund, which, the Institute contends, is exactly what the Trust amounts to. . . . Second, under [*ICI I*], the term "security" includes any "undivided and redeemable interest in the assets of a common trust fund."

A

The strength of the Institute's first argument lies in its intuitive appeal, for [*ICI I*] indeed overturned the Comptroller's earlier attempt to authorize Citibank's operation of what amounted to a mutual fund. Now Citibank–again with the Comptroller's approval–is attempting to offer a service that, in the eyes of many customers and, apparently, Citibank's marketing and advertising departments, looks very much like a mutual fund. To call Citibank's fund anything but a mutual fund, according to the Institute, is to exalt form over substance.

In our view, however, [*ICI I*] cannot fairly be read to prohibit any financial service that some actors in the marketplace view as functionally similar to a mutual fund. [*ICI I*] nowhere states that all such services are prohibited. To be sure, the Court found significant the fact that the fund at issue there was "in direct competition with the mutual fund industry." . . . But the mere existence of such competition was not the decisive element in the Court's analysis.

More fundamentally, Citibank's Trust is, upon close analysis, quite distinct from the fund at issue in [*ICI I*]. As the Comptroller found, the principal difference is that Citibank serves as trustee of its IRA funds rather than as managing agent, the situation before the Court in [*ICI I*]. Although the Institute devotes considerable energy to arguing why this distinction is irrelevant, . . . , [*ICI I*] itself suggests otherwise. After expressly observing that "the investment fund plan as established does not provide that the bank receives the investor's money in trust," . . . the Court stated:

> For at least a generation . . . there has been no reason to doubt that a national bank can, consistently with the banking laws, commingle trust funds on the one hand, and act as managing agent on the other. No provision of the banking law suggests that it is improper for a national bank to pool trust assets, or to act as a managing agent for individual customers, or to purchase stock for the account of its customers. But the union of these powers gives birth to an investment fund whose activities are of a different character.

401 U.S. at 624-25. According to the Court, then, it was the combination of the bank's commingling of trust assets and its acting as managing agent (rather than trustee) that spawned Glass-Steagall concerns. Here, by contrast, Citibank is seeking to exercise only one of the two powers which [*ICI I*] held could not be joined: the power to commingle trust funds. The existence of a trust relationship is sufficient, by itself, to take this case out of [*ICI I*]'s express teaching.

But even if the investment fund at issue in [*ICI I*] had employed a trust device, our case would still not be on all fours. [*ICI I*] evinces the Court's concern with the risks to which a national bank might subject itself in offering a new, unconventional product. In the Court's analysis, whether such a product is a "security" depends to some extent on whether, from the bank's perspective, the product entails the relatively small risks presumably characteristic of commercial banking or, as in [*ICI I*], the relatively large risks (either real or apparent) usually associated with investment banking. . . . This concern also appears to underlie the [*ICI I*] Court's attempt to determine whether a financial service represents a "fiduciary" service or a run-of-the-mill "investment." . . . The Court in [*ICI I*] was constrained to undertake an analysis of economic effects since, as discussed more fully below, the Comptroller in that case had not bothered to shed any light whatever as to Glass-Steagall's meaning. . . . In order to determine whether [*ICI I*] controls this case, we are obliged to examine some of the economic effects of Citibank's Trust.

We see four reasons why, from a banking perspective, the Citibank Trust is likely to be less risky than the investment fund at issue in [*ICI I*]. First, customers of the [*ICI I*] investment fund were permitted to invest between $10,000 and $500,000. . . . Here, by contrast, ERISA imposes a limit of $2,000 per person per year. 26 U.S.C. § 408(a)(1). This limitation, it seems to us (as it seemed to the Comptroller), makes it less likely that Citibank would be tempted to engage in unsound lending practices in order to attract or retain particularly valued customers. This was one of the "subtle hazards" identified in [*ICI I*]. . . .

Second, Citibank's units may not be used as collateral, unlike the investment fund shares in [*ICI I*]. This, again, is assured by ERISA. See 26 U.S.C. § 408(e)(4). One would expect this limitation to reduce Citibank's risk by preventing it from selling its units "on the margin," that is, financing a portion of the purchase price with a loan secured by the shares. Margin selling was, of course, one of the lending abuses widely thought to have contributed to the unhappy events of 1929.

Third, unlike the investment fund shares in [*ICI I*], Citibank's units are non-transferable. . . . This restriction naturally impedes formation of an independent "market" in the units, and thereby allows Citibank more control over the aggregate size of the Trust. For example, if Citibank decides that its Trust is becoming too risky, or is perceived by the public as too risky, the bank can gradually scale down the program by the simple expedient of diminishing its marketing efforts and retiring any units presented for redemption. By contrast, if the units were transferable, owners wishing to trade their units for cash could do so by selling them to a third party rather than redeeming them at Citibank.

Finally, the ten percent income tax penalty imposed by ERISA for early redemption would seem to reduce the risk that Citibank will be called upon to redeem large numbers of units at any one time. This was another concern animating the Court in [*ICI I*]. The Court feared that, if confronted with such circumstances, "a bank might find itself under pressure to rescue the fund through measures inconsistent with sound banking.". . .

For all these reasons, we believe the Trust at issue here is distinguishable in significant respects from the managing-agent fund in [*ICI I*].

B

The Institute's second argument under [*ICI I*] is less plausible. The Institute cites that case for the proposition that the term "security" necessarily includes any "undivided and redeemable interest in the assets of a common trust fund." . . . [*ICI I*] will be searched in vain for any statement of this sweeping proposition. The Institute has arrived at this understanding by splicing together unrelated phrases from different parts of the [*ICI I*] opinion. This effort, albeit creative, is unavailing.

The Institute's argument, moreover, proves far too much. If the term "security" were indeed interpreted as broadly as the Institute suggests, then any ownership interest in a bank's common trust fund would constitute a security, and all commingling of trust funds by national banks would be effectively prohibited. We are at a loss to determine how a national bank could pool the assets of various trusts without creating some kind of certificates or other instruments setting forth the ownership interests of each of the participating trusts in the common trust assets. But such commingling, as we have seen, has historically been permitted and is clearly sanctioned by [*ICI I*]. . . .

III

Over the years, the Supreme Court has frequently stated that courts should defer to reasonable interpretations of statutes by the administrative agencies charged with their administration. . . .

Notably, the [*ICI I*] majority reaffirmed this principle. The Court's declination to defer to the Comptroller signaled no departure from this settled principle, but was occasioned instead by the Comptroller's complete silence as to the meaning of the governing statute. That is to say, there was in [*ICI I*] no explicit interpretation of the Glass-Steagall Act to which the Court could appropriately defer. . . .

. . . Here, in the administrative proceedings, the Comptroller provided a thorough, explicit interpretation of Glass-Steagall as it applies to this case. We are therefore duty bound, as [*ICI I*] teaches us, to give "great weight" to that interpretation. . . .

A

. . . [T]he [first] inquiry before us is whether the framers of Glass-Steagall intended to prohibit national banks from engaging in activities like that at issue here. Although both the Comptroller and Citibank vigorously urge us to consider ERISA's legislative history, that history is not relevant here for two reasons: first, in enacting ERISA, Congress in no wise purported to amend Glass-Steagall; second, nothing in ERISA or its legislative history suggests that Congress as a whole had any view, let alone a clear intent, on the applicability of Glass-Steagall to the operation of IRA collective trusts by national banks. . . .

1

. . . Inasmuch as the term "security" is not defined in the Act, we must "'start with the assumption that the legislative purpose is expressed by the ordinary meaning of the words used.'" *Securities Industry Ass'n v. Board of Governors*, 468 U.S. 137, ----, 104 S.Ct. 2979, 2986 (1984) (*Becker*) (quoting *Richards v. United States*, 369 U.S. 1, 9 (1962)). The Institute urges us simply to borrow the definition used in the federal securities laws. Under this view, any instrument registered as a security with the SEC would be considered a security for Glass-Steagall purposes.

The Institute relies heavily upon the Supreme Court decision in *Becker, supra*, for this argument. There, the issue was whether the term "security" includes commercial paper, which all parties to that litigation agreed is simply an unsecured promissory note. The Court held that commercial paper falls within the plain meaning of the term "note," and since the term "security" explicitly includes all notes, commercial paper is therefore a "security." . . . The Institute interprets *Becker* as holding that SEC registration itself constitutes "considerable evidence" that the instruments at issue are "securities" within the meaning of Glass-Steagall. . . .

Fairly read, however, *Becker* does not stand for this proposition. To be sure, the Court found that Congress' explicit inclusion of commercial paper as a "security" for purposes of the securities laws was an indication that Congress considered commercial paper to be a "security" for Glass-Steagall purposes as well. But the Court did not indicate that SEC registration by itself bears on the classification of a financial instrument as a "security" within the meaning of the banking statute.[7] Nor did *Becker*, as the Institute suggests, hold as

---

7. As the *Becker* dissent pointed out, the definition of the term for securities law purposes should be different from that used in a Glass-Steagall analysis because (1) "the purposes of the banking and securities laws are quite different," and (2) some instruments, for example, bankers' acceptances, are securities for purposes of the securities laws but "plainly do not constitute securities under the Glass-Steagall Act." 104 S.Ct. at 2999-3000 (O'Connor, J., dissenting). Nothing in the majority

a general matter that the term "security" itself has an ascertainable ordinary meaning in all contexts.[8] As already noted, the majority opinion in *Becker* relied primarily on the plain meaning of the term "note," not on the plain meaning of the term "security."[9]

As we see it, the statutory language is of limited help in divining Congressional intent in this case. The term "security" clearly encompasses instruments like stocks, bonds, notes, and mutual fund shares, which have traditionally been underwritten and marketed by members of the securities industry. As [*ICI I*] teaches, moreover, the term may include other financial interests that are functionally equivalent to these traditional kinds of securities. But, as we have also seen, the term cannot be interpreted to include all financial interests in assets or in a business venture, lest traditional common trust funds be rendered invalid. Although interests in Citibank's Trust share some of the features of traditional mutual fund shares -- for example, they permit diversification of risk and can be widely marketed -- they are, as we have seen, quite different from traditional mutual fund shares in several important respects. Obviously, interests in IRA trust funds did not exist in 1933 when Congress passed Glass-Steagall; the term Congress employed to identify the financial instruments it had in mind, moreover, is not sufficiently precise as to clearly encompass such interests.

2

Unfortunately, the legislative history is also of limited usefulness in illuminating Congress' intent. The Institute has uncovered only two relevant aspects of Glass-Steagall's legislative history, both of which have been discussed in prior Supreme Court decisions.

The first is that, as noted in [*ICI I*], the Glass-Steagall Act was in part the product of Congressional investigations into the activities of bank security affiliates, including their operation of investment trusts. . . . The Court reasoned that, "[s]ince Congress generally intended to divorce commercial banking from the kinds of activities in which bank security affiliates engaged, there is reason to believe that Congress explicitly intended to prohibit a national bank from operating an investment trust." *Id.* (footnote omitted).

[*ICI I*] did not, however, hold that the term "security" includes interests in any kind of fund consisting of pooled assets. It held, rather, that Congress intended to prohibit the kind of investment fund at issue there, which the Court believed was nearly identical to the investment funds operated by bank security affiliates in the pre-Depression era. IRA trusts, with all the limitations imposed by ERISA, did not exist, of course, in 1933. More to the point, as we have already discussed, Citibank's Trust is much less like a traditional mutual fund than was the investment fund at issue in [*ICI I*]. We are not persuaded that Congress' concern with the activities of banks' securities affiliates would extend to the kinds of ERISA-related activities at issue here.

The second potentially relevant aspect of legislative history is the fact, noted in *Becker*, that in drafting the Glass-Steagall Act Congress rejected a regulatory approach in favor of a set of "flat prohibitions," thereby evincing a desire to "separat[e] as completely as possible commercial from investment banking." . . . The Institute seems to interpret this as an indication that national banks should be prohibited from intruding onto what the securities industry considers its own turf. The Institute reasons that since many mutual funds have

---

opinion contradicts these specific points; the Court, rather, divided over the clarity of Congressional intent as to commercial paper's falling within the statutory terms "note" or "security." *See infra* n. 9.

8. Indeed, the *Becker* dissent explicitly stated that it does not. *Id.* at 2994.

9. Although the *Becker* opinion stated that the "ordinary meaning of the terms 'security' and 'note' as used by the 1933 Congress encompasses commercial paper," 104 S.Ct. at 2987, the Court did not articulate any broad definition of the term "security." Rather, it relied upon the plain meaning of the statutory definition which, as we have seen, clearly encompasses "notes," and hence commercial paper. *See* 104 S.Ct. at 2986-88.

been offering their own IRA trusts, . . . prohibiting Citibank's entry into the field would be in keeping with Congress' apparent desire to keep commercial banking separated as much as possible from investment banking.

The problem with this argument, however, is that it is not entirely clear who is intruding onto whose turf. It is true, as we have already observed, that Citibank's fund represents something of a departure from the traditional role of a commercial bank in that it allows small account holders to benefit from the diversification that was previously available only to relatively large customers of the bank's trust department. But operation of an IRA trust by a mutual fund, which necessarily puts the mutual fund in the position of serving as trustee of its customers' money, also would seem to represent something of an intrusion into the traditional domain of commercial banking. Citibank's Trust, then, like the IRA trust offered by mutual funds, falls somewhere between the traditional activities of commercial and investment banking.

B

. . . [A]s long as Congress has no clearly discernible intent on the point in question, it is the agency which is vested with primary responsibility for interpreting the statute. . . .

This broad principle has two corollaries. First, an agency interpretation may be reasonable even if it is one which the court would not have rendered had it been interpreting the statute in the first instance. . . . But the reviewing court may not simply substitute its own reading for that of the agency.

Second, an agency interpretation may not be branded as unreasonable simply because the court doubts the wisdom of the policy choice embodied in the agency's interpretation. . . . It is true, as the Institute points out, that a court must reject administrative interpretations that "frustrate the policy Congress sought to implement." . . . But ... a court can lawfully overturn an agency interpretation on this ground only if the Congressional policy is sufficiently clear, and the agency's interpretation so inconsistent with that policy, that the court can conclude that Congress' clear intent has been violated. Absent a violation of clear Congressional intent, it is for the agency, not the reviewing court, "to make such policy choices–resolving the competing interests which Congress itself either inadvertently did not resolve, or intentionally left to be resolved." . . .

C

With these principles in mind, we turn in the final phase of our analysis to an examination of the Institute's attack on the reasonableness of the Comptroller's interpretation. We observe first that the Comptroller, in determining whether ownership interests in Citibank's Trust constitute "securities" for Glass-Steagall purposes, employed the analytical framework fashioned by the Supreme Court in [*ICI I*]. The Comptroller first analyzed the transaction to determine whether Citibank would be receiving funds for a true fiduciary purpose; he then examined the transaction in light of each of the Congressional concerns identified in [*ICI I*]. . . . On the basis of that analysis, the Comptroller concluded that the units of participation are not "securities" and that the Act's prohibitions are therefore inapplicable. Since the Comptroller's analytical framework was the very one employed in [*ICI I*], we find that framework, needless to say, eminently reasonable.

The Institute, however, challenges the Comptroller's application of this framework. It first contends that the Comptroller erroneously found Citibank's Trust to have a bona fide fiduciary purpose. Second, according to the Institute, the Comptroller erroneously concluded either that the Trust did not raise the Congressional concerns identified in [*ICI I*] or, alternatively, that he could adequately address those concerns through the exercise of his regulatory powers.

1

The Institute advances two distinct reasons why it believes Citibank's Trust represents an investment rather than a fiduciary service. First, according to the Institute, the Comptroller granted an exemption to his own "fiduciary regulations," allowing Citibank to vest management of the fund in an independent supervisory committee. According to those regulations, a common trust fund must be under the "exclusive management" of the sponsoring bank. *See* 12 CFR s 9.18(12) (1984).

To be sure, the existence of a non-bank supervisory committee renders the Trust at issue here more akin to a traditional mutual fund.[11] Yet the regulations at issue merely prescribe standards or requirements for collective investments by national banks; they do not purport to define when a particular service will be deemed "fiduciary" in nature. More fundamentally, vesting control over the Trust in an independent supervisory committee does not dilute the legal effects of the bank's fiduciary obligations to its IRA customers. . . . This feature, we are satisfied, does not take the Citibank Fund out of the domain of "fiduciary" services and propel it into the mutual fund business.

Second, the Institute points out that Citibank is not merely commingling assets of pre-existing trusts, but is actively marketing its Trust to the public as an investment. According to the Institute's interpretation of a 1940 Federal Reserve Board regulation cited in [*ICI I*], this aggressive marketing campaign disqualifies the Trust as a bona fide fiduciary service. *See* 26 Fed. Reserve Bull. 393, 394 (1940).

We agree with the Institute that, in light of [*ICI I*]'s concern with "promotional pressures," . . . Citibank's marketing strategy might provide one indication that its Trust falls on the wrong side of the line between investments and bona fide fiduciary services. We cannot agree, however, that this consideration is dispositive in this case. The passages of the 1940 regulation in which the Institute relies were not themselves quoted or cited in [*ICI I*], and we have discerned no indication that the Supreme Court intended to elevate this regulation to the status of binding precedent. Quite apart from the regulation itself, the Comptroller carefully considered each of the promotional pressures that Citibank's marketing strategy might arguably create, and concluded that in this case those pressures are not sufficiently strong to warrant concern. . . . This evaluation seems to us eminently reasonable.

Finally, we do not believe that Citibank's characterization of the Trust as an "investment opportunity" should bear on whether the Trust constitutes a bona fide fiduciary service. The two terms are not mutually exclusive. Any fiduciary service is also an investment opportunity if by that one means an opportunity to earn a return on one's money; very few customers would likely be satisfied with the services of a bank's trust department if the bank did no more than safekeep their funds. We agree with the Comptroller that the proper inquiry is whether the bank is offering a genuine fiduciary service in addition to an opportunity to earn a return. Banks can appropriately provide more than vaults and safety deposit boxes and still remain faithful to the demands of federal law. . . .

2

The Institute contests the Comptroller's treatment of the potential economic hazards of Citibank's Trust on a number of grounds. It first advances an argument which it successfully asserted in the California litigation, . . . namely that the Comptroller's findings exhibit a disagreement with Congress and the Court in [*ICI I*] about the potential dangers of entry by commercial banks into the investment banking business. . . . In our view, this is

---

11. We note again that Citibank's Trust is directed by a non-bank supervisory committee only because, according to Citibank, it is required to do so by virtue of the SEC's interpretation of federal securities laws. Citibank also contends, as already pointed out, that it complied with the SEC's requirement only to avoid a protracted legal battle with that agency, a not uncommon tactic in the arena of securities regulation.

not a fair reading of the Comptroller's opinion. Rather, that opinion reflects a belief that this particular arrangement does not raise the concerns identified in [*ICI I*], and that the arrangement is therefore not the kind of activity Congress intended to proscribe through Glass-Steagall's prohibitions.

The Institute next argues that the Comptroller simply dismissed all of the potential dangers identified in [*ICI I*] based upon a belief that his general regulatory power under 12 U.S.C. § 92a and other statutes would be sufficient to curb any abuses that might arise. ... Upon analysis, this is likewise a mischaracterization of the Comptroller's ruling. The Comptroller nowhere even mentions 12 U.S.C. § 92a, and does not rely upon any general regulatory power in minimizing the importance of the dangers identified in [*ICI I*]. Rather, the Comptroller points to specific, existing regulations that would obviate some of those dangers. For example, one regulation relied upon by the Comptroller, 12 C.F.R. § 9.18(B)(8)(I) (1982), prevents Citibank from lending money to the Trust itself or to any individual participant. Fairly read, the Comptroller's decision does not run afoul of *Becker*'s teaching that a bank regulator may not rely upon its general regulatory powers in order to circumvent the "broad prohibition" of the Glass-Steagall Act. . . .

The Institute's remaining arguments reflect, at bottom, disagreement with the Comptroller's judgment about the potential economic effects of Citibank's Trust on Citibank and on the banking industry.[12] We concede the apparent plausibility of the Institute's view. On the other hand, the Comptroller has advanced plausible reasons for his view that such concerns are misplaced in this particular instance given the entire set of circumstances before him. Any assessment of the dangers foreseen by the Institute would involve judgments about complex economic phenomena related to the banking industry. Congress has charged the Comptroller with making those judgments in the first instance. We may overturn the Comptroller's judgments only if they are unreasonable. We are unable to conclude that they are.

Notes and Comments 5.109. Is *Conover* reading *ICI I* fairly? In light of its extremely deferential approach to the Comptroller's interpretive authority, what is left of *ICI I*?

5.110. Is *Conover* using the "subtle hazards" discussion of *ICI I* as a test of the validity of the challenged collective investment activity? Is that consistent with *ICI I*? With *Securities Industry Association, infra*?

5.111. On the issue of the meaning of the term "security," is *Conover* reading the Supreme Court's decision in *Securities Industry Association v. Board of Governors* ("SIA I"), *infra*, fairly? If, as would seem obvious from a balanced reading of the latter case, "security" has the same technical meaning in the federal securities laws and the Glass-Steagall Act, what happens to the analysis in *Conover*? Notice also that *Conover* repeatedly relies on the

---

12. The Institute advances an additional argument unrelated to these economic effects, namely that the Comptroller's action "subverts the legislative process." . . . The Institute observes that members of the banking industry have unsuccessfully sought legislation that would explicitly permit the kind of service at issue here. Thus, according to the Institute, "the Comptroller simply and unlawfully has attempted, by administrative fiat, to 'enact' the very legislation Congress repeatedly has refused to enact." . . . In our view, however, these facts do not establish that the Comptroller has in any way subverted the legislative process. Elementary principles of law teach that current legislative activity is irrelevant in determining . . . whether Congress in 1933 expressed any clear intent with respect to the issue before us or, if it did not, whether the Comptroller's interpretation of Congress' language is reasonable. Congress, moreover, remains free to address the issue if it finds itself in disagreement with the actions of the Comptroller or the courts.

dissent in *SIA I* (which it refers to as "*Becker*"). The majority opinion does not appear to square with *Conover*, does it?

Securities Industry Association v. Board of Governors

468 U.S. 137 (1984)

Justice BLACKMUN delivered the opinion of the Court.

This case involved a challenge to the efforts of a state commercial bank to enter the business of selling third-party commercial paper. The Board of Governors of the Federal Reserve System (Board) concluded that such activity by state member banks is not prohibited by the . . . Glass-Steagall Act because commercial paper is neither a "security" nor a "note" within the meaning of that Act and therefore falls outside the Act's proscriptions. The District Court disagreed with the Board, but the Court of Appeals deferred to the Board's interpretation and reversed the judgment of the District Court. Because commercial paper falls within the plain language of the Act, and because the inclusion of commercial paper within the terms of the Act is fully consistent with the Act's purposes, we conclude that commercial papers is a "security" under the Glass-Steagall Act, and we reverse the judgment of the Court of Appeals.

I.

During 1978 Bankers Trust Company (Bankers Trust), a New York-chartered member bank of the Federal Reserve System, began serving as agent for several of its corporate customers in placing their commercial paper[1] in the commercial-paper market. Petitioners, the Securities Industry Association (SIA), a national securities-industry trade association, and A.G. Becker Inc. (Becker), a dealer in commercial paper, informally expressed concern to the Board about Bankers Trust's commercial-paper activities. SIA and Becker subsequently petitioned the Board for, among other things, a ruling that Bankers Trust's activities are unlawful under §§ 16 and 21 of the Act, 12 U.S.C. §§ 24 Seventh and 278(a)(1). . . .

. . . The Board acknowledged that Congress enacted the Act to prevent commercial banks from engaging in certain investment-banking activities, but explained that Congress did not intend the Act's prohibitions to cover every instrument that could be characterized as a "note" or "security." The Board expressed concern that such a broad interpretation might preclude commercial banks from maintaining many of their traditional activities. Accordingly, the Board took the position that "if a particular kind of financial instrument evidences a transaction that is more functionally similar to a traditional commercial banking operation than to an investment transaction, then fidelity to the purposes of the Act would dictate that the instrument should not be viewed as a security." . . . Applying this "functional analysis" to commercial paper, the Board concluded that such paper more closely resembles a commercial bank loan than an investment transaction and that it is not a "security" for purposes of the Glass-Steagall Act. Because of this determination, the Board did not consider whether Bankers Trust's involvement with commercial paper constitutes "underwriting," within the meaning of the Act.

II.

The Board is the agency responsible for federal regulation of the national banking system, and its interpretation of a federal banking statute is entitled to substantial deference.

1. "Commercial paper" refers generally to unsecured, short-term promissory notes issued by commercial entities. Such a note is payable to the bearer on a stated maturity date. Maturities vary considerably, but typically are less than nine months. . . .

As the Court states elsewhere today, "the Board has primary responsibility for implementing the Glass-Steagall Act, and we accord substantial deference to the Board's interpretation of that Act whenever its interpretation provides a reasonable construction of the statutory language and is consistent with legislative intent." *Securities Industry Assn. v. Board of Governors of Federal Reserve System* [468 U.S. 207 (1984) ("*SIA II*")]. We also have made clear, however, that deference is not to be a device that emasculates the significance of judicial review. Judicial deference to an agency's interpretation of a statute "only sets the 'framework for judicial analysis; it does not displace it.'" ... A reviewing court "must reject administrative constructions of [a] statute, whether reached by adjudication or by rulemaking, that are inconsistent with the statutory mandate or that frustrate the policy that Congress sought to implement." ...

... At the administrative level, the Board took the position that commercial paper was not a "security" within the meaning of the Act, and that, therefore, it did "not appear necessary to examine the dangers that the Act was intended to eliminate."[2] ... Before this Court, however, the Board appears to have changed somewhat the nature of its argument. The Board's counsel now insists that the activities of Bankers Trust "involv[e] none of the 'hazards' that this Court identified" as the concerns at which the Act is aimed. ... We previously have stated that post hoc rationalizations by counsel for agency action are entitled to little deference: "It is the administrative official and not appellate counsel who possesses the expertise that can enlighten and rationalize the search for the meaning and intent of Congress." [*ICI I*, 401 U.S. at 628.] ... As a result, the Board's presentation here of the policies behind the Act as they apply to this case is of less significance than it would be if it had occurred at the administrative level. Because of this apparent shift, moreover, the contours of the Board's present position are somewhat unclear; much of the Board's argument now addresses the particular characteristics of the commercial paper in this case, apparently leaving open the possibility that commercial paper with different characteristics would qualify as a "security" and be subject to the Glass-Steagall Act's proscriptions. ... To the extent that the Board has changed its position from that adopted at the administrative level, its interpretation is entitled to less weight.

III.

A.

In [*ICI I*] this Court explored at some length the congressional concerns that produced the Glass-Steagall Act. ...

The Act's design reflects the congressional perception that certain investment-banking activities are fundamentally incompatible with commercial banking. After hearing much testimony concerning the appropriate form of a legislative response to the problems, Congress rejected the view of those who preferred legislation that simply would regulate the underwriting activities of commercial banks. Congress chose instead a broad structural approach that would "surround the banking business with sound rules which recognize the imperfection of human nature that our bankers may not be led into temptation, the evil effect of which is sometimes not so subtle as not to be easily recognized by the most honorable man." ... Through flat prohibitions, the Act sought to "separat[e] as completely as possible commercial from investment banking." ... Such an approach was not without costs in terms of efficiency and competition, but the Act reflects the view that the subtle risks created by mixing the two activities justified a strong prophylaxis. ...

---

2. Despite this conclusion, the Board responded to concerns that activity similar to that of Bankers Trust might give rise to the problems that the Act sought to avoid, and issued a policy statement with "guidelines" imposing conditions as to when state member banks may sell third-party commercial paper. ...

B.

Sections 16 and 21 of the Act are the principal provisions that demarcate the line separating commercial and investment banking. . . . Bankers Trust may not underwrite commercial paper if commercial paper is a "security" within the meaning of the Act.

Section 21 also separates investment and commercial banks, but does so from the perspective of investment banks. Congress designed § in specific investment-banking activities from entering the commercial-banking business. The section prohibits any person "engaged in the business of issuing, underwriting, selling, or distributing . . . stocks, bonds, debentures, notes, or other securities" from receiving deposits. Bankers Trust receives deposits, and it therefore is clear that § 21's prohibitions apply to it.

Because § 16 and § 21 seek to draw the same line, the parties agree that the underwriting prohibitions described in the two sections are coextensive, and we shall assume that to be the case. In any event, because both § 16 and § 21 apply to Bankers Trust, its activities in this case are unlawful if prohibited by either section. The language of § 21 is perhaps the more helpful, however, because that section describes in greater detail the particular activities of investment banking that Congress found inconsistent with the activity of commercial banks.

It is common ground that the terms "stocks," "bonds," and "debentures" do not encompass commercial paper. The dispute in this case focuses instead on petitioners' claims that commercial paper constitutes a "note" within the meaning of § 21, and, if not, that it is nevertheless encompassed within the inclusive term "other securities." Thus, petitioners claim that the plain language of the Act makes untenable the Board's conclusion that commercial paper is not a "security" within the meaning of the Act. Petitioners contend further that the role played by Bankers Trust in placing the commercial paper of third parties is precisely what the Glass-Steagall Act sought to prohibit.

C.

Neither the term "notes" nor the term "other securities" is defined by the statute. "This silence compels us to 'start with the assumption that the legislative purpose is expressed by the ordinary meaning of the words used.'" . . . Respondents do not dispute that commercial paper consists of unsecured promissory notes and falls within the general meaning of the term "notes." . . . Respondents assert, however, that the context in which the term is used suggests that Congress intended a narrower definition. Because the term appears in a phrase that includes "stocks, bonds, [and] debentures," the Board insists that the Act's prohibitions apply only to "notes [and] other securities" that resemble the enumerated financial instruments. The Board's position seems to be that because "stocks, bonds, [and] debentures" normally are considered "investments," the Act is meant to prohibit the underwriting of only those notes that "shar[e] the characteristic of an investment that is the common feature of each of the other enumerated instruments." . . . Applying that criterion to commercial paper, the Board maintains that commercial paper more closely resembles a commercial loan and that it is therefore not an investment of the kind that qualifies as a "security" under the Act.

For a variety of reasons, we find unpersuasive the notion that Congress used the terms "notes . . . or other securities" in the narrow sense that respondents suggest. First, the Court noted in [*ICI I*] that "there is nothing in the phrasing of either § 16 or § 21 that suggests a narrow reading of the word 'securities.' To the contrary, the breadth of the term is implicit in the fact that the antecedent statutory language encompasses not only equity securities but also securities representing debt." . . .

There is, moreover, considerable evidence to indicate that the ordinary meaning of the terms "security" and "note" as used by the 1933 Congress encompasses commercial paper. Congress enacted the Glass-Steagall Act as one of several pieces of legislation collectively designed to restore public confidence in financial markets. . . . In each of these other statutes, the definition of the term "security" includes commercial paper, and each statute contains explicit exceptions where Congress meant for the provisions of an Act not to apply to commercial paper.[7] These explicit exceptions demonstrate congressional cognizance of commercial paper and Congress' understanding that, unless modified, the use of the term "security" encompasses it.

The Securities Act of 1933, for example, defines the term "security" to include "any note." 15 U.S.C. § 77b(1). During the hearings on that Act, Senator Glass-expressed dissatisfaction with that definition because it plainly did encompass commercial paper. With the support of the Board, he sought to amend the definition of the term to exclude commercial paper, but Congress chose instead to exempt commercial paper from only the registration requirements of the statute, *see* 15 U.S.C. § 77c(a)(3),[9] while preserving application of the statute's antifraud provisions to all commercial-paper "securities." §§ 77*l*, 77q(c). Congress passed the Glass-Steagall Act two weeks later, and throughout consideration of that Act by the same Committees of the same Congress, the eponymous Senator Glass-displayed no similar concern over the ordinary meaning of the broad phrase "notes . . . or other securities" in § 21.

The difficulty with the Board's attempt to narrow the ordinary meaning of the statutory language is evidenced by the Board's unsuccessful efforts to articulate a meaningful distinction between notes that the Act purportedly covers and those it does not. In other statutes in which commercial paper is exempted from securities regulation, Congress either has identified a particular feature, such as maturity period, that defines the exempted class of "notes," or it has authorized a federal agency to define it through regulations. . . . The Glass-Steagall Act does neither, and the efforts by the Board and the Court of Appeals to provide a workable definition that excludes commercial paper have been fraught with uncertainty and inconsistency. The Court of Appeals concluded that the Act applies only to notes that are issued "to raise money available for an extended period of time as part of the corporation's capital structure." . . . It is not clear that such a distinction finds support even with reference to the statutory language from which it purportedly derives. There is no requirement, for example, that stocks, bonds, and debentures be used only to meet the capital requirements of a corporation, and, even if there were, the legislative history provides little evidence to suggest that such a distinction was one that Congress found significant.

The Board, in contrast, seems to have concluded that a note is covered by the Act only if the note is properly viewed as an "investment." The Board contends that this approach requires it to consider a "cluster" of the note's features, . . . such as its maturity period, its risk features, and its prospective purchasers. Stocks, bonds, and debentures display a wide range of each of these characteristics, however, and the Act's underwriting prohibition does not demonstrate any sensitivity to the characteristics of a particular issue; the Act simply prohibits commercial banks from underwriting them all. Without some clearer directive from Congress that it intended the statutory terms to involve the nebulous inquiry described by the Board, we cannot endorse the Board's departure from the literal meaning of the Act. . . .

---

7. *See* 15 U.S.C. § 77c(a)(3) (exempting certain "note[s]" with maturities of less than nine months from the definition of "security" for certain provisions of the Securities Act of 1933); 15 U.S.C. § 79i(c)(3) (exempting "commercial paper and other securities" specified by the Securities and Exchange Commission from the Public Utility Holding Company Act's restriction prohibiting acquisition by a holding company of "securities").

9. It is significant that the exemption for commercial paper is described using the term "note," plainly indicating that Congress understood the ordinary meaning of that term to encompass commercial paper.

In this respect, we find ourselves in substantial agreement with petitioners' suggestion that the Board's interpretation effectively converts a portion of the Act's broad prohibition into a system of administrative regulation. By concluding that commercial paper is not covered by the Act, the Board in effect has obtained authority to regulate the marketing of commercial paper under its general supervisory power over member banks. The Board acknowledges that "the sale of third party commercial paper by a commercial bank could involve, at least in some circumstances, practices that are not consistent with principles of safe banking." . . . In response to these concerns, the Board issued guidelines for state member banks explaining the circumstances in which they properly may place the commercial paper of third parties. . . .

Although the guidelines may be a sufficient regulatory response to the potential problems, Congress rejected a regulatory approach when it drafted the statute, and it has adhered to that rejection ever since. In 1935, for example, Congress refused to amend the Act to permit "national banks under regulations by the Comptroller of the Currency . . . to underwrite and sell bonds, debentures, and notes." . . . As recently as 1980, Congress extended to the Comptroller of the Currency authority to issue such rules as were needed to "carry out the responsibilities of the office," but expressly continued to withhold from the Comptroller the authority to issue regulations concerning "securities activities of National Banks under the Act commonly known as the 'Glass-Steagall Act.'" Depository Institutions Deregulation and Monetary Control Act of 1980, § 708, 94 Stat. 188, 12 U.S.C. § 93a. When Congress has concluded that a particular form of notes should not be covered by the Act's prohibitions, it has amended the statute accordingly. *See* Banking Act of 1935, § 303(a), 49 Stat. 707, 12 U.S.C. § 378(a)(1) (exempting mortgage notes from the coverage of § 21). In the face of Congress' refusal to give the Board any rulemaking authority over the activities prohibited by the Act, we find it difficult to imagine that Congress intended the Board to engage in the subtle and ad hoc "functional analysis" described by the Board.

D.

By focusing entirely on the nature of the financial instrument and ignoring the role of the bank in the transaction, moreover, the Board's "functional analysis" misapprehends Congress' concerns with commercial bank involvement in marketing securities. Both the Board and the Court of Appeals emphasized that Congress designed the Act to prevent future bank losses arising out of investments in speculative, long-term investments. This description of the Act's underlying concerns is perhaps accurate but somewhat incomplete. "[I]n enacting the Glass-Steagall Act, Congress contemplated other hazards in addition to the danger of banks using bank assets in imprudent securities investments." [*ICI I*], 450 U.S., at 66. The concern about commercial-bank underwriting activities derived from the perception that the role of a bank as a promoter of securities was fundamentally incompatible with its role as a disinterested lender and adviser. . . .

At the administrative level, the Board expressly chose not to consider whether these concerns are present when a commercial bank has a pecuniary interest in promoting commercial paper. . . . Although the Board indicates before this Court that such activities do not implicate the concerns of the Act, we are unpersuaded by this belated assertion. In adopting the Act, for example, Congress concluded that a bank's "salesman's interest" in an offering "might impair its ability to function as an impartial source of credit." . . . In the commercial-paper market, where the distribution of an issue depends heavily on the creditworthiness of the issuer, a bank presumably can enhance the marketability of an issue by extending backup credit to the issuer. Similarly, as a commercial bank finds itself in direct competition with other commercial-paper dealers, it may feel pressure to purchase unsold notes in order to demonstrate the reliability of its distribution system, even if the paper does not meet the bank's normal credit standards. Recognizing these pressures, this

Court stated in [*ICI I*]: "When a bank puts itself in competition with [securities dealers], the bank must make an accommodation to the kind of ground rules that Congress firmly concluded could not be prudently mixed with the business of commercial banking." . . .

The 1933 Congress also was concerned that banks might use their relationships with depositors to facilitate the distribution of securities in which the bank has an interest, and that the bank's depositors might lose confidence in the bank if the issuer should default on its obligations. . . . This concern would appear fully applicable to commercial-paper sales, because banks presumably will use their depositor lists as a prime source of customers for such sales. To the extent that a bank sells commercial paper to large bank depositors, the result of a loss of confidence in the bank would be especially severe.

By giving banks a pecuniary incentive in the marketing of a particular security, commercial-bank dealing in commercial paper also seems to produce precisely the conflict of interest that Congress feared would impair a commercial bank's ability to act as a source of disinterested financial advice. . . .

This conflict of interest becomes especially acute if a bank decides to distribute commercial paper on behalf of an issuer who intends to use the proceeds of the offering to retire a debt that the issuer owes the bank.

In addressing these concerns before this Court, the Board focuses primarily on the extremely low rate of default on prime-quality commercial paper. We do not doubt that the risk of default with commercial paper is relatively low–lower perhaps than many bank loans. For several reasons, however, we find reliance on this characteristic misplaced. First, it is not clear that the Board's exemption of commercial paper from the proscriptions of the Act is limited to commercial paper that is "prime." The statutory language admits of no distinction in this respect, and the logic of the Board's opinion must exempt all commercial paper from the prohibition on underwriting by commercial banks. Second, as described above, it appears that a bank can make a particular issue "prime" simply by extending backup credit to the issuer. Such a practice would seem to fit squarely within Congress' concern that banks would use their credit facilities to aid in the distribution of securities.

More importantly, however, there is little evidence to suggest that Congress intended the Act's prohibitions on underwriting to depend on the safety of particular securities. Stocks, bonds, and debentures exhibit the full range of risk; some are less risky that many of the loans made by a bank. And while the risk features of a security presumably affect whether it qualifies as an "investment security" that a commercial bank may purchase for its own account,[10] the Act's underwriting prohibition displays no appreciation for the features of a particular issue; the Act just prohibits commercial banks from underwriting any of them, with an exception for certain enumerated governmental obligations that Congress specifically has chosen to favor. *See* 12 U.S.C. § 24 Seventh. The Act's prophylactic prohibition on underwriting reflects Congress' conclusion that the mere existence of a securities operation, "'no matter how carefully and conservatively run, is inconsistent with the best interests'" of the bank as a whole. . . .

In this regard, the Board's focus on the fact that commercial banks traditionally have acquired commercial paper for their own accounts is beside the point. It is clearly true, as the Board asserts before this Court, that Congress designed the Glass-Steagall Act to cause banks to invest more of their funds in short-term obligations like commercial paper instead

---

10. It is clear that Congress' concern with commercial-bank purchases of securities was different from its concern about commercial-bank involvement in securities underwriting activities. In 1938 Congress refused to report out of committee legislation that would have allowed national banks to "underwrite or participate in the underwriting of new issues of such securities as [they] may otherwise lawfully purchase for its own account." H.R. 9441, § 1(b), 75th Cong., 3d Sess. (1938).

of in longer term and more speculative securities. By so doing, Congress hoped to enhance the liquidity of funds and protect bank solvency. But the authority to discount commercial paper is very different from the authority to underwrite it. The former places banks in their traditional role as a prudent lender. The latter places a commercial bank in the role of an investment banker, which is precisely what Congress sought to prohibit in the Act.[11]

The Board also seeks comfort in the fact that commercial paper is sold largely to "sophisticated" investors. Once again, however, the Act leaves little room for such an ad hoc analysis. In its prohibition on commercial-bank underwriting, the Act admits of no exception according to the particular investment expertise of the customer. The Act's prohibition on underwriting is a flat prohibition that applies to sales to both the knowledgeable and the naive. Congress expressed concern the commercial-bank involvement in securities operations threatened the ability of commercial banks to act as "financial confidant and mentor" for both "the poor widow" and "the great corporation." . . . Even if purchaser-sophistication is relevant under the Act, moreover, it is not clear that commercial paper is sold only in large denominations. . . .

Finally, it is certainly not without some significance that Bankers Trust's commercial-paper placement activities appear to be the first of that kind since the passage of the Act. The history of commercial-bank involvement in commercial paper prior to the Act is not well documented; evidently, commercial banks occasionally dealt in commercial paper, but their involvement was overwhelmingly in the role of discounter rather than dealer. ... Since enactment of the Act, however, there is no evidence of commercial-bank participation in the commercial-paper market as a dealer. The Board has not offered any explanation as to why commercial banks in the past have not ventured to test the limits of the Act's prohibitions on underwriting activities. Although such behavior is far from conclusive, it does support the

---

11. The Board makes an additional argument based on § 16's restrictions on securities purchases by commercial banks. Section 16 prohibits commercial banks from "dealing in securities" on their own account altogether, and permits them to "purchase for [their] own account" only "investment securities." The Board argues that commercial paper does not constitute an "investment security" within the meaning of that term in § 16, and hence that § 16 would not permit commercial banks to purchase commercial paper for their own account if commercial paper were classified as a "security." Because commercial banks traditionally *have* acquired commercial paper for their own account, and because that practice universally has been assumed not to run afoul of the Glass-Steagall Act, the Board argues that the practice cannot be reconciled with § 16 unless commercial paper is not deemed a "security." . . .

Even if the Board is correct that commercial paper is not an "investment security" under § 16, something that we need not decide, we find the Board's argument unpersuasive because it rests on the faulty premise that the process of acquiring commercial paper necessarily constitutes "the business of dealing" in securities. The underlying source of authority for national banks to conduct business is the first sentence of § 16, which originated as § 8 of the National Bank Act of 1864, ch. 106, 13 Stat. 101. That provision grants national banks the authority to exercise "all such incidental powers as shall be necessary to carry on the business of banking" and enumerates five constituent powers that constitute "the business of banking." One of those powers is "discounting and negotiating promissory notes." 12 U.S.C. § 24 Seventh. The Board appears to concede that the authority for national banks to acquire commercial paper is grounded in this authorization to discount promissory notes. . . . The subsequent prohibition on engaging in "[t]he business of dealing in securities" does not affect this authority; while the Glass-Steagall Act does not define the term "business of dealing" in securities, the term clearly does not include the activity of "discounting" promissory notes because that activity is defined to be a part of the "business of banking." In short, the fact that commercial banks properly are free to acquire commercial paper for their own account implies not that commercial paper is not a "security," but simply that the process of extending credit by "discounting" commercial paper is not part of the "business of dealing" in securities. . . .

view that when Congress sought to "separat[e] as completely as possible commercial from investment banking," . . . the banks regulated by the Act universally recognized that underwriting[12] commercial paper falls on the investment-banking side of the line. . . .

Justice O'CONNOR, with whom Justice BRENNAN and Justice STEVENS join, dissenting.

The question in this case is whether the Board of Governors of the Federal Reserve System (Board) adopted an erroneous interpretation of law when it concluded that commercial paper is not a "security" under, and hence is not subject to the proscriptions of, §§ 16 and 21 of the Glass-Steagall Act. . . . The area of banking law in which this question arises is as specialized and technical as the financial world it governs, and the relevant statutes are far from clear or easy to interpret. The question is accordingly one on which this Court must give substantial deference to the Board's construction. Because of the Board's expertise and experience in this complicated area of law, and because of its extensive responsibility for administering the federal banking laws, the Board's interpretation of the Glass-Steagall Act must be sustained unless it is unreasonable. . . .

Analysis of this case requires simply an examination of the usual sources of statutory interpretation–primarily the statutory language–to determine whether the Board's reading is a reasonable one, even if it is not the only reasonably one. The Court of Appeals departed from this approach when it limited its approval of the Board's position to certain kinds of sales of certain kinds of commercial paper that it thought did not present certain dangers addressed by the Glass-Steagall Act, . . . and the Solicitor General, though not actually adopting a similarly limited position on behalf of the Board, has devoted a significant portion of his brief in this Court to elaborating the safety analysis underlying the Court of Appeals' limitation. . . . It is the Board's position, however, and not that of the Court of Appeals or of the Solicitor General, to which deference is due. It is the Board that has the experience, expertise, and responsibility that require us to give it "considerable deference it its interpretation of the statute." . . .

The Board's own careful and thorough opinion, I believe, amply demonstrates the reasonableness–perhaps the inevitability–of its construction of the critical statutory language. Moreover, the Court's construction of the statute and petitioners' objections to the Board's position are unpersuasive. In these circumstances, the Court should defer to the Board and uphold its ruling. Because the Court does not do so, I respectfully dissent. . . .

[T]he Board's view that §§ 16 and 21, as amended in 1935, were intended to apply only to investment instruments akin to stocks, bonds, and debentures . . . also comports with what the legislative history reveals to have been of concern to the Congress enacted Glass-Steagall. During the extensive legislative hearings and debates leading up to the enactment of the Glass-Steagall Act, Congress focused its attention on commercial banks' participation in the markets for long-term and speculative securities, and commercial paper was distinguished from the investment securities that Congress was worried about. . . . Moreover, although commercial banks' purchasing activities were a major subject of congressional concern, and although commercial banks were the dominant buyers of commercial paper at the time, no one in Congress, as far as anything brought to this Court's attention shows, ever adverted to banks' commercial paper activities as contributing to the difficulties at which the

12. Because of its conclusion that the commercial paper in this case was not a "security" under the Act, the Court of Appeals did not consider whether the activity of Bankers Trust constitutes "underwriting" within the meaning of § 16, or "the business of issuing, underwriting, selling, or distributing" within the meaning of § 21. We express no opinion on these matters, leaving them to be decided on remand.

Act was aimed. . . . Thus, the legislative history shows Congress to have been concerned with investment instruments, as the Board contends, and not with their involvement with commercial paper.

In sum, the language of §§ 16 and 21 strongly supports the Board's interpretation. Indeed, petitioners have suggested no other construction that can be accommodated by the language of the statute. Since the legislative history makes it impossible to argue that Congress intended something contrary to the statutory language, the Board's conclusion about legislative intent concerning commercial paper appears to be compelled by statute. In any event, it is certainly "a reasonable construction of the statutory language and is consistent with legislative intent." . . .

II.

Petitioners advance several arguments in an effort to demonstrate the error of the Board's reading of the Glass-Steagall Act, but these arguments are unavailing. It is worth noting at the outset that I have no quarrel with the Court's extensive discussion of the general policies behind the Glass-Steagall Act. . . . None of that discussion, however, speaks to the threshold question whether commercial paper is among the "securities" to which Congress thought those policies would apply when it adopted the Act. For all of the reasons given above, the Board's negative answer to that question is all but mandated by the statutory language and is not contradicted by anything in the legislative history. The Board came to the reasonable conclusion that Congress simply had no intention to apply its policies to commercial paper. . . .

III.

The dangers that Congress sought to eliminate when it enacted the Glass-Steagall Act are easily stated at a level of generality that might make the Board's ruling appear inconsistent with congressional policies. The translation of policy into legislation, however, is always complicated by the necessity of taking into account potentially competing and overlapping laws and policies. The task of this Court, therefore, is to interpret the statutory language that Congress enacted into law. Careful attention to the statutory language is especially important in an area as technical and complex as banking law, where the policies actually enacted into law are likely to be complicated and difficult for a nonspecialist judiciary to discern in their proper perspective.

In this case, the statutory language strongly supports the construction adopted by the Board, and it cannot bear the only construction proposed by petitioners and adopted by the Court. The Board's construction is also wholly consistent with the legislative history. It is singularly inappropriate for this Court, reasoning from the general policies it finds in the statute and with little regard for the statutory language, to reject the construction of the statute adopted by the Board after careful consideration and with full explanation. It is the Board, and not this Court, that has both responsibility for the oversight of much of our Nation's banking system and expertise and experience in applying the arcane body of law that governs it. When the statutory support for the Board's position is as strong as it is in this case, the Court's rejection of the agency's position is unjustified.

Notes and Comments 5.112. In *SIA I*, is "subtle hazards" a test of the validity of a bank's securities activity? Is that the issue in the challenge to the Fed's administrative action? What is the majority's view on this issue? What is Justice O'Connor's view?

5.113. Is Justice O'Connor correct in treating the disputed issue in the case as one involving the validity of the Fed's interpretation, or is the issue whether the Fed, as a matter of administrative procedure, properly developed its reasoning for allowing the challenged activity? Consider what difference this makes in *SIA I* on remand.

Securities Industry Association v. Board of Governors

807 F.2d 1052 (D.C.Cir. 1986), *cert. denied*, 483 U.S. 1005 (1987)

BORK, Circuit Judge.

This is an appeal from an order of the district court invalidating under the Glass-Steagall Act a decision of appellant Board of Governors of the Federal Reserve System that permitted appellant Bankers Trust Company, a state-chartered commercial bank and a member of the Federal Reserve System, to place commercial paper issued by third parties. The Act prohibits commercial banks from engaging in investment banking. The Board of Governors determined that Bankers Trust's activities did not cross into investment banking, but the district court concluded that they did. After considering the language and history of the Act and the applicable case law, we reverse the judgment of the district court and reinstate the Board's decision.

I.

. . . Upon remand, the Board of Governors found that Bankers Trust's placement of commercial paper constituted the "selling" of a security without recourse and solely upon the order and for the account of customers, a practice permitted by section 16 of the Act, 12 U.S.C. § 24 (Seventh) (1982). . . . The district court reviewed the Board's decision on the petition of the SIA and granted SIA summary judgment, holding that Bankers Trust's activities involved the "underwriting" and "distributing" prohibited by section 21(a)(1) of the Act, 12 U.S.C. § 378(a)(1) (1982). . . .

II.

In reviewing the Board's decision, we owe the agency's determination "the greatest deference." . . . In [*SIA I*], the Board had provided an opinion explaining its view of whether commercial paper constituted "securities" for purposes of the Glass-Steagall Act but failed to analyze the legislative purposes behind the Act. Because of this omission, the Court gave "little deference" to the Board's position that its interpretation ran afoul of none of the purposes of the Act. . . . The Court at the same time observed generally that because "[t]he Board is the agency responsible for federal regulation of the national banking system, . . . its interpretation of a federal banking statute is entitled to substantial deference."

In the present case, . . . the Board has comprehensively addressed the language, history, and purposes of the Act that bear on whether commercial banks should be able to place commercial paper. We consequently owe the Board's determination "substantial deference" or "significant weight." . . . Since Congress has not clearly addressed the question of whether activities such as those conducted by Bankers Trust fall within the prohibitions of the Act, we must examine whether the agency, in filling the statutory gap left by Congress, has acted reasonably. . . .

III.

The question in this case involves the interplay of sections 16 and 21 of the Glass-Steagall Act. These provisions implement what the Supreme Court has described as the Act's "general purpose of separating as completely as possible commercial from investment banking." Section 16, 12 U.S.C. § 24 (Seventh) (1982), draws the line between permissible and impermissible activities for commercial banks, while section 21(a)(1), 12 U.S.C. § 378(a)(1) (1982), draws this line for investment banks. The Supreme Court has found that "§ 16 and § 21 seek to draw the same line." [*SIA I*], 468 U.S. at 149. The issue before us is whether the Board has reasonably determined that the activities of Bankers Trust do not cross that line between commercial and investment banking. . . .

. . . Because no one disputes that Bankers Trust constitutes a commercial bank within the meaning of these sections, we must determine, first, if the Board has reasonably concluded that the commercial paper placement activities of Bankers Trust fall within the permissive language of section 16. To determine this, we must look at the question of what the statute means by "underwrite," for underwriting not only triggers section 21's prohibitions but defeats section 16's permissive effect. We must, in contrast, address the meaning of section 21's terms "issuing, . . . selling, or distributing" only if section 16 is inapplicable. In other words, section 21 cannot be read to prohibit what section 16 permits. . . . Therefore, if we find that the Board acted reasonably in concluding that section 16 permits Bankers Trust's activities, that is the end of our analysis.

While this proposition seems obvious, SIA nonetheless argues that we must examine both the prohibitions of section 21 and the permissive phrase of section 16 to determine if the Board has erred. SIA seeks to restrict the scope of section 16 by relying on language (added to section 21 in 1935) that expressly refers to section 16 as an exception to section 21's restrictions, stating that "the provisions of this paragraph shall not prohibit national banks or State banks . . . from dealing in, underwriting, purchasing, and selling investment securities, or issuing securities, to the extent permitted to national banking associations by the provisions of [section 16 of the Act.]" 12 U.S.C. § 378(a)(1) (1982). SIA directs our attention to a passage in the House Report accompanying the 1935 amendments stating that this language was added to "make it clear that [section 21] does not prohibit any financial institution or private banker from engaging in the securities business to the limited extent permitted to national banks under [section 16]." H.R. Rep. No. 742, 74th Cong., 1st Sess. 16 (1935). The Report goes on to say parenthetically that this provision permits commercial banks to deal in or underwrite only certain enumerated government obligations not at issue in this case. *Id.* SIA has suggested that the overlap between sections 16 and 21 is restricted to this narrow context, and that we must affirm the district court if we find, as SIA argues, that the language of section 21 covers the transaction permitted by the Board in this case.

SIA's argument is wholly unpersuasive for several reasons. First, the House Report said that the cross-reference to section 16 was being added to "make it clear" that commercial banks could underwrite and deal in certain government obligations, and the title of the relevant passage in that Report was "Section 21 of the Banking Act Clarified." H.R.Rep. No. 742, *supra*, at 16. That this amendment sought merely to *clarify* the relationship between section 16 and section 21 necessarily implies that before the amendment the two provisions by their own force had to be read together. Congress amended section 21 simply to leave no doubt of the need to read the two sections harmoniously in a matter of particular congressional concern. Moreover, apart from this apparent purpose, the sweeping and comprehensive language employed explicitly provides that any restriction on the activities of a commercial bank that may arise because of the prohibitions of section 21 is relieved insofar as the activity is permitted by section 16. This unambiguous language controls our reading of the statute.

We reject SIA's position for a second and independently decisive reason. If section 21 prohibited what section 16 explicitly permits, section 21 would render section 16's permissive language entirely nugatory -- an absurd result. Section 16 allows a commercial bank to sell securities "without recourse, solely upon the order, and for the account of, customers, and in no case for its own account." Section 21, in sharp contrast, flatly prohibits a commercial bank from "selling" securities. If we permitted the restrictions of section 21 to control, the "selling" of securities would be entirely proscribed, despite the explicit permission contained in the statute. If, on the other hand, we read section 16's permissive provisions as an exception to section 21, the restriction on selling in section 21 would retain its force for all activities not permitted by section 16. We must therefore read section 21's operative terms (issuing, underwriting, selling, distributing) to exclude any activity section

16 allows. (We discuss below the prohibition of underwriting by a commercial bank contained in section 16 itself.)

Finally, because the Supreme Court has stated that sections 16 and 21 "seek to draw the same line" between commercial and investment banking, . . . those activities of commercial banks that section 16 places on the acceptable commercial banking side of the line cannot be placed by section 21 on the impermissible investment banking side of the line. Thus, if the Board reasonably found that section 16 permits Bankers Trust's activities, our inquiry ends there.

IV.

We believe that the Board's determination is reasonable. The Board found that Bankers Trust's activities fell within section 16's requirement that "[t]he business of dealing in securities and stock by the [bank] shall be limited to purchasing and selling securities and stock without recourse, solely upon the order, and for the account of, customers, and in no case for its own account, and the [bank] shall not underwrite any issue of securities of stock." 12 U.S.C. § 24 (Seventh) (1982). While the district court did not dispute the Board's finding that Bankers Trust's activities "fit neatly within the literal language of section 16's permissive phrase," and relied instead on an analysis of the legislative purposes of the Act to reverse the Board's holding, . . . SIA vigorously disputes on several grounds the conclusion that the bank's activities come within the permissive language of that section. We take up these arguments in turn.

A.

SIA argues that section 16's permissive language does not apply to the activities of Bankers Trust because the section 16 exception applies only to "the business of dealing in securities and stock," while SIA asserts that the term "dealing" is typically understood to encompass the purchasing and selling of securities only in the secondary trading market. In support of this argument, SIA cites the definition of "dealer" contained in the Securities Act of 1933. In fact, the Securities Act undercuts SIA's position by defining a "dealer" as "any person who engages . . . as agent, broker, or principal, in the business of offering, buying, selling, or otherwise dealing or trading in securities issued by another person," without any exclusion of the primary offering market. 15 U.S.C. § 77b(12) (1982). Moreover, the so-called "dealer's exemption" to registration of securities under the Securities Act makes it clear that one may be a dealer under that statute in both secondary and primary markets. This exemption from registration, contained in section 4(3) of the Securities Act, 15 U.S.C. § 77d(3) (1982), applies to "transactions by a dealer (including an underwriter no longer acting as an underwriter in respect of the security involved in [the] transaction." This language necessarily implies that one may be a dealer -- "in the business of offering, buying, selling, or otherwise dealing or trading in securities"–and still act as an underwriter–one who unquestionably may participate in the primary or new issue market. Congress' ordinary understanding of "the business of dealing" clearly was not restricted to secondary trading; SIA's argument on this point is insupportable.

B.

SIA also contends that the Board erred in concluding that the activities of Bankers Trust are "upon the order . . . of . . . customers," claiming that Congress imposed this restriction to make it clear that banks could perform the transactions permitted by section 16 only as an accommodation to the existing customers of the bank. In support of this proposition, SIA relies almost exclusively on the Supreme Court's recent opinion in [*Securities Industry Ass'n v. Board of Governors*, 468 U.S. 207 (1984) (*SIA II*)], in which SIA unsuccessfully challenged a bank holding company's retail brokerage operations under section 20 of the Glass-Steagall Act. *See* 12 U.S.C. § 377 (1982) (prohibiting bank affiliation with any firm "engaged principally in the issue, flotation, underwriting, public sale, or distribution" of securities). In approving the retail brokerage operation, run by a non-bank affiliate of the bank holding company as an accommodation to the affiliate's customers, the Court relied in part on the fact that section 16 "allows banks to engage directly in the kind of [retail] brokerage activities at issue here, to accommodate [their] customers." . . . SIA suggests that this statement amounted to an interpretation of section 16 requiring banks to provide securities services under the relevant language only as an accommodation to the bank's preexisting customers. This argument misses the mark. While the Court did state that section 16 permitted retail brokerage as an accommodation to customers of the bank's other services, it specifically left open the question whether such securities brokerage, if more broadly available, would still satisfy that provision. . . . Thus, the Court did not, as we must, decide whether section 16 allows the placement of securities only as an accommodation to existing customers of other bank services.

While the meaning of "upon the order . . . of . . . customers" is decidedly ambiguous, we defer . . . to the Board's reasonable conclusion that section 16 should not be given such a narrow reading. The Board below correctly observed that "[n]othing in the literal terms of section 16 requires a preexisting customer relationship." . . . According to SIA, however, the legislative history makes it clear that Congress had such a relationship in mind when it included the language "upon the order, and for the account of, customers." In support of its thesis, SIA directs us to a remark in the committee reports that the purpose of section 16 was to permit "[n]ational banks . . . to purchase and sell investment securities for their customers to the same extent as heretofore." . . . Because the Supreme Court in [*SIA II*] stated that "[b]anks long have arranged the purchase and sale of securities as an accommodation to their customers," and that section 16, read in conjunction with the above-cited legislative history, "expressly endorsed this traditional banking service," . . . SIA contends that section 16 was intended *only* to permit such services as had been traditionally performed as an accommodation to preexisting customers of the bank.

SIA again reads too much into [*SIA II*]. Congress, in enacting section 16, may well have intended to endorse traditional banking services as they existed before 1933. This does not mean, however, that section 16 permits the transactions covered by its language *only* to the extent that identical transactions occurred prior to the enactment of Glass-Steagall. Since nothing in the language or legislative history of section 16 even remotely suggests that the Act meant to freeze particular functions in place as of 1933, we decline to read that meaning into the Act.

Moreover, the history of commercial banking shows that, prior to the Glass-Steagall Act, banks offered the securities brokerage services at stake in [*SIA II*] both to existing customers and to persons with no preexisting relationship to the banks. . . . Thus, we may not construe "upon the order . . . of . . . customers" to require a preexisting relationship between the bank and the user of the services permitted under section 16, since Congress intended that language to ratify banking practices that served at least some persons without any relationship to the bank except as "customers" of the services permitted by section 16.

Despite the conclusion that section 16 requires no preexisting customer relationship as a matter of law, we still must inquire whether the Board reasonably concluded that Bankers Trust places commercial paper solely on the order of the issuer. The Board stated that "[a]ccording to Bankers Trust's submission, the issuer, not the bank, decides whether to raise funds by issuing commercial paper and, if so, in what amount." . . . The Board concluded that this meant that "the bank places commercial paper solely on the request and on the order of its customer, the commercial paper issuer." . . . SIA counters that the bank solicits the business of issuers and gives financial advice about the terms and timing of the potential issue of commercial paper. Neither point upsets the Board's conclusion.

SIA offers no support for its claim that Bankers Trust recruits or solicits the business of issuers beyond the assertion that the bank "touts" its placement services in advertisements.[1] . . .

Nor are we convinced that the rendering of financial advice itself removes Bankers Trust's placements from the category transactions made solely upon the order of customers. Nothing in section 16 suggests that the bank may not advise issuers who have decided that they may or do want to raise money by issuing commercial paper. If a customer asks the advice of Bankers Trust but makes its own decision about whether and in what amount to issue commercial paper, the transaction is made solely on the order of that customer. Consider, by contrast, a case in which an investment bank decides that the market is favorable to the refinancing of a bond issue or the conversion of debt to equity and initiates discussions with its customer leading up to the eventual transaction. In such a situation, the initiative of the investment banker itself creates the very demand for the particular transaction. This is a far cry from the type of passive advice that Bankers Trust renders after the issuer has decided that it needs to raise capital and must only decide the best way to do it. Indeed, the legislative history provides support for just this distinction, evincing a concern about bankers who found it "necessary . . . to seek for customers to become makers of issues of securities when the needs of those customers for long-term money were not very pressing." 75 Cong. Rec. 9911 (1932) (remarks of Sen. Bulkley). We cannot conclude that the Board acted unreasonably in deciding that the danger identified by Senator Bulkley does not characterize the financial advice rendered by Bankers Trust.

SIA also argues that, because section 16 applies both to "purchasing and selling" of securities, the solicitation of buyers of commercial paper by Bankers Trust means that its activities are not "upon the order . . . of . . . customers." This argument is meritless. Since Bankers Trust acts as sales agent for the issuer, it is clearly engaged in "selling" securities for its customers and necessarily finds and solicits buyers for those securities, buyers who may be customers of other bank services. This does not mean, however, that Bankers Trust is "purchasing" securities for those investors who buy the paper. The buyers decide upon and make their own purchases, while Bankers Trust has an explicit policy against purchasing for

1. SIA directs us to an advertisement in which Bankers Trust claims credit for "initiat[ing]" an issuer's commercial paper placement program to show that the bank's placement activities are not solely upon the order of customers. SIA may not seek by this proffer of facts not before the Board to refute the Board's factual premise that the issuer decides whether and in what amount to raise funds by offering commercial paper. While the case comes to us on a review of a grant of summary judgment in which the district court relied on facts, like the foregoing, that were not before the Board, such reliance was improper. The questions before us is whether, on the facts supplied to the Board by Bankers Trust or by the Board's own assumptions, the Board reasonably determined the applicability of the relevant provisions of the Glass-Steagall Act. To the extent that the parties attempt to introduce new facts not before the Board, they mistake the function and scope of our review. Even if the facts upon which the Board relied are not accurate, this does not affect our review of the Board's decision; any inaccuracy will properly be remedied by the Board's enforcement of the Act on the facts that exist at that point.

Moreover, even if Bankers Trust did "initiate" the particular issuer's commercial paper program, as stated in the advertisement, it is not at all clear that this would defeat the exemption. If the customer decided to inquire about commercial paper and, on a rational assessment of the facts and advice supplied by the bank, decided to place successive issues of paper using Bankers Trust as its agent, the sale of those issues would still be solely upon the order of the issuer, even though Bankers Trust might fairly claim that as advisor and agent, it "initiated" the program. "Touting" is not enough to render the Board's conclusion unreasonable. Although the bank may generally solicit customers for its placement services by making it known that such services are available, either in the so-called "tombstone ads" or in more general advertisements (for example, "What do you get when you combine an investment bank with a commercial bank? Bankers Trust Company.")

any account that it manages, advises, or serves as trustee–the only accounts for which the bank would even have the authority to make such purchases.

Moreover, no sensible construction of the statute could say that otherwise permissible selling activities cannot involve the solicitation of buyers. The seller's very purpose in engaging a selling agent any paying a commission is to acquire that agent's superior ability to place the product with buyers. If placement of the product with buyers did not require any solicitation of buyers, no rational business would pay another firm to do what it could without cost to itself: passively wait for orders. This construction of "upon the order . . . of . . . customers," therefore, would lead to the absurd statutory result of allowing a seller-agent relationship to arise only in circumstances that not only would never actually exist but that also would strip the relationship itself of its purpose. The Board's rejection of such a construction appears eminently reasonable.

C.

The final assault on the Board's conclusion that the activities of Bankers Trust fit within the terms of section 16 suggests that these activities amount to "underwriting" and thus divest Bankers Trust of its exemption. Although the Act and its legislative history are barren of any definition of the term "underwriting," the parties and the district court have spent much effort considering whether the term "underwriting" includes agency, as well as principal, transactions, and whether what is commonly called "best efforts" underwriting, in which the selling group assumes none of the risk of its failure fully to distribute the issue, amounts to statutory underwriting for purposes of the exemption.[3] These efforts were needless, since we find that the Board reasonably concluded that an "underwriting" defeats the section 16 exemption only if it includes a public offering; private placements therefore do not for this purpose constitute statutory "underwriting." The Board's reliance on the distinction between public offerings and private placements is reasonable because the distinction derives support from congressional intent embodied in contemporaneous securities legislation and reasonably related to concerns that the Glass-Steagall Act sought to meet.

1. Contemporaneous Securities Legislation–The Glass-Steagall Act nowhere defines "underwriting," and the legislative history contains nothing to clarify the term. When in [*SIA I*] the Supreme Court reviewed the case we now consider on remand, similar ambiguity surrounded the definition of the terms "security" and "note." The Court in [*SIA I*] made it very plain that the meaning of a term in other legislation passed roughly at the same time as the Glass-Steagall Act with the shared purpose of restoring confidence in the nation's financial markets provided "considerable evidence" of the "ordinary meaning" Congress attached to the same term in the Glass-Steagall Act itself. . . .

Only the Securities Act of 1933 defines the term "underwriter" (although the Securities Exchange Act of 1934 provides useful evidence on the meaning of that term as

---

3. We do not believe that § 16 gives unlimited rein to banks in the performance of agency transactions, as Bankers Trust suggests. We instead read the restriction against underwriting contained in § 16 as an independent restriction on the bank's securities operations that applies even to agency transactions. While some have questioned whether a best efforts underwriting, performed solely on an agency basis, is technically an "underwriting," *see* 1 L. LOSS, SECURITIES REGULATION 172 (2D ED. 1961), this point seems to relate to underwriting in its strict sense of insurance against risk, and not as a term of art in the securities industry. The securities industry and the Securities Act of 1933, 15 U.S.C. § 77b(11) (1982), treat "best efforts" participation in a distribution as "underwriting." Thus, we cannot read § 16's proscription against underwriting as merely addressing the distinction between principal and agent. Such a construction would make little sense, since the main phrase of § 16 makes it abundantly clear that the bank may engage only in agency, not principal, transactions in securities. We need not decide this question, however, since the prohibition against underwriting does not appear to cover the kind of private offering activities at stake here. . . .

used in the Securities Act). While the evidence of the ordinary congressional cognizance of the term "underwrite" or "underwriter" thus comes from only one piece of similar legislation, that legislation, the Securities Act of 1933, is the closest to Glass-Steagall in time and purpose of the various statutes relied on in [*SIA I*]. . . .

SIA contends that the significance of the Securities Act for this case is that it provides an express exemption from registration for "transactions by an issuer not involving any public offering." 15 U.S.C. § 77d(2) (1982). SIA asserts that this exemption demonstrates Congress' ability knowingly to provide an exemption from statutory requirements for private offerings; Congress' failure so to provide in section 16 of the Glass-Steagall Act means that the Board acted unreasonably when by interpreting the term "underwrite" it effectively read such a private offering into the act. This point would have considerable force, except that the history of the Securities Act's exemption betrays SIA's argument and, in fact, establishes the converse–that Congress did understand the concept of underwriting to connote involvement in a public offering of securities.

The Securities Act in section 2(11) defines an "underwriter" as "any person who has purchased from an issuer with a view to, or offers or sells for an issuer in connection with, the distribution of any security, or participates or has a direct or indirect participation in any such undertaking, or participates or has a direct participation in the direct or indirect underwriting of any such undertaking." 15 U.S.C. § 77b(11) (1982). An "underwriter" thus cannot exist unless a "distribution" exists.

As originally introduced in the House bill that was to become the Securities Act of 1933, the exemption relied on by SIA applied to "transactions by an issuer not with or through an underwriter." *See* H.R. 5480, 73d Cong., 1st Sess. § 4(1) (1933). The House Committee added to this language the phrase "and not involving any public offering." H.R.Rep. No. 85, 73d Cong., 1st Sess. 1 (1933). While the deliberate inclusion of both "not with or through an underwriter" and "not involving a public offering" would ordinarily support the conclusion that Congress viewed the coverage of the two phrases as being different, other legislative history shows that, in fact, both phrases had the same coverage. In interpreting the statute contemporaneously with its passage, the Federal Trade Commission, the agency originally charged with administering the securities laws, observed that a statutory "distribution" necessarily involved a "public offering," thus making it clear that one could not be an "underwriter" in the absence of a public offering. *See* H.R.Conf.Rep. No. 1838, 73d Cong., 2d Sess. 41 (1934). Acknowledging the correctness of the Commission's interpretation, the same Congress that had passed the Securities Act of 1933 eliminated as "superfluous" the language "not with or through an underwriter" when it amended the Securities Act in Title II of the Securities Exchange Act of 1934. *Id.*, *see* ch. 404, § 203(a)(1), 48 Stat. 881, 906 (1934); *see also* 1 L. LOSS, SECURITIES REGULATION 551 and n. 307 (2d ed. 1961) (distribution "more or less synonymous with" public offering). While by no means conclusive, this history offers support for the reasonableness of the Board's view that Congress understood "underwriting" (and, for that matter, "distribution") of securities to connote a public offering, and that the private offerings of commercial paper effected by Bankers Trust do not come within the Glass-Steagall Act's meaning of "underwriting." At the least, it refutes SIA's contention that the Securities Act undercuts the Board's conclusion in this regard. . . .

The Board's responsibility in this case was to arrive at a reasonable determination of what should constitute a private offering under the Glass-Steagall Act. The Board found Bankers Trust's activities to constitute a private offering because (1) the bank "places commercial paper by separately contacting large financial and non-financial institutions," (2) the bank "does not place commercial paper with any individuals," (3) "the maximum number of offerees and purchasers of commercial paper place by the bank in any given case is relatively limited," (4) the bank "makes no general solicitation or advertisement to the public" with respect to the placement of particular paper (though it does advertise its activities in business publications to publicize its availability as an agent to issuers), and (5) "the commercial paper placed with the bank's assistance is issued in very large average minimum denominations, which are not a likely investment of the general public." ... Such considerations properly determine what distinguishes a private from a public offering of securities; we shall shortly see that they also have a strong relationship to one of the principal concerns that animated the Glass-Steagall Act.

2. Legislative Purposes–As the Supreme Court has amply documented, the legislative history of the Glass-Steagall Act shows that, besides "the obvious risk that a bank could lose money by imprudent investment of its funds in speculative securities," Congress sought to address "'the more subtle hazards that arise when a commercial bank goes beyond the business of acting as fiduciary or managing agent and enters in investment banking business.'" ... The hazards identified by the Court included danger to the impartiality of the bank as a dispenser of financial advice. ...

Congress recognized that these pressures largely resulted from the heavy fixed costs incurred by commercial banks in running investment banking operations. In the period immediately preceding the financial collapse that precipitated the enactment of Glass-Steagall, the distribution of an issue of securities took place through an elaborate syndication involving various tiers of purchase, banking, and selling groups managed by an originating banker who handled the negotiations with the issuer. *See* L. LOSS, SECURITIES REGULATION 164-66 (2d ed. 1961). The precise details of the distribution process, as it then existed, are not important for our purposes. What is important is that "a large number of the leading originators of securities, particularly the security affiliates of commercial banks," developed "large selling organizations" in this period. ... Indeed, the "bank affiliates were particularly active in constructing substantial retail organizations" to distribute the securities to which they had committed themselves as originators or members of a purchase group.

Congress was well aware of these developments. The heavy overhead incurred by banks to carry these large retail operations caused much of the congressional concern about "subtle hazards" that animated the sponsors of the Glass-Steagall Act. ...

The distinction between public and private offerings meshes well with the congressional goal of eliminating the "subtle hazards" of conflicts of interest and abuse of fiduciary relationships in banking. Senator Bulkley's remarks show a concern with the development of a vast selling apparatus necessary to participate in the distribution of "great security issues needed for the development of the country: and mirror the unchallenged evidence in the literature that banks in the early twentieth century were building that type of large selling organization.

In light of the specific congressional focus on the large fixed costs that accompanied retail participation in public distributions, it seems highly plausible that one line Congress might have drawn in adopting the permissive language of section 16 of the Glass-Steagall Act was at the point of public offering, a line which could well explain the prohibition against underwriting. While regular involvement in private offerings of securities undoubtedly produces some fixed costs and some attendant pressures, it seems reasonable to think that Congress might have found these relatively minor expenses acceptable when compared with the much heavier fixed burden of having a far-flung retail network to distribute securities to the public. Although implementation of this distinction through the prohibition of commercial-bank underwriting would not address all the "subtle hazards" with which Congress was concerned (for example, it would do nothing to meet the fear that a bank would sell securities for an issuer to help the issuer repay loans to the bank), the prohibition of underwriting is only one of the limitations that section 16 imposes on banks that desire to deal in securities. We believe that the distinction between public and private offerings as drawn by the Board reasonably interprets the prohibition of underwriting and reasonably relates to the elimination of some of those hazards.

V.

While SIA has not met its burden of refuting the reasonableness of the Board's conclusion that Bankers Trust's activities fit within the literal terms of section 16, SIA mounts a final, sweeping challenge to the reasonableness of the Board's interpretation of the Act. SIA asks the court to analyze the activities approved by the Board to determine whether they pose the "subtle hazards" that the Act seeks to eliminate. The district court relied on the potential for these hazards to conclude that, while the activities of Bankers Trust come within the literal terms of section 16, those terms should be construed narrowly to exclude an otherwise permissible arrangement that frustrates the policies of the Act. In other words, although the language and history of the specific provisions support the reasonableness of the Board's construction of those provisions, the Board might nonetheless be obligated to adopt a different construction if the background policies of the Act as interpreted by the Supreme Court in cases like [*ICI I*] and [*SIA I*] conflict with that construction and render it unreasonable. This admittedly seems at odds with the recent statement by the Supreme Court that

> [a]pplication of "broad purposes" of legislation at the expense of specific provisions ignores the complexity of the problems Congress is called upon to address and the dynamics of legislative action. Congress may be unanimous in its intent to stamp out some vague social or economic evil; however, because its Members may differ sharply on the means for effectuating that intent, the final language of the legislation may reflect hard fought compromises. Invocation of the "plain purpose" of legislation at the expense of the terms of the statute itself takes no account of the processes of compromise and, in the end, prevents the effectuation of congressional intent.

Board of Governors of the Fed. Reserve Sys. v. Dimension Fin. Corp., --- U.S. ---, 106 S.Ct. 681, 689 (1986). But the Supreme Court's Glass-Steagall Act cases uniformly consider "subtle hazards" and examine background purposes of the Act. Until the Court indicates that it no longer employs this analysis to interpret the Glass-Steagall Act, we too must take such considerations into account. We therefore turn to that analysis.

We believe that the district court erred in concluding that the private placement of commercial paper by Bankers Trust creates the kind of "subtle hazards" that would require the Board to construe section 16 narrowly to exclude that activity. Since the Supreme Court has already undertaken a "subtle hazards" analysis with respect to commercial paper, albeit without the benefits of the Board's analysis of that issue, we know precisely the concerns the Court has identified in this area. What we must decide is whether the practices of Bankers Trust at issue here sufficiently differ from those in the last round of this litigation to justify concluding that the hazards identified are no longer present, or whether the Board has presented new considerations that were not before the Court in [*SIA I*] and that meet the concerns expressed by the Court.

Initially, it bears noting that the most obvious hazard reached by the Act–the investment of banks funds in speculative securities–is not at issue in this case. Bankers Trust does not purchase the commercial paper of its customers; it does not inventory the paper overnight; and it makes no loans to provide financing to an issuer when an offering of paper falls short of its goal. Nothing in Bankers Trust's services puts its own resources at risk.

This takes us directly to the "subtle hazards" analysis, which catalogues the various conflicts of interest and dangers that may result from a commercial bank's dealing in "particular" securities. The first set of potential conflicts involves the bank in its role as a lender, raising the dual specter of the bank's making loans to the issuer (to ensure the success of its issue) or to the purchasers of commercial paper placed by the bank. . . . The Board's analysis adequately answers those concerns.

To avoid any danger of making unsound loans to an issuer, Bankers Trust has, since the Supreme Court decided [*SIA I*] adopted a policy of providing no back- up credit or guarantees to facilitate the acceptance of commercial paper, any line of credit now granted to an issuer must have "substantially different timing, terms, conditions and maturities from the commercial paper being place." . . . SIA does not dispute the salutary nature of this change, but argues that the Board's reliance on such representations amounts to "regulation" in a statute that Congress meant to operate through "flat prohibitions." This argument is without merit. The Glass-Steagall Act does impose a system of flat "prohibitions" and "prophylactic" measures, . . . but this cannot obviate the need to examine particular factual situations to determine on which side of the prohibitory line they fall. Although the Act may seek to prevent even "potential" conflicts, . . . this does not foreclose the Board from deciding that the realities of a situation make even the potential for conflict substantially unlikely. Bankers Trust has made representations about the conduct of its loan department that seem to meet the congressional concerns identified by the Supreme Court; it is perfectly appropriate for the Board to credit the bank's new policies. Moreover, we do not believe that the Board's assumption that Bankers Trust will keep adequate records to substantiate its contentions transforms the Board's decision into an instance of "regulation." If a member of the industry were to file charges with the Board, claiming that Bankers Trust was not adhering to its stated policies, the availability of Bankers Trust's records would facilitate the Board's investigation of that charge. It is in no way an impermissible "regulation" to require Bankers Trust to keep adequate records.

The Board has also advanced an argument not considered by the Court in [*SIA I*] to explain why the arrangement adopted by Bankers Trust will not lead to the lending of money to "shore up" customers of the bank's commercial paper service. The Board points out that the profit from the placement of commercial is small, amounting to a commission on the order of one-eighth of one percent of the total amount of the issuer's commercial paper, computed on an annualized basis. The rewards from these commissions are so small compared to the cost of the loans the bank would have to write to make an unsound issuer's paper more attractive to the market that writing such loans would not be worth the risk. ... A judgment such as this, that the economic realities of the financial marketplace would preclude banks from making loans to shore up troubled issuers, is precisely the kind of exercise of delegated expertise that deserves our full deference.

The Board has also concluded that there is no appreciable risk of the bank's placing commercial paper to enable a debtor of the bank to repay its loans. The Board's opinion reasons that an issuer unable to repay bank loans will probably be unable to raise money in the commercial paper market in any case; Bankers Trust furthermore has adopted a policy of not providing letters of credit or guarantee arrangements to make such paper more attractive. . . . Moreover, the antifraud provisions of the securities laws would compel the disclosure of the intended use of the proceeds to satisfy a potentially bad debt owed to the bank, providing an obvious disincentive to such a transaction. . . . Finally, empirical evidence indicates that the proceeds of private placements by banks have not been used to pay off any loans involving a material risk of nonpayment. . . . The Board's findings as to these factors, which the [*SIA I*] court apparently did not consider, are reasonable and accordingly receive our deference.

As for the second "subtle hazard," the possibility of the bank's making self-interested loans to finance the purchase of commercial paper it helps issue, the Board provides a persuasive argument, again not before the Supreme Court in [*SIA I*], that no such hazard arises here. Turning again to an analysis of financial markets, the Board asserts that it is wholly impractical for a commercial bank to make such loans because the yields on commercial paper are generally lower than the interest rates the loans would have to bear. . . . In the absence of any evidence that this conclusion is wrong, the Board is again entitled to our deference.

Another category of concerns involves the bank's role as disinterested financial advisor to its customers. First, there is the potential that the bank will give unsound financial advise to the issuer in order to reap the profits from placement of the issuer's commercial paper. . . . The Board found any such risk to be insignificant because the profit from such placements is so low that the bank has no incentive to offer deliberately unsound advice. . . . This rationale, not considered by the Supreme Court, seems consistent with the notion that much of the concern with banks' giving self-interested advice was based on the banks' need to meet the fixed costs of far-flung distribution networks. . . . When the rewards and incentives are lower, the potential benefits from rendering unsound and self-interested advice seem likely to be outweighed by the damage to the bank's reputation and goodwill that would arise from giving bad advice. The Board's conclusion that bad advice will not result from the scheme at issue here is rational.

The role of disinterested financial advisor to depositors presents different concerns. Congress feared that depositors purchasing securities through their bank might lose confidence in their bank if an issuer using the bank's securities services defaulted on their securities. . . . Although Bankers Trust has prevented any conflict of interest concerning any account managed or advised by the bank or its affiliates or for any account in the bank's trust department by adopting a flat rule that it will purchase none of the commercial paper it places for these accounts, . . . Bankers Trust does otherwise place commercial paper with its depositors. The Board argues that because the depositors who purchase commercial paper are large, sophisticated business institutions, they would be unlikely to blame their bank for what really amounts to their own error in judgment, while any harm to the bank that did result would not affect its public reputation. . . . Though this assessment seems entirely realistic, the Supreme Court in [*SIA I*] clearly rejected these arguments, stating that the Act makes no distinctions on the basis of financial expertise and that the loss of confidence of a few large depositors might, in fact, prove "especially severe." . . . While the Board also argues that an empirical study has indicated no harm to the reputation of commercial banks form their private placements of securities, . . . nowhere does the Board's analysis indicate that the study specifically addressed the effect of issuer defaults on depositor/purchaser confidence in commercial banks.

We believe, however, the despite the existence of this one "subtle hazard," we must still affirm the Board. There are several reasons for that conclusion. First, the "subtle hazards" . . . have never alone cause the Supreme Court to hold that Glass-Steagall permits or prohibits any particular banking practice. Rather, analysis of the hazards in those cases simple reinforced the Court's conclusion that, as a matter of statutory interpretation, Glass-Steagall permitted or prohibited the questioned practice. Moreover, the Court has concluded that "subtle hazards" counsel prohibition of a banking practice only when the practice gave rise to each and every one of the hazards. . . . Nor must a hazard be "totally obliterated" to permit a banking practice–avoidance of the hazard "to a large extent" suffices. . . . Finally, our conclusion is reinforced by our view that the "subtle hazards" analysis as a whole is a specific instance of the . . . principle that requires our deference to an agency's reasonable construction of its statute's ambiguities, . . . since an agency's statutory interpretation that impairs one of the statute's purposes but not others may surely nonetheless be reasonable.

(Indeed, the binding force of the Supreme Court's "subtle hazards" analysis in [*SIA I*] is unclear, since, as we have already noted, . . . the Board failed to offer the Court any rationale concerning those hazards to which the Court could defer. . . . We think, in short, that the Board reasonably concluded not only that Bankers Trust's placements of commercial paper meet the literal requirements of section 16, but also that those placements are consistent with the panoply of the Act's purposes.

Notes and Comments 5.114. How does Judge Bork use the "subtle hazards" concept, as an explanatory device or as a "test" of the validity of the activity? Or as either, depending upon what suits his result-oriented analysis?

5.115. Should it have made a difference that Bankers Trust advertised its service as involving the "initiation" of placement of commercial paper? Is Judge Bork's treatment of this issue, in note 1 of the opinion, adequate?

5.116. Is Judge Bork's analysis of the securities regulation concepts correct? Consider the following excerpt in reaching a conclusion on this issue.

2 Michael P. Malloy, Banking Law and Regulation

§ 7.03[G] (2d ed., Aspen Publishers, 2011)

The Fed had determined that the commercial paper placement activities fell within the permissive terms of section 16, and the court found this determination to be reasonable.[1] The Securities Industry Association had argued to the contrary that section 16 permission for dealing in securities applied to the secondary trading market, in transactions undertaken as an accommodation to bank customers, whereas the placement activities were in the distribution market, outside of the contemplation of section 16.[2] The court rejected this argument, reasoning that, under the 1933 Act,

> one may be a dealer . . . and still act as an underwriter–one who may unquestionably participate in the primary or new issue market. Congress' ordinary understanding of "the business of dealing" clearly was not restricted to secondary trading. . . .[3]

Unfortunately, this reasoning comes close to missing the point entirely. A firm may be at one time or another both a dealer and underwriter, but it is clear that, to the extent the firm is active as an underwriter in a given security in distribution, the 1933 Act exemption for *dealers* is simply not available as to that security.[4] Thus, though one firm may be both an underwriter and a dealer, that does not mean that the two functions of underwriting and dealing cannot (or should not) be distinguished.

Having blurred this distinction, the court then goes on to broaden the range of the permissive language in section 16 with respect to "accommodation" transactions.[5] Thus,

---

1. *See* [*Securities Indus. Assn.*, 807 F.2d at 1058].

2. *See id.* at 1058-1059.

3. *Id.* at 1059.

4. *See* 15 U.S.C. § 77d(3), which exempts from the 1933 Act requirements "transactions by a dealer (including an underwriter *no longer acting as an underwriter in respect of the security* involved in [the] transaction)." (Emphasis added.)

5. [*I.e.*, securities transactions undertaken by a bank purely as an "accommodation" to banking customers, but not as an independent business activity of the bank.]

reaching well beyond the Supreme Court's holding in *SIA II* permitting bank discount brokerage services, the court holds that the modest language of section 16 encompasses private placements in the distribution market as well as retail brokerage in the secondary trading market.[6] One may wonder what is left of the prohibitions in section 21 of the act.

On the evidence of this case, the answer would appear to be, very little. The court apparently absorbs all of the prohibitory terms into the single term "underwriting," and then narrowly interprets that term to include no more than underwriting in a public offering.[7] So, for example, the court states:

> we find that the [Fed] reasonably concluded that an "underwriting" defeats the section 16 exemption only if it includes a public offering; private placements therefore do not for this purpose constitute statutory "underwriting."[8]

The court went on to argue that its narrow reading of the term "underwriting" in the Glass-Steagall Act was supported by the legislative history of the contemporaneous 1933 Act.[9] While the court admitted that the aspects of legislative history on which it relied were "by no means conclusive,"[10] it offered sufficient support to lead the court to conclude that the Fed's understanding of the relevant statutory terms was at least reasonable enough to withstand judicial review.[11] The court's understanding of the legislative purposes of the Glass-Steagall Act itself,[12] and its assessment of the possibility that the placement activities in question might trigger the "subtle hazards" that the act sought to prevent,[13] also reinforced its conclusion that the Fed's interpretation was a sufficiently reasonable one to withstand review.[14]

It may be significant, however, that the Fed, in reaching its determination, and the court, in upholding it, were dealing with what had evolved into a very narrow range of activities. The conclusion that the placement activities in question constituted a "private offering," not subject to the Glass-Steagall Act's prohibitions, rested upon a constricted

---

6. *See Securities Indus. Assn.*, 807 F.2d at 1059-1060.

7. To its credit, the court does resist the temptation to resolve the question before it by simply confining the concept of "underwriting" as used in the act to "classic" underwriting, exclusive of "best efforts" underwriting. . . . In this regard, the court states:

> While some have questioned whether a best efforts underwriting . . . is technically an "underwriting," *see* 1 L. Loss, Securities Regulation 172 (2d ed. 1961), this point seems to relate to underwriting in the strict sense of insurance against risk, and not as a term of art in the securities industry. The securities industry and the [1933 Act], 15 U.S.C. § 77b(11) (1982), treat "best efforts" participation in a distribution as "underwriting." Thus we cannot read § 16's proscription against underwriting as merely addressing the distinction between principal and agent. Such a construction would make little sense, since the main phrase of § 16 makes it abundantly clear that the bank may engage only in agency, not principal, transactions in securities.

Securities Indus. Assn., 807 F.2d at 1062 n. 3.

8. *Securities Indus. Assn.*, 807 F.2d at 1062.

9. *See id.* at 1062-1065.

10. *Id.* at 1064.

11. *See id.*

12. *See id.* at 1065-1066.

13. *See id.* at 1066-1070.

14. *See id.* at 1069-1070.

operating plan in which

1. The bank would place commercial paper through separate contacts with institutional investors only;[15]

2. The maximum number of purchasers *and offerees*[16] of the commercial paper in any offering would be relatively limited;[17]

3. No general solicitation or advertisement would be made to the public with respect to any particular placement;[18] and,

4. The paper would be issued in large minimum denominations, unsuited for non-institutional investors.[19]

10. Financial Activities

The Gramm-Leach-Bliley Act (GLBA) permits a national bank to engage, through a subsidiary in "financial activities"[68] authorized by the act,[69] subject to specified conditions. Review 12 U.S.C. § 24a and the following excerpt before considering the questions presented by Notes 5.117-5.120, *infra.*

2 Michael P. Malloy, Banking Law and Regulation

§ 6.08 (2d ed., Aspen Publishers, 2011)

[The following specified conditions apply under § 24a.] First, a national bank may control such a subsidiary (or hold an interest therein) only if the financial subsidiary engages only in activities that are financial in nature or incidental to a financial activity pursuant to subsection (b), and activities that are permitted for national banks to engage in directly (subject to the same terms and conditions that govern the conduct of the activities by a national bank).[1]

Second, the GLBA specifically excludes certain types of activities for such a

---

15. In contrast, the SEC's rules concerning permissible private offerings do not restrict an offering from being made to individuals. *See* 17 C.F.R. § 230.506(b)(2)(i).

16. In contrast, the SEC's rules concerning permissible private offerings are framed in terms of the number of purchasers only, not offerees. *See id.* §§ 230.501(e), 230.506(b)(2)(i).

17. While the SEC's rules similarly limit the number of purchasers (but not offerees) to 35 purchasers (*see id.* § 230.506(b)(2)(i)), institutional investors -- the sort to whom a bank private placement would be made -- are not included in the SEC's limit of 35 and placements may therefore be made with such institutional purchasers without limit. *See, e.g., id.* §§ 230.501(a)(1)-(3), 230.501(e)(1)((iv) ("accredited investors" excluded from calculation of number of purchasers).

18. Similar limitations apply to private offerings under the SEC rules. *See id.* § 230.502(c).

19. *See Securities Indus. Assn.*, 807 F.2d at 1064. No such restriction is imposed under the SEC rules with respect to private offerings, but there is a restriction on resales which would in practice have a similar effect, namely, limiting the distribution of the securities involved to a relatively discrete primary group. *See* 17 C.F.R. § 230.502(d).

68. On the meaning of the term "financial activity" for these purposes, see *id.* §§ 24a(b), 1843(k)(4).

69. 12 U.S.C. § 24a(a)(1).

1. 12 U.S.C. § 24a(a)(2)(A)(i)-(ii).

subsidiary, acting as principal. These include: (*i*) insurance or annuity underwriting;[2] (*ii*) real estate investment and development;[3] (*iii*) insurance company portfolio investments;[4] and, (*iv*) merchant banking.[5] These types of financial activities would only be permitted when undertaken by an affiliate of a financial holding company (FHC).[6] However, after a five-year period from enactment of the GLBA, the Fed and the Secretary of the Treasury are authorized jointly to adopt rules permitting merchant banking by financial subsidiaries, subject to the conditions that the agencies may jointly determine.[7]

Third, the national bank and each depository institution affiliate of the national bank must be well capitalized[8] and well managed.[9] Failure by the national bank or its affiliate to

---

2. *Id.* § 24a(a)(2)(B)(i).

3. *Id.* § 24a(a)(2)(B)(ii).

4. *Id.* § 24a(a)(2)(B)(iii).

5. *Id.* § 24a(a)(2)(B)(iii). [On the meaning of the term "merchant banking," see Note 1.60, *supra*, at n. 21.]

6. *See id.* § 1843(k)(4) (specifying financial activities of FHCs). Insurance companies have shown increasing interest in acquiring or establishing de novo banking and financial services affiliates under the FHC structure. *See* Shefali Anand, *U.S. Insurers Acquire A Foothold in Banking*, Wall St. J. Europe, July 18, 2005, at M1, col. 5 (discussing insurance companies establishing retail banking units). Since 1998, over fifteen insurance companies have established such affiliates-including State Farm Group (State Farm Bank), MetLife (MetLife Bank NA), American International Group (AIG Federal Savings Bank), and Allstate Corp. (Allstate Bank)-with total assets of $28 billion. *Id.* With large bank-based FHCs possibly withdrawing from the insurance sector and selling off insurance assets (see id. at M1, col. 6, M5, col. 5, describing movement of banks away from insurance), insurance companies have an opportunity to diversify into a sector with higher return on equity. Efficiencies are also being achieved by the insurance companies by maintaining their banking affiliates as virtual banks, accessed by customers through the Internet, ATMs, and mail. *Id.* at M5, col. 6.

7. GLBA, § 122 (codified at 12 U.S.C. § 1843 note). *Cf.* 65 Fed. Reg. 16,460 (2000) (codified at 12 C.F.R. §§ 225.1(c)(9)-(15), 225.170-225.175, 1500.1-1500.7; redesignating §§ 225.1(c)(9)-(13) as (c)(11)-(15); reserving §225.1(c)(9)) (permitting FHCs to engage in securities underwriting, merchant banking, and investment banking activities pursuant to joint Fed-Treasury rules).

8. For these purposes, the term "well capitalized" is given the same meaning as in section 38 of the Federal Deposit Insurance Act. *Id.* § 24a(g)(5). *See id.* § 1831o. *Cf. id.* 24a(c)(1)(A) (requiring deduction of aggregate amount of outstanding equity investment, including retained earnings, in all financial subsidiaries from assets and tangible equity of national bank, in determining compliance with applicable capital standards). Assets and liabilities of financial subsidiaries and parent bank are not to be consolidated for purposes of capital requirements. *Id.* § 24a(c)(1)(B). Published financial statements must include separate financial information for the parent bank, in addition to any information prepared in accordance with GAAP. *Id.* § 24a(c)(2).

9. *Id.* § 24a(a)(2)(C). For these purposes, the term "well managed" is defined to mean:

> (A) in the case of a depository institution that has been examined, unless otherwise determined in writing by the appropriate Federal banking agency--
>
> (i) the achievement of a composite rating of 1 or 2 under the Uniform Financial Institutions Rating System (or an equivalent rating under an equivalent rating system) in connection with the most recent examination or subsequent review of the depository institution; and
>
> (ii) at least a rating of 2 for management, if such rating is given; or
>
> (B) in the case of any depository institution that has not been examined, the existence and use of managerial resources that the appropriate Federal banking agency determines are satisfactory.

continue to meet these requirements would result in issuance of a notice by the Comptroller of the Currency to the national bank, describing the conditions that triggered the notice.[10] Within 45 days of receipt of the notice,[11] the national bank must execute an agreement with the Comptroller,[12] and any other involved insured depository institution affiliate must execute an agreement with its appropriate federal banking agency to comply with these requirements.[13] Until the deficiencies are corrected, the Comptroller may impose limits on the conduct or activities of the national bank or any subsidiary thereof, as the Comptroller deems appropriate under the circumstances and consistent with the statutory purposes.[14] Other appropriate federal banking agencies may impose similar limits on the conduct or activities of other involved insured depository institution affiliates or subsidiaries, as such agencies deem appropriate.[15] If the conditions are not corrected within 180 days of receipt of the notice, the Comptroller may require the national bank, under terms, conditions and timing imposed by the Comptroller, to divest control of any financial subsidiary.[16]

Fourth, aggregate consolidated total assets of all financial subsidiaries of the national bank may not exceed the lesser of 45 percent of consolidated total assets of the parent bank,[17] or $50,000,000,000.[18] This dollar amount will be indexed and adjusted in accordance with a mechanism to be established jointly by regulation by the Secretary of the Treasury and the Fed.[19]

Fifth, the national bank must meet certain rating requirements made applicable by the act.[20] In general, if the national bank is one of the fifty largest insured banks,[21] then it must have no fewer than one issue of outstanding eligible debt[22] currently rated within the three highest investment grade rating categories by a nationally recognized statistical rating

---

Id. § 24a(g)(6).

10. *Id.* § 24a(e)(1).

11. The Comptroller may permit an "additional period." *Id.* § 24a(e)(2).

12. Any action under this provision by the Comptroller requires consultation "with all relevant Federal and State regulatory agencies and authorities." *Id.* § 24a(e) (5).

13. *Id.* § 24a(e)(2).

14. *Id.* § 24a(e)(3)(A).

15. *Id.* § 24a(e)(3)(B).

16. *Id.* § 24a(e)(4).

17. *Id.* § 24a(a)(2)(D)(i).

18. *Id.* § 24a(a)(2)(D)(ii).

19. *Id.* § 24a(a)(6).

20. *Id.* § 24a(a)(2)(E).

21. For these purposes, the size of an insured bank is to be determined on the basis of consolidated total assets of the bank as of calendar-year-end. *Id.* § 24a(a) (3)(B).

22. For these purposes, the term "eligible debt" is defined to mean

> unsecured long-term debt that–
>
> (A) is not supported by any form of credit enhancement, including a guarantee or standby letter of credit; and
>
> (B) is not held in whole or in any significant part by any affiliate, officer, director, principal shareholder, or employee of the bank or any other person acting on behalf of or with funds from the bank or an affiliate of the bank.

Id. § 24a(g)(4). . . .

organization.[23] If it is is one of the second fifty largest insured banks, then it must meet either the foregoing criteria "or such other criteria as the Secretary of the Treasury and the [Fed] may jointly establish by regulation and determine to be comparable to and consistent with the purposes of" those criteria.[24] This rating requirement does not apply to financial subsidiaries that engage in financial activities solely as agent and not directly or indirectly as principal.[25] A national bank's failure to maintain the public rating or to meet other applicable criteria would effectively bar the bank, directly or through a subsidiary, from purchasing or acquiring any additional equity capital[26] of any financial subsidiary until the bank again meets the requirements.[27]

Sixth, the national bank must receive approval of the Comptroller of the Currency before its subsidiary may engage in financial activities.[28] The Comptroller has nine months (270 days) to promulgate regulations prescribing implementing procedures.[29]

Seventh, no approval of a financial subsidiary's financial activities is permitted if the parent bank, its holding company, or any insured depository institution affiliate has received in its most recent CRA examination a rating of less than "satisfactory."[30]

The GLBA mandates risk-analysis safeguards.[31] Failure by a national bank or its

---

23. *Id.* § 24a(a)(3)(A)(i).

24. *Id.* § 24a(a)(3)(A)(ii). *See* 65 Fed. Reg. 15,050 (2000) (codified at 12 C.F.R. §§ 208.71(c), 208.77(e)-(g), 1501.2; redesignating § 208.77(e)-(f) as (f)-(g)) (setting forth joint Fed-Treasury alternative criteria); 65 Fed. Reg. 16,460 (2000) (codified at 12 C.F.R. pts. 208, 1501) (interim rule establishing alternative criteria), *superseded by* 66 Fed. Reg. 8748 (2001) (codified at 12 C.F.R. pts. 208, 1501) (promulgating joint Fed-Treasury rules permitting national bank or state member bank in second 50 largest insured banks to own or control a financial subsidiary only if bank meets section 121 eligible debt requirement or alternative criteria of current long-term issuer credit rating from nationally recognized statistical rating organization within organization's three highest investment grade rating categories).

25. *Id.* § 24a(a)(4).

26. For these purposes, the term "equity capital" is defined to include

> in addition to any equity instrument, any debt instrument issued by a financial subsidiary, if the instrument qualifies as capital of the subsidiary under any Federal or State law, regulation, or interpretation applicable to the subsidiary.

Id. § 24a(f)(2).

27. *Id.* § 24a(f)(1).

28. *Id.* § 24a(a)(2)(F).

29. *Id.* § 24a(a)(5). *See* 65 Fed. Reg. 3157 (2000) (proposing OCC rules concerning financial subsidiaries and operating subsidiaries *per* § 24a); 65 Fed. Reg. 12,905 (2000) (codified at 12 C.F.R. §§ 5.24(d)(2)(ii)(G), 5.33(e)(3)(i)-(ii), 5.34, 5.35(e), (f)(1)-(5), (g)(2), (h), (i)(2), 5.36(c)-(f), 5.39; removing § 5.35(f)(3); redesignating § 5.35(f)(4)-(6) as (f)(3)-(5); redesignating § 5.36(c)-(d) as (d), (f)) (implementing GLBA).

30. *Id.* §§ 24a(a)(7), 1843(*l*)(2) (applying CRA requirements of § 1843(*l*) to national bank that controls financial subsidiary).

31. *See id.* § 24a(d), which requires that a national bank establishing or maintaining a financial subsidiary assure that:

> (1) the procedures of the national bank for identifying and managing financial and operational risks within the national bank and the financial subsidiary adequately protect the national bank from such risks;
>
> (2) the national bank has, for the protection of the bank, reasonable policies and

affiliate to continue to meet these safeguards requirements would trigger the notice and correction procedures discussed previously.

The GLBA also establishes substantial "firewalls" intended to limit exposure of a state or national bank to the risk of the activities of the bank's financial subsidiary.[32] In addition, in determining what activities may be considered "financial activities" for purposes of the GLBA provision, the Secretary of the Treasury–*not* the Comptroller–is required to interpret the provision consistent with the purpose of the GLBA.[33]

Notes and Comments 5.117. In the next chapter, we shall examine in detail the kinds of activities that are considered "financial in nature" for purposes of the GLBA.[70] To what extent does this concept overlap with the concept of incidental powers discussed in § 7, *supra*? Why are two such concepts needed?

5.118. Assume that Quarter National Bank (QNB) is well capitalized and well managed. It wants to create a wholly-owned subsidiary that will publicly market to sophisticated investors "participations" in the ownership of high-velocity competitive biological entities (HVCBEs). Is it likely that the Comptroller would approve QNB's proposal? What other information do you need to resolve this issue?

5.119. QNB is also considering the establishment of a subsidiary that would provide venture capital to newly formed high-tech companies that wish to develop Internet products and services. It is assumed that such companies would eventually "go public"–*i.e.*, sell shares in the company to investors in a public offering of newly issued securities–and that the QNB subsidiary would then eventually cash out its investment in the high-tech company. Is it likely that the Comptroller would approve this proposal?

5.120. Despite the characterization of the GLBA as reforming and streamlining financial services regulation, § 24a seems to complicate regulation. Three agencies–the Comptroller, the Treasury Secretary and the Fed–each has a role to play in regulation of financial subsidiaries of national banks. What are these roles, and why are they necessary? If the Comptroller is primarily responsible for supervising the financial services activities of national bank subsidiaries, why is it the the Treasury Secretary who gets to decide what kind of activities are "financial in nature"?

5.121. What exactly is the relationship between powers authorized under 12 U.S.C. § 24(Seventh) and those authorized under § 24a? Does the following case help in answering the question?

---

procedures to preserve the separate corporate identity and limited liability of the national bank and the financial subsidiaries of the national bank; and

(3) the national bank is in compliance with this section.

32. GLBA, §§ 121(b)-(d) (codified at 12 U.S.C. §§ 335, 371c(b)(11), (e)-(f), 1831w, 1971).

33. 12 U.S.C. § 24a(b)(2)(A), (b)(3). *See, e.g.*, 66 Fed. Reg. 257 (2001) (codified at 12 C.F.R. pts. 225, 1501) (promulgating joint Fed-Treasury interim rule finding three general types of activities to be "financial in nature" and creating mechanism by which FHCs, financial subsidiaries of national banks, and others may request that Fed or Treasury Secretary define particular activities within one of three categories); 66 Fed. Reg. 307 (2001) (to be codified at 12 C.F.R. pts. 225, 1501) (proposing joint Fed-Treasury rule determining that real estate brokerage is activity "financial in nature" or incidental to financial activity).

70. *See* Chapter 6, *infra*, comment **6.10** (discussing activities that are "financial in nature").

Watters v. Wachovia Bank, N.A.
550 U.S. 1 (2007)

Justice GINSBURG delivered the opinion of the Court.

[Wachovia, a national bank, and its state-chartered mortgage company subsidiary sued the Michigan Commissioner of Insurance and Financial Services seeking declaratory and injunctive relief from state registration and inspection requirements, based on preemption of the state law by the NBA. The Court's discussion of the substantive issues raised by the case is excerpted at other appropriate points in this supplement. However, in the course of upholding the preemption argument, the Court considered the types of subsidiaries that a national bank might have and the statutory authority that supported them.]

The NBA . . . provides that [federally chartered] banks shall have power "[t]o exercise ... all such incidental powers as shall be necessary to carry on the business of banking." § 24 Seventh. Among incidental powers, national banks may conduct certain activities through "operating subsidiaries," discrete entities authorized to engage solely in activities the bank itself could undertake, and subject to the same terms and conditions as those applicable to the bank. See § 24a(g)(3)(A); 12 CFR § 5.34(e) (2006). . . .

II

B

In 1999, Congress defined and regulated "financial" subsidiaries; simultaneously, Congress distinguished those national bank affiliates from subsidiaries-typed "operating subsidiaries" by OCC-which may engage only in activities national banks may engage in directly, "subject to the same terms and conditions that govern the conduct of such activities by national banks." Gramm-Leach-Bliley Act (GLBA), § 121(a)(2), 113 Stat. 1378 (codified at 12 U.S.C. § 24a(g)(3)(A)).[9] . . .

. . . In *NationsBank of N. C., N. A.*, 513 U.S., at 256-261, . . . we upheld OCC's determination that national banks had "incidental" authority to act as agents in the sale of annuities. It was not material that the function qualifying as within "the business of banking," § 24 Seventh, was to be carried out not by the bank itself, but by an operating subsidiary, *i.e.*, an entity "subject to the same terms and conditions that govern the conduct of [the activity] by national banks [themselves]." § 24a(g)(3)(A); 12 CFR § 5.34(e)(3) (2006).

. . . [U]nlike affiliates that may engage in functions not authorized by the NBA, *e.g.*, financial subsidiaries, an operating subsidiary is tightly tied to its parent by the specification that it may engage only in "the business of banking" as authorized by the Act. § 24a(g)(3)(A); 12 CFR § 5.34(e)(1) (2006). . . . Notably, when Congress amended the NBA confirming that operating subsidiaries may "engag[e] solely in activities that national banks are permitted to engage in directly," 12 U.S.C. § 24a(g)(3)(A), it did so in an Act, the GLBA, providing that other affiliates, authorized to engage in nonbanking financial activities, *e.g.*, securities and insurance, are subject to state regulation in connection with those activities. See, *e.g.*, §§ 1843(k), 1844(c)(4). See also 15 U.S.C. § 6701(b) (any person who sells insurance must obtain a state license to do so).

Justice THOMAS took no part in the consideration or decision of this case.

Justice STEVENS, with whom THE CHIEF JUSTICE and Justice SCALIA join, dissenting. . . .

---

9. OCC subsequently revised its regulations to track the statute. See § 5.34(e)(1), (3); Financial Subsidiaries and Operating Subsidiaries, 65 Fed.Reg. 12905, 12911 (2000).

. . . Congress . . . neither disavowed nor endorsed the Comptroller's position on national bank ownership of operating subsidiaries. Notwithstanding the congressional silence, in 1996 the OCC once again attempted to expand national banks' ownership powers. The agency issued a regulation permitting national bank operating subsidiaries to undertake activities that the bank was *not* allowed to engage in directly. 12 CFR §§ 5.34(d), (f) (1997) (authorizing national banks to "acquire or establish an operating subsidiary to engage in [activities] different from that permissible for the parent national bank," so long as those activities are "part of or incidental to the business of banking, as determined by the Comptroller of the Currency"); see also 61 Fed.Reg. 60342 (1996).

Congress overruled this OCC regulation in 1999 in the Gramm-Leach-Bliley Act (GLBA), 113 Stat. 1338. The GLBA was a seminal piece of banking legislation inasmuch as it repealed the Glass-Steagall Act's ban on affiliations between commercial and investment banks. See § 101, *id.,* at 1341. More relevant to this case, however, the GLBA addressed the powers of national banks to own subsidiary corporations. The Act provided that any national bank subsidiary engaging in activities forbidden to the parent bank would be considered a "financial subsidiary," § 121, *id.,* at 1380, and would be subjected to heightened regulatory obligations, see, *e.g.,* 12 U.S.C. § 371c-1(a)(1). The GLBA's definition of "financial subsidiaries" excluded those subsidiaries that "engag[e] solely in activities that national banks are permitted to engage in directly and are conducted subject to the same terms and conditions that govern the conduct of such activities by national banks." § 24a(g)(3).

By negative implication, then, only subsidiaries engaging in purely national bank activities-which the OCC had termed "operating subsidiaries," but which the GLBA never mentions by name-could avoid being subjected to the restrictions that applied to financial subsidiaries. Compare § 371c(b)(2) (exempting subsidiaries from certain regulatory restrictions) with § 371c(e) (clarifying that financial subsidiaries are not to be treated as "subsidiaries"). Taken together, these provisions worked a rejection of the OCC's position that an *operating* subsidiary could engage in activities that national banks could not engage in directly. See § 24a(g)(3). Apart from this implicit rejection of the OCC's 1996 regulation, however, the GLBA does not even mention operating subsidiaries.

In sum, Congress itself has never authorized national banks to use subsidiaries incorporated under state law to perform traditional banking functions. Nor has it authorized OCC to "license" any state-chartered entity to do so. The fact that it may have acquiesced in the OCC's expansive interpretation of its authority is a plainly insufficient basis for finding preemption.

Notes and Comments 5.122. The Court accepts the OCC argument that Congress distinguished national bank "affiliates" from "operating subsidiaries," citing § 24a(g)(3)(A). Does this distinction make sense? Is it useful in trying to understand the difference between "incidental powers" and "financial activities"? Between "financial subsidiaries" and "operating subsidiaries"?

5.123. The Court also seems to suggest that there are distinct statutory authorities for "financial" and "operating" subsidiaries. Is that correct? What about 12 U.S.C. § 24a(a)(1), (2)(A)(ii)?

Chapter 6

Holding Company Activities

1. Introduction

In addition to restricting entry into the banking industry, the Bank Holding Company Act (BHCA)[1] also regulates the activities of bank holding companies created in accordance with the Act. These holding companies are generally limited to the narrow role of serving as *bank* holding companies. The provisions of 12 U.S.C. § 1843(a) basically prohibit acquisition of non-bank subsidiaries. However, attention should be focused upon § 1843(c), which sets forth a series of exemptions from this general prohibition. Until 1999, the key provision was § 1843(c)(8), which contemplated an exemption for the acquisition of a nonbank subsidiary the activities of which were "so closely related to banking or managing or controlling banks as to be a proper incident thereto. . . ." However, this provision is no longer operative prospectively, and has been displaced by § 1843(k). (*See* Note 6.3, *infra.*)

Notes and Comments 6.1. Consider the text of 12 U.S.C. § 1843. Subsection (a) contains the basic prohibition against nonbanking activities, applicable as of May 9, 1956 (the original effective date),[2] or two years after the date at which any company subsequently becomes a "bank holding company" for purposes of the BHCA.[3] It is also riddled with exceptions and limitations. What are they? Do they frustrate the overall prohibition of the section?

6.2. Most of the express exceptions to the prohibition against nonbanking activities are contained in subsection (c). The most important exception, however, is now contained in 12 U.S.C. § 1843(k), which is discussed at length in the following section of this chapter. How significant are the other exceptions? To what extent do they frustrate the general prohibition of the section?

6.3. *Effect of the GLBA on holding company activities.* The Gramm-Leach-Bliley Act of 1999 (GLBA),[4] has a significant effect on the scope of permissible activities of bank holding companies (BHCs). The act permits BHCs that qualify as financial holding companies (FHCs) to engage in activities, and acquire companies engaged in activities, that are

---

1. 12 U.S.C. §§ 1841 *et seq.*

2. *Id.* § 1843(a)(1).

3. *Id.* § 1843(a)(2).

4. Pub. L. No. 106-102, Nov. 12, 1999, 113 Stat. 1338 (1999) (codified at scattered sections of 12, 15, 16, 18 U.S.C.).

"financial in nature" or that are incidental to such activities.[5] This authority for FHCs broadly parallels the authority for direct financial subsidiaries that the GLBA established for national banks.[6] The GLBA permits a national bank to engage through a financial subsidiary only in activities that are "financial in nature,"[7] subject to the Comptroller's approval, with certain specified exceptions.[8] However, insurance or annuity underwriting, insurance company portfolio investments, real estate investment and development, and merchant banking[9] may only be done in FHC affiliates.[10]

6.4. Could an investment bank become an FHC? In late 2008, two major investment banks, Goldman Sachs and Morgan Stanley, reorganized their operations to convert to bank holding company status, with a full service bank as an operating subsidiary. *See* Stephen Joyce, *Last Two Investment Banks Receive Charters, Foreshadow Regulatory Debate*, BNA BANKING DAILY (Dec. 1, 2008), *available at* http://news.bna.com (discussing approvals of reorganizations and conversions by state and federal authorities). Goldman Sachs converted some of its operations to full service bank approved by New York State, and Morgan Stanley similarly converted some of its operations to a national bank approved by the Comptroller of the Currency.

6.5. The savings & loan holding company provisions of the Home Owners' Loan Act, 12 U.S.C. § 1467a, also contemplate continuing regulation of SLHCs after formation. To what extent do the SLHC provisions parallel those of the BHCA in this regard?

6.6. *Supervision of SLHC Activities*. The OTS has traditionally supervised SLHCs, but the Dodd-Frank Act abolished the OTS and the position of the DOTS,[11] effective October 19, 2011. On July 21, 2011, the Fed began to exercise the functions and authority of the OTS and the DOTS with respect to SLHC activities.[12] In February 2011, the Fed announced its intention to require the use of *BHC* reporting forms for *SLHCs*, beginning with the March 31, 2012, reporting period.[13] In April 2010, the Fed announced that it would apply elements of its consolidated supervisory program currently applicable to BHCs to SLHCs after it assumed supervisory responsibility for SLHCs.[14] It invited comments on this notice by May 23, 2011.[15] The Fed's position is that any company that owns and operates a depository institution – not just a bank – should be held to appropriate standards of capitalization, liquidity, and risk management consistent with the principles of safety and soundness. Hence, to the greatest extent possible, while taking into account any characteristics of SLHCs that

---

5. GLBA, § 103(a), 113 Stat. at 1342 (codified at 12 U.S.C. § 1843(k)).

6. *See* Chapter 5, § 10, *supra* (discussing direct financial subsidiaries under GLBA).

7. Activities are "financial in nature" if they are defined as such in the BHCA, 12 U.S.C. § 1843(k)(4), or the Secretary of the Treasury in consultation with the Fed determines that the activity is financial in nature. *Id.* § 24a(b)(1)(A)-(B).

8. GLBA § 121(a)(2), 113 Stat. at 1373-1378 (codified at 12 U.S.C. § 24a).

9. On the meaning of the term "merchant banking," see Note 1.60, *supra*, at note 21.

10. 12 U.S.C. § 24a(a)(2)(B)(i)-(iii). However, after a five-year period from enactment of the GLBA, the Fed and the Secretary of the Treasury are authorized jointly to adopt rules permitting merchant banking by financial subsidiaries, subject to the conditions that the agencies may jointly determine. GLBA, § 122, 113 Stat. at 1381-1382 (codified at 12 U.S.C. § 1843 note).

11. Dodd-Frank Act § 313 (codified at 12 U.S.C. § 5413).

12. *See id.* § 312(b) (codified at 12 U.S.C. § 5412(b)) (mandating transfer of functions).

13. 76 Fed. Reg. 7091 (2011).

14. 76 Fed. Reg. 22,662 (2011).

15. 76 Fed. Reg. at 22,662.

would distinguish them from BHCs and allowing for specific HOLA requirements, the Fed wants to assess the condition, performance, and activities of SLHCs on a consolidated risk-based basis in a manner that is consistent with its established approach to BHC supervision. The supervisory objectives would be to ensure (i) that the SLHC and its nondepository subsidiaries are effectively supervised, (ii) that the SLHC serves as a source of strength for subsidiary depository institutions, and (iii) that the SLHC does not threaten the soundness of its subsidiary depository institutions.

6.7. *Further effects of the Dodd-Frank Act.* In February 2011, the Fed adopted an amendment to the regulations[16] that, *inter alia*, implemented a two-year period during which "banking entities"[17] must bring their activities and investments into compliance with the prohibitions and restrictions on proprietary trading and relationships with hedge funds and private equity funds[18] imposed by Dodd-Frank Act § 619[19] – the so-called "Volcker Rule." Section 619 generally prohibits banking entities from engaging in proprietary trading or from investing in, sponsoring, or having certain relationships with a hedge fund or private equity fund. The amendment also provides that "nonbank financial companies" supervised by the Fed – like systemically significant investment firms – that engage in such activities or have such investments are subject to additional capital requirements, quantitative limits, or other restrictions.

---

16. 76 Fed. Reg. 8265 (2011) (codified at 12 C.F.R. §§ 225.1(c)(11), 225.180-225.182; reorganizing existing 12 C.F.R. § 225.200 as Subpart L).

17. The term *banking entity* is defined in 12 U.S.C. § 1851(h)(1) to mean any insured depository institution (other than certain limited-purpose trust institutions), any company that controls an insured depository institution, any company that is treated as a bank holding company under section 8 of the International Banking Act of 1978, 12 U.S.C. § 3106, and any affiliate or subsidiary of any of these specified entities.

18. 12 C.F.R. § 225.181. *See* 12 U.S.C. § 1851(h)(2) (defining *hedge fund* and *private equity fund* for purposes of Dodd-Frank Act provisions). Basically,

> [a] hedge fund is an investment fund, usually organized as a private investment partnership, open to a limited number of investors and requiring a very large initial minimum investment committed to the fund for a relatively long period, typically at least one year. The fund's investment strategies are usually very aggressive, making use of leveraged and derivative trading in targeted securities in order to increase the rate of return when the securities perform well. (This also means, of course, that losses can be exacerbated if the securities perform poorly.) A private equity fund is an investment fund that specializes in investments not quoted on public exchanges. The fund typically makes an investment directly into an existing private company or it may buy up a public company and take it private, "delisting" it from public exchanges in the process. Participants in a private equity fund are typically high-end investors (institutions and sophisticated, wealthy individuals) who commit a relatively large amount to the fund for a long period of time.

1 MICHAEL P. MALLOY, BANKING LAW AND REGULATION § 1.04[K][10] (2d ed., Aspen Publishers, 2011) (footnote omitted).

19. 12 U.S.C. § 1851. This conformance period generally extends two years after the date on which the prohibitions become effective – July 12, 2012 – or, in the case of a nonbank financial company supervised by the Fed, two years after the company is designated for supervision by the Fed, if that period is later. *See generally* 76 Fed. Reg. at 8266-8267 (discussing conformance period).

2. Bank Holding Company Act

a. Regulation of Nonbanking Activities

Notes and Comments 6.8. *Pre-GLBA activities*. BHC nonbanking activities require the prior approval of the Fed in many instances, depending upon the BHCA exception or exemption relied upon. However, the most important exemption pre-GLBA–§ 1843(c) (8), authorizing activities that are "so closely related to banking or managing or controlling banks as to be a proper incident thereto"–was frozen in place by the GLBA, and so is not available prospectively. Consider the following excerpts from the Fed's Regulation Y dealing with nonbanking activities. What is the statutory authority for each of the provisions?

Board of Governors of the Federal Reserve System

12 C.F.R. pt. 225

§ 225.2 Definitions.

Except as modified in this regulation or unless the context otherwise requires, the terms used in this regulation have the same meaning as set forth in the relevant statutes.

(a) Affiliate means any company that controls, is controlled by, or is under common control with, another company. . . .

(r) Well-capitalized– [a]

(1) Bank holding company. In the case of a bank holding company, well-capitalized means that:

(i) On a consolidated basis, the bank holding company maintains a total risk-based capital ratio of 10.0 percent or greater . . . ;

(ii) On a consolidated basis, the bank holding company maintains a Tier 1 risk-based capital ratio of 6.0 percent or greater . . . ; and

(iii) The bank holding company is not subject to any written agreement, order, capital directive, or prompt corrective action directive issued by the Board to meet and maintain a specific capital level for any capital measure.

(2) Insured and uninsured depository institution–(i) Insured depository institution. In the case of an insured depository institution, "well capitalized" means that the institution has and maintains at least the capital levels required to be well capitalized under the capital adequacy regulations or guidelines applicable to the institution that have been adopted by the appropriate Federal banking agency for the institution under section 38 of the Federal Deposit Insurance Act (12 U.S.C. 1831o).

(ii) Uninsured depository institution. In the case of a depository institution the deposits of which are not insured by the Federal Deposit Insurance Corporation, "well capitalized" means that the institution has and maintains at least the capital levels required for an insured depository institution to be well capitalized.

(s) Well managed–(1) In general. Except as otherwise provided in this part, a company or depository institution is well managed if:

(i) At its most recent inspection or examination or subsequent review by the appropriate Federal banking agency for the company or institution (or the appropriate state banking agency in an examination described in section 10(d) of the Federal Deposit Insurance Act (12 U.S.C. 1820(d)), the company or institution received:

---

a. On risk-based capital ratios, alluded to in this section, see Chapter 7, *infra*, § 5.

(A) At least a satisfactory composite rating; and

(B) At least a satisfactory rating for management, if such rating is given.

(ii) In the case of a company or depository institution that has not received an inspection or examination rating, the Board has determined, after a review of the managerial and other resources of the company or depository institution and after consulting with the appropriate Federal and state banking agencies, as applicable, for the company or institution, that the company or institution is well managed.

(2) Merged depository institutions–(i) Merger involving well managed institutions. A depository institution that results from the merger of two or more depository institutions that are well managed shall be considered to be well managed unless the Board determines otherwise after consulting with the appropriate Federal and state banking agencies, as applicable, for each depository institution involved in the merger.

(ii) Merger involving a poorly rated institution. A depository institution that results from the merger of a depository institution that is well managed with one or more depository institutions that are not well managed or have not been examined shall be considered to be well managed if the Board determines, after a review of the managerial and other resources of the resulting depository institution and after consulting with the appropriate Federal and state banking agencies for the institutions involved in the merger, as applicable, that the resulting institution is well managed. . . .

§ 225.21 Prohibited nonbanking activities and acquisitions; exempt bank holding companies.

(a) Prohibited nonbanking activities and acquisitions. Except as provided in § 225.22 of this subpart, a bank holding company or a subsidiary may not engage in, or acquire or control, directly or indirectly, voting securities or assets of a company engaged in, any activity other than:

(1) Banking or managing or controlling banks and other subsidiaries authorized under the BHC Act; and

(2) An activity that the Board determines to be so closely related to banking, or managing or controlling banks as to be a proper incident thereto, including any incidental activities that are necessary to carry on such an activity, if the bank holding company has obtained the prior approval of the Board for that activity in accordance with the requirements of this regulation.

(b) Exempt bank holding companies. The following bank holding companies are exempt from the provisions of this subpart:

(1) Family-owned companies. Any company that is a "company covered in 1970" (as defined in [12 U.S.C. § 1841(b)]), more than 85 percent of the voting securities of which was collectively owned on June 30, 1968, and continuously thereafter, by members of the same family (or their spouses) who are lineal descendants of common ancestors.

(2) Labor, agricultural, and horticultural organizations. Any company that was on January 4, 1977, both a bank holding company and a labor, agricultural, or horticultural organization exempt from taxation under section 501 of the Internal Revenue Code (26 U.S.C. 501(c)).

(3) Companies granted hardship exemption. Any bank holding company that has controlled only one bank since before July 1, 1968, and that has been granted an exemption by the Board under [12 U.S.C. § 1843(d)], subject to any conditions imposed by the Board.

(4) Companies granted exemption on other grounds. Any company that acquired control of a bank before December 10, 1982, without the Board's prior approval under [12 U.S.C. § 1842], on the basis of a narrow interpretation of the term demand deposit or

commercial loan, if the Board has determined that:

(i) Coverage of the company as a bank holding company under this subpart would be unfair or represent an unreasonable hardship; and

(ii) Exclusion of the company from coverage under this part is consistent with the purposes of the BHC Act and section 106 of the Bank Holding Company Act Amendments of 1970 (12 U.S.C. 1971, 1972(1)). The provisions of § 225.4 of subpart A of this part do not apply to a company exempt under this paragraph.

§ 225.22 Exempt nonbanking activities and acquisitions.

(a) Certain de novo activities. A bank holding company may, either directly or indirectly, engage de novo in any nonbanking activity listed in § 225.28(b) (other than operation of an insured depository institution) without obtaining the Board's prior approval if the bank holding company:

(1) Meets the requirements of paragraphs (c) (1), (2), and (6) of § 225.23;

(2) Conducts the activity in compliance with all Board orders and regulations governing the activity; and

(3) Within 10 business days after commencing the activity, provides written notice to the appropriate Reserve Bank describing the activity, identifying the company or companies engaged in the activity, and certifying that the activity will be conducted in accordance with the Board's orders and regulations and that the bank holding company meets the requirements of paragraphs (c)(1), (2), and (6) of § 225.23.

(b) Servicing activities. A bank holding company may, without the Board's prior approval under this subpart, furnish services to or perform services for, or establish or acquire a company that engages solely in servicing activities for:

(1) The bank holding company or its subsidiaries in connection with their activities as authorized by law, including services that are necessary to fulfill commitments entered into by the subsidiaries with third parties, if the bank holding company or servicing company complies with the Board's published interpretations and does not act as principal in dealing with third parties; and

(2) The internal operations of the bank holding company or its subsidiaries. Services for the internal operations of the bank holding company or its subsidiaries include, but are not limited to:

(i) Accounting, auditing, and appraising;

(ii) Advertising and public relations;

(iii) Data processing and data transmission services, data bases, or facilities;

(iv) Personnel services;

(v) Courier services;

(vi) Holding or operating property used wholly or substantially by a subsidiary in its operations or for its future use;

(vii) Liquidating property acquired from a subsidiary;

(viii) Liquidating property acquired from any sources either prior to May 9, 1956, or the date on which the company became a bank holding company, whichever is later; and

(ix) Selling, purchasing, or underwriting insurance, such as blanket bond insurance, group insurance for employees, and property and casualty insurance.

(c) Safe deposit business. A bank holding company or nonbank subsidiary may, without the Board's prior approval, conduct a safe deposit business, or acquire voting securities of a company that conducts such a business.

(d) Nonbanking acquisitions not requiring prior Board approval. The Board's prior approval is not required under this subpart for the following acquisitions:

(1) DPC acquisitions.

(i) Voting securities or assets, acquired by foreclosure or otherwise, in the ordinary course of collecting a debt previously contracted (DPC property) in good faith, if the DPC property is divested within two years of acquisition.

(ii) The Board may, upon request, extend this two-year period for up to three additional years. The Board may permit additional extensions for up to 5 years (for a total of 10 years), for shares, real estate or other assets where the holding company demonstrates that each extension would not be detrimental to the public interest and either the bank holding company has made good faith attempts to dispose of such shares, real estate or other assets or disposal of the shares, real estate or other assets during the initial period would have been detrimental to the company.

(iii) Transfers of DPC property within the bank holding company system do not extend any period for divestiture of the property.

(2) Securities or assets required to be divested by subsidiary. Voting securities or assets required to be divested by a subsidiary at the request of an examining federal or state authority (except by the Board under the BHC Act or this regulation), if the bank holding company divests the securities or assets within two years from the date acquired from the subsidiary.

(3) Fiduciary investments. Voting securities or assets acquired by a bank or other company (other than a trust that is a company) in good faith in a fiduciary capacity, if the voting securities or assets are:

(i) Held in the ordinary course of business; and

(ii) Not acquired for the benefit of the company or its shareholders, employees, or subsidiaries.

(4) Securities eligible for investment by national bank. Voting securities of the kinds and amounts explicitly eligible by federal statute (other than section 4 of the Bank Service [Company] Act, 12 U.S.C. 1864) for investment by a national bank, and voting securities acquired prior to June 30, 1971, in reliance on [12 U.S.C. § 1843(c)(5)] and interpretations of the Comptroller of the Currency under section 5136 of the Revised Statutes (12 U.S.C. 24(7)).

(5) Securities or property representing 5 percent or less of a company. Voting securities of a company or property that, in the aggregate, represent 5 percent or less of the outstanding shares of any class of voting securities of a company, or that represent a 5 percent interest or less in the property. . . .

(6) Securities of investment company. Voting securities of an investment company that is solely engaged in investing in securities and that does not own or control more than 5 percent of the outstanding shares of any class of voting securities of any company.

(7) Assets acquired in ordinary course of business. Assets of a company acquired in the ordinary course of business . . . if the assets relate to activities in which the acquiring company has previously received Board approval under this regulation to engage.

(8) Asset acquisitions by lending company or industrial bank. Assets of an office(s) of a company, all or substantially all of which relate to making, acquiring, or servicing loans if:

(i) The acquiring company has previously received Board approval under this regulation or is not required to obtain prior Board approval under this regulation to engage in lending activities or industrial banking activities;

(ii) The assets acquired during any 12-month period do not represent more than 50 percent of the risk-weighted assets (on a consolidated basis) of the acquiring lending company or industrial bank, or more than $100 million, whichever amount is less;

(iii) The assets acquired do not represent more than 50 percent of the selling company's consolidated assets that are devoted to lending activities or industrial banking business;

(iv) The acquiring company notifies the Reserve Bank of the acquisition within 30 days after the acquisition; and

(v) The acquiring company, after giving effect to the transaction, meets the Board's Capital Adequacy Guidelines . . .[b] and the Board has not previously notified the acquiring company that it may not acquire assets under the exemption in this paragraph.

(e) Acquisition of securities by subsidiary banks–(1) National bank. A national bank or its subsidiary may, without the Board's approval under this subpart, acquire or retain securities on the basis of [12 U.S.C. § 1843(c)(5)] in accordance with the regulations of the Comptroller of the Currency.

(2) State bank. A state-chartered bank or its subsidiary may, insofar as federal law is concerned, and without the Board's prior approval under this subpart:

(i) Acquire or retain securities, on the basis of [12 U.S.C. § 1843(c)(5)], of the kinds and amounts explicitly eligible by federal statute for investment by a national bank; or

(ii) Acquire or retain all (but, except for directors' qualifying shares, not less than all) of the securities of a company that engages solely in activities in which the parent bank may engage, at locations at which the bank may engage in the activity, and subject to the same limitations as if the bank were engaging in the activity directly.

(f) Activities and securities of new bank holding companies. A company that becomes a bank holding company may, for a period of two years, engage in nonbanking activities and control voting securities or assets of a nonbank subsidiary, if the bank holding company engaged in such activities or controlled such voting securities or assets on the date it became a bank holding company. The Board may grant requests for up to three one-year extensions of the two-year period.

(g) Grandfathered activities and securities. Unless the Board orders divestiture or termination under [12 U.S.C. § 1843(a)(2)], a "company covered in 1970," as defined in [12 U.S.C. § 1841(b)], may:

(1) Retain voting securities or assets and engage in activities that it has lawfully held or engaged in continuously since June 30, 1968; and

(2) Acquire voting securities of any newly formed company to engage in such activities. . . .

§ 225.23 Expedited action for certain nonbanking proposals by well-run bank holding companies.

(a) Filing of notice–

(1) Information required. A bank holding company that meets the requirements of paragraph (c) of this section may satisfy the notice requirement of this subpart in connection with the acquisition of voting securities or assets of a company engaged in nonbanking activities that the Board has permitted by order or regulation (other than an insured depository institution), or a proposal to engage de novo, either directly or indirectly, in a nonbanking activity that the Board has permitted by order or by regulation, by providing the appropriate Reserve Bank with a written notice containing the following:

(i) A certification that all of the criteria in paragraph (c) of this section are met;

(ii) A description of the transaction that includes identification of the companies involved in the transaction, the activities to be conducted, and a commitment to conduct the

---

b. *See* note a, *supra*.

proposed activities in conformity with the Board's regulations and orders governing the conduct of the proposed activity;

(iii) If the proposal involves an acquisition of a going concern:

(A) If the bank holding company has consolidated assets of $150 million or more, an abbreviated consolidated pro forma balance sheet for the acquiring bank holding company as of the most recent quarter showing credit and debit adjustments that reflect the proposed transaction, consolidated pro forma risk-based capital ratios for the acquiring bank holding company as of the most recent quarter, a description of the purchase price and the terms and sources of funding for the transaction, and the total revenue and net income of the company to be acquired;

(B) If the bank holding company has consolidated assets of less than $150 million, a pro forma parent-only balance sheet as of the most recent quarter showing credit and debit adjustments that reflect the proposed transaction, a description of the purchase price and the terms and sources of funding for the transaction and the sources and schedule for retiring any debt incurred in the transaction, and the total assets, off-balance sheet items, revenue and net income of the company to be acquired;

(C) For each insured depository institution whose Tier 1 capital, total capital, total assets or risk-weighted assets change as a result of the transaction, the total risk-weighted assets, total assets, Tier 1 capital and total capital of the institution on a pro forma basis;[c]

(iv) Identification of the geographic markets in which competition would be affected by the proposal, a description of the effect of the proposal on competition in the relevant markets, a list of the major competitors in that market in the proposed activity if the affected market is local in nature, and, if requested, the market indexes for the relevant market; and

(v) A description of the public benefits that can reasonably be expected to result from the transaction.

(2) Waiver of unnecessary information. The Reserve Bank may reduce the information requirements in paragraphs (a)(1) (iii) and (iv) of this section as appropriate.

(b)(1) Action on proposals under this section. The Board or the appropriate Reserve Bank shall act on a proposal submitted under this section, or notify the bank holding company that the transaction is subject to the procedure in § 225.24, within 12 business days following the filing of all of the information required in paragraph (a) of this section.

(2) Acceptance of notice if expedited procedure not available. If the Board or the Reserve Bank determines, after the filing of a notice under this section, that a bank holding company may not use the procedure in this section and must file a notice under § 225.24, the notice shall be deemed accepted for purposes of § 225.24 as of the date that the notice was filed under this section.

(c) Criteria for use of expedited procedure. The procedure in this section is available only if:

(1) Well-capitalized organization–[c]

(i) Bank holding company. Both at the time of and immediately after the proposed transaction, the acquiring bank holding company is well-capitalized;

(ii) Insured depository institutions. Both at the time of and immediately after the transaction:

(A) The lead insured depository institution of the acquiring bank holding company is well-capitalized;

(B) Well-capitalized insured depository institutions control at least 80 percent of the total risk-weighted assets of insured depository institutions controlled by the acquiring bank

---

c. *See* note a, *supra*.

holding company; and

(C) No insured depository institution controlled by the acquiring bank holding company is undercapitalized;

(2) Well managed organization–(i) Satisfactory examination ratings. At the time of the transaction, the acquiring bank holding company, its lead insured depository institution, and insured depository institutions that control at least 80 percent of the total risk-weighted assets of insured depository institutions controlled by the holding company are well managed and have received at least a satisfactory rating for compliance at their most recent examination if such rating was given;

(ii) No poorly managed institutions. No insured depository institution controlled by the acquiring bank holding company has received 1 of the 2 lowest composite ratings at the later of the institution's most recent examination or subsequent review by the appropriate federal banking agency for the institution.

(iii) Recently acquired institutions excluded. Any insured depository institution that has been acquired by the bank holding company during the 12-month period preceding the date on which written notice is filed under paragraph (a) of this section may be excluded for purposes of paragraph (c)(2)(ii) of this section if:

(A) The bank holding company has developed a plan acceptable to the appropriate federal banking agency for the institution to restore the capital and management of the institution; and

(B) All insured depository institutions excluded under this paragraph represent, in the aggregate, less than 10 percent of the aggregate total risk-weighted assets of all insured depository institutions controlled by the bank holding company;

(3) Permissible activity.

(i) The Board has determined by regulation or order that each activity proposed to be conducted is so closely related to banking, or managing or controlling banks, as to be a proper incident thereto; and

(ii) The Board has not indicated that proposals to engage in the activity are subject to the notice procedure provided in § 225.24;

(4) Competitive criteria–

(i) Competitive screen. In the case of the acquisition of a going concern, the acquisition, without regard to any divestitures proposed by the acquiring bank holding company, does not cause:

(A) The acquiring bank holding company to control in excess of 35 percent of the market share in any relevant market; or

(B) The Herfindahl-Hirschman index to increase by more than 200 points in any relevant market with a post-acquisition index of at least 1800; and

(ii) Other competitive factors. The Board has not indicated that the transaction is subject to close scrutiny on competitive grounds;

(5) Size of acquisition–

(i) In general–

(A) Limited growth. Except as provided in paragraph (c)(5)(ii) of this section, the sum of aggregate risk-weighted assets to be acquired in the proposal and the aggregate risk-weighted assets acquired by the acquiring bank holding company in all other qualifying transactions does not exceed 35 percent of the consolidated risk-weighted assets of the acquiring bank holding company. . . .

(B) Consideration paid. The gross consideration to be paid by the acquiring bank holding company in the proposal does not exceed 15 percent of the consolidated Tier 1 capital of the acquiring bank holding company; and

(C) Individual size limitation. The total risk-weighted assets to be acquired do not exceed $7.5 billion;

(ii) Small bank holding companies. Paragraph (c)(5)(i)(A) of this section shall not apply if, immediately following consummation of the proposed transaction, the consolidated risk-weighted assets of the acquiring bank holding company are less than $300 million;

(6) Supervisory actions. During the 12-month period ending on the date on which the bank holding company proposes to consummate the proposed transaction, no formal administrative order, including a written agreement, cease and desist order, capital directive, prompt corrective action directive, asset maintenance agreement, or other formal enforcement order is or was outstanding against the bank holding company or any insured depository institution subsidiary of the holding company, and no formal administrative enforcement proceeding involving any such enforcement action, order, or directive is or was pending; and

(7) Notification. The bank holding company has not been notified by the Board, in its discretion, prior to the expiration of the period in paragraph (b) of this section that a notice under § 225.24 is required in order to permit closer review of any potential adverse effect or other matter related to the factors that must be considered under this part. . . .

§ 225.24 Procedures for other nonbanking proposals.

(a) Notice required for nonbanking activities. Except as provided in § 225.22 and § 225.23, a notice for the Board's prior approval under s 225.21(a) to engage in or acquire a company engaged in a nonbanking activity shall be filed by a bank holding company (including a company seeking to become a bank holding company) with the appropriate Reserve Bank in accordance with this section. . . .

(1) Engaging de novo in listed activities. A bank holding company seeking to commence or to engage de novo, either directly or through a subsidiary, in a nonbanking activity listed in § 225.28 shall file a notice containing a description of the activities to be conducted and the identity of the company that will conduct the activity.

(2) Acquiring company engaged in listed activities. A bank holding company seeking to acquire or control voting securities or assets of a company engaged in a nonbanking activity listed in § 225.28 shall file a notice containing the following:

(i) A description of the proposal, including a description of each proposed activity, and the effect of the proposal on competition among entities engaging in each proposed activity in each relevant market with relevant market indexes;

(ii) The identity of any entity involved in the proposal, and, if the notificant proposes to conduct the activity through an existing subsidiary, a description of the existing activities of the subsidiary;

(iii) A statement of the public benefits that can reasonably be expected to result from the proposal;

(iv) If the bank holding company has consolidated assets of $150 million or more:

(A) Parent company and consolidated pro forma balance sheets for the acquiring bank holding company as of the most recent quarter showing credit and debit adjustments that reflect the proposed transaction;

(B) Consolidated pro forma risk-based capital and leverage ratio calculations for the acquiring bank holding company as of the most recent quarter; and

(C) A description of the purchase price and the terms and sources of funding for the transaction;

(v) If the bank holding company has consolidated assets of less than $150 million:

(A) A pro forma parent-only balance sheet as of the most recent quarter showing credit and debit adjustments that reflect the proposed transaction; and

(B) A description of the purchase price and the terms and sources of funding for the transaction and, if the transaction is debt funded, one-year income statement and cash flow projections for the parent company, and the sources and schedule for retiring any debt incurred in the transaction;

(vi) For each insured depository institution whose Tier 1 capital, total capital, total assets or risk-weighted assets change as a result of the transaction, the total risk-weighted assets, total assets, Tier 1 capital and total capital of the institution on a pro forma basis;[d] and

(vii) A description of the management expertise, internal controls and risk management systems that will be utilized in the conduct of the proposed activities; and

(viii) A copy of the purchase agreements, and balance sheet and income statements for the most recent quarter and year-end for any company to be acquired.

(3) [Deleted.[e]]

(b) Notice provided to Board. The Reserve Bank shall immediately send to the Board a copy of any notice received under paragraph[ ] (a)(2) . . . of this section.

(c) Notice to public–

(1) Listed activities and activities approved by order–

(i) In a case involving an activity listed in § 225.28 or previously approved by the Board by order, the Reserve Bank shall notify the Board for publication in the Federal Register immediately upon receipt by the Reserve Bank of:

(A) A notice under this section; or

(B) A written request that notice of a proposal under this section or § 225.23 be published in the Federal Register. Such a request may request that Federal Register publication occur up to 15 calendar days prior to submission of a notice under this subpart.

(ii) The Federal Register notice published under this paragraph shall invite public comment on the proposal, generally for a period of 15 days.

(2) New activities–

(i) In general. In the case of a notice under this subpart involving an activity that is not listed in § 225.28 and that has not been previously approved by the Board by order, the Board shall send notice of the proposal to the Federal Register for publication, unless the Board determines that the notificant has not demonstrated that the activity is so closely related to banking or to managing or controlling banks as to be a proper incident thereto. The Federal Register notice shall invite public comment on the proposal for a reasonable period of time, generally for 30 days.

(ii) Time for publication. The Board shall send the notice required under this paragraph to the Federal Register within 10 business days of acceptance by the Reserve Bank. The Board may extend the 10-day period for an additional 30 calendar days upon notice to the notificant. In the event notice of a proposal is not published for comment, the Board shall inform the notificant of the reasons for the decision.

---

d. *See* note a, *supra*.

e. The Fed explained the deletion of this provision, which concerned procedures for engaging in unlisted activities, as follows:

> The Board has deleted the existing text of subsection (a)(3), which discusses the information requirements for proposals to engage in activities that are not listed in §225.28. The GLB Act amends section 4(c)(8) to remove the Board's authority to authorize additional nonbanking activities for bank holding companies under that section. Therefore, subsection (a)(3) is unnecessary and has been deleted.

65 Fed. Reg. 14,433, 14,437 (2000).

(d) Action on notices–

(1) Reserve Bank action–

(i) In general. Within 30 calendar days after receipt by the Reserve Bank of a notice filed pursuant to paragraphs (a)(1) or (a)(2) of this section, the Reserve Banks shall:

(A) Approve the notice; or

(B) Refer the notice to the Board for decision because action under delegated authority is not appropriate.

(ii) Return of incomplete notice. Within 7 calendar days of receipt, the Reserve Bank may return any notice as informationally incomplete that does not contain all of the information required by this subpart. The return of such a notice shall be deemed action on the notice.

(iii) Notice of action. The Reserve Bank shall promptly notify the bank holding company of any action or referral under this paragraph.

(iv) Close of public comment period. The Reserve Bank shall not approve any notice under this paragraph (d)(1) of this section prior to the third business day after the close of the public comment period, unless an emergency exists that requires expedited or immediate action.

(2) Board action; internal schedule. The Board seeks to act on every notice referred to it for decision within 60 days of the date that the notice is filed with the Reserve Bank. If the Board is unable to act within this period, the Board shall notify the notificant and explain the reasons and the date by which the Board expects to act.

(3)(i) Required time limit for System action. The Board or the Reserve Bank shall act on any notice under this section within 60 days after the submission of a complete notice.

(ii) Extension of required period for action.

(A) In general.–The Board may extend the 60-day period required for Board action under paragraph (d)(3)(i) of this section for an additional 30 days upon notice to the notificant.

(B) Unlisted activities. If a notice involves a proposal to engage in an activity that is not listed in § 225.28, the Board may extend the period required for Board action under paragraph (d)(3)(i) of this section for an additional 90 days. This 90-day extension is in addition to the 30-day extension period provided in paragraph (d)(3)(ii)(A) of this section. The Board shall notify the notificant that the notice period has been extended and explain the reasons for the extension.

(4) Requests for additional information. The Board or the Reserve Bank may modify the information requirements under this section or at any time request any additional information that either believes is needed for a decision on any notice under this section.

(5) Tolling of period. The Board or the Reserve Bank may at any time extend or toll the time period for action on a notice for any period with the consent of the notificant.

§ 225.25 Hearings, alteration of activities, and other matters.

(a) Hearings–

. . .

(2) Determination to hold hearing. The Board may order a formal or informal hearing or other proceeding on a notice. . . . The Board shall order a hearing only if there are disputed issues of material fact that cannot be resolved in some other manner.

(3) Extension of period for hearing. The Board may extend the time for action on any notice for such time as is reasonably necessary to conduct a hearing and evaluate the hearing record. Such extension shall not exceed 91 calendar days after the date of submission to the Board of the complete record on the notice. . . .

(b) Approval through failure to act.

(1) Except as provided in paragraph (a) of this section or § 225.24(d)(5), a notice under this subpart shall be deemed to be approved at the conclusion of the period that begins on the date the complete notice is received by the Reserve Bank or the Board and that ends 60 calendar days plus any applicable extension and tolling period thereafter.

(2) Complete notice. For purposes of paragraph (b)(1) of this section, a notice shall be deemed complete at such time as it contains all information required by this subpart and all other information requested by the Board or the Reserve Bank.

(c) Notice to expand or alter nonbanking activities–

(1) De novo expansion. A notice under this subpart is required to open a new office or to form a subsidiary to engage in, or to relocate an existing office engaged in, a nonbanking activity that the Board has previously approved for the bank holding company under this regulation, only if:

(i) The Board's prior approval was limited geographically; . . . or

(iii) The Board or appropriate Reserve Bank has notified the company that a notice under this subpart is required. . . .

(3) Alteration of nonbanking activity. Unless otherwise permitted by the Board, a notice under this subpart is required to alter a nonbanking activity in any material respect from that considered by the Board in acting on the application or notice to engage in the activity.

(d) Emergency savings association acquisitions. In the case of a notice to acquire a savings association, the Board may modify or dispense with the public notice and hearing requirements of this subpart if the Board finds that an emergency exists that requires the Board to act immediately and the primary federal regulator of the institution concurs.

§ 225.26 Factors considered in acting on nonbanking proposals.

(a) In general. In evaluating a notice under § 225.23 or § 225.24, the Board shall consider whether the notificant's performance of the activities can reasonably be expected to produce benefits to the public (such as greater convenience, increased competition, and gains in efficiency) that outweigh possible adverse effects (such as undue concentration of resources, decreased or unfair competition, conflicts of interest, and unsound banking practices).

(b) Financial and managerial resources. Consideration of the factors in paragraph (a) of this section includes an evaluation of the financial and managerial resources of the notificant, including its subsidiaries and any company to be acquired, the effect of the proposed transaction on those resources, and the management expertise, internal control and risk-management systems, and capital of the entity conducting the activity.

(c) Competitive effect of de novo proposals. Unless the record demonstrates otherwise, the commencement or expansion of a nonbanking activity de novo is presumed to result in benefits to the public through increased competition.

(d) Denial for lack of information. The Board may deny any notice submitted under this subpart if the notificant neglects, fails, or refuses to furnish all information required by the Board.

(e) Conditional approvals. The Board may impose conditions on any approval, including conditions to address permissibility, financial, managerial, safety and soundness, competitive, compliance, conflicts of interest, or other concerns to ensure that approval is consistent with the relevant statutory factors and other provisions of the BHC Act. . . .

§ 225.28 List of permissible nonbanking activities.

(a) Closely related nonbanking activities. The activities listed in paragraph (b) of this section are so closely related to banking or managing or controlling banks as to be a proper incident thereto, and may be engaged in by a bank holding company or its subsidiary in accordance with the requirements of this regulation.

(b) Activities determined by regulation to be permissible–

(1) Extending credit and servicing loans. Making, acquiring, brokering, or servicing loans or other extensions of credit (including factoring, issuing letters of credit and accepting drafts) for the company's account or for the account of others.

(2) Activities related to extending credit. Any activity usual in connection with making, acquiring, brokering or servicing loans or other extensions of credit, as determined by the Board. The Board has determined that the following activities are usual in connection with making, acquiring, brokering or servicing loans or other extensions of credit:

(i) Real estate and personal property appraising. Performing appraisals of real estate and tangible and intangible personal property, including securities.

(ii) Arranging commercial real estate equity financing. Acting as intermediary for the financing of commercial or industrial income-producing real estate by arranging for the transfer of the title, control, and risk of such a real estate project to one or more investors, if the bank holding company and its affiliates do not have an interest in, or participate in managing or developing, a real estate project for which it arranges equity financing, and do not promote or sponsor the development of the property.

(iii) Check-guaranty services. Authorizing a subscribing merchant to accept personal checks tendered by the merchant's customers in payment for goods and services, and purchasing from the merchant validly authorized checks that are subsequently dishonored.

(iv) Collection agency services. Collecting overdue accounts receivable, either retail or commercial.

(v) Credit bureau services. Maintaining information related to the credit history of consumers and providing the information to a credit grantor who is considering a borrower's application for credit or who has extended credit to the borrower.

(vi) Asset management, servicing, and collection activities. Engaging under contract with a third party in asset management, servicing, and collection of assets of a type that an insured depository institution may originate and own, if the company does not engage in real property management or real estate brokerage services as part of these services.

(vii) Acquiring debt in default. Acquiring debt that is in default at the time of acquisition, if the company:

(A) Divests shares or assets securing debt in default that are not permissible investments for bank holding companies, within the time period required for divestiture of property acquired in satisfaction of a debt previously contracted . . . ;

(B) Stands only in the position of a creditor and does not purchase equity of obligors of debt in default (other than equity that may be collateral for such debt); and

(C) Does not acquire debt in default secured by shares of a bank or bank holding company.

(viii) Real estate settlement servicing. Providing real estate settlement services.

(3) Leasing personal or real property. Leasing personal or real property or acting as agent, broker, or adviser in leasing such property if:

(i) The lease is on a nonoperating basis;[5]

5. The requirement that the lease be on a nonoperating basis means that the bank holding company may not, directly or indirectly, engage in operating, servicing, maintaining, or repairing leased property during the lease term. For purposes of the leasing of automobiles, the requirement that

(ii) The initial term of the lease is at least 90 days;

(iii) In the case of leases involving real property:

(A) At the inception of the initial lease, the effect of the transaction will yield a return that will compensate the lessor for not less than the lessor's full investment in the property plus the estimated total cost of financing the property over the term of the lease from rental payments, estimated tax benefits, and the estimated residual value of the property at the expiration of the initial lease; and

(B) The estimated residual value of property for purposes of paragraph (b)(3)(iii)(A) of this section shall not exceed 25 percent of the acquisition cost of the property to the lessor.

(4) Operating nonbank depository institutions–

(i) Industrial banking. Owning, controlling, or operating an industrial bank, Morris Plan bank, or industrial loan company, so long as the institution is not a bank.

(ii) Operating savings association. Owning, controlling, or operating a savings association, if the savings association engages only in deposit-taking activities, lending, and other activities that are permissible for bank holding companies under this subpart C.

(5) Trust company functions. Performing functions or activities that may be performed by a trust company (including activities of a fiduciary, agency, or custodial nature), in the manner authorized by federal or state law, so long as the company is not a bank for purposes of [12 U.S.C. § 1841(c)].

(6) Financial and investment advisory activities. Acting as investment or financial advisor to any person, including (without, in any way, limiting the foregoing):

(i) Serving as investment adviser (as defined in section 2(a)(20) of the Investment Company Act of 1940, 15 U.S.C. 80a-2(a)(20)), to an investment company registered under that act, including sponsoring, organizing, and managing a closed-end investment company;

(ii) Furnishing general economic information and advice, general economic statistical forecasting services, and industry studies;

(iii) Providing advice in connection with mergers, acquisitions, divestitures, investments, joint ventures, leveraged buyouts, recapitalizations, capital structurings, financing transactions and similar transactions, and conducting financial feasibility studies;

(iv) Providing information, statistical forecasting, and advice with respect to any transaction in foreign exchange, swaps, and similar transactions, commodities, and any forward contract, option, future, option on a future, and similar instruments;

(v) Providing educational courses, and instructional materials to consumers on individual financial management matters; and

(vi) Providing tax-planning and tax-preparation services to any person.

(7) Agency transactional services for customer investments–

(i) Securities brokerage. Providing securities brokerage services (including securities clearing and/or securities execution services on an exchange), whether alone or in combination with investment advisory services, and incidental activities (including related securities credit activities and custodial services), if the securities brokerage services are restricted to buying and selling securities solely as agent for the account of customers and

---

the lease be on a nonoperating basis means that the bank holding company may not, directly or indirectly: (1) Provide servicing, repair, or maintenance of the leased vehicle during the lease term; (2) purchase parts and accessories in bulk or for an individual vehicle after the lessee has taken delivery of the vehicle; (3) provide the loan of an automobile during servicing of the leased vehicle; (4) purchase insurance for the lessee; or (5) provide for the renewal of the vehicle's license merely as a service to the lessee where the lessee could renew the license without authorization from the lessor. The bank holding company may arrange for a third party to provide these services or products.

do not include securities underwriting or dealing.

(ii) Riskless principal transactions. Buying and selling in the secondary market all types of securities on the order of customers as a "riskless principal" to the extent of engaging in a transaction in which the company, after receiving an order to buy (or sell) a security from a customer, purchases (or sells) the security for its own account to offset a contemporaneous sale to (or purchase from) the customer. This does not include:

(A) Selling bank-ineligible securities[7] at the order of a customer that is the issuer of the securities, or selling bank-ineligible securities in any transaction where the company has a contractual agreement to place the securities as agent of the issuer; or

(B) Acting as a riskless principal in any transaction involving a bank-ineligible security for which the company or any of its affiliates acts as underwriter (during the period of the underwriting or for 30 days thereafter) or dealer.[8]

(iii) Private placement services. Acting as agent for the private placement of securities in accordance with the requirements of the Securities Act of 1933 (1933 Act) and the rules of the Securities and Exchange Commission, if the company engaged in the activity does not purchase or repurchase for its own account the securities being placed, or hold in inventory unsold portions of issues of these securities.

(iv) Futures commission merchant. Acting as a futures commission merchant (FCM) for unaffiliated persons in the execution, clearance, or execution and clearance of any futures contract and option on a futures contract traded on an exchange in the United States or abroad if:

(A) The activity is conducted through a separately incorporated subsidiary of the bank holding company, which may engage in activities other than FCM activities (including, but not limited to, permissible advisory and trading activities); and

(B) The parent bank holding company does not provide a guarantee or otherwise become liable to the exchange or clearing association other than for those trades conducted by the subsidiary for its own account or for the account of any affiliate.

(v) Other transactional services. Providing to customers as agent transactional services with respect to swaps and similar transactions, any transaction described in paragraph (b)(8) of this section, any transaction that is permissible for a state member bank, and any other transaction involving a forward contract, option, futures, option on a futures or similar contract (whether traded on an exchange or not) relating to a commodity that is traded on an exchange.

(8) Investment transactions as principal–

(i) Underwriting and dealing in government obligations and money market instruments. Underwriting and dealing in obligations of the United States, general obligations of states and their political subdivisions, and other obligations that state member banks of the Federal Reserve System may be authorized to underwrite and deal in under 12 U.S.C. 24 and 335, including banker's acceptances and certificates of deposit, under the same limitations as would be applicable if the activity were performed by the bank holding company's subsidiary member banks or its subsidiary nonmember banks as if they were

---

7. A bank-ineligible security is any security that a State member bank is not permitted to underwrite or deal in under 12 U.S.C. 24 and 335.

8. A company or its affiliates may not enter quotes for specific bank-ineligible securities in any dealer quotation system in connection with the company's riskless principal transactions; except that the company or its affiliates may enter "bid" or "ask" quotations, or publish "offering wanted" or "bid wanted" notices on trading systems other than NASDAQ or an exchange, if the company or its affiliate does not enter price quotations on different sides of the market for a particular security during any two-day period.

member banks.

(ii) Investing and trading activities. Engaging as principal in:

(A) Foreign exchange;

(B) Forward contracts, options, futures, options on futures, swaps, and similar contracts, whether traded on exchanges or not, based on any rate, price, financial asset (including gold, silver, platinum, palladium, copper, or any other metal approved by the Board), nonfinancial asset, or group of assets, other than a bank-ineligible security, if:

(1) A state member bank is authorized to invest in the asset underlying the contract;

(2) The contract requires cash settlement; or

(3) The contract allows for assignment, termination, or offset prior to delivery or expiration, and the company makes every reasonable effort to avoid taking or making delivery; and

(C) Forward contracts, options, futures, options on futures, swaps, and similar contracts, whether traded on exchanges or not, based on an index of a rate, a price, or the value of any financial asset, nonfinancial asset, or group of assets, if the contract requires cash settlement.

(iii) Buying and selling bullion, and related activities. Buying, selling and storing bars, rounds, bullion, and coins of gold, silver, platinum, palladium, copper, and any other metal approved by the Board, for the company's own account and the account of others, and providing incidental services such as arranging for storage, safe custody, assaying, and shipment.

(9) Management consulting and counseling activities–

(i) Management consulting.

(A) Providing management consulting advice:

(1) On any matter to unaffiliated depository institutions, including commercial banks, savings and loan associations, savings banks, credit unions, industrial banks, Morris Plan banks, cooperative banks, industrial loan companies, trust companies, and branches or agencies of foreign banks;

(2) On any financial, economic, accounting, or audit matter to any other company.

(B) A company conducting management consulting activities under this subparagraph and any affiliate of such company may not:

(1) Own or control, directly or indirectly, more than 5 percent of the voting securities of the client institution; and

(2) Allow a management official . . . of the company or any of its affiliates to serve as a management official of the client institution, except where such interlocking relationship is permitted pursuant to an exemption . . . or otherwise permitted by the Board.

(C) A company conducting management consulting activities may provide management consulting services to customers not described in paragraph (b)(9)(i)(A)(1) of this section or regarding matters not described in paragraph (b)(9)(i)(A)(2) of this section, if the total annual revenue derived from those management consulting services does not exceed 30 percent of the company's total annual revenue derived from management consulting activities.

(ii) Employee benefits consulting services. Providing consulting services to employee benefit, compensation and insurance plans, including designing plans, assisting in the implementation of plans, providing administrative services to plans, and developing employee communication programs for plans.

(iii) Career counseling services. Providing career counseling services to:

(A) A financial organization[12] and individuals currently employed by, or recently displaced from, a financial organization;

(B) Individuals who are seeking employment at a financial organization; and

(C) Individuals who are currently employed in or who seek positions in the finance, accounting, and audit departments of any company.

(10) Support services–

(i) Courier services. Providing courier services for:

(A) Checks, commercial papers, documents, and written instruments (excluding currency or bearer-type negotiable instruments) that are exchanged among banks and financial institutions; and

(B) Audit and accounting media of a banking or financial nature and other business records and documents used in processing such media.

(ii) Printing and selling MICR-encoded items. Printing and selling checks and related documents, including corporate image checks, cash tickets, voucher checks, deposit slips, savings withdrawal packages, and other forms that require Magnetic Ink Character Recognition (MICR) encoding.

(11) Insurance agency and underwriting–

(i) Credit insurance. Acting as principal, agent, or broker for insurance (including home mortgage redemption insurance) that is:

(A) Directly related to an extension of credit by the bank holding company or any of its subsidiaries; and

(B) Limited to ensuring the repayment of the outstanding balance due on the extension of credit in the event of the death, disability, or involuntary unemployment of the debtor.

(ii) Finance company subsidiary. Acting as agent or broker for insurance directly related to an extension of credit by a finance company that is a subsidiary of a bank holding company, if:

(A) The insurance is limited to ensuring repayment of the outstanding balance on such extension of credit in the event of loss or damage to any property used as collateral for the extension of credit; and

(B) The extension of credit is not more than $10,000, or $25,000 if it is to finance the purchase of a residential manufactured home and the credit is secured by the home; and

(C) The applicant commits to notify borrowers in writing that:

(1) They are not required to purchase such insurance from the applicant;

(2) Such insurance does not insure any interest of the borrower in the collateral; and

(3) The applicant will accept more comprehensive property insurance in place of such single-interest insurance.

(iii) Insurance in small towns. Engaging in any insurance agency activity in a place where the bank holding company or a subsidiary of the bank holding company has a lending office and that:

(A) Has a population not exceeding 5,000 (as shown in the preceding decennial census); or

(B) Has inadequate insurance agency facilities, as determined by the Board, after notice and opportunity for hearing.

(iv) Insurance-agency activities conducted on May 1, 1982. Engaging in any

---

12. Financial organization refers to insured depository institution holding companies and their subsidiaries, other than nonbanking affiliates of diversified savings and loan holding companies that engage in activities not permissible under section 4(c)(8) of the Bank Holding Company Act (12 U.S.C. 1842(c)(8)).

specific insurance-agency activity if the bank holding company, or subsidiary conducting the specific activity, conducted such activity on May 1, 1982, or received Board approval to conduct such activity on or before May 1, 1982. A bank holding company or subsidiary engaging in a specific insurance agency activity under this clause may:

(A) Engage in such specific insurance agency activity only at locations:

(1) In the state in which the bank holding company has its principal place of business (as defined in 12 U.S.C. 1842(d));

(2) In any state or states immediately adjacent to such state; and

(3) In any state in which the specific insurance-agency activity was conducted (or was approved to be conducted) by such bank holding company or subsidiary thereof or by any other subsidiary of such bank holding company on May 1, 1982; and

(B) Provide other insurance coverages that may become available after May 1, 1982, so long as those coverages insure against the types of risks as (or are otherwise functionally equivalent to) coverages sold or approved to be sold on May 1, 1982, by the bank holding company or subsidiary.

(v) Supervision of retail insurance agents. Supervising on behalf of insurance underwriters the activities of retail insurance agents who sell:

(A) Fidelity insurance and property and casualty insurance on the real and personal property used in the operations of the bank holding company or its subsidiaries; and

(B) Group insurance that protects the employees of the bank holding company or its subsidiaries.

(vi) Small bank holding companies. Engaging in any insurance-agency activity if the bank holding company has total consolidated assets of $50 million or less. A bank holding company performing insurance-agency activities under this paragraph may not engage in the sale of life insurance or annuities except as provided in paragraphs (b)(11) (i) and (iii) of this section, and it may not continue to engage in insurance-agency activities pursuant to this provision more than 90 days after the end of the quarterly reporting period in which total assets of the holding company and its subsidiaries exceed $50 million.

(vii) Insurance-agency activities conducted before 1971. Engaging in any insurance-agency activity performed at any location in the United States directly or indirectly by a bank holding company that was engaged in insurance-agency activities prior to January 1, 1971, as a consequence of approval by the Board prior to January 1, 1971.

(12) Community development activities–

(i) Financing and investment activities. Making equity and debt investments in corporations or projects designed primarily to promote community welfare, such as the economic rehabilitation and development of low-income areas by providing housing, services, or jobs for residents.

(ii) Advisory activities. Providing advisory and related services for programs designed primarily to promote community welfare.

(13) Money orders, savings bonds, and traveler's checks. The issuance and sale at retail of money orders and similar consumer-type payment instruments; the sale of U.S. savings bonds; and the issuance and sale of traveler's checks.

(14) Data processing.

(i) Providing data processing and data transmission services, facilities (including data processing and data transmission hardware, software, documentation, or operating personnel), data bases, advice, and access to such services, facilities, or data bases by any technological means, if:

(A) The data to be processed or furnished are financial, banking, or economic; and

(B) The hardware provided in connection therewith is offered only in conjunction with software designed and marketed for the processing and transmission of financial, banking, or economic data, and where the general purpose hardware does not constitute more than 30 percent of the cost of any packaged offering.

(ii) A company conducting data processing and data transmission activities may conduct data processing and data transmission activities not described in paragraph (b)(14)(i) of this section if the total annual revenue derived from those activities does not exceed 30 percent of the company's total annual revenues derived from data processing and data transmission activities.

Notes and Comments 6.9. Quarter National Bank (QNB) is controlled by Forth Corp. Forth has decided that it needs to diversify significantly. It is considering the following proposals: (*i*) creating a new subsidiary that would specialize in real estate and personal property appraising; (*ii*) acquiring control of Altered State Savings and Loan Association as a subsidiary; (*iii*) acquiring control of Moorless Safe Deposit Company as a subsidiary; or, (*iv*) creating a new subsidiary that would operate as a full-service travel agency. In accordance with the regulations excerpted above, which of these activities is authorized?

b. Financial Holding Companies

Notes and Comments 6.10. *Financial holding companies and activities "financial in nature".* As to nonbanking activities of BHCs, the GLBA has decisively shifted the center of gravity in the BHCA from the "closely related" exemption of § 1843(c)(8) to the "financial in nature" concept of the FHC authorization.[20] The GLBA permits BHCs that qualify as FHCs to engage in activities, and acquire companies engaged in activities, that are "financial in nature" or incidental to such activities,[21] or that are complementary to financial activities.[22] The Fed is required, by regulation or order, to define, consistent with the purposes of the GLBA, the activities described as financial in nature, and the extent to which such activities are financial in nature or incidental to a financial activity.[23] The GLBA itself lists the following described activities: (i) lending, exchanging, transferring, investing for others, or safeguarding financial assets other than money or securities; (ii) providing any device or other instrumentality for transferring money or other financial assets; (iii) arranging,

20. 12 U.S.C. § 1843(k)(1) (authorizing activities "financial in nature").

21. *Id.* § 1843(k)(1)(A).

22. *Id.* § 1843(k)(1)(B). A complementary activity is permitted only if it does not pose a substantial risk to the safety or soundness of depository institutions or the financial system in general. *Id.* For an example of the Fed's implementation of the authority for "complementary" activities, see 65 Fed. Reg. 80,384 (2000) (to be codified at 12 C.F.R. pt. 225) (proposing to allow FHC to own company engaged in specified types of data storage, internet and portal hosting activities, and broad advisory activities involving data processing activities, if company also provides financial data processing or other financial products and services; also considering whether to permit FHC to invest in company engaged in developing new technologies that might support the sale and availability of financial products and services, company providing communication links for delivery of financial products and services, and/or company engaged in electronic sale and delivery of products and services).

23. 12 U.S.C. § 1843(k)(5)(A). On the implementation of § 1843(k)(5), see 66 Fed. Reg. 257 (2001) (codified at 12 C.F.R. pts. 225, 1501) (joint Fed-Treasury interim rule identifying three general types of activities as "financial in nature;" creating mechanism for FHCs, financial subsidiaries of national banks, and others to request that Fed or Treasury Secretary define particular activities within one of three categories).

effecting, or facilitating financial transactions for the account of third parties.[24] In determining whether proposed activities are financial in nature or incidental, the Fed must notify the Secretary of the Treasury of applications or requests to engage in new financial activities.[25] The Fed is prohibited from determining that an activity is financial or incidental to a financial activity if the Secretary objects in accordance with the procedure outlined in the GLBA.[26] The Secretary may also propose to the Fed that the latter find that a particular activity is financial in nature or incidental.[27] Section 1843(k)(4) does contain a list of activities that are *per se* considered to be financial in nature. An FHC may engage in such "K4 activities" without obtaining prior approval from the Fed,[28] but with notice to the Fed within 30 days after the activity is commenced or a company is acquired.[29]

6.11. *FHC approval procedures*. To engage in the new financial activities and affiliations,[30] a BHC may elect to become an FHC, if all of its subsidiary banks are well capitalized and well managed.[31] A BHC that meets these requirements may file a certification to that effect with the Fed and a declaration electing to be an FHC.[32] After this filing an FHC may engage, either *de novo* or by acquisition, in any activity that has been determined by the Fed to be financial in nature or incidental.[33] BHCs that elect to become FHCs are not required to file a duplicative BHC registration statement under section 1844(a). FHCs may engage in K4 activities (and any other financial activity approved by the Fed) without prior notice.[34] Complementary activities must be approved by the Fed case-by-case under BHCA notice procedures.[35]

6.12. *FHC enforcement procedures*. If the Fed finds that an FHC is engaged in an activity financial in nature (other than a "closely related" activity) at a time when it is not well capitalized or well managed, or before it has filed an FHC election and certification, the Fed is required to give notice to the FHC to that effect, describing the conditions giving rise to the notice.[36] Within 45 days of receipt of the notice,[37] the FHC must execute an agreement with the Fed[38] to comply with these requirements.[39] Until the deficiencies are corrected, the Fed may impose limits on the conduct or activities of the FHC or any affiliate thereof, as the

---

24. 12 U.S.C. § 1843(k)(5)(B)(i)-(iii).

25. *Id.* § 1843(k)(2)(A)(i).

26. *Id.* § 1843(k)(2)(A)(ii).

27. *Id.* § 1843(k)(2)(B).

28. *Id.* § 1843(k)(6)(B).

29. *Id.* § 1843(k)(6)(A).

30. For limited grandfathering authority as to activities lawfully engaged in as of 30 September 1999, see *id.* § 1843(n)-(o).

31. *Id.* § 1843(*l*)(1)(A)-(B).

32. *Id.* 1843(*l*)(1)(C).

33. *Id.* § 1843(*l*)(1).

34. *Id.* § 1843(k)(6)(B).

35. *Id.* § 1843(j).

36. *Id.* § 1843(m)(1).

37. The Fed may permit an "additional period." *Id.* § 1843(m)(2).

38. Any action under this provision by the Fed requires consultation "with all relevant Federal and State regulatory agencies and authorities." *Id.* § 1843(m)(5).

39. *Id.* § 1843(m)(2).

Fed deems appropriate under the circumstances and consistent with the statutory purposes.[40] If the conditions are not corrected within 180 days of receipt of the notice, the Fed may require the FHC, under terms, conditions and timing imposed by the Fed, to divest control of any depository institution subsidiary[41] or to cease activities that are not "closely related" to banking.[42]

6.13. *Implementing regulations*. On 25 January 2000, the Fed published an interim final rule under the GLBA implementing the new authority for such activities,[43] effective 11 March 2000. In January 2001, the Fed adopted a final rule[44] implementing the FHC provisions and replacing three interim rules that it had adopted in early 2000.[45] Among other things, the final rule establishes procedures domestic BHCs and foreign banking organizations must follow, and the capital, management, and CRA requirements that they must meet in order to qualify as an FHC. It also contains provisions that apply to an FHC that subsequently ceases to meet the applicable requirements. In addition, the final rule lists the activities that the GLBA defines as "financial in nature" and thus authorized for an FHC to conduct. It contains procedures that apply to an FHC that conducts those activities, a procedure that allows any interested party to request the to Fed determine, in consultation with the Secretary of the Treasury, that additional activities are "financial in nature" or incidental to a financial activity and thus permissible for an FHC, and a procedure that allows an FHC to request Fed prior approval to conduct an activity that is complementary to a financial activity. Review the implementing regulations excerpted below and the provisions of 12 U.S.C. § 1843, in order to answer the problems in Notes 6.14-6.20, *infra*.

Board of Governors of the Federal Reserve System

12 C.F.R. pt. 225

Subpart I–Financial Holding Companies

Sec.

---

40. *Id.* § 1843(m)(3).

41. *Id.* § 1843(m)(4)(A).

42. *Id.* § 1843(m)(4)(B).

43. 65 Fed. Reg. 3785 (2000).

44. 66 Fed. Reg. 400 (2001) (codified at 12 C.F.R. pt. 225).

45. 65 Fed. Reg. 3785 (2000); 65 Fed. Reg. 14,433 (2000); 65 Fed. Reg. 15,053 (2000).

. . .

§ 225.81 What is a financial holding company?

(a) Definition. A financial holding company is a bank holding company that meets the requirements of this section.

(b) Requirements to be a financial holding company. In order to be a financial holding company:

(1) All depository institutions controlled by the bank holding company must be and remain well capitalized;

(2) All depository institutions controlled by the bank holding company must be and remain well managed; and

(3) The bank holding company must have made an effective election to become a financial holding company.

(c) Requirements for foreign banks that are or are owned by bank holding companies–(1) Foreign banks with U.S. branches or agencies that also own U.S. banks. A foreign bank that is a bank holding company and that operates a branch or agency or owns or controls a commercial lending company in the United States must comply with the requirements of this section, § 225.82, and §§ 225.90 through 225.92 in order to be a financial holding company. After it becomes a financial holding company, a foreign bank described in this paragraph will be subject to the provisions of §§ 225.83, 225.84, 225.93, and 225.94.

(2) Bank holding companies that own foreign banks with U.S. branches or agencies. A bank holding company that owns a foreign bank that operates a branch or agency or owns or controls a commercial lending company in the United States must comply with the requirements of this section, § 225.82, and §§ 225.90 through 225.92 in order to be a financial holding company. After it becomes a financial holding company, a bank holding company described in this paragraph will be subject to the provisions of §§ 225.83, 225.84, 225.93, and 225.94.

§ 225.82 How does a bank holding company elect to become a financial holding company?

(a) Filing requirement. A bank holding company may elect to become a financial holding company by filing a written declaration with the appropriate Reserve Bank. A declaration by a bank holding company is considered to be filed on the date that all information required by paragraph (b) of this section is received by the appropriate Reserve Bank.

(b) Contents of declaration. To be deemed complete, a declaration must:

(1) State that the bank holding company elects to be a financial holding company;

(2) Provide the name and head office address of the bank holding company and of each depository institution controlled by the bank holding company;

(3) Certify that each depository institution controlled by the bank holding company is well capitalized as of the date the bank holding company submits its declaration;

(4) Provide the capital ratios as of the close of the previous quarter for all relevant capital measures, as defined in section 38 of the Federal Deposit Insurance Act (12 U.S.C. 1831o), for each depository institution controlled by the company on the date the company submits its declaration; and

(5) Certify that each depository institution controlled by the company is well managed as of the date the company submits its declaration.

(c) Effectiveness of election. An election by a bank holding company to become a financial holding company shall not be effective if, during the period provided in paragraph (e) of this section, the Board finds that, as of the date the declaration was filed with the appropriate Reserve Bank:

(1) Any insured depository institution controlled by the bank holding company (except an institution excluded under paragraph (d) of this section) has not achieved at least a rating of "satisfactory record of meeting community credit needs" under the Community Reinvestment Act at the institution's most recent examination; or

(2) Any depository institution controlled by the bank holding company is not both well capitalized and well managed.

(d) Consideration of the CRA performance of a recently acquired insured depository institution. Except as provided in paragraph (f) of this section, an insured depository institution will be excluded for purposes of the review of the Community Reinvestment Act rating provisions of paragraph (c)(1) of this section if:

(1) The bank holding company acquired the insured depository institution during the 12-month period preceding the filing of an election under paragraph (a) of this section;

(2) The bank holding company has submitted an affirmative plan to the appropriate Federal banking agency for the institution to take actions necessary for the institution to achieve at least a rating of "satisfactory record of meeting community credit needs" under the Community Reinvestment Act at the next examination of the institution; and

(3) The appropriate Federal banking agency for the institution has accepted the plan described in paragraph (d)(2) of this section.

(e) Effective date of election–(1) In general. An election filed by a bank holding company under paragraph (a) of this section is effective on the 31st calendar day after the date that a complete declaration was filed with the appropriate Reserve Bank, unless the Board notifies the bank holding company prior to that time that the election is ineffective.

(2) Earlier notification that an election is effective. The Board or the appropriate Reserve Bank may notify a bank holding company that its election to become a financial holding company is effective prior to the 31st day after the date that a complete declaration was filed with the appropriate Reserve Bank. Such a notification must be in writing.

(f) Requests to become a financial holding company submitted as part of an application to become a bank holding company–(1) In general. A company that is not a bank holding company and has applied for the Board's approval to become a bank holding company under section 3(a)(1) of the BHC Act (12 U.S.C. 1842(a)(1)) may as part of that application submit a request to become a financial holding company.

(2) Contents of request. A request to become a financial holding company submitted as part of an application to become a bank holding company must:

(i) State that the company seeks to become a financial holding company on consummation of its proposal to become a bank holding company; and

(ii) Certify that each depository institution that would be controlled by the company on consummation of its proposal to become a bank holding company will be both well capitalized and well managed as of the date the company consummates the proposal.

(3) Request becomes a declaration and an effective election on date of consummation of bank holding company proposal. A complete request submitted by a company under this paragraph (f) becomes a complete declaration by a bank holding company for purposes of section 4(l) of the BHC Act (12 U.S.C. 1843(l)) and becomes an effective election for purposes of § 225.81(b) on the date that the company lawfully consummates its proposal under section 3 of the BHC Act (12 U.S.C. 1842), unless the Board notifies the company at any time prior to consummation of the proposal and that:

(i) Any depository institution that would be controlled by the company on consummation of the proposal will not be both well capitalized and well managed on the date of consummation; or

(ii) Any insured depository institution that would be controlled by the company on consummation of the proposal has not achieved at least a rating of "satisfactory record of meeting community credit needs" under the Community Reinvestment Act at the institution's most recent examination.

(4) Limited exclusion for recently acquired institutions not available. Unless the Board determines otherwise, an insured depository institution that is controlled or would be controlled by the company as part of its proposal to become a bank holding company may not be excluded for purposes of evaluating the Community Reinvestment Act criterion described in this paragraph or in paragraph (d) of this section.

(g) Board's authority to exercise supervisory authority over a financial holding company. An effective election to become a financial holding company does not in any way limit the Board's statutory authority under the BHC Act, the Federal Deposit Insurance Act, or any other relevant Federal statute to take appropriate action, including imposing supervisory limitations, restrictions, or prohibitions on the activities and acquisitions of a bank holding company that has elected to become a financial holding company, or enforcing compliance with applicable law.

§ 225.83 What are the consequences of failing to continue to meet applicable capital and management requirements?

(a) Notice by the Board. If the Board finds that a financial holding company controls any depository institution that is not well capitalized or well managed, the Board will notify the company in writing that it is not in compliance with the applicable requirement(s) for a financial holding company and identify the area(s) of noncompliance. The Board may provide this notice at any time before or after receiving notice from the financial holding company under paragraph (b) of this section.

(b) Notification by a financial holding company required–(1) Notice to Board. A financial holding company must notify the Board in writing within 15 calendar days of becoming aware that any depository institution controlled by the company has ceased to be well capitalized or well managed. This notification must identify the depository institution involved and the area(s) of noncompliance.

(2) Triggering events for notice to the Board–(i) Well capitalized. A company becomes aware that a depository institution it controls is no longer well capitalized upon the occurrence of any material event that would change the category assigned to the institution for purposes of section 38 of the Federal Deposit Insurance Act (12 U.S.C. 1831o). . . .

(ii) Well managed. A company becomes aware that a depository institution it controls is no longer well managed at the time the depository institution receives written notice from the appropriate Federal or state banking agency that either its composite rating or its rating for management is not at least satisfactory.

(c) Execution of agreement acceptable to the Board–(1) Agreement required; time period. Within 45 days after receiving a notice from the Board under paragraph (a) of this section, the company must execute an agreement acceptable to the Board to comply with all applicable capital and management requirements.

(2) Extension of time for executing agreement. Upon request by a company, the Board may extend the 45-day period under paragraph (c)(1) of this section if the Board determines that granting additional time is appropriate under the circumstances. A request by a company for additional time must include an explanation of why an extension is necessary.

(3) Agreement requirements. An agreement required by paragraph (c)(1) of this section to correct a capital or management deficiency must:

(i) Explain the specific actions that the company will take to correct all areas of noncompliance;

(ii) Provide a schedule within which each action will be taken;

(iii) Provide any other information that the Board may require; and

(iv) Be acceptable to the Board.

(d) Limitations during period of noncompliance–Until the Board determines that a company has corrected the conditions described in a notice under paragraph (a) of this section:

(1) The Board may impose any limitations or conditions on the conduct or activities of the company or any of its affiliates as the Board finds to be appropriate and consistent with the purposes of the BHC Act; and

(2) The company and its affiliates may not commence any additional activity or acquire control or shares of any company under section 4(k) of the BHC Act without prior approval from the Board.

(e) Consequences of failure to correct conditions within 180 days–(1) Divestiture of depository institutions. If a company does not correct the conditions described in a notice under paragraph (a) of this section within 180 days of receipt of the notice or such additional time as the Board may permit, the Board may order the company to divest ownership or control of any depository institution owned or controlled by the company. Such divestiture must be done in accordance with the terms and conditions established by the Board.

(2) Alternative method of complying with a divestiture order. A company may comply with an order issued under paragraph (e)(1) of this section by ceasing to engage (both directly and through any subsidiary that is not a depository institution or a subsidiary of a depository institution) in any activity that may be conducted only under section 4(k), (n), or (o) of the BHC Act (12 U.S.C. 1843(k), (n), or (o)). The termination of activities must be completed within the time period referred to in paragraph (e)(1) of this section and in accordance with the terms and conditions acceptable to the Board.

(f) Consultation with other agencies. In taking any action under this section, the Board will consult with the relevant Federal and state regulatory authorities.

§ 225.84 What are the consequences of failing to maintain a satisfactory or better rating under the Community Reinvestment Act at all insured depository institution subsidiaries?

(a) Limitations on activities–(1) In general. Upon receiving a notice regarding performance under the Community Reinvestment Act in accordance with paragraph (a)(2) of this section, a financial holding company may not:

(i) Commence any additional activity under section 4(k) or 4(n) of the BHC Act (12 U.S.C. 1843(k) or (n)); or

(ii) Directly or indirectly acquire control, including all or substantially all of the assets, of a company engaged in any activity under section 4(k) or 4(n) of the BHC Act (12 U.S.C. 1843(k) or (n)).

(2) Notification. A financial holding company receives notice for purposes of this paragraph at the time that the appropriate Federal banking agency for any insured depository institution controlled by the company or the Board provides notice to the institution or company that the institution has received a rating of "needs to improve record of meeting community credit needs" or "substantial noncompliance in meeting community credit needs" in the institution's most recent examination under the Community Reinvestment Act.

(b) Exceptions for certain activities–(1) Continuation of investment activities. The prohibition in paragraph (a) of this section does not prevent a financial holding company from continuing to make investments in the ordinary course of conducting merchant banking activities under section 4(k)(4)(H) of the BHC Act (12 U.S.C. 1843(k)(4)(H)) or insurance company investment activities under section 4(k)(4)(I) of the BHC Act (12 U.S.C. 1843(k)(4)(I))if:

(i) The financial holding company lawfully was a financial holding company and commenced the merchant banking activity under section 4(k)(4)(H) of the BHC Act (12 U.S.C. 1843(k)(4)(H)) or the insurance company investment activity under section 4(k)(4)(I) of the BHC Act (12 U.S.C. 1843(k)(4)(I)) prior to the time that an insured depository institution controlled by the financial holding company received a rating below "satisfactory record of meeting community credit needs" under the Community Reinvestment Act; and

(ii) The Board has not, in the exercise of its supervisory authority, advised the financial holding company that these activities must be restricted.

(2) Activities that are closely related to banking. The prohibition in paragraph (a) of this section does not prevent a financial holding company from commencing any additional activity or acquiring control of a company engaged in any activity under section 4(c) of the BHC Act (12 U.S.C. 1843(c)), if the company complies with the notice, approval, and other requirements of that section and section 4(j) of the BHC Act (12 U.S.C. 1843(j)).

(c) Duration of prohibitions. The prohibitions described in paragraph (a) of this section shall continue in effect until such time as each insured depository institution controlled by the financial holding company has achieved at least a rating of "satisfactory record of meeting community credit needs" under the Community Reinvestment Act at the most recent examination of the institution.

§ 225.85 Is notice to or approval from the Board required prior to engaging in a financial activity?

(a) No prior approval required generally–(1) In general. A financial holding company and any subsidiary (other than a depository institution or subsidiary of a depository institution) of the financial holding company may engage in any activity listed in § 225.86, or acquire shares or control of a company engaged exclusively in activities listed in § 225.86, without providing prior notice to or obtaining prior approval from the Board unless required under paragraph (c) of this section.

(2) Acquisitions by a financial holding company of a company engaged in other permissible activities. In addition to the activities listed in § 225.86, a company acquired or to be acquired by a financial holding company under paragraph (a)(1) of this section may engage in activities otherwise permissible for a financial holding company under this part in accordance with any applicable notice, approval, or other requirement.

(3) Acquisition by a financial holding company of a company engaged in limited nonfinancial activities–(i) Mixed acquisitions generally permitted. A financial holding company may under this subpart acquire more than 5 percent of the outstanding shares of any class of voting securities or control of a company that is not engaged exclusively in activities that are financial in nature, incidental to a financial activity, or otherwise permissible for the financial holding company under section 4(c) of the BHC Act (12 U.S.C. 1843(c)) if:

(A) The company to be acquired is substantially engaged in activities that are financial in nature, incidental to a financial activity, or otherwise permissible for the financial holding company under section 4(c) of the BHC Act (12 U.S.C. 1843(c));

(B) The financial holding company complies with the notice requirements of § 225.87, if applicable; and

(C) The company conforms, terminates, or divests, within 2 years of the date the financial holding company acquires shares or control of the company, all activities that are not financial in nature, incidental to a financial activity, or otherwise permissible for the financial holding company under section 4(c) (12 U.S.C. 1843(c))of the BHC Act.

(ii) Definition of "substantially engaged." Unless the Board determines otherwise, a company will be considered to be "substantially engaged" in activities permissible for a financial holding company for purposes of paragraph (a)(3)(A) of this section if at least 85 percent of the company's consolidated total annual gross revenues is derived from and at least 85 percent of the company's consolidated total assets is attributable to the conduct of activities that are financial in nature, incidental to a financial activity, or otherwise permissible for a financial holding company under section 4(c) of the BHC Act (12 U.S.C. 1843(c)).

(b) Locations in which a financial holding company may conduct financial activities. A financial holding company may conduct any activity listed in § 225.86 at any location in the United States or at any location outside of the United States subject to the laws of the jurisdiction in which the activity is conducted.

(c) Circumstances under which prior notice to the Board is required–(1) Acquisition of more than 5 percent of the shares of a savings association. A financial holding company must obtain Board approval in accordance with section 4(j) of the BHC Act (12 U.S.C. 1843(j)) and either § 225.14 or § 225.24, as appropriate, prior to acquiring control or more than 5 percent of the outstanding shares of any class of voting securities of a savings association or of a company that owns, operates, or controls a savings association.

(2) Supervisory actions. The Board may, if appropriate in the exercise of its supervisory or other authority, including under § 225.82(g) or § 225.83(d) or other relevant authority, require a financial holding company to provide notice to or obtain approval from the Board prior to engaging in any activity or acquiring shares or control of any company.

§ 225.86 What activities are permissible for any financial holding company?

The following activities are financial in nature or incidental to a financial activity:

(a) Activities determined to be closely related to banking. (1) Any activity that the Board had determined by regulation prior to November 12, 1999, to be so closely related to banking as to be a proper incident thereto, subject to the terms and conditions contained in this part, unless modified by the Board. These activities are listed in § 225.28.

(2) Any activity that the Board had determined by an order that was in effect on November 12, 1999, to be so closely related to banking as to be a proper incident thereto, subject to the terms and conditions contained in this part and those in the authorizing orders. These activities are:

(i) Providing administrative and other services to mutual funds (Societe Generale, 84 Federal Reserve Bulletin 680 (1998));

(ii) Owning shares of a securities exchange (J.P. Morgan & Co, Inc., and UBS AG, 86 Federal Reserve Bulletin 61 (2000));

(iii) Acting as a certification authority for digital signatures and authenticating the identity of persons conducting financial and nonfinancial transactions (Bayerische Hypo- und Vereinsbank AG, et al., 86 Federal Reserve Bulletin 56 (2000));

(iv) Providing employment histories to third parties for use in making credit decisions and to depository institutions and their affiliates for use in the ordinary course of business (Norwest Corporation, 81 Federal Reserve Bulletin 732 (1995));

(v) Check cashing and wire transmission services (Midland Bank, PLC, 76 Federal Reserve Bulletin 860 (1990) (check cashing); Norwest Corporation, 81 Federal Reserve Bulletin 1130 (1995) (money transmission));

(vi) In connection with offering banking services, providing notary public services, selling postage stamps and postage-paid envelopes, providing vehicle registration services, and selling public transportation tickets and tokens (Popular, Inc., 84 Federal Reserve Bulletin 481 (1998)); and

(vii) Real estate title abstracting (The First National Company, 81 Federal Reserve Bulletin 805 (1995)).

(b) Activities determined to be usual in connection with the transaction of banking abroad. Any activity that the Board had determined by regulation in effect on November 11, 1999, to be usual in connection with the transaction of banking or other financial operations abroad (see § 211.5(d) of this chapter), subject to the terms and conditions in part 211 and Board interpretations in effect on that date regarding the scope and conduct of the activity. In addition to the activities listed in paragraphs (a) and (c) of this section, these activities are:

(1) Providing management consulting services, including to any person with respect to nonfinancial matters, so long as the management consulting services are advisory and do not allow the financial holding company to control the person to which the services are provided;

(2) Operating a travel agency in connection with financial services offered by the financial holding company or others; and

(3) Organizing, sponsoring, and managing a mutual fund, so long as:

(i) The fund does not exercise managerial control over the entities in which the fund invests; and

(ii) The financial holding company reduces its ownership in the fund, if any, to less than 25 percent of the equity of the fund within one year of sponsoring the fund or such additional period as the Board permits.

(c) Activities permitted under section 4(k)(4) of the BHC Act (12 U.S.C. 1843(k)(4)). Any activity defined to be financial in nature under sections 4(k)(4)(A) through (E), (H) and (I) of the BHC Act (12 U.S.C. 1843(k)(4)(A) through (E), (H) and (I)).

§ 225.87 Is notice to the Board required after engaging in a financial activity?

(a) Post-transaction notice generally required to engage in a financial activity. A financial holding company that commences an activity or acquires shares of a company engaged in an activity listed in § 225.86 must notify the appropriate Reserve Bank in writing within 30 calendar days after commencing the activity or consummating the acquisition by using the appropriate form.

(b) Cases in which notice to the Board is not required–(1) Acquisitions that do not involve control of a company. A notice under paragraph (a) of this section is not required in connection with the acquisition of shares of a company if, following the acquisition, the financial holding company does not control the company.

(2) No additional notice required to engage de novo in an activity for which a financial holding company already has provided notice. After a financial holding company provides the appropriate Reserve Bank with notice that the company is engaged in an activity listed in § 225.86, a financial holding company may, unless otherwise notified by the Board, commence the activity de novo through any subsidiary that the financial holding company is authorized to control without providing additional notice under paragraph (a) of this section.

(3) Conduct of certain investment activities. Unless required by paragraph (b)(4) of this section, a financial holding company is not required to provide notice under paragraph (a) of this section of any individual acquisition of shares of a company as part of the conduct by a financial holding company of securities underwriting, dealing, or market making activities as described in section 4(k)(4)(E) of the BHC Act (12 U.S.C. 1843(k)(4)(E)),

merchant banking activities conducted pursuant to section 4(k)(4)(H) of the BHC Act (12 U.S.C. 1843(k)(4)(H)), or insurance company investment activities conducted pursuant to section 4(k)(4)(I) of the BHC Act (12 U.S.C. 1843(k)(4)(I)), if the financial holding company previously has notified the Board under paragraph (a) of this section that the company has commenced the relevant securities, merchant banking, or insurance company investment activities, as relevant.

(4) Notice of large merchant banking or insurance company investments. Notwithstanding paragraph (b)(1) or (b)(3) of this section, a financial holding company must provide notice under paragraph (a) of the section if:

(i) As part of a merchant banking activity conducted under section 4(k)(4)(H) of the BHC Act (12 U.S.C. 1843(k)(4)(H)), the financial holding company acquires more than 5 percent of the shares, assets, or ownership interests of any company at a total cost that exceeds the lesser of 5 percent of the financial holding company's Tier 1 capital or $200 million;

(ii) As part of an insurance company investment activity conducted under section 4(k)(4)(I) of the BHC Act (12 U.S.C. 1843(k)(4)(I)), the financial holding company acquires more than 5 percent of the shares, assets, or ownership interests of any company at a total cost that exceeds the lesser of 5 percent of the financial holding company's Tier 1 capital or $200 million; or

(iii) The Board in the exercise of its supervisory authority notifies the financial holding company that a notice is necessary.

§ 225.88 How to request the Board to determine that an activity is financial in nature or incidental to a financial activity?

(a) Requests regarding activities that may be financial in nature or incidental to a financial activity. A financial holding company or other interested party may request a determination from the Board that an activity not listed in § 225.86 is financial in nature or incidental to a financial activity.

(b) Required information. A request submitted under this section must be in writing and must:

(1) Identify and define the activity for which the determination is sought, specifically describing what the activity would involve and how the activity would be conducted;

(2) Explain in detail why the activity should be considered financial in nature or incidental to a financial activity; and

(3) Provide information supporting the requested determination and any other information required by the Board concerning the proposed activity.

(c) Board procedures for reviewing requests--(1) Consultation with the Secretary of the Treasury. Upon receipt of the request, the Board will provide the Secretary of the Treasury a copy of the request and consult with the Secretary in accordance with section 4(k)(2)(A) of the BHC Act (12 U.S.C. 1843(k)(2)(A)).

(2) Public notice. The Board may, as appropriate and after consultation with the Secretary, publish a description of the proposal in the Federal Register with a request for public comment.

(d) Board action. The Board will endeavor to make a decision on any request filed under paragraph (a) of this section within 60 calendar days following the completion of both the consultative process described in paragraph (c)(1) of this section and the public comment period, if any.

(e) Advisory opinions regarding scope of financial activities–(1) Written request.

A financial holding company or other interested party may request an advisory opinion from the Board about whether a specific proposed activity falls within the scope of an activity listed in § 225.86 as financial in nature or incidental to a financial activity. The request must be submitted in writing and must contain:

(i) A detailed description of the particular activity in which the company proposes to engage or the product or service the company proposes to provide;

(ii) An explanation supporting an interpretation regarding the scope of the permissible financial activity; and

(iii) Any additional information requested by the Board regarding the activity.

(2) Board response. The Board will provide an advisory opinion within 45 calendar days of receiving a complete written request under paragraph (e)(1) of this section.

§ 225.89 How to request approval to engage in an activity that is complementary to a financial activity?

(a) Prior Board approval is required. A financial holding company that seeks to engage in or acquire more than 5 percent of the outstanding shares of any class of voting securities of a company engaged in an activity that the financial holding company believes is complementary to a financial activity must obtain prior approval from the Board in accordance with section 4(j) of the BHC Act (12 U.S.C. 1843(j)). The notice must be in writing and must:

(1) Identify and define the proposed complementary activity, specifically describing what the activity would involve and how the activity would be conducted;

(2) Identify the financial activity for which the proposed activity would be complementary and provide detailed information sufficient to support a finding that the proposed activity should be considered complementary to the identified financial activity;

(3) Describe the scope and relative size of the proposed activity, as measured by the percentage of the projected financial holding company revenues expected to be derived from and assets associated with conducting the activity;

(4) Discuss the risks that conducting the activity may reasonably be expected to pose to the safety and soundness of the subsidiary depository institutions of the financial holding company and to the financial system generally;

(5) Describe the potential adverse effects, including potential conflicts of interest, decreased or unfair competition, or other risks, that conducting the activity could raise, and explain the measures the financial holding company proposes to take to address those potential effects;

(6) Describe the potential benefits to the public, such as greater convenience, increased competition, or gains in efficiency, that the proposal reasonably can be expected to produce; and

(7) Provide any information about the financial and managerial resources of the financial holding company and any other information requested by the Board.

(b) Factors for consideration by the Board. In evaluating a notice to engage in a complementary activity, the Board must consider whether:

(1) The proposed activity is complementary to a financial activity;

(2) The proposed activity would pose a substantial risk to the safety or soundness of depository institutions or the financial system generally; and

(3) The proposal could be expected to produce benefits to the public that outweigh possible adverse effects.

(c) Board action. The Board will inform the financial holding company in writing of the Board's determination regarding the proposed activity within the period described in section 4(j) of the BHC Act (12 U.S.C. 1843(j)). . . .

Notes and Comments 6.14. QuarterCorp is the holding company of Quarter National Bank. It is interested in acquiring a controlling interest in Fellow Travellers Insurance Corp. Would it be permitted to do so under § 1843(c)(8)?

6.15. QuarterCorp is also interested in acquiring a controlling interest in the Jaccuse Investment Bank. Would it be permitted to do so under § 1843(c)(8)?

6.16. Would QuarterCorp be permitted to acquire a controlling interest in Fellow Travellers or Jaccuse under 1843(k)? If so, with what procedures would QuarterCorp be required to comply?

6.17. In what other financial services could QuarterCorp invest under 1843(k)?

6.18. Assume that Stranglehold Corporation is a financial holding company under 1843(k), and that it has complied with the required procedures under that subsection. Because of losses in one of its subsidiaries, the subsidiary has written off certain assets and is no longer well capitalized. What are the possible consequences for Stranglehold under these circumstances?

6.19. Would it make a difference to your analysis if the result of the write-off was that Stranglehold was no longer a well capitalized company?

6.20. DotCorp is a newly formed corporation in Palo Alto, California. It plans to apply for a charter for a Cyber National Bank, the activities of which would be limited to offering banking services over the Internet. It also intends to incorporate a subsidiary, ComCorp, that will market over the Internet ownership interests in high-velocity competitive biological entities (HVCBEs). Each HVCBE valued at $1 million or more would be offered to the public in 1000 equal ownership interest units, with a minimum required purchase of 100 units. DotCorp expects to use Cyber's website and database of customers in its marketing efforts with respect to ComCorp. What is the likelihood that DotCorp's proposals would be approved under the BHCA?

6.21. As originally enacted, 12 U.S.C. § 1843(n)(5) imposed restrictions on certain cross-marketing activities between a depository institution affiliated with an FHC and the FHC's affiliates identified in § 1843(k)(4)(I), but not in (H). Are these restrictions the same with respect to both securities and insurance affiliates? Can you explain any differences? Section 611 of the Financial Services Regulatory Relief Act of 2006, Pub. L. No. 109-351, 120 Stat. 1966, 1984 (2006) (codified at 12 U.S.C. § 1843(n)(5)(B)), modifies the cross marketing restrictions, allowing an FHC's depository institution subsidiary to engage in cross-marketing with affiliates that are merchant banking firms to the same extent that cross-marketing is currently permissible for affiliates that are insurance firms. *See* 12 U.S.C. § 1843(n)(5)(A)-(B). What is the effect of the current version of the cross-marketing restrictions?

6.22. *Relationship between Comptroller's power under the NBA and Fed's power under BHCA*. When a national bank is acquired by a BHC, what approvals are necessary? *See* 12 U.S.C. § 215a-2. What about approval of activities of the bank? One complexity that arose under § 1843(c)(8) involved applications by national banks to conduct an activity as an "incidental power" in a wholly owned subsidiary, which might be indirectly controlled by such a bank's BHC parent. Did the Comptroller get to approve the activity, or must it also (or first) be approved by the Fed under the BHCA? Under the GLBA, however, activities are "financial in nature" (and thus permissible for national bank subsidiaries) if they are defined as such in the BHCA, 12 U.S.C. § 1843(k)(4), or the Secretary of the Treasury (and not the Comptroller) in consultation with the Fed determines that the activity is financial in nature. *Id.* § 24a(b)(1)(A)-(B). Thus, unlike the pre-GLBA situation concerning direct national bank subsidiaries engaging in "incidental powers," policy in this area is now seems to be centered upon the BHCA, not the NBA, with the primary policy role within the purview of the Fed. How would the GLBA have affected the following case?

American Ins. Ass'n v. Clarke

865 F.2d 278 (D.C.Cir. 1989)

BUCKLEY, Circuit Judge:

[For the court's discussion of the background of the case, see Chapter 5, § .b, *supra*.]

II. Discussion

A. Standard of Review

[T]he Board of Governors of the Federal Reserve System has exclusive jurisdiction to interpret and apply the BHCA. *See generally Whitney Nat'l Bank v. Bank of New Orleans & Trust Co.*, 379 U.S. 411 (1965). . . . "[W]hen an agency interprets a statute other than that which it has been entrusted to administer, its interpretation is not entitled to deference." *Department of the Treasury v. FLRA*, 837 F.2d 1163, 1167 (D.C.Cir.1988). . . .

C. Bank Holding Company Act

The BHCA, administered by the Board of Governors of the Federal Reserve System ("Board"), limits the nonbanking activities of bank holding companies (entities that control banks). A bank holding company may not "acquire direct or indirect ownership or control of any voting shares of any company which is not a bank," 12 U.S.C. § 1843(a)(1) (1982), subject to a number of statutory exceptions, 12 U.S.C. § 1843(c). The most commonly invoked exception is 12 U.S.C. § 1843(c)(8). . . .

Citicorp, a bank holding company, controls Citibank, a national bank. Citibank in turn controls AMBAC, which is not itself a bank.

Appellant argues that the Comptroller should not have concurred in Citibank's proposal without requiring Citicorp to obtain the Board's approval under the BHCA. Appellant claims the proposal raised a substantial question under the BHCA because AMBAC would be engaged in insurance, an activity specifically excluded from the "closely related to banking" standard. The Comptroller was obliged, this argument concludes, to defer his final approval pending the Board's resolution of that issue.

Although the Board has exclusive jurisdiction to administer the BHCA, *Whitney Nat'l Bank v. Bank of New Orleans & Trust Co.*, 379 U.S. 411, 419 (1965), the Comptroller may, in "exceptional circumstances," be required to defer his final approval under the NBA pending completion of the Board's inquiry under the BHCA. *Id.* at 426 n. 7. In *Whitney*, a bank sought to form a bank holding company that would own the establishing bank and form a new bank in a different Louisiana parish. The Comptroller gave preliminary approval, subject to the action of the Board. The Board then approved the plan under the BHCA, and competitor banks petitioned for review in the Fifth Circuit. After the Board's decision, Louisiana adopted a law prohibiting bank holding companies from opening banking subsidiaries. The competitors then sought to enjoin the Comptroller from issuing a certificate authorizing the opening of the new bank, arguing that the BHCA prohibited approval of actions proscribed by state law.

The Supreme Court concluded that the suit against the Comptroller was improper because the Board had the responsibility in the first instance to determine the merits of a BHCA challenge. The Court noted that the Comptroller's decision was not a final action subject to review: even if he approved the transaction, his action "would be completely negated" if the Board's approval was reversed by the Fifth Circuit. . . . The Court declined, however, to rule that BHCA issues are always irrelevant to the Comptroller's decision:

> [T]here may be exceptional circumstances under which equity may stay the hand of the Comptroller in issuing a certificate to a new bank. Obviously if the holding company application has not been acted upon by the Board, the Comptroller would have no power to issue the certificate and his persistence in doing so would subject him to the temporary orders of a court of competent jurisdiction.

... *Whitney*, as then before the Court, was not such a case. The Court therefore dismissed the complaint against the Comptroller, but stayed its judgment for sixty days to permit the parties to move in the Fifth Circuit for a remand to the Board to consider the effect of the new Louisiana statute.

Whitney has been interpreted as requiring the Comptroller to defer the issuance of a bank charter pending completion of an inquiry by the Board when the transaction presents a "substantial" question under the BHCA. *American Bank of Tulsa v. Smith*, 503 F.2d 784, 789 (10th Cir.1974). We are aware of no case that applies the substantial question doctrine outside the context of the chartering of a new bank, and we do not decide that question today. It is perfectly clear, however, that the Comptroller, if he so chooses, may condition any approval on subsequent action by the Board. *See, e.g., Gravois Bank v. Board of Governors*, 478 F.2d 546, 548 (8th Cir.1973).

In this case, the Comptroller did not exercise his discretion to condition his approval on subsequent Board approval because he thought the BHCA did not apply. The Comptroller gave two reasons for his conclusion: (1) the BHCA limits only the non-bank subsidiaries of bank holding companies themselves, not of their banking subsidiaries, and (2) AMBAC's standby credits were not insurance under the BHCA. The district court affirmed the Comptroller's conclusion for a different reason: section 4(c)(5) of the BHCA permits any investments approved by the Comptroller. We reject each of these arguments.

First, the Comptroller thought that the BHCA did not limit the subsidiaries of national banks that are in turn owned by bank holding companies. A bank holding company, however, is prohibited from acquiring "direct or indirect ownership or control of any voting shares of any company which is not a bank," unless an exception applies. 12 U.S.C. § 1843(a)(1) (1982).... Shares owned or controlled by any subsidiary of a holding company are "deemed to be indirectly owned or controlled by such bank holding company." 12 U.S.C. § 1841(g)(1) (1982). Citicorp manifestly exercises indirect control over AMBAC because AMBAC's parent is Citicorp's subsidiary. *See* 12 C.F.R. § 225.101(c) (1988) (BHCA's investment prohibitions apply to holding company's indirect ownership of shares in nonbanking company owned directly by banking subsidiary). The Board has repeatedly held that "the acquisition of voting shares by a subsidiary bank of a bank holding company is treated as an acquisition by the parent bank holding company and, on this basis, is subject to the nonbanking limitations of section 4 of the [BHCA]." *Security Pacific Corp.*, 72 Fed.Res.Bull. 800, 801 (1986); *see also Merchants Nat'l Corp.*, 73 Fed. Res. Bull. 876, 880 (1987), *vacated in part on other grounds sub nom. Independent Ins. Agents of Am. v. Board of Governors*, 838 F.2d 627 (2d Cir.1988).

The Comptroller's second rationale, that AMBAC's standby credits were not insurance under the BHCA, was not his judgment to make. The Comptroller could conclude that the standby credits were part of the business of banking under the NBA even though they resemble insurance in some respects, as the district court observed.... Unlike the NBA, however, the BHCA specifically provides that bank holding companies cannot acquire nonbank companies that provide insurance. 12 U.S.C. § 1843(c)(8). Whether AMBAC's standby credits constitute insurance under the BHCA therefore requires a different analysis than that employed under the NBA. That analysis must be undertaken by the Board in the first instance.

Although the Comptroller may, in the exercise of his discretion, conclude that the questions under the BHCA are so frivolous that he should not await the Board's judgment, this was not such a case. While we do not decide whether the Comptroller must await the Board's approval whenever a substantial BHCA question is presented, it was inappropriate for the Comptroller to fail to consider that possibility by concluding that there was no substantial BHCA question in this case.

The district court thought the BHCA inapplicable for another reason. It relied on 12 U.S.C. § 1843(c)(5) (1982), which permits a bank holding company to own "shares which are of the kinds and amounts eligible for investment" by national banks under 12 U.S.C. § 24. The Board's regulation provides: "A national bank or its subsidiary may, without the Board's approval . . . , acquire or retain securities on the basis of section 4(c)(5) of the BHC Act in accordance with the regulations of the Comptroller of the Currency." 12 C.F.R. § 225.22 (d)(1) (1988). The Board's contemporaneous explanation of the regulation states that it permits banks to "acquire or retain *subsidiaries*" in accordance with the Comptroller's rules. . . . In the district court's view, "a bank holding company may own through its subsidiaries any operating subsidiary whose activities are deemed permissible under the [NBA] by the Comptroller." . . .

We disagree with this aspect of the district court's otherwise excellent analysis. Section 1843(c)(5) permits bank holding companies to own shares "eligible for *investment*" by national banks under 12 U.S.C. § 24. Section 24 (Seventh) permits a national bank to "purchase for its own account investment securities," defined as "marketable obligations, evidencing indebtedness. . . ." The "investment securities" exception in section 24 simply does not apply to a bank's ownership of the *stock* of an *operating* subsidiary, nor does section 1843(c)(5) exempt such interests from the BHCA. These interests are neither an "investment" nor a "security" as defined in section 24 (Seventh).

This reading of the plain language of the statutes is confirmed by two additional considerations. First, section 24 (Seventh) permits banks to acquire investment securities "under such limitations and restrictions as the Comptroller of the Currency may *by regulation* prescribe" (emphasis added); *see also* 12 C.F.R. § 225.22 (d)(1) (1988) (under section 1843(c)(5), Board permits banks to acquire securities "in accordance with the regulations of the Comptroller"). This clearly refers to the Comptroller's general regulatory classification of debt securities in which banks may invest. *See* 12 C.F.R. Part 1 (1988). It does not apply to the Comptroller's *adjudicative* determination that a particular activity by a bank's subsidiary is permissible under the NBA.

Second, 12 U.S.C. § 1843(a)(2) (1982), prohibits certain bank holding companies from retaining

> direct or indirect ownership or control of any voting shares of any company which is not a bank or a bank holding company or engage in any activities other than (A) those of banking . . . , and (B) those permitted under [§ 1843(c)(8)].

If section 1843(c)(5) permits bank holding companies to acquire a subsidiary engaged in activities approved by the Comptroller, section 1843(a)(2) becomes difficult to understand. A bank holding company could acquire a non-bank subsidiary of a bank, but would be prohibited from retaining it if subject to section 1843(a)(2). This irrational result would be avoided if section 1843(c)(5) were read as overriding section 1843(a)(2), but then all of section 1843(c), including 1843(c)(8), necessarily would override section 1843(a) (2). The specific reference in section 1843(a)(2) to section 1843(c)(8) would be surplusage;

Congress would not have mentioned only section 1843(c)(8) if it intended subsection (c)(5) and (c)(8) to be treated identically.

We recognize that the Board interpreted its regulation implementing section 1843(c)(5) as permitting a national bank subsidiary of a holding company to acquire subsidiaries in accordance with the Comptroller's rules. . . . As this interpretation conflicts with the plain meaning of the BHCA, however, we decline to enforce it. . . .

The upshot is that Citicorp must obtain Board approval under 12 U.S.C. § 1843(c)(8). The Comptroller did not consider what effect the applicability of the BHCA would have on his decision because he mistakenly thought the BHCA did not apply. Accordingly, we direct the district court to return the case to the Comptroller for further action consistent with this opinion.

III. Conclusion

The judgment of the district court upholding the Comptroller's action under the National Bank Act is affirmed. The judgment as to the Bank Holding Company Act is reversed and remanded for further action consistent with our opinion.

On Petitions for Rehearing

PER CURIAM.

On August 23, 1988, this panel issued its decision ("Initial Decision"). On October 24, 1988, the panel granted the petitions for rehearing filed by appellees (the Comptroller of the Currency, the United States, and Citibank) on two questions:

1. Was it appropriate for this court to address the Comptroller of the Currency's interpretation of the Bank Holding Company Act?

2. Did Citibank's acquisition of the American Municipal Bond Assurance Corporation require the prior approval of the Federal Reserve Board under section 4(c)(8) of the Bank Holding Company Act, 12 U.S.C. § 1843(c)(8)? . . .

In Part II.B. of our Initial Decision, we held that the Comptroller had properly found that Citibank's acquisition of AMBAC was authorized under the NBA. In Part II.C., however, we ruled that the Comptroller had erred in construing the BHCA as permitting the establishment of the municipal bond insurance subsidiary.

On reviewing the supplemental briefs submitted by the parties, we now conclude that it was inappropriate for us to have reached the latter question. Although the Comptroller concluded, inter alia, that section 4(c)(8) of the BHCA, 12 U.S.C. § 1843(c)(8), did not prohibit Citibank's acquisition of AMBAC, that finding was not essential to his determination that the acquisition was permitted by the NBA. Furthermore, because the Comptroller's jurisdiction arises under the NBA rather than the BHCA, his interpretation of the latter statute is without precedential effect and will not prevent the AIA from petitioning the Board for a ruling on the propriety of the acquisition. Indeed, Congress has granted the Board initial jurisdiction to conduct an administrative hearing to decide BHCA issues, 12 U.S.C. § 1842(b), and has provided for direct judicial review of Board decisions in a court of appeals. *Id.* § 1848.

We recognize that the Comptroller and the Board have overlapping jurisdiction in certain situations. For example, in *Whitney National Bank v. Bank of New Orleans & Trust Co.*, 379 U.S. 411 (1965), the Comptroller preliminarily approved a national bank's proposal to open a new bank as part of a complex holding company transaction that was subject to the Board's final approval under the BHCA, which was granted. Competitor banks sought to enjoin the Comptroller from issuing a certificate chartering the new bank, claiming that a state law enacted after the Board's approval nullified the Board's action. The Supreme Court dismissed the suit against the Comptroller in the district court as improper because the Board had exclusive jurisdiction in the first instance to determine the merits of a BHCA challenge with judicial review only in a court of appeals. . . . The Court noted, however, that "there may be *exceptional circumstances* under which equity may stay the hand of the Comptroller in issuing a certificate to a new bank." *Id.* at 426 n. 7 (emphasis added).

While declining to decide the precise scope of *Whitney*, we conclude that the facts of this case do not present the "exceptional circumstances" that would warrant our reaching the merits of the AIA's contention that the challenged acquisition is prohibited by the BHCA. Accordingly, we affirm Part II.B. of our Initial Decision and vacate Part II.C.

3. Home Owners' Loan Act

Notes and Comments 6.23. Holding companies of savings and loan associations are subject to federal regulation under the savings and loan holding company provisions of the Home Owners' Loan Act (HOLA), 12 U.S.C. § 1467a. How do these provisions compare with the corresponding provisions of the BHCA? Consider the following excerpt.

Michael P. Malloy, Principles of Bank Regulation

§ 6.6 (3d ed., West, 2011)

The savings and loan holding company provisions of the [HOLA][1] generally parallel the [BHCA] provisions, although there are some significant differences. Figure 6-5, *infra*, gives a schematic comparison of the two sets of provisions.

Figure 6-5
Holding Company Activities: BHCA and HOLA

Provision	*BHCA Section*	*HOLA Section*
General prohibition on non-banking/non-S&L activities	§ 1843(a)	§ 1467a(c)(1), (4)
Treatment of share certificates	§ 1843(b)	
Exceptions	§ 1843(c)	§ 1467a(c)(2)
Special organizations	§ 1843(c)(i)	[§ 1467a(c)(2)(F), (4)]
Family companies	§ 1843(c)(ii)	[§ 1467a(c)(2)(F), (4)]
Special services	§ 1843(c)(1)	§ 1467a(c)(2)(A), (C), (D), (F), (4)
Debt previously contracted	§ 1843(c)(2)	§ 1467a(c)(2)(F), (4)
Divesting subsidiaries	§1843(c)(3)	§1467a(c)(2)(C), (F), (4)

1. 12 U.S.C. § 1467a.

Fiduciary activities	§ 1843(c)(4)	§ 1467a(c)(2)(E), (F), (4)
Investment securities	§ 1843(c)(5)	§ 1467a(c)(2)(F), (4)
Five percent holdings	§ 1843(c)(6)	§ 1467a(c)(2)(F), (4)
Diversified investment company	§ 1843(c)(7)	§ 1467a(c)(2)(F), (4)
Closely related activities	§ 1843(c)(8)	§ 1467a(c)(2)(B), (F), (4)
Foreign corporation	§ 1843(c)(9)	§ 1467a(c)(2)(F), (4)
Grandfathered bank subsidiary	§ 1843(c)(10)	[§ 1467a(c)(2)(F), (4)]
Grandfathered 1970 activities	§ 1843(c)(11)	[§ 1467a(c)(2)(F), (4)]
Transition for 1970 companies	§ 1843(c)(12)	[§ 1467a(c)(2)(F), (4)]
Foreign-based company activities	§ 1843(c)(13)	§ 1467a(c)(2)(F), (4), (7)
Export trading company	§ 1843(c)(14)	§ 1467a(c)(2)(F), (4)
Financial holding company	§ 1843(k)-(o)	[2]
unitary holding companies		§ 1467a(c)(3)(A)
qualified thrift lender holding companies		§ 1467a(c)(3)(B)
bank holding companies		§ 1467a(c)(8), (t)
Grace period for compliance		§ 1467a(c)(5)
Special provisions for 1987 amendments		§ 1467a(c)(6)

2. In a memorandum publicly released on 15 May 2001, the OTS Chief Counsel has taken the position that multiple SLHCs had authority to engage in activities that are permissible for FHCs. *FHC Activities Allowed for Thrift Firms, Federal Savings and Loan Regulator Says*, BNA Banking Daily, May 16, 2001, at d4. The text of the OTS document is available online at http://www.ots.treas.gov/docs/56102.pdf. Arguably, the authority is to be found in HOLA § 10(c), 12 U.S.C.A. § 1467a(c), as amended by the GLBA. The OTS has since proposed amendments to its regulation to authorize certain S & L holding companies to engage in financial activities post-GLBA. 66 Fed. Reg. 56,488 (2001) (to be codified at 12 C.F.R. §§ 584.1-584.2a, 584.100, 584.110, 584.120, 584.130).

Judicial review	§ 1848	§ 1467a(j)
Mutual holding companies		§ 1467a(o)(5), (6)

One important structural difference is that the HOLA incorporates by reference activities approved by the Fed for bank holding companies.[3] These activities are authorized for savings and loan holding companies unless the [OTS, and after July 2011 the Fed] prohibits or limits such an activity by regulation for savings and loan holding companies.[4] However, BHCA-authorized activities still require the prior approval of the OTS.[5]

In reviewing an application for approval of such activities, the [regulator] is required to consider the following statutory factors: (1) Whether the performance of the activity described in the application by the company or the subsidiary can reasonably be expected to produce benefits to the public (such as greater convenience, increased competition, or gains in efficiency) that outweigh possible adverse effects of such activity (such as undue concentration of resources, decreased or unfair competition, conflicts of interest, or unsound financial practices).[6] (ii) The managerial resources of the companies involved.[7] (3) Finally, the adequacy of the financial resources, including capital, of the companies involved.[8]

Unlike the situation under the BHCA, the HOLA exempts from regulation the non-savings association activities of any holding company that controls only one savings association.[9] This exemption is available so long as the savings association subsidiary is a "qualified thrift lender"[10]–in effect, an association specializing to a significant degree in traditional savings association activities of home mortgage lending and savings deposits.[11] However, in 1999 the Gramm-Leach-Bliley Act ("GLBA")[12] prohibited *new* unitary savings and loan holding companies from engaging in nonfinancial activities or affiliating with nonfinancial entities.[13] The prohibition applies to a company that becomes a unitary savings and loan holding company pursuant to an application filed with the OTS after 4 May 1999[,][14] [or, after July 21 2011, the Fed]. A grandfathered unitary thrift holding company retains its authority to engage in nonfinancial activities.[15] In addition, the prohibition does not apply to corporate reorganizations.[16]

---

3. [12 U.S.C.] § 1467a(c)(2)(F)(i).

4. *Id.*

5. *Id.* § 1467a(b)(4)(A).

6. *Id.* § 1467a(c)(4)(B)(i).

7. *Id.* § 1467a(c)(4)(B)(ii).

8. *Id.* § 1467a(c)(4)(B)(iii).

9. 12 U.S.C. § 1467a(c)(3)(A).

10. *Id.*

11. *See id.* § 1467a(m) (establishing qualified thrift lender test).

12. Pub. L. No. 106-102, Nov. 12, 1999, 113 Stat. 1338 (1999) (codified at scattered sections of 12, 15, 16, 18 U.S.C.A.).

13. GLBA, § 401(a) (codified at 12 U.S.C.A. § 1467a(c)(9)).

14. 12 U.S.C.A. § 1467a(c)(9)(A).

15. *Id.* § 1467a(c)(9)(C).

16. *Id.* § 1467a(c)(9)(D).

An exemption from the application requirement is also available for a holding company controlling more than one savings association, on the following conditions.[17] (1) All or all but one of the savings association subsidiaries must have been acquired initially by the holding company, or an individual controlling the company, either in an FDIC-assisted transaction,[18] an emergency acquisition,[19] or an FSLIC-approved acquisition;[20] or in an acquisition in which capital assistance to the savings association was continued under the FDIA.[21] (2) All of the savings association subsidiaries must be qualified thrift lenders.[22]

One final set of differences between the BHCA and HOLA provisions concerns the applicability of HOLA to certain entities. First, upon application, a savings bank or cooperative bank[23] may be treated as a savings association for purposes of the holding company provisions of the HOLA, if the [regulator] determines that the bank is a qualified thrift lender.[24] Second, a bank holding company subject to the BHCA, or a company controlled by such a bank holding company, is exempt from the HOLA provisions.[25]

4. State Law

Notes and Comments 6.24. Forth Corp is the holding company of a *national* bank. Does this mean that Forth Corp is not subject to state regulation? If Forth Corp's banking subsidiary were a state chartered bank, would Forth Corp nevertheless escape direct regulation by the chartering state, since the holding company is fully subject to the federal BHCA? *See* 12 U.S.C. § 1846(a). *See also Security Nat. Bank & Trust Co. v. First W. Va. Bancorp., Inc.*, 277 S.E.2d 613 (W.Va. 1981), *appeal dismissed*, 454 U.S. 1131 (1982) (finding state authority not preempted).

6.25. Could a state be more restrictive, as to formation or activities of bank holding companies, than the Fed is under the BHCA? *Cf., e.g., Commercial Nat. Bank of Little Rock v. Board of Governors*, 451 F.2d 86 (8th Cir. 1971) (finding state free to prohibit formation of bank holding companies).

---

17. *Id.* § 1467a(c)(3)(B).

18. *Id.* § 1823(c) (providing for FDIC "open bank" assistance).

19. *Id.* § 1823(k) (providing for FDIC-approved emergency acquisitions).

20. *Id.* § 1467a(c)(3)(B)(i)(I). *See* 12 U.S.C. § 1730a(m) (1988) (providing since repealed emergency acquisitions for now abolished FSLIC).

21. 12 U.S.C. § 1467a(c)(3)(B)(i)(II). *See id.* § 1823(i) (concerning purchase of "net worth certificates" from troubled depository institution by FDIC as support for institution's capital position).

22. *Id.* § 1467a(c)(3)(B)(ii).

23. *See id.* § 1813(h) (defining "cooperative bank").

24. *Id.* § 1467a(*l*)(1). However, failure to maintain qualified thrift lender status will disqualify the bank for treatment as such a lender (and, hence, as a savings association for these purposes) for a period of five years. *Id.* § 1467a(*l*)(2).

25. *Id.* § 1467a(t).

Chapter 7

Securities Regulation

1. Introduction

Aside from regulatory restrictions on securities activities,[1] banks and other depository institutions are also subject to securities regulation, like other issuers and traders in securities. However, as issuers, they are not fully subject to federal regulations generally applicable to the issuance of securities, 15 U.S.C. §§ 77a *et seq.*[2] Until 1964, much the same could be said for generally applicable federal regulations governing periodic disclosure and trading in securities in the secondary market.[3] Since 1964, banks and savings associations with publicly traded securities are subject to the requirements of the Securities Exchange Act of 1934 (1934 Act), but these requirements are administered in their case *not* by the Securities and Exchange Commission (SEC), but by their respective primary federal regulators.[4]

Depository institutions may also be securities market professionals, entities that underwrite, purchase, sell and otherwise deal in securities in the securities markets, subject to the limits of the Glass-Steagall Act.[5] However, before 1999 banks acting as market professionals were rarely subject to SEC supervision of their activities in that capacity.[6]

This chapter will try to make sense of the peculiar version of securities regulation that applies to depository institutions. You should keep in mind, however, that to some

---

1. *See supra* Chapter 5, § 9 (discussing securities activities of financial institutions); *id.* § 10 (discussing regulation of activities "financial in nature").

2. *See* 12 U.S.C. § 77c(a)(2), (5) (exempting bank- and thrift-issued securities from registration requirements of Securities Act of 1933).

3. *See* 2 MICHAEL P. MALLOY, BANKING LAW AND REGULATION § 8.02[A] (2d ed., Aspen Publishers, 2011) (discussing pre-1964 scope of Securities Exchange Act of 1934, 15 U.S.C. §§ 78a *et seq.*).

4. 15 U.S.C. § 78*l*(i).

5. *See supra* Chapter 5, § 9 (discussing Glass-Steagall limitations).

6. Under the Gramm-Leach-Bliley Act, Pub. L. No. 106-102, Nov. 12, 1999, 113 Stat. 1338 (1999) (codified at scattered sections of 12, 15, 16, 18 U.S.C.) (GLBA), securities activities of banks generally are to supervised by federal and state securities regulators, not bank regulators. GLBA, §§ 201-202 (codified at 15 U.S.C. § 78c(a)(4)-(5)). *See also id.*, §§ 221(a) (codified at 15 U.S.C. § 77c(a)(2)) (treatment of bank common trust funds under Securities Act of 1933); 221(b) (codified at 15 U.S.C. § 78c(a)(12)(A)(iii)) (treatment under Securities Exchange Act).

degree the securities regulation regime that applies to depository institution defies logical explanation.[7] It has also been significantly modified under the 1999 Gramm-Leach-Bliley Act (GLBA).[8]

Issuance of securities in a public offering, involving the use of interstate instrumentalities, normally is subject to regulation by the Securities and Exchange Commission under the Securities Act of 1933 (1933 Act), 15 U.S.C. §§ 77a *et seq*. However, bank- and thrift-issued securities are exempt from the registration requirements of the 1933 Act. *Id.* § 77c(a)(2), (5).

Section 3(a)(2) of the 1933 Act exempts any security issued by a "bank" from the registration requirements of the Act.[9] Section 3(a)(5) exempts any security issued by a savings and loan association, building and loan association, cooperative bank, homestead association or similar thrift institution.[10] The reason for these exemptions seems to be that Congress assumed that depository institutions would be adequately supervised by their primary federal and state regulators, making application of the 1933 Act requirements unnecessary.[11]

Notes and Comments 7.1. Federal statutes and regulations have created a parallel system of securities regulation for issuance and trading of bank and thrift securities in the public market. Taken as a whole, the parallel system that applies to depository institutions is broader than that of the 1933 Act and 1934 Act, and many of its elements are informed primarily by policy concerns peculiar to the depository institutions regulators–namely, maintenance of safety and soundness of the depository institutions sector, not protection of investors and stability of the securities markets. With these institutional priorities, can the depository institutions regulators be effective securities regulators?

2. Securities Disclosure Requirements

Notes and Comments 7.2. The first element of this parallel system is in fact concerned with adequate public disclosure with respect to bank- and thrift-issued securities. As to the issuance of securities to the public, this parallel system is, in most respects, almost identical to the SEC's regulations under the 1933 Act. *Compare, e.g.*, 17 C.F.R. pt. 230 (SEC 1933 Act regulations) *with* 12 C.F.R. pts. 16 (OCC securities disclosure regulations), 563g (OTS securities disclosure regulations). To the extent these sets of regulation are identical–so

---

7. *See, e.g.*, Michael P. Malloy, *The 12(i)'ed Monster: Administration of the Securities Exchange Act of 1934 by the Federal Bank Regulatory Agencies*, 19 HOFSTRA L. REV. 269 (1991) (criticizing bank regulators' administration of 1934 Act).

8. *Supra* note 6. For discussion of the effects of the GLBA, see § 6, *infra*. *See also* Note 1.60, *supra* (discussing GLBA).

9. "Bank" these purposes means "any national bank, or any banking institution organized under the laws of any State, territory, or the District of Columbia, the business of which is substantially confined to banking and is supervised by the State or territorial banking commission or similar official." *Id.* § 77c(a)(2).

10. *Id.* § 77c(a)(5)(A). An institution must be "supervised and examined by State or Federal authority having supervision over such institution" to qualify for the exemption. *Id.*

11. *See Dougherty v. Carver Fed. Sav. Bank, infra* (discussing exemption). *See also* 2 MICHAEL P. MALLOY, BANKING LAW AND REGULATION §§ 7.02[A]-[B] (2d ed., Aspen Publishers, 2011) (discussing exemption and legislative history of 1933 Act).

that as a practical matter issuers subject to each are subject to the same disclosure requirements–what is the point of exempting bank- and thrift-issued securities from the 1933 Act?

7.3. Initial securities disclosure requirements under the depository institutions regulatory system can be illustrated by the regulations of the Comptroller of the Currency. As regulator of national banks, the Comptroller has promulgated detailed Securities Offering Disclosure Rules that require material disclosure in connection with the issuance of securities by national banks. 12 C.F.R. pt. 16. These regulations generally require that any direct or indirect offer or sale by a national bank of any security[12] issued by it be made through the use of an "offering circular" filed with and declared effective by the Comptroller. *Id.* § 16.3(a). Like the 1933 Act regulations applicable to non-bank issuers, *see* 15 U.S.C. § 77e, the offering circular requirements contemplate three separate stages in the process leading to distribution of securities: (*i*) prior to filing the circular, offers and sales are prohibited, *compare* 12 C.F.R. § 16.3(a)-(b) *with* 15 U.S.C. § 77e(a), (c); (*ii*) between filing and the effective date of the circular, offers to sell, but not sales, may be made through underwriters, under certain conditions, *compare* 12 C.F.R. § 16.3(b) *with* 15 U.S.C. § 77e(b)(1), (c);[13] and, (*iii*) after the effective date of the offering circular, offers and sales of the securities may generally be made. *Compare* 12 C.F.R. § 16.3(a), (e) *with* 15 U.S.C. § 77e. The effective period of the offering circular is generally six months. 12 C.F.R. § 16.3 (e). The Office of Thrift Supervision ("OTS") has had a corresponding set of regulations[14] requiring material disclosure in the issuance of securities by savings associations subject to its supervision.

7.4. If bank- and thrift-issued securities are exempt from the registration requirements of the 1933 Act, then on what authority did the Comptroller and the OTS impose virtually identical, detailed requirements on depository institutions subject to their supervision? *See* 42 Fed. Reg. 2200 (1977) (promulgating Comptroller regulations, citing 12 U.S.C. § 57 as statutory authority).[15]

7.5. Quarter National Bank (QNB) issued shares of stock to the general public, using the mails and interstate telephone lines. The "offering circular" that it used in soliciting purchasers for its stock contains statements concerning management of its loan portfolio that arguably are materially misleading. When QNB thereafter charges off a substantial amount of loans that have defaulted, some of the purchasers of the securities sue QNB under the antifraud provisions of the 1933 Act, 15 U.S.C. §§ 77*l*, 77q. Since QNB's shares are exempt under 15 U.S.C. § 77c(a)(2), does that mean that it is exempt from suit under the antifraud

---

12. The regulations define "security" to mean:

> any common stock, preferred stock, or other equity security, or right to subscribe to any of the foregoing, or subordinated note or debenture. The term "security" shall not include any deposit loan, participation, letter of credit or other form of bank indebtedness incurred in the ordinary course of business.

12 C.F.R. § 16.2(d).

13. The conditions are as follows: (*i*) prior authorization must be obtained from the Comptroller, 12 C.F.R. § 16.3(b)(1), and an appropriate "preliminary offering circular" can be used, *id.* § 16(b); (*ii*) prior to consummation of the actual sale, a copy of the offering circular as finally effective, must be furnished to each purchaser, *id.* § 16.3(b)(2).

14. 12 C.F.R. pt. 563g (2010). The OTS was replaced by the OCC, the Fed, and the FDIC as to its functions and authority on July 21, 2011. Dodd-Frank Act §312(b) (codified at 12 U.S.C. §5412(b)) (mandating transfer of functions).

15. *See* 2 MICHAEL P. MALLOY, BANKING LAW AND REGULATION § 5.03[B] (2d ed., Aspen Publishers, 2011) (discussing basis of authority).

provisions? *See Dougherty v. Carver Fed. Sav. Bank, infra* (discussing application of antifraud provisions).

7.6. Proposals have been made to eliminate the Comptroller and OTS securities disclosure regulations. (Post-July 2011, the Comptroller has responsibility for federal savings associations.) Does the following excerpt make a convincing case for such proposals?

2 Michael P. Malloy, Banking Law and Regulation

§ 7.04[A] (2d ed., Aspen Publishers, 2011)[a]

. . . What is particularly noteworthy about [the OCC and OTS regulations] is the degree to which they resemble, and in many respects directly incorporate, the coordinate provisions of the regulations promulgated by the Securities and Exchange Commission ("SEC") under the Securities Act of 1933 ("1933 Act"). . . .

. . . [S]ecurities disclosure would appear to be "an area of unnecessary duplication of government resources."[1] In an effort to promote more consistent functional regulation of financial services generally and to streamline unnecessary regulatory controls, . . . the Task Group [on Regulation of Financial Services] made the recommendation that "[t]he registration requirements of the [1933 Act] should be made applicable to publicly offered securities of banks and thrifts (but not deposit instruments)."[2] However, the Task Group would allow the FHLBB [*i.e.*, Federal Home Loan Bank Board, predecessor to OTS] to continue to exercise securities jurisdiction over the conversion of S&L's and federal savings banks from mutual to stock form of organization.[3] In addition, the Task Group would leave such jurisdiction with the FHLBB with respect to "other matters involving the safety and soundness of [FSLIC-]insured [thrift] thrift institutions or affecting the operations of the [FSLIC]."[4]

The Task Group offered no cogent reason why it would split off securities jurisdiction for conversions. As to the retention of this jurisdiction by the FHLBB with respect to safety and soundness matters and FSLIC operations, the Task Group argued as follows:

> The issuance of securities by thrift institutions sometimes differs from securities offerings by other financial institutions because of the unique mortgage-related nature of many types of thrift securities. For example, thrifts issue a variety of securities that represent interests in pools of mortgages, or that are collateralized by mortgages. Thrifts also have developed other debt and equity financing techniques that use mortgage-related securities that have been obtained in exchange for mortgages in their portfolio.
>
> While other types of firms issue mortgage- backed securities that are registered with the SEC under the 1933 Act, such issuances by thrifts are unique because the mortgages backing such securities issued by thrifts may directly affect the assets available to the FSLIC in the event of insolvency or have other direct impacts on safety and soundness. Therefore, the FHLBB should have authority to

---

a. Reprinted with permission. Footnotes have been renumbered.

1. *Report of the Task Group on Regulation of Financial Services* 93 (1984) (hereinafter "*Task Group Report*").

2. *Task Group Report* at 91. In light of the Supreme Court's holding in *Marine Bank v. Weaver*, 455 U.S. 551 (1982), that a bank-issued certificate of deposit was not a "security" for purposes of the Securities Exchange Act of 1934, 15 U.S.C. §§ 78a *et seq.*, it seems doubtful whether the parenthetical limitation in the quoted text is necessary. . . .

3. *Task Group Report* at 91. . . .

4. [*Id.*]

limit securities offerings by thrift institutions that would adversely affect thrift safety and soundness or the FSLIC [insurance] fund.[5]

This purported distinction between thrifts and other issuers seems rather thin. Realignment of securities disclosure regulation under the administration of the SEC need not have any impact upon thrift regulatory considerations such as safety and soundness and the integrity of the FSLIC's deposit insurance fund. Indeed, since securities regulation is disclosure-oriented, not primarily substantive, it appears to be a weak argument to assert that the FHLBB needs to retain disclosure regulation authority in order to "to limit [certain] securities offerings by thrift institutions." Such direct authority does not exist under the federal securities laws; it remains with the regulator of the substantive activities of the depository institution in question.

Notes and Comments 7.7. Prior to 1964, most depository institutions were not subject to the *periodic* disclosure rules of 1934 Act, though they were subject to the antifraud prohibitions administered by the SEC. Until 1964, the 1934 Act did not cover over-the-counter securities (*i.e.*, securities not listed on a national securities exchange) except for the antifraud provisions of Section 10(b), 15 U.S.C. § 78j(b), which covers all securities, whether listed or not. As a matter of fact, most if not all bank-issued securities fell into this over-the-counter category, and hence they were not generally subject to the 1934 Act. Based on a special study performed by the SEC,[16] Congress decided to bring over-the-counter securities–and specifically, bank-issued securities–under the 1934 Act. *See* 15 U.S.C. § 78*l*(g). The bank regulators resisted this change in the law.[17] Their efforts were unsuccessful, but the bank regulators did extract one concession: they were granted administrative authority over the 1934 Act provisions that applied to depository institutions, with one important exception. With respect to bank- and thrift-issued securities, the registration[18] reporting,[19] proxy[20] and insider reporting provisions[21] of the 1934 Act are administered by the bank regulatory agencies, not by the Commission.[22] Section 12(i) of the Act, also added in 1964, contains a statutory mandate to the bank regulatory agencies to issue regulations substantially similar to those issued by the Commission, under Section 12, 13, 14(a), 14(c), 14(d), 14(f) and 16, unless such regulations would not be "necessary or appropriate in the public interest or for the protection of investors," within 60 days of any amendments to pertinent Commission

5. *Id.* at 93.

16. REPORT OF THE SPECIAL STUDY OF THE SECURITIES MARKETS OF THE SECURITIES AND EXCHANGE COMMISSION, H.R. Doc. No., 95, 88th Cong., 1st Sess. (1963).

17. *See, e.g., Letter from the Federal Reserve Board to the Chairman, House Interstate and Foreign Commerce Committee*, June 21, 1963, reprinted in H.R. Rep. No. 1418, 88th Cong., 1st Sess. (1963). *See also Report on Bank Securities Activities of the Securities and Exchange Commission*, 95th Cong., 1st Sess. 307-8 (1977).

18. 15 U.S.C. § 78*l*.

19. *Id.* § 78m.

20. *Id.* § 78n.

21. *Id.* § 78p.

22. *Id.* § 78*l*(i). *See* Michael P. Malloy, *The 12(i)'ed Monster: Administration of the Securities Exchange Act of 1934 by the Federal Bank Regulatory Agencies*, 19 HOFSTRA L. REV. 269 (1991) (discussing § 78*l*(i) and its implementation by depository institution regulators).

rules.[23] Despite this statutory mandate, by the end of the 1980s, the regulatory agencies were generally at least one year, and often as much as seven years, behind in adopting appropriate analogs to Commission amendments, with one longstanding exception: the FHLBB (and, since 1989, its successor the OTS), whose 1934 Act regulations simply incorporated by reference the SEC regulations.[24] Neither the FHLBB nor the OTS ever had occasion to amend this section. In 1988, the Fed followed the FHLBB's lead, and converted to an incorporation-by-reference approach as well.[25] The Fed was later joined by the OCC,[26] and, in February 1997, by the FDIC.[27]

7.8. If the federal regulators are simply incorporating SEC 1934 Act rules into their own regulations, what is the point of delegating authority to them under 15 U.S.C. § 78*l*(i)? The SEC administers the 1934 Act with respect to bank and savings and loan holding companies. Could it not do the same directly with respect to banks and savings associations?

7.9. Quarter National Bank (QNB) is a publicly traded banking corporation. With what agency must it file its periodic reports under 15 U.S.C. § 78m? What if QNB was a state-chartered bank? What if Quarter was Quarter Bank Holding Corp.? *See* 12 U.S.C. § 78*l*(i).

7.10. QNB's annual report contained statements that may have been materially inaccurate. Certain members of QNB's board of directors, knowing that the report will be corrected shortly and that the market price of QNB common stock will decline in value when the correction is made public, sell off a substantial amount of their holdings of QNB common stock. What agency has the authority to bring action against the directors for violations of 15 U.S.C. § 78j(b)? Does 12 U.S.C. § 1818(b)(1) have any bearing on this issue? *Cf. Peoples Bank of Danville v. Williams*, 449 F. Supp. 254 (W.D.Va. 1978).

7.11. *The Sarbanes-Oxley Act.* On 30 July 2002, President Bush signed into law the Sarbanes-Oxley Act of 2002 (Sarbanes-Oxley).[28] Largely in response to the corporate accounting scandals that erupted during late 2001,[29] titles III and IV of Sarbanes-Oxley include a number of provisions designed to improve the corporate governance and financial disclosures of issuers that have a class of securities registered under sections 12(b) or 12(g) of the 1934 Act,[30] or that are required to file periodic reports with the SEC under section 15(d)[31] of the act. Sarbanes-Oxley also amended section 12(i) of the 1934 Act to vest the banking agencies with authority to administer and enforce Sarbanes-Oxley §§ 302-304, 306(a), 401(b), 404 and 406-407, as well as 1934 Act § 10A(m) (added by Sarbanes-Oxley § 301), with respect to insured banks and savings associations registered under the 1934 Act.[32] The Fed's implementing regulations are illustrative. In September 2002, the Fed

---

23. 15 U.S.C. § 78*l*(i).

24. 12 C.F.R. § 563d.1.

25. *See id.* § 208.16.

26. *See id.* pt 11 (incorporating SEC 1934 Act rules into OCC rules).

27. *See* 62 Fed. Reg. 6852 (1997) (codified at 12 C.F.R. pt. 335) (incorporating SEC 1934 Act rules into FDIC rules).

28. Pub. L. 102-204, 116 Stat. 745 (2002).

29. For background on the scandals, see *Special Report Enron: One Year On*, THE ECONOMIST, Nov. 30, 2002, at 59.

30. 15 U.S.C. § 78*l*(a), (g).

31. *Id.* § 78o(d).

32. As of December 2002, seventeen state member banks had a class of securities registered under section 12(b) or 12(g) of the Exchange Act. 68 Fed. Reg. 4092, 4093 n. 1 (2003).

adopted an interim rule amending 12 C.F.R. § 208.36(a) to implement the revisions made by Sarbanes-Oxley to 1934 Act § 12(i).[33] On January 28, 2003, the Fed published an identical final rule.[34] The rule is effective as of April 1, 2003.[35] As required by § 12(i), the final rule provides that the Fed will administer and enforce the Sarbanes-Oxley provisions with respect to registered member banks. The final rule also generally requires registered member banks to comply with any rules, regulations and forms adopted by the SEC to implement the Sarbanes-Oxley sections, unless such rules, regulations or forms are modified by the Fed. If the SEC rules require the filing of any documents with the SEC, registered member banks must file such documents with the Fed, rather than the SEC, in accordance with § 208.36.

3. Minimum Capital Requirements

Notes and Comments 7.12. The second element of securities regulation affecting depository institutions is concerned with minimum capital requirements for entry into the industry. Until 2001, national banks were required to be organized with no less than a statutorily required amount of capital,[36] but now minimum capital requirements for formation are found only in the OCC regulations. Assume that a group of investors seek to organize a new national bank in San Francisco. What would be the minimum capital required for approval of this proposal? *See* 12 C.F.R. § 5.20(f)(2)(i)(C), (h)(4) (pages 90, 92, *supra*).

7.13. The Fed also imposes minimum capital requirements for Fed membership.[37] To be eligible for membership, state-chartered banks must possess capital and surplus adequate for their assets and deposit liabilities and other obligations. 12 C.F.R. pt. 208. Similarly, for state-chartered banks to be eligible for deposit insurance, adequacy of capital is also a requirement. 12 U.S.C. § 1816.

4. Regulation of Capital Formation ("Merit Review")

Notes and Comments 7.14. The third element of securities regulation in the depository institutions system is the regulation of capital formation itself. Capital formation by a depository institution is subject to prior approval by its chartering authority, on the merits of the proposed securities offering, quite apart from any applicable public disclosure

33. 67 Fed. Reg. 57,938 (2002) (codified at 12 C.F.R. § 208.36(a)) (Fed interim final rule modifying regulations implementing 1934 Act § 12(i) to reflect Sarbanes-Oxley Act amendments to § 12(i)). The Fed also issued supervisory guidance designed to assist registered member banks and other public banking organizations supervised by the Fed in understanding and complying with the requirements of Sarbanes-Oxley. *See The Sarbanes-Oxley Act of 2002*, SR Letter 02-20 (Oct. 29, 2002).

34. 68 Fed. Reg. 4092 (2003) (codified at 12 C.F.R. § 208.36(a)).

35. *Id.* at 4092.

36. 12 U.S.C. § 51, *repealed*, American Homeownership and Economic Opportunity Act of 2000, Pub. L. No. 106-569, § 1233(c), 114 Stat. 2944 (2000).

37. *See Continental Bank & Trust Co. of Salt Lake City v. Woodall*, 239 F.2d 707 (10th Cir. 1957), *cert. denied*, 353 U.S. 909 (1957) (upholding Fed membership requirements).

requirements imposed in connection with the issuance of the securities. The practices of agencies vary. In the case of national banks, for example, the Comptroller's regulations require substantive approval of securities issuances by national banks. *See, e.g.*, 12 C.F.R. §§ 5.46, 5.47 (providing for approval of changes in permanent capital; subordinated debt).

7.15. What is the relationship between securities disclosure requirements and capital formation requirements? Capital formation requires approval of the proposed issuance on the merits. What, then, are we to make of the provision in the Comptroller's offering circular rules requiring that the circular include a boldface disclaimer to the effect that

> **THE MERITS OF THESE SECURITIES HAVE NOT BEEN PASSED UPON BY THE COMPTROLLER OF THE CURRENCY. . . .**

12 C.F.R. § 16.7(c), Item 1(d). In this regard, consider the following case.

Dougherty v. Carver Fed. Sav. Bank

112 F.3d 613 (2d Cir. 1997)

CARDAMONE, Circuit Judge.

This appeal arises out of the conversion by defendant Carver Federal Savings Bank (Carver or Bank) from the mutual to the stock form of ownership in the fall of 1994.[a] In connection with that transaction, Carver issued 2,314,375 shares of common stock to investors at a price of $10 per share. Plaintiffs . . . each subscribed for and purchased Carver stock . . . , only to see the stock lose a substantial portion of its value in the first week of public trading. Plaintiffs then brought separate securities fraud class actions . . . alleging that the offering circular used by Carver to sell its stock contained material misstatements and omissions in violation of federal and state securities laws. Because the Office of Thrift Supervision (OTS) approved Carver's application to convert to stock form, the district court, relying on 12 U.S.C. § 1464(i)(2)(B), which designates the Court of Appeals as the exclusive forum for judicial review of final OTS conversion approvals, dismissed the plaintiffs' claims for lack of subject matter jurisdiction. . . . OTS approval of Carver's conversion from mutual form to stock form did not decide the issues raised by plaintiffs' securities fraud claims. Hence, we reverse. . . .

In early 1994, defendant Carver was one of the largest African-American owned financial institutions in the United States, but had not yet converted from mutual to stock form. Although the mutual form of ownership has certain advantages–among other things, it offers near-complete takeover protection–Carver, like many other mutual banks, decided to convert to stock form to raise capital by selling its stock to investors. Converting to stock form allows a savings bank to operate in a more traditional manner, provides the capital necessary to acquire branches more readily and strengthens the bank's ability to recruit and retain quality managers using stock-based incentives such as employee stock option plans. . . .

As a federally-chartered savings bank, Carver could not convert from mutual to stock form without securing the prior written approval of the OTS. Under the OTS regulations in effect in 1994, a mutual savings association seeking such approval was required to submit an application to the OTS containing the formal written plan of conversion, a draft proxy statement, a preliminary form of the offering circular to be used to sell the stock issued

---

a. On conversions, see *supra* Chapter 2, § 4.

upon conversion, and information relating to the valuation of the stock to be issued. *See* 12 C.F.R. § 563b.100 (1994) (conversion application). To assist in the valuation of the stock, OTS regulations further required the bank to obtain an appraisal of the bank's market value, prepared by "persons independent of the applicant." § 563b.7(f). On June 21, 1994 Carver's Board of Directors unanimously approved a plan of conversion.To assist in implementing the plan, the Bank hired defendant Capital Resources, Inc. as "financial consultant and sales agent."

In July 1994 Carver submitted its conversion application to the OTS, which subsequently advised Carver to publish a notice of the filing. . . . The application thus submitted, OTS began its review of the matter and could either approve or reject the plan. This determination is made in a non-judicial capacity–the regulations make no provision for an evidentiary hearing, or any other opportunity to present witnesses. If the plan were approved, the bank would then make a subscription offering to members of the association, selling any securities remaining to the public in the community and then elsewhere. . . .

In anticipation of the eventual subscription offering, Carver prepared an offering circular relating to the stock that would be sold under the conversion. Under OTS regulations, the capital stock issued upon a conversion cannot be issued and sold "except by means of a final offering circular . . . declared effective by the [OTS]." . . . As a savings association, Carver was exempt from the registration requirements of the Securities Act of 1933, and thus was not required to register its capital stock with the Securities and Exchange Commission. . . .

[Carver used Capital Resources Group, an affiliate of its underwriter Capital Resources, to prepare the appraisal of estimated market value of the stock to be issued in the conversion. Under current OTS regulations, this practice is generally not permitted, but it was permitted under regulations in effect at the time of the appraisal. *Compare* 12 C.F.R. § 563b.7(f)(2) (1996) (affiliate of an appraiser generally not permitted to act as underwriter or selling agent) *with* 12 C.F.R. § 563b.7(f)(2) (1994) (practice permitted). Carver's offering circular did not disclose the relationship between the underwriter and the appraiser. Instead, the offering circular referred to Carver's appraiser as "independent," and it advised potential investors that the aggregate offering price of Carver's stock would be based on an "independent appraisal."]

On August 12, 1994 the OTS approved the conversion application, and on August 15, 1994 it cleared Carver's offering circular. . . . Carver distributed the offering circular to its members and received a strong response. At the close of the subscription period on September 22, 1994, the offering was oversubscribed. Thereafter, . . . Capital Resources Group performed an updated appraisal. That appraisal, dated September 23, 1994, increased the estimated pro forma market value to the maximum amount possible without requiring a resolicitation of subscribers. . . . The updated appraisal was submitted to and approved by the OTS on October 4, 1994. On October 24, 1994 Carver converted to stock form and issued 2,314,375 shares of common stock at $10 per share.

Carver's stock opened for trading on NASDAQ under the symbol "CARV" on October 25, 1994. By the end of the first day of trading, the price had plummeted over 23 percent from the initial $10 price–it closed at $7.66 per share. The stock price continued its downward spiral, and by mid-March 1995, it had fallen to $6.625–nearly 34 percent below its subscription price. . . .

. . . Each of the complaints alleges that the offering circular was misleading in that (1) it represented that the number of shares to be issued in the offering would be based upon an independent valuation, yet it omitted to disclose the nature of Capital Resources Group's affiliation with Capital Resources; (2) it represented that Capital Resources Group's initial appraisal was reliable when in fact defendants knew or should have known that it was not; (3) it represented that the updated appraisal would be increased only if "changing market conditions and other factors" warranted such increase when in fact the defendants knew or should have known that the offering would be increased by 15 percent regardless of market conditions; and (4) it failed to disclose the degree to which the bank was subject to losses in the event of a rise in interest rates due to the percentage of mortgage-backed securities in its portfolio. . . . [I]n addition, [one plaintiff alleged] that certain favored depositors were allowed to rescind their subscription orders despite the representation in the offering circular that such subscriptions once made could not be rescinded. . . .

The defendants moved . . . to dismiss the complaints for lack of subject matter jurisdiction, arguing that the plaintiffs' claims, although couched in terms of securities fraud, were in reality nothing but attacks on the OTS's approval of the conversion application. Because judicial review of OTS conversion decisions may only be obtained in the courts of appeals, the defendants reasoned that the district court could not hear the case.

The district court . . . dismissed the claims for lack of subject matter jurisdiction. . . .

Because of the regulatory controls imposed on savings institutions by banking legislation and the jurisdiction exercised over such institutions by bank regulatory agencies like the OTS, Congress has expressly exempted securities issued by savings and loan banks from registration with the SEC as a condition to their offer and sale under the Securities Act of 1933. . . . Carver was thus not required to register the stock issued in its conversion with the SEC. However, Carver's stock is not exempt from the securities law antifraud provisions, including § 12(2) of the Securities Act, 15 U.S.C. § 77*l*(a)(2), and § 10(b) of the Exchange Act, 15 U.S.C. § 78j(b), and Rule 10b-5, 17 C.F.R. § 240.10b-5. *See Tcherepnin* v. *Knight*, 389 U.S. 332, 340-41 (1967); *see also* §§ 12(2) and 17(c) of the Securities Act, 15 U.S.C. 77l(a)(2), 77q(c) (expressly including these exempted securities within antifraud coverage). Savings association spokesmen appearing before Congress in the 1930s "emphatically endorsed the coverage of [savings] associations under the . . . antifraud provisions," *Tcherepnin*, 389 U.S. at 340, and when it enacted the Exchange Act, Congress intended the antifraud provisions to act as a "shield" to protect savings association investors against "unscrupulous or unqualified promoters," *id.* at 345-46. . . .

[12 U.S.C. § 1464(i)(2)(B)] was not intended to deny investors purchasing stock pursuant to a conversion the protections of the securities laws. The statute does not purport on its face to affect–let alone extinguish–securities fraud claims. Nor have we found anything in the legislative history to suggest that by enacting this provision, Congress sought to relieve converting federal savings associations of the general obligation to offer and sell securities honestly. *See Rembold* v. *Pacific First Fed. Sav. Bank*, 798 F.2d 1307, 1310 (9th Cir.1986) (noting no intent to repeal securities laws protection in legislative history); *see also* 12 U.S.C. § 1467a(k) (conversion provisions not intended to approve any conduct previously prohibited by law). Simply put, OTS approval of a conversion does not lift from the shoulders of the bank, its managers and agents the obligation to conduct the sale of its stock in an honest and straightforward manner so that investors are not mislead. *See Ordower* [v. *Office of Thrift Supervision*, 999 F.2d 1183, 1188 (7th Cir. 1993)].

However, because every conversion involves the preparation of an offering circular and a proxy statement, there is a danger that some litigants seeking review of the OTS decision to approve or disapprove the plan of conversion will recast the allegations in their complaints to assert securities fraud claims in order to circumvent the exclusive review provisions contained in the conversion statute. To prevent this end-run around § 1464(i)(2)(B), other circuits have cautioned trial courts to review carefully the substance of securities fraud causes of action allegedly arising out of a conversion in order to ensure that by means of artful pleading litigants do not obtain prohibited district court review of an OTS conversion approval. *Ordower*, 999 F.2d at 1188 (instructing district court on remand to ensure that securities fraud claims in complaint did not amount to "collateral attack" on decision of the OTS); *Craft v. Florida Fed. Sav. & Loan Ass'n*, 786 F.2d 1546, 1553-54 (11th Cir. 1986) (plaintiffs could not use "bare bones allegations [of securities fraud] made to escape the exclusive review provisions"); *Harr v. Prudential Fed. Sav. & Loan Ass'n*, 557 F.2d 751, 754 (10th Cir. 1977) (litigants could not circumvent exclusive review provisions of statute by putting "a Rule 10b-5 gloss" on their attacks on the agency decision). . . .

. . . [S]ecurities fraud claims alleging misstatements or omissions in offering materials should rarely divest the district court of subject matter jurisdiction under the conversion statute's exclusive review provisions because the OTS does not pass upon the adequacy or accuracy of offering materials when giving its approval. 12 C.F.R. § 563b.7(d) (1994). . . .

. . . To ensure that investors do not misinterpret the order approving the plan of conversion to constitute approval of the adequacy and accuracy of the offering materials, the OTS prohibits issuers from making representations to that effect, 12 C.F.R. § 563b.7(d) (1994), and requires that each offering circular contain on its cover the following disclaimer in capital letters and bold-face type:

> THESE SHARES HAVE NOT BEEN APPROVED OR DISAPPROVED BY THE OFFICE OF THRIFT SUPERVISION NOR HAS SUCH OFFICE PASSED UPON THE ACCURACY OR ADEQUACY OF THIS OFFERING CIRCULAR. ANY REPRESENTATION TO THE CONTRARY IS UNLAWFUL.

12 C.F.R. § 563b.102 Item 3 (1994). Because the agency expressly disclaims any intent to decide whether or not the disclosure contained in an offering circular is adequate or accurate, a district court is ordinarily free to decide those issues without fear of contravening 12 U.S.C. § 1464(i)(2)(B). . . .

Recognizing that it is the responsibility of the investor, not the OTS, to decide whether the stock represents a good investment, the OTS expressly prohibits issuers from representing to investors that the OTS has approved the price of the shares. The OTS does not (and has no authority to) make binding determinations as to whether stock is fairly priced from the investor's point of view. Nor does the OTS pass upon the adequacy or accuracy of the information disclosed in the offering circular. We therefore agree with the [*amicus*] SEC that an investor can allege fraud in a conversion appraisal without running afoul of the exclusive review provisions.

A different result would fail to protect investor interests. First, when it comes to evaluating the price at which the converted institution's stock will be sold, the OTS and investors have different objectives. In conducting its review of the appraisal methodology, the OTS's primary aim is to ensure that the converted institution's stock is not underpriced. . . .

Overvaluing of the stock, rather than undervaluing, is the subscriber's primary concern.

As a practical matter, then, potential investors in the stock issued by a converted institution may be reluctant to rely on the OTS to protect their interests fully. *See* 2 MICHAEL P. MALLOY, BANKING LAW AND REGULATION § 5.3, AT 5.46 (1995) (noting that banking regulators like the OTS focus their primary attention on the "safety and soundness of [depository] institutions rather than . . . adequate disclosure to the investing public.").

Second, requiring an investor defrauded by misrepresentations or omissions relating to an appraisal to seek recourse exclusively under 12 U.S.C. § 1467a(j) would deprive the investor of a meaningful opportunity to pursue a valid securities fraud claim. . . .

Finally, as the SEC notes in its amicus brief, it is doubtful that defrauded investors can discover the existence of fraud in an appraisal within the short time frame provided to seek judicial review of the conversion decision, particularly where, as here, the stock offering does not occur until after that 30-day period has expired. . . .

Because OTS approval does not require an investor to purchase the savings association's stock, the investor is free to make independent decisions as to matters relevant to the investment. Thus, the fact that the OTS, in approving the conversion, may have concluded that the appraiser was sufficiently independent does not mean an investor must reach the same conclusion. Investors are free to make their own determinations as to the independence of conversion appraisers and are entitled to the protections of the securities laws when doing so. The OTS does not make binding determinations with respect to the adequacy of the appraiser's independence from the investor's point of view or the adequacy of the offering circular's disclosure on such matters. Absent such determinations, resolving the issues raised by the plaintiffs' complaint with regard to the appraiser's independence requires no judicial review of an OTS decision, and the district court, which was free to decide the issue, erred in dismissing it.

5. Capital Adequacy

Notes and Comments 7.16. The fourth element of securities regulation under the depository institutions system–and the most recent development–is concerned with supervision of the capital adequacy of existing institutions (usually measured in relation to the assets of the institutions). The regulators have increased their attention to capital adequacy of depository institutions. If inadequate capital maintenance constitutes an "unsafe and unsound practice," the bank regulators have broad statutory authority progressively to define and remedy capital inadequacy.[38] This authority was questioned in *First National Bank of Bellaire v. Comptroller of the Currency*, 697 F.2d 674 (5th Cir. 1983), but the authority was confirmed by congressional action. Pub. L. No. 98-181, tit. IX, S 908, 97 Stat. 1280 (1983) (codified at 12 U.S.C. § 3907). The following material discusses the regulators' use of that authority.

Development of the Basel Methodology[39]

Capital adequacy has long been a concern of bank supervisors worldwide, but it has often been expressed simply as a supervisory concern over insufficient capital to support a bank's operations. If inadequate capital maintenance constitutes an "unsafe and unsound practice," bank supervisors may have broad authority progressively to define and remedy

38. 12 U.S.C. §§ 1818(b)(1), 3907(b). *Cf., e.g., Groos Nat. Bank v. Comptroller of the Currency*, 573 F.2d 889 (5th Cir. 1978); *First Nat. Bank of Eden v. Department of the Treasury*, 568 F.2d 610 (8th Cir. 1978). Similar authority exists in the bank holding company context. *See Board of Governors v. First Lincolnwood Corp.*, 439 U.S. 234 (1978).

39. This material is based upon Michael P. Malloy, *Capital Regulation and International Banking: A Questionable Strategy*, in GREGORY T. PAPANIKOS (ed.), ESSAYS ON THE ECONOMICS OF LAW AND INDUSTRIAL ORGANIZATION 155 (2006).

such problems.[40] By the early 1980s, however, capital maintenance began to be viewed not simply as an enforcement issue but as an ongoing feature of basic bank supervisory policy.

During the period 1982-1988, capital adequacy was gauged using a simple required ratio of capital-to-assets that varied from one nation to the next. (In the United States, this simple ratio was fixed at 6 percent.) This was a crude method; two banks of approximately the same asset size–one embracing risk for access to higher rates of return, the other almost entirely risk-averse–would be subject to the same capital requirement.

To the extent that U.S. supervisors applied capital requirements aggressively, they were placing U.S. banks at a competitive disadvantage in international markets. Competing non-U.S. banks would be subject to widely differing capital requirements, depending upon the policies of their respective home states. Assuming that capital adequacy served a legitimate regulatory purpose, however, U.S. supervisors would be ill advised to ameliorate this competitive disadvantage simply by lowering U.S. capital requirements.

Basel I

By the mid-1980s, U.S. supervisors openly admitted that their rules did not adequately or efficiently promote capital adequacy goals.[41] They began directing their attention to the establishment of a multilateral capital adequacy regime among the United States and its major trading partners, under a new approach that, *within* the capital ratio, would quantify and account for financial factors that significantly affected capital adequacy, but that were not necessarily apparent from the face of the balance sheet.[42] This technical objective was joined to a broader one–reaching multilateral convergence of capital requirements and supervision for banks participating in the international market.

Guidelines for international convergence of capital measurement and capital standards, now known as Basel I, were finalized in 1988 and became fully effective in 1992.[43] Basel I, developed under the auspices of the BIS Committee (formerly the Committee on Banking Supervisory Practices), set forth "the details of the agreed framework for measuring capital adequacy and the minimum standard to be achieved which the national supervisory authorities represented on the Committee intend to implement in their respective countries."[44] The basic focus of this multilateral framework was "assessing capital in relation to credit risk (the risk of counterparty failure)."[45] However, the framework acknowledged that

---

40. *See, e.g.*, 12 U.S.C. §§ 1818(b)(1), 3907(b). *Cf., e.g., Groos Nat. Bank v. Comptroller of the Currency*, 573 F.2d 889 (5th Cir. 1978) (noting "progressive definition" of unsafe and unsound practices under § 1818(b)); *First Nat. Bank of Eden v. Department of the Treasury*, 568 F.2d 610 (8th Cir. 1978). Similar authority exists in the bank holding company context. *See Board of Governors v. First Lincolnwood Corp.*, 439 U.S. 234 (1978).

41. For example, in issuing its 1985 capital adequacy regulations, the Office of the Comptroller or the Currency ("OCC"), the supervisor of U.S. national banks, acknowledged that the minimum capital ratio rules did not rigorously account either for differences in a given bank's balance sheet composition or for the presence of off-balance-sheet activities that contributed to risk. *See* 50 Fed. Reg. 10,207, 10,214 (1985).

42. *See* Michael P. Malloy, *U.S. International Banking and the New Capital Adequacy Requirements: New, Old and Unexpected*, 7 ANN. REV. BANKING L. 75 (1988) (discussing transition from pre-1998 U.S. regulatory practice to multilateral rules).

43. BANK FOR INTERNATIONAL SETTLEMENTS, FINAL REPORT FOR INTERNATIONAL CONVERGENCE OF CAPITAL MEASUREMENT AND CAPITAL STANDARDS, *reprinted in* 4 Fed. Banking L. Rep. (CCH) ¶ 47-105 (Mar. 15, 1996) [hereinafter "Basel I"]. *See* Michael P. Malloy, *Capital Adequacy and Regulatory Objectives*, 25 SUFFOLK TRANSNAT'L L. REV. 299 (2002) (discussing Basel I).

44. Basel I at 51,166.

45. *Id.* at 51,167.

"other risks, notably interest rate risk and the investment risk on securities, need[ed] to be taken into account by supervisors in assessing overall capital adequacy."[46] The framework consisted of a minimum required ratio of specified constituents of capital to *risk-weighted* assets.

Basel I established a relatively simple methodology for risk-weighting, employing only five risk weights.[47] Essentially, the methodology effectively captured only credit risk.[48] It was left to the discretion of individual supervisory authorities to decide whether to attempt to account for more methodologically difficult types of risk, such as investment risk, interest rate risk, exchange rate risk or concentration risk.[49] Furthermore, the individual supervisory authorities also retained discretion to supplement the framework's risk-weighted methodology with "other methods of capital measurement,[50] such as the mandated capital-assets ratios previously established by individual national regulators. Further, to account for country transfer risk, the Committee ultimately adopted an approach that applied differing risk weights to defined groups of countries.[51]

Basel I also recognized the importance of bringing off-balance-sheet risk into the analysis of capital adequacy.[52] All categories of off-balance-sheet risk were brought within the framework, by conversion into appropriate credit risk equivalents.[53] Uncertainty remained about the appropriate approach to items exposed to significant interest-rate and exchange-rate related risk, such as swaps, options and futures.[54] As to these contingencies, the framework took the position that special treatment was necessary, "because banks are not exposed to credit risk for the full face value of their contracts, but only to the cost of replacing the cash flow if the counterparty defaults."[55]

---

46. *Id.*

47. *See id.* at 51,175-51,176, Annex 2 (establishing risk weights by categories of on-balance-sheet asset).

48. *Id.* at 51,169.

49. *Id.* at 51,169-51,170.

50. *Id.* at 51,169.

51. *Id.* at 51,170-51,171:

> [T]he Committee has concluded that a defined group of countries should be adopted as the basis for applying differential weighting coefficients[.] The framework also recognizes the importance of and that this group should be full members of the OECD or countries which have concluded special arrangements with the [International Monetary Fund] associated with the Fund's General Arrangements to Borrow. . . .
>
> . . . This decision has the following consequences for the weighting structure. Claims on central governments within the OECD will attract a zero weight (or a low weight if the national supervisory authority elects to incorporate interest rate risk); and claims on OECD non-central government public-sector entities will attract a low weight. . . . Claims on central governments and central banks outside the OECD will also attract a zero weight (or a low weight if the national supervisory authority elects to incorporate investment risk), provided such claims are denominated in the national currency and funded by liabilities in the same currency. . . .
>
> . . . As regards the treatment of interbank claims, in order to preserve the efficiency and liquidity of the international interbank market[,] there will be no differentiation between short-term claims on banks incorporated within or outside the OECD. However, the Committee draws a distinction between . . . short-term placements with other banks . . . and . . . longer-term cross-border loans to banks which are often associated with particular transactions and carry greater transfer and/or credit risks. A 20 per cent [*sic*] weight will therefore be applied to claims on all banks, wherever incorporated, with a residual maturity of up to an[d] including one year; longer-term claims on OECD incorporated banks will be weighted at 20 per cent [*sic*]; and longer-term claims on banks incorporated outside the OECD will be weighted at 100 percent.

52. *See id.* at 51,171-51,172 (discussing treatment of off-balance-sheet engagements).

53. *See id.* at 51,176, Annex 3 (establishing credit conversion factors for off-balance-sheet items).

54. *See id.* at 51,172.

55. *Id.*

Once the credit equivalent amounts of such contingencies have been calculated, the amounts are to be weighted in accordance with the risk weights applicable to the category of counterparties involved. However, in anticipation of the fact that most counterparties in the market for such contingencies, particularly long-term contracts, "tend to be first-class names,"[56] Basel I reflected general agreement that such contingencies would be assigned a 50 percent risk weight, rather than the 100 percent risk weight that might otherwise be applicable.[57]

The final element in the risk-weighted methodology, as with any capital-assets ratio requirement, was the required minimum level of the ratio. It was generally agreed that specifying a target ratio was desirable before the proposed framework was circulated at the national level for consultation and discussion. After further consultations and study, final agreement was reached, and the framework adopted a target standard ratio of eight percent, of which core capital must constitute at least four percent.[58] This target ratio became fully applicable at year-end 1992.[59]

The Committee continued to refine the details and mechanics of risk management and supervision,[60] an extremely important task. While BIS guidelines are only directly relevant to states that participate in the BIS Committee–namely, the "Group of Ten" large industrialized democracies ("G-10"),[61] plus Luxembourg, Spain, and Switzerland, nevertheless "[i]n many cases, supervisory authorities in non-G-10 countries have seen fit publicly to associate themselves with the Committee's initiatives."[62] Basel I is currently used by supervisors in over 100 countries to determine minimum capital reserves of banks subject to their jurisdiction.[63]

Shortcomings of Basel I

It should be evident, however, that the Basel I methodology exhibited some serious shortcomings. First, the framework recognized only a narrow, though very significant, type of risk–credit risk, *i.e.*, the risk of counterparty failure.[64] Over time, the methodology was

56. *Id.* at 51,178.

57. *Id.* However, some member countries apparently reserved the right to apply the full 100 percent risk weight. *See id.* n. 9.

58. *Id.* at 51,172.

59. *Id.* at 51,172-51,173.

60. *See, e.g.*, 2 MICHAEL P. MALLOY, BANKING LAW AND REGULATION § 7.04[C][4][b] (2d ed., Aspen Publishers, 2011) (discussing refinements of Basel I).

61. Belgium, Canada, France, Germany, Italy, Japan, the Netherlands, Sweden, United Kingdom, and the United States. On the BIS and the G-10, see Michael P. Malloy, *Emerging International Regime of Financial Services Regulation*, 18 TRANSNAT'L LAW. 327 (2005).

62. Bank for International Settlements, *The Basel Committee on Banking Supervision*, available at http://www.bis.org/ bcbs/aboutbcbs.htm.

63. Daniel Pruzin, *Basel Committee Cites Mixed Results for Meeting Proposed Capital Accord*, BNA Int'l Bus. & Fin. Daily, Apr. 24, 2001, at d2.

64. For contrasting discussion of the types of risk relevant to the conduct of the business of banking, see Committee on Banking Supervision, Bank for International Settlements, *Core Principles for Effective Banking Supervision* principles 7-16 (revised version, Oct. 2006), *reprinted in*, MICHAEL P. MALLOY, INTERNATIONAL BANKING: 2010-2011 SUPPLEMENT 266-267 (2010) (hereinafter "CORE PRINCIPLES").

refined to fold in other types of risk, namely, interest-rate, exchange-rate, and market risks.[65] Nevertheless, there was still no calibration within the methodology for internal or "operational" risk–broadly speaking, the risks attendant upon poor management of asset risks–yet surely this type of risk was important for safety and soundness purposes.[66]

Second, the methodology for risk-weighting was technically rudimentary. Five risk weights–0, 10, 20, 50 and 100 percent of asset value–were available for *all* types of assets and *all* types of counterparties. This arrangement produced such anomalous results as the application of the same risk weight to a commercial loan to a small business operating a local retail computer store and a commercial loan to a major dot.com corporation, despite the obvious differences in the relative risks involved in the two borrowers.

Third, the framework did not take into account the dramatic changes in the contours of the banking market itself. These changes included consolidation in holding company patterns of ownership and control of increasingly diversified financial services enterprises. Consolidation and diversification were taking place in a markedly more globalized market environment.

Fourth, the methodology tended to be insensitive to the individual experience and operational qualities of banks. The framework had one size to fit all banks subject to capital adequacy requirements.[67] Thus, greater reliance on standardized capital adequacy calculations–a tendency clearly exhibited by U.S. statutes[68]–carries with it the danger of neglecting individualized safety-and-soundness assessment of particular banks.

Basel II

Over the past decade, the BIS Committee began working on amendments to Basel I in order to take account of new globalized financial practices and to create a more flexible, risk-sensitive framework for determining minimum capital requirements.[69] In June 1999, the BIS issued a proposal that would significantly revise the capital adequacy accord, in two basic ways: by extensively refining Basel I guidelines, and by providing a dramatic alternative approach. The new approach had three basic principles: (*i*) International banks would be required to establish their own internal methods for assessing the relative risks of their assets. (*ii*) Supervisory authorities would be expected to exercise greater oversight of these

---

65. *See, e.g.*, 61 Fed. Reg. 33,166 (1996) (publishing OCC, FRS & FDIC joint policy statement providing guidance on sound practices for managing interest rate risk); 66 Fed. Reg. 15,049 (2001) (to be codified at 12 C.F.R. §§ 567.1, 567.5(b)(4), (c)(2)(i)-(ii), 567.6(a)(1)(ii)(H), (a)(1)(iv)(G)-(H); removing 12 C.F.R. §§ 567.5(c)(2)(iii), (c)(3), 567.7) (proposing 50 percent risk weight for certain qualifying mortgage loans; eliminating interest rate risk component of risk-based capital regulations; proposing technical changes); 62 Fed. Reg. 68,064 (1997) (codified at 12 C.F.R. pts. 3, 208, 225, 325) (amending market risk provisions in risk-based capital standards)

66. The term *operational risk* may be defined as "the risk of direct or indirect loss resulting from inadequate or failed internal processes, people and systems or from external events." BIS Committee on Banking Supervision, *Consultative Document: The New Capital Accord* 94 (Jan. 2001) [hereinafter "*Consultative Document*"]. The term does not include strategic and reputational risk. *Id.* For discussion of reputational risk, see CORE PRINCIPLES at 137.

67. This was particularly true of U.S. application of Basel I. While Basel I by its own terms applied only to international banks, U.S. statutes and implementing regulations apply the capital adequacy regime to *all* banks subject to federal regulation.

68. *See, e.g.*, 2 MALLOY, BANKING LAW AND REGULATION, *supra*, § 7.03[A] (discussing use of capital supervision as central focus of U.S. bank supervisory policy).

69. *See* Daniel Pruzin, *Basel Committee Sets Out Changes to Risk Calculations Under Capital Accord*, BNA Int'l Bus. & Fin. Daily, Oct. 3, 2001, at d3 (discussing BIS motivations for proposed Capital Accord).

capital assessments by banks. (*iii*) Greater transparency in banking operations would be required, *e.g.*, the creditworthiness of borrowing governments and corporations would be assessed by credit-rating agencies, and these ratings would be used by banks in pricing loans to such borrowers. The BIS anticipated that the new accord, which came to be known as "Basel II," would be effective no sooner than 2001.[70]

A revised version of the proposal was issued for comment in January 2001.[71] This version retained the three-pronged approach of the original proposal, referred to as the three "pillars" of minimum capital requirements, enhanced supervision, and market discipline.

Of the three pillars, by far the most extensively discussed was the first pillar, which would involve significant changes in capital adequacy regulation. First, capital requirements would be extensively revised from the Basel I version and would offer banks two alternative approaches to capital adequacy. The *standardized approach*[72] is essentially Basel I, as revised.[73] The revisions represent refinements, for example, including more articulated risk weights with respect to claims on sovereign borrowers based upon their credit assessments by export credit agencies.[74] Further, the revision would impose a requirement that internationally active banks account for operational risk (arising from poor documentation, fraud, infrastructural failure and the like), in addition to credit and market risk.[75] Generally, the proposed charge for operational risk would be approximately 20 percent of overall capital requirements.[76] The capital requirements would be applied to consolidated and sub-consolidated elements of larger financial services enterprises.[77]

As an alternative to the standardized approach, banks that demonstrated to their supervisors an internal methodology for assigning exposures to different classes of assets consistently over time[78] would be permitted to maintain capital in accordance with an internal credit ratings system (the so called "*internal ratings based*," or "*IRB*" *approach*).[79] The IRB approach was to be based upon sophisticated computer modeling or other in-house analytical tools to determine credit risk, on a borrower-by-borrower basis that includes an estimate of future losses on assets.[80] Two methodologies are available in this regard. The *foundation methodology* would allow the bank to estimate internally the probability of default on the

70. Alan Cowell, *An International Banking Panel Proposes Ways to Limit Risk*, N.Y. Times, June 4, 1999, at C4, col. 4.

71. *Consultative Document, supra.*

72. *Id.* at 7-31.

73. *Id.* at 7.

74. *Id.* at 7-8.

75. *Id.* at 95.

76. *Id.* at 95 n.51.

77. *Id.* at 1:

> 1. The New Basel Capital Accord . . . will be applied on a consolidated basis to internationally active banks.
>
> . . .
>
> 2. The scope of application of the Accord will be extended to include, on a fully consolidated basis, holding companies that are parents of banking groups to ensure that it captures risks within the whole banking group. ...
>
> 3. The Accord will also apply to all internationally active banks at every tier within a banking group. ...

(Footnote omitted.) However, the parent holding company of a banking group's holding company may not itself be subject to the revised rules if it is not viewed as a parent of a banking group. *Id.* at 1 n.1.

78. *Id.* at 32.

79. *Id.* at 32-86.

80. *Id.* at 34.

asset, while using supervisor-imposed analysis of other risk components associated with the asset.[81] Under the *advanced methodology*, a sophisticated bank would be permitted to use internally generated estimates for other risk components.[82]

The revised proposal was highly criticized by banking industry commentators,[83] mainly because of reporting requirements perceived as excessive, and the level of capital charges viewed as unnecessarily high. In addition, in the Spring 2001, the annual report of the BIS Committee, reviewing the public disclosure practices of international banks, criticized the relative lack of disclosure in areas related to credit risk modeling and use of internal and external ratings by major banks.[84] This problem seriously implicated the proposed Basel II, since disclosure of information with respect to use of internal ratings was necessary for banks to qualify for the IRB approach proposed in "Pillar 1" of the new accord.[85]

In fact, as a result of its assessment of the critical comments that were received in response to the 2001 proposal, in June 2001 the BIS Committee decided to delay implementation of Basel II until 2005.[86]

In a working paper issued 28 September 2001, the Risk Management Group of the BIS Committee outlined changes to the proposed Basel II.[87] The proposed changes to "Pillar 1" would include, *inter alia*, a significant lowering of the operational risk charge as a percentage of a bank's overall capital set-aside requirements and greater flexibility in the use of advanced internal risk estimate methods for determining a bank's minimum capital requirements.[88]

On 5 October 2001, the BIS Committee released another working paper, proposing further changes to Basel II.[89] The working paper focused on issues concerning the application of IRB approaches to risk assessment, and specifically on the treatment of "specialized loans" such as project finance undertakings.[90] The working paper proposed a specific framework for treatment of specialized loans that relied upon a stream of income generated by an asset rather than the creditworthiness of the borrower for repayment of the loan. Such

---

81. *Id.* In October 2001, a task force of the BIS Committee questioned whether the foundation approach was necessary and asked for comment from the banking industry on this issue. Models Task Force, BIS Committee on Banking Supervision, *Working Paper on the Internal Ratings-Based Approach to Specialized Lending Exposures*, *available at*, http://www.bis.org [hereinafter *MTF Working Paper*].

82. *Consultative Document* at 34.

83. *See* Daniel Pruzin, *supra* at d3 (noting industry opposition).

84. Daniel Pruzin, *Basel Committee Cites Mixed Results for Meeting Proposed Capital Accord*, BNA Int'l Bus. & Fin. Daily, Apr. 24, 2001, at d2.

85. *Id.*

86. Daniel Pruzin, *Capital Accord Draft Completion Delayed as Basel Committee Eyes New Revisions*, BNA Int'l Bus. & Fin. Daily, June 26, 2001, at d3.

87. Risk Management Group, BIS Committee on Banking Supervision, *Working Paper on the Regulatory Treatment of Operational Risk*, *available at*, http://www.bis.org [hereinafter *RMG Working Paper*].

88. Daniel Pruzin, *supra* d3 (discussing proposed changes).

89. *MTF Working Paper, supra*. *See* Daniel Pruzin, *Basel Committee Outlines Further Changes to IRB Approach in Proposed Capital Accord*, Int'l Bus. & Fin. Daily, Oct. 10, 2001, at d5 (reporting on *MTF Working Paper*).

90. *See* Michael P. Malloy, *International Project Finance: Risk Analysis and Regulatory Concerns*, 18 TRANSNAT'L LAW. 89 (2004) (discussing Basel II treatment of project finance).

a loan arrangement does not conform to assumptions underlying the IRB approach of the 2001 revision, which tended to focus on the ongoing operations of the borrower as the source of repayment.[91]

Thus began a repeated round of revised proposals, public and often strenuous criticism, and further delays in the expected effective date. By the Summer of 2003–while Basel II was still in process–the U.S. Congress had already begun to cool on the idea of the IRB approach,[92] as had British bankers.[93] These attitudes would continue up to the moment that Basel II was finalized,[94] and beyond.[95] On 11 May 2004, the BIS Committee announced that it had reached agreement on outstanding issues that had impeded finalizing Basel II.[96] The Committee stated that it would adhere to a proposed year-end 2006 target date for banks to adopt the more basic standardized and foundation IRB approaches for assessing minimum capital charges.[97] However, for banks adopting the most advanced IRB approaches–most, if not all, major internationally-active banks–the Committee expected that a year-end 2007 target date was necessary to allow further impact analysis and parallel running before full implementation.[98] On 26 June 2004, the Committee approved the final version of the Basel II. The Committee emphasized that it would continue to review the calibration of the new requirements prior to implementation and to adjust Basel II as necessary to ensure that the new capital rules did not result in a sharp increase in overall minimum capital requirements.

Notes and Comments 7.17. What do capital adequacy requirements add to the supervision of safety and soundness of depository institutions? To pose the question in different terms, what does the current required ratio of capital to assets indicate about the soundness of a depository institution?

7.18. Assume that Quarter National Bank had only cash and cash-like assets.[99] (Under the BIS guidelines, cash is "risk-weighted" at 0 percent.) According to the guidelines,

---

91. *See, e.g., Consultative Document, supra* at 50-51 (discussing risk assessment criteria applicable to corporate exposures).

92. *See, e.g.*, R. Christian Bruce, *Regulators Must Supply More Answers Before Basel Can Be Adopted, Shelby, Sarbanes Say*, BNA BANKING DAILY, June 19, 2003, at 1 (reporting on congressional dissatisfaction with Basel II deliberations).

93. *See* Patrick Tracey and Karen Werner, *British Banking Groups Seek Delay In Basel II Capital* Accord *Until 2010*, BNA BANKING DAILY, Aug. 11, 2003, at 1 (reporting on request by British Bankers' Association and London Investment Banking Association for "less prescriptive and more principles-based" rules).

94. Committee on Banking Supervision, Bank for International Settlements, *International Convergence of Capital Measurement and Capital Standards: A Revised Framework* (June 26, 2004), *available at* http://www.bis.org/publ /bcbs107.htm (hereinafter "Basel II").

95. Richard Cowden, *Regulators, Lawmakers, Industry Cautious As Basel II Accord Staggers to Finish Line*, BNA BANKING DAILY, April 26, 2004 (reporting on preference of U.S. banks, regulators, and lawmakers to delay Basel II implementation past 2006).

96. Daniel Pruzin, *Basel Committee Announces Deal On Key Remaining Accord Issues*, BNA Banking Daily, May 12, 2004. These issues included calibration of minimum capital requirements, the proposed capital charge for operational risk, and the use of advanced internal ratings-based (IRB) systems for assessing bank capital charges. *Id.*

97. *Id.*

98. *Id.*

99. This is a practical impossibility, since QNB would in reality necessarily have some other, physical assets somewhere. But assume it anyway.

how much capital must QNB maintain in order to meet the requirement of a minimum capital/assets ratio of eight percent?

7.19. One fundamental question was not explicitly addressed by the original Basel I, nor has it been the subject of deliberations over Basel II: Why use capital as the basic measuring tool of safety and soundness in banking supervision? In traditional corporate law terms, capital serves at least four distinct roles, among others. First, capital is the source of the primary (or, at least, the most significant) operational financial resources for the corporate enterprise. Second, it is the marker for the competing property interests in the enterprise, indicating the ultimate (*i.e.*, liquidational) property rights of various classes of investors. Third, capital serves as a marker for associational rights and obligations, indicating, for example, the relative voting rights of different classes of investors. Fourth, capital deterioration is the primary measure or precondition of insolvency. Banking enterprises tend to be atypical and asymmetrical with respect to the corporate roles of capital. This is particularly true of the first and fourth roles just identified. So, why use the capital-assets ratio as the basic measure of safety and soundness?

7.20. For three decades, capital supervision has been a key strategy in bank regulatory policy, but the emphasis on capital supervision is not intuitively justifiable. Even banks that fully comply with capital requirements are still highly leveraged, far beyond the levels of viable general business corporations. (Thus, in a capital-intensive industry like automotive manufacturing debt-to-equity ratios might be above 2/1, but in a "well capitalized" bank, it would not be surprising to find a debt-to-equity ratio of 9/1.) This prompts the question whether the capital levels of banks are an appropriate benchmark at all for judging the safety and soundness of banks.[100]

7.21. As with Basel I, the BIS Committee expected that Basel II would become the global standard for minimum capital requirements.[101] However, India and China, among other major developing countries, had already indicated that they did not intend to adopt Basel II,[102] and U.S. supervisors–including the SEC as well as the four principal federal bank supervisors–have decided that Basel II will only be applied to the relatively small number of the largest internationally-active U.S. banks.[103] The vast majority of U.S. financial institutions will continue to be governed by a modified version of Basel I, now referred to as "Basel IA." This could stratify U.S. bank supervision, as between the largest banks and all other financial institutions, for the first time in the history of modern U.S. bank supervision. Exacerbating concerns about regulatory stratification, the most recent BIS quantitative impact study ("QIS 4") indicated that Basel II would significantly reduce aggregate bank regulatory capital of the banks to which it applied. As a result, supervisors must consider whether to add capital charges under "pillar 2"–the enhanced supervisory review process–for noncredit risks (*e.g.*, interest rate risk, concentration risk, strategic risk,

---

100. See, e.g., Michael P. Malloy, *Capital Regulation and International Banking: A Questionable Strategy*, in GREGORY T. PAPANIKOS (ed.), ESSAYS ON THE ECONOMICS OF LAW AND INDUSTRIAL ORGANIZATION 155 (2006) (expressing doubts about efficacy of capital supervision).

101. *Id.*

102. *Id.* However, in April 2006, the head of China's Banking Regulatory Commission stated that China would adopt Basel II standards within four to six years for domestic banks with substantial numbers of overseas branches. Kathleen E. McLaughlin, *CBRC Chair Says China Will Adopt Basel II Standards Starting in 2010*, BNA BANKING DAILY (April 13, 2006), *available at* http://pubs.bna.com/ip/bna/bbd.nsf/ eh/A0B2Q6C7R7.

103. *Five Federal Agencies Announce Plans to Implement Basel II over Four-year Period*, BNA Banking Daily, June 29, 2004.

liquidity risk).[104] If you were a U.S. policy maker, would you still be in support of the BIS capital adequacy regime? How–if at all–would you want Basel II changed?

7.22. The QIS 4 data indefinitely delayed the plans of U.S. supervisors to ask for comment on proposed rules implementing Basel II during the Summer 2005. The data also raised questions about the ability of banks relegated to Basel IA to compete with banks that are permitted to adopt the Basel II methodologies. This situation would give Basel II banks significant competitive advantages over Basel IA banks, and might leave the latter vulnerable to acquisition by the former, a result that would be politically unacceptable to many in the U.S. Congress. As a result, the supervisors put their plans on hold in May 2005, to allow more time to analyze the QIS 4 results. In September 2005, after further congressional hearings on Basel II, U.S. supervisors announced that they would delay implementation by at least one year and would develop extra safeguards to address the problems identified by the QIS 4.[105]

7.23. *Further delays in U.S. implementation.* European competitors had already begun implementing the EU version of Basel II as of January 1, 2007. It was not until September 2006 that the U.S. regulators even issued a joint notice proposing a new risk-based capital adequacy framework that would require some, and permit other, qualifying depository institutions (*i.e.*, banks, savings associations and bank holding companies) to use an internal ratings-based approach to calculate regulatory capital requirements and advanced measurement approaches to calculate regulatory operational risk capital requirements.[106] The proposed rule described the qualifying criteria for banks required or seeking to operate under the proposed framework and the applicable risk-based capital requirements for banks that operate under the framework. Comments on the proposal were due January 23, 2007.[107] However, on November 1, 2006, the American Bankers Association requested more time to comment on the proposed Basel II rules, in light of the delay in issuing a proposal for Basel IA rules.[108] (Federal regulators had planned overlapping comment periods for the Basel II and Basel IA rules, but issuance of the Basel IA proposal had been delayed by a review by the Office of Management and Budget, which conceivably could last for as long as 90 days.) In December 2006, the regulators announced proposed Basel IA rules,[109] and extended the

---

104. Also in July 2005, the Basel Committee and the International Organization of Securities Commissions (IOSCO) finalized rules on capital set-aside requirements for bank exposures related to trading in securities, derivatives, and other financial instruments, as well as the treatment of "double default effects," *i.e.*, the risk that both a borrower and guarantor could default on the same obligation. Daniel Pruzin, *Basel Committee, IOSCO Finalize Rules On Treatment of Trade-Related Exposures*, BNA Banking Daily, July 19, 2005, *available at* http://pubs.bna.com/ip/BNA/bbd.nsf/is/A0B1D1N8C5. The Basel Committee/IOSCO paper, *The Application of Basel II to Trading Activities and the Treatment of Double Default Effects*, is available at http://www.bis.org. The new rules amend several aspects of Basel II, to increase significantly the risk-sensitivity of capital requirements for these exposures.

105. R. Christian Bruce, *Regulators Delay Basel II Implementation, Promising New Roadmap, Extra Safeguards*, BNA BANKING DAILY (Oct. 3, 2005), *available at* http://pubs.bna.com/ip/BNA/bbd.nsf/is/A0B1P0X1Q1.

106. 71 Fed. Reg. 55,830 (2006) (to be codified at 12 C.F.R. pts. 3 (OCC rules), 208, 225 (Fed rules), 325 (FDIC rules), 566 (OTS rules)).

107. *Id.* at 55,830.

108. R. Christian Bruce, *ABA Asks Regulators for More Time To File Comments on Basel II Proposal* (Nov. 2, 2006), *available at* http://pubs.bna.com/ip/bna/ibd.nsf/eh/A0B3P9T7A5.

109. 71 Fed. Reg. 77,446 (2006) (to be codified at 12 C.F.R. pts. 3 (OCC rules), 208, 225 (Fed rules), 325 (FDIC rules) 567 (OTS rules)); *as corrected*, 72 Fed. Reg. 1266 (2007).

comment period on the Basel II proposed rules an additional two months.[110] The regulators were specifically seeking comment on the question whether Basel II banks–the largest internationally active banks–should have the option of adopting Basel IA rules instead of being required to follow Basel II.[111] If adopted as proposed, the Basel IA revisions would apply to banks, bank holding companies, and savings associations (collectively, "banking organizations"). A banking organization would be permitted to elect to comply with the proposed Basel IA revisions or remain subject to the existing risk-based capital rules, unless it uses the Basel II Advanced Capital Adequacy Framework proposed in September 2006.[112] The extended comment period for the proposal ended on March 26, 2007. By July 2007, the regulators announced that they had reached a compromise agreement on a final rule that cleared the way for U.S. implementation of Basel II in early 2008.[113] In December 2007 the four regulators jointly published final rules implementing Basel II for the largest, internationally active U.S. banks.[114] The final rules were effective April 1, 2008.[115] Banks were to start a preliminary phase of the U.S. implementation effort early in 2008, but required Basel II compliance does not initiate until January 1, 2009, when the new standards will begin to be phased in over a three-year period.[116] At that point, it is anticipated that only about twenty-five U.S. banking institutions will be required to adopt Basel II, with another small group of relatively large U.S. banking institutions having the option to do so.[117] The overwhelming majority of U.S. banking institutions will be required either to continue to apply the 1988 Basel I standards, or the new and more risk-sensitive Basel IA standards still to be proposed by the regulators.[118]

7.24. *Introducing Basel III.* Technically, the Basel II Capital Accord was incorporated — but not fully implemented — into domestic regulations in the United States on December 7, 2007.[119] In the wake of the financial collapse, however, a cascading series of efforts to refine the Accord ensued.[120] Among those efforts, the Basel Committee has

---

110. 71 Fed. Reg. 77,518 (2006) (extending comment period until March 26, 2007).

111. R. Christian Bruce, *Regulators Unveil Basel IA Proposal, Will Consider Adoption by Basel II Banks* (Dec. 6, 2006), *available at* http://pubs.bna.com/ip/bna/bbd.nsf/eh/A0B3U6D7U2.

112. 71 Fed. Reg. at 77,446.

113. R. Christian Bruce, *Regulators Reach Agreement on Basel II, Clearing Path for 2008 U.S. Implementation*, BNA BANKING DAILY (July 23, 2007), available at http://pubs.bna.com/ip/bna/bbd.nsf/125731d8816a84d385256297005f336a/c228220131a5bb868525731f000184b5?OpenDocument.

114. 72 Fed. Reg. 69,288 (2007) (codified at 12 C.F.R. pts. 3 (OCC rules), 208, 225 (Fed rules), 325 (FDIC rules), 559-560, 563, 567 (OTS rules)). For simplicity, the final rule uses the term "bank" to include banks, savings associations, and bank holding companies (BHCs). 72 Fed. Reg. at 69,288 n.1. The terms "bank holding company" and "BHC" do not include savings and loan holding companies regulated by the OTS. *Id.*

115. 72 Fed. Reg. at 69,288.

116. *See* R. Christian Bruce, *Fed's Governors, Eyeing Credit Turmoil, Welcome New Capital Rules Under Basel II*, BNA BANKING DAILY (Nov. 5, 2007), *available at*, http://pubs.bna.com/ip/bna/bbd.nsf/eh/A0B5H8M7E8.

117. *Id.*

118. *Id.*

119. 72 Fed. Reg. 69,288 (2007).

120. For a summary, *see* Basel Committee on Banking Supervision, *Strengthening the Resilience of the Banking Sector (Consultative Document*, Dec. 17, 2009) (including proposed changes to definition of capital, proposed introduction of leverage ratio, and proposed changes to treatment of

produced revisions to the market risk framework,[121] and guidelines on incremental risk in an institution's trading book,[122] including incremental risk capital charge, a comprehensive risk measure for correlation trading portfolios, new rules for securitization exposures in the trading book, and revised capital charges for equity exposures subject to a standardized measurement method for market risk. Given the significance of securitization in the collapse, enhancements to the Basel II framework included revised risk weights for re-securitizations held in the banking book.[123] Finally, in December 2009 the Committee raised the issue of the need to increase liquidity in institutions subject to the Accord.[124] It was becoming clearer that a new "Basel III" arrangement was emerging from the consultative process.

7.25. *Killer Capital.* To assist in building liquidity, the Basel Committee's December 2009 Basel III proposals include a new global leverage ratio, together with a series of measures to promote the retention of capital liquidity buffers to be drawn upon in periods of economic stress, and a required "liquidity coverage" ratio to ensure that banks have sufficient high-quality liquidity to survive an acute financial stress lasting for one month. There is no question that reliable liquidity measures need to be developed post-meltdown, but there is cause for concern whether the relatively inflexible measures now being proposed are appropriate as broadly applicable requirements.[125] For one thing, the cost of capital under these measures is likely to be high, perhaps prohibitively so for many banks.[126]

6. Market Activities under the GLBA

Notes and Comments 7.26. *Effect of GLBA on securities activities of banks.* The 1999 Graham-Leach-Bliley Act (GLBA)[127] is one of the most significant pieces of federal banking legislation since the Banking Act of 1933 itself. Among other things, it works a fundamental change in the scheme of regulation of securities activities of depository institutions. The GLBA eliminates prohibitions on affiliations between commercial and investment banking enterprises and on interlocking directorates between such enterprises by

---

counterparty credit risk).

121. Basel Committee on Banking Supervision, *Revisions to the Basel II Market Risk Framework* (July 2009).

122. Basel Committee on Banking Supervision, *Guidelines for Computing Capital for Incremental Risk in the Trading Book* (July 2009).

123. *See* Basel Committee on Banking Supervision, *Enhancements to the Basel II Framework* (July 2009).

124. *See* Basel Committee on Banking Supervision, *International Framework for Liquidity Risk Measurement, Standards and Monitoring* (Consultative Document, Dec. 17, 2009).

125. *See* Daniel Pruzin, *Research Group Says Banks Would "Struggle" To Meet Liquidity Standards of Basel III Draft*, BNA INT'L BUS. & FIN. DAILY (May 10, 2010), *available at* http://www.bna.com (reporting on analysts' concerns about consequences of "Basel III" liquidity proposals).

126. Estimates suggest that over the first five years of implementation, banks would be forced to raise $700 billion in new equity and $5.4 trillion in long-term debt to meet the proposed liquidity requirements. Daniel Pruzin, *Panel Chief Cites Long-Term Benefits From Basel III, Indicates Deadline Flexibility*, BNA Int'l Bus. & Fin. Daily (June 6, 2010), *available at* http://www.bna.com.

127. Pub. L. No. 106-102, Nov. 12, 1999, 113 Stat. 1338 (1999) (codified at scattered sections of 12, 15, 16, 18 U.S.C.).

repealing sections 20 and 32 of Glass-Steagall.[128] It also authorizes national banks to deal in, underwrite, and purchase municipal bonds for their own investment accounts.[129] As dramatic as the Glass-Steagall repeals may be, however, GLBA effects an even more fundamental re-alignment of securities and bank regulatory regimes. For example, the GLBA endorses the principle of functional regulation, positing that similar activities should be regulated by the same regulator.[130] Accordingly, securities activities generally are to be supervised by federal and state securities regulators, not bank regulators.

7.27. *Broker-dealer activities of banks.* Prior to the enactment of the GLBA, banks were excluded from the definition of "broker" and "dealer" under the 1934 Act, and their securities broker-dealer activities were therefore not subject to regulation by the SEC.[131] The GLBA imposes functional regulation on bank securities activities by generally eliminating the "bank exception" from the definitions of "broker" and "dealer" in the 1934 Act.[132] However, the GLBA retains limited exemptions for banks from the definition of "broker" to facilitate certain traditional bank activities such as third-party networking arrangements, trust activities, commercial paper and exempted securities, employee and shareholder benefit plans, sweep accounts, affiliate transactions, private placements, safekeeping and custody services, asset-backed securities, derivatives, and "identified banking products."[133] Similar limited exemptions are available for banks from the definition of the term "dealer."[134] The exemptions in each of these definitional provisions seem to leave a fairly significant range of bank activities outside SEC regulation of broker-dealers. What kind of activities conducted by banks would actually be subject to SEC supervision?

7.28. *Treatment of banks as investment advisers.* Similarly, the GLBA amends the Investment Company Act of 1940, 15 U.S.C. §§ 80a-1 *et seq.*, and the Investment Advisers Act of 1940, 15 U.S.C. §§ 80b-1 *et seq.*, to subject banks that advise mutual funds to the same regulatory scheme, administered by the SEC, as other advisers to mutual funds.[135]

7.29. *Treatment of new hybrid products.* For new hybrid products that emerge in the securities markets, the GLBA establishes in the federal securities laws a process that requires the SEC to act by rulemaking (with notice of proposed rulemaking and opportunity for public

---

128. GLBA, § 101, 113 Stat. at 1341 (repealing 12 U.S.C. §§ 78 & 377).

129. GLBA, § 151, 113 Stat. at 1384 (codified at 12 U.S.C. § 24).

130. *See* Note 1.60.a, *supra* (discussing functional regulation under GLBA).

131. *See American Bankers Ass'n v. S.E.C.*, 804 F.2d 739 (D.C.Cir. 1986) (striking down SEC rule attempting to regulate bank broker-dealer activities). *See also* Michael P. Malloy, *The Regulation of Bank Brokerage Activities: Was Rule 3b-9 Benign?* 6 ANN. REV. BANKING L. 181 (1987) (discussing and criticizing *American Bankers Ass'n*).

132. GLBA, §§ 201-202, 113 Stat. at 1385-1391 (codified at 15 U.S.C. § 78c(a)(4)-(5)). *See also* GLBA, § 221(a), 113 Stat. at 1401 (codified at 15 U.S.C. § 77c(a)(2)) (treatment of bank common trust funds under Securities Act of 1933); GLBA, § 221(b), 113 Stat. at 1401 (codified at 15 U.S.C. § 78c(a)(12)(A)(iii)) (treatment of bank common trust funds under Securities Exchange Act of 1934).

133. *See* 15 U.S.C. § 78c(a)(4)(B) (excepting from 1934 Act definition of "broker" bank that engages in specified activities under certain conditions).

134. *See id.* § 78c(a)(5)(C)(i)-(iv) (exempting banks from definition of "dealer" where bank engages in specified activities under certain conditions).

135. GLBA, §§ 211-220, 222-224, 113 Stat. at 1396-1402, (codified at 15 U.S.C. §§ 80a-2(a)(5), (a)(6), (a)(11), (a)(19)(A)(v)-(vii), (a)(19)(B)(v)-(vii), 80a-9(a)(1)-(2), 80a-10(c), 80a-17(a)(4), (f)(1)-(6), 80a-26(b)-(f), 80a-34(a), 80b-2(a)(3), (a)(7), (a)(11)(A), (a)(26), (c), 80b-10a). *See also* GLBA, § 221(c), 113 Stat. at 1401 (codified at 15 U.S.C. § 80a-3(c)(3)) (treatment of bank common trust funds under Investment Company Act of 1940).

comment) prior to seeking to regulate any bank sales of such new products.[136] The legislative history of the GLBA indicates that this rulemaking process is intended to give notice to the banking industry in an area that might involve complex new products.[137]

7.30. *Safety and soundness concerns.* Should functional regulation of securities activities of depository institutions and BHCs eclipse traditional bank regulatory policy concerning institutional safety and soundness or public confidence in the banking system? The GLBA requires the SEC to consult and coordinate with the appropriate federal banking regulators before taking any action or rendering any opinion with respect to reporting of loan loss reserves by any insured depository institution or insured depository holding company.[138] What is the justification for this requirement?

7.31. *Implementing regulations.* In October 2007, the Fed and the SEC published a single set of jointly adopted rules[139] to implement GLBA exceptions for banks from the definition of the term "broker."[140] The rules define terms used in these statutory exceptions and include certain related exemptions. The rules became fully effective in December 2007, as did the amendments removing and reserving certain superseded provisions of 17 C.F.R. pt. 240.[141] The effective dates of the rules do not control the date of required compliance, however. A bank is exempt from complying with the rules and the "broker" exceptions in 1934 Act until the first day of its first fiscal year commencing after September 30, 2008.[142]

7.32. *Related regulatory amendments.* At the same time, the SEC adopted rules and rule amendments regarding exemptions from the definitions of "broker" and "dealer" under the 1934 Act for bank securities activities.[143] These new rules and rule amendments are effective November 2, 2007.[144] Intended to complement Regulation R, the rules and rule amendments for the most part reflect changes that the GLBA made to the 1934 Act with respect to the status of banks as "dealers."[145] In particular, the SEC adopted a conditional exemption[146] that will allow banks to effect riskless principal transactions with non-U.S.

136. GLBA, § 205, 113 Stat. at 1391 (codified at 15 U.S.C. § 78o(i)).

137. *See Conference Report on S. 900, reprinted in* 145 Cong. Rec. H11255-01, H11297 (1999) (discussing congressional intent concerning GLBA section 205).

138. GLBA, § 241, 113 Stat. at 1407 (codified at 15 U.S.C. § 78m note).

139. 72 Fed. Reg. 56,514 (2007) (codified at 12 C.F.R. §§ 218.100, 218.700-218.701, 218.721-218.723, 218.740-218.741, 218.760, 218.771-218.772, 218.775-218.776, 218.780-218.781; 12 C.F.R. §§ 247.100, 247.700-247.701, 247.721-247.723, 247.740-247.741, 247.760, 247.771-247.772, 247.775-247.776, 247.780-247.781; *removing* 17 C.F.R. §§ 240.3a4-2 - 240.3a4-6, 240.3b-17, 240.15a-7, 240.15a-8). Identical sets of the final rules were adopted by the Fed and the SEC, codified by the Fed in 12 C.F.R. pt. 218 and by the SEC in 17 C.F.R. pt. 247. The final rules adopted by the two agencies within their respective C.F.R. titles were intentionally numbered identically from § ---.100 to § ---.781. 72 Fed. Reg. 56,514, 56,516 & n.27 (2007).

140. 15 U.S.C. § 78c(a)(4). Pursuant to the FSRRA § 101, this single set of final rules supersedes any and all other proposed or final rules issued by the SEC on or after the date of enactment of the GLBA with regard to the definition of "broker." 72 Fed. Reg. at 56,516.

141. *Id.*

142. 72 Fed. Reg. at 56,514.

143. 72 Fed. Reg. 56,562 (2007).

144. 72 Fed. Reg. at 56,562.

145. 72 Fed. Reg. at 56,562-56,563.

146. *See* 17 C.F.R. § 240.3a5-2 (providing conditional exemption from definition of "dealer" to allow banks to engage in certain transactions involving securities exempted from registration by Reg S). This new 1934 Act rule corresponds to Rule 771 of Regulation R under the 1933 Act, which

persons pursuant to Regulation S[147] under the 1933 Act. The exemption will apply only to purchases and sales of "eligible securities,"[148] *i.e.*, securities that are not in the inventory of the bank or an affiliate, and that are not underwritten by the bank or an affiliate on a firm commitment basis (apart from securities acquired from an unaffiliated distributor). In addition, this exemption will apply only to Reg S transactions that a bank makes on a "riskless principal" basis.[149] This focus permits U.S. banks to sell securities overseas that foreign banks themselves sell, "thus helping to avoid placing U.S. banks at a competitive disadvantage with respect to eligible securities, while also helping to safeguard against investor protection risks associated with unregistered entities distributing eligible securities."[150] The exemption is available when a bank purchases a newly issued eligible security from an issuer or a broker-dealer and sells that security in compliance with the requirements of Rule 903[151] to a purchaser who is not in the United States.[152] The exemption is also available when a bank purchases, from a person who is not a "U.S. person" under Reg S,[153]

---

permits banks to engage in certain Regulation S transactions on an agency basis without being "brokers." Rule 771 "recognizes that non-U.S. persons generally will not rely on the protections of the U.S. securities laws when purchasing Regulation S securities from U.S. banks, and that non-U.S. persons can purchase the same securities from banks located outside of the U.S." 72 Fed. Reg. at 56,563 (citing 71 Fed. Reg. at 77,552, discussing proposed version).

147. 17 C.F.R. §§ 230.901 *et seq.*

148. The rule specifically defines an "eligible security" as a security that is not being sold from the inventory of the bank or an affiliate of the bank, and not being underwritten by the bank or an affiliate of the bank on a firm-commitment basis unless the bank acquired the security from an unaffiliated distributor that did not purchase the security from the bank or an affiliate of the bank. 17 C.F.R. § 240.3a5-2(b)(2). For these purposes, the term "distributor" is defined to have the same meaning as in Rule 902(d). *Id.* § 230.902(d) (defining "distributor" to mean any underwriter, dealer, or other person who participates, pursuant to contractual arrangement, in distribution of securities offered or sold in reliance on Regulation S).

149. The rule defines a "riskless principle transaction" as a transaction in which, after receiving an order to buy from a customer, the bank purchased the security from another person to offset a contemporaneous sale to such customer or, having received an order to sell from a customer, the bank sold the security to another person to offset a contemporaneous purchase from such customer. *Id.* § 3a5-2(b)(4).

150. 72 Fed. Reg. at 56,563.

151. *Id.* § 230.903. Rule 903 provides that an offer or sale of securities by the issuer, a distributor, or an affiliate or a person acting on their behalf shall be deemed to occur outside the U.S. within the meaning of Rule 901 if the offer or sale is made in an offshore transaction, and no directed selling efforts are made in the U.S. by the issuer, a distributor, affiliate, or person acting on their behalf. However, other conditions may also apply, depending upon the place of incorporation and reporting status of the issuer, and the amount of U.S. market interest in the securities. *Cf. id.* § 230.901 (providing generally that, for purposes of 1933 Act § 5, the terms "offer," "offer to sell," "sell," "sale" and "offer to buy" include offers and sales that occur within United States, and excludes those occurring outside United States).

152. *Id.* § 240.3a5-2(a)(1).

153. *See id.* § 230.902(k) (defining "U.S. person" to mean: (*i*) any natural person resident in United States; (*ii*) any partnership or corporation organized or incorporated under the U.S. laws; (*iii*) any estate of which any executor or administrator is U.S. person; (*iv*) any trust of which any trustee is U.S. person; (*v*) any agency or branch of foreign entity located in United States; (*vi*) any non-discretionary account or similar account (other than estate or trust) held by dealer or other fiduciary for benefit or account of U.S. person; (*vii*) any discretionary account or similar account (other than estate or trust) held by dealer or other fiduciary organized, incorporated, or (if individual) resident in United

an eligible security after its initial sale with a reasonable belief that the eligible security was initially sold outside of the United States within the meaning of and in compliance with the requirements of Rule 903, and resells that security to a purchaser who is not in the United States or to a registered broker-dealer.[154] If that resale is made prior to any applicable distribution compliance period specified in Rules 903(b)(2) or (b)(3),[155] the resale must be made in compliance with the requirements of Rule 904.[156] Finally, the exemption is available when a bank purchases, from a registered broker-dealer, an eligible security after its initial sale with a reasonable belief that the eligible security was initially sold outside of the United States within the meaning of and in compliance with the requirements of Rule 903, and resells that security to a purchaser who is not in the United States.[157] This provision also requires compliance with Rule 904 if the resale is made prior to the expiration of the security's distribution compliance period. It should be emphasized that nothing in these amendments modifies the 1934 Act § 3(a)(6) definition of "bank"[158] as it applies to foreign banks. "Generally, foreign banks doing business with U.S. customers will not meet this definition and would be considered broker-dealers under the U.S. securities laws."[159] Accordingly, a foreign bank would generally be required to register as a U.S. broker-dealer unless it qualified for an exemption from registration under Rule 15a-6.[160]

7.33. *Conforming amendments*. The SEC also amended and redesignated an existing exemption from the definition of "dealer"[161] for bank securities lending activities as a conduit

---

States; and, (*viii*) any partnership or corporation if organized or incorporated under laws of any foreign jurisdiction and formed by U.S. person principally for purpose of investing in securities not registered under 1933 Act, unless organized or incorporated, and owned, by accredited investors (as defined in *id.* § 230.501(a)) who are not natural persons, estates or trusts).

154. *Id.* § 240.3a5-2(a)(2).

155. Rules 903(b)(2) and (b)(3), *id.* § 230.903(b)(2)-(3), subject "Category 2" securities and "Category 3" debt securities to a 40-day distribution compliance period, and subject "Category 3" equity securities to a one-year distribution compliance period. Under Rule 903, "Category 1" encompasses certain securities (*i*) issued by a foreign issuer, for which there is no substantial U.S. market interest; (*ii*) that are offered and sold in an overseas directed offering; (*iii*) that are backed by the full faith and credit of a foreign government; or, (*iv*) that are offered and sold to employees of the issuer or its affiliates pursuant to certain foreign employee benefit plans. "Category 2" encompasses securities not eligible for Category 1 that are equity securities of a reporting foreign issuer, or debt securities of a reporting issuer or of a non-reporting foreign issuer. "Category 3" applies to all offerings of securities that do not fall within Category 1 or 2.

156. Rule 904, *id.* § 230.904, provides that an offer or sale of securities by any person other than the issuer, a distributor, an affiliate (except an officer or director who is an affiliate solely by virtue of that position) or person acting on their behalf will be deemed to occur outside the United States within the meaning of Rule 901 if the offer or sale are made in an offshore transaction, and no directed selling efforts are made in the U.S. by the seller, an affiliate or person acting on their behalf. Additional conditions apply in the case of resales of Category 2 or 3 securities by dealers and persons receiving selling concessions, and in the case of resales by certain affiliates of the issuer or a distributor.

157. *Id.* § 240.3a5-2(a)(3).

158. 15 U.S.C. § 78c(a)(6).

159. 72 Fed. Reg. at 56,565.

160. *See id.* (expressing SEC view to this effect).

161. *See id.* § 240.3a5-3 (former Rule 15a-11, concerning bank securities lending activities). In February 2003, the SEC adopted 1934 Act Rule 15a-11 to provide an exemption from the definitions of both "broker" and "dealer" for banks engaging in securities lending transactions. *See* 68

lender.[162] In addition, the SEC conformed the rule[163] that grants a limited exemption from U.S. broker-dealer registration for foreign broker-dealers to the amended definitions of "broker" and "dealer" under the 1934 Act.[164]

7.34. *Eliminated rules*. The SEC withdrew three rules under the 1934 Act as either unnecessary or superseded by circumstance. First, an earlier rule defining the term "bank" for purposes of the 1934 Act definitions of "broker" and "dealer" was withdrawn due to judicial invalidation.[165] Second, the time-limited exemption for bank securities activities was withdrawn due to the passage of time.[166] Third, the exemption from the definitions of "broker" and "dealer" for savings associations and savings banks was withdrawn, since the exemption was no longer necessary in light of enactment of the FSRRA.[167]

7.35. *Impact of Dodd-Frank Act.* The Dodd-Frank Wall Street Reform and Consumer Protection Act,[168] the most significant structural response so far to the ongoing financial crisis precipitated by the failure of the subprime mortgage market,[169] will have a significant impact on U.S. securities regulation and practice once it is fully implemented. The following excerpt examines the Dodd-Frank measures that are intended to strengthen regulation of the financial services sector. How likely is it that the new Dodd-Frank measures will actually result in a more stable financial services sector?

Fed. Reg. 8686 (2003) (codified at 17 C.F.R. § 240.15a-11). As applicable to bank broker activities, the Rule 15a-11 exemption was never operable, because of the temporary exemptions applicable to all bank broker activities. In accordance with the mandate of the FSRRA, the SEC and the Fed jointly proposed rules governing bank broker activities, and the SEC adopted Rule 772 of Regulation R jointly with the Fed to exempt banks from the "broker" definition for certain securities lending activities. However, the FSRRA did not directly affect the operation of the rules the SEC adopted concerning banks' dealer activities.

162. Rule 3a5-3(d) defines the term "conduit lender" to mean a bank that borrows or loans securities, as principal, for its own account, and contemporaneously loans or borrows the same securities, as principal, for its own account. The rule further states that a bank that qualifies under this definition as a conduit lender at the commencement of a transaction will continue to qualify, notwithstanding whether (*i*) the lending or borrowing transaction terminates and so long as the transaction is replaced within one business day by another lending or borrowing transaction involving the same securities; and, (*ii*) any substitutions of collateral occur. 17 C.F.R. § 240.3a5-3(d).

163. *Id.* § 240.15a-6(a)(4)(i).

164. The amendment "does not change the substance of Rule 15a-6." 72 Fed. Reg. at 56,565.

165. 17 C.F.R. § 240.3b-9 (2007). *See American Bankers Ass'n v. S.E.C.*, 804 F.2d 739 (D.C.Cir. 1986) (striking down Rule 3b-9 regulating bank broker-dealer activities). *See also* Michael P. Malloy, *The Regulation of Bank Brokerage Activities: Was Rule 3b-9 Benign?* 6 ANN. REV. BANKING L. 181 (1987) (discussing and criticizing *American Bankers Ass'n*).

166. 17 C.F.R. § 240.15a-8 (2007).

167. *Id.* § 240.15a-9.

168. Pub. L. No. 111-203, 124 Stat. 1376 (2010) (codified at scattered sections of 2, 5, 7, 11, 12, 15, 18, 20, 22, 26, 28, 31, 42, 44 U.S.C.).

169. For background on the subprime mortgage crisis, *see* MICHAEL P. MALLOY, ANATOMY OF A MELTDOWN (Aspen 2010). . . . For a timeline of the current financial crisis, *see* http://www.stlouisfed.org/timeline/default.cfm.

1 Michael P. Malloy, Banking Law and Regulation

§ 1.04[K] (2d ed., Aspen Publishers, 2011)

Proprietary Securities Trading

[The Dodd-Frank Act (DFA)] restricts, but does not eliminate, proprietary securities trading by banks.[1] For these purposes, proprietary trading is defined to mean:

> engaging as a principal for the trading account of the banking entity or nonbank financial company supervised by the [Fed] in any transaction to purchase or sell, or otherwise acquire or dispose of, any security, any derivative, any contract of sale of a commodity for future delivery, any option on any such security, derivative, or contract, or any other security or financial instrument that the appropriate Federal banking agencies, the Securities and Exchange Commission, and the Commodity Futures Trading Commission may, by rule as provided in [§ 1851(b)(2)], determine.[2]

DFA § 619 requires the [newly created Financial Stability Oversight Council (FSOC)] to study and make recommendations on implementing these restrictions,[3] known as the "Volcker Rule," for former Fed Chairman Paul Volcker, who first recommended the inclusion of a broader prohibition in the draft that eventually became the DFA. The implementing agencies—OCC, FDIC, the Fed, SEC, and the Commodity Futures Trading Commission (CFTC)—must consider the FSOC recommendations coming out of this study in developing and adopting regulations to implement the Volcker Rule. To assist the FSOC in conducting the study and formulating its recommendations, in October 2010 the FSOC issued a request for public comment and information relevant to the study.[4] The FSOC study was issued in January 2011.[5]

In late November 2010, the Fed proposed a rule that would implement the conformance period during which banking entities and nonbank financial companies supervised by the Fed would be required to bring their activities and investments into compliance with the prohibitions and restrictions on proprietary trading and relationships with hedge funds and private equity funds imposed by DFA § 619.[6] In February 2011, the Fed issued a final rule to implement the conformance period.[7] The final rule is similar to the proposal version, but with some modest changes to address issues raised by commenters, to reduce potential regulatory burdens, and to clarify the rule's application. It is effective on April 1, 2011. . . .[8]

Securitization of Financial Instruments

DFA does not confine itself to the application of securities regulation to banks

---

1. DFA §619 (codified at 12 U.S.C. §1851).

2. 12 U.S.C. § 1851(h)(4).

3. DFA § 619(b).

4. 75 Fed. Reg. 61,758 (2010).

5. *See* FSOC, *Study & Recommendations on Prohibitions on Proprietary Trading Certain Relationships with Hedge Funds & Private Equity Funds* (Jan. 18, 2011). . . .

6. 75 Fed. Reg. 72,741 (2010) (to be codified at 12 C.F.R. §§ 225.180–225.182, redesignating 12 C.F.R. § 225.200).

7. 76 Fed. Reg. 8265 (2011) (codified at 12 C.F.R. §§ 225.180–225.182, redesignating 12 C.F.R. § 225.200).

8. 76 Fed. Reg. at 8265.

alone. For all market participants, it imposes new standards with respect to securitization of pools of financial instruments.[9] Prior to the 2008 collapse of the mortgage market, securitization, the process in which interests in a pool of obligations or rights are marketed to investors as pro rata securities, was one of the critical processes for moving mortgage obligations into the capital markets as securities.

SEC Enforcement Powers

DFA enhances the enforcement powers of the Securities and Exchange Commission (SEC).[10] It also provides for the SEC to maintain an additional $100 million of its revenues in a separate fund, which the SEC could use as necessary, with a full accounting to Congress.[11]

Supervision of Hedge and Private Equity Fund Advisers

DFA requires hedge fund and private equity fund advisers to register with the SEC, and will subject them to SEC inspection and examination.[12] A hedge fund is an investment fund, usually organized as a private investment partnership, open to a limited number of investors and requiring a very large initial minimum investment committed to the fund for a relatively long period, typically at least one year. The fund's investment strategies are usually very aggressive, making use of leveraged and derivative trading in targeted securities in order to increase the rate of return when the securities perform well. (This also means, of course, that losses can be exacerbated if the securities perform poorly.) A private equity fund is an investment fund that specializes in investments not quoted on public exchanges. The fund typically makes an investment directly into an existing private company or it may buy up a public company and take it private, "delisting" it from public exchanges in the process. Participants in a private equity fund are typically high-end investors (institutions and sophisticated, wealthy individuals) who commit a relatively large amount to the fund for a long period of time.[13]

---

9. DFA §§ 941–945 (codified at 15 U.S.C. §§ 77d(5), 77g(c)-(d), 78c(a)(4)(B)(vii)(I), 78c(a)(77), 78o(d), 78o-11). See also DFA § 621(a) (codified at 15 U.S.C.A. § 77z-2a) (concerning conflicts of interest with respect to securitizations). Cf. DFA § 619(g)(2) (codified at 12 U.S.C. § 1851(g)(2)) (protecting otherwise authorized sale or securitization of loans by banking entity or systemically significant nonbank financial company from prohibitions on proprietary trading).

10. DFA §§912, 919, 921–929X (codified at 5 U.S.C. §§3101, 3114(a); 15 U.S.C. §§77h-1(g), 77o, 77s(e), 77t(d)(3)(A), 77v(a), 78d-5, 78g(c)(1)(A), 78i(d)-(j), 78j(a)(1), 78m, 78m(f), 78o(b)(6)(A), (c)(1)(A), (e)-(j), (n)-(o), 78o-4(c)(4), (8), 78o-5(c), 78p(a), 78q(f)(1)-(2), 78q-1(c)(4)(C), (g), 78s(h)(4), 78t(a), (e), 78u(a)(1), 78u-1, 78u-2(a), 78u-6, 78u-7, 78x, 78aa, 78cc(a), 78ddd(d)(1)(C), (h), 78eee(a)(3), 78fff-3(a)(1), (d)-(e), 78jjj(c)-(d), 80a-9(d)(1), 80a-30, 80a-35(a), 80a-41(e)(3)(A), 80a-43, 80a-48, 80b-3(f), (i)(1), 80b-4, 80b-5(a), (f), 80b-9(d)(3)(C)(i), (f), 80b-10(d), 80b-14, 7201(9), 7215(c)(6), 7216, 7217(d)(3), 7246(a)-(b), (h); 18 U.S.C. §§1514A(a), (b)(2), (e)).

11. *See* DFA §991 (codified at 15 U.S.C. §§77f(b), 78d(i), 78m(e), 78n(g), 78ee(m), 78kk (match funding).

12. Id. §§ 401-412, 419 (codified at 15 U.S.C.A. §§ 80b-2(a)(11), (29)-(30), 80b-3(b), (l)-(n), 80b-3a(a), 80b-4, 80b-10(c), 80b-11, 80b-18b). As a general rule, these registration requirements are effective as of 21 July 2011, except that an investment adviser may, in its discretion, register with the SEC under the Investment Advisers Act of 1940 during this one-year transition period, subject to rules to be promulgated by the SEC. 15 U.S.C.A. § 80b-2 note.

13. The DFA treats these definitional issues less helpfully. *See* DFA § 619 (codified at 12 U.S.C.A. § 1851), which defines both terms as follows:

> The terms "hedge fund" and "private equity fund" mean an issuer that would be an investment company, as defined in the Investment Company Act of 1940 (15 U.S.C.A. 80a-1 *et seq.*), but for [the Investment Company Act exemptive provisions in 15 U.S.C.A. § 80a-

Regulation of Swaps and Security-Based Swaps

DFA provides for comprehensive regulation of swaps and security-based swaps by the Commodity Futures Trading Commission (CFTC) and the SEC[14] in consultation with the Fed.[15] The SEC and the CFTC have joint responsibility for swap products, to be allocated between the two agencies depending on whether the underlying product is a "security" or not.[16] Institutions deemed to be swap dealers – typically, large banks that make markets in swaps by creating and selling them[17] – as well as "major swap participants" are required to register with either the SEC or CFTC, depending on the nature of their products.[18]

Similarly, despite the welcome imposition of disclosure requirements with respect to, and federal supervision over, derivatives and derivatives markets, there are still no clearly

---

> 3(c)(1) or (c)(7)], or such similar funds as the appropriate Federal banking agencies, the Securities and Exchange Commission, and the Commodity Futures Trading Commission may, byrule, as provided in subsection (b)(2), determine.

12 U.S.C.A. § 1851(h)(2). The exemptive provisions referred to in the quoted excerpt actually provide a more informative description of these types of funds as follows:

> [N]one of the following persons is an investment company within the meaning of [the Investment Company Act]:
>
> (1) Any issuer whose outstanding securities (other than short-term paper) are beneficially owned by not more than one hundred persons and which is not making and does not presently propose to make a public offering of its securities. . .
>
> (7)(A) Any issuer, the outstanding securities of which are owned exclusively by persons who, at the time of acquisition of such securities, are qualified purchasers [*i.e.*, sophisticated investors], and which is not making and does not at that time propose to make a public offering of such securities. . .
>
> (E) For purposes of determining compliance with this paragraph and paragraph (1), an issuer that is otherwise excepted under this paragraph and an issuer that is otherwise excepted under paragraph (1) shall not be treated by the Commission as being a single issuer for purposes of determining whether the outstanding securities of the issuer excepted under paragraph (1) are beneficially owned by not more than 100 persons or whether the outstanding securities of the issuer excepted under this paragraph are owned by persons that are not qualified purchasers. . . .

See Clemente Global Growth Fund, Inc. v. Pickens, 705 F. Supp. 958 (S.D.N.Y. 1989) (interpreting § 80a-3(c)(1)).

14. DFA §§711–716, 718 (codified at 7 U.S.C. §§6d(h), 24(c); 15 U.S.C. §§78o(c)(3)(C), 8301–8306).

15. *Id.* §712(a)(8) (codified at 15 U.S.C. §8302(a)(8)).

16. *Id.* §717 (codified at 7 U.S.C. §2(a)(1)(C)7a-2(c)(1); 15 U.S.C. §§78c-1, 78s(b)(10)). Cf. DFA §720 (codified at 15 U.S.C. §8308) (memorandum of understanding to be negotiated between CFTC and Federal Energy Regulatory Commission). The SEC and the CFTC have already jointly issued proposed rules "further defining" key terms and regulating "mixed swaps." 75 Fed. Reg. 51,429 (2010) (to be codified at 17 C.F.R. pt. 1 (CFTC rules); *id.* pt. 240 (SEC rules)). Public comments were due September 20, 2010. 75 Fed. Reg. at 51,429.

17. At the same time, a "de minimis" exception from designation as a swap dealer is available to "an entity that engages in a de minimis quantity of swap dealing in connection with transactions with or on behalf of customers." DFA §721(a)(49)(D) (codified at 7 U.S.C. § 1a(a)(49)(D)). This clause is important for regional banks and other smaller financial institutions such as savings associations and credit unions and will enable them to avoid the regulatory burdens likely to be associated with being identified as a swap dealer.

18. DFA §§721–724 (codified at 7 U.S.C. §§1a, 1b, 2(a)(1), (c)(2)(A), (i)-(j), 6(c)(1), (6), 6d(f) 6m, 6q, 6s(l), 7-7a-1, 13-1(a), 16(h), 27; 11 U.S.C. 761; 15 U.S.C. §§78f, 8321-8322).

established jurisdictional lines between the SEC and the CFTC over derivatives. For example, equity swaps and their dealers are under CFTC jurisdiction, not that of the SEC, because equity swaps are still considered commodities, not securities. The DFA provides for the SEC and the CFTC, in consultation with the Fed, jointly to "further define" certain key terms (specifically, "swap," "security-based swap," "swap dealer," "security-based swap dealer," "major swap participant," "major security-based swap participant," "eligible contract participant," and "security-based swap agreement"), and jointly prescribe regulations regarding "mixed swaps," as that term is used in DFA Title VII. Hence, at the statutory level there remains fundamental uncertainty about the scope of the new derivatives approach.

Credit Rating Agencies

DFA imposes disclosure requirements on credit rating agencies, and requires their registration with and supervision by the SEC.[19] DFA also expands the availability of private rights of action against credit rating agencies. It eliminates an explicit exclusion of private rights of action arising out of 1934 Act,[20] requiring registration of nationally recognized statistical rating organizations.[21] It also allows for potential liability under the 1933 Act, by eliminating an SEC rule[22] that deemed credit ratings not to be a part of the registration statement "prepared or certified" by a person within the meaning of the private right of action under 1933 Act §11.[23] Hence, credit ratings are now part of the "expertised" portions of a 1933 Act registration statement filed with the SEC, giving rise to an express private right of action against a credit rating agency for materially false or misleading ratings prepared by it and contained in such a statement.[24]

Corporate Governance

Arguably, extravagant executive compensation practices were a contributing cause of the financial crisis. DFA requires companies registered pursuant to 1934 Act §12[25] to permit their shareholders to have a nonbinding vote, at least once every three years,[26] on executive compensation.[27] The DFA also requires disclosure by any person soliciting proxies

---

19. DFA §§931-939B, 939F (codified at 12 U.S.C. §§24a, 1817(b)(1)(E)(i), 1831e, 4519; 15 U.S.C. §§78a(3)(a), 78c(a)(62), 78o-7(m), (u)-(v), 78o-8, 78u-4(b)(2), 80a-6(a)(5)(A)(iv)(I); 22 U.S.C. §286hh(a)(6)).

20. 15 U.S.C. §78o-7(m)(2) (2009) (foreclosing implication of private right of action resulting from registration of statistical rating agency).

21. DFA §933(a) (codified at 15 U.S.C. §78o-7(m)) (applying 1934 Act enforcement and penalty provisions to statements made by a credit rating agency).

22. 17 C.F.R. §230.436(g) (2009), nullified by DFA §939G, 124 Stat. 1376, 1890 (2010).

23. 15 U.S.C. §77k.

24. Pre-Dodd-Frank litigation attempts to impose liability on credit rating agencies that provided misleading favorable ratings for securitized subprime mortgage pools have generally been unsuccessful. *See, e.g., Public Employees' Ret. Sys. of Mississippi v. Merrill Lynch & Co., Inc.*, — F. Supp. 2d —, 2010 WL 2175875 (S.D.N.Y. 2010), at *3–4 (dismissing 1933 Act §11 action against credit rating agencies; holding agencies not "underwriters" for §11 purposes); *Teamsters Allied Benefit. Funds v. McGraw-Hill Cos., Inc.*, — F. Supp. 2d —, 2010 WL 882883 (S.D.N.Y. 2010) (dismissing derivative suit by shareholders of parent company of credit rating agency for failure to state adequate claim under 1934 Act §10(b)).

25. 15 U.S.C. §78l.

26. The DFA allows for more frequent nonbinding votes, upon the approval of the shareholders in that regard. *See* DFA §951 (codified at 15 U.S.C. §78n-1(a)(2)) (permitting, at least once every six years, shareholder vote on frequency of compensation votes).

27. 15 U.S.C. §78n-1(a)(1).

in favor of a merger or other acquisition of any "golden parachute" agreement or understanding in favor of departing executives in connection with the merger or acquisition.[28] These provisions of DFA do not appear to supersede substantive guidance previously issued by the regulators.[29]

---

28. *Id.* §78n-1(b)(1). For these purposes, the term "golden parachute" is characterized by the statute as "any type of compensation (whether present, deferred, or contingent) that is based on or otherwise relates to the acquisition, merger, consolidation, sale, or other disposition of all or substantially all of the assets of the issuer and the aggregate total of all such compensation that may (and the conditions upon which it may) be paid or become payable to or on behalf of such executive officer." *Id.*

29. For example, in late June 2010, the OCC, the Fed, the FDIC, and the OTS adopted final guidance designed to ensure that "incentive compensation policies" at banking organizations did not encourage imprudent risk-taking, and that they were consistent with safety and soundness. Guidance on Sound Incentive Compensation Policies, 75 Fed. Reg. 36,395, 36,405–36,414 (2010). The guidance was effective June 25, 2010. 75 Fed. Reg. at 36,395.

Chapter 8

Resolution of Institution Failures

1. Introduction

This chapter examines the ways in which the supervisory agencies regulate troubled depository institutions (*i.e.*, those in danger of failing if their financial condition continues to deteriorate) and failing depository institutions (*i.e.*, those that are "in default"). Behind a failure, as in the case of the bankruptcy of a general business corporation, is a situation of insolvency.[1] Determination of insolvency or default by the institution's primary regulator may result in the institution being placed into receivership[2] or conservatorship.[3]

A preliminary definitional question may underscore some of the uncertainty and delicacy of regulatory action in this regard. What precisely is a "troubled" institution, and how does it differ from a "failing" institution? The short answer is, quite simply, that as a matter of law a troubled institution is one that has not yet "failed," but is in danger of doing so if current trends in its financial condition continue.[4] However, an institution is "failing" only if it has been declared insolvent by its primary regulator.[5] Accordingly, an institution which has, in any common-sense understanding of the term, failed may continue operating so long as the primary regulator declines to declare it insolvent, and so long as short-term funds continue to be provided to it.

Failure of a financial institution is generally viewed as a situation presenting fundamentally dangerous implications for public confidence in the integrity of the banking system as a whole.[6] The crisis in confidence may also make large-denomination depositors,

---

1. *See, e.g.*, 12 U.S.C. § 191 (grounds for appointment of receiver of national bank).

2. *See, e.g.*, *id.* §§ 191-199 (receivership rules for national bank). *See also id.* §§ 91 (transfers in contemplation of insolvency), 288 (cancellation of stock), 501a (forfeiture of charter).

3. *See, e.g.*, *id.* §§ 202-206, 209, 211 (conservatorship rules for national bank).

4. In current statutory terminology, since the passage of the Financial Institutions Reform, Recovery, and Enforcement Act of 1989 (FIRREA), Pub. L. No. 101-73, 103 Stat. 183 (1989) (codified at scattered sections of, *inter alia*, 12, 15 & 18 U.S.C.), the technical terms for "troubled" and "failing" institutions are institutions "in danger of default" and institutions "in default," respectively.

5. In the case of a state-chartered bank, insolvency would be declared by the state chartering authority. In the case of a national bank, the Comptroller has the sole authority to declare the bank insolvent. *See, e.g.*, 12 U.S.C. § 191.

6. There is increasingly empirical evidence, much of it anecdotal, for the proposition that confidence in the banking system is eroding, in the wake of recent failures of financial institutions. *See, e.g.*, *Faith in Banking Wanes, Poll of U.S. Investors Says*, Wall St. J., July 11, 1984, at 49, col.

typically uninsured, very sensitive to potential financial problems of their depository banks. The end result is that they may be likely to pull out their deposits at the first sign of financial trouble, thus exacerbating any difficulty the institution may be experiencing.[7] In the past, the natural inclination of chartering authorities has therefore been to avoid legal recognition of failure if it is possible to reform the institution in any feasible way short of determination of insolvency.

An actual bank failure can also have fairly specific and disastrous implications for the community served by the failing institution. As a result, the primary goal of the regulation of troubled institutions is to identify the problem at the earliest possible moment and rectify the problem with the minimum of dislocation to the interests of the bank and those who deal with it.[8] The effectiveness with which this policy goal is implemented should be judged against the statutory powers available to the regulators and the ways in which they invoke these powers.

2. Institutions in Danger of Default

There are a range of statutory powers available to the federal bank regulatory agencies to deal with the problems of troubled institutions. This section surveys some of the principal sources of authority in this regard and some of the supervisory devices employed in dealing with troubled or potentially troubled institutions.

Notes and Comments 8.1. If the Comptroller of the Currency is concerned about the long-term stability of Quarter National Bank (QNB), what statutory powers are available to deal with these concerns? Review 12 U.S.C. §§ 55, 57, 91, 93, 161, 1818, 3907.

8.2. What if QNB were a state-chartered, Fed member bank? Review 12 U.S.C. §§ 503, 504, 1818.

8.3. What if QNB were a state-chartered, nonmember insured bank? Review 12 U.S.C. §§ 1817, 1818, 1823(c).

8.4. *Federal enforcement practice.* In fact, there is now a more or less unified body of enforcement provisions collected in one place in federal statutory law, and applicable regardless of the type of depository institution is involved.[9] These enforcement provisions include the power to issue administrative cease and desist orders against violations of law or unsafe and unsound banking practices, the power to suspend or remove members of management, and the power to impose civil money penalties.[10]

8.5. Hiram Forth, a controlling shareholder of QNB, has pressured the president of QNB to grant loans on very favorable terms to certain business associates of Forth. The loans

---

6.

7. *See Big Depositors' Runs on Beleaguered Banks Speed the Failure Rate*, Wall St. J., Aug. 23, 1984, at 1, col. 6.

8. *See, e.g., Continental Examiners Criticized*, N.Y. Times, Sept. 19, 1984, at D18, col. 1; *'Timid Regulation' of Continental Illinois Alleged as Congressional Hearings Begin*, Wall. St. J., Sept. 19, 1984, at 7, col. 1.

9. The single exception is credit unions, which are subject to a parallel set of enforcement powers contained in the Federal Credit Union Act, 12 U.S.C. § 1786, administered by the National Credit Union Administration.

10. For discussion of these enforcement powers, see Note 8.11, *infra*, and the material following the note.

have since gone into default, resulting in considerable losses for QNB. Can a shareholder of QNB bring a derivative action against Forth and the president for the losses sustained by QNB, claiming violations of fiduciary duties of due care and good faith and loyalty? *See* 12 U.S.C. § 93(a). *Cf. Harmsen v. Smith*, 542 F.2d 496 (9th Cir. 1976).

8.6. Would it make any difference if the bank involved had been Fourth State Bank (FSB), a member of the Federal Reserve System? *See* 12 U.S.C. § 503. *Cf. Fitzpatrick v. Federal Deposit Ins. Corp.*, 765 F.2d 569 (6th Cir. 1985); *Lode v. Leonardo*, 557 F. Supp. 675 (D.Ill. 1982).

8.7. What action might QNB's or FSB's primary federal regulator take in response to the actions of Forth and the bank president? Supervisory responses to troubled institutions operate along a continuum, from relatively informal techniques through formal, statutorily established enforcement measures. The administrative practice of the Office of the Comptroller of the Currency with respect to examination and supervision is representative of the corresponding practice of the other regulators. Consider the following excerpt with a view to answering the questions raised in Notes 8.8-8.10, *infra*.

Office of the Comptroller of the Currency
The Director's Book

70-75 (1987)

The OCC has several tools available to carry out its supervisory responsibilities, and Congress has given the agency broad discretion in the use of these tools. Although the OCC may sue bank directors in federal court for statutory violations, most often it uses an administrative action when dealing with such violations or with other breaches of duty and improper practices. The more commonly used actions vary in severity, ranging from the least severe commitment letters to cease and desist orders. The OCC also has the authority to impose civil money penalties and to order the removal of bank officers and directors. Finally, in appropriate circumstances, it can revoke a bank's charter.

The OCC decides whether to bring an action against a bank or an individual, and what the nature of such action should be, on a case-by-case basis, giving consideration to the need to correct current violations and prevent future bank problems. Key factors in its decisions are the seriousness of the safety and soundness concerns and the violations of law and the bank's history of cooperation with the OCC in working out the bank's problems. Since the OCC and the bank's management and directors have a mutual interest in improving the condition of a bank in which problems have been identified or administrative actions brought, it is in both parties' best interests that corrective action be taken expeditiously. A bank's failure to respond promptly and decisively to correct cited problems likely will result in a severe OCC action.

A bank may first become aware that the OCC is considering an action at the examiner's exit interview, when the examiner in charge of the bank's examination meets with management, and often with the board of directors, to discuss generally the agency's concerns. Directors should actively participate in this meeting, making sure the examiner is aware of the bank's current strengths and successes and seeking advice in correcting existing problems or potential problems.

The period between the end of an examination and the time the findings are formalized in a written communication to the board provides a good opportunity for the bank to formulate and begin to carry out a reasonable plan to correct the problems the examiners noted. The OCC encourages banks to submit responses stating the bank's commitment to a corrective plan and specifying the terms of the plan. It also is advisable during this period for the bank to keep in contact, either by telephone or in writing, with the appropriate OCC district office personnel to expedite the corrective process and to show the OCC that it is responding promptly and positively to the agency's concerns. Actions proposed and taken to deal with these concerns should be documented in the board minutes.

If the OCC decides to bring an actions, the bank's directors usually will receive a request to meet with district personnel who will present to them the course of action the OCC has chosen. If the directors disagree with the OCC's position on certain aspects of the proposed action and differences cannot be resolved at the meeting, the board will be given a reasonable amount of time to propose changes and to discuss alternatives with the district.

Good faith discussions between the board and the OCC generally are highly useful in bringing about a speedy and mutually acceptable resolution of differences. The emphasis in these proceedings should be on devising a realistic and reassonable method to restore the bank to good condition.

Remedial Actions

Remedial actions are actions the OCC takes to correct specific problems that have been identified at a particular bank. They may take the form of commitment letters, memoranda of understanding, formal agreements, capital directives, cease and desist orders, and removals. Typically, a remedial actions specifies several things the bank or individuals need to do to correct identified problems, such as devising a plan to increase capital or to provide for management succession, or disposing of a piece of real property held by the bank in violation of applicable law.

Such actions may be imposed on a bank or individual either through the bank's directors consenting to comply with the items in the proposed document or, absent consent, through an administrative proceeding. In either case, the directors are ultimately responsible for seeing that the bank complies with the action.

A remedial action is terminated when the OCC determines that the overall condition of the bank is significantly improved, and the bank has substantially complied with the terms of the document.

Commitment Letter

A commitment letter is the least severe tool used by the OCC. In fact, a commitment letter may be initiated by a bank's board of directors that has identified or been advised of a problem, such as a deficiency in the bank's lending policy that needs to be corrected for the bank to avoid serious loan problems in the future. The letter, signed by the board, enumerates the problems that require corrective action and lays out the plan and timetable established to remedy the problems. A commitment letter may be used by a bank that has been responsive and does not have a history of serious problems and when the problems identified do not pose an immediate or serious threat to the bank's health.

Memorandum of Understanding

A memorandum of understanding (MOU) is initiated by the OCC and entered into between a bank's board of directors, or an individual, and the agency. Unlike a commitment letter, the MOU is a formally drafted OCC document that sets forth the bank's agreement to take certain actions within specified time periods to correct violations of law or unsafe and unsound conditions. Generally, the OCC will consider using an MOU only when the problems do not pose an immediate or serious threat to the bank and when the agency expects that the bank will cooperate in correcting the problems so that legal enforcement will not be required to achieve compliance. If a bank fails to comply with an MOU, the OCC will consider a stronger action.

Formal Agreement

A formal agreement is similar in form to the MOU. Like the MOU and the commitment letter, it requires agreement between the OCC and the bank, or individual, as to the remedial action necessary to correct the cited conditions. It is proposed when the problems in the bank are not too severe and management is cooperative. The formal agreement differs from an MOU, however, because the OCC may order compliance with a formal agreement through a cease and desist order and may seek judicial enforcement of any failure to respond to the order.

Cease and Desist Order

Through cease and desist orders (C & Ds), the OCC has broad authority to fashion appropriate remedies for abuses. Using a C & D, the OCC may require banks, or persons participating in the bank's affairs, that violate the law or a formal agreement or engage in an unsafe and unsound practice, to stop the proscribed activities and to take affirmative action to remedy conditions resulting from the violations or practices. For instance, individuals who received excessive bonuses from a national bank have been ordered to return those sums to the bank. Affirmative actions designed to prevent future violations may also be ordered. For example, to ensure that future abuses would not occur, insiders who have abused their account relationships with a bank have been prohibited from maintaining accounts at the institution.

Cease and desist orders are issued most often when the agency is not confident that bank management will take the necessary corrective action or when the problems are so severe that a lesser action cannot be justified. Cease and desist orders are also used to compel compliance with enforcement documents.

When the OCC determines that a cease and desist order is required, it will bring the problems to the directors' attention and serve upon the directors an order specifying the corrective actions to be taken. Usually, the order will be served at a board meeting. At that time, the OCC will ask for consent of the board to the order. Consent requires the signatures of the majority of the board. Once an order becomes effective, all the directors are responsible for compliance with it.

If consent to a cease and desist order is not obtained, the OCC will serve a notice of charges identifying the problems and setting out the basis for the action and the parties against whom the action is being brought. . . .

A cease and desist order remains in effect until the OCC terminates it.

Temporary Cease and Desist Order

The OCC may issue a temporary cease and desist order before a cease and desist proceeding is completed when one of the following is likely to occur: bank insolvency; substantial dissipation of bank assets or earnings; serious progressive weakening of the bank's condition; or prejudice to the interests of the depositors. The temporary order may require the bank or other party to cease and desist from the violation or practice and/or to take affirmative corrective action. Unless the temporary cease and desist order is set aside by court order, it is effective on service and remains in effect until the administrative proceedings leading to a cease and desist order are complete.

Capital Directive

Because of the critical importance of adequate capital, capital requirements have been established for all national banks. When necessary or appropriate, the OCC may issue to an individual bank a capital directive, which establishes higher capital requirements for the individual bank and requires the bank to achieve these levels. The directive is a form of order that the OCC may issue when a national bank is not maintaining its capital at or above the required level. A directive also may be issued when a bank has failed to submit or is not in compliance with a reasonable plan to achieve required capital levels.

When a bank is notified that the OCC intends to issue a capital directive, the bank may consent to the directive or notify the OCC in writing of its objection. If the bank objects, the OCC will review the bank's response and determine whether to issue the directive or require the bank to submit an acceptable plan of its own. A capital directive, or any plan submitted pursuant to a directive, may be enforced by the OCC in the same manner as a cease and desist order.

Removal and Suspension

The OCC also may initiate action to remove and, if necessary to protect the bank, may suspend a national bank director or officer for a particularly serious violation of law, unsafe and unsound practice, violation of a cease and desist order, or other breach of duty. A suspension is an interim procedure the OCC may use while removal proceedings are underway to protect the bank and its depositors from an immediate threat. Unless stayed by a court, a suspension is effective upon written notice by the OCC and remains in effect until the removal proceedings are completed or until the OCC dismisses the charges. . . .

The OCC may also protect the bank by removing or suspending on written notice a bank officer or director charged with or convicted of a felony involving dishonesty or breach of trust if continued service to the bank may threaten the depositors' interests or impair public confidence in the bank. . . .

Notes and Comments 8.8. QNB is being examined by district examiners from the OCC. QNB's executive vice president, who is also a member of the board of directors, is preparing for the exit interview with the lead examiner. She suspects that the bank is going to be criticized for a series of loans that it granted to Mr. Forth and several of his business associates. She has asked you, a member of the bank's legal staff for advice on what she may expect at the exit interview. Should she refuse to discuss the matter with the lead examiner, and say that the matter is now in the hands of the bank's attorneys? Should she come to the exit interview prepared to dispute the criticism? Should she start off with a conciliatory approach to the exit interview? What are the likely legal consequences of the exit interview, if in fact the loans are criticized by the examiner?

8.9. Assume that the examiner does criticize the Forth group loans, and also criticizes the lack of adequate documentation in many of QNB's loan files. You have been asked to prepare a letter to the OCC responding to these criticisms. What should you include in the response? Would it be a tactical mistake for the bank to concede that documentation practices in the loan department may be less than adequate?

8.10. If QNB concedes that documentation is inadequate, what is likely to be the OCC's response?

Chavers v. Fleet Bank (RI), N.A.

844 A.2d 666 (R.I. 2004)

WILLIAMS, Chief Justice.

[Credit card holders brought an action against the national bank that had issued their cards, alleging breach of contract and violations of the Rhode Island Deceptive Trade Practices Act (DTPA), R.I.G.L.1956, § 6-13.1-4, after the bank increased annual percentage rates. The trial court granted the bank summary judgment, and the plaintiffs appealed. The Rhode Island Supreme Court affirmed in part, reversed in part, and remanded, holding *inter alia* that: (*i*) the bank's practices regarding credit card solicitations were exempted from the DTPA; and, (*ii*) the trial court had equitable jurisdiction over the contract claim. In this excerpt, the court considers the Comptroller's authority under 12 U.S.C. § 1818.]

II

Summary Judgment . . .

A

Deceptive Trade Practices Act . . .

2. *Specific Acts* . . .

The OCC is charged with the primary responsibility of regulating national banks, such as Fleet. *See Roberts* [*v. Fleet Bank (R.I.),*] 342 F.3d [260,] 269 n. 5 [(3d Cir.2003)]. In carrying out its supervisory responsibilities, the OCC operates under a comprehensive statutory framework set forth in 12 U.S.C. § 1818. Section 1818 provides the OCC with "wideranging supervisory and enforcement authority over our nation's banking system." *First National Bank of Scotia v. United States,* 530 F.Supp. 162, 166 (D.D.C.1982). Under 12 U.S.C. §§ 1818(b) and (c), the OCC is authorized to initiate cease-and-desist proceedings and issue temporary cease-and-desist orders against national banks for violation of any "law, rule, or regulation." *See also Roberts,* 342 F.3d at 270.

The OCC has used cease-and-desist orders "to regulate all areas of a bank's operations." *First Union National Bank v. Burke,* 48 F.Supp.2d 132, 137 (D.Conn.1999) (quoting *In re Franklin National Bank Securities Litigation,* 478 F.Supp. 210, 217 (E.D.N.Y.1979)). In addition to its use of cease-and-desist proceedings, the OCC employs informal procedures to induce national banks' compliance with laws, rules and regulations. *Id.* at 137-38 (quoting *United States v. Philadelphia National Bank,* 374 U.S. 321, 330 (1962) (noting that most banks follow "[r]ecommendations by the agencies concerning banking practices * * * without the necessity of formal compliance procedings") and *In re Franklin National Bank Securities Litigation,* 478 F.Supp. at 218 ("Achieving voluntary compliance with laws, recommendations and agreements is often the rule rather than the exception.")). For example, the OCC frequently issues commitment letters, memoranda of understanding and enters formal agreements[7] with banks "to achieve expeditious corrective and remedial action to return the bank to a safe and sound condition." *Special Supervision/Fraud and Enforcement Activities,* 21-1 O.C.C. Q.J. 21 (2002).

Drawing on its power to obtain compliance with any "law, rule, or regulation" under 12 U.S.C. § 1818, the OCC has routinely taken steps to enforce various state and federal statutes. *See, e.g., First National Bank of Gordon v. Department of Treasury, Office of the Comptroller of the Currency,* 911 F.2d 57, 59 (8th Cir.1990) (issuing cease-and-desist order for violations of 12 U.S.C. §§ 18 and 161(a)); *First National Bank of Bellaire v. Comptroller of the Currency,* 697 F.2d 674, 688 (5th Cir.1983) (affirming OCC's cease-and-desist order for violations of 12 U.S.C. § § 29, 375a and 30); *National State Bank, Elizabeth, N.J. v. Long,* 630 F.2d 981, 989 (3d Cir.1980) (holding that the OCC was responsible for enforcing a state antiredlining statute). We are of the opinion that the OCC's authority to enforce such laws includes the power to regulate Fleet's credit-card solicitations pursuant to the [Federal Trade Commission Act, 15 U.S.C. § 45].

The Third Circuit has recognized the OCC's power to take . . . action to prevent unfair and deceptive credit card solicitations. In *Roberts,* the court was presented with factual allegations that were identical to the allegations in this case. *See Roberts,* 342 F.3d at 262-64. . . . The court held that, pursuant to its regulatory powers set forth in 12 U .S.C. § 1818, the OCC was authorized to bring enforcement actions against Fleet to prevent violations of 15 U.S.C. § 45. *Roberts,* 342 F.3d at 269-70. . . .

This Court is not persuaded by plaintiffs' argument that the OCC is powerless to

7. Formal agreements are similar in content to cease and desist orders, but do not carry the threat of contempt or civil money penalties as a remedy for a breach. *Special Supervision/Fraud and Enforcement Activities,* 21-1 O.C.C. Q.J. 21, 22 (2002).

regulate Fleet's credit-card solicitations under 15 U.S.C. § 45(a)(1). Citing 15 U.S.C. § 45(a)(2), plaintiffs contend that the prohibitions set forth in § 45(a)(1) do not apply to banks. Under 15 U.S.C. § 45(a)(2), "[t]he [FTC] is hereby empowered and directed to prevent persons, partnerships, or corporations, except banks, savings and loan institutions [and] *** Federal credit unions * * * from using unfair methods of competition in or affecting commerce and unfair or deceptive acts or practices in or affecting commerce." The limiting provisions of 15 U.S.C. § 45(a)(2), however, expressly apply to the FTC's enforcement power. That section has no effect on the OCC's ability to prevent violations of 15 U.S.C. § 45(a)(1) as a consequence of its power to enforce any "law, rule, or regulation" under 12 U.S.C. § 1818.

The plaintiffs further argue that the prohibitions of 15 U.S.C. § 45(a)(1) cannot be enforced against Fleet because the Board of Governors of the Federal Reserve System (Federal Reserve Board) has not issued regulations defining what acts or practices shall be deemed unfair or deceptive. Under 15 U.S.C. § 57a(f), the Federal Reserve Board is required to take steps to "prevent unfair or deceptive acts or practices in or affecting commerce" by issuing regulations "defining with specificity such unfair or deceptive acts or practices, and containing requirements prescribed for the purpose of preventing such acts or practices." The ability of the Federal Reserve Board to promulgate such regulations, however, does not eviscerate the OCC's authority to classify a particular act or practice as unfair or deceptive on a case-by-case basis.

In the absence of regulations specifically defining which acts or practices could be deemed unfair or deceptive under 15 U.S.C. § 45(a)(1), the OCC properly could make such a determination through informal adjudication. Congress did not provide strict guidance on what particular acts violate that section. Indeed, the phrase "unfair or deceptive acts or practices" does not easily lend itself to precise definition. Rather, "the meaning and application of [the phrase 'unfair or deceptive'] must be arrived at by the gradual process of inclusion and exclusion." *In the Matter of The American Bank of the South Merritt Island, Florida,* FDIC Enf. Dec. Lexis 512, FDIC-92-17b at 13 (November 24, 1992). The broad prohibitions outlined in 15 U.S.C. § 45(a)(1) leave room for interpretations by implementing agencies such as the OCC. The fact that Congress directed the Federal Reserve Board to enact corresponding regulations did not strip the OCC of its power to adjudicate such issues and make appropriate determinations on a case-by-case basis. *See Teambank, N.A. v. McClure,* 279 F.3d 614, 619 (8th Cir.2002) (recognizing the OCC's power to fill gaps in a particular statute through informal adjudication).

Regulations promulgated by the Federal Reserve Board pursuant to 15 U.S.C. § 57a(f) merely serve to further identify deceptive acts or practices. The Federal Reserve Board's responsibility for issuing regulations pursuant to 15 U.S.C. § 57a(f) in no way curtails the OCC's broad enforcement power under 12 U.S.C. § 1818. Rather, regulations issued pursuant to 15 U.S.C. § 57a(f) would only increase the reach of the OCC's authority because they would constitute specific regulations that the OCC could enforce pursuant to 12 U.S.C. § 1818.

Next, plaintiffs argue that the OCC has no power to enforce the provisions of 15 U.S.C. § 45(a)(1) against Fleet in this case because even deceptive credit-card solicitations do not affect Fleet's financial stability, which is a requirement for the OCC to invoke its enforcement authority under 12 U.S.C. § 1818. *See First National Bank of Bellaire,* 697 F.2d at 681. The OCC has taken steps to stop such solicitations, thereby clearly evincing the OCC's position on the matter. The OCC has, on numerous occasions, initiated enforcement actions and entered consent orders with national banks whereby the bank agreed to cease certain credit-card solicitations. *See, e.g., In the matter of: net 1st National Bank Boca Raton,*

Florida, OCC Enf. Dec., Lexis 93, OCC EA No.2000-88 (issued September 25, 2000); *In the matter of: Providian National Bank, Tilton, New Hampshire,* OCC Enf. Dec., Lexis 54, OCC EA No.2000- 53 (issued June 28, 2000).[8] The initiation of an informal enforcement proceeding that resulted in the consent order in those cases presumably was triggered by concerns that such credit-card solicitations could undermine the credibility of the banking institution, thereby triggering a wave of instability throughout the banking industry. Moreover, by monitoring national banks' credit-card solicitations to ensure that they are truthful and trustworthy, the OCC is able to take proactive steps to shield such banks from large-scale civil liability under various statutory and common law causes of action. . . .

FLANDERS, Justice, dissenting. . . .

Neither the Office of the Comptroller of the Currency (OCC) nor any other regulatory agency permits or regulates the activity in question (the issuing and marketing of credit cards). Although the OCC contends that it has the power to review national banks' alleged unfair and deceptive credit-card activity on an ad-hoc basis to determine whether to initiate the enforcement of any alleged violation of law, such episodic, ad-hoc enforcement, under a questionable grant of authority to do so, does not constitute the kind of permissive regulation and continuing monitoring of an activity that is necessary to qualify for the statutory exemption under DTPA. . . .

Although the Third Circuit has held in *Roberts v. Fleet Bank R .I.),* 342 F.3d 260, 270 (3d Cir.2003) that section 8(b)(1) of the Federal Deposit Insurance Act (FDIA)–codified at 12 U.S.C. § 1818(b)(1)–authorizes the OCC to initiate enforcement activity with respect to national banks' alleged unfair and deceptive acts, national banks do not have to register with the OCC or to obtain its permission before they can issue or market credit cards. Thus, whatever review OCC may undertake of national banks' credit-card activities is strictly to decide whether to initiate enforcement actions and not to monitor or regulate their compliance with any federal authorization to engage in such activity. Moreover, the Third Circuit has previously restricted 12 U.S.C. § 1818(b)(1)'s grant of authority to situations that threaten the financial stability of the bank in question. *See, e.g., National State Bank v. Long,* 630 F.2d 981, 988 (3d Cir.1980) (holding that 12 U.S.C. 1818(b)(1) is applicable to a violation of state law that directly implicates concerns in the banking field). Thus, given that the OCC does not authorize and monitor the credit-card activity of national banks as a regulator and given the murky scope of any authority it might have to initiate enforcement actions against illegal credit-card activity by national banks, we should not exempt this defendant from DTPA. . . .

Nevertheless, it is certainly true that national banks are federal instrumentalities that are subject to OCC enforcement actions. . . . For example, under 12 U.S.C. § 1818(b)(1) of the FDIA, the OCC can issue cease-and-desist orders when a national bank engages in an "unsafe or unsound" practice, or violates a law, rule or regulation. 12 U.S.C. § 1818(b)(1). *E.g., Branch v. FDIC.,* 825 F.Supp. 384, 391 (D.Mass.1993). When a cease-and-desist order is premised on an unsafe or unsound banking practice, however, the OCC's enforcement authority is limited to acts directly affecting the bank's financial stability. See *First National*

8. Although "consent orders need not be supported by findings or opinion, they do express a good deal of the law of the agency." 2 Charles H. Koch, Jr. et al., *Administrative Law and Practice* § 5 .43[2] (2d ed.1997). Because practitioners pay considerable attention to consent orders, it has been "alleged that agencies intentionally make law through the consent process" by negotiating a "consent settlement with a small violator [to] establish a principle whereas a larger perpetrator might have fought the case * * *." *Id.*

Bank of Bellaire v. Comptroller of Currency, 697 F.2d 674, 681 (5th Cir.1983); see also *Gulf Federal Savings and Loan Association v. Federal Home Loan Bank Board,* 651 F.2d 259, 264, 267 (5th Cir.1981) (interpreting cease-and-desist authority of former FHLLB over federally chartered thrifts). But when the order is based on an asserted violation of a law, rule, or regulation, the alleged violation need not threaten the banks financial soundness for the OCC to properly exercise its authority under 12 U.S.C. 1818(b)(1). Arthur E. Wilmarth, Jr., *The Expansion of State Bank Powers, the Federal Response, and the Case for Preserving the Dual Banking System,* 58 Fordham L.Rev. 1133, 1205 (1990). *But see First National Bank of Bellaire,* 697 F.2d at 681 (citing *Gulf Federal Savings and Loan Association,* 651 F.2d at 264, 265 n. 5). And the OCCs power to enforce [section] 5 of the Federal Trade Commission Act against national banks is questionable at best, given the absence of any specific regulations or laws promulgated by the Federal Reserve Board concerning the alleged bait-and-switch tactics used to market credit cards that are at issue here. *See* 15 U.S.C. 57a(f)(1) (empowering the board to prescribe regulations defining unfair and deceptive bank practices).

. . . The Fifth Circuit has interpreted 12 U.S.C. 1818(b)(1) more narrowly than its sister circuits, requiring that the alleged violation must actually threaten the banks financial soundness. See *First National Bank of Bellaire,* 697 F.2d at 681 (12 U.S.C. 1818(b) applies only to violations of law "with a reasonably direct effect on a banks financial stability"). ...

Despite the *Roberts* court's reliance on the facial language of 12 U.S.C. § 1818(b)(1), the Third Circuit previously suggested that the OCC may issue a cease-and-desist order pursuant to a violation of law only when the purpose of the law is to further the financial stability of the banking institution or when the law directly implicates concerns in the banking field. *See National State Bank,* 630 F.2d at 988.[14] This view is followed by the Ninth Circuit in *Saratoga Savings and Loan Association v. Federal Home Loan Bank Board,* 879 F.2d 689, 693 (9th Cir.1989), and the Fifth Circuit, which has adopted an even more restrictive interpretation, ruling that the alleged violation of law must actually threaten the banks financial soundness. *First National Bank of Bellaire,* 697 F.2d at 681.

Notes and Comments 8.11. Assume that QNB's board of directors has signed a commitment letter, acknowledging that there appears to be a problem with maintaining adequate documentation in loan files, and describing the steps the board intends to take to correct the problem. The letter indicates that a new written policy will be in place in this regard within four weeks, and that full, accurate documentation for all outstanding loans will be in place within three months. However, at the end of two months from the date of the letter, the draft of the new written policy is still being worked on by QNB's outside counsel, and no steps have yet been taken to improve loan documentation. Would these circumstances be legally sufficient to justify the issuance of a cease and desist order against the bank?

8.12. Would it make any difference to your answer to the last question if QNB had entered into a formal agreement with the OCC, rather than signing a commitment letter?

---

14. Specifically, the Third Circuit stated:

"[Section 1818(b)(1)] provides that the appropriate federal banking agency may initiate cease and desist proceedings against any insured bank that violates '*a law.*' 12 U.S.C. 1818(b)(1). The legislative history of the Act indicates that Congress was concerned not only with federal but with state law as well, particularly as it might bear on corruption of bank officials *or the financial stability of the institution.* It may be that the word 'law' as used in the statute is not all encompassing and may exclude matters of purely local concern. However, when state law prohibits the practice of redlining, its enforcement so *directly implicates concerns in the banking field* that the appropriate federal regulatory agency has jurisdiction." *National State Bank v. Long,* 630 F.2d 981, 988 (3d Cir.1980). (Emphases added.)

2004 WL 249605, 2004 WL 249605 (R.I.).

8.13. What if the OCC and QNB had been unable to agree upon a suitable commitment letter or formal agreement? What procedures would be involved in the issuance of a cease and desist order? If QNB's board believed that the bank's loan documentation was adequate and that any changes in its current practice would be too expensive, how could they resist the issuance of the order?

8.14. Assume that the OCC has issued a notice indicating that it is seeking to impose a cease and desist order against QNB, on the grounds that the bank's current loan documentation policies constituted an unsafe and unsound banking practice. QNB's general counsel has asked you to explain what an "unsafe and unsound banking practice" means. Is it statutorily defined? *See Groos Nat. Bank v. Comptroller of the Currency*, 573 F.2d 889 (5th Cir. 1978) (concept left to "progressive definition" administratively). *See also* Malloy, *Balancing Public Confidence and Confidentiality: Adjudication Practices and Procedures of the Federal Bank Regulatory Agencies*, 61 TEMP. L. REV. 723, 769-74 (1988) (discussing meaning of term; collecting cases). *But see First Nat. Bank of Bellaire v. Comptroller of the Currency*, 697 F.2d 674 (5th Cir. 1983) (limiting concept to issues of financial soundness); *Gulf Fed. Sav. & Loan Assn. v. Federal Home Loan Bank Bd.*, 651 F.2d 259 (5th Cir. 1981), *cert. denied*, 458 U.S. 1121 (1982) (same).

8.15. If, in response to examiner criticism of its lending policies and practices, QNB stopped such practices and began improving those policies on the initiative of its Board of Directors, would that prevent the Comptroller, as a legal matter, from issuing a cease and desist order, ordering QNB not to engage in such practices in the future? *See First State Bank of Wayne County v. Federal Deposit Ins. Corp.*, 770 F.2d 81 (6th Cir. 1985).

8.16. Could the cease and desist order legally include a requirement that Hiram Forth reimburse QNB for all losses and costs in connection with the defaulted loans to his business associates? Or should such relief be confined to 12 U.S.C. § 93(a)? *See Citizens State Bank of Marshfield, Mo. v. Federal Deposit Ins. Corp.*, 751 F.2d 209 (8th Cir. 1984); *Larimore v. Comptroller of the Currency*, 789 F.2d 1244 (7th Cir. 1986). *But cf.* 12 U.S.C. §§ 1786(e)(3)(A)(i)-(ii), 1818(b)(6)(A)(i)-(ii) (FIRREA amendments).

8.17. An "institution-affiliated party" (IAP) of an insured depository institution as defined in 12 U.S.C. § 1813(u)(4) is subject to administrative enforcement just as the institutions themselves are. The next case is a significant decision, because it is one of only a few cases considering the application of the IAP definition to independent contractors of insured depository institutions,[11] a definition that on its own terms could apply to outside counsel of such an institution, thus putting counsel at risk of administrative enforcement action for its representation. Review the excerpt in preparation for the questions that follow.

Grant Thornton, LLP v. Office of Comptroller of the Currency

514 F.3d 1328 (D.C.Cir. 2008)

WILLIAMS, Senior Circuit Judge:

Grant Thornton, LLP, an accounting firm, appeals a final decision and order of the

---

11. *Cf. Oberstar v. F.D.I.C.*, 987 F.2d 494 (8th Cir. 1993) (holding potential investor in bank granted proxies to vote controlling shareholders' shares at bank shareholders' meeting constituted "institution-affiliated party"); *Paul v. Office of Thrift Supervision*, 763 F.Supp. 568 (S.D.Fla. 1990), *affirmed sub nom. Paul v. Ryan*, 948 F.2d 1297 (1991) (holding definition of "institution affiliated party" encompassed depository institution officer-shareholder even after OTS had appointed Resolution Trust Corporation as receiver for institution, institution had been closed, and OTS had issued temporary cease and desist order).

Comptroller of the Currency that requires the firm to pay $300,000 in civil penalties for recklessly failing to meet Generally Accepted Auditing Standards ("GAAS") in its audit of the First National Bank of Keystone. Grant Thornton also appeals the Comptroller's cease and desist order mandating that the firm comply with a host of conditions whenever it audits depository institutions. We vacate the final decision and both orders, finding that when an accounting firm merely performs an external audit aimed solely at verifying the accuracy of a bank's books, it is not "participat[ing]" or "engaging" in "an unsafe or unsound practice in conducting the business" or "the affairs" of the bank, as those terms are used in 12 U.S.C. §§ 1813(u)(4)(c), 1818(b)(1), and 1818(i)(2)(B)(i)(II). . . .

In 1992 the First National Bank of Keystone, then a small rural bank in West Virginia, sought to increase its revenues, launching an ambitious loan securitization program. The bank bought subprime or high loan-to-value loans from large originators throughout the country. It then pooled these loans with loans it had originated itself. The bank bundled the loans into securities and sold them to institutional investors. Keystone hired asset servicers to collect the principal, interest, and penalties on the loans and to issue monthly checks of interest income to Keystone. By 1999 the bank's assets of approximately $100 million had apparently skyrocketed to about $1 billion.

Examiners from the Office of the Comptroller of Currency ("OCC") scrutinized the bank's records periodically from 1992 through 1999. In a 1997 report, the examiners criticized the accuracy of the bank's statements and the effectiveness of the securitization program's management. Using a standard rating system, the OCC gave the bank very low marks for its overall condition and management quality.

Because of Keystone's failure to address these concerns, the OCC initiated an enforcement action against the bank in May 1998. As a result, Keystone and the OCC formally agreed that the bank would retain a nationally recognized independent accounting firm to audit the bank's mortgage operations, assess the accuracy of its financial statements, and determine the validity of the bank's accounting for loans it purchased and bundled into securities. In July 1998 the bank hired Grant Thornton to conduct the agreed-upon external audit. In April 1999 Grant Thornton issued its audit opinion. The opinion acknowledged the firm's duty to "obtain reasonable assurance about whether [Keystone's] financial statements [for 1997 and 1998] are free of material misstatement," and in effect stated that it had found such assurance.

In August 1999 OCC examiners uncovered Keystone's fraud. The bank had inflated its interest income by nearly $98 million and its assets by about $450 million. These $450 million in assets supposedly belonging to Keystone were in reality those of another bank. The scheme masked the fact that Keystone had been insolvent since 1996. Several members of Keystone management were convicted of felonies for falsifying bank financial records, loan servicer reports, and remittances, as well as lying to auditors and regulators. After the OCC determined that Keystone was insolvent, it closed the bank.

On March 5, 2004 the OCC invoked the Financial Institutions Reform, Recovery, and Enforcement Act ("FIRREA") of 1989, Pub.L. No. 101-73, 103 Stat. 183, and initiated an administrative proceeding claiming that Grant Thornton, in auditing Keystone's financial statements, had "recklessly engag[ed] in an unsafe or unsound practice in conducting [Keystone's] affairs." 12 U.S.C. § 1818(b)(1); see also §§ 1813(u)(4), 1818(i)(2)(B). The government's evidence showed, among other things, that Grant Thornton had relied on oral representations as to Keystone's ownership of approximately $236 million of the $450 million at issue, even in the face of written communications suggesting the opposite. At the end of the hearing, however, the administrative law judge recommended that all charges be dismissed because she found that Grant Thornton had not acted recklessly.

On December 7, 2006 the Comptroller rejected the ALJ's recommendation and fined Grant Thornton. Relying or purporting to rely on the evidence introduced by Harry Potter, the OCC's audit wizard, the Comptroller found that Grant Thornton participated in an unsafe or unsound practice by recklessly failing to comply with GAAS in planning and conducting the Keystone audit. In a cease and desist order, the Comptroller limited Grant Thornton's freedom to accept and conduct audits independently, hire accountants, and handle working papers.

. . . We find that the Comptroller exceeded his statutory authority in characterizing Grant Thornton's external auditing activity as "participat[ing] in ... [an] unsafe or unsound [banking] practice," see § 1813(u)(4), and as "engaging ... in an unsafe or unsound practice in conducting [Keystone's] business," see § 1818(b)(1), and in "conducting [Keystone's] affairs," see § 1818(i)(2)(B)(i)(II). Those conclusions end the case. . . .

The relevant statutory structure is unusual to say the least. It is a bit as if provisions penalizing theft started by defining a "thief" as "a person who commits theft, to wit, one who intentionally takes away the property of another," etc., and then imposed penalties on any "thief who intentionally takes away the property of another," etc. The upshot obviously involves a good deal of linguistic duplication; and imposition of a penalty requires that the accused be shown both to fit the statutory definition and to have committed the acts actually triggering punishment.

Here the crucial *definition* is that of an "institution-affiliated party" ("IAP"), which includes

> (4) any independent contractor (including any attorney, appraiser, or accountant) who knowingly or recklessly participates in-
>
> ...
>
> (C) any unsafe or unsound practice, which caused or is likely to cause more than a minimal financial loss to or a significant adverse effect on, the insured depository institution.

12 U.S.C. § 1813(u)(4). We assume without deciding that an accounting firm like Grant Thornton can qualify as an independent contractor.

The relevant *substantive* provisions of FIRREA echo the definition. Under 12 U.S.C. § 1818(b)(1), the Comptroller of the Currency may issue a cease-and-desist order if a bank or IAP "is engaging or has engaged ... in an unsafe or unsound practice in conducting the business of [an] insured depository institution"; and under § 1818(i)(2)(B)(i)(II) the Comptroller may impose civil monetary penalties when a depository institution or IAP "recklessly engages in an unsafe or unsound practice in conducting the affairs of [an] insured depository institution" which causes a more than minimal loss to the bank or meets other aggravating circumstances.

While the definitional section doesn't specify that the accused must have engaged in the "unsafe or unsound practice" in *"conducting the business of"* the bank, § 1818(b)(1), or in *"conducting the affairs of"* the bank, § 1818(i)(2)(B)(i)(II), the OCC doesn't dispute that, to prevail under the substantive provisions, it must show that Grant Thornton's audit activity amounted to such "conducting." . . .

Nor does the Comptroller contest that the phrase "unsafe or unsound practices," in all its appearances here, means "unsafe or unsound *banking* practices." The latter is, indeed, the formulation that the Comptroller uses in his Notice of Assessment of a Civil Monetary Penalty, at 17-18 and his Final Decision and Order, at 17. That reading (besides being undisputed and according with conventional banking terminology) harmonizes the definitional section, § 1813(u)(4), with the two substantive sections penalizing one who recklessly participates or engages in "an unsafe or unsound practice in conducting the business" or "the affairs" of a depository institution. § 1818(b)(1), (i)(2)(B)(i)(II).

Although the OCC's Notice of Charges for Issuance of an Order to Cease and Desist might be read as claiming that the "unsafe or unsound practice" in which Grant Thornton allegedly engaged was Keystone's own fraud, . . . its final decision identified the practice as Grant Thornton's conduct of the audit: "Clearly, Grant Thornton itself 'participated' in an unsafe or unsound practice when it violated GAAS in carrying out its audit." . . . Thus, the Comptroller's orders rest on the idea that recklessly conducting a non-GAAS audit of a bank constitutes participation in an unsafe or unsound practice in conducting the business or affairs of the bank. But however incompetently or recklessly the audit may have been performed, conduct of the audit cannot be shoehorned into the controlling statutory language.

First, Grant Thornton didn't participate in an "unsafe or unsound [banking] practice" because an audit of the sort conducted here is not a banking practice. Grant Thornton was fulfilling the classic reporting function of external auditors-examining the company's books from the outside and verifying the accuracy of its records and the adequacy of its internal controls. This sort of outside look into a bank's activity is not a "practice" of a depository institution or bank. FIRREA defines a "depository institution" as "any bank or savings association." § 1813(c)(1). It defines a "bank" as "any national bank and State bank, and any Federal branch and insured branch." § 1813(a)(1)(A). As this definition is in part circular, itself depending on the meaning of the word "bank," Congress evidently relied on common understanding to fill the gap. The language of *Webster's Third New International Dictionary* (1981), identifying a bank as "an establishment for the custody, loan, exchange, or issue of money, for the extension of credit, and for facilitating the transmission of funds by drafts or bills of exchange," *id.* at 172, seems apt. A review of a bank's books is quite distinct from the "custody, loan, exchange, or issue ... of money" or "facilitating the transmission of funds." *Id.* We do not attempt to define the full universe of activities that encompass "banking practices." Yet we are certain that an *external* auditor whose sole role is to verify a bank's books cannot be said to be engaging in a "banking practice." We do not answer the question of whether an *internal* auditor with an equally limited role (if there be any such) is conducting the bank's business.

In oral argument, Comptroller's counsel advanced the idea that because § 1831m(f)(1) requires that banks, in order to stay in business, undergo GAAS-compliant audits on an annual basis, it follows that such audits are necessarily part of a bank's business. . . . This seems to us a complete non-sequitur. That a bank must engage outsiders to perform services does not necessarily turn such providers into bankers. In the case of auditors, of course, the need to enlist their services comes in part from the law, in part from the practicalities of raising the bank's own capital, but it is hard to see why the element of legal compulsion should change the matter. It makes as much sense to say that Grant Thornton was conducting Keystone's business as it is to say that an Underwriters Laboratories representative who inspects a toaster is "engaged in conducting the manufacture of toasters," or that a Department of Agriculture representative checking a smokehouse for compliance with meat safety laws is "engaged in conducting the operation of a smokehouse."

Second, we have some assistance from the Supreme Court on the meaning of a phrase closely parallel to those in question here. In *Reves v. Ernst & Young,* 507 U.S. 170 (1993), the Court construed the following language from RICO: "to conduct or participate, directly or indirectly, in the conduct of [an enterprise's] affairs." *Id.* at 177-79 (discussing 18 U.S.C. § 1962(c)). Reasoning that Congress meant something broader than "conduct [the enterprise's] affairs," but narrower than merely "participate in [its] affairs," the Court concluded that a covered party "must have some part in directing [the enterprise's] affairs." *Id.* at 179. Grant Thornton played no such directive role in Keystone's affairs.

A directing role can, of course, be a minor one. In *Cavallari v. Office of Comptroller of the Currency,* 57 F.3d 137, 140-41 (2d Cir.1995), the court affirmed the Comptroller's classification of an attorney as an IAP because he provided oral and written advice to a bank that exchanging loan guaranties, resulting in the bank's gaining an interest in a financially unsound company, was in the bank's best interest. The court's holding also rested on the fact that the lawyer drafted the paperwork needed to complete the transaction. Thus he advised the bank, in a forward-looking capacity, on how to conduct the bank's own business-lending. By actively encouraging a dubious transaction, he played a part in conducting the bank's business in a way that was "contrary to accepted standards for banking operations." *Id.* at 143.In contrast, while Grant Thornton's audit may have been "strikingly incompetent," as described at length by the concurring opinion, it neither proffered advice on nor assumed any directive role in Keystone's conduct of its affairs. The Comptroller nowhere suggests that Grant Thornton was in cahoots with Keystone's fraudulent managers. . . .

Finally, we note that Congress has given the Comptroller wide latitude to punish accountants who transgress GAAS in their audits of depository institutions:

> In addition to any authority contained in [12 U.S.C. § 1818], the Corporation or an appropriate Federal banking agency may remove, suspend, or bar an independent public accountant, upon showing of good cause, from performing audit services required by this section.

12 U.S.C. § 1831m(g)(4)(A). While Congress added this provision after adoption of FIRREA (as part of the Federal Deposit Insurance Corporation Improvement Act, Pub.L. No. 102-242, § 36, 105 Stat. 2236, 2244 (1991)), its presence makes clear that giving the words of FIRREA their ordinary meaning leaves the banking authorities ample power to sanction delinquent auditors. Here, of course, we need not address the application of § 1831m(g)(4)(A) to Grant Thornton, as the Comptroller has not tried to rest its case on that section.

KAREN LECRAFT HENDERSON, Circuit Judge, concurring in the judgment:

I agree with my colleagues that we should vacate the civil monetary penalty and cease and desist order the Office of the Comptroller of the Currency (OCC) imposed on Grant Thornton; however, I am not persuaded by their reasoning and therefore concur in the judgment only. The Congress enacted the Financial Institution Reform, Recovery and Enforcement Act of 1989 (FIRREA), Pub.L. 101-73, 103 Stat. 183 (1989), as a direct response to the savings and loan crisis of the late 1980s. *See* H.R. Rep. No 101-54, at 291-92 (1989), *as reprinted in* 1989 U.S.C.C.A.N. 87. The House Banking, Finance and Urban Affairs Committee Report (House Report) accompanying the legislation discusses the causes of that crisis. Among them, the Report highlights "poor quality audit work" as one of the primary ones. . . .

. . . 12 U.S.C. § 1818(b)(1) and 12 U.S.C. § 1818(i)(2)(B)(i)(II) expressly include an Institution Affiliated Party (IAP) within their respective sanctions so that there must be *some* way in which an IAP accountant "participates" or "engage[s]" in "an unsafe or unsound practice in [the] conduct[ ]" of the "business"/"affairs" of a bank. The Second Circuit has decided as much with regard to an IAP attorney. *Cavallari v. OCC,* 57 F.3d 137, 142-43 (2d Cir.1995). Because an IAP accountant *can* be sanctioned under section 1818(b)(1) and section 1818(i)(2)(B)(i)(II), I believe that the majority's rejection of such a result here is wrong.

The OCC's sanctions levied against Grant Thornton should nonetheless be vacated. The same House Report makes clear that the Congress did not intend FIRREA to be used to levy a *firm-wide* penalty against an IAP unless "most or many of the managing partners or senior officers of the entity have participated in some way in the egregious misconduct." H.R.Rep. No. 101-54, at 467. . . .

Notes and Comments 8.18. If QNB's outside counsel had actively advised the bank and its president, and assisted the bank in structuring the series of loans to Forth's business associates, could the Comptroller impose civil money penalties on counsel? *Cf. Cavallari v. Office of Comptroller of Currency*, 57 F.3d 137 (2d Cir. 1995).

8.19. If instead QNB's outside counsel had actively advised the bank and its president, and assisted the bank in challenging the Comptroller's efforts to issue a cease and desist order against and to impose civil money penalties on the bank, could the Comptroller impose civil money penalties on counsel and bar it from further involvement with QNB? *Cf. Lindquist & Vennum v. F.D.I.C.*, 103 F.3d 1409 (8th Cir. 1997), *cert. denied sub nom. Donohoo v. Federal Deposit Ins. Corp.*, 522 U.S. 821.

8.20. Instead of a cease and desist order, could the Comptroller impose civil money penalties on Hiram Forth and QNB's president in amounts equal to the losses and costs? *Cf. Abercrombie v. Office of Comptroller of Currency*, 641 F. Supp. 598 (S.D.Ind. 1986), *affirmed*, 833 F.2d 672 (7th Cir. 1987).

8.21. Could the Comptroller remove or bar Forth and the QNB president from management or control of the bank? If they resisted, what procedures would the Comptroller be required to comply with?

8.22. Could the Comptroller remove or bar them from management or control of *any* national bank in the future? From management or control of *any depository institution*? *Cf. Anonymous v. Federal Deposit Ins. Corp.*, 619 F. Supp. 866 (D.D.C. 1985). *But see* 12 U.S.C. §§ 1786(g)(7), 1818(e)(7) (FIRREA amendments).

8.23. What if Forth had already sold all his shares in QNB and the bank's president had already resigned? As a legal matter, could the Comptroller bar them from any future involvement in QNB? *See Stoddard v. Board of Governors*, 868 F.2d 1308 (D.C.Cir. 1989). *But cf.* 12 U.S.C. §§ 1786(k)(3), 1818(i)(3) (FIRREA amendments). *See generally Greenberg v. Comptroller of the Currency*, 938 F.2d 8 (2d Cir. 1991) (noting that *Stoddard* is superseded by statute).

8.24. *Changes in supervision under the Federal Deposit Insurance Corporation Improvement Act of 1991 (FDICIA).* The FDICIA, Pub. L. No. 102-242, 105 Stat. 2236 (December 19, 1991) (codified at scattered sections of 12 U.S.C.), contains a series of provisions intended to improve supervision of insured depository institutions. The principal provisions in this regard are as follows:

> **a.** *Annual examinations.* The FDICIA has adopted a general rule requiring annual on-site examinations of all insured depository institutions,[12] effective one year after enactment (December 19, 1991).[13] In addition, the federal bank regulatory agencies, acting through the Federal Financial Institutions Examination Council, are required to establish a "comparable examination

---

12. FDICIA, § 111(a) (codified at 12 U.S.C. § 1820(d) (1)-(3)). Certain specified small institutions (well-capitalized and well-managed institutions with total assets of less than $100 million with no recent change in control) are to be examined every eighteen months. *Id.* (codified at 12 U.S.C. § 1820(d)(4)).

13. *Id.* § 111(b).

improvement program,"[14] meeting certain specified requirements.[15]

b. *Independent audits.* As a general rule, the FDICIA requires independent audits of insured depository institutions.[16]

c. *Accounting.* The FDICIA establishes specific accounting objectives, standards and requirements generally applicable to all insured depository institutions.[17] These include uniform standards for accounting of capital.[18]

d. *Prompt "corrective action".* The Act generally requires prompt "corrective action"[19] intended to "resolve the problems of insured depository institutions at the least possible long-term loss to the deposit insurance fund."[20] Such action includes the implementation of capital standards.[21] A related amendment affects the conservatorship and receivership provisions of the FDIA,[22] the National Bank Act,[23] the Bank Conservation Act,[24] the Home Owners' Loan Act,[25] and the Federal Reserve Act[26] to facilitate prompt regulatory action.

e. *Safety and soundness concerns.* The FDICIA contains several provisions focusing on the safety and soundness of insured depository institutions. It authorizes federal bank regulatory agencies to impose more stringent treatment of capital of institutions that are determined to be in an unsafe and unsound condition or to be engaged in an unsafe and unsound practice.[27] It also requires the creation by the federal bank regulatory agencies of detailed standards for safety and soundness of insured depository institutions and their holding companies,[28] in specified areas of concern such as operational and managerial standards,[29] asset quality, earnings and stock valuation standards,[30] and compensation standards.[31]

f. *Risk-based insurance assessments.* FDICIA also requires the es-

---

14. *Id.* § 111(d)(1).

15. *See id.* § 111(d)(2).

16. *Id.* § 112(a) (codified at 12 U.S.C. § 1831m).

17. *Id.* § 121(a) (codified at 12 U.S.C. § 1831n).

18. *Id.* (codified at 12 U.S.C. § 1831n(b)).

19. *Id.* § 131 (codified at 12 U.S.C. § 1831o(a)(2)).

20. 12 U.S.C. § 1831o(a)(1). *Cf. id.* § 1823(c)(4)-(11) (mandating least-cost resolution of failing institution problems). On principles of early resolution, see FDICIA, § 143. *See also* 12 U.S.C. § 1821(d)(5)(D) (authorizing disallowance by receiver of secured claims in excess of collateral); *id.* §§ 347a, 347b(a)-(b), (n) (limiting Federal Reserve discount window advances).

21. *Id.* § 1831o(c)-(f), (h)-(i), (k), (n). These rules do not apply to depository institutions in conservatorship, or to bridge banks the stock of which is owned only by the FDIC or RTC. *Id.* § 1831o(j). The Act also contains provisions requiring the periodic review and improvement of applicable capital standards. *See* FDICIA, § 305.

22. 12 U.S.C. § 1821 (c)(5), (9)-(13).

23. *Id.* § 191.

24. *Id.* § 203(a).

25. *Id.* § 1464(d)(2)(A)-(F).

26. *Id.* § 248(p).

27. *Id.* § 1831o(g).

28. *Id.* § 1831s.

29. *Id.* § 1831s(a).

30. *Id.* § 1831s(b).

31. *Id.* § 1831s(c).

tablishment of a riskbased assessment system for federal deposit insurance.[32] This potentially powerful tool of supervision may have extremely significant effects on management decisionmaking, imposing tangible costs on risk-sensitive activities. For example, the risk-based assessment system is intended to calculate a depository institution's semiannual deposit insurance assessment by reference to, among other things, any risks attributable to different categories and concentrations of assets and of liabilities, both insured and uninsured, contingent and noncontingent.[33] For a risk-sensitive depository institution, such considerations would presumably translate directly into a higher cost of doing business, unless management were to incline towards a more risk-averse business policy.

g. *Extensions of credit to insiders.* FDICIA recodifies the statutory provisions restricting extensions of credit to insiders of depository institutions.[34]

3. Institutions in Default

Notes and Comments 8.25. What is the relationship between the elaborate set of statutory provisions governing federal regulation of failing depository institutions and the generally applicable federal bankruptcy law? Consider the following case.

MCorp Financial, Inc. v. Board of Governors

900 F.2d 852 (5th Cir. 1990)
reversed on other grounds, 502 U.S. 32 (1991)

W. Eugene Davis, Circuit Judge:

The Board of Governors of the Federal Reserve appeals an order of the district court, sitting in bankruptcy, enjoining the Board from pursuing its enforcement actions against MCorp without district court approval. . . . Because the Board's source of strength proceedings exceed its statutory authority, we remand with instructions to enjoin the Board from further prosecution of these charges. Because the district court lacks subject matter jurisdiction to enjoin the Board's actions on the remaining charges, we vacate the injunction as to these charges. . . .

In October 1988, the Board of Governors of the Federal Reserve (the Board), the primary regulator for bank holding companies, issued a notice of charges and of hearing against MCorp, a Texas-based bank holding company. The Board alleged that MCorp was engaging in unsafe and unsound practices, "likely to cause substantial dissipation of the assets of MCorp that could be used to allow MCorp to serve as a source of financial strength for the subsidiary Banks." A week later the Board issued an Amended Notice of Charges, which sought, among other things, to require MCorp to "implement[] an acceptable capital plan that would ensure that all of MCorp's available assets are used to recapitalize the Subsidiary Banks that are suffering capital deficiencies." MCorp's subsidiary banks were suffering heavy losses from real estate and energy loans.

In March 1989, three creditors of MCorp commenced an involuntary bankruptcy proceeding against MCorp in the U.S. bankruptcy court for the Southern District of New York. The Comptroller of the Currency (OCC), the primary regulator for national banks, subsequently declared a total of 20 of MCorp's subsidiary banks (MBanks) insolvent; OCC

32. *Id.* § 1817(b).

33. *Id.* § 1817(b)(1)(C)(i)(I)-(II).

34. *Id.* § 375b.

appointed the Federal Deposit Insurance Corporation (FDIC) as receiver, divesting MCorp of control of these banks. MCorp was left with 5 banks. MCorp and two of its subsidiaries, MCorp Financial and MCorp Management then filed voluntary Chapter 11 bankruptcy petitions in U.S. Bankruptcy Court for the Southern District of Texas. The bankruptcy proceedings against MCorp and its subsidiaries (hereafter collectively referred to as MCorp), were consolidated into one jointly administered proceeding in the Texas forum.

In March 1989, by notice of charges and hearing the Board also commenced further administrative proceedings against MCorp. The March charges accused MCorp and MCorp management of violations of § 23A of the Federal Reserve Act, alleging MCorp caused MBank Houston and MBank Preston, two of the closed banks, to provide Mcorp management "unsecured extensions of credit." In late May the Board issued a second amended notice of charges, relating to the October notice of charges, alleging that MCorp had failed to act as a source of financial strength to its remaining subsidiary banks.

MCorp initiated an adversary proceeding against the Board in May 1989, and filed an Emergency Motion for a TRO and preliminary injunction, seeking to enjoin the Board from prosecuting its administrative proceedings against the debtors, and from initiating further administrative proceedings against the debtors without prior approval of the bankruptcy court. The bankruptcy court denied the TRO request. The Board moved the district court to withdraw the reference of the adversary proceeding to the bankruptcy court. The district court granted the Board's motion and placed the case on its own docket.

In June 1989, the district court entered a preliminary injunction granting the relief sought by the debtors. The district court preliminarily enjoined the Board from prosecuting its pending administrative proceedings and using its authority over bank holding companies or banks to attempt to effect, directly or indirectly, a reorganization of the MCorp group or its components or to interfere, except through participation in the bankruptcy proceedings, with the restructuring being developed in the bankruptcy proceeding.

The district court stated that the preliminary injunction left completely unaffected the Board's "general execution, supervisory and examination duties of the operations of MCorp and its bank subsidiaries and . . . central bank duties as they affect Mcorp in common with all other institutions." The court established a procedure for future Board proceedings, where the Board was first required to present to MCorp any new administrative proceedings, notices of charges or temporary cease and desist orders before their issuance. If the Board and MCorp could not agree whether a proposed proceeding was subject to the preliminary injunction, the Board could then present that issue to the district court. If the court decided the Board's proposed action related to the banks' "operations," the court proposed to exempt this action from the restraint of the preliminary injunction; if however the Board's proposed action affected the reorganization, the district court proposed to stay this action in deference to the Bankruptcy Court. . . .

The Board contends first that the district court, sitting in bankruptcy, has no jurisdiction to enjoin the Board's prosecution of its administrative actions, because of 12 U.S.C. § 1818(i) (the Financial Institutions Supervisory Act of 1966 (FISA) as amended), which provides:

> . . . except as otherwise provided in this section no court shall have jurisdiction to affect by injunction or otherwise the issuance or enforcement of any notice or order under this section, or to review, modify, suspend, terminate, or set aside any such notice or order.

As we stated in *Groos National Bank v. Comptroller of Currency*, 573 F.2d 889 (5th Cir.1978), "section 1818(i) in particular evinces a clear intention that this regulatory process is not to be disturbed by untimely judicial intervention, at least where there is no 'clear departure from statutory authority.' " *Id.* at 895, *quoting Manges v. Camp*, 474 F.2d 97, 99 (5th Cir. 1973). Thus, under 12 U.S.C. § 1818(h) and the Administrative Procedure Act (APA), a bank holding company is not ordinarily entitled to judicial review until the Board issues a final order.

MCorp's principal argument that the district court properly exercised subject matter jurisdiction is predicated on 28 U.S.C. §§ 1334(b) and (d) of the Bankruptcy Code. MCorp argues that these sections of the Bankruptcy Code effectively supersede the Board's exclusive jurisdiction under § 1818(i)(1) to prosecute its enforcement actions, and therefore empower the court to enjoin prosecution of those actions. The district court presumably agreed and concluded that § 1818(i) conflicted with sections 1334(b) and (d) of the Bankruptcy Code.

Section 1334(b) provides:

> Notwithstanding any Act of Congress that confers exclusive jurisdiction on a court or courts other than the district courts, the district courts shall have original but not exclusive jurisdiction of all civil proceedings arising under title 11, or arising in or related to cases under title 11.

The plain language of Section 1334(b) does not purport to give the district court exclusive jurisdiction over matters arising under Chapter 11 to the exclusion of administrative agencies; rather, § 1334(b) grants the district court concurrent jurisdiction over matters that otherwise would lie within the exclusive jurisdiction of another court.

The legislative history of § 1334(b) also supports the view that the section was intended to prevent another court from exercising exclusive jurisdiction over a matter brought within the Bankruptcy Code. The Commission on the Bankruptcy Laws of the United States, quoted at length in the House Judiciary Committee report, stated that "The first and most important objection to the present dispensation is the division of labor between the bankruptcy court and other courts." . . . Under the prior bankruptcy law, the jurisdiction of the bankruptcy court was limited by the concepts of possession and consent. The House report adopted the reasoning of the Commission that the old law was undesirable because of "the frequent, time-consuming, and expensive litigation of the question whether the bankruptcy court has jurisdiction of a particular proceeding." . . . Under the prior jurisdictional scheme, " 'When a "summary" proceeding in the bankruptcy court is appropriate and when a plenary suit is required is one of the most involved and controversial questions in the entire field of bankruptcy,' " the Committee observed. . . . We are persuaded therefore that it was this division of jurisdiction between bankruptcy courts and other courts which the jurisdictional changes of the new law were intended to address.

MCorp argues that the legislative history explains that § 1334(b) grants bankruptcy courts pervasive jurisdiction over all matters and proceedings that arise in or in connection with bankruptcy cases. Yet the legislative history reflects no intent that the bankruptcy court's jurisdiction supersede the exclusive jurisdiction of an administrative agency, or reinvest the courts with jurisdiction barred by § 1818.

In holding that § 1334 superseded § 1818(i), the district court did not harmonize the two statutes, but effectively repealed § 1818(i), and negated its basic sense and purpose of preventing early interference with administrative proceedings. This interpretation invested the district court, sitting in bankruptcy, with equitable power withheld from every other court by the language of § 1818(i). Implied repeals are highly disfavored, and one statute will not be considered to impliedly repeal another unless there is a "positive repugnancy" between the two. . . . We find no such irreconcilable conflict here. [The court then quotes the Supreme Court's "plain purpose" language from *Board of Governors v. Dimension Financial Corp.*,

474 U.S. 361, 373-74 (1986), excerpted after Note 4.15, *supra*.]

MCorp further contends that courts consistently have held that the phrase in § 1334(b), "Notwithstanding any act of Congress that confers exclusive jurisdiction on [any other] court," was expressly intended to confer on the bankruptcy courts jurisdiction over all matters related to a debtor's chapter 11 case, including administrative proceedings. ... [The court rejected this argument.]

MCorp argues next that the bankruptcy court has exclusive jurisdiction over the Board's enforcement proceeding based on § 1334(d). . . .

According to MCorp, because the bankruptcy court has exclusive control of MCorp's assets, it necessarily follows from the above section that the Board had no jurisdiction over MCorp. But the Board has not sought control over the property of Mcorp's estate in this action, only the opportunity to go forward in its administrative proceedings. Nor at this early stage do we find the Board's enforcement actions to be sham proceedings, brought as a means of controlling the debtor's assets. We therefore do not consider § 1334 (d) to grant the district court exclusive jurisdiction here. . . .

MCorp also argues that because the above Bankruptcy Code provisions were enacted after § 1818, and do not exempt bank holding company administrative actions from the comprehensive jurisdiction of the bankruptcy court, Congress must have intended no such exemptions. MCorp contends that this is especially true in view of the express exemption granted banks from recourse to bankruptcy protection in § 109 of the Bankruptcy Code. Absent some clear intention to the contrary, however, a specific statute will not be controlled by a general one regardless of the priority of enactment. . . . Congress revealed no intent to supersede the specific jurisdictional bar of § 1818(i) in the legislative history of the Bankruptcy Reform Act, nor in the recently enacted Financial Institutions Reform, Recovery, and Enforcement Act (FIRREA) of 1989, Pub.L. No. 101-73, 103 Stat. 183. We decline to imply any affirmative powers to the bankruptcy court from Congress' failure to act in this area. . . .

MCorp asserts that the Board lacks authority to proceed against banks in FDIC receivership, that the Board's self-dealing charges are a pretext for avoiding the exclusive jurisdiction of the bankruptcy court over MCorp's assets, and that the Board's source of strength policy is without statutory authority.

In *Manges v. Camp*, 474 F.2d 97 (5th Cir. 1973), we recognized that the statute at issue here, § 1818, that withdraws the jurisdiction of the court in deference to an agency, is not effective when the agency exceeds its authority under that statute. There is "a very strong court created exception to withdrawal statutes. This exception comes into play when there has been a clear departure from statutory authority, and thereby exposes the offending agency to review of administrative action otherwise made unreviewable by statute." *Manges*, 474 F.2d at 99. If the Board's proceedings exceed its statutory authority, we may review the Board's action prior to a final order despite the jurisdictional bar of § 1818; if the Board "was not acting within [the] authority granted by Congress, then 12 U.S.C. § 1818(i) could not withdraw jurisdiction." *Manges*, 474 F.2d at 99. . . .

MCorp argues that the Board exceeded its authority in three respects because it has no authority to (1) regulate MCorp's relationships with former MBanks, now under FDIC receivership, which are the subject of the administrative proceedings; (2) assist the FDIC, as receiver of the closed MBanks, to obtain damages under the pretext of punishing MCorp for violations of § 23A of the Federal Reserve Act,[1] which concerns self-dealing among holding

---

1. Section 23A of the Federal Reserve Act, 12 U.S.C. § 371c, prohibits a bank from extending credit to a nonbank affiliate unless the extension of credit is secured by collateral having a market value of at least 100 percent of the loan. The Board has charged that MCorp violated this

company subsidiaries; and (3) compel a bank holding company to transfer its funds to subsidiary banks.

MCorp argues first that the Board lacks authority to regulate MCorp's relationships with former subsidiary banks now under FDIC receivership. Both the "source of strength" charges and the self dealing charges, as initially set out by the Board, were levelled in part to the relationship between MCorp and MBanks which were later closed and placed under FDIC receivership. We are persuaded that the Board is at least entitled to make a determination on the legitimacy of the credit transaction with the closed banks at issue to allow it to evaluate what remedy it wants to pursue against MCorp. Certainly the Board's attempt to do that is not facially invalid.

MCorp next argues that the Board's § 23A proceeding is simply an attempt to assist the FDIC to obtain MCorp's property under the guise of remedying a violation of § 23A of the Reserve Act. We disagree. The Board is well within its authority in seeking an order against MCorp to cease and desist any transactions which violate the provisions of § 23A, or "to take affirmative action" as may be appropriate. 12 U.S.C. § 1818(b)(1). The notice of charges relating to the appropriateness of the credit transactions between an MCorp nonbank subsidiary and two of MCorp's former subsidiary banks is not on its face a sham proceeding initiated only to assist the FDIC to collect damages; at least a fact issue is presented on the merits of the § 23A charges. The mere prosecution of the charges before the Board does not in itself disturb the Bankruptcy Court's alleged exclusive jurisdiction over MCorp's property under § 1334(d) of the Bankruptcy Code.

We are persuaded, however, that a serious legal issue is presented as to whether the Board has statutory authority to pursue its source of strength charges. Before turning to that problem, we address a threshold argument of the Board that we are precluded from considering the Board's authority to proceed.

The Board contends that MCorp may not judicially challenge at this stage the Board's authority to proceed with its charges because MCorp has not exhausted its administrative remedies. . . .

The question of the Board's authority to impose its source of strength requirement is quite a different issue. No facts are in dispute. The sole question presented is a legal one: whether the Board has authority to order a holding company to transfer its funds to its troubled subsidiary banks. The Board has instituted proceedings to require the holding company to transfer those funds. The legal issue of the Board's authority can be resolved without further factual development. "[P]rompt resolution will eliminate uncertainty and be in the interest of efficient judicial administration." *Indep. Bankers Ass'n v. Heimann*, 613 F.2d 1164, 1167 (D.C.Cir. 1979), *cert. denied*, 449 U.S. 823 (1980). Because we conclude that MCorp is not required to exhaust its administrative remedies in this circumstance, we turn to the merits of whether the Board has authority to require the holding company to transfer its funds to troubled subsidiary banks.

The Board contends it has authority to issue the source of strength charges under §§ 1818(b)(1) and (3), which empower it to file charges against a bank holding company which the Board believes (1) has violated or is about to violate a "law, rule or regulation"; or (2) is engaging in an "unsafe or unsound" practice. The Board contends that MCorp has failed to act as a source of strength for its bank subsidiaries in violation of the Board's regulations and policy statements. The Board also contends that this failure constitutes an unsafe

---

requirement by causing two of its former subsidiary banks to extend $63.7 million of unsecured credit to an affiliated subsidiary of MCorp, and failing to make timely repayments to the subsidiary banks that extended the credit.

or unsound practice in violation of § 1818.[3]

[The court first considered whether the Fed had valid statutory authority to issue its source-of-strength regulation and policy statement. It concluded that the Fed was without such authority under the BHCA. Excerpts from the court's discussion in this regard are set forth in Chapter 4, § 2, *supra*.]

The Board asserts as an independent basis for its source of strength regulation, policy statement and enforcement proceedings its broad authority under § 1818(b)(1) and (3) of FISA to order a holding company to cease and desist from any activity that, in the Board's judgment, constitutes an unsafe or unsound practice. The Board argues that MCorp's failure to provide capital to its subsidiary banks is an unsafe or unsound practice which the Board may act to restrain under § 1818. . . .

The Congress has not spoken clearly to what constitutes an unsafe or unsound practice, leaving the development of the phrase to the regulatory agencies. As we stated in *Groos Nat'l Bank v. Comptroller of Currency*, 573 F.2d 889, 897 (5th Cir. 1978), "[t]he phrase 'unsafe or unsound banking practice' is widely used in the regulatory statutes and in case law, and one of the purposes of the banking acts is clearly to commit the progressive definition and eradication of such practices to the expertise of the appropriate regulatory agencies." Thus, . . . in the absence of clear congressional intent on the meaning of this language, we must examine the "reasonableness" and "permissibility" of the Board's interpretation that the failure of the holding company to inject capital into subsidiary banks is an "unsafe or unsound" practice.

In *Gulf Federal Sav. & Loan Ass'n v. Federal Home Loan Bank Bd.*, 651 F.2d 259 (5th Cir. 1981), *cert. denied*, 458 U.S. 1121 (1982), the Federal Home Loan Bank Board found that Gulf Federal's contracting practice was an "unsafe or unsound" practice within the meaning of § 1818. We disagreed and concluded that the FHLBB's finding that Gulf Federal's use of inconsistent contract terms was an unsafe or unsound practice was not a reasonable interpretation of the "unsafe or unsound practice" provision.

We also noted in *Gulf Federal* that the "unsafe or unsound practice" provision was the subject of lively congressional debate at the time the statute was enacted. . . .

Enforcement of the Board's source of strength requiring MCorp to transfer MCorp's funds to the troubled subsidiary banks can hardly be considered a "generally accepted standard[] of prudent operation." Such a transfer of funds would require MCorp to disregard its own corporation's separate status; it would amount to a wasting of the holding company's assets in violation of its duty to its shareholders. Also, one of the fundamental purposes of the BHCA is to separate banking from commercial enterprises. That purpose is obviously not served if the Board is permitted to treat a holding company as merely an extension of its subsidiary bank.

Congress first under the BHCA in 1956 and later in amendments to the Federal Reserve Act in 1966 has generally defined with specificity the dealings between subsidiary banks and nonbank affiliates, including holding companies, it considered unsafe and unsound. . . . Congress made no effort in any of this legislation to require holding companies to make capital injections into subsidiary banks as part of these safeguards. Congress noted only that the provision enacted as part of the BHCA "does not prohibit the borrowing of funds by any subsidiary in the system from the parent bank holding company." S. Rep. No. 1095, 84th Cong., 2nd Sess., *reprinted in* 1956 U.S. Code Cong. & Admin. News 2482, 2496. In sum, Congress set forth detailed limits on transactions considered unsound between

3. Because we conclude that the source of strength proceedings exceed the Board's statutory authority, we need not resolve whether the source of strength charges relating to MCorp's former subsidiary banks are beyond the Board's authority.

subsidiary banks and holding companies, without mentioning the infusion of capital by holding companies into subsidiaries. This strongly supports MCorp's argument that Congress never intended to grant authority to the Board to require a holding company to inject capital into subsidiary banks as a safeguard against "unsafe or unsound" practices.

This is consistent with the conclusion reached by the Shadow Financial Regulatory Committee,[6] responding to the Board's source of strength policy. The Committee stated that, "while Congress has empowered regulators of banks to issue capital directives to institutions in their charge, it has not authorized the Fed to issue capital directives to bank holding companies." 48 Banking Rep. (BNA) No. 21, at 923 (May 25, 1987).

Thus, we conclude that the Board's determination that the holding company's failure to transfer its assets to a troubled subsidiary was an "unsafe or unsound practice" under §§ 1818(b)(1) and (3) is an unreasonable and impermissible interpretation of that term.

It is not our role to pass judgment on the wisdom of the scheme Congress put in place to regulate bank holding companies. Similarly, the Board cannot exceed the authority Congress granted to it to correct perceived flaws in the congressional scheme. . . .

Notes and Comments 8.26. On certiorari, the Supreme Court reversed the Fifth Circuit's decision enjoining the "source of strength" proceeding, on narrow grounds that did not determine the validity of the doctrine. Rather, the Court focused on the independence of these administrative proceedings from judicial intervention, in the following terms:

Board of Governors v. MCorp Financial, Inc.

502 U.S. 32 (1991)

Justice Stevens delivered the opinion of the Court.

In June 1989, the District Court ruled that it had jurisdiction to enjoin the Board from prosecuting both administrative proceedings against MCorp and entered a preliminary injunction halting those proceedings. The injunction restrained the Board from exercising "its authority over bank holding companies . . . to attempt to effect, directly or indirectly, a reorganization of the MCorp group [of companies] except through participation in the bankruptcy proceedings." . . .

Although the District Court did not differentiate between the two Board proceedings, the Court of Appeals held that the § 23A proceeding could go forward but that the source of strength proceeding should be enjoined. The court reasoned that the plain language of the judicial review provisions of the Financial Institutions Supervisory Act of 1966 (FISA), 80 Stat. 1046, *as amended*, 12 U.S.C. § 1818, *et. seq*. (1988 ed. and Supp. I), particularly § 1818(i)(1), deprived the District Court of jurisdiction to enjoin either proceeding, but that our decision in *Leedom v. Kyne*, 358 U.S. 184 (1958), nevertheless authorized an injunction against an administrative proceeding conducted without statutory authorization. The Court of Appeals ruled that the Board's promulgation and enforcement of its source of strength regulation exceeded its statutory authority. . . .

The Board's petition challenges the Court of Appeals' interpretation of *Leedom v. Kyne*, as well as its invalidation of the source of strength regulation. MCorp's petition challenges the Court of Appeals' interpretation of the relationship between the provisions governing judicial review of Board proceedings and those governing bankruptcy proceedings.

---

6. Formed in February 1986, the Shadow Financial Regulatory Committee (SFRC) meets periodically to monitor regulations of the financial services industry. The SFRC is composed of economists, academics and former financial regulators.

We first address the latter challenge. . . .

A series of federal statutes gives the Board substantial regulatory power over bank holding companies and establishes a comprehensive scheme of judicial review of Board actions. *See* FISA; the Bank Holding Company Act of 1956 (BHCA), 12 U.S.C. § 1841 *et seq*. (1988 ed. and Supp. I); and the International Lending Supervision Act of 1983, 12 U.S.C. § 3901 *et seq*. In this litigation, the most relevant of these is FISA.

FISA authorizes the Board to institute administrative proceedings culminating in cease-and-desist orders, 12 U.S.C. §§ 1818(a)-(b) (1988 ed., Supp. I), and to issue temporary cease-and-desist orders that are effective upon service on a bank holding company. § 1818(c). In addition, FISA establishes a tripartite regime of judicial review. First, § 1818 (c)(2) provides that, within 10 days after service of a temporary order, a bank holding company may seek an injunction in district court restraining enforcement of the order pending completion of the related administrative proceeding. Second, § 1818(h) authorizes court of appeals review of final Board orders on the application of an aggrieved party.[8] Finally, § 1818(i)(1) provides that the Board may apply to district court for enforcement of any effective and outstanding notice or order.

None of these provisions controls this litigation: The action before us is neither a challenge to a temporary Board order, nor a petition for review of a final Board order, nor an enforcement action initiated by the Board. Instead, FISA's preclusion provision appears to speak directly to the jurisdictional question at issue in this litigation. . . .

Notwithstanding this plain, preclusive language, MCorp argues that the District Court's injunction against the prosecution of the Board proceedings was authorized either by the automatic stay provision in the Bankruptcy Code, 11 U.S.C. § 362, or by the provision of the Judicial Code authorizing district courts in bankruptcy proceedings to exercise concurrent jurisdiction over certain civil proceedings. 28 U.S.C. § 1334(b). We find no merit in either argument.

The filing of a bankruptcy petition operates as an automatic stay of several categories of judicial and administrative proceedings. . . . The Board's planned actions against MCorp constitute the "continuation . . . [of] administrative . . . proceeding[s]" and would appear to be stayed by 11 U.S.C. § 362(a)(1). However, the Board's actions also fall squarely within §362(b)(4), which expressly provides that the automatic stay will not reach proceedings to enforce a "governmental unit's police or regulatory power."

MCorp contends that in order for § 362(b)(4) to obtain, a court must first determine whether the proposed exercise of police or regulatory power is legitimate and that, therefore, in this litigation the lower courts did have the authority to examine the legitimacy of the Board's actions and to enjoin those actions. We disagree. MCorp's broad reading of the stay provisions would require bankruptcy courts to scrutinize the validity of every administrative or enforcement action brought against a bankrupt entity. Such a reading is problematic, both because it conflicts with the broad discretion Congress has expressly granted many administrative entities and because it is inconsistent with the limited authority Congress has vested in bankruptcy courts. We therefore reject petitioner's reading of § 362(b)(4).

MCorp also argues that it is protected by §§ 362(a) (3) and 362(a)(6) of the Bankruptcy Code. Those provisions stay "any act" to obtain possession of, or to exercise control over, property of the estate, or to recover claims against the debtor that arose prior to the filing of the bankruptcy petition. MCorp contends that the ultimate objective of the source of strength proceeding is to exercise control of corporate assets and that the §23A proceeding

8. The statute characterizes such review of final Board orders as "exclusive" and provides: [quoting 12 U.S.C. § 1818(h)(2)].

seeks enforcement of a prepetition claim.

We reject these characterizations of the ongoing administrative proceedings. At this point, the Board has only issued "Notices of Charges and of Hearing" and has expressed its intent to determine whether MCorp has violated specified statutory and regulatory provisions. It is possible, of course, that the Board proceedings, like many other enforcement actions, may conclude with the entry of an order that will affect the Bankruptcy Court's control over the property of the estate, but that possibility cannot be sufficient to justify the operation of the stay against an enforcement proceeding that is expressly exempted by subsection (b)(4). To adopt such a characterization of enforcement proceedings would be to render §362(b)(4)'s exception almost meaningless. If and when the Board's proceedings culminate in a final order, and if and when judicial proceedings are commenced to enforce such an order, then it may well be proper for the Bankruptcy Court to exercise its concurrent jurisdiction under 28 U.S.C. § 1334(b). We are not persuaded, however, that the automatic stay provisions of the Bankruptcy Code have any application to ongoing, nonfinal administrative proceedings.[11]

MCorp's final argument rests on 28 U.S.C. § 1334(b). That section authorizes a district court to exercise concurrent jurisdiction over certain bankruptcy-related civil proceedings that would otherwise be subject to the exclusive jurisdiction of another court. MCorp's reliance is misplaced. Section 1334(b) concerns the allocation of jurisdiction between bankruptcy courts and other "courts," and, of course, an administrative agency such as the Board is not a "court." Moreover, contrary to MCorp's contention, the prosecution of the Board proceedings, prior to the entry of a final order and prior to the commencement of any enforcement action, seems unlikely to impair the Bankruptcy Court's exclusive jurisdiction over the property of the estate protected by 28 U.S.C. § 1334(d). In sum, we agree with the Court of Appeals that the specific preclusive language in 12 U.S.C. § 1818(i)(1) (1988 ed., Supp. I) is not qualified or superseded by the general provisions governing bankruptcy proceedings on which MCorp relies. . . .

Although the Court of Appeals found that § 1818(i) (1) precluded judicial review of many Board actions, it exercised jurisdiction in this litigation based on its reading of *Leedom v. Kyne*, 358 U.S. 184 (1958). *Kyne* involved an action in District Court challenging a determination by the National Labor Relations Board that a unit including both professional and nonprofessional employees was appropriate for collective-bargaining purposes–a determination in direct conflict with a provision of the National Labor Relations Act. The Act, however, did not expressly authorize any judicial review of such a determination. Relying on *Switchmen v. National Mediation Board*, 320 U.S. 297 (1943), the Board argued that the statutory provisions establishing review of final Board orders in the courts of appeals indicated a congressional intent to bar review of any Board action in the District Court. The Court rejected that argument, emphasizing the presumption that Congress normally intends the federal courts to enforce and protect the rights that Congress has created. Concluding that the Act did not bar the District Court's jurisdiction, we stated: "This Court cannot lightly infer that Congress does not intend judicial protection of rights it confers against agency action taken in excess of delegated powers." 358 U.S., at 190.

In this litigation, the Court of Appeals interpreted our opinion in *Kyne* as authorizing judicial review of any agency action that is alleged to have exceeded the agency's

11. The Board suggests that the automatic-stay provisions of § 362 do not themselves confer jurisdiction on the bankruptcy court, and thus that the filing of a bankruptcy petition operates as an automatic stay only where the bankruptcy court's jurisdiction has not already been precluded by a statute like § 1818(i)(1). We need not address this question in light of our determination that the automatic stay does not apply to the Board's ongoing administrative proceedings.

statutory authority. *Kyne*, however, differs from this litigation in two critical ways. First, central to our decision in *Kyne* was the fact that the Board's interpretation of the Act would wholly deprive the union of a meaningful and adequate means of vindicating its statutory rights.

> "Here, differently from the Switchmen's case, 'absence of jurisdiction of the federal courts' would mean 'a sacrifice or obliteration of a right which Congress' has given professional employees, for there is no other means, within their control . . . to protect and enforce that right." *Ibid.*

The case before us today is entirely different from Kyne because FISA expressly provides MCorp with a meaningful and adequate opportunity for judicial review of the validity of the source of strength regulation. If and when the Board finds that MCorp has violated that regulation, MCorp will have, in the Court of Appeals, an unquestioned right to review of both the regulation and its application.

The second, and related, factor distinguishing this litigation from *Kyne* is the clarity of the congressional preclusion of review in FISA. In *Kyne*, the Board contended that a statutory provision that provided for judicial review implied, by its silence, a preclusion of review of the contested determination. By contrast, in FISA Congress has spoken clearly and directly: "[N]o court shall have jurisdiction to affect by injunction or otherwise the issuance or enforcement of any [Board] notice or order under this section." 12 U.S.C. § 1818(i)(1) (1988 ed., Supp. I). . . . In this way as well, this litigation differs from *Kyne*. ...

Notes and Comments 8.27. *Source of strength doctrine revisited.* The 1999 Gramm-Leach-Bliley Act (GLBA)[35] enhances the source of strength doctrine (and clarifies situations like that involved in *MCorp*, where a holding company is in bankruptcy proceedings to which its banking subsidiaries are not directly subject). In certain circumstances, the GLBA protects the federal banking agencies and the deposit insurance funds from claims brought by the bankruptcy trustee of the holding company or other persons for the return of capital infusions made by the company to the banking subsidiaries. GLBA, § 730 (codified at 12 U.S.C. § 1828(t)). To qualify for this protection, the transferred assets must be those of an affiliate or a controlling shareholder of an insured depository institution, and the transfer must be made by an affiliate or controlling shareholder of such insured depository institution. 12 U.S.C. § 1828(t)(1). The transfer must be to or for the benefit of an insured depository institution. *Id.* Barred claims would include a claim against a federal banking agency for monetary damages, return of assets, or for other legal or equitable relief in connection with such transfer, consistent with certain limitations. *Id.* For purposes of this provision, a "claim" is defined as a cause of action based on federal or state law providing for the avoidance of preferential or fraudulent transfers or conveyances, or providing for similar remedies. The definition, however, explicitly excepts any claim based on actual intent to hinder, delay or defraud pursuant to such fraudulent transfer or conveyance law. *Id.* § 1828(t)(2). The legislative history of the GLBA indicates that this provision is not intended to limit any right to seek direct review of an order or directive of a federal banking agency under the APA in accordance with various banking statutes, or to limit the rights of a claimant to bring suit against the United States for a breach of contract or for a taking under the Fifth Amendment to the Constitution. *See Conference Report on S. 900, reprinted in* 145 Cong. Rec. H11255-01, H11302 (1999) (discussing effect of GLBA § 730). For other

35. Pub. L. No. 106-102, Nov. 12, 1999, 113 Stat. 1338 (1999) (codified at scattered sections of 12, 15, 16, 18 U.S.C.).

indications in the GLBA of congressional support for the source of strength doctrine, see Note 4.19, *supra*.

8.28. *"Failing" institutions: Statutory alternatives.* When faced with a failing depository institution, what statutory alternatives are available to regulators to deal with the situation? Consider the following excerpt.

3 Michael P. Malloy, Banking Law and Regulation

§§ 14.03[B], [D]-[D][3], [D][5] (2d ed., Aspen Publishers, 2011)[a]

The ultimate liability of the federal government in a situation involving a failed depository institution is the obligation for insured deposits of the institution.[1] In fact, the way in which the FDIC has handled failures has varied from situation to situation, and at least since 1945 the insured deposit payoff approach has not been favored.[2] . . .

a. *Insured deposit payoff.* Originally, the FDIC tended to resolve failures by either paying off its deposit insurance obligation or by allowing the failing bank to be acquired by another institution.[3] In a deposit payoff transaction . . . , the FDIC as receiver would hold any net assets of the failed institution, against which uninsured depositors, other unsecured creditors, and the FDIC itself as insurer became general creditors.

b. *Modified insured deposit payoff.* In 1984, the FDIC initiated a "modified payoff" approach as a variation on the traditional insured deposit payoff.[4] Under this approach, insured deposits would be paid off, and a sum equal to a "conservative" estimate of the funds to be realized from the assets left in receivership would be paid out to the uninsured deposits, with additional payments to be made in the future if collections exceeded the conservative estimate. This approach eventually led to the development of the "insured deposit transfer,"[5] in which an acquiring bank would pay a premium for insured deposits and certain assets of a failed bank which would otherwise be subject to an insured deposit payoff.

c. *Purchase and assumption.* Originally, the typical acquisition transaction involving a failed bank was not a merger, strictly speaking, but was in fact structured as a purchase of assets (*i.e.*, loans) and assumption of liabilities (*i.e.*, deposits) of the failing bank by the acquiring bank, with the FDIC making up the shortfall between the value of liabilities assumed and assets purchased.[6] Before the 1960s, these resolutions took place without the creation of a receivership, and so approval of the shareholders and the chartering authority

---

a. Footnotes have been renumbered in this excerpt.

1. *See* 12 U.S.C. § 1821(a)(1), as amended, Dodd-Frank Wall Street Reform and Consumer Protection Act (DFA) §§ 343(a), 363(5), Pub. L. No. 111-203, 124 Stat. 1376, 1544-1545, 1552-1553 (2010) (codified at 12 U.S.C. §§ 1821, 1821(a)(1)) (providing for insurance of deposit to statutory maximum).

2. *See generally* U.S. DEPARTMENT OF THE TREASURY, MODERNIZING THE FINANCIAL SYSTEM, Discussion Chapter I, at I-30 - I-45 (February 1991), *reprinted in* Fed. Banking L. Rep. (CCH) No. 1377, Pt. II (Feb. 14, 1991) (hereinafter "*Modernizing*") (discussing FDIC treatment of bank failures). *But cf.No Buyer for Utah Bank; FDIC to Mail Checks; Va. Bank Takes Over Failed Maryland Thrift*, BNA Banking Daily (Feb. 2, 2009), available at http://www.bna (reporting on FDIC decision to perform insured deposit payout as to closed MagnetBank of Salt Lake City, Utah). . . .

3. *Modernizing* at I-30. Between 1935 to 1945, approximately 390 failures were resolved by either payoff or merger. *Id.*

4. *Id.* at I-32.

5. *Id.*

6. *Id.* at I-30.

of the acquired bank would be required. . . .[7] During the latter part of the 1960s, the FDIC adopted a different approach to these transactions, first placing the institution into receivership, so that the FDIC as receiver could proceed with the transaction without the costly delays of shareholder and chartering authority approval. . . .[8]

If successful, the effect of these transactions was very much like a payoff of *all* depositors, not just insured depositors.[9] On the other hand, assuming that the cost of the "sweetener" provided by the FDIC to the acquiror bank was less than the potential total insured depositor liability, the purchase and assumption method could be less costly to the FDIC. (However, the FDIC as receiver was left, almost inevitably, with a nearly worthless shell within the receivership.) Furthermore, from 1968, the FDIC sought premiums from potential acquiror banks in proposed purchase and assumption transactions, through an explicit bidding process.[10]

d. *"Open-bank" assistance*. In many of the approaches adopted by the FDIC,[11] one goal has been to avoid the rigors of insured deposit payoff, and the resulting disruption of the local economy that a closing of a bank would cause. An important device in this regard, not used until 1971,[12] is "open-bank assistance."[13] This approach proceeds on the assumption that it will be less costly to the FDIC to lend financial assistance to a troubled bank than to close and liquidate it in receivership.

e. *Other variations*. Two variations on this "walking dead" approach to failing bank resolution should be mentioned. One was the "capital forbearance" program, in which capital and other supervisory requirements were not enforced against financially troubled institutions viewed as viable by the FDIC.[14] This approach has been severely criticized as increasingly the ultimate cost of unavoided (and possibly unavoidable) collapse of such "viable" but troubled institutions.[15]

Until recently, the other "walking dead" approach involved an FDIC equity investment in the troubled institution.[16] This often involved extreme, and arguably questionable measures, such as the 75 to 80 percent equity interests assumed by the FDIC in large, failing

---

7. *Id.* at I-31.

8. *Id.*

9. *Cf. id.* (describing similar criticism by Senator Fulbright in 1951).

10. *Id.*

11. For a recent case discussing alternative methods of fulfilling the FDIC's obligation to depositors, including deposit payoffs and purchase-and-assumption transactions, see *NCNB Texas Nat. Bank v. Cowden*, 895 F.2d 1488 (5th Cir. 1990).

12. *See Modernizing,* Discussion Chapter I, at I-34.

13. *See* 12 U.S.C. § 1823(c), *as amended*, Riegle Community Development and Regulatory Improvement Act of 1994 (CDRIA), Pub. L. No. 103-325, Sept. 23, 1994, § 602(a)(34)-(35), 108 Stat. 2160, 2289-2290 (1994) (codified at 12 U.S.C. § 1823(c)(1)(B), (c)(2)(A)) (technical amendments); Economic Growth and Regulatory Paperwork Reduction Act, Pub. L. No. 104-208, title II, §2704(d)(14)(M) 110 Stat. 3009 (1996) (codified at 12 U.S.C. §1823) (technical and conforming amendment. . . .

14. *See Modernizing*, Discussion Chapter I, at I-37 - I-38. *See also* 12 U.S.C. § 1823(i) (purchase of "net worth certificates" from troubled depository institution by FDIC as support for institution's capital position).

15. *See Modernizing*, Discussion Chapter I, at I-37.

16. *See id.* at I-38 - I-39. *But see* 12 U.S.C. § 1823(c)(5), (i)(11) (limiting FDIC authority to make equity investments).

regional banks such as the MCorp subsidiary and Continental Illinois.[17] . . .

Current Statutory Approaches

Fears about the implications of these trends have triggered increasing attention from Congress. The most recent results of this attention have been provisions of the Financial Institutions Reform, Recovery, and Enforcement Act of 1989[18] and the Federal Deposit Insurance Corporation Improvement Act of 1991.[19] . . .

Financial Assistance

To prevent the default of an insured depository institution,[20] to restore a closed insured bank to normal operation,[21] or to lessen the risk to the FDIC from the instability of a significant number of insured depository institutions or of institutions with significant financial resources,[22] the FDIC has the sole authority and discretion to give financial assistance to such institutions.[23] Such assistance may take the form of loans to, deposits in, purchase of assets or securities of, assumption of liabilities of, or contributions to any such institution.[24] FDIC financial assistance may also take the form of assistance to facilitate a merger, consolidation or other acquisition of a troubled or closed insured depository institution by another insured institution.[25] FDIC decisions to render assistance are generally subject to a requirement that the FDIC make a determination that the assistance provided be "necessary to meet the obligation of the [FDIC] to provide insurance coverage,"[26] and that

---

17. MODERNIZING THE FINANCIAL SYSTEM, *supra* note 2, Discussion Chapter I, at I-39.

18. Pub. L. No. 101-73, 103 Stat. 183 (1989) (codified at scattered sections of, *inter alia*, 12 U.S.C.).

19. Pub. L. No. 102-242, 105 Stat. 2236 (1991) (codified at scattered sections of 12 U.S.C.).

20. 12 U.S.C. § 1823(c)(1)(A), as amended, Economic Growth and Regulatory Paperwork Reduction Act (EGRPR Act), Pub. L. No. 104-208, title II, §2704(d)(14)(M) 110 Stat. 3009 (1996) (codified at 12 U.S.C. §1823).

21. *Id.* § 1823(c)(1)(B), *as amended,* Riegle Community Development and Regulatory Improvement Act of 1994 (CDRIA), Pub. L. No. 103-325, Sept. 23, 1994, § 602(a)(34), 108 Stat. 2160, 2289 (1994) (codified at 12 U.S.C. § 1823(c)(1)(B)) (technical amendment).

22. *Id.* § 1823(c)(1)(C), *as amended.*

23. *Id.* § 1823(c)(1). For a discussion of the implications of an open bank assistance arrangement, see *Senior Unsecured Creditors' Committee v. FDIC*, 749 F. Supp. 758 (N.D.Tex. 1990). In December 1992, the FDIC published a policy statement indicating the circumstances under which it would extend assistance to a troubled insured depository institution that was still open. 57 Fed. Reg. 60,203 (1992). In July 1996, the FDIC published a proposed revision of the policy statement. 61 Fed. Reg. 34,814 (1996).

24. 12 U.S.C. § 1823(c)(1). On purchase of assets by the FDIC, see *id.* § 1823(d). On parallel FDIC assistance authority for savings associations, see *id.* § 1823(k)(5). Section 111 of the Garn-St. Germain Act, Public Law 97-320, § 111, 96 Stat.1469 (1982), fundamentally amended the formerly narrow option presented by 12 U.S.C. § 1823(c). Previously, § 1823(c) had only authorized loans, deposits, and purchase of assets by the FDIC to prevent closing or to reopen a bank. The amended section also explicitly authorized the FDIC to engage in a range of actions in order to facilitate a merger or consolidation of an insured bank, or to arrange a purchase and assumption transaction. *See* 12 U.S.C. § 1823(c)(2), *as amended*, CDRIA, § 602(a)(35), 108 Stat. at 2289-2290 (codified at 12 U.S.C. § 1823(c)(2)(A)) (technical amendment).

25. 12 U.S.C. § 1823(c)(2). For SEC discussion of the accounting treatment of an acquisition of a troubled financial institution, see 68 Fed. Reg. 26,840, 26,854-26,855 (2003) (codified at 17 C.F.R. pt. 211) (Staff Accounting Bulletin No. 103, "Update of Codification of Staff Accounting Bulletins").

26. 12 U.S.C. § 1823(c)(4)(A)(i).

it be the least-cost approach to resolving the problem; that is, that

> the total amount of the expenditures by the [FDIC] and obligations incurred by the [FDIC] (including any immediate and long-term obligation of the [FDIC] and any direct or contingent liability for future payment by the [FDIC]) in connection with the exercise of any such [assistance] authority with respect to such institution is the least costly to the deposit insurance fund of all possible methods for meeting the [FDIC's] obligation. . . .[27]

The FDIC may not use its assistance authority to purchase voting or common stock of an insured depository institution.[28] Assistance provided may be made subordinate to the rights of depositors and other creditors.[29]

Appointment of Conservator of receiver

It is generally within the discretion of the chartering authority[30] of a failing depository institution to determine whether or not to place it in conservatorship or receivership.[31]

---

27. *Id.* § 1823(c)(4)(A)(ii). See 58 Fed. Reg. 67,662 (1993) (codified at 12 C.F.R. pt. 360) (FDIC least-cost resolution rules, implementing §141). See also Federal Deposit Insurance Corporation, Statement of Policy on Assistance to Operating Insured Depository Institutions, reprinted in 58 Fed. Reg. 60,203 (1993) (FDIC policy with respect to statutory cost test for FDIC-assisted resolutions, and requirements for FDIC assistance to operating institutions prior to appointment of conservator or receiver).

28. 12 U.S.C. § 1823(c)(5).

29. *Id.* § 1823(c)(9).

30. *But see id.* § 1821(c)(4) (FDIC appointment of itself as conservator or receiver, notwithstanding other state or federal law, under specified statutory conditions). On judicial review of these FDIC self-appointments, see *id.* § 1821(c)(7). On FDIC replacement of itself as conservator in such situations, see *id.* § 1821(c)(8). *See also id.* § 1821(c)(10) (other grounds for FDIC self-appointment as conservator or receiver of insured depository institution). Heightened involvement of the regulators in the burgeoning thrift crisis beginning in the early 1980s placed additional strains on the regulatory system and raised questions about the discretion and good faith of the regulators themselves. For a case considering a challenge to federal regulatory discretion in the face of claims of basic property rights of thrift owners, see *Biscayne Fed. S. & L. v. Federal Home Loan Bank Bd.*, 720 F.2d 1499 (11th Cir. 1983), *cert. denied*, 467 U.S. 1215 (1984). *Cf.Hindes v. F.D.I.C.*, 137 F.3d 148 (3d Cir. 1998) (barring actions affecting FDIC exercise of powers as receiver, where claims based on allegedly improper notification by FDIC in corporate capacity that bank was operating in unsafe and unsound condition); *Auction Co. of America v. F.D.I.C.*, 132 F.3d 746 (D.C. Cir. 1998), clarified on denial of rehearing, 141 F.3d 1198 (allowing breach of contract action where auction company was to auction assets of failed thrifts for FDIC receiver; reading statutory reference to FDIC "as receiver" to mean as receiver for specific institution, not situation under auctioneer's contract); *Bolduc v. Beal Bank, SSB*, 994 F. Supp. 82 (D.N.H. 1998) (allowing certain affirmative claims of debtors' invalid indorsement relating to transfers arising long after FDIC received promissory notes at issue); *First Pacific Bancorp, Inc. v. Helfer*, 224 F.3d 1117 (9th Cir. 2000) (contra *Hindes*; allowing private action under § 1821(d)(15) against FDIC to compel financial accounting in conformity with FDIC accounting and reporting practices and procedures; barring corresponding private action under state law).

31. *See, e.g.*, 12 U.S.C. §§ 191 (Comptroller; declaration with respect to national bank), 1464(d)(2)(A) (DOTS; declaration with respect to federal savings association). *See Sinclair v. Hawke*, 314 F.3d 934 (8th Cir. 2003) (affirming dismissal of claim by owner of failed national bank declared insolvent by Comptroller). On the procedures governing a conservatorship, *see generally In re Conservatorship of Wellsville Nat. Bank*, 407 F.2d 223 (3d Cir. 1969),), *cert. denied sub nom.Miller v. Camp,* 396 U.S. 832, reh'g denied, 396 U.S. 949. *See also Central W. Rental Co. v. Horizon Leasing*, 740 F. Supp. 1109 (E.D. Pa. 1990) (challenge to conservator's actions, despite §1464(d)(7)(C)

In a conservatorship, the basic statutory assumption is that the institution may well return to the transaction of its business.[32] In a receivership, the basic statutory assumption is that the institution will be merged with or otherwise acquired by a healthy depository institution or liquidated.[33] In either event, a conservator or receiver, respectively, will be appointed. Almost inevitably in either case, this will be the FDIC.[34]

The statutory rules governing the appointment of the FDIC in either capacity override any contrary provision of federal law, state constitution or state law.[35] In the case of federal depository institutions,[36] appointment of the FDIC as conservator is within the discretion of the institution's supervisor.[37] Appointment of the FDIC as receiver is mandatory whenever the institution's supervisor decides to place it in receivership.[38] When acting as conservator or receiver, the FDIC is not subject to the direction or supervision of any other state or federal agency in the exercise of its rights, powers or privileges.[39] However, in the

---

prohibition on judicial action restraining or affecting conservator's power). On the procedures governing the decision to place an institution in receivership, see generally *Federal Deposit Ins. Corp. v. McKnight*, 769 F.2d 658 (10th Cir. 1985), cert. denied, 475 U.S. 1010. The receivership process has primarily been an administrative one, with a limited role for courts. *See Shemonsky v. Office of Thrift Supervision*, 733 F. Supp. 892 (M.D. Pa. 1990), aff'd, 922 F.2d 833 (3d Cir.), *cert. denied*, 499 U.S. 965 (1991); *Matter of Receivership of Penn Square Bank, N.A.*, 556 F. Supp. 494 (D. Okla. 1983). On conservatorship and liquidation procedures for insured credit unions, see, e.g., 66 Fed. Reg. 40,574 (2001) (codified at 12 C.F.R. §§709.0, 709.12) (clarifying that, as conservator or liquidating agent of federally insured credit union, NCUA will honor claim for prepayment fees by FHLBank under specified circumstances); 68 Fed. Reg. 32,355 (2003) (codified at 12 C.F.R. §709.13) (amending NCUA involuntary liquidation regulation to designate swap agreements as "qualified financial contracts," limiting swap counterparty exposure when federally-insured credit union is placed in involuntary liquidation or conservatorship).

32. *See, e.g.*, 12 U.S.C. § 205(a)(1) (termination of conservatorship of a national bank permitting the bank "to resume the transaction of its business subject to such terms, conditions, and limitations as the Comptroller may prescribe"). *See also Minichello v. Saxon*, 337 F.2d 75 (3d Cir. 1964), *cert. denied*, 380 U.S. 952, 393 U.S. 849, *rehearing denied*, 393 U.S. 992 (Comptroller's authority and minority shareholder rights). *Cf.* 12 U.S.C. § 1821(d)(2)(D) (general power of FDIC as conservator to put institution on sound and solvent condition and to conserve its assets). *But see* note 33, *infra*.

33. *See, e.g.*, 12 U.S.C. § 1821(c)(2)(A)(ii) (appointment of FDIC as receiver "for the purpose of liquidation or winding up the affairs of an insured Federal depository institution"). *See also id.* § 1821(d)(2)(E) (general power of FDIC as receiver to place institution in liquidation). Despite its starting assumption (*see* text and accompanying note 32, *supra*), a conservatorship may also ultimately conclude with the liquidation or winding up of the affairs of the institution in conservatorship. *See* 12 U.S.C. § 205(a)(2).

34. *See generally* 12 U.S.C. § 1821(c) (appointment of FDIC as conservator or receiver).

35. *See id.* § 1821(c)(1).

36. For these purposes, the term *federal depository institution* is defined by the FDIA to mean "any national bank, any Federal savings association, and any Federal branch" of a foreign bank. *Id.* § 1813(c)(4). On the meaning of *Federal savings association*, see *id.* § 1813(b)(2). On the meaning of the term *Federal branch*, see *id.* § 1813(s)(2).

37. *Id.* § 1821(c)(2)(A)(i) (in general), (c)(6)(A) (DOTS appointment of FDIC or RTC as conservator; FDIC acceptance of appointment). *But see id.* § 1821(c)(11) (FDIC opportunity to appoint itself as receiver, under certain conditions, before federal agency may appoint conservator).

38. *Id.* § 1821(c)(2)(A)(ii) (in general), (c)(6)(B)(i)-(ii) (DOTS appointment of RTC during three-year period beginning August 9, 1989; DOTS appointment of FDIC thereafter).

39. *Id.* § 1821(c)(2)(C).

conservatorship context, the institution in conservatorship itself remains subject to the supervision of its appropriate federal banking agency, *i.e.*, the Comptroller (for national banks and District banks) and, until at least July 2011, the Director of the Office of Thrift Supervision (DOTS) (for federal savings associations).[40] Under the Dodd-Frank Act (DFA) § 312,[41] the functions and authority of the DOTS and the OTS will be transferred to the other federal regulators on the "transfer date,"[42] *i.e.*, 21 July 2011. Under DFA § 313,[43] the OTS and the position of the DOTS are then scheduled to be abolished 90 days after the transfer date.

In the case of insured state depository institutions,[44] appointment of the FDIC as conservator or receiver is within the discretion of the appropriate state authority.[45] When acting as conservator or receiver under appointment by the state authority, the FDIC is not subject to the direction or supervision of any other state or federal agency in the exercise of its rights, powers or privileges.[46] However, in the conservatorship context, the institution in conservatorship itself remains subject to the supervision of its state authority.[47]

As conservator or receiver, the FDIC has a wide range of statutory powers.[48] The FDIC gains control of the entity as its successor by operation of law.[49] As such, the FDIC has

---

40. Id. §1821(c)(2)(D).

41. *See id.* § 312(b) (codified at 12 U.S.C. § 5412(b)) (mandating transfer of functions).

42. *Id.* §§ 311(a), 313 (codified at 12 U.S.C. §§ 5411(a), 5413).

43. DFA § 313 (codified at 12 U.S.C. § 5413).

44. For these purposes, the term *insured State depository institution* is derived from two terms defined by the FDIA: *insured depository institution*, defined to mean "any bank or savings association the deposits of which are insured by the [FDIC]" and *State depository institution*, defined to mean "any State bank, any State savings association and any insured branch which is not a Federal branch" of a foreign bank. *Id.* § 1813(c)(2), (c)(4). On the meaning of the term *State bank*, see *id.* § 1813(a)(2). On the meaning of the term *State savings association*, see *id.* § 1813(b)(3). On the meaning of the term *insured branch*, see *id.* § 1813(s)(3).

45. *Id.* § 1821(c)(3)(A). In the past, this discretionary aspect of the appointment of a federal agency as receiver has occasionally created tension between the state authority and the federal agency. *See, e.g., Fidelity Sav. & Loan Ass'n v. Federal Home Loan Bank*, 689 F.2d 803 (9th Cir. 1982) (describing tension between California Savings and Loan Commissioner and now defunct FSLIC). For grounds for appointment of FDIC as conservator or receiver of state depository institution by its appropriate *federal* banking agency (after consultation with the state authority), see 12 U.S.C. § 1821(c)(9).

46. 12 U.S.C. § 1821(c)(3)(C).

47. *Id.* § 1821(c)(3)(D).

48. This grant of authority includes all incidental powers "as shall be necessary to carry out [its] powers" as conservator or receiver. *Id.* § 1821(d)(2)(I). *See also id.* § 1821(c)(2)(B), (c)(3)(B) (additional powers available to FDIC as conservator or receiver), (c)(13) (additional powers where FDIC is self-appointed under § 1821(c)(4), appointed by the DOTS under § 1821(c)(6), appointed because of undercapitalization under § 1821(c)(9), or self-appointed because of potential loss to deposit fund under § 1821(c)(10)). The FDIC resolution and receivership rules are contained in 12 C.F.R. pt. 360. For a case discussing the applicability of pt. 360, see *Waterview Management Co. v. FDIC*, 257 F. Supp. 2d 31 (D.D.C. 2003) (holding judgment awarding customer of savings bank in receivership prejudgment interest not superseded by FDIC claim-prioritizing regulation; requiring FDIC to pay customer post-judgment interest).

49. *Id.* § 1821(d)(2)(A).

full authority to operate the institution.[50] Whether serving as conservator or receiver, it also has the power to effect the merger of the institution with another insured depository institution,[51] or arrange a purchase or assumption transaction with another insured depository institution.[52] The FDIC may, where it determines that it is "practicable, efficient, and cost effective"[53] utilize the resources of the private sector to carry out its responsibilities for management and disposition of the assets of an insured depository institution. In addition to these general powers, there is also a range of specific powers available to the FDIC in either of its capacities.

As conservator, the FDIC has the power to take any action necessary to put the institution in a sound and solvent condition.[54] It also has the power to take any action appropriate to carry on the institution's business and to preserve or conserve the institution's assets.[55]

As receiver, the FDIC has the power to liquidate the institution and realize on the institution's assets, "having due regard [for] the conditions of credit in the locality" of the institution.[56] In this respect, it may organize a new savings association,[57] a new national bank,[58] or transitional "bridge bank"[59] to take over assets and liabilities of the institution in receivership, as it deems appropriate. . . .

In addition, the FDIC as receiver has authority to determine the validity of claims against the institution in accordance with an elaborate statutory procedure.[60] As was demonstrated in *First Empire Bank-New York v. FDIC*,[61] resolving the problems of a failing institution has often been considerably often complicated, and the costs markedly increased, by the claims of third parties that have dealt with the institution. In this regard, the now defunct Federal Home Loan Bank Board and the FSLIC experienced great difficulty in attempting to deal with such claims by way of an expedited administrative process for claims

---

50. *Id.* § 1821(d)(2)(B), *as amended*, CDRIA, § 602(a)(22), 108 Stat. at 2289 (codified at 12 U.S.C. § 1821(d)(2)(B)(iii)) (technical amendment). On the functions of the institution's directors, officers and shareholders by FDIC regulation or order, see *id.* § 1821(d)(2)(C). In operating the institution, the FDIC also has the responsibility to pay all valid obligations of the institutions, "in accordance with the prescriptions and limitations of [the FDIA]." *Id.* § 1821(d)(2)(H).

51. *Id.* § 1821(d)(2)(G)(i)(I).

52. *Id.* § 1821(d)(2)(G)(i)(II). *See SCFC ILC, Inc. v. Visa USA, Inc.*, 936 F.2d 1096, 1099-1100 (11th Cir. 1991) (interpreting statute). This transaction would be subject to the approval of the appropriate federal banking agency that supervises the acquiring institution. 12 U.S.C. § 1821(d)(2)(G)(ii). The FDIC also has the authority to purchase assets of an insured depository institution in default from any conservator, receiver or liquidator, including itself, or to take assets as security for loans from the FDIC. *Id.* § 1823(d)(2)(D).

53. 12 U.S.C. § 1821(d)(2)(K).

54. *Id.* § 1821(d)(2)(D)(i).

55. *Id.* § 1821(d)(2)(D)(ii).

56. *Id.* § 1821(d)(2)(E). On the status of the FDIC as receiver, see *id.* § 1822.

57. *See id.* § 1821(d)(2)(F)(i).

58. *See id.* § 1821(d)(2)(F)(ii), (m).

59. *See id.* § 1821(d)(2)(F)(ii), (n). *See generally Bell & Murphy and Associates, Inc. v. Interfirst Bank Gateway, N.A.*, 894 F.2d 750 (5th Cir.), *cert. denied*, 498 U.S. 895 (1990) (discussing role of bridge banks).

60. *See* 12 U.S.C. § 1821(d)(3)-(10). . . .

61. 572 F.2d 1361 (9th Cir. 1978)), *aff'd after remand*, 634 F.2d 1222 (9th Cir. 1980), cert. denied, 452 U.S. 906 (1981).

resolution.[62] The FDIA was subsequently amended to provide an elaborate procedure for the resolution of third-party claims.[63] The FDIA was also amended in August 1993, to provide

62. *See Coit Independence Joint Venture v. FSLIC*, 489 U.S. 561 (1988) (invalidating administrative claims process). *See also Carrollton-Farmers Branch Independent School District v. Johnson & Cravens*, 889 F.2d 571 (5th Cir. 1989) (rehearing on claims following *Coit*); *Triland Holding & Co. v. Sunbelt Service Corp.*, 884 F.2d 205 (5th Cir. 1989) (remand under *Coit*). . . . *See generally* Baxter, *Life in the Administrative Track: Administrative Adjudication of Claims against Savings Institution Receivers*, 1988 DUKE L.J. 422 (discussing *Coit* and making recommendations for reform).

63. *See* Pub. L. No. 101-73, § 212(a), 103 Stat. 183, 225-234 (1989) (codified at 12 U.S.C. § 1821(d)), *as amended*, Pub. L. No. 102-242, §§ 123(a), 141(b), 161(a)(1)-(2), 416, 105 Stat. 2236 (1991) (codified at 12 U.S.C. § 1821(d)(3)(A), (d)(4), (d)(5)(D), (d)(11)(B), (d)(13)(E)); CDRIA, § 602(a)(22)-(25), 108 Stat. at 2289 (codified at 12 U.S.C. § 1821(d)(2)(B)(iii), (d)(8)(B)(ii), (d)(14)(B), (d)(16)(B)(iv)). *See Tuxedo Beach Club Corp. v. City Federal Sav. Bank*, 737 F. Supp. 18 (D.N.J. 1990) (discussing statutory policy and legislative intent of 1989 amendments); *Meliezer v. RTC*, 952 F.2d 879 (5th Cir. 1992) (discussing administrative claims procedures).

Generally, the 1989 legislation is retroactively applicable to cases pending at the time of its enactment. *Demars v. First Service Bank for Savings*, 907 F.2d 1237 (1st Cir. 1990). However, the claims determination provisions, and specifically § 1821(d)(13)(D), do not require dismissal of all pending claims against failed institutions at the time of the enactment of the legislation. *Marquis v. FDIC*, 965 F.2d 1148 (1st Cir. 1992) (efficiency goal of statute promoted by this approach). Proceedings may be stayed under 12 U.S.C. § 1821(d)(12) pending the completion of the administrative claims process. *Id.* (interpreting § 1821(d) to allow more than one 90-day stay). *But cf. Praxis Properties, Inc. v. Colonial S.B., SLA*, 947 F.2d 49 (3d Cir. 1991) (stay expires 90 days after FDIC appointment); *Hunter's Run v. Arapahoe County Public Trustee*, 741 F. Supp. 207 (D.Colo. 1990) (stay of proceedings under § 1821(d)(12) inappropriate where FDIC has had sufficient time to prepare case and plaintiff will suffer irreparable harm); *Tuxedo Beach Club Corp. v. City Federal Sav. Bank*, 729 F. Supp. 1508 (D.N.J. 1990) (same result as to RTC as receiver); *FDIC v. Taylor*, 727 F. Supp. 326 (S.D.Tex. 1989) (same; FDIC as receiver).

Failure to file a timely claim bars the claim before the administrative agency and the courts. *Althouse v. RTC*, 969 F.2d 1544, 1546 (3d Cir. 1992). On the relationship between the administrative claims procedure and pending litigation involving the claim, see *RTC v. Mustang Partners*, 946 F.2d 103 (10th Cir. 1991). On the necessity of exhausting remedies under the administrative review process of claims or filing claims in an appropriate district court, see *Village of Oakwood v. State Bank and Trust Co.*, 519 F. Supp. 2d 730 (N.D. Ohio 2007).

State law claims may be preempted by the administrative claims provisions. Meliezer, 952 F.2d at 883 (involving negligence claim by home mortgage owners against failed bank that issued loan); Bueford v. Resolution Trust Corp., 991 F.2d 481, 484 (8th Cir.1993) (employment discrimination claims by former employees of failed bank); Henderson v. Bank of New England, 986 F.2d 319, 321 (9th Cir.1993) (claims by denied credit card applicant); McCarthy v. FDIC, 348 F.3d 1075, 1081 (9th Cir.2003) (claims by debtors of failed bank arising out of acts of receiver, rather than bank in receivership); Freeman v. FDIC, 56 F.3d 1394, 1402 (D.C.Cir.1995) (claims by debtors of failed bank alleging fraudulent restructuring of home mortgage loan). There are few types of claims that the courts have retained for judicial resolution. See, e.g., Homeland Stores, Inc. v. Resolution Trust Corp., 17 F.3d 1269, 1273-75 (10th Cir.1994) (holding claims against receiver, not failed bank, in connection with receiver's management of shopping center asset of failed institution, not subject to administrative claims process); Rosa v. Resolution Trust Corp., 938 F.2d 383, 394-95 (3d Cir.1991), cert. denied, 502 U.S. 981, 112 S.Ct. 582 (1991) (claim by pension plan participants seeking order barring retroactive termination of plan). *RTC v. Elman*, 949 F.2d 624, 627 (2d Cir. 1991) (involving attorney retaining lien). *FDIC v. Shain, Schaffer & Rafenello*, 944 F.2d 129 (3d Cir. 1991) (same). *See also Circle Industries v. City F.S.B.*, 931 F.2d 7 (2d Cir. 1991).

As to standing under the administrative claims procedure, it has been held that a union has standing to represent claims of its members, pursuant to 12 U.S.C. § 1821(d)(6). *Transohio S.B. v.*

a national depositor preference for amounts realized from the liquidation or other resolution of FDIC-insured depository institutions.[64]

Claims Against Third Parties

As conservator or receiver, the FDIC stands in a position to prosecute claims of the depository institution against third parties.[65] The current FDIA contains a provision[66] that

---

Director, OTS, 967 F.2d 598 (D.C.Cir. 1992); *Office of Professional Employees International Union, Local 2 v. FDIC*, 962 F.2d 63, 67 (D.C.Cir. 1992).

64. Pub. L. No. 103-66, 107 Stat. 312 (1993) (codified at 12 U.S.C. §1821(d)(11)). The amendment requires that distributions from all future receivership estates be made in the following order:

i) administrative expenses of the receiver;
ii) deposit liability claims;
iii) other general or senior liabilities of the institution, other than subordinated obligations or shareholder claims;
iv) subordinated obligations; and,
v) shareholder claims.

Id. The legislation applies to all receiverships of insured institutions established after its enactment date (August 10, 1993), 12 U.S.C. §1821 note, and it supersedes any inconsistent state or other federal distribution provisions. *Id.* §1821(d)(11). For FDIC rules interpreting and implementing the amendment, see 58 Fed. Reg. 43,069 (1993) (codified at 12 C.F.R. pt. 360) (interim rule); 58 Fed. Reg. 67,662 (1993) (redesignating 12 C.F.R. §§360.1-360.3 as §§360.2-360.4) (final rule), as amended, 60 Fed. Reg. 35,487 (1995) (codified at 12 C.F.R. §§360.3(f), 360.4). For discussion of the applicability of sections 1821(d) and (e), see *Battista v. FDIC*, 195 F.3d 1113 (9th Cir. 1999), *cert. denied,* 531 U.S. 812 (2000) (holding that severance pay claims arising from FDIC repudiation, as receiver, of insolvent bank's employment contracts were subject to distribution priority scheme under section 1821(e), not distribution priority under section 1821(d)(11)(A)); *Bank of New York v. F.D.I.C.*, 453 F. Supp. 2d 82 (D.D.C. 2006) (upholding broad FDIC power to repudiate contracts of bank in receivership). See also 67 Fed. Reg. 34,385 (2002) (codified at 12 C.F.R. §360.7) (providing for payment of post-insolvency interest in receiverships with surplus funds). *Cf. Golden Pac. Bancorp. v. FDIC*, 375 F.3d 196 (2d Cir. 2004) (holding that FDIC, as insured depositors' subrogee, was entitled to post-insolvency interest on funds previously paid to cover insurance obligations).

65. *See, e.g.*, 12 U.S.C. § 1821(d)(2)(B)(ii) (power of FDIC as conservator or receiver to collect obligation and money due the institution). *See also FDIC v. Schuchmann*, 235 F.3d 1217 (10th Cir. 2000) (acknowledging limitation of negligence theories in FDIC suit against director of failed savings association for director's alleged breach of fiduciary duty and negligence in allegedly causing association to enter into transactions in which director had personal interest); *In re Sunrise Sec. Litig.*, 916 F.2d 874, 889 (3d Cir. 1990) (FDIC as receiver has power to pursue derivative claims against directors and officers of failed institution); *Hindes v. FDIC*, 137 F.3d 148 (3d Cir. 1998) (barring derivative actions by shareholders); *Pareto v. FDIC*, 139 F.3d 696 (9th Cir. 1998) (holding that claims asserted by stockholders were derivative to which FDIC had acceded; stockholders lacked standing to sue). *But see Hayes v. Gross*, 982 F.2d 104 (3d Cir. 1992) (1989 legislation did not amend or subordinate federal securities law cause of action). *See generally Telematics Intl. v. NEMLC Leasing Corp.*, 967 F.2d 703 (1st Cir. 1992) (FDIC attachment of certificate of deposit as security for loan agreement within FDIC's discretion under §1821(j)). Under 12 U.S.C. §1821(j), courts are generally prohibited from taking "any action, except at the request of the [FDIC] Board of Directors by regulation or order, to restrain or affect the exercise of power or functions of the [FDIC] as a conservator or a receiver." The provision has been interpreted to restrict injunctions and other equitable relief against the FDIC (or the now defunct RTC) when it acts as a receiver or conservator, even if it were to violate its own procedures or to behave unlawfully. *Bank of America National Association v. Colonial Bank*, 604 F.3d 1239 (11th Cir. 2010); *281-300 Joint Venture v. Onion*, 938 F.2d 35, 39 (5th Cir. 1991), *cert. denied*, 502 U.S. 1057 (1992); *Rosa*, 938 F.2d at 397-400 (3d Cir. 1991), *cert. denied*, 502 U.S. 981 (1991); *In re Landmark Land Co. of Oklahoma*, 973 F.2d 283 (4th Cir. 1992); *Gross v.*

continues in expanded form the original codification of the rule of *D'Oench, Duhme & Co., Inc. v. FDIC*[67] against secret agreements against the interests of the FDIC.[68] Under the

---

Bell Sav. Bank PaSA, 974 F.2d 403 (3d Cir. 1992); *Telematics Int'l, Inc. v. NEMLC Leasing Corp.*, 967 F.2d 703, 705-706 (1st Cir. 1992); *United Liberty Life Ins. Co. v. Ryan*, 985 F.2d 1320, 1328-1329 (6th Cir. 1993); *Harkness Apartment Owners Corp. v. FDIC*, 999 F.2d 538 (2d Cir. 1993); *National Trust for Historic Preservation v. FDIC*, 21 F.3d 469 (D.C. Cir. 1994); *Bursik v. One Fourth St. North, Ltd.*, 84 F.3d 1395 (11th Cir. 1996); *Hindes v. FDIC,* 137 F.3d 148 (3d Cir. 1998) (barring actions affecting FDIC exercise of powers as receiver, where claims based on allegedly improper notification by FDIC in corporate capacity that bank was operating in unsafe and unsound condition). *But cf. Auction Co. of America v. FDIC*, 132 F.3d 746 (D.C. Cir. 1998), *clarified on denial of rehearing*, 141 F.3d 1198 (allowing breach of contract action where auction company was to auction assets of failed thrifts for FDIC receiver; reading statutory reference to FDIC "as receiver" to mean as receiver for specific institution, not situation under auctioneer's contract); *Bolduc v. Beal Bank, SSB*, 994 F. Supp. 82 (D.N.H. 1998) (allowing certain affirmative claims of debtors' invalid indorsement relating to transfers arising long after FDIC received promissory notes at issue); *National Loan Investors L.P. v. Town of Orange*, 204 F.3d 407 (2d Cir. 2000), *cert. denied*, 531 U.S. 828 (holding municipal water pollution control authority's assessment of additional fee for late sewer charges, for period when FDIC was receiver for an insolvent mortgagee-bank, not a "penalty"; FDIC exemption from liability for penalties under FIRREA not applicable); *FDIC v. Ernst & Young LLP*, 374 F.3d 579 (7th Cir. 2004) (holding that FDIC could not sue in corporate capacity to avoid limitations on FDIC as receiver).

66. 12 U.S.C. § 1823(e). . . .

67. 315 U.S. 447 (1942) (holding such agreements unenforceable against the FDIC). Section 1823(e) codifies but does not preempt the D'Oench, Duhme decision. *Murphy v. FDIC,* 208 F.3d 959 (11th Cir. 2000), *cert. granted sub nom. Murphy v. Beck*, 530 U.S. 1306, *cert. dismissed*, 531 U.S. 1107 (2001), *FSLIC v. Griffin*, 935 F.2d 691, 698 (5th Cir. 1991), *cert. denied sub nom. Griffin v. First Gibraltar Bank, FSB*, 502 U.S. 1092 (1992); *Adams v. Madison Realty and Dev., Inc.*, 746 F. Supp. 419 (D.N.J. 1990), aff'd, 937 F.2d 845 (3d Cir. 1991). But see Murphy v. FDIC, 829 F. Supp. 3 (D.D.C. 1993), *aff'd in part and rev'd in part*, 61 F.3d 34 (D.C. Cir. 1995) (holding contra). *See also Central W. Rental Co. v. Horizon Leasing*, 967 F.2d 832, 840 (3d Cir. 1992) (doctrine prevents use of "oral undocumented agreements" as defense against enforcement of FDIC judgment); *FDIC v. Kasal,* 913 F.2d 487 (8th Cir. 1990), *cert. denied,* 498 U.S. 1119 (1991) (applying §1823(e)); *Oliver v. RTC*, 747 F. Supp. 1351 (E.D. Mo. 1990), *aff'd*, 955 F.2d 583 (8th Cir. 1992) (applying §1823(e)); *Morgan v. Heights Sav. Assn.*, 741 F. Supp. 620 (E.D. Tex. 1990) (applying doctrine to alleged pre-insolvency settlement of action on mortgage); *Mery v. Universal Sav. Assn.*, 737 F. Supp. 1000 (S.D. Tex. 1990) (applying §1823(e) to partner's liability for partnership notes to failed institution); *Carico v. First Natl. Bank of Bogota*, 734 F. Supp. 768 (S.D. Tex. 1990) (applying §1823(e)); *FDIC v. Wainer*, 124 N.E.2d 29 (Ill. App. Ct. 1955) (interpreting §1823(e)). The doctrine applies to affirmative claims as well as to defenses. *Jackson v. FDIC*, 981 F.2d 730 (5th Cir. 1992). *Accord, Bruneau v. FDIC*, 981 F.2d 175 (5th Cir. 1992); *FDIC v. Byrne*, 736 F. Supp. 727 (N.D. Tex. 1990) (rule precludes affirmative claims as well as defenses). *But cf. Murphy v. FDIC, supra* (suggesting that §1823(e) supersedes *D'Oench, Duhme*). *See generally FDIC v. Kucera Builders, Inc.*, 503 F. Supp. 967, 970 (N.D. Ga. 1980) (collecting cases); Skillern, *Federal Deposit Insurance Corporation and the Failed Bank: The Past Decade*, 99 BANKING L.J. 292, 295-305 (1982) (discussing cases interpreting §1823(e)); J. Michael Echevarria, *A Precedent Embalms a Principle: The Expansion of the D'Oench, Duhme Doctrine,* 43 CATH. U. L. REV. 745 (1994) (review and critique of litigation).

68. 12 U.S.C. § 1823(e), *as amended*, Pub. L. No. 101-73, § 217(4), 103 Stat. at 256. *See Timberland Design v. FDIC*, 745 F. Supp. 784 (D.Mass. 1990) (applying amended § 1823(e) retroactively to the benefit of FDIC as receiver); *FDIC v. Sullivan*, 744 F. Supp. 239 (D.Colo. 1990) (applying amended § 1823(e) retroactively); RTC v. Camp, 965 F.2d 25, 31 (5th Cir. 1992) (avoiding question of retroactivity). *Cf. RTC v. Murray*, 935 F.2d 89, 94 (5th Cir. 1991) (extension of doctrine to RTC claims); *Olney S&L Ass'n v. Trinity Banc Savings Ass'n*, 885 F.2d 266 274 (5th Cir. 1989), *rehearing denied*, 892 F.2d 78 (extension of doctrine to FSLIC claims).

D'Oench, Duhme doctrine, any agreement between a depository institution and a third party that would tend to diminish or defeat the interest of the FDIC in any asset acquired by it under the financial assistance provisions of the FDIA[69] or the conservatorship and receivership provisions of the FDIA[70] (either as security for a loan, by purchase, or asxreceiver) is invalid unless it meets certain specified conditions.[71] [These conditions are as follows:]

> (1) The agreement must be in writing.[72]
>
> (2) The agreement must have been executed by the depository institution and the third party contemporaneously with the acquisition by the institution of the asset in question.[73]
>
> (3) The agreement must have been approved by the institution's board of directors or its loan committee.[74]
>
> (4) The agreement must have been, continuously from the time of its execution, an official record of the institution.[75] . . .

Emergency Interstate Acquisitions

One technique of particular importance in the interstate market of depository institutions is the arranged acquisition, typically through a bidding process, of a troubled depository institution by an institution not within the same state. Despite longstanding federal statutory bias against interstate acquisitions,[76] in emergency circumstances an out-of-state

---

69. 12 U.S.C. § 1823(c). . . .

70. 12 U.S.C. § 1821, *as amended*, Dodd-Frank Wall Street Reform and Consumer Protection Act (DFA) §§ 335(a), 343(a), 363(5), Pub. L. No. 111-203, 124 Stat. 1376, 1540, 1544-1545, 1552-1553 (2010) (codified at 12 U.S.C. §§ 1821, 1821(a)(1)(E)).

71. 12 U.S.C. § 1823(e). . . . The doctrine may even be raised in the first instance on appeal in exceptional circumstances. *In re 604 Columbus Avenue Realty Trust*, 968 F.2d 1332, 1343-1344 (1st Cir. 1992) (discussing circumstances).

72. *Id.* § 1823(e)(1)(A).

73. *Id.* § 1823(e)(1)(B). . . .

74. *Id.* § 1823(e)(1)(C). This approval must be reflected in the minutes of the board or committee. *Id.*

75. *Id.* § 1823(e)(1)(D).

76. *See, e.g.*, 12 U.S.C. § 1842(d) (prohibition on interstate acquisitions by bank holding companies where law of the home state of the target is contrary). This restriction on interstate acquisitions is removed by the Riegle-Neal Interstate Banking and Branching Efficiency Act of 1994 (IBBEA), Pub. L. No. 103-328, Sept. 29, 1994, 108 Stat. 2338 (1994) (codified at scattered sections of 12 U.S.C.). . . .

A further complication was caused by a particularly strong bias against cross-industry acquisitions of failed savings associations by bank holding companies. As late as March 1981, the Fed was still denying such applications. *See National Detroit Corp.*, FRB Press Release (March 6, 1982). Staff studies by the Fed, OCC, FDIC and the FHLBB during 1981 and 1982, however, took the position generally that such acquisitions might, under appropriate circumstances, be in the public interest and might be permissible under current law. (Assuming, of course, that the Fed was willing to swallow its earlier position.) There was some reluctance to changing the position, since Congress had not acted and had the "Garn proposal" (later to become the Garn-St. Germain Act, Pub. L. No. 97-320, *supra*) under review. Before the final struggles of the large California S&L Fidelity Savings & Loan Association even began, . . . the Fed had reevaluated its position with respect to thrift acquisitions by BHCs. A key change of policy was finally indicated in a letter from the Fed Chairman, December 23, 1981, indicating that "The force of events could require the Board to consider using its authority under existing law to approve acquisitions of failing thrifts by bank holding companies." This acquiror may be the only feasible candidate to take over the ailing institution and avoid an expensive regulatory resolution of the institution's eventual default. The FDIA provides for such acquisitions.

In the case of an insured bank or a holding company, assisted[77] emergency interstate acquisitions by an out-of-state bank, savings association or holding company are authorized under certain specified conditions.[78] If the target insured bank is in default, the target must have total assets of $500 million or more.[79] The FDIC must consult the target's state bank supervisor before making a determination to take action.[80] The supervisor must be given a reasonable opportunity (not less than 48 hours) to object to the proposed acquisition.[81] The FDIC may still proceed, but only on an affirmative vote of 75 percent of the FDIC Board of Directors.[82] Assuming all applicable conditions are met, the FDIC is authorized to arrange a purchase and assumption transaction involving the insured bank in default.[83] Such transactions are also generally subject to the approval of the primary federal or state supervisor of each party to the transaction.[84]

In determining whether or not to arrange such a transaction, in its discretion, the FDIC is specifically authorized to solicit offers or acquisition proposals from any prospective purchasers or merger partners.[85] Intra-industry in-state bidders are favored in this process.[86]

The FDIC is to give consideration to minimizing the cost of its financial assistance

---

change in policy led to a resolution of the Fidelity crisis in advance of the changes in "existing law" effected by Public Law 97-320. *See* Bennett, *Citicorp Acquires Fidelity: New York Bank Allowed Into California*, N.Y. Times, Sept. 29, 1982, at D1. . . .

77. That is, financially assisted by the FDIC under § 1823(c). *See* 12 U.S.C. § 1823(f)(1).

78. *Id.* § 1823(f)(1). Under certain circumstances, an emergency interstate acquisition may be authorized even though the § 1823(c) financial assistance preceded the proposed acquisition, rather than being an integral part of it. *See id.* § 1823(f)(3)(D). The FDIC may require consideration for its previous assistance as a condition for approval of such an acquisition. *Id.* § 1823(f)(3)(G).

79. *Id.* § 1823(f)(2)(A). Total assets are to be determined from the most recent report of condition. *Id.*

80. *Id.* § 1823(f)(2)(B)(i), *as amended*, Riegle Community Development and Regulatory Improvement Act of 1994 (CDRIA), Pub. L. No. 103-325, Sept. 23, 1994, § 602(a)(36), 108 Stat. 2160, 2290 (1994) (codified at 12 U.S.C. § 1823(f)(2)(B)(i)) (technical amendment).

81. *Id.* § 1823(f)(2)(B)(ii).

82. *Id.* § 1823(f)(2)(B)(iii), *as amended*, CDRIA, § 602(a)(37), 108 Stat. at 2290 (codified at 12 U.S.C. § 1823(f)(2)(B)(iii)) (technical amendment).

83. *Id.* § 1823(f)(2)(A).

84. *Id.* However, these transactions are generally not subject to prohibitions of the Bank Holding Company Act, state law, or the S&L holding company provisions of the Home Owner's Loan Act. *Id.* § 1823(f)(4)(A), (E). Any subsidiary created as a result of the transaction may retain existing branches of the target institution. *Id.* § 1823(f)(4)(B). (This does not authorize any move of a principal office or branch. *Id.* § 1823(f)(4)(C).) Subsequent nonemergency interstate acquisitions would be subject to applicable state law. *Id.* § 1823(f)(4)(D).

85. *Id.* § 1823(f)(5). Such prospective purchasers or partners must be "both qualified and capable of acquiring the assets and liabilities of the bank in default or in danger of default." *Id.*

86. *See, e.g., id.* § 1823(f)(6)(A), *as amended*, CDRIA, § 602(a)(39), 108 Stat. at 2290 (codified at 12 U.S.C. § 1823(f)(6)(A)) (technical amendment). . . .

and to the maintenance of specialized depository institutions.[87] . . .

Coordinate rules apply to emergency acquisitions of savings associations.[88] . . .

Notes and Comments 8.29. The relevant statutory provisions with respect to insolvency and receivership were subjected to amendment by FIRREA. Review 12 U.S.C. §§ 1821, 1823. What is the extent of the FDIC's authority under these amended sections?

8.30. QNB has fallen on hard times. Its loan portfolio, heavily concentrated in real estate lending and foreign government loans, is not performing adequately. As a result, it has increasingly been forced to charge off these loans against its relatively small loan loss reserve, and its surplus accounts. It also appears that recently issued capital stock has not been paid up in full. What will be the consequences for QNB under 12 U.S.C. § 1818? What about under 12 U.S.C. § 55? If it wished to dissolve and go into liquidation, what procedures would it be required to follow? *See id.* §§ 181-182.

8.31. Assuming that QNB is experiencing a serious impairment of capital, could the Comptroller force it into receivership? *See* 12 U.S.C. § 191. What procedures would govern? *See id.* §§ 193-197, 198-199. *See generally Federal Deposit Ins. Corp. v. McKnight*, 769 F.2d 658 (10th Cir. 1985), *cert. denied*, 475 U.S. 1010. The receivership process is primarily an administrative one, with a limited role for courts. *See Matter of Recevie rship of Penn Square Bank, N.A.*, 556 F. Supp. 494 (D.Okla. 1983). What would the FDIC's role be in the receivership? *See* 12 U.S.C. §§ 1819(a)(Ninth) (FDIC authority to be receiver), 1822 (FDIC powers as receiver).

8.32. Assume that a number of QNB shareholders were willing to purchase additional shares in the bank and pay up the outstanding shares. Could they bring QNB out of receivership, or must it be liquidated? *See* 12 U.S.C. § 197a.

8.33. As an alternative, could the Comptroller put QNB into a conservatorship? What is the difference between this procedure and a receivership? *See* 12 U.S.C. §§ 202-203, 206. *See generally In re Conservatorship of Wellsville Nat. Bank*, 407 F.2d 223 (3d Cir. 1969), *cert. denied sub nom. Miller v. Camp*, 396 U.S. 832, *rehearing denied*, 396 U.S. 949. What role would the FDIC play in a conservatorship? *See* 12 U.S.C. § 1821(c)(2).

8.34. Once the Comptroller had placed QNB into conservatorship, under what circumstances could the Comptroller terminate the conservatorship? *See* 12 U.S.C. § 205. *See also Minichello v. Saxon*, 337 F.2d 75 (3d Cir. 1964), *cert. denied*, 380 U.S. 952, 393 U.S. 849, *rehearing denied*, 393 U.S. 992 (Comptroller's authority and minority shareholder rights).

8.35. Consider § 1821(j). What if a depository institution *A* is holding the property of another bank *B* in trust for *B* and *B*'s customer? Could *B* obtain injunctive relief, to

---

87. *Id.* § 1823(f)(6)(B), *as amended*, CDRIA, § 602(a)(40), 108 Stat. at 2290 (codified at 12 U.S.C. § 1823(f)(6)(B)(i)) (technical amendment). In other words, the FDIC is directed to consider favorably transactions that would not result in a savings association from being absorbed by a commercial bank. . . .

Generally, a disappointed bidder for bank assets does not have standing to challenge the FDIC's selection of the successful bidder. *Gosnell v. FDIC*, 938 F.2d 372, 376 (2d Cir. 1991).

88. 12 U.S.C. § 1823(k), *as amended*, Dodd-Frank Wall Street Reform and Consumer Protection Act (DFA) § 363(6), Pub. L. No. 111-203, 124 Stat. 1376, 1553 (2010) (codified at 12 U.S.C. § 1823(k)(1)(A)(iv)). Unlike the corresponding provisions with respect to emergency acquisitions of insured banks and holding companies, these provisions do not specifically require that the acquisition transaction involve financial assistance by the FDIC under § 1823(c). However, they do include specific provisions for financial assistance before grounds exist for appointment of a conservator or receiver. *See id.* § 1823(k)(5).

preserve the trust, if *A* were placed in an FDIC receivership? Would it make any difference if the petition for injunctive relief related to *A*'s acts prior to the receivership, rather than anything that the FDIC was doing? In answering these questions, consider the following case.

Bank of America National Association v. Colonial Bank

604 F.3d 1239 (11th Cir. 2010)

ANDERSON, Circuit Judge:

[Bank of America was a trustee for customers who had purchased interests in mortgage loans originated by a mortgage banker, but held in trust by Colonial Bank. Bank of America sued Colonial, alleging that Colonial had wrongfully refused to return the loans and their proceeds, to which Bank of America had legal title. The FDIC was appointed as receiver for Colonial and was substituted as defendant. The Southern District of Florida issued a preliminary injunction against the FDIC, preventing it from controlling and disposing of the loans and proceeds. The FDIC appealed the preliminary injunction order and petitioned for writ of mandamus to dissolve the preliminary injunction. In the excerpt that follows, the Eleventh Circuit vacated and remanded, holding that the anti-injunction provision of FIRREA deprived the district court of jurisdiction to issue the preliminary injunction.]

. . . Because we conclude that the FDIC's proposed actions with respect to the loans and loan proceeds at issue fall squarely within its statutory receivership powers and functions, we hold that 12 U.S.C. § 1821(j) stripped the district court of its jurisdiction to enter the preliminary injunction. Accordingly, we vacate the district court's order and remand with instructions to dismiss Bank of America's motion for a preliminary injunction for lack of jurisdiction.

I. FACTS AND PROCEDURAL HISTORY

The loans and loan proceeds at issue in this case originated from a series of June 2008 agreements between LaSalle Bank N.A. ("LaSalle"), Ocala Funding, LLC ("Ocala"), and Taylor, Bean & Whitaker Mortgage Corp. ("Taylor Bean"). LaSalle, representing certain secured parties as their custodian and collateral agent, provided capital for Ocala to purchase various mortgage notes originated and serviced by Taylor Bean for the benefit of the secured parties. Bank of America, as LaSalle's successor-in-interest, became the trustee and collateral agent for the secured parties and perfected its security interest by taking possession of the loans and loan documents.

From June to August 2009, Bank of America then issued a series of Transmittal Letters to Colonial, which provided notice of its security interest in the loans and established that Bank of America would deliver the loans to Colonial and in return Colonial would hold the loans in trust and serve as custodian, agent, and bailee for and on behalf of the secured parties. Under the agreement, Colonial was also obligated to facilitate the sale of the loans to Freddie Mac. Upon Colonial's receipt of the loans, it had fifteen days either to remit sale proceeds or return unsold loans to Bank of America. Freddie Mac, in connection with its purchase of more than 6,000 of these loans, delivered over $1 billion in loan proceeds to Colonial.

In early August 2009, with the news of Colonial's demise spreading, Bank of America requested that Colonial return the loans and loan proceeds. When Colonial refused, Bank of America presented Colonial with a Demand for Documents and Proceeds, which attempted to revoke the governing Transmittal Letters and terminate Colonial's rights to continued possession of the loans. Colonial again refused to comply with Bank of America's demand. On August 12, 2009, Bank of America filed its complaint in federal court, setting forth five causes of action – replevin, imposition of constructive trust, breach of bailee letters, unjust enrichment, and civil theft – and filed an accompanying motion for a TRO and preliminary injunction against Colonial.

On August 13, 2009, the district court granted Bank of America's motion, issued an *ex parte* TRO, and enjoined Colonial from selling, pledging, assigning, liquidating, encumbering, transferring, or otherwise disposing of all or any portion of the loans and loan proceeds related to the loans. The following day, the Alabama State Banking Department appointed the FDIC as receiver for Colonial, and the FDIC subsequently moved to be substituted for Colonial in this lawsuit. On August 21, 2009, the FDIC filed an emergency motion to dissolve the TRO, arguing that 12 U.S.C. § 1821(j) stripped the court of jurisdiction to restrain or affect the exercise of its powers or functions as receiver. In its motion, the FDIC asserted that Bank of America could pursue its claim through the administrative claims procedures set forth in FIRREA. *See* 12 U.S.C. § 1821(d)(3)-(13). In response, Bank of America argued that it was not a creditor subject to the claims administration process; that the loans never belonged to Colonial and were therefore not a part of the receivership estate; and, thus, that § 1821(j)'s jurisdictional bar did not apply.

The district court rejected the FDIC's jurisdictional challenge and converted the TRO into a preliminary injunction against the FDIC in a final order on September 8, 2009, determining that "assets possessed by, but not belonging to, the failed bank are outside the receivership estate, and the FDIC's attempts to dispose of these assets is therefore not protected by the jurisdiction-stripping provisions of FIRREA." The district court reasoned that the FDIC's attempt to control such assets constituted an act beyond its receivership powers, and FIRREA's jurisdictional prohibitions do not "extend to situations in which the FDIC as receiver asserts authority beyond that granted to it as receiver." . . .

II. DISCUSSION . . .

Section 1821(j) of FIRREA provides in relevant part:

> no court may take any action ... to restrain or affect the exercise of powers or functions of the [FDIC] as a conservator or a receiver.

12 U.S.C. § 1821(j). This provision has been interpreted broadly to bar judicial intervention whenever the FDIC is acting in its capacity as a receiver or conservator, even if it violates its own procedures or behaves unlawfully in doing so. *Bursik v. One Fourth St. N., Ltd.,* 84 F.3d 1395, 1397 (11th Cir.1996); *Nat'l Trust for Historic Pres. v. FDIC,* 995 F.2d 238, 240 (D.C.Cir.1993), *vacated,* 5 F.3d 567 (D.C.Cir.1993), *reinstated in relevant part,* 21 F.3d 469 (D.C.Cir.1994). *See also RPM Invs., Inc. v. Resolution Trust Corp.,* 75 F.3d 618, 620 n. 2 (11th Cir.1996) ("The 'exceptions' to § 1821(j)'s jurisdictional bar are extremely limited."). Therefore, our jurisdictional inquiry under § 1821(j) is quite narrow. First, we evaluate whether the FDIC's challenged actions constitute the exercise of a receivership power or function. *See RPM Invs., Inc.,* 75 F.3d at 620. If so, the FDIC is protected from all court action that would "restrain or affect" the exercise of those powers or functions pursuant to § 1821(j), and we proceed to the secondary inquiry of whether the district court's actions do in fact restrain or affect the FDIC as receiver. *Id.*

The district court found and Bank of America argues that the FDIC would exceed its statutory powers and functions as receiver by controlling and disposing of the loans and loan proceeds at issue. We disagree. Such actions fall squarely within the powers and functions granted to the FDIC by Congress in FIRREA. For example, § 1821(d)(2)(G) grants the receiver the power to "transfer any asset or liability of the institution in default (including assets and liabilities associated with any trust business) without any approval, assignment, or consent with respect to such transfer." Section 1821(d)(2)(H) grants the receiver the broad power to "pay all valid obligations" of the failed financial institution. And § 1821(d)(3) grants the receiver the power to determine all claims against the institution in accordance with the comprehensive administrative claims procedures set forth in § 1821(d)(3)-(13). Further, under § 1821(d)(2)(J)(i), the FDIC also enjoys "such incidental powers" as shall be necessary to carry out those powers expressly granted by statute.

By marshaling the items found on hand at Colonial at the time of its failure, including custodial items held in trust, beginning the process of identifying their proper nature and ownership, and ultimately disposing of these items to parties with valid claims, the FDIC would engage in at least one if not all of these statutory receivership functions. Not only do these functions fall squarely within the FDIC's statutory powers contained in FIRREA, common sense and common experience make plain that such functions are routinely undertaken by receivers. Indeed, there is no other party, except the FDIC as receiver, that could perform such functions. And Congress expressly mandated that no court-at the behest of other parties-may take any action to restrain or affect the exercise of the FDIC's powers or functions as receiver. 12 U.S.C. § 1821(j).

Moreover, as previously noted, "the availability of injunctive relief does not hinge on our view of the proper exercise of otherwise-legitimate powers." *Gross v. Bell Sav. Bank PaSA,* 974 F.2d 403, 408 (3d Cir.1992). *See also Bursik,* 84 F.3d at 1397. Thus, Bank of America's fear that the FDIC will make an erroneous determination of ownership is immaterial to our analysis because it is merely a fear of the FDIC's improper performance of its legitimate receivership functions. Congress contemplated the reality that the FDIC may err in its determination of receivership claims and provided all claimants with the remedy of *de novo* review in federal court of the FDIC's claims determination. 12 U.S.C. § 1821(d)(6) (providing for the option of filing suit after the FDIC's initial determination to allow or disallow a claim in one of two specified federal courts); *id.* § 1821(d)(7)(A) (providing for judicial review of the FDIC's final administrative determination).

There can also be no question that the district court would "restrain or affect" the exercise of these powers or functions by enjoining the FDIC from "selling, pledging, assigning, liquidating, encumbering, transferring, or otherwise disposing of all or any portion of the loans and loan proceeds related to the Ocala loans." Under this broad injunction, the FDIC is left solely to possess the loans, unable to exercise the congressional mandate that it "shall pay all valid obligations" of the failed bank, 12 U.S.C. § 1821(d)(2)(H), or process any administrative claims relating to the loans. In essence, injunctive relief, like that issued here, violates the heart of what is commonly termed FIRREA's "anti-injunction provision." *See, e.g., Hindes v. FDIC,* 137 F.3d 148, 160 (3d Cir.1998); *Sharpe v. FDIC,* 126 F.3d 1147, 1154 (9th Cir.1997); *Elmco Props., Inc. v. Second Nat'l Fed. Sav. Ass'n,* 94 F.3d 914, 923 (4th Cir.1996). *See also, e.g., Nat'l Trust for Historic Pres.,* 995 F.2d at 239 (concluding that an injunction against a planned sale of an historic property of the failed bank would "surely 'restrain or affect' the FDIC's exercise of those powers or functions"); *Gross,* 974 F.2d at 408 (concluding that an injunction requiring the receiver to release certain deposits would "restrain or affect" the receiver's exercise of its powers and functions); *Tillman v. Resolution Trust Corp.,* 37 F.3d 1032, 1036 (4th Cir.1994) (concluding that an injunction restraining a foreclosure sale violated FIRREA's anti-injunction provision).

Nor is our analysis affected by Bank of America's argument that the disputed items were custodial assets, unowned by Colonial, much like the contents of a safe deposit box. Even assuming *arguendo* that the nature of the assets at issue is purely custodial and that title to the loans and their proceeds never transferred to Colonial, § 1821(j) would still clearly bar judicial restraint of the FDIC as long as it acts in its receivership capacity. In interpreting a statutory provision, "we must presume that Congress said what it meant and meant what it said." *United States v. Steele,* 147 F.3d 1316, 1318 (11th Cir.1998) (en banc). "Additionally, we must assume that the ordinary meaning of a statute's language accurately expresses [its] legislative purpose." *Yu v. U.S. Att'y Gen.,* 568 F.3d 1328, 1332 (11th Cir.2009) (quotation marks and citation omitted). Applying these presumptions, the plain language of § 1821(j) clearly and unambiguously reflects congressional intent to bar courts from granting the precise type of injunctive relief sought here so long as the receiver is not acting in some capacity other than receiver or conservator or attempting to exercise powers and functions beyond those granted by FIRREA. Thus, we decline to carve out an "non-owned assets" exception to § 1821(j) that stands in direct contradiction to the statute's plain meaning. No language in § 1821(j) so limits the breadth of its jurisdictional bar or the "powers and functions" of the FDIC. To the contrary, at least one subsection expressly includes non-owned custodial assets associated with trust business among the FDIC's powers and functions as receiver. *See* § 1821(d)(2)(G) ("including assets and liabilities associated with any trust business").

Furthermore, no circuit court case has ever limited the application of § 1821(j) to assets "owned" by a failed financial institution. The only two district court opinions addressing § 1821(j) that arguably support Bank of America's position have only recognized such a limitation implicitly. *See Cummings Props. Mgmt., Inc. v. FDIC,* 786 F.Supp. 144, 145-46 (D.Mass.1992) (holding that the threshold issue of whether an ATM situated on property leased to a failed bank is a fixture, and thus whether it may be removed by the FDIC as part of liquidation, was appropriate for judicial review), *vacated as moot due to settlement,* No. 92-1504, 1992 WL 366909 (1st Cir. Sept. 1, 1992); *Steamboat Ventures v. FDIC,* No. 1:09-cv-01399, 2009 WL 4797832, at *3 (N.D.Ga. Dec. 8, 2009) (holding that § 1821(j) does not deprive a court of jurisdiction to enjoin the FDIC from initiating foreclosure proceedings where the failed bank's security interest in the property proposed for sale had been extinguished prior to the FDIC's takeover). However, neither of these two cases involved cash or loan documents contained in the failed bank's accounts, whether general or custodial, upon the bank's failure. In addition, neither case examined whether the injunction sought would restrain the FDIC's exercise of a proper receivership power or function. To the extent that these two lower court cases support the broad "non-owned assets" exception advanced by Bank of America, we do not find them persuasive. . . .

. The operation of § 1821(j) does not leave Bank of America without a remedy. Its claim is one that can and should be pursued through the administrative claims process. *See* 12 U.S.C. § 1821(d)(3)-(13). The FDIC has consistently maintained in its pleadings before the district court and submissions to this court that it will adjudicate Bank of America's claim administratively. The FDIC's position is consistent with the case law, which illustrates that claims similar to Bank of America's have been subject to FIRREA's administrative claims process. *See Merrill Lynch Mortgage Capital, Inc. v. FDIC,* 293 F.Supp.2d 98, 101-03 (D.D.C.2003) (reviewing *de novo* the FDIC's administrative claims determination with respect to large pools of residential mortgages held in custodial counts and serviced by a failed bank). . . .

Notes and Comments 8.36. There is another jurisdictional bar in the FDIA, 12 U.S.C. § 1821(d)(13)(D), which is contained in the administrative claims procedures mentioned by the *Bank of America* court. Section 1821(d)(13)(D) states:

> [N]o court shall have jurisdiction over ... (i) any claim or action for payment from, or any action seeking a determination of rights with respect to, the assets of any depository institution for which the Corporation has been appointed receiver ... or

(ii) any claim relating to any act or omission of such institution or the Corporation as receiver.

What is the difference between the two jurisdictional bars? The *Bank of America* court declined to pursue this second line of argument, because § 1821(j) seemed to provide all the authority needed to justify the FDIC's jurisdictional defense.

8.37. The exclusive administrative claims process has received broad support from the circuit courts that have considered challenges to the FDIA provisions. *See, e.g., Resolution Trust Corp. v. Elman,* 949 F.2d 624, 628 (2d Cir.1991) (holding claim by attorney of failed bank for return of bank's files subject to administrative claims process); *Meliezer v. Resolution Trust Co.,* 952 F.2d 879, 883 (5th Cir.1992) (negligence claim by home mortgage owners against failed bank that issued loan); *Bueford v. Resolution Trust Corp.,* 991 F.2d 481, 484 (8th Cir.1993) (employment discrimination claims by former employees of failed bank); *Henderson v. Bank of New England,* 986 F.2d 319, 321 (9th Cir.1993) (claims by denied credit card applicant); *McCarthy v. FDIC,* 348 F.3d 1075, 1081 (9th Cir.2003) (claims by debtors of failed bank arising out of acts of receiver, rather than bank in receivership); *Freeman v. FDIC,* 56 F.3d 1394, 1402 (D.C.Cir.1995) (claims by debtors of failed bank alleging fraudulent restructuring of home mortgage loan). There are in fact few types of claims that the courts have *not* committed to the administrative claims process. *See, e.g., Homeland Stores, Inc. v. Resolution Trust Corp.,* 17 F.3d 1269, 1273-75 (10th Cir.1994) (holding claims against receiver, not failed bank, in connection with receiver's management of shopping center asset of failed institution, not subject to administrative claims process); *Rosa v. Resolution Trust Corp.,* 938 F.2d 383, 394-95 (3d Cir.1991), *cert. denied,* 502 U.S. 981, 112 S.Ct. 582 (1991)(claim by pension plan participants seeking order barring retroactive termination of plan).

8.38. What if it was Quarter State Bank (QSB) that was experiencing difficulty? *See* 12 U.S.C. § 1821(c)(3) (FDIC and state-chartered institutions). Under what circumstances could the FDIC intervene and appoint itself as receiver or conservator of a state bank? *See id.* § 1821(c)(4)-(5).

8.39. As an alternative, could the FDIC simply terminate Quarter's deposit insurance? *See* 12 U.S.C. § 1818(a)(2).

8.40. *Liability of FDIC for its discretionary actions.* There is much talk of the FDIC's broad discretion in the receivership context. *See, e.g., supra* at 593 n.30. To what extent, however, might the FDIC be liable for actions undertaken in its discretion? Is it responsible to shareholders and other creditors of a failing bank if its supervision of the receivership itself results in further financial harm to them? Consider the following two cases in answering this question.

Hindes v. Federal Deposit Insurance Corporation

137 F.3d 148 (3d Cir. 1998)

GREENBERG, Circuit Judge.

[The Pennsylvania Secretary of Banking seized Meritor Savings Bank, the largest savings bank in Pennsylvania, and appointed the FDIC receiver. Shareholders of the bank brought action against the Secretary, the FDIC in its corporate and receivership capacities, and unidentified FDIC agents and employees, alleging that defendants had deprived them of their substantive due process rights and engaged in a conspiracy to close the bank. The District Court dismissed the claims, on motions to dismiss or for summary judgment. The shareholders appealed.]

I. Introduction

[A]ppellants allege that the FDIC reneged on an agreement with Meritor with respect to the computation of its capital base, ignored Meritor's actual financial condition when seizing Meritor, and engaged in a conspiracy with state officials to close the bank. Appellants also assert that the FDIC violated certain of its statutory duties as receiver. ...

II. Facts and Procedural History

. . . In 1982, at the FDIC's request, Meritor assumed the deposit liabilities of Western Savings Fund Society of Philadelphia ("Western"). To induce Meritor to assume these liabilities, the FDIC granted Meritor the right to amortize, over a 15-year period, $796 million of "goodwill" resulting from the Western transaction ("grandfathered goodwill"), thereby increasing Meritor's regulatory capital base. This transaction saved the FDIC and its Bank Insurance Fund $400 million. The FDIC and Meritor evidenced this regulatory goodwill inducement in a written agreement dated April 3, 1982. For over ten years, the FDIC and Meritor abided by that agreement.

In an agreement dated April 5, 1991, the FDIC reaffirmed the 1982 agreement and further agreed to renegotiate Meritor's capital requirements if at any time Congress prohibited Meritor from considering this goodwill as a capital component. . . .

On December 19, 1991, Congress adopted the FDIC Improvements Act of 1991, requiring the FDIC to adopt new rules regulating bank capital. The FDIC published draft regulations in the summer of 1992 which clearly permitted Meritor's grandfathered goodwill to continue to be included in its capital. When the FDIC adopted final regulations in September 1992, however, the regulations differed from the proposals so as to create doubt as to whether Meritor's grandfathered goodwill would remain as capital. The FDIC refused Meritor's request to clarify the uncertainty. The confusion created by the regulations resulted in a withdrawal of over $300 million in deposits from Meritor.

The appellants allege that, by mid-September, the FDIC and the Secretary had begun to devise a plan to seize Meritor in mid-December 1992, which was approximately the time the new regulations would take effect, and to sell its assets to one of Meritor's most aggressive competitors.

On December 11, 1992, the FDIC hand-delivered a letter to Meritor reneging on its 1982 agreement and formally notifying Meritor that, under the new regulations, the grandfathered goodwill no longer would be included in its capital base. On the same day, the FDIC also hand-delivered Meritor a "Notification to Primary Regulator" ("Notification") which stated that the FDIC Board of Directors had found that Meritor was in violation of its 1991 agreement regarding capital maintenance, was in an unsound condition, and had inadequate capital. In the Notification, the FDIC asserted that it immediately would institute proceedings to cancel Meritor's insurance if Meritor did not promptly satisfy certain capitalization requirements. Because insurance was a prerequisite to Meritor's continued operation, the demand created a crisis. The Secretary, who the FDIC notified of these matters prior to notifying Meritor, used the crisis to justify the immediate closing of the bank on the same afternoon. At that time, he appointed the FDIC as receiver of Meritor. Neither Meritor nor the appellants challenged the appointment under the state procedure available for that purpose. . . .

The appellants also allege that the FDIC and the Secretary disregarded circumstances which rendered the closing of Meritor inappropriate. In particular, eight days before the closing of the bank, Meritor sold a subsidiary bringing in capital which put it in compliance with the capital maintenance agreement. In addition, on December 9, 1992, two days prior to the closing of the bank, the FDIC received a bid of $181.3 million for Meritor's remaining operations and deposits. . . .

III. Discussion

. . .

B. Due Process and APA Claims

On March 1, 1995, the district court held that 12 U.S.C. § 1821(j) deprived it of jurisdiction over appellants' due process and APA [Administrative Procedure Act] claims, Counts I and IV respectively, and therefore dismissed those counts against all appellees. . . .

Count I seeks the following remedies based upon an alleged due process violation: (1) a declaration that the FDIC, Doe defendants and the Secretary violated appellants' substantive due process rights; (2) a declaration that the FDIC's notification is void and a rescission thereof; (3) a declaration of the invalidity of the Secretary's orders closing Meritor and appointing FDIC as receiver and rescissions thereof; and (4) the imposition of a constructive trust for Meritor's benefit nunc pro tunc. This count, however, does not identify the source of the substantive cause of action for the alleged constitutional violation as against each appellee. . . .

1. Section 1983 Claim

. . .

Section 1983 creates a cause of action against "[e]very person who, under color of any [state law] ... subjects, or causes to be subjected, any citizen of the United States or other person within the jurisdiction thereof to the deprivation of any rights, privileges, or immunities secured by the Constitution." 42 U.S.C. § 1983. Because section 1983 provides a remedy for violations of federal law by persons acting pursuant to state law, federal agencies and officers are facially exempt from section 1983 liability inasmuch as in the normal course of events they act pursuant to federal law. . . .

It is a well-established principle, however, that federal officials are subject to section 1983 liability when sued in their official capacity where they have acted under color of state law, for example in conspiracy with state officials. . . .

The allegations in the section 1983 claim, however, are against a federal agency, the FDIC, not federal officials. We find no authority to support the conclusion that a federal agency is a "person" subject to section 1983 liability, whether or not in an alleged conspiracy with state actors. We, therefore, hold that federal agencies are not "persons" subject to section 1983 liability.

. . . [O]ur dismissal of the section 1983 claim makes it unnecessary to discuss whether 12 U.S.C. § 1821(j) would preclude the district court from granting the declaratory and injunctive relief requested in Count I to the extent it would operate against the FDIC....

3. APA Claim

a. 12 U.S.C. § 1821(j)

We turn next to Count IV of appellants' complaint, which seeks APA review of the FDIC's issuance of the Notification finding that Meritor was operating in an unsafe and unsound condition. Count IV alleges that the FDIC's determinations, as embodied in the Notification, were arbitrary, capricious, an abuse of discretion and in violation of appellants' constitutional rights. Appellants thus seek the following remedies: (1) a declaration that the findings are null and void; (2) a rescission of the declarations; and (3) the imposition of a constructive trust. The district court dismissed this claim as precluded by 12 U.S.C. § 1821 (j). We agree.

The Financial Institutions, Reform, Recovery, and Enforcement Act of 1989 ("FIRREA") establishes a comprehensive scheme for conservatorships and receiverships of insured financial institutions. . . . The FDIC may be appointed as a conservator or receiver of an insured financial institution if, inter alia, the institution becomes insolvent. *See* 12 U.S.C. § 1821(c). . . . FIRREA also includes an anti-injunction provision intended to permit the FDIC to perform its duties as conservator or receiver promptly and effectively without judicial interference. . . .

In making the determinations and issuing the Notification, the FDIC clearly was acting in its corporate capacity. Appellants argue that the district court erred in dismissing the APA claim based upon section 1821(j) because the section does not preclude judicial intervention where the FDIC acts in its corporate capacity. Thus, appellants would have us interpret section 1821(j) to preclude only those orders directly against the FDIC as receiver or as conservator.

We find, however, that the plain language of the statute is not so limited. Rather, the statute, by its terms, can preclude relief even against a third party, including the FDIC in its corporate capacity, where the result is such that the relief "restrain[s] *or affect[s]* the exercise of powers or functions of the [FDIC] as a conservator or a receiver." 12 U.S.C. § 1821(j) (emphasis added). After all, an action can "affect" the exercise of powers by an agency without being aimed directly at it. . . .

The Court of Appeals for the First Circuit has indicated quite clearly that a court order which operates against a third party is precluded by section 1821(j) if the order would have the same effect from the FDIC's perspective as a direct action against it precluded by section 1821(j). *See Telematics International, Inc. v. NEMLC Leasing Corp.*, 967 F.2d 703, 707 (1st Cir.1992). The *Telematics* court held that the district court could not enjoin the FDIC from foreclosing on a security interest. *See id.* at 705. . . .

The relief appellants seek in this case clearly would "affect the exercise of powers or functions of the [FDIC] as conservator or receiver." Appellants' Count IV seeks a declaration that the Notification was void *ab initio* and a rescission thereof. Because the FDIC's findings directly and proximately caused the Secretary to close Meritor, the appellants also seek the imposition of a constructive trust as of the date Meritor was seized. Here, the requested relief against the FDIC-Corporate clearly would affect the FDIC's continued functioning as receiver and it effectively would throw into question every act of FDIC-Receiver.

. . . We do not suggest that we would reach the same result in a case in which the effect on the FDIC of an order against a third party would be of little consequence to its overall functioning as receiver. That type of situation is not before us.

We reject appellants' contention that section 1821(j) cannot be interpreted to bar their constitutional claims because Congress did not express a clear intent for the section to preclude review of constitutional claims. . . . Our interpretation of section 1821(j) only denies appellants the declaratory and injunctive relief they now seek, but does not deny them judicial review for their constitutional claims. Courts uniformly have held that the preclusion of section 1821(j) does not affect a damages claim. . . .

b. Availability of APA Review

Even if we agreed that section 1821(j) did not preclude the relief appellants seek, we would affirm the district court's dismissal of their claim for review under the APA because such review is not available in this instance. The APA grants a right of judicial review of an agency action to "[a] person suffering legal wrong because of any agency action, or adversely affected or aggrieved by agency action within the meaning of a relevant statute." 5 U.S.C. § 702. This right of review, however, is limited. First, the APA only provides for review of those actions "made reviewable by statute and final agency action for which there is no other adequate remedy in a court." 5 U.S.C. § 704. Second, the APA withdraws the right of review "to the extent that statutes preclude judicial review." 5 U.S.C. § 701(a)(1).

We find that the district court did not have jurisdiction to review the FDIC-Corporate's issuance of the Notification because (1) it was not a final agency action, and (2) review expressly is barred by 12 U.S.C. § 1818(i)(1) and jurisdiction therefore is withdrawn pursuant to 5 U.S.C. § 701(a)(1). . . .

APA review is unavailable in this case also because 12 U.S.C. § 1818(i) precludes judicial review of the Notification, and the APA does not allow judicial review where another statute specifically prohibits it, *see* 5 U.S.C. § 701(a)(1). Section 1818(i) precludes review of orders and notices except as specifically provided elsewhere in section 1818. ...

The Supreme Court has found that th[e] language [of 1818(i)(1)] is clear. *See Board of Governors of the Federal Reserve System v. MCorp Financial, Inc.*, 502 U.S. 32, 39 (1991). In *MCorp*, the Court held that section 1818(i)(1) "provides us with clear and convincing evidence that Congress intended to deny the District Court jurisdiction to review and enjoin the Board's ongoing administrative proceedings." *MCorp*, 502 U.S. at 44; *see also Groos Nat'l Bank v. Comptroller of the Currency*, 573 F.2d 889, 895 (5th Cir.1978) (noting that the section "in particular evinces a clear intention that this regulatory process is not to be disturbed by untimely judicial intervention, at least where there is no 'clear departure from statutory authority'").

The question we now face is whether section 1818(i) applies only where there is such an ongoing administrative proceeding. As discussed above, here there is no such proceeding because the Secretary's decision to close Meritor based upon the Notification eviscerated the need for further proceedings to terminate Meritor's insured status. Moreover, to our knowledge, the only case law involving section 1818(i) is in the context of an ongoing administrative proceeding.

Yet the plain language of section 1818(i) broadly precludes the review of the issuance of any notice under any subsection. *See* 12 U.S.C. § 1818(i)(1); *Henry v. Office of Thrift Supervision*, 43 F.3d 507, 512 (10th Cir.1994) (rejecting contention that the "orders" referred to in section 1818(i) are limited to those issued after administrative hearings). Further, while section 1818 provides for review of certain notices and orders, such as those issued after a hearing, *see* 12 U.S.C. § 1818(a)(5) (providing for review of an order terminating an institution's insured status); 12 U.S.C. § 1818(h) (providing for review of orders and notices issued after required hearings), it does not provide for review of the issuance of this Notification, which was issued pursuant to section 1818(a)(1). Thus, by its terms section 1818(i) applies to this case and is not restricted to precluding judicial review which would interfere with an ongoing administrative proceeding. Based upon this plain meaning, we conclude that the district court did not have jurisdiction to review the issuance of the Notification.

Courts, however, have recognized a limited exception to a statute's specific withdrawal of jurisdiction where the plaintiff claims that the agency acted in a blatantly lawless manner or contrary to a clear statutory prohibition. *See, e.g., Abercrombie v. Office of the Comptroller of Currency*, 833 F.2d 672, 674-75 (7th Cir.1987); *First Nat'l Bank of Grayson v. Conover*, 715 F.2d 234, 236 (6th Cir.1983); *Groos Nat'l Bank*, 573 F.2d at 895. The roots of this so-called "statutory-authority" exception are in *Leedom v. Kyne*, 358 U.S. 184 (1958).

The Supreme Court has considered the application of this exception to section 1818(i). *See Board of Governors of the Federal Reserve System v. MCorp Financial, Inc.*, 502 U.S. 32. In *MCorp*, the Court declined to apply the exception, distinguishing it in two respects from the situation in *Kyne*. First, the Court found that there were adequate means of review available upon a final determination by the agency. Second, the Court held that *Kyne* did not apply because there the preclusion was implied from congressional silence, whereas the preclusion of section 1818(i) was express and clear. *See id.* at 43-44. . . .

C. Enforcement of FDIC's Statutory Obligations

The district court also dismissed Counts V and VI, in which appellants sought to enforce certain statutory duties of the FDIC. We affirm the dismissal of these counts because there is no implied private right of action to enforce the FDIC's duty to maximize gain and minimize loss in its disposition of assets and the shareholders have no enforceable right to an accurate accounting.

1. FDIC's Duty to Maximize Gain and Minimize Loss in its Disposition of Assets

In its September 6, 1995 order, the district court dismissed appellants' claim for money damages for the FDIC-Receiver's alleged failure to comply with its statutory duty to maximize the gain and minimize the loss in the disposition of Meritor's assets. *See* 12 U.S.C. § 1821(d)(13)(E). The district court held that this provision neither expressly nor impliedly grants a private right of action to individual shareholders.

The standard announced in *Cort v. Ash*, 422 U.S. 66 (1975), guides our inquiry into whether section 1821(d)(13)(E) impliedly grants shareholders of a failed financial institution a private right of action to enforce the FDIC-Receiver's statutory obligations. In *Cort*, the Court announced that courts should consider the following four factors to determine whether a statute impliedly grants a private right of action: (1) whether the plaintiff is a member of the class for whose special benefit the statute was created; (2) whether there is either an explicit or implicit legislative intent to create or deny a private remedy; (3) whether an implied remedy is consistent with underlying policies of the statute; and (4) whether the cause of action is one that traditionally is relegated to state law and the area is a state concern so that it would be inappropriate to imply a federal cause of action. *See id.* at 78. . . .

Appellants contend that the district court erred by failing to give proper consideration of two circumstances which distinguish this case from others involving receiverships: (1) the existence of a surplus in the Meritor receivership; and (2) the appellants, as shareholders, have an express statutory right to distribution of this surplus. According to appellants, in the context of a receivership operating with a surplus, the *Cort* factors are met and thus we should imply the existence of a private right of action in their favor.

We disagree. Our analysis of the *Cort* factors, with an emphasis on the first two, . . . leads us to the conclusion that there is no evidence of a congressional intent to provide for a private remedy. Because such intent is our ultimate guidepost, we find that the shareholders of a failed financial institution do not have a private right of enforcement of the FDIC's duty to maximize gain and minimize loss in its disposition of the institution's assets.

First, appellants, as shareholders, are not members of a class for whose special benefit Congress created section 1821(d)(13)(E). The duty to maximize gain in the disposition of assets has implications broader than to benefit shareholders. The FDIC's duty to maximize gain and minimize loss primarily is intended to benefit the insurance fund by minimizing the claims against it, thereby reducing the cost to the taxpayers. Thus, the benefits gained by the shareholders and other claimants are incidental to the primary intended beneficiaries, the insurance fund and the taxpayers. . . .

In addition, the duty to maximize gain and minimize loss does not operate for the special benefit of shareholders where the receivership is operating with a surplus. Section 1821(d)(11)(B) establishes a shareholder right to distribution of funds in a case where there is a surplus after the payment of all claimants and administrative expenses. Given this right to distribution, appellants argue that the FDIC fulfills its statutory duty to maximize gain in order to preserve the surplus, thus for the sole benefit of the shareholders. We disagree.

We recognize that the express right to distribution of surplus granted under section 1821(d)(11)(B) creates a direct interest in shareholders. . . . This right, however, does not transform the FDIC's duty to maximize gain and minimize loss into one inuring solely to the benefit of the shareholders. The FDIC performs its section 1821(d)(13)(E) duty to maximize gain intending to reduce the claims against the insurance fund, not to ensure that shareholders receive distribution.

. . . Turning to the second *Cort* factor, the parties agree that there is no statement in the legislative history which suggests that Congress intended either to create or deny a private right of action to enforce the FDIC's duty to maximize gain and minimize loss. While congressional silence does not preclude a court from implying a private right of action where the other factors are satisfied, . . . here we find that the other factors do not support finding a private right of action.

While we acknowledge that an action against a federal entity to enforce rights expressly granted under federal law traditionally is not relegated to state law, our inquiry ends upon our conclusion that the first two *Cort* factors are not met. . . .

2. FDIC's Duty to Provide Annual Accounting

The district court dismissed appellants' claim for a full and fair accounting from the FDIC-Receiver, to which appellants alleged they were entitled under 12 U.S.C. § 1821 (d)(15)(A)-(C). The court found that the FDIC-Receiver had complied with the literal requirements of the provision by providing a copy of the annual accounting report to appellants upon their request, and refused to engraft an enforceable duty to provide a correct accounting to shareholders.

We again part with the district court's approach, but not its result. While the district court focused on whether an accuracy requirement is implicit in the statute, we find the more appropriate inquiry to be whether the statute grants shareholders an implied private right of enforcement. We hold that it does not. . . .

Although appellants urge us to imply a requirement of accuracy, they cite no authority which directly supports this view. Rather, they cite analogous authority, which we find unpersuasive in this context. *See First Nat'l Bank of Gordon v. Department of Treasury*, 911 F.2d 57, 62-63 (8th Cir.1990).[20] Despite this lack of authority, we recognize that, in a practical sense, at some point the right to an accounting may be rendered meaningless if the accounting is not accurate. Nevertheless, even if we were to imply an accuracy requirement, we must affirm the district court's dismissal of this claim because our analysis of the *Cort* factors establishes that the shareholders do not have a private right of action to enforce the FDIC duty.

The shareholders are not members of a special class for whose benefit the statute was created. Rather, the plain language of the statute puts shareholders on par with members of the general public. The statute gives shareholders and members of the public identical rights–the FDIC must make the annual report available to either upon request–and the statute establishes these rights in the same subsection. We see no reason, therefore, to distinguish between shareholders and members of the general public for purposes of this statute.

Further, the legislative history is silent as to whether Congress intended to create a private remedy. Because the first two *Cort* factors are not satisfied, our inquiry ends here....

ROTH, Circuit Judge, concurring and dissenting:

I concur for the most part with the majority's thorough and thoughtful opinion. I cannot, however, agree with their conclusion in Part III.C.2. that the appellants do not have a right to demand an annual accounting beyond what the FDIC might choose to provide to them. . . .

---

20. In *First National*, the court addressed the interpretation of a statute which requires financial associations to make reports of condition in accordance with 12 U.S.C. § 1811 *et seq*. *See* 12 U.S.C. § 161(a). The court found that a bank violated section 161(a) where the report of its condition was not accurate. Section 161(a) includes a requirement that the report be accurate to the best knowledge and belief of the officers who sign it, but does not expressly make the bank responsible for an inaccurate report. In contrast, section 1821(d) does not include language concerning accuracy. Thus, *First National* is distinguishable.

I conclude from the . . . statutory language that the shareholders, as well as the general public, have the right to an annual report which has been prepared in a manner which is consistent with the accounting and reporting practices established by the FDIC. It has not been documented on the record here that the annual reports supplied to appellants by the FDIC do conform to such practices. I would therefore remand this issue to the district court for a determination whether the reports in question meet the required statutory standard. . . .

First Pacific Bancorp, Inc. v. Helfer

224 F.3d 1117 (9th Cir. 2000)

MOLLOY,* District Judge.

[Following termination of the FDIC's receivership of First Pacific Bank, the Bank, its holding company First Pacific Bancorp, Inc. ("Bancorp"), and shareholders of Bancorp brought suit seeking an accounting of the bank's financial condition beginning with FDIC's appointment as receiver (*Bancorp I*). The District Court granted summary judgment for FDIC. Plaintiffs appealed, and the appeal was consolidated with appeal of a judgment in a removed action, dismissing the bank's suit against the FDIC for alleged breach of fiduciary duty, unjust enrichment and intentional misrepresentation (*Bancorp II*).]

On August 7, 1990, the California Department of Banking appointed the . . . FDIC as Receiver for the Bank. Sometime around May 7, 1996, nearly six years after the Bank went into receivership, the FDIC notified Plaintiffs that it was terminating its receivership of the Bank. Along with the notice, the FDIC gave Plaintiffs two pages of unaudited financial information covering the period from August 10, 1990, through December 31, 1995. One report was entitled "Statement of Financial Condition," and reported the assets, liabilities, and equity of the bank as of August 10, 1990 and as of December 31, 1995. The other statement, "Financial Condition and Liquidation Activity," reported aggregated amounts of receipts and disbursements of the Bank between August 10, 1990, and December 31, 1995.[1] The information contained in these two skeletal reports spanned a period of over five years. No detailed information was given for interim dates or time periods.

Struck by the lack of meaningful information within the reports, the Plaintiffs requested additional financial information from the FDIC. . . . Plaintiffs sought additional information not only to better comprehend the financial position of the Bank, but also to assist in defending a directors' and officers' liability suit brought against them by the FDIC. [T]he FDIC provided the Plaintiffs with four additional pages of information: an unaudited, one-page "Statement of Income and Expenses," detailing total liquidation income and expense, loss on assets, and net loss from liquidation; an unaudited, one-page "Statement of Cash Receipts and Disbursements," detailing liquidation receipts and disbursements; and an unaudited, two-page document entitled "Supplemental Information." All documents involved the period from August 10, 1990 through December 31, 1995.

---

*. The Honorable Donald W. Molloy, United States District Judge for the District of Montana, sitting by designation.

1. The statement broke down the total amount of money received by the FDIC during the five-plus year period into only two categories: "Principal Collections and Interest Income on Assets, Net of Participation," reported at nearly $83 million, and "Receipts from FDIC and Others," reported at over $20 million. The disbursements received similar treatment, reported in only two aggregate amounts: "Liquidation and Other Disbursements" at nearly $84 million, and "Payments to FDIC" totalling over $18 million.

. . . The issue we confront [in *Bancorp I*] is whether 12 U.S.C. § 1821(d)(15) gives Bancorp, as shareholder of a bank in receivership,[2] a private right of action against the FDIC to compel it to provide a financial accounting in conformity with the FDIC's own accounting and reporting practices and procedures.

. . . [*Bancorp II*] rais[es] the issue of whether Bancorp's claims for relief under state law are barred by the doctrine of res judicata because they mirror the federal law claims in *Bancorp I*. . . .

Analysis

I. *Bancorp I*

. . .

The statute in question here is 12 U.S.C. § 1821(d) and is a part of the statutory scheme governing the FDIC. . . . The specific language in § 1821(d)(15)(B) was inserted as part of the Financial Institutions Reform, Recovery, and Enforcement Act of 1989 ("FIRREA").

Generally, the Act vests the FDIC, in its capacity as receiver, with a broad range of powers and duties designed to ensure maintenance of the going concern value of failed banks and to avoid significant disruption in banking services. . . . For example, the FDIC has the power to make rules governing the conduct of conservatorships or receiverships, to take title to the assets and assume the rights of the shareholders, depositors, officers, and directors of the institution, to operate the institution in receivership, to liquidate the institution, to organize a new one, to effect mergers, and to determine claims. *See* 12 U.S.C. § 1821(d)(1), (2)(A), (B), (E), (G), and (3). The FDIC also has the duty, in its capacity as receiver, to pay all valid claims made against the bank "in accordance with the prescriptions and limitations of this Act." *Id.* § 1821(d)(2)(H).

Measured against these broad powers are certain accounting and reporting requirements that strike a balance between power and duty. For example, the priority for payment of claims against the institution is set forth at § 1821(d)(11)(A). In connection with that prioritization, subsection (d)(11)(C) requires that "the report described in subsection (d)(15)(B)" accompany distributions to shareholders or members of the bank. Independently of any payment of claims, § 1821(d)(15) imposes accounting and recordkeeping requirements. . . .

. . . Shareholders of an institution in receivership, therefore, have a right to receive the reports prepared in accordance with subparagraph (15)(B) both under subparagraph (15)(C) and under subparagraph (11)(C), along with any payment of claims.

In this case, Plaintiffs complain that the FDIC did not compile reports on the statutorily required annual basis and did not comply with its own accounting and reporting requirements. None of the entities named in subsection (d)(15)(B) has attempted to compel the FDIC to prepare and file conforming reports. This lack of oversight raises a perplexing problem for Plaintiffs and others similarly situated. They are entitled to receive annual reports that conform to the FDIC's own accounting and reporting requirements, yet they have no means to compel the FDIC to produce or provide the reports. The question, then, is whether Congress intended to give shareholders a private right of action to compel the FDIC to produce the annual reports required by subsection (d)(15)(B), pursuant to their statutory right to receive such reports under subsections (d)(11)(C) and (d)(15)(C).

A violation of a federal statute which results in harm to an individual "does not

2. Although all the Plaintiffs are parties to the appeal, we find that only Bancorp can be treated as a "shareholder" within the meaning of the statute. Only Bancorp is a "shareholder of the depository institution for which the Corporation was appointed . . . receiver," 12 U.S.C. § 1821(d)(15)(C). The individual plaintiffs are shareholders of Bancorp, not First Pacific Bank.

automatically give rise to a private cause of action in favor of that person." *Cannon v. University of Chicago*, 441 U.S. 677, 688 (1979). To determine whether a given statute creates a private right of action, the Supreme Court prescribed a four-factor test in *Cort v. Ash*, 422 U.S. 66 (1975). . . .

Though the Supreme Court never indicated that the four *Cort* factors carried different weight, subsequent decisions have emphasized that the key inquiry is whether Congress intended to provide the plaintiff with a private right of action. . . . Indeed, there has even been some suggestion that Cort has been overruled. *Compare Touche Ross & Co. v. Redington*, 442 U.S. 560, 575-76 (1979) (stating that *Cort*'s first three factors–the language and focus of the statute, its legislative history, and its purpose–are traditional considerations in determining congressional intent), *with Thompson v. Thompson*, 484 U.S. 174, 189 (1988) (Scalia, J., concurring) (suggesting that *Touche Ross* focuses attention on the second *Cort* factor, denominated "legislative intent," and subsumes the others). Nevertheless, we still find the four-factor test helpful in determining whether a statute provides a private right of action. . . .

A. Is Bancorp a member of the class for whose especial benefit the statute was enacted?

The district court held that, under the first factor, Plaintiffs are not part of the class sought to be protected by the statute. The district court found that the statute was enacted to benefit depositors, the insurance fund, and the public at large, but not the shareholders of the failed institution.

In this instance, the district court painted with too broad a brush. While the over-arching goal of the Act is to protect faith and confidence in the banking system and to ensure adequate protection of depositors through the insurance fund, shareholders are the specifically named beneficiaries in the subsection at issue here. Section 1821(d)(15)(B) requires the FDIC to provide an annual accounting or report, "as appropriate," to certain governmental authorities. Pursuant to subparagraph (C), that same report must be made available on request to "any shareholder of the depository institution for which [the FDIC] was appointed . . . receiver." Thus, this subsection places the shareholders on the same footing with the governmental authorities and with the general public named in subparagraph (15)(B). The distinction is that the FDIC has a burden of production under subparagraph (15)(B) and the shareholder or citizen has a burden of request under subparagraph (15)(C). Furthermore, § 1821(d)(11)(C) requires the same report to accompany distributions to shareholders made pursuant to § 1821(d)(11)(A)(v). We conclude that the Plaintiffs are members of the class for whose benefit the statute was enacted. . . .

In this case, 12 U.S.C. § 1821(d)(15) does more than simply provide a "generic imperative" mandating that the FDIC prepare certain reports. Instead, "shareholders of the depository institution for which the Corporation was appointed ... receiver" are specifically named as persons for whose benefit the FDIC must prepare annual accountings and reports. The annual reports statutorily required to be prepared by the FDIC "shall be made available" to the shareholders. Because shareholders of the institution in receivership are given, as a special class, a statutory right of access to the required information, we conclude that "the customary legal incidents," *see Transamerica Mortgage Advisors, Inc. v. Lewis*, 444 U.S. 11, 19 (1979), of a specific class's right to a report would follow. We believe the first factor of the Cort test is met.

We note that the district court, agreeing with the FDIC, reasoned that subsection (15)(C) places the shareholders on the same footing as the public in general. According to the district court, this eliminates the possibility that the statute was enacted for the benefit of the shareholders. This view is not correct. Both shareholders and the general public are given a right of access to the information that the FDIC is required to compile.

B. Is there any indication of Congressional intent to create or deny a remedy?

The district court found no evidence that Congress intended to create a private cause of action under this statute, and consequently found the second *Cort* factor was not met. We disagree with that finding. While we have not located any explicit statement of Congress's intent to create a remedy in the event the FDIC fails to comply with its statutorily mandated accounting and reporting practices and procedures, neither have we located any statement that Congress intended to deny such a remedy.[3] The absence of a statement of intent to create a remedy does not necessarily mean that no remedy is available. Indeed, if that were the case, the Supreme Court would not have developed a test for an implied private right of action. . . .

Within the Act at issue here, there is no explicit indication that Congress intended either to permit or to bar an individual shareholder from enforcing the statutory requirement for an accounting. The legislative history on this point reveals nothing. . . . Congress' silence does not, however, answer the question, because we have found in the statutory language concerning shareholders' entitlement to reports evidence in favor of a private remedy. *See* Section I.A, *supra*. . . .

Moreover, because the remedy at hand is an equitable one, we are more inclined to perceive in Congress' silence a presumption that an individual may pursue a claim. In fact, the Supreme Court has observed:

> [u]nless a statute in so many words, or by a necessary and inescapable inference, restricts the court's jurisdiction in equity, the full scope of that jurisdiction is to be recognized and applied. The great principles of equity, securing complete justice, should not be yielded to light inferences, or doubtful construction.

Weinberger v. Romero-Barcelo, 456 U.S. 305, 313 (1981) (internal citations and quotations omitted). The remedy sought here is an equitable one, an accounting. We will not assume that Congress intended to strip away our power to do equity in the absence of either specific statutory language or a "necessary and inescapable inference" from the language of the statute. Such a limit is not present in the language of the statute or in the legislative history in this case. . . .

C. Is a private right of action consistent with the purposes of the Act?

The third inquiry is whether implying the equitable remedy of an accounting is consistent with the underlying purposes of the legislative scheme. The FDIC argues that the

---

3. The only legislative history we have discovered states the purpose of subsection (d)(15) as follows:

> The amendment makes it clear that the FDIC may use its ordinary accounting procedures and schedules when making reports regarding liquidations to the shareholders of the failed institution, to the Secretary of the Treasury and to the Comptroller General. The amendment also specifies that such reports will be prepared on an annual basis and will be made available to the specified parties on request.

Technical Amendments to S. 413, Federal Deposit Insurance Corporation Act, 101st Cong. (1989), reprinted in Arnold & Porter Legislative History for Specific Acts, Financial Institutions Reform, Recovery and Enforcement Act, Pub.L. No. 101-73 Mat'l. 53, at ¶ 15 (1989), available in Westlaw, FIRREA-LH.

Despite use of the word "may," the language of the statute, both as it is expressed in the proposed technical amendment and as ultimately codified, contains the word "shall." Given that, we construe "may" in the legislative history to mean that the FDIC need not develop special procedures or schedules for its annual reports, and not to mean that the FDIC need not use its ordinary procedures and schedules and need not prepare annual reports.

purpose of the Act is to enhance its power to preserve the solvency of its insurance fund. To that end, the Act requires every institution insured by the FDIC to submit an audited annual report to the FDIC. *See* 12 U.S.C. § 1831m. Thus, before the Bank went into receivership in 1990, it was required to submit annual reports, audited by independent public accountants, to the FDIC. This requirement advances the purpose of preserving solvency of the insurance fund by allowing for early detection of institutions in financial trouble.

A somewhat different purpose is advanced by requiring the FDIC to continue the annual reporting of the financial activities of a failed institution for which it has been appointed receiver. Not only is the FDIC required to maintain a "full accounting of each receivership," it is also required to make an annual accounting or report of those matters to three specified entities, *id.* § 1821(d)(15)(A), (B), and to make that accounting or report available on request, *id.* § 1821(d)(15)(C). This requirement is consistent with at least one of the stated purposes of FIRREA, *viz*., "to improve the supervision of savings associations by strengthening capital, accounting, and other supervisory standards." H.R. Conf. Rep. No. 101-222, at 393 (1989), *reprinted in* 1989 U.S.C.C.A.N. 432, 432. Strengthened accounting standards elevate sunlight over secrecy.

While the Supreme Court has found that implying a private right of action in a statute that is part of an "elaborate administrative scheme" can undercut legislative goals, *see, e.g., Universities Research Ass'n, Inc. v. Coutu*, 450 U.S. 754, 783 (1981) (holding that a private right of action under the Davis-Bacon Act would disrupt the balance between the interests of contractors and the interests of their employees), the lack of any enforcement mechanism can also undercut legislative goals. Courts properly defer to remedies put in place by Congress or by administrative agencies. *See, e.g., Massachusetts Mut. Life Ins. Co. v. Russell*, 473 U.S. 134, 146 (1985) (the presence of six statutory enforcement provisions provided evidence that Congress did not intend any other means of enforcement). However, where no enforcement mechanism is explicitly provided by Congress or an administrative agency, it is appropriate to infer that Congress did not intend to enact unenforceable requirements. Thus, it is fair to imply a private right of action from the statute at issue.

In this case, there is no alternative remedy or means to enforce § 1821(d)(15) apart from an implied right of action. There is no separate enforcement provision within the statutory scheme, nor is there any indication of what entities might compel an accounting. Although the FDIC must submit annual reports to the Secretary of the Treasury, the Comptroller General of the United States, and the appointing authority, the language of the statute gives none of these entities any greater right to compel production of the reports than we recognize today as implied in the shareholders. . . .

D. Is this cause of action traditionally relegated to state law?

While the utility of the fourth *Cort* factor is in doubt, we note that the claim here is not traditionally relegated to state law. . . . [I]n the instant case, the FDIC's duty to make an accounting arises under federal law. Thus, the fourth and final factor of the *Cort* test, whatever its weight, must be answered in favor of the Plaintiffs.

We recognize that our decision conflicts with that of a divided panel of the Third Circuit in *Hindes v. FDIC*, 137 F.3d 148 (3d Cir.1998). . . .

As we have already pointed out, silence does not necessarily mean that no remedy is intended. For that reason, the other *Cort* factors remain instructive.

Moreover, the *Hindes* majority's analysis of the first *Cort* factor does not consider two other plausible readings of the statute's reference to both shareholders and the general public. One possibility is that the right to an accounting is not limited to shareholders but may be maintained by any member of the general public. *See Hindes*, 137 F.3d at 172 (Roth, J., dissenting). The other is that the statute's mention of both shareholders and members of the general public distinguishes shareholders from the general public to the extent that shareholders have a private right of action for an accounting in conformity with the FDIC's own requirements, while members of the general public do not.

It can hardly be denied that reference to both shareholders and the general public tends to make the term "shareholders" superfluous. Nonetheless, the term is in the statute, and we must avoid construing a statute's terms in such a way that they become surplusage. In our view, the inclusion of the term "shareholders" indicates that shareholders are members of a special class for whose benefit the reports required by subparagraph (A) are intended.[6] Thus, contrary to the *Hindes* majority, we find that the first two Cort factors are satisfied and that Congress intended to give shareholders a private right of action to compel an accounting.

[W]e neither imply nor suggest that 12 U.S.C. § 1821(d)(15) creates a private right of action for monetary damages. Our holding is limited to a finding that when inadequate or meaningless information is provided to a shareholder of a bank in receivership with the FDIC, the shareholders may sue for an accounting "consistent with the accounting practices and procedures established by the [FDIC]."

We remand *Bancorp I* to the district court for a determination whether the six pages provided to Plaintiffs by the FDIC comply with the annual accounting and reporting practices and procedures required by the statute. If those six pages are sufficient, then Plaintiffs have received everything to which the statute entitles them. If they are not, the FDIC must perform the accounting required by the statute.

II. *Bancorp II*

[After summary judgment in favor of the FDIC in *Bancorp I*, the Bank had filed a second action in state court, *Bancorp II*, alleging the same misconduct by the FDIC, but raising only state law claims against the FDIC, for breach of fiduciary duty, unjust enrichment, intentional misrepresentation, and an accounting. The FDIC removed the action to federal court, and the district court dismissed the action, concluding that they were barred by res judicata. The Ninth Circuit agreed.]

[T]he central question is whether the Bank had a right to proceed in state court when a federal court had already entered judgment. Thus, we ask whether the two causes of action are the same for purposes of claim preclusion. . . .

The two actions in these consolidated cases arise from the same transactional nucleus of facts. The Bank's dissatisfaction with the FDIC's accounting reports of its receivership lies at the heart of both actions. *Bancorp I* is based on Plaintiffs' attempt to force the FDIC to produce the accounting reports required by 12 U.S.C. § 1821(d) (15), and every cause of action brought in *Bancorp II* is based on alleged defects in the reports appellants actually received. Plaintiffs could have brought in *Bancorp I* the claims asserted in *Bancorp II*. Claim preclusion bars grounds for recovery which could have been asserted in a prior suit between the same parties on the same cause of action. . . . The district court correctly dismissed *Bancorp II*.

8.41. *Liability of OCC for its discretionary actions.* The OCC has broad discretion to decide whether or not to place a national bank in conservatorship or receivership, with the FDIC as conservator or receiver. To what extent, however, might the OCC be liable for actions undertaken in its discretion–or for the subsequent discretionary actions of the FDIC? Is the OCC responsible to shareholders of a failing bank if its actions–or the FDIC's supervision of the receivership itself–result in further financial harm to them? Consider the following case in answering this question.

---

6. We leave for another day the question whether a member of the public, such as the individual plaintiffs in this case or a watchdog organization, might have the same statutory right.

Sinclair v. Hawke

314 F.3d 934 (8th Cir. 2003)

LOKEN, Circuit J.

[For background on the litigation in this case, see Chapter 1, § 3, *supra*. The owner of a failed national bank filed an amended complaint against the Comptroller and certain employees of the Office of the Comptroller of the Currency (OCC) claiming constitutional or statutory standing to sue the defendants for indirect monetary loss for regulatory actions against the bank, for constitutional damage claims (asserted by the bank), 42 U.S.C. §§ 1981, 1982, and for a violation of the Racketeer Influenced and Corrupt Organizations Act, 18 U.S.C. §§ 1961 *et seq*. In the following excerpt from the court's opinion, the Eighth Circuit considers each of these claims.]

Exercising his comprehensive authority to regulate national banks, the Comptroller of the Currency declared Sinclair National Bank (SNB) insolvent and appointed the Federal Deposit Insurance Corporation (FDIC) as SNB's receiver under the national banking laws. *See* 12 U.S.C. §§ 191, 1821(c)(2)(A)(ii). SNB and its owner, Damian Sinclair, sued the Comptroller in his official capacity, the FDIC, and certain employees of the Office of the Comptroller of the Currency (OCC) seeking an order removing the FDIC as receiver and other equitable relief. The district court denied plaintiffs' motion for a temporary restraining order, and the FDIC sold the assets of SNB to another Arkansas bank.

Mr. Sinclair, acting individually and as assignee of SNB, then filed an amended complaint, dropping the agency defendants and the claims for equitable relief and asserting damage claims against the Comptroller and eight other OCC employees, in their individual capacities, for violating the First and Fifth Amendments; two federal civil rights laws, 42 U.S.C. §§ 1981 and 1982; and the Racketeer Influenced and Corrupt Organizations Act (RICO), 18 U.S.C. § 1962(c). The district court granted defendants' motion to dismiss, concluding that District Deputy Comptroller John Bodnar is entitled to qualified immunity regarding his action in approving Mr. Sinclair's change-of-control application, and that all defendants are entitled to absolute immunity regarding the other regulatory actions challenged in the amended complaint. Mr. Sinclair appeals the court's absolute immunity ruling. Concluding that the amended complaint fails to state a claim upon which relief can be granted, we affirm without reaching the absolute immunity issue. . . .

I. Background.

In 1999, Northwest National Bank was a distressed bank operating in Gravette, Arkansas, under a Memorandum of Understanding with the OCC. Mr. Sinclair filed a change-in-control application[a] with the OCC, stating his intent to purchase the bank and submitting a business plan in which the bank would purchase large pools of non-prime consumer loans to low-income borrowers from Stevens Financial Group, Inc., a company formerly owned by Mr. Sinclair. The OCC approved the change of ownership provided the bank would maintain enhanced capital ratios. In March 2000, Mr. Sinclair agreed to that condition, purchased the bank for $2.75 million, changed the bank's name to SNB, and contributed an additional $2 million to the bank's capital. The District Deputy Comptroller primarily responsible for oversight of SNB immediately received a letter from the FDIC criticizing the OCC for approving the change in ownership without considering the FDIC's negative comments regarding Mr. Sinclair's business plan. Thus began a contentious two-year regulatory relationship during which, the amended complaint alleges, OCC officials

---

a. On change-in-bank-control requirements, see Chapter 4, § 4, *supra*.

took the following actions against SNB:

• In April 2000, OCC began "a persistent series of directives and criticisms, each of increasing severity, none of which was based on a comprehensive examination of the actual loan files." A May 17 OCC letter alleged that the bulk loans purchased by SNB violated the legal lending limit.[b]
• On June 28, 2000, the OCC issued a Safety and Soundness Notice of Deficiency criticizing SNB's management and monitoring of its non-prime loans and containing "numerous contrived and specious allegations." The statute authorizes the OCC to commence cease-and-desist proceedings if "in the opinion of" the agency, a national bank "is engaging or has engaged ... in an unsafe or unsound practice." 18 U.S.C. § 1818(b)(1). The Comptroller's regulations authorize the OCC to issue a Notice of Deficiency to request a compliance plan. *See* 12 C.F.R. § 30.3(b).[2]
• In September 2000, OCC officials demanded that SNB limit non-prime minority and low-income loans to one-hundred percent of the bank's capital. OCC threatened to issue a safety and soundness order if SNB did not comply. Because this "patently punitive demand" would leave SNB unable to implement its business plan, SNB sued the OCC in the United States Court of Federal Claims for breach of an alleged contract defining the capital requirements OCC would impose. SNB also sued various OCC officials in the District of Columbia District Court, asserting the constitutional violations alleged in this lawsuit and seeking declaratory and injunctive relief from the threatened regulatory action.[3]
• The OCC conducted two lengthy on-site examinations of SNB in late 2000 and early 2001 that "totally paralyzed SNB's activities by virtue of the [examiners'] constant and deliberate interference." The National Bank Act authorizes the Comptroller to "appoint examiners who shall examine every national bank as often as the Comptroller ... shall deem necessary." 12 U.S.C. § 481.
• In December 2000, the OCC concluded that SNB's proposed compliance plan was inadequate and issued a Notice of Intent to Issue a Safety and Soundness Order, a regulatory action authorized by 12 C.F.R. § 30.5(a). In response, SNB submitted another compliance plan. In March 2001, the OCC criticized that plan and imposed "restrictions on non-prime lending that made it impossible for SNB to carry out the business plan that the OCC had expressly approved just one year earlier."
• In April 2001, the OCC issued a Cease and Desist Consent Order. When SNB refused to consent, the agency issued a Notice of Charges on June 7, 2001, as authorized by 12 U.S.C. § 1818(b)(1). SNB answered the Charges, and an administrative law judge set a discovery schedule.
• In early August 2001, the OCC reclassified SNB's loan portfolio, declared SNB "critically undercapitalized," and issued a Prompt Corrective Action Directive requiring SNB to submit a capital restoration plan and take other corrective

---

b. On lending limits applicable to national banks, see Chapter 5, *supra*, § 2.a.

2. Congress did not define unsafe and unsound banking practices in the statute. "[T]he Comptroller suggests that these terms encompass ... conduct deemed contrary to accepted standards of banking operations which might result in abnormal risk or loss to a banking institution or shareholder." *First Nat'l Bank of Eden v. Dept. of the Treasury,* 568 F.2d 610, 611 n. 2 (8th Cir.1978).

3. On February 27, 2001, the District of Columbia District Court denied SNB's emergency motion to stay regulatory action, concluding that the bank was unlikely to prevail in the litigation. SNB dismissed this lawsuit one month later, allegedly because Mr. Bodnar told Mr. Sinclair that the OCC would not approve SNB's compliance plan with the action pending. The Court of Claims action was not dismissed. *See Sinclair v. United States,* 49 Fed. Cl. 274 (2001) (denying the OCC's motion to dismiss). The record on appeal does not disclose the status of that action.

actions, a directive authorized by statute, *see* 12 U.S.C. § 1831o (e)(2) & (i), and by the Comptroller's regulations, which provide for a prompt administrative appeal, *see* 12 C.F.R. § 6.21(a)(2). SNB filed a capital restoration plan and an administrative appeal. In addition, the Chapter 11 trustee for Stevens Financial Group submitted a change-of-control application to the OCC, seeking to purchase SNB from Mr. Sinclair for $2 million. When the OCC denied SNB's request for a hearing and more time to respond, SNB and Mr. Sinclair filed their initial Petition for Review of Agency Action and Complaint in the district court. After a telephonic hearing the next day, the district court denied plaintiffs' motion for a temporary restraining order.

• In early September 2001, the OCC declared SNB insolvent, appointed the FDIC as SNB'sstatutory receiver, and terminated the pending administrative proceeding as moot. *See* 12 U.S.C. §§ 191, 1821(c)(2)(A)(ii). The district court declined to enjoin the receivership, the FDIC sold SNB's assets to another bank, and Mr. Sinclair alleges he lost the ability to recover his investment in SNB.

After setting forth the above-summarized dispute in great detail, the amended complaint asserts the following compensatory and punitive damages claims on behalf of Mr. Sinclair personally and as SNB's assignee:

1. Fifth Amendment equal protection and procedural and substantive due process claims under *Bivens v. Six Unknown Named Agents of the Fed. Bureau of Narcotics,* 403 U.S. 388 (1971), alleging that the OCC officials took the above regulatory actions for retaliatory and vindictive purposes and to discriminate against minority borrowers.
2. First Amendment *Bivens* claims alleging that, beginning in December 2000, all the OCC regulatory actions were taken in retaliation for SNB's exercise of its First Amendment right to file the two lawsuits SNB filed that fall.
3. Claims of race discrimination under 42 U.S.C. §§ 1981 and 1982. In support of these claims, the amended complaint alleges that various OCC officials made statements over the course of the two-year dispute evidencing their hostility toward minority borrowers, statements of the kind we have called "stray remarks" in the more familiar context of employment discrimination disputes.
4. RICO claims alleging that defendants "conspired to fraudulently approve the charter for SNB and then institute a program of regulatory action to force SNB to abandon its non-prime lending programs" as part of a pattern of racketeering activity "designed to deprive minorities from having ownership of significant national banks and to prevent minority and low-income borrowers from having access to credit."

By these claims, Mr. Sinclair seeks to have a jury decide whether defendants' facially lawful regulatory actions were the product of an unlawful motive. To our knowledge, such judicial review of the actions of federal bank regulators would be unprecedented. The issue, broadly stated, is whether Congress has authorized wide-ranging judicial review of regulators' motives in personal damage actions that might have a chilling effect on their willingness to aggressively attack unsafe and unsound banking practices.

II. The Constitutional and Civil Rights Act Claims.

A. Mr. Sinclair's Individual Claims. The amended complaint alleges that Mr. Sinclair was sole shareholder and chairman of the board of SNB and "was damaged in his business or property" by defendants' alleged unlawful regulatory conduct. The pleading is defective for failing to allege Mr. Sinclair's constitutional and prudential standing to assert these claims. His only financial injury was to the value of his investment in SNB resulting from adverse actions taken against SNB. Thus, Mr. Sinclair "falls squarely within the prudential standing rule that normally bars litigants from asserting the rights or legal interests of others in order to obtain relief from injury to themselves." *Warth v. Seldin,* 422 U.S. 490, 509 (1975).

In *Potthoff v. Morin,* 245 F.3d 710, 716 (8th Cir.2001), we dismissed a sole shareholder's First Amendment claim for lack of standing, applying the longstanding principle that "[a]ctions to enforce corporate rights or redress injuries to the corporation cannot be maintained by a stockholder in his own name ... even though the injury to the corporation may incidentally result in the depreciation or destruction of the value of the stock" (quotation omitted). *Accord Gregory v. Mitchell,* 634 F.2d 199, 202 (5th Cir.1981) (dismissing bank shareholders' equal protection and due process claims against the FDIC and state regulators); *Des Vergnes v. Seekonk Water Dist.,* 601 F.2d 9, 16 (1st Cir.1979) (dismissing developer's § 1981 claim against local regulator). Here, too, Mr. Sinclair's indirect monetary loss simply does not give him constitutional or statutory standing to sue the OCC defendants for their regulatory actions against SNB.

B. SNB's Bivens Claims. In *Bivens,* the Supreme Court held that private citizens have a cause of action for damages against federal agents who violate their Fourth Amendment rights. The Court has since declined to extend this nonstatutory damages remedy to contexts in which it may be inferred that Congress has spoken to the contrary. For example, in *Bush v. Lucas,* 462 U.S. 367, 368 (1983), the Court held that the elaborate and comprehensive statutory remedies available under the civil service system precluded a *Bivens* damage action by a federal employee who was allegedly disciplined for exercising his First Amendment rights. In *Schweiker v. Chilicky,* 487 U.S. 412, 414 (1988), the Court held that Social Security claimants may not sue government officials under *Bivens* for alleged due process violations in denying or delaying benefits. And in *FDIC v. Meyer,* 510 U.S. 471, 473 (1994), and *Corr. Servs. Corp. v. Malesko,* 534 U.S. 61, 63 (2001), the Court refused to extend *Bivens* to claims against federal agencies and private government contractors, as opposed to individual federal officials. The issue in this case is whether to extend *Bivens* to Mr. Sinclair's claims for damages against OCC officials for their adverse regulatory actions against SNB.[4]

In *Chilicky,* 487 U.S. at 423, the Supreme Court stated that a "special factor" precluding a *Bivens* action is the existence of a statutorily created remedy, even if that remedy does not provide complete relief. . . .

When Congress has created a comprehensive regulatory regime, the existence of a right to judicial review under the Administrative Procedure Act is sufficient to preclude a *Bivens* action. . . .

We conclude that [the] comprehensive statutory regime [applicable to banks] precludes the *Bivens* damage claims asserted by SNB. All the adverse regulatory actions at issue fell within the OCC's express statutory powers to regulate national banks, to take action against unsafe and unsound banking practices, and to appoint a receiver for insolvent banks. The OCC actions up to the declaration of SNB's insolvency were subject to administrative and judicial review processes that SNB invoked. To the extent these APA remedies are limited, the long history of congressional regulation of national banks confirms that the limitations are not inadvertent. Rather, Congress has repeatedly adjusted, and at times overhauled, these statutory remedies in a continuing effort to resolve–

4. SNB assigned its claims to Mr. Sinclair after the FDIC was appointed SNB's receiver. Defendants argue that the assigned claims must be dismissed because only the FDIC as receiver has standing to assert them on behalf of SNB. *See* 12 U.S.C. §§ 91, 1821(d)(2)(A)(i). We need not consider this issue.

> a difficult and delicate problem of reconciling conflicting interests–on one hand, the interests of depositors and savers who have their money in these insured institutions, the interests of well-run banks and savings and loan associations who contribute substantial premiums to the reserve funds of the insuring agencies, and the interests of the Government which underwrites the insuring agencies–in preventing irresponsible or even criminal individuals from looting or otherwise wrecking insured banks and savings and loan associations through improper activities; on the other hand, the interests of insured banks and savings and loan associations and their officials in receiving fair treatment from the Government, and in receiving a reasonable degree of protection from Government actions which might at times, for one reason or another, degenerate into arbitrary, capricious, and overbearing tactics.

S.Rep. No. 1482, 1966-3 U.S.C.C.A.N. at 3534-35. In this complex regulatory environment, it is for Congress to decide whether the public interest in a sound national banking system would be furthered by a cause of action requiring bank regulators to pay damages personally unless they can convince a jury that their conduct in aggressively regulating a national bank was not the product of an unconstitutional motive. Because Congress has not created that cause of action, we decline to extend *Bivens* so as to create it by implication, just as many circuits have declined to permit *Bivens* damage actions against agents of the Internal Revenue Service, who administer another comprehensive federal regulatory regime in which relationships between the regulator and the regulated are frequently hostile and adversarial. . . .

SNB's § 1981 and § 1982 Claims. These civil rights statutes grant causes of action to persons who, on account of race, are denied the right to make and perform contracts (§ 1981) or to buy, hold, and sell property (§ 1982). . . . The amended complaint alleges that defendants, on account of race, took regulatory actions "to deny creditworthy, non-white and minority borrowers and potential borrowers of loans purchased or financed by Plaintiff Sinclair," thereby depriving those persons of their "equal right to make and enter into contracts with qualified buyers to buy, own and sell real property on account of Plaintiffs' association with persons who are non-white."

SNB did not lend directly to non-white borrowers. Rather, SNB purchased large pools of non-prime loans from a company owned or formerly owned by Mr. Sinclair. The FDIC criticized SNB's high-risk business plan, the OCC demanded increased equity capital to protect the bank's insured depositors, and ultimately the OCC placed SNB in receivership as insolvent. In response to defendants' motion to dismiss in the district court, plaintiffs cited no case imposing § 1981 or § 1982 liability on federal regulators for regulatory actions taken within their statutory authority. Here, it is not enough for SNB to allege and prove that the pools of non-prime loans included a disproportionate number of loans to non-white borrowers. . . . In these circumstances, we doubt that SNB has stated a claim under § 1981 or § 1982, but in any event it is clear that defendants are entitled to qualified immunity from these damage claims. . . .

III. The RICO Claims.

"The major purpose behind RICO is to curb the infiltration of legitimate business organizations by racketeers." *Atlas Pile Driving Co. v. DiCon Fin. Co.,* 886 F.2d 986, 990 (8th Cir.1989). To establish a RICO violation, a plaintiff must allege and prove "(1) the existence of an enterprise; (2) defendant's association with the enterprise; (3) defendant's participation in predicate acts of racketeering; and (4) defendant's actions constitute a pattern of racketeering activity." *United Healthcare Corp. v. Amer. Trade Ins. Co.,* 88 F.3d 563, 570 (8th Cir.1996). In his lengthy response to defendants' motion to dismiss in the district court, Mr. Sinclair asserted that the nine defendants, all employees of the OCC, functioned as an enterprise and that their above-described conduct in regulating SNB constituted a pattern of racketeering activity intended to "persecute national banks that seek to make minority lending a primary focus of their activities and force these institutions out of business." Mr. Sinclair has cited no authority for the proposition that federal employees who take regulatory action consistent with their statutory powers engage in a "pattern of racketeering activity" if those actions are adverse to a particular industry or business activity. In our view, the proposition is ludicrous on its face. "Bankers do not become racketeers by acting like bankers." *Terry A. Lambert Plumbing, Inc. v. Western Sec. Bank,* 934 F.2d 976, 981 (8th Cir.1991). Likewise, bank regulators do not become racketeers by acting like aggressive regulators.

Notes and Comments 8.42. To what extent would directors, officers, and other insiders be liable for the losses experienced by the now failing QNB? *See* 12 U.S.C. § 1821(k)-(*l*). What effect would the following case have on your answer?

Atherton v. Federal Deposit Insurance Corporation

519 U.S. 213 (1997)

Justice BREYER delivered the opinion of the Court.

The Resolution Trust Corporation (RTC) sued several officers and directors of City Federal Savings Bank, claiming that they had violated the legal standard of care they owed that federally chartered, federally insured institution. The case here focuses upon the legal standard for determining whether or not their behavior was improper. It asks where courts should look to find the standard of care to measure the legal propriety of the defendants' conduct–to state law, to federal common law, or to a special federal statute (103 Stat. 243, 12 U.S.C. § 1821(k)) that speaks of "gross negligence"?

We conclude that state law sets the standard of conduct as long as the state standard (such as simple negligence) is stricter than that of the federal statute. The federal statute nonetheless sets a "gross negligence" floor, which applies as a substitute for state standards that are more relaxed. . . .

In 1989, City Federal Savings Bank (City Federal), a federal savings association, went into receivership. The RTC, as receiver, brought this action in the bank's name against officers and directors. (Throughout this opinion, we use the more colloquial term "bank" to refer to a variety of institutions such as "federal savings associations.") The complaint said that the defendants had acted (or failed to act) in ways that led City Federal to make various bad development, construction, and business acquisition loans. It claimed that these actions (or omissions) were unlawful because they amounted to gross negligence, simple negligence, and breaches of fiduciary duty.

The defendants moved to dismiss. They pointed to a federal statute, 12 U.S.C. § 1821(k), that says in part that a "director or officer" of a federally insured bank "may be held personally liable for monetary damages" in an RTC-initiated "civil action . . . for gross negligence" or "similar conduct . . . that demonstrates a greater disregard of a duty of care (than gross negligence). . . ." . . . They argued that, by authorizing actions for gross negligence or more seriously culpable conduct, the statute intended to forbid actions based upon less seriously culpable conduct, such as conduct that rose only to the level of simple negligence. The District Court agreed and dismissed all but the gross negligence claims.

The Third Circuit, providing an interlocutory appeal . . . reversed. It interpreted the federal statute as simply offering a safeguard against state legislation that had watered down applicable state standards of care–below a gross negligence benchmark. As so interpreted, the statute did not prohibit actions resting upon stricter standard of care rules– whether those stricter standard of care rules originated in state law (which the Circuit found applicable in the case of state-chartered banks) or in federal common law (which the Circuit found applicable in the case of federally chartered banks). *Resolution Trust Corp.* v. *Cityfed Financial Corp.*, 57 F.3d 1231, 1243-1244, 1245-1249 (1995). Noting that City Federal is a federally chartered savings institution, the Circuit concluded that the RTC was free "to pursue any claims for negligence or of breach of fiduciary duty available as a matter of federal common law." *Id.*, at 1249.

The defendants, pointing to variations in the Circuits' interpretations of the "gross negligence" statute, sought certiorari. *Compare Resolution Trust Corp. v. Frates*, 52 F.3d 295 (C.A.10 1995) (§ 1821(k) prohibits federal common-law actions for simple negligence) with *Cityfed, supra*, at 1246-1249 (§ 1821(k) does not prohibit federal common-law actions for simple negligence). And we granted review. . . .

We begin by temporarily setting the federal "gross negligence" statute to the side, and by asking whether, were there no such statute, federal common law would provide the applicable legal standard. We recognize, as did the Third Circuit, that this Court did once articulate federal common-law corporate governance standards, applicable to federally chartered banks. *Briggs v. Spaulding*, 141 U.S. 132 (1891). *See also Martin v. Webb*, 110 U.S. 7, 15 (1884) (directors must "use ordinary diligence . . . and . . . exercise reasonable control"); *Bowerman v. Hamner*, 250 U.S. 504 (1919). But the Court found its rules of decision in federal common law long before it held, in *Erie R. Co. v. Tompkins*, 304 U.S. 64 (1938), that "[t]here is no federal general common law." *Id.*, at 78. The Third Circuit, while considering itself bound by *Briggs*, asked whether relevant federal common-law standards could have survived *Erie*. We conclude that they did not and that (except as modified . . . *infra*) state law, not federal common law, provides the applicable rules for decision.

This Court has recently discussed what one might call "federal common law" in the strictest sense, *i.e.*, a rule of decision that amounts, not simply to an interpretation of a federal statute or a properly promulgated administrative rule, but, rather, to the judicial "creation" of a special federal rule of decision. *See Texas Industries, Inc. v. Radcliff Materials, Inc.*, 451 U.S. 630, 640-643 (1981). The Court has said that "cases in which judicial creation of a special federal rule would be justified . . . are . . . 'few and restricted.'" *O'Melveny & Myers v. FDIC*, 512 U.S. 79, 87 (1994) (quoting *Wheeldin v. Wheeler*, 373 U.S. 647, 651 (1963)). "Whether latent federal power should be exercised to displace state law is primarily a decision for Congress," not the federal courts. *Wallis v. Pan American Petroleum Corp.*, 384 U.S. 63, 68 (1966). Nor does the existence of related federal statutes automatically show that Congress intended courts to create federal common-law rules, for " 'Congress acts . . . against the background of the total corpus juris of the states. . . .' " *Id.*, at 68 (quoting H. HART & H. WECHSLER, THE FEDERAL COURTS AND THE FEDERAL SYSTEM 435 (1953)). Thus, normally, when courts decide to fashion rules of federal common law, "the guiding principle is that a significant conflict between some federal policy or interest and the use of state law . . . must first be specifically shown." *Ibid.* Indeed, such a "conflict" is normally a "precondition." *O'Melveny, supra*, at 87. *See also United States v. Kimbell Foods, Inc.*, 440 U.S. 715, 728 (1979); *Kamen v. Kemper Financial Services, Inc.*, 500 U.S. 90, 98 (1991).

No one doubts the power of Congress to legislate rules for deciding cases like the one before us. . . . Other federal statutes regulate the activities of federally chartered savings associations in various ways. . . . No one argues, however, that either these statutes, or federal regulations validly promulgated pursuant to statute, set forth general corporate governance standards of the sort at issue applicable to a federally chartered savings association such as City Federal. *Cf.* 12 C.F.R. § 7.2000 (1996) (discussed *infra*) (describing governance procedures applicable to federally chartered national banks, but not federal savings associations). Consequently, we must decide whether the application of state-law standards of care to such banks would conflict with, and thereby significantly threaten, a federal policy or interest.

We have examined each of the basic arguments that the respondent implicitly or explicitly raises. In our view, they do not point to a conflict or threat that is significant, and we shall explain why. (The respondent, by the way, is now the Federal Deposit Insurance Corporation–the FDIC–which has replaced the Resolution Trust Corporation pursuant to a new federal statute. 12 U.S.C. § 1441a(b)(4)(A).)

First, the FDIC invokes the need for "uniformity." Federal common law, it says, will provide uniformity, but "[s]uperimposing state standards of fiduciary responsibility over standards developed by a federal chartering authority would . . . 'upset the balance' that the federal chartering authority 'may strike. . . .'" . . . To invoke the concept of "uniformity," however, is not to prove its need. *Cf. Kimbell Foods*, *supra*, at 730 (rejecting "generalized pleas for uniformity"); *O'Melveny*, *supra*, at 88 (same).

For one thing, the number of federally insured banks is about equally divided between federally chartered and state-chartered banks, Federal Deposit Insurance Corporation, 1 Statistics on Banking: A Statistical History of the United States Banking Industry, Table SI9, p. B-9 (Aug.1995) (showing that, in 1989, there were 1,595 federally chartered institutions and 1,492 state chartered ones); and a federal standard that increases uniformity among the former would increase disparity with the latter.

For another, our Nation's banking system has thrived despite disparities in matters of corporate governance. Consider, for example, the divergent state law governance standards applicable to banks chartered in different States, *e.g.*, Ind.Code Ann. § 23-1-35-1(e)(2) (1994) (directors not liable unless conduct constitutes at least "willful misconduct or recklessness"); Iowa Code § 524.605 (1995) (providing ordinary negligence standard), as well as the different ways in which lower courts since 1891 have interpreted *Briggs*' "federal common law" standard. *Compare Federal Deposit Insurance Corporation v. Mason*, 115 F.2d 548, 551-552 (C.A.3 1940) (applying standard similar to simple negligence) *with Washington Bancorporation v. Said*, 812 F.Supp. 1256, 1266 (D.D.C. 1993) (*Briggs* did not apply "simple negligence" standard of care). *See* R. Stevens & B. Nielson, *The Standard of Care for Directors and Officers of Federally Chartered Depository Institutions: It's Gross Negligence Regardless of Whether Section 1821(k) Preempts Federal Common Law*, 13 ANN. REVIEW BANKING L. 169, 172 (1994) (in part because of "widely varying results, the federal common law standard of care is neither fully developed, nor well settled"). ... Indeed, the Comptroller of the Currency, acting through regulation, permits considerable disparity in the standard of care applicable to federally chartered banks other than savings banks (which are under the jurisdiction of the Office of Thrift Supervision, 12 U.S.C. §§ 1462a, 1463(a)). *See* 12 C.F.R. § 7.2000 (1996) (permitting banks, within broad limits, "to follow the corporate governance procedures of the law of the state in which the main office of the bank is located . . . [or] the Delaware General Corporation Law . . . or the Model Business Corporation Act").

Second, the FDIC at times suggests that courts must apply a federal common-law standard of care simply because the banks in question are federally chartered. This argument, with little more, might have seemed a strong one during most of the first century of our Nation's history, for then state-chartered banks were the norm and federally chartered banks an exception–and federal banks often encountered hostility and deleterious state laws. . . .

. . . To point to a federal charter by itself shows no conflict, threat, or need for "federal common law." It does not answer the critical question.

Third, the FDIC refers to a conflict of laws principle called the "internal affairs doctrine"–a doctrine that this Court has described as

> "a conflict of laws principle which recognizes that only one State should have the authority to regulate a corporation's internal affairs–matters peculiar to the relationships among or between the corporation and its current officers, directors, and shareholders–because otherwise a corporation could be faced with conflicting demands." *Edgar v. MITE Corp.*, 457 U.S. 624, 645 (1982).

States normally look to the State of a business' incorporation for the law that provides the relevant corporate governance general standard of care. Restatement (Second) Conflict of Laws § 309 (1971). And by analogy, it has been argued, courts should look to federal law to find the standard of care governing officers and directors of federally chartered banks. *See Resolution Trust Corporation v. Chapman*, 29 F.3d 1120, 1123-1124 (C.A.7 1994).

To find a justification for federal common law in this argument, however, is to substitute analogy or formal symmetry for the controlling legal requirement, namely, the existence of a need to create federal common law arising out of a significant conflict or threat to a federal interest. *O'Melveny*, 512 U.S., at 85, 87. The internal affairs doctrine shows no such need, for it seeks only to avoid conflict by requiring that there be a single point of legal reference. Nothing in that doctrine suggests that the single source of law must be federal. *See Chapman*, *supra*, at 1126-1127 (Posner, C.J., dissenting). In the absence of a governing federal common law, courts applying the internal affairs doctrine could find (we do not say that they will find) that the State closest analogically to the State of incorporation of an ordinary business is the State in which the federally chartered bank has its main office or maintains its principal place of business. *Cf.* 12 C.F.R. § 7.2000 (1996) (federally chartered commercial banks may "follow the corporate governance procedures of the law of the state in which the main office of the bank is located"). So to apply state law, as we have said, would tend to avoid disparity between federally chartered and state-chartered banks (that might be next door to each other). And, of course, if this approach proved problematic, Congress and federal agencies acting pursuant to congressionally delegated authority remain free to provide to the contrary.

Fourth, the FDIC points to statutes that provide the Office of Thrift Supervision, a federal regulatory agency, with authority to fine, or to remove from office, savings bank officers and directors for certain breaches of fiduciary duty. The FDIC adds that in "the course of such proceedings, the OTS, applying the ordinary-care standard [of *Briggs*] . . . has spoken authoritatively respecting the duty of care owed by directors and officers to federal savings associations." . . . The FDIC does not claim, however, that these OTS statements, interpreting a pre-existing judge-made federal common-law standard (*i.e.*, that of *Briggs*) themselves amounted to an agency effort to promulgate a binding regulation pursuant to delegated congressional authority. Nor have we found, in our examination of the relevant OTS opinions, any convincing evidence of a relevant, significant conflict or threat to a federal interest.

Finally, we note that here, as in *O'Melveny*, the FDIC is acting only as a receiver of a failed institution; it is not pursuing the interest of the Federal Government as a bank insurer–an interest likely present whether the insured institution is state, or federally, chartered.

In sum, we can find no significant conflict with, or threat to, a federal interest. The federal need is far weaker than was present in what the Court has called the "few and restricted instances," *Milwaukee v. Illinois*, 451 U.S. 304, 313 (1981), in which this Court has created a federal common law. Consider, for example, *Hinderlider v. La Plata River &*

Cherry Creek Ditch Co., 304 U.S. 92 (1938) (controversy between two States regarding apportionment of streamwater); *Boyle v. United Technologies Corp.*, 487 U.S. 500 (1988) (Federal Government contractors and civil liability of federal officials); *United States v. Standard Oil Co. of Cal.*, 332 U.S. 301, 305 (1947) (relationship between Federal Government and members of its armed forces); *Howard v. Lyons*, 360 U.S. 593, 597 (1959) (liability of federal officers in the course of official duty); *Banco Nacional de Cuba v. Sabbatino*, 376 U.S. 398, 425 (1964) (relationships with other countries). *See also Texas Industries, Inc. v. Radcliff Materials, Inc.*, 451 U.S. 630, 641 (1981) ("[A]bsent some congressional authorization to formulate substantive rules of decision, federal common law exists only in such narrow areas as those concerned with the rights and obligations of the United States, interstate and international disputes implicating the conflicting rights of States or our relations with foreign nations, and admiralty cases"). Indeed, the interests in many of the cases where this Court has declined to recognize federal common law appear at least as strong as, if not stronger than, those present here. . . .

We conclude that the federal common-law standards enunciated in cases such as *Briggs* did not survive this Court's later decision in *Erie R. Co. v. Tompkins*. There is no federal common law that would create a general standard of care applicable to this case. ...

We now turn to a further question: Does federal statutory law (namely, the federal "gross negligence" statute), supplant any state-law standard of care? [The opinion quotes 12 U.S.C. § 1821(k).]

Lower courts have taken different positions about whether this statute, in stating that directors and officers "may be held personally liable" for conduct that amounts to "gross negligence" or worse, immunizes them from liability for conduct that is less culpable than gross negligence such as simple negligence. . . .

In our view, the statute's "gross negligence" standard provides only a floor–a guarantee that officers and directors must meet at least a gross negligence standard. It does not stand in the way of a stricter standard that the laws of some States provide.

For one thing, the language of the statute contains a savings clause that, read literally, preserves the applicability of stricter state standards. . . . The petitioner, in contending that the statute displaces federal common law, says that "any right" means only a right created elsewhere in the same Act of Congress, for example, by various regulatory enforcement provisions. *E.g.*, § 1818(b) (cease-and-desist provision). But that is not what the Act says nor does its language compel so restrictive a reading. That language, read naturally, suggests an interpretation broad enough to save rights provided by other state, or federal, law.

For another thing, Congress enacted the statute against a background of failing savings associations . . . , large federal payments to insured bank depositors, and recent changes in state law designed to limit preexisting officer and director negligence liability. . . . The state-law changes would have made it more difficult for the Federal Government to recover, from negligent officers and directors, federal funds spent to rescue failing savings banks and their depositors. And the background as a whole supports a reading of the statute as an effort to preserve the Federal Government's ability to recover funds by creating a standard of care floor.

The legislative history, insofar as it is relevant, supports this conclusion. . . . To have pre-empted state law with a uniform federal "gross negligence" standard would have cured the problem in some instances (where state law was weaker) but would have aggravated it in others (where state law was stronger).

In fact, the legislative history says more. The relevant Senate Report addresses the point specifically. It says:

> "This subsection does not prevent the FDIC from pursuing claims under State law or under other applicable Federal law, if such law permits the officers or directors of a financial institution to be sued (1) for violating a lower standard of care, such as simple negligence." S.Rep. No. 101-19, p. 318 (1989).

This Report was not published until two weeks after Congress enacted the law. But . . . the Report was circulated within Congress several weeks before Congress voted. . . .

The history is not all on one side. The Congressional Record contains one statement that suggests a competing congressional purpose, namely to protect bank officers and directors from too strict a liability standard. . . . But we have not found other such statements. And that statement is inconsistent with the language of the Senate Report. It suggests an interpretation of the statute largely rejected in the lower courts, namely that it pre-empts stricter state law as applied to state-chartered, as well as to federally chartered, institutions. . . .

The petitioner, in the courts below and as an alternative ground in this Court, made a final complicated argument to explain why § 1821(k) displaces federal common law. He points to the universally conceded fact that the "gross negligence" statute applies to federal, as well as to state, banks. He then assumes, for sake of the argument, that in the absence of the statute, federal common law would determine liability for federal banks. He then asks why Congress would have applied the "gross negligence" statute to federal banks unless it wanted that statute to set an absolute standard, not a floor. After all, on the assumption that, without the statute, federal common law would hold federal directors and officers to a standard as strict, or stricter, there would have been no need for the statute unless (as applied to federal banks) it intended to set a universal standard, freeing officers and directors from the potentially less strict standard of the common law, and not what, given the assumptions, would be a totally unnecessary floor. This argument, taken to its logical conclusion, would also suggest that state standards of simple negligence would be displaced by the federal gross negligence statute.

One obvious short answer to this ingenious argument lies in the fact that our conclusion in Part II runs contrary to the argument's critical assumption, namely that federal common law sets the standard of liability applicable to federal banks. State law applies. Without that assumption, the need for a "gross negligence" floor in the case of federally chartered banks, is identical to the need in the case of state-chartered banks. In both instances, the floor is needed to limit state efforts to weaken liability standards; in both instances a floor serves that purpose; and the reasons for believing the statute only sets such a floor are equally strong.

A more thorough answer lies in the fact that Congress nowhere separated its consideration of federally chartered, from that of state-chartered, banks. Congress did not ask whether one looked to federal common law or to state law to find the liability standard applicable to federally chartered banks. Nor did it try to determine the content of federal common law. One can reconcile congressional silence on the matter with a "gross negligence" statute, the language of which brings all banks (federal and state-chartered) within its scope, simply by assuming that Congress, when enacting the statute, wanted to leave other law, including the law applicable to federally chartered banks, exactly where Congress found it. That, after all, is what the statute says. And the savings clause language taken at face value permits Congress to achieve its basic objective (providing a "gross negligence" floor) without having to unravel the arcane intricacies of federal common law. In our view, this understanding of congressional intent better explains the statute's language and history than the petitioner's interpretation, imputing to Congress an intent to apply a uniform "gross negligence" standard to federally chartered, but not state chartered, institutions.

For these reasons, the judgment of the Court of Appeals is vacated, and the case is remanded for proceedings consistent with this opinion.

Justice O'CONNOR, with whom Justice SCALIA and Justice THOMAS join, concurring in part and concurring in the judgment.

I join all of the Court's opinion, except to the extent that it relies on the notably unhelpful legislative history to 12 U.S.C. § 1821(k). . . . As the Court correctly points out, the most natural reading of the savings clause in § 1821(k) covers both state and federal rights. . . . With such plain statutory language in hand, there is no reason to rely on legislative history that is, as the majority recognizes, "not all on one side."

Notes and Comments 8.43. Could a new bank be created to take over QNB's business? What would be the procedure for creation of the new bank? *See* 12 U.S.C. § 1821 (m).

8.44. Several banks in QNB's area are experiencing similar difficulties and are in danger of failing. Could these be cumulated into a single new entity to take over the ongoing business of the failing entities? *See* 12 U.S.C. § 1821(n). *See generally Bell & Murphy and Associates, Inc. v. Interfirst Bank Gateway, N.A.*, 894 F.2d 750 (5th Cir. 1990), *cert. denied*, 498 U.S. 895 (discussing role of bridge banks).

8.45. Assume that QNB is in danger of closing because of its inability to meet the future demands of its depositors and other creditors. What action, if any, could the FDIC take, short of conservatorship or receivership, to assist it? *See* 12 U.S.C. § 1823(c).

8.46. An August 1993 amendment[36] to section 11(d)(11) of the FDIA, 12 U.S.C. § 1821(d)(11), provides for a national depositor preference for amounts realized from the liquidation or other resolution of any depository institution insured by the FDIC. The amendment provides that distributions shall be made from all future receivership estates in the following order:

1. Administrative expenses of the receiver;
2. Deposit liability claims;
3. Other general or senior liabilities of the institution, other than subordinated obligations or shareholder claims;
4. Subordinated obligations; and,
5. Shareholder claims.

The legislation applies to all receiverships of insured institutions established after its enactment date (August 10, 1993) and supersedes any inconsistent state or other federal distribution provisions. The language of the statute explicitly covers post-appointment obligations incurred by a receiver as part of the liquidation of an institution. The FDIC Board of Directors has determined that this priority also covers certain expenses incurred prior to the appointment of the receiver. Such expenses include obligations which may have been incurred prior to the closing of the institution, but which the receiver determines should be paid to facilitate the smooth and orderly transfer of banking operations to a purchasing institution or to obtain an accounting and orderly disposition of the assets of the institution.

These expenses may include, but are not limited to, for example, the payment of the institution's last payroll, guard services, data processing services, utilities and expenses related to leased facilities. They do not include expenses such as severance pay claims,

36. Pub. L. No. 103-66, 107 Stat. 312 (1993).

golden parachute claims and claims arising from contract repudiations. The FDIC's implementing rules[37] limit the inclusion of expenses within the scope of "administrative expenses" to those that the receiver determines are necessary and appropriate for the orderly liquidation or resolution of the institution.

The legislative history of the amendment is explicit on the coverage of certain pre-receivership obligations within the scope of the "administrative expenses" priority of the receivership. The House/Senate Conference Report on the legislation noted that

> it is the conferees' intent that the FDIC interpret the depositor preference provision for the payment of administrative expenses of the receiver as including ordinary and necessary expenses of the institution that are unpaid at the time of failure, but only those that the receiver determines are necessary to maintain services and facilities to effect an orderly resolution of the institution.

H.R. Rep. No. 213, § 3001, Omnibus Budget Reconciliation Act of 1993, 103rd Cong., 1st Sess. (1993). The conferees noted that such coverage of expenses is the FDIC's current practice, in its role as receiver of failed insured institutions, and that the FDIC should continue its current practice of paying these expenses prior to paying deposits or other expenses if it determines such payment is required for an orderly resolution of the institution". *Id.*

8.47. *Collapse of the thrift industry.* One of the most singular events in the recent history of depository institutions regulation is the collapse of the savings and loan industry during the 1980s. What caused this extraordinary melt-down? For one perspective, consider the following excerpt.

United States v. Winstar Corporation

518 U.S. 839 (1996)

Justice SOUTER announced the judgment of the Court and delivered an opinion, in which Justice STEVENS and Justice BREYER join, and in which Justice O'CONNOR joins except as to Parts IV-A and IV-B.

I

* * *

A

* * *

. . . When the costs of short-term deposits overtook the revenues from long-term mortgages, some 435 thrifts failed between 1981 and 1983. . . .

While the regulators tried to mitigate the squeeze on the thrift industry generally through deregulation, the multitude of already-failed savings and loans confronted [the Federal Savings and Loan Insurance Corporation (FSLIC)] with deposit insurance liabilities that threatened to exhaust its insurance fund. *See Olympic Federal Savings and Loan Assn. v. Director, Office of Thrift Supervision*, 732 F.Supp. 1183, 1185 (D.C. 1990). According to the General Accounting Office, FSLIC's total reserves declined from $6.46 billion in 1980 to $4.55 billion in 1985, . . . when the [Federal Home Loan] Bank Board estimated that it would take $15.8 billion to close all institutions deemed insolvent under generally accepted accounting principles. . . . By 1988, the year of the last transaction involved in this case, FSLIC was itself insolvent by over $50 billion. . . . And by early 1989, the GAO estimated that $85 billion would be needed to cover FSLIC's responsibilities and put it back on the road

37. 60 Fed. Reg. 35,487 (1995) (codified at 12 C.F.R. §§ 360.3(f), 360.4).

to fiscal health. . . . In the end, we now know, the cost was much more even than that. *See, e.g.*, Horowitz, *The Continuing Thrift Bailout*, Investor's Business Daily, Feb. 1, 1996, p. A1 (reporting an estimated $140 billion total public cost of the S & L crisis through 1995).

Realizing that FSLIC lacked the funds to liquidate all of the failing thrifts, the Bank Board chose to avoid the insurance liability by encouraging healthy thrifts and outside investors to take over ailing institutions in a series of "supervisory mergers." . . . Such transactions, in which the acquiring parties assumed the obligations of thrifts with liabilities that far outstripped their assets, were not intrinsically attractive to healthy institutions; nor did FSLIC have sufficient cash to promote such acquisitions through direct subsidies alone, although cash contributions from FSLIC were often part of a transaction. . . . Instead, the principal inducement for these supervisory mergers was an understanding that the acquisitions would be subject to a particular accounting treatment that would help the acquiring institutions meet their reserve capital requirements imposed by federal regulations. . . .

B

Under Generally Accepted Accounting Principles (GAAP) there are circumstances in which a business combination may be dealt with by the "purchase method" of accounting. . . . The critical aspect of that method for our purposes is that it permits the acquiring entity to designate the excess of the purchase price over the fair value of all identifiable assets acquired as an intangible asset called "goodwill." [Goodwill would then be "amortized" over time; the value of this intangible asset would be gradually reduced.]

. . . In [the] case [of failed savings associations], the disparity between assets and liabilities from which the accounting goodwill was derived was virtually equal to the value of the discount from face value of the thrift's outstanding loans. [The discount adjusted the book value of the loans in light of their market value. The amount of the discount would be reduced (or "accreted") and the loan as accounted for would approximate full value as its maturity approached.] Thrift regulators, however, typically agreed to supervisory merger terms that allowed acquiring thrifts to accrete the discount over the average life of the loans (approximately seven years), . . . while permitting amortization of the goodwill asset over a much longer period. Given that goodwill and discount were substantially equal in overall values, the more rapid accrual of capital gain from accretion resulted in a net paper profit over the initial years following the acquisition. . . . The difference between amortization and accretion schedules thus allowed acquiring thrifts to seem more profitable than they in fact were.

Some transactions included yet a further inducement, described as a "capital credit." Such credits arose when FSLIC itself contributed cash to further a supervisory merger and permitted the acquiring institution to count the FSLIC contribution as a permanent credit to regulatory capital. By failing to require the thrift to subtract this FSLIC contribution from the amount of supervisory goodwill generated by the merger, regulators effectively permitted double counting of the cash as both a tangible and an intangible asset. . . . Capital credits thus inflated the acquiring thrift's regulatory capital and permitted leveraging of more and more loans.

. . . [T]he accounting treatment to be accorded supervisory goodwill and capital credits was the subject of express arrangements between the regulators and the acquiring institutions. . . . Although GAAP demonstrably permitted the use of the purchase method in acquiring a thrift suffering no distress, the relevant thrift regulations did not explicitly state that intangible goodwill assets created by that method could be counted toward regulatory capital. . . . Indeed, the rationale for recognizing goodwill stands on its head in a supervisory merger: ordinarily, goodwill is recognized as valuable because a rational purchaser would not pay more than assets are worth; here, however, the purchase is rational only because of the accounting treatment for the shortfall. . . . In the end, of course, such reasoning circumvented the whole purpose of the reserve requirements, which was to protect depositors and the deposit insurance fund. . . .

C

. . . [I]t is relatively clear that the overall regulatory response of the early and mid-1980's was unsuccessful in resolving the crisis in the thrift industry. . . . As a result, Congress enacted the Financial Institutions Reform, Recovery, and Enforcement Act of 1989 (FIRREA), Pub.L. 101-73, 103 Stat. 183, with the objects of preventing the collapse of the industry, attacking the root causes of the crisis, and restoring public confidence.

Notes and Comments 8.48. The use of the purchase method of accounting in the acquisition of a failing savings association was doubtful at the beginning of the 1980s.[38] By 1983, however, it was beyond any dispute that the accounting devices permitted by the FSLIC in the acquisitions of failing thrifts were inconsistent with GAAP. In another portion of his plurality opinion, Justice Souter explained the situation as follows:

> In 1983, the Financial Accounting Standards Board (the font of GAAP) promulgated Statement of Financial Accounting Standards No. 72, which applied specifically to the acquisition of a savings and loan association. SFAS 72 provided that "[i]f, and to the extent that, the fair value of liabilities [*e.g.*, deposits] assumed exceeds the fair value of identifiable assets [*e.g.*, mortgages and other loans] acquired in the acquisition of a banking or thrift institution, the unidentifiable intangible asset recognized generally shall be amortized to expense by the interest method over a period no longer than the discount on the long-term interest-bearing assets acquired is to be recognized as interest income." Accounting Standards, Original Pronouncements (July 1973-June 1, 1989), p. 725. In other words, SFAS 72 eliminated any doubt that the differential amortization periods on which acquiring thrifts relied to produce paper profits in supervisory mergers were inconsistent with GAAP. SFAS 72 also barred double-counting of capital credits by requiring that financial assistance from regulatory authorities must be deducted from the cost of the acquisition before the amount of goodwill is determined.

Winstar, 518 U.S. at 855.

8.49. One of the ways FIRREA went about "attacking the root causes of the crisis" was to mandate the use of GAAP in accounting by savings associations. One preliminary question might be, was this mandate prospective or retroactive? If it was intended to be retroactive, then it would affect the outstanding supervisory merger agreements. There was extensive litigation concerning this provision of FIRREA, and the circuit courts appear to have been in agreement that Congress did intend to abrogate agreements that had allowed non-GAAP accounting. *See Transohio Sav. Bank v. Director, Office of Thrift Supervision*, 967 F.2d 598, 617 (D.C.Cir. 1992); *Carteret Sav. Bank v. Office of Thrift Supervision*, 963 F.2d 567, 581-582 (3d Cir. 1992); *Security Sav. & Loan v. Director, Office of Thrift Supervision*, 960 F.2d 1318, 1322 (5th Cir. 1992); *Far West Federal Bank v. Director, Office of Thrift Supervision*, 951 F.2d 1093, 1098 (9th Cir. 1991); *Guaranty Financial Services, Inc.*

---

38. *See Winstar*, 518 U.S. 839, 855 n.10 (1996):

> [T]he proper amortization period for goodwill under GAAP was uncertain prior to th[e] time [of the Glendale transaction]. According to one observer, "when the accounting profession designed the purchase accounting rules in the early 1970s, they didn't anticipate the case of insolvent thrift institutions. . . . The rules for that situation were simply unclear until September 1982." . . . [M. LOWY, HIGH ROLLERS: INSIDE THE SAVINGS AND LOAN DEBACLE 39-40 (1991).]

v. Ryan, 928 F.2d 994, 1006 (11th Cir. 1991); *Franklin Federal Sav. Bank v. Director, Office of Thrift Supervision*, 927 F.2d 1332, 1341 (6th Cir.), *cert. denied*, 502 U.S. 937 (1991). *Cf. Resolution Trust Corp. v. FSLIC*, 25 F.3d 1493, 1502 (10th Cir. 1994) (observing that Congress gave OTS authority to exempt thrifts until 1991); *Charter Federal Sav. Bank v. Office of Thrift Supervision*, 976 F.2d 203, 210 (4th Cir. 1992) (*dicta*) (accepting view of other circuits), *cert. denied*, 507 U.S. 1004 (1993).

8.50. *FIRREA and the response to the S&L crisis.* Largely in response to the S&L disaster, FIRREA significantly realigned the structure of regulation as it applies to troubled and failing institutions. Consider in that regard the following excerpts.

Michael P. Malloy, Nothing to Fear but FIRREA Itself: Revising and Reshaping the Enforcement Process of Federal Bank Regulation

50 Ohio St. L. J. 1117, 1134-39 (1989)[a]

. . . [T]o wrap up the affairs of the FSLIC, an FSLIC Resolution Fund has been established, to be managed and separately maintained by the FDIC, consisting of assets and liabilities transferred from the FSLIC.[1] The FSLIC Resolution Fund is to be dissolved upon the satisfaction of all debts and liabilities and sale of all assets.[2]

The FDIC's powers as conservator or receiver have also been expanded and include appointment as receiver for any insured depository institution.[3] Likewise, provisions concerning the use of FDIC funds with respect to insured banks closed or in danger of closing have been correspondingly amended to cover the authority of the FDIC to respond to the problem of insured depository institutions in default.[4]

Certainly the most dramatic indications of structural realignment will be seen in the immediate abolition of the FSLIC[5] and, effective 60 days after the enactment of the FIRREA, the abolition of the FHLBB and the position of Chairman of the FHLBB.[6] In addition, the Home Owners' Loan Act (HOLA) has been completely revised by the FIRREA.[7] An Office

---

a. Footnotes have been renumbered in this excerpt.

1. [FIRREA] § 215 (codified at 12 U.S.C. § 1821a).

2. *Id.* (codified at 12 U.S.C. § 1821a(f)).

3. *See id.* §§ 212 (codified at 12 U.S.C. § 1821(c)-(*l*)) (appointment of FDIC as conservator or receiver), 216 (codified at 12 U.S.C. § 1822) (FDIC as receiver).

4. *See id.* § 217(3)-(8) (codified at 12 U.S.C. § 1823(c)-(f), (i), (k)).

5. *Id.* § 401(a)(1). *But see id.* §§ 401(b) (disposition and winding up of affairs of the FSLIC and FHLBB), (c) (transitional authority and status of FHLBB Chairman), (d) (status of employees), (e) (continuation of services), (f) (savings provisions relating to FSLIC), (h)-(i) (continuation of orders, resolutions, determinations and regulations of FSLIC and FHLBB), 402(a)-(b) (continuation and coordination of certain regulations).

6. *Id.* § 401(a)(2). *But see id.* §§ 401(b) (disposition and winding up of affairs of the FSLIC and FHLBB), (c) (transitional authority and status of FHLBB Chairman), (e) (continuation of services), (g) (savings provisions relating to FHLBB), (h)-(i) (continuation of orders, resolutions, determinations and regulations of FSLIC and FHLBB), 402(a)-(b) (continuation and coordination of certain regulations).

7. *See id.* § 301 (amending the Home Owners Loan Act, 12 U.S.C. §§ 1461 *et seq.*) (hereinafter HOLA).

of Thrift Supervision has been established within the Treasury Department,[8] and the DOTS[9] effectively replaces the FHLBB and the Chairman of the FHLBB,[10] except to the extent that any powers of the FHLBB or the Chairman have been transferred to other agencies.[11] . . .

The DOTS is now included in the FDIA definition as the "appropriate Federal banking agency" with respect to any savings association or any savings and loan holding company (SLHC).[12] . . .

The DOTS is also given exclusive power and jurisdiction to appoint a conservator or receiver for a federally chartered savings association,[13] and the DOTS has authority to promulgate regulations for the reorganization, consolidation, liquidation and dissolution of savings associations, for mergers between insured savings associations, and for savings associations in conservatorship or receivership and the conduct thereof.[14] In addition, under statutorily specified grounds, the DOTS has the power and jurisdiction to appoint a conservator or receiver for an insured state-chartered savings association.[15] . . .

[T]he FDIC has authority, by regulation or order, to determine that any specific activity poses a serious threat to the SAIF and to order that no SAIF member engage directly in any such activity.[16] This provision does not limit the authority of the DOTS to issue safety and soundness regulations generally, or to enforce compliance with other laws as applicable.[17] . . .

To "resolve" all cases involving FSLIC-insured institutions placed in conservatorship or receivership between January 1, 1989, and the date of enactment of the FIRREA, or to be so placed within the three-year period following that enactment, three new regulatory entities have been created. The Resolution Trust Corporation (RTC) has been established[18] for the express purpose, inter alia, of managing and resolving such cases.[19] The RTC is under the exclusive management of the FDIC.[20]

In addition, the FIRREA has established the Oversight Board[21] to oversee and be

---

8. HOLA § 3(a).

9. *See id.* § 3(b) (establishment of position of the DOTS).

10. *Id.* § 3(e)(1).

11. *Id.* § 3(e)(2).

12. FIRREA § 204(f)(4) (codified at 12 U.S.C. § 1813(q)(4)).

13. *Id.* § 5(d)(2)(E). On the grounds for appointment of a conservator or receiver for a federally chartered savings association, see *id.* § 5(d)(2)(A) (mandatory grounds), 5(d)(2)(B) (additional grounds; consent of the association, or removal from membership in a federal home loan bank or from status as insured institution).

14. *Id.* § 5(d)(3)(A). In cases where the FDIC or the RTC is the conservator or receiver, DOTS regulations must be consistent with regulations prescribed by the FDIC. *Id.* § 5(d)(3)(B). ...

15. HOLA § 5(d)(2)(C). Written approval of the state official with jurisdiction over the insured association, indicating that one or more of the statutory grounds exists, is generally necessary for the exercise of this authority by the DOTS. *Id.* § 5(d)(2)(D)(i). *But cf. id.* § 5(d)(2)(D)(ii) (authority of DOTS to proceed with appointment under certain circumstances).

16. *Id.* § 221(4) (codified at 12 U.S.C. § 1828(m) (3)(A)). *See also id.* (codified at 12 U.S.C. § 1828(m)(3)(C)) (additional authority of FDIC; serious risks to SAIF and BIF).

17. *See id.* § 221(4) (codified at 12 U.S.C. § 1828(m)(3)(B)).

18. *Id.* § 501(a) (codified at 12 U.S.C. § 1441a(b)(1)).

19. *Id.* (codified at 12 U.S.C. § 1441a(b)(3)).

20. *Id.* (codified at 12 U.S.C. § 1441a(b)(1)(C)).

21. *Id.* (codified at 12 U.S.C. § 1441a(a)(1)).

accountable for the RTC.[22] . . . While the FDIC has management responsibility for the RTC, the Oversight Board has the responsibility, inter alia, to develop and establish overall strategies, policies and goals of the RTC's activities, in consultation with the RTC,[23] to approve, prior to their implementation, periodic financing request developed by the RTC,[24] and to authorize the use of proceeds from funds provided by the Treasury Department and from any financing by the newly created Resolution Funding Corporation (REFCO) and to oversee collection of funds by the REFCO.[25]

Finally, the FIRREA has established the REFCO,[26] as the mechanism for providing funds to the RTC. REFCO will issue nonvoting capital stock to the federal home loan banks[27] as well as debt obligations,[28] and purchase capital certificates issued by the RTC[29] and in addition transfer statutorily specified amounts to the RTC.[30]

United States v. Winstar Corporation

518 U.S. 839 (1996)

Justice SOUTER announced the judgment of the Court and delivered an opinion, in which Justice STEVENS and Justice BREYER join, and in which Justice O'CONNOR joins except as to Parts IV-A and IV-B.

I

* * *

C

* * *

FIRREA made enormous changes in the structure of federal thrift regulation by (1) abolishing FSLIC and transferring its functions to other agencies; (2) creating a new thrift deposit insurance fund under the Federal Deposit Insurance Corporation (FDIC); (3) replacing the Bank Board with the Office of Thrift Supervision (OTS), a Treasury Department office with responsibility for the regulation of all federally insured savings associations; and (4) establishing the Resolution Trust Corporation (RTC) to liquidate or otherwise dispose of certain closed thrifts and their assets. *See* note following 12 U.S.C. § 1437, §§ 1441a, 1821. More importantly for the present case, FIRREA also obligated OTS to "prescribe and maintain uniformly applicable capital standards for savings associations" in accord with strict statutory requirements. 12 U.S.C. § 1464(t)(1)(A). In particular, the statute required thrifts to "maintain core capital in an amount not less than 3 percent of the savings association's total assets," 12 U.S.C. § 1464(t)(2)(A), and defined "core capital" to exclude "unidentifiable intangible assets," 12 U.S.C. § 1464(t)(9)(A), such as goodwill. Although the reform

---

22. *Id.* (codified at 12 U.S.C. § 1441a(a)(2)).

23. *Id.* (codified at 12 U.S.C. § 1441a(a)(6)(A)).

24. *Id.* (codified at 12 U.S.C. § 1441a(a)(6)(B)).

25. *Id.* (codified at 12 U.S.C. § 1441a(a)(6)(G).

26. *Id.* § 511(a) (codified at 12 U.S.C. § 1441b(b)).

27. *See id.* (codified at 12 U.S.C. § 1441b(d)(1)). *See also id.* (codified at 12 U.S.C. § 1441b(e)) (capitalization of REFCO).

28. *Id.* (codified at 12 U.S.C. § 1441b(d)(3)). *See also id.* (codified at 12 U.S.C. § 1441b(f)) (obligations of the REFCO).

29. *Id.* (codified at 12 U.S.C. § 1441b(d)(2)).

30. *See id.* (codified at 12 U.S.C. § 1441b(d)(2), (e)(8)).

provided a "transition rule" permitting thrifts to count "qualifying supervisory goodwill" toward half the core capital requirement, this allowance was phased out by 1995. 12 U.S.C. § 1464(t)(3)(A). According to the House Report, these tougher capital requirements reflected a congressional judgment that "[t]o a considerable extent, the size of the thrift crisis resulted from the utilization of capital gimmicks that masked the inadequate capitalization of thrifts." . . .

The impact of FIRREA's new capital requirements upon institutions that had acquired failed thrifts in exchange for supervisory goodwill was swift and severe. OTS promptly issued regulations implementing the new capital standards along with a bulletin noting that FIRREA "eliminates [capital and accounting] forbearances" previously granted to certain thrifts. . . . OTS accordingly directed that "[a]ll savings associations presently operating with these forbearances . . . should eliminate them in determining whether or not they comply with the new minimum regulatory capital standards." . . . Despite the statute's limited exception intended to moderate transitional pains, many institutions immediately fell out of compliance with regulatory capital requirements, making them subject to seizure by thrift regulators. . . .

Notes and Comments 8.51. In the post-FIRREA world of failing savings associations, both the FDIC and the OTS have roles to play. Among other things, the DOTS now has the full range of enforcement authority under section 8 of the FDIA. *See* 12 U.S.C. §§ 1464(d)(1)(A), 1813(q)(4), 1818. Does this make any material difference to the DOTS's authority, as compared with that of the predecessor agencies, the Federal Home Bank Board and the Federal Savings and Loan Insurance Corporation?

8.52. What authority does the DOTS have with respect to conservatorship and receivership of failing federal savings associations? *See* 12 U.S.C. § 1464(d)(2)(A)-(B), (3)(E)-(I). What authority does the FDIC have in this regard? *See id.* §§ 1821(c)(2), (6)(A)-(B), 1822.

8.53. What authority does the DOTS have with respect to conservatorship and receivership of failing state-chartered savings associations? *See* 12 U.S.C. § 1464(d)(2)(C)-(D), (F)-(I), (3). How does this compare with its authority with respect to failing federal savings associations? What authority does the FDIC have with respect to state-chartered savings associations? *See, e.g., id.* § 1821(c)(3).

8.54. Under what circumstances could the FDIC terminate the deposit insurance of a troubled or failing savings association? *See* 12 U.S.C. § 1818(a)(2).

8.55. Assume that Twentififth State Savings Association is in danger of closing because of an accumulation of bad loans and poor investments that may have impaired its ability to pay depositors in the near future. What assistance, if any, could the FDIC offer Twentififth, in order to aid it in avoiding failure? *See* 12 U.S.C. § 1823(c).

8.56. Could the FDIC purchase net worth certificates issued by Twentififth in order to assist its capital position and allow it to continue to meet its current obligations? *See* 12 U.S.C. § 1823(i).

8.57. Forth Corp, a bank holding company located in a neighboring state, has expressed an interest in acquiring Twentififth as a subsidiary, and possibly merging it into QNB. Under what circumstances could the FDIC authorize this acquisition? *See* 12 U.S.C. § 1823(f), (k). Would the Federal Reserve permit the acquisition of Twentififth as a subsidiary of Forth Corp? *See id.* § 1843(i).

8.58. Would it make any difference to your answer to the previous question if it appeared that Twentififth was in immediate danger of failing, absent a swift takeover by a financially strong acquirer? *See* 12 U.S.C. § 1823(k).

8.59. *Judicial limits on the FIRREA reforms.* The *Winstar* litigation has indicated that there are some significant limits on the reforms established by FIRREA, particularly as to their retroactive application to depository institutions already in danger of default or in default at the time FIRREA was enacted. To what extent does *Winstar* frustrate the legislative objectives of FIRREA? Consider the following excerpt from the case.

United States v. Winstar Corporation

518 U.S. 839 (1996)

Justice SOUTER announced the judgment of the Court and delivered an opinion, in which Justice STEVENS and Justice BREYER join, and in which Justice O'CONNOR joins except as to Parts IV-A and IV-B.

The issue in this case is the enforceability of contracts between the Government and participants in a regulated industry, to accord them particular regulatory treatment in exchange for their assumption of liabilities that threatened to produce claims against the Government as insurer. Although Congress subsequently changed the relevant law, and thereby barred the Government from specifically honoring its agreements, we hold that the terms assigning the risk of regulatory change to the Government are enforceable, and that the Government is therefore liable in damages for breach.

I

* * *

D

. . . Respondents Glendale Federal Bank, FSB, Winstar Corporation, and The Statesman Group, Inc. acquired failed thrifts in 1981, 1984, and 1988, respectively. After the passage of FIRREA, federal regulators seized and liquidated the Winstar and Statesman thrifts for failure to meet the new capital requirements. Although the Glendale thrift also fell out of regulatory capital compliance as a result of the new rules, it managed to avoid seizure through a massive private recapitalization. Believing that the Bank Board and FSLIC had promised them that the supervisory goodwill created in their merger transactions could be counted toward regulatory capital requirements, respondents each filed suit against the United States in the Court of Federal Claims, seeking monetary damages on both contractual and constitutional theories. . . .

[The Court of Federal Claims granted the plaintiffs' motions for partial summary judgment on contract liability. On interlocutory appeal, a divided panel of the Federal Circuit reversed, but the Federal Circuit *en banc* reversed the panel decision and affirmed the Court of Federal Claims' rulings on liability.]

II

[Justice Souter would not consider the "anterior question of whether there were contracts at all between the Government and respondents dealing with regulatory treatment of supervisory goodwill and capital credits," because the Court "ordinarily does not consider questions outside those presented in the petition for certiorari," *citing* Sup. Ct. Rule 14.1 (a).]

* * *

A

[Justice Souter then reviewed "the relevant circumstances and documents" of each of the three transactions before the Court, "although each of these transactions was fundamentally similar" to the others.

[As to each transaction, Justice Souter accepted "the Federal Circuit's conclusion that 'the government was contractually obligated to recognize the capital credits and the supervisory goodwill generated by the merger as part of the Statesman's regulatory capital requirement and to permit such goodwill to be amortized on a straight line basis over 25 years.'"]

* * *

B

[Viewing the matter before the Court essentially as an issue of contract law, Justice Souter then took the position that the Government's contractual undertaking to recognize the supervisory goodwill and the amortization periods should be treated "as a promise to insure the promisee against loss arising from the promised condition's nonoccurrence."]

When the law as to capital requirements changed in the present instance, the Government was unable to perform its promise and, therefore, became liable for breach. We accept the Federal Circuit's conclusion that the Government breached these contracts when, pursuant to the new regulatory capital requirements imposed by FIRREA, 12 U.S.C. § 1464(t), the federal regulatory agencies limited the use of supervisory goodwill and capital credits in calculating respondents' net worth. . . .

III

The Government argues for reversal, first, on the principle that "contracts that limit the government's future exercises of regulatory authority are strongly disfavored; such contracts will be recognized only rarely, and then only when the limitation on future regulatory authority is expressed in unmistakable terms." . . . Hence, the Government says, the agreements between the Bank Board, FSLIC, and respondents should not be construed to waive Congress's authority to enact a subsequent bar to using supervisory goodwill and capital credits to meet regulatory capital requirements.

The argument mistakes the scope of the unmistakability doctrine. The thrifts do not claim that the Bank Board and FSLIC purported to bind Congress to ossify the law in conformity to the contracts; they seek no injunction against application of FIRREA's new capital requirements to them and no exemption from FIRREA's terms. They simply claim that the Government assumed the risk that subsequent changes in the law might prevent it from performing, and agreed to pay damages in the event that such failure to perform caused financial injury. The question, then, is not whether Congress could be constrained but whether the doctrine of unmistakability is applicable to any contract claim against the Government for breach occasioned by a subsequent act of Congress. The answer to this question is no.

A

. . . The impetus for the modern unmistakability doctrine was . . . Chief Justice Marshall's application of the Contract Clause to public contracts [in *Fletcher v. Peck*, 6 Cranch 87, 3 L.Ed. 162 (1810)]. Although that Clause made it possible for state legislatures to bind their successors by entering into contracts, it soon became apparent that such contracts could become a threat to the sovereign responsibilities of state governments. Later decisions were accordingly less willing to recognize contractual restraints upon legislative freedom of action, and two distinct limitations developed to protect state regulatory powers. One came to be known as the "reserved powers" doctrine, which held that certain substantive powers of sovereignty could not be contracted away. . . . The other . . . was a canon of construction disfavoring implied governmental obligations in public contracts. Under this rule that "[a]ll public grants are strictly construed," . . . we have insisted that "[n]othing can be taken against the state by presumption or inference," . . . and that "neither the right of taxation, nor any other power of sovereignty, will be held . . . to have been surrendered, unless such surrender has been expressed in terms too plain to be mistaken." . . .

The posture of the Government in these early unmistakability cases is important. In each, a state or local government entity had made a contract granting a private party some concession (such as a tax exemption or a monopoly), and a subsequent governmental action had abrogated the contractual commitment. In each case, the private party was suing to invalidate the abrogating legislation under the Contract Clause. A requirement that the government's obligation unmistakably appear thus served the dual purposes of limiting contractual incursions on a State's sovereign powers and of avoiding difficult constitutional questions about the extent of State authority to limit the subsequent exercise of legislative power. . . .

The same function of constitutional avoidance has marked the expansion of the unmistakability doctrine from its Contract Clause origins dealing with state grants and contracts to those of other governmental sovereigns, including the United States. . . . Although the Contract Clause has no application to acts of the United States, it is clear that the National Government has some capacity to make agreements binding future Congresses by creating vested rights. . . . The extent of that capacity, to be sure, remains somewhat obscure. . . .

[The] collective holding [of the precedents] is that a contract with a sovereign government will not be read to include an unstated term exempting the other contracting party from the application of a subsequent sovereign act (including an act of Congress), nor will an ambiguous term of a grant or contract be construed as a conveyance or surrender of sovereign power. The cases extending back into the 19th-century thus stand for a rule that applies when the Government is subject either to a claim that its contract has surrendered a sovereign power (e.g., to tax or control navigation), or to a claim that cannot be recognized without creating an exemption from the exercise of such a power (e.g., the equivalent of exemption from social security obligations). The application of the doctrine thus turns on whether enforcement of the contractual obligation alleged would block the exercise of a sovereign power of the Government.

Since the criterion looks to the effect of a contract's enforcement, the particular remedy sought is not dispositive and the doctrine is not rendered inapplicable by a request for damages, as distinct from specific performance. . . .

The Government argues that enforcement of the contracts in this case would implicate the unmistakability principle. . . . The Government's position is mistaken, however, for the complementary reasons that the contracts have not been construed as binding the Government's exercise of authority to modify banking regulation or of any other sovereign power, and there has been no demonstration that awarding damages for breach would be tantamount to any such limitation.

. . . The contracts have been read as solely risk-shifting agreements and respondents seek nothing more than the benefit of promises by the Government to insure them against any losses arising from future regulatory change. They seek no injunction against application of the law to them, . . . and they acknowledge that the Bank Board and FSLIC could not bind Congress (and possibly could not even bind their future selves) not to change regulatory policy.

Nor do the damages respondents seek amount to exemption from the new law. ... Once general jurisdiction to make an award against the Government is conceded, a requirement to pay money supposes no surrender of sovereign power by a sovereign with the power to contract. . . . Even if the respondents were asking that the Government be required to make up any capital deficiency arising from the exclusion of goodwill and capital credits from the relevant calculations, such relief would hardly amount to an exemption from the capital requirements of FIRREA. . . .

We recognize, of course, that while agreements to insure private parties against the costs of subsequent regulatory change do not directly impede the exercise of sovereign power, they may indirectly deter needed governmental regulation by raising its costs. But all regulations have their costs, and Congress itself expressed a willingness to bear the costs at issue here when it authorized FSLIC to "guarantee [acquiring thrifts] against loss" that might occur as a result of a supervisory merger. 12 U.S.C. § 1729(f)(2) (1988 ed.) (repealed 1989). Just as we have long recognized that the Constitution "'bar[s] Government from forcing some people alone to bear public burdens which, in all fairness and justice, should be borne by the public as a whole,'" . . . so we must reject the suggestion that the Government may simply shift costs of legislation onto its contractual partners who are adversely affected by the change in the law, when the Government has assumed the risk of such change. . . .

. . . We accordingly hold that the Federal Circuit correctly refused to apply the unmistakability doctrine here. . . . There being no need for an unmistakably clear "second promise" not to change the capital requirements, it is sufficient that the Government undertook an obligation that it subsequently found itself unable to perform. This conclusion does not, of course, foreclose the assertion of a defense that the contracts were ultra vires or that the Government's obligation should be discharged under the common-law doctrine of impossibility, . . . but nothing in the nature of the contracts themselves raises a bar to respondents' claims for breach. . . .

B

The answer to the Government's unmistakability argument also meets its two related contentions on the score of ultra vires: that the Bank Board and FSLIC had no authority to bargain away Congress's power to change the law in the future, and that we should in any event find no such authority conferred without an express delegation to that effect. The first of these positions rests on the reserved powers doctrine, developed in the course of litigating claims that States had violated the Contract Clause. . . . It holds that a state government may not contract away "an essential attribute of its sovereignty." . . .

The Government says that "[t]he logic of the doctrine . . . applies equally to contracts alleged to have been made by the federal government." . . . This may be so but is also beside the point, for the reason that the Government's ability to set capital requirements is not limited by the Bank Board's and FSLIC's promises to make good any losses arising from subsequent regulatory changes. . . .

The same response answers the Government's demand for express delegation of any purported authority to fetter the exercise of sovereign power. . . .

There is no question, conversely, that the Bank Board and FSLIC had ample statutory authority to . . . promise to permit respondents to count supervisory goodwill and capital credits toward regulatory capital and to pay respondents' damages if that performance became impossible. The organic statute creating FSLIC as an arm of the Bank Board, 12 U.S.C. § 1725(c) (1988 ed.) (repealed 1989), generally empowered it "[t]o make contracts," and § 1729(f)(2), enacted in 1978, delegated more specific powers in the context of supervisory mergers:

> "Whenever an insured institution is in default or, in the judgment of the Corporation, is in danger of default, the [FSLIC] may, in order to facilitate a merger or consolidation of such insured institution with another insured institution ... guarantee such other insured institution against loss by reason of its merging or consolidating with or assuming the liabilities and purchasing the assets of such insured institution in or in danger of default."

12 U.S.C. § 1729(f)(2) (1976 ed. Supp. V) (repealed 1989). Nor is there any reason to suppose that the breadth of this authority was not meant to extend to contracts governing treatment of regulatory capital. Congress specifically recognized FSLIC's authority to permit thrifts to count goodwill toward capital requirements when it modified the National Housing

Act in 1987: "No provision of this section shall affect the authority of the [FSLIC] to authorize insured institutions to utilize subordinated debt and goodwill in meeting reserve and other regulatory requirements." 12 U.S.C. § 1730h(d) (1988 ed.) (repealed 1989). . . . There is no serious question that FSLIC (and the Bank Board acting through it) was authorized to make the contracts in issue.

IV

The Government's final line of defense is the sovereign acts doctrine, to the effect that "'[w]hatever acts the government may do, be they legislative or executive, so long as they be public and general, cannot be deemed specially to alter, modify, obstruct or violate the particular contracts into which it enters with private persons.'" . . . Because FIRREA's alteration of the regulatory capital requirements was a "public and general act," the Government says, that act could not amount to a breach of the Government's contract with respondents.

The Government's position cannot prevail, however, for two independent reasons. The facts of this case do not warrant application of the doctrine, and even if that were otherwise the doctrine would not suffice to excuse liability under this governmental contract allocating risks of regulatory change in a highly regulated industry. . . .

As an initial matter, we have already expressed our doubt that a workable line can be drawn between the Government's "regulatory" and "nonregulatory" capacities. In the present case, the Government chose to regulate capital reserves to protect FSLIC's insurance fund, much as any insurer might impose restrictions on an insured as a condition of the policy. The regulation thus protected the Government in its capacity analogous to a private insurer, the same capacity in which it entered into supervisory merger agreements to convert some of its financial insurance obligations into responsibilities of private entrepreneurs. In this respect, the supervisory mergers bear some analogy to private contracts for reinsurance. On the other hand, there is no question that thrift regulation is, in fact, regulation, and that both the supervisory mergers of the 1980's and the subsequent passage of FIRREA were meant to advance a broader public interest. The inescapable conclusion from all of this is that the Government's "regulatory" and "nonregulatory" capacities were fused in the instances under consideration, and we suspect that such fusion will be so common in the modern regulatory state as to leave a criterion of "regulation" without much use in defining the scope of the sovereign acts doctrine. . . .

An even more serious objection is that allowing the Government to avoid contractual liability merely by passing any "regulatory statute," would flaunt the general principle that, "[w]hen the United States enters into contract relations, its rights and duties therein are governed generally by the law applicable to contracts between private individuals." . . .

A

If the Government is to be treated like other contractors, some line has to be drawn in situations like the one before us between regulatory legislation that is relatively free of government self-interest and therefore cognizable for the purpose of a legal impossibility defense and, on the other hand, statutes tainted by a governmental object of self-relief. Such an object is not necessarily inconsistent with a public purpose, of course, and when we speak of governmental "self-interest," we simply mean to identify instances in which the Government seeks to shift the costs of meeting its legitimate public responsibilities to private parties. . . . Hence, while the Government might legitimately conclude that a given contractual commitment was no longer in the public interest, a government seeking relief from such commitments through legislation would obviously not be in a position comparable to that of the private contractor who willy-nilly was barred by law from performance. There would be, then, good reason in such circumstance to find the regulatory and contractual characters of the Government fused together, . . . so that the Government should not have the benefit of the defense. . . .

. . . Hence, governmental action will not be held against the Government for purposes of the impossibility defense so long as the action's impact upon public contracts is, as in Horowitz, merely incidental to the accomplishment of a broader governmental objective. . . . The greater the Government's self-interest, however, the more suspect becomes the claim that its private contracting partners ought to bear the financial burden of the Government's own improvidence, and where a substantial part of the impact of the Government's action rendering performance impossible falls on its own contractual obligations, the defense will be unavailable. . . .

B

In the present case, it is impossible to attribute the exculpatory "public and general" character to FIRREA. Although we have not been told the dollar value of the relief the Government would obtain if insulated from liability under contracts such as these, the attention given to the regulatory contracts prior to passage of FIRREA shows that a substantial effect on governmental contracts is certain. The statute not only had the purpose of eliminating the very accounting gimmicks that acquiring thrifts had been promised, but the specific object of abrogating enough of the acquisition contracts as to make that consequence of the legislation a focal point of the congressional debate. . . .

C

Even if FIRREA were to qualify as "public and general," however, other fundamental reasons would leave the sovereign acts doctrine inadequate to excuse the Government's breach of these contracts. . . . [T]hat defense simply relieves the Government as contractor from the traditional blanket rule that a contracting party may not obtain discharge if its own act rendered performance impossible. But even if the Government stands in the place of a private party with respect to "public and general" sovereign acts, it does not follow that discharge will always be available, for the common-law doctrine of impossibility imposes additional requirements before a party may avoid liability for breach. As the Restatement puts it,

> "[w]here, after a contract is made, a party's performance is made impracticable without his fault by the occurrence of an event the non-occurrence of which was a basic assumption on which the contract was made, his duty to render that performance is discharged, unless the language or the circumstances indicate the contrary."

Restatement (Second) of Contracts § 261. *See also* 2 Farnsworth on Contracts § 9.6, at 543-544 (listing four elements of the impossibility defense). Thus, since the object of the sovereign acts defense is to place the Government as contractor on par with a private contractor in the same circumstances, . . . the Government, like any other defending party in a contract action, must show that the passage of the statute rendering its performance impossible was an event contrary to the basic assumptions on which the parties agreed, and must ultimately show that the language or circumstances do not indicate that the Government should be liable in any case. While we do not say that these conditions can never be satisfied when the Government contracts with participants in a regulated industry for particular regulatory treatment, we find that the Government as such a contractor has not satisfied the conditions for discharge in the present case.

1

For a successful impossibility defense the Government would have to show that the nonoccurrence of regulatory amendment was a basic assumption of these contracts. . . . The premise of this requirement is that the parties will have bargained with respect to any risks that are both within their contemplation and central to the substance of the contract; as Justice Traynor said, "[i]f [the risk] was foreseeable there should have been provision for it in the contract, and the absence of such a provision gives rise to the inference that the risk was assumed." *Lloyd v. Murphy*, 25 Cal.2d 48, 54, 153 P.2d 47, 50 (1944). That inference is particularly compelling, where, as here, the contract provides for particular regulatory treatment (and, a fortiori, allocates the risk of regulatory change). Such an agreement reflects the inescapable recognition that regulated industries in the modern world do not live under the law of the Medes and the Persians, and the very fact that such a contract is made at all is at odds with any assumption of regulatory stasis. In this particular case, whether or not the reach of the FIRREA reforms was anticipated by the parties, there is no doubt that some changes in the regulatory structure governing thrift capital reserves were both foreseeable and likely when these parties contracted with the Government, as even the Government agrees. . . .

2

Finally, any governmental contract that not only deals with regulatory change but allocates the risk of its occurrence will, by definition, fail the further condition of a successful impossibility defense, for it will indeed indicate that the parties' agreement was not meant to be rendered nugatory by a change in the regulatory law. . . . The mere fact that the Government's contracting agencies (like the Bank Board and FSLIC) could not themselves preclude Congress from changing the regulatory rules does not, of course, stand in the way of concluding that those agencies assumed the risk of such change, for determining the consequences of legal change was the point of the agreements. It is, after all, not uncommon for a contracting party to assume the risk of an event he cannot control, even when that party is an agent of the Government. . . .

As to each of the contracts before us, our agreement with the conclusions of the Court of Federal Claims and the Federal Circuit forecloses any defense of legal impossibility, for those courts found that the Bank Board resolutions, Forbearance Letters, and other documents setting forth the accounting treatment to be accorded supervisory goodwill generated by the transactions were not mere statements of then-current regulatory policy, but in each instance were terms in an allocation of risk of regulatory change that was essential to the contract between the parties. . . .

We affirm the Federal Circuit's ruling that the United States is liable to respondents for breach of contract. Because the Court of Federal Claims has not yet determined the appropriate measure or amount of damages in this case, we remand for further proceedings consistent with our opinion. . . .

Justice BREYER, concurring.

I join the plurality opinion because, in my view, that opinion is basically consistent with the following understanding of what the dissent and the Government call the "unmistakability doctrine." The doctrine appears in the language of earlier cases, where the Court states that

> "sovereign power, even when unexercised, is an enduring presence that governs all contracts subject to the sovereign's jurisdiction, and *will remain intact unless surrendered in unmistakable terms*." *Merrion v. Jicarilla Apache Tribe*, 455 U.S. 130, 148 (1982) (emphasis added). . . .

Both common sense and precedent make clear that an "unmistakable" promise to bear the risk of a change in the law is not required in every circumstance in which a private party seeks contract damages from the Government. Imagine, for example, that the General Services Administration or the Department of Defense were to enter into a garden variety contract to sell a surplus commodity such as oil, under circumstances where (1) the time of shipment is critically important, (2) the parties are aware that pending environmental legislation could prevent the shipment, and (3) the fair inference from the circumstances is that if the environmental legislation occurs and prevents shipment, a private seller would incur liability for failure to ship on time.

Under ordinary principles of contract law, one would construe the contract in terms of the parties' intent, as revealed by language and circumstance. . . . If the language and circumstances showed that the parties intended the seller to bear the risk of a performance-defeating change in the law, the seller would have to pay damages. . . .

The Court has often said, as a general matter, that the "rights and duties" contained in a government contract "are governed generally by the law applicable to contracts between private individuals." . . .

The Court has also indicated that similar principles apply in certain cases where courts have had to determine whether or not a government seller is liable involving contracts resembling the ones before us. . . .

This approach is unsurprising, for in practical terms it ensures that the Government is able to obtain needed goods and services from parties who might otherwise, quite rightly, be unwilling to undertake the risk of government contracting. . . . This is not to say that the Government is always treated just like a private party. The simple fact that it is the Government may well change the underlying circumstances, leading to a different inference as to the parties' likely intent–say, making it far less likely that they intend to make a promise that will oblige the government to hold private parties harmless in the event of a change in the law. But to say this is to apply, not to disregard, the ordinary rule of contract law.

This approach is also consistent with congressional intent, as revealed in Congress' determination to permit, under the Tucker Act, awards of damages and other relief against the United States for "any claim . . . founded . . . upon any express or implied contract." 28 U.S.C. § 1491(a)(1). The thrifts invoked this provision in their complaints as the basis for jurisdiction to adjudicate their claims in the lower courts, . . . and, as the majority [*sic*] explains, . . . the lower courts held that each proved the existence of an express promise by the Government to grant them particular regulatory treatment for a period of years. For my purposes, the provision is relevant only to show that Congress clearly contemplated the award of damages for breach against the Government in some contexts where the Government's promises are far from "unmistakable" as the Government defines that term. ...

There are, moreover, at least two good reasons to think that the cases containing special language of "unmistakability" do not, as the Government suggests, impose an additional "clear-statement" rule, . . . that shields the Government from liability here. First, it is not clear that the "unmistakability" language was determinative of the outcome in those cases. In two of the three cases in which that language appears (and several of the older cases from which it is derived), the private parties claimed that the sovereign had effectively promised not to change the law in an area of law not mentioned in the contract at issue. ...

A second reason to doubt the Government's interpretation of the "unmistakability" language is that, in all these cases, the language was directed at the claim that the sovereign had made a broad promise not to legislate, or otherwise to exercise its sovereign powers. Even in the cases in which damages were sought . . . the Court treated the claimed promise as a promise not to change the law, rather than as the kind of promise more normally at issue in contract cases, including this one–namely, a promise that obliges the government to hold a party harmless from a change in the law that the government remains free to make. . . . It is difficult to believe that the Court intended its "unmistakability" language in these unusual cases to disable future courts from inferring, from language and circumstance under ordinary contract principles, a more narrow promise in more typical cases–say, a promise not to abrogate, or to restrict severely through legislation and without compensation, the very right that a sovereign explicitly granted by contract. . . .

The Government attempts to answer this objection to its reading of the "unmistakability" language by arguing that any award of "substantial damages" against the government for breach of contract through a change in the law "unquestionably carries the danger that needed future regulatory action will be deterred," and thus amounts to an infringement on sovereignty requiring an "unmistakable" promise. . . . But this rationale has no logical stopping point. . . . It is difficult to see how the Court could, in a principled fashion, apply the Government's rule in this case without also making it applicable to the ordinary contract case . . . which, for the reasons explained above, are properly governed by ordinary principles of contract law. To draw the line–i.e., to apply a more stringent rule of contract interpretation–based only on the amount of money at stake, and therefore (in the Government's terms) the degree to which future exercises of sovereign authority may be deterred, seems unsatisfactory. . . .

The Government attempts to show that . . . special circumstances, warranting application of an unmistakability principle, are present in this case. To be sure, it might seem unlikely, in the abstract, that the Government would have intended to make a binding promise that would oblige it to hold the thrifts harmless from the effects of future regulation (or legislation) in such a high- risk, highly regulated context as the accounting practices of failing savings and loans. But, as the plurality's careful examination of the circumstances reveals, that is exactly what the Government did. The thrifts demonstrate that specific promises were made to accord them particular regulatory treatment for a period of years, which, when abrogated by subsequent legislation, rendered the Government liable for breach of contract. These promises affect only those thrifts with pre-existing contracts of a certain kind. They are promises that the banks [*sic*] seek to infer from the explicit language of the contracts, not ones they read into contracts silent on the matter. And, there is no special policy reason related to sovereignty which would justify applying an "unmistakability" principle here. For these reasons, I join the plurality opinion.

Notes and Comments 8.60. Justice Souter's opinion refuses to address the question whether these supervisory merger agreements were contracts. Would it make a difference to the case if they were *not* contracts? Assume that the LossStar Corporation owns DrawStar Federal Savings Association, which has insufficient capital and surplus. LossStar, DrawStar, and the OTS enter into a formal agreement,[39] under which the parties agree to a eighteen-month plan for LossStar to recapitalize DrawStar. Six months later, new federal legislation is enacted requiring the FDIC to revoke the insurance of any depository institution that does not have adequate capital within six months. Does LossStar have a viable cause of action in contract against the OTS?

8.61. In the LossStar litigation, would it make a difference whether LossStar was suing for injunctive relief or damages?

8.62. Does it make a difference if the new legislation is characterized as "regulatory"? Does that give the legislation a "public" character that would insulate it from a *Winstar* cause of action?

8.63. The legislation did not identify or refer to LossStar or DrawStar. Does that fact give the legislation a "public" character that would insulate it from a *Winstar* cause of action?

39. Pursuant to 12 U.S.C. § 1818(b)(1).

Justice Souter responded to a similar argument in the following terms:

> Nor is Congress's own judgment neutralized by the fact, emphasized by the Government, that FIRREA did not formally target particular transactions. Legislation can almost always be written in a formally general way, and the want of an identified target is not much security when a measure's impact nonetheless falls substantially upon the Government's contracting partners.

Winstar, 518 U.S. at 902-903.

8.64. Winstar *and contract analysis*. Would it make any difference in a *Winstar*-related case if the issue of the status of the supervisory agreements as contracts were actually put in question? How far could traditional contract analysis affect the outcome in such a case? Consider the following cases in answering these questions.

Admiral Financial Corp. v. United States

378 F.3d 1336 (Fed. Cir. 2004)

BRYSON, Circuit Judge.

[Admiral Financial, a holding company that owned a thrift created through a supervisory merger, brought suit against the United States alleging that enactment of the FIRREA breached the government's contractual promise that supervisory goodwill could be counted toward regulatory capital requirements. After initially finding that FIRREA and its implementing regulations breached the contract, the Court of Federal Claims entered judgment for the Government, holding that prior to any breach by the Government, Admiral Financial anticipatorily breached the contract. The court also held that, even if Admiral Financial did not anticipatorily breach the contract, Admiral Financial could not recover because it was not harmed by the Government's breach. Admiral Financial appealed.]

This is a *Winstar*-related breach of contract case. *See United States v. Winstar Corp.,* 518 U.S. 839 (1996). . . . For the reasons set forth below, we affirm.

I . . .

In February 1987, William Lee Popham contacted the Federal Home Loan Bank Board ("Bank Board") to discuss acquiring a failing savings and loan institution, or "thrift." In exchange for acquiring ownership, Mr. Popham offered to contribute assets to the thrift. ... The Bank Board suggested Haven Federal Savings & Loan as a candidate for acquisition. In April 1987, Mr. Popham formed Admiral Financial Corp. for the purpose of acquiring Haven. In August 1987, Admiral and Haven entered into an acquisition agreement under which Admiral agreed to contribute $6.4 million in real estate and cash in order to bring Haven into compliance with the Bank Board's minimum capital requirements. The agreement was conditioned on the Bank Board's giving Admiral certain forbearances in connection with the regulatory oversight of Haven.

In September 1987, Admiral applied for Bank Board approval of its merger with Haven. After several iterations, the Bank Board deemed the application complete in February of 1988. The Bank Board issued a resolution in April 1988 formally approving the merger. The resolution incorporated a business plan under which Admiral agreed to liquidate . . . contributed real estate according to a schedule. The resolution also contemplated that the Bank Board would treat Haven's negative net worth as "goodwill," an asset, rather than as a liability. Haven initially recorded nearly $9 million of goodwill based on its negative net worth. In May 1988, additional terms were incorporated by letter into the resolution, including the Bank Board's agreement to allow the goodwill to be amortized over a period of 25 years using the straight-line method of depreciation.

In June 1988, the Bank Board and Admiral executed a Regulatory Capital Maintenance/Dividend Agreement ("RCMA"). The RCMA bound Admiral to maintain a certain level of capital in Haven, and it obligated Admiral to make up any capital shortfall. The agreement provided that if Haven's capital fell below the level specified in the RCMA, Admiral would have 90 days to infuse enough capital into Haven to make up the shortfall. If Admiral failed to make up the shortfall, it would be in default.

Things did not go well for Haven after its acquisition by Admiral. In March 1989, Haven sold a portion of the contributed real estate at substantially below the appraised value that had been accepted by the Bank Board. In addition, the equity interest in a business that Admiral had contributed to Haven and had valued at $4.1 million turned out to be valueless. By the end of March 1989, Haven was out of regulatory capital compliance by approximately $580,000. Pursuant to the RCMA, Admiral was obligated within 90 days to infuse enough capital into Haven to make up the shortfall. Admiral did not do so. Instead, Haven's financial condition further deteriorated, resulting in a shortfall of approximately $2.3 million by June 1989. On July 17, 1989, the Bank Board provided Admiral with an official notice of default.

According to the RCMA, Admiral was entitled to 90 days from the date of the default notice to cure the default. On August 2, 1989, the Bank Board removed Mr. Popham from his role as Haven's executive vice president and chief financial officer, but allowed him to remain a member of the Haven board of directors at no compensation. On August 9, 1989, nearly a month into the 90-day cure period, Congress enacted the Financial Institutions Reform, Recovery, and Enforcement Act, Pub.L. No. 101-73, 103 Stat. 183 (1989) ("FIRREA"), which limited Admiral's ability to count Haven's goodwill as an asset and to amortize it over a lengthy time period. FIRREA, however, did not take effect until December 7, 1989, and as of September 30, 1989, Haven was more than $4 million out of compliance under the pre-FIRREA accounting methods.

In March 1990, the Office of Thrift Supervision ("OTS"), the Bank Board's successor under FIRREA, placed Haven in receivership. At that time, Haven was more than $22 million out of regulatory capital compliance under FIRREA. It was approximately $12 million out of compliance under pre-FIRREA accounting methods. . . .

II

The government argues that by the terms of its contract Admiral assumed the risk of the regulatory changes brought about by FIRREA and that the enactment of FIRREA therefore did not breach the government's contractual obligations. The government did not prevail on that argument in the trial court, but it advances the argument here as an alternative ground for affirmance.

In a section entitled "Miscellaneous Provisions," the RCMA included clause VI(D), which provided as follows:

> All references to regulations of the Board or the FSLIC used in this Agreement shall include any successor regulation thereto, it being expressly understood that subsequent amendments to such regulations may be made and that such amendments may increase or decrease the Acquirors' obligation under this Agreement.

On its face, clause VI(D) contemplated that the government might alter the regulations governing the supervision of thrifts such as Haven; by agreeing to the clause, Admiral acknowledged that its obligations might change if the regulatory regime changed.

In *Guaranty Financial Services, Inc. v. Ryan,* 928 F.2d 994, 999 (11th Cir.1991), the Eleventh Circuit found that an identical clause in the RCMA at issue in that case shifted to the acquirer the risk of a regulatory change of the kind effected by FIRREA and the regulations promulgated pursuant to FIRREA. The court explained that the clause "unmistakably warn[ed] Guaranty that its obligations under the contract may be increased by subsequent regulation." *Id.* The court held that "the agencies, at the same time they made that promise [of regulatory forbearances], also unambiguously warned Guaranty that the rules might later change to Guaranty's detriment," and that "[b]y signing the contract, Guaranty took that chance, in effect wagering the chance that the rules would be changed against the potential return if they were not ." *Id.* The court's analysis in *Guaranty,* if applied in this case, would lead to the conclusion that Admiral assumed the risk of a regulatory change such as the one brought about by FIRREA, and that the enactment of FIRREA and the promulgation of regulations pursuant to that statute did not constitute a breach of the government's contractual obligations. . . .

. . . [This court's decision] in *Castle* [*v. United States,* 301 F.3d 1328 (Fed.Cir. 2002),] addressed a takings claim made by a party that acquired a thrift with a promise of regulatory forbearances similar to those at issue in this case. 301 F.3d at 1341-42. The acquirer alleged that the enactment of FIRREA constituted a taking of its contract with the government. *Id.* at 1341. The court in *Castle* disagreed and ruled that "[t]he breach-of-contract based takings claim fails because even assuming it was breached, the alleged contract did not create a reasonable expectation that the government would cease regulating the thrift industry, or any particular thrift therein." *Id.* at 1342. To support the conclusion that regulatory changes were common in the banking industry, the court referred to a clause in the contract similar to clause VI(D) in this case. *Id.* The court then held that the government was not liable for a taking of the acquirer's contract because the enactment of FIRREA had not deprived the plaintiffs of any remedy they previously had, including a cause of action for damages. *Id.* . . .

. . . Clause VI(D) does not contain any qualifications of the sort to which the trial court referred. The clause states that the government might make changes to the regulations that could increase Admiral's obligation under the contract. It does not limit those changes to increasing or decreasing the level of capital that thrifts must maintain, as opposed to changing the accounting methods the Bank Board requires. And as for the trial court's concern that the government's interpretation of the clause would render the contract illusory, the government's reservation of the right to change the extent of its performance as to some of its promises does not render the contract illusory as long as the government has otherwise given consideration, as is plainly the case here. *Restatement (Second) of Contracts* § 80(2) (1979) ("The fact that part of what is bargained for would not have been consideration if that part alone had been bargained for does not prevent the whole from being consideration.").

The trial court relied on *Sterling Savings v. United States,* 53 Fed. Cl. 599 (2002), and *Southern California Federal Savings & Loan Ass'n v. United States,* 52 Fed. Cl. 531 (2002), as support for the proposition that the purported risk-shifting clause should not be interpreted to shift the risk of regulatory change from the government to the private party. *Admiral I,* 54 Fed. Cl. at 257. The contract at issue in *Sterling* included language similar to the language of clause VI(D) in Admiral's contract. The *Sterling* court read *Guaranty* as not holding that the purported risk-shifting clause mandated that the risk of regulatory change was shifted to the plaintiffs. Instead, the court in *Sterling* ruled that the risk-shifting clause meant that the acquirer could be required to comply with regulations regarding maintenance of capital levels, payment of dividends, and reporting of deviations from the business plan, but that the clause did not alter the government's obligation to allow the plaintiff to treat supervisory goodwill as an asset and amortize it over the period set forth in the contract. 53 Fed. Cl. at 614.

We do not believe *Guaranty* can be distinguished in that manner. The court in *Guaranty* found that the language in question altered the government's obligations with respect to the regulatory capital and amortization issues and shifted to Guaranty the risk of FIRREA's regulatory change with respect to those issues. The *Guaranty* court "interpret[ed] the contract to mean that Guaranty had the right to treat its goodwill as regulatory capital and amortize it over a twenty-five year period for so long as the statutes and regulations governing the area remained as they were when the agreement was signed." *Guaranty,* 928 F.2d at 1001.

In the other case on which the trial court relied, *Southern California Federal Savings & Loan Ass'n v. United States,* the language of the purported risk-shifting clause was significantly different from the language of the clause at issue here. The clause at issue in *Southern California* merely stated that the acquirer was obligated to maintain capital in compliance with existing or future regulations. 52 Fed. Cl. at 545. The court in *Southern California* held that, while the clause at issue in that case bound the acquirer to follow the regulations, it did not preclude a finding of breach by the government if the regulations changed. *Id.* at 545-56. Thus, the provision stated the obvious--that the acquirer was bound by the law--without providing for any shift of risk in the event of a change in the law.

Language similar to that in the *Southern California* contract was included in the contract at issue in *California Federal Bank v. United States,* 39 Fed. Cl. 753, 778 (1997). The court in *California Federal Bank,* like the court in the *Southern California* case, held that the contract language before it was sufficiently similar to the contract language at issue in *United States v. Winstar Corp.,* 518 U.S. 839 (1996), to be governed by the Supreme Court's conclusion that such language does not shift the risk of regulatory change to the acquirer. 39 Fed. Cl. at 779. The language of clause VI(D), on the other hand, is far more explicit with respect to the issue of regulatory change and makes clear that Admiral's obligations may increase or decrease under successor regulations.

The plurality opinion in *Winstar* addressed contract language similar to the language of the contracts in *Southern California* and *California Federal Bank* as follows:

> The Government also cites a provision requiring Statesman to "comply in all material respects with all applicable statutes, regulations, orders of, and restrictions imposed by the United States or ... by any agency of [the United States]," but this simply meant that Statesman was required to observe FIRREA's new capital requirements once they were promulgated. The clause was hardly necessary to oblige Statesman to obey the law, and nothing in it barred Statesman from asserting that passage of that law required the Government to take action itself or be in breach of its contract.
>
> ....
>
> We read this promise as the law of contracts has always treated promises to provide something beyond the promisor's absolute control, that is, as a promise to insure the promisee against loss arising from the promised condition's nonoccurrence.

518 U.S. at 868-69. Importantly, the opinion continued:

> To be sure, each side could have eliminated any serious contest about the correctness of their interpretive positions by using clearer language. *See, e.g., Guaranty Financial Services, Inc. v. Ryan,* 928 F.2d 994, 999-1000 (C.A.11 1991) (finding, based on very different contract language, that the Government had expressly reserved the right to change the capital requirements without any responsibility to the acquiring thrift). The failure to be even more explicit is perhaps more surprising here, given the size and complexity of these transactions. But few contract cases would be in court if contract language had articulated the parties' postbreach positions as clearly as might have been done, and the failure

> to specify remedies in the contract is no reason to find that the parties intended no remedy at all.

Winstar, 518 U.S. at 869 n. 15. As noted above, the "clearer language" that the opinion referred to as being used in the *Guaranty* case is identical to the risk-shifting language in clause VI(D) of the Admiral contract.

Thus, *Winstar* stands for the proposition that the government is still obligated to honor its contracts even if the governing regulations change. *See* 518 U.S. at 869-70 ("The drafters of the Restatement attested to this when they explained that, 'with the trend toward greater governmental regulation ... parties are increasingly aware of such risks, and a party may undertake a duty that is not discharged by such supervening governmental actions....' *Restatement (Second) of Contracts* § 264, Comment a. 'Such an agreement,' according to the Restatement, 'is usually interpreted as one to pay damages if performance is prevented rather than one to render a performance in violation of law.' "). However, the plurality opinion in *Winstar* also recognized that the government could address the risk-shifting issue in bargaining and could even "reserve the right to change the capital requirements without any responsibility to the acquiring thrift." 518 U.S. at 869 n. 15. Moreover, the example used by the plurality opinion for language that would have the effect of shifting the risk of a regulatory change to the private contractor was the contract language used both in *Guaranty* and in the contract with Admiral. Thus, following the lead of the Eleventh Circuit in *Guaranty* and the Supreme Court plurality in *Winstar,* we hold that Admiral assumed the risk of a regulatory change such as that brought about by FIRREA. For that reason, Admiral cannot recover damages based on the enactment of FIRREA and the promulgation of regulations pursuant to that statute that altered Admiral's obligations under the contract.

III

Although the trial court did not agree with the government that the contract shifted the risk of regulatory change to Admiral, the court nonetheless rejected Admiral's claim for damages. The trial court based its ruling in part on its conclusion that even if the government breached a contract with Admiral, the enactment of FIRREA did not cause Admiral harm. *Admiral III,* 57 Fed. Cl. at 434-35. We uphold the trial court's disposition of the no-injury issue. Accordingly, on that ground as well, we affirm the trial court's ruling denying Admiral's claim for damages.

The trial court's no-injury finding was based on a detailed analysis of the financial status of Admiral and Haven and a careful assessment of the likely impact of the enactment of FIRREA on their fortunes. In particular, the court found that Haven was running operational deficits long before FIRREA was proposed, and that Haven was likely to continue running deficits in the future regardless of whether FIRREA was enacted. 57 Fed. Cl. at 434. The court also found that the real estate that Admiral contributed to Haven was selling at far below its appraised value at the time it was contributed, and that the goodwill for the contributed business was going to be written off, since the business did not actually exist. *Id.*

The court concluded that Haven "was in such dire straits that it was failing under pre-FIRREA capital requirements," and that

> [h]ad all its goodwill been counted toward its regulatory capital, Haven would still have been insolvent: Haven had negative core capital as of December 31, 1989. This means that even if Admiral had been able to replace all of Haven's goodwill with cash on September 30, 1989, Haven would still have been at least $4 million formally below its minimum capital requirement, and perhaps more than $10 million, counting expected real estate losses, and a write-off of the TSC business.

57 Fed. Cl. at 435. . . .

In this case, as noted above, the trial court found that at the time of the breach Admiral was in such dire straits that it would not have been able to recover, even absent a breach. Thus, the court found that even under the pre-FIRREA requirements Admiral would not have been able to infuse enough capital in the thrift to avoid receivership. Given Haven's condition in 1989 and 1990, the trial court found that the enactment of FIRREA had no practical effect on Admiral's ability to find the necessary additional funding for the thrift. Therefore, the government's action did not "substantially impair[ ] the value of the contract to the injured party at the time of the breach" so as to make rescission an appropriate remedy. *Mobil Oil,* 530 U.S. at 608. As the trial court stated, "[t]he fact that FIRREA was passed in the middle of Admiral's cure period is sheer happenstance." *Admiral III,* 57 Fed. Cl. at 432. . . .

IV

Admiral asserts that the trial court erred in concluding that Admiral anticipatorily breached the contract. Because we decide that Admiral may not recover on the contract both because it assumed the risk of regulatory change and because the enactment of FIRREA did not harm Admiral, we need not reach the issue of anticipatory breach. In light of our rulings on those two issues, we also find it unnecessary to address the government's argument that no enforceable contract was formed between the government and Admiral.

Fifth Third Bank v. United States

518 F.3d 1368 (Fed. Cir. 2008)

PLAGER, Senior Circuit Judge.

[Citizens Federal Bank FSB ("Citizens") had entered into supervisory transactions with failing thrifts. Its successor in interest, Fifth Third Bank ("Fifth Third"),* sued the United States, alleging that the government had breached a contractual promise to allow special accounting treatment and effected a taking through enactment of FIRREA. The Court of Federal Claims entered judgment for government. The plaintiff appealed, and the Federal Circuit affirmed in part, reversed in part, and remanded. On remand, the Court of Federal Claims entered judgment for plaintiff, and the parties cross-appealed. On appeal, the Federal Circuit affirmed, holding that: (*i*) the finding that the government's breach of contract was the but-for cause of Fifth Third's sale of a division and its premature conversion from mutual to stock organization was not clearly erroneous; (*ii*) the finding that its damages from breach were foreseeable at the time of contracting was not clearly erroneous; (*iii*) the finding that damages arising from its sale of branches were established to a reasonable certainty was not clearly erroneous; (*iv*) the finding that its lost profit damages were too speculative was not clearly erroneous; and, (*v*) the proceeds that Fifth Third lost by converting to stock organization earlier than it would have, had the breach not occurred, were an appropriate

---

*. In the interests of clarity, the court refers to "Citizens" when necessary, but otherwise it referred to the plaintiff as "Fifth Third." If you are wondering how the bank came to be named "Fifth Third," the origins of the name go back to 1863, when Third National Bank was organized in Ohio. In 1888 Queen City National Bank of Cincinnati was renamed Fifth National Bank. The two banks merged in 1908 to become the Fifth Third National Bank of Cincinnati. Today, Fifth Third Bank is owned by Fifth Third Financial Corporation which is owned by Fifth Third Bancorp (both Ohio corporations). The extensive history of the bank's changes in name and size through mergers and acquisitions, of which its acquisition of Citizens Bank is a part, is detailed on the bank's website, *www.53.com.*

measure of expectancy damages.]

This is another *Winstar*-related case, in which a banking institution alleges that it was financially injured, wrongfully, by actions of the United States Government and its regulatory agencies. . . .

Fifth Third sought damages from the Government for breach of contract related to the savings and loan debacle arising out of the enactment of [FIRREA]. FIRREA negatively affected the way certain financial institutions could utilize what was called "supervisory goodwill," an accounting method that earlier had been promised to them by federal regulators who sought their help in salvaging failing savings and loan institutions ("S & Ls") in the 1980s. FIRREA caused these rescuing and once-healthy S & Ls to suffer significant losses, for which the United States Government was eventually held liable.

Since this court's 1995 opinion in *Winstar Corp. v. United States,*[3] affirmed by the Supreme Court, these injured financial institutions have sought damages for the losses; the Government's litigators have doggedly fought them every step of the way. This court has been called upon to issue a number of opinions further defining the terms of the Government's liability and settling the theories underlying and the scope of the issues for which damages were to be paid. This case is one more in that long-running tail,[5] and the Government again insists on challenging virtually every finding and conclusion reached by the trial judge after extensive hearings and multiple carefully reasoned opinions. Because the trial judge in this case did not err, we affirm.

BACKGROUND . . .

The issue regarding liability was whether, at the Government's urging, Citizens in acquiring four failing thrifts between 1982 and 1985 had relied on a promise from the Government that it would have the supervisory goodwill accounting method to keep itself in regulatory compliance over the years, despite the book deficits the acquisitions caused. In short, was there a binding contractual promise by the Government which was breached by the enactment of FIRREA, the enforcement of which denied the longterm use of that accounting method?

Much of the evidence at trial regarding liability was based on witnesses' recollections, with oral and deposition testimony describing the communications between Citizens and FHLB-Cincinnati that led to Citizens' acquisition of the failing thrifts. There was testimony that both parties believed they had entered into a contract concerning the special accounting treatment of supervisory goodwill. The somewhat sparse written documentation was consistent with this understanding.

The trial court, however, was concerned that the witnesses' testimony seemed to be rote in nature and that the written evidence supporting the testimony was contained in what the court described as routine agency documents. Based on its consideration of the evidence, the trial court concluded that the parties had not formed a contractual relationship.

When the case was appealed to this court, we reversed the trial court's ruling on liability.[10] We concluded that, when viewed in the light of the regulatory and economic context in which the parties negotiated and in which their understandings were reached, the evidence was sufficient to establish that the parties created contractual obligations which included the extended amortization of supervisory goodwill and the counting of supervisory goodwill as an asset for capital compliance purposes. We therefore held that the Government

---

3. 64 F.3d 1531 (Fed.Cir.1995) (en banc).

5. There indeed is a tail on this tale-the Government's brief reports that there are still some twenty-six remaining cases in dispute that have been designated as *Winstar*-related cases.

10. *Fifth Third Bank of W. Ohio v. United States,* 402 F.3d 1221 (Fed.Cir.2005) ("*Fifth Third VIII*").

was liable for breach of contract as a result of the enactment and enforcement of FIRREA.

We addressed two additional issues on appeal. First, we agreed with the trial court that FHLB-Cincinnati had actual authority to bind the Government to a contract involving supervisory goodwill. We also affirmed the trial court's ruling on summary judgment barring Fifth Third's cover damages claim as speculative because it was based entirely on hypothetical costs of issuing preferred stock, and unrealistic because at the time Citizens was a mutual organization and could not issue stock. The case was remanded to the trial court for a determination of damages, if any, to be awarded.

A second trial took place in early 2006, now eleven years after the original complaint was filed. The trial resumed where the first trial ended, i.e., with the Government's case-in-chief, followed by Fifth Third's rebuttal. Because all of Fifth Third's other damages theories had been precluded by the earlier rulings, the trial focused on the claim for incidental damages.

As noted earlier, the claim for incidental damages was based on two specific events that occurred in the early 1990s, shortly after the enactment of FIRREA. They involved, first, the sale by Citizens of its branches in Cincinnati, and second, a conversion of Citizens' ownership from mutual form to stock form. Both events were the result of a capital plan agreed upon by Citizens and the Office of Thrift Supervision, a government agency established by FIRREA as the primary thrift regulator. The purpose of the plan was to restore Citizens to profitability and to compliance with the federal minimum regulatory capital requirements imposed by FIRREA.

The dispute that Fifth Third and the Government are now engaged in is whether these events – the Cincinnati branch sale and the mutual-to-stock conversion – were caused by the Government's breach of the promises earlier made by the Government regulators regarding accounting of supervisory goodwill, and, if so, how any damages should be measured. Fifth Third's position is that the sale and conversion would have occurred, if they occurred at all, at a time of Citizens' own choosing when market conditions were favorable, rather than at the times imposed upon the bank by the regulators in response to the requirements of FIRREA. Having been forced to sell the Cincinnati branches and convert from a mutual to a stock organization prematurely, Citizens allegedly suffered substantial losses in the form of reduced proceeds and other lost profits.

After trial on these issues, the trial court published a 45-page opinion with extensive findings of fact and a thorough legal analysis of Fifth Third's damages claims. The court awarded Fifth Third substantial damages for the losses sustained by Citizens, including about $8.5 million for lost profits from the sale of the Cincinnati division (after certain adjustments) and about $44.2 million for premature conversion. Following an adjustment to compensate for the taxes Fifth Third will owe on the premature conversion damages, the total damages award came to about $76.5 million, which, as the trial court noted, is a relatively modest sum in the context of *Winstar* litigation. . . .

DISCUSSION

A. Overview

Expectancy damages are intended to make a non-breaching party whole by providing the benefits expected to be received had the breach not occurred. *Glendale Fed. Bank, FSB v. United States,* 239 F.3d 1374, 1379 (Fed.Cir.2001) (citing Restatement (Second) of Contracts § 344(a) (1981)). Expectancy damages include lost profits but are not limited to them. *Id.* As a general proposition, a party is entitled to expectancy damages if the party satisfies three requirements. First, the party must show that the claimed damages were within the realm of reasonable foreseeability at the time the contract was entered into (the foreseeability requirement). *Cal. Fed. Bank v. United States,* 395 F.3d 1263, 1267 (Fed.Cir. 2005). Second, the party must establish that the damages would not have occurred but for the breach (the causation requirement). *Id.* Third, "the measure of damages must be reasonably certain, although if 'a reasonable probability of damage can be clearly established, uncertainty as to the amount will not preclude recovery' " (the proof of damages to a reasonable certainty requirement). *Id.* (quoting *Glendale Fed. Bank v. United States,* 378 F.3d 1308, 1313 (Fed.Cir.2004)).

In the *Winstar* litigation context, foreseeability, causation, and proof of damages to a reasonable certainty are all issues of fact that we review for clear error. *Home Sav. of Am., FSB v. United States,* 399 F.3d 1341, 1347 (Fed.Cir.2005).[11] Clear error is among the more deferential standards an appellate court applies to the work of a trial court – a finding is clearly erroneous only when "the reviewing court on the entire evidence is left with the definite and firm conviction that a mistake has been committed." *United States v. U.S. Gypsum Co.,* 333 U.S. 364, 395 (1948). In the case before us, the liability issues were settled by our prior opinion. The damages issues, to the extent there are questions about the applicable rules, fall within the well-established principles of our prior cases. The only issues then on appeal are whether the trial court in its extensive and thorough fact findings and conclusions committed clear error. Given the deference we grant to trial courts in their fact-finding role, this is a heavy burden for the Government to carry.

B. Causation

We examine first the Government's arguments regarding causation. The Government argued at trial that several factors other than FIRREA, such as alleged mismanagement of the thrift and overall lack of profitability, led to Citizens' actions and the times they were taken, and that in any event the regulatory pressure to raise capital and downsize would have been the same absent the breach. The trial court disagreed, finding that Citizens would not have sold the Cincinnati division in 1991 or converted to stock form in January 1992 but for the breach caused by FIRREA. *Fifth Third IX,* 71 Fed.Cl. at 87-90.

On appeal, the Government asserts that the trial court erred in concluding that regulators would not have been concerned with Citizens' level of tangible capital even in the absence of the breach, and would not have required Citizens to take steps to recapitalize or downsize when they did. Recreating the past – who thought what, when, and why – is quintessentially a question of fact. Though, as in most fact-based trials, one could read the evidence different ways and reach different conclusions, the trial court's findings are supported by ample evidence, including the contemporaneous circumstances, documentation, and witness testimony expressly credited by the trial judge. On this record there is clearly no basis on which we could say that the trial court committed clear error in its finding of but-for causation.

C. Foreseeability

The trial court found that the damages caused by the sale of the Cincinnati branches and the reduced conversion damages were reasonably foreseeable at the time of the contract, based on the following analysis. *Id.* at 88-90. First, the court found that a prudent regulator would have been aware that removal of supervisory goodwill would cause Citizens to become capital deficient, which would require Citizens to raise capital to comply with capital requirements. The court found that a prudent regulator would have known that the principal ways of raising capital were sales of assets and conversion of ownership to stock form, and would have understood that the timing of these actions could affect the amount of proceeds received. Thus, the trial court concluded, a prudent regulator would have foreseen that a

11. *But cf. Home Sav. of Am.,* 399 F.3d at 1347 (suggesting that we review the trial court's methodology for calculating damages for abuse of discretion). Since in most respects the clear error and abuse of discretion standards are similarly deferential, we need not try in this case to separate the applied methodology from the process of fact-finding.

breach of the accounting method promise and the consequences thereof would take away Citizens' ability to choose the timing of its sale of the Cincinnati division and its conversion to stock form, and that this could cause damages. Furthermore, the trial court found that the regulators in this case actually knew what would happen if the Government breached its contract, and therefore actual foresight existed.

The Government contends that damages based on the 1991 sale of the Cincinnati branches were not reasonably foreseeable because the higher deposit premium[12] Citizens was able to obtain in 1998 was due to an improvement in the economy, an event that was unforeseeable at the time of the contract. Similarly, the Government argues that the damages resulting from the reduced conversion proceeds were not reasonably foreseeable at the time of the contract because the calculation of reduced proceeds was based on the increase in the thrift stock price market index between January 1992 and August 1993. In the Government's view, regulators could not have foreseen that the conversion market would improve during that time period.

At times the Government couches this argument in terms of proximate causation – the damages were caused by changed economic conditions and thus were not proximately caused by the breach. Since both arguments relate to the ability of the Government to contemplate at the time of the contract the nature of Citizens' injuries, we will address both in terms of foreseeability. *See Old Stone Corp. v. United States,* 450 F.3d 1360, 1375 (Fed.Cir.2006) ("Because these two doctrines are not meaningfully distinct, at least in the context of the case before us, we analyze them under the rubric of foreseeability.").

The trial court did not clearly err in concluding that the damages in this case were foreseeable. The trial court's basic findings, supported by the record and unchallenged by the Government, are sufficient to show foreseeability. Fifth Third was not required to demonstrate that the Government could have foreseen at the time of contracting that the market conditions might be less than favorable when it later breached the contract. We recently rejected a similar argument in *Citizens Federal Bank v. United States,* 474 F.3d 1314 (Fed.Cir.2007). In that case, we affirmed the trial court's finding that the plaintiff was entitled to compensation for the negative tax consequences incurred in raising capital to replace lost goodwill. *Id.* at 1321. We held that the plaintiff was not required to prove that the tax consequences were foreseeable; all that was necessary was a showing that the need to raise capital in the event of a breach was foreseeable. *Id.* ("If it was foreseeable that the breach would cause the other party to obtain additional capital, there is no requirement that the particular method used to raise that capital or its consequences also be foreseeable."). Fifth Third has made that showing here and is not required also to show that the precise economic conditions at the time regulators forced Citizens to raise capital were foreseeable.

As the trial court correctly held, *Old Stone* does not support the Government's cause. The plaintiff bank in that case was forced to raise capital after FIRREA by selling assets, and we affirmed the trial court's award of damages associated with that activity. 450 F.3d at 1367-70. But the bank had other problems unrelated to the loss of goodwill and was eventually seized. The trial court awarded damages related to the seizure; we reversed that award because the seizure was not a foreseeable result of the breach. *Id.* at 1376. We explained that for the seizure to be foreseeable, a number of specific facts had to be established. *Id.* Based on the lack of evidence in the record, we concluded that the bank had failed to prove that the extended chain of causation was foreseeable. *Id.* Here, in contrast,

12. In a branch sale, the seller theoretically gives the buyer the branch's deposit liabilities (e.g., savings accounts) and an amount of cash equal to these liabilities. However, depending on the negotiated value of the liabilities, the buyer may agree to take something less than the full amount of cash. In that case, the difference is the deposit premium.

Fifth Third is not claiming damages due to a seizure or other comparable event far removed from the breach; the damages compensate directly for the steps taken by Citizens to achieve regulatory compliance in the wake of FIRREA. *See also Citizens,* 474 F.3d at 1321-22 (distinguishing *Old Stone* on similar grounds).

The Government's reliance on *Estate of Berg v. United States,* 231 Ct.Cl. 466, 687 F.2d 377 (1982), is also misplaced. That case is not about foreseeability or proximate causation at all, but instead deals with the proper time for measuring damages. Moreover, it does not stand for the proposition that an upswing in the market value of an asset following a breach is irrelevant to the damages caused by the breach. The court in *Berg* noted two general rules. First, the goal of expectancy damages is to place the injured party in as good a position as he would have been had the breaching party performed the contract. *Id.* at 379; *see also* Restatement (Second) of Contracts § 344(a) (1981). Second, the proper date for measuring damages is usually the date of the breach. *Berg,* 687 F.2d at 380. In *Berg,* the plaintiff was made whole by valuing the bonds at issue as of the date of the breach; calculating the bonds' fair market value as of the later date urged by the Government would have reduced the damages award and would not have fully compensated the plaintiff for the Government's breach. *Id.*

In some cases, however, strict application of the second rule may not result in the most accurate assessment of expectancy damages. *See Energy Capital Corp. v. United States,* 302 F.3d 1314, 1330 (Fed.Cir.2002) ("That rule does not apply, however, to anticipated profits or to other expectancy damages that, absent the breach, would have accrued on an ongoing basis over the course of the contract."). A court may consider post-breach evidence when determining damages in order to place the non-breaching party in as good a position as he would have been had the contract been performed. *See id.*; *Castle v. United States,* 48 Fed.Cl. 187, 207 n. 16 (2000), *aff'd in part, rev'd in part on other grounds,* 301 F.3d 1328 (Fed.Cir.2002); *see also* Restatement (Second) of Contracts § 352 cmt. b, illus. 6 (1981) (using post-breach evidence to establish lost profits). Here the trial court found that, but for the breach, Citizens would have sold the Cincinnati division in 1998 rather than 1991, and converted to stock ownership in August 1993 rather than January 1992. Therefore it was appropriate, and certainly not clear error, for the court to consider the improved markets for conversion and branch sales in order to compensate Citizens for the damage sustained.

D. Proof of Damages

1. Damages Related to the Sale of the Cincinnati Division

For calculating the damages associated with the forced sale of the Cincinnati division, Fifth Third's expert, Dr. Brumbaugh, created a model that restored to Citizens the assets that had been transferred to Banc One in 1991 as well as additional assets to account for the loss of deposits caused by the breach, for a total of $400 million in assets associated with the Cincinnati division. *Fifth Third IX,* 71 Fed.Cl. at 77-78. Next he divided the damages calculation into two parts. The first was a calculation of lost operating profits on the restored Cincinnati assets for the period between 1992 and 1998. Based on Citizens' actual return on assets for that time period with certain adjustments, he calculated lost profits of approximately $10.5 million. *Id.* at 78-79. The second part of the damages calculation assumed that the Cincinnati division would have been sold in 1998 to Fifth Third when the other Citizens branches were sold. Conservatively using a 7% deposit premium, which was somewhat lower than the average deposit premium Citizens actually received in the 1998 sale, Dr. Brumbaugh calculated that the proceeds from selling the Cincinnati branches in 1998 would have been $11.1 million greater than the proceeds of the sale to Banc One in 1991. *Id.* at 79-80.

The trial court awarded Fifth Third damages for the lost profits Citizens would have made on the sale of the Cincinnati branches in 1998 but not for the lost operating profits from

1992 to 1998. The trial court found that, though lost profit claims are often not susceptible to proof due to their speculative nature, this claim for lost profits on the sale of the Cincinnati division was based on a specific investment opportunity-Citizens' 1998 sale of assets to Fifth Third. The court concluded that these damages had been proven to a reasonable certainty. *Id.* at 90-91.

In contrast, the trial court determined that Fifth Third's claim for lost operating profits for the Cincinnati division had not been established to a reasonable certainty. Fifth Third's model applied a hypothetical rate of return on assets to the restored Cincinnati asset base. The trial court found that this method was too speculative because there is no evidence that the thrift's expanded asset base, including the Cincinnati assets, would have realized profits at a similar rate to the thrift's actual profits during that period. *Id.* at 91.

On appeal, the Government challenges the award based on the 1998 branch sale on the grounds that it was based on a hypothetical transaction, and thus is too speculative. There are two flaws in the Government's argument. First, although we have noted that damages claims based on hypothetical events often are difficult to prove, they are not barred as a matter of law. *See Granite Mgmt. Corp. v. United States,* 416 F.3d 1373, 1381-83 (Fed.Cir.2005); *Fifth Third VIII,* 402 F.3d at 1236-37; *Glendale,* 378 F.3d at 1313. Second, the Cincinnati division award was not entirely hypothetical since it relied on two *actual* transactions-the 1991 sale of the Cincinnati branches to Banc One and the 1998 sale of the remaining branches to Fifth Third, albeit without the Cincinnati division. We see no clear error in the trial court's finding that the award was established to a reasonable certainty, which the record fully supports.

In its cross-appeal, Fifth Third argues that the trial court erred in rejecting its claim for lost operating profits of the Cincinnati division between 1992 and 1998. It first asserts legal error, alleging that the trial court incorrectly applied the "reasonable certainty" standard to the *amount* of damages, rather than just to the *fact* that damages occurred. We agree with Fifth Third that some courts, including this one, have interpreted the "reasonable certainty" standard to apply only to the *fact* of damages, after which the court may "make a fair and reasonable approximation of the damages." *Bluebonnet Sav. Bank, F.S.B. v. United States,* 266 F.3d 1348, 1356-57 (Fed.Cir.2001) (quoting *Locke v. United States,* 151 Ct.Cl. 262, 283 F.2d 521, 524 (1960)); *see also* 1 Robert L. Dunn, *Recovery of Damages for Lost Profits* § 1.8 (6th ed. 2005) ("While the proof of the *fact* of damages must be certain, proof of the *amount* may be an estimate, uncertain or inexact."). Nevertheless, we do not understand the trial court's decision as having misapplied that standard when the court found that the claim for lost operating profits from 1992 to 1998 was not established. Rather, the opinion can be fairly read as finding it was not reasonably certain that the Cincinnati assets would have earned profits during the entire period in question.

Fifth Third also argues that the trial court made a factual error by assuming that Citizens invested its funds separately by division, as indicated by the court's reference to a "Dayton" rate of return, *Fifth Third IX,* 71 Fed.Cl. at 78-79, 91, when in fact the thrift's assets were pooled for investment purposes. It appears, however, that for at least part of the 1992-1998 time period, Citizens consisted of only a Dayton division, so the rate of return on pooled assets was indeed a Dayton rate of return for some of those years. Thus it is not clear that the trial court made an erroneous assumption.

What is evident is that the trial court rejected the notion that the bank's expanded asset base (which would have included the Cincinnati branches in the absence of the breach) would have realized profits at a rate similar to that of the actual bank's profits. The trial court found that determining hypothetical Cincinnati profits in the absence of the breach was too speculative an endeavor to result in a reasonable approximation of lost profits damages. The record supports that finding, and we are unconvinced that the trial court committed clear error in holding against Fifth Third's claim for lost operating profits in this context.

2. Damages Related to the Mutual-to-Stock Conversion

Fifth Third's other damages claim related to its conversion from mutual to stock form. Its expert testified that absent the breach Citizens would have converted in August 1993 because that was the first date when the three conditions set out by Citizens' management for conversion were satisfied. He then calculated the damages as the difference between the proceeds that would have resulted from a hypothetical conversion in August 1993 and those received when Citizens converted in January 1992. His results ranged from about $30 million to about $47 million, depending on whether the Cincinnati division was restored, and, if so, whether its operating profits were also restored.

The Government argued before the trial court that no damages were sustained as a result of the conversion in January 1992 because the conversion was successful. In addition, the Government's outside experts were of the view that conversion proceeds were a liability that had to be paid back to the shareholders, similar to a loan. Thus, the Government argued, damages could only result from the loss of investment opportunities due to the lesser equity raised from the conversion. Because Fifth Third had not identified any clearly defined investment opportunities that Citizens had foregone, the Government believed there were no damages from reduced conversion proceeds.

Fifth Third responded that the sale of stock was analogous to a sale of property, not a loan, a view of the transaction with which the trial court agreed. *Id.* at 75-77, 92-94. Fifth Third's expert testified that generally corporations have no obligation to pay dividends or for that matter repurchase shares. More specifically, Citizens' conversion prospectus for the sale of its stock did not mention a requirement to pay dividends, or any other liability or debt to the shareholders. The trial court therefore found that the sale of stock at the conversion of ownership form had the characteristics of equity, not of debt. Thus the court treated the sale of stock like the sale of property and concluded that reduced conversion proceeds were a proper measure of damages. Accepting the model that assumed the Cincinnati division had been restored before the conversion, but without the division's hypothetical operating profits, the trial court awarded approximately $44.2 million in damages for lost conversion proceeds. *Id.* at 93-94.

On appeal, the Government repeats many of the arguments it made below. Its first argument – that reduced conversion proceeds are too speculative – is unpersuasive, just as it was unpersuasive with respect to the damages for the sale of the Cincinnati division. Unlike some damages claims that we have rejected previously, *see, e.g., Fifth Third VIII,* 402 F.3d at 1237 (affirming trial court's conclusion that cover damages claim based on hypothetical costs of issuing preferred stock was too speculative), this claim does not depend only on a hypothetical capital-raising transaction. Instead, Citizens actually converted in January 1992, and the trial court specifically found that, absent the breach, Citizens would have converted in August 1993, a finding supported by the record and not challenged by the Government on appeal.

The heart of the Government's argument on appeal is that reduced conversion proceeds are not a proper measure of expectancy damages, and an award of these damages would result in a windfall to Fifth Third. The Government's position rests on the notion that investors who purchase stock have an expectation of repayment of their investment. Thus, the argument goes, the investors who would have provided the additional capital if Citizens had converted in August 1993 would have expected a return on their investment. If, instead, the Government provides the additional capital in the form of contract damages, the Government would have no expectation of repayment. Therefore Fifth Third will be in a better position with a damages award for breach of contract than it would have been had the contract been performed, a result not contemplated by the recovery principle of expectancy damages. The Government's conclusion, as was explained at the trial, is that the only damages to which Fifth Third might be entitled are the profits that would have been earned on the lost conversion proceeds, not the lost proceeds themselves.

The trial court heard extensive expert testimony from both sides and ultimately determined that Fifth Third's experts held the correct view of the transaction. We agree. In the first place, whether the investors who purchased the stock when Citizens converted expected a return on their investment is immaterial because they had no legally enforceable right of repayment. As the trial court found, there was no formal obligation on the part of Citizens to pay dividends or to repurchase the shares. The conversion prospectus explicitly stated that Citizens would not issue an initial dividend, and it contained no guarantees of future dividends. The windfall theory does not hold air-we see no error in the trial court's conclusion that the proceeds Citizens lost by converting earlier than it would have in the absence of the breach were an appropriate measure of expectancy damages. . . .

The trial court also found that, even if reduced conversion proceeds were not an acceptable measure of damages, they are a "fair and reasonable approximation" of damages under the so-called jury verdict method. We need not address the Government's challenge to this alternative finding because we affirm the trial court's decision that the lost conversion proceeds were a suitable form of expectancy damages.

Notes and Comments 8.65. Does *Admiral Financial* read *Winstar* correctly? Is the language of RCMA clause VI(D) sufficiently different from the corresponding language at issue in *Winstar* to justify a different result in *Admiral Financial*?

8.66. Each post-*Winstar* dispute over accounting standards tends to be highly "fact-specific."[40] What should be the result in a case in which the pertinent language of the agreement between the acquiror of a failing savings association and the now-defunct Federal Home Bank Board:

> Pursuant to Subpart C of Part 563b of the Rules and Regulations for Insurance of Accounts, . . . for purposes of reporting to the Board, *X* Savings Association may amortize the value of any intangible asset resulting from the purchase over a period not to exceed 35 years by the straight-line method.

Cf. La Van v. United States, 382 F.3d 1340 (Fed.Cir. 2004) (holding *inter alia* that investors could recover expectancy damages under implied-in-fact contract, but that post-FIRREA government action did not constitute taking); *Slattery v. United States*, 583 F.3d 800 (Fed.Cir. 2009) (upholding failed bank shareholder derivative action against FDIC for breach of contract).

8.67. The contract analysis in *Admiral Financial* is obviously much more extensive than the *Winstar* case. Do you agree with the Federal Circuit's contract analysis? Is it reconcilable with *Winstar*?

8.68. In the first phase of *Fifth Third Bank*, the Federal Circuit gave considerable attention to traditional contract analysis in determining whether a contract was formed in the situation before it. Likewise, in the opinion excerpted above, the court focuses on contract measures of damages. Is its analysis of applicable principles of contract law correct?

8.69. As *Fifth Third Bank* illustrates, the persuasive emerging strategy for the Government, if – as seems likely – it loses the argument about contract formation, is to pur-

---

40. *See, e.g., La Van v. United States*, 382 F.3d 1340, 1342 (Fed.Cir. 2004) (characterizing dispute as "another fact-specific dispute following the seminal decision of *United States v. Winstar Corp.*").

sue vigorously other principles of contract law with respect to interpretation of contract terms, the existence of breach, causation, or available remedies. How does the Government fare with respect to such arguments in *Fifth Third Bank*?

8.70. *Responses to the Subprime Mortgage Crisis*. U.S. Government responses to the financial crisis that resulted from the failure of the subprime mortgage market have generally fallen into one of three categories. The Government initiated certain transactional responses to assuage the crisis by injecting credit into the financial markets. The Government also launched certain regulatory responses that tweak regulatory requirements in an effort to ease the situation of market participants or to encourage private parties to participate in troubled markets. Finally, the Government has fashioned certain supervisory responses, in which regulators invoke their supervisory power over regulated entities to correct conditions or behavior in the financial markets. The following excerpt examines these responses in detail.

3 Michael P. Malloy, Banking Law and Regulation

§§ 14.04[A]-[C] (2d ed., Aspen Publishers, 2011)

U.S. Government responses to the financial crisis generally have fallen into one of three categories. First, the Government has initiated certain transactional responses to assuage the crisis by injecting credit into the financial markets. Second, the Government has launched certain regulatory responses that tweak regulatory requirements in an effort to ease the situation of market participants or to encourage private parties to participate in troubled markets. Third, the Government has fashioned certain supervisory responses, in which regulators invoke their supervisory power over regulated entities to correct conditions or behavior in the financial markets. . . .

Transactional responses

Much of the national response so far has been a series of fatalistic attempts to spend our way out of the crisis. For example, on September 7, 2008, the Treasury Department entered into senior preferred stock purchase agreements with the Federal National Mortgage Association (Fannie Mae) and the Federal Home Loan Mortgage Corporation (Freddie Mac), providing in effect protection to the holders of senior debt, subordinated debt, and mortgage-backed securities (MBS) issued or guaranteed by Fannie and Freddie.[1] . . .

On October 3, 2008, Title I of the Emergency Economic Stabilization Act of 2008 (EESA)[2] created the Troubled Assets Relief Program [(TARP)] for the purchase of troubled assets of financial institutions. The EESA granted the Secretary of the Treasury emergency authorities and facilities to help restore liquidity and stability to the U.S. financial system. ...

From the onset of the TARP, Treasury appeared to be improvising, unsure of even basic issues such as how to price the targeted assets.[3] By mid-October 2008, Treasury shifted

---

1. U.S. Department of Treasury Office of Public Affairs, Fact Sheet: Treasury Senior Preferred Stock Purchase Agreement (Sept 7, 2008) available at http://www.treas.gov/press/releases/reports/pspa--factsheet--090708hp1128.pdf.

2. Pub. L. No. 110-343, tit. I, §§ 101-136. 122 Stat. 3765, 3767-3800 (2008) (codified at 5 U.S.C. § 5315, 12 U.S.C. §§ 461 note, 1715z-23, 1823(c)(11), 1828(a), (c), 5211-5241, 15 U.S.C. § 1638 note, 1638(b)(2), 31 U.S.C. §§ 301, 3101).

3. *See, e.g.*, Stephen Joyce, *Treasury Official Discusses Implementation of $700 Billion Program to Buy Bad Assets*, BNA Banking Daily (Oct. 7, 2008), *available at* http://news.bna.com (reporting on efforts of Treasury to implement TARP). For discussion of the evolution of TARP strategy and the status of TARP programs, as of September 25, 2009, see U.S. Government

direction[4] and began using TARP funds to purchase equity in troubled financial institutions (primarily nine large institutions) rather than purchasing troubled assets.[5] Treasury adopted this approach arguably on the basis of its EESA authority.[6] The new approach prompted criticism[7] that Treasury has failed to require beneficiaries of its funding to use the capital infusions to strengthen the weak credit market.[8] Cluelessly, Treasury officials insisted that the Capital Purchase Program (CPP), under which Treasury was buying shares of preferred stock in selected financial institutions,[9] taking, in most cases, a 5 percent dividend for the first few years, with an increase to 9 percent, would be profitable in the long run.[10] More

---

Accountability Office, *Troubled Asset Relief Program: One Year Later, Actions Are Needed to Address Remaining Transparency and Accountability Challenges* (GAO-10-16, Oct. 08, 2009).

4. *Cf.* Thecla Fabian, *Senate Finance Ranking Member Hammers Paulson on EESA Implementation*, BNA Banking Daily (Nov. 14, 2008), available at http://news.bna.com (criticizing "repeated[] change[s] [of] direction" by Treasury and the Fed under EESA).

5. Thus, in October 2008, the Fed issued an interim final rule allowing BHCs that issued senior perpetual preferred stock to Treasury under a Capital Purchase Program to include such securities in Tier 1 capital for purposes of risk-based and leverage capital guidelines for bank holding companies. 73 Fed. Reg. 62,851 (2008) (codified at 12 C.F.R. pt. 225, App. A), corrected, 73 Fed. Reg. 63,624 (2008). In June 2009, the Fed adopted the rule as a final rule without any substantive changes. 74 Fed. Reg. 26,081 (2009).

6. *Cf.* R. Christian Bruce & Aaron Lorenzo, *Banks Receiving Treasury Investments See New Opportunities for Acquisitions,* BNA Banking Daily (Oct. 28, 2008), *available at* http://news.bna.com (discussing allocation of $250 billion of EESA funding for capital injections under Treasury Capital Purchase Program (CPP)). For discussion of the CPP, see Stephen Joyce & Nora Macaluso, *Government Officials Say TARP Eligibility May Expand to Additional Types of Firms*, BNA Banking Daily (Oct. 29, 2008), *available at* http://news.bna.com.

7. *See, e.g.*, Levin, *Treasury Needs Firm Commitment From Banks to Use New Funds for Loans*, BNA Banking Daily (Oct. 20, 2008), *available at* http://news.bna.com; Malini Manickavasagam, *Pelosi, Reid, Other Lawmakers Share Concern Over Banks' Possible TARP Misuse*, BNA Banking Daily (Oct. 30, 2008), *available at* http://news.bna.com.

8. For contrary studies, arguing that bank lending had increased during the credit crisis, see V. Chari, L. Christiano, & P. Kehoe, *Facts and Myths about the Credit Crisis* (Federal Reserve Bank of Minneapolis Working Paper 666, Oct. 2008), *available at* http://www.minneapolisfed.org/publications_papers/pub_display.cfm?id=4062; Octavio Marenzi *et al.*, *Flawed Assumptions about the Credit Crisis:A Critical Examination of US Policymakers* (Celent, Dec. 2009) (arguing that U.S. government responses to credit crisis based on assumptions contradicted by government's own data), *available at* http://www.celent.com/PressReleases/20081210/CreditCrisis20081212DRAFT.pdf. *But see* Ethan Cohen-Cole, Burcu Duygan-Bump, Jose Fillat, & Judit Montoriol-Gerriga, *Minneapolis: Looking Behind the Aggregates: A Reply to* "Facts and Myths About the Financial Crisis of 2008" (Federal Reserve Bank of Boston Working Paper No. QAU08-5, Nov. 2008) (disputing Minneapolis Fed paper), *available at* http://www.bos.frb.org/bankinfo/qau/wp/2008/qau0805.htm.

9. Independent mutual banks and savings associations may apply for CPP investments in amounts up to $25 billion under terms set by Treasury. For the basic terms applied to mutual depository institutions, see http://www.treasury.gov/press/releases/reports/ccptermsheet/mutual-banks.pdf Each approved institution would be eligible to sell debt in a total amount equal to 1 to 3 percent of its risk-weighted assets. *See Treasury Announces Capital Purchase Terms for Mutual Banks; Sets May 14 Deadline*, BNA Banking Daily (Apr. 15, 2009), *available at* http://www.bna.com (reporting on CPP for mutual institutions). The institution would be subject to Treasury rules on transparency, monitoring, and executive compensation. *Id.*

10. The text of prepared remarks on the CPP by Interim Assistant Secretary for Financial Stability Neel Kashkari is available at http://www.treas.gov/press/releases/hp1314.htm. *See also Capital Purchases Will Turn a Profit For Taxpayers, Treasury's Kashkari Says*, BNA Banking Daily

recently, congressional concern has grown over the excessive levels of executive compensation at institutions benefitting from the CPP.[11] Whether as a result of the intense criticism of its use of the TARP or because of its own meandering approach to responding to the financial crisis, by mid-November 2008, Treasury was publicly moving away from its plan to buy mortgage-related assets; instead, it was reportedly considering other uses for what remained of the original $700 billion in TARP funds.[12] Coincidentally, on November 14, 2008, the Administration reached agreement with congressional leaders to establish a TARP inspector general, and congressional leaders appointed three experts to the Congressional Oversight Panel, another EESA-mandated watchdog.[13] The CPP officially ended on December 29, 2009, after Treasury closed the last ten CPP investments, worth about $29.3 million.[14]

In the meantime, on January 8, 2009, Treasury released the latest in a series of reports required under EESA concerning TARP expenditures.[15] Recent transactions have raised total TARP transactions to $266.9 billion, including $177.54 billion under CPP.[16] According to a Financial Services Roundtable Lending Report, 9 of the 20 recipients of the

---

(Dec. 8, 2008), available at http://news.bna.com (reporting on Assistant Secretary Kashkari's remarks).

11. *See Pelosi, Reid Concerned About Excessive CEO Compensation at Banks Getting EESA Funds*, BNA Banking Daily (Oct. 30, 2008), *available at* http://news.bna.com (reporting on congressional criticism of CEO compensation at EESA-aided firms participating in CPP). Criticism was exacerbated by the apparent failure of CPP-assisted banks to increase lending. Treasury's Bank Lending Survey indicated that overall lending by financial institutions that received the largest amount of government investment under CPP declined in February 2009. Mike Ferullo, *Survey Shows Slight Decline in Lending Among Banks Receiving Government Capital,* BNA Banking Daily (Apr. 16, 2009), *available at* http://www.bna.com. The February lending survey is *available at* http://www.financialstability.gov/latest/tg_041509.html. Concern over excessive executive competition in financial services firms led Treasury to issue an interim final rule, pursuant to EESA §§101 and 111, 12 U.S.C. §§5211, 5221, providing "guidance" about the EESA executive compensation and corporate governance provisions that apply to entities that receive TARP assistance. 74 Fed. Reg. 28,394 (2009) (codified at 31 C.F.R. pt. 30).

12. Aaron Lorenzo & R. Christian Bruce, *Treasury Pulls Back From TARP Purchase Of Mortgage-Related Assets, Paulson Says*, BNA Banking Daily (Nov. 13, 2008), *available at* http://news.bna.com. Controversy has grown over whether or not repaid TARP funds created renewed authority to initiate fresh rescues, i.e., whether TARP was a revolving fund. Aaron Lorenzo, *Sens. Hatch, Lincoln, Corker Push to Block Treasury From Recycling Repaid TARP Funds*, BNA Banking Daily (June 23, 2009), *available at* http://www.bna.com.

13. R. Christian Bruce, Oversight of TARP Comes into Focus with Action by White House, Pelosi, Reid, BNA Banking Daily (Nov. 17, 2008), *available at* http://news.bna.com. The members of the five-member TARP Congressional Oversight Panel are appointed by Speaker of the House (who appointed Richard H. Neiman, the N.Y. Superintendent of Banks), the House Republican Leader (appointing Rep. Jeb Hensarling (R-Texas)), the Senate Majority Leader (appointing Harvard Law Professor Elizabeth Warren, who serves as chair), and the Senate Republican Leader (appointing former Sen. John Sununu) each selecting one member. The fifth member is jointly selected by the Speaker and the Majority Leader (who jointly appointed Damon Silvers, AFL-CIO associate general counsel). *See* R. Christian Bruce, *McConnell Names Sununu to TARP Panel; Thacher, Proffitt Tapped to Advise Treasury*, BNA Banking Daily (Dec. 18, 2008), *available at* http://news.bna.com (reporting on TARP panel).

14. Aaron Lorenzo, Treasury Closes CPP Program with 10 Final Investments in Community Banks, BNA Banking Daily (Jan. 5, 2010), *available at* http://www.bna.com.

15. http://www.treas.gov/initiatives/eesa/docs/Fourth-Tranche-Report.pdf.

16. *Id.*

largest amount of CPP financing increased lending in February 2009 as compared to January 2009.[17] Mortgage originations for the period increased 30 percent overall (from $78 billion to $102 billion) among those 20 recipients. All other lending decreased during the period, from $243 billion to $231 billion. However, efforts to oversee the use of TARP aid delivered to financial institutions has been impeded by Treasury, according to Prof. Warren, chair of the Congressional Oversight Panel, and others charged with overseeing TARP.[18] TARP recipients have been paying back TARP loans in full since April 2009.[19] In June, American Express Co. repurchased a warrant it had issued to Treasury as a condition for receiving a total of $3.39 billion in TARP funds, including $74.4 million in dividends (an annualized return on investment of approximately 26 percent).[20] In August 2009, Morgan Stanley announced that it would pay $950 million for warrants that it had issued to Treasury in exchange for TARP funds, a 20 percent annualized return.[21] With TARP funds being repaid, by November, the Administration was beginning to consider other use of TARP proceeds.[22]

In accordance with Treasury's determination of systemic risk under FDIA §13(c)(4)(G),[23] the FDIC initiated the Temporary Liquidity Guarantee Program (TLGP) in October 2008.[24] The program has two components: (i) the debt guarantee program, which guaranteed newly issued senior unsecured debt[25] of insured depository institutions and most U.S. holding companies of such institutions;[26] and, (ii) the transaction account guarantee

---

17. http://www.fsround.org/askew/pdfs/LendingSurveyforFebruary2009.doc.pdf. *See also* Thecla Fabian, *Almost Half of Top 20 CPP Recipients Increased Lending; Mainly in Mortgages,* BNA Banking Daily (Apr. 21, 2009), *available at* http://www.bna.com (discussing Financial Services Roundtable survey).

18. Brett Ferguson, *Auditors Blast Treasury as Uncooperative in Efforts to Improve TARP Accountability,* BNA Banking Daily (Apr. 1, 2009), *available at* http://www.bna.com.

19. Stephen Joyce, *American Express Fully Repays TARP Loan By Making $340 Million Warrant Payment*, BNA Banking Daily (July 31, 2009), *available at* http://www.bna.com.

20. *Id.*

21. Mike Ferullo, Morgan Stanley Buys TARP Warrants From Treasury Department for $950 Million, BNA Banking Daily (Aug. 10, 2009), *available at* http://www.bna.com.

22. Jonathan Nicholson, *OMB's Orszag Says Administration Mulling 'Reorienting' TARP to Help Cut Debt Load,* BNA Banking Daily (Nov. 13, 2009), *available at* http://www.bna.com. Under EESA §120(b), 12 U.S.C. §5230(b). the TARP would expire on December 31, 2009, unless the Secretary of the Treasury submits to Congress a written certification extending the program for two years from the date of enactment, i.e., October 3, 2010. On December 9, 2009, the Secretary extended TARP. http://www.treasury.gov/press/releases/tg433.htm.

23. 12 U.S.C. §1823(c)(4)(G). FDICIA §141 added §13(c)(4)(G) to the FDIA, 12 U.S.C. §1823(c)(4)(G). The section authorizes action by the federal government in circumstances involving a systemic risk to the nation's financial system.

24. 73 Fed. Reg. 64,179 (Oct. 29, 2008), *amended,* 73 Fed. Reg. 66,160 (2008). For background on the TLG Program, see 73 Fed. Reg. at 66, 160-66,162.

25. For these purposes, the term "newly issued senior unsecured debt" was defined to mean senior unsecured debt issued by a participating entity on or after October 14, 2008, and on or before: (i) the earlier of November 12, 2008 or the date an eligible entity opts out, for an eligible entity that opts out of the debt guarantee program; or, (ii) June 30, 2009, for an eligible entity that does not opt out of the debt guarantee program. 12 C.F.R. §370.2(f). Based on the public comments received, the FDIC revised the definition in the final version of the rule to exclude debt with a stated maturity of thirty days or less. 73 Fed. Reg. 72,244, 72,267 (Nov. 26, 2008) (codified at 12 C.F.R. §370.2(f)).

26. *See* 74 Fed. Reg. 54,743 (2009) (codified at 12 C.F.R. pt. 370) (establishing limited six-month emergency guarantee facility for debt guarantee component of TLGP).

program (TAG), which guaranteed certain non-interest-bearing transaction accounts at insured depository institutions.[27] In early November 2008, the FDIC amended the interim TLGP rule,[28] by extending the opt-out date for eligible entities until December 5, 2008, extending the deadline for complying with certain disclosure requirements related to the TLGP until December 19, 2008, and establishing assessment procedures to accommodate the extended opt out period. The amended interim rule generally became effective November 4, 2008.[29] The final version of the rule was published on November 26, 2008.[30]

In June 2009, the FDIC proposed two alternatives for phasing out the TAG component of the TLGP.[31] Under the first proposed alternative, the FDIC guarantee of deposits held in qualifying noninterest-bearing transaction accounts subject to the TAG program would continue until December 31, 2009. There would be no modification of the existing fee structure or any other change in the FDIC's guarantee of noninterest-bearing transaction accounts, as provided for in the current regulation. Under the second proposed alternative, the TAG program would be extended for six months until June 30, 2010. Insured depository institutions that are currently participating in the TAG program would be provided a single opportunity to opt out of the extended TAG program. Those that choose to participate in the extended TAG program, would be subject to increased fees for the FDIC extended guarantee of its qualifying noninterest-bearing transaction accounts, and might be required to update their disclosures related to the TAG program. Those that opt out would be required to update their disclosure postings and notices to indicate that they are no longer participating in the program. Comments were due by July 30, 2009.[32] . . .

In mid-November 2008, the Fed provided nearly $50 billion in options for loans through the Term Securities Lending Facility (TSLF), under which options are offered to primary government securities dealers-banks and securities broker-dealers that trade with the Federal Reserve Bank of New York-to draw upon short-term, fixed-rate loans in exchange for program-eligible collateral.[33]

By late November 2008, Treasury had completed a $40 billion purchase of

---

27. *See* 74 Fed. Reg. 45,093 (2009) (codified at 12 C.F.R. §§370.2(g), (h)(4), 370.4(a), 370.5(c), (g), (h)(5), 370.7(c)) (extending Transaction Account Guarantee component of TLGP until June 30, 2010).

28. 73 Fed. Reg. 66,160 (Nov. 7, 2008) (codified at 12 C.F.R. §§370.2, 370.3, 370.5(a), (c), (f), (j), (h), 370.6(a), (b)(1), (b)(2), (c), 370.7(a), (b)).

29. 73 Fed. Reg. at 66,160. The effective date of §370.5(h)(2)- (3) (the TLG Program disclosure requirements), added by 73 Fed. Reg. 64,186 (Oct. 29, 2008), was delayed from December 1 until December 19, 2008.

30. 73 Fed. Reg. 72,244 (Nov. 26, 2008) (codified at 12 C.F.R. §§370.1-370.12), amended, 74 Fed. Reg. 12,078 (2009), 74 Fed. Reg. 26,521 (2009) (extending Debt Guarantee Program), modified, 74 Fed. Reg. 26,941 (2009) (making permanent a minor modification to TLGP to include certain issuances of mandatory convertible debt Debt Guarantee Program). For discussion of the changes from the interim to the final version of the rule, see 73 Fed. Reg. at 72,260-72,264.

31. 74 Fed. Reg. 31,217 (2009) (to be codified at 12 C.F.R. pt. 370).

32. 74 Fed. Reg. at 31,217.

33. For results of the TSLF program, see http://www.newyorkfed.org/markets/top/topseclending.cfm. *See also* Aaron Lorenzo, *Fed Extends Almost $50 Billion in Options for Loans Through TSLF Options Program*, BNA Banking Daily (Nov. 12, 2008), *available at* http://news.bna.com (discussing TSLF program).

American International Group (AIG) preferred stock and warrants through the TARP.[34] That transaction was part of a restructured rescue of AIG, in which the Fed reworked loans to the insurance company, relaxing some terms and offered two new lending facilities. In effect, AIG would use the proceeds from the Treasury transaction to reduce the credit extended by the Fed in September 2008.[35] By September 2009, a GAO report indicated that the sustainability of AIG operations and repayment efforts was still not clear, and recouping the federal assistance to AIG would depend upon the long-term changes in and reorganization of AIG.[36]

In the meantime, the Fed initiated two programs to boost lending and limit damage from the weakening economy-(i) the Term Asset-Backed Securities Loan Facility (TALF), a $200 billion lending facility to facilitate purchases of loan-backed securities, with a Treasury pledge of $20 billion to assist the Fed in hedging the credit risk of possible defaults on the underlying credit exposure;[37] and, (ii) a program to purchase up to $600 billion in mortgage-related assets, involving a commitment to buy up to $100 billion in direct debt issued by Fannie Mae, Freddie Mac, and the FHLBanks, and a commitment to purchase up to $500 billion in MBS guaranteed by Fannie Mae, Freddie Mac, and the Government National Mortgage Association (Ginnie Mae).[38] The TALF program was to continue to operate through the Federal Reserve Bank of New York until Dec. 31, 2009,[39] but the program is now operative through June 2010.[40] It was not until December 30, 2008 that the Fed announced the selection of four private investment firms to implement the new MBS purchase program.[41] The Fed selected BlackRock Inc, Goldman Sachs Asset Management, PIMCO, and Wellington Management Co. to act as government agents in the purchase of up

34. Aaron Lorenzo, *Treasury Completes $40 Billion Equity Buy in AIG; Transaction Proceeds to Repay Fed*, BNA Banking Daily (Nov. 28, 2008), *available at* http://news.bna.com (reporting on AIG rescue).

35. For details concerning Treasury transactions conducted under the Emergency Economic Stabilization Act of 2008 see http://www.treasury.gov/initiatives/eesa/transactions.shtml.

36. U.S. Government Accountability Office, Troubled Asset Relief Program: Status of Government Assistance Provided to AIG (GAO-09-975, Sept. 21, 2009), reprinted in 2009 WL 2993017.

37. The TALF program since has been expanded to cover a wider class of collateral and extended maturities. Five-year loans for commercial mortgage-backed securities (CMBS) will be eligible, in addition to securities backed by insurance premium finance loans. Aaron Lorenzo, *Fed to Use TALF to Aid CMBS Markets, Aaron Lorenzo Allowing Five-Year Loans in the Process,* BNA Banking Daily (May 4, 2009), *available at* [[xrefpub="internet"root="http"normval="http://www.bna.com"link-status="active"effect="default"relate="no"]] http://www.bna.com. For the terms and conditions of CMBS TALF, see http://www.newyork_fed.org/markets/talf_cmbs_terms.html.

38. *See* R. Christian Bruce & Aaron Lorenzo, *Fed, Treasury Announce New Actions*, BNA Banking Daily (Nov. 26, 2008), *available at* http://news.bna.com (reporting on TALF and MBS facility). For background information on Ginnie Mae, see www.ginniemae.gov.

39. Bruce & Lorenzo, *supra.*

40. In August 2009, the Fed and Treasury announced the extension of the TALF program through June 30, 2010, *available at* http://www.federalreserve.gov/newsevents/press/monetary/20090817a.htm.

41. Mike Ferullo, *Federal Reserve Selects Investment Firms for $500 Billion MBS Purchase Program,* BNA Banking Daily (Dec. 31, 2008), *available at* http://www.bna.com/corp/index.html.

to $500 billion of MBS by the end of June 2009.[42]

Also in November 2008, an economic assistance package for ailing Citigroup was finalized.[43] It involved an agreement by the government to purchase approximately $27 billion in Citigroup stock, and the issuance of over $300 billion in guarantees with respect to mortgage-back securities. Combining features of the CPP, financial assistance such as AIG received, and troubled asset purchases under the TARP, the transaction requires Citigroup to assume up to $29 billion in portfolio losses, and 10 percent of all losses thereafter, with Treasury, the FDIC, and the Fed each successively responsible for all remaining losses. ...

On February 17, 2009, the President signed the American Recovery and Reinvestment Act (ARRA) into law.[44] The ARRA is primarily a $787 billion economic stimulus package intended to create or preserve approximately 3.5 million jobs and to jump start the failing economy, but it does not address the serious problems affecting regulatory and supervisory structure applicable to the financial services industry. Even Title V of the ARRA,[45] specifically dealing with financial services and general government, has no intended effect on the regulatory structure itself.

Regulatory Responses

In some instances, the regulatory responses have adjusted regulatory requirements to create incentives for private firms to invest in troubled financial assets. For example, in September 2008, the Fed established a special lending facility that enabled depository institutions and BHCs to borrow from the Federal Reserve Bank of Boston on a nonrecourse basis if they use the proceeds of the loan to purchase certain types of asset-backed commercial paper (ABCP) from money market mutual funds.[46] To support this program, the Fed adopted, on an interim final basis, an exemption from its leverage and risk-based capital rules for ABCP held by a state member bank or BHC as a result of participation in the program.[47] Effective January 30, 2009, the exemption was made permanent.[48] To facilitate national bank participation in the program, the OCC adopted on an interim final basis an exemption from its risk-based capital guidelines for ABCP held by any national bank as a result of its participation in the program.[49] In March 2009, the OCC finalized the risk-based capital exemption and extended it to ABCP purchased beyond the original January 30, 2009, date.[50] The OCC final rule applies to any ABCP purchased as a result of a national bank's participation in the facility. The risk-based capital exemption will continue to apply as long

---

42. *Id. See* http://www.newyorkfed.org/markets/mbs_faq.html (providing details of MBS purchase program).

43. R. Christian Bruce, *Regulators Unveil Assistance Package To Back $300 Billion in Citigroup Assets*, BNA Banking Daily (Nov. 25, 2008), *available at* http://news.bna.com.

44. Pub. L. No. 111-5, 111th Cong., 1st. Sess., 123 Stat. 115 (2009) (codified at scattered sections of 1, 6, 7, 12, 15, 16, 19, 20, 26, 28, 29, 31, 33, 38, 42, 47 U.S.C.) (ARRA).

45. ARRA, tit. V, 123 Stat. at 148-161 (2009) (codified at scattered sections of 15 U.S.C.).

46. *See* 73 Fed. Reg. 55,706 (2008) (discussing ABCP lending facility). *See also* 73 Fed. Reg. 55,708 (2008) (codified at 12 C.F.R. §§223.42(o), 223.56) (exempting on interim basis member banks from certain provisions of FRA §§23A, 23B to increase authority of member bank to purchase ABCP from affiliated money market mutual funds in connection with ABCP Lending Facility).

47. 73 Fed. Reg. at 55,707 (codified at 12 C.F.R. pt. 208, app. A, §III.C.1, app. B, §II; *id.* pt. 225, app. A, §III.C.1, app. D, §II (implementing ABCP purchase policy for member banks and BHCs, respectively).

48. 74 Fed. Reg. 6226 (2009) (codified at 12 C.F.R. §§223.42(o), 223.56).

49. 73 Fed. Reg. 55,704 (2008) (codified at 12 C.F.R. pt. 3, app. A, §3(a)(1)(ix)).

50. 74 Fed. Reg. 13,336 (2009) (codified at 12 C.F.R. pt. 3, App. A, §3(a)(1)(ix)).

as the lending facility remains in effect. The effective date of this OCC final rule was March 27, 2009. However, in light of June 2009 changes in generally accepted accounting principles (GAAP),[51] in January 2010, the agencies made a number of changes to their capital rules in light of these changes in GAAP, including the elimination of the exclusion of certain consolidated ABCP programs from risk-weighted assets.[52]

Similarly, in October 2008 the Fed issued an interim final rule allowing BHCs that issued senior perpetual preferred stock to Treasury under the CPP to include such capital instruments in tier 1 capital for purposes of risk-based and leverage capital guidelines for bank holding companies.[53] In June 2009, the Fed adopted the rule as a final rule without any substantive changes.[54]

At the same time, the Fed published an interim final rule to support full implementation of the CPP by permitting BHCs that had made a valid election to be taxed as S Corps and BHCs organized in mutual form to include the full amount of any new subordinated debt securities issued to Treasury under the CPP in tier 1 capital for purposes of the risk-based and leverage capital guidelines, provided that the subordinated securities count toward the limit on the amount of other restricted core capital elements includable in tier 1 capital.[55] The interim rule also allows BHCs subject to the Small Bank Holding Company Policy Statement and that are S Corps or mutual BHCs to exclude the subordinated securities from treatment as debt for purposes of the debt-to-equity standard under the policy statement. The interim final rule became effective June 1, 2009.[56]

In light of the continuing unusual and exigent circumstances in the financial markets, the Fed also adopted a regulatory exemption for member banks permitting them to enter into securities financing transactions with affiliates, such as an SEC-registered broker-dealer, that the affiliate ordinarily would have financed through the U.S. tri-party repurchase agreement market.[57] The exemption is subject to the following conditions: (i) the member bank may use the exemption only to finance asset types that the affiliate financed in the U.S. tri-party repurchase agreement market during the week of September 8-12, 2008;[58] (ii) the transactions must be marked to market daily and subject to daily margin maintenance

---

51. *See* Statement of Financial Accounting Standards No. 166, Accounting for Transfers of Financial Assets, an Amendment of FASB Statement No. 140; Statement of Financial Accounting Standards No. 167, Amendments to FASB Interpretation No. 46(R) (modifying accounting treatment under GAAP of certain structured finance transactions involving special purpose entity).

52. 75 Fed. Reg. 4636 (2010) (codified at 12 C.F.R. pt. 3, App. A §3(a)(5), App. C §42(l) (OCC ABCP rules); id. pt. 208, App. A §III.B.6.b, App. F §42(l); id. pt. 225, App. A §III.B.6.b, App. G §42(l) (Fed rules); id. pt. 325, App. A §II.B.6.b, App. D §42(l) (FDIC rules); id. §567.6(a)(2)(vi)(E), pt. 567, App. C §42(l) (OTS rules)).

53. 73 Fed. Reg. 62,851 (2008) (codified at 12 C.F.R. pt. 225, App. A), corrected, 73 Fed. Reg. 63,624 (2008).

54. 74 Fed. Reg. 26,081 (2009).

55. 74 Fed. Reg. 26,077 (2009) (codified at 12 C.F.R. pt. 225, App. A).

56. 74 Fed. Reg. at 26,077.

57. 74 Fed. Reg. 6225 (2009) (codified at 12 C.F.R. §223.42(n)) The term "U.S. tri-party repurchase agreement market" means "the U.S. market for securities financing transactions in which the counterparties use custodial arrangements provided by JPMorgan Chase Bank or Bank of New York or another financial institution approved by the [Fed]." 12 C.F.R. §223.42(n)(2)(ii).

58. 12 C.F.R. §223.42(n)(1)(i).

requirements;[59] (iii) the aggregate risk profile of the exempt securities financing transactions must be no greater than the aggregate risk profile of the affiliate's U.S. tri-party repurchase agreement transactions on September 12, 2008;[60] (iv) the member bank's top-tier holding company must guarantee the obligations of the affiliate under the securities financing transactions (or provide other security to the bank that is acceptable to the Fed);[61] and (v) a member bank may use the exemption only if the bank has not been specifically informed by the Fed, after consultation with the bank's appropriate federal banking agency, that the bank may not use this exemption.[62]

Finally, the Fed also adopted an exemption from its leverage and risk-based capital rules for ABCP held by any state member bank or BHC as a result of its participation in the program.[63] . . .

The SEC has taken multiple actions to protect investors and ensure the integrity of U.S. securities markets in response to the turmoil in the financial markets.[64] Most recently, the SEC adopted interim final temporary rules providing exemptions under the Securities Act of 1933, the Securities Exchange Act of 1934, and the Trust Indenture Act of 1939 for certain credit default swaps (CDS),[65] to facilitate the operation of one or more central counterparties for these instruments.[66] The rules define such credit default swaps as "eligible credit default

---

59. *Id.* §223.42(n)(1)(ii). The member bank must be at least as over-collateralized in its securities financing transactions with the affiliate as the affiliate's clearing bank was in its U.S. tri-party repurchase agreement transactions with the affiliate on September 12, 2008. *Id.*

60. *Id.* §223.42(n)(1)(iii).

61. *Id.* §223.42(n)(1)(iv).

62. *Id.* §223.42(n)(1)(v).

63. 74 Fed. Reg. 6223 (2009) (codified at 12 C.F.R. pts. 208, app. A, §III.C.1, app. B, §II; 225, app. A, §III.C.1, app. D, §II).

64. For a selective list of major SEC actions taken in an effort to stabilize financial markets during the credit crisis, see Securities & Exchange Commission, Temporary Exemptions for Eligible Credit Default Swaps To Facilitate Operation of Central Counterparties To Clear and Settle Credit Default Swaps, 74 Fed. Reg. 3967, 3968 n.4 (2009).

65. A CDS is a bilateral financial contract between two parties, known as counterparties. For the basic structure of the CDS, see Figure 1, *infra*. CDS were initially created to meet the demand of banking institutions looking to hedge and diversify the credit risk related to with their lending activities. More recently, financial institutions such as insurance companies, pension funds, securities firms and hedge funds have entered the CDS market. See Bank for International Settlements, Semiannual OTC derivatives statistics at end-December 2007, available at http:// www.bis.org/statistics/otcder/dt1920a.pdf (noting recent rapid increase in CDS market volumes). The value of the contract is based on underlying obligations ("reference obligations") of a single entity (a "reference entity") or on a particular security or other debt obligation ("reference security"), or an index of several such entities, securities, or obligations. The obligation of the seller to make payments under a CDS contract is triggered by a default or other credit event as to such entity or entities or such security or securities. Investors may use CDS for a variety of reasons, for example to offset or insure against risk in their fixed-income portfolios, to take synthetic positions in bonds or in segments of the debt market as represented by an index, or to capitalize on the volatility in credit spreads during times of economic uncertainty.

66. 74 Fed. Reg. 3967 (2009) (codified at 17 C.F.R. pts. 230, 240, 260). For recent specific orders of exemption in this regard, see Order Pursuant to Section 36 of the Securities Exchange Act of 1934 Granting Temporary Exemptions From Sections 5 and 6 of the Exchange Act for Broker-Dealers and Exchanges Effecting Transactions in Credit Default Swaps, Release No. 34-59165 (Dec. 24, 2008) 74 Fed. Reg. 133 (Jan. 2, 2009); Order Granting Temporary Exemptions Under the Securities Exchange Act of 1934 in Connection with Request of Liffe Administration and Management

swaps"[67] and exempt them from all provisions of the Securities Act[68] – other than the anti-fraud provisions § 17(a) – as well as from Exchange Act registration requirements[69] and the provisions of the Trust Indenture Act,[70] provided certain conditions are met. The rules also define as a "qualified purchaser," for purposes of the "covered securities" provisions of Securities Act § 18, any "eligible contract participant," as defined in Commodity Exchange Act (CEA) § 1a(12), other than a person who is an eligible contract participant under CEA § 1a(12)(c), to whom a sale of a eligible credit default swap is made in reliance on the interim final temporary Securities Act exemption.

Figure 1: Overview of a CDS Contract

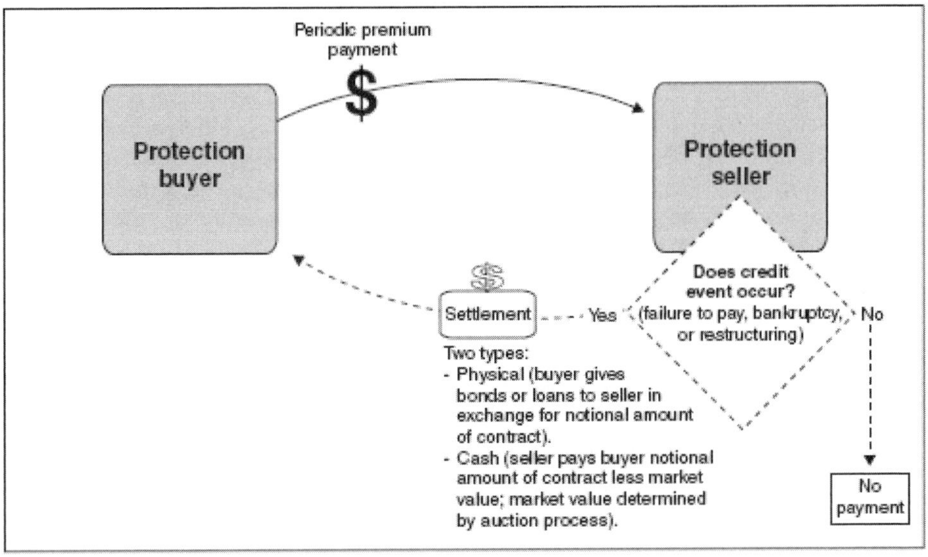

Source: GAO.

The OTC market for CDS – operating without meaningful regulation, transparen-

---

and Lch.Clearnet Ltd. Related to Central Clearing of Credit Default Swaps, Release No. 34-59164 (Dec. 24, 2008), 74 Fed. Reg. 139 (Jan. 2, 2009).

67. However, for those CDS that are "swap agreements" as defined in GLBA § 206A, 15 U.S.C. §§ 77b(b)-1, 78c-1, SEC authority is limited, since those swap agreements are excluded from the definition of "security," and the interim final temporary rules do not apply to them. GLBA § 206A defines a "swap agreement" as "any agreement, contract, or transaction between eligible contract participants (as defined in section 1a(12) of the Commodity Exchange Act . . .) . . . the material terms of which (other than price and quantity) are subject to individual negotiation. . . ." 15 U.S.C. § 78c note.

68. 17 C.F.R. §§ 230.146(c)T, 230.239T (providing temporary exemption for eligible credit default swaps).

69. Id. §§ 240.12a-10T, 240.12h-1(h)T (providing temporary exemption of eligible credit default swaps from Exchange Act registration requirements).

70. Id. § 260.4d-11T (providing temporary exemption for eligible credit default swaps offered and sold in reliance on Rule 239T).

cy,[71] or central counterparties (CCPs) – has been a source of interrelated concerns for the SEC and the other financial regulators, including the systemic risk posed by CDS, the possible inability of counterparties to meet their obligations, the potential adverse effects on other markets and the financial system as a whole, in addition to operational risks, risks relating to manipulation and fraud, and regulatory arbitrage risks.[72] Recent credit market events have emphasized the need for CCPs to help mitigate systemic impacts.[73] In pursuit of this objective, the SEC, the Fed and the CFTC signed a Memorandum of Understanding[74] establishing a framework for consultation and information-sharing on issues related to CCPs for CDS. The interim final temporary rules are intended to facilitate the ability of one or more CCPs for CDS to operate, by providing exemptions from regulatory provisions that might otherwise prevent them from engaging in such activities.

The operation of a well-regulated CCP could significantly reduce counterparty risks by preventing the failure of a single market participant from having a disproportionate effect on the overall market. A CCP would novate[75] bilateral trades, resulting in separate contractual arrangements undertaken by the CCP with each of the counterparties – becoming buyer to one and seller to the other. In contrast, contemporary CDS agreements usually are negotiated and entered into bilaterally, though both parties may agree that one party may novate the agreement and substitute another party to take responsibility for performance, by acting as the counterparty under the agreement.

In March 2009, the SEC published an order granting temporary exemptions to ICE U.S. Trust LLC, relating to central clearing of CDS.[76] Initially, ICE Trust's business will be limited to the provision of clearing services for the OTC CDS market.[77] ICE Trust will act as a central counterparty for ICE Trust participants by assuming through novation the obligations of all eligible CDS transactions accepted by it for clearing and collecting margin

---

71. *Cf.* President's Working Group on Financial Markets, Policy Objectives for the OTC Derivatives Market, (Nov. 14, 2008), *available at* http://www.ustreas.gov/press/releases/reports/policyobjectives.pdf (calling for "[p]ublic reporting of prices, trading volumes and aggregate open interest . . . to increase market transparency for participants and the public") (hereinafter "Policy Objectives").

72. *See* The Role of Credit Derivatives in the U.S. Economy Before the House Agriculture Comm., 110th Cong. (2008) (Statement of Erik Sirri, Director, SEC Division of Trading and Markets) (discussing seriousness of risks in CDS market).

73. *See* Policy Objectives, *supra* (identifying implementation of CCP for CDS as top priority). *See also* President's Working Group on Financial Markets, Policy Statement on Financial Market Developments, (Mar. 13, 2008), *available at* http://www.treas.gov/press/releases/reports/pwgpolicystatemktturmoil--03122008.pdf; President's Working Group on Financial Markets, Progress Update on March Policy Statement on Financial Market Developments (October 2008), *available at* http://www.treas.gov/press/releases/reports/q4progressüpdate.pdf.1.

74. Memorandum of Understanding Between the Board of Governors of the Federal Reserve System, the U.S. Commodity Futures Trading Commission and the U.S. Securities and Exchange Commission Regarding Central Counterparties for Credit Default Swaps (Nov. 14, 2008), *available at* http://www.treas.gov/press/releases/ reports/finalmou.pdf (hereinafter MOU).

75. "Novation" is a "process through which the original obligation between a buyer and seller is discharged through the substitution of the CCP as seller to buyer and buyer to seller, creating two new contracts." Committee on Payment and Settlement Systems, Technical Committee of the International Organization of Securities Commissioners, Recommendations for Central Counterparties 66 (Nov. 2004).

76. 74 Fed. Reg. 10,791 (Mar. 12, 2009).

77. 74 Fed. Reg. at 10,793.

and other credit support from ICE Trust participants to collateralize their obligations to ICE Trust. ICE Trust's trade submission process is designed to ensure that it maintains a matched book of offsetting CDS contracts.[78] A similar order was issued a week later to Chicago Mercantile Exchange Inc. and Citadel Investment Group, L.L.C. [79]

Of related interest, the Commodity Futures Trading Commission (CFTC) has taken similar action by order with respect to the clearing activities of Eurex as a multilateral clearing organization in the United States for over-the-counter derivative instruments.[80] The CFTC order, which became effective July 31, 2009,[81] finds, in accordance with FDICIA §409(a),[82] that Eurex is subject to appropriate supervision by the Bundesanstalt für Finanzdienstleistungaufsicht (commonly referred to as BaFin), in conjunction with the German Central Bank.[83]

Section 626 of the 2009 Omnibus Appropriations Act,[84] signed by the President on March 11, 2009, introduced a new regulatory approach to the crisis. The provision directed the Federal Trade Commission (FTC) to initiate, within 90 days of the date of enactment, a rulemaking proceeding with respect to mortgage loans. On May 22, 2009, the President signed the Credit Card Accountability and Responsibility and Disclosure Act of 2009 (Credit CARD Act) into law.[85] Credit CARD Act §511 clarifies that FTC rulemaking under Omnibus Appropriations Act §626 "shall relate to unfair or deceptive acts or practices regarding mortgage loans, which may include unfair or deceptive acts or practices involving loan modification and foreclosure rescue services."[86] Even as clarified by the Credit CARD Act, however, the Omnibus Appropriations Act does not specify any particular type of provision that the FTC should include in a mortgage loan or loan servicing rule.[87] As a result, the FTC has interpreted the Omnibus Appropriation Act as allowing it to issue rules prohibiting or restricting conduct not unfair or deceptive in itself that would be reasonably related to the goal of preventing unfairness or deception.[88] Credit CARD Act §511 also clarifies that FTC rulemaking authority is limited to entities that are subject to FTC enforcement under the FTC

---

78. For a fuller explanation of the operation of the clearing services and the conditions imposed by the SEC, see 74 Fed. Reg, at 10,796-10,799.

79. 74 Fed. Reg. 11,781 (March 19, 2009).

80. 74 Fed. Reg. 39,303 (2009).

81. *Id* at 39,303.

82. 12 U.S.C. §4422(a).

83. *Id.* 74 Fed. Reg. at 39,304.

84. Omnibus Appropriations Act of 2009, Pub. L. No. 111-8, §626, 123 Stat. 524 (Mar. 11, 2009).

85. Pub. L. No. 111-24, 123 Stat. 1734 (2009).

86. Credit CARD Act §511(a)(1)(B).

87. Unlike, for example, FTC Act §18, 15 U.S.C. 57, the Omnibus Appropriations Act – as clarified by the Credit CARD Act – does not require the FTC to identify with specificity the unfair or deceptive acts or practices that the prohibition will prevent. *See* Omnibus Appropriations Act §626(a); Credit CARD Act §511(a)(1)(B). *Cf. Katharine Gibbs Sch. v. FTC*, 612 F.2d 658 (2d Cir. 1979) (requiring specificity in definition of unfair or deceptive acts or practices under FTC Act §18).

88. 75 Fed. Reg. 10,707, 10,707 (2010).

Act.[89] Hence, the implementing FTC rules cannot cover the practices of certain nonprofits,[90] or of banks, thrifts, federal credit unions.[91]

Accordingly, in June 2009, the FTC commenced a two-part rulemaking. The Mortgage Acts and Practices Rulemaking (MAP)[92] targets activities that occur throughout the life cycle of a mortgage loan (*i.e.*, practices with regard to mortgage loan advertising and marketing, origination, appraisals, and servicing). A separate rulemaking proceeding, the Mortgage Assistance Relief Services Rulemaking (MARS),[93] focuses on the practices of entities (other than mortgage servicers) that offer assistance to consumers in dealing with owners or servicers of their loans to modify them or avoid foreclosure. The FTC is seeking comment with regard to unfair and deceptive acts and practices that should be prohibited or restricted pursuant to any rules adopted in either of these proceedings. Rules adopted in these proceedings would apply to entities other than banks, thrifts, federal credit unions, and non-profits that are engaged in such acts and practices.[94] . . .

In March 2010, pursuant to Omnibus Appropriations §626, the FTC proposed a rule concerning the practices of for-profit companies that, in exchange for a fee, offer to work with lenders and servicers on behalf of consumers to modify the terms of mortgage loans or to avoid foreclosure on those loans.[95] Among other things, the rule would prohibit service providers from making false or misleading claims,[96] mandate certain disclosures about the services,[97] and prohibit advance fees for these services.[98] The rule would also prohibit persons from providing substantial assistance or support to an entity they know or consciously avoid knowing is engaged in a violation of the rule.[99] Finally, the rule would impose recordkeeping and compliance requirements.[100] . . .

On March 4, 2009, Treasury announced guidelines under the Home Affordable Mortgage Program (HAMP) to promote sustainable loan modifications for homeowners at risk of losing their homes due to foreclosure.[101] The HAMP provides a detailed framework

---

89. Credit CARD Act §511(a)(1)(B).

90. 15 U.S.C. §44. The FTC does, however, have jurisdiction over for-profit entities that provide mortgage-related services as a result of a contractual relationship with a nonprofit organization. *See Nat'l Fed'n of the Blind v. FTC*, 420 F.3d 331, 334-335, 341 (4th Cir. 2005), *cert. denied,* 547 U.S. 1128 (2006) (upholding "narrowly tailored" rule as applied to nonprofit telemarketers). In addition, the Commission asserts jurisdiction over "sham charities" that operate as for-profit entities in practice. *See, e.g., AMA v. FTC*, 638 F.2d 443 (2d Cir. 1980), *affirmed,* 455 U.S. 676 (1982) (equally divided court) (upholding FTC order against AMA restraints on doctor advertisements); *FTC v. Ameridebt, Inc.*, 343 F. Supp. 2d 451 (D. Md. 2004) (holding nonprofit credit counseling service subject to FTC Act jurisdiction).

91. 15 U.S.C. §45.

92. 74 Fed. Reg. 26,118 (2009) (to be codified at 16 C.F.R. pts. 321–322).

93. 74 Fed. Reg. 26,130 (2009) (to be codified at 16 C.F.R. pts. 321–322).

94. 74 Fed. Reg. at 26,118.

95. 75 Fed. Reg. 10,707 (2010) (to be codified at 16 C.F.R. §§322.1-322.11).

96. 16 C.F.R. §322.3 (proposed rule).

97. *Id.* §322.4.

98. *Id.* §322.5.

99. *Id.* §322.6.

100. *Id.* §322.9.

101. *See* http://www.makinghomeaffordable.gov (announcing HAMP; providing HAMP terms and borrower eligibility criteria). For detailed discussion of the operation and procedures of the HAMP, see *Williams v. Geithner*, — F. Supp. 2d —, 2009 WL 3757380 (D.Minn. 2009), at *1-*3

for loan servicers to modify mortgages on owner-occupied residential properties and offers financial incentives to lenders and servicers that participate in the program. The HAMP also provides financial incentives for homeowners whose mortgages are modified pursuant to program guidelines to remain current on their mortgages after modification.

In November 2009, agencies adopted a final rule allowing banks, savings associations, and bank holding companies to risk-weight mortgage loans modified pursuant to HAMP with the same risk weight assigned to the loan prior to the modification, so long as the loan continues to meet other applicable prudential criteria.[102] . . . So, for example, a qualifying mortgage loan is risk-weighted at 50 percent, as are a first-lien mortgage and a junior-lien mortgage on the same property held by one banking organization with no intervening liens.[103]

Supervisory responses

While much of U.S. policymakers' attention has naturally been focused on short-term steps to address the immediate nature of the financial crisis, the crisis has served to demonstrate that the current U.S. financial regulatory system is in need of substantial reform. Indeed, as a January 2009 GAO study cogently argued, the current U.S. financial services regulatory system requires a significant restructuring.[104] The system involves a fragmented and complex set of federal and state regulations, rooted in a situation arising over 150 years ago, that has not kept pace with major developments in the financial services sector in recent decades.[105] While the government has generally been reluctant to take pervasive supervisory responses to the crisis – an apparent result of the "too-big-to fail"rationale transformed into a "too-big-to-touch" excuse[106] – certain supervisory actions have been undertaken. For example, in early September 2008, the Government placed the Federal National Mortgage Association (Fannie Mae), and the Federal Home Loan Mortgage Corporation (Freddie Mac) in conservatorship and replaced their management.[107] As in a bank conservatorship or receivership, the end result of the process could be the elimination of the value of private

---

(denying preliminary injunction in suit challenging constitutionality of HAMP as violating due process).

102. 74 Fed. Reg. 60,137 (2009) (codified at 12 C.F.R. pt. 3, App. A, §3(a)(3)(iii) (OCC rule); *id.* pt. 208, App. A §III. C.3; pt. 225, App. A §III.C.3. (Fed rules); pt. 325, App. A (FDIC rule); *id.* §567.1(4) (OTS rule)); *interim rule corrected*, 74 Fed. Reg. 34,499 (2009) (codified at 12 C.F.R. pt. 3, App. A §3(a)(3)(iii)) (reinstating language inadvertently omitted).

103. *See, e.g.*, 12 C.F.R. pt. 3, App. A §3(a)(3)(iii) (OCC rule). Other junior-lien mortgage loans would be risk-weighted at 100 percent. *Id.* pt. 3, App. A §3(a)(3)(iii); *id.* pt. 208, App. A §III.C.4; pt. 225, App. A §III.C.4 (Fed rules); *id.* pt. 325, App. A §II.C. (FDIC rule); *id.* §567.6(1)(iv) (OTS rule).

104. U.S. Government Accountability Office, *Financial Regulation: A Framework for Crafting and Assessing Proposals to Modernize the Outdated U.S. Financial Regulatory System* (GAO-09-216, Jan. 8, 2009), available at 2009 WL 52168.

105. *Id.* at 2.

106. In March 2009 testimony before a Senate Banking Committee hearing and in a speech before the national convention of the Independent Community Bankers of America, FDIC Chairman Sheila Bair criticized the "too big to fail" concept and argued that it should be eliminated. *See* Thecla Fabian, *Bair Seeks New Playbook to Resolve Plight Of 'Too Big to Fail' Financial Institutions*, BNA Banking Daily (Mar. 23, 2009), *available at* http://www.bna.com (reporting on Chairman Bair's remarks).

107. Stephen Labaton & Edmund L. Andrews, *In Rescue to Stabilize Lending, U.S. Takes Over Mortgage Finance Titans,* N.Y. Times, Sept. 8, 2008, at A1.

investment in the each of the two enterprises.[108]

On September 22, 2008, the Fed announced that Morgan Stanley and Goldman Sachs Group would convert immediately from investment banks to BHCs.[109] The move would, on the one hand, subject the firms to Fed supervision, but it would also give them access to Fed credit facilities, and the extensive liquidity and funding resource of deposit-taking. There is no indication so far that the Fed has utilized its extensive supervisory authority over BHCs to shape the behavior of these investment banks. American Express followed the same path to BHC status in November 2008, again with no specific constraints on its behavior.[110]

The first major congressional response to the crisis, the Housing and Economic Recovery Act of 2008 (HERA)[111] evidences a concern with all three aspects. The principal supervisory response of the HERA was the transfer of the supervisory and oversight responsibilities of the Office of Federal Housing Enterprise Oversight (OFHEO) over Fannie Mae and Freddie Mac[112] and the oversight responsibilities of the [Federal Housing Finance Board] over the [Federal Home Loan Banks (FHLBanks)] and the Office of Finance (which

---

108. *Id.*

109. Malini Manickavasagam & Joe Tinkelman, *Changing Face of Wall Street, Goldman, Morgan Become Banks*, BNA Banking Daily, Sept. 23, 2008, *available at* http://pubs.bna.com/ip/-bna/bbd.nsf/eh/ A0B7C3F1Y3.

110. *See* Eric Dash, *American Express to Become A Bank to Access the Bailout,* N.Y. Times, Nov. 11, 2008, at B2 (reporting on American Express reorganization as BHC, in order to gain eligibility to Fed financial assistance).

111. Pub. L. 110-289, div. A (Federal Housing Finance Regulatory Reform Act of 2008), §§ 1001-1605, 122 Stat. 2654, 2659-2830 (July 30, 2008) (codified at 5 U.S.C. §§ 3132 note, 3132(a)(1)(B), (D)-(F), 5313, app. 3 § 11, 11 U.S.C. § 783, 12 U.S.C. §§ 250, 1422(11)-(12), 1423-1424, 1426(a)(3)(A), (B), (b)(1), (c)(4)(B), (d)(2), 1426a, 1427(a)-(d), (f), (i)(1), (l), 1428, 1430(a)-(b), (j)(2)(A), (B)-(C), (12)(C)-(D), (k), 1430c, 1431(b)-(c), (f), (l), 1432, 1435, 1436, 1440, 1440a, 1441(b)(5), 1441a-1441b, 1442-1446, 1452 note, 1452(a)(2)(A)-(C), (b)(2), (d)(4), (h)(2), (4), 1454 note, 1454(a)(2), 1455(c)(2), (i), (j)(2), (l), 1456(e)-(f), 1701 note, 1701x note, 1708(e)(5), 1715z-23, 1717 note, 1717(b)(2), 1718(c)(2), 1719(g), 1723 note, 1723(b), 1723a(d)(3)(B), (k)(1), (m)-(n), 1787(c)(10(C)(i), 1813(I), 1820(d)(5)(B), 1821(d)(2)(F), (G), (e)(10)(C)(i), (m)(1), (6), (9), (15)-(16), (18), (n)(1)(A)-(B)(i), (E), (2)(A), (4)(C)-(D), (H), (5)(D), (8)(A)-(B), (11)-(13), (t)(2)(A)(vii), 1822, 1831o(j)(2), 1833(a)(3), (b)-(c), 3413(o), 4501 note, 4502(2), (8)-(11), (13), (19)-(20), (24), (25)-(31), 4511 note, 4511-4513, 4513a, 4513b, 4514, 4514a, 4515(a), (c)-(f), 4516-4521, 4523-4526, 4541-4548, 4561-4569, 4581-4588, 4588(c), 4611, 4612(a)-(f), 4613 note, 4613(a)-(b), 4614 note, 4614(a)-(f), 4615(b)(1)-(2), (c), 4616(a)(2), (b)(5), (7), (c), 4617, 4618, 4619(a)(3), 4622-4623(a)(1), 4624 note, 4624, 4631(a)-(e), 4632(a)-(e), 4633, 4634(a), 4635(a)-(b), 4636(a)-(d), (g), 4636a, 4636b, 4637-4642, 4715(a)(1), (4)-(5), 4716, 5101 note, 5101-5116, 15 U.S.C. §§ 78oo, 1639a, 7215(b)(5)(B)(ii)(II), 18 U.S.C. §§ 212, 657, 1006, 1014, 1905, 26 U.S.C. § 414(l)(2)(G), 42 U.S.C. §§ 1437f note, 4012a(f)(3)(A), 44 U.S.C. § 3502(5); redesignating 12 U.S.C. § 1422(2)-(9), (12)-(13) as § 1422(1)-(10); redesignating 12 U.S.C. § 4502(2)-(7), (8)-(12), (16)-(19) as § 4502(5)-(7), (12), (14)-(18), (21)-(23); redesignating 12 U.S.C. § 4614(c)-(d) as § 4614(d), (f); redesignating 12 U.S.C. § 4616(b)(5) as § 4616(b)(6); redesignating 12 U.S.C. § 4715(a)(1)-(2) as § 4715(a)(2)-(3); repealing 12 U.S.C. §§ 1422(1), (9)-(10), 1422a-1422b, 1427(f)(2), 1438(b), 1451 note, 4502(13)-(15), 4520(b), 4541, 4542, 4547-4548, 4562 note, 4589, 4616(b)(6), 4619-4621, 42 U.S.C. § 3534(d)). . . .

112. See, e.g.,74 Fed. Reg. 2347 (Jan 15, 2009) (codified at 12 C.F.R. pt. 1250) (codifying FHFA authority and responsibility to oversee and enforce statutory requirements affecting flood insurance operations of Federal National Mortgage Association and Federal Home Loan Mortgage Corporation under the Flood Disaster Protection Act of 1973 (FDPA); implementing congressionally mandated adjustments to the civil money penalties applicable to violations of FDPA; replacing prior HUD regulations, 12 C.F.R. pt. 1773).

acts as the FHLBanks' fiscal agent) to a new independent executive branch agency, the Federal Housing Finance Agency (FHFA).[113] . . .

In February 2009, the interested regulators – Treasury, the OCC, the Fed, the FDIC, and the OTS, but not the NCUA – unveiled the details of Treasury's Capital Assistance Plan (CAP),[114] which required "stress testing"[115] of, primarily, the 19 largest U.S. banking enterprises that hold more than $100 billion in assets. The release of the results of the stress tests on May 7, 2009, indicated that ten of the largest U.S. banking enterprises would need more capital to withstand worse-than-expected economic conditions . . . , assuming a requirement of a tier 1 risk-based ratio of at least 6 percent, of which at least 4 percent must be common equity by the end of 2010.[116] The banks have 30 days to develop capital plans and six months to complete recapitalization. Stressed banking enterprises that fail to raise enough private capital would then be eligible for a federal capital injection if the pertinent supervisor approved. Enterprises that have already received funds under the CPP, which involved Treasury purchases of nonvoting preferred bank shares with a 5 percent dividend, will be permitted to exchange those shares for the new CAP instruments – 9 percent preferred shares, convertible, at the issuer's option, to common stock equity. . . .

All of these administrative attempts at supervisory responses were merely hanging fire, waiting for a significant statutory initiative with respect to regulatory reform. Most observers stopped holding their breath in expectation of substantial reform long since the Administration announced in mid-June 2009 the broad outline of proposed comprehensive reform legislation. By late June 2009, the Administration announced that it would soon send to Congress legislative language for a proposed Consumer Financial Protection Agency (CFPA), as part of "a broad, still-evolving overhaul of the regulatory system." Unfortunately, this overhaul effort was about six months too late in starting, and about eighteen months too late in finishing. . . .

. . . [T]he Dodd-Frank Wall Street Reform and Consumer Protection Act ("Dodd-Frank Act") was approved by both houses and signed into law by the President on July 21, 2010.[117]

Notes and Comments 8.71. Of these three types of governmental response to the financial crisis – transactional, regulatory, and supervisory – which, if any, seems to be effective?

8.72. One neglected aspect of the response to the subprime crisis is state consumer protection law. The sad irony is that the federal government's aggressive preemption initia-

---

113. For discussion of the FHFA and its functions, see [Note 1.68, *supra*].

114. For background information on the CAP, see http://www.treas.gov/press/releases/-tg40.htm. *See also* R. Christian Bruce, *Capital Plan Gives Bank Firms Six Months To Raise Private Funds Following New Tests*, BNA Banking Daily (Feb. 26, 2009), *available at* http://news.bna.com (discussing CAP).

115. I.e., submission to "forward-looking economic assessments" that will test the ability of a subject enterprise to function and lend under two different macroeconomic scenarios: (i) a "consensus estimate" that forecasts an economic upturn in 2010; and (ii) a further significant economic downturn, factoring in an environment with unemployment as high as 10.3 percent. . . .

116. For stress test results, see http://www.federalreserve.gov/newsevents/press/bcreg/bcreg20090507a1.pdf.

117. Pub. L. No. 111-203, 124 Stat. 1376 (2010) (codified at scattered sections of 2, 5, 7, 11, 12, 15, 18, 20, 22, 26, 28, 31, 42, 44 U.S.C.) (DFA). . . .

tive against state regulation of financial services[41] may have blunted any "early warning response" that state regulation might have provided. The following case illustrates how state consumer protection regulation – here vindicated in private litigation – would apply to subprime mortgage programs.

LaSalle Bank, N.A. v. Shearon

19 Misc.3d 433, 850 N.Y.S.2d 871 (N.Y.Sup. 2008),
adhered to on reargument, 23 Misc.3d 959, 881 N.Y.S.2d 599 (N.Y.Sup. 2009)

JOSEPH J. MALTESE, J.

This court has denied the plaintiff bank's summary judgment motion in a mortgage foreclosure action because it has found that the original lender has violated the "predatory lending" statutes found in New York Banking Law § 6L. As a result of the findings of violations of the predatory lending sections of the New York Banking Law this court grants the defendant home owner summary judgment wherein he may be entitled to damages to include the voiding of the mortgage and loan, along with the return of all mortgage payments, the expenses of obtaining the loans and attorney fees.

Facts

In the summer of 2005, after living in a rental home for three years, the Shearons, as first time home buyers, decided to purchase a house in Staten Island, New York. After searching for the "right" home, they executed a contract of sale for real property located at 33 Westport Lane in Staten Island, New York.

To locate this home, the Shearons utilized the services of a real estate agent from Coldwell Banker. After finding their home, they utilized the services of Glen DeLuca and Michael Farber, mortgage brokers associated with Liberty Capital Mortgage [doing business as (d/b/a) HCI Mortgage Company located in Lake Ariel, Pennsylvania], to provide them with all necessary financial information and potential lenders in order to obtain financing for the purchase. In August and September 2005, Michael Farber advised the Shearons that they would qualify for traditional loan products with fixed interest rates and that he was "shopping around for the best rates." At the time the Shearons were applying for financing, as husband and wife, in connection with purchasing their home, David Shearon's credit score was 696 and Karen Shearon's credit score was 760 on a scale where 800 is the maximum score.

The Shearons presented a joint tax return which shows a combined adjusted gross income of $29,567. On October 17, 2005 the Shearons entered into a contract of sale to purchase the house for $335,000. However, the Contract listed a purchase price of $355,100 with a "Seller's Concession" of $20,100. At the execution of the contract, the Shearons deposited $5,000 with the seller's attorneys, which would leave a balance of $350,100. But the financing was for the full $355,000, implying that it would be a "no money down" purchase at closing where arguably that amount should have reflected a deduction of the $5,000 deposit that the Shearons paid at the contract signing.

From the time of the contract until closing in January 2006, Michael Farber advised the Shearons that WMC Mortgage Corp. would be able to finance the entire $355,100 of the purchase price in two loans. The plaintiff, LaSalle Bank, N.A., (hereinafter "lender") was the trustee and successor for WMC. The first mortgage was for $284,000 and the second mort-

---

41. On the effect of federal preemption policies on state financial services regulation, see Chapter 5, § 2.d, *supra*. *See generally* Mark E. Budnitz, *The Federalization and Privatization of Public Consumer Protection Law in the United States: Their Effect on Litigation and Enforcement*, 24 GA. ST. U. L. REV. 663 (2008).

gage was for $71,000. . . . However, David Shearon was listed as the sole purchaser and sole borrower on all closing documents.

Shearon, in his answer alleges that he has been the victim of "*Predatory Lending*" practices by the mortgage brokers and the lender regarding the finance of his home. Shearon alleges the following six separate and distinct acts to justify his claim of predatory lending:

> 1) Excessive financing was approved and extended to 106% of the purchase price, which permitted Shearon to finance the points, broker fees and costs;
>
> 2) Improper, inadequate or non-existent lender due diligence regarding Shearon's ability to repay the high cost home loan given;
>
> 3) The intentional and improper placement of Shearon into sub-prime loan products with excessively high interest rates, longer loan terms and impaired refinancing flexibility to the sole benefit of the lender;
>
> 4) Absent or inadequate state and federally mandated truth-in-lending ("TILA") disclosures regarding material elements of the financing being obtained including, without limitation, matters relating to closing costs and fees, counseling services, loan terms, amortization schedules and balloon payment requirements;
>
> 5) Forgeries of numerous loan-related documents, including without limitation the (i) Residential Loan Application, dated November 7, 2005; (ii) undated "Addendum to Contract of Sale"; and (iii) "Request for Verification of Rent", dated January 3, 2006 (purportedly signed by Jennifer Ogman) reflecting inaccurate information used to underwrite the Loans; and
>
> 6) The employment of repeated and continuous coercive and concerted tactics by plaintiff and other non-parties who stood to benefit from the loan process, which successfully targeted and forced Shearon to close on the loans and the property or face significant and dire financial consequences (i.e. losing the loan commitment, defaulting under the purchase contract, losing the down-payment/deposit).

New York Banking Law

Predatory lending practices are prohibited by both New York State and Federal laws. Here, the "home loans"[3] in question are governed by New York Banking Law § 6-L(1)(d) which governs "High Cost Home Loans" which are classified as such by the scheme provided for in Banking Law § 6-L(1)(g). New York Banking Law § 6-L(2) prohibits certain practices by lending institutions when offering High Cost Loans. The statute also provides for a six year statute of limitations accruing from the origination of the loan, as well as remedies for violations of the statute. A court may also award reasonable attorneys fees to the prevailing borrower. And the Court may grant the borrower injunctive, declaratory and such other equitable relief to enforce compliance with this section.

However, the most drastic remedies provided are found in Banking Law §§ 10 and 11 of the statute. Banking Law § 6-L(10) states:

> "Upon a finding by the court of an intentional violation by the lender of this section, or regulation thereunder, the home loan agreement shall be rendered void, and the lender shall have no right to collect, receive or retain any principal, interest, or other charges whatsoever with respect to the loan, and the borrower may recover any payments made under the agreement."

New York Banking Law 6-L(11) states: "Upon a judicial finding that a high-cost

3. "Home Loans" are defined in N.Y. Banking Law § 6-L(1)(e).

home loan violates any provision of this section, whether such violation is raised as an affirmative claim or as a defense, the loan transaction may be rescinded. Such remedy of rescission shall be available as a defense without time limitation."

Discussion

. . . Specifically, Shearon alleges that he was given excessive financing on a High Cost Loan without the lenders inquiry as to his ability to pay, which is mandated by N.Y. Banking Law § 6-L(2)(k). The lender alleges that loans of 7.65% and 10.5 % are less than the 16% usury statute and hence are not "high cost" loans. But the home loans were considered high cost loans by the lender because the lender prepared the following forms dated December 8, 2005: a New York High Cost Loan Disclosure; New York High Cost Loan Payment Disclosure; and New York High Cost Loan Insurance.

It is undisputed that Shearon was given $355,000 to finance the purchase of a $335,000 house, where the extra $20,000 or 6% of the purchase price was used to pay points and fees associated with the closing on the property. Specifically, when examining the HUD-1 closing statement prepared at the time of closing, it is apparent that $19,145.69 was used to pay all costs and fees associated with securing the High Cost Loans. These monies were paid from financing received above and beyond the contract price of $335,000. This ultimately left Shearon with negative equity in the property.

The financing of the fees and points associated with the loan is also a violation of Banking Law 6-L(2)(m) which states:

> "In making a high-cost home loan, a lender shall not, directly or indirectly, finance any points and fees as defined in paragraph (f) of subdivision one of this section, in an amount that *exceeds three percent* of the principal amount of the loan" (emphasis added).

Here, the amount financed to cover the fees are in violation of the statute because the points and fees exceed 3% of the principal amount of the loan. Three percent of the loan equates to $10,650. However, the expenses of the loan were $19,145.69, which equates to about 5.4% ($19,145.69 / $355,000 = .0539) which is more than the 3% allowed by the statute. What is more egregious is that $19,145.69 in expenses is 5.72% of the original cost of the $335,000 house ($19,145.69 / $335,000 = .0572).

Shearon also alleges that the Lender did not conduct a "due diligence" or any inquiry into their ability to repay the High Cost Loan. The plaintiff argues in its motion for summary judgment that David Shearon stated that he reported $7,200 as monthly income when he first applied for the loan. The plaintiff then states in paragraph 25 of their attorney's affirmation that Mr. Shearon "cannot argue that his annual income of $86,400 places him in a category of low-income."

If David Shearon and his wife stated on the original loan application that their monthly income was $7,200, the lender's statutory requirement is to make an inquiry as to the truth of the statement and the borrower's ability to repay the loan. While this court will not condone fraud by the borrower, New York Banking Law § 6-L(2)(k) states that:

> "A lender or mortgage broker shall not make or arrange a high-cost home loan without due regard to repayment ability, based upon consideration of the resident borrower or borrowers' current and expected income, current obligations, employment status, and other financial resources (other than the borrower's equity in the dwelling which secures repayment of the loan), *as verified by detailed documentation of all sources of income and corroborated by independent verification.*" (*emphasis added*).

Here, plaintiff's counsel states in both the moving papers and reply papers that "Based on Defendant's income, credit history, and the low interest rate on the Mortgage loan, along with the Defendant's lack of evidence supporting predatory lending, the Defendant is precluded from alleging the same. As such, the Defendant's mortgage loan was in compliance with all applicable laws, including, but not limited to, all anti-predatory lending laws ."

While statements contained in an attorney's affirmation are not proper evidence before the court, the plaintiffs do not offer one scintilla of evidence as to their required "due diligence" inquiry regarding David Shearon's ability to pay, which is a violation of New York's Banking Law governing High Cost Loans.

Shearon also alleges that he and his wife were intentionally placed into a sub-prime loan product. He bases the argument upon two facts. First, David Shearon and his wife originally applied jointly for the loans where he had a credit score of 696 and his wife had a score of 760 on a scale of 800. The Shearons jointly were considered "A paper," a term given to those loan applicants that are deemed to have the highest level of credit-worthiness.[9] Shortly before the closing, Karen Shearon was removed as a borrower for the loans. The Lender claimed that since no loan terms were modified, the application was not subject to any new underwriting or analysis and the closing occurred without any apparent change to the entire financing process. However, removing the higher rated borrower from the loan would require a new underwriting inquiry, but none was conducted. Therefore, the Shearons argue that they were intentionally placed into a sub-prime loan product.

The second factor that the Lender used to place the Shearons into a sub-prime product was an adjustable rate mortgage. Throughout the process, Michael Faber from Liberty Capital stated that the Shearons would be placed into a traditional loan product with fixed interest rates. However, when Shearon closed title, he obtained the First Loan with a 7.59% rate for the first 2 years, which would thereafter re-adjust and rise to no more than 10.59% in February 2008. However, every six (6) months thereafter it was subject to increase with a ceiling of 14.09% with anticipated finance charges over the life of the loan of $682,821.49. The Second Loan had a fixed rate of 10.750% for the life of the loan with anticipated finance charges over the life of the loan of $121,861.87. Therefore, Shearon would be obligated to pay up to $804,683.36 for a house that sold for $335,000. At the time of closing, these loans were considered sub-prime products, even though they had qualified for traditional fixed loan products at lower rates, because of their "A paper" credit worthiness.

Shearon also alleges a violation of Banking Law § 6-L(2)(l)(I), which has been dubbed the "*Counseling Statute.*" This section provides that a lender or mortgage broker must deliver, place in the mail, fax or electronically transmit the following notice in at least twelve point type[a] to the borrower at the time of application: "You should consider financial counseling prior to executing loan documents. The enclosed list of counselors is provided by the New York State Banking Department." Banking Law § 6-L(2)(l)(ii) requires that the lender or mortgage broker within three days after determining that the loan is a high-cost loan, but no less that ten days before closing, give the "Consumer Caution and Home Ownership Counseling Notice" to the borrower. This was not done.

David Shearon states in his affidavit that: 1) he has never been provided with, nor did Liberty Capital ever advise him of the nature of the loans and or the disclosures regarding counseling services available; and 2) the repercussions of the loans on his credit or that a

---

9. *See EMC Mortg. Corp. v. Batista* 15 Misc.3d 1143(A) [Sup.Ct. Kings County].

a. This footnote is in 8-point type. The text of the excerpted case is in 10-point type. By contrast, this is 12-point type.

balloon payment was required in connection with the loan. Moreover, the plaintiff fails to provide any evidence of the required disclosure in any of their papers. Their attorney simply states that their loans were sold in compliance with the various regulating statutes including *RESPA, TILA, HOEPA, New York State Banking law and Federal Statutory Law* prohibiting predatory lending.

. . . As is relevant, summary judgment is a drastic remedy that should be granted only if no triable issues of fact exist and the movant is entitled to judgment as a matter of law. On a motion for summary judgment, the function of the court is to issue findings, and not to issue a determination. In making such an inquiry, the proof must be scrutinized carefully in the light most favorable to the party opposing the motion. Here, the plaintiff has put forth a plethora of documentary evidence that, at the very least, precludes summary judgment on behalf of the plaintiff; and accordingly, their motion is denied.

However, when making a motion for summary judgment, the movant always runs the risk that the court may search the record, and in the absence of a cross-motion, award summary judgment on behalf of the non-moving party. When doing so, the court must offer the same careful scrutinization of the proof in the light most favorable to [the] party which summary judgment is being sought against. In moving for summary judgment, the plaintiff was required to assemble and lay bare its proof entitling it to summary judgment.

Here, the voluminous documentary evidence demonstrates violations of New York Banking Law § 6-L(2)(k), which deals with the plaintiff's due diligence into the ability of the defendants to repay the loan. The plaintiff has not offered one scintilla of evidence of any inquiry into the defendants ability to repay the loan. New York Banking Law § 6-L(2)(k) requires this inquiry to be "verified by detailed documentation of all sources of income and corroborated by independent verification." This failure to inquire is a violation of New York's Banking Law. Therefore, summary judgment on this affirmative defense is granted in favor of the defendant.

The plaintiff apparently also violated N.Y. Banking Law § 6-L(2)(l)(I), which requires the lending institution to provide a list of credit counselors licensed in New York State to any recipient of a High Cost Loan. David Shearon states in his affidavit that he never received the notice for required counseling. This document was also not provided to the court by plaintiff, although a copy of the entire origination file was provided. Failure to provide this notice is a violation of N.Y. Banking Law § 6-L(2)(l)(I).

In this action, clearly the most egregious violation of N.Y. Banking Law is the violation of § 6-L(2)(m) which states that no more than 3 percent of the amount financed is eligible to pay the points and fees associated with closing the loans on the real property. The amount financed to cover the fees are violative of the statute because more than 3% of the amount financed was used to pay the fees and points associated with the loan. The $19,145.69 in expenses equates to almost 5.4% of the High Cost Loan and is a clear violation of the statute.

After searching the record, it is clear that the lending institution, in providing home financing to David Shearon, violated, at least three provisions of New York's Banking Law. Therefore, summary judgment is granted in favor of the defendant, David Shearon, on his counter claims for violations of N.Y. Banking Law §§ 6-L(2)(k); 6-L(2)(l)(I); and 6-L(2)(m). Consequently, the finding of these violations now triggers N.Y. Banking Law § 6-L(7) through § 6-L(10) which is the remedy and damages provisions of the statute.

New York Banking Law § 6-L(7) provides in pertinent part that: "Any person found by a preponderance of the evidence to have violated this section shall be liable to the borrower for the following:

> (a) actual damages, including consequential and incidental damages; and

(b) statutory damages as follows (i) all of the interest, earned or unearned, points and fees, and closing costs charged on the loan shall be forfeited and any amounts paid shall be refunded; except that this element of statutory damages shall not be awarded for violations of:

(1) paragraph (i) of subdivision two of this section regarding loan flipping; and

(2) paragraph (k) of subdivision two of this section regarding ensuring the borrower's ability to repay the loan, so long as the lender demonstrates that at the time of the loan, it verified by detailed documentation all sources of the borrower's income and corroborated it with independent verification; or

(ii) five thousand dollars per violation or twice the amount of points and fees and closing costs as defined in this section, whichever is greater, for violations of:

(1) paragraph (i) of subdivision two of this section regarding loan flipping; and

(2) paragraph (k) of subdivision two of this section regarding ensuring the borrower's ability to repay the loan, where the borrower is not entitled to relief under subparagraph (i) of this paragraph."

In this case, the defendant David Shearon demonstrated by a preponderance of the evidence that the Lender violated the anti-predatory lending statutes of New York's Banking Law. Therefore, David Shearon may be entitled to receive: actual, consequential and incidental damages, as well as all of the interest, earned or unearned, points, fees, the closing costs charged for the loan; and a refund of any amounts paid.

This court will hold a hearing where all parties shall present any evidence as to actual damages and any other evidence not otherwise mentioned herein that may mitigate the findings of this court pertaining to the alleged intentional behavior of the Lender who violated several sections of the New York Banking Law § 6-L. The finding of intentional violation renders the home loan agreement (mortgage) void, and strips the lender from having a right to collect, receive or retain any principal, interest, or other charges whatsoever with respect to the loan, as well as giving the borrower the ability to recover any payments made under the agreement.[19] The hearing shall also be used to determine the amount of damages.

Additionally, the defendant is entitled to receive reasonable attorneys fees in conjunction with the defense of this action.[20]

Notes and Comments 8.73. LaSalle Bank tried to argue that the Shearon home loan could not be a "high cost loan" because it did not violate the N.Y. usury prohibition. How did the court deal with that argument? What is the relationship, if any, between the predatory lending and usury prohibitions?

8.74. How would the court define "subprime loan"? If the Shearon home loan is a "high cost loan," does that alone make it a "subprime loan"?

8.75. What sort of "due diligence" inquiry is a lender supposed to make under the state law? Is it the lender's responsibility to determine whether or not the loan is appropriate for the borrower?

8.76. LaSalle Bank seems to be arguing that Shearon is estopped from arguing that he was a "low-income" borrower, and therefore he cannot trigger the "due diligence" pro-

---

19. NY Banking Law § 6-L(10).

20. NY Banking Law § 6-L(8).

visions. Is that a relevant argument? How does the court respond to the argument?

8.77. State consumer protection statutes often provide very significant prohibitions and protections that would be applicable to the typical subprime loan situation – prohibitions on excessive financing, lender due diligence requirements, prohibitions on "intentional and improper placement," disclosure requirements, and prohibitions on "coercive and concerted tactics." In addition to actual damages, they also provide other rather significant remedies for victimized borrowers – statutory damages, forfeiture or cancellation provisions, and other equitable relief. *But cf. Hill v. Mr. Money Finance Co.*, 491 F.Supp.2d 725 (N.D.Ohio 2007) (denying whistle-blower protection to dismissed executive of subprime lender). What consumer protection prohibitions, requirements, and remedies are at issue in *LaSalle Bank*, and which of these seem most effective in controlling predatory subprime loan practices?

8.78. *Impact of Dodd-Frank Act.* Almost two years into the financial crisis, Congress enacted the Dodd-Frank Act, the most significant structural response so far to the ongoing financial crisis precipitated by the failure of the subprime mortgage market.[42] Among other things, Dodd-Frank is supposed to correct certain "structural" weaknesses in the financial services regulatory system, so that future systemic crises – financial crises triggered not by the failure of individual firms but by flaws in the structure of the financial services sector – can be anticipated or decisively contained. The following excerpt examines the Dodd-Frank measures that are intended to make these adjustments in the regulation of the financial services sector. How likely is it that the new Dodd-Frank measures will actually result in a safer and more stable financial services sector?

1 Michael P. Malloy, Banking Law and Regulation

§ 14.03[D][6] (2d ed., Aspen Publishers, 2011)

Traditionally, failures in the financial services sector have been divided along broad regulatory lines. Depository institutions were subject to an administratively supervised resolution process, while holding companies of depository institutions — as well as securities and insurance enterprises — were subject to the generally applicable federal bankruptcy law. In the wake of the failure of the subprime mortgage market in 2008, the question naturally arises whether it makes sense to organize the financial services sector in this way for purposes of failure and resolution. An April 2009 report issued by the Congressional Research Service[1] argued that Congress must consider whether there was a better way to handle the failure of "systemically significant financial companies" (SSFCs) that are not themselves depository institutions. Congressional proposals for regulatory reform included such measures.[2]

. . . The [Dodd-Frank Act] has as its twin themes new supervision and controls over

---

42. For background on the subprime mortgage crisis, *see* MICHAEL P. MALLOY, ANATOMY OF A MELTDOWN (Aspen 2010). . . . For a timeline of the current financial crisis, *see* http://www.stlouisfed.org/timeline/default.cfm.

1. David H. Carpenter, *Insolvency of Systemically Significant Financial Companies: Bankruptcy vs. Conservatorship/Receivership* (Cong. Res. Serv. Apr. 20, 2009).

2. Both H.R. 4173, the Wall Street Reform and Consumer Protection Act of 2009, and the Administration's proposed Resolution Authority for Systemically Significant Financial Companies Act of 2009 contemplated resolution procedures modeled on FDIC conservatorship/receivership authority under 12 U.S.C. § 1821. *See* Diane Davis, *CRS Report Compares Bankruptcy Process With Conservatorship/Receivership Regimes*, BNA Banking Daily, Jan. 19, 2010, available at http://www.bna.com (discussing proposals).

large and "systemically significant" financial institutions and creation of genuine consumer protection mechanisms at the federal level.

In terms of the supervision of troubled financial institutions, the Dodd-Frank Act includes the following principal features. First, it mandates the transfer of enforcement functions and responsibilities of the Office of Thrift Supervision to the other federal regulators,[3] effective July 21, 2011.[4] The abolishment of the OTS and the position of its director follows 90 days after that effective date.[5]

Second, the act establishes a new Financial Stability Oversight Council (FSOC), a committee of financial services regulators[6] to identify systemic risks, to promote market discipline, and to respond to emerging threats to the U.S. financial system.[7] Under Dodd-Frank § 113[8] the FSOC has the authority to require that a nonbank financial company be supervised by the Fed and subject to prudential standards, if the FSOC determines that material financial distress at such a firm, or the nature, scope, size, scale, concentration, interconnectedness, or mix of the activities of the firm, could pose a threat to the financial stability of the United States. In October 2010, the FSOC issued a proposed rule identifying the criteria that should inform its designation of nonbank financial companies under the DFA.[9] In addition, under Dodd-Frank § 619[10] the FSOC is required to study and make recommendations on implementing the "Volcker Rule," which prohibits banking entities from engaging in proprietary trading and from maintaining certain relationships with hedge funds and private equity funds. Accordingly, in October the FSOC published a notice initiating that study.[11]

Third, the Dodd-Frank Act gives the Fed authority to supervise the nonbank financial companies[12] identified by the FSOC as systemically significant.[13] This authority is in addition to Fed authority over bank holding companies and financial holding companies.[14]

---

3. DFA §§ 312(b), 314 (codified at 12 U.S.C.A. §§ 1, 4a, 11 5412(b)(2)(B) (OCC authority); 12 U.S.C. 5412(b)(1), (2)(A) (Fed authority); 12 U.S.C.A. § 5412(b)(2)(C) (FDIC authority)).

4. DFA § 311(a) (codified at 12 U.S.C. § 5411(a)). The effective date may be extended under certain specified circumstances. 12 U.S.C. § 5411(b). Technical details of the transfer are handled by DFA §§ 302, 312(a)-(b), 317, 319, 322-327.

5. DFA § 313 (codified at 12 U.S.C. 5413).

6. DFA § 111(a)-(h) (codified at 12 U.S.C. § 5321(a)-(h)).

7. DFA § 112(a)(1) (codified at 12 U.S.C. § 5322(a)(1)).

8. DFA § 113 (codified at 12 U.S.C. § 5323).

9. DFA § 113 (codified at 12 U.S.C. § 5323).

10. DFA § 619 (codified at 12 U.S.C. § 1851).

11. Financial Stability Oversight Council, *Public Input for the Study Regarding the Implementation of the Prohibitions on Proprietary Trading and Certain Relationships With Hedge Funds and Private Equity Funds*, 75 Fed. Reg. 61,758 (October 6, 2010).

12. DFA §§ 161-169 (codified at 12 U.S.C. §§ 5361-5369). *See also id.* § 170 (codified at 12 U.S.C. § 5370) (providing for safe harbor exemptions for certain types or classes of U.S. nonbank financial companies or foreign nonbank financial companies from supervision by Fed).

13. DFA § 113 (codified at 12 U.S.C. § 3523).

14. *See* 12 U.S.C. §§ 1841 *et seq., as amended*, Dodd-Frank Wall Street Reform and Consumer Protection Act (DFA), §§ 354(1)-(3), 355, 604(a)-(b), (c)(1)-(2), (d), (e)(1)-(2), 606(a), 607(a), 616(a), 618-619, 622, 623(b)(1)(A)-(B), (b)(2), 628, Pub. L. No. 111-203, 124 Stat. 1376, 1546-1547 1599-1602, 1607, 1615-1635 1640-1641 (2010) (codified at 12 U.S.C. §§ 1841(c)(2)(F)(v), 1841(j)(3), 1841(o)(4), 1842(c)(7), 1842(d)(1)(A), 1843(i)(8), 1843(j)(2)(A), 1843(k)(6)(B), 1843(l)(1), 1844(b), 1844(c)(1)-(2), 1844(c)(5)(B), 1850a, 1851, 1852, 1872(1); repealing 12 U.S.C.

Fourth, the act gives the FDIC authority to supervise the "orderly liquidation" of any systemically significant financial company that is at risk.[15] This authority is in addition to the separate and distinct FDIC resolution authority over insured depository institutions.[16] In October 2010, the FDIC published a proposed rule to implement its authority to "resolve" the failure of any covered financial companies.[17]

---

§ 1848a).

15. DFA §§ 201-214 (codified at 12 U.S.C. §§ 4403, 5381-5394; 18 U.S.C. § 1032(1)).

16. DFA § 201(a)(8)(B) (codified at 12 U.S.C. § 5381(a)(8)(B)).

17. Federal Deposit Insurance Corporation, *Notice of Proposed Rulemaking Implementing Certain Orderly Liquidation Authority Provisions of the Dodd-Frank Wall Street Reform and Consumer Protection Act*, 75 Fed. Reg. 64,173 (October 19, 2010) (to be codified at 12 C.F.R. pt. 380). Comments on the proposal were due by November 18, 2010. 75 Fed. Reg. at 64,173. Written responses to certain additional questions posed by the FDIC were due by January 18, 2011. *Id.*

Chapter 9

International Financial Services Policy

1. Introduction

International financial services regulatory policy is a complex field, quite capable of occupying its own casebook.[1] This chapter seeks simply to identify significant issues for the U.S. regulatory agenda affecting international banking. During the past twenty years, the international financial services industry, and financial services in general, have faced tremendous opportunity and challenge.[2] Many unresolved issues remain for the coming years.[3] In fact, the United States has entered the twenty-first century with a regulatory structure patched together from over one hundred years of historical accidents.[4]

---

1. *See, e.g.*, MICHAEL P. MALLOY, INTERNATIONAL BANKING: CASES, MATERIALS AND PROBLEMS (Carolina Academic Press: 2d ed., 2005) (examining international financial services regulatory policy).

2. *See* Michael P. Malloy, *Double, Double Toil and Trouble: Bank Regulatory Policy at Mid-Decade*, 63 FORDHAM L. REV. 2031 (1995) (assessing significant statutory changes in U.S. bank regulatory policy); Gary N. Kleiman, *Banking Law Is Good, as Far as It Goes*, N.Y. Times, Oct. 9, 1994, § 3, at 9 (discussing progress in U.S. bank regulation and contrasting it with advances in other banking markets).

3. *See* Michael P. Malloy, *Banking in the Twenty-First Century*, 25 J. CORP. L. 787 (2000) (discussing regulatory issues remaining after enactment of 1999 Gramm-Leach-Bliley Act). On the Gramm-Leach-Bliley Act, see Note 1.60, *supra*. *See also Bush Task Group on Regulation of Financial Services: Blueprint for Reform: Hearings Before a Subcomm. of the Comm. on Government Operations*, 99th Cong., 1st Sess. (1985) (recommending fundamental changes in bank regulatory structure to eliminate duplicative regulation); U.S. DEPARTMENT OF THE TREASURY, MODERNIZING THE FINANCIAL SYSTEM: RECOMMENDATIONS FOR SAFER, MORE COMPETITIVE BANKS (1991), *reprinted in* [1990-1991 Transfer Binder] Fed. Banking L. Rep. (CCH) ¶ 88,367, at 97,335 (Feb. 8, 1991) (advancing recommendations intended to make U.S. banks more competitive internationally) [hereinafter Modernization Study].

4. On the current regulatory environment, see 1 MICHAEL P. MALLOY, BANKING LAW AND REGULATION §§ 1.1-1.3.8 (1994 & Cum. Supp.). *See also* Gail & Norton, *A Decade's Journey from "Deregulation" to "Supervisory Regulation": The Financial Institutions Reform, Recovery, and Enforcement Act of 1989*, 45 BUS. LAW. 1103 (1990) (discussing the movement away from a U.S. policy of "deregulation" in the wake of the collapse of the savings and loan industry); Cynthia C. Lichtenstein, *U.S. Restructuring Legislation: Revising the International Banking Act of 1978, For the*

While financial services regulation faces a broad range of challenges in the new millennium, we focus here on issues of international regulation that illustrate two interrelated themes. First, "international" financial services regulation[5] presents a conceptual and practical dilemma: this area of regulatory concern consists primarily not of international regulatory institutions but of national systems of regulation responding to transborder enterprises and activities. Second, international competitiveness, rather than safety and soundness, has become a fundamental goal when formulating international banking policy within domestic policy.

The next section examines these two themes as they affect the agenda of U.S. international financial services regulation. Domestic regulatory strategies may not adequately or effectively deal with transborder problems. Moreover, increasing regulatory concern over the international competitiveness of U.S. banks may further complicate the situation, by requiring regulators to strike a balance between the traditional domestic objective of safety and soundness and the new concern with competitiveness.

The third section then examines five specific areas of concern that the agenda in the new millennium should encompass. These include areas of domestic concern with international consequences, such as capital adequacy supervision and artificial domestic barriers to the delineation of commercial and investment banking product markets. These specific areas also include external regulatory concerns with domestic consequences, such as transborder bank failures, U.S. national treatment policy with respect to foreign bank entrants into the U.S. banking market, and multilateral responses to terrorism.

The final section offers some suggestions for future approaches to these areas of concern. While noting the progress that has already occurred in some of these areas, the section emphasizes some problem areas of the agenda remaining substantially unresolved.

2. Basic Themes

a. "International" Financial Services Regulation

Banking first flourished in the post-medieval period in part because of the emerging needs of transborder commerce. Yet, banking activity remained based in individual national systems, governed by national law. This, of course, mirrored traditional or classical international law, grounded on the principle of absolute sovereign equality of individual states.[6] This traditional principle, however, has suffered considerable strain in contemporary

---

Worse?, 60 FORDHAM L. REV. 37 (1992) (discussing 1991 legislation revising U.S. regulation of international banking).

5. "International" financial services regulation in the context of national policy may be no more than public policy towards international banking formulated in a domestic context. However, there are some narrow examples of "supervisory initiatives arising out of a multilateral or international undertaking," that we might accurately identify as international bank regulation. *Cf., e.g.*, § 3.a, *infra* (discussing multilateral initiatives of the Bank for International Settlements (BIS)).

6. *See, e.g.*, Claudio Grossman & Daniel D. Bradlow, *Are We Being Propelled Towards a People-Centered Transnational Legal Order?* 9 AM. U. J. INT'L L. & POL'Y 1, 1 (1993) ("[I]nternational law has traditionally been concerned with the relations between coequal sovereign states.").

times.[7] For example, the fact that financial services increasingly transcend national boundaries strains the traditional principle of absolute sovereign equality of individual states. Distinctly global methods of communication and information transfer now underlie the business of major financial services firms.[8] Patterns of finance and investment, and the organization and structure of capital and secondary markets have an increasingly interdependent, transborder character.[9] The structure and focus of international banking in particular follow these markets in similar patterns of development.[10]

In theory, therefore, regulation of such activity should have an international or transborder character as well.[11] Although this observation appears cogent in the abstract, the fact remains that individual nation states have, for almost all intents and purposes, retained domestically grounded regulatory systems. For example, despite the increasingly transborder character of banking activity taken as a whole, banking policy remains a prominent national concern for individual nation states.[12]

b. Competitiveness and Safety and Soundness Concerns

Before attempting to balance competitiveness and safety and soundness concerns as objectives of international financial services regulation, we should first consider whether financial services activity requires regulation at all. Assuming regulation can be justified, we must also consider whether that regulation should try to keep pace with evolving banking behavior or simply wither away. The alternative would be to allow the operation of market forces to self-regulate the market for financial services and products.

For example, U.S. regulators and their critics have hotly debated the justifications for banking regulation in the United States,[13] one of the most thoroughly regulated banking

---

7. Grossman and Bradlow describe this strain in the following terms: "The principle of a state-grounded jurisprudence became less satisfactory as technological and socio-economic developments expanded the range of activities whose causes or effects transcended national boundaries and increased national interdependence." *Id.* at 2.

8. *Cf., e.g.*, Stephen Zamora, *Regulating the Global Banking Network–What Role (If Any) for the IMF?* 62 FORDHAM L. REV. 1953, 1957 (1994) (claiming that due to "dramatic technological advances in trading systems, foreign currency trading has become the hot international banking market of the 1990s).

9. *See generally Determinants and Systemic Consequences of International Capital Flows*, IMF Occasional Paper No. 77, at 4-19 (1991) (discussing international capital flows).

10. *See, e.g.*, Zamora, *supra* at 1968 ("[The] global banking network is merely the circuit in which market forces operate").

11. Grossman and Bradlow have argued that the banking industry is "[a] good example of an area where the desirability of an international regulatory body is clear. . . . As banks now have the ability and the client-driven need to move instantaneously funds around the world, it is no longer possible for each individual nation state to regulate effectively its banks." Grossman & Bradlow, *supra* at 13 (footnotes omitted).

12. *See, e.g.*, Malloy, *supra* at 2082 (discussing domestic policy concerns that affect treatment of international banking).

13. For an interesting interchange of views on the subject of market discipline as a regulating device, see Helen A. Garten, *Banking on the Market: Relying on Depositors to Control Bank Risks*, 4 YALE J. REG. 129 (1986) (criticizing "market discipline" device as a substitute for regulation); Jonathan R. Macey & Elizabeth H. Garrett, *Market Discipline by Depositors: A Summary of the Theoretical and Empirical Arguments*, 5 YALE J. REG. 215 (1988) (arguing for increased reliance on market discipline); Helen A. Garten, *Still Banking on the Market: A Comment on the Failure of Market*

markets in the world. Commentators often advance the argument that the danger of systemic failure in the banking sector justifies regulation.[14] Because the banking sector fundamentally affects the entire economy, it requires external regulation to maintain its safety and soundness.[15] Like other sectors, the financial services industry provides products and services to the economy. Beyond that characteristic, however, banking is also the mechanism for transfers for all sectors, at every level of the economy. In addition, unlike most sectors, banking is critically vulnerable to the vagaries of public confidence.[16] Thus, while banks provide credit, they can only operate effectively to the extent that they retain the credit[17] of the community in which they operate.

This concern with public confidence lies at the heart of the current policy debate in the United States. To compete effectively in the transborder market, banks must expand the range of risks they undertake.[18] However, banks must continue to maintain a public perception as systemically safe and sound to retain the confidence of the broad retail market that serves as their basic source of funding.[19] Thus, the fundamental policy objective in contemporary U.S. international bank regulatory policy is to maintain the balance between competitiveness, which necessarily involves risk, and public confidence, which is inherently skeptical of risk.

Discipline, 5 YALE J. REG. 241 (1988) (responding to market discipline arguments). *See also* Helen A. Garten, *Whatever Happened to Market Discipline of Banks?* 1991 ANN. SURV. AM. L. 749 (1992) (reviewing the demise of market discipline arguments).

14. *See, e.g.*, Michael P. Battin, Note, *Bank Director Liability under FIRREA*, 63 FORDHAM L. REV. 2347, 2383 (1995) ("[B]ecause banks today still serve unique functions, when a bank encounters problems or fails, the rest of the banking system must fill the void left by the problem bank. . . .").

15. *See id.* at 2383-84 (discussing effects of bank failure on the banking system as a whole).

16. *See, e.g.*, Michael P. Malloy, *Balancing Public Confidence and Confidentiality: Adjudication Practices and Procedures of the Federal Bank Regulatory Agencies*, 61 TEMP. L. REV. 723, 797 (1988) ("Confidentiality in formal enforcement adjudications does, in the abstract, serve to foster public confidence in the safety and soundness of the banking system, particularly by avoiding precipitous and unwarranted public reactions against target institutions and their management officials"). For discussion of some of the ambiguities surrounding the application of disclosure principles to depository institutions that are generally regulated under a principle of confidentiality, see Michael P. Malloy, *Public Disclosure as a Tool of Federal Bank Regulation*, 9 ANN. REV. BANKING L. 229 (1990); Alfred D. Mathewson, *From Confidential Supervision to Market Discipline: The Role of Disclosure in the Regulation of Commercial Banks*, 11 J. CORP. L. 139 (1986).

17. "Credit" in this sense is a pun. Banks require the credit of the community in which they operate, in the sense that their business essentially involves the performance of the "credit function," *i.e.*, taking money and credit in (as deposits) and putting money back into the financial system (as loans). The aggregate amount of loans will be exponentially greater than the aggregate amount of deposits from which loan funds are generated; this is the basis for the "credit function" performed by modern depository institutions. *See* Chapter 1, § 1, *supra* (discussing credit function). However, to keep this credit function operating successfully, banks depend upon the "credit" of their communities, in the root sense of the term, "believe, trust; good reputation." THE LITTLE OXFORD DICTIONARY 124 (4TH ED. 1977).

18. *See* MODERNIZATION STUDY, *supra* at 97,336-97,337.

19. *See id.*

3. The Emerging Agenda for International Financial Services

Five specific areas of regulatory concern reflect this balancing, particularly with respect to international banking policy. The first two arise from internal factors that have external consequences. First, the supervision of capital adequacy of depository institutions is undergoing further–seemingly continuous–refinement.[20] Second, former artificial divisions between commercial and investment banking are in the process of change.[21]

The last three concerns arise from external factors that have internal consequences. First, national and multilateral responses to bank failures must continue to improve,[22] particularly in light of the looming dangers of derivative trading.[23] Second, policymakers must address the occlusion of the U.S. banking market.[24] Third, more effective multilateral safeguards must be developed in response to the exploitation of the international financial sector by terrorists and those who facilitate terrorism.[25]

a. Capital Adequacy

The search for "[a] sound, internationally competitive banking system"[26] has focused on the maintenance of adequate capital. In its February 1991 MODERNIZATION STUDY, the Treasury Department identified the competitive undercutting of the U.S. banking industry as a problem requiring attention by policymakers.[27] The MODERNIZATION STUDY concluded

---

20. For problems and materials concerning international capital adequacy policy, see Chapter 7, § 5, *supra*. *See also* Zamora, *supra* at 1958-1959 (discussing capital adequacy initiatives of the BIS).

21. *See* Chapter 5, § 10, *supra*; Chapter 6, § 2.b, *supra* (discussing legislative and regulatory progress toward elimination of such divisions).

22. For examples of "multilateral responses" to transborder bank failures, see INTERNATIONAL BANKING, *supra* at 80-94.

23. For an excellent and exhaustive introduction to the study of derivatives, see Adam R. Waldman, *OTC Derivatives & Systemic Risk: Innovative Finance or the Dance into the Abyss?* 43 AM. U. L. REV. 1023 (1994) (assessing the risks posed by derivative trading). *See also* Zamora, *supra* at 1956-1958 (discussing derivatives trading in the global banking network); Saul S. Cohen, *The Challenge of Derivatives*, 63 Fordham L. Rev. 1993 (1995) (arguing against federal regulation of derivatives). Unfortunately, the provocative subject of derivatives and their regulation has attracted much secondary literature marred by simplistic and unproductive commentary. *See, e.g.*, Marc Levy, Note, *Japanese and U.S. Financial Derivatives Markets: Recommendations for Loosening Japan's Tightly Regulated Market*, 18 Fordham Int'l L.J. 1970 (1995) (purporting to provide comparative analysis of derivatives regulation).

24. *See, e.g.*, INTERNATIONAL BANKING, *supra* at 225-226 (discussing effects of 1991 federal legislation on openness of U.S. banking market).

25. *See, e.g.*, *id.* at 541-555 (discussing multilateral responses to international terrorism).

26. MODERNIZATION STUDY, *supra* at 97,336.

27. *See* MODERNIZATION STUDY, *supra* at 97,336 ("[T]he competitiveness of the banking industry has been undercut by our failure to adapt our banking laws to the evolution of financial markets, which has brought vigorous new competition to markets traditionally served by banks").

that the U.S. banking industry must increase its level of competitiveness.[28] Policymakers could achieve this goal if they permitted greater geographic and product diversification.[29] However, "[a]ppropriate safety and soundness limitations must accompany any such change."[30] Because supervision of capital plays a crucial role in assuring safety and soundness,[31] this view has increased the attention of the banking regulators with respect to capital maintenance.[32]

The MODERNIZATION STUDY advanced a formidable array of recommendations,[33] some of which have proven to be provocative.[34] The Federal Deposit Insurance Corporation Improvement Act of 1991 (FDICIA)[35] only enacted a limited number of these recommendations.[36] The provisions enacted by the FDICIA include more frequent on-site examinations, specific accounting requirements, and prompt corrective action, among other things.

FDICIA generally[37] requires annual on-site examinations of all insured depository

---

28. *Id.*

29. *Id.*

30. *Id.* at 97,337.

31. *See id.* ("Capital is a crucial tool for making banks safer. The role of capital in the supervisory system [should] be strengthened"). Specifically, the MODERNIZATION STUDY recommended that regulators impose increasingly stringent restrictions on activities to prevent the relative undercapitalization of banking institutions, assess deposit insurance premiums on the basis of risk in relation to the level of capitalization, permit newly authorized financial activities only through separately capitalized affiliates of banks, and include interest-rate risk in calculating the amount of capital required of individual banks. *Id.*

32. *See* Office of the Comptroller of the Currency, Board of Governors of the Federal Reserve System, Federal Deposit Insurance Corporation & Office of Thrift Supervision, *Joint Report to Congressional Committees: Differences in Accounting and Capital Standards Among the Federal Banking and Thrift Agencies*, 68 Fed. Reg. 5976 (2003) (discussing capital adequacy regulations).

33. For discussion of the MODERNIZATION STUDY recommendations, see BANKING LAW AND REGULATION, *supra*, §§ 1.42, 2.5, 3.5, 7.4.3, 8.5.

34. *Cf.* Jill M. Considine, *A State's Response to the United States Treasury Department Proposals to Modernize the Nation's Banking System*, 59 Fordham L. Rev. S243 (1991) (discussing New York State Superintendent of Banks' critique of MODERNIZATION STUDY).

35. Pub. L. No. 102-242, 105 Stat. 2236 (1991) (codified in scattered sections of 12 U.S.C.).

36. One recommendation the FDICIA did not address, the elimination of artificial geographic barriers to banking, has since been acted upon by the Riegle-Neal Interstate Banking and Branching Act Efficiency Act of 1994 (IBBEA), Pub. L. No. 103-328, 108 Stat. 2338 (1994) (codified in scattered sections of 12 U.S.C.). *See* Chapter 3, §4, *supra*; Notes 4.27-4.31, 4.47-4.51, *supra* (discussing and analyzing IBBEA). The provisions of the IBBEA permit geographic expansion by banks and holding companies without regard to artificial barriers to interstate expansion heretofore imposed by the Douglas Amendment (12 U.S.C. § 1842(d) (1988) to the Bank Holding Company Act (12 U.S.C. §§ 1841 *et seq.* (1988)) and the branching provisions of state law and the National Bank Act (NBA). *See* 3 BANKING LAW AND REGULATION, *supra*, § 8.2.1 (discussing legislative history and applicability of Bank Holding Company Act); 12 U.S.C. § 36(c) (1988) (NBA provision limiting branching by national banks to branching permitted to state banks in same state). *See generally First Nat'l Bank of Logan v. Walker Bank & Trust Co.*, 385 U.S. 252 (1966) (construing 12 U.S.C. § 36(c)); *First Nat'l Bank in Plant City v. Dickinson*, 396 U.S. 122 (1969) (defining "branch" for purposes of 12 U.S.C. § 36(c)).

37. Regulators will examine certain specified small institutions (well-capitalized and well-managed institutions with total assets of less than $100 million with no recent change in control) every eighteen months. Pub. L. No. 102-242, 105 Stat. 2236 (1991) (codified at 12 U.S.C. § 1820(d)

institutions.[38] FDICIA also requires independent audits of insured depository institutions.[39] Further, for a depository institution to receive FDIC insurance, it must apply to, and receive approval from the FDIC.[40]

FDICIA established specific accounting objectives, standards, and requirements. These are applicable to all insured depository institutions.[41] They include uniform standards for accounting of capital.[42]

FDICIA requires "prompt corrective action"[43] by regulators. Such action is intended to "resolve the problems of insured depository institutions at the least possible long-term loss to the deposit insurance fund."[44] "Prompt corrective action" generally[45] includes the implementation of capital standards.[46]

Consistent with the MODERNIZATION STUDY, FDICIA also focused on the safety and soundness of insured depository institutions in several ways. It authorized federal bank regulatory agencies to impose more stringent treatment of the capital of institutions that regulators determine are in an unsafe and unsound condition or are engaged in an unsafe and unsound practice.[47] FDICIA required that federal bank regulatory agencies create detailed safety and soundness standards for insured depository institutions and their holding companies.[48] Most significantly, the FDICIA required the establishment of a risk-based assessment system for federal deposit insurance.[49]

A new capital adequacy accord for internationally active banks, popularly known as "Basel II" was approved by the Committee on Banking Supervision of the Bank for International Settlements (BIS Committee) in June 2004.[50] By year-end 2007, Basel II was to

---

(4)).

38. FDICIA § 111(a) (codified at 12 U.S.C. § 1820(d)(1)-(3)).

39. *Id.* § 112(a) (codified at 12 U.S.C. § 1831m).

40. *Id.* § 115(a) (codified at 12 U.S.C. § 1815(a)).

41. *Id.* § 121(a) (codified at 12 U.S.C. § 1831n).

42. 12 U.S.C. § 1831n(b).

43. FDICIA § 131 (codified at 12 U.S.C. § 1831o(a) (2)).

44. *Id.* (codified at 12 U.S.C. § 1831o(a)(1)). *Cf. id.* § 141(a), (e) (codified at 12 U.S.C. § 1823(c)(4) (11)) (mandating least-cost resolution of failing institution problems). *See* Federal Deposit Insurance Corporation, *Statement of Policy on Assistance to Operating Insured Depository Institutions*, 57 Fed. Reg. 60,203 (1992) (explaining FDIC policy concerning statutory cost test for FDIC-assisted resolutions and requirements for FDIC assistance to operating institutions prior to appointment of conservator or receiver).

45. These rules do not apply to depository institutions in conservatorship, or to FDIC wholly-owned bridge banks. 12 U.S.C. § 1831o(j).

46. FDICIA § 131(a) (codified at 12 U.S.C. § 1831o(c)-(f), (h)-(i), (k), (n) (1994)). FDICIA also contains provisions requiring the periodic review and improvement of applicable capital standards. *See id.* § 305(b)(1) (codified at 12 U.S.C. § 1828 note) (requiring federal bank regulatory agencies to consider interest-rate, concentration and other forms of risk).

47. *Id.* § 131(a) (codified at 12 U.S.C. § 1831o(g)).

48. *Id.* § 132(a) (codified at 12 U.S.C. § 1831s).

49. *Id.* § 302 (codified at 12 U.S.C. § 1817(b)). *See* 58 Fed. Reg. 29,952 (1993) (codified at 12 C.F.R. pt. 330) (FDIC insurance coverage rules).

50. Committee on Banking Supervision, Bank for International Settlements, *International Convergence of Capital Measurement and Capital Standards: A Revised Framework* (June 26, 2004), *available at* http://www.bis.org/publ/bcbs107.htm (hereinafter "Basel II"). The BIS Committee is a committee of banking supervisory authorities, which was established by the central bank governors

replace international capital adequacy guidelines ("Basel I") that have been in operation since 1992,[51] but Basel II essentially collapsed in the wake of the meltdown of international markets in 2008. The BIS and national regulators have been scrambling since then to construct a credible post-meltdown replacement – popularly known as Basel III.[52] I remains to be seen whether these efforts will be successful.

b. Commercial and Investment Banking Barriers

For more than sixty years, an almost complete separation of commercial and investment banking characterized the U.S. banking system. However, with the enactment of the Gramm-Leach-Bliley Act (GLBA),[53] a more integrated approach to the regulation of financial services was undertaken by the United States.[54] While this development addresses the main concerns about the previous artificial separation of commercial and investment banking, much work remains in terms of implementation, interpretation and refinement of the new regulatory regime.[55]

c. Responses to Transborder Bank Failures

Banks operating transborder have occasionally encountered significant financial difficulty, and even failure, but the response of the international community has tended to be *ad hoc* and episodic.[56] Development by the BIS of the Basle Concordat of 1975, followed by the revised Concordat of 1983,[57] reflects some progress. The Concordat seeks to identify basic principles governing the responsibilities of host and home country regulators in the

---

of the Group of Ten countries in 1975. Currently, it consists of senior representatives of bank supervisory authorities and central banks from Argentina, Australia, Belgium, Brazil, Canada, China, France, Germany, Hong Kong SAR, India, Indonesia, Italy, Japan, Korea, Luxembourg, Mexico, the Netherlands, Russia, Saudi Arabia, Singapore, South Africa, Spain, Sweden, Switzerland, Turkey, the United Kingdom and the United States. It usually meets at the Bank for International Settlements (BIS) in Basel, Switzerland, where its permanent Secretariat is located.

51. BANK FOR INTERNATIONAL SETTLEMENTS, FINAL REPORT FOR INTERNATIONAL CONVERGENCE OF CAPITAL MEASUREMENT AND CAPITAL STANDARDS, *reprinted in* 4 Fed. Banking L. Rep. (CCH) ¶ 47-105 (Mar. 15, 1996) [hereinafter "Basel I"]. *See* Michael P. Malloy, *Capital Adequacy and Regulatory Objectives*, 25 SUFFOLK TRANSNAT'L L. REV. 299 (2002) (discussing Basel I).

52. *See* notes 7.24-7.25, *supra* (discussing Basel III).

53. Pub. L. No. 106-102, Nov. 12, 1999, 113 Stat. 1338 (1999) (codified at scattered sections of 12, 15, 16, 18 U.S.C.).

54. *See* Note 1.60 (discussing GLBA).

55. *See* Michael P. Malloy, *Banking in the Twenty-First Century*, 25 J. Corp. L. 787 (2000) (discussing regulatory issues remaining after enactment of GLBA).

56. For a discussion of the problem of transborder bank failures and the BIS response, see INTERNATIONAL BANKING, *supra* at 80-94.

57. BIS, Committee on Banking Regulations and Supervisory Practices, *Principles for the Supervision of Banks' Foreign Establishments* (1983), *reprinted in* INTERNATIONAL BANKING, *supra* at 81-85 (Basle Concordat).

event of the failure or threatened failure of a bank operating transborder.[58] Unfortunately, the Concordat evidences two shortcomings that may in fact be typical of international bank regulation.

First, bank regulation remains almost exclusively domestic-based in character and orientation, even when the regulated bank or regulated banking activity is international. Hence, the Concordat's principles are explicitly nonbinding.[59] Second, regulatory initiatives that are international in character have tended to have a limited scope. The Concordat, on its own terms, embodies only the expression of (nonbinding) views of those states that participated in its development. Nevertheless, even the formal expression of nonbinding principles provides a starting point for discussion and negotiation between states concerned with a transborder bank failure.

Since the issuance of the revised Concordat in 1983, the BIS has provided further guidance with respect to transborder bank failures. For example, in April 1990, it issued a Supplement to the Concordat that sought to ensure an adequate flow of information between bank supervisors in different states.[60] Like the Concordat itself, however, the Supplement is merely hortatory, providing only a series of non-binding recommendations.

Following the international failure of the Bank of Credit and Commerce International (BCCI),[61] the BIS did issue a report containing minimum standards for the supervision of transborder banking enterprises, which it urged states to adopt as binding.[62] These standards mandate consolidated supervision of transborder banking enterprises by the home state regulator, prior consent for establishment of operations by both home and host states, and mandatory provision of information about banking enterprises from the home to the host state.[63] A host state would also have the explicit right to impose restrictive measures on a banking enterprise seeking to operate within its jurisdiction if the enterprise's home state did not adhere to these minimum standards.[64] Unfortunately, the report and its recommendations

---

58. *See* Basle Concordat, *reprinted in* INTERNATIONAL BANKING, *supra* at 82:

> Effective co-operation between host and parent authorities is a central prerequisite for the supervision of banks' operations. . . . In giving effect to these principles, host authorities should ensure that parent authorities are informed immediately of any serious problems which arise in a parent bank's foreign establishment. Similarly, parent authorities should inform host authorities when problems arise in a parent bank which are likely to affect the parent bank's foreign establishment.

59. *Id.* at 81 ("The principles set out in the [Concordat] are not necessarily embodied in the laws of the countries represented on the [BIS] Committee [on Banking Regulations and Supervisory Practices]. Rather they are recommended guidelines of best practices in this area, which all members have undertaken to work towards implementing, according to the means available to them").

60. BIS, Committee on Banking Regulations and Supervisory Practices, Supplement to the Basle Concordat Ensuring of Adequate Information Flows between Banking Supervisory Authorities (April 1990), *reprinted in* INTERNATIONAL BANKING, *supra* at 86-89.

61. On the BCCI scandal and the regulatory responses thereto, see RAJ K. BHALA, FOREIGN BANK REGULATION AFTER BCCI (1994).

62. BIS, Committee on Banking Regulations and Supervisory Practices, *Report on Minimum Standards for the Supervision of International Banking Groups and Their Cross-Border Establishment* (June 1992), *reprinted in*, INTERNATIONAL BANKING, *supra* at 89-93.

63. *Id.*

64. *Id.*

remain subject to individual implementation at the decision of national governments.[65]

Coordinated, binding rules concerning the supervision of failing banks are essential. This need becomes even more critical after the meltdown of the capital markets following the subprime mortgage crisis, in which extraordinary risks related to trading in volatile instruments like mortgage-backed securities and other derivatives endangered substantial institutions.

d. National Treatment Policy

1. Introduction

The United States has traditionally espoused a policy of national treatment[66] with respect to direct foreign investment, a policy formally adopted with respect to international banking under the IBA.[67] Three factors have caused an increasingly pronounced trend away from national treatment in U.S. bank regulatory policy. First, discriminatory policies in other states persist.[68] Second, the relatively slow progress of the General Agreement on Trade in Services (GATS)[69] to rationalize the rules governing domestic regulation of international banking may have dampened hopes for coordinated, multilateral solutions.[70] Third, the threat of international bank failures such as the BCCI scandal has strained U.S. adherence to the principle of national treatment.[71]

By the time the GATS was established, FDICIA had already significantly altered the rules governing the establishment and operation of federal branches and agencies of foreign-based banks. For the first time, Congress has given the Board of Governors of the Federal Reserve System (the Fed), in addition to the Comptroller of the Currency (the Comptroller), authority to approve or disapprove the establishment of any U.S. branch or agency, or the acquisition or control of any commercial lending company, by a non-U.S.-

---

65. *See generally* 12 U.S.C. §§ 1842(c)(3)(B) (application for bank holding company involving foreign bank denied if bank not subject to comprehensive supervision or regulation on consolidated basis by home state authorities); 3105(d)(2)(A) (establishment of U.S. office of foreign bank denied in absence of comprehensive home state supervision); 3105(d)(3)(A) (standards of approval for establishment of U.S. office of foreign bank to include whether home state consents to proposed establishment); 3105(e)(1)(A) (termination of U.S. office of foreign bank in absence of comprehensive home state supervision).

66. "National treatment" is a policy intended "to provide to the extent possible or appropriate equal treatment for foreign and domestic banks operating in the United States." H.R. Rep. No. 910, 95th Cong., 2d Sess. 5 (1978) (describing one objective behind International Banking Act of 1978).

67. 12 U.S.C. §§ 3101 *et seq. See Conference of State Bank Supervisors v. Conover*, 715 F.2d 604 (D.C. Cir. 1983), *cert. denied*, 466 U.S. 927 (1984) (discussing national treatment policy and IBA). *See also* INTERNATIONAL BANKING, *supra* at 72-75 (discussing national treatment and post-IBA Treasury studies of national treatment in other states).

68. *See* Gary N. Kleiman, *Banking Law Is Good, as Far as It Goes*, N.Y. Times, Oct. 9, 1994, § 3, at 9 (citing discriminatory bank regulatory policies of Brazil, China and Russia).

69. General Agreement on Trade in Services, 15 April 1994, Agreement Establishing the World Trade Organization, Annex 1B, 33 Int'l Leg. Materials 1167 (1994) (GATS).

70. *See* MICHAEL P. MALLOY, PRINCIPLES OF BANK REGULATION § 9.10 (2d ed. 2004) (discussing GATS).

71. *See* Zamora, *supra* at 1959-1960 (discussing effects of BCCI scandal).

based bank.[72] The Fed also has the authority, under specified circumstances, to order the closing of any state-licensed office of a foreign-based bank,[73] and to recommend to the Comptroller the termination of the license of any federally-licensed office of a foreign-based bank.[74] The FDICIA also gives the Fed broad authority to examine U.S. branches, agencies and affiliates of non-U.S. based banks, whether state- or federally-approved.[75]

FDICIA has also imposed limitations on the powers of state-licensed branches and agencies of foreign banks, prohibiting them from engaging in any activity that is not permissible for a federally-licensed branch.[76] However, the Fed may determine that the activity is consistent with sound banking practice.[77] Nevertheless, FDICIA allows the Fed or the state supervisory authority to impose more stringent restrictions on state-licensed branches and agencies of foreign banks than those that apply to federally-licensed branches and agencies.[78] In addition, the same limits on lending to a single borrower that apply to federally-licensed branches and agencies apply to these branches and agencies.[79]

FDICIA also imposed new requirements regarding the establishment and supervision of U.S. representative offices of non-U.S.-based banks.[80] Prior to enactment of FDICIA, the IBA required a non-U.S.-based bank operating a representative office in the United States to register with the Department of the Treasury.[81] Under FDICIA, establishment of a representative office now requires approval by the Fed.[82] The Fed also has the authority to examine representative offices,[83] and to terminate their activities.[84]

Departing decisively from the relatively benign policy of national treatment is the most provocative provision of FDICIA, which restricts retail deposit-taking by non-U.S.-based banks. To engage in the retail deposit business (*i.e.*, to accept deposits under $100,000), foreign banks must establish a U.S. banking subsidiary for that purpose, and obtain federal deposit insurance for the subsidiary.[85] Only time will tell whether the United

---

72. 12 U.S.C. § 3105(d)(1), (g).

73. *Id.* § 3105(e)(1)-(4), (g).

74. *Id.* § 3105(e)(5).

75. *Id.* § 3105(c)(1).

76. *Id.* § 3105(h)(1).

77. *Id.* § 3105(h)(1)(A). In the case of an insured branch of a non-U.S.-based bank, the FDIC must also determine that the activity would pose no significant risk to the deposit insurance fund. *Id.* § 3105(h)(1)(B).

78. *Id.* § 3105(h)(3).

79. *Id.* § 3105(h)(2).

80. On the limited role and functions of representative offices, see INTERNATIONAL BANKING, *supra* at 128.

81. 12 U.S.C. § 3107 (1988).

82. 12 U.S.C. § 3107(a)(1). Compliance with any applicable state law requirements is still required. *Id.* § 3107(d).

83. *Id.* § 3107(c), *as amended*, Gramm-Leach-Bliley Act, § 142, Pub. L. No. 106-102, Nov. 12, 1999, 113 Stat. 1338, 1384 (1999) (codified at 12 U.S.C. §§ 3101(b)(15), 3107(c)).

84. *Id.* § 3107(b).

85. *Id.* § 3104(d)(1)(B). However, non-U.S.-based banks with U.S. branches that were insured prior to FDICIA are grandfathered. *Id.* § 3104(d)(2). IBBEA extends the requirement of subsidiary operations for retail deposit taking, under certain specified circumstances, to interstate operations of any non-U.S.-based bank. *Id.* § 3103(a)(6). Furthermore, if the Fed or the Comptroller finds that, in light of differing regulatory or accounting standards in the bank's home country, adherence by

States will continue to move away from the policy of national treatment, into a more confrontational approach to international bank regulation.

2. National Treatment and the GATS

The experience to date with the GATS would seem to suggest that U.S. policy with respect to national treatment will continue to be guarded at best. The GATS established "a multilateral framework of principles and rules for trade in services with a view to the expansion of such trade under conditions of transparency and progressive liberalization,"[86] by applying the nondiscrimination principles of the General Agreement on Tariffs and Trade (GATT) to trade in services.[87] The GATS specifically applies to financial services.[88] The requirements of nondiscriminatory treatment do not, however, prevent states that are members of the World Trade Organization (WTO) from enforcing domestic regulations for "prudential reasons, including for the protection of . . . depositors, . . . or persons to whom a fiduciary duty is owed by a financial service supplier, or to ensure the integrity and stability of the financial system."[89]

As a transitional matter, a second Annex to the GATS, concerning financial services, permitted temporary withdrawal from the GATS commitments.[90] Nevertheless, it was anticipated that inclusion of financial services under the GATS regime would "likely . . . result in increased market access"[91] for international banks. This expectation received a setback when the United States withdrew from the GATS transitional process with respect to the Agreement on Financial Services in June 1995.[92]

In withdrawing from the transitional arrangement, the U.S. Government opted for a policy of measured reciprocity, prospectively limiting access to U.S. markets to financial

---

the bank to applicable U.S. capital requirements could only be verified if it carried out its U.S. banking activities in a separate U.S. subsidiary, the agencies have the authority to require that the bank (or the company controlling the bank) establish a U.S. subsidiary to carry out the interstate operations. *Id.* § 3103(a)(6).

86. GATS, preamble.

87. *See, e.g.*, GATS, art. II, ¶ 1 (applying most-favored-nation treatment to services and service suppliers); GATS, art. XVII, ¶ 1 (applying national treatment to services and service suppliers of other WTO member states).

88. GATS, Annex on Financial Services.

89. GATS, Annex on Financial Services, § 2(a).

90. GATS, Second Annex on Financial Services. One commentator has suggested that temporary withdrawal or modification is permitted in the Second Annex to allow for continued negotiation on market liberalization "because at the conclusion of the Uruguay Round, the United States was unsatisfied with other countries' commitments. The United States was not willing to lock in its own liberal policies without reciprocal guarantees of full market access on a most-favored nation basis." Kristin Leigh Case, Recent Development, *The Daiwa Wake-Up Call: The Need for International Standards for Banking Supervision*, 26 GA. J. INT'L & COMP. L. 215, 220 n.32 (1996) (citing Joel P. Trachtman, *Trade in Financial Services Under GATS, NAFTA and the EC: A Regulatory Jurisdiction Analysis*, 34 COLUM. J. TRANSNAT'L L. 37, 54 (1995)).

91. Case, *supra* at 221.

92. *See* Paul Lewis, *Trade Accord Without U.S. Set in Geneva*, N.Y. Times, July 27, 1995, at D1, col. 6 (reporting U.S. refusal to join transitional arrangement). In July 1995, over 80 states–including Japan, but not the United States–concluded a transitional agreement to liberalize international trade in financial services. *Id.*

services firms from home countries that provided reciprocal treatment to U.S. firms.[93] Essentially, the government had decided to seek market-access liberalization through bilateral negotiations, rather than through the multilateral mechanism of the WTO and the GATS.[94]

Matters remained in play, however, because the commitments of WTO member states participating in the transitional arrangement were to expire at the end of 1997.[95] Thereafter, WTO member states were expected to renegotiate GATS financial services commitments.[96] In advance of the expiration date, however, the United States joined in the signing of a global accord to govern international trade in services.[97] While the United States made no concessions, in light of the relatively open access to U.S. markets already permitted to non-U.S. firms, the initiation of the accord should result in significant opening of banking, insurance and securities service markets in such countries as Argentina, Brazil, India and Indonesia, among others, that have traditionally been relatively opaque.[98] However, other target markets, such as Malaysia and South Korea, have made no concessions for expansion of access.[99] On the other hand, Japan did agree to significant concessions in terms of opening its domestic financial services markets to international competition.[100]

If the accord is successfully implemented,[101] its effects on international trade in financial services would be dramatic. Under the GATS, each WTO member is required to accord most-favored-nation treatment to services and service suppliers of other WTO members.[102] Current restrictions on trade in services of each member must be transparent.[103] Members are also required to administer current restrictions "in a reasonable, objective and impartial manner."[104]

A series of general exceptions do apply to GATS obligations, similar to the general exceptions under the GATT.[105] More importantly, perhaps, the GATS includes a self-judging special exception for essential security interests of member states, similar to the special

93. Bob Davis & John R. Wilke, *Trade Official Is 'Close' to Limited Pact To Liberalize Global Financial Services*, Wall St. J., July 25, 1995 at A2.

94. *See, e.g.*, Frances Williams, *EU Eager to Salvage Financial Services Pact*, Fin. Times, July 1, 1995, at A1 (noting U.S. position).

95. Joel P. Trachtman, *Trade in Financial Services Under GATS, NAFTA and the EC: A Regulatory Jurisdiction Analysis*, 34 Colum. J. Transnat'l L. 37, 55 (1995).

96. *Id.*

97. *See* Edmund L. Andrews, *Accord Is Reached To Lower Barriers In Global Finance*, N.Y. Times, Dec. 13, 1997, at A1, col. 6 (discussing GATS accord).

98. *Id.*

99. *Id.*

100. *Id.* at B2.

101. *Cf. id.* at A1 (citing possible Congressional criticism of accord, but noting existing authorization for immediate effectiveness of accord under U.S. law).

102. GATS, art. II, ¶ 1.

103. *See* GATS, art. III (requiring publication and reporting of restrictive measures).

104. GATS, art. VI, ¶ 1. *Cf.* GATS, art. X, ¶ 1 (requiring that any emergency safeguard measures be administered in a nondiscriminatory manner).

105. *Compare, e.g.*, GATT, art. XX (excepting from GATT requirements measures undertaken for morals, life or health, precious metals, compliance with certain regulatory laws, products of prison labor, national treasures or patrimony, conservation, certain commodity agreements, world-price adjustment, and short-supply materials) *with* GATS, art. XIV (excepting from GATS requirements measures undertaken for morals or public order, life or health, compliance with certain regulatory laws, and taxation).

security exception contained in the GATT.[106] Presumably, this exception would shield U.S. international economic sanctions measures from the requirements and strictures of the GATS.[107]

3. National Treatment and the NAFTA

In 1994 the North American Free Trade Agreement (NAFTA) entered into force, creating a free trade area that eliminates tariffs on trade in goods among the member states, Canada, Mexico and the United States.[108] NAFTA was the first regional trade agreement to include financial services within its scope.[109] NAFTA Chapter 14 mandates access for financial services firms of each member state in the markets of the other member states, although it tolerates differences in methods of entry. While "[e]vidence of growth exists in cross border financial services provision"[110] under NAFTA, there is as yet little credible concrete data as to the specific effects of NAFTA on financial services.

Chapter 14 applies to national measures relating to financial institutions of any NAFTA member state operating in another member state, to nationals of one member state who are investors in financial institutions in another member state, and to cross-border trade

---

106. *Compare* GATT, art. XXI (providing exceptions from GATT obligations with respect to any measure undertaken that a member "considers necessary for the protection of its essential security interests") *with* GATS, art. XIV *bis*, ¶ 1 (providing exceptions from GATS obligations with respect to any measure undertaken that a member "considers necessary for the protection of its essential security interests"). *But cf.* GATS, art. XIV *bis*, ¶ 2 (requiring reporting of certain excepted measures and of their termination to WTO Council for Trade in Services).

107. *Cf. Panel Report on Nicaraguan Complaint*, GATT ACTIVITIES 1986 58-59 (1987) (noting that GATT panel examining complaint by Nicaragua concerning U.S. trade sanctions not authorized to examine U.S. invocation of GATT, art. XXI). For analysis of the effect of national security exceptions on unilateral economic sanctions programs of the United States, see Michael P. Malloy, Où est votre chapeau*? Economic Sanctions and Trade Regulation*, 4 CHI. J. INT'L L. 371 (2003).

108. North American Free Trade Agreement (NAFTA), Dec. 8, 1993, 107 Stat. 2057, 32 INT'L LEGAL MAT. 289, 605 (1993) [hereinafter NAFTA].

109. For NAFTA purposes, the term "financial services" is broadly defined to mean "a service of a financial nature, including insurance, and a service incidental or auxiliary to a service of a financial nature." NAFTA, art. 1416. For analysis of the effect of NAFTA on financial services, see Bradly Condon, *Smoke and Mirrors: a Comparative Analysis of WTO and NAFTA Provisions Affecting the International Expansion of Insurance Firms in North America*, 8 CONN. INS. L.J. 97 (2001/2002) (analyzing interaction of NAFTA and WTO with U.S. federal and state regulation affecting risk reduction and market entry strategies in North American insurance market); Art Alcausin Hall, *International Banking Regulation into the 21st Century: Flirting With Revolution*, 21 N.Y.L. SCH. J. INT'L & COMP. L. 41, 56 (2001); Valerie J. McNevin, *Policy Implications of the NAFTA for the Financial Services Industry*, 5 COLUM. J. INT'L ENVTL. L. & POL'Y 369, 380 (1994); Anna V. Morner, *Financial Services and Regional Integration: A Comparative Snapshot*, 7 L. & BUS. REV. AM. 549 (2001) (providing comparative analysis of regional strategies for harmonization of financial services regulation). The *locus classicus* in this regard remains Joel P. Trachtman, *Trade in Financial Services under GATS, NAFTA and the EC: A Regulatory Jurisdiction Analysis*, 34 COLUM. J. TRANSNAT'L L. 37 (1995).

110. Morner, *Financial Services and Regional Integration*, 7 L. & BUS. REV. AM. at 579.

in financial services.[111] It does not impose any binding market access requirements,[112] although Article 1403(1) does recognize in principle that an investor of a member state should be permitted to establish a financial institution in another member state's territory.[113] Article 1403(2) recognizes "the principle that an investor of another [member state][[114]] should be permitted to participate widely in a [member state's] market."[115] The article lists specific rights to be accorded to foreign investors–the right to provide a range of financial services through separate entities as required by regulation; the right to expand geographically; and, the right to own financial institutions notwithstanding otherwise applicable limitations on foreign ownership.

NAFTA does freeze barriers to *cross-border* trade in financial services.[116] Member states are required to permit their respective residents and nationals to purchase financial services cross-border.[117] However, they are not required to permit cross-border financial service providers to do business or solicit in their respective territories.[118] Furthermore, if a member state does permit such activity, it may require registration of such providers and of

111. NAFTA, art. 1401, ¶ 1(a)-(c).

112. In this regard, Trachtman describes the provisions of NAFTA article 1403 as "weak market access requirements." Trachtman, *Trade in Financial Services*, 34 COLUM. J. TRANSNAT'L L. at 81. In any event, the market access provisions of article 1403 do not apply to (*i*) existing or promptly renewed non-conforming measures specified in Section A of each party's schedule to Annex VII or to non-conforming local government measures, *per* NAFTA, art. 1409, ¶ 1; or, (*ii*) reservations under Annex VII, Section B, *per id.*, art. 1409, ¶ 2.

113. However, NAFTA art. 1403, ¶ 4 authorizes member states to require local incorporation (as opposed to direct cross-border branching) as the method of entry and to impose terms and conditions on entry consistent with the national treatment requirements of article 1405. *But cf. id.*, ¶ 3 (requiring member states to review market access provisions "with a view to adopting arrangements permitting investors of another [member state] to choose the juridical form of establishment of commercial banks," when United States allows *interstate* banking in substantially all of U.S. market). On the current U.S. rules with respect to interstate banking, see note 36, *supra*.

114. Article 1403 uses the term "investor of another Party," which for these purposes is defined to mean "an investor of another Party engaged in the business of providing financial services in the territory of that Party." NAFTA, art. 1403, ¶ 5. In turn, for purposes of Chapter 14 generally, the term "investor of a Party" is defined to mean "a Party or state enterprise thereof, or a person of that Party, that seeks to make, makes, or has made an investment." *Id.*, art. 1416.

115. Presumably, this participation would include newly developed financial services. *See* notes 130-131, *infra* (discussing national treatment with respect to new financial services under article 1407).

116. NAFTA, art. 1404, ¶ 1. "Cross-border trade" in financial services is defined for these purposes as financial services provided from a home member state to a person of another member state, or by a national of a member state in the territory of another member state. *Id.*, art. 1416. The provisions of article 1404 do not apply to (*i*) existing or promptly renewed non-conforming measures specified in Section A of each party's schedule to Annex VII or to non-conforming local government measures, *per id.*, art. 1409, ¶ 1; or, (*ii*) reservations under Annex VII, Section B, *per id.*, art. 1409, ¶ 2. Canada and the United States reserved against each other with respect to cross-border trade in securities services. *Id*, Annex VII, Schedule of Canada, Section B; *id.*, Annex VII, Schedule of the United States, Section B.

117. *Id.*, art. 1404, ¶ 2.

118. *Id.* The parties agreed to consult on further liberalization of such cross-border trade by the year 2000. *Id.*, art. 1404, ¶ 4.

financial instruments.[119]

Chapter 14 requires national treatment with respect to financial services,[120] subject to significant exceptions.[121] This obligation applies in favor of investors from any other NAFTA member state,[122] as well as to financial institutions from any other member state and investments made by investors of any other member state in financial institutions.[123] The national treatment obligation applies to the establishment, acquisition, expansion, management, conduct, operations and sale or other disposition of any member state financial institution, and any investment in a financial institution in the territory of another member state.[124] These obligations apply both at the level of national regulation and at the level of state or provincial regulation.[125] A member state's national treatment obligation is satisfied, "whether different or identical" treatment is accorded to financial institutions or cross-border

---

119. *Id.*, art. 1404, ¶ 3. This authority is in addition to any prudential regulation imposed on cross-border service providers pursuant to article 1410, ¶ 1. On the effect of article 1410, see text and accompanying notes 138-141, *infra.*

120. NAFTA, art. 1405, ¶ 1. On application of the national treatment obligation to cross-border provision of financial services (*i.e.*, without establishment of a local office), see *id.*, arts. 1404, 1405, ¶ 3. Specifically, a member state "may require the registration of cross-border financial service providers of another [member state] and of financial instruments." *Id.*, art. 1404, ¶ 3. A national treatment obligation would apply to types of financial services that may not yet exist. Article 1407, ¶ 1, provides that financial institutions of another member state are to be permitted to provide any new financial service of a type similar to what a member state permits its own financial institutions to provide in like circumstances under its domestic law. For these purposes, "new financial service" is defined to mean

> a financial service not provided in the Party's territory that is provided within the territory of another Party, and includes any new form of delivery of a financial service or the sale of a financial product that is not sold in the Party's territory.

Id., art. 1416. A member state may determine the institutional form in which the service may be provided, and may also require prior local authorization, which may only be denied for prudential reasons. *Id.*, art. 1407, ¶ 1. Presumably, this provision will become of increasing significance in light of the authorization of "activities financial in nature" contained in the Gramm-Leach-Bliley Act, Pub. L. No. 106-102, Nov. 12, 1999, §§ 103(a), 205, 113 Stat. 1338, 1342-1350, 1391 (1999) (codified at 12 U.S.C. §§ 1843(k)-(o), 15 U.S.C. § 78o(i)) (GLBA). For analysis and discussion of the GLBA financial activities provisions, see Chapter 5, § 10, *supra*; Chapter 6, § 2.b, *supra*. Note that, like the provisions of article 1405, the "new financial service" provisions of article 1407 are limited by the reservations specified in article 1409, ¶¶ 1-2.

121. The national treatment provisions of article 1405 do not apply to (*i*) existing or promptly renewed non-conforming measures specified in Section A of each party's schedule to Annex VII or to non-conforming local government measures, *per* NAFTA, art. 1409, ¶ 1; or, (*ii*) reservations under Annex VII, Section B, *per id.*, art. 1409, ¶ 2.

122. *Id.*, art. 1405, ¶ 1.

123. *Id.*, art. 1405, ¶ 2.

124. *Id.*, art. 1405, ¶¶ 1, 2.

125. *Id.*, art. 1405, ¶ 4. Where operations take place in more than one state or province, the article requires application of "the most favorable treatment" as the baseline for the national treatment obligation. *Id.*, art. 1405, ¶ 4(c)-(d).

service providers, so long as "the treatment affords equal competitive opportunities."[126]

NAFTA also contains a "most-favored-nation" (MFN) obligation running in favor of each of the other two member states, with respect to the treatment of non-members.[127] However, NAFTA Article 1410(1)(a) allows a NAFTA host state to invoke prudential concerns related to protection of depositors and financial markets, maintenance of safe and sound financial institutions, and integrity and stability of the host state's financial system in adopting measures that might otherwise violate NAFTA investment protections. Obviously, as affirmative defenses available to a host state regulating entry into its financial services market by foreign firms that are NAFTA country residents, these exceptions suggest a serious potential for non-tariff barriers to trade in services that may be practically impervious to redress under NAFTA.[128] The affirmative defenses thus preserved under NAFTA Chapter 14 do invite manipulation as non-tariff barriers to trade in financial services.[129] If such issues

---

126. *Id.*, art. 1405, ¶ 5. For these purposes, defines the term "equal competitive opportunities" to mean "treatment that does not disadvantage financial institutions of another party in their ability to provide financial services as compared with the ability of the party's own financial institutions, in like circumstances." *Id.*, art. 1405, ¶ 6. Note that "[d]ifferences in market share, profitability or size do not in themselves establish a denial of equal competitive opportunities, but such differences may be used as evidence regarding whether a Party's treatment affords equal competitive opportunities." *Id.*, art. 1405, ¶ 7.

127. *Id.*, art. 1406. The MFN obligations of article 1406 do not apply to (*i*) existing or promptly renewed non-conforming measures specified in Section A of each party's schedule to Annex VII or to non-conforming local government measures, *per id.*, art. 1409, ¶ 1; or, (*ii*) reservations under Annex VII, Section B, *per id.*, art. 1409, ¶ 2. In addition, reservations to articles 1102, 1103, 1202 and 1203 are deemed to be reservations to article 1406. *Id.*, art. 1409, ¶ 4. With respect to the United States, and with respect to cross-border trade in securities services, Canada reserved against the MFN requirement. *Id.*, Annex VII, Schedule of Canada, Section B, ¶ 1.

128. See Constance Z. Wagner, *The New WTO Agreement on Financial Services and Chapter 14 of NAFTA: Has Free Trade in Banking Finally Arrived?*, 5 NAFTA: L. & BUS. REV. AM. 5, 23 (1999) (stating that non-tariff barriers to trade are much less transparent than barriers caused by tariffs). Such non-tariff barriers would include, *inter alia*, licensing procedures and requirements and differing regulatory standards. *Id. See also* Eric J. Gouvin, *Cross-Border Bank Branching Under the NAFTA: Public Choice and the Law of Corporate Groups*, 13 Conn. J. Int'l L. 257, 259 (1999) (suggesting that bank regulators and financial services firms will seek to preserve existing non-tariff barriers).

129. *Cf.* Trachtman, *Trade in Financial Services*, 34 COLUM. J. TRANSNAT'L L. at 121 (arguing that "[t]he most intractable barrier to trade in financial services is varying and overlapping prudential or protective regulation"). This problem does not even take into account the additional opacity added to trade in financial services under NAFTA as a result of Canadian and Mexican reservations with respect to financial services. Gouvin has observed:

> When representatives of the United States, Canada, and Mexico signed [NAFTA] in 1992, the schedule of reservations and commitments on the annex relating to financial services gave the distinct impression that Mexico and Canada were not inclined to embrace fully the idea of free and unfettered trade in banking services. While NAFTA broke new ground by setting out a principles-based approach to liberalized trade in financial services, Canada and Mexico made it clear that they intended to keep in place the non-tariff barriers that ensured that their largest banks would remain under domestic control.

Eric J. Gouvin, *The Political Economy of Canada's "Widely Held" Rule for Large Banks*, 32 L. & POL'Y INT'L BUS. 391, 391 (2001) (footnotes omitted).

are raised in a NAFTA arbitration, on request of a member state the arbitral tribunal[130] is required to refer the question of the validity of the defenses to an investor's claim to the NAFTA Financial Services Committee.[131] The Committee's decision as to the validity of the defenses is binding on the tribunal.[132] If the Committee does not render a decision within sixty days of the referral, either the host state or the investor's home state may request the convening of an arbitral panel[133] under the institutional (*i.e.*, state-to-state) dispute resolution provisions of NAFTA to resolve the question of validity of defenses.[134] The panel's report is binding on the tribunal.[135]

NAFTA jurisprudence is already beginning to develop with respect to national treatment obligations in the context of trade in services generally[136] and in the context of cross-border investment.[137] So far, however, it is unclear whether the national treatment obligation of NAFTA article 1405 would prevail over "prudential" concerns of a member state seeking to restrict cross-border investment in the financial services sector.

e. Terrorism and International Financial Services

The tragic events of September 11, 2001, reinvigorated unilateral and multilateral responses against terrorism. Some of these responses are explicitly intended to have serious effects on transborder financial activities, in order to deny terrorists access to financial services that are essential to their continued attacks. Thus, anti-terrorism measures may impose substantial compliance burdens and risks on financial services firms, while failure to enforce compliance may carry fatal consequences for potential targets of terrorism.

On September 23, 2001, the President issued Executive Order No. 13,224,[138] blocking the property of, and prohibiting transactions with, persons who commit, threaten to commit, or support terrorism. The order declared a national emergency to deal with the "unusual and extraordinary threat to the national security, foreign policy, and economy of the United States" posed by the terrorist attacks. On September 28, 2001, the U.N. Security

---

130. The term "tribunal" refers generically to whatever body of arbitrators is deciding the particular dispute. *Compare* NAFTA, art. 1126, *with* NAFTA, art. 1415(2).

131. The various committees to which particular matters can be referred are listed in NAFTA, Annex 2001.2(A), 32 INT'L LEGAL MAT. at 698. The Financial Services Committee is provided for in NAFTA, art. 1414, but its function is relatively unspecified. It consists of officials of the governmental agencies responsible for financial services. *Id.*

132. NAFTA, art. 1415(2).

133. This arbitral panel must be constituted in accordance with article 1414, chosen from a special financial services roster. NAFTA, art. 1415(3).

134. NAFTA, arts. 1415(3), 2008-2022.

135. In the absence of such a dispute resolution request within ten days of the expiration of the sixty-day period, the tribunal may itself adjudicate the claim.

136. *See In Re Cross-border Trucking Services* (United States v. Mexico) USA-MEX-98-2008-01 (NAFTA Arbitral Panel, Feb. 6, 2001) (determining that national treatment obligations of NAFTA article 1202 prevail over U.S. concerns about highway safety and environmental impact).

137. *See The Loewen Group, Inc. v. United States of America*, International Centre for Settlement of Investment Disputes, Case No. ARB(AF)/98/3, *reprinted in* 42 INT'L LEGAL MAT. 811 (2003) (concerning claim of violation of national treatment under NAFTA. article 1102).

138. 66 Fed. Reg. 49,079 (2001).

Council unanimously adopted a U.S.-sponsored resolution[139] requiring all U.N. member states to sanction the financing, training and movement of terrorists–and requiring that they cooperate in any campaign against terrorists, including military action. The U.N. sanctions required the immediate freezing of the financial resources of terrorists and their organizations. Once fully implemented by the member states, the U.N. sanctions will also include required efforts at preventing and suppressing terrorism, prohibitions against making funds available to terrorist organizations, and the suppression of recruitment by such organizations and the elimination of their weapon supplies. In addition, the member states are required to deny safe havens to anyone who finances, plans, supports or commits terrorist acts, or who provides safe havens to terrorists. They are also committed to providing assistance in criminal investigations of terrorism and to preventing the movement of terrorists and terrorist groups through more effective control over borders and travel documents.

The implications for transborder banking are obviously serious. Section 1 of the order blocks "all property and interests in property" of persons targeted by the order if the property is in the United States or later comes within the United States, or within the possession or control of a U.S. person (which is defined to include a foreign branch of a U.S.-based bank). Presumably, blocked assets would include such items as bank accounts, assets held in trust, and funds in the course of transaction through the banking system. Section 2(a) goes on to prohibit any "transaction or dealing" in blocked assets by any U.S. person or within the United States. The blocking applies even if a preexisting contract with respect to the property or transaction requires the U.S. party to perform, and even if the property or transaction was covered by a preexisting license or permit from the U.S. Government.[140]

Under section 1(d) of the order, targeted persons include those determined by the Treasury Secretary (in consultation with the Secretary of State and the Attorney General) to be assisting in, sponsoring, or providing financial, material, or technological support for, or financial or other services to or in support of, terrorism or persons listed in the annex to the order or otherwise determined to be subject to the order. Persons may also be blocked if the Secretary determines that they are "otherwise associated with" persons listed or determined to be subject to the order. These provisions dramatically widen the scope of the blocking to include a broad range of financial intermediaries and other international middlemen–perhaps even banks themselves. However, for this class of potentially blockable persons, section 5 of the order authorizes the Treasury Secretary to take steps in his discretion short of a complete blocking. This could mean, for example, selective blocking of accounts, reversal of transactions, restrictions on operations, and the like.

Targeted persons also include persons determined by the Secretary of the Treasury (in consultation with the Secretary of State and the Attorney General) to be owned or controlled by, or to act for or on behalf of, any other targeted person.[141] In many if not most situations, this provision will make it very difficult for a bank to preplan and monitor

---

139. U.N. Security Council Res. No. 1373, Sept. 28, 2001, S/RES/1373 (2001).

140. In addition, notwithstanding any preexisting contract or any preexisting license or permit, the order prohibits any transaction by a U.S. person or within the United States that evades or avoids, or has the purpose of evading or avoiding, or attempts to violate, any of the prohibitions of the order. Ex. Order No. 13,224, *supra*, § 2(b). It also prohibits any conspiracy formed to violate any of the prohibitions of the order. *Id.* § 2(c).

141. *Id.*, § 1(c).

compliance with the sanctions, absent prior notice from Treasury.[142]

The Uniting and Strengthening America by Providing Appropriate Tools Required to Intercept and Obstruct Terrorism Act of 2001[143]–usually referred to by its acronym, USA PATRIOT Act–also creates major compliance burdens and risks for banks involved in international financial services. Title III of the act, accounting for approximately one-third of its entire text, most directly affect financial services firms.[144] Among other things, Title III enhances anti-money laundering provisions of U.S. law that are applicable to financial services firms. Extensive amendments to the Bank Secrecy Act[145] are apparently intended to align reporting, disclosure and other anti-money laundering requirements to the provisions of the new act.

For example, under § 311,[146] the Secretary of the Treasury is authorized to designate non-U.S. jurisdictions, classes of transactions, financial institutions or types of accounts as being of "primary money laundering concern," and as to any of these designated jurisdictions, the Secretary can require domestic financial institutions and domestic financial agencies to take a variety of specified measures to detect and prevent money laundering. Under § 312,[147] financial institutions are required to establish "appropriate, specific, and, where necessary, enhanced, due diligence policies, procedures, and controls" as to money laundering for U.S. correspondent accounts and private banking accounts of non-U.S. persons (*including* a foreign individual visiting the United States, or a U.S. representative of a non-U.S. person). Furthermore, if a foreign bank with an "offshore" banking license, or licensed by a country designated as "noncooperative" by certain intergovernmental organizations[148] requests or maintains a correspondent account with a U.S. financial institution, the latter is required to establish additional due diligence standards. Under § 313,[149] financial institutions are prohibited from maintaining correspondent accounts for shell banks–banks with no physical presence in any country–and must take reasonable steps to ensure that correspondent accounts of foreign banks are not used to provide banking services to shell banks. Under § 325,[150] the Secretary is given authority to issue rules regulating the maintenance of concentration accounts[151] by financial institutions, to ensure that these

142. Prior notice may well be absent, however. The order eliminates the necessity of prior notice of any "listing or determination made" pursuant to the order, at least as to any person who has "a constitutional presence in the United States." *Id.*, § 10.

143. Pub.L. 107-56, Oct. 26, 2001, 115 Stat. 280 (codified at scattered sections of, *inter alia*, 12, 18, 31 U.S.C.).

144. For example, under § 327 a financial institution's effectiveness in combating money-laundering is now an explicit factor in considering approval of bank holding company status under 12 U.S.C. § 1842(c)(6), or approval of a bank or savings association merger under the Bank Merger Act, *id.* § 1828(c)(11). For extended discussion of the effect of USA PATRIOT Act Title III on financial services firms, see INTERNATIONAL BANKING, *supra*, at 452-460, 544-555.

145. 31 U.S.C §§ 5311 *et seq.*

146. 31 U.S.C. § 5318A.

147. *Id.* § 5318(i).

148. *E.g.*, the Paris-based Financial Action Task Force on Money Laundering.

149. *Id.* § 5318(j).

150. *Id.* § 5318(h)(3).

151. The term "concentration account" is not defined by Title III. The legislative history of the USA PATRIOT Act seems to suggest that concentration accounts "are used to commingle related funds temporarily in one place pending disbursement or the transfer of funds into individual client accounts." 147 Cong. Rec. S11,041 (Oct. 25, 2001)(statement of Sen. Sarbanes).

accounts are not used to mask the interest of any person in the movement of funds.

4. Possible Future Approaches

U.S. financial services policy is currently in a state of significant change. As a result, it presents great uncertainty as to its contours in the new millennium. Regulators remain committed to capital adequacy as a primary technique of safety and soundness regulation, but the refinement of capital requirements is still at an early stage.[152] The regulators must broaden the distinct categories of risk weights to recognize the differences in risk of various types of assets.[153] The regulators must continue to refine their techniques for the measurement of other types of risk, such as interest-rate and exchange-rate risks, that are of particular importance to international banks.[154] Finally, regulators must continue to emphasize direct supervision of the asset management policies of international banks, rather than rely on the indirect technique of capital adequacy measurement as an indicator of the safety and soundness of banks.

Three substantial problems in U.S. international banking policy remain unresolved. First, the effective treatment of transborder bank failures eludes the grasp of bank regulators.[155] In this regard, the U.S. regulators should seek direct, bilateral, binding commitments of cooperation from major trading partners, perhaps modeled on the nonbinding principles of the BIS guidelines. Unilaterally, U.S. regulators should provide greater vigilance as well.[156]

Second, the openness of the U.S. market to the rest of international banking is no longer a basic assumption of U.S. international banking policy. The United States and its trading partners need to renew a firm understanding of and commitment to the idea that in international financial services policy, open competitiveness and safety and soundness are inextricably bound together.

Third, the enforcement of U.N. and U.S. sanctions against terrorists and states and persons facilitating terrorism must be reinforced. For international financial services policy, such sanctions have a two-fold significance. Obviously, the effectiveness of unilateral and multilateral responses to terrorism is compromised if access by terrorists to international financial services and payment systems is not frustrated. Furthermore, to the extent that the facilities of the international financial services sector remain available to terrorists, the integrity–and the safety and soundness of international financial services enterprises–will be compromised.

---

152. *Cf.* Jaret Seiberg, *N.Y. Fed Chief Urges Review Of '88 Global Capital Rules*, Am. Banker, Sept. 23, 1998, at 1 (discussing criticisms of current capital rules).

153. *See supra* at 548-549 (criticizing the present system of five broad categories of risk weights).

154. *See id.* (discussing relatively narrow scope of capital adequacy supervision).

155. *See, e.g., Former Daiwa Official Talks Of a Cover-Up*, N.Y. Times, Oct. 23, 1995, at D3 (reporting that Japanese bank with significant trading losses in its U.S. operations may have attempted to conceal losses from U.S. officials). Japanese regulators may have assisted or at least allowed this concealment for some six weeks. Sheryl WuDunn, *Daiwa Affair Turns Up Heat on Japan's Finance Ministry*, N.Y. Times, Oct. 26, 1995, at D4.

156. *See* Peter Truell, *Fed Missed Big Opportunity on Daiwa, Ex-Officials Say*, N.Y. Times, Oct. 19, 1995, at A1 (reporting that Fed officials failed to supervise adequately New York operations of Daiwa Bank Ltd., missing opportunity to expose unauthorized bond trading as early as 1993).

Selected Bibliography

1. The Regulated Environment for Financial Services

Anderson, *Federal Deposit Insurance Assessments–1950 Act and Regulations*, 73 Banking L. J. 701 (1956).

Baxter, *Judicial Responses to the Recent Enforcement Activities of the Federal Banking Regulators,* 59 Fordham L. Rev. S193 (1991).

________, *Life in the Administrative Track: Administrative Adjudication of Claims against Savings Institution Receivers,* 1988 Duke L.J. 422.

Bell, *Branches of National Banks–Recent Cases on Review of Decisions of Comptroller of the Currency,* 16 Bus. Law. 386 (1961), *reprinted in*, 78 Banking L. J. 220 (1961).

Boudreau, *Developments in Banking and Financial Law: 2006-2007*, 26 Ann. Rev. Banking & Fin. L. 176 (2007).

Brown, *E Pluribus Unum–Out of Many, One: Why the United States Needs a Single Financial Services Agency*, 14 U. Miami Bus. L. Rev. 1 (2005).

Budnitz, *The Federalization and Privatization of Public Consumer Protection Law in the United States: Their Effect on Litigation and Enforcement*, 24 Ga. St. U. L. Rev. 663 (2008).

Clarke, *The Futility of Current Approaches to Bank Regulation,* 4 J. L. Com. 213 (1984).

Colombo, *The Role of Trust in Financial Regulation*, 55 Vill. L. Rev. (2010)

Comment, *The Dangers of Piecemeal Reformation of the United States Banking Industry,* 39 St. Louis U. L.J. 1099 (1995).

Considine, *A State Response to the United States Treasury Department Proposals to Modernize the Nation's Banking System,* 59 Fordham L. Rev. S243 (1991).

Coyne, *Deregulation of the Banking Industry in the 1980's,* 86 W. Va. L. Rev. 189 (1983).

Cunningham & Zaring, *The Three or Four Approaches to Financial Regulation: A Cautionary Analysis Against Exuberance in Crisis Response*, 78 Geo. Wash. L. Rev. 39 (2009).

Davis, *Administrative Procedure in the Regulation of Banking,* 31 Law & Contemp. Prob. 713 (1966).

________, *Banking Agencies' Secrecy,* 31 Law & Contemp. Prob. 731 (1966).

Davis, *Banking Regulation Today: A Banker's View*, 31 Law & Contemp. Prob. 639 (1966).

DiNuzzo, *The Depository Institutions Deregulation Committee: Did it Achieve the Goal?* 101 Banking L. J. 100 (1984).

Engelke & Bridges, *Savings and Loans: An Industry in Transition*, 161 J. Accountancy 101 (1986).

Englert, *Bank Supervision in Historical Perspective*, 34 Bus. Law. 1659 (1979).

Fanto, *Paternalistic Regulation of Public Company Management: Lessons from Bank Regulation*, 58 Fla. L. Rev. 859 (2006).

Fanto, *Paternalistic Regulation of Public Company Management: Lessons from Bank Regulation*, 58 Fla. L. Rev. 859 (2006).

Fein, *Fragmented Depository Institutions Systems: A Case for Unification*, 29 Am. U. L. Rev. 633 (1980).

Felsenfeld & Bilali, *Business Divisions from the Perspective of the U.S. Banking System*, 3 Hous. Bus. & Tax. L.J. 66 (2003).

________, *Is There a Dual Banking System?* 2 J. Bus. Entrepreneurship & L. 30 (2008).

Fisher, *Orphan of Invention: Why the Gramm-Leach-Bliley Act was Unnecessary*, 80 Or. L. Rev. 1301 (2002).

Frankel, *The Dual State-Federal Regulation of Financial Institutions–A Policy Proposal*, 53 Brooklyn L. Rev. 53 (1987).

Friedman & Friesen, *A New Paradigm for Financial Regulation: Getting from Here to There*, 43 Md. L. Rev. 413 (1984).

Garten, *Banking on the Market: Relying on Depositors to Control Bank Risks*, 4 Yale J. Reg. 129 (1986).

________, *Devolution and Deregulation: The Paradox of Financial Reform*, 14 Yale L. & Pol'y Rev. 65 (1996).

________, *Market Discipline Revisited*, 14 Ann. Rev. Banking L. 187 (1995).

________, *Regulatory Growing Pains: A Perspective on Bank Regulation in a Deregulatory Age*, 57 Fordham L. Rev. 501 (1989).

________, *Subtle Hazards, Financial Risks, and Diversified Banks: An Essay on the Perils of Regulatory Reform*, 49 Md. L. Rev. 314 (1990).

Ginsberg, *An Idea for a Modified Dual Banking System*, 53 Brooklyn L. Rev. 23 (1987).

Golembe, *Our Remarkable Banking System*, 53 Va. L. Rev. 1091 (1967).

Gorinson, *Depository Institution Regulatory Reform in the 1980's: The Issue of Geographic Restrictions,* 28 Antitrust Bull. 227 (1983).

Hackley, *Our Discriminatory Banking Structure,* 55 Va. L. Rev. 1421 (1969).

________, *Our Baffling Banking System,* 52 Va. L. Rev. 565, 771 (1966).

Hanauer, *A Brave New World for Banking Law,* 4 Cal. Law. 24 (1984).

Herron, *Federal Home Loan Board: Pre-emptive Rights or Unbridled Powers?* 12 Cap. U. L. Rev. 529 (1983).

Indick, Greene & Squire, *The Economic Growth and Regulatory Paperwork Reduction Act of 1996*, 114 Banking L.J. 298 (1997).

Isaac, *The Role of Deposit Insurance in the Emerging Financial Services Industry,* 1 Yale J. Reg. 195 (1984).

Karr & Rhoads, *DIDC and Premiums,* 98 Banking L.J. 700 (1981).

Kreider, *American Banking: Structure, Supervision, and Strengths,* 92 Banking L.J. 437 (1975).

Kreps, *Modernizing Banking Regulation,* 31 Law & Contemp. Prob. 648 (1966).

Lagomarcino, *Federal Income Taxation Shapes the Banking Structure and Competitive Relationships Within It,* 15 Bus. Law. 404 (1960).

Lapidus, *State and Federal Deposit Insurance Schemes,* 53 Brooklyn L. Rev. 45 (1987).

Litan, *Evaluating and Controlling the Risks of Financial Product Deregulation,* 3 Yale J. Reg. 1 (1985).

Loring & Brundy, *The Deregulation of Banks,* 42 Wash. & Lee L. Rev. 347 (1985).

Lovett, *Federalism, Boundary Conflicts and Responsible Financial Regulation,* 18 Loy.-L.A. L. Rev. 1053 (1985).

Lund, *Federally Chartered Corporations and Federal Jurisdiction*, 36 Fla. St. U. L. Rev. 317 (2009).

Lybecker, *The "South Dakota" Experience and the Bush Task Group's Report: Reconciling Perceived Overlaps in the Dual Regulation of Banking,* 53 Brooklyn L. Rev. 71 (1987).

Malloy, *Balancing Public Confidence and Confidentiality: Adjudication Practices and Procedures of the Federal Bank Regulatory Agencies,* 61 Temple L. Rev. 723 (1988).

________, *Banking in the Twenty-First Century*, 25 J. Corp. L. 787 (2000).

________, *Double, Double Toil and Trouble: Bank Regulatory Policy at Mid-Decade*, 63 Fordham L. Rev. 2031 (1995), *reprinted in* 9 Banking L. Anth. 269 (1995).

________, *Foreword: . . . And Backward: Death and Transfiguration among the Savings Associations*, 59 Fordham L. Rev. S1 (1991).

________, *Nothing to Fear but FIRREA Itself: Revising and Reshaping the Enforcement Process of Federal Bank Regulation*, 50 Ohio St. L.J. 1117 (1989).

________, *Public Disclosure as a Tool of Federal Bank Regulation*, 9 Ann. Rev. Banking L. 229 (1990).

Mathewson, *From Confidential Disclosure to Market Discipline: the Role of Disclosure in the Regulation of Commercial Banks*, 11 J. Corp. L. 139 (1986).

Michael, *Self-Regulation for Safety and Security: Final Minutes or Finest Hour?*, 36 Seton Hall L. Rev. 1075 (2006).

Miller, *The Future of the Dual Banking System,* 53 Brooklyn L. Rev. 1 (1987).

Murane, *FDIC and Bank Regulation,* 89 Banking L.J. 483 (1972).

________, *SEC, FTC, and the Federal Bank Regulators: Emerging Problems of Administrative Jurisdictional Overlap,* 61 Geo. L.J. 37 (1972).

Murphy, *What Reason for the Quest?: A Response to Professor Scott,* [*In Quest of Reason, infra*] 42 U. Chi. L. Rev. 299 (1975).

Nguyen & Watkins, *Financial Services Reform*, 37 Harv. J. Legis. 579 (2000).

Norton, *The 1982 Banking Act and the Deregulation Scheme,* 38 Bus. Law. 1627 (1983).

Note, *Conflicts of Jurisdiction Between the Comptroller of the Currency and the Federal Reserve Board,* 65 Col. L. Rev. 660 (1965).

Note, *Efficiency or Principle?: A Model for Judicial Review of Federal Banking Agency Decisions,* 2 Ann. Rev. Banking L. 235 (1983).

Note, *Federal Bank Commission Act: A Proposal to Consolidate the Federal Banking Agencies,* 25 Clev. St. L. Rev. 475 (1976).

Note, *The Federal Open Market Committee and the Sharing of Governmental Power with Private Citizens,* 75 Va. L. Rev. 111 (1989).

Note, *The Office of Thrift Supervision,* 59 Fordham L. Rev. S363 (1991).

Note, *Playing with FIRREA, Not Getting Burned: Statutory Overview of the Financial Institutions Reform, Recovery, and Enforcement Act of 1989,* 59 Fordham L. Rev. S323 (1991).

Note, *Too Many Consonants and not Enough Consonance: The Development of the S&L Regulatory Framework,* 59 Fordham L. Rev. S263 (1991).

Oedel, *Puzzling Banking Law: Its Effects and Purposes*, 67 U. Colo. L. Rev. 477 (1996).

Peters & Powers, *Functional Regulation: Looking Ahead,* 18 Loy.-L.A. L. Rev. 1075 (1985).

Randall, *The Federal Deposit Insurance Corporation: Regulatory Functions and Philosophy,* 31 Law & Contemp. Prob. 696 (1966).

Redford, *Dual Banking: A Case Study in Federalism,* 31 Law & Contemp. Prob. 749 (1966).

Robertson, *Federal Regulation of Banking: A Plea for Unification,* 31 Law & Contemp. Prob. 673 (1966).

Roster, *The Modern Role of Thrifts,* 18 Loy.-L.A. L. Rev. 1099 (1985).

Schiltz, *The Amazing, Elastic, Ever-expanding Exportation Doctrine and Its Effect on Predatory Lending Regulation*, 88 Minn. L. Rev. 518 (2004).

Schweitzer, *Banks and Banking–A Review of the Definition,* 94 Banking L.J. 6 (1977).

Schwind & O'Leary, *Are National Banks Federal Instrumentalities Today?* 86 Banking L.J. 99 (1969).

Schwinger, *Banking Law: Preemptive Effect of Federal Banking Regulations; Depository Institutions Act of 1982; and Electronic Fund Transfers,* 1983 Ann. Sur. Am. L. 741 (1984).

Scott, *Deposit Insurance–The Appropriate Roles for State and Federal Governments,* 53 Brooklyn L. Rev. 27 (1987).

________, *Dual Banking System: Model of Competition in Regulation,* 30 Stan. L. Rev. 1 (1977).

________, *In Quest of Reason: The Licensing Decisions of the Federal Banking Agencies,* 42 U. Chi. L. Rev. 235 (1975).

________, *Patchwork Quilt: State and Federal Roles in Bank Regulation,* 32 Stan. L. Rev. 687 (1980).

Shay, *Emerging Federal Reserve Primacy in Bank Supervision*, 90 Banking L. J. 649 (1973).

Smith, *Retail Delivery of Financial Services after the Gramm-Leach-Bliley Act: How Will Public Policy Shape the "Financial Services Supermarket"?* 4 N.C. Banking Inst. 39 (2000).

Sperry, *Selective Bibliography on the Federal Deposit Insurance Corporation and the Guaranty of Bank Deposits,* 87 Banking L. J. 791 (1970).

Treiber, *Federal Reserve System after Fifty Years,* 20 Bus. Law. 247 (1965).

Vestner, *Trends and Developments in State Regulation of Banks,* 90 Banking L.J. 464 (1973).

Wille, *State Banking: A Study in Dual Banking,* 31 Law & Contemp. Prob. 734 (1966).

Wilmarth, *The Expansion of State Bank Powers, the Federal Response, and the Case for Preserving the Dual Banking System,* 58 Fordham L. Rev. 1133 (1990).

________, *The Transformation of the U.S. Financial Services Industry, 1975-2000: Competition, Consolidation, and Increased Risks*, 2002 U. Ill. L. Rev. 215.

Wynne & Spagnola, *The Myth of Bank Deregulation: For Every Action There is an Equal and Opposite Reaction,* 42 Wash. & Lee L. Rev. 383 (1985).

2. Entry Rules

Allister, *Federal Charter vs. State Charter: New Opportunities for Savings Banks,* 98 Banking L. J. 908 (1981).

Bierman, *et al.*, *Regulatory Change and the Availability of Banking Facilities in Low-Income Areas: A Texas Empirical Study*, 49 S.M.U. L. Rev. 1421 (1996).

________, *Community Reinvestment Act: A Preliminary Empirical Analysis*, 45 Hastings L.J. 383 (1994).

Carstensen, *Regulating Banking in the Public Interest: The Case for an Open Approach to Chartering and Branching,* 57 Tex. L. Rev. 1085 (1979).

Cohen, *The Community Reinvestment Act–Asset or Liability?*, 75 Marquette L. Rev. 599 (1992).

Comment, *Standing to Challenge Unlawful Competition under the National Bank Act,* 10 B.C. Ind. & Com. L. Rev. 421 (1969).

Curry & Rose, *Diversification and Barriers to Entry: Some Evidence from Banking,* 29 Antitrust Bull. 759 (1984).

Edminster, *Bank Deregulation and Deposit Reform: Some Hard Questions for Congress,* 104 Banking L.J. 42 (1987).

Edmonds, *Credit Unions: Legislative Approaches to Greater Freedom and a Competitive Advantage,* 90 Banking L.J. 952 (1973).

Garten, *Banking on the Market: Relying on Depositors to Control Bank Risks,* 4 Yale J. Reg. 129 (1986).

________, *Market Discipline Revisited,* 14 Ann. Rev. Banking L. 187 (1995).

Goodman & Shaffer, *The Economics of Deposit Insurance: A Critical Evaluation of Proposed Reforms,* 2 Yale L.J. Reg. 145 (1984).

Howell-Best, Note, *Universal Charter Options: Providing a Competitive Advantage for State Financial Institutions*, 6 N.C. Banking Inst. 487 (2002).

Isaac, *The Role of Deposit Insurance in the Emerging Financial Services Industry,* 1 Yale J. Reg. 195 (1984).

Kreider, *Who Owns the Mutuals? Proposals for Reform of Membership Rights in Mutual Insurance and Banking Companies,* 41 Cin. L. Rev. 275 (1972).

Lapidus, *State and Federal Deposit Insurance Schemes,* 53 Brooklyn L. Rev. 45 (1987).

Lund, *Federally Chartered Corporations and Federal Jurisdiction*, 36 FLA. ST. U. L. REV. 317 (2009).

Malloy, *Banking in the Twenty-First Century*, 25 J. Corp. L. 787 (2000).

________, *Seeing the Light: Savings Associations Conversions and Regulatory Realignment*, 10 Ann. Rev. Banking L. 189 (1991).

Murane, *FDIC and Bank Regulation,* 89 Banking L.J. 483 (1972).

Note, *Bank Charter, Branching, Holding Company and Merger Laws: Competition Frustrated,* 71 Yale L.J. 502 (1962), *reprinted in*, 79 Banking L.J. 553, 645 (1962).

Note, *The FDIC's Enhanced Powers over Savings Associations: Does FIRREA Make it "SAIF"?,* 59 Fordham L. Rev. S381 (1991).

Note, *A Note to Congress and the FDIC: After FIRREA, Where is the BIF?,* 59 Fordham L. Rev. S411 (1991).

Peltzman, *Entry in Commercial Banking,* 8 J. L. & Econ. 11 (1965).

Randall, *The Federal Deposit Insurance Corporation: Regulatory Functions and Philosophy,* 31 Law & Contemp. Prob. 696 (1966).

Robertson & Phillips, *Are Uniform Reserve Requirements Really Necessary?* 91 Banking L.J. 403 (1974).

Rose, *Entry in U.S. Banking Markets: Dimensions and Implications of the Charter Process,* 25 Antitrust Bull. 195 (1980).

Schrader, *Competition and Convenience: The Emerging Role of Community Reinvestment,* 67 Ind. L.J. 331 (1992).

Schwind, *Conversion and Acquisition of Savings Institutions,* 82 Banking L.J. 847 (1966).

Scott, *Deposit Insurance–The Appropriate Roles for State and Federal Governments,* 53 Brooklyn L. Rev. 27 (1987).

Scott & Mayer, *Risk and Regulation in Banking: Some Proposals for Federal Deposit Insurance Reform,* 23 Stan. L. Rev. 857 (1971).

Sperry, *Selective Bibliography on the Federal Deposit Insurance Corporation and the Guaranty of Bank Deposits,* 87 Banking L. J. 791 (1970).

Stokes, *Public Convenience and Advantage in Applications for New Banks and Branches,* 74 Banking L. J. 921 (1957).

Teitelbaum & Casanova, *Regulatory Reform or Retread? The New Community Reinvestment Act Regulations*, 51 Bus. Law. 831 (1996).

Wilmarth, *The Transformation of the U.S. Financial Services Industry, 1975-2000: Com-*

petition, Consolidation, and Increased Risks, 2002 U. Ill. L. Rev. 215.

Zinnecker, *When a Hundred Grand Just Isn't Enough: Fifty Hypotheticals That Explore the Contours of FDIC Deposit Insurance Coverage*, 72 TENN. L. REV. 1005 (2005).

3. Branching

Bell, *Branches of National Banks–Recent Cases on Review of Decisions of Comptroller of the Currency,* 16 Bus. Law. 386 (1961), *reprinted in*, 78 Banking L. J. 220 (1961).

Butler, *The Competitive Equality Doctrine and the Demise of Intrastate Bank Branching Restrictions*, 55 Tenn. L. Rev. 703 (1988).

Carstensen, *Regulating Banking in the Public Interest: The Case for an Open Approach to Chartering and Branching,* 57 Tex. L. Rev. 1085 (1979).

Gorinson, *Depository Institution Regulatory Reform in the 1980's: The Issue of Geographic Restrictions,* 28 Antitrust Bull. 227 (1983).

Huffstutler, *Bank Holding Company Restructuring Alternatives Following the Enactment of the Riegle-Neal Interstate Banking and Branching Efficiency Act of 1994*, Practicing Law Institute, Corporate Law and Practice Course Handbook Series (December 1996).

Lund, *National Banks and Diversity Jurisdiction*, 46 U. Louisville L. Rev. 73 (2007).

Malloy, *Banking in the Twenty-First Century*, 25 J. Corp. L. 787 (2000).

________, *Double, Double Toil and Trouble: Bank Regulatory Policy at Mid-Decade*, 63 Fordham L. Rev. 2031 (1995), *reprinted in*, 9 Banking L. Anth. 269 (1995).

Note, *Bank Charter, Branching, Holding Company and Merger Laws: Competition Frustrated,* 71 Yale L.J. 502 (1962), *reprinted in*, 79 Banking L.J. 553, 645 (1962).

Regan, *Circumventing the McFadden Act: The Comptroller of the Currency's Efforts to Broaden the Branching Capabilities of National Banks,* 72 Ky. L. J. 707 (1983-84).

Reardon, Note, *An Examination of Recent Preemption Issues in Banking Law*, 90 Iowa L. Rev. 347 (2004).

Rollinger, *Interstate Banking and Branching Under the Riegle-Neal Act of 1994*, 33 Harv. J. on Legis. 183 (1996).

Ross, Comment, *Around the Corner but Still Out-of-State? Whether National Banks' Branches Destroy Diversity Jurisdiction*, 52 Loy. L. Rev. 195 (2006).

Wilmarth, *The OCC's Preemption Rules Exceed the Agency's Authority and Present a Serious Threat to the Dual Banking System and Consumer Protection*, 23 Ann. Rev. Banking & Fin. L. 225 (2004).

4. Control Transactions

Alcaly, *Neither Convenient nor Needed: the Convenience and Needs and Public Benefits Tests of the Bank Holding Company Act,* 96 Banking L.J. 325 (1979).

Alcaly & Nelson, *Will Including Thrifts in the Banking Market Affect Mergers?* 97 Banking L.J. 346 (1980).

Alcorn, *Merger Analysis for Banks and Others–Marine Bancorporation and Connecticut National Bank,* 12 Houston L. Rev. 539 (1975).

________, *Phillipsburg and Beyond–Developing Trends in Substantive Standards for Bank Mergers,* 9 Houston L. Rev. 417 (1972).

Alhadeff & Alhadeff, *Bank Entry and Bank Concentration,* 20 Antitrust Bull. 471 (1975).

Aronowitz, *Retracing the Antitrust Roots of Section 1972 of the Bank Holding Company Act,*

44 Vand. L. Rev. 865 (1991).

Austin, *Commercial Bank Dissenters Appraisals,* 101 Banking L.J. 302 (1984).

________, *Evolution of Commercial Bank Merger Antitrust Law,* 36 Bus. Law. 297 (1981).

Austin & Bires, *Dissenters' Appraisals,* 111 Banking L.J. 393 (1994).

Austin & Hakala, *Bank Holding Company Formation and Acquisitions: How to Tell if the Fed is Likely to Say No,* 95 Banking L.J. 213 (1978).

Austin & Nigem, *Dissenters' Appraisals Revisited,* 106 Banking L.J. 246 (1989).

Austin & Solomon, *New Antitrust Problem: Vertical Integration in Correspondent Banking,* 122 U. Pa. L. Rev. 366 (1973).

Baker, *Potential Competition in Banking: After Greeley What?* 90 Banking L.J. 362 (1973).

Balamut, *A Morality Tale: Everything's Got a Moral if Only You Can Find It,* 27 Ad. L. Rev. 343 (1975).

Baxter & Shah, *Department of Justice Competitive Factors Reports,* 101 Banking L.J. 692 (1984).

Benson, *Economic Theory of Regulation as an Explanation of Policies Toward Bank Mergers and Holding Company Acquisitions,* 28 Antitrust Bull. 839 (1983).

Bintz, *The Change in Bank Control Act–A Line of Defense for Target Banks?* 52 Geo. Wash. L. Rev. 459 (1984).

Bleier & Eisenbeis, *Commercial Banking as the "Line of Commerce" and the Role of Thrifts,* 98 Banking L. J. 374 (1981).

Bloom, *Changes in Control of Banks,* 2 Ann. Rev. Banking L. 21 (1983).

Bransilver, *Failing Banks–FDIC's Options and Constraints,* 27 Ad. L. Rev. 327 (1975).

Brimmer, *Market Structure, Public Convenience and the Regulation of Bank Mergers,* 86 Banking L.J. 773 (1969).

Broome, *Private Market Solutions to the Savings and Loan Crisis: Bank Holding Company Acquisitions of Savings Associations,* 59 Fordham L. Rev. S111 (1991).

Buchalter & Allen, *Bank Insider Abuses: Where Does the Ax Fall?* 96 Banking L. J. 804 (1979).

Butler & Dugan, *The Impact of Recent Banking Regulations on the Market for Corporate Control,* 68 Wash. U. L.Q. 861 (1990).

Carlson, *The Case Against Cash-outs in National Bank Mergers: A Critical Analysis of NoDak Bancorporation v. Clarke,* 79 Minn. L. Rev. 173 (1994).

Carstensen, *Public Policy Toward Interstate Bank Mergers: The Case for Concern,* 49 Ohio St. L.J. 1397 (1989).

________, *Restricting the Power to Promote Competition in Banking: A Foolish Consistency among the Circuits,* 1983 Duke L.J. 580 (1983).

Carter, *Bank Mergers: the New Law and Renewed Litigation,* 12 Antitrust Bull. 109 (1967).

______, *Commercial Banking and the Antitrust Laws,* 11 Antitrust Bull. 141 (1966).

Case Comment, *Monopolies: Clayton Section 7 and the Potential Competition Doctrine–What Sort of Standards for Commercial Banks?* 27 U. Fla. L. Rev. 574 (1975).

Casenote, *Antitrust–Bank Mergers–Section 7 of the Clayton Act Applies to Banks and Bank Holding Company Mergers. Mercantile Texas Corporation v. Board of Governors,* 638 F.2d 1255, 13 St. Mary's L.J. 1013 (1982).

Chase, *Emerging Financial Conglomerate: Liberalization of the Bank Holding Company Act,* 60 Geo. L.J. 1225 (1972).

Cimeno & Brady, *Bank Holding Companies and the Regulatory Process,* 9 Suffolk U. L. Rev. 1213 (1975).

Cohen, *Interstate Banking: Myth and Reality,* 18 Loy.-L.A. L. Rev. 965 (1985).

Cohen & Sullivan, *The Herfindahl-Hirschman Index and the New Antitrust Merger Guide-*

lines: Concentrating on Concentration, 62 Tex. L. Rev. 453 (1983).
Collins, *Application of Bank Holding Company Act Discussed,* 10 Pers. F. L. Q. Rep. 94 (1956).
Comizio, *Post-FIRREA "Cross-Industry" Depository Institution Transactions: Current Regulatory Issues in Industry Consolidation,* 45 Consumer Fin. L.Q. Rep. 275 (1991).
Comment, *Antitrust: The Supreme Court Recognizes "Economic Realities" in the Banking Industry,* 59 Minn. L. Rev. 609 (1975).
Comment, *Bank Mergers: Agency Review and the Changing Line of Commerce,* 11 Fordham Urb. L.J. 307 (1982/83).
Comment, *Bank Mergers: A New Standard of Evaluation?* 46 Tex. L. Rev. 81 (1967).
Comment, *Bank Mergers and Potential Competition,* 43 Fordham L. Rev. 767 (1975).
Comment, *Bank Mergers and the Six-Headed Monster,* 15 Cath. U. L. Rev. 69 (1966).
Comment, *The Change in Bank Control Act of 1978: Does it give rise to a Private Cause of Action?* 72 Ky. L. J. 671 (1983-84).
Comment, *Management Interlocks between Banks and Other Financial Institutions: United States v. Crocker National Corporation,* 2 Ann. Rev. Banking L. 355 (1983).
Comment, *National Bank–Bank Holding Company Act–State Regulation of Intrastate National Bank Holding Companies,* 33 N.Y.U. L. Rev. 889 (1958).
Comment, *1966 Amendment to the Bank Merger Act,* 66 Col. L. Rev. 764 (1966).
Comment, *One-Bank Holding Companies: The Case Against a Legislative Roadblock,* 36 U. Chi. L. Rev. 803 (1969).
Comment, *Potential Competition in Bank Mergers under Section 7 of the Clayton Act,* 44 U. Cin. L. Rev. 314 (1975).
Comment, *Standing to Challenge Emergency Acquisitions: Marshall & Isley Corporation v. Heimann,* 2 Ann. Rev. Banking L. 373 (1983).
Conner & Hable, *Selected Tax Consequences in Bank Holding Company Formations: Charting a Course through the Section 304/351 Labyrinth,* 72 Ky. L. J. 595 (1983-84).
Current Legislation, *Proposed Amendment to the Bank Merger Act of 1960,* 7 B.C. Ind. & Com. L. Rev. 302 (1966).
Darnell, *Bank Holding Companies and Competition: The First National Bancorporation Case,* 89 Banking L.J. 291 (1972).
________, *Phillipsburg National Bank*, 16 Antitrust Bull. 33 (1971).
DeVolder, *Expansionary Possibilities for Affiliated Commercial Banks: A Current Dilemma,* 12 Pac. L.J. 895 (1985).
Dorset, *Bank Mergers and Holding Companies and the Public Interest,* 18 Bus. Law. 703 (1963), *reprinted in*, 80 Banking L.J. 755 (1963).
Dunlap, *Interstate Banking Developments in Florida: Pushing Through the Legal Barriers and Toward a Level Playing Field*, 9 Nova L.J. 1 (1984).
Edwards, *Bank Mergers and the Public Interest: A Legal and Economic Analysis of the 1966 Bank Merger Act,* 85 Banking L.J. 753 (1968).
________, *One-Bank Holding Company Conglomerate: Analysis and Evaluation,* 22 Vand. L. Rev. 1275 (1969).
________, *Tie-in Sales in Banking and One-Bank Holding Companies,* 14 Antitrust Bull. 587 (1969).
Eisen, *Banking Acquisition Procedures by Holding Companies,* 101 Banking L. J. 681 (1984).
Evans, *Disclosure through a Glass Darkly,* 27 Ad. L. Rev. 357 (1975).
Fiechter, *Another Year of American Antitrust Law Regarding Bank Merger,* 17 Bus. Law. 906 (1962).

Ford, *One-Bank Holding Companies for Community Banks,* 14 Tex. Tech. L. Rev. 739 (1983).

Franck, *Keeping Kentucky Banks Competitive in the Financial Industry: The Multibank Holding Company Statute,* 72 Ky. L. J. 689 (1983-84).

Friedlander & Slayton, *Determination of the Relevant Product Market in Bank Mergers: A Time for Reassessment?* 36 Bus. Law. 1537 (1981).

Funk, *Antitrust Legislation affecting Bank Mergers,* 12 Bus. Law. 496 (1957), *reprinted in,* 75 Banking L.J. 369 (1958).

Ginsburg, *Bank Holding Company Expansion Strategies: the Illinois Bank Holding Company Act,* 99 Banking L.J. 598 (1982).

Golden, *Corporate Law For Financial Institutions: Directors' Duties when Forming a Bank Holding Company,* 99 Banking L. J. 146 (1982).

________, *Preparing the Convenience and Needs Defense under the Bank Merger Act of 1966,* 96 Banking L.J. 100 (1979).

________, *Regulation of Commercial Banking under the Bank Merger Act and Bank Holding Company Act as Amended,* 36 Tenn. L. Rev. 706 (1969).

Golembe & Kumin, *Regional Interstate Banking Compacts: Ill-conceived and Unconstitutional Anomalies,* 18 Loy.-L.A. L. Rev. 993 (1985).

Gorinson, *Depository Institution Regulatory Reform in the 1980's: The Issue of Geographic Restrictions,* 28 Antitrust Bull. 227 (1983).

Gouvin, *Bank Mergers in North America: Comparing the Approaches in the United States and Canada*, 18 Transnat'l Law. 245 (2005).

Greenspan, *Bank Holding Companies: Competition, Capital and Nonbanking Acquisitions,* 90 Banking L.J. 560 (1973).

Gruis, *Antitrust Laws and their Application to Banking,* 24 Geo. Wash. L. Rev. 89 (1955), *reprinted in,* 73 Banking L.J. 793 (1956).

Hakala & Austin, *Denials of BHC Formations and Acquisitions: Has There been a Shift in Policy?* 99 Banking L. J. 947 (1982).

Hakala & Austin, *Denials of Bank Holding Company Formations and Acquisitions: New Issues, New Criteria,* 105 Banking L.J. 19 (1988).

Hale, *Comment on Dr. Austin's Article, "The Evolution of Commercial Bank Merger Antitrust Law",* 36 Bus. Law. 1557 (1981).

Heggestad & Wolken, *Mergers and Acquisitions in Commercial Banking: Economic and Financial Considerations,* 18 Loy.-L.A. L. Rev. 1165 (1985).

Helfer & Bruemmer, *Federal Banking Law Considerations in Unfriendly Takeovers of Depository Institutions,* 33 Am. U. L. Rev. 309 (1984).

________, *Interstate Nonvoting Equity Agreements and "Control" under the Bank Holding Company Act: the Impact of the Federal Reserve Board's 1982 Policy Statement,* 39 Bus. Law. 383 (1984).

Hoffman & Edge, *State Regulation of Bank Holding Companies and the Future of Interstate Banking, A Tennessee Perspective,* 51 Tenn. L. Rev. 383 (1984).

Holland, *$500 Limitation on BHC Acquisition?* 97 Banking L. J. 884 (1980).

Horsley, *Marine Bancorporation, Connecticut National Bank and Potential Competition: A Critique,* 55 B.U. L. Rev. 3 (1975).

Horvitz & Shull, *Bank Merger Act of 1960: a Decade After,* 16 Antitrust Bull. 859 (1971).

________. *Reply* [to Reid, *Comment, infra*], 19 Antitrust Bull. 321 (1974).

James, *An Analysis of the Effect of State Acquisition Laws on Managerial Efficiency: The Case of the Bank Holding Company Acquisitions,* 27 J. L. & Econ. 211 (1984).

Joseph & Mountz, *The Justice Department Guidelines: Impact on Horizontal Mergers between Commercial Banks,* 72 Ky. L. J. 505 (1983-84).

Katz, *The Determination of the Line of Commerce for Bank Mergers: A Contemporary View,* 5 J. L. & Com. 155 (1984).

Kintner & Hansen, *Review of the Law of Bank Mergers,* 14 B.C. Ind. & Com. L. Rev. 213 (1972).

Klebaner, *Bank Merger Policy and the Third National Bank Decision,* 22 Vand. L. Rev. 531 (1969).

________, *Federal Control of Commercial Bank Mergers,* 37 Ind. L.J. 287 (1962).

________, *Lexington Merger Decision and its Significance for Commercial Banking,* 11 Antitrust Bull. 897 (1966).

________, *Potential Competition in Banking and the Supreme Court,* 92 Banking L.J. 545 (1975).

________, *Recent Changes in United States' Commercial Banking Structure in Perspective,* 18 Antitrust Bull. 759 (1973).

Lagomarcino, *Federal Income Taxation Shapes the Banking Structure and Competitive Relationships Within It,* 15 Bus. Law. 404 (1960).

Lee, *Acquisitions of Financial Institutions,* 17 Inst. Sec. Reg. 231 (1986).

Legislation, *1966 Amendment to the Bank Merger Act: Economic Perspective and Legal Analysis,* 20 Vand. L. Rev. 200 (1966).

Lehr & Hammond, *Regulating the Foreign Acquisition of U.S. Banks: the CBCA and the BHCA,* 97 Banking L. J. 100 (1980).

Lifland, *Banking Practices and the Antitrust Laws,* 42 Notre Dame Law 465 (1967).

Loeys, *Bank Acquisitions: The Mitigating Factors Defense,* 103 Banking L.J. 427 (1986).

Lobell, *Nonbank Banks: Controversy over a New Form of Consumer Bank,* 39 Bus. Law. 1193 (1984).

Loumiet, *Florida's Reciprocal Banking Act of 1984,* 14 Stetson L. Rev. 1 (1984).

Malloy, *Balancing Public Confidence and Confidentiality: Adjudication Practices and Procedures of the Federal Bank Regulatory Agencies*, 61 Temple L. Rev. 723 (1988), *reprinted in*, 4 BANKING L. ANTH. 631 (1988).

________, *Double, Double Toil and Trouble: Bank Regulatory Policy at Mid-Decade*, 63 Fordham L. Rev. 2031 (1995), *reprinted in*, 9 Banking L. Anth. 269 (1995).

________, *Nonbanks and Nondefinitions: New Challenges in Bank Regulatory Policy*, 10 Seton Hall Leg. J. 1 (1986), *reprinted in*, 3 Banking L. Anth. 531 (1986-87).

________, *Nothing to Fear but FIRREA Itself: Revising and Reshaping the Enforcement Process of Federal Bank Regulation*, 50 Ohio St. L.J. 1117 (1989).

________, *State Change-in-Bank-Control Statutes: Does* MITE *Make Light of Recent Trends?*, 5 Ann. Rev. Banking L. 29 (1986).

Mann, *The Reality and the Promise of Bank Holding Companies,* 90 Banking L.J. 181 (1973).

Marcus, *Undermining of an Antitrust Bank Merger Policy,* 16 DePaul L. Rev. 59 (1966).

Marshall, *Legal Factors Underlying Bank Mergers,* 75 Banking L.J. 553 (1958).

Mastens & Severiens, *Bank Holding Company Regulatory Experience since 1970,* 8 Ind. L. Rev. 942 (1975).

Mayne, *New Directions in Bank Holding Company Supervision,* 95 Banking L. Rev. 729 (1978).

McCall & Steinhour, *Issuance of Debt Securities in Connection with the Formation of Bank Holding Companies,* 105 Banking L.J. 52 (1988).

McCarthy, Note, *Refining Product Market Definition in the Antitrust Analysis of Bank Mergers*, 46 Duke L.J. 865 (1997).

McDonald & Staff, *Bank Mergers after Omnibus Banking Bill: Is Philadelphia National Bank Finally Dead?* 20 Am. Bus. L.J. 421 (1982).

McHatton, *Bank Holding Company and the Sherman Act: The Validity of Cooperation among Held Banks,* 18 Ariz. L. Rev. 147 (1976).

McKenna, *Federal Preemption of State Anti-Trust Law in Transactions of Federally Chartered Banks,* 58 Conn. B. J. 355 (1984).

Meigher, *Bank Mergers and the Clayton Act: Some Chips in the Doctrine of Potential Competition?* 16 B.C. Ind. & Com. L. Rev. 705 (1975).

Metzger, *A Reply* [to Reid, *Legislation, infra*], 92 Banking L.J. 427 (1975).

Metzger & Greenfield, *Agency Discretion to Deny Bank Mergers: What are the Limits?* 98 Banking L.J. 838 (1981).

Miller, *Interstate Branching and the Constitution,* 41 Bus. Law. 337 (1986).

Mogel, *Bank Mergers and the Antitrust Laws,* 17 Am. U. L. Rev. 57 (1967).

Murane, *SEC, FTC, and the Federal Bank Regulators: Emerging Problems of Administrative Jurisdictional Overlap,* 61 Geo. L.J. 37 (1972).

Nash & Shapiro, *Control Relationships under the Bank Holding Company Act,* 92 Banking L.J. 618 (1975).

Nimkin, *Legal Problems in the Acquisition by Bank Holding Companies of Additional Banks and Non-Banks,* 89 Banking L.J. 387 (1972).

Noble, *Antitrust Consideration Affecting Bank Growth: Greeley and Beyond,* 90 Banking L.J. 381 (1973).

Note, *Antitrust–Banking–Federal Reserve Board may not Apply Competitive Standards more Stringent than the Antitrust Laws in Reviewing Bank Merger Applications– County National Bancorporation v. Board of Governors of the Federal Reserve System, 654 F.2d 1253,* 55 Temp. L. Q. 210 (1982).

Note, *Antitrust–The Clayton Act–The Regulation of Interlocking Directorates Between Competing Banks and Insurance Companies, BankAmerica Corporation v. United States,* 51 Tenn. L. Rev. 599 (1984).

Note, *Antitrust Law–Banks–Legal Barriers to Market Entry Means no Elimination of Potential Competition,* 26 Mercer L. Rev. 975 (1975).

Note, *Applicability of the Antitrust Laws to Combinations Approved under the Bank Merger Act, Federal Power Act and Natural Gas Act,* 37 N.Y.U. L. Rev. 735 (1962).

Note, *Approaches to Regulation of One-Bank Holding Companies,* 55 Va. L. Rev. 952 (1969).

Note, *Bank Charter, Branching, Holding Company and Merger Laws: Competition Frustrated,* 71 Yale L.J. 502 (1962), *reprinted in*, 79 Banking L.J. 553, 645 (1962).

Note, *Bank Merger Act and the Antitrust Law: Hopeless Conflict?* 32 U. Cin. L. Rev. 505 (1963).

Note, *Bank Mergers and Potential Competition after Marine Bancorporation: the Role of Regulatory Entry Barriers,* 5 New Mexico L. Rev. 139 (1974).

Note, *Commercial Bank Mergers: The Case for Procedural and Substantive Deregulation,* 95 Harv. L. Rev. 1914 (1982).

Note, *Conflicts of Jurisdiction Between the Comptroller of the Currency and the Federal Reserve Board,* 65 Col. L. Rev. 660 (1965).

Note, *The Demise of the Bank/Nonbank Distinction: An Argument for Deregulating the Activities of Bank Holding Companies,* 98 Harv. L. Rev. 650 (1985).

Note, *Jurisdiction over State Banks: Does the Bank Holding Company Act Preempt State Regulation,* 36 Ohio St. L.J. 114 (1975).

Note, *Legislative History of the 1960 Bank Merger Act and its 1966 Amendment: Judicial*

Misuse and a Suggested Approach, 44 Ind. L.J. 596 (1969).

Note, *1966 Amendment to the Bank Merger Act,* 83 Banking L.J. 753 (1966).

Note, *Potential Competition and Bank Mergers: Recent Supreme Court Decisions,* 9 Suffolk U. L. Rev. 1372 (1975).

Note, *Regional Banking Laws: An Analysis of Constitutionality Under the Commerce Clause,* 60 N. Dame L. Rev. 548 (1985).

Note, *Reorganization Treatment of Acquisitions of Stock Savings and Loan Institutions by Mutual Savings and Loan Associations,* 52 Fordham L. Rev. 1261 (1984).

Note, *States May Selectively Authorize Regional Bank Holding Company Acquisitions,* 17 Seton Hall L. Rev. 106 (1987).

Notes & Comments, *Banks & Banking: The 1956 Bank Holding Company Act and the Development of One-Bank Holding Companies,* 23 Okla. L. Rev. 73 (1970.

O'Brien, *Federal Reserve: Administrative Procedure and the Right to be Heard under the Bank Holding Company Act,* 91 Banking L.J. 856 (1974).

Phillips, *Bank Mergers, Branch Banking and Bank Holding Companies in Pennsylvania,* 115 U. Pa. L. Rev. 560 (1967).

Pinto, *Takeover Statutes: The Dormant Commerce Clause and State Corporate Law,* 41 U. Miami L. Rev. 473 (1987).

Pitts & Cranmore, *Considerations under the Federal Banking and Securities Laws with Respect to Bank Mergers or Takeovers,* 36 Okla. L. Rev. 789 (1983).

Recent Decisions, *Antitrust–Bank Mergers: State Banking Restrictions on de novo Expansion must be considered in the Determination of Whether a Market Extension Merger between Commercial Banking Organizations is Proscribed by Federal Antitrust Legislation,* 41 Brooklyn L. Rev. 711 (1975).

Recent Decisions, *Banks and Banking–Antitrust Law–Mergers–Pursuant to Bank Merger Act, Comptroller Will Consider Factors Other than Anticompetitive Effects When Determining Desirability of Bank Merger,* 54 Geo. L.J. 686 (1966).

Recent Developments, *Antitrust Laws and One-Bank Holding Companies: Breaking into the Piggy Bank,* 18 Cath. U. L. Rev. 524 (1969).

Recent Developments, *Bank Merger Approved by Federal Banking Agency under Bank Merger Act Held not Exempt from Attack under Sherman Act,* 62 Colum. L. Rev. 716 (1962).

Reid, *Comment* [on Horvitz & Shull, *Bank Merger Act, supra*], 18 Antitrust Bull. 449 (1974).

________, *Legislation, Regulation, Antitrust, and Bank Mergers,* 92 Banking L.J. 6 (1975).

Reycraft, *Bank Merger Compliance with the Antitrust Laws,* 12 Antitrust Bull. 445 (1967).

Rhoades, *Aggregate Concentration: An Emerging Issue in Bank Merger Policy,* 24 Antitrust Bull. 1 (1979).

________, *Impact of Bank Mergers and Laws on Statewide Banking Structure,* 25 Antitrust Bull. 377 (1980).

________, *Impact of Foothold Acquisitions on Bank Market Structure,* 22 Antitrust Bull. 119 (1977).

________, *Interstate Banking and Product Line Expansion: Implications from Available Evidence,* 18 Loy.-L.A. L. Rev. 1115 (1985).

Rhoades & Yeats, *Evaluation of Recent Evidence Advanced in Support of the Potential Competition Doctrine,* 19 Antitrust Bull. 543 (1974).

Robinson, *Antitrust Developments Affecting Banks in General,* 86 Banking L.J. 980 (1969).

Rollinger, *Interstate Banking and Branching Under the Riegle-Neal Act of 1994*, 33 Harv. J. on Legis. 183 (1996).

Rose & Fraser, *Bank Holding Company Diversification into Mortgage Banking and Finance Companies,* 91 Banking L.J. 976 (1974).

Rose & Savage, *Bank Holding Company de novo Entry and Market Share Accumulation,* 26 Antitrust Bull. 753 (1981).

Rosenblum, *et al.*, *On Banks, Non Banks, and Overlapping Markets: A Reassessment of Commercial Banking as a Line of Commerce,* 51 Tenn. L. Rev. 401 (1984).

Roster, *Acquisitions of Savings and Loan Associations by Holding Companies,* 37 Bus. Law. 875 (1982).

Rutz, *Chain Banking, Competition and the Change in Bank Control Act of 1978,* 59 Neb. L. Rev. 234 (1980).

________, *The Tax Benefits of Forming One-Bank Holding Companies Under the Fed's New Guidelines,* 98 Banking L. J. 24 (1981).

Saxon, *Bank Expansion and Economic Growth: A New Perspective,* 8 Antitrust Bull. 597 (1963).

Schellie, *Nonbank Banks: Current Status and Opportunities,* 102 Banking L.J. 142 (1985).

Searls & Reasoner, *Bank Merger Act of 1966–Its Strange and Fruitless Odyssey,* 25 Bus. Law. 133 (1969).

Seeley, *Banks and Antitrust*, 21 Bus. Law. 917 (1966), *reprinted in*, 83 Banking L.J. 1035 (1966).

Shapiro, *One-Bank Holding Company Movement: An Overview,* 86 Banking L.J. 291 (1969).

Shay, *Bank Holding Companies and the Fed: Whose Board?* 91 Banking L. J. 332 (1974).

Sheehan, *Acquisitions of Financial Institutions,* 16 Inst. on Sec. Reg. 149 (1985).

Shull, *The Separation of Banking and Commerce: Origin, Development and Implications for Antitrust,* 28 Antitrust Bull. 255 (1983).

Silver & Norman, *The Trust Company: A Means of Entering the Financial Services Market or Positioning for Interstate Banking,* 101 Banking L. J. 216 (1984).

Simms, *Control and Ownership of Banks by Individuals,* 17 S.T. L. Rev. 189 (1976).

Solomon, *Bank Merger Policy and Problems: A Linkage Theory of Oligopoly,* 89 Banking L.J. 116 (1972).

Vartanian, *Potential Competition and Bank Mergers: Defense Blueprint for the 1980's,* 99 Banking L.J. 882 (1982).

Velk, *Estimate of the Federal Reserve Board of Governors' Policy Role in Merger and Holding Company Cases, 1966-1970,* 21 Antitrust Bull. 537 (1976).

Via, *Administration of the Bank Merger and Holding Company Acts: Confusion Compounded,* 51 Va. L. Rev. 1517 (1965).

________, *Antitrust and the Amended Bank Merger and Holding Company Acts: The Search for Standards,* 53 Va. L. Rev. 1115 (1967).

________, *Commerical Banking as the "Line of Commerce" in Bank Amalgamations: A Reexamination,* 99 Banking L.J. 326 (1982).

Waxberg & Robinson, *Chaos in Federal Regulation of Bank Mergers: A Need for Legislative Revision,* 82 Banking L.J. 377 (1965).

Weiss, *Competitive Standards Applied to Foreign and Domestic Acquisitions of U.S. Banks,* 25 Antitrust Bull. 701 (1980).

Wemple & Cutler, *Federal Bank Merger Law and the Antitrust Laws,* 16 Bus. Law. 994 (1961), *reprinted in*, 79 Banking L.J. 461 (1962).

Whitesell, *Potential Competition and Bank Mergers,* 88 Banking L.J. 387 (1971).

Willacy & Willacy, *Conglomerate Bank Mergers and Clayton 7: Is Potential Competition the Answer?* 93 Banking L.J. 148 (1976).

Williams, *Bank Mergers and the Antitrust Laws–Recent Developments,* 12 Antitrust Bull.

427 (1967).

________, *New Dimensions to Bank Merger Law, the Supreme Court in the Mid-Seventies,* 20 Antitrust Bull. 699 (1975).

Wilmarth, *The Case for the Validity of State Regional Banking Laws,* 18 Loy.-L.A. L. Rev. 1017 (1985).

________, *The Transformation of the U.S. Financial Services Industry, 1975-2000: Competition, Consolidation, and Increased Risks*, 2002 U. Ill. L. Rev. 215.

Wilson, *Separation Between Banking and Commerce under the Bank Holding Company Act–A Statutory Objective under Attack,* 33 Cath. U. L. Rev. 163 (1983).

Wu & Connell, *Merger Myopia: An Economic View of Supreme Court Decisions on Bank Mergers,* 59 Va. L. Rev. 860 (1973).

Zak, *Regional Banking Statutes and the Equal Protection Clause,* 84 Colum. L. Rev. 2025 (1984).

5. Transactional Rules

Abney & Nadeau, *National Banks, the Impassable "Chinese Wall," and Breach of Trust: Shaping a Solution,* 10 Banking L.J. 251 (1990).

Ahart, *Advising the Individual Investor: Comparing the Federal Regulation of Investment Advisers, Banks and Broker-Dealers,* 6 Pepperdine L. Rev. 31 (1978).

Anderson, *Federal Deposit Insurance Assessments–1950 Act and Regulations,* 73 Banking L. J. 701 (1956).

Aronowitz, *Retracing the Antitrust Roots of Section 1972 of the Bank Holding Company Act,* 44 Vand. L. Rev. 865 (1991).

Bell & Yen, *Federal & State Insider Constraints,* 98 Banking L. J. 796 (1981).

Bell & Oliver, *Correspondent Bank Loans after the Financial Institutions Regulatory and Interest Rate Control Act of 1978,* 34 Bus. Law. 1347 (1979).

Bevan, *et al.*, *Corporate Securities Underwriting and Broker-Dealer Services by Banks,* 2 Ann. Rev. Banking L. 111 (1983).

Broome, *The Influence of Enhanced Thrift Institution Powers on Commercial Bank Market Expansion,* 67 N.C. L. Rev. 795 (1989).

Broome & Markham, *Banking and Insurance: Before and After the Gramm-Leach-Bliley Act*, 25 J. Corp. L. 723 (2000).

Church & Seidel, *Entrance of Banks into the Field of Mutual Funds,* 13 B.C. Ind. & Com. L. Rev. 1175 (1972).

Clark & Saunders, *Judicial Interpretation of Glass-Steagall: The Need for Legislative Action,* 97 Banking L. J. 721 (1980).

Comment, *Correspondent Banking and Insider Loans after the Financial Institutions Regulatory and Interest Rate Control Act of 1978,* 37 Wash. & Lee L. Rev. 1327 (1980).

Comment, *Expansion of National Bank Powers: Regulatory and Judicial Precedent under the National Bank Act, Glass-Steagall Act, and Bank Holding Company Act,* 36 S.W. L.J. 765 (1982).

Comment, *Banking Law–A.G. Becker v. Board of Governors Federal Reserve System: Commercial Paper is not a Security under the Glass-Steagall Act,* 9 J. Corp. L. 321 (1984).

Comment, *Banking Law–Fiduciary Activity–National Bank's Operation of Commingled Managing Agency Account Held not to Contravene Federal Reserve Act or Glass-Steagall Act,* 44 N.Y.U. L. Rev. 1135 (1969).

Comment, *Banks, Trusts, and Investment Companies: The Commingled Investment Fund,* 115 U. Pa. L. Rev. 1276 (1967).

Comment, *Expansion of National Bank Powers: Regulatory and Judicial Precedent under the National Bank Act, Glass-Steagall Act, and Bank Holding Company Act,* 36 S.W. L.J. 765 (1982).

Comment, *Fifty-two Years After the Glass-Steagall Act: Do Commercial Bank Securities Activities Merit a Second Look?* 1984 Det. C. L. Rev. 933.

Comment, *Glass-Steagall: Section 16 and the Authority of a National Bank to Accept the Common Stock Purchase Warrants of the Debtor-Issuer,* 51 Tenn. L. Rev. 535 (1984).

Comment, *National Bank-Sponsored Investment Companies,* 65 Nw. U. L. Rev. 93 (1970).

Comment, *Of Banks and Mutual Funds: The Collective Investment Trusts,* 20 Sw. L.J. 334 (1966).

Deal, *Regulation of Bank Subsidiaries: The FDIC Stakes a Claim,* 7 J. L. & Com. 1 (1987).

DiLorenzo, *Public Confidence and the Banking System: The Policy Basis for Continued Separation of Commercial and Investment Banking,* 35 Am. U. L. Rev. 647 (1986).

Edminster, *Bank Deregulation and Deposit Reform: Some Hard Questions for Congress,* 104 Banking L.J. 42 (1987).

Edwards, *Economics of "Tying" Arrangements: Some Proposed Guidelines for Bank Holding Company Regulation,* 6 Antitrust L. & Econ. Rev. 87 (1973).

Farrar, *Commerical Banks, Trust Departments, and Concentration of Power: A Legacy of Glass-Steagall,* 4 J. Comp. Corp. L. & Sec. Reg. 237 (1982).

Faucette, *The Impact of Convergence and the Gramm-Leach-Bliley Act on the Insurance Industry*, 8 Geo. Mason L. Rev. 623 (2000).

Fischer, *et al., The Securities Activities of Commercial Banks: A Legal and Economic Analysis,* 51 Tenn. L. Rev. 383 (1984).

Fisher, *Toward a Basal Tenth Amendment: A Riposte to National Bank Preemption of State Consumer Protection Laws*, 29 Harv. J.L. & Pub. Pol'y 981 (2006).

Friedman, *et al., Mutual Fund Underwriting by Banks,* 2 Ann. Rev. Banking L. 81 (1983).

Garten, *Banking on the Market: Relying on Depositors to Control Bank Risks,* 4 Yale J. Reg. 129 (1986).

________, *Market Discipline Revisited,* 14 Ann. Rev. Banking L. 187 (1995).

________, *Subtle Hazards, Financial Risks, and Diversified Banks: An Essay on the Perils of Regulatory Reform,* 49 Md. L. Rev. 314 (1990).

Glidden, *Bank Sales of Commercial Paper under the Glass-Steagall Act: The Hazards of the Bankers Trust Decisions,* 42 Bus. Law. 1 (1986).

Glidden, *The Regulation of National Banks' Subsidiaries,* 40 Bus. Law. 1299 (1985).

Golembe, *Calm before the Storm: The Washington Outlook for Bank Trust Departments,* 111 Trusts & Est. 636 (1972).

Hamilton, *Why the Check Cashers Win: Regulatory Barriers to Banking the Unbanked*, 30 W. New Eng. L. Rev. 119 (2007).

Harrell, *Some Surprising New (And Old) Perspectives on Check-Kiting*, 57 Consumer Fin. L.Q. Rep. 214 (2003).

Huck, *What is the Banking Business?* 21 Bus. Law. 537 (1966), *reprinted in*, 83 Banking L.J. 491 (1966).

Ianni, *"Security" under the Glass-Steagall Act and the Federal Securities Acts of 1933 and 1934: The Direction of the Supreme Court's Analysis,* 100 Banking L. J. 100 (1983).

Isaac, *The Role of Deposit Insurance in the Emerging Financial Services Industry,* 1 Yale

J. Reg. 195 (1984).

Janvey, *Securities Activities of Banks: Life Beyond Lending,* 14 Sec. Reg. L.J. 315 (1987).

Johnson, *Wild Card Statutes, Parity, and National Banks–The Renascence of State Banking Powers,* 26 Loy. U. Chi. L.J. 351 (1995).

Lance, *Can the Glass-Steagall Act be Justified under the Global Free Market Policies of the Nafta?,* 34 Washburn L.J. 297 (1995).

Lane, *Will Credit Cardholders Default over Minimum Payment Hikes?* 18 Loy. Consumer L. Rev. 331 (2006).

Lapidus, *Commerical Banks and Thrift Institutions: The Differing Portfolio Powers,* 92 Banking L.J. 450 (1975).

________, *State and Federal Deposit Insurance Schemes,* 53 Brooklyn L. Rev. 45 (1987).

Ledwidge, *Loan Participation Among Commercial Banks,* 51 Tenn. L. Rev. 519 (1984).

Leslie & Cain, *Financial Institutions and Insurance in 1995: State Insurance Regulators Assert Authority over Banks*, 51 Bus. Law. 909 (1996).

Lybecker, *Bank Collective Investment Management Activities,* 15 Inst. on Sec. Reg. 347 (1984).

________, *Bank Investment Management Activities: The Current Regulatory Environment,* 113 Banking L.J. 970 (1996).

________, *Bank-Sponsored Investment Management Services: Consideration of the Regulatory Problems,* 1977 Duke L.J. 983.

________, *Bank-Sponsored Investment Management Services: A Legal History and Statutory Interpretative Analysis,* 5 Sec. Reg. L.J. 110 (1977).

________, *Regulation of Bank Trust Department Investment Activities,* 82 Yale L.J. 977 (1973).

Malloy, *The Sound of Two Hands Flapping: Insurance-Related Activities of National Banks*, 41 St. Louis U. L.J. 75 (1997).

Malloy & Pitts, *Post-Mortem on Retail Repurchase Agreements: Where were the Regulators?* 3 Ann. Rev. Banking L. 89 (1984).

Markham & Gilberg, *Federal Regulation of Bank Activities in the Commodities Markets,* 39 Bus. Law. 1719 (1984).

Marler, *American Deposit Corp. v. Schacht: Yet Another Attempt to Limit National Banks' Powers to Sell Nondeposit Investment Products*, 74 Wash. U. L.Q. 841 (1996).

Matarese, *Has the Chevron Deference Made a Difference When Courts Review Federal Banking Agency Interpretations of the Glass-Steagall Act?,* 33 How. L.J. 195 (1990).

Mathewson, *From Confidential Disclosure to Market Discipline: The Role of Disclosure in the Regulation of Commercial Banks*, 11 J. Corp. L. 139 (1986).

McClatchey, *Commercial Banks Need Not be Crowded Out of the Market for Savings Accounts,* 15 Bus. Law. 879 (1960).

Meaney, *et al., Revenue Bond Underwriting by Banks*, 2 Ann. Rev. Banking L. 53 (1983).

Miller, *Participation of National Banks in Private Placements of Corporate Securities,* 13 New England L. Rev. 63 (1977).

Morse, *Bank Insiders and the Wilfull Misapplication Statute: Toward More Effective Protections from Self-Dealing*, 92 Banking L. J. 715 (1975).

Mulhern, *Bank-Brokerage Activities,* 14 Inst. on Sec. Reg. 413 (1983).

Murane, *FDIC and Bank Regulation,* 89 Banking L.J. 483 (1972).

Nichols, *Bank Underwriting,* 17 Inst. Sec. Reg. 341 (1986).

Norton, *The 1982 Banking Act and the Deregulation Scheme,* 38 Bus. Law. 1627 (1983).

Note, *Avoiding the Glass-Steagall Act and Bank Holding Company Acts: an Option for Bank*

Product Expansion, 59 Ind. L. J. 89 (1983-84).

Note, *A Banker's Adventures in Brokerland: Looking through Glass Steagall at Discount Brokerage Services,* 81 Mich. L. Rev. 1498 (1983).

Note, *Bank-Sponsored Investment Services: Statutory Proscriptions, Jurisdictional Conflicts, and a Legislative Proposal,* 27 U. Fla. L. Rev. 776 (1975).

Note, *Diversification by National Banks,* 21 Stan. L. Rev. 650 (1969).

Note, *Glass-Steagall: A Proposal for Regulation rather than Prohibition,* 47 Alb. L. Rev. 1378 (1983).

Note, *Insider Loans: How Restricted is the Banker?* 9 Fordham Urban L.J. 431 (1980/81).

Note, *Legality of Bank-Sponsored Investment Services,* 84 Yale L.J. 1477 (1975).

Note, *The Merger of Banking and Insurance: Will Congress Close the South Dakota Loophole?* 60 N. Dame. L. Rev. 762 (1985).

Note, *National Banks and the Brokerage Business: the Comptroller's New Reading of the Glass-Steagall Act,* 69 Va. L. Rev. 1303 (1983).

Note, *Ownership of Member Bank by Mutual Fund Advisers under the Glass-Steagall Act,* 52 Fordham L. Rev. 691 (1984).

Note, *Regulation of Bank Securities Transactions*, 41 Wash. & Lee L. Rev. 1187 (1984).

Note, *Restrictions on Bank Underwriting of Corporate Securities: A Proposal for a more Permissive Regulation,* 97 Harv. L. Rev. 720 (1984).

Note, *Tender Offers and "Chinese Walls": A Bank's Duty of Confidentiality when Financing Acquisitions of a Customer,* 12 Akron L. Rev. 689 (1979).

Note, *Washington Steel Corp. v. TW Corp.: Bank Confidentiality in Corporate Takeovers,* 68 Cal. L. Rev. 1257 (1978).

Notes & Comments, *Regulation of Bank-Operated Collective Investment Funds–Judicial or Legislative Resolution of an Administrative Controversy?* 73 Yale L.J. 1249 (1964).

Norton, *Up Against "The Wall": Glass-Steagall and the Dilemma of a Deregulated ("Re-regulated") Banking Environment,* 42 Bus. Law. 327 (1987).

Omarova, *The Quiet Metamorphosis: How Derivatives Changed the "Business of Banking"*, 63 U. Miami L. Rev. 1041 (2009).

Orbe, *Glass-Steagall: Lest We Forget,* 11 Fla. St. U. L. Rev. 163 (1983).

Osborn, *Discount Brokerage Services, the Glass-Steagall Act, and Branch Banking in Texas,* 16 St. Mary's L.J. 185 (1984).

Perkins, *The Divorce of Commercial and Investment Banking: A History,* 88 Banking L.J. 483 (1971).

Pitt & Williams, *The Convergence of Commercial and Investment Banking: New Directions in the Financial Services Industry,* 5 J. Comp. Bus. & Cap. Market L. 233 (1983).

Pitt & Williams, *The Glass-Steagall Act: Key Issues for the Financial Services Industry,* 11 Sec. Reg. L.J. 234 (1983).

Plotkin, *What Meaning Does Glass-Steagall Have for Today's Financial World?* 95 Banking L.J. 404 (1978).

Randall, *The Federal Deposit Insurance Corporation: Regulatory Functions and Philosophy,* 31 Law & Contemp. Prob. 696 (1966).

Reardon, Note, *An Examination of Recent Preemption Issues in Banking Law*, 90 Iowa L. Rev. 347 (2004).

Ritchie, *Banks Should be Able to Offer Financial Services Nationally,* 124 Tr. & Est. 18 (1985).

Rowen, *The Emerging Financial Services Industry,* 14 Inst. on Sec. Reg. 423 (1983).

Saba, *Regulation of State Nonmember Insured Banks' Securities Activities: A Model for the Repeal of Glass- Steagall?* 23 Harv. J. Legis. 211 (1986).

Schiltz, *The Amazing, Elastic, Ever-expanding Exportation Doctrine and Its Effect on Predatory Lending Regulation*, 88 MINN. L. REV. 518 (2004).

Schweitzer & Halbrook, *Insurance Activities of Banks and Bank Holding Companies: A Survey of Current Issues and Regulations,* 29 Drake L. Rev. 743 (1979/80).

Scott, *Deposit Insurance–The Appropriate Roles for State and Federal Governments,* 53 Brooklyn L. Rev. 27 (1987).

Scott & Mayer, *Risk and Regulation in Banking: Some Proposals for Federal Deposit Insurance Reform,* 23 Stan. L. Rev. 857 (1971).

Sinder, *The Gramm-Leach-Bliley Act and State Regulation of the Business of Insurance–Past, Present and . . . Future?* 5 N.C. Banking Inst. 49 (2001).

Sosa-Llorens, *Glass-Steagall Limitations on Puerto Rican Banking: Loopholes, Auto-Limitations and Opportunities,* 60 Rev. Jur. U. Puerto Rico 329 (1991).

Smoot, *Financial Institutions Reform in the Wake of VALIC*, 29 Creighton L. Rev. 691 (1996).

Spencer, *Regulation of Bank Securities Activities: The Effects of the SEC Bank Study,* 95 Banking L.J. 616 (1978).

Sperry, *Selective Bibliography on the Federal Deposit Insurance Corporation and the Guaranty of Bank Deposits,* 87 Banking L. J. 791 (1970).

Symons, *The "Business of Banking" in Historical Perspective,* 51 Geo. Wash. L. Rev. 676 (1983).

Wade, *Bank-Sponsored Collective Investment Funds: An Analysis of Applicable Federal Banking and Securities Laws,* 35 Bus. Law. 361 (1980).

Wagner, *Structuring the Financial Service Conglomerates of the Future: Does the Choice of Corporate Form to House New Financial Activities of National Banks Matter?* 19 Ann. Rev. Banking L. 329 (2000).

Wallace, *National Bank Insurance Agency Powers: What Law Controls?*, 113 Banking L.J. 138 (1996).

Whitesell & Kelly, *Is the Glass-Steagall Act Obsolete?* 87 Banking L.J. 387 (1970).

Willin, *Commercial Banks and the Glass-Steagall Act: A Survey of New Products and Activities,* 104 Banking L.J. 5 (1987).

Wilmarth, *The Expansion of State Bank Powers, the Federal Response, and the Case for Preserving the Dual Banking System,* 58 Fordham L. Rev. 1133 (1990).

________, *The OCC's Preemption Rules Exceed the Agency's Authority and Present a Serious Threat to the Dual Banking System and Consumer Protection*, 23 Ann. Rev. Banking & Fin. L. 225 (2004).

________, *The Transformation of the U.S. Financial Services Industry, 1975-2000: Competition, Consolidation, and Increased Risks*, 2002 U. Ill. L. Rev. 215.

Wilson & Johnson, *Legal Limitations on Real-Estate Loans by National Banks and Some Suggested Changes in the Present Limitations,* 11 Bus. Law. 15 (1956), *reprinted in*, 74 Banking L.J. 196 (1957).

Wook Bai Kim, *Challenging the Roots of the Subprime Mortgage Crisis: The OCC's Operating Subsidiaries Regulations and Watters v. Wachovia Bank*, 21 Loy. Consumer L. Rev. 278 (2009).

Zaitzeff & Mette, *Investment Powers of Federal Savings and Loan Associations After Garn-St Germain,* 36 U. Fla. L. Rev. 591 (1984).

Zinnecker, *When a Hundred Grand Just Isn't Enough: Fifty Hypotheticals That Explore the Contours of FDIC Deposit Insurance Coverage*, 72 Tenn. L. Rev. 1005 (2005).

6. Holding Company Activities

Bailey, Note, *Tearing Down the Wall Between Banking and Commerce: An Evaluation of the Federal Reserve Board's Implementation of the New Standard for Permissible Non-Banking Activities*, 91 KY. L.J. 205 (2002-2003).

Blaine, *Bank Holding Companies in a Year of Slowdown,* 92 Banking L.J. 674 (1975).

Broeckel, *Regulation of Bank Holding Companies' State Bank Subsidiaries that Engage in Nonbanking Activities: An Unjustified Extension of the Federal Reserve Board's Regulatory Power,* 4 Admin. L.J. 169 (1990).

Broome, *The Influence of Enhanced Thrift Institution Powers on Commercial Bank Market Expansion,* 67 N.C. L. Rev. 795 (1989).

________, *Private Market Solutions to the Savings and Loan Crisis: Bank Holding Company Acquisitions of Savings Associations,* 59 Fordham L. Rev. S111 (1991).

Comment, *Expansion of National Bank Powers: Regulatory and Judicial Precedent under the National Bank Act, Glass-Steagall Act, and Bank Holding Company Act,* 36 S.W. L.J. 765 (1982).

Comment, *Implementation of the Bank Holding Company Act Amendments of 1970: The Scope of Banking Activities,* 71 Mich L. Rev. 1170 (1973).

Deal, *Regulation of Bank Subsidiaries: The FDIC Stakes a Claim,* 7 J. L. & Com. 1 (1987).

Edwards, *Economics of "Tying" Arrangements: Some Proposed Guidelines for Bank Holding Company Regulation,* 6 Antitrust L. & Econ. Rev. 87 (1973).

Garten, *Subtle Hazards, Financial Risks, and Diversified Banks: An Essay on the Perils of Regulatory Reform,* 49 Md. L. Rev. 314 (1990).

________, *Market Discipline Revisited,* 14 Ann. Rev. Banking L. 187 (1995).

Glidden, *The Regulation of National Banks' Subsidiaries,* 40 Bus. Law. 1299 (1985).

Helfer & Morse, *Hearings under Section 4(c)(8) of the Bank Holding Company Act,* 101 Banking L. J. 50 (1984).

Hemmer, *Insurance Underwriting Activities of BHCs,* 100 Banking L.J. 700 (1983).

Johnson, *Rationale for Acquisition of Finance Companies by Holding Companies,* 92 Banking L.J. 304 (1975).

Malloy, *Double, Double Toil and Trouble: Bank Regulatory Policy at Mid-Decade*, 63 Fordham L. Rev. 2031 (1995), *reprinted in*, 9 Banking L. Anth. 269 (1995).

Mastens & Severiens, *Bank Holding Company Regulatory Experience since 1970,* 8 Ind. L. Rev. 942 (1975).

Mayne, *New Directions in Bank Holding Company Supervision,* 95 Banking L. Rev. 729 (1978).

Note, *Approval of Citicorp's Application to Expand Data Services Activities: the Federal Reserve Board's Policies Regarding Nonbanking Activities,* 1983 Duke L. J. 423.

Note, *Conflicts of Jurisdiction Between the Comptroller of the Currency and the Federal Reserve Board,* 65 Col. L. Rev. 660 (1965).

Schweitzer & Halbrook, *Insurance Activities of Banks and Bank Holding Companies: A Survey of Current Issues and Regulations,* 29 Drake L. Rev. 743 (1979/80).

Wagner, *Structuring the Financial Service Conglomerates of the Future: Does the Choice of Corporate Form to House New Financial Activities of National Banks Matter?* 19 Ann. Rev. Banking L. 329 (2000).

Wilmarth, *The Transformation of the U.S. Financial Services Industry, 1975-2000: Competition, Consolidation, and Increased Risks*, 2002 U. Ill. L. Rev. 215.

7. Securities Regulation

Ahart, *Advising the Individual Investor: Comparing the Federal Regulation of Investment Advisers, Banks and Broker-Dealers,* 6 Pepperdine L. Rev. 31 (1978).

Arnold, *Guidelines for the Banker "Insider" or "Tippee": The Texas Gulf and Merrill Lynch Decisions,* 86 Banking L.J. 319 (1969).

Azar, *FIRREA: Controlling Savings and Loan Association Credit Risk Through Capital Standards and Asset Restrictions,* 100 Yale L.J. 149 (1990).

Barr, *Public Disclosure for Investors in Bank Securities,* 82 Banking L.J. 960 (1965).

Bialkin, *Banks and Investment Managers as Institutional Investors,* 89 Banking L.J. 883 (1972).

Boyle, *Greenspan's Lament: Incentive Mechanisms and the Contamination of the Safety and Soundness of Depository Institutions from Risky Derivative Securities*, 10 Transactions: Tenn. J. Bus. L. 199 (2009).

Bruzda & Seidel, *Bank Trust Departments and the 10b-5 Dilemma,* 21 Vill. L. Rev. 367 (1976).

Butera, *Bank Exemption from the 1933 Securities Act,* 93 Banking L.J. 432 (1976).

Carter, *Bank Loans and Bank Credit Agreements: Federal Securities Law Status,* 93 Banking L.J. 1020 (1976).

Comment, *Bank Loan Participations as Securities: Notes, Investment Contracts, and the Commerical/Investment Dichotomy*, 15 Duquesne L. Rev. 261 (1976/77).

Comment, *Banks and the Securities Act of 1933,* 52 Va. L. Rev. 117 (1966), *reprinted in*, 84 Banking L.J. 95 (1967).

Comment, *Legal Aspects of Commercial Bank Issuance of Subordinated Debt,* 17 Cath. U. L. Rev. 61 (1967), *reprinted in*, 10 Banking L.J. 847 (1968).

Comment, *Securities Regulation–Proxy Solicitations–Federal Reserve Board Omits Shareholder Proposal Rule from Regulations Governing Member Banks,* 41 N.Y.U. L. Rev. 451 (1966).

Conroy, *Note, Risk-Based Capital Adequacy Guidelines: A Sound Regulatory Policy or a Symptom of Regulatory Inadequacy?,* 63 Fordham L. Rev. 2395 (1995).

Cook, *S.E.C. and Banks,* 89 Banking L.J. 499 (1972).

Dombalagian, *Requiem for the Bulge Bracket?: Revisiting Investment Bank Regulation*, 85 Ind. L.J. 777 (2010).

Eason, *Bank Acquisitions–SEC Problems on Issuance and Resale of Securities,* 14 Ga. St. B. J. 114 (1978).

Epstein, *Bank Participation Agreements as Securities,* 87 Banking L.J. 99 (1970).

Finn, *The Impact of the Proposed Federal Securities Code Upon the Banking Industry,* 36 Bus. Law. 397 (1981).

Greenberg, *Banks and the Federal Securities Laws: Some Recent Developments,* 49 So. Calif. L. Rev. 665 (1976).

Greenberg, *et al.*, *Obligations of Banks in the Public Securities Markets,* 1980 Duke L. J. 1063 (1980).

Hacker & Rotunda, *SEC's Ectoplasmic Theory of an Issuer as Applied to Educational and Charitable Institutions, Bank Trustees and other Exempt Issuers,* 65 Cal. L. Rev. 1181 (1977).

Harfield, *Texas Gulf Sulphur and Bank Internal Procedures between the Trust and Commercial Departments,* 86 Banking L.J. 869 (1969).

Herman & Safanda, *The Commercial Bank Trust Department and the "Wall"*, 14 B.C. Ind. & Comm. L. Rev. 21 (1972).

________, *Proxy Voting by Commercial Bank Trust Departments,* 90 Banking L.J. 91 (1973).

Herzel & Colling, *Chinese Wall Revisited,* 6 Corp. L. Rev. 116 (1983).

Huber, *Mandatory Disclosure of Information About Banks,* 6 Ann. Rev. Banking L. 53 (1987).

Huck, *The Fatal Lure of the "Impermeable Chinese Wall,"* 94 Banking L.J. 100 (1977).

Ianni, *"Security" under the Glass-Steagall Act and the Federal Securities Acts of 1933 and 1934: the Direction of the Supreme Court's Analysis,* 100 Banking L. J. 100 (1983).

Israels, *Banks and Federal Securities Regulation,* 85 Banking L.J. 1 (1968).

Jacobsohn, *Bank Securities–Offering Circular Requirements,* 92 Banking L.J. 244 (1975).

________, *Banks and Securities: the Regulatory Agencies Get Tougher,* 6 Sec. Reg. L.J. 213 (1978).

Kettering, *Securitization and its Discontents: The Dynamics of Financial Product Development*, 29 Cardozo L. Rev. 1553 (2008).

Klein, *Certificates of Deposit as Securities: State Law Considerations,* 5 Ann. Rev. Banking L. 55 (1986).

Lovett, *Moral Hazard, Bank Supervision and Risk- Based Capital Requirements,* 49 Ohio St. L.J. 1365

Lybecker, *Securities Law Aspects of a Bank-Account-Related Money Market Fund,* 14 Inst. on Sec. Reg. 363 (1983).

Malloy, *Can 10b-5 for the Banks? The Effect of an Antifraud Rule on the Regulation of Banks*, 61 Fordham L. Rev. S23 (1993), *reprinted in*, 8 Banking L. Anth. 257 (1994).

________, *Public Disclosure as a Tool of Federal Bank Regulation*, 9 Ann. Rev. Banking L. 229 (1990).

________, *The Regulation of Bank Brokerage Activities: Was Rule 3b-9 Benign?* 6 Ann. Rev. Banking L. 181 (1987).

________, *The 12(i)'ed Monster: Administration of the Securities Exchange Act of 1934 by the Federal Bank Regulatory Agencies*, 19 Hofstra L. Rev. 269 (1990), *reprinted in*, 1992 Sec. L. Rev.

________, *U.S. International Banking and the New Capital Adequacy Requirements: New, Old and Unexpected*, 7 Ann. Rev. Banking L. 75 (1988).

________, *U.S. International Banking Policy: Prospects and Problems in a New Millennium*, 15 Ann. Rev. Banking L. 277 (1996).

Malloy & Pitts, *Post-Mortem on Retail Repurchase Agreements: Where were the Regulators?* 3 Ann. Rev. Banking L. 89 (1984).

Méndez-Penato, *Bank "Chinese Wall": Resolving and Contending with Conflicts of Duties,* 93 Banking L.J. 674 (1976).

Murane, *SEC, FTC, and the Federal Bank Regulators: Emerging Problems of Administrative Jurisdictional Overlap,* 61 Geo. L.J. 37 (1972).

Note, *Bank Loan Participations: the Affirmative Duty to Disclose under SEC Rule 10b-5,* 27 Syracuse L. Rev. 807 (1976).

Note, *The Proposed Risk-Based Capital Framework: A Model of International Banking Cooperation?* 11 Ford. Int'l L.J. 777 (1988).

Note, *Retail Repurchase Agreements: Overcoming Insecurity within the Securities Laws,* 2 Ann. Rev. Banking L. 257 (1983).

Note, *Securities Regulation–Sale-of-Business Doctrine Does Not Exempt Sale of 100% of Corporate Stock from Provisions of Federal Securities Acts,* 16 Seton Hall L. Rev. 811 (1986).

Norton, *Capital Adequacy Standards: A Legitimate Regulatory Concern for Prudential Supervision of Banking Activities?* 49 Ohio St. L.J. 1299 (1989).

Omarova, *The Quiet Metamorphosis: How Derivatives Changed the "Business of Banking"*, 63 U. Miami L. Rev. 1041 (2009).

Quinn, *After Reves v. Ernst & Young, When Are Certificates of Deposit "Notes" Subject to Rule 10b-5 of the Securities Exchange Act [sic]*, 46 Bus. Law. 173 (1990).

Scholl & Weaver, *Loan Participations: Are they "Securities"?* 10 Fla. St. U. L. Rev. 215 (1982).

Weber, *New Governance, Financial Regulation, and Challenges to Legitimacy: The Example of the Internal Models Approach to Capital Adequacy Regulation*, 62 Admin. L. Rev. 783 (2010).

8. Resolution of Institution Failures

Alper, *FDIC Suspension and Removal Powers: An Industry-wide Bar,* 104 Banking L.J. 539 (1987).

Banks & Hoskins, *Liability and Responsibility of Bank Directors: Being Alert in Troubled Times,* 72 Ky. L. J. 639 (1983-84).

Barr, *The Last Days of Franklin National Bank,* 27 Ad. L. Rev. 301 (1975).

Barrett, *Comptroller's Shift to a Stronger Enforcement Posture: Self-Dealing and Unsound Banking Practices are the Targets,* 94 Banking L.J. 725 (1977).

Battin, Note, *Bank Director Liability Under FIRREA,* 63 Fordham L. Rev. 2347 (1995).

Batton, *Duties and Liabilities of Bank Directors,* 73 Banking L. J. 1 (1956).

Baxter, *Administrative and Judicial Review of Prompt Corrective Action Decisions by Federal Banking Regulators,* 7 Ad. L.J. Am. U. 505 (1994).

________, *Judicial Responses to the Recent Enforcement Activities of the Federal Banking Regulators,* 59 Fordham L. Rev. S193 (1991).

________, *Life in the Administrative Track: Administrative Adjudication of Claims against Savings Institution Receivers,* 1988 Duke L.J. 422.

Bebchuk & Spamann, *Regulating Bankers' Pay*, 98 Geo. L.J. 247 (2010).

Bishop, *Derivative Suits against Bank Directors: New Problems, New Strategies,* 97 Banking L.J. 158 (1980).

Block, *Measuring the True Cost of Government Bailout*, 88 Wash. U. L. Rev. 149 (2010).

Bloom, *Hearing Procedures of the Office of the Comptroller of the Currency,* 31 Law & Contemp. Prob. 723 (1966).

Boltz & Ludolph, *Serving at the Pleasure: Termination of Officers and Employees of Financial Institutions,* 104 Banking L.J. 553 (1987).

Boyle, *Greenspan's Lament: Incentive Mechanisms and the Contamination of the Safety and Soundness of Depository Institutions from Risky Derivative Securities*, 10 Transactions: Tenn. J. Bus. L. 199 (2009).

Bratter, *Degree of Care and Diligence Expected of Bank Directors*, 73 Banking L. J. 311 (1956).

Breeden, *Thumbs on the Scale: The Role that Accounting Practices Played in the Savings and Loan Crisis,* 59 Fordham L. Rev. S71 (1991).

Broome, *Private Market Solutions to the Savings and Loan Crisis: Bank Holding Company Acquisitions of Savings Associations,* 59 Fordham L. Rev. S111 (1991).

Budnitz, *The Federalization and Privatization of Public Consumer Protection Law in the United States: Their Effect on Litigation and Enforcement*, 24 Ga. St. U. L. Rev. 663 (2008).

Cahill, Note, *The Supreme Court's Decision in Hudson v. United States: One Step Up and Two Steps Back for Multiple Punishment Protection under the Double Jeopardy Clause*, 33 Wake Forest L. Rev. 439 (1998).

Case, *Deregulation: Invitation to Disaster in the S&L Industry*, 59 Fordham L. Rev. S93 (1991).

Clark, *et al.*, *Regulation of Savings Associations under the Financial Institutions Reform, Recovery, and Enforcement Act of 1989*, 45 Bus. Law. 1013 (1990).

Class, Note, *The Precarious Position of the Federal Deposit Insurance Corporation after O'Melveny & Myers v. FDIC*, 9 Admin. L.J. Am. U. 373 (1995).

Cobb, *New Clout in Federal Bank Regulatory Agencies,* 96 Banking L.J. 512 (1979).

Comment, *A Realistic Duty of Care for Outside Bank Directors,* 51 Tenn. L. Rev. 569 (1984).

Cunningham & Zaring, *The Three or Four Approaches to Financial Regulation: A Cautionary Analysis Against Exuberance in Crisis Response*, 78 Geo. Wash. L. Rev. 39 (2009).

Deal, *Bank Regulatory Enforcement–Some New Dimensions,* 40 Bus. Law. 1319 (1985).

Dore, *Presumed Innocent? Financial Institutions Professional Malpractice Claims, and Defenses Based on Management Misconduct,* 1995 Colum. Bus. L. Rev. 127.

Durkin, *Duties and Liabilities of Bank Directors,* 9 N.H.B.J. 146 (1967).

Echevarria, *A Precedent Embalms a Principle: The Expansion of the D'Oench, Duhme Doctrine,* 43 Cath. U. L. Rev. 745 (1994).

Felsenfeld, *The Savings and Loan Crisis,* 59 Fordham L. Rev. S7 (1991).

Fisher, *Bank Enforcement Actions: Usurping Legislative Prerogatives,* 104 Banking L.J. 215 (1987).

Gabilondo, *So Now Who Is Special?: Business Model Shifts Among Firms That Borrow to Lend*, 4 J. Bus. & Tech. L. 261 (2009).

Galbraith & Seidel, *FDIC vs. Imprudent Banking Officials: the Enforcement Apparatus,* 104 Banking L.J. 92 (1987).

Galves, *Might Does Not Make Right: The Call for Reform of the Federal Government's D'Oench, Duhme and 12 U.S.C. § 1823(e) Superpowers in Failed Bank Litigation,* 80 Minn. L. Rev. 1323 (1996).

Garten, *Banking on the Market: Relying on Depositors to Control Bank Risks,* 4 Yale J. Reg. 129 (1986).

________, *Market Discipline Revisited,* 14 Ann. Rev. Banking L. 187 (1995).

________, *Regulatory Growing Pains: A Perspective on Bank Regulation in a Deregulatory Age,* 57 Fordham L. Rev. 501 (1989).

________, *Subtle Hazards, Financial Risks, and Diversified Banks: An Essay on the Perils of Regulatory Reform,* 49 Md. L. Rev. 314 (1990).

Glidden, *National Bank Directors' Liability: The Case for Private Rights of Action,* 102 Banking L.J. 142 (1985).

Gonzales, *FDIC–Insured Bank Failures: Let the Makers Beware,* 17 Colo. Law. 2357 (1988).

Gorman, Note, *Liability of Directors and Officers Under FIRREA: The Uncertain Standard of Section 1821(k) and the Need for Congressional Reform,* 88 Kentucky L.J. 653 (1994-1995).

Green, *After the Fall: The Criminal Law Enforcement Response to the S&L Crisis,* 59 Fordham L. Rev. S155 (1991).

Grunewald & Golden, *Bank Director Liability post-FIRA: How to Avoid it,* 98 Banking L. J. 412 (1981).

Head, *The Global Financial Crisis of 2008-2009 in Context–Reflections on International Legal and Institutional Failings, "Fixes," and Fundamentals*, 23 Pac. McGeorge Global Bus. & Dev. L.J. 43 (2010).

Kawasaki, *Liability of Attorneys, Accountants, Appraisers, and Other Independent Contractors under the Financial Institutions Reform, Recovery, and Enforcement Act of 1989,* 42 Hastings L.J. 249 (1990).

Kull, *Disgorgement for Breach, the "Restitution Interest," and the Restatement of Contracts*, 79 Tex. L. Rev. 2021 (2001).

Labovitz, *FIRREA: The Risks Involved in Being a Nonemployee "IAP"*, 113 Banking L.J. 803 (1996).

Lee, *Risk Management and the Role of the Board of Directors: Regulatory Expectations and Shareholder Actions*, 125 Banking L.J. 679 (2008).

Leibell, *Accountants Liability in the Savings and Loan Crisis: An Argument in Favor of Affirmative Defenses,* 1991 Colum. Bus. L. Rev. 71 (1991).

Mayer, *Civil and Criminal Liability of Directors of California Banks and Savings and Loan Associations,* 41 Calif. S.B.J. (1966).

Malloy, *Balancing Public Confidence and Confidentiality: Adjudication Practices and Procedures of the Federal Bank Regulatory Agencies,* 61 Temple L. Rev. 723 (1988).

________, *Foreword: . . . And Backward: Death and Transfiguration among the Savings Associations*, 59 Fordham L. Rev. S1 (1991).

________, *Nothing to Fear but FIRREA Itself: Revising and Reshaping the Enforcement Process of Federal Bank Regulation,* 50 Ohio St. L.J. 1117 (1989).

________, *When You Wish Upon Winstar: Contract Analysis and the Future of Regulatory Action*, 42 St. Louis U. L.J. 409 (1998).

McKenna, *Control and Management of Federal Savings and Loan Associations,* 27 So. Cal. L. Rev. 47 (1953).

McLaughlin *et al.*, *Financial Institutions Fraud*, 35 Am. Crim. L. Rev. 789 (1998).

Michael, *Self-Regulation for Safety and Security: Final Minutes or Finest Hour?*, 36 Seton Hall L. Rev. 1075 (2006).

Murphy, *Assuring Responsible Risk Management in Banking: the Corporate Governance Dimension*, 36 Del. J. Corp. L. 121 (2011).

Nelson, *Director Liability and the Insolvent, Federally Chartered Financial Institution: A Standard Emerges*, 73 Wash. U. L.Q. 1477 (1995).

Newman, *Reducing the Risk of Bank Director Liability,* 96 Banking L.J. 418 (1979).

Note, *Borrower Beware: D'Oench, Duhme and Section 1823 Overprotect the Insurer When Banks Fail,* 62 So. Cal. L. Rev. 253 (1988).

Note, *Causes of the Savings and Loan Debacle,* 59 Fordham L. Rev. S301 (1991).

Note, *The FDIC's Enhanced Powers Over Savings Associations: Does FIRREA Make It "SAIF"?* 59 Fordham L. Rev. S381 (1991).

Note, *A Note to Congress and the FDIC: After FIRREA Where's the BIF?* 59 Fordham L. Rev. S411 (1991).

Note, *The Office of Thrift Supervision,* 59 Fordham L. Rev. S363 (1991).

Note, *Playing with FIRREA Not Getting Burned: Statutory Overview of the Financial Institutions Reform, Recovery, and Enforcement Act of 1989,* 59 Fordham L. Rev. S323 (1991).

Note, *The Resolution Trust Corporation: Waste Management and the S&L Crisis,* 59 Fordham L. Rev. S339 (1991).

Note, *Too Many Consonants and Not Enough Consonance: The Development of the S&L Regulatory Framework,* 59 Fordham L. Rev. S263 (1991).

Note, *Civil Money Penalties in the Financial Institutions Reform, Recovery, and Enforcement Act of 1989: An Analysis*, 12 Geo. Mason U. L. Rev. 289 (1990).

Note, *The Resolution Trust Corporation: Waste Management and the S&L Crisis,* 59 Fordham L. Rev. S339 (1991).

Oltman, *Failing Banks–The Role of the Fed,* 27 Ad. L. Rev. 317 (1975).

O'Malley, *The Federal Criminal Liability of Bank Personnel Under the Misapplication Statute,* 99 Banking L.J. 100 (1982).

Pasley, *Double Jeopardy and Civil Money Penalties*, 114 Banking L.J. 4 (1996).

Phillips, *The Jumbled Alphabet Soup of the Collapsed Home Mortgage Market: ABCP, CDO, CDS and RMBS*, 18 U. Miami Bus. L. Rev. 143 (2010).

Pratt, *Legal Responsibilities of Bank Directors,* 75 Banking L.J. 645 (1958).

Ramirez, *The Chaos of 12 U.S.C. Section 1821(k): Congressional Subsidizing of Negligent Bank Directors and Officers?*, 65 Fordham L. Rev. 625 (1996).

Recent Developments, *Criminal Prosecution of Bank Personnel under the Misapplication Statute: The Proper Mens Rea Standard for Establishing Intent,* 37 Vand. L. Rev. 1397 (1984).

Rose-Ackerman & Rossi, *Disentangling Deregulatory Takings*, 86 Va. L. Rev. 1435 (2000).

Sabado, Note, *Adopting a Jurisdictional Approach to the Rights of Asset Purchasers from the FDIC*, 69 Fordham L. Rev. 287 (2000).

Schaller, *FSLIC Federal Receivership Appointments for Allegedly Insolvent State Savings and Loan Associations: A Plot to Federalize State Savings and Loans Against Their Will,* 33 DePaul L. Rev. 783 (1984).

Schwind, *Removal of National Bank Directors,* 85 Banking L.J. 313 (1968).

Scott, *Introduction, Franklin National Bank and its Progeny: the Procedural Road to Bank Failure: Montreal Meeting Panel,* 27 Ad. L. Rev. 299 (1975).

________, *Never Again, The S&L Bailout Bill,* 45 Bus. Law. 1883 (1990).

Skillern, *Federal Deposit Insurance Corporation and the Failed Bank: The Past Decade (Parts I & II),* 99 Banking L.J. 233, 292 (1982).

Snyder & Zully, *Management Powers and Obligations of Officers, Directors, and Trustees of Banking Corporations,* 76 Banking L.J. 921 (1959).

Spencer, *Directors' Duties and Responsibilities,* 76 Banking L.J. 645 (1959).

Staffenberg, Note, *Treacherous Terrain for In-House Bank Attorneys,* 14 Ann. Rev. Banking L. 405 (1995).

Stowman, *Savings and Loan Director Liability in Kansas After O'Melveny & Myers*, 6 Kan. J. L. & Pub. Pol'y 199 (1996).

Torrie, *Weathering the Global Financial Crisis: An Overview of the Canadian Experience*, 16 L. & Bus. Rev. Am. 25 (2010).

Tussig, *The Case for Bank Failure,* 10 J. L. & Econ. 129 (1967).

Via, *Antitrust and the Rescue of Distressed Banks by Acquisition*, 94 Banking L.J. 508 (1977).

White, *The S&L Debacle,* 59 Fordham L. Rev. S57 (1991).

Wilson, *Responsibilities of a Bank Director,* 72 Banking L.J. 171 (1955).

Wook Bai Kim, *Challenging the Roots of the Subprime Mortgage Crisis: The OCC's Operating Subsidiaries Regulations and Watters v. Wachovia Bank*, 21 Loy. Consumer L. Rev. 278 (2009).

Zinman, Note, *Diamond is the RTC's Best Friend: Federal Preemption and the Balance of the Term of Rent Regulated Leases in Resolution Trust Corporation v. Diamond,* 22 Fordham Urb. L. J. 1295 (1995).

Zou, Note and Comment, *United States v. Winstar Corporation: Implications for the*

Regulated Industries, 16 St. Louis U. Pub. L. Rev. 477 (1997).

9. International Financial Services Policy

Alford, *Core Principles for Effective Banking Supervision: An Enforceable International Financial Standard?*, 28 B.C. Int'l & Comp. L. Rev. 237 (2005).

Asiedu-Akrofi, *Sustaining Lender Commitment to Sovereign Debtors,* 30 Colum. J. Transnat'l L. 1 (1992)

Bhala, *Equilibrium Theory, the FICAS Model, and International Banking Law*, 38 Harv. Int'l L.J. 1 (1997).

Blau, *The Federal Reserve and European Central Bank as Lenders-of-Last-Resort: Different Needles in Their Compasses*, 21 N.Y. Int'l L. Rev. 39 (2008).

Bloom, Note, *Plurality and Precedence: Judicial Reasoning, Lower Courts, and the Meaning of United States v. Winstar Corp.*, 85 Wash. U. L. Rev. 1373 (2008).

Brown, *A Comparison of the Handling of the Financial Crisis in the United States, the United Kingdom, and Australia*, 55 Vill. L. Rev. 509 (2010).

Burand, *Regulation of Foreign Banks' Entry into the United States under the FBSEA: Implementation and Implications,* 24 L. & Pol'y Int'l Bus. 1089 (1993).

Cleveland, *Norm Internationalization and U.S. Economic Sanctions*, 26 Yale J. Int'l L. 1 (2001).

Comment, *United States Foreign Banking and Investment Opportunities: Branching Out to the Russian Federation*, 8 Transnat'l Law. 159 (1995).

Crimm, *High Alert: The Government's War on the Financing of Terrorism and Its Implications for Donors, Domestic Charitable Organizations, and Global Philanthropy*, 45 Wm. & Mary L. Rev. 1341 (2004).

Dowling, Comment, *Fatal Broadside: the Demise of Caribbean Offshore Financial Confidentiality Post USA PATRIOT Act*, 17 Transnat'l Law. 259 (2004).

Fanikos, Note, *The Foreign Bank Supervision Enhancement Act of 1991: Necessary Additions and Amendments to the International Banking Act of 1978 or Legislative Overreaction to Recent Foreign Bank Scandals?* 16 Suffolk Transnat'l L. Rev. 482 (1993).

Fisher, *In Rem Alternatives for Money Laundering*, 25 Loy. L.A. Int'l & Comp. L. Rev. 409 (2003).

Folendorf, *Breaking Terror's Bank Without Breaking the Law: A Comment on the USA PATRIOT Act and the United States Financial War on Terrorism*, 23 J. Nat'l Ass'n Admin. L. Judges 481 (2003).

Frenkel, *Russian Commercial Banking following the Currency Crisis*, 13 Int'l Banking L. 375 (1998).

Gouvin, *Are There Any Checks and Balances on the Government's Power to Check Our Balances? The Fate of Financial Privacy in the War on Terrorism*, 14 Temp. Pol. & Civ. Rts. L. Rev. 517 (2005).

________, *Bank Mergers in North America: Comparing the Approaches in the United States and Canada*, 18 Transnat'l Law. 245 (2005).

________, *Cross-Border Bank Branching under NAFTA: Public Choice and the Law of Corporate Groups*, 13 Conn. J. Int'l L. 257 (1999).

Gruson & Nikowitz, *The Second Banking Directive of the European Economic Community and its Importance for Non-EEC Banks,* 12 Fordham Int'l L.J. 205 (1989).

Head, *The Global Financial Crisis of 2008-2009 in Context-Reflections on International Legal and Institutional Failings, "Fixes," and Fundamentals,* 23 Pac. McGeorge

Global Bus. & Dev. L.J. 43 (2010).

Hipp, Comment, *Defending Expanded Presidential Authority to Regulate Foreign Assets and Transactions*, 17 Emory Int'l L. Rev. 1311 (2003).

Karmel, *The Blame Game*, New York Law Journal, Oct. 16, 2008, at 3.

Kim, *Markets, Financial Institutions, and Corporate Governance: Perspectives from Germany*, 26 Law & Pol'y Int'l Bus. 371 (1995).

Kuan-Chun Chang, *From Zero to Something: The Necessity of Establishing a Regulatory System of Financial Conglomerates in China*, 11 Asian-Pac. L. & Pol'y J. 1 (2010).

Lance, *Can the Glass-Steagall Act be Justified under the Global Free Market Policies of the Nafta?,* 34 Washburn L.J. 297 (1995).

Lehr & Hammond, *Regulating the Foreign Acquisition of U.S. Banks: the CBCA and the BHCA,* 97 Banking L. J. 100 (1980).

Lehrer, Comment, *Unbalancing the Terrorists' Checkbook: Analysis of U.S. Policy in its Economic War on International Terrorism*, 10 Tulane J. Int'l & Comp. L. 333 (2002).

Lucio, *Establishment of a Banking Presence in the United States by Foreign Banks,* 11 N.C. J. Int'l L. & Com. Reg. 583 (1986).

Malloy, *Bumper Cars: Themes of Convergence in International Regulation*, 60 Fordham L. Rev. S1 (1992).

________, *U.S. International Banking and the New Capital Adequacy Requirements: New, Old and Unexpected*, 7 Ann. Rev. Banking L. 75 (1988).

________, *U.S. International Banking and Treasury's Foreign Assets Controls: Springing Traps for the Unwary*, 8 Ann. Rev. Banking L. 181 (1989).

________, *U.S. International Banking Policy: Prospects and Problems in a New Millennium*, 15 Ann. Rev. Banking L. 277 (1996).

Matthews, *Emerging Public International Banking Law? Lessons from the Law of the Sea Experience*, 10 Chi. J. Int'l L. 539 (2010).

Misuraca, Comment, *Foreign Banking in the United States: An Objective Study of the International Banking Act of 1978,* 4 J. Int'l L. & Prac. 539 (1995).

Note, *The Proposed Risk-Based Capital Framework: A Model of International Banking Cooperation?* 11 Ford. Int'l L.J. 777 (1988).

Nunes, *Foreign Banks Come Sailing in as United States Banks Tack Slowly Upwind,* 13 Hous. J. Int'l L. 39 (1990).

Singh, *U.K. Approach to Financial Crisis Management*, 19 Transnat'l L. & Contemp. Probs. 868 (2011).

Stutts & Watts, *Of Herring and Sausage: Nordic Responses to Banking Crises as Examples for the United States*, 44 Tex. Int'l L.J. 577 (2009).

Taylor, *Islamic Banking–The Feasibility of Establishing an Islamic Bank in the United States*, 40 Am. Bus. L.J. 385 (2003).

Weida, *Reaching Multinational Corporations: A New Model for Drafting Effective Economic Sanctions*, 30 Vt. L. Rev. 303 (2006).

Westbrook, *What's in Your Portfolio? U.S. Investors Are Unknowingly Financing State Sponsors of Terrorism*, 59 DePaul L. Rev. 1151 (2010)

Windsor, *The WTO Committee on Trade in Financial Services: The Exercise of Public Authority Within an Informational Forum*, 9 German L.J. 1805 (2008).

Zheng, *Management of Lenders' Currency Exposure in Multicurrency Financings: Structural and Documentational Considerations,* 22 L. & Pol'y Int'l Bus. 213 (1991).

Index

D

E

F